Spain

Damien Simonis
John Noble
Susan Forsyth
Tim Nollen
Fionn Davenport

LONELY PLANET PUBLICATIONS
Melbourne • Oakland • London • Paris

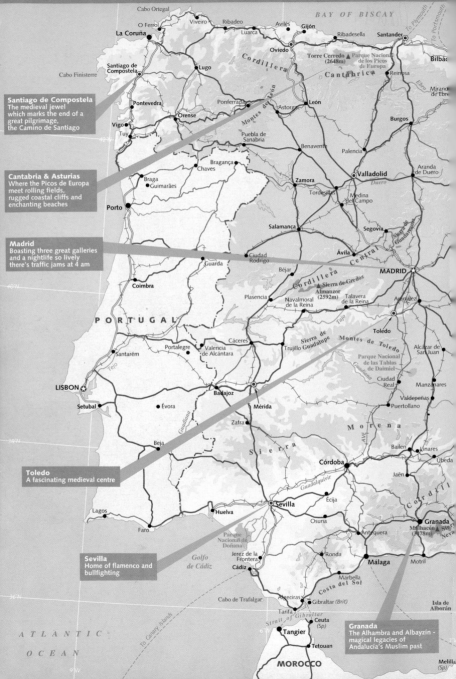

SPAIN

Santiago de Compostela
The medieval jewel which marks the end of a great pilgrimage, the Camino de Santiago

Cantabria & Asturias
Where the Picos de Europa meet rolling fields, rugged coastal cliffs and enchanting beaches

Madrid
Boasting three great galleries and a nightlife so lively there's traffic jams at 4 am

Toledo
A fascinating medieval centre

Sevilla
Home of flamenco and bullfighting

Granada
The Alhambra and Albayzín - magical legacies of Andalucía's Muslim past

BAY OF BISCAY

Cabo Ortegal
O Ferrol
Viveiro
Ribadeo
Avilés
Gijón
Luarca
Ribadesella
Santander
To Plymouth
To Portsmouth
La Coruña
Oviedo
Ribadesella
Bilbao
Santiago de Compostela
Cabo Finisterre
Lugo
Torre Cerredo (2648m)
Parque Nacional de los Picos de Europa
Reinosa
Miranda de Ebro
Pontevedra
Ponferrada
Cordillera
Cantábrica
Astorga
León
Burgos
Vigo
Tuy
Orense
Montes de León
Puebla de Sanabria
Benavente
Palencia
Aranda de Duero
Bragança
Chaves
Zamora
Valladolid
Braga
Guimarães
Tordesillas
Medina del Campo
Segovia
Sierra de Guadarrama
Duero
Porto
Salamanca
Ávila
MADRID
PORTUGAL
Coimbra
Ciudad Rodrigo
Guarda
Béjar
Cordillera
Sierra de Gredos
Almanzor (2592m)
Central
Aranjuez
Plasencia
Navalmoral de la Reina
Talavera de la Reina
Toledo
Alcázar de San Juan
Cáceres
Sierra de Guadalupe
Montes de Toledo
Portalegre
Valencia de Alcántara
Trujillo
Parque Nacional de las Tablas de Daimiel
Santarém
Ciudad Real
Manzanares
LISBON
Tejo
Badajoz
Mérida
Guadiana
Valdepeñas
Puertollano
Setúbal
Évora
Zafra
M o r e n a
Beja
Sierra
Bailén
Linares
Úbeda
Córdoba
Jaén
Cord
Guadalquivir
Lagos
Huelva
Sevilla
Écija
Granada
Mulhacén Sierra (3478m) Nevada
Faro
Osuna
Antequera
Málaga
Motril
Parque Nacional de Doñana
Golfo de Cádiz
Jerez de la Frontera
Cádiz
Ronda
Marbella
Costa del Sol
Cabo de Trafalgar
Algeciras
Gibraltar (Brit)
Isla de Alborán
Tarifa
Strait of Gibraltar
Ceuta (Sp)
Melilla (Sp)
ATLANTIC OCEAN
To Canary Islands
Tangier
Tetouan
MOROCCO

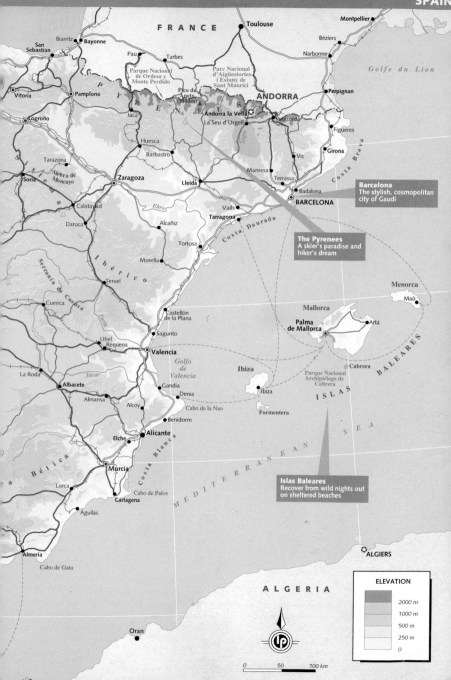

FRANCE

Montpellier

Toulouse

Béziers

San Sebastián
Biarritz
Bayonne

Narbonne

Pau
Tarbes

Golfe du Lion

Vitoria

Pamplona

Parque Nacional
de Ordesa y
Monte Perdido

Parc National
d'Aigüestortes
i Estany de
Sant Maurici

ANDORRA

Perpignan

Logroño

Pico del
Aneto
(3404m)

Andorra la Vella

Figueres

Jaca

La Seu d'Urgell

Tarazona

Huesca

Vic

Girona

Costa Brava

Soria
Sierra de
Moncayo

Barbastro

Manresa

Terrassa

Barcelona
The stylish, cosmopolitan
city of Gaudí

Calatayud

Zaragoza

Lleida

Badalona

BARCELONA

Daroca

Ebro

Valls

Tarragona

The Pyrenees
A skier's paradise and
hiker's dream

Serranía de Cuenca

Teruel

Alcañiz

Morella

Costa Daurada

Tortosa

Ibérico

Menorca

Maó

Cuenca

Turia

Castellón
de la Plana

Mallorca

Artá

Sagunto

Palma
de Mallorca

Utiel
Requena

Valencia

*Golfo
de
Valencia*

Ibiza

La Roda

Júcar

Gandia

Islas Baleares

Albacete

Almansa

Alcoy

Denia

Ibiza

Parque Nacional
Archipiélago de
Cabrera

Cabrera

ISLAS

BALEARES

Benidorm

Cabo de la Nao

Formentera

Elche

Alicante

Costa Blanca

Bética

Murcia

MEDITERRANEAN SEA

Lorca

Cabo de Palos

Islas Baleares
Recover from wild nights out
on sheltered beaches

Águilas

Cartagena

ALGIERS

Almería

Cabo de Gata

ALGERIA

ELEVATION	
	2000 m
	1000 m
	500 m
	250 m
	0

Oran

LP

0   50   100 km

Spain
2nd edition – April 1999
First published – May 1997

Published by
Lonely Planet Publications Pty Ltd A.C.N. 005 607 983
192 Burwood Rd, Hawthorn, Victoria 3122, Australia

Lonely Planet Offices
Australia PO Box 617, Hawthorn, Victoria 3122
USA 150 Linden St, Oakland, CA 94607
UK 10a Spring Place, London NW5 3BH
France 1 rue du Dahomey, 75011 Paris

Photographs
Many of the images in this guide are available for licensing from
Lonely Planet Images.
email: lpi@lonelyplanet.com.au

Front cover photograph
Flamenco dancer (Reimund Zunde)

ISBN 0 86442 633 X

text & maps © Lonely Planet 1999
photos © photographers as indicated 1999

Printed by Colorcraft Ltd, Hong Kong

Contents – Text

1

COMUNIDAD DE MADRID   245

CASTILLA Y LEÓN   255

CASTILLA-LA MANCHA   323

BARCELONA   355

CATALUNYA (CATALUÑA)   417

EXTREMADURA
936

LANGUAGE
967

GLOSSARY
973

FOOD GLOSSARY
977

ACKNOWLEDGMENTS
980

INDEX
994

MAP LEGEND
back page

METRIC CONVERSION
inside back cover

Contents – Maps

CAMINO DE SANTIAGO SPECIAL SECTION

PAÍS VASCO, NAVARRA & LA RIOJA

CANTABRIA & ASTURIAS

GALICIA

VALENCIA

ISLAS BALEARES (BALEARIC ISLANDS)

MURCIA

ANDALUCÍA

EXTREMADURA

8 Contents – Maps

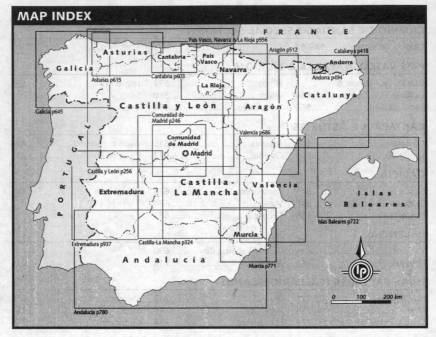

MAP INDEX

The Authors

Damien Simonis

With a degree in languages and several years' reporting and sub-editing on several Australian newspapers (including the *Australian* and the *Age*), Sydney-born Damien left the country in 1989. He has lived, worked and travelled extensively throughout Europe, the Middle East and North Africa. Since 1992, Lonely Planet has kept him busy in *Jordan & Syria*, *Egypt & the Sudan*, *Morocco*, *North Africa*, *Italy* and the *Canary Islands*. The ink wasn't dry on this edition of *Spain* when he returned to Barcelona to write Lonely Planet's forthcoming guide to that city. He has also written and snapped for other publications in Australia, the UK and North America. When not on the road, Damien resides in splendid Stoke Newington, in deepest north London.

John Noble

John comes from the Ribble Valley in northern England. After a Cambridge University degree he embarked on a newspaper journalism career, but increasing interruptions for travel to various bits of the globe saw him eventually abandon Fleet Street for a Lonely Planet trail that has taken him to four continents via over a dozen LP books, from *Indonesia* and *Sri Lanka* to *Mexico* and *Andalucía*. John was also a pioneer of Lonely Planet's coverage of the former Soviet Union, co-authoring *USSR*, *Russia*, *Ukraine & Belarus* and *Central Asia* and writing *Baltic States* solo. Since 1994 he has enjoyed living in southern Spain, together with his wife and co-author Susan Forsyth and their children Jack and Isabella.

Susan Forsyth

Susan hails from Melbourne and survived a decade teaching in the Victorian state education system before activating long-postponed travel plans and heading off for a year as a volunteer lecturer in Sri Lanka, where she met her future husband John Noble. Susan has since helped to update LP's *Australia*, *Indonesia*, *Mexico* and *Sri Lanka*, *Travel With Children*, co-written *Andalucía* with John, given birth to and nurtured two little rubios (blondies) and weathered five years in England's cold, wet but beautiful Ribble Valley. Since 1994 the family has lived in southern Spain.

Tim Nollen

Tim comes from Washington, DC. After university work, he settled in Prague in the early 90s – just before it was hip, of course. There he taught primary school English for a spell and dealt property on the burgeoning real estate market. He has also studied music at the conservatory and graduate school levels. This is his first job for Lonely Planet but he has written and updated guidebooks to several European countries for various publishers, and has had articles published on subjects as diverse as the Dead Sea, the Trans-Siberian railroad and a Czech piano manufacturer. For some reason, he currently lives in Philadelphia.

Fionn Davenport

Fionn is an Irish freelance writer and editor with a degree in history and nomadic wanderlust. His post-college travels eventually brought him to New York, where he worked for a number of years as a travel guide editor (as well as a lucrative stint as a bartender and a not-so-successful career as an actor). Itchy feet finally dragged him from behind his desk and he resumed travelling, making a career out of his favourite pastime. Currently residing in his native Dublin, he has spent the past couple of years travel-writing his way through Europe. He has written about Italy, France, Britain, Ireland and, now, Spain. This is his first job for Lonely Planet.

FROM THE AUTHORS

Damien Simonis People all over the place have helped me out on this job in many different ways.

On the home front, Sam Carew and Cathy Lanigan in particular and all the gang in general at LP London have helped me keep things ticking over – especially in times of national emergency! In LP Aus, Mary Neighbour, Marcel Gaston and the team have all been fine fellows (not to mention abundantly patient) and thanks to Leonie Mugavin for help with the Australasia Getting There & Away info. Same to Sacha Pearson in the USA for similar aid.

In Madrid, Debby, Gary and Alex Luhrman rolled out the welcome mat and allowed me free run of their home. As usual, a gaggle of friends in Madrid made my time there not only productive, but also fun (maybe too much fun). They include Bárbara Azcona, David Ing, Arancha Lamela Ruiz, Diane Palumbo, Ángeles Sánchez Caballero, Jean-Marc Simon and Luis Soldevila.

Geoff Leaver Heaton and Lola down in Málaga gave Gnomo the valiant Renault 5 a temporary home when I was not thrashing the poor beasty.

Up in Barcelona, I owe a lot to Susana Pellicer, Rafa Perera (who became my temporary landlord on the 4th floor at Gran Vía), Álvaro Picardo (in London, thanks for the contacts), Max Jacobson (also in London, with more contacts) and Susan Kempster and the gang from Carrer de Sant Pere més alt (Michael, Paloma, Natalia), who welcomed me into their labyrinthine home on more than one occasion and kept a watchful eye on Gnomo during his well-earned rest periods in Catalunya.

In Ibiza, I was ably assisted in clacking style for a couple of days by Kate Walsh, Claire England and Elaine Dempster. Across the water, Raquel Evans behind the bar at Texas not only poured fine cañas but also wisdom on Menorca as well. Her pal Big Ál(varo) was also full of good advice. Thanks also to Miles Roddis in Valencia for passing on some tips.

The staff at several tourist offices were very obliging, but none more than those in the provincial office in Alicante – they deserve a medal! Following close behind were: Oficina d'Informació i Turisme staff in Andorra la Vella; the park officers at Espot; and the staff at Ibiza city's and Ciutadella's tourist offices (Islas Baleares).

Last but not least, thanks to John Noble, Susan Forsyth, Tim Nollen and Fionn Davenport (the A-team) for helping to reconstruct this tome and get it in by deadline. John also provided me with a lot of info for the introductory chapters.

John Noble & Susan Forsyth We owe thanks to everyone who answered our questions, gave us tips and shared their experiences and knowledge of Spain. Particularly: Nick and Corinna Selby for a great deal of help with Algeciras, Gibraltar, Tarifa, technology and other things; Patricia Luce for being a constant source of information and pointing us in some interesting directions; Tony and Jean Allsop for Ronda help; Jane Warnick for tips on the Granada coast; Damien Simonis for all sorts of bits and pieces; and the many helpful staff in Andalucian and Extremaduran tourist offices, especially María Angustias Maldonado in Granada.

Tim Nollen Thanks to the many tourist office staff who were too modest to give their names, especially the Polish woman at Toledo's *ayuntamiento* and the energetic assistant in Aínsa. A big *gracías* to John and Susan for the hospitality provided and a much-needed break. I appreciate the help of the music department faculty and staff at U Penn in enabling the early departure. And thanks to Mom, Dad and 'Tine for the support and to Ája for somehow not minding me doing this!

Fionn Davenport Fionn would like to thank the staff at all of the tourist offices for their invaluable help. They patiently explained everything he needed to know and made his job a whole lot easier. A big thanks to Paul 'Scorchio' Rooney, whose company and humour throughout the long drives and tiring walks made travelling all the more pleasurable. And no, I didn't mind driving halfway across the country just to pick you up in Madrid!

This Book

Foreword

Spain was first written by John Noble, Damien Simonis, Mark Armstrong, Susan Forsyth and Corinne Simcock.

This second edition was researched and written by Damien (co-ordinating author), John, Susan, Tim Nollen and Fionn Davenport. Damien wrote the Madrid, Comunidad de Madrid, Barcelona, Catalunya, Andorra, Valencia, Islas Baleares and Murcia chapters, and contributed to the introductory chapters. John and Susan updated Andalucía and Extremadura, and contributed to the introductory chapters. Tim researched the Aragón, Castilla-La Mancha and País Vasco, Navarra & La Rioja chapters. Fionn updated the Castilla y León, Cantabria & Asturias and Galicia chapters.

From the Publisher

This second edition was produced at Lonely Planet's Melbourne office and coordinated by Helen Rowley (mapping and design) and Rebecca Turner (editorial).

On the editing and proofing front, Rebecca was helped by Ada Cheung, Carolyn Bain, Ron Gallagher, Martine Lleonart (who also created the Camino de Santiago special section), Arabella Bamber and Jocelyn Harewood. Ada also helped with the index.

Helen was assisted in mapping matters by Piotr Czajkowski, Paul Dawson, Mark Griffiths, Jenny Jones and Andrew Smith. Anthony Phelan produced the climate charts and a team of illustrators – Trudi Canavan, Marcel Gaston, Errol Hunt, Ann Jeffree, Nick Kelly, Kath Nolan and Mick Weldon – produced some fine creations.

Muchas gracias to Quentin Frayne for the language section, Simon Bracken for the cover design, Matt King for his illustration know-how, the folks at Lonely Planet Images for help with the photographs and Katie Cody, Liz Filleul, Mary Neighbour, Kristin Odijk and Chris Wyness for the final checks.

And the final slaps on the back go to Katie, Marcel Gaston and Mary for their help and support, Tim 'Quark' Uden for his endless good humour and bad puns and Adrian Persoglia for his last-minute help.

THANKS
Many thanks to the travellers who used the last edition and wrote to us with helpful hints, advice and interesting anecdotes. Your names appear in the back of this book.

Foreword

ABOUT LONELY PLANET GUIDEBOOKS

The story begins with a classic travel adventure: Tony and Maureen Wheeler's 1972 journey across Europe and Asia to Australia. Useful information about the overland trail did not exist at that time, so Tony and Maureen published the first Lonely Planet guidebook to meet a growing need.

From a kitchen table, then from a tiny office in Melbourne (Australia), Lonely Planet has become the largest independent travel publisher in the world, an international company with offices in Melbourne, Oakland (USA), London (UK) and Paris (France).

Today Lonely Planet guidebooks cover the globe. There is an ever-growing list of books and there's information in a variety of forms and media. Some things haven't changed. The main aim is still to help make it possible for adventurous travellers to get out there – to explore and better understand the world.

At Lonely Planet we believe travellers can make a positive contribution to the countries they visit – if they respect their host communities and spend their money wisely. Since 1986 a percentage of the income from each book has been donated to aid projects and human rights campaigns.

Updates Lonely Planet thoroughly updates each guidebook as often as possible. This usually means there are around two years between editions, although for more unusual or more stable destinations the gap can be longer. Check the imprint page (following the colour map at the beginning of the book) for publication dates.

Between editions up-to-date information is available in two free newsletters – the paper *Planet Talk* and email *Comet* (to subscribe, contact any Lonely Planet office) – and on our Web site at www.lonelyplanet.com. The *Upgrades* section of the Web site covers a number of important and volatile destinations and is regularly updated by Lonely Planet authors. *Scoop* covers news and current affairs relevant to travellers. And, lastly, the *Thorn Tree* bulletin board and *Postcards* section of the site carry unverified, but fascinating, reports from travellers.

Correspondence The process of creating new editions begins with the letters, postcards and emails received from travellers. This correspondence often includes suggestions, criticisms and comments about the current editions. Interesting excerpts are immediately passed on via newsletters and the Web site, and everything goes to our authors to be verified when they're researching on the road. We're keen to get more feedback from organisations or individuals who represent communities visited by travellers.

> Lonely Planet gathers information for everyone who's curious about the planet – and especially for those who explore it first-hand. Through guidebooks, phrasebooks, activity guides, maps, literature, newsletters, image library, TV series and Web site we act as an information exchange for a worldwide community of travellers.

Research Authors aim to gather sufficient practical information to enable travellers to make informed choices and to make the mechanics of a journey run smoothly. They also research historical and cultural background to help enrich the travel experience and allow travellers to understand and respond appropriately to cultural and environmental issues.

Authors don't stay in every hotel because that would mean spending a couple of months in each medium-sized city and, no, they don't eat at every restaurant because that would mean stretching belts beyond capacity. They do visit hotels and restaurants to check standards and prices, but feedback based on readers' direct experiences can be very helpful.

Many of our authors work undercover, others aren't so secretive. None of them accept freebies in exchange for positive write-ups. And none of our guidebooks contain any advertising.

Production Authors submit their raw manuscripts and maps to offices in Australia, USA, UK or France. Editors and cartographers – all experienced travellers themselves – then begin the process of assembling the pieces. When the book finally hits the shops, some things are already out of date, we start getting feedback from readers and the process begins again ...

WARNING & REQUEST

Things change – prices go up, schedules change, good places go bad and bad places go bankrupt – nothing stays the same. So, if you find things better or worse, recently opened or long since closed, please tell us and help make the next edition even more accurate and useful. We genuinely value all the feedback we receive. Julie Young coordinates a well travelled team that reads and acknowledges every letter, postcard and email and ensures that every morsel of information finds its way to the appropriate authors, editors and cartographers for verification.

Everyone who writes to us will find their name in the next edition of the appropriate guidebook. They will also receive the latest issue of *Planet Talk*, our quarterly printed newsletter, or *Comet*, our monthly email newsletter. Subscriptions to both newsletters are free. The very best contributions will be rewarded with a free guidebook.

Excerpts from your correspondence may appear in new editions of Lonely Planet guidebooks, the Lonely Planet Web site, *Planet Talk* or *Comet*, so please let us know if you *don't* want your letter published or your name acknowledged.

Send all correspondence to the Lonely Planet office closest to you:

Australia: PO Box 617, Hawthorn, Victoria 3122
USA: 150 Linden St, Oakland, CA 94607
UK: 10A Spring Place, London NW5 3BH
France: 1 rue du Dahomey, 75011 Paris

Or email us at: talk2us@lonelyplanet.com.au

For news, views and updates see our Web site: www.lonelyplanet.com

HOW TO USE A LONELY PLANET GUIDEBOOK
The best way to use a Lonely Planet guidebook is any way you choose. At Lonely Planet we believe the most memorable travel experiences are often those that are unexpected, and the finest discoveries are those you make yourself. Guidebooks are not intended to be used as if they provide a detailed set of infallible instructions!

Contents All Lonely Planet guidebooks follow the same format. The Facts about the Country chapters or sections give background information ranging from history to weather. Facts for the Visitor gives practical information on issues like visas and health. Getting There & Away gives a brief starting point for researching travel to and from the destination. Getting Around gives an overview of the transport options when you arrive.

The peculiar demands of each destination determine how subsequent chapters are broken up, but some things remain constant. We always start with background, then proceed to sights, places to stay, places to eat, entertainment, getting there and away, and getting around information – in that order.

Heading Hierarchy Lonely Planet headings are used in a strict hierarchical structure that can be visualised as a set of Russian dolls. Each heading (and its following text) is encompassed by any preceding heading that is higher on the hierarchical ladder.

Entry Points We do not assume guidebooks will be read from beginning to end, but that people will dip into them. The traditional entry points are the list of contents and the index. In addition, however, there is a complete list of maps and an index map illustrating map coverage.

There's also a colour map that shows highlights. These highlights are dealt with in greater detail in the Facts for the Visitor chapter, along with planning questions and suggested itineraries. Each chapter covering a geographical region begins with a locator map and another list of highlights. Once you find something of interest in a list of highlights, turn to the index.

Maps Maps play a crucial role in Lonely Planet guidebooks and include a huge amount of information. A legend is printed on the back page. We seek to have complete consistency between maps and text, and to have every important place in the text captured on a map. Map key numbers usually start in the top left corner.

Although inclusion in a guidebook usually implies a recommendation we cannot list every good place. Exclusion does not necessarily imply criticism. In fact there are a number of reasons why we might exclude a place – sometimes it is simply inappropriate to encourage an influx of travellers.

Introduction

It has been said that Europe ends at the Pyrenees. While that has always been an exaggeration, any journey south of those mountains proves that, as an old tourism promotion campaign had it, Spain *is* different. With its plethora of colourful fiestas and indefatigable nightlife, its complete spectrum of scenery and its unique, well-preserved architectural and artistic heritage, Spain provides a variety of fun and fascination that few countries can match.

Travel is easy, accommodation plentiful, the climate generally benign, the people relaxed and fun-loving, the beaches long and sandy, and food and drink easy to come by and full of regional variation. More than

60 million foreigners a year visit Spain, yet you can also travel for days and hear no other tongue but Spanish. Once away from the holiday *costas*, you could only be in Spain. In the cities, narrow, twisting old streets suddenly open out to views of daring modern architecture, while spit-and-sawdust bars serving wine from the barrel rub shoulders with blaring, glaring discos. Travel out into the back country and you'll find, an hour or two from some of Europe's most stylish and sophisticated cities, villages where time has done its best to stand still since the Middle Ages.

Geographically, Spain's diversity is immense. In Andalucía, for example, you could ski in the Sierra Nevada and later the

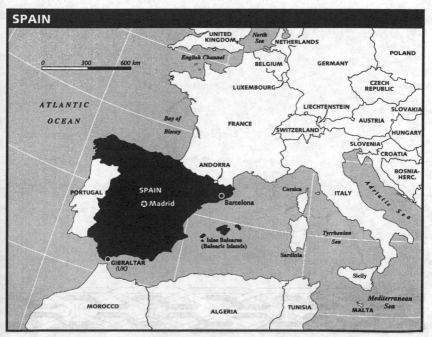

SPAIN

same day recline on a Mediterranean beach or traverse the deserts of Almería. There are endless tracts of wild and crinkled *sierra* to explore, as well as some spectacularly rugged stretches of coast between the beaches – many of which are far less crowded and developed than you might imagine.

Culturally, the country is littered with superb old buildings, from Roman aqueducts and Islamic palaces to Gothic cathedrals. Almost every second village has a medieval castle. Spain has been the home of some of the world's great artists – El Greco, Goya, Dalí, Picasso and more – and has museums and galleries to match. The country vibrates with music of every kind.

The more you travel in Spain, the bigger it seems to get. It's surprising just how many Spains there are. Cool, damp, green Galicia is a world away from hot, dry Andalucía, home of flamenco and bullfighting. Fertile Catalunya in the north-east, with its separate language and independent spirit, seems a different nation from the Castilian heartland on the austere *meseta* at the centre of the Iberian Peninsula. Once you leave the beaten track, it can take as long to wind your way through a couple of remote valleys and over the sierra between them as it would to travel the highway or railway from Madrid to Barcelona. All you need to do is get out there and enjoy it!

Facts about Spain

HISTORY

The ancestors of today's Spaniards included Stone Age hunters from Africa, Phoenicians, Visigoths from the Balkans, Berber tribes from Morocco, Jews and Arabs from the Middle East, and numerous other European peoples. The ancestors of a good half of the people of the Americas today – and others dotted across the rest of the globe – were Spaniards. The key to this ebb and flow of peoples, cultures and empires is Spain's location: on both the Mediterranean Sea and the Atlantic Ocean, in Europe yet a stone's throw from Africa and as near to America as anywhere in the Old World. This pivotal position has entangled Spain in the affairs of half the world and half the world in Spain's.

In the Beginning

Caves throughout the country tell us plenty about Spain's earliest inhabitants. The most impressive, at Altamira near Santander, date from around 12,000 BC. Altamira's sophisticated, colourful paintings of bison, stag, boar and horses show confident brush strokes and realistic perspective – not primitive efforts!

Altamira was part of the Magdalenian hunting culture of southern France and northern Spain, a Palaeolithic (Old Stone Age) culture that lasted from around 20,000 BC to the end of the Ice Age about 8000 BC. One of the many theories about the origins of the Basque people of northern Spain and south-western France is that they are descended from the Magdalenians.

But the story goes much further back. In recent years archaeologists have discovered two lots of human bone fragments reckoned to be older than any others found in Europe. Those found in 1994 in the Sierra de Atapuerca near Burgos are widely accepted to be about 780,000 years old and probably come from ancestors of the later Neanderthals. The second set of bones, from Orce near Granada and Cueva Victoria in Murcia, are reckoned to be the remains of meals eaten by giant hyenas 1.2 to 1.6 million years ago, although some experts are sceptical that there were people in Spain so long ago.

From the later Neanderthal era comes 'Gibraltar Woman', a skull from about 50,000 BC, which was found in 1848. Current thinking is that the Neanderthals were displaced in about 40,000 BC, during the last Ice Age, by waves of migrants of African origin. The Cueva de Nerja in Andalucía is one of many Spanish sites of these Cro-Magnons, the first real modern humans, who hunted mammoth, bison and reindeer. After the Ice Age, new peoples known as Iberians or proto-Berbers arrived, probably from North Africa. Their rock-shelter paintings of hunting and dancing survive on the east coast.

The Neolithic (New Stone Age) reached eastern Spain from Mesopotamia and Egypt about 6000 BC, bringing innovations such as the plough, crops, livestock raising, pottery, textiles and permanent villages. Out of this arose, between 3000 and 2000 BC, the country's first metalworking culture, based at Los Millares near Almería.

The beginnings of Spanish art – a detail from the 14,000-year-old paintings at Altamira

Spanish History at a Glance

BC

c 12,000 Stone Age hunters at Altamira, near Santander, paint some of Europe's most sophisticated cave art

c 3000-2000 Spain's first metalworking culture flourishes at the Copper Age site of Los Millares, near Almería

c 1900 El Argar, Almería province, becomes probably Spain's first Bronze Age settlement

c 1100-600 Phoenician traders, with colonies at Cádiz and elsewhere, influence the culture of western Andalucía, probably the Tartessos referred to by later writers as a source of fabulous riches; the Iron Age starts around 700

c 1000-500 Celts settle north of the Ebro, bringing iron technology to the north

c 600 Greek traders start to found colonies on the Mediterranean coast

237 Carthage invades the Iberian Peninsula

218 Rome defeats Carthage in the Second Punic War and begins a 600-year occupation of the Iberian Peninsula

1st century Rome organises the peninsula into three provinces: Baetica (capital: Córdoba), Lusitania (capital: Mérida) and Tarraconensis (capital: Tarragona)

AD

3rd century Christianity reaches Spain

3rd to 8th centuries Roman power wanes and a series of Germanic tribes invade the Iberian Peninsula, which culminates in rule by the Christian Visigoths from the 6th century until 711

711 Muslims invade the peninsula from North Africa, overrunning it within a few years, except for small areas in the Asturian mountains in the north

c 722 Christians score a victory over the Muslims at Covadonga in Asturias, the first success in the eight-centuries-long Reconquista (Reconquest) of the peninsula by Christians

756-929 The Emirate of Córdoba dominates the Muslim areas of the peninsula, known as Al-Andalus

929-1031 Under the Caliphate of Córdoba, Al-Andalus reaches its peak of power and cultural and scientific achievement; the caliphate collapses into civil war after 1008 and splits into dozens of *taifas* (small kingdoms)

1085 The northern Christian kingdom of Castilla captures Toledo

1091-1140s The Almoravids, a fanatical Muslim sect from North Africa, rule Al-Andalus

1137 The north-eastern kingdoms of Aragón and Catalunya unite to form a powerful new Christian state, the Kingdom of Aragón

1160-73 The Almohads, another North African Muslim sect, conquer Al-Andalus

1195 The Almohads rout Castilla's army at Alarcos, south of Toledo

1212 The combined armies of three Spanish Christian states (Castilla, Aragón and Navarra) rout the Almohads at Las Navas de Tolosa, Andalucía

1248 Sevilla falls to Fernando III of Castilla

1248-1492 The Nasrid Emirate of Granada, comprising about half of Andalucía, survives as the last Muslim state on the peninsula

1469 Isabel, heir to the Castilian throne, marries Fernando, heir to the Aragonese throne, uniting the peninsula's two most powerful Christian states

Spanish History at a Glance

1478 Isabel and Fernando, the Reyes Católicos (Catholic Monarchs), set up the Spanish Inquisition

1492 (January) Isabel and Fernando capture Granada, the last Muslim possession on the
peninsula

1492 (April) Isabel and Fernando expel Jews who refuse Christian baptism

1492 (October) Christopher Columbus, funded by the Catholic Monarchs, lands on the island
of Guanahaní, Bahamas, opening the way for Spanish conquest and colonisation of the
Americas

1500 Muslims revolt in Andalucía and are ordered to convert to Christianity or leave Spain

1512 Fernando annexes Navarra, uniting Spain under one rule

1517-56 Reign of Carlos I (also Holy Roman Emperor Charles V), who also ruled the Low
Countries, much of Central Europe and parts of Italy, France and Germany, involving
Spain in wars that absorbed much of the new wealth from the Americas

1556-98 Reign of Felipe II: Spain absorbs Portugal but loses Holland; the Spanish navy defeats
the Ottoman Turks at Lepanto (1571) but its 1588 Armada is routed by the English;
Madrid is made national capital (1561)

17th century Silver shipments from the Americas shrink and Spain enters economic decline;
Spain loses Portugal (1641)

1609-14 The *moriscos* (converted Muslims) are expelled from Spain

1702-13 War of the Spanish Succession: Spain loses possessions in Italy and the Low Countries (to Austria) and Gibraltar and Menorca (to Britain)

1746-88 Bourbon kings Fernando VI and Carlos III try to modernise Spain; industry in
Catalunya and the Basque Country prospers

1805 Spanish sea power is terminated when a Spanish-French fleet is defeated by Britain at
Trafalgar

1808 French troops occupy Spain: Napoleon installs his brother Joseph as King José I

1808-13 Spanish War of Independence (Peninsular War): Spanish guerrillas, with British and
Portuguese support, drive out the French

1812 The liberal Cádiz Constitution proclaims sovereignty of the people, but is soon revoked
by the conservative Fernando VII (1814-33)

1813-25 Most of Spain's American colonies win independence

1833-39 First Carlist War: liberals defeat conservatives and northern regional rebels

1868 Septembrina Revolution: liberals led by General Juan Prim overthrow Queen Isabel II

late 1860s Anarchist ideas reach Spain and soon gain a wide following among marginalised
industrial workers and peasants

1872-76 Second Carlist War: a three-way affair between liberals and two factions of conservatives backing rival claimants to the throne

> **1873** First Republic: liberals declare Spain a federal republic of 17 states, resulting in
> chaos and restoration of the monarchy

> **1876** A new constitution recognises both the monarchy and parliament

1888 The UGT, the powerful socialist union, is formed

Late 19th century Strong Catalan and Basque separatist movements emerge

1898 Spanish-American War: Spain loses its last overseas possessions (Cuba, Puerto Rico,
Guam and the Philippines)

Spanish History at a Glance

1909 The 'Tragic Week' in Barcelona: a general strike turns into a frenzy of violence.

1910 The CNT, the powerful anarchist union, is formed

1917 A general strike is crushed by the army; the anarchist and socialist movements grow; political violence escalates.

1923-30 Mild dictatorship of General Miguel Primo de Rivera

1931 King Alfonso XIII goes into exile

1931-36 Second Republic

> **1931-33** A left-centre government outrages Catholics, gives Catalunya autonomy and introduces universal suffrage
>
> **1933-36** Under a right-wing government, political violence spirals and a workers' take over in Asturias (1934) is viciously quashed by the military
>
> **1936 (February)** The left-wing Popular Front wins a general election; political violence continues and extremist groups grow

1936-39 Spanish Civil War: about 350,000 Spaniards are killed

> **1936 (July)** The Spanish garrison in Melilla in North Africa revolts against the Republi can government, starting the civil war
>
> **1936 (October)** General Francisco Franco is confirmed as leader of the rebels (Nation alists) who, with German and Italian support, control over half the country by the end of the year
>
> **1936 (November)-1939** Nationalists besiege communist-led Madrid
>
> **1937 (May)** Communists crush anarchists and Trotskyites during internecine Republi can fighting in Barcelona
>
> **1938 (February)** Franco repulses a Republican offensive in Aragón then moves east, cutting off Republican Barcelona and Valencia from each other
>
> **1938 (July)** The Nationalists defeat the Republicans' last big offensive, in the Ebro valley, resulting in 20,000 dead
>
> **1938 (September)** The USSR ceases to help the Republicans
>
> **1939 (January)** Nationalists enter Barcelona
>
> **1939 (March)** Nationalists enter Madrid
>
> **1939 (April)** Franco declares the civil war over

1939-75 The Franco dictatorship: after the civil war, Nationalist repression continues (an es timated 100,000 are killed or die in prison)

> **Late 1940s** A UN-sponsored trade boycott helps to turn these years into Spain's *años de hambre* (years of hunger)
>
> **1960s** Economic boom: industry and agriculture are modernised, while tourism takes off spectacularly

1975 Franco dies and is succeeded by King Juan Carlos I

1975-81 Juan Carlos' prime minister, Adolfo Suárez, engineers and consolidates a return to democracy; Spain becomes a parliamentary monarchy with no official religion

1982-96 Spain is governed by the centre-left PSOE party led by Felipe González, which in troduces a national health system, improves education and takes Spain into the EC (1986), bringing on an economic boom till 1991, but is eventually unseated by a slump and a series of scandals

1996 The centre-right PP party, led by José María Aznar, takes power

The Los Millares people's ability to smelt and shape local copper deposits was a big breakthrough in agricultural and military terms. The same era also saw the building of megalithic tombs (dolmens), made of large rocks, in many parts of the Iberian Peninsula's perimeter. The best examples are at Antequera in Andalucía.

The next big technological advance was bronze – an alloy of copper and tin, and stronger than copper. About 1900 BC El Argar in Almería province became probably the first Bronze Age settlement on the Iberian Peninsula.

Celts

From around 1000 to 500 BC, Celts (originally from Central Europe) and other tribes from beyond the Pyrenees started to settle north of the Río Ebro. In contrast to the dark-featured Iberians, the Celts were fair, drank beer and ate lard. The Celts and Iberians who merged on the *meseta* (the high tableland of central Spain) became the Celtiberians. Celts and Celtiberians typically lived in sizable hill fort towns called *castros*. The Celts introduced iron technology to the north about the same time the Phoenicians brought it to the south.

Phoenicians & Greeks

By about 1000 BC there was a flourishing culture in the lower Guadalquivir valley in Andalucía. The development of this and other societies in the south and east was influenced by Phoenician and, later, Greek traders, who exchanged oils, textiles, jewels and ivory for local copper, silver and tin. The Phoenicians, a Semitic people from present-day Lebanon, set up permanent trading colonies including Cádiz (which they called Gadir), Huelva (Onuba), Málaga (Malaca) and Almuñécar (Sexi). Cádiz's supposed founding date of 1100 BC may make it the oldest city in Europe. Greek settlements, which began around 600 BC, tended to be farther north on the Mediterranean coast. The main one was Emporion (Empúries), Catalunya.

These incomers brought the potter's wheel, writing, coinage, some musical instruments, the olive tree and vine, and domestic animals like the donkey and hen. Around 700 BC iron replaced bronze in the lower Guadalquivir valley. This Phoenician-influenced culture was very likely the fabled Tartessos, which later Greek, Roman and Biblical writers mythologised as a place of unimaginable wealth. No one knows whether Tartessos was a city or a state. If it was a city, it has vanished. Some believe it may lie beneath the delta of the Río Guadalquivir.

Carthaginians

From about the 6th century BC the Phoenicians and Greeks were pushed out of the western Mediterranean by Carthage, a former Phoenician colony in modern Tunisia. Cádiz became the Carthaginians' main Iberian settlement, but there was a flourishing colony on Ibiza too.

The Carthaginians came into conflict with the next rising Mediterranean power – Rome. After losing the First Punic War (264-241 BC) fought against Rome for control of Sicily, Carthage responded by invading the Iberian Peninsula under generals Hamilcar Barca, Hasdrubal and Hannibal. The first landing was in 237 BC.

The Second Punic War (218-201 BC) not only saw Hannibal march his elephants over the Alps towards Rome but also brought Roman legions to Spain to open up another theatre of war. Hannibal was eventually forced to retreat, finally being routed in North Africa in 202.

Romans

Though the Romans held sway on the peninsula for 600 years, it took them 200 years to subdue the fiercest of the local tribes.

The Basques in the north, though defeated, were never Romanised like the rest of Hispania, as the Romans called the peninsula. Legendary stands against the Romans included the eight-year revolt led by the shepherd-turned-guerrilla Virathius in the west and centre from around 150 BC and the siege of Numancia near Soria in 133 BC. Rome had to bring in its most illustrious generals to deal with these and other insubordinations.

By 50 AD most of the peninsula, particularly the south, had adopted the Roman way of life. This was the time of the Pax Romana, a long, prosperous period of stability. Hispania became urbanised and highly organised. The early Roman provinces were called Hispania Citerior and Hispania Ulterior, with their capitals at Carthago Nova (Cartagena) and Corduba (Córdoba), but in the 1st century BC they were reorganised into Baetica (most of present-day Andalucía plus southern Extremadura and south-western Castilla-La Mancha), with its capital at Corduba; Lusitania (Portugal and northern Extremadura), with its capital at Augusta Emerita (Mérida), the greatest Roman city on the peninsula; and Tarraconensis (the rest), with its capital at Tarraco (Tarragona).

Rome gave the peninsula a road system, aqueducts, theatres, temples, amphitheatres, circuses, baths and the basis of its legal system and languages. The Roman era also brought many Jews, who spread throughout the Mediterranean part of the empire, and Christianity, which probably came with soldiers from North Africa and merchants in the 3rd century AD, taking root first in Andalucía. Hispania gave Rome gold, silver, grain, wine, soldiers, emperors (Trajan, Hadrian and Theodosius) and even some of the greatest Latin literature – that of Seneca, Martial, Quintilian and Lucan. Another notable export was *garum*, a spicy sauce derived from fish and used as a seasoning. The finest of Spain's Roman ruins are at Empúries, Itálica, Mérida, Tarragona and Segovia.

The Pax Romana started to crack when two Germanic tribes, the Franks and the Alemanni, swept across the Pyrenees in the late 3rd century AD, causing devastation. The end came when the Huns arrived in Eastern Europe from Asia a century later. Germanic peoples displaced by the Huns moved west, among them the Suevi and Vandals, who overran the Iberian Peninsula around 410 AD.

Visigoths

Another Germanic people, the Visigoths, sacked Rome itself in 410 AD. Within a few years, however, the Visigoths had become Roman allies, being granted lands in southern Gaul (France) and fighting on the emperor's behalf against other barbarian invaders on the Iberian Peninsula. But in the 6th century the Franks pushed the Visigoths out of Gaul. The Visigoths penetrated more deeply into the Iberian Peninsula and Toledo became their capital.

The rule of the roughly 200,000 long-haired Visigoths, who had a penchant for gaudy jewellery, over the several million more sophisticated Hispano-Romans was precarious and undermined by strife among their own nobility. The Hispano-Roman nobles still ran the fiscal system and their anachronistic bishops were the senior figures in urban centres. Town life declined in quality under Visigothic rule.

Ties between the Visigoth monarchy and the Hispano-Romans were greatly strengthened in 587 AD, when King Reccared converted to orthodox Christianity from the Visigoths' Arian version which denied that Christ was identical with God. But the Visigoth kings still had to contend with regular revolts by nobles, bishops and others.

The Visigoths had no long-standing culture of their own and tended to ape Roman ways. A few Visigothic churches can be seen today in northern Spain. One at Baños de Cerrato near Palencia, dating from 661, is probably the oldest church in the country.

The Muslim Conquest

By 700, with famine and disease in Toledo, strife among the aristocracy and chaos throughout the peninsula, the Visigothic kingdom was falling apart. This paved the way for the Muslim invasion of 711, which set Spain's destiny quite apart from that of the rest of Europe.

Following the death of Mohammed in 632, Arabs had spread through the Middle East and North Africa, taking Islam with them. If you believe the myth, they were ushered on to the Iberian Peninsula by the sexual exploits of the last Visigoth king, Roderick. Ballads and chronicles written long after the event relate how Roderick seduced (to put it mildly) young Florinda, the daughter of Count Julian, the Visigothic governor of Ceuta in North Africa, and how her father sought revenge by approaching the Muslims with a plan to invade Spain. In dull fact Julian probably just wanted outside help in a struggle for the Visigothic throne.

In 711 Musa, the Arab governor of northwest Africa, ordered the governor of Tangier, Tariq ibn Ziyad, across the Strait of Gibraltar. Tariq landed at Gibraltar with around 10,000 men, mostly Berbers (indigenous North Africans). He had some of Roderick's Visigoth rivals as allies. Roderick's army was decimated, probably near the Río Guadalete in Andalucía, and he is thought to have drowned while fleeing the scene. Visigothic survivors fled north.

Within a few years the Muslims had conquered the rest of the Iberian Peninsula, except small areas in the Asturian mountains in the north. In many places they were welcomed by Jews and slaves, who had been badly treated under Visigothic rule. The Muslims even pushed on over the Pyrenees, but were driven back by the Franks.

Muslim Spain

The Muslims (often referred to as Moors) were the dominant force on the Iberian Peninsula for nearly four centuries, a potent force for 170 years after that and a lesser one for a further 250 years. Between wars and rebellions, Al-Andalus, the name given to Muslim territory on the peninsula, developed the most highly cultured society of medieval Europe.

Al-Andalus' frontiers were constantly shifting as the Christians strove to regain territory in the stuttering 800-year Reconquista (Reconquest). But up to the mid-11th century the frontier lay across the north of the Iberian Peninsula, roughly from just south of Barcelona to northern Portugal, with a protrusion up to the central Pyrenees. Al-Andalus also suffered internal conflicts and at times Muslims and Christians even struck up alliances in the course of quarrels with their own co-religionists.

Muslim political power and cultural developments centred initially on Córdoba (756-1031), then Sevilla (c 1040-1248) and lastly Granada (1248-1492). In these cities the Muslims built beautiful palaces, mosques and gardens, established bustling markets (zocos) and opened universities and public baths. They developed the Hispano-Roman agricultural base by improving irrigation and introducing new fruits and crops (oranges, lemons, peaches, sugar cane, rice and more).

Though military campaigns against the northern Christians could be bloodthirsty affairs, Al-Andalus' rulers allowed freedom of worship to Jews and Christians (mozárabes, or Mozarabs) under their rule. Jews mostly flourished, but Christians had to pay a special tax, so most either converted to Islam (to be known as muladíes, or muwallads) or left for the Christian north.

The Muslim settlers themselves were not a homogeneous group: beneath the Arab ruling class was a larger group of Berbers and tension between these two groups broke into Berber rebellion numerous times.

The Arabs and Berbers didn't seem to bring many women with them, and before long Muslim and local blood merged. This applied as much to the rulers as the ruled, for, as well as the acquisition of women for royal harems, there was frequent intermarriage with the Christian royalty and aristocracy of the north – for tribute, appeasement or even alliance.

The Cordoban Emirate & Caliphate

Initially Muslim Spain was a province of the Emirate of Ifriqiya (North Africa), part of the Caliphate of Damascus which ruled the Muslim world. In 750 the Omayyad caliphal dynasty was overthrown by a rival clan, the Abbasids, who shifted the caliphate to Baghdad. But an Omayyad survivor managed to establish himself in 756 in Córdoba as the independent emir of Al-Andalus, Abd ar-Rahman I. He began the construction of the Córdoba Mezquita (Mosque), one of the world's greatest Muslim monuments. Most of Al-Andalus was more or less unified under Cordoban rule for some fairly long periods. In 929 Abd ar-Rahman III bestowed on himself the title caliph, launching the Caliphate of Córdoba (929-1031), during which Al-Andalus reached its peak of power and lustre.

At this time Córdoba was the biggest and most dazzling city in Western Europe, thriving on a productive agriculture sector and the work of its skilled artisans. Astronomy, medicine, mathematics and botany flourished and one of the greatest Muslim libraries was established in the city. Abd ar-Rahman III's court was frequented by Jewish, Arab and Christian scholars.

Later in the 10th century the fearsome Cordoban general Al-Mansour (or Almanzor) terrorised the Christian north with 50-odd forays in 20 years. He destroyed the cathedral at Santiago de Compostela in north-western Spain in 997 and forced Christian slaves to carry its doors and bells to Córdoba, where they were incorporated into the great mosque. But after the death of Al-Mansour's son in 1008, rival claimants to the caliphate indulged in a devastating civil war. In 1031 the caliphate broke up into dozens of *taifas* (small kingdoms), with Sevilla, Granada, Toledo and Zaragoza among the most powerful.

Almoravids & Almohads Political unity was restored to Al-Andalus by the Almoravid invasion of 1091. The Almoravids, a fanatical Muslim sect of Saharan nomads who had conquered North Africa, were initially invited on to the Iberian Peninsula to help the Sevilla taifa against the growing Christian threat from the north. Seventy years later another Berber sect, the Almohads, invaded the peninsula after overthrowing the Almoravids in Morocco. Both sects soundly defeated the Christian armies they encountered.

Under the Almoravids and the Almohads, religious intolerance sent Christian refugees fleeing north. But in time both mellowed in their adopted territory and Almohad rule saw a revival of the cultural achievements that the Almoravids had interrupted in Sevilla. In Córdoba the philosopher Averroës (1126-98) wrote commentaries on Aristotle, trying to reconcile science with religious faith, which had great influence on European Christian thought in the 13th and 14th centuries.

The Nasrid Emirate of Granada Almohad power eventually disintegrated in the face of internal disputes and Christian advances. After Sevilla fell to the Christians in 1248, Muslim territory on the Iberian Peninsula was reduced to the Emirate of Granada, comprising about half of modern Andalucía and ruled from the lush Alhambra palace by the Nasrid dynasty. Granada saw Muslim Spain's final cultural flowering, prospering with an influx of refugees from the Reconquista. It reached its peak in the 14th century under Yousouf I and Mohammed V, both of whom contributed to the splendours of the Alhambra.

Granada survived by playing off rival Spanish Christian states and Muslim Morocco against each other. Christian armies eventually started nibbling at its borders in the 15th century.

Muslim Legacy The Muslims left a deep imprint on Spain – and not just in terms of the palaces, castles and mosques which rank among its greatest monuments today. For one thing, many Spaniards today are partly descended from the Muslims. For another, the narrow, labyrinthine street plan of many old villages and towns is of Muslim origin. Muslim crafts and architectural tastes, too, were adopted by Christians both inside and outside Al-Andalus. The Spanish language is rich in words of Arabic origin – including *arroz* (rice), *alcalde* (mayor), *naranja* (orange) and *azúcar* (sugar). Many foods eaten in Spain today were introduced by the Muslims. Many churches are converted mosques. And so on.

It was also through Al-Andalus that much of the learning of ancient Greece was transmitted to Christian Europe. Arabs absorbed the Greek scientific and philosophical traditions in the eastern Mediterranean, and there were two meeting points in Europe between the Islamic and Christian worlds where this knowledge could find its way north – one was southern Italy, the other was Al-Andalus.

The Reconquista

The Christian reconquest of the peninsula began about 722 at Covadonga and ended with the fall of Granada in 1492. It was a stuttering affair, conducted by a tangled sequence of emerging, merging and demerging Christian states that were as often at war with each other as with the Muslims. But the Muslims were gradually pushed south as the northern kingdoms of Asturias, León, Navarra, Castilla and Aragón developed and ultimately forged a sufficiently united front to oust Muslim rule from the peninsula.

Santiago Matamoros An essential ingredient in the Reconquista was the cult of Santiago (St James), one of the 12 apostles. In 813, strange celestial happenings were reported at the saint's supposed tomb in Galicia. The town of Santiago de Compostela grew around the church that was built on the spot, eventually to become the third most popular medieval Christian pilgrimage goal after Rome and Jerusalem. Visions of Santiago 'appeared' to Christian leaders before forays against the Muslims and he became the inspiration and special protector of soldiers in the Reconquista, earning the sobriquet 'Matamoros' (Moorslayer). Today he is the patron saint of Spain.

The First 500 Years – the Rise of Castilla Covadonga lies in the Picos de Europa in Asturias, where Visigothic nobles took refuge after the Muslim conquest. Christian versions of what happened there tell of a small band of fighters under their leader, Pelayo, crushing an enormous force of Muslims; Muslim accounts make it a rather less important skirmish. Whatever the facts of Covadonga, by 757 Christians occupied nearly a quarter of the peninsula. Progress thereafter was a lot slower.

The Asturian kingdom eventually moved its capital to León, which spearheaded the Reconquista until the Christians were set on the defensive by Al-Mansour in the 10th century. Castilla, originally a small principality in the east of the kingdom of León, developed as the dominant Reconquista force. Taking its name from the castles built by its Christian conquerors, Castilla grew from the 11th century as hardy adventurers set up towns in the no-man's-land of the Duero basin, spurred on by land grants in conquered territory and other rights and privileges *(fueros)*. The capture of Toledo by Alfonso VI of Castilla in 1085 led the Sevilla Muslims to call in the Almoravids.

Alfonso I of Aragón, on the southern flank of the Pyrenees, led the counterattack against the Almoravids, taking Zaragoza in 1118. After his death Aragón was united through royal marriage with Catalunya, creating a formidable new Christian power block (known to history as the Kingdom of Aragón although Catalunya was the stronger partner). Portugal, too, emerged as an independent Christian kingdom in the 12th century.

Castilla suffered a terrible defeat by the Almohads at Alarcos, south of Toledo, in 1195, but in 1212 the combined Christian armies of Castilla, Aragón and Navarra routed a large Almohad force at Las Navas de Tolosa in Andalucía. This was the beginning of the end for Al-Andalus.

León took the key towns of Extremadura in 1229 and 1230; Aragón took the Balearic Islands and Valencia in the 1230s; Fernando III El Santo (the Saint) of Castilla took Córdoba in 1236 and Sevilla (with help from the rival Muslim state of Granada) in

1248; and Portugal expelled the Muslims in 1249. The sole surviving Muslim state on the peninsula was the Emirate of Granada.

The Lull (1250-1479) Fernando III's son, Alfonso X El Sabio (the Learned; 1252-84), proclaimed Castilian the official language of his realm. At Toledo he gathered around him scholars regardless of their religion, particularly Jews who knew Arabic and Latin. Muslims who stayed on in Christian territory were known as *mudéjares*. Many from western Andalucía were expelled and sent to Granada or North Africa, after a 1264 rebellion in Jerez de la Frontera sparked by new taxes and rules requiring them to celebrate Christian feasts and live in ghettoes. Alfonso was plagued by further uprisings and plots, even from within his own family. This unrest continued in Castilla until the 15th century, with the nobility repeatedly challenging the crown.

The late 13th and the 14th centuries were a time of cultural malaise in Castilla, although architecture, the great art of the late Middle Ages, was an exception, reaching its heights in great cathedrals such as those at Toledo and León. This was also an era of growing intolerance towards the Jews and Genoese who were taking over Castilian commerce and finance, while the Castilians were preoccupied with their low effort-high profit wool production. Jews were blamed for economic crises and even for the Black Death in the mid-14th century. Anti-Jewish feeling culminated in pogroms around the peninsula in the 1390s.

Aragón, meanwhile, looked outwards to the Mediterranean, taking Sardinia and Sicily, from where Catalan soldiers went off to fight the Ottoman Turks.

Both Castilla and Aragón laboured under a series of ineffectual monarchs from the late 14th century until the time of Isabel and Fernando, whose marriage in Segovia Castle in 1469 would merge the two kingdoms. Isabel succeeded to the Castilian throne in 1474 and Fernando to Aragón's in 1479, both coming through civil wars to

Isabel I of Castille: her marriage to Fernando II of Aragón created an unbeatable team

claim their inheritances. The joint rule of the Reyes Católicos (Catholic Monarchs), as they are known, dates from 1479.

The Fall of Granada After Emir Abu al-Hasan of Granada refused in 1476 to pay any more tribute to Castilla, Isabel and Fernando launched the final crusade of the Reconquista in 1482, with an army largely funded by Jewish loans and the Catholic church.

By now Granada's rulers had retreated to a pleasure-loving existence in the Alhambra and were riven by internal feuds. Matters degenerated into a confused civil war, of which the Castilians took full advantage. Fernando and Isabel entered Granada, after a long siege, on 2 January 1492 – an appropriate start for what turned out to be the most momentous year in Spanish history.

The surrender terms were fairly generous to Boabdil, the last emir, who got the Alpujarras valleys south of Granada and 30,000 gold coins. The remaining Muslims were promised respect for their religion, culture and property, but this didn't last long.

The Catholic Monarchs

The pious Isabel and the Machiavellian Fernando were an unbeatable team. The war against Granada was just one of several steps they took to unify Spain. They checked the power of the Castilian nobility, granting Andalucian land to their supporters and excluding aristocrats from their administration. They also reformed a corrupt, immoral clergy. By the time Fernando died in 1516 (12 years after Isabel) all of Spain was under single rule for the first time since Visigothic days.

Jews & the Inquisition The urge for unity was not just territorial. The Catholic Monarchs revived the almost extinct Inquisition – founded earlier to deal with heretics in France – to root out those who didn't practise Christianity as the Catholic church wished them to. The Spanish Inquisition focused most of all on *conversos*, Jews who had converted to Christianity, accusing many of continuing to practise Judaism in secret. Despite Fernando's part-Jewish background and Jewish loans for the Granada war, Jews were considered Muslim allies on top of their other problems. The Inquisition was responsible for perhaps 12,000 deaths over 300 years, 2000 of them in the 1480s.

Under the influence of Grand Inquisitor Tomás de Torquemada, Isabel and Fernando in April 1492 ordered the expulsion from their territories of all Jews who refused Christian baptism. Around 50,000 to 100,000 Jews converted, but some 200,000 – the first Sephardic Jews – left for other Mediterranean destinations. The bankrupt monarchy seized all unsold Jewish property. A talented middle class was decimated.

Persecution of the Muslims Cardinal Cisneros, Isabel's confessor and overseer of the Inquisition, tried to eradicate Muslim culture. Given the task of converting the Muslims of the former Granada emirate, he carried out forced mass baptisms, had Islamic books burnt and banned the Arabic language. This, combined with seizures of

Muslim land, sparked a revolt in Andalucía in 1500. Afterwards, Muslims were ordered to convert to Christianity or leave. Most (an estimated 300,000) underwent baptism and stayed, to be known as *moriscos* (converted Muslims), but their conversion was barely skin-deep and they never assimilated. The moriscos were finally expelled between 1609 and 1614.

Christopher Columbus In April 1492 the Catholic Monarchs granted Christopher Columbus (Cristóbal Colón to Spaniards) funds for his long-desired voyage across the Atlantic in search of a new trade route to the Orient. Isabel and Fernando were motivated by the need to fill empty coffers and the possibility of more Christian conversions.

Columbus set off from Palos de la Frontera (Andalucía) on 3 August with three small ships and 120 men. They stopped at the Canary Islands, then sailed west for 31 days, sighting no land. The rebellious crew gave Columbus two more days. He sighted the island of Guanahaní (Bahamas), which he named San Salvador, went on to discover Cuba and Hispaniola and returned to a hero's welcome from the monarchs in Barcelona eight months after his departure.

Columbus made three more voyages, founding Santo Domingo on Hispaniola, discovering Jamaica, Trinidad and other Caribbean islands, and reaching the mouth of the Orinoco and the coast of Central

Columbus' reception with the Reyes Católicos, as shown in Antonio Susillo's 1893 relief

America. But he proved an unsuccessful administrator and was shipped home as a prisoner from his third voyage, though released on his return. He died poor, and apparently still believing he had reached Asia, in Valladolid in 1506.

After Isabel Fernando entangled Spain in European affairs by marrying his and Isabel's four children into the royal families of Portugal, Burgundy and England and the powerful Habsburg family of Central Europe. (The English connection failed when the youngest, Catalina, or Catherine of Aragón, was cast aside by Henry VIII.) The early death of two children left the third, Princess Juana, heir to the Castilian throne when Isabel died in 1504. Juana's husband, Felipe El Hermoso (the Handsome), was heir to the Low Countries and to the Habsburg lands in Central Europe. But Juana, dubbed Juana la Loca (the Mad), was unfit to rule and, when Felipe died soon after, Fernando took over as regent of Castilla until his own death in 1516.

The Habsburgs

Carlos I In 1517, 17-year-old Carlos I, son of Juana la Loca and Felipe El Hermoso, came from Flanders to take up his Spanish inheritance. In 1519 Carlos also succeeded to the Habsburg lands in Austria and managed to win election as Holy Roman Emperor (as Charles V). Carlos now ruled more of Europe than anyone since the 9th century – all of Spain, the Low Countries, Austria, several Italian states and parts of France and Germany – plus the Spanish colonies in the Caribbean and Panama. To these he would add more of Central Europe and big slices of the Americas.

Carlos spent only 16 years of his 40-year reign in Spain. At first the Spanish did not care for a king who spoke no Castilian, nor for his appropriating their wealth. Castilian cities revolted in 1520-21 (the Guerra de las Comunidades, or War of the Communities) but were crushed. Eventually the Spanish came round to him, at least for his strong stance against emerging Protestantism and

his learning of Castilian. Under Carlos, Spain could have developed into an early industrial power, but he spent the bulk of the monarchy's new American wealth on an endless series of European conflicts. War weary, Carlos abdicated shortly before his death in 1556, dividing his territories between his son Felipe and his brother Fernando. Felipe got the lion's share, including Spain, the Low Countries and the American possessions.

The American Empire Carlos I's reign saw Spain take over vast tracts of the American mainland. Ruthless but brilliant conquistadors such as Hernán Cortés (who subdued the Aztec empire with a small band of adventurers in 1519-21) and Francisco Pizarro (who did the same to the Inca empire in 1531-33) were, with their odd mix of brutality, bravery, gold lust and piety, the natural successors to the crusaders of the Reconquista.

By 1600 Spain controlled Florida, all the biggest Caribbean islands, nearly all of present-day Mexico and Central America and a strip of South America from present-day Venezuela to Argentina. The new colonies sent huge cargoes of silver, gold and other riches back to Spain, where the crown was entitled to one-fifth of the bullion (the *quinto real*, or royal fifth). Sevilla enjoyed a monopoly on this trade and grew into one of Europe's richest cities by 1600.

Whether the Spanish empire was any more or less greedy and cruel than comparable enterprises is a topic of much pointless debate. The conquistadors sprang from one war culture and confronted others – which also indulged in practices such as slavery and mass human sacrifice. Many Spaniards considered the conquest to have as much a moral as an economic and political mission – that of winning new Christian souls. The clergy managed to spare the indigenous people some of the worst excesses of other colonists. At the instigation of the friar Bartolomé de Las Casas, Spain enacted laws that gave some protection to the indigenous people. Decimation of the native populations was at least as much a result of new diseases as of colonial oppression.

Felipe II Carlos I's son, Felipe II (1556-98), presided over the zenith of Spanish power. His reign is a study in contradictions. He enlarged the overseas empire but lost wealthy Holland to a long drawn-out rebellion. He thrashed the Ottoman Turks, Spain's great Mediterranean rivals, at the sea battle of Lepanto (Greece) in 1571, but saw his Spanish Armada in 1588 routed by England. He received greater flows of silver than ever from the Americas, but went bankrupt. He was a fanatical Catholic who spurred the Inquisition to new persecutions, yet readily allied Spain with Protestant England against Catholic France when it suited Spain's interests.

When Felipe claimed Portugal on its king's death in 1580, he not only united the Iberian Peninsula but also Europe's two great overseas empires. But there was no plan to absorb the new wealth. The Castilian gentry's disdain for commerce and industry allowed foreign merchants to dominate trade. Money that didn't find its way into foreign pockets or wasn't owed for European wars went towards building churches, palaces and monasteries. Spain, it was said, had discovered the magic formula for turning silver into stone.

One of Felipe's most lasting decisions, made in 1561, was to turn the minor country town of Madrid into a new capital from which to mould his kingdom.

The 17th Century Under a trio of ineffectual kings, Spain saw its chickens come home to roost. Felipe III (1598-1621) preferred hunting to ruling and left government to the self-seeking Duke of Lerma. Felipe IV (1621-65) concentrated on a long line of mistresses and handed over affairs of state to Count-Duke Olivares, who tried bravely but retired a broken man in 1643. Spain fought unsuccessful wars with France and Holland, lost Portugal and faced revolts in Sicily, Naples and Catalunya. Silver ship-

ments from the Americas shrank disastrously. The feeble Carlos II (1665-1700), who liked picking strawberries and was unable to produce children, bequeathed only the War of the Spanish Succession.

The gentry and the church, which was entitled to one-tenth of all production, led a comfortable existence, but for most Spaniards life was decidedly underprivileged.

The Cultural Golden Age Mid-16th to late 17th century Spain was like a gigantic artisans' workshop, in which architecture, sculpture, painting and metalwork consumed around 5% of the nation's income. The age was immortalised on canvas by artists such as Velázquez, El Greco, Zurbarán, Murillo and Ribera, and in words by Miguel de Cervantes, the mystics Santa Teresa of Ávila and San Juan de la Cruz (St John of the Cross) and the prolific playwright Lope de Vega.

The 18th Century

Under the new Bourbon dynasty, still in place today, the 18th century saw limited recovery from the decline of the 17th.

Felipe V Carlos II bequeathed his throne to his young relative Felipe V (1701-46), who also happened to be second in line to the French throne. The Austrian emperor Leopold, however, wanted to see his son Charles, a nephew of Carlos II, on the Spanish throne. The resulting War of the Spanish Succession (1702-13) was a contest for the balance of power in Europe, involving England, Holland and even a rebellious Catalunya. In the end Felipe V held on to Spain but renounced his right to the French throne. Spain lost several Italian states and its last possessions in the Low Countries to Austria, and Gibraltar and Menorca to Britain.

Felipe, with many French and Italian advisers, instituted reforms in economy and government, but land reform proved impossible. Two-thirds of the land was in the hands of the nobility and church and was underproductive, and large numbers of males, from nobles to vagrants, were unwilling to work.

This was the age of the Enlightenment, but Spain's powerful church and Inquisition were at odds with the rationalism that trickled in from France.

Fernando VI & Carlos III Fernando VI (1746-59) replaced all foreign advisers with Spaniards, strengthened the navy and ended the Inquisition's dreaded *autos de fe* (elaborate execution ceremonies). The economy was on an upturn largely due to a revitalised Catalunya and the Basque shipbuilding industry. But agricultural Castilla and Andalucía were left behind, unable to increase yields due to a lack of land reforms.

Carlos III (1759-88) was an enlightened despot. He expelled the backward-looking Jesuits, transformed Madrid, sent a new road system spoking out to the provinces and tried to improve agriculture. But food shortages fuelled unrest among the masses.

French Revolution & Spanish War of Independence (Peninsular War)

Carlos IV (1788-1808) was dominated by his Italian wife, Maria Luisa of Parma; she hooked up with a handsome royal guard called Manuel Godoy, who became chief minister. This unholy trinity was ill suited to coping with the crisis presented by the French Revolution of 1789.

When Louis XVI of France (Carlos' cousin) was guillotined in 1793, Spain declared war on France. Two years later, with France's Reign of Terror spent, Godoy made peace, pledging military support for France against Britain. In 1805 a combined Spanish-French navy was beaten by the British fleet under Nelson off Cape Trafalgar (between Cádiz and Gibraltar). This put an end to Spanish sea power and sealed Spain's colonial decline.

Two years later, Napoleon and Godoy agreed to divide Britain's ally Portugal between them. French forces poured into Spain, supposedly on the way to northern

Portugal. By 1808 this had become a French occupation of Spain. The king, queen and Godoy fled. Carlos abdicated in favour of his son Fernando. Napoleon then summoned the royal family and Godoy to Bayonne (France) and forced Fernando to abdicate in favour of Carlos, who was then made to abdicate to let Napoleon's brother Joseph Bonaparte (José I) take the crown.

In Madrid crowds revolted, and countrywide the Spanish populace took up arms in guerrilla fashion, reinforced by British and Portuguese forces led by the Duke of Wellington. By 1812, Napoleon's attention was diverted to his Russian campaign and the French withdrew in large numbers. They were finally expelled following their defeat at Vitoria in the Basque Country in 1813.

The 19th Century

Liberals vs Conservatives During the war, a national Cortes (Parliament), meeting at Cádiz in 1812, had drawn up a new liberal constitution which incorporated many of the principles of the American and French prototypes. This upset the church and monarchy, setting the pattern for a contest lasting most of the 19th century between conservatives, who liked the status quo, and liberals, who wanted vaguely democratic reforms.

Fernando VII (1814-33) took the throne to popular acclaim but revoked the Cádiz constitution, persecuted liberal opponents, re-established the Inquisition and invited the Jesuits back. In 1820 Colonel Rafael de Riego made the first of the 19th century's many *pronunciamientos* (pronouncements of military rebellion), in the name of liberalism. But French troops put Fernando back on the throne in 1823. Severe reprisals and corrupt government drastically cut the king's popularity before his death.

Meanwhile the restless American colonies had taken advantage of Spain's problems to strike out on their own. By 1824 only Cuba and Puerto Rico remained Spanish.

First Carlist War Fernando's dithering over the succession to the throne resulted in the First Carlist War (1833-39), between supporters of his brother Don Carlos and his infant daughter Isabel. Don Carlos was supported by the church, other conservatives, and regional rebels in the Basque Country, Navarra, Catalunya and Aragón – together known as the Carlists. The Isabel faction had the support of liberals and the army.

During the war violent anticlericalism emerged. Religious orders were closed and, in the Disamortisation of 1836, church property and lands were seized and auctioned off by the government. As usual, only the wealthy benefited. The army emerged victorious.

Isabel II In 1843 Isabel, now all of 13, declared herself Queen Isabel II (1843-68). One achievement of sorts during her inept reign was the creation of a rural police force, the Guardia Civil, mainly to protect the wealthy in the bandit-ridden countryside. There was an upturn in the economy, with progress in business, banking, mining and railways, plus some reforms in education, but the benefits accrued to few. Eventually radical liberals, and discontented soldiers led by General Juan Prim, overthrew Isabel in the Septembrina Revolution of 1868.

Second Carlist War & First Republic
Spain still wanted a monarch and eventually Amadeo of Savoy, a son of the Italian king and known for his liberal sentiments, accepted the job in 1870. The aristocracy, who opposed Amadeo, split into two camps: one favouring Isabel II's teenage son Alfonso, the other backing Don Carlos' grandson Carlos. Thus began the three-way Second Carlist War (1872-76).

With the Carlists holding most of the north, Barcelona a law unto itself and anarchism making strides in Andalucía, Amadeo abandoned Spain in 1873. The liberal-dominated Cortes immediately proclaimed Spain a federal republic of 17 states. But this First Republic, riven by internal divisions and unable to keep a grip on the regions, lasted only 11 months. In the end the army, no longer liberal, put Alfonso on the throne as Alfonso XII (1874-85), in a coalition with the church and landowners. The 1876 constitution, recognising both monarchy and parliament, produced a sequence of orderly changes of government *(turnos)* between supposed conservatives and liberals. Little actually separated their political persuasions and electoral rigging was the norm.

Social Unrest

The 1890s brought economic growth, improved schools and rumblings among the industrial working class. In the humiliating Spanish-American War of 1898, Spain lost the last of its once vast overseas possessions – Cuba, Puerto Rico, the Philippines and Guam.

Alfonso XIII (1902-1930) was initially sensitive to the liberal mood but became fed up with constitutional government and started interfering. There were 33 different governments during his reign. His friends were among the military, church and wealthy landowners.

At the other end of the social scale, a powder keg was forming. Industry had brought both prosperity and squalid slums to cities which attracted large-scale migration from the country: Barcelona, Madrid and some Basque cities. In the country, the old problems of underproduction and land ownership by the few persisted. Many Spaniards left for Latin America. The working class increasingly gravitated towards Marxism and anarchism. The wealthy, powerful church had failed them.

Anarchism The anarchist ideas of the Russian Mikhail Bakunin reached Spain in the 1860s and gained support rapidly. Bakunin advocated replacing the state and church with a free society in which people would voluntarily cooperate with each other – a state of affairs to be prepared for by strikes, sabotage and revolts and ultimately achieved by a spontaneous, angry revolution of the oppressed. In the 1890s and 1900s anarchists bombed Barcelona's Liceu opera house, assassinated two prime ministers and detonated a bomb at Alfonso XIII's wedding in 1906 and killed 24 people.

Anarchism appealed to the peasants of Andalucía, Aragón, Catalunya and the north-west and to workers living in appalling conditions in Barcelona and other cities. In 1910, the anarchist unions were organised by the syndicalists (anarchist trade unionists) into the powerful CNT (Confederación Nacional del Trabajo, or National Confederation of Work). The syndicalists saw organisation of labour as the way to an anarchist society, their main weapon being the general strike.

Socialism This grew more slowly than anarchism because of its strategy of steady change through parliamentary processes. Spanish socialists rejected Soviet-style communism. The UGT (Unión General de Trabajadores, or General Union of Workers), established in 1888, was moderate and disciplined. Its appeal was greatest in Madrid and Bilbao, where people were fearful of Catalan separatism. Its sharpest growth was between 1906 and 1910.

Regionalism Parallel with the rise of the left was the growth of Basque and Catalan separatism. In Catalunya, this was led by big business interests. Basque nationalism emerged in the 1890s largely due to the perceived threat to Basque identity from the many Castilians who had flocked to work in Basque industries.

Semana Trágica & General Strikes
When in 1909 Berbers wiped out a contingent of Spanish troops in Morocco, part of which was a Spanish protectorate, the government called up Catalan reserves to go to Morocco. The result was the so-called Semana Trágica (Tragic Week) in Barcelona, which began with a general strike and turned into a frenzy of violence. The government responded by executing many workers.

Spain stayed neutral during WWI (1914-18) and enjoyed an economic boom. When the king and the right refused widespread demands for parliamentary reforms in 1917, a general strike ensued but was later crushed by the army. Anarchist and socialist numbers grew, inspired by the Russian Revolution, and political violence and general mayhem continued, especially in lawless Barcelona.

Primo de Rivera's Dictatorship
In 1921, 10,000 Spanish soldiers were killed by a small force of Berbers at Anual in Morocco. The finger of blame was pointed at King Alfonso, who had intervened to select the Spanish commander for the Moroccan campaign. But just as a report on the event was to be submitted to parliament in 1923, General Miguel Primo de Rivera, an eccentric Andalucian aristocrat, led an army rising in support of the king, then launched his own mild six-year dictatorship.

Primo was a centralist who censored the press and upset intellectuals but gained the cooperation of the socialist UGT. Anarchists went underground. Primo founded new industries, improved roads, made the trains run on time and built dams and power plants. But, facing an economic downturn following the Wall Street crash and discontent in the army, Alfonso eventually took the chance to return to dismiss him.

The Second Republic (1931-36)
Alfonso had brought the monarchy into too much disrepute to last long himself. When a new republican movement scored sweeping victories in municipal elections in 1931, the king left for exile in Italy. The Second Republic that followed was an idealistic, tumultuous period which polarised Spain and ended in civil war.

The Left in Charge (1931-33) La Niña Bonita (the Pretty Child), as the Second Republic was called by its supporters, was welcomed by leftists and the poor masses, but conservatives were alarmed. Strife began within a month of the king's departure. In Navarra a new Carlist pretender, Don Jaime, called on anti-Republicans. There were church burnings and lootings, mostly initiated by anarchists but also by those in the pay of the right.

Elections during 1931 brought in a government composed of socialists led by Francisco Largo Caballero, the so-called Radicals (actually more like centrists) led by Alejandro Lerroux and the Republican Action Party led by Manuel Azaña. The Cortes contained few workers and no-one from the anarchist CNT, which continued with strikes and violence to bring on the revolution.

A new constitution in December 1931 outraged Catholics: it ended Catholicism's status as the official religion, disbanded the Jesuits, stopped government payment of priests' salaries, legalised divorce and banned clerical orders from teaching. The constitution gave autonomy-minded Catalunya its own parliament in return for ultimate support of the republic, but socialists and the right saw this as a threat to national unity. The constitution also promised land redistribution, which pleased the Andalucian landless, but failed to deliver much. Even new universal suffrage rebounded on the republic because newly enfranchised women led a swing to the right in the next elections in 1933.

The Right in Charge (1933-36)
Anarchist disruption, an economic slump, alienation of big business and disunity on the left all helped the right win the 1933 election. The new Catholic party CEDA (Confederación Española de Derechas Autónomas, or Spanish Confederation of Autonomous Rights) won the most seats. Other new forces on the right included the fascist Falange, led by José Antonio Primo de Rivera, son of the 1920s dictator. The Falange practised blatant street violence. The left, including the emerging communists (who, unlike the socialists, supported the Russian Revolution), now called increasingly for revolution.

By 1934 violence was spiralling out of control. The socialist UGT called for a general strike, Catalunya's president declared Catalunya independent (albeit within a federal Spanish republic) and workers' committees took over the northern mining region of Asturias after attacking police and army posts. All these moves were quashed, but in Asturias it took a campaign of violent repression by the Spanish Foreign Legion (set up to fight Moroccan tribes in the 1920s), led by generals Francisco Franco and José Millán Astray. The events in Asturias firmly divided the country into left and right.

Popular Front Government & Army Uprising
In the February 1936 elections the Popular Front, a left-wing coalition with communists at the fore, narrowly defeated the right-wing National Front. Now the left feared an army coup, the right a revolution. Catalan autonomy was restored. Suspect generals were moved out of the way (Franco to the Canary Islands).

Violence continued on both sides. Extremist groups grew (the anarchist CNT now had over a million members) and peasants were on the verge of revolution.

On 17 July 1936 the Spanish army garrison in Melilla in North Africa revolted against the government, followed the next day by some garrisons on the mainland. The leaders of the plot were five generals, among them Franco, who on 19 July flew from the Canary Islands to Morocco to lead his legionnaires. The civil war had begun.

The Civil War (1936-39)
The Spanish Civil War split communities, families and friends. Both sides committed atrocious massacres and reprisals and employed death squads to eliminate members of opposition organisations, in the early weeks especially. The rebels, who called themselves Nationalists because they thought they were fighting for Spain, shot or hanged tens of thousands of supporters of the republic. Republicans did likewise to Franco sympathisers, including some 7000

priests, monks and nuns. Political affiliation often provided a convenient cover for settling old scores. In the whole war an estimated 350,000 Spaniards died.

Much of the military and the Guardia Civil went over to the Nationalists, whose campaign quickly took on overtones of a holy crusade against the enemies of God. In Republican areas, anarchists, communists or socialists ended up running many towns and cities. Social revolution followed.

Nationalist Advance The basic battle lines were drawn within a week of the rebellion in Morocco. Cities whose military garrisons backed the rebels (most did), and were strong enough to overcome any resistance, fell immediately into Nationalist hands. North of Madrid, everywhere except Catalunya, eastern Aragón, the Basque coast, Cantabria and Asturias was in Nationalist hands, as were western Andalucía and Granada in the south. Franco's force of legionnaires and Moroccan mercenaries was airlifted from Morocco to Sevilla by German warplanes in August. Essential to the success of the revolt, they moved northwards through Extremadura towards Madrid, wiping out fierce resistance in some cities. At Salamanca in October, Franco pulled all the Nationalists into line behind him, styling himself as Generalísimo (Supreme General). Before long he was to declare himself head of state and adopt the title *caudillo*, roughly equivalent to the German *Führer*.

Madrid, reinforced by the first battalions of the International Brigades (armed foreign idealists and adventurers organised by the communists) battalions, repulsed Franco's first assault in November then endured, under communist inspiration, over two years siege.

Foreign Intervention From autumn 1936 the International Brigades arrived to aid the Republicans, but they never numbered more than 20,000 and couldn't turn the tide against the better armed and organised Nationalist forces.

What really tipped the scales in the Nationalists' favour was support from Nazi Germany and Fascist Italy – weapons, planes and men (75,000 from Italy, 17,000 from Germany) – which turned the war into a rehearsal for WWII. The Republicans had some Soviet support – planes, tanks, artillery and advisers – but the rest of the international community refused to get involved, although 25,000 or so French fought on the Republican side. The war came to be seen internationally as a struggle between fascism and communism, but it was a more complex conflict than that – and an essentially Spanish one, which evolved from centuries-old tensions.

Republican Quarrels The Republican government, with Largo Caballero now prime minister, moved to Valencia in late 1936 to continue trying to preside over the diversity of political persuasions on the Republican side, from anarchists and communists to moderate democrats and regional secessionists. Barcelona was even more revolutionary than Madrid, with anarchists and the POUM (Partido Obrero de Unificación Marxista, or Workers' Marxist Unification Party) Trotskyite militia running it for nearly a year. The Basques supported the Republic because it promised them autonomy.

Italian and Nationalist troops took Málaga in February 1937. In April German planes bombed the Basque town of Gernika (Guernica), causing terrible casualties; this became the subject of Picasso's famous pacifist painting. All the north coast fell in the summer, giving the Nationalists control of Basque industry. Republican counterattacks near Madrid and in Aragón failed.

Meanwhile tensions among the Republicans erupted into fierce street fighting in Barcelona in May 1937, with the communists, who under growing Soviet influence were trying to unify the Republican war effort, crushing the anarchists and Trotskyites. Largo Caballero was replaced as prime minister by Juan Negrín. The Republican government moved to Barcelona in autumn 1937.

Nationalist Victory In early 1938 Franco repulsed a Republican offensive at Teruel, Aragón, then swept eastward with 100,000 troops, 1000 planes and 150 tanks, isolating Barcelona from Valencia. Italian bombers from Mallorca started battering Barcelona. In July the Republicans launched a last offensive as the Nationalists moved through the Ebro valley. The bloody encounter, won by the Nationalists, resulted in 20,000 dead.

The USSR withdrew from the war in September 1938. In January 1939 the Nationalists took Barcelona unopposed. The Republican government and hundreds of thousands of supporters fled to France.

However, the Republicans still held Valencia and Madrid and had 500,000 people under arms but internecine squabbling continued. In the end the Republican army simply evaporated. The Nationalists entered Madrid on 28 March 1939 and Franco declared the war over on 1 April.

General Francisco Franco, Spain's absolute ruler from 1939 until his death in 1975

Franco's Spain (1939-75)

War's Aftermath The Nationalist victors were merciless, so more bloodletting ensued. Informing, private vendettas and executions were rife. An estimated 100,000 people were killed or died in prison after the war. The hundreds of thousands imprisoned included many artists, intellectuals and teachers; others fled abroad, depriving Spain of a generation of scientists, artists, writers, educationalists and more.

Dictatorship Franco ruled absolutely. He was commander of the army and leader of both the government and the sole political party, the Movimiento Nacional (National Movement), a development of the Falange. The Cortes was merely a rubber stamp for decrees Franco chose to submit to it. Regional autonomy aspirations were not tolerated.

Franco hung on to power by never allowing any single powerful group – the church, the Movimiento, the army, monar-

chists or bankers – to dominate. The army provided many ministers and enjoyed a generous budget. Catholic orthodoxy was fully restored, with most secondary schools entrusted to the Jesuits, divorce made illegal and church weddings compulsory. The Movimiento was given control of press, propaganda and unions, with labour organised into 'vertical' unions covering entire sectors of the economy. Franco won some working-class support with carrots such as job security, paid holidays and social security, but there was no right to strike.

WWII & After WWII began a few months after the civil war ended. Franco kept Hitler at bay by promising an alliance but never committing himself to a date. Spanish communists and Republicans who had been in the French Resistance crossed the Pyrenees to attack Franco's Spain but failed in September 1944; they continued their hopeless struggle in small guerrilla units in the north,

Extremadura and Andalucía right up to 1951.

Franco's ambiguous stance during WWII won him no friends abroad. Spain was excluded from the United Nations and NATO and suffered a UN-sponsored trade boycott that helped turn the late 1940s into the *años de hambre* (years of hunger). With the onset of the Cold War, Franco's anticommunism gained him some support. In 1953 he agreed to the USA's request for four bases in Spain in return for large sums in aid. In 1955 Spain was admitted to the UN.

Economic Miracle Spain was on the brink of insolvency by the late 1950s but the Stabilisation Plan of 1959, with its devaluation of the peseta as well as other deflationary measures, brought an economic upswing. The plan was engineered by a new breed of technocrats linked to the powerful lay Catholic group Opus Dei (see the boxed text later in this chapter).

Spanish industry boomed. Thousands of young Spaniards went abroad to study and returned with a new attitude of teamwork. Modern machinery, techniques and marketing were introduced, transport was modernised and even agriculture moved forward with new dams providing irrigation (as well as hydro power) and conservation and reforestation schemes reclaiming land from civil war blight and sheep grazing.

The recovery was funded in part by US aid and remittances from more than a million Spaniards working abroad, but above all by tourism. From 1960 to 1965, the annual number of tourists arriving in Spain jumped from four to 14 million.

Social Change A massive population shift from impoverished rural regions to the cities and tourist resorts took place. Many Andalucians went to Barcelona, with Sevilla, Valencia, Madrid and Bilbao also attracting people; elegant suburbs developed, as did shantytowns and, later, high-rise housing for the workers.

The Final Decade In 1964 Franco celebrated 25 years of peace, order and material progress. But the jails were still full of political prisoners and large garrisons were maintained outside every major city. Over the next decade, as the European economic boom faltered, labour strife grew and there were political rumblings in the universities and even the army and church.

Regional problems resurfaced. The Basque terrorist group ETA (Euskadi Ta Askatasuna, or Basques and Freedom), founded in 1959, gave cause for the declaration of six states of emergency between 1962 and 1975; heavy-handed police tactics won it support from Basque moderates who normally eschewed violence.

Looming over everything was the question of what would happen after Franco. The dictator chose as his successor the Spanish-educated Prince Juan Carlos, grandson of Alfonso XIII (who had died in 1941). In 1969 Juan Carlos swore loyalty to Franco and the Movimiento Nacional.

Cautious reforms by Franco's last prime minister, Carlos Arias Navarro, produced violent reactions from right-wing extremists. By 1975 Spain seemed to be descending into chaos as Franco's health declined. Franco gave a final faltering speech, characteristically warning of a 'Judaeo-Masonic-Marxist conspiracy', in Madrid in October. On 20 November he died.

Transition to Democracy

Juan Carlos I & Adolfo Suárez Juan Carlos I, aged 37, took the throne two days later. The new king's links with Franco inspired little confidence in a Spain now clamouring for democracy. But Juan Carlos had kept his cards close to his chest and earned much of the credit for the successful transition to democracy that followed. He sacked prime minister Arias Navarro in July 1976, replacing him with Adolfo Suárez, a 43-year-old former Franco apparatchik with film-star looks. To general surprise, Suárez railroaded through the Francoist-filled Cortes a proposal for a new, two-chamber parliamentary system. In early 1977 political parties, trade unions and strikes were all legalised and the Movimiento Nacional abolished.

New Constitution Suárez's centrist UCD (Unión del Centro Democrático) won nearly half the seats in the new Cortes in 1977. The left-of-centre PSOE (Partido Socialista Obrero Español, or Spanish Socialist Worker Party), led by a charismatic young lawyer from Sevilla, Felipe González Márquez, came in second. In 1978 the Cortes passed a new constitution, which made Spain a parliamentary monarchy with no official religion. In response to the regional autonomy fever that gripped Spain after the stiflingly centralist Franco era, the constitution also provided for a large measure of devolution. By 1983 this resulted in the country being divided into 17 'autonomous communities' with their own regional governments controlling a range of policy areas.

Social Liberation Spaniards' personal and social life also enjoyed a rapid liberation after Franco. Contraceptives, homosexuality and divorce were legalised and during this era the *movida* (the late-night bar and disco scene that enables people almost anywhere in Spain to party till dawn or after) emerged. But Prime Minister Suárez faced mounting resistance from within his own party to further reforms in areas such as the police, army, education and legal system. In 1981 he resigned.

Attempted Coup During the investiture of Suárez's UCD successor, Leopoldo Calvo Sotelo, Lieutenant-Colonel Antonio Tejero Molina of the Guardia Civil marched with an armed detachment into the Cortes and held it captive for almost 24 hours. This attempted military putsch was snuffed out by the king, who made clear to any wavering generals that Tejero did not have his support. The nightmarish images of the wing-helmeted Tejero waving his pistol at cowering deputies proved to be the last spasm of Francoism's corpse.

The PSOE Years

In 1982 Spain made a final break with the past by voting the PSOE into power with a sizable overall majority. González was to be prime minister for 14 years.

Squeeze & Boom The PSOE's young, educated leadership came from the generation that had opened the cracks in the Franco regime in the late 1960s and early 70s. It legalised narcotics use in 1983 and abortion in 1985 (though in the face of major drug and alcoholism problems, public narcotics use was banned in 1992). On the economic front, the PSOE persuaded the unions to accept wage restraint and job losses to streamline industry. Unemployment rose from 16% to 22% by 1986. But in 1986 Spain joined the European Community (now the European Union), bringing on its second post-civil war boom, which lasted till 1991 and cut unemployment back to 16%. Most Spaniards now had more money than ever before and flung it about lavishly. The middle class grew ever bigger and Spain's traditionally stay-at-home women poured into higher education and jobs.

The PSOE put a proper national health system in place by the early 1990s and made big improvements in state education, raising the university population to well over a million.

Rumblings of Discontent It was around halfway through the boom that the good life began to go a bit sour. People observed that many of the glamorous new rich were making their money by property or share speculation, or plain corruption. Meanwhile the government had failed to improve welfare provision for those left out of the fun. The PSOE began to figure in a series of scandals. Most of these were matters of petty abuse of privilege, but the ultimately far more serious GAL affair (see later in this section) first came to light in 1988.

Slump & Scandal In 1992 – five centuries after the country's pivotal year – Spain celebrated its return to the modern world in style with the Barcelona Olympics and the Expo 92 world fair in Sevilla. But the economic boom had now turned into a slump and the PSOE was increasingly mired in scandals. Questions were asked about how it got hold of its substantial party funds. González's long-standing No 2, Alfonso Guerra, had resigned as deputy prime minister in 1991 over an affair involving his wheeler-dealer brother's use of a government office.

By 1993 unemployment was back up to 22.5%. It was a testament partly to González's personal appeal that the PSOE government survived that year's election. It lost its overall majority and had to rely on support from the moderate Catalan nationalist party Convergència i Unió (CiU).

The slump bottomed out in 1993, but the scandals multiplied. Among the most bizarre was the case of Luis Roldán, the González-appointed head of the Guardia Civil from 1986 to 1993, who suddenly vanished in 1994 after being charged with embezzlement and bribery. He was arrested the following year in Bangkok and jailed in Spain.

Most damaging of all was the affair of the GAL (Grupos Antiterroristas de Liberación) death squads that had murdered 28 suspected ETA terrorists (several of whom were innocent) in France in the mid-1980s. In 1998 a dozen senior police and PSOE men were jailed in connection with the affair. José Luis Barrionuevo, who was González's interior minister in the mid-1980s, received a 10-year sentence for authorising the kidnap of a suspect who turned out to be innocent. The GAL affair seemed to be mixed up with other scandals too. The interior ministry, it appeared, had operated a huge slush fund in its fight against the ETA and organised crime. In 1997 Luis Roldán was tried for a raft of alleged crimes including taking 352.4 million pesetas from secret slush funds to fight terrorism and organised crime. He was jailed for 28 years the following year.

The PP Takes Over

In the face of all this CiU withdrew parliamentary support for the PSOE, forcing an election in March 1996. The winner was the centre-right PP (Partido Popular, or People's Party), led by José María Aznar, an Elton John fan and former tax inspector. The PP, however, failed to get an overall majority and Aznar was forced to stitch together a coalition with the CiU and moderate Basque and Canary Islands nationalists. One of the concessions he made in return for these parties' support was to allow Spain's 17 regional governments to collect and spend 30% of the income tax raised in their regions (up from 15%), a move which pleased wealthy regions such as Catalunya but not the poorer ones.

Aznar's main policy thrusts were economic – cuts in public investment, sell-offs of state enterprises and liberalisation of sectors such as telecommunications. In 1997 employers and unions signed a deal reforming Spain's cumbersome employment contract and dismissal system: sackings were made easier but it was expected that more jobs would be created. Unemployment fell from 23% in 1996 to 19.2% in 1998, but was still easily the highest in the EU and an alarming 40% among under-26s. (Spain's tradition of family support and a big black economy may make the situation less horrendous than the figures show.) By 1998 the economy was purring along and Spain met the criteria for launching the new European currency, the euro, in 1999. The euro bloc accounts for almost one-fifth of world production and will be a major economic force.

The Basque terrorist organisation ETA, thought to have been all but dismantled in the early 90s, returned to the forefront of national attention in 1997 and 1998 with a chilling assassination campaign aimed largely at local PP councillors. By 1998 ETA had murdered over 750 people in 30 years. Some of its recent killings, however, had provoked widespread outrage and in September 1998, following a call for talks and peace by moderate Basque nationalists, ETA announced its first-ever ceasefire without a time limit. The government initially responded coolly, aware that previous ETA ceasefires had led nowhere and that heavy regional autonomy concessions would probably be demanded in return for a permanent end to violence.

Joaquín Almunia replaced Felipe González as secretary-general of the PSOE leadership in 1997. The following year, the party introduced a primaries voting system that was widely expected to confirm him as the Socialist candidate to face off Aznar in the next elections, due by 2000. In an upset, a Catalan, Josep Borrell, won the vote and became the party's election candidate. Borrell decided to retain Almunia as party secretary-general while concentrating his own efforts on the elections, effectively creating a dual party leadership. It is too early to know how this odd bicephalous arrangement will work out.

GEOGRAPHY

Spain is probably Europe's most geographically diverse country, ranging from the near-deserts of eastern Andalucía to the green countryside and deep coastal inlets of Galicia, and from the sunbaked uplands of Castilla-La Mancha to the rugged, snow-capped Pyrenees. It covers 84% of the Iberian Peninsula and spreads over nearly 505,000 sq km, making it the biggest country in Western Europe after France.

Uplands

Spain is a mountainous country and with an average altitude of 650m it's the highest European country after Switzerland. In the past this rugged topography not only separated Spain's destiny from that of the rest of Europe, but encouraged the rise of separate small states in both the Christian and Islamic parts of medieval Spain.

Meseta & Cordillera Central At the heart of Spain and occupying 40% of the country is the meseta – a tableland of boundless horizons, 400 to 1000m high. It covers most of Castilla y León, Castilla-La Mancha and Extremadura. Apart from a handful of major cities (including Madrid), the meseta is sparsely populated and much given over to grain-growing, although vineyards and long lines of olive trees stretch across the south, while Extremadura boasts extensive pastures. Contrary to what Henry Higgins taught Eliza Dolittle, the meseta is not where most of Spain's rain falls, nor is it really a plain! Much of Castilla y León is rolling plains and hills, and the meseta is split in two by the Cordillera central mountain chain, running from north-east of Madrid to the Portuguese border. Its two main ranges are the Sierra de Guadarrama north of Madrid and the Sierra de Gredos to the west, both of which reach above 2400m. South of the cordillera are the lower Montes de Toledo and Sierra de Guadalupe.

Mountains around the Meseta On all sides except the west (where it slopes gradually down across Portugal), the meseta is bounded by mountain chains.

Across the north, close to the Bay of Biscay (Mar Cantábrico), is the damp Cordillera Cantábrica, straddling Castilla y León's borders with Cantabria and Asturias and rising above 2500m in the spectacular Picos de Europa. In the north-west the Montes de León and associated ranges cut off Galicia from the meseta.

The Sistema Ibérico runs down from wine-growing La Rioja to the olive orchards of southern Aragón, peaks at 2316m in the Sierra de Moncayo, and varies from plateaus and high moorland to deep gorges and strangely eroded rock formations as in the Serranía de Cuenca.

The southern boundary of the meseta is the low, wooded Sierra Morena running across northern Andalucía.

Outlying Mountains Spain's highest mountains, however, lie on or towards its edges. The Pyrenees stretch 400km along the French border, from the Mediterranean

Sea to the Bay of Biscay, and reach down into Catalunya, Aragón and Navarra, with the foothills extending west into the País Vasco. There are numerous 3000m peaks in Catalunya and Aragón, the highest being Aragón's Pico de Aneto (3408m).

Across southern and eastern Andalucía stretches the Cordillera Bética, a rumpled mass of ranges that includes mainland Spain's highest peak, Mulhacén (3478m), in the Sierra Nevada south-east of Granada. This system continues east into Murcia and southern Valencia, dips under the Mediterranean, then re-emerges as the Balearic islands of Ibiza and Mallorca. On Mallorca it rises to over 1400m in the Serra de Tramuntana. The other main Balearic island, Menorca, is a tip of the same underwater massif as Sardinia and Corsica.

Lowlands

Around and between all the mountains are five main lower-lying areas.

Fertile Catalunya, in the north-east, is composed mainly of ranges of lower hills.

The Ebro basin, between the Sistema Ibérico to its south and the Cordillera Cantábrica and Pyrenees to its north, supports wine production in La Rioja, grain-growing in Navarra, and horticulture in eastern Aragón, although other parts of Aragón are near-desert.

Galicia in the north-west is hilly and green with mixed farming, and reminiscent of other Celtic lands like Ireland or Brittany.

The coastal areas of Valencia and Murcia are dry plains transformed by irrigation into green *huertas* (market gardens and orchards). Similar areas farther south, around Almería in eastern Andalucía, are virtually desert.

The Guadalquivir basin, stretching across Andalucía between the Sierra Morena and Cordillera Bética, is a highly fertile zone where a wide range of produce, from grain to olives and citrus fruit, is grown.

Rivers

The major rivers are the Ebro, Duero, Tajo (Tagus), Guadiana and Guadalquivir, each draining a different basin between the mountains. All of these, and many of their tributaries, are dammed here and there into long, snaking reservoirs to provide much of Spain's water and electricity.

The Ebro is the largest in volume, rising in the Cordillera Cantábrica and draining the southern side of the Pyrenees and the northern side of the Sistema Ibérico. It flows across north-eastern Castilla y León, La Rioja, Navarra and Aragón to enter the Mediterranean Sea in southern Catalunya.

All the other major rivers empty into the Atlantic Ocean. The Duero flows west from the northern Sistema Ibérico and drains the northern half of the meseta, then continues across Portugal as the Douro.

The Tajo and the Guadiana rise in the southern Sistema Ibérico and flow across the southern half of the meseta, the Tajo draining the part north of the Montes de Toledo and the sluggish Guadiana draining the southern part. The Tajo continues west across Portugal to Lisbon as the Tejo, while the Guadiana turns south: its last stretch into the Golfo de Cádiz forms the Portuguese border.

The Guadalquivir flows from east to west across the middle of Andalucía.

Coasts

Spain's coasts are as varied as its interior.

Mediterranean Coast The long Mediterranean coast begins in the north with Catalunya's Costa Brava (Rugged Coast), pockmarked with rocky coves and inlets that have to some extent restricted the growth of concrete tourist resorts. The Costa Daurada, south of Barcelona, and the Costa del Azahar, north of Valencia, are flatter, with some long, sandy beaches and fairly mundane resorts (lively Sitges excepted). Sea temperatures on the *costas* average 19°C or 20°C in June and October and a comfortable 22°C to 24°C from July to September.

South of Valencia, there are some attractive coves around Denia and Jávea, before the coast travels around Cabo La Nao to the infamous Costa Blanca, whose good, sandy beaches are disfigured by concrete package resorts like Benidorm and Torrevieja. Alicante, in the same way as Málaga on the Costa del Sol, is a refreshingly Spanish city amid all this. Murcia's Mar Menor lagoon has warm waters, more good beaches and more high-rise development, but the hard-to-reach beaches on the Golfo de Mazarrón, west of Cartagena, are almost undeveloped. Sea temperatures on the Costa Blanca and the Murcian coast are mainland Spain's warmest: a degree or two higher than farther north.

Entering Andalucía, there's more resort development at Mojácar before you reach the rugged, beautiful 50km coast around Cabo de Gata, where near-desert and mountains come right down to beaches lapped by warm, turquoise waters. Several beaches here can only be reached by foot or boat. Immediately west of Almería is a narrow coastal plain covered by hideous plastic greenhouses. Beyond here the Costa del Sol stretches between Málaga and Gibraltar, where the package-tourism pressure cookers of Torremolinos, Fuengirola and Marbella form an almost continuously built-up strip 70km long. Surprisingly, Andalucian coastal waters are generally a couple of degrees cooler than Catalunya's.

Atlantic Coasts The Atlantic coasts have a wilder climate and colder seas than the Mediterranean.

The Costa de la Luz, much less developed than the Costa del Sol, stretches north-west from Tarifa, west of Gibraltar, to the Portuguese border. It has some fine, wide, dune-backed beaches, especially south of Cádiz and west of the Guadalquivir delta, which is an important water-bird and wildlife habitat.

Galicia's coast is Spain's most rugged, deeply indented with majestic estuaries called *rías*, dotted with appealing coves, beaches and fishing villages, and almost ignored by foreign package tourism. The Rías Bajas on the west-facing coast are the best known, but the Rías Altas on the north-

facing coast are just as impressive in decent weather and include Spain's most awesome cliffs, at Cabo Ortegal and Serra de la Capelada.

All along the Bay of Biscay, the Cordillera Cantábrica comes almost down to the coast, providing a fine backdrop for resorts big and small (the biggest are Santander and San Sebastián), many of which have good beaches, and surfing centres like Zarautz and Mundaka.

Islas Baleares The waters here are warmer than on the mainland, averaging 21°C in June and October and 25°C in August. The north coast of Mallorca is lined with high, wild cliffs and the hard-to-reach beaches on its coves are much quieter than those around Palma de Mallorca, on Mallorca's lower-lying east coast. Menorca is perhaps the islands' best-kept secret, peppered with deserted coves and beaches awash in limpid unspoiled waters. Ibiza and Formentera too are dotted by little beaches, but few with the stunning pristine beauty encountered in Menorca.

CLIMATE

The meseta and the Ebro basin have a continental climate: scorching in summer, cold in winter and dry. Madrid regularly freezes in December, January and February and temperatures climb above 30°C in July and August (locals describe it as: *nueve meses de invierno y tres de infierno* – nine months of winter and three of hell). Valladolid on the northern meseta and Zaragoza in the Ebro basin are even drier, with only around 300mm of rain a year (little more than Alice Springs in Australia). The Guadalquivir basin in Andalucía is only a little wetter and positively broils in high summer, with temperatures of 35°C-plus in Sevilla that kill people every year. This area doesn't get as cold as the meseta in winter.

The Pyrenees and the Cordillera Cantábrica backing the Bay of Biscay coast bear the brunt of cold north and north-western airstreams, which bring moderate temperatures and heavy rainfall (three or

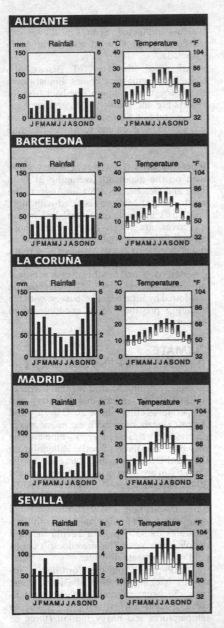

four times as much as Madrid's) to the northern and north-western coasts. Even in high summer you never know when you might get a shower.

The Mediterranean coast as a whole, and the Islas Baleares, get a little more rain than Madrid and the south can be even hotter in summer. The Mediterranean also provides Spain's warmest waters (reaching 27°C or so in August) and you *can* swim as early as April or even late March in the south-east.

In general you can rely on pleasant or hot temperatures just about everywhere from April to early November (plus March in the south, but minus a month at either end on the northern and north-western coasts). In Andalucía there are plenty of warm, sunny days right through winter. In July and August, temperatures can get unpleasant, even unbearable, anywhere inland (unless you're high enough in the mountains). Spaniards abandon their cities in droves for the coast and mountains at this time.

Snowfalls in the mountains start as early as October and some snow cover lasts all year on the highest peaks.

ECOLOGY & ENVIRONMENT

Spain's environment has been radically altered by human hands over two millennia. The Romans began to cut, for timber, fuel and weapons, the country's extensive woodlands and forests, which until then even covered half the meseta. Over the next 2000 years further deforestation, along with overtilling and overgrazing (especially by huge sheep herds), brought substantial topsoil erosion: most of the 300 sq km delta of the Río Ebro has been formed by eroded deposits in the past 600 years. Many animal species were drastically depleted by hunting. Urban and industrial growth, joined in the 20th century by the construction of numerous dams for hydroelectricity and irrigation, caused further change.

Considering how well the resulting system can sustain human, animal and plant life, on the whole things today don't seem too bad. Despite uncertain rainfall and, in many areas, impoverished soils, the country supports a varied, often low-tech and mostly healthy agriculture, although the irrigation and chemicals on which this in part depends have brought problems. By European standards Spain is sparsely populated and most of its people live in towns and cities, which reduces their impact on the countryside. There's still lots of wilderness. Serious urban pollution is limited, since Spain is relatively lightly industrialised and urban authorities have taken appropriate action in many places. Protection given to many animal and bird species has brought big increases in numbers for some, although it's probably too late for others (see Other Problems in this section and Fauna in the Flora & Fauna section).

Conservation

Environmental awareness took a huge leap forward in the post-Franco 1980s. The PSOE government made environmental pollution a crime and spurred a range of actions by regional governments, which now have responsibility for most environmental matters. In 1981 Spain had just 35 environmentally protected areas, covering 2200 sq km. Now there are over 400, covering more than 25,000 sq km (see Reserves & National Parks under Flora & Fauna).

Different regions give conservation different priorities: Andalucía has over 80 protected areas, while neighbouring Extremadura has just three. Nor are protected areas always well protected, often because their ecosystems extend beyond their own boundaries. Most notoriously, in 1998 the vital wetlands of the Doñana national and natural parks in Andalucía were damaged by a huge spill of acids and heavy metals into a river that feeds them. Other wetlands, such as Catalunya's Ebro delta and Valencia's Albufera, have been severely damaged by pesticide pollution.

Drought

Potentially Spain's worst environmental problem is drought. It struck in the 1950s and 60s, and again in the first half of the 1990s, despite huge investment in reservoirs (which cover a higher proportion of Spain than of any other country in the world) and projects like the Tajo-Segura water diversion system. This project can transfer 600 million cubic metres of water a year from the Tajo basin in central Spain to the heavily irrigated Valencia and Murcia regions on the Mediterranean coast. The 1990s drought damaged southern agriculture, brought water rationing for 10 million people by 1995, and even led to talk of water being shipped in by sea to keep tourism going on the Costa del Sol. However disaster was staved off by three wet winters from 1995-96 to 1997-98, which broke the drought and filled up the reservoirs – for a while, at least.

Water is money in Spain and, when it's in short supply, local politicians often aren't keen to see it transferred out of their regions. In 1994 the government had to intervene to compel Castilla-La Mancha to transfer 55 million cubic metres to Murcia and Valencia. Plans for a 6000 billion peseta investment to ensure that all Spain has adequate water supplies face similar political hurdles. The 'dry' regions are Andalucía, Castilla-La Mancha, Extremadura, Valencia, Murcia and parts of the Ebro basin in Aragón.

Other Problems

Although Spain's many dams and reservoirs provide irrigation and hydroelectricity (reducing the need for nuclear or dirtier forms of power) and conserve water, they inevitably destroy habitats.

Vegetables growing under huge areas of plastic in the south-east and plantations of thirsty eucalyptus (now going out of fashion) threaten to destroy the natural vegetation of some areas.

Intensive agriculture and the spread of towns and cities (including tourist resorts) have lowered water tables in some areas, threatening vegetation and the quality of water supplies. Growing coastal urban areas add to the pollution of the seas, although sewage treatment facilities are being constantly improved. Spain gets creditable numbers of EU 'blue flags' for its beaches, indicating that they meet certain minimal standards of hygiene and facilities.

Hunting is deeply ingrained in Spanish life. Over 15,000 sq km are set aside as national hunting reserves and over 1.25 million shooting licences are issued annually. Many species are now protected, but a lot of illegal shooting and trapping of animals and birds goes on. Nevertheless, species like the wild boar and red deer have recovered in some areas to the point where they are now legally culled. The Spanish ibex, a species of mountain goat, was almost extinct by 1900 but protection has since raised its numbers to around 10,000.

Industrial pollution is probably at its worst around Bilbao in the País Vasco and the small chemical-producing town of Avilés in Asturias.

FLORA & FAUNA
Flora

The variety of Spain's flora is astonishing, as anyone who witnesses the spectacular wildflower displays on roadsides and pastures in spring and early summer will testify. Spain has around 8000 plant species, many unique to the Iberian Peninsula. This abundance is largely due to the fact that the last Ice Age did not cover the entire peninsula, enabling plants killed off farther north to survive in Spain.

High-Altitude Plants Spain's many mountain areas claim a lot of the variety. The Pyrenees have about 150 unique species and even the Sierra Nevada in the south, covering a much smaller area, has about 60. When the snows melt, the alpine and subalpine zones (above the tree line) bloom spectacularly with some small rock-clinging plants and gentians, orchids, crocuses, narcissi and sundews. Particularly good orchid areas are the alpine meadows of the Picos de Europa (with 40 species) and the Serranía de Cuenca in the Sistema Ibérico.

Mountain Forests Higher mountain forests tend to be coniferous and are often commercial. The silver fir is common in the Pyrenees and Sistema Ibérico, while the Spanish fir is confined to the Ronda area in Andalucía. The Scots pine, with its flaking red bark, is common on the cooler northern mountains; the umbrella pine, with its large spreading top and edible kernel, is more common near the coast. Many pine forests are threatened by the pine processionary moth, whose hairy caterpillars devour pine needles. The caterpillars' large silvery nests are easy to spot in the trees; touching the caterpillars can provoke a nasty allergic reaction (see Cuts, Stings & Bites under Health in Facts for the Visitor). Deciduous forests – predominantly beech but also Pyrenean oak and other trees – are found mainly on the lower slopes of the damp northern mountains. Many orchids grow on forest floors.

Lowland Forests Mixed forests are dotted over the lowlands and meseta, and occasionally elsewhere, such as around Ronda in Andalucía. Many contain two useful evergreen oaks: the cork oak (alcornoque), whose thick bark is stripped every nine years for cork (corcho), and the holm or ilex oak (encina), whose acorns are gobbled up by pigs destined to become jamón ibérico (see Food in Facts for the Visitor). Where the tree cover is scattered, the resulting combined woodland-pastures are known as dehesas. These mostly occur in the south-western meseta and bloom with flowers in early summer. Mixed forests may also contain conifers for timber or eucalyptus grown for wood pulp.

Scrub & Steppe Where there's no woodland and no agriculture, the land is often maquis scrub or steppe. Maquis occurs where forests were felled and the land was then abandoned. Herbs like lavender, rosemary and thyme are typical maquis plants, as are shrubs of the cistus family in the south and gorse, juniper, heather and the strawberry tree in the north. If the soil is acidic, there may also be broom. Orchids, gladioli and irises may flower beneath these shrubs, which are colourful in spring.

Steppe is produced by overgrazing or occurs naturally in hot, dry climates. Much of the Ebro valley and Castilla-La Mancha are steppe, as is the almost desert-like Cabo de Gata in Andalucía. These areas burst into colour after rain.

Fauna

Spain's wildlife is among the most varied in Europe thanks to its wild terrain, which has allowed the survival of several species that have died out in many other countries, though some are now in perilously small numbers. Many of Spain's wild animals are nocturnal and you need to be both dedicated and lucky to track them down.

Mammals There are about 50 brown bears *(oso pardo)* in the Picos de Europa and farther west in the Cordillera Cantábrica, and a few in the Pyrenees (mostly on the French side). Though hunting or killing these bears has been banned since 1973, their numbers have continued to decline. The Pyrenean population is effectively extinct (although the French are attempting to boost the population by importing bears from Slovenia) and its Cantabrian counterpart may be going that way too. In 1900 Spain had about 1000 brown bears: hunting and poisoning (accidental and deliberate) have been the main reasons for their decline.

Up to 1000 wolves *(lobo)* survive, mostly in the mountains of the north-west, though there are a few in the south-western meseta and the Sierra Morena. Though heavily protected, they're still regarded as an enemy by many local people.

Things look better for the ibex *(cabra montés)*, a stocky high-mountain goat whose males have distinctive, long horns. It spends summer hopping agilely around high crags and descends to pastures in winter. Almost hunted to extinction by 1900, the ibex was protected by royal decree a few years later. There are an esti-

mated 70,000, the main populations being in the Sierra de Gredos and Andalucía.

The pardel lynx *(lince ibérico)*, a uniquely Spanish wild feline smaller than the lynx of northern Europe, has been reduced to 600 or 800 by hunting and a decline in the numbers of rabbits, its staple diet. Now stringently protected, it lives in wild southern and western woodlands, including Doñana National Park and Monfragüe Natural Park.

Less uncommon beasts – though you'd still need to go looking for them – include the mainly nocturnal wild boar *(jabalí)*, which likes thick woods, marshes and farmers' root crops; the red, roe and fallow deer *(ciervo, corzo, gamo)* found in forests and woodlands of all types; and the nocturnal genet *(gineta)*, rather like a short-legged cat with a white coat spotted with black, and a long, striped tail, living in woodland and scrub in the south and north. The chamois *(rebeco, sarrio, isard* or *gamuza)*, not unlike a smaller, shorter-horned ibex but actually a member of the antelope family, lives above and just within the tree line in the Pyrenees and the Cordillera Cantábrica, descending to pastures in winter. There are also the red squirrel *(ardilla)* in mountain forests; the mainly nocturnal Egyptian mongoose *(meloncillo)* in woods, scrub and

The pardel lynx is unique to Spain, where it is a protected species

marshes in the southern half of the country; the otter *(nutria)*; the beech marten *(garduña)* in scattered deciduous forests and on rocky outcrops and cliffs; and the pine marten *(marta)* in some Pyrenees pine forests.

Birds of Prey Spain has around 25 breeding species of birds of prey, some of them summer visitors from Africa. In the mountains or on the meseta you'll often see them circling or hovering. Monfragüe Natural Park and the Serranía de Cuenca are two places particularly noted for birds of prey. (Identifying them is a different matter! See Books in Facts for the Visitor for some useful field guides.)

The threatened lammergeier, with its majestic 2m-plus wingspan, is recovering slowly in the high Pyrenees (to 55 pairs in 1996) and is being reintroduced in its other Spanish habitat, the Sierra de Cazorla. Poisoned food and furtive hunting have been its main threats. Its Spanish name, *quebrantahuesos* (bone-breaker), reflects its habit of smashing bones, by dropping them on to rocks, so it can get at the marrow.

Spain's few hundred pairs of black vulture *(buitre negro)*, Europe's biggest bird of prey, are probably the world's biggest population. Its strongholds are in the Sierra Morena, Monfragüe Natural Park in Extremadura, the Montes de Toledo in Castilla-La Mancha and the Sierra de la Peña de Francia in Castilla y León.

Another emblematic bird is the Spanish imperial eagle *(águila imperial)*, which was almost killed off by hunting and the decline in the rabbit population. Its white shoulders distinguish it from other imperial eagles. Around 100 pairs remain, about 20 of them in Doñana National Park and others in Monfragüe Natural Park, the Pyrenees and Cantabria.

Other notable large birds of prey include the golden eagle *(águila real)*, griffon vulture *(buitre leonado)* and Egyptian vulture *(alimoche)*, all found in high mountain regions. Smaller birds of prey include the kestrel *(cernícalo)* and buzzard *(ratonero)*,

which are both common, the sparrowhawk *(gavilán)*, various harriers *(aguiluchos)* and the acrobatic red kite *(milano real)* and black kite *(milano negro)*; many of them are found around deciduous or lowland woods and forests. Black kites may be seen over open ground near marshes and rubbish dumps.

Water Birds Spain is a haven for numerous water birds, thanks to some large wetland areas. The most famous and important of the wetlands is the Guadalquivir delta in Andalucía, large sections of which are included in the Doñana National Park and its buffer zones. Hundreds of thousands of birds winter here and many more call in during spring and autumn migrations. Other important coastal wetlands are the Albufera de Valencia, and the Ebro delta and Aiguamolls de l'Empordà in Catalunya.

Inland, thousands of ducks *(pato)* winter on the Tablas de Daimiel wetlands, in Castilla-La Mancha, and, with cranes *(grulla)* too, at Laguna de Gallocanta, Spain's biggest natural lake (though it can virtually dry up in summer), 50km south of Calatayud in Aragón. Laguna de Fuente de Piedra near Antequera in Andalucía is Europe's main breeding site for the greater flamingo *(flamenco)*, with as many as 13,000 pairs rearing chicks in spring and summer. This beautiful pink bird can be seen in many other saline wetlands along the Mediterranean and southern Atlantic coasts, including the Ebro delta, Cabo de Gata and Doñana National Park.

Other Birds Two species of rare large birds famous for their elaborate male courtship displays are the great bustard *(avutarda)*, which inhabits the plains of the meseta, and the capercaillie *(urogallo)*, a kind of giant black grouse, in the northern mountain woodlands. Spain has perhaps 8000 great bustards, more than the rest of Europe combined, though the bird is under pressure from the modernisation of agriculture. Weighing up to 14kg, the male in flight

Flying High

Being the white stork's summer holiday destination can sometimes overwhelm a Spanish *pueblo*. Malpartida de Cáceres (population 2500) in Extremadura found itself virtually under siege in 1997: 534 storks came to stay that summer.

Look atop a church bell tower, tree or pylon and you'll probably find one of the huge nests in which the white stork *(ciconia ciconia)*, known as a *cigüeña blanca*, makes its summer home. These majestic birds do not chirp cheerfully (they don't have sufficiently developed vocal cords), but rather clap their long bills.

Spain is the first leg in one of two migration routes for the stork from Africa. Crossing at the Strait of Gibraltar, flocks of as many as 3000 sweep northwards. These graceful beasts of the air rely heavily on thermals and up-draughts to soar along their way – wing flapping is strictly for the (other) birds. As they pair off to breed, they abandon the crowd, settle down, build their impressive, 60cm high nests and hunker down to raise a family.

Many content themselves with a Spanish summer holiday, particularly in Andalucía, Extremadura and the two Castillas. But some don't even bother returning to Africa for the winter. They're a protected species in Spain, where their population has quadrupled to about 16,000 since the mid-1980s, but their numbers in Europe are decreasing as their natural habitat is destroyed. In Spain the main stork route and biggest concentration of nests lies across Extremadura. You'll be hard pressed *not* to see them around Mérida, Cáceres, Trujillo, Plasencia and Jarandilla.

The white stork is one of 17 species of stork, closely related to herons, ibises and flamingos, and grows to about one metre, is white with black flight feathers and sports a dark red bill and red legs. The only other species in Europe is the less gregarious *cigüeña negra*, or black stork *(ciconia nigra)*. They too cross at the Strait of Gibraltar, but tend to nest on cliff ledges and shy away from people – with good reason. Their population has dropped to as few as 200 pairs, as people have polluted watering and feeding places, but seems stable. Their stronghold is the western part of the southern meseta, especially Monfragüe natural park.

has been compared to a goose with eagle's wings.

Among the most colourful of Spain's many other birds are the golden oriole *(oropéndola)* in orchards and deciduous woodlands in summer (the male has an unmistakable, bright-yellow body); the orange, black and white hoopoe *(abubilla)*, with its distinctive crest, which is common in open woodlands, on farmland and golf courses; and the gold, brown and turquoise bee-eater *(abejaruco)*, which nests in sandy banks in summer. All three are more common in the south. Various woodpeckers *(pitos* or *picos)* and owls *(búhos)* inhabit mountain woodlands.

Other Fauna Most of Europe's butterflies are found in Spain, including some unique to the Iberian Peninsula. There are also 20-odd bat species, four types of salamander, midwife toads, chameleons in Andalucía's Axarquía region, snakes and numerous lizards. Gibraltar is famous for its Barbary macaques, the only wild monkeys in Europe.

Twenty-seven species of marine mammals, including several each of whale and dolphin, live off Spain's shores. Cabo de Peñas, near Gijón on the Bay of Biscay, is a noted gathering ground. In the Mediterranean, some species are threatened by driftnet fishing (though this is not practised by Spanish fishing boats). Dolphin-spotting boat trips are a popular attraction at Gibraltar.

See Health in Facts for the Visitor for information on Spain's few dangerous beasts.

National Parks & Reserves

Much of Spain's most spectacular and ecologically important country – about 40,000 sq km if you include national hunting reserves – is under some kind of official protection. Nearly all these areas are at least partly open to visitors, but degrees of conservation and access vary. *Parques naturales* (natural parks), for instance, the largest category of protected area, may include villages with hotels, *hostales*

(budget hotels) and camp sites, or may limit access to a few walking trails with the nearest accommodation 10km away. A few reserves require special permits and others include sections with no public access. Fortunately, the most interesting usually have visitor centres with ample suggestions about how to spend your time. You'll find information on access, accommodation etc under specific destinations in this book.

National Parks *Parques nacionales* are areas of exceptional importance for their fauna, flora, geomorphology or landscape and are generally the most strictly controlled protected areas. They are declared by the national parliament and administered by the national and regional governments. Mainland Spain and the Balearic Islands have, at the time of writing, five national parks: Picos de Europa, a mountain refuge for endangered species which straddles Asturias, Cantabria and Castilla y León; Ordesa y Monte Perdido, a spectacular section of the Aragón Pyrenees, with over 30 mammal species and bird life including the lammergeier; the Tablas de Daimiel wetlands in Castilla-La Mancha; Doñana in Andalucía's Guadalquivir delta, a vital haven for birds and mammals with a unique variety of ecosystems; and Archipiélago de Cabrera, a group of rocky islets in the Balearics. Several other areas are due to be upgraded to national park status, including the higher slopes of the Sierra Nevada in Andalucía, Galicia's Islas Cíes, and Aigüestortes i Estany de Sant Maurici in the Catalan Pyrenees. The latter has been a Catalan 'Parc Nacional' for years but hasn't (yet) been recognised as a *Spanish* national park.

Other Protected Areas These are administered by Spain's 17 regional governments. There are literally hundreds of them, falling into at least 16 classifications and ranging in size from 100 sq m rocks off the Balearics to the mountainous 2140 sq km Parque Natural de Cazorla in Andalucía.

A few of the other most important and interesting reserves are: Parque Natural de Monfragüe in Extremadura, with spectacular birds of prey; Catalunya's Parc Natural Delta de l'Ebre, a wetland vital for birds; mountainous Parque Natural Sierra de Grazalema in Andalucía, one of Spain's wettest areas, with a rich bird life; the Áreas Naturales de la Serra de Tramuntana, covering most of this spectacular mountain range on Mallorca; and Menorca's S'Albufera des Grao wetlands, which were central to the whole of Menorca being declared a UNESCO biosphere reserve in 1993.

Reservas Nacionales de Caza Some 15,000 sq km of wilderness areas around the country are Reservas Nacionales de Caza (National Hunting Reserves). These areas are usually well-conserved for the sake of the wildlife which will be hunted. Their animal stocks must be exploited in a 'rational' manner and hunting is controlled by a fairly strict licence system. Public access is usually pretty open (some hunting reserves include villages or towns) and you may well hike or drive across one without even knowing it. If you hear shots, though, be careful!

GOVERNMENT & POLITICS

Since 1978, three years after the death of Franco, Spain has been a constitutional monarchy. The king is commander of the armed forces, a role that proved decisive in the February 1981 coup attempt, when Juan Carlos I came down unequivocally against any move to impose a military government.

The Cortes Generales, or parliament, is bicameral, with the Congreso de los Diputados (lower house) and Senado (upper house). Both houses are elected through free, universal suffrage. From December 1982 until March 1996, the PSOE ruled modern Spain's destinies, guided by the seemingly invincible Felipe González. His fall in 1996 in an atmosphere of scandal and disillusion ushered in a shift to the right as José María Aznar's PP entered government supported by pacts with Catalan,

Basque and Canary Islands nationalists (although not covered in this book, the Canary Islands, off the Moroccan Atlantic coast, are an integral part of Spain – see Lonely Planet's *Canary Islands* guide).

The most fundamental change in recent Spanish history has been the devolution of power from the central state to the 17 regions, known as *comunidades autónomas*, (autonomous communities or regions), under the 1978 constitution. What began as a response to long-standing desires for greater self-rule by the obviously distinct communities of Catalunya, the País Vasco and Galicia has become a generalised decentralisation from Madrid to all the regions. It could hardly be claimed that, for instance, Castilla-La Mancha has a historical or cultural identity and heritage terribly distinct from that of Castilla y León. And yet both regions now have their own autonomous governments. The city-enclaves of Melilla and Ceuta in North Africa were granted a degree of autonomy in 1995.

The physiognomy of the regions in fact changed after the demise of the Francoist state. Castilla y León is made up of what were the separate regions of León (even today you can see graffiti in León calling for separation from Castilla) and Castilla la Vieja. The latter lost the coastal province of Cantabria, which became a separate region, and the province of Logroño, which in turn became the region of La Rioja. Castilla la Nueva absorbed Albacete province to its south-east from the region of Murcia and was renamed Castilla-La Mancha.

One result of the autonomous regions policy has been a massive duplication of bureaucracy, with each comunidad having its own parliament, while the central state also has separate representation in each comunidad.

Article 148 of the constitution lists areas of power which are eligible for transfer to the comunidades. These include transport, agriculture, tourism, health policy and the environment. Negotiations on the transfer of powers continue even now, with Catalunya and the País Vasco particularly eager to attain as much elbowroom as possible. In September 1998, nationalist parties from Catalunya, the País Vasco and Galicia approved a common front to work for greater devolution through a change of the autonomy statutes.

The País Vasco is leading this particular charge and it has caused a storm of protest from other regions. They say that, yet again, the historically distinct regions are attempting to become more equal than the others. Re-writing the autonomy statute could open

some unpleasant cans of worms but is unlikely to happen tomorrow.

In Catalunya more central money has been allocated to its health services and Barcelona has managed to win increases in the amount of tax it is allowed to collect and spend directly. Catalunya and the País Vasco are pushing to have regional sports teams represent them in international competitions, in much the same way as Scotland, Wales and England often appear as separate teams at major events such as the soccer World Cup.

AUTONOMOUS COMMUNITIES & PROVINCES

Aznar is a centralist: he and the PP have pooh-poohed the sports teams initiatives. He has pushed for a uniform history curriculum in schools across Spain and has made no secret of his opposition to Catalan moves to promote the local language to the detriment of Castilian.

The 17 autonomous regions are divided into provinces, most of which are named after their capital city (eg Segovia is the capital of Segovia province). The provinces are divided into town and district administrative units, called *municipios*.

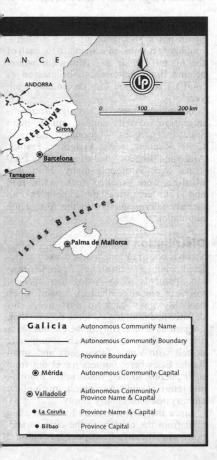

Galicia	Autonomous Community Name
———	Autonomous Community Boundary
———	Province Boundary
◉ Mérida	Autonomous Community Capital
◉ Valladolid	Autonomous Community/Province Name & Capital
● La Coruña	Province Name & Capital
● Bilbao	Province Capital

ECONOMY

By the time the Spanish Civil War ended in 1939, the country's already weak economy had been devastated. Throughout WWII and into the early 1950s, the country laboured under a self-sufficiency program that appealed to the nationalist sensibilities of the country's more comfortably placed political elite but did little to alleviate the extreme poverty in which many Spanish people languished.

US economic aid from the early 1950s and a 1959 stabilisation plan helped the wheels turn a little faster. From the early 1960s an unprecedented boom was soon touted as a Francoist-inspired economic 'miracle'. Up until the world oil crisis in 1973-74, the miracle was in fact fuelled largely by growing foreign investment (Spain was the land of cheap labour *par excellence*), tourism and remittances from emigrant Spaniards; almost two million left the country to work abroad between 1959 and 1973.

Tourism has since the early 1960s played a key role in boosting the economy. Throughout the 1960s and into the 1970s it was the single most important pillar in Spain's spectacular growth.

The oil crisis hit Spain hard and by 1982 inflation and unemployment had reached crippling levels. The arrival in power of the Socialists ushered in a period of renewed, if more modest, growth with inflation coming down to single figures but unemployment remaining high. A new period of stagnation which began in 1989 has since 1994 shown signs of reversal but, in spite of the Aznar's declaration that *España va bien* (Spain's going well), the country has serious problems to deal with.

Agriculture accounts for some 4.5% of Spain's GDP, well above the EU average. The most profitable farming is carried out along the Mediterranean coast and the Río Ebro. Intense plasticulture (hothouse agriculture using plastic) farming on the south coast, particularly around Almería and Huelva, contributes year-round high yields of everything from tomatoes to strawberries and cucumbers. Inland, farmers have to contend with extreme conditions in winter and summer and persistent rainfall shortages and drought. The main products are wine, olives, citrus fruit, almonds, wheat and rice.

Fishing is another traditionally important sector. Spain's fleet, the largest in the EU, has to cast its nets far and wide to maintain its activities. The biggest fleets operate out of Galicia and Andalucía.

Some 35% of Spain's GDP comes from industry but, although Spain is among the top 10 industrialised nations in the world, much of the production is fuelled by sometimes fickle foreign investment (which in 1997 was up 8%). Aside from motor vehicles, other major products include steel (mostly in the north), textiles, chemicals and ships.

Of the services sector, tourism remains a huge component. In the first nine months of 1997 (the latest figures available at the time of writing), 51 million visitors poured into Spain, bringing some US$40 billion into the economy. The previous year all records were broken and in 1998 the authorities were expecting more of the same.

Spain joined the then EC in 1986 and has always been an enthusiastic member of the European club, largely because it has been a net beneficiary of EU funds. The gravy train has brought problems though, and sectors traditionally hard-hit by new competition and quotas imposed from Brussels, such as wine production and fishing, have recently been joined by another pillar of Spanish industry – the olive.

Signing up for the first wave of the single currency (the euro) has forced a tough austerity policy on the Spanish economy. Inflation has been crunched to 1.8%, the public sector deficit is low at 2.3% of GDP and interest rates have reached their lowest level since the days of Franco at 4.7%.

This is all well and good but the open sore of unemployment continues to plague Madrid. Official figures of *registered* unemployed were as low as 12.14% in 1998 (the lowest since 1981). While it is true that the real figure has been falling steadily for more than three years, it remains the EU's highest at 19.2%.

Of those with jobs, many struggle on part-time and temporary contract arrangements. And the average wage for full-time professionals is considerably lower than elsewhere in Western Europe, hovering at around 150,000 ptas (US$1200) a month – not a lot if you live in Madrid and have a family to look after.

Still, when all is said and done, Spain is enjoying a minor boom; growth was tipped to remain high at 3.7% until well into 1999.

POPULATION & PEOPLE

Spain has a population of 39.7 million – roughly two-thirds of a Spaniard for each of the 60 million or so visitors (of whom around three-quarters can be classed as tourists) who flood into the country each year!

Spain never received any significant immigration from its empire and its main ancestral peoples – Iberians, Basques, Celts, Romans, Jews, Visigoths, Franks, Arabs and Berbers – had all arrived by 1000 years ago. Although many Jews and Muslims were expelled in the 15th, 16th and 17th centuries, these peoples had already intermingled with the rest of the population.

Distribution

Spain is one of Europe's least densely populated countries, with about 77 people per sq km. Spaniards like to live together, in cities, towns or *pueblos* (villages), a habit which probably goes back to past needs for defence and must have a lot to do with their gregarious nature. Only in the Basque lands are you likely to see much countryside dotted with single farmsteads and small fields. Elsewhere, farmers travel out from their pueblos to their fields in the morning and return at night. As a result, much of the countryside looks oddly empty.

Since the civil war there has been a big shift from the country to the cities – and, more specifically, from poor agricultural regions like Andalucía, the meseta and Galicia to industrialised areas in Catalunya, the País Vasco and elsewhere. More than half of all Spaniards live in cities and most of the rest live in towns of 10,000 or more people. Most major cities, past and present, grew up as ports (Barcelona, Tarragona, Valencia, Cartagena, Málaga, La Coruña, Cádiz and even Sevilla, which is linked to the Atlantic by the Río Guadalquivir) or at strategic sites on major rivers (Zaragoza, Valladolid, Mérida, Badajoz and Córdoba). The major exception is Madrid, which was chosen in the 16th century, mainly for its central location, as the country's new capital.

The biggest cities are Madrid (population: 2.9 million), Barcelona (1.5 million), Valencia (746,000), Sevilla (697,000), Zaragoza (602,000) and Málaga (549,000). Greater Madrid and greater Barcelona each number about four million people and there are sizable conurbations around Bilbao, Valencia, Zaragoza and Sevilla. At the other end of the scale are Aragón, with only around 20 people per sq km outside its capital, Zaragoza, and the three meseta regions of Castilla-La Mancha (21 people per sq km, even including cities), Extremadura (25) and Castilla y León (27).

The most striking thing about the Spanish population is its slow rate of growth. Along with that other great bastion of Catholicism and seemingly child-friendly society, Italy (and remember, the Pope doesn't view contraception kindly), Spain has the lowest birth rate in the world – the annual population increase is just 1.2%.

Regional Differences

The peoples with the strongest local identities – the Catalans, Basques and, to a lesser extent, the Galicians – owe a lot of their sense of differentness to 19th century cultural and political reawakenings and a reaction to decades of rigid centralist rule under Franco. These regions are on the fringes of the country, whose heartland is Castilla. Some Basques and Catalans, and a handful of Galicians, feel so strongly about their identity that they don't consider themselves Spaniards. All these peoples have their own languages, and minority independence movements, the Basque terrorist organisation ETA being the most infamous.

Ethnic Minorities

Some consider Spain's *gitanos* (formerly called Gypsies but now known as the Roma) to be its only true ethnic minority, as interbreeding has made the rest of the population fairly homogeneous. Generally reckoned to be the originators – as well as the best performers – of flamenco, the gitanos are thought to have originated in India and reached Spain in the 15th century. As elsewhere, they have suffered discrimination. There are about 500,000 gitanos in Spain, more than half of them in Andalucía. Some still lead a wandering existence but most are settled. Barcelona, Granada, Madrid, Murcia and Sevilla all have sizable gitano communities.

Spain has about 200,000 permanent residents, and perhaps 250,000 semipermanent ones, from other EU countries, mostly Britain, Germany, Holland, Belgium and Scandinavia. They are concentrated mainly on the Costa del Sol and Costa Blanca and a good proportion of them are retired. In the past decade or two there has been a trickle of immigrants from North Africa and the Caribbean, although on a smaller scale than in other European countries such as France.

EDUCATION

Education is free and compulsory in Spain from the age of six to 14. About one-third of pupils attend Catholic schools, which are often subsidised by the state.

Upon matriculation, students must also sit entrance exams for university. Students tend to study for six or so years, taking out qualifications such as the *diplomada* after three years and the *licenciado* after another two or three years' study. There are 33 universities across Spain.

An estimated 96% of the population aged 15 and over are literate.

ARTS
Dance

Mention dance and Spain together and what traditionally springs to mind is flamenco and its associated forms (see Music later in this section). However, dance and ballet are alive and well too. Although contemporary dance pops up all round the country, Barcelona is its capital, with several shows to choose from almost any week of the year. Nacho Duato, head of and principal dancer of the Madrid-based Compañía Nacional de Baile since 1990, transformed it from a low-profile classical company into one of the world's most technically dazzling and accomplished contemporary dance groups. The Ballet Nacional de España, founded in 1978, mixes classical ballet with Spanish dance.

Here and there you'll find the occasional regional folk dance, such as Catalunya's *sardana* or the Málaga area's unique *verdiales* flag dances, done to exhilarating fiddle-and-percussion music.

Music

Spain pulsates with music. As if awakened from a long torpor, all the elements that make up the patchwork quilt of the country's musical geography seem to be gathering force. Flamenco, revived earlier this century but subsequently much ignored by most Spaniards, is undergoing a startling transformation. No longer the preserve of the initiated or dished up sloppily for tourists, it has become increasingly fashionable among locals as it has demonstrated greater innovation. The country's rock and pop scene, while not wildly successful beyond Spanish shores, is nonetheless busy and vibrant – and a good deal more so than in other European countries. Folk music peculiar to the many different regions of Spain is also blossoming, and even on the classical front there are stirrings.

Classical Of the great or once great European nations, Spain has been noticeable in the realm of classical music by its absence. Rather, it has generally fallen to outsiders to pick up the country's vibrant rhythms and translate them into lasting homages. Who has not at least heard of *Carmen*, an opera whose leading lady epitomises all the fire, guile and flashing beauty of Andalucía and its women? Its composer, Frenchman Georges Bizet (1838-75), had been mesmerised by Moorish-influenced melodies of southern Spain in much the same way as Claude Debussy (1862-1918), whose penchant for the peninsula found expression in *Iberia*. Another Frenchman, Emmanuel Chabrier (1841-94), immortalised his love for the country's sounds in *España*, while Maurice Ravel (1875-1937) whipped up his *Bolero* almost as an aside in 1927. Russians, too, have been swept away by the Hispanic. Mikhail Glinka (1804-57) arrived in Granada in 1845 and his resulting compositions inspired a new movement in Russian folk music. Nicolai Rimsky-Korsakov (1844-1908) popped into Spain on shore leave while in the Russian navy. At heart more composer than captain, he penned his delightful *Capriccio Espagnol*.

Spain itself was bereft of composers until the likes of Cádiz-born Manuel de Falla (1876-1946) and Enrique Granados (1867-1916) came onto the scene early in the 20th century. Granados and Isaac Albéniz (1860-1909) became great pianists and interpreters of their own compositions, such as the latter's *Iberia* cycle. Joaquín Rodrigo (1902-) is another composer of note.

The best known of Spain's operatic performers is Plácido Domingo (1934-), followed closely by José Carreras (1946-). Joined by Italian tenor Luciano Pavarotti (1935-), they form the big three of contemporary male opera singers. One of the world's most outstanding sopranos is Catalunya's Montserrat Caballé (1933-). Teresa Berganza (1935-) is a well-known mezzo.

Classical Guitar To many purists, the words 'classical' and 'guitar' cannot stand together. The guitar, they will explain, is not a noble instrument, but rather a popular expedient – folksy and highly enjoyable, but by no means elevated. Be that as it may, a school of Spanish musicians has taken the humble guitar to dizzying heights of virtuosity and none more so than the great Andrés Segovia (1893-1987), born in Linares and steeped in the roots of flamenco and the passionate temperament of the south. He studied cello and piano, but his soul was in the guitar. Since it was hard to find a decent teacher of the instrument, he taught himself. He transcribed 150 works for other instruments into pieces for guitar and by the time he performed in Paris in 1924 he had established an international reputation for himself and his guitar.

Flamenco This generic term covers a broad range of music and dance. It is rooted in the *cante hondo* (deep song) of the gitanos of Andalucía and probably influenced by North African rhythms (or, indeed, music of Al-Andalus). The poet García Lorca and composer Manuel de Falla helped keep the genre alive with their grand competition in 1922, but by then it already had a well-established history. The gitanos had settled in Andalucía early in the 15th century, and by the end of the 18th century several centres of cante hondo (also known as *cante jondo*) had emerged, among them Cádiz, Jerez de la Frontera and the Triana area of Sevilla.

The guitar was invented in Andalucía: its origin lay in Arab lutes and about the 1790s a sixth string was added, probably by a Cádiz guitar-maker called Pagés. In the 1870s Antonio de Torres of Almería gave the instrument its modern shape and sonority.

The melancholy cante hondo is performed by a singer, who may be male *(cantaor)* or female *(cantaora)*, to the accompaniment of a blood-rush of guitar from the *tocaor*. Although in its pure, traditional form this is sometimes a little hard for the uninitiated to deal with, it is difficult not to be moved by the very physical experience. The accompanying dance is performed by one or more *bailaores*. The *sevillana* (Andalucian classical dance) closely resembles, but should not be confused with, the bailaores' dance. Girls all over the country try to learn sevillanas at some time during their school careers.

It is impossible in this limited space to delve into the intricacies of the various orthodox schools of flamenco that have emerged over the past century (schools of Cádiz, Sevilla, Jerez, Córdoba and so on) or of the different kinds of song and music (ranging from the most anguished *siguiriyas* and *soleás* to the more lively *bulerías*, *boleros*, *fandangos*, *alegrías* and *farrucas*). Suffice to say that there is more to it than meets the eye.

Although flamenco's home turf is in the south, many artists establish themselves in other major cities, especially Madrid, with

Flamenco song and dance have their origins in the anguished lament of Spain's marginalised gitanos, like those shown in this 19th century illustration

its gitano *barrios* or districts and long-time flamenco bars. Indeed, in the 1950s musicians streamed from the impoverished south to seek a better life in Madrid. One of the best known dance studios in the country is an unnamed place on Calle del Amor de Dios, near Huertas.

Some of the greatest figures around the turn of the century, to some the *Edad de Oro* (Golden Age) of flamenco, include the guitarist Ramón Montoya and the singer Silverio Franconetti. Manolo Caracol joined the great singer Lola Flores (died 1995) to introduce theatrical elements and even orchestral accompaniment, which injected new life into the genre but was not welcomed by purists.

Flamenco's real golden age may well be opening up before us. Never has it been so popular both in Spain and abroad, and never has there been such a degree of innovation. Strangely, the most successful proponents of modern flamenco (or flamenco-style) music are the Gipsy Kings, who are from southern France, not Spain.

Paco de Lucía (1947-), also known as Paco Peña, is doubtless the best known flamenco guitarist internationally. He has a virtuosity few would dare to claim they can match and is the personification of *duende*, that indefinable capacity to transmit the power of flamenco. There is a wealth of albums to choose from; the double album *Paco de Lucía Antología* is a good introduction to his work, ranging from 1967 to 1990.

Paco de Lucía spends more time abroad than in Spain, but plenty of other good musicians fill the gap at home. The list of fine flamenco guitarists is long, among them the Montoya family (some of whom are better known by the sobriquet of *los Habichuela*), especially Juan (1933-) and Pepe (1949-). Other artists to watch for include El Tomatito (1947-), Manolo Sanlúcar (1943-) and Moraíto Chico (1956-).

Paco de Lucía's friend El Camarón de la Isla was, until his death in 1992, the leading light of contemporary cante hondo; plenty of flamenco singers today try to emulate him. Another who has reached the level of cult

figure is Enrique Morente (1942-), referred to by a Madrid paper as 'the last Bohemian'. Among other leading vocalists figure such greats as Carmen Linares (1951-), from the province of Jaén, and the Sevillano José Menese (1941-). El Camarón's successors include Antonio Vargas (known as El Potito), Juan Cortés Duquende, Miguel Poveda and José Parra. Rising female vocalists include Aurora (1972-) and the Cádiz-born Niña Pastori (1978-), who fronts an electric jazz-rock band.

Of Spain's flamenco dancers and choreographers, the greatest name this century is with little doubt Antonio Ruiz Soler (1921-96). Leading contemporary figures include Joaquín Cortés and Manuela Vargas. Traditionalists dislike fashionable attempts to mix flamenco dance with ballet and other forms. One of the great traditional bailaores, Farruco, died in late 1997. A wild gitano soul, he argued that performers such as Cortés don't really dance flamenco. The only *'puro masculino'* bailaor these days,

Paco de Lucía, world famous virtuoso flamenco guitarist

Farruco used to say, was his teenage grandson Farruquito.

Antonio Canales, Antonio Gades, Cristina Hoyos, Miguel El Funi and Concha Vargas are other top-notch dancers, some with their own successful companies.

If you want to give yourself a general introduction to the best of flamenco, try to see Carlos Saura's 1995 flick, *Flamenco*. A double-CD set of the music is also available.

Tourist-oriented flamenco shows, called *tablaos*, lack the genuine emotion of real flamenco, although a few are worth seeing if you have no alternative. The show-cum-vaudeville atmosphere will not be to everyone's taste.

For hints on where and when to catch good live flamenco in Spain, see Entertainment in the Facts for the Visitor chapter. Some venues which stage regular flamenco are mentioned in city sections later in this guide.

Nuevo Flamenco & Fusion Possibly the most exciting developments in flamenco have taken it to other musical shores. Two of the best-known groups that have experimented with flamenco-rock fusion since the 1980s are Ketama and Pata Negra, whose music is labelled by some as Gypsy rock. One of Ketama's best albums is *Canciones Hondas*, while Pata Negra's seventh, *Como Una Vara Verde*, is a good choice. A former member of Pata Negra, Raimundo Amador (1960-), has gone his own way and in 1996 made a CD with the American blues master BB King.

In the early 1990s, Radio Tarifa emerged with a mesmerising mix of flamenco, North African and medieval sounds. The first CD, *Rumba Argelina*, was a great hit. A more traditional flamenco performer, Juan Peña (El Lebrijano), has done some equally appealing combinations with classical Moroccan music. His CD *Encuentros*, recorded with the Andalusian Orchestra of Tangier, is a good sample.

Pop & Rock In purely monetary terms, Julio Iglesias must be the country's most successful performer ever. Long a resident of the USA, he has for many years had millions swooning with his crooning in Spanish and various other languages. Apart from Iglesias, the success of Spanish popular music abroad has been limited. In the mid-1990s, however, the Sevilla duo Los del Río's song *Macarena* was a hit around the world.

Kiko Veneno is one of the durables of Spanish rock. Catalan by birth but raised in Andalucía, his music is rooted in flamenco, but in no way detracts from his crisp rock sound. Although he's been around for quite a while, he has cut few albums, all of them good. Danza Invisible is another long-time mainstream band from Málaga. One of the country's more popular groups at home and abroad is Mecano, two male musicians fronted by a powerful woman singer.

A couple of male vocalists with a big following are Miguel Bosé and Madrid-born Antonio Vega.

Moving up the rock scale a little, El Último de la Fila was, until it broke up in 1997, a fine Barcelona duo and one of the best musical products of the city. Another duo worth catching is Amistades Peligrosas: Cristina del Valle and Alberto Comesaña do some great harmonies. *La Última Tentación* is one of their better albums. They also decided to split up for a while in the summer of 98.

For something a little racier, Celtas Cortos has a sound reminiscent of the Pogues (some would say too much so and with less inspired lyrics). If this sort of music appeals, *Cuéntame un Cuento* is a good choice of CD.

The Madrid quartet Dover is an emerging indie band, competing with the Granada-based Los Planetas. The latter's third album, *Una Semana en el Motor de un Autobús*, came out in April 1998.

Def Con Dos, Extremoduro, Ska-P, Reincidentes, Soziedad Alkohólika, Molotov and the Pleasure Fuckers are just a few other popular rock bands touring around the country. Members of Mojinos Escozíos, a Catalan-Sevilla group, describe themselves as 'fat, ugly and heavy [as in heavy metal] to the death'. Their lyrics prove that PC is not a concern – and they have been selling CDs like there's no tomorrow.

Techno If techno is your thing, the Barcelonese trio Vanguard and compatriot An Der Beat are both riding high – more to be danced to than listened to.

In a more extreme vein is the world of loud and, for many, unbearable dance noise commonly known as *bakalao*. For this ear-splitting Spanish contribution to the wonderful world of techno, Valencia seems to be something of a headquarters. A sub-category (for those capable of discerning a difference) is *mákina*.

Folk Although the odd group playing traditional folk music can be found across several regions, the best and most prolific source of folk is Galicia. The area's rich heritage is closely related to that of its Celtic cousins in Brittany and Ireland and has nothing at all in common with what might be considered quintessential 'Spanish' music, such as flamenco. Emblematic of the music is the *gaita*, Galicia's version of the bagpipes. The most successful purveyor of Galicia's Celtic tradition is the highly polished group Milladoiro, which has cut many fine CDs.

Another group worth seeking out is Palla Mallada, from Santiago de Compostela, which does a mix of instrumental pieces, dances and traditional songs. Others include Na Lua, Berrogüetto, Chouteira and Luar Na Lubre. Santiago's Fía Na Roca combines traditional sounds with original compositions.

Among soloists, Uxía is an enchanting female vocalist, a gutsy version of Enya, who also seeks her inspiration in traditional *gallego* (Galician) folk music.

A highly versatile gallego performer of gaita and wind instruments is Carlos Núñez. He presents a slick show, involving violins, percussion, guitar and lute, and often invites a wide range of guest artists to play at his concerts, providing for a highly entertaining and eclectic mix of styles.

The Celtic tradition is also alive in Asturias and even Cantabria, but not to nearly the same extent as in Galicia.

From the País Vasco, Oskorri is a fine electrical and acoustic band and one of the best folk-inspired groups to emerge from the region.

Cantautores Some of the great singer-songwriters of the *movida* are still in circulation. People like Pedro Guerra and Javier Krahe, who might loosely be compared with France's Georges Brassens or Germany's Wolf Biermann, still cover the late-night circuit in Madrid with their witty ballads of protest and mordant social commentary and are even experiencing something of a revival. For non-Spaniards they are the most challenging, for it is their lyrics that matter, not the music. Luis Pastor is a younger member of this crowd.

Festivals For information on when and where to catch some of the more important music festivals, see Public Holidays & Special Events in the Facts for the Visitor chapter.

Literature
Medieval Works It is difficult to talk of a 'Spanish' literature much earlier than the 13th century, if you mean literature in Castilian. Before this, troubadours working in Vulgar Latin, Arabic and other tongues were doing the rounds of southern Europe and the great writers and thinkers in a Spain largely dominated by Muslims produced their treatises more often than not in Arabic or Hebrew.

Among the latter, the best known was the Muslim philosopher Averroës or Ibn Rushd (1126-98), from Córdoba. His commentaries on Aristotle, trying to reconcile science with religious faith, had great influence on European Christian thought in the 13th and 14th centuries.

Alfonso X, king of Castilla and León (1252-84) and known as El Sabio (the

Learned), did much to encourage the use of Castilian as a language of learning and literature, himself writing on diverse subjects.

Of all the works produced in Spanish in the Middle Ages, the *Poema de Mio Cid*, which has survived in a version penned in 1307 (although first written in 1140), is surely the best known. The epic tale of El Cid Campeador, or Rodrigo Díaz, whose exploits culminated in mastery over Valencia, bears little resemblance to the facts. Rather, it is concerned with telling a good story in which a towering figure overcomes all odds by his prowess and so attains glory.

This was an age of didactic writing, of poetry and injunctions working at once on a literal, moral and allegorical level. Gonzalo de Berceo, who died in the late 1200s, composed some of the most elegant writing in this genre, culminating in his *Milagros de Nuestra Señora* (Miracles of Our Lady). Juan Ruiz, who wrote in the first half of the 14th century, was one of the period's finest poets and something of a humorist, often descending into the downright bawdy. His *Buen Amor* (1330) leads the reader along paths of Good and Evil, with a less constrained view of earthly peccadillos than usually propounded in the edifying literature of the day.

El Siglo de Oro The end of the Reconquista in 1492 and the glory days of the Catholic Monarchs imbued with optimism the writing of the first half of the 16th century. Garcilaso de la Vega (1501-36), steeped in Italian literary sensibilities and *au fait* with the likes of Ariosto and Bembo, left behind sonnets and eclogues of unparalleled beauty. His successor and perhaps the greatest of all Spanish poets was Luis de Góngora (1561-1627). Unconcerned by theories, morals or high-minded sentiments, Góngora manipulated words with a majesty that has largely defied attempts at critical 'explanation'; his verses are above all intended as a source of sensuous pleasure. With Góngora we are in the greatest period of Spanish letters; *El Siglo de Oro* (the Golden Century), which stretched roughly

from the middle of the 16th century to the middle of the 17th.

This was equally the age of some of the country's greatest mystics. For San Juan de la Cruz (St John of the Cross), poetry, especially of a lightly erotic flavour, served as the best of imperfect tools to render the ecstasy of union between God and the soul. His works, such as *Noche Oscura* and *Llama de Amor Viva*, didn't appear until well after his death in 1591. His contemporary, Santa Teresa de Ávila (1515-82), headed down another road, capturing in evocative, if not always strictly correct, prose accounts of her explorations of her spiritual life, including *Camino de Perfección* and *Las Moradas o el Castillo Interior*.

Histories were gaining in popularity; the Jesuit Juan de Mariana (1535-1624) was a meticulous compiler.

The advent of the *comedia* in the early 17th century in Madrid produced some of the country's greatest playwrights. Lope de Vega (1562-1635), also an outstanding lyric poet, was perhaps the most prolific: more than 300 of the 800 plays and poems attributed to him remain. He explored the falseness of court life and roamed political subjects with his imaginary historical plays. Less playful and perhaps of greater substance is the work of Tirso de Molina (1581-1648), in whose *El Burlador de Sevilla* we meet the immortal character of Don Juan, a likable seducer who meets an unhappy end.

Yet another great name of the period is Pedro Calderón de la Barca (1600-81). The beauty of this grand master of the stage's works lies in his agile language and inventive techniques as a dramatist. The themes and story lines of his work were, however, comparatively run-of-the-mill. His more powerful pieces are *La Vida es Sueño* and *El Alcalde de Zalamea*; in both Calderón upholds an idea of righteousness and justice irrespective of class and caste.

Also noteworthy is Francisco de Quevedo (1580-1645), an accomplished poet working in almost diametric opposition to Góngora. He is perhaps best known today for his prose – a sparkling virtuoso game of metaphor and wordplay, but often laden with a heavy dose of bitter and unforgiving social commentary. His *La Historia de la Vida del Buscón Llamado Don Pablos*, tracing the none too elevating life of an antihero, El Buscón, is laced with especial venom for the lower classes.

Cervantes & the Novel His life something of a jumbled obstacle course of trials, tribulations and peregrinations, Miguel de Cervantes Saavedra (1547-1616) had little success with his forays into theatre and verse. But today he is commonly thought of as the man who gave modern literature a new genre: the novel.

El Ingenioso Hidalgo Don Quijote de la Mancha started life as a short story, designed to make a quick peseta, but Cervantes found himself turning it into an epic tale by the time it appeared in 1605. The ruined *ancien régime* knight and his equally impoverished companion, Sancho Panza, embark on a trail through the foibles of his era – a journey whose timelessness and universality marked the work out for greatness. *Don Quijote* would a century later be a fundamental source of inspiration for the further development of the modern novel, particularly in France and Britain.

18th & 19th Centuries The 18th century was not exactly a halcyon period for Spanish letters. Its greatest figure was Juan Meléndez Valdés (1754-1817). His *Poesías* bring together his finest work, ranging from the humanistic and even a hint of the coming romanticism through to a more personal, sometimes erotic verse. Another outstanding figure of the times was the Benedictine monk Benito Jerónimo Feijóo (1676-1764), an enlightened essayist whose defence of rational thought and the diffusion of culture is summed up in the eight volume collection of his finest essays, the *Teatro Crítico Universal*.

The age of the romantics touched Spain less than much of Europe. Its greatest poetic exponent, José de Espronceda (1788-1842),

reached the pinnacle of his often anguished work with *El Diablo Mundo*, an unfinished history of man that incites people to feverish life in the face of the enigma of existence and death. Less tortured but with a fine sense of nuance was Gustavo Adolfo Becquer (1836-70). Galicia's Rosalía de Castro (1837-85) was another bright light of the age.

One novelist towers above the rest through to the end of the 19th century. Benito Pérez Galdós (1843-1920) is the closest Spain produced to a Dickens or a Balzac. His novels and short stories ranged from social critique to the simple depiction of society through the lives of its many players. His more mature works, such as *Fortunata y Jacinta*, display a bent towards naturalism and, in the early 20th century, even symbolism. Another harsh realist and early feminist was Doña Emilia, Condesa de Pardo-Bazán. Her *Los Pazos de Ulloa* is a masterpiece.

From 1900 to Franco Miguel de Unamuno (1864-1936) was one of the leading figures of the so-called Generation

Miguel de Cervantes Saavedra, the foremost figure in Spanish literature

of 98, a group of writers and artists working around and after 1898 (a bad year for Spain with the loss of its last Caribbean colonies and an economic crisis at home). Unamuno's work is difficult, but among his most enjoyable prose is the *Tres Novelas Ejemplares*, imbued, like most of his novels and theatre, with a disquieting existentialism.

The greatest poet of the era was Antonio Machado. Steeped in symbolism, his poetry moves towards the metaphysical in his mature years, particularly in *Proverbios y Cantares*. *Nuevas Canciones* were written from 1917 to 1930. Machado's friend Juan Ramón Jiménez (1881-1958) won the 1956 Nobel literature prize for a poetic oeuvre *Platero y Yo*, a prose-poem telling of his childhood wanderings with his donkey.

The leading light in early 20th century modernist poetry was the Nicaraguan Rubén Darío (1867-1916). Another experimental writer of note was Ramón María del Valle Inclán (1869-1936).

A little later came the brief flourishing of Andalucía's Federico García Lorca (1898-1936), whose verse and theatre leaned towards surrealism, leavened by a unique musicality and visual sensibility. His many offerings include *Canciones*, *Poema del Cante Jondo* and plays such as the powerful *Bodas de Sangre* (Blood Wedding). His career was cut short by Nationalist executioners in the early stages of the civil war. Associated with Lorca in the so-called 'Generation of 27' of Andalucian writers were the poets Rafael Alberti, Vicente Aleixandre (the 1977 Nobel literature laureate) and Luis Cernuda.

The Franco Years The censors of Fascist Spain kept a lid, albeit far from watertight, on literary development in Spain.

One of the few writers of quality who managed to work throughout the years of the dictatorship, and who continues to thrive, is the Galician Nobel prize-winning novelist Camilo José Cela (1916-). His most important novel, *La Familia de Pascual Duarte*, appeared in 1942 and marked a rebirth of the Spanish realist novel.

Much of worth was also produced by writers in exile, among them Francisco Ayala, Max Aub, Juan Larrea and Mercé Rodoreda.

Contemporary Writing The death of Franco in 1975 signalled the end of the constraints placed on Spanish writers. Many of those now able to work in complete freedom were already active in exile during the Franco years and some choose to remain outside Spain. Juan Goytisolo (1931-) started off in the neorealist camp but his more recent works, such as *Señas de Identidad* and *Juan sin Tierra*, are decidedly more experimental.

A highly accessible writer is Barcelona-born José Luis Sampedro (1917-). A professor of structural economics (!) and one-time senator, he writes wide-ranging and thought-provoking novels. He considers *Octubre, Octubre* his life testament. *La Sonrisa Etrusca* is a touching account of the loves and death of a Calabrian peasant in Milan – other works take Sampedro from the Baltic to the South Seas.

Jorge Semprún (1923-), who lost his home and family in the civil war, ended up in a Nazi concentration camp for his activities with the French Resistance in WWII. He writes mostly in French. His first novel, *Le Grand Voyage*, is one of his best.

Of course, younger authors are emerging all the time. One to note is Antonio Muñoz Molina (1956-), whose *El Invierno en Lisboa* is a touching novel which won him considerable acclaim when it first appeared in 1987.

Notable female writers to emerge in the past 30 years include Adelaida García Morales, Ana María Matute and Montserrat Roig. Rosa Montero (1951-) is a prominent journalist who has had considerable success with her novels, such as *Te Trataré Como a una Reina* (I'll Treat You Like a Queen) and *La Hija del Caníbal* (The Cannibal's Daughter).

Painting

The Beginnings Humans have been creating images in Spain for as long as 14,000 years, as the cave paintings in Altamira (Cantabria) attest.

Later, the Celt-Iberian tribes were producing some fine ceramics and statuary, perhaps influenced by the presence of Greeks, Carthaginians and ultimately Romans.

More strictly speaking, the origins of Spanish painting lie in the early Middle Ages. From this period some magnificent frescoes have been preserved. Although much-faded examples remain visible in some of the pre-Romanesque churches of Asturias, among the oldest and most invaluable frescoes to have survived are those in the 11th century Mozarabic Ermita de San Baudelio, near Berlanga de Duero (Castilla y León). In the same unique building is a rich serving of Romanesque frescoes from the following century.

The single most outstanding collection of 12th century Romanesque frescoes can be seen in Museu Nacional d'Art de Catalunya in Barcelona. It is a collection of pieces taken from churches and chapels across northern Catalunya and carefully preserved and presented in a unique display. The most outstanding frescoes of the same era still in situ are those of the Panteón Real of the Real Basílica de San Isidoro in León.

Catalan & Valencian Schools Much of the painting to emerge from medieval Spain has remained anonymous, but a few leading lights managed to get some credit. Ferrer Bassá (c1290-c1348) is considered one of the country's first masters. Influenced by the Siennese school, his only surviving works are murals with a slight caricatural touch in Barcelona's Pedralbes convent. He is considered the Spanish creator of the Italo-Gothic style.

The style soon displayed a more international flavour, best embodied in the work of Bernat Martorell (?-1452), a master of chiaroscuro. As the Flemish school gained influence, painters like Jaume Huguet

(1415-92) adopted the sombre realism, lightened with Hispanic splashes of gold, as can be seen from his *San Jorge* in the Museu Nacional d'Art de Catalunya.

Closely linked to Catalunya was the school of painters that emerged in neighbouring Valencia. Its major exponents included Lorenzo Zaragoza (1365-1402), Pere Nicolau (died 1410) and Andrés Marzal de Sax (died 1410), but Bartolomé Bermejo (died 1495) was the most interesting of the lot, incorporating Flemish influences and exploring the use of oil. Nothing better illustrates the Córdoba-born artist's gifts than the *Pietà* in Barcelona's cathedral museum.

Castilla Local artists tended to be passed over in favour of foreigners in 15th century Castilla. Their 'surnames' often give this away: Nicolás Florentino (from Florence; born Dello Delli, he did the retablo in the Catedral Vieja in Salamanca), Nicolás Francés (from France) and Juan de Flandes (Flemish).

One local exception was Fernando Gallego (1466-1507), heavily influenced by Flanders' Rogier van der Weyden. Zamora's cathedral houses altarpieces by him; others can be seen in the Prado.

Also initially imbued with Hispano-Flemish thinking, Pedro Berruguete (1438-1504) is said to have done a stint in Urbino, Italy. Although there is no direct proof of this, his later work as court painter to Fernando and Isabel tends to support the claim. His son, Alonso (1488-1561), definitely enjoyed an extended stay in Urbino and, although a fine painter, is remembered for his sculpture. His alabaster *Resurrección* in Valencia's cathedral is a master work.

16th Century One of the most remarkable artists at work in Spain in the latter half of the 16th century was an 'adopted' Spaniard. Domenikos Theotokopoulos (1541-1614), known as El Greco (literally 'the Greek'), was schooled in both Crete and Italy, but spent his productive working life in Toledo.

(continued on page 77)

SPANISH ARCHITECTURE

DAMIEN SIMONIS

SPANISH ARCHITECTURE

Spain's place on the 'edge' of Europe and centuries of Muslim rule left an indelible imprint on the country's architectural heritage, setting it apart from the rest of Europe. Phoenicia, Carthage, Greece, Rome and the Visigoths all left their mark. But they were overshadowed by the genius of the Arabs, who not only left behind extraordinary monuments, but also an artistic legacy that would continue to find expression long after the last Muslim kingdom had fallen to the Reconquista.

All the great European architectural movements – from Romanesque to Gothic, from the baroque to neoclassicism – seeped into Spain, although usually later than elsewhere and often altered to suit local tastes. But no other European country can boast the diversity of Spain. While the towering Gothic cathedrals of Burgos, León and Toledo were being raised to the greater glory of God in the first half of the 13th century, Granada became home to the Alhambra, one of the most remarkable visual delights the Muslim world has ever produced.

Across the country, countless magnificent churches and monasteries vie for your attention with castles and palaces of all shapes and sizes. The range, from startling feats of Roman engineering to the caprice of Gaudí, can seem overwhelming but is never tiresome.

Facing page 64: Chimney pots à la Gaudí at La Pedrera (Casa Milà), Barcelona

Opposite: Gaudí's modernisme gingerbread house – Casa Batlló, Barcelona

Below: Roman bridge at Burgui (Navarra)

TIM NOLLEN

Celtiberians & Greeks

The tribes that first inhabited the Iberian Peninsula, collectively known as Celtiberians, left behind a wealth of evidence of their existence. The most common living arrangement, called the *castro*, was a hamlet surrounded by stone walls and made up of circular stone houses. Several have been partly preserved in locations as disparate as La Guardia, on Galicia's southern coast, and Vinaceite, deep in Aragón. One of the best is near Coaña, in Asturias.

The Greeks and Carthaginians rarely made it far into the Spanish interior. Apart from some Carthaginian necropolises in Ibiza, a couple of spots in Andalucía and some Greek remains at Empúries (Catalunya), little is left to remind you of their presence.

Romans

The Roman legacy in Spain is not as great as in some other of the empire's former provinces. Spectacular exceptions include the aqueduct in Segovia (Castilla y León), the bridge at Alcántara (Extremadura) and the stout walls of Lugo (Galicia), while other charming Roman remnants include the bridge over the Río Esca at Burgui.

Vestiges of Roman towns can also still be seen. Among the more important are: the ancient town of Augusta Emerita in Mérida (Extremadura); ancient Tarraco at Tarragona (Catalunya); the amphitheatre and other ruins at Itálica (near Sevilla, Andalucía); and Sagunto (Valencia). Modest remains have been imaginatively converted into underground museums in Barcelona and Zaragoza. Ancient Numancia, north of Soria (Castilla y León), is largely Roman, although it was preceded by a Celtiberian city that for a long time resisted imperial rule.

DAMIEN SIMONIS

Left: What remains of a once 15km long, 1st century Roman aqueduct, Segovia (Castilla y León)

Visigoths

Filling the vacuum left by the departing Romans, the Visigoths employed a more humble but remarkably attractive style, which survives in a handful of small churches. The 7th century Ermita de Santa María de Lara, at Quintanilla de las Viñas in Burgos province (Castilla y León) is one of the best. Fragments of this unique style can be seen in several cities across Spain, including Toledo.

Reputedly the oldest church in Spain is that of the 7th century San Juan, in Baños de Cerrato, while the cathedral in nearby Palencia (Castilla y León) has Visigothic origins in the crypt. The horseshoe arch, later perfected by the Arabs, is characteristic of the Visigothic aesthetic.

Below left: The Iglesia de Santa María del Naranco near Oviedo is an evocative example of pre-Romanesque architecture (Asturias)

Below right: The 9th century Iglesia de Valdediós, near Villaviciosa (Asturias)

Pre-Romanesque

When Spain was swamped by the Muslim invasion of 711, only the unruly northern strip of the country in what is today Asturias held out. During the 9th century, a unique building style emerged in this green corner of Spain cut off from the rest of Christian Europe. Of the 30-odd examples of pre-Romanesque architecture scattered about the Asturian countryside, the little Iglesia de Santa María del Naranco and Iglesia de San Miguel de Lillo (Oviedo) are the finest. The complete vaulting of the nave, the semicircular arches in the windows and porches and the angular simplicity of these churches are a foretaste of Romanesque style.

DAMIEN SIMONIS

DAMIEN SIMONIS

Muslim Architecture

Meanwhile, the Muslims were settling in for a long occupation: they would remain for almost 800 years in their longest-lasting enclave, Granada. Córdoba was the centre of Muslim political power and culture for the first 300 years.

The Syrian Omayyad dynasty that set up shop here brought with it architects imbued with ideas and experience won in Damascus. This was soon put to use in the construction of the Mezquita (mosque) in Córdoba, whose style was echoed across Muslim Spain. Horseshoe-shaped and lobed arches; the use of exquisite tiles in the decoration – mostly calligraphy (usually verses from the Qur'an) and floral motifs; peaceful inner courtyards; complex stucco work; and stalactite ceiling adornments are all features easily recognisable and comparable with buildings raised in Damascus. Just outside Córdoba, the now ruined city of Medina Azahara was built in similar style.

Remnants of this Muslim legacy abound across Spain, although many grand examples have been lost. The most striking piece of Islamic architecture in northern Spain is the palace of the Aljafería in Zaragoza, a proud residence subsequently much altered by the Christians.

Throughout Andalucía and parts of central Spain towns and villages retain a labyrinthine air characteristic of medieval Islamic towns. Toledo, Granada's Albayzín area and the Muslim quarters of Córdoba are all fascinating reminders of this chapter in Spanish urban history.

In the 12th century, the armies of Morocco's Almohad dynasty stormed across the by now hopelessly divided lands of Muslim Spain. To them we owe some of the marvels of Sevilla, in particular the square-based minaret known as the Giralda, which is even more beautiful than their minaret of the Koutoubia mosque in Marrakesh.

SUSAN FORSYTH

Left: An example of the intricate stucco work and elegant arches of the Alhambra in Granada, the pinnacle of Muslim architecture in Spain (Andalucía)

Opposite: Qur'anic calligraphy in stucco in the Alhambra's Patio de los Leones (Andalucía)

Muslim art reached new heights of elegance with the construction of the Alhambra palace in Granada. Built from the 13th to the 15th centuries, it is symptomatic of the direction taken by Islamic art at the time. Eschewing innovation, the Alhambra expresses a desire to refine already well-tried forms. In this it is an unqualified success and surely one of the Muslim world's most beautiful creations.

About the same time, Pedro I decided to build himself a new palace in the *alcázar* (fortress) of what was by now Christian-controlled Sevilla. Granada's Mohammed V sent artisans to help out and the result is a jewel of Iberian Islamic architecture – built for a Christian monarch!

In places such as Girona (Catalunya), Cáceres (Extremadura), Jaén and Ronda (Andalucía) you can visit well-preserved Muslim bathhouses.

SUSAN FORSYTH

Mozarabic & Mudéjar

What sets much of Christian Spain's architecture apart from its counterparts elsewhere in Europe is the deep-seated influence exercised over it by Islamic styles.

Already in the 10th century, Christians practising in Muslim territory – known as *Mozárabes* (Mozarabs) – began to adopt elements of classic Islamic construction and export them to Christian-held territory. Although Mozarabic artisans contributed to many buildings, 'purely' Mozarabic structures are few and far between. Among the outstanding examples are: the Iglesia de San Miguel de Escalada (east of León), the Ermita de San Baudelio (in Soria province) and the Iglesia de Nuestra Señora de Lebeña (on the eastern side of the Picos de Europa).

More important was the *mudéjar* influence, that of Muslims who remained behind in the lands of the Reconquista. Their skills were found to be priceless (but cheap) and throughout Spain their influence is evident.

One unmistakable mudéjar feature was the preponderance of brick: castles, churches and mansions all over the country were built of this material.

Another telltale feature is in the ceilings. Extravagantly decorated timber creations, often ornately carved, are a mark of the mudéjar hand. Several different types get constant mention. The term *armadura* refers to any of these wooden ceilings, especially when they have the appearance of being an inverted boat. *Artesonado* ceilings are characterised by interlaced beams leaving regular spaces (triangular, square or polygonal) for the insertion of decorative *artesas*. The truly mudéjar ones generally bear floral or simple geometric patterns, but Renaissance variations also abound, with less Oriental patterns.

SPANISH ARCHITECTURE

DAMIEN SIMONIS

TIM NOLLEN

Far left: Detail from the Iglesia de San Miguel de Escalada, east of León, an outstanding Mozarabic structure (Castilla y León)

Left: A 13th century fantasy of brick and ceramics – the mudéjar Torre de San Salvador, near Teruel (Aragón)

The term *techumbre* (which can simply mean 'roof') applies more specifically to the most common of armaduras, where the skeleton of the ceiling (looked at from the end) looks like a series of 'A's.

In the Convento de Santa Clara in Salamanca ramps have been installed, allowing close inspection of the original ceiling.

Romanesque

As the Muslim tide was turned back and the Reconquista gathered momentum, the first great medieval European movement in design began to take hold in Spain, spreading from Italy and France. From about the 11th century, churches, monasteries, bridges, pilgrims' hospices and other buildings in the Romanesque style mushroomed in the north.

The first wave came in Catalunya, where Lombard artisans influenced by Byzantine building techniques soon covered the countryside with comparatively simple churches – the church of Sant Climent in Taüll is emblematic of this. Another outstanding example is the Monestir de Santa Maria in Ripoll; some 2000 Romanesque buildings survive in Catalunya. Soon more home-grown styles began to emerge across the rest of northern Spain.

Romanesque is easily identified by a few basic characteristics. The exterior of most edifices bears little decoration and they tend to be simple, angular structures. In the case of churches in particular, the concession to curves comes with the semicylindrical apse – or, in many cases, triple apse. The single most striking element of decoration is the semicircular arch or arches that grace doorways, windows, cloisters and naves. The humble church of the Monasterio de Sigena, east of Zaragoza, has a doorway boasting 14 such arches, one encased in the other.

Romanesque bridges abound in northern Spain, but the most impressive is the Puente de los Peregrinos at Puente de la Reina, a key point along the Camino de Santiago in Navarra.

With all the baroque baubles, you could be excused for overlooking that the cathedral in Santiago de Compostela is itself a seminal work of Romanesque design, much imitated, for instance in Orense and Tuy.

The Camino de Santiago is studded with Romanesque beauties. These include (from east to west) the Monasterio de Santo Domingo de Silos, the smaller cloister (Las Claustrillas) in the Monasterio de las Huelgas in Burgos and the restored Iglesia de San Martín in Frómista.

South of this line, the Romanesque mantle thins out – for the simple reason that no-one was building Romanesque churches in Muslim territory. Segovia is an island of a peculiar style, with arcaded porches added to the sides of its churches and in Ávila the Basílica de San Vicente is largely Romanesque. What really stands out in Ávila, however, are the Romanesque walls that still surround the city.

Right: The charming Romanesque-mudéjar Iglesia de San Tirso, Sahagún, was built in the 12th century (Castilla y León)

DAMIEN SIMONIS

The Transition

During the 12th century, modifications in the Romanesque recipe became apparent. The pointed arch and ribbed vault of various kinds are clear precursors of the Gothic revolution to come.

The Monasterio de Santa María de la Oliva in Navarra was among the first to incorporate such features and other buildings followed. Cathedrals in Ávila (part-fortress), Sigüenza (Castilla-La Mancha), Tarragona (Catalunya) and Tudela (Navarra) all display at least some transitional elements.

A peculiar side development affected south-western Castilla. The cathedrals in Salamanca, Zamora and Toro all boast Byzantine lines, particularly in the cupola.

Gothic

In northern Europe, everyone marvelled at the towering new cathedrals made possible by the use of flying buttresses and other technical innovations.

The idea caught on later in Spain, but three of the most important Gothic cathedrals in the country, in Burgos, León and Toledo, went up in the 13th century. The former two owe much to French models, but the Spaniards soon introduced other elements. The choirstalls *(coro)* in the centre of the nave and huge decorative *retablos* (altarpieces) towering over the high altar were just two such innovations.

The main structural novelty in Spanish Gothic was star-vaulting (a method of weight distribution in the roof in which ribbed vaults project outwards from a series of centre points), while a clearly Hispanic touch is the cloister and gardens.

A problem with identifying to what style a monument belongs is that often they belong to several. Many great buildings begun at the height of Romanesque glory were only completed long after Gothic had gained the upper hand. And although, for instance, the cathedral in Burgos was one of the first to go up, its magnificent spires were a result of German-inspired Late Gothic imagination. In many cases, these Gothic or Romanesque-Gothic buildings received a plateresque or baroque overlay at a later date. Sevilla's immense cathedral was completed in 1507 and betrays not a few Renaissance touches.

Mudéjar influences were also alive and well, most easily recognised in the giveaway penchant for working in brick rather than stone. Toledo is covered in Gothic-mudéjar combinations, while Aragón was blessed with a singular version of the theme. Zaragoza, Teruel, Tarazona and Calatayud all contain marvellous works.

Finally, the so-called Isabelline style was a late addition to the cocktail. Taking some decorative cues from the more curvaceous traits of Islamic design, it was in some ways an indirect precursor to plateresque. Perhaps its ultimate expression is Toledo's San Juan de los Reyes, originally destined to be the final resting place of the Catholic

Below: The intricate ceiling of the León cathedral cloisters (Castilla y León)

DAMIEN SIMONIS

Right: A masterpiece of Gothic grandeur – the cathedral in Burgos took three centuries to build (Castilla y León)

DAMIEN SIMONIS

Monarchs. Designed by French-born Juan Güas (1453-96), it is a medley of earlier Gothic and mudéjar elements, with a final decorative Isabelline flourish. The Catholic Monarchs actually ended up in Granada's Capilla Real, another fine example of the genre.

The 16th century saw a revival of pure Gothic, perhaps best exemplified in the new cathedral in Salamanca, although the Segovia cathedral was about the last, and possibly most pure, Gothic house of worship to be constructed in Spain.

Not only religious buildings flourished. Most of the innumerable castles scattered across the country went up in Gothic times. Many never saw action and were not intended to – a couple of the more extraordinary samples of mudéjar castle-building from this era are the Castillo de la Mota (Medina del Campo, Castilla y León) and the sumptuous castle at Coca, not far away. Others intended more for warfare were built of sturdier materials, such as the one at Peñafiel on the Río Duero, long the front line between Muslim and Christian Spain. A long way farther south, near Almagro (Castilla-La Mancha), the knights of Calatrava built a castle in a stunning position controlling a valley into what was by then left of Muslim territory – the kingdom of Granada.

Renaissance

The Renaissance in Spain can be roughly divided into three distinct styles. First was the Italian-influenced special flavour of plateresque. To visit Salamanca is to receive a concentrated dose of the most splendid work in the genre, which refers more to decoration than to structure. The university façade especially is a virtuoso piece, featuring busts, medallions and swathes of complex floral design. It is busy but controlled, and the Italian influence is clearly evident. Not far behind in intensity comes the façade of the Convento de San Esteban. Little of the work can be convincingly traced to any one hand and it appears that the principal exponent of plateresque, Alonso de Covarrubias (1488-1570), was busier in places such as his home city of Toledo (the Alcázar and the Capilla de los Nuevos Reyes in the cathedral).

Next was the more purist Renaissance style that prevailed in Andalucía and had its maximum expression in the Palacio de Carlos V in Granada's Alhambra. Diego de Siloé (1495-1563) and his followers are regarded as masters. Siloé made his mark with Granada's cathedral; others followed him with such masterpieces as the Jaén cathedral and the Capilla de El Salvador in Úbeda (although this leans more to plateresque). The latter was designed by Andrés de Vandelvira (1509-75).

Juan de Herrera (1530-97) is the last and perhaps greatest figure of the Spanish Renaissance, but his work bears almost no resemblance to anything else of the period. His austere masterpiece was the palace-monastery complex of San Lorenzo de El Escorial. Even after his death, Herrera's style lived on. Madrid's Plaza Mayor and *ayuntamiento* (town hall) were built pretty much in imitation of his work.

Below: The Italian-influenced Palacio de Vázquez de Molina (now Úbeda's town hall) is one of Andrés de Vandelvira's Renaissance buildings in Úbeda (Andalucía)

JOHN NOBLE

DAMIEN SIMONIS

Baroque

The heady frills and spills of baroque can be seen all over Spain, but usually in the form of additions rather than complete buildings. Cádiz's baroque cathedral is an exception (although some neoclassical work was added). Three loose phases can be identified, starting with a sober baroque still heavily influenced by Herrera (see earlier), followed by a period of greater architectural exuberance (some would say, a sickening amount) and finally running into a mixture of baroque with the beginnings of neoclassicism.

The leading exponents of this often overblown approach to building and decoration were the Churriguera brothers. Alberto (1676-1750) designed Salamanca's Plaza Mayor, but he and José (1665-1735) are best known for their extraordinary retablos, huge carved wooden backdrops for altars, with twisting gilded columns and burdened with all manner of angels and saints.

Baroque reached heights of opulence with the Sagrario in Granada's La Cartuja monastery and the Transparente in Toledo's cathedral. Sevilla is jammed with baroque gems. But baroque appears elsewhere too: the façade superimposed over the Romanesque original in the cathedral of Santiago de Compostela and the cathedral in Murcia are notable examples.

Neoclassicism

In Spain as elsewhere, the pendulum swung away from the gaudy extremes of baroque as the 18th century closed. Tastes became more sober and the cleaner, restrained lines of neoclassicism came into fashion. In Spain, minor churches, bullrings and public buildings were built in this style, but little of greatness was achieved.

Modernisme

The end of the 19th century ushered in arguably one of the most imaginative periods in Spanish building. Catalunya was home to the *modernistas*, whose master was Antoni Gaudí (1852-1926). Although he exercised his fantasy outside Catalunya (in Astorga, León and Comillas), he and his peers left their most singular mark in Barcelona. Work continues even now on his most exciting project, the immense La Sagrada Família church. Other jewels in the Gaudí crown include the Casa Battló and La Pedrera, not to mention the Parc Güell.

Modern

The main boulevards of Madrid are filled with the portentous façades, owned by banks and ministries, from around the turn of the century. Together they make an agreeable impression, without being of any notable architectural worth.

DALE BUCKTON

Left: La Pedrera's grey-stone façade ripples around a Barcelona corner

(continued from page 64)

His slender, exalted figures and, in the latter part of his career, a striking simplicity of colour and fluidity of movement are hallmarks that many tried to imitate but none emulated. One of his earlier works is also one of his greatest – *El Entierro del Conde de Orgaz* (The Burial of the Count of Orgaz) in Toledo's Iglesia de Santo Tomé.

El Greco and Spanish artists in general had a hard time raising interest in their material at the court of Felipe II, who above all preferred Titian and a series of lesser Italian Mannerists. Holding up the Spanish side to a certain extent was El Mudo (the Mute), Juan Navarrete (1526-79), who became one of Spain's first practitioners of 'tenebrism', a fashion that largely aped Caravaggio's chiaroscuro style.

The Golden Age As the 16th century gave way to the 17th, a remarkably fecund era in the history of Spanish painting dawned.

One of Navarrete's protégés was Francisco Ribalta (1565-1628). He ended up in Valencia, where he turned out mostly religious portraiture in which he deployed to great effect the tenebrist methods he had learned.

Across the Mediterranean in Italy, José (Jusepe) de Ribera (1591-1652) also came under the influence of Caravaggio. Many of his works found their way back to Spain and are now scattered about various galleries, but he remained in Naples until the end of his days. It is odd that a Spaniard who spent most of his life in Italy should be known today as a Spanish artist, while El Greco is *not* known as Cretan! Ribera's mastery of light was bettered perhaps only by his contemporary Velázquez.

In Sevilla, meanwhile, another school gathered momentum under Francisco Pacheco (1564-1654). A true Renaissance man, he had an alumnus whom he set in the right direction. Not only did Diego Rodríguez de Silva Velázquez (1599-1660) marry Pacheco's daughter, but he also soon rose to prominence after leaving his native Sevilla for Madrid. Within a year he was admitted to the magic circle of court painters, where he stayed for the rest of his life.

Velázquez stands in a class of his own. He composed scenes that owe their life not only to his photographic eye for light and contrast but to a compulsive interest, not unlike Ribera's, in the humanity of his subjects. With him any trace of the idealised stiffness which characterised a by-now spiritless Mannerism fell by the wayside. Realism became a key and the majesty of his royal subjects springs from a capacity to capture the essence of the person – king or *infanta* – and the detail of their finery. And between commissions he'd take just as sympathetic a view of less fortunate members of the royal menagerie, like court jesters and dwarfs.

His masterpieces include *Las Meninas* and *La Rendición de Breda* (The Surrender of Breda), both on view in the Prado, and a portrait of Pope Innocent X he carried out while in Rome in 1650.

A less exalted contemporary and close friend of Velázquez, Francisco de Zurbarán moved *to* Sevilla as an official painter. Probably of Basque origin but born in Extremadura, he is best remembered for the startling clarity and light in his portraits of monks. He travelled a great deal and in Guadalupe a series of eight portraits can still be seen hanging where Zurbarán left them in the Hieronymite monastery. Zurbarán fell on hard times in the 1640s and was compelled by the plague to flee Sevilla. He died in poverty.

Zurbarán has come to be seen as one of the masters of the Spanish canvas, but in his lifetime it was a younger and less inspired colleague who won all the prizes. Bartolomé Esteban Murillo (1618-82) took the safe road and turned out stock religious pieces and images of beggar boys and the like with technical polish but little verve.

Yet another solid artist of the same period and a student of Pacheco was Alonso Cano (1601-67), who spent his working life in Granada. Also a gifted sculptor and architect, he is sometimes referred to as the Michelangelo of Spain. Not a great deal of his work remains and his stormy life didn't help matters. He might well have joined the Velázquez gravy train in Madrid had he not been accused of his second wife's murder and been obliged to leave.

A parade of late baroque artists working over the course of the century have been loosely lumped together as the 'Madrid school'. Among their number, a few names stand out. They include Antonio de Pereda, the monk Fray Juan Rizi, Juan Carreño de Miranda and Francisco Rizi (the monk's younger brother). The last of them, and the most gifted, was Claudio Coello (1642-93). He specialised in the big picture, literally. Some of his enormous decorative canvases decorate El Escorial, among them his magnum opus, *La Sagrada Forma*.

18th Century The Bourbon kings had little interest in sponsoring Spanish talent, being obsessed, rather, with all things French and, to a lesser extent, Italian. Carlos III had Anton Raphael Mengs (1728-79) brought from Bohemia as court painter and he became the maker and breaker of rising artists. Aided by Francisco Bayeu (1734-95), he was a gifted if unexciting portraitist.

Goya Mengs could spot talent. He encouraged Francisco José de Goya y Lucientes (1746-1828), a provincial hick from Fuendetodos in Aragón, as a cartoonist in the Fábrica Real de Tapices in Madrid. Here began the long and varied career of Spain's only truly great artist of the 18th (and, indeed, even the 19th) century.

In the early stages of his rise, Goya's portrayals of everyday scenes appeared to owe something to the candour of Hogarth and in some cases also to the influence of Tiepolo, whom Carlos III attracted to Spain to work on the Palacio Real.

Before his arrival in Madrid, married to Francisco Bayeu's sister, Goya had managed to finance a trip to study art in Italy and carried out some commissions in Zaragoza, notably frescoes depicting the lives of Christ and the Virgin Mary in the

Cartuja de Auli, a monastery just outside the city. They have been restored and can be seen today.

In 1776 he began designing for the tapestry factory and by 1799 was appointed Carlos IV's court painter. Illness in 1792 left him deaf. This perhaps influenced his style, which was increasingly unshackled by convention and often merciless.

Several distinct series and individual paintings mark the progress of his life and work. In the last years of the century he painted such enigmatic masterpieces as *La Maja Vestida* and *La Maja Desnuda*, identical portraits but for the lack of clothes in the latter. At about the same time he did the frescoes in Madrid's Ermita de San Antonio de la Florida and *Los Caprichos*, a biting series of 80 etchings lambasting the follies of court life and ignorant clergy.

The arrival of the French and war in 1808 profoundly affected his work. Unforgiving portrayals of the brutality of war are *El Dos de Mayo* and, more dramatically, *El Tres de Mayo*. The latter depicts the execution of Madrid rebels by French troops.

With the return of Fernando VII at the end of the war, Goya's position became more tenuous. After he retired to the Quinta del Sordo (Deaf Man's House), as he called his modest lodgings west of the Manzanares in Madrid, age and perhaps a bitterness prompted the creation of his most extraordinary paintings, the nightmarish *Pinturas Negras* (Black Paintings). Done on the walls of the house, they were later removed and now hang in the Prado. *Saturno Devorando a Su Hijo* (Saturn Devouring his Son) is emblematic of the hallucinatory horror of these works. He spent the last years of his life in voluntary exile in France, where he continued to paint until his death.

It is difficult to do justice to Goya's role in the evolution of European painting. An obvious precursor to many subsequent strands of modern art, he was an island of grandeur in a sea of mediocrity in Spain.

Late 19th Century Although no-one of the stature of Goya can be cited, new trends were noticeable in the latter decades of the century. For the first time in centuries the focus shifted, briefly, back to Valencia. A trio from this region merit a mention: Ignacio Pinazo (1849-1916), Francisco Domingo (1842-1920) and Emilio Sala (1850-1910). Sala, who was clearly influenced by Degas, and Domingo lived and worked in Paris, but neither achieved great success. More successful in the long run was the Basque Ignacio Zuloaga (1870-1945).

Joaquín Sorolla (1863-1923), if anything, flew in the face of the French impressionists, preferring the blinding sunlight of the Valencian coast to the muted tones favoured in Paris. He is known for his cheerful, large-format images of beach life. His work can be studied at the Museo de Sorolla, Madrid.

20th Century In a sense, the history of Spanish art turned full circle at the close of the 19th century, returning to Catalunya. Barcelona, a hothouse of social agitation and the home of Spanish modernism (see the Architecture special section), was about the only environment in an otherwise depressed and sluggish Spain in which artists could hope to flourish. It was the perfect place for someone like Pablo Ruiz Picasso (1881-1973), born in Málaga, to come and flex his brushes.

Picasso is one of the monumental characters of Western European art. Having shown prodigious aptitude at an early age, he started visiting Paris in 1900. He had already absorbed lessons from his greatest forerunners – Goya, Velázquez and El Greco – and in Paris opened himself to the riches of Gauguin, Toulouse-Lautrec and Van Gogh.

Picasso was a turbulent character and gifted not only on canvas, but also as a sculptor, graphic designer and ceramicist. His work knew many abruptly changing periods. His Blue Period, until 1904, is characterised by rather sombre renditions of the lives of the down and out. The common denominator was the preponderance of blues in his palette. After his definitive move to Paris in 1904, he began the so-called Pink Period; the subjects became merrier and the colouring leaned towards light pinks and greys.

Picasso remained ever in search of new forms. *Les Demoiselles d'Avignon* (1907) broke with all forms of traditional representation, introducing a deformed perspective that would spill into cubism, of which he and Georges Braque were the pioneers. Picasso experimented continually with different methods and by the mid-1920s was dabbling with surrealism. His best-known work is *Guernica*, a complex canvas portraying the horror of war and inspired by the German aerial bombing of the Basque town Gernika in 1937.

Picasso's output during and after WWII remained prolific and indeed he was cranking out paintings, sculptures, ceramics and etchings until the day he died.

While Picasso went his way, his friend and compatriot Juan Gris (1887-1927) remained faithful to cubist orthodoxy and, among

Pablo Ruiz Picasso changed the face of Western European art

other strong works produced an intriguing portrait of Picasso.

Separated from Picasso by barely a generation, two other artists reinforced the Catalan contingent in the vanguard of first-class Spanish contributions to this century's art: Dalí and Miró. Although he started off dabbling in cubism, Salvador Dalí (1904-89) became more readily identified with the surrealists. This complex character's 'hand-painted dream photographs', as he called them, are virtuoso executions brimming with fine detail and nightmare images dragged up from a feverish and Freud-fed imagination. Preoccupied with Picasso's fame, Dalí built himself a reputation as an outrageous showman and self-promoter. The single best display of his works can be seen at the 'theatre-museum' he created in Figueres (Catalunya).

Slower to find his feet, Joan Miró (1893-1983) developed a joyous and almost childlike style that earned him the epithet 'the most surrealist of us all' from André Breton. His later period is his best known, characterised by simple use of bright colours and forms.

Picasso, Dalí and Miró were a pretty hard act to follow and contemporary painters lack the greatness of this extraordinary trio.

In the wake of the civil war, Fernando Zobel collected his own works and those of his contemporaries in the 1950s 'Generación Abstracta' under one roof in a private museum in Cuenca. Gustavo Torner and Eusebio Sempere feature among those on display. Other names worth looking for include Antonio Saura, Manuel Millares and Antoni Tàpies.

The art of Madrid's Eduardo Arroyo (1937-) is steeped in the radical spirit that kept him in exile from Spain for 15 years from 1962.

Cinema

While a handful of directors and actors keep the modern Spanish cinema industry ticking over, occasionally with some success beyond their own shores, the history of film in Spain has been a largely barren expanse with the occasional burst of brilliance.

Way back in 1897 a short film was made showing people at Zaragoza's basilica and later studios were set up in Barcelona.

Luis Buñuel The man now universally regarded as the greatest Spanish film maker emerged with the surrealist movement in the 1920s. Luis Buñuel, born in Teruel in 1900, only developed an interest in film after moving to Paris in 1926. By then he had already established himself in Spanish literary and art circles and for a long time was a close friend of Salvador Dalí.

Buñuel's first full attempt at film production, made when he was already under the sway of the surrealists, was *Un Chien Andalou* (1929), followed a year later by *L'Age d'Or*. Both were made with Dalí. They have lived on as classics, as has his next effort, a hard-hitting account of the desperation of rural life for which he returned to Spain. *Las Hurdes – Terre Sans Pain*, filmed in the hilly Las Hurdes region of Extremadura and the surrounding area, was banned in Spain and hence originally appeared in its French version. Buñuel remained in Spain, dubbing for Warner Brothers. He did not really move back into film-making until winding up in Mexico in the mid-1940s, an exile from Francoist Spain. Mexico City then became his base, although he also continued to work in France. *Belle de Jour* (1966) was a big success.

The Civil War & the Franco Years Meanwhile, in Spain itself, censorship tended to stifle most creative impulses. During the civil war, the Republican side had beaten the Nationalists in the use of film as a propaganda tool, but this didn't prevent them from losing the war. Once Franco installed himself in power in 1939, a tight if not always consistent clamp was applied to the industry.

There were exceptions to the rule. Luis García Berlanga's *Bienvenido Mr Marshall* (Welcome Mr Marshall), made in 1952, was a breath of Italian-style neorealism that managed to get through the net. It observes the belated agreement on US aid to Spain under the Marshall Plan (in which the USA ignored its own disapproval of Franco in return for military bases) from a small Spanish village; about the only tangible result for the villagers is a rain of dust as Marshall's cavalcade of VIP cars charges through the town.

Juan Antonio Bardem followed in 1955 with *Muerte de un Ciclista* (Death of a Cyclist) and Berlanga chimed in again with *El Verdugo* (The Executioner) in 1964. Buñuel was asked back to Spain at this time to produce a film. *Viridiana* was a biting performance deemed worthy of a Palme d'Or at Cannes and subsequently banned by Franco.

The next star to emerge was Carlos Saura, whose first film, *Los Golfos* (The Scoundrels), came out in 1959. He developed a more subversive style in the early 1970s, peaking with *Ana y los Lobos* (1973), in which the power of the church and army in Francoist Spanish society comes under attack. In the same year, Victor Erice's *El Espíritu de la Colmena* (The Spirit of the Beehive) hit the screen; it is a quiet and beautifully crafted picture in which one of the cinema's outcast figures, Frankenstein's monster, becomes real for a beekeeper's little daughter.

Cinema after Franco The late 1970s and the 1980s breathed new life into Spanish cinema, with a few directors producing work appreciated not only in Spain, but also abroad. Pedro Almodóvar is Spain's best-known cinema export, having won many fans with such quirkily comic looks at modern Spain as *Átame* (Tie Me Up, Tie Me Down) and *Mujeres al Borde de un Ataque de Nervios* (Women on the Edge of a Nervous Breakdown). Darker sentiments are explored in productions like *Matador*, where the blood lust of the *corrida* (bullfight) and the lust of the bed are closely tied together.

Ten years after his success with *El Espíritu de la Colmena*, Erice brought another

classic to the screen with *El Sur*. Saura had another popular success in 1990 with *¡Ay Carmela!*. Set in the civil war, it is a clever balance of tragedy and comedy that follows a roving theatre duo around the country as they unwittingly stumble from Republican to Nationalist zones. A completely different turn came in 1995 with *Flamenco*, not so much a film as an exciting review of the best in this vein of Spanish dance and song.

Vicente Aranda has been less prolific than Almodóvar, but found acclaim with *Amantes* (1991), set in the Madrid of the 1950s and based on the real story of a love triangle that ends particularly badly. The following year, Fernando Trueba brought out *Belle Epoque*, which examines the melancholy underside to bliss through the story of four sisters' pursuit of a young chap. It won an Oscar.

Almodóvar in particular has moved away from the deadening burden of Franco and the civil war years (although even he falls occasionally into the trap) and other directors are following suit. That said, British director Ken Loach tried his hand in 1995 at the war theme. The UK-Spanish production that resulted is probably one of the most successful treatments of the subject on film to date – *Tierra y Libertad* (Land and Freedom).

Spanish cinema continues to show some encouraging signs of creative life. Almodóvar's latest, *Carne Trémula* (Live Flesh; 1997), was perhaps not his best. A typically fraught love story set in Madrid, it still sparkles with his trademark quirky approach to birth, death and discomfort.

Moving to Barcelona, Ventura Pons' *Caricias* (Caresses; 1997) slides through a loveless urban jungle, only allowing a glimmer of humanity to poke through the gloom towards the end.

Quite another world is conjured up in *La Novia de Medianoche* (The Midnight Fiancée; 1997). Antonio Simón sets his first work using a script by Buñuel in the brooding, misty cliff country of Galicia, creating a dark story of love enveloped in sombre Celtic tragedy.

What's in an Apellido?

You may soon notice that there's something not quite straightforward about Spaniards' names. María García and Pedro Blanco present no problem, but what to make of Almudena López López, Francisco Sánchez G or Isabel de Colón Villalobos?

A Spaniard has three names: a given name *(nombre)* and two surnames *(apellidos)*. The first of the surnames is the person's father's first surname. The second surname is the mother's first surname. So Isabel, the daughter of Antonio Romero Cervantes and Alicia Ruiz Álvarez, is Isabel Romero Ruiz.

In practice many people don't bother with their second surname or occasionally just shorten it to an initial – so our Isabel is simply Isabel Romero or maybe Isabel Romero R. But if the first surname is a particularly common one (García, Fernández, López, González and Rodríguez are the most common), a person is more likely to keep the second one in use too – and may even, when a short version of their name is wanted, use only the second surname. A famous case of this is the writer Federico García Lorca, who is known as either García Lorca or just Lorca, but never as García.

Women don't change their names when they marry, but may tack their husband's surnames (preceded by de) on to the end of their own. So if Isabel Romero Ruiz were to marry Pedro Colón Villalobos, she could call herself Isabel Romero Ruiz de Colón Villalobos – and, for short, she might end up being called anything from Isabel Romero to Isabel de Colón!

Theatre

Thanks mainly to a big theatre development program by the PSOE governments of the 1980s and 90s, most cities have a theatre. Productions range from old classics to modern comedy or avant-garde fare, with a fair swag of foreign drama in translation. Madrid and Barcelona are the epicentres, with Barcelona having an edge when it comes to avant-garde productions. Straight theatre is unlikely to appeal, however, if your understanding of Spanish – or, in Barcelona, Catalan – is less than fluent.

SOCIETY & CONDUCT

Spaniards can be economical with etiquette and thank-yous but this does not signify unfriendliness. One way in which you may notice people expressing their fellow feeling is the general *'Buenos días'* they often utter to all present when they enter a small shop or bar and the *'Adiós'* when they leave. Spaniards don't expect foreigners to speak much Spanish – although you need some words to get by outside tourist centres and of course it helps a lot if you *can* communicate in Spanish.

Most Spaniards don't really show much interest in communicating more than superficially with transient visitors. Invitations to Spanish homes are rare enough to be a mark of true friendship.

But they are famous for being gregarious and the family is of paramount importance, with children adored and always a good talking point. At the same time they're an individualistic, proud people.

Day, Night & Time

The Spanish attitude to time *is* more relaxed than in most western cultures. But things that need a fixed time – trains, buses, cinemas, football matches – get one and it's generally stuck to. Things that need to get done, get done. Waiters may not always be in a hurry, but they come before too long.

What's different is the daily timetable. The Spanish *tarde* (afternoon) doesn't really start until 4 pm or so and goes on until 9 pm or later. Shops and offices close from around 2 to 5 pm, then mostly open again until around 8 pm. In hot summer months people stay outside late, enjoying the coolness. At fiestas don't be surprised to see merry-go-rounds packed with children at 3 am. And of course Friday and Saturday nights, all year round, barely begin until midnight for those doing the rounds of bars and discos.

Siesta Contrary to popular opinion, most Spaniards do not have a sleep in the afternoon. The siesta is generally devoted to a long, leisurely lunch and lingering conversation. But then again, if you've stayed out until 6 am ...

RELIGION
Roman Catholicism

It's impossible not to notice the importance of the Roman Catholic church in Spain. So many of the country's great occasions are

religious fiestas; so many of its most magnificent buildings are cathedrals or churches, lavishly adorned and lovingly tended by the faithful. The great majority of Spaniards have church baptisms, weddings and funerals. According to surveys, around 90% of them say they are Catholics. Spain has around 20,000 Catholic priests, over 15,000 monks and 50,000 nuns.

All this is hardly surprising in a country whose very existence is the result of a series of medieval anti-Muslim crusades and which gave the world the Jesuits to fight the Protestant Reformation in the 16th century. Under Franco the church and state were so closely tied that the Vatican allowed the government to appoint Spanish bishops,

---

Opus Dei

Although the lay Catholic organisation Opus Dei (Work of God) hasn't had quite the influence on post-Franco Spain that it did during the dictatorship, it remains powerful in areas like the media, education and business (at least two cabinet members in the present government are Opus Dei members). Founded in 1928 by an Aragonese, Josemaría Escrivá (1902-75), Opus Dei now has members in 80 countries around the world. Its basic philosophy is salvation through work. Escrivá noticed that economic progress tended to turn people away from Catholicism. He attempted to reverse this by inspiring Catholics with a new ethic of work and self-reliance, concentrating Opus Dei's efforts in influential areas like higher education, in a successful effort to gain support among the country's elite.

The organisation sees itself as nonpolitical, but it is religiously conservative – with a strong emphasis on confession, for instance – and its philosophy lends itself to conservative economic policies. Opus Dei members and supporters were at the forefront of Spain's 1960s economic takeoff under Franco. Partly because of its rather clandestine nature, the fellowship is the subject of all sorts of conspiracy theories among people at the other end of the political spectrum.

Senior members of Opus Dei live in communities, take vows of poverty, chastity and obedience and practise self-mortification, yet they do normal (often senior) jobs in the outside world and don't wear any kind of special clothing. They hand over most of their often large earnings to their communities. Only a few are priests.

Opus Dei, which has its headquarters in Rome, found early favour with Pope John Paul II and in 1993 was made a 'personal prelature' answerable directly to him. Only one year earlier, Escrivá had been beatified (a step towards canonisation) in record time. Opus Dei apologists tend to dismiss criticism as the work of Jesuits and other 'competitors'.

Opus Dei runs eight universities and 250 schools around the world. It's also said to control a significant number of TV networks, newspapers, press agencies and publishing houses. For more on Opus Dei, see the Torreciudad section in the Aragón chapter.

while the government paid priests' salaries and granted the church numerous other privileges, including lots of money. The government still subsidises the church heavily and one-sixth of schools are still run by religious orders and groups, even though Spain has had no official religion since 1978. Only about half the Spaniards go to church regularly. The numbers of priests, monks and nuns are all falling.

Spain has a long-standing anticlerical tradition too, originating in the 19th century when the church became identified with conservative opposition to political change. Liberal and left-wing movements were often accompanied by church-burnings and killings of priests, monks and nuns. This reached a bloody crescendo in the civil war, when some 7000 were killed.

But so deeply is Catholicism ingrained in the Spanish way of life that men who hardly ever go to church vie for membership of the brotherhoods that carry holy images round the streets in Easter processions, while thousands of less than pious folk take part in giant pilgrimages to holy sites and other religion-based fiestas. The early 20th century philosopher Miguel Unamuno's quip, 'Here in Spain we are all Catholics, even the atheists', is still largely true.

Other Faiths

Protestantism was eradicated by the Inquisition in the 16th century before it could even get a toehold. Today there are only around 60,000 active Protestants in Spain, many of them in Catalunya. The Jehovah's Witnesses are one of the leading Protestant churches.

Muslims and Jews played enormous roles in medieval Spain but were stamped on at the end of that period (see History earlier).

Spain has around 150,000 to 200,000 Muslims; half of them live in the North African enclaves, Ceuta and Melilla. Most of the others are Muslim immigrants, although there are about 1000 Spanish-born converts, many of whom live in Granada.

The Jewish community numbers about 15,000, many of them from Morocco. Franco allowed Jewish refugees to enter Spain in WWII and in 1982 Sephardic Jews (Jews of Spanish and North African origin) were officially invited to return to Spain, 490 years after their expulsion by the Catholic Monarchs.

LANGUAGE

Spanish, or Castilian *(castellano)*, as it is often and more precisely called, is spoken throughout Spain, but there are also three widely spoken regional languages: Catalan *(català*; another Romance language, with close ties to French) is spoken in Catalunya, the Islas Baleares and Valencia; Galician *(galego*; similar enough to Portuguese to be regarded by some as a dialect) is spoken in Galicia; and Basque *(euskara*; of obscure, non-Latin origin) is spoken in the País Vasco and Navarra.

English isn't as widely spoken as many travellers expect. It's easier to find people who speak some English in the cities and tourist areas, but you'll be better received if you try to communicate in Spanish.

See the Language section at the back of this book for pronunciation details and useful phrases. The glossary, also at the back, contains some common words in Castilian, Basque, Catalan and Galician Spanish. It is followed by the food glossary – a handy menu decoder.

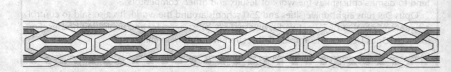

Facts for the Visitor

SUGGESTED ITINERARIES

Where you should go depends on what you like doing. Every part of Spain has its own compelling reasons to be visited. Nor does it matter much in which order you take your chosen destinations: Spain is easy enough to travel around for you to make up your itinerary as you go.

The basic choice is between a wide-ranging tour that takes you to as many varied parts of the country as you can manage or a narrower focus on a smaller number of places to explore in greater depth. Following are a few highlights to help you start planning. Also check the Public Holidays & Special Events and Activities sections of this chapter for further ideas on places and events you might like to work into your timetable.

Cities & Towns

Madrid and Barcelona are obviously the most vibrant cities, with the most to see and do. They're a strong contrast but both are essential experiences if you want a feel for the country.

Sevilla, with its exciting southern atmosphere, isn't far behind the 'big two' for excitement and introduces you to the distinctive region of Andalucía. Other cities and towns with a particularly strong pull include Santiago de Compostela and Pontevedra in Galicia; San Sebastián in the País Vasco; Segovia, Ávila, Salamanca, León, Toledo and Cuenca in the old Castilian heartland; Trujillo in Extremadura; Valencia on the Mediterranean coast; and Granada and Ronda in Andalucía.

Coasts

The Costa Brava in Catalunya is rugged enough not to have been completely overwhelmed by tourist development and still secretes many pretty coves, villages and beaches. The Islas Baleares have many fine, isolated little beaches, especially on

Menorca, while Mallorca's cliff-strewn northern coast is one of the most spectacular in the country. Cabo de Gata in eastern Andalucía is lined with excellent, isolated and, by Spanish standards underpopulated beaches, backed by some fine, rugged coastal scenery. The Costa de la Luz on Andalucía's Atlantic coast has more good beaches and is relatively underdeveloped; Tarifa at its southern end is one of Europe's top windsurfing centres.

In Galicia, the Rías Bajas and Rías Altas are two series of majestic estuaries not unlike the Norwegian fjords, dotted with good beaches, fishing villages and low-key resorts. Spain's most awesome coastal scenery is here too. On the Bay of Biscay coast are the country's best surf beaches and, at San Sebastián, probably its most beautiful city beach.

Countryside & Wilderness

The Pyrenees, especially in Catalunya and Aragón, are strung with imposing peaks and lovely valleys. Two of the best areas to head for are the national parks: Aigüestortes i Estany de Sant Maurici in Catalunya and Ordesa y Monte Perdido in Aragón.

In the north-west, the Picos de Europa range, which straddles Cantabria, Asturias and Castilla y León, is justly famous for its wild and beautiful mountain scenery. Galicia is Spain's greenest area – rolling countryside abutting a dramatic coast.

In the central west, the Sierra de Gredos and its western offshoots, such as the Sierra de Peña de Francia, contain further impressive ranges and charming, remote valleys, such as those of La Vera and the Jerte and Ambroz rivers in northern Extremadura. There's yet more impressive mountainous terrain in the Serranía de Cuenca area on the borders of Castilla-La Mancha and Aragón, and in Mallorca's Serra de Tramuntana.

In Andalucía, the mountains around Ronda, the Alpujarras valleys south of the Sierra Nevada and the sierras of Cazorla and Segura east of Baeza stand out for their beauty, while the semidesert scenery east of

Almería is weird enough to have been used as the setting for dozens of western movies.

PLANNING
When to Go

Spain can be enjoyable any time of year. The *ideal* months to visit are May, June and September (plus April and October in the south). At these times you can rely on good to excellent weather, yet avoid the sometimes extreme heat – and the main crush of Spanish and foreign tourists – of July and August, when temperatures may climb to 45°C in inland Andalucía and Madrid is unbearable and almost deserted.

But there's decent weather in some parts of Spain virtually year-round. Winter along the southern and south-eastern Mediterranean coasts is mild, while in the height of summer you can retreat to the north-west or to beaches or high mountains anywhere to escape excessive heat.

The best festivals are mostly concentrated between Semana Santa (the week leading up to Easter Sunday) and September/October. See this chapter's Public Holidays & Special Events section for more details.

If you plan to pursue some specific activity, you may need to choose your time carefully. See Activities later in this chapter and destination sections in the regional chapters.

Maps

Small-Scale Maps Some of the best maps for travellers are published by Michelin, which produces the 1:1,000,000 *Spain Portugal* map and six 1:400,000 regional maps covering the whole country. These are all pretty accurate, even down to the state of minor country roads, frequently updated and detailed yet easy to read. They're widely available in Spain if you don't manage to pick them up before you go. Also good are the GeoCenter maps published by Germany's RV Verlag.

Probably the best physical map of Spain is *Península Ibérica, Baleares y Canarias* published by the Centro Nacional de Información Geográfica (CNIG). Ask for it in good bookshops or map shops.

Large-Scale Maps Two organisations publish detailed close-up maps of small parts of Spain. The CNIG covers most of the country in 1:25,000 (1cm to 250m) sheets, most of which are recent. The CNIG and the Servicio Geográfico del Ejército (SGE; Army Geographic Service) each publish a 1:50,000 series; the SGE's tend to be more up to date. The CNIG also has a *Mapa Guía* series of maps of national and natural parks, mostly at 1:50,000 or 1:100,000 and published in the 1990s. Until a few years ago the CNIG was called the IGN (Instituto Geográfico Nacional) and some of its maps still bear that name.

Also useful for hiking and exploring some areas are Editorial Alpina's *Guía Cartográfica* and *Guía Excursionista y Turística* series. The series combines information booklets in Spanish (or sometimes Catalan) with detailed maps at scales ranging from 1:25,000 to 1:50,000. They're worth their price (around 500 ptas), although the maps have their inaccuracies. The Institut Cartogràfic de Catalunya does good 1:50,000 maps for each of the 41 *comarcas* (districts) of Catalunya, but there's no equivalent for other parts of Spain.

For SGE maps, contact the service (Departamento de Venta de Cartografía y Publicaciones; ☎ 91 711 50 43, fax 91 711 50 32, Calle de Darío Gazapo 8, 28024 Madrid). This Madrid office is its only official outlet, where maps are sold for the interesting price of 303 ptas a piece.

Editorial Alpina publications and CNIG and SGE maps are often available in town bookshops near hiking and trekking areas. But to make sure you get them visit a specialist map or travel bookshop such as La Tienda Verde in Madrid, or Altaïr or Quera in Barcelona. Some map specialists in other countries, such as Stanfords (12-14 Long Acre, London WC2E 9LP), also have good ranges of Spain maps. The CNIG (☎ 91 554 14 50, Calle del General Ibáñez de Íbero 3,

28003 Madrid) can supply you with a free catalogue of its maps.

City Maps For finding your way around cities, the free maps handed out by tourist offices are often adequate. If you want something more comprehensive, most cities are covered by one or another of the Spanish series such as Telstar, Alpina and Everest, which have street indexes; they're available in bookshops. Check their publication dates as some are rather out of date.

Road Atlases See under Car & Motorcycle in the Getting Around chapter.

What to Bring
Bring as little as possible. Everything you bring, you have to carry. You can buy just about anything you need in Spain, in any case.

Luggage If you'll be doing any walking with your luggage, even just from stations to hotels and back, a backpack is the only sensible answer. One whose straps and openings can be zipped inside a flap is more secure. If you'll be using taxis, or your own car, you might as well take whatever luggage is easiest to open and shut, unpack and pack. Either way, a small day pack is a useful addition.

Inscribing your name and address on the inside of your luggage, as well as labelling it on the outside, increases your chances of getting it back if it's lost or stolen. Packing things in plastic bags inside your backpack/ suitcase is a good way of keeping them organised and, if it rains, dry.

Clothes & Shoes In high summer you may not need more than one layer of clothing, even at 4 am. At cooler times, layers of thin clothing, which trap warm air and can be peeled off if necessary, are better than a single thick layer. See Climate in the Facts about Spain chapter for the kind of temperatures and rainfall you can expect. It's a good idea to pack some good clothes (something other than jeans and T-shirts)

some good clothes (something other than jeans and T-shirts) for some clubs and smart restaurants – they don't have to be too formal, though.

You need a pair of strong shoes, even strong trainers, no matter what type of trip you're making. You'll probably also appreciate having a lighter pair sometimes. And if you plan on going to smart clubs or restaurants, you'll need something other than trainers. If you can combine these requirements into two pairs or even one, you'll save space in your luggage!

Useful Items Apart from any special personal needs, or things you might require for particular kinds of trips (camping gear, hiking boots, surfboard etc), consider the following:

* an under-the-clothes money belt or shoulder wallet, useful for protecting your money and documents in cities
* a towel and soap, often lacking in cheap accommodation
* sunscreen lotion, which can be more expensive in Spain than elsewhere
* a small Spanish dictionary and/or phrasebook
* books, which can be expensive and hard to find outside main cities and tourist resorts
* photocopies of your important documents, kept separate from the originals
* a Swiss army knife
* minimal unbreakable cooking, eating and drinking gear if you plan to prepare your own food and drinks
* a medical kit (see Health later in this chapter)
* a padlock or two to secure your luggage to racks and to lock hostel lockers
* a sleeping sheet to save on sheet rental costs if you're using youth hostels (a sleeping bag is unlikely to be useful unless you're camping)
* an adapter plug for electrical appliances
* a torch (flashlight)
* an alarm clock
* sunglasses
* binoculars, if you plan to do any wildlife spotting

TOURIST OFFICES
Local Tourist Offices

All cities and many smaller towns have an *oficina de turismo* or *oficina de informa-*

ción turística. In provincial capitals you'll sometimes find more than one office – one specialising in information on the city alone, the other carrying mostly provincial or regional information. There seems, however, to be no set rule on this division of labour. National and natural parks also often have visitor centres offering useful information. Their opening hours and quality of info vary widely.

Tourist Offices Abroad

Get information from the Spanish national tourist offices in 19 countries, including:

Belgium
(☎ 02-280 19 26) Avenue des Arts 21, B-1040 Brussels

Canada
(☎ 416-961-3131) 2 Bloor St West, 34th floor, Toronto M4W 3E2

Denmark
(☎ 33 15 11 65) Store Kongensgade 1-3, DK-1264 Copenhagen

France
(☎ 01 45 03 82 50) 43, rue Decamps, 75784 Paris, Cedex 16

Germany
(☎ 030-8 82 65 43) Kurfürstendamm 180, D-10707 Berlin
(☎ 0211-6 80 39 80) Grafenberger Allee 100, 'Kutscherhaus', D-40237 Düsseldorf
(☎ 069-72 50 33) Myliusstrasse 14, D-60325 Frankfurt am Main
(☎ 089-5 38 90 75) Schubertstrasse 10, D-80336 Munich

Italy
(☎ 06-678 31 06) Via del Mortaro 19, interno 5, 00187 Rome
(☎ 02-72 00 46 17) Piazza del Carmine 4, 20121 Milan

Netherlands
(☎ 070-346 59 00) Laan Van Meerdervoort 8-8a, 2517 The Hague

Portugal
(☎ 01-354 1992) Edificio Monumental, Avenida Fontes Pereira de Melo 51-4° andar D, 1000 Lisbon

UK
(☎ 0171-486 8077, from 22 April 2000 ☎ 020-7486 8077; brochure request ☎ 0891 669920 at 50p a minute) 22-23 Manchester Square, London W1M 5AP

USA
    (☎ 212-265-8822) 666 Fifth Ave, 35th floor, New York, NY 10103
    (☎ 213-658-7188) 8383 Wilshire Blvd, Suite 960, Beverly Hills, Los Angeles, CA 90211
    (☎ 312-642-1992) 845 North Michigan Ave, Chicago, IL 60611
    (☎ 305-358-1992) 1221 Brickell Ave, Suite 1850, Miami, FL 33131

VISAS & DOCUMENTS
Passport
Citizens of the 15 European Union (EU) member states and Switzerland can travel to Spain with their national identity card alone. If such countries do not issue ID cards – as in the UK – travellers must carry a full valid passport (UK visitor passports are not acceptable). All other nationalities must have a full valid passport.

Check that your passport's expiry date is at least some months away, otherwise you may not be granted a visa, should you need one.

By law you are supposed to have your passport or ID card with you at all times in Spain. It doesn't happen often, but it could be embarrassing if you are asked by the police to produce a document and you don't have it with you. You will usually need one of these documents for police registration when you take a hotel room.

Visas
For tourist visits to Spain of up to 90 days, nationals of many countries – including the EU states, Australia, Canada, Israel, Japan, New Zealand, Norway, Switzerland and the USA – require no visa.

South Africans are nationalities who *do* need a visa for Spain – unless they are residents of a Schengen country (see the boxed text 'The Schengen System'). Options include 30-day and 90-day single-entry visas (in London these cost UK£17.75 and UK£21.30 respectively), 90-day multiple-entry visas (UK£24.85) and various transit visas (nationalities needing visas for Spain may need them even if they are just changing planes at a Spanish airport, especially if they are heading for another Schengen country – see the boxed text). A multiple-entry visa will save you a lot of time and trouble if you plan to leave Spain – say to go to Gibraltar or Morocco – and then re-enter. You are allowed to use only one 90-day visa of either type in any six-month period.

You usually have to supply your passport-size photos with your visa application form.

If you apply in person in your country of residence, the process should take from 24 to 48 hours.

If you apply for the visa in a country where you are *not* resident, your request may be forwarded to Madrid and a reply could take weeks. You may also be asked to present tickets for onward or return flights, evidence of hotel accommodation and solvency or even an invitation from someone in Spain. Finally, you may not be allowed the option of the 90-day three-entry visa.

Visa Extensions & Residence Nationals of EU countries, Norway and Iceland can virtually (if not technically) enter and leave Spain at will. Those wanting to stay in Spain longer than 90 days are supposed to apply during their first month for a residence card *(tarjeta de residencia)*. This is a lengthy bureaucratic procedure: consult a Spanish consulate before you go to Spain, as you will need to take certain documents with you.

Other nationalities who want to stay in Spain longer than 90 days are also supposed to get a residence card. For them it's a truly nightmarish process, starting with a residence visa issued by a Spanish consulate in your country of residence: start the process light years in advance.

Non-EU citizen spouses of EU citizens resident in Spain can apply for residence too. The process is lengthy and those needing to travel in and out of the country in the meantime could ask for an *exención de visado* (visa exemption). In most cases, the spouse is obliged to make the formal application in their country of residence, which is a real pain.

Travel Insurance
A travel insurance policy to cover theft, loss of luggage or tickets, medical problems and

The Schengen System

Spain is one of the Schengen countries that have theoretically done away with passport control on travel between them. (The others are Austria, Belgium, France, Germany, Italy, Luxembourg, the Netherlands and Portugal. Denmark, Finland, Greece, Iceland, Norway and Sweden are expected to join up before long.) The Schengen countries reserve the right to make spot passport checks, which occur fairly regularly at Spanish airports and have been known on Lisbon-Madrid trains.

Nationals of Australia, Canada, Israel, Japan, New Zealand, Norway, Switzerland, the USA and the non-Schengen EU countries require no visa for tourist visits of up to 90 days to any Schengen country. South Africans do. You *could* avoid the visa if you are willing to gamble. Travelling from the UK by boat or train there is a chance your passport will not be checked on entering France or Belgium. From there you could travel overland with some hope of not having your passport checked. Travelling by air, however, you have no chance. Take this seriously, as travellers have been bundled on to planes back to the country they flew from.

Coming from Morocco, you are unlikely to get into Spain's North African enclaves of Ceuta or Melilla without a Spanish visa (if you are supposed to have one), and passports are generally checked again when you head on to the peninsula. You may well be able to board a boat from Tangier (Morocco) to Algeciras, and certainly to Gibraltar, but, again, passports are generally closely checked by the Spaniards at Algeciras and you could find yourself being sent back to Morocco. If you go via Gibraltar, you may just sneak across at La Línea without having your passport checked – but you can't bank on it.

One saving grace of the Schengen system is that a visa for one Schengen country is valid for all other Schengen countries too – so, for instance, a French visa is good for Spain and vice versa. Compare validity periods, prices and the number of permitted entries from the respective embassies before you apply. Schengen visas are free for spouses and children of EU nationals.

If you are going to visit more than one Schengen country that requires you to obtain a visa, you should apply for the visa at an embassy of your main destination country.

Legal residents of one Schengen country do not require a visa for another Schengen country.

---

perhaps cancellation or delays in your travel arrangements, is a very good idea (see Health later in this chapter for more on medical insurance).

A wide variety of policies is available and your travel agent will be able to make recommendations. The international student travel policies handled by STA Travel or other student travel organisations are usually good. Check the small print:

- Some policies exclude 'dangerous activities', which can include scuba diving, motorcycling, even trekking.

- Some policies may impose a surcharge for expensive photo equipment and the like.
- Check whether the policy covers ambulances or an emergency flight home.
- Policies often require you to pay up front for medical expenses, then to claim from the insurance company afterwards, showing receipts, but you might prefer to find a policy which involves the insurance company paying the doctor or hospital direct.

Buy travel insurance as early as possible. If you buy it in the week before you leave home, you may find, for example, that you are not covered for delays to your trip caused by industrial action.

Paying for your ticket with a credit card often provides limited travel accident insurance and you may be able to reclaim payment if the operator doesn't deliver. Ask your credit card company what it will cover.

Insurance papers, and the international medical aid numbers that generally accompany them, are valuable documents, so treat them like air tickets and passports. Keep the details (photocopies or handwritten) in a separate part of your luggage.

Driving Licence & Permits

For information on driving licences, International Driving Permits and vehicle papers and insurance see under Car & Motorcycle in the Getting There & Away chapter.

Hostel Cards

A valid HI (Hostelling International) card or youth hostel card from your home country is required at most HI youth hostels in Spain. If you don't already have one, you can get an HI card, valid till 31 December of the year you buy it in, at most HI hostels in Spain. You pay in instalments of 300 ptas for each night you spend in a hostel, up to 1800 ptas. The cards are also available from the TIVE youth travel organisation, which has offices in many of Spain's regional and some provincial capitals (see Useful Organisations later in this chapter).

Student, Teacher & Youth Cards

These cards can get you worthwhile discounts on travel and reduced prices at some museums, sights and entertainments.

The International Student Identity Card (ISIC), for full-time students, and the International Teacher Identity Card (ITIC), for full-time teachers and professors, are issued by over 5000 organisations world-wide, mostly student travel-related and often selling student tickets. They include:

Australia
    (☎ 03-93492411) STA Travel, 222 Faraday St, Carlton, Victoria 3053
    (☎ 02-9360 1822) STA Travel, 9 Oxford Street, Paddington, Sydney, NSW 2021

Canada
    (☎ 416-979-2406) Travel CUTS, 187 College St, Toronto M5T 1P7
    (☎ 514-398-0647) Voyages Campus, Université McGill, 3480 rue McTavish, Montreal H3A 1X9
UK
    Get cards from STA Travel and Campus Travel offices (see under Air in the Getting There & Away chapter)
USA
    (☎ 212-822-2700) Council Travel, 205 East 42nd St, New York, NY 10017
    (☎ 310-208-3551) Council Travel, 10904 Lindbrook Drive, Los Angeles, CA 90024
    (☎ 415-421-3473) Council Travel, 530 Bush St, San Francisco, CA 94108

The fake student card business is alive and well and some travel agents will even issue cards with certain discounted air tickets without asking to see any proof of student status.

Anyone under 26 can get a GO25 card or a Euro<26 card. Both these give similar discounts to the ISIC and are issued by most of the same organisations. The Euro<26 has a variety of names including the Under 26 Card in England and Wales and the Carnet Joven Europeo in Spain. For information you can contact Under 26 (☎ 0171-730 7285, from 22 April 2000 ☎ 020-7730 7285, 52 Grosvenor Gardens, London SW1W 0AG, UK). In Spain, the Euro<26 is issued by various youth organisations, including TIVE (see Hostel Cards earlier in this section) and the Dirección General de Juventud (☎ 91 580 41 96, Calle Alcalá 30, 28014 Madrid) for 1000 ptas. You don't have to be Spanish to get the card in Spain.

As an example of the sort of discounts you can expect in Spain, the better things on offer for Euro<26 card holders include 20% or 25% off most 2nd-class train fares, 10% or 20% off many Trasmediterránea ferries and some bus fares, good discounts at some museums and discounts of up to 20% at some youth hostels.

Photocopies

Keep photocopies of the data pages of your passport and other identity cards, and even your birth certificate if you can manage it. This will help speed up the replacement process if the originals go missing. If your passport is stolen or lost, notify the police, get a statement and then contact your embassy or consulate as soon as possible.

Other worthwhile things to photocopy include airline tickets, travel insurance documents with emergency numbers, credit cards (and phone numbers to contact in case of card loss), driving licence and vehicle documentation. Keep all of this, and a list of your travellers cheque numbers, separate from the originals. Leave extra copies with someone reliable at home.

EMBASSIES & CONSULATES
Spanish Embassies & Consulates Abroad
Spanish embassies and consulates can be found in:

Andorra
(☎ 82 00 13) Carrer Prat de la Creu 34, Andorra la Vella
Australia
(☎ 02-6273 3555) 15 Arkana St, Yarralumla, Canberra, ACT 2600
Consulates in Brisbane (☎ 07-3221 8571), Melbourne (☎ 03-9347 1966), Perth (☎ 09-9322 4522) and Sydney (☎ 02-9261 2433)
Canada
(☎ 613-747-2252) 74 Stanley Avenue, Ottawa, Ontario K1M 1P4
Consulates in Toronto (☎ 416-977-1661) and Montreal (☎ 514-935-5235)
France
(☎ 01 44 43 18 00) 22, avenue Marceau, 75008 Paris, Cedex 08
Germany
(☎ 0228-21 70 94) Schlossstrasse 4, 53115 Bonn
Consulates in Berlin (☎ 030-2 61 60 81), Düsseldorf (☎ 0211-43 90 80), Frankfurt am Main (☎ 069-96 10 41) and Munich (☎ 089-98 50 27)
Ireland
(☎ 01-269 1640) 17A Merlyn Park, Balls Bridge, Dublin 4
Morocco
(☎ 07-707600, ☎ 07-707980) 105 Ave Allal ben Abdellah, 3 Zankat Madnine, Rabat
Netherlands
(☎ 070-364 38 14) Lange Voorhout 50, 2514 EG The Hague

New Zealand
Spain has no diplomatic representation here
Portugal
(☎ 01-347 2381) Rua do Salitre 1, 1200 Lisbon
Tunisia
(☎ 01-280 613) 22 Avenue Dr Ernest Conseil, Cité Jardin, 2001 Tunis
UK
(☎ 0171-235 5555, from 22 April 2000 ☎ 020-7235 5555) 39 Chesham Place, London SW1X 8SB
(☎ 0171-581 7888, from 22 April 2000 ☎ 020-7581 7888) 20 Draycott Place, London SW3 2RZ (consulate)
(☎ 0161-236 1233) Suite 1A, Brook House, 70 Spring Gardens, Manchester M2 2BQ (consulate)
(☎ 0131-226 4568, ☎ 0131-220 1843) 63 North Castle St, Edinburgh EH2 3LJ (consulate)
USA
(☎ 202-728-2330) 2375 Pennsylvania Ave NW, Washington, DC 20037
Consulates in Boston (☎ 617-536-2506), Chicago (☎ 312-782-4588), Houston (☎ 713-783 6200), Los Angeles (☎ 213-938-0158), Miami (☎ 305-446-5511), New Orleans (☎ 504-525-4951), New York (☎ 212-355-4080) and San Francisco (☎ 415-922-2995)

Embassies & Consulates in Spain
The main embassies are in Madrid. Some countries also maintain consulates in major cities. Embassies and consulates in Madrid (Madrid map references are listed after addresses – see that chapter) include:

Australia
(☎ 91 441 93 00) Plaza del Descubridor Diego de Ordás 3-2, Edificio Santa Engrácia 120 (map: North)
Canada
(☎ 91 431 43 00) Calle de Núñez de Balboa 35 (map: Sal)
France
(☎ 91 435 55 60) Calle de Salustiano Olózaga 9 (map: Central)
(☎ 91 597 32 67) Paseo de la Castellana 79 (consulate; map: North)
Germany
(☎ 91 557 90 00) Calle de Fortuny 8 (map: Mal & Ch)
Ireland
(☎ 91 576 35 00, 91 435 16 77) Calle de Claudio Coello 73 (map: Sal)

Morocco
(☎ 91 563 79 28, 91 563 10 90) Calle de
Serrano 179 (map: North)
(☎ 91 561 89 12, 91 561 21 45)
Calle de Leizaran 31 (consulate; map: North)
Netherlands
(☎ 91 359 09 14) Avenida del Comandante
Franco 32 (map: North)
New Zealand
(☎ 91 523 02 26, 91 531 09 97) Plaza de la
Lealtad 2 (map: Central)
Portugal
(☎ 91 561 78 00) Calle del Castillo 128
(☎ 91 445 46 00) Paseo del General Martínez
Campos 11 (consulate; map: Madrid)
Tunisia
(☎ 91 447 35 08) Plaza de Alonso Martínez 3
(map: Mal & Ch)
UK
(☎ 91 319 02 00) Calle de Fernando el Santo
16 (map: Mal & Ch)
(☎ 91 308 52 01) Calle del Marqués Ensenada
16 (consulate; map: Mal & Ch)
USA
(☎ 91 587 22 00) Calle de Serrano 75 (map: Sal)

CUSTOMS

People entering Spain from outside the EU
are allowed to bring in duty-free one bottle
of spirits, one bottle of wine, 50ml of
perfume and 200 cigarettes. If you are travelling from one EU country to another, you
can bring 2L of wine *and* 1L of spirits, with
the same limits on the rest. But duty-free allowances for travel between EU countries
are due to be abolished on 30 June 1999.
For *duty-paid* items bought at normal shops
in one EU country and taken into another,
the allowances are 90L of wine, 10L of
spirits, unlimited quantities of perfume and
800 cigarettes.

There are duty-free shops at all main
Spanish airports.

MONEY

A combination of travellers cheques and
credit or cash cards is the best way to take
your money.

Currency

Spain's currency, the peseta (pta), comes in
coins of one, five, 10, 25, 50, 100, 200 and

500 ptas and notes of 1000, 2000, 5000 and
10,000 ptas.

A 5 ptas coin is widely known as a *duro*
and it's fairly common for small sums to be
quoted in duros: *dos duros* for 10 ptas,
cinco duros for 25 ptas, even *veinte duros*
for 100 ptas.

Sometimes it's hard to get change for a
5000 or 10,000 ptas note. If you're getting
cash from a bank or ATM, a sum that's not
a multiple of 5000 ptas will prevent you
from being stuck with 5000 or 10,000 ptas
notes only.

The Euro The new common currency for
most EU countries, the euro, was launched
on 1 January 1999. Spain was among the
first wave of countries to adopt it. However,
use of the euro will at first be restricted to
finance matters like share prices and inter-
bank transfers. Euro coins and notes will
not appear until 1 January 2002, although
euro equivalents for some shop prices, exchange rates etc may be quoted before then
to get people used to the idea. The euro will
then circulate alongside the peseta for a few
months. By 1 July 2002 the peseta will
cease to be legal tender.

The euro will have a fixed peseta value
(about 165 ptas) and be divided into 100
cents.

Exchange Rates

Exchange rates fluctuate, of course, but the
peseta has been fairly stable since its last
devaluation in 1993.

Australia	A$1	=	87 ptas
Canada	C$1	=	92 ptas
EU	1€	=	167 ptas
France	1FF	=	25 ptas
Germany	DM1	=	85 ptas
Japan	¥100	=	119 ptas
Morocco	Dr1	=	15 ptas
New Zealand	NZ$1	=	73 ptas
Portugal	100$00	=	83 ptas
UK	UK£1	=	235 ptas
USA	US$1	=	142 ptas

Exchanging Money

You can change cash or travellers cheques at virtually any bank or exchange office. International airports and major train stations usually have both and road border crossings will have one or the other close by. Banks tend to offer the best rates, with minor differences between them; they're common in cities and even small villages often have one. They're mostly open Monday to Friday from 8.30 am to 2 pm, and Saturday from 9 am to 1 pm, though some don't bother with Saturday opening in summer. Many banks have ATMs.

Exchange offices, usually indicated by the word *cambio* (exchange), exist mainly in tourist resorts and other places that attract high numbers of foreigners. Generally they offer longer opening hours and quicker service than banks, but worse exchange rates (though American Express exchange offices are an honourable exception).

Travellers cheques usually bring a slightly better exchange rate than cash and, in many places, the more money you change the better the exchange rate.

Wherever you change, ask about commissions first, and confirm that exchange rates are as posted (in other words, that they haven't changed since the sign was last updated). Also make sure that the exchange rate posted up is for *buying* pesetas, not for selling them. Commissions vary from bank to bank. They may be different for travellers cheques and cash and may depend on how many cheques or how much money you're cashing. A typical commission is 3%, with a minimum of 300 to 500 ptas, but there are places with a minimum commission of 1000 or even 2000 ptas. Places that advertise 'no commission' may offer poor exchange rates to start with (American Express is again an honourable exception).

Cash Currencies of the developed world can be changed without problems (except sometimes queues!) in any bank or exchange office. If you're coming from Morocco, get rid of any dirham before you leave Morocco. You can change them for pesetas in Ceuta and Melilla but rates are worse than in Morocco.

Travellers Cheques These protect your money because they can be replaced if they are lost or stolen. In Spain they can be cashed at the many banks and exchange offices and usually attract a higher exchange rate than cash. American Express and Thomas Cook are widely accepted brands with efficient replacement policies. For American Express travellers cheque refunds you can call ☎ 900-99 44 26 from anywhere in Spain.

It doesn't really matter whether your cheques are denominated in pesetas or in the currency of the country you buy them in: Spanish exchange outlets will change most nonobscure currencies. Get most of your cheques in fairly large denominations (the equivalent of 10,000 ptas or more) to save on any per-cheque commission charges. American Express exchange offices charge no commission to change travellers cheques (even other brands). Take along your passport when you cash travellers cheques.

It's vital to keep your initial receipt, and a record of your cheque numbers and the ones you have used, separate from the cheques themselves.

ATMs & Credit, Debit & Charge Cards

You can use plastic to pay for many purchases (including meals and rooms at many establishments, especially those in the middle and upper price ranges, and long-distance trains) and you can use it to withdraw cash pesetas from banks and automatic teller machines (ATMs). Among the most widely usable cards are American Express, Cirrus, Diners Club Eurocard, Eurocheque, JCB, MasterCard, Plus and Visa.

Once you consider the exchange rates and commissions involved in exchanging travellers cheques or cash, you'll find that you usually win by using plastic, even taking into account any charges levied on foreign transactions and cash advances. Some foreign cash cards, for accessing money in personal bank accounts, can also be used in Spain and do not attract any cash-advance fees.

A high proportion of Spanish banks, even in small towns and villages, have an ATM *(cajero automático)* that will dispense cash pesetas at any time if you have the right piece of plastic to slot into it – *and* will save you from queuing at a bank counter.

Check with your card's issuer before you come to Spain on how widely usable your card will be, how to report and replace a lost card, withdrawal/spending limits and whether your personal identification number (PIN) will be acceptable (some European ATMs don't accept PINs of more than four digits).

American Express card-holders can get cash or at least travellers cheques (up to various maximums depending on the type of card) from American Express offices around Spain by writing a personal cheque drawn on their home bank account.

American Express are among the easiest cards to replace: call ☎ 91 572 03 03 or ☎ 91 572 03 20 (in Madrid) at any time. Always report a lost card straight away; you can ring the following Madrid telephone numbers: ☎ 91 519 21 00 (Visa, MasterCard or Access), ☎ 91 519 60 00 (Eurocard) and ☎ 91 547 40 00 (Diners Club).

A recently introduced option worth considering, for travellers from Britain at least, is Visa TravelMoney, a prepaid disposable credit card that you can buy from selected banks or travel agencies for amounts from £100 to £5000. It works for ATM withdrawals wherever the Visa sign is displayed. Inquire at Thomas Cook or call Visa before you travel.

International Transfers To have money transferred from another country, you need to organise someone to send it to you (through a bank there or a money-transfer service such as Western Union or MoneyGram) and a bank (or Western Union or MoneyGram office) in Spain at which to collect it. If there's money in your bank account back at home, you may be able to instruct the bank yourself.

For information on Western Union services, you can call free on ☎ 900-63 36 33 from anywhere in Spain. MoneyGram (☎ 900-20 10 10) has offices in Madrid,

Barcelona, Sevilla, Málaga, Benidorm and Alicante, and in other cities throughout the world.

To set up a transfer through a bank, either get advice from the bank at home on a suitable pick-up bank in Spain or ask a Spanish bank how to organise it. You'll need to let the sender have full details of the Spanish bank branch (its name, full address, city and any contact or code numbers required).

A bank-to-bank telegraphic transfer typically costs the equivalent of about 3000 or 4000 ptas and should take about a week. Western Union is likely to be quicker but a bit more expensive. For sums of up to US$400, MoneyGram charges the sender US$20; the money can supposedly be handed over to the recipient within 10 minutes of being sent.

It's also possible to have money sent by American Express.

Security

Spain has a high rate of theft from tourists. According to the British organisation Card Protection Plan, no fewer than 200,000 British credit cards and cash cards went missing in Spain in just four months (June to September) in 1995. Barcelona was ranked Europe's worst city for card theft and Madrid the third worst.

Keep only a limited amount as cash and the bulk in more easily replaceable forms such as travellers cheques or plastic. If your accommodation has a safe, use it. If you have to leave money in your room, divide it into several stashes and hide them in different places.

For carrying money on the street – take particular care in cities and tourist resorts – the safest thing is a shoulder wallet or under-the-clothes money belt. An external money belt is only safe if it can't be sliced off by a quick knife cut. Watch out for people who touch you or seem to be getting unwarrantedly close, in any situation.

Some spare cash tucked away into a money belt, stuffed into a pair of socks or otherwise concealed could come in handy if you lose your wallet, purse and/or money pouch.

Costs

Spain is one of Western Europe's more affordable countries, with costs of accommodation, eating out and train and bus travel considerably lower than in, for instance, Britain or France. If you are particularly frugal, it's just about possible to scrape by on 2500 to 3000 ptas a day; this would involve staying in the cheapest possible accommodation, not eating in restaurants or going to museums or bars, and not moving around too much. Places like Madrid, Barcelona, Sevilla and San Sebastián will place a greater strain on your money belt.

A more comfortable budget would be 5000 ptas a day. This could allow you 1500 to 2000 ptas for accommodation; 300 ptas for breakfast (coffee and a pastry); 800 to 1000 ptas for a set lunch; 250 ptas for public transport (two metro or bus rides); 500 ptas for a major museum; and 600 ptas for a light dinner, with a bit left over for a drink or two and intercity travel.

With 20,000 ptas a day you can stay in excellent accommodation, rent a car and eat some of the best food Spain has to offer.

Ways to Save Two people can travel more cheaply (per person) than one by sharing rooms. You'll also save money by avoiding the peak tourist seasons, when most room prices go up. The seasons vary from place to place, depending on local festivals and climate, but run from about July to mid-September in most places (sometimes plus a month or two either side). A student or youth card, or a document such as a passport proving you're over 60, brings worthwhile savings on some travel costs and entry to some museums and sights (see Visas & Documents earlier in this chapter). Some museums and sights have free days occasionally and a few have cheaper entry for EU passport holders.

Prolific letter-writers can save a few pesetas on long-distance mail by sending aerograms instead of standard letters or postcards (this does not apply to letters under 20g posted to Europe).

More info on accommodation, food and travel costs can be found under Accommodation in this chapter, in the Food & Wine special section and in the Getting Around chapter.

Tipping & Bargaining

In restaurants, the law requires menu prices to include service charge. Tipping is a matter of personal choice – most people leave some small change if they're satisfied and 5% is usually plenty. It's common to leave small change at bar and café tables. Hotel porters will generally be happy with 200 ptas and most won't turn their noses up at 100 ptas.

The only places in Spain where you're likely to bargain are markets – though even there most things have fixed prices – and, occasionally, cheap hotels, particularly if you're staying for a few days.

Taxes & Refunds

In Spain, value-added tax (VAT) is known as IVA (pronounced `EE-ba'; *impuesto sobre el valor añadido*). To accommodation and restaurant prices add 7% IVA; IVA is usually – but not always – included in quoted prices. On retail goods and car hire IVA is 16%. To check whether a price includes IVA, you can ask '*¿Está incluido el IVA?*' ('Is IVA included?').

Visitors are entitled to a refund of the 16% IVA on purchases costing more than 15,000 ptas from any shop if they are taking them out of the EU within three months. Ask the shop for an invoice showing the price and IVA paid for each item and identifying the vendor and purchaser. Then present the invoice to the customs booth for IVA refunds when you leave Spain. The officer will stamp the invoice and you hand it in at a bank in the airport or port for the reimbursement.

(continued on page 105)

THE BULLFIGHT

DAMIEN SIMONIS

THE BULLFIGHT

The low-lying sun floods the arena with heavy summer light from the west. There is a buzz as places fill. Families jostle for space with older, beret-bearing enthusiasts, their faces creased with years of farm toil, and bright young things sporting sky-blue sunglasses. Some clutch plastic cups of beer, others swig red wine from animal-hide botas. All but those who have paid for the comfort of real seats in the shade *(sombra)* have brought some kind of cushion: bare concrete or wooden slats can pall after a while on unprotected behinds. Many have chosen to huddle on the cheap benches facing the unforgiving midsummer sun *(sol)*. At one end of the ring, high up in the top rows, a brass band strikes up a stirring pasodoble, while on the opposite side the president of the fight and his adjutants await the arrival of the toros (bulls).

The *corrida* (bullfight) is a spectacle with a long history. It is not, as some suggest, simply a ghoulish alternative to the slaughter-house (itself no pretty sight). Aficionados say the bull is better off dying at the hands of a *matador* (killer) than in the *matadero* (abattoir). The corrida is about many things – death, bravery, performance. No doubt, the fight is bloody and cruel. To witness it is not necessarily to understand it, but might give an insight into some of the thought and tradition behind it. Many Spaniards loathe the bullfight, but there is no doubting its overall popularity. If on a bar-room TV there is football on one channel and a corrida on another, the chances are high that football fever will cede to the fascination of the fiesta.

Contests of strength, skill and bravery between man and beast are no recent phenomenon. The ancient Etruscans liked a good bullfight, and the Romans caught on. Of course things got a little kinky under the Romans and half the time there was no fight at all, merely the merciless butchery of Christians and other criminal fodder.

La lidia, as the art of bullfighting is also known, really took off in an organised fashion in Spain in the mid-18th century. In the 1830s, Pedro Romero, the greatest *torero* (bullfighter) of the time, was at the age of 77 appointed director of the Escuela de Tauromaquia de Sevilla, the country's first bullfighters' college. It was around this time too that breeders succeeded in creating the first reliable breeds of *toro bravo*, or fighting bull.

Facing page:
Toreros in action at the
Plaza de Toros in Valencia

El Matador & La Cuadrilla

Traditionally, young men have aspired to the ring in the hope of fame and fortune, much as boxers have done. Most attain neither one nor the other. Only champion matadors make good money and some make a loss. For the matador must rent or buy his outfit and equipment, pay for the right to fight a bull and also pay his *cuadrilla* (team).

If you see a major fight, you will notice this team is made up of quite a few people. Firstly there are several *peones*, junior bullfighters under the orders of the main torero, who is the matador. The peones come out to distract the bull with great capes, manoeuvre him into the desired position and so on. Then come the horseback-mounted *picadores*. Charged by the bull, which tries to eviscerate the horse, the picador shoves his lance into the withers of the bull – an activity that weakens and angers the bull. Animal-lovers may take some small consolation from the fact that since the 19th century the horses at least have been protected by heavy padding. The peones then return to the scene to measure their courage against the (hopefully) charging bull. The picador is shortly followed by the *banderilleros*. At a given moment during the fight, one or two banderilleros will race towards the bull and attempt to plunge a pair of colourfully decorated *banderillas* (short prods with harpoon-style ends) into the bull, again aiming for the withers. This has the effect of spurring the animal into action – the matador will then seek to use this to execute more fancy manoeuvres.

Then there is the matador himself. His dress could be that of a flamenco dancer. At its simplest, in country fiestas, it is generally a straightforward combination of black trousers or tights, white shirt and black vest. At its most extravagant, the *traje de luces* (suit of lights) can be an extraordinary display of bright, spangly colour – the name is apt. All the toreros, with the occasional exception of the matadors, wear the black *montera* (the Mickey Mouse ears hat). The torero's standard weapons are the *estoque* or *espada* (sword) and the heavy silk and percale *capa* (cape). You will notice, however, that the matador, and the matador alone, employs a different cape with the sword – a smaller piece of cloth held with a bar of wood called the *muleta* and used for a number of different passes.

La Corrida

To summarise all that takes place on the day of a corrida is no easy task. In many cases, corridas are held over several days, or even weeks, and the whole fiesta is known as the *feria*. The bulls are transported from their farms to a location near the ring, often days in advance. In Madrid, they are kept at an Andalucian-style ranch in the Casa de Campo known as Batán.

In some towns, the bulls are brought to another point in town from where they are let loose on the morning of the corrida to charge to the ring. The *encierro*, as it is known, in Pamplona was made famous by Ernest Hemingway, but scores of towns across the country celebrate it. Barriers are set up along a route to the ring, and some people feel inclined to run with the bulls (see the boxed text 'The Running of the Bulls' in the País Vasco, Navarra & La Rioja chapter). It's a dangerous business and people get hurt, sometimes mortally.

Right: The mounted picador goads and tries to weaken the bull by stabbing it in the withers

DAMIEN SIMONIS

When the bulls arrive, the cuadrillas, president and breeders get together to look over the animals and draw lots to see who is going to fight which one. It depends a little on how many breeders are represented, how many matadors and teams there are and so on. The selected bulls are later huddled into darkened *corrals*, where they await their moment.

The bullfight generally begins at 6 pm, hence the title of Hemingway's manual on the subject, *Death in the Afternoon*. As a rule, six toros and three matadors are on the day's card, although small country fiestas may feature only four. If any are considered not up to scratch, they are booed off (at this point the president will display a green handkerchief) and replacements brought on. Each fight takes about 10 to 15 minutes.

When the fateful moment comes, the corral is opened, light gushes in and the bull charges out, sensing a chance to escape. You wonder if it feels disappointment as it barrels out into the ring to be confronted by the peones, darting about and flashing their rose-and-yellow coloured capes at the heaving beast. The matador then appears and executes his *faenas* (moves) with the bull. To go into the complexities of what constitutes fine faenas would require a book.

Suffice to say, the more closely and calmly the torero works with the bull, pivoting and dancing before the bull's horns, the greater will be the crowd's approbation. After a little of this, the matador strides off and leaves the stage first to the picadores, then the banderilleros, before returning for another session. At various moments during the fight, the brass band will hit some stirring notes, adding to the air of grand spectacle. The various moves must be carried out in certain parts of the ring, which is divided into three parts: the *medios* (centre); *tercios* (an intermediate, chalked-off ring); and *tablas* (the outer ring).

When the bull seems tired out and unlikely to give a lot more, the matador chooses his moment for the kill. Placing himself head-on, he aims to sink the sword cleanly into the animal's neck *(estocada)* for an instant kill. It's easier said than done.

A good performance followed by a clean kill will have the crowd on its feet waving handkerchiefs in the air in clear appeal to the president to award the matador an *oreja* (ear) of the animal. The president usually waits to assess the crowd's enthusiasm before flopping a white handkerchief onto his balcony. If the fight was exceptional, the matador might *cortar dos orejas* – cut two ears off. On rare occasions the matador may be awarded the tail as well. What he does with them when he gets home is anyone's guess.

The sad carcass is meanwhile dragged out by a team of dray-horses and the sand raked about in preparation for the next toro. The meat ends up in the butcher shop.

When & Where

Bullfights are mainly a spring and summer activity, but it is occasionally possible to see them at other times. The season begins more or less officially in the first week of February with the fiestas of Valdemorillo and Ajalvir, near Madrid, to mark the feast day of San Blas. Virtually all encierros and corridas are organised as part of one town's fiesta or other.

In the Comunidad de Madrid, for instance, there are any number of local fiestas and the encierros can be a wild and unpredictable affair. In many towns the *plaza mayor* serves as a makeshift bullring. Often the small-town fights are amateurish affairs known as *capeas*.

The most prestigious feria in the world is that held in Madrid over four weeks from mid-May as part of the Fiesta de San Isidro.

Local tourist offices can tell you if any bullfights are going on in nearby towns, but a tip is to keep an eye out for town fiestas. Where there's a fiesta there's often a corrida and maybe an encierro.

Below:
Sevilla's Plaza de Toros – one of Spain's oldest and most elegant bullrings (Andalucía)

MARK DAFFEY

THE BULLFIGHT

DAMIEN SIMONIS

Left: The matador

Right: A toro bravo in pastures south of Salamanca (Castilla y León)

The Matadors

If you are spoiling for a fight, look out for the big names. A big name is no guarantee you'll see a high quality corrida, as that depends in no small measure on the animals themselves, but it is a good sign. The last true star of the fiesta, Luis Miguel Dominguin, a hero of the 1940s and 50s, died in 1996. Another maestro was Rafael Ortega (1921-1997). Their present-day successors count among their number some fine performers, but perhaps none of their stature.

Names to look for include: Jesulín de Ubrique, a true macho whose attitudes to women don't go down well with everyone; Enrique Ponce, a serious class act; Joselito; and Manuel Diaz (El Cordobés), one of the biggest names, although for some tastes his style borders on mocking the animal and is thus considered unnecessarily cruel.

Ethics of the Fight

'Is the bullfight 'right'? Passions are frequently inflamed by the subject. Many people feel ill at the sight of the kill, although this is a merciful relief and surely no worse than being lined up for the production-line kill in an abattoir. The preceding 10 or so minutes torture are cruel. The animal is frightened and in pain. Let there be no doubt about that. Aficionados will say, however, that these bulls have been bred for conflict and that their lives before this fateful day are better by far than those of any other farm animals. Toros bravos are treated like kings. To other western cultures – and to many Spaniards too – the bullfight is 'uncivilised'. Yet there is something about this direct confrontation with death that invites reflection. As an integral part of Spanish culture, it deserves to be experienced; there is nothing to say that anyone should also *like* it.

Beyond Spain

La lidia is not merely a Spanish preoccupation. It is a regular, if lower-profile, part of the calendar of events in southern France and Portugal. The Portuguese specialise in horseback toreros, known in Spanish as *rejoneadores*. *Corridas de rejones*, still occasionally seen in Spain, served as a kind of cavalry training.

The bullfight has a big following in Latin America, particularly in Mexico, although Spaniards consider the quality there to be inferior.

DAMIEN SIMONIS

THE BULLFIGHT

Women's Touch

The rising star in the ring today is not another brash *don* from the south, but a young *torera* from outside Madrid – Cristina Sánchez. She carries a double burden: not only must she face the danger of the bulls, but also the potential wave of derision that could crash upon her at any moment for simply being a woman in a man's world. She represents not only herself but also the claim of women to be taken seriously in this man's arena. For women, the fight has always been as intense outside the ring as in.

Nicolasa Escamilla, 'La Pajuelera', was the first woman to take on the bulls seriously, back in the late 18th century. Goya was so impressed that he left behind a sketch of her in combat in Zaragoza. Martina García, born in 1814, was fighting until the age of 66. As often as she killed her toros she found herself being flipped by them. Towards the end of the century, Sevilla's Dolores Sánchez, 'La Fragosa', became one of the first toreras to don the traje de luces and abandon the skirt. Machismo and the fight go hand in hand; the former caught up with the handful of active toreras in 1908, when a law was promulgated forbidding women to fight bulls, considering it 'improper and contrary to civilised manners and all delicate sentiment'.

Only in 1974 did Ángela Hernández succeed in having the law repealed, but this did little to change attitudes. Maribel Atiénzar began her career in 1977 and found she could only appear if she renounced the right to take on mature bulls as a fully recognised matador. In the language of the bullring, she was unable to *tomar la alternativa*. In this ritual the senior matador acknowledges a junior's capacity as a full matador in the ring and hands him the sword and cape. With this a torero's right to fight as a full matador (and hence be paid considerably more) is recognised everywhere in Spain but Madrid – the mecca of the corrida, which has its own qualifying hurdle. Maribel 'took the alternative' in Mexico, an achievement not recognised at all in Spain.

Cristina Sánchez, born in 1972, has achieved the unimaginable, taking the alternative in Madrid's Las Ventas – the ultimate achievement for any bullfighter – in mid-1996. She had a bad year touring South America in 1997 but in May 1998 confirmed the alternative in Madrid – another first.

(continued from page 96)

POST & COMMUNICATIONS
Postal Rates

To send a postcard or letter weighing up to 20g costs 70 ptas from Spain to other European countries, 115 ptas to North America, and 185 ptas to Australia, New Zealand or Asia. Three A4 sheets in an air-mail envelope weigh between 15g and 20g. To send an aerogram to anywhere in the world costs 85 ptas.

Certificado (registered mail) costs an extra 175 ptas for international mail.

Urgente service, which means your letter may arrive two or three days quicker, costs an extra 230 ptas for international mail. You can send mail both urgente and certificado.

A day or two quicker than urgente service – but a lot more expensive – is Postal Exprés, sometimes called Express Mail Service (EMS). This is available at most post offices and uses courier companies for international deliveries. Packages weighing up to 1kg cost 3780 ptas to send to the EU or Norway, 6300 ptas to North America and 8015 ptas to Australia or New Zealand.

Getting Addressed

You might think that if you have the address of a hotel, office or café, you should have little trouble locating it. But if the Pensión España should turn out to be at C/ Madrid 2°D Int, not far from Gta Atocha and just round the corner from P° del Prado, you could be forgiven for being a little confused. Here's a key to common abbreviations used in addresses:

Almd	Alameda	P° or Po	Paseo
Av or Avda	Avenida	Pje	Pasaje
C/	Calle	Pl or Pza or Pª	Plaza
Cllj	Callejón	Pllo	Pasillo
Cno	Camino	Pte	Puente
Cril	Carril	Rda	Ronda
Ctra or Ca	Carretera	s/n	*sin número*
Gta	Gloria		(without number)
	(major roundabout)	Urb	Urbanización

The following are used where there are several flats, hostales, offices etc in a building. They're often used in conjunction, eg 2°C or 3°I Int:

2°	2nd floor	I or izq	*izquierda* (left-hand side)
3°	3rd floor	Int	interior (a flat or office too
4°	4th floor		far inside a building to
C	*centro* (middle)		look on to any street –
D or dcha	*derecha* (right-hand side)		the opposite is Ext, *exterior*)

If someone's address is Apartado de Correos 206 (which might be shortened to Apdo Correos 206 or even just Apdo 206), don't bother going looking for it at all. An *apartado de correos* is a post-office box.

Note also that the word *de* is often omitted: Calle de Madrid (literally 'Street of Madrid') may be truncated to C/ Madrid. In fact it's not uncommon for streets to be referred to by their names alone: Calle de Alfonso Rodríguez will just as likely be referred to as Alfonso Rodríguez.

Sending Mail

Stamps are sold at most *estancos* (tobacconist shops with '*Tabacos*' in yellow letters on a maroon background), as well as at all post offices *(oficinas de correos y telégrafos)*. Cities have quite a lot of post offices and most villages have one too. Main post offices in cities and towns are usually open Monday to Friday from about 8.30 am to 8.30 pm, Saturday from about 9 am to 1.30 pm. Smaller offices may be open shorter hours. Estancos are usually open during normal shop hours.

It's quite safe and reliable to post your mail in the yellow street postboxes *(buzones)* as well as at post offices.

Delivery times are erratic but ordinary mail to other Western European countries normally takes up to a week; to North America up to 10 days; and to Australia or New Zealand up to two weeks.

Receiving Mail

Delivery times are similar to those for outbound mail. All Spanish addresses have five-digit postcodes; using postcodes may help your mail arrive a bit quicker.

Poste restante mail can be addressed to you at poste restante (or better, *lista de correos*, the Spanish name for it) at any place in Spain that has a post office. It will be delivered to the place's main post office unless another is specified in the address. Take your passport when you pick up mail. It helps if people writing to you capitalise or underline your surname and include the postcode in the address. Postcodes for poste restante at some main post offices are given in this book's destination sections. A typical lista de correos address looks like this:

Jane SMITH
Lista de Correos
29780 Nerja
Málaga
Spain

For some quirks of address abbreviations, see the boxed text 'Getting Addressed'. American Express card or travellers cheque holders can use the free client mail-holding service at American Express offices in Spain. You can get a list of these from American Express offices inside or outside Spain. Take your passport when you pick up mail.

Telephone

Spain has many street pay phones, which are blue and easy to use for both international and domestic calls. They accept coins and phonecards *(tarjetas telefónicas)* issued by the national phone company Telefónica or Printelcard Optima cards issued by an independent company that give useful discounts on some international calls (at the time of writing it was most common on the Costa del Sol). Tarjetas telefónicas come in 1000 and 2000 ptas denominations and, like postage stamps, are sold at post offices and estancos. Printelcard Optima cards (2000 ptas), sold at newsstands, require you to follow a special dialling procedure that is explained on the card.

Public phones inside bars and cafés, and phones in hotel rooms, are nearly always a good deal more expensive than street pay phones.

Costs Domestic and international calls from pay phones cost 30 to 35% more than from private phones. A three-minute pay phone call using coins or a tarjeta telefónica costs around 20 ptas to other places within your local area, 75 ptas to other places in the same province, 180 ptas to other Spanish provinces, 260 ptas to other EU countries, 350 ptas to North America and 600 ptas to Australia. All these calls are cheaper (around 15% cheaper for international calls) between 10 pm and 8 am and on Sundays and holidays. Domestic calls are also cheaper after 2 pm on Saturday. Printelcard Optima rates appear to be better for intercontinental calls (to North America, for instance) but no better for calls to Spanish or EU numbers.

Calls to Spanish numbers starting ☎ 900 are free, while calls to numbers starting ☎ 902 cost around 140 ptas for three minutes. Calls to mobile phones – numbers starting ☎ 907, ☎ 908, ☎ 909, ☎ 929, ☎ 939 or ☎ 970 – cost about 200 ptas for three minutes.

Domestic Calls Since 1998, Spain has had no telephone area codes. All numbers now have nine digits and you just dial that number, no matter where in the country you are calling from. Some people still give their number in the old style of area code followed by the number (eg ☎ 95-345 67 89), but this isn't a problem, as the new numbers simply consist of the old area code followed by the old number. So the old ☎ 95-345 67 89 is now just ☎ 95 345 67 89.

Dial ☎ 1009 to speak to a domestic operator, including for a domestic reverse-charge (collect) call (una llamada por cobro revertido). For directory inquiries dial ☎ 1003; calls cost about 60 ptas.

International Calls The access code for international calls is ☎ 00. To make an international call dial the access code, wait for a new dialling tone, then dial the country code, area code and number you want.

International collect calls are simple: dial ☎ 900 99 00, followed by a code for the country you're calling (☎ 61 for Australia, ☎ 44 for the UK, ☎ 64 for New Zealand, ☎ 15 for Canada and, for the USA, ☎ 11 for AT&T or ☎ 14 for MCI). Codes for other countries – usually the normal country code – are sometimes posted up in pay phones. You'll get straight through to an operator in the country you're calling. The same numbers can be used with direct-dial calling cards.

If for some reason the above doesn't work, in most places you can get an English-speaking Spanish international operator on ☎ 1008 (for calls within Europe) or ☎ 1005 (rest of the world).

For international directory inquiries dial ☎ 025 and be ready to pay about 150 ptas.

Retevisión Some phone users subscribe to a private-enterprise competitor to Telefónica called Retevisión, which offers lower costs on inter-provincial and international calls. To make a Retevisión inter-provincial

or international call you dial ☎ 050, then continue as with a normal call. Other competitor services are likely to appear.

Calling Spain from Other Countries
Spain's country code is ☎ 34. Follow this with the full nine-digit number you are calling.

Fax
Most post offices have a fax service: sending one page costs about 350 ptas within Spain, 920 ptas to elsewhere in Europe and 1700 to 2000 ptas to other countries. However you'll often find cheaper rates at shops or offices with 'Fax Público' signs.

Email & Internet Access
If you plan to carry a portable computer with you and the Spanish power supply voltage (see Electricity later in this chapter) is different from that in your home country, your best investment is a universal AC adapter for your appliance, which will enable you to plug it in anywhere without frying the innards. You'll also need a plug adapter (see Electricity) – often it's easiest to buy this before you leave home.

Also, your PC-card modem may or may not work once you leave your home country – and you won't know for sure until you try. The safest option is to buy a reputable 'global' modem before you leave home, or buy a local PC-card modem if you're spending an extended time in Spain. Keep in mind that Spanish telephone sockets may be different from those at home, so ensure that you have at least a US RJ-11 telephone adapter that works with your modem. You can almost always find an adapter that will convert from RJ-11 to the local variety. For more information on travelling with a portable computer, see www.teleadapt.com or www.warrior.com.

Major Internet service providers (ISP) such as AOL (www.aol.com), CompuServe (www.compuserve.com) and IBM Net (www.ibm.net) have dial-in nodes throughout Europe; it's best to download a list of the dial-in numbers before you leave home. CompuServe has four direct nodes (33,600bps) in Barcelona (☎ 93 487 3888), Madrid (☎ 91 575 90 30 and ☎ 91 577 06 86) and Valencia (☎ 96 351 01 33). A further nine access numbers are less reliable and may involve extra charges.

If you access your Internet email account at home through a smaller ISP or your office or school network, your best option is either to open an account with a global ISP, like those mentioned above, or to rely on cybercafés and other public access points to collect your mail.

Spain also has a number of Internet cafés and other public Internet and email services, which you can use for a few hundred pesetas an hour. You'll find some mentioned in city sections of this guide or check these Web sites:

EuroCyberCafes
    www.xs4all.nl/~bertb/cybercaf.html
Guía de los CiberCafés de España (in Spanish)
    www.andal.es/guiaCiberCafes

If you do intend to rely on cybercafés, you'll need to carry three pieces of information with you to enable you to access your Internet mail account: your incoming (POP or IMAP) mail server name, your account name and your password. Your ISP or network supervisor will be able to give you these. Armed with this information, you should be able to access your Internet mail account from any net-connected machine in the world, provided it runs some kind of email software (remember that Netscape and Internet Explorer both have mail modules). It pays to become familiar with the process for doing this before you leave home.

Another option for collecting mail through cybercafés is opening a free Web-based email account, using services such as HotMail (www.hotmail.com) or Yahoo! Mail (www.mail.yahoo.com). You can then get access to your email from anywhere in the world from any machine connected to the Internet and running a standard Web browser.

INTERNET RESOURCES

A search of the World Wide Web under 'Spain, travel' will reveal dozens of sites including the national tourist office's useful, although not too frequently updated, site called Discover Spain at www.spaintour.com. It provides all sorts of links to specific sites. A handy one for tracking tour organisations is www.okspain.org. Another site for the Spanish Board of Tourism (Turespaña) is www.tourspain.es/inicioi.htm.

Lonely Planet's enormously popular site (www.lonelyplanet.com) has a 'Destination Spain' page, which includes recent travellers tips and links to a number of other sources of information on Spain.

CompuServe's Spanish Forum has a data library with copious info on various aspects of Spanish travel; you can post messages asking for specific tips.

For a couple of hints on access to the Internet in Spain, see Email & Internet Access earlier in this chapter.

BOOKS

Most books are published in different editions by different publishers in different countries. As a result, a book might be a hardcover rarity in one country and readily available in paperback in another. Fortunately, bookshops and libraries search by title or author, so they are best placed to advise you on the availability of the listed recommendations.

Spain has inspired a deep fascination among foreign writers for two centuries. There's a huge wealth of literature in English on the country – and obviously plenty in Spanish too.

In London there are several good bookshops devoted to the business of travel. For guidebooks and maps, Stanfords bookshop (☎ 0171-836 2121, from 22 April 2000 ☎ 020-7836 2121, 12-14 Long Acre WC2E 9LP), is acknowledged as one of the better first ports of call. A well-stocked source of travel literature is Daunts Books for Travellers (☎ 0171-224 2295, from 22 April 2000 ☎ 020-7224 2295, 83 Marylebone High Street W1M 4AL).

Books on Spain (☎ /fax 0181-898 7789, from 22 April 2000 ☎ 020-8898 7789, PO Box 207, Twickenham TW2 5BQ) can send you a catalogue of hundreds of old and new titles available by mail order. For books in Spanish, one of the best options is Grant & Cutler (☎ 0171-734 2012, from 22 April 2000 ☎ 020-7734 2012, 55-57 Great Marlborough St, London W1V 2AY).

In Australia, the Travel Bookshop (☎ 02-9241 3554), 20 Bridge Street, Sydney, is worth a browse. In the USA, try Book Passage (☎ 415-927-0960), 51 Tamal Vista Boulevard, Corte Madera, California, and The Complete Traveler Bookstore (☎ 212-685-9007), 199 Madison Ave, New York. In France, L'Astrolabe rive gauche (☎ 01 46 33 80 06), 14 rue Serpente, Paris, is recommended.

Lonely Planet

If trekking or hiking is on your agenda, you'll find a wealth of route descriptions for all the main areas and lots of practical and informative background in Lonely Planet's *Walking in Spain*. Lonely Planet also publishes companion guides on *Andalucía*, *Canary Islands* and *Barcelona* (forthcoming).

For people travelling on from Spain, other Lonely Planet travel guides include *France*, *Portugal* and *Morocco*.

Guidebooks

Blue Guide Spain isn't a bad companion if you want lots of detail about the country's architecture and art in historical context. For walking guides, see the Activities section later in this chapter.

Of the many guides in Spanish to different parts of Spain, those published by El País/Aguilar stand out for their concise, intelligent and honest coverage and handy format. There are around 60 guides in various series, covering provinces, cities, routes such as the Camino de Santiago, tapas bars in various cities, and one-offs such as the excellent *Pequeños Hoteles con Encanto* (Small Hotels with Charm), *Alojamientos en Monasterios* (Lodgings in Monasteries) and *Pequeños Pueblos con Encanto* (Small Villages with Charm).

Yachties might want the bilingual *Yachtsman's Guide* to Spain and Portugal, updated annually and available in Spain in specialist bookstores, yacht clubs and El Corte Inglés.

Travel

19th Century Classics Washington Irving was an American who took up residence in Granada's Alhambra palace when it was in an abandoned state in the early 19th century. His *Tales of the Alhambra* (1832) weaves a series of still-enchanting stories around the folk with whom he shared his life and was largely responsible for the romantic image of Al-Andalus – and, by extension, of Spain – which persists to this day.

A Handbook for Travellers in Spain by Richard Ford (1845) set standards that few guidebook writers have matched since. It remains a classic not only for telling us how things were in places we see now, but also for its irascible English author, who is by turns witty, prejudiced, highly informative and downright rude.

The Bible in Spain by George Borrow is an English clergyman's view of the 19th century Spain in which he tried to spread the Protestant word. It's an amusing read both for the man himself and for his experiences.

20th Century In the 1920s Gerald Brenan settled in a remote village south of Granada, aiming to educate himself unimpeded by his British mores and traditions. *South from Granada* (1957) is his absorbing account of local life and visits from members of the Bloomsbury set with whom he was associated. In 1949 Brenan returned to explore Franco's Spain, an experience recounted in *The Face of Spain* (1950).

Meanwhile Laurie Lee, aged 19, walked off from his Gloucestershire home in 1934. He arrived by boat at Vigo, then walked the length of Spain, playing his fiddle for a living. *As I Walked Out One Midsummer Morning* (1969) is a delightful account of his adventures that also records the sights, smells and contrasting moods of turbulent pre-civil war Spain. *A Moment of War*

(1991) describes Lee's bizarre experiences in the International Brigades during the civil war. In the third of his Spanish 'trilogy', *A Rose for Winter*, Lee tells of his return to Andalucía 15 years later.

If you can trace Rose Macauley's out-of-print *Fabled Shore*, which recounts a trip along the coast from Catalunya to the Algarve in 1949, it will leave you wondering if she is really writing about the same seaboard that spawned the Costa Blanca and Costa del Sol.

Of recent travel writings, David Gilmour's *Cities of Spain* and Adam Hopkins' *Spanish Journeys*, both culture and history focused, and Michael Jacobs' amusing *Between Hopes and Memories: A Spanish Journey* stand out. Travels along the Camino de Santiago are recounted by Robin Hanbury-Tenison in *Spanish Pilgrimage – A Canter to St James* and Bettina Selby in *Pilgrim's Road*. He had a penchant for white horses; she did it by bike.

History & Politics

For a colourful but thorough and not overlong survey of Spanish history, *The Story of Spain* by Mark Williams is hard to beat. Also concise and worthwhile is Juan Lalaguna's *A Traveller's History of Spain*.

John A Crow's *Spain: the Root and the Flower* is an American Hispanophile's insightful, scholarly, but rarely dry, ramble through history and culture from early times to the 1980s.

Moorish Spain by Richard Fletcher is one of the best histories of Spain's fascinating Islamic era. *Imperial Spain, 1469-1716* by JH Elliot is probably the best single book covering the country's golden age and its immediate aftermath.

Gerald Brenan's *The Spanish Labyrinth* (1943) is an in-depth but readable unravelling of the tangle of political and social movements in the half-century or so before the civil war.

If you are looking for a more detailed and somewhat academic exploration of Spanish history, the series *A History of Spain*, edited by John Lynch, covers the subject in more than a dozen separate volumes by various authors.

Civil War & Franco Era The civil war is said to be the second most written-about conflict in history (after WWII) and has spawned some wonderful books. *The Spanish Civil War* by Hugh Thomas is probably the classic account of the conflict in any language, long and dense with detail, yet readable, even-handed and humane. Raymond Carr's more succinct *The Spanish Tragedy* is another well-written and respected account.

Homage to Catalonia is George Orwell's story of his involvement in the civil war, moving from the euphoria of the early days in Barcelona to disillusionment with the disastrous infighting on the Republican side.

The murky story of one of the war's more infamous atrocities, the murder near Granada of the poet and playwright Lorca, is chillingly pieced together in *The Assassination of Federico García Lorca* by noted Lorca scholar (and now Spanish citizen) Ian Gibson; the book also gives background on Lorca and the war. Ronald Fraser's *Blood of Spain* is a fascinating collection of eyewitness accounts of the war.

Paul Preston's *Franco* is the big biography of one of history's little dictators.

Regions

Andalucía and Catalunya, two strongly contrasting regions at opposite ends of the country, seem to have inspired foreigners more than any other part of Spain.

The Sierras of the South by Alastair Boyd is a vivid story of life around Ronda in the Andalucian hill country in the 1950s and 60s. (The same author also penned *The Essence of Catalonia*.) Nicholas Luard does a similar job for the valleys behind Tarifa in *Andalucía: A Portrait of Southern Spain* (1984). *Inside Andalusia* by David Baird (1993) is an always interesting collection of portraits of people and places in this region.

Michael Jacobs' *A Guide to Andalusia* runs comprehensively through all the important cultural and historical aspects of Andalucía, from Muslim architecture to Lorca and the Sevillan golden age to flamenco.

Homage to Barcelona by Colm Tóibín (1990) is an excellent personal introduction to the city's modern life and artistic and political history; Tóibín is an Irish journalist who lived there. *Barcelona* by Robert Hughes (1992) goes into more depth, approaching the city's past and art with mordant wit and a keen eye.

Two books give a revealing insight into Spanish attitudes to the changes of the past decades (notably tourism): Ronald Fraser's *The Pueblo*, about the village of Mijas on the Costa del Sol, and Norman Lewis' semifictional *Voices of the Old Sea*, set on the Costa Brava.

Un Hiver À Majorque (A Winter in Mallorca) is George Sand's account of an 1830s sojourn in an abandoned monastery on the island with her lover, the composer Chopin, and her two children. There was little love lost between the locals and the French writer.

Hemingway

Ernest Hemingway's *For Whom the Bell Tolls* (1941) is probably the most-read of all English-language books set in Spain. This terse tale of the civil war is full of Spanish atmosphere and all the emotions unleashed in the war. Its plot keeps you hanging on until the last sentence. Hemingway's earlier novel *Fiesta* made the Sanfermines bull-running festival at Pamplona world famous; it's also published under the title *The Sun Also Rises. Death in the Afternoon* is his book on bullfighting.

Society, Culture & Arts

The two best overall introductions to modern Spain are *The New Spaniards* by John Hooper, a former *Guardian* Madrid correspondent, whose writings range comprehensively from the arts through politics and bullfighting to sex, and the more controversial and personal *Fire in the Blood* by Ian Gibson, based on a British TV series. Gibson has written weighty biographies of Lorca and Salvador Dalí.

Titus Burckhardt's *Moorish Culture in Spain* is a classic book on the unique architecture and culture of Islamic Spain. In the handy Thames & Hudson series on artistic movements, *Romanesque Art* by Meyer Schapiro covers this pre-Gothic architectural and artistic era, while *The Arts of Spain* by José Guidol ranges from cave paintings to the 20th century.

It would be hard to better James Woodall's *In Search of the Firedance* as an introduction to flamenco.

Food & Wine

There are dozens of books on Spanish cookery. Three of the best are *The Foods and Wines of Spain* by Penelope Casas, *Cooking in Spain* by Janet Mendel and the slimmer *Spain on a Plate* by María-José Sevilla. All have good background on the country's widely varied regional cuisines as well as recipes.

Flora & Fauna

Wildlife Travelling Companion Spain by John Measures is a good traveller's guide, focusing on 150 of the best sites for viewing flora and fauna, with details of how to reach them and what you can hope to see.

Spain's Wildlife by Eric Robins covers the country's most interesting animals and birds – and their prospects for survival – in an informative way, spiced with plenty of personal experience and some good photos.

Serious birdwatchers in Andalucía and Extremadura will find *Where to Watch Birds in Southern Spain* by Ernest Garcia and Andrew Paterson invaluable. But they will also want a field guide such as the *Collins Field Guide to the Birds of Britain and Europe* by Roger Peterson, Guy Mountfort & PAD Hollom, or *Collins Pocket Guide Birds of Britain and Europe* by H Heinzel, RSR Fitter & J Parslow.

The single best guide to flowers and shrubs in Spain is *Flowers of South-West Europe, A Field Guide* by Oleg Polunin & BE Smythies.

FILM

See Cinema under Arts in the Facts about Spain chapter for a discussion of Spanish cinema.

CD ROM

There are some interesting CD ROMs available on Spain, but most of them have text and any voice-over in Spanish only and could be hard to come by outside Spain.

A few examples include:

- AND Route 98 (España y Portugal) – similar to E-Atlas (see later), only instead of Spanish cities you get Portugal thrown in, and often comes as a package with a general European route planner (7990 ptas)
- Descubre Madrid y Sus Museos – a tourist guide concerned mainly with introductory info on what's in Madrid's museum, plus other sights and information (Power CD sells it for 1995 ptas)
- E-Atlas – contains maps of Spain and major cities, allows you to plan routes, zooming in on areas of interest etc (4995 ptas)
- El Greco – lets you get to know the Cretan-born and Spanish adopted master's work from the comfort of your own ergonomically correct work station chair (Biblioteca Multimedia; 4950 ptas)
- Esqui en Ruta – a guide which contains info on all the ski resorts in Spain and Andorra, but you should check the edition year before buying (2990 ptas)
- España en Fiestas – lets you know the when and where of Spanish fiestas and what they look like handy for planning trips around local events (Indes Media; 1495 ptas)
- Flamenco – Biblioteca Multimedia's fairly basic guide to the wonders of flamenco song and dance (4950 ptas)
- Historia de España – a series of CD ROMs dealing with various aspects of Spanish history (4990 ptas each)
- Museos en Ruta '98 – a guide to museums (what they contain, when they open etc) throughout Spain (2990 ptas)
- Tauromaquia – all you ever needed to know about bullfighting, even if the idea of the real thing puts you off (Biblioteca Multimedia; 4950 ptas)
- Visual Map Sevilla – has Sevilla maps and walks, as well as potted summaries of information on on the city's sites, restaurants and the like (5990 ptas)

NEWSPAPERS & MAGAZINES
Spanish Press

Spain has a thriving and free press. Daily newspapers sell around four or five million copies between them, working out at one for every eight to 10 people (a similar figure to Italy), compared to one for every 2½ people in Britain. The sales figures in part reflect the Spanish habit of sharing newspapers; it's actually reckoned that about one-third of Spaniards read papers regularly.

For some reason Spaniards have never taken to the idea of what's generously called a 'popular' press. There's no equivalent of the *Sun* or the *New York Daily News* here. However, one of the best-selling dailies is *Marca*, which is devoted exclusively to sport.

The major daily newspapers are the liberal *El País*, the conservative *ABC*, and *El Mundo*, which specialises in breaking political scandals. For solid reporting of national and international events, *El País* is hard to beat.

There's also a welter of regional dailies, some of the best being Barcelona's *La Vanguardia* and *El Periódico* (both in Spanish, although the latter also does a Catalan edition) and *Avui* (in Catalan) and Andalucía's *Sur* and *El Correo*. The País Vasco has two papers produced partly in the Basque language: *Deia* and ETA's mouthpiece, *Egin*.

Foreign-Language Press

Coastal areas with large expatriate populations have a few mainly English-language publications. Some of them are best for wrapping your fish and chips in, but in Andalucía the free weekly *Sur in English* reviews local news quite thoroughly and has good small ads, while *Lookout* is a glossy monthly magazine with some interesting features.

International press such as the *International Herald Tribune*, *Time* and *Newsweek*, and newspapers from Western European countries, reach major cities and tourist areas on the day of publication; elsewhere they're a bit harder to find and a day or two late.

RADIO & TV
Radio

There are several hundred radio stations around the country, mainly on FM, and they run the gamut from a lot of loud babble interspersed with silly noises to nonstop good music. Many are independent but some are run by town councils. The state network, Radio Nacional de España (RNE), has four stations. RNE 1, with general interest and current affairs programs, and RNE 5, with sport and entertainment, are on AM (medium wave); RNE 2, with classical music, and RNE 3 (or 'Radio d'Espop'), with admirably varied pop and rock music, are on FM (VHF). The most popular is commercial pop and rock station 40 Principales, on FM. Frequencies vary from place to place: El País publishes local wavelength guides in its Cartelera what's-on section.

Some of the expat-populated costas have the odd foreign-language station, such as the English-language Onda Cero International (101.6 MHz FM) on the Costa del Sol. These stations' programming is mostly middle-of-the-road, though they often carry BBC World Service news (on the hour), with better reception than the BBC itself.

The BBC World Service broadcasts its services to Spain on 3.955, 6.195, 7.150, 9.410, 12.095, 15.070 and 15.400 MHz (short wave). There's transmission on one or other of these frequencies from 4.30 am to 11.15 pm GMT/UTC. Voice of America can be found on various short-wave frequencies, including 9.700, 15.205 and 15.255 MHz, depending on the time of day.

TV

Spaniards are Europe's greatest TV watchers after the British, but do some of their watching in bars and cafés, which makes it more of a social activity.

Most TVs receive between five and seven channels. Two come from the state-run Televisión Española (TVE1 and La 2) and three are independent (Antena 3, Tele 5 and Canal Plus). In some areas one or two stations are run by regional governments, such as Madrid's Telemadrid, Catalunya's TV-3 and Canal 33, Galicia's TVG, the País Vasco's ETB-1 and ETB-2, Valencia's Canal 9 and Andalucía's Canal Sur. Apart from news (of which there's a respectable

amount), TV programming consists largely of game and talk shows, sport, telenovelas (soap operas) and English-language films dubbed into Spanish.

Canal Plus is a pay channel, however non-subscribers can get most programs except films (which is what the channel specialises in), for which you need a decoder.

Satellite TV is popular too – mainly in private homes, although some bars, cafés and top-end hotels have it too. Foreign channels you may come across include BBC World (mainly news and travel), BBC Prime (other BBC programs), CNN, Eurosport, Sky News, Sky Sports, Sky Sports 2, Sky Movies and the German SAT 1.

VIDEO SYSTEMS

If you want to record or buy video tapes to play back home, you won't get a picture if the image registration systems are different. Spanish TVs, and nearly all prerecorded videos on sale in Spain, use the PAL (phase alternation line) system common to most of Western Europe and Australia. France uses the incompatible SECAM system and North America and Japan use the incompatible NTSC system. PAL videos can't be played back on a machine that lacks PAL capability.

PHOTOGRAPHY

Most main brands of film are widely available and processing is fast and generally efficient. A roll of print film (36 exposures, ISO 100) costs around 650 ptas and can be processed for around 1700 ptas, though there are often better deals if you have two or three rolls developed together. The equivalent in slide (diapositiva) film is around 850 ptas plus 850 ptas for processing.

Some museums and galleries ban photography, or at least flash photography, and soldiers can be touchy about it. It's common courtesy to ask – at least by gesture – when you want to photograph people, unless perhaps when they're in some kind of public event like a procession.

Bright middle-of-the-day sun tends to bleach out your shots. You get more colour and contrast earlier and later in the day.

TIME

Spain is on GMT/UTC plus one hour during winter and GMT/UTC plus two hours during the daylight-saving period, from the last Sunday in March to the last Sunday in October. Most other Western European countries have the same time as Spain year round, the major exceptions being Britain, Ireland and Portugal. Add one hour to these three countries' times to get Spanish time.

Morocco is on GMT/UTC year round. From the last Sunday in March to the last Sunday in October, subtract two hours from Spanish time to get Moroccan time; the rest of the year, subtract one hour.

Spanish time is normally USA Eastern Time plus six hours and USA Pacific Time plus nine hours. But the USA tends to start daylight saving a week or two later than Spain (meaning you must add one hour to the time differences in the intervening period).

In the Australian winter (Spanish summer), subtract eight hours from Australian Eastern Standard Time to get Spanish time; in the Australian summer subtract 10 hours. The difference is nine hours for a few weeks in March.

ELECTRICITY

Electric current in Spain is 220V, 50 Hz, as in the rest of continental Europe, but a few places are still on 125V or 110V (sockets are often labelled when this applies). The voltage may even vary in the same building. Don't plug 220V (or British 240V) appliances into 125V or 110V sockets unless they have a transformer. Several countries outside Europe (such as the USA and Canada) use 60 Hz, which means that appliances from those countries with electric motors (such as some CD and tape players) may perform poorly.

Plugs have two round pins, again like the rest of continental Europe.

WEIGHTS & MEASURES

The metric system is used. Like other continental Europeans, the Spanish indicate decimals with commas and thousands with points.

LAUNDRY

Self-service laundrettes are rare. Small laundries *(lavanderías)* are fairly common; staff will usually wash, dry and fold a load for 1000 to 1200 ptas. Some youth hostels and a few budget hostales have washing machines for guests' use.

TOILETS

Public toilets are not particularly common in Spain, but it's OK to wander into most bars and cafés to use their toilet even if you're not a customer. It's worth carrying some loo paper with you as many toilets lack it. If there's a bin beside the loo, put paper etc in it – it's there because the local sewerage system couldn't cope otherwise.

HEALTH

Spain is a pretty healthy country. Your main risks are likely to be sunburn, dehydration, foot blisters, insect bites, or mild gut problems at first if you're not used to a lot of olive oil. Most travellers experience no problems.

Predeparture Planning

Health Insurance Make sure that you have adequate health insurance. See Travel Insurance under Visas & Documents earlier in this chapter for more information on health, theft and loss insurance for travellers.

EU citizens are entitled to free medical care under the Spanish national health system on presentation of an E111 form, which you must get in your country. Even with an E111, you will still have to pay for any medicines bought from pharmacies, even if a doctor has prescribed them, and perhaps for a few tests and procedures.

An E111 is no good, however, for private medical consultations or treatment in Spain, which includes virtually all dentists, some of the better clinics and surgeries and emergency flights home. If you want to avoid paying for these, you'll need medical as well as theft and loss insurance on your travel policy (see Travel Insurance under Visas & Documents earlier in this chapter).

In Britain, E111s are issued free by post offices; all you need to supply is your name, address, date of birth and National Insurance number. In other EU countries ask your doctor or health service how to get the form.

Most, but not all, US health insurance policies stay in effect, at least for a limited period, if you travel abroad. Most non-European national health plans (including Australia's Medicare) don't, so you must take out special medical as well as theft and loss insurance.

Travel Health Guides If you are planning to be away or travelling in remote areas for a long time, you may like to consider taking a more detailed health guide:

Travellers' Health by Dr Richard Dawood, Oxford University Press, 1995. It's comprehensive, easy to read, authoritative and highly recommended, though rather large to lug around.

Travel with Children by Maureen Wheeler, Lonely Planet Publications, 1995. It includes advice on travel health for younger children.

Immunisations No jabs are normally needed to visit Spain, but the odd one might be required if you're coming from an infected area – yellow fever is the most likely one. You can check with your travel agent or Spanish embassy.

There are, however, a few routine vaccinations that are recommended whether you're travelling or not. They include polio, tetanus and diphtheria and sometimes measles, mumps and rubella (German measles). All these are usually administered in childhood, but some require later booster shots. For details, check with your doctor or nearest health agency.

All vaccinations should be recorded on an International Health Certificate, which is available from your physician or government health department.

Other Preparations Make sure you're healthy before you start travelling. If you are going on a long trip make sure your teeth are OK. If you wear glasses take a spare pair and your prescription.

If you require a particular medication take an adequate supply, as it may not be available locally. Take part of the packaging showing the generic name, rather than the brand, which will make getting replacements easier. It's a good idea to have a legible prescription or letter from your doctor to show that you use the medication legally.

Basic Rules

Food If you're travelling hard and fast and missing meals, or if you simply lose your appetite, you can soon start to lose weight and place your health at risk. Make sure your diet is well balanced. Eggs, meat, pulses and dairy products are all safe ways of getting protein. Fruit and vegetables are good sources of vitamins. Try to eat plenty of grains (including rice) and bread.

In hot weather make sure you drink enough; don't rely on feeling thirsty to indicate when you should drink. Not needing to urinate, or very dark yellow urine, is a danger sign. Carry a water bottle on long trips. Excessive sweating can lead to loss of salt and therefore muscle cramping.

Water Domestic, hotel and restaurant tap water is safe to drink virtually everywhere in Spain. In places with water shortages you might want to check if the water's OK: lowering of water tables might introduce some undesirable ingredients into the supply. Ask '*¿Es potable el agua?*' if you're in any doubt. Water from public spouts and fountains is not reliable unless it has a sign saying '*Agua Potable*'. Often there are signs saying '*Agua No Potable*: Don't Drink Here'.

Natural water, unless it's straight from a definitely unpolluted spring or running off snow or ice without interference from people or animals, is also not safe to drink unpurified.

Safe bottled water is available everywhere, generally for 40 to 75 ptas for a 1.5L bottle in shops and supermarkets.

Medical Kit Check List

Following is a list of items you should consider including in your medical kit – consult your phamacist for brands available in your country.

☐ **Aspirin** or **paracetamol** (acetaminophen in the USA) – for pain or fever.

☐ **Antihistamine** – for allergies, eg hay fever; to ease the itch from insect bites or stings; and to prevent motion sickness.

☐ **Antibiotics** – consider including these if you're travelling well off the beaten track; see your doctor, as they must be prescribed, and carry the prescription with you.

☐ **Loperamide** or **diphenoxylate** – 'blockers' for diarrhoea; **prochlorperazine** or **metaclopramide** for nausea and vomiting.

☐ **Rehydration mixture** – to prevent dehydration, eg due to severe diarrhoea; particularly important when travelling with children.

☐ **Insect repellent, sunscreen, lip balm** and **eye drops**.

☐ **Calamine lotion, sting relief spray** or **aloe vera** – to ease irritation from sunburn and insect bites or stings.

☐ **Antifungal cream** or **powder** – for fungal skin infections and thrush.

☐ **Antiseptic** (such as povidone-iodine) – for cuts and grazes.

☐ **Bandages, elastic plasters** and other wound dressings.

☐ **Water purification tablets** or **iodine**.

☐ **Scissors, tweezers** and a **thermometer** (note that mercury thermometers are prohibited by airlines).

☐ **Syringes** and **needles** – in case you need injections in a country with medical hygine problems. Ask your doctor for a note explaining why you have them.

☐ **Cold** and **flu tablets, throat lozenges** and **nasal decongestant**.

☐ **Multivitamins** – consider for long trips, when dietary vitamin intake may be inadequate.

The simplest way of purifying water is to boil it vigorously for five minutes. However, at high altitude water boils at a lower temperature, so germs are less likely to be killed. If you can't boil water it should be treated chemically. Chlorine tablets (Puritabs, Steritabs or other brand names) will kill many pathogens. Iodine is also effective in purifying water and is available in tablet form (such as Potable Aqua).

Medical Problems & Treatment

For serious medical problems and emergencies, the Spanish public health service provides care to rival that of anywhere in the world. Seeing a doctor about something more mundane can be less than enchanting, because of obscure appointment systems, queues and sometimes grumpy personnel, though you should get decent attention in the end. The expense of going to a private clinic or surgery often saves time and frustration: you'll typically pay between 3000 and 6000 ptas for a consultation (not counting medicines). All dental practices are private in any case.

If you want see a doctor quickly, or need emergency dental treatment, try going along to the *urgencias* (emergency) section of the nearest hospital. Many towns also have a *centro de salud* (health centre) with an urgencias section.

Take along as much documentation (passport, E111, insurance papers, ideally photocopies too) as you can muster when you deal with medical services. Tourist offices, the police and usually your accommodation can tell you where to find doctors, dentists and hospitals, or how to call an ambulance. You could also contact your country's nearest consulate in Spain for advice. Many major hospitals and emergency medical services are mentioned and/or shown on maps in this book's city sections.

Pharmacies *(farmacias)* can help with many ailments. A system of duty pharmacies *(farmacias de guardia)* ensures that each town or district of a city has a pharmacy open all the time. When a pharmacy is closed, it posts the name of the nearest open one on the door. Lists of farmacias de guardia are often in local papers.

Environmental Hazards

Altitude Sickness Lack of oxygen at high altitudes (over 2500m) affects most people to some extent. The effect may be mild or severe and occurs because less oxygen reaches the muscles and the brain, requiring the heart and lungs to work harder. Symptoms of Acute Mountain Sickness (AMS) usually develop during the first 24 hours at altitude but may be delayed by up to three weeks. Mild symptoms include headache, lethargy, dizziness, difficulty sleeping and loss of appetite. There is no hard-and-fast rule on what is too high: AMS has been fatal at 3000m, although 3500 to 4500m is the usual range. The only mountains higher than 3000m in mainland Spain are in the Pyrenees and Andalucía's Sierra Nevada. None of these exceeds 3500m.

Treat mild symptoms by resting at the same altitude until recovery, usually a day or two. Paracetamol or aspirin can be taken for headaches. If symptoms persist or become worse, *immediate descent is necessary*; even 500m can help. Drug treatments should never be used to avoid descent or to enable further ascent.

Fungal Infections Fungal infections occur more commonly in hot weather and are usually found on the scalp, between the toes or fingers, in the groin and on the body (ringworm). You get ringworm (which is a fungal infection, not a worm) from infected animals or other people. Moisture encourages these infections.

To prevent fungal infections wear loose, comfortable clothes, avoid artificial fibres, wash frequently and dry carefully. If you get an infection, wash the area at least daily with a disinfectant or medicated soap and water, and rinse and dry well. Apply an antifungal cream or powder like tolnaftate (Tinaderm). Try to expose the area to air or sunlight as much as possible and wash all towels and underwear in hot water, change them often and let them dry in the sun.

Heat Exhaustion Dehydration and salt deficiency can cause heat exhaustion. Take time to acclimatise to high temperatures, drink sufficient liquids and don't do anything too physically demanding.

Salt deficiency is characterised by fatigue, lethargy, headaches, giddiness and muscle cramps; salt tablets may help, but adding extra salt to your food is better.

Heat Stroke This serious, occasionally fatal, condition can occur if the body's heat-regulating mechanism breaks down and the body temperature rises to dangerous levels. Long, continuous periods of exposure to high temperatures and insufficient fluids can leave you vulnerable to heat stroke.

The symptoms are feeling unwell, not sweating very much (or at all) and a high body temperature (39°C to 41°C, 102°F to 106°F). Where sweating has ceased, the skin becomes flushed and red. Severe, throbbing headaches and a lack of coordination will occur and the sufferer may be confused or aggressive. Eventually the victim will become delirious or convulse. Hospitalisation is essential, but meanwhile

Everyday Health

Normal body temperature is up to 37°C or 98.6°F; more than 2°C (4°F) higher than this indicates a high fever. The normal adult pulse rate is 60 to 100 per minute (children 80 to 100, babies 100 to 140). As a general rule the pulse increases about 20 beats per minute for each 1°C (2°F) rise in fever.

Respiration (breathing) rate is also an indicator of illness. Count the number of breaths per minute: between 12 and 20 is normal for adults and older children (up to 30 for younger children, 40 for babies). People with a high fever or serious respiratory illness breathe more quickly than normal. More than 40 shallow breaths a minute may indicate pneumonia.

get victims out of the sun, remove their clothing, cover them with a wet sheet or towel and then fan continually. Give them fluids if they are conscious.

Hypothermia Too much cold can be just as dangerous as too much heat. Though unlikely in Spain, it could occur in the mountains in winter. If trekking at high altitudes, be prepared.

Hypothermia occurs when the body loses heat faster than it can produce it and the body's core temperature falls. It's surprisingly easy to progress from very cold to dangerously cold due to a combination of wind, wet clothing, fatigue and hunger. It is best to dress in layers: silk, wool and some of the new artificial fibres are good insulating materials. A hat is important. A strong, waterproof outer layer (and a 'space' blanket for emergencies) are essential. Carry basic supplies, including food containing simple sugars to generate heat quickly and fluids to drink.

Symptoms of hypothermia are exhaustion, numb skin (particularly toes and fingers), shivering, slurred speech, irrational or violent behaviour, lethargy, stumbling, dizzy spells, muscle cramps and violent bursts of energy. Irrationality may take the form of sufferers claiming they are warm and trying to take off their clothes.

To treat mild hypothermia, first get the person out of the wind and/or rain, and replace wet clothes with dry, warm ones. Give them hot liquids – not alcohol – and some high-kilojoule, easily digestible food. Do not rub victims; instead allow them to slowly warm themselves. The early recognition and treatment of mild hypothermia is the only way to prevent severe hypothermia, a critical condition.

Jet Lag Jet lag is experienced when a person travels by air across more than three time zones. Many of the functions of the human body (such as temperature, pulse rate and emptying of the bladder and bowels) are regulated by internal 24-hour cycles. When we travel long distances

rapidly, our bodies take time to adjust to the 'new time' of our destination and we may experience fatigue, disorientation, insomnia, anxiety, impaired concentration and loss of appetite. These effects will usually be gone within three days of arrival, but to minimise the impact of jet lag:

- Rest for a couple of days before departure.
- Try to select flight schedules that minimise sleep deprivation; arriving late in the day means you can go to sleep soon after you arrive. For very long flights, try to organise a stopover.
- During the flight, avoid excessive eating (which bloats the stomach) and alcohol (which causes dehydration). Instead, drink plenty of noncarbonated, nonalcoholic drinks such as fruit juice or water.
- Avoid smoking.
- Make yourself comfortable by wearing loose-fitting clothes and perhaps bringing an eye mask and ear plugs to help you sleep.
- Try to sleep at the appropriate time for the time zone you are travelling to.

Motion Sickness Eating lightly before and during a trip will reduce the chances of motion sickness. If you are prone to this, try to find a place that has minimal movement – near the wing on aircraft, close to midships on boats, near the centre on buses. Fresh air usually helps; reading and cigarette smoke don't. Commercial motion-sickness preparations, which can cause drowsiness, have to be taken before the trip commences.

Ginger (available in capsule form) and peppermint (including mint-flavoured sweets) are natural preventatives.

Prickly Heat This itchy rash, caused by excessive perspiration trapped under the skin, usually strikes people who have just arrived in a hot climate. Keeping cool, bathing often, drying the skin and using a mild talcum or prickly heat powder, or resorting to air-conditioning, may help.

Sunburn You can get sunburnt surprisingly quickly, even through cloud. Use sunscreen, a hat and barrier cream for your nose and lips. Calamine lotion or Stingose is good for mild sunburn. Protect your eyes with good quality sunglasses, particularly if you will be near water, sand or snow.

Infectious Diseases

Diarrhoea Simple things like a change of water, food or climate can all cause a mild bout of diarrhoea, but a few rushed toilet trips with no other symptoms are not indicative of a major problem.

Dehydration is the main danger with any diarrhoea, particularly in children or the elderly, as it can occur quite quickly. Under all circumstances *fluid replacement* (at least equal to the volume being lost) is the most important thing to remember. Weak black tea with a little sugar, soda water, or soft drinks allowed to go flat and diluted 50% with clean water are all good.

Hepatitis Hepatitis is a general term for inflammation of the liver. Its symptoms are fever, chills, headache, fatigue, feelings of weakness and aches and pains, followed by loss of appetite, nausea, vomiting, abdominal pain, dark urine, light-coloured faeces and jaundiced (yellow) skin. The whites of the eyes may turn yellow.

There are almost 300 million chronic carriers of hepatitis B in the world and Spanish children are routinely vaccinated against it. Hepatitis B can lead to long-term problems such as irreparable liver damage or even liver cancer. It is spread through contact with infected blood, blood products or body fluids, for example through sexual contact, unsterilised needles, blood transfusions or contact with blood via small breaks in the skin. Other risk situations include having a shave, a tattoo or your body pierced with contaminated equipment. A hepatitis B vaccination is available. It involves three injections, the quickest course being over three weeks, with a booster at 12 months.

Hepatitis C, which can lead to chronic liver disease, is spread by contact with blood usually via contaminated transfusions or shared needles. Avoiding these is the only means of prevention.

HIV & AIDS HIV, the Human Immunodeficiency Virus, develops into the fatal disease AIDS, Acquired Immune Deficiency Syndrome. There is no cure for AIDS.

Any exposure to blood, blood products or body fluids may put the individual at risk. The disease is often transmitted through sexual contact or dirty needles – vaccinations, acupuncture, tattooing and body piercing can be potentially as dangerous as intravenous drug use. HIV/AIDS can also be spread through infected blood transfusions. Intravenous drug use is the major reason for Spain having the highest AIDS rate in Europe: 6680 new cases in 1996 and about 50,000 cases since 1981. The number of new cases reported in 1997 was 21% lower than in 1996.

If you do need an injection, ask to see the syringe unwrapped in front of you or take a needle and syringe pack with you. Fear of HIV infection should never preclude treatment for serious medical conditions.

HIV and AIDS are VIH and *sida*, respectively, in Spanish. The Fundación Anti-Sida de España (Calle de Juan Montalvo 6, 28040 Madrid) has a free information line (☎ 900-11 10 00). Many gay organisations, including Coordinadora Gai-Lesbiana (☎ 93 309 79 97, Carrer Buenaventura Muñoz 4, 08018 Barcelona) can provide AIDS information and advice. Coordinadora Gai-Lesbiana's Web site at www.pangea.org/org/cgl/inde.htm has a long list of Spanish AIDS information and support organisations under 'Information & Services'.

Sexually Transmitted Diseases Gonorrhoea, herpes and syphilis are sexually transmitted diseases (STDs); common symptoms are sores, blisters or rashes around the genitals, discharges or pain when urinating. With some STDs, such as the wart virus or chlamydia, symptoms may be less marked or not observed at all, especially in women. Syphilis symptoms eventually disappear but the disease continues and can cause severe problems in later years. While abstinence from sexual contact is the only 100% effective prevention from STDs, using condoms (condones, preservativos), available in pharmacies, is also effective. Gonorrhoea and syphilis are treated with antibiotics, but each disease requires specific antibiotics. There is no cure for herpes.

Cuts, Bites & Stings

Cuts & Scratches Skin punctures can easily become infected in hot climates and may be difficult to heal. Wash well and treat any cut with an antiseptic such as povidone-iodine. Where possible avoid bandages and elastic plasters, which can keep wounds wet.

Insects, Scorpions & Centipedes Bee and wasp stings are usually painful rather than dangerous. But people who are allergic to them may have severe breathing difficulties and require urgent medical care. Calamine lotion or Stingose spray will give relief and ice packs will reduce the pain and swelling.

Scorpion stings are notoriously painful but the stings of Spanish scorpions are not considered fatal. Scorpions often shelter in shoes or clothing, so shake these out before you put them on when camping. Some Spanish centipedes (escolopendras) also have a very nasty, but not fatal, sting. Steer clear of scorpions composed of clearly defined segments, which may be marked by, for instance, alternate black and yellow stripes.

Also beware of the hairy, reddish-brown caterpillars (procesionarias) of the pine processionary moth, which live in easily discernible silvery nests in pine trees in many parts of Spain, and have a habit of walking around in long lines (hence the name). Touching the caterpillars' hairs sets off a severely irritating allergic skin reaction. It's even more harmful to animals, which get gangrene of the tongue if not treated straight away.

Mosquito and other insect bites can be a nuisance – in the Pyrenees, for instance – but none of the mosquitoes in Spain carry malaria. You can avoid bites by covering your skin and using an insect repellent.

Leishmaniasis Leishmaniasis is a group of parasitic diseases found in many parts of the Mediterranean. The strain found in Spain, mainly in country areas near the Mediterranean coasts, is a form of visceral leishmaniasis called leishmania infantum. Visceral leishmaniasis is characterised by irregular bouts of fever, substantial weight loss, anaemia and swelling of the spleen and liver. It can be fatal for children under five and people with immune system deficiencies, such as AIDS sufferers. It's transmitted when sandflies bite dogs carrying leishmaniasis and then bite humans. Avoiding sandfly bites is the best precaution: cover up and apply repellent. Sandflies are most active at dawn and dusk. The bites are usually painless but itchy. If you suspect leishmaniasis, seek medical advice as laboratory testing is required for diagnosis and treatment.

Snakes The only venomous snake that is even relatively common in Spain is the hog-nosed viper (vibora hocicuda). This is a smallish, triangular-headed creature, rarely more than 50cm long, which is coloured grey with a zigzag pattern along its back. It lives in dry, rocky areas, away from humans. Its bite can be fatal and needs to be treated as soon as possible with a serum kept by state clinics in major towns. Also to be avoided are the Montpellier snake (culebra bastarda), which is blue with a white underside and prominent ridges over the eyes, and Lataste's viper. These two live mainly in scrub and sandy areas but keep a low profile and are unlikely to be a threat unless trodden on. To minimise your chances of being bitten, always wear boots, socks and long trousers when walking through undergrowth where snakes may be present. Don't put your hands into holes and crevices and be careful when collecting firewood.

Snake bites do not cause instantaneous death and antivenenes are usually available. Immediately wrap the bitten limb tightly, as you would for a sprained ankle, and then attach a splint to immobilise it. Keep the victim still and seek medical help, if possible with the dead snake for identification.

Don't attempt to catch the snake if there is a possibility of being bitten again. Tourniquets and sucking out the poison are now comprehensively discredited methods of treating snakebite.

Jellyfish Heeding local advice is the best way of avoiding stinging and biting sea creatures. Jellyfish *(medusas)*, with their stinging tentacles, generally occur in large numbers or hardly at all. Dousing in vinegar will deactivate any jellyfish stingers that have not 'fired'. Calamine lotion, antihistamines and analgesics may reduce the reaction and relieve the pain.

Ticks Check for ticks all over your body if you have been walking through a potentially tick-infested area, as ticks can cause skin infections and other more serious diseases. If a tick is found attached, press down around its head with tweezers, grab the head and gently pull upwards. Avoid pulling the rear of the body as this may squeeze the tick's gut contents through the attached mouth parts into the skin, increasing the risk of infection and disease. Smearing chemicals on the tick will not make it let go and is not recommended.

Women's Health

Gynaecological Problems Sexually transmitted diseases are a major cause of vaginal problems. Symptoms include a smelly discharge, painful intercourse and sometimes a burning sensation when urinating. Male sexual partners must also be treated. Medical attention should be sought and remember that HIV or hepatitis B may also be acquired during exposure. Besides abstinence, the best thing is safe sex using condoms.

Antibiotic use, wearing synthetic underwear, sweating and taking the contraceptive pill can lead to fungal vaginal infections in hot climates. Good personal hygiene, loose-fitting clothes and cotton underwear will help to prevent them.

Fungal infections, characterised by a rash, itch and discharge, can be treated with a vinegar or lemon-juice douche or with yoghurt. Nystatin, miconazole or clotrimazole pessaries or vaginal cream are the usual treatment.

Pregnancy Most miscarriages happen during the first three months of pregnancy. Miscarriage is not uncommon and can occasionally lead to severe bleeding. The last three months should also be spent within reasonable distance of good medical care. A baby born as early as 24 weeks stands a chance of survival, but only in a good modern hospital. Pregnant women should avoid all unnecessary medication and vaccinations. Additional care should be taken to prevent illness and particular attention should be paid to diet and nutrition. Alcohol and nicotine, for example, should be avoided.

WOMEN TRAVELLERS

Women travellers should be ready to ignore stares, catcalls and unnecessary comments, though harassment is much less frequent than you might expect. Men under about 30, who have grown up in the post-Franco era, conform less to sexual stereotypes. They are less diverted by foreign women than their older counterparts (though you might notice that sexual stereotyping becomes more pronounced as you move from north to south and from city to country).

You still need to exercise common sense about where you go on your own. So think twice about going by yourself to isolated stretches of beach, lonely country areas or down empty city streets at night. Where there are crowds you are safer. It's highly inadvisable for a woman to hitchhike alone – and not a great idea even for two women together.

Topless bathing and skimpy clothes are in fashion in many coastal resorts, but people tend to dress more modestly elsewhere.

Spain's women's liberation movement, after the amazingly constrictive Franco era (when wives could not legally take a job or even go on a long journey without their husband's permission), took the form less of radical feminism than of sexual permissiveness. Women flooded into the workforce and higher education. Some of the causes – and leaders – of the 1970s women's movement were taken up by the PSOE (Partido Socialista Obrero Español, or Spanish Socialist Worker Party) governments of the 1980s and the movement fizzled out as a major independent force. Today it's stronger in the north than in the south. Many women who go out to work still run the household and take most of the responsibility for the children. One consequence is that they're having fewer children.

Organisations

The Comisión de Investigación de Malos Tratos a Mujeres (Commission of Investigation into Abuse of Women) has a free 24-hour national emergency line for victims of physical abuse: ☎ 900-10 00 09. The Asociación de Asistencia a Mujeres Violadas (Association for Assistance to Raped Women; ☎ 91 574 01 10), Calle O'Donnell 42, Madrid, offers advice and help to rape victims and can refer you to similar centres in other cities, though only limited English may be spoken. The phone line is open Monday to Friday from 10 am to 2 pm and from 4 to 7 pm; there's a recorded message in Spanish at other times.

There are women's bookshops in Madrid, Barcelona and a few other cities (see these chapters) that are also useful sources of information on women's organisations and activities. Many women's organisations are listed (though not usually in English) at www.secociti.org/Dona/Dona.htm on the Web. Recommended reading is the *Handbook for Women Travellers* by M & G Moss.

GAY & LESBIAN TRAVELLERS

Gay and lesbian sex are legal in Spain and the age of consent is 16 years, the same as for heterosexuals. In 1996 the conservative Partido Popular (PP) government put the brakes on a law intended to establish the legal rights of gay couples. By 1998 the law still had not passed, although some civil registrars were recording de facto gay/lesbian couples.

The gay male scene is more developed than the lesbian one, though the latter certainly exists. Lesbians and gay men generally take a fairly low profile, but can be more open in the cities. Madrid, Barcelona, Sitges, Torremolinos and Ibiza have particularly lively scenes. Sitges is a major destination on the international gay party circuit; gays take a leading role in the wild *carnaval* there in February/March. As well, there are gay parades, marches and events in several cities on and around the last Saturday in June, when Madrid's gay & lesbian pride march takes place.

You'll find gay and lesbian bars, discos, bookshops and information or social centres listed in some city sections of this book.

Guía Gay Visado is a guide to gay and lesbian bars, discos, contacts etc in Spain. You can find it, along with one or two similar publications, at some of the newsstands on La Rambla in Barcelona and in lesbian/gay bookshops. *Entiendes*, a gay magazine, is on sale at some newsstands for 500 ptas and has a quarterly English edition; see both at www.ctv.es/USERS/cogam/entint on the Internet (in Spanish). International gay and lesbian guides worth tracking down are the *Spartacus Guide for Gay Men* (the Spartacus list also includes the comprehensive *Spartacus National Edition España*, in English and German), published by Bruno Gmünder Verlag (Mail Order, PO Box 11 07 29, D-1000 Berlin 11); *Places for Women*, published by Ferrari Publications in Phoenix, Arizona, in the USA; and *Women Going Places*, published in London by Women Going Places.

Organisations

A good source of information on gay places and organisations throughout Spain is the Coordinadora Gai-Lesbiana (☎ 93 309 79 97, fax 93 309 78 40, Carrer de Buenaventura Muñoz 4, 08018 Barcelona, cogailes@pangea.org). In Madrid, the equivalent is Cogam (☎ /fax 91 532 45 17, Calle del Fuencarral 37, 2804 Madrid); see its site at www.ctv.es/USERS /cogam on the Web. Both can provide info on help groups, AIDS, places to go, bars and just about anything else you might want to know.

DISABLED TRAVELLERS

Some Spanish tourist offices in other countries can provide a basic information sheet with some useful addresses for disabled travellers and give details of accessible accommodation in specific places.

You'll find some accessible accommodation in main centres but it may not be in the budget category, though some 25 Spanish youth hostels are classed as suitable for wheelchair users. One Sevilla disabled association estimates that 80% of Spanish hotels that claim to be accessible actually retain problem features. All new public buildings are required to have wheelchair access, but most public buildings predate the law.

The Royal Association for Disability & Rehabilitation (RADAR; ☎ 0171-250 3222, from 22 April 2000 ☎ 020-7250 3222, 12 City Forum, 250 City Rd, London EC1V 8AF), based in the UK, publishes the useful *Holidays & Travel Abroad*, with a section on Spain covering contact addresses, transport, services and accommodation. Mobility International (☎ 02-410 6274, Rue de Manchester 25, Brussels 1070, Belgium, mobint@dproducts.be) has researched facilities for disabled tourists in Spain.

ECOM (☎ 93 451 55 50, fax 93 451 69 04), Gran Via de les Corts Catalanes 562, 08011 Barcelona, is Spain's federation of private organisations for the disabled; staff can send you listings of accessible hotels (mainly in Catalunya) and transport information.

Organisations

Cruz Roja Española, the Spanish Red Cross (☎ 91 522 22 22), Calle del Doctor Santero 18, 28039 Madrid, may be able to help with travel arrangements. INSERSO (☎ 91 347 88 88), Calle de Ginzo de Limea 58, 28029 Madrid, is the Spanish government department for the disabled, with branches in all 50 provinces. ONCE (☎ 91 597 47 27), Planta 28, Paseo de la Castellana 95, Madrid, is the Spanish association for the blind.

SENIOR TRAVELLERS

There are reduced prices for people over 60, 63 or 65 (depending on the place) at some museums and attractions and occasionally on transport (see the Getting There & Away and Getting Around chapters). Some of the luxurious *paradores* (see Accommodation later in this chapter) offer discounts for people over 60.

TRAVEL WITH CHILDREN

Spaniards as a rule are very friendly to children. Any child whose hair is less than jet black will get called *rubia* (blonde) if she's a girl or *rubio* if he's a boy. Accompanied children are welcome at all kinds of accommodation, and in virtually every café, bar and restaurant, where outside tables often allow kids a bit of space and freedom while their grown-ups sit and eat or drink. Spanish children stay up late and at fiestas it's common to see even tiny ones toddling the streets at 2 or 3 am. Visiting kids like this idea too – but can't cope with it quite so readily.

Most children don't like moving around too much but are happier if they can settle into places and make new friends. It's easier on the parents too if you don't have to pack up all their gear and move on every day or two. Children are also likely to need extra time to acclimatise and extra care to avoid sunburn. Be prepared for minor health effects brought on by change of diet or water or disrupted sleeping patterns.

Spanish street life and bustle, and the novelty of being in new places, provide some distraction for most kids but they'll get bored unless some of the time is devoted to their favoured activities. Apart from the obvious attractions of beaches, playgrounds are fairly plentiful and in many places you can find excellent special attractions such as amusement parks (such as Catalunya's Port Aventura and Sevilla's Isla Mágica), aquaparks, boat and train rides, child-friendly museums, zoos, aquariums – and let's not forget Mini Hollywood and other western movie sets in the Almería desert. Bring some of the children's own toys, books etc and let them have time to get on with some of the activities they are used to back at home.

Most children are fascinated by the ubiquitous street-corner *kioscos* selling sweets or *gusanitos* (corn puffs) for a few pesetas. The magnetism of these places often overcomes a child's inhibitions enough for them to carry out their own first Spanish transactions there.

Nappies, creams, lotions, baby foods etc are as easily available in Spain as in any other western country, but if there's some particular brand you swear by it's best to bring it with you. Calpol, for instance, isn't easily found.

Children benefit from cut-price or free entry at many sights and museums. Those under four travel free on Spanish trains and those aged four to 11 normally pay 60% of the adult fare.

Lonely Planet's *Travel with Children* has lots of practical advice and first-hand stories from many Lonely Planet authors and others.

USEFUL ORGANISATIONS

The Instituto Cervantes, with branches in over 30 cities around the world, exists to promote the Spanish language and the cultures of Spain and other Spanish-speaking countries. It's mainly involved in Spanish teaching and library and information services. The library at the London branch (☎ 0171-486 4350, from 22 April 2000 ☎ 020-7486 4350, 102 Eaton Square, London SW1 W9AN) has a wide range of reference books, literature, books on history and the arts, periodicals, over 1000 videos including feature films, language-teaching material, electronic databases and music CDs. In New York, the institute (☎ 212-689 4232) is at 122 East 42nd St, suite 807, New York, NY 10168.

TIVE, the Spanish youth and student travel organisation, is good for reduced-price youth and student travel tickets. It also issues various useful documents such as HI youth hostel cards and ISIC cards (see Visas & Documents earlier in this chapter). TIVE has branches in many cities and its head office is at Calle de José Ortega y Gasset 71, 28006 Madrid (☎ 91 347 77 00).

DANGERS & ANNOYANCES

Spain is generally a pretty safe country. The main thing you have to be wary of is petty theft (which may of course not seem so petty to you if your passport, cash, travellers cheques, credit card and camera all go missing). But with a few simple precautions you can minimise the risk and any worries.

For some specific hints about looking after your luggage and money and on safety for women, see the What to Bring, Money and Women Travellers sections, respectively, earlier in this chapter.

Before you leave home, inscribe your name, address and telephone number *inside* your luggage and take photocopies of the important pages of your passport, travel tickets and other important documents. Keep the copies separate from the originals and ideally leave one set of copies at home. These steps will make things easier if you do suffer a loss or theft.

Travel insurance against theft and loss is another good idea; see the Health section in this chapter.

Theft & Loss

Theft is most a risk in tourist resorts, big cities and when you first arrive in the country or at a new city and may be off your guard. Barcelona, Madrid and Sevilla have the worst reputations for theft and, occasionally, muggings.

The main things to guard against are pickpockets, bag snatchers and theft from cars. Carry valuables under your clothes if possible – not in a back pocket, a day pack or anything that could be snatched away easily – and keep your eyes open for people who get unnecessarily close to you on the streets and in public transport. Don't leave baggage unattended and avoid crushes.

Also be cautious with people who come up to offer or ask you something (like the time or directions) or start talking to you for no obviously good reason. These could be attempts to distract you and make you an easier victim.

Always remove the radio and cassette player from your car and never leave any belongings visible when you leave the car. Better still, don't leave anything in an unattended car (which is often harder than it sounds).

Anything left lying on the beach can disappear in a flash when your back is turned. Also avoid dingy, empty city alleys and backstreets, or anywhere that just doesn't feel 100% safe, at night.

You can also help yourself by not leaving anything valuable lying around your room, above all in any hostel-type place. Use a safe if one is available.

If anything valuable does go missing, you'll need to report it to the police and get a copy of the report if you want to make an insurance claim. Occasionally, this might even help you get it back. If your passport has gone, contact your embassy or consulate for help in issuing a replacement. Many countries have consulates in a few cities around Spain (such as Barcelona, Valencia, Alicante, Málaga and Sevilla) and your embassy can tell you where the nearest one is. Embassies and consulates can also give help of various kinds in other emergencies, but as a rule cannot advance you money to get home.

Other Emergencies

A new single emergency telephone number for ambulance, police or fire (☎ 112) will be used throughout Spain some time soon, but no-one knows when.

In the meantime, ☎ 061 is the number for an ambulance in many, but not all, places. Other medical emergency numbers and the locations of many hospitals and clinics are given in this book's city and town sections. See the Health section earlier in this chapter for more on Spanish medical facilities and health problems. If you're seriously ill or injured, someone should let your embassy or consulate know.

In many places the fire brigade *(bomberos)* is on ☎ 080 or ☎ 085, but in others it's on some completely different number.

Terrorism

Throughout the mid-1990s the Basque terrorist organisation ETA has maintained its campaign of terror, striking as far away from its home territory as Sevilla. In 1997 and 1998 the main victims were, above all, PP politicians. As a rule, foreigners are not targeted.

Annoyances

Spain is a mellow place and there ain't much to get annoyed about. That said, you should expect a few attempts to short-change you and you've got to be prepared for more noise than you're probably used to! While a certain amount of noise and crowds can make anybody feel more alive, it can be hard to understand why young Spanish males deliberately tinker with their motorbike exhausts to make the blessed things even noisier than they need to be. There's some sort of legislation about silencers but no-one dreams of enforcing it.

LEGAL MATTERS

If you're arrested you will be allotted the free services of a duty solicitor *(abogado de oficio)*, who may speak only Spanish. You're also entitled to make a phone call. If you use this to contact your embassy or consulate, the staff will probably be able to do no more than refer you to a lawyer who speaks your language. If you end up in court, the authorities are obliged to provide a translator.

Drugs

Spain's liberal drug laws were severely tightened in 1992. The only legal drug is cannabis and it's only legal in amounts for personal use, which means very small amounts.

Public consumption of any drug is apparently illegal, yet there are still some

La Policía – Who's Who

Spanish police are on the whole more of a help than a threat to the average law-abiding traveller. Most are certainly friendly enough to be approached for directions on the street. Highway police can be hard on locals but tend to steer clear of foreign vehicles unless they stop to give help (but see the Getting Around chapter for the list of documents and equipment you should carry in your vehicle). Unpleasant events such as random drug searches do occur, but not with great frequency.

There are three main types of *policía*: the Policía Nacional, the Policía Local (aka Policía Municipal) and the Guardia Civil (the words policía and *guardia* refer to the forces, but also stand for each individual member).

Guardia Civil Most numerous are the green-uniformed members of the Guardia Civil, 70,000 strong. Their main responsibilities are roads, the countryside, villages, prisons, international borders and some environmental protection. These are the guys who used to wear those alarming winged helmets, which were phased out in the 1980s but still resurface on some ceremonial occasions.

The Guardia Civil was set up in the 19th century to quell banditry but soon came to be regarded as a politically repressive force that clamped down on any challenge to established privilege. Although its image has softened since responsibility for it has been switched from the defence ministry to the interior ministry, it's still a military body in some ways: most officers have attended military academy and members qualify for military decorations.

Policía Nacional This force, 50,000 strong, covers cities and bigger towns and is the main crime-fighting body because most crime happens on its patch. Those who wear uniforms are in blue. There is also a large contingent in plain clothes, some of whom form special squads dealing with drugs, terrorism and the like. Most of them will be found in large bunker-like police stations called *comisarías*, shuffling masses of paper dealing with things like issuing passports, DNIs (*documentos nacionales de identidad*, or national identity cards) and residence cards for foreigners who like Spain enough to opt for long-term entanglement with its bureaucracy.

Policía Local The 35,000 members of the Policía Local are controlled by city and town councils and deal mainly with minor matters such as parking, traffic and bylaws. They wear blue-and-white uniforms. In Catalunya the equivalent force is called the Guàrdia Urbana. Spain has no real equivalent of 'bobby on the beat' street-patrol police.

Regional Police Finally, four of Spain's 17 autonomous communities have their own police forces in addition to the above three: Catalunya (where it's called the Mossos d'Esquadra), the País Vasco (the Ertzaintza), Valencia and Galicia.

Contacting the Police If you need to go to the police, any of them will do, but you may find the Policía Local are the most helpful.

Anywhere in Spain you can call ☎ 091 for the Policía Nacional or ☎ 092 for the Policía Local. Guardia Civil numbers vary from place to place. Some further police numbers and locations of main stations are given in the city and town sections of this book.

bars where people smoke joints openly. Other bars will ask you to step outside if you light up. The only sure moral of these stories is to be very discreet if you do use cannabis. There is a reasonable degree of tolerance when it comes to people having a smoke in their own home, but it would be unwise in hotel rooms or guesthouses and could be risky in even the coolest of public places.

Travellers entering Spain from Morocco should be prepared for intensive drug searches, especially if they have a vehicle.

BUSINESS HOURS

Generally, Spaniards work Monday to Friday from about 9 am to 2 pm and then again from 4.30 or 5 pm for another three hours. Shops and travel agencies are usually open these hours on Saturday too, though some may skip the evening session. Big supermarkets, and department stores, such as the nationwide El Corte Inglés chain, often stay open Monday to Saturday from about 9 am to 9 pm. A few shops in tourist resorts open on Sunday in the summer. A lot of government offices don't bother opening in the afternoon any day of the year.

Museums all have their own opening hours: major ones tend to open for something like normal Spanish business hours (with or without the afternoon break), but often have their weekly closing day on Monday, not Sunday.

See Money and Post & Communications earlier in this chapter for bank and post office hours, respectively.

PUBLIC HOLIDAYS & SPECIAL EVENTS
Public Holidays

There are at least 14 official holidays a year – some observed nationwide, some local.

When a holiday falls close to a weekend, Spaniards like to make a *puente* (bridge), meaning they take the intervening day off too. On the odd occasion when some holidays fall close, they make an *acueducto* (aqueduct)!

National holidays are:

Año Nuevo (New Year's Day)
  1 January
Viernes Santo (Good Friday)
  March/April
Fiesta del Trabajo (Labour Day)
  1 May
La Asunción (Feast of the Assumption)
  15 August
Fiesta Nacional de España (National Day)
  12 October
La Inmaculada Concepción (Feast of the Immaculate Conception)
  8 December
Navidad (Christmas)
  25 December

Regional governments set five holidays and local councils two more. Common dates include:

6 January
  Epifanía (Epiphany) or *Día de los Reyes Magos* (Three Kings' Day), when children receive presents; observed everywhere

19 March
  Día de San José (St Joseph's Day)

March/April
  Jueves Santo (Maundy Thursday, the day before Good Friday); observed everywhere except Catalunya and Valencia

June
  Corpus Christi (the Thursday after the eighth Sunday after Easter Sunday); observed widely

24 June
  Día de San Juan Bautista (Feast of St John the Baptist), King Juan Carlos' saint's day; observed widely

25 July
  Día de Santiago Apóstol (Feast of St James the Apostle), Spain's patron saint's day; observed widely

6 December
  Día de la Constitución (Constitution Day)

Holiday Times

The two main periods when Spaniards go on holiday are Semana Santa (the week leading up to Easter Sunday) and during August. At these times accommodation in resorts can be scarce and transport heavily booked, but other cities are often half-empty.

Festivals

Spaniards indulge in their love of colour, noise, crowds, dressing up and partying at innumerable local fiestas and *ferias* (fairs): even small villages will have at least one, probably several, in the year, all with their own unique twists. Many fiestas are religion-based but are celebrated with a party spirit. Main local festivals are noted in city and town sections of this book and tourist offices can supply more detailed info. A few of the most outstanding include:

January
Festividad de San Sebastián
Everyone in San Sebastián dresses up and goes berserk (20 January).

February/March
Carnaval
Several days of fancy-dress parades and merrymaking in many places, usually ending on the Tuesday 47 days before Easter Sunday (wildest in Cádiz and Sitges, also good in Ciudad Rodrigo).

March
Las Fallas
Several days of all-night dancing and drinking, first-class fireworks and processions; in Valencia, but also celebrated in Gandía and Benidorm (15-19 March).

March/April
Semana Santa (Holy Week)
Parades of holy images and huge crowds, notably in Sevilla, but also big in Málaga, Córdoba, Toledo, Ávila, Valladolid and Zamora (the week leading up to Easter Sunday).

April
Moros y Cristianos
Colourful parades and 'battles' between Christian and Muslim 'armies' in Alcoy, near Alicante, make this one of the best of several similar events in Valencia and Alicante provinces through the year (22-24 April).

Feria de Abril
A week-long party in Sevilla after the religious fervour of Semana Santa (late April).

Romería de la Virgen de la Cabeza
Hundreds of thousands of people make a mass pilgrimage to the Santuario de la Virgen de la Cabeza near Andújar, Jaén province (last Sunday in April).

May
Feria del Caballo (Horse Fair)
Colourful equestrian and other festivities in Andalucía's horse capital, Jerez de la Frontera (early May).

Concurso de Patios Cordobeses
Scores of beautiful private courtyards are open to the public for two weeks in Córdoba (early/mid-May).

Fiestas de San Isidro
Madrid's major fiesta, with bullfights, parades, concerts and more (third week of May).

May/June
Romería del Rocío
Festive pilgrimage by up to one million people to the shrine of the Virgin at the Andalucian village of El Rocío (focused on Pentecost weekend, the seventh after Easter).

Corpus Christi
Religious processions and celebrations in Toledo and other cities (on or shortly before the ninth Sunday after Easter Sunday).

June
Hogueras de San Juan
Midsummer bonfires and fireworks, notably along the south-eastern and southern coasts (around 24 June).

July
Sanfermines
Festival with the famous Running of the Bulls in Pamplona, an activity also pursued in dozens of other cities and towns through the summer (6-14 July).

Día de la Virgen del Carmen
On or near this day of the patron of fisherfolk, her image is carried into the sea or paraded on it amid a flotilla of small boats at most coastal towns (16 July).

Día de Santiago (Feast of St James)
The national saint's day, spectacularly celebrated in Santiago de Compostela, site of his tomb (25 July).

August
Semana Grande or Aste Nagusia
A week of general celebration, heavy drinking and hangovers on the north coast (dates vary from place to place).

La Tomatina
Wild tomato-throwing festival in Buñol, Valencia (last Wednesday in August).

September
Festes de la Mercè
A week-long party in Barcelona (around 24 September).

Arts Festivals Spain's calendar also abounds in arts festivals (any excuse for a party!). These festivals will enliven visits to their host cities: Mérida's Festival de Teatro of drama and dance from late June to August; Barcelona's concurrent Grec festival of music, dance and theatre; Córdoba's two-week Festival Internacional de Guitarra starting in late June; San Sebastián's International Jazz Festival in July; Santander's mainly musical Festival Internacional in July and August; Sevilla's Bienal de Flamenco in the September of even-numbered years; and the November Festival Internacional de Jazz de Barcelona, which also includes blues.

Rock, Pop & Dance Festivals Music festivals are growing in number and popularity with the young crowd. Summer is busy with festivals. In July 1997 more than 90 acts (ranging from dinosaurs of rock like Alice Cooper to heavy metal's Megadeth to the more mellow Sheryl Crow) turned up for the Doctor Music Festival (also affectionately known, perhaps for the setting, as *las vacas*), the country's biggest musical event near Esterri d'Aneu in the Catalan Pyrenees.

Madrid's big one is Festimad, an early-May orgy of varied music in bars, halls and open-air stages.

The Benicasim festival north of Valencia is a long-weekend indie get-together in early August.

There are many other smaller-scale festivals in summer, some just one night long. You'll see plenty of posters telling you about them. Outside the s…… Granada holds the weekend-long …… Rock festival in late March or early …… highlighting Spanish and foreign alternati…… rock. Just down the road in Málaga, the annual World Dance festival sees the port area turned into a massive dance venue for one Saturday night in May, with more than 100,000 people enjoying live international dance music.

The biggest numbers get together for modern dance gatherings with DJs *(pinchadiscos)* and bands pumping out techno, house, eurobeat, euroenergy and their relatives for a night or two. Barcelona's June Festival Sonar is the main annual event of this kind.

For any of these festivals expect to pay a minimum of 10,000 ptas to get in.

ACTIVITIES
Spanish tourist offices can provide quite detailed information on possibilities for many activities from hiking, skiing, mountaineering or windsurfing to horse riding, birdwatching, golf or wine tours. If you fancy going in a guided group, see the Organised Tours section of the Getting There & Away chapter for a few pointers. Spanish tourist offices can also usually tell you about tour companies running a vast range of activity holidays.

Cycling
Mountain biking is popular among both Spaniards and foreigners. There are kilometre upon kilometre of good and bad tracks and roads for biking in many areas, including Andalucía and Catalunya. Tourist offices often have info on routes. A good general source for mountain bikers who can read Spanish is *100 Rutas en Bicicleta de Montaña* by Juanjo Pedales (Espasa Calpe, 1995). Some tourist offices in Andalucía sell an English-language booklet, *120 Itineraries around Andalusía on a Mountain bike*, for 400 ptas. The Spanish for mountain bike is *bici todo terreno* (BTT).

See the Getting Around chapter for info on cycle touring in Spain.

...to rent is a hit-
...oth availability
...ary enormously.
...ovided with rental
...n bikes and touring
...ou should bring your
...t on the idea.

Skiing

Spain is not the first country that leaps to
mind when talk turns to Europe's ski
centres, but its profile was significantly
lifted by the world skiing championships in
the Sierra Nevada near Granada in 1996.
Andorra is much better known and has
several good, well-established resorts.

The skiing facilities and conditions in
Spain are surprisingly good and the costs
are low, although in general the snow is not
quite up to the standards of the Alps or even
the French side of the Pyrenees. The season
normally runs from December to April,
with the best snow in February, but snow
cover can be unpredictable, even in the
higher altitude resorts.

Spain's main ski resorts are in the Pyrenees and include: La Molina and
Baquiera-Beret in Catalunya; Candanchú,
Formigal and Cerler in Aragón; and five
resorts in Andorra. The other major resort is
in the Sierra Nevada, outside Granada in the
south. Minor ski fields (with unreliable
snowfall) cater to locals in the Sierra de
Guadarrama north of Madrid, the Cordillera
Cantábrica and even La Rioja and southern
Aragón.

Ski package holidays from other countries are a novelty to Spain (but not to
Andorra). Travel agencies in Spanish cities
offer affordable packages for one day or
longer. If you prefer to organise it yourself
on the spot, a day's ski pass (forfait) at the
better resorts in Spain and Andorra costs up
to 3900 ptas a day (depending on resort and
season) or up to 17,000 ptas for five days;
equipment rental is usually around 1500 to
2000 ptas a day. Ski school costs anything
up to 3725 ptas an hour for individual
tuition or around 12,000 ptas for 15 hours of
group lessons.

You can find a range of accommodation,
from mid-priced hostales up, in or near
most resorts.

The high season – when the slopes are
most crowded and prices for lift passes, ski
school and accommodation are at their
highest – generally means the Christmas-
New Year holiday period, February,
Semana Santa and weekends almost all
season long. At these times, the slopes are
emptiest from 9 to 11 am and from 1 to 3
pm while the Spanish skiers take breakfast
and lunch.

Spanish and Andorran pistes are all
graded green (verde) for beginners, blue
(azul) for easy, red (rojo) for intermediate
and black (negro) for difficult, although
there's some variation in criteria between
resorts.

Good resorts for cross-country skiing
include Baqueira-Beret (Catalunya), Candanchú (Aragón) and several in Andorra.
Snowboarding is growing fast in popularity
at many ski resorts.

Spanish tourist offices in other countries
and tourist offices in Spanish and Andorran cities and towns near the ski resorts
usually have fairly detailed information on
skiing.

Hiking & Trekking

With its large tracts of wilderness, Spain
offers limitless opportunities for short and
long walks. Some wonderful areas are
easily accessible and can be enjoyed on day
or half-day walks, as well as by committed
trekkers.

Trekking Trekking is popular among
Spaniards as well as foreigners. Outstanding mountain areas are the Pyrenees in
Aragón and Catalunya, the Picos de Europa
straddling Cantabria, Asturias and León
provinces, the Sierra de Gredos west of
Madrid, the Sierra Nevada and Alpujarras
valleys in Andalucía and the Serra de Tramuntana on Mallorca.

GRs, PRs & Other Paths Spain, particularly the north, has an extensive network of

long-distance footpaths, the s... *Gran Recorrido* (GRs). Where... these cross-country routes, so... hundred kilometres long, avoi... tracks used by vehicles. Not a... are marked or maintained fo... length – or even for much of th... some cases.

Among the longest of the GF...

- the well-marked, well-establish... tacular GR-11 or Senda Pirenáic... the length of the Spanish Pyren... de Creus on the coast of Catalun... ribia (Fuenterrabía) on the Bay o... País Vasco
- the GR-10 from Puçol on the coa... to La Alberca, just 70km from th... border (though the stretch a... province doesn't yet exist)
- the GR-7 from Andorra all the... Murcia and Andalucía, which f... route forms part of the so-called E4 Mediterranean Arc, a footpath from Greece to Algeciras via Bulgaria, Romania, Hungary, Austria, Germany, Switzerland and France; it's nearly all open, except for sections in Bulgaria, Romania and Andalucía

Spain's most famous long walk is the Camino de Santiago (part of which forms the GR-65). This ancient pilgrim route, in use since the 11th century, can be started at various places in France. It then crosses the Pyrenees at Roncesvalles and runs across Navarra, La Rioja, Castilla y León and Galicia to the cathedral in Santiago de Compostela, shrine of Spain's patron saint Santiago (St James). See the Camino de Santiago special section.

Of course most people don't walk the full length of these long-distance paths. Most are quite easily accessible by road (and often public transport) at many points and it's perfectly feasible to join them for just a few hours amble if you're not committed to more serious walking.

Spain also has many *senderos de Pequeño Recorrido* (PRs), shorter footpaths suitable for day or weekend hikes. Like GRs, these vary widely in quality of trails and markings. There's also lots of good paths that haven't become either GRs or PRs.

and September through mid-October are the most pleasant, but the high Sierra Nevada is only really accessible from mid-July to September; in the Picos de Europa May, June and September are good. The weather in high mountains is never predictable at any time, however.

Sources of Information Tourist offices can often help with trekking information. There are many Spanish mountain walking and climbing clubs that can give information on routes, refuges and equipment shops, including the Federación Española de Montañismo (☎ 91 445 13 82) in Madrid. Others are mentioned in regional chapters.

Hiking guides to parts of Spain are available in English, French and other languages, as well as in Spanish. Lonely Planet's *Walking in Spain* covers routes in all the main trekking areas and has plenty of advice on equipment, preparation, seasons, accommodation etc.

A good companion on the Camino de Santiago is *The Way of St James – The Pilgrimage Route to Santiago de Compostela* by Dr Elias Valiña Sampedra, a book of detailed colour maps. Mountain guides worth tracking down include *Walks & Climbs in*

the Pyrenees by Kev Reynolds, and *Walks & Climbs – Picos de Europa* by Robin Walker. In Spanish, the Colección El B... Viajero series of hiking and walking... published by Libros Penthalon cove... regions of Spain in detail. Detail... walking guides are gene... *topoguías*. It's best to get... head off; try specialist... own country or book... Quera in Barcelona... Madrid.

For inform... the Plannin... Referen... specifi... of...

Ribadesella on the coast, on the first weekend in August.

Diving & Snorkelling

Some of the rockier parts of the Mediterranean coast – notably the Illes Medes off L'Estartit, Catalunya, but also San Sebastián, Cadaqués, Isla de Tabarca, Cabo de Gata and Almuñecar – are good. Snorkelling and diving trips and diving gear rental are available at all these places.

COURSES

A spot of study in Spain is a great way not only to learn something but also to meet people – Spaniards as well as other travellers – and get more of an inside angle on local life than the average visitor.

Language

Branches of the Instituto Cervantes (see Useful Organisations earlier in this chapter) can send you long lists of places offering Spanish-language courses in Spain. Some Spanish embassies and consulates also have information on courses. In Spain you can contact the Servicio Central de Cursos de Español (☎ 91 593 19 49, fax 91 445 69 60, Calle de Trafalgar 32, 1º D, 28010 Madrid).

Universities, which exist in most sizable cities, offer some of the best-value language courses: those at Salamanca, Santiago de Compostela and Santander have good reputations. Sevilla, Granada, Madrid and Barcelona are also popular places to study Spanish. Private language schools as well as universities cater for a wide range of levels (from beginners up), course lengths, times of year, intensity and special requirements. Many courses have a cultural component as well as pure language. University courses often last a term, although some are as short as two weeks or as long as a year. Private colleges can be more flexible. One with a good reputation is ¿Don Quijote?, with branches in Salamanca, Barcelona and Granada. There's further information on some courses in the city sections of this book.

---

ution on maps for hikers, see

g section earlier in this chapter.

es to some appropriate maps for

c areas are made in regional chapters

his guide.

Surfing

The País Vasco has some good waves at San Sebastián, Zarautz, which stages a round of the world championship each September, and Mundaka, with its legendary left, among others. Santander in Cantabria also attracts surfers in force and there are other good spots in Cantabria and Asturias. You'll find boards (and wet suits) available in most surf spots if you're not carrying your own.

Windsurfing

Tarifa, Spain's southernmost point, is a windsurfer's heaven, with strong breezes all year, a big windsurfing scene and long, uncrowded beaches. In Galicia, Praia de Lariño on the Ría de Muros and La Lanzada beach on the Ría de Pontevedra can be good.

Rafting, Canoeing & Hydrospeed

The turbulent Noguera Pallaresa in northwestern Catalunya is Spain's top whitewater river, with a string of grade III and IV drops. Rafting, canoeing and hydrospeed (water-tobogganing) are at their best here in May and June. Numerous local companies offer outings. The Río Sella in Asturias also has some good white water and more than 1000 canoeists from around the world take part in the 22km Descenso del Sella race, from Arriondas in the Picos de Europa to

Costs vary widely. A typical four-week course at a university, with 20 one-hour classes a week, will be around 40,000 or 50,000 ptas. Many places offer accommodation with families, in student lodgings or in flats if you want it. Accommodation offers generally range from around 30,000 ptas a month with no meals to about 60,000 ptas for full board.

Other things to think about when you're weighing up your choice of course include its intensity (*intensivo* means different things at different schools), class sizes, who the other students are likely to be and whether you want organised extracurricular social activities. It's also worth asking whether your course will lead to any formal certificate of competence. The Diploma de Español como Lengua Extranjera (DELE) is recognised by Spain's Ministry of Education and Science.

It's also easy to arrange private classes in many places: check notice boards in universities, language schools and foreign cultural institutes, or small ads in the local press. Expect to pay around 2000 ptas per hour for individual private lessons.

Other Courses

You can take courses in lots of other subjects too. Some places offering language courses also offer courses in other aspects of Spanish culture. The Instituto Cervantes and Spanish tourist offices are good places to start asking about possibilities.

See the Sevilla, Granada, Las Alpujarras and Jerez de la Frontera sections for information on some courses in Spanish dance or guitar.

A number of foreigners living in Spain have set up residential centres where you can combine your learning experience with comfortable surroundings, company and, often, extras like excursions. These include:

Can Xanet School of Painting
    workshops and courses, some led by guest tutors, in country homes in Pollensa, Mallorca; contact Sheila Peczenik (☎ 0171-937 0727, from 22 April 2000 ☎ 020-7937 0727, 8 Pitt St, Kensington, London W8 4NX, UK)

Castillo San Rafael
    (☎ /fax 958 64 02 47, 18697 La Herradura, Granada) two-week painting or ceramics courses near the coast for around 160,000 ptas
Cortijo Romero
    (☎ 958 78 42 52) personal development and alternative living centre in the Alpujarras area south of Granada, with vegetarian food and week-long programs ranging from dance to yoga, walking to clowning (typical price around 60,000 ptas); contact Janice Gray (☎ 01494-782720, Little Grove, Grove Lane, Chesham, Bucks HP5 3QQ, UK)
Learning for Pleasure
    (☎ 956 64 01 02, fax 956 64 09 34, apartado 25, 11330 Jimena de la Frontera, Cádiz) courses include painting, wildlife, Spanish cooking (led by well-known cooks) and herbal medicine at a restored farmhouse
Los Pinos Centro de Fotografía
    (☎ 95 203 02 90, Molino Becerril, 29710 Periana, Málaga) one-week workshop-holiday led by well-known British photographers, emphasising architecture, festivals, landscape and nature (around 90,000 ptas)
The Spirit of Andalucía
    (☎/fax 95 215 13 03, apartado 20, 29480 Gaucín, Málaga) cooking courses with 'name' cooks, painting and interior decorating courses

WORK

With the EU's highest unemployment rate, Spain doesn't exactly have a labour shortage. Unlike in France, there's no casual work for foreigners in fruit picking or harvests. But there are a few ways of earning your keep (or almost) while you're here.

Nationals of EU countries, Norway and Iceland may work in Spain without a visa, but for stays of more than three months they are supposed to apply within the first month for a tarjeta de residencia (residence card); for information on this laborious process, see Visas & Documents earlier in this chapter. Virtually everyone else is supposed to get, from a Spanish consulate in their country of residence, a work permit and, if they plan to stay more than 90 days, a residence visa. These procedures are well-nigh impossible unless you have a job contract lined up before you begin them; in any case you should start the processes a long time before you aim to go to Spain. That said, quite a few people do work, discreetly, without bothering to tangle with the bureaucracy.

Language Teaching

This is an obvious option, for which language-teaching qualifications are a big help. There are lots of language schools in all the big cities, and often one or two in smaller towns. They're listed under 'Academias de Idiomas' in the Páginas Amarillas (Yellow Pages). Getting a job in one is harder if you're not an EU citizen. Some schools do employ people without work papers, usually at lower than normal rates. Giving private lessons is another worthwhile avenue, but is unlikely to bring you a living wage straight away.

Sources of information on possible teaching work – school or private – include foreign cultural centres (the British Council, Alliance Française etc), foreign-language bookshops, universities and language schools. Many have notice boards where you may find work opportunities or can advertise your own services.

Tourist Resorts

Summer work on the Mediterranean costas is another possibility, especially if you get in there early in the season and are prepared to stay awhile. Many bars, restaurants and other businesses are run by foreigners. Check any local press in foreign languages, such as the Costa del Sol's *Sur In English*, which carries some ads for waiters, nannies, chefs, baby-sitters and cleaners, as well as 'closers', 'liners' and others wanted to hawk time-share properties to foreign holiday-makers.

Busking

A few travellers earn a crust (but not much more) busking in the main tourist cities.

Yacht Crewing

It is possible to stumble upon work as crew on yachts and cruisers. The best ports to look are, in descending order: Palma de Mallorca, Gibraltar and Puerto Banús.

In summer the voyages tend to be restricted to the Mediterranean, but from about November to January quite a few boats head for the Caribbean. Such work is usually unpaid.

ACCOMMODATION

Virtually all accommodation prices are subject to IVA, the Spanish version of value-added tax, at a rate of 7%. This is often included in the quoted price at cheaper places, but less often at more expensive ones. To check, ask: '*¿Está incluido el IVA?*' ('Is IVA included?').

Room prices given in this book include IVA unless stated otherwise.

Camping

Spain has something like 1000 officially graded camp sites *(campings)*. Some are well located in woodland or near beaches or rivers, but others are stuck away on the unattractive edges of towns and cities. Very few are near city centres, and camping isn't particularly convenient if you're relying on public transport.

Sites are officially rated as 1st class (1ª C), 2nd class (2ª C) or 3rd class (3ª C). There are also a few nonofficially graded sites, usually equivalent to 3rd class. The facilities generally range from reasonable to very good, though any site can be crowded and noisy at busy times. Even a 3rd-class site is likely to have hot showers, electrical hook-ups and a cafeteria. The best sites have heated swimming pools, supermarkets, restaurants, travel agencies, a laundry service, children's playgrounds and tennis courts. Sizes range from a capacity of under 100 people to over 5000.

Camp sites usually charge per person, per tent and per vehicle – anywhere between 250 and 800 ptas for each, though 500 ptas is typical. Children usually pay a bit less than adults. Many sites are open all year, though quite a few close from around October to Easter. Some are crowded in July and August.

The annual *Guía Oficial de Campings*, available in bookshops for about 800 ptas, lists most of the country's sites and their facilities and prices. Tourist offices can always direct you to the nearest camp site.

You sometimes come across a *zona de acampada* or *área de acampada*, a country site often used by local campers but with no facilities, no supervision and no charge.

With certain exceptions – such as many beaches and environmentally protected areas and a few municipalities which ban it – it is legal to camp outside camp sites (though not within 1km of official ones!). Signs usually indicate where wild camping is not allowed. If in doubt you can always check with tourist offices. You'll need permission to camp on private land.

Note that Camping Gaz is the only common brand of camping gas; screw-on canisters are near-impossible to find.

Hostels

Spain's 180 or so youth hostels (*albergues juveniles*, not be confused with *hostales*, budget hotels) are often the cheapest places for lone travellers, but two people can usually get a double room elsewhere for a similar price. Many hostels are only moderate value, with night-time curfews, daytime closing hours and no cooking facilities (though if there is nowhere to cook there is usually a cafeteria). They can, too, be rather spartan, lacking in privacy and often heavily booked by school groups. Others, however, are conveniently located, relaxed about curfews, composed mainly of double rooms or small dorms, or even sited in fine historic buildings. Hostels can be good places for meeting people.

Most youth hostels are members of the Red Española de Albergues Juveniles (REAJ, or Spanish Youth Hostel Network), the Spanish affiliate of Hostelling International, which used to be called the International Youth Hostel Federation. REAJ's head office (☎ 91 347 77 00, fax 91 401 81 60) is at Calle de José Ortega y Gasset 71, 28006 Madrid.

Most hostels, however, are actually managed by regional governments. Each region usually sets its own price structure.

Some have central booking services where you can make reservations for most hostels in the region. These include Andalucía (☎ 95 455 82 93, fax 95 455 82 92), Catalunya (☎ 93 483 83 63, fax 93 483 83 50) and Valencia (☎ 96 386 92 52, fax 96 386 99 51).

HI's annual Europe hostels directory contains details of all REAJ hostels; the REAJ also publishes an annual list. Some of the autonomous regions publish their own hostel guides, too.

Just a few hostels are run by other organisations or as private concerns, in which case they probably won't appear in regional guides – although they may still be REAJ members and appear in REAJ and HI directories!

Prices often depend on the season or whether or not you're under 26: typically you pay 900 to 1500 ptas a night. In some hostels the price includes breakfast. If there's an age distinction, 26 and overs will usually pay 300 or 400 ptas more. Many hostels require you to rent sheets (around 300 ptas for your stay) if you don't have your own or a sleeping bag.

Some hostels require an HI card or membership card from your home country's youth hostel association; others don't (even though they may be HI hostels) but may charge more if you don't have one. You can buy HI cards for 1800 ptas at many hostels, at REAJ or regional youth hostel offices, or at branches of the youth travel agency TIVE (see Useful Organisations earlier in this chapter). If you like, you can pay your 1800 ptas in 300 ptas nightly instalments. All you need to show is your passport. HI cards are valid until 31 December in the year of purchase.

Only five hostels throughout the country are in HI's International Booking Network (IBN), which enables you to book through about 200 other HI hostels and booking centres around the world.

Hostales, Hospedajes, Pensiones, Hotels & Paradores

Officially, *hoteles* are places with from one to five stars, *hostales* have one to three stars

Seasonal Variations

Prices at any type of accommodation may vary with the season. Many places have separate price structures for the high season *(temporada alta)*, mid-season *(temporada media)* or low season *(temporada baja)*, all usually displayed on a notice in the reception or close by. (Although these notices look official and the prices on them have been registered, hoteliers are not bound by them. They are free to charge less, which they quite often do, or more, which happens fairly rarely.)

What the high season is depends on where you are, but in most places it's summer – which can mean a period as short as mid-July to the end of August or as long as Easter to October. The Christmas-New Year period and Semana Santa are also high, or at least mid, season in some places. Local festivals that attract lots of visitors often count as high season too.

Differences between low-season and high-season prices vary widely around the country. They tend to be biggest – typically 30% or 50% – in coastal resorts and other places that attract a lot of tourism in summer. But even in these places you may still find some accommodation that keeps virtually the same prices year round. Occasionally there are bigger differences. Some hotels and hostales in Sevilla, for instance, charge three times as much during the city's Semana Santa and the Feria de Abril festivities as they do in the preceding winter months. On the coast some hotels seem to create a kind of 'super' high season within high season, usually lasting from mid-July to mid-August. This can express itself in still higher prices than the average high-season ones or obligatory half or full board arrangements.

Major seasonal price variations are noted in Places to Stay sections through this book.

Another problem that often comes with the high season is the shortage of single rooms. Indeed, many hotels and *pensiones* actually have few single rooms, but would rather let out doubles at reduced rates. In the low season that is no problem but, when things get tight, singles or reduced-rate doubles can become as rare as hen's teeth.

In the low season there's generally no need to book ahead, but when things get busier it's advisable and at peak periods it can be essential if you want to avoid a wearisome search for a room. At most places a phone call is all that's needed, giving your approximate time of arrival. Many hotels will help you book ahead to a hotel in your next destination.

and *pensiones* have one or two stars. These are the categories used by the annual *Guía Oficial de Hoteles* (1000 ptas), which lists many of these places in Spain (but not one-star places), with approximate prices.

In practice, places to stay use all sorts of overlapping categories to describe themselves, especially at the budget end of the market. In broad terms, the cheapest are usually places just advertising *camas* (beds), *fondas* (traditionally a basic eatery and inn combined, though one of these functions is now often missing), and *casas de huéspedes* or *hospedajes* (guesthouses).

A pensión (basically a small private hotel) is usually a small step up, but you're

likely to share bathrooms in any of these and pay 1000/2000 to 1500/3000 ptas for a single/double room. They'll be bare and basic, and your room may be small and even lack a window and towel, but most of them are pretty clean. Most discomfort is likely to come from lumpy beds, failure of hot water supplies, or insufficient bedding to keep you warm in winter (ask for more).

Next up the scale are hostales, which are little different from pensiones, except that some are considerably more comfortable and more rooms tend to have their own bathrooms. Hostales may have more lounge space too. Hostal prices range from pensión levels up to 6000 ptas or so for a double in the better ones. Some hostales are bright, modern and pleasant places to stay; others are less so. A *hostal-residencia* is a hostal without any kind of restaurant – but since this is the case at a lot of 'hostales' too, the extra label seems a bit pointless.

Establishments calling themselves hotels range from simple places, where a double room could cost 4000 ptas or less, up to wildly luxurious, five-star places where you could pay 60,000 ptas or more. Even in the cheapest ones rooms are likely to have an attached bathroom and there'll probably be a restaurant.

In a special category are the *paradores*, officially *paradores de turismo*, a state-run chain of 80-odd high-class hotels around the country. Many are in converted castles, palaces, mansions, monasteries or convents. These can be wonderful places to stay if you have 14,000 ptas or more (sometimes a lot more) for a double room. Occasional special offers, such as discounts of 35% for people aged 60 or more, may make paradores more affordable. You can book a room at any parador through their Central de Reservas (Reservation Centre; ☎ 91 516 66 66, fax 91 516 66 57), Calle de Requena 3, 28013 Madrid. The Amigos de Paradores plan allows you to collect loyalty points for staying in or eating at paradores. Each 500 ptas spent gets a point and a night in a three-star parador is worth 250 points; 600 points gets you a night in Granada's parador. For information call ☎ 91 374 26 00. Another possibility is the Libreta 5 Noches, a discounted book giving you five nights in paradores of your choice (subject to some limitations).

Many places listed under this heading have a range of rooms at different prices. At the bottom end prices will vary according to whether the room has a washbasin *(lavabo)*, shower *(ducha)* or full bathroom *(baño completo)*, which includes toilet, bath and/or shower and basin. At the top end you may pay more for a room on the outside *(exterior)* of the building or with a balcony *(balcón)* and will often have the option of a suite.

Casas Rurales

Spaniards' burgeoning interest in their own countryside and environment has brought a boom in recent years in rural tourism, with many small new places to stay there. These *casas rurales* are usually comfortably renovated country houses or farmhouses, with just a handful of rooms. Some have meals available, while at some you'll have to self-cater. A double room costs from 3000 to 8000 ptas or so. Tourist offices can usually provide leaflets listing casas rurales and other country accommodation in their areas.

Refugios

Refugios are mountain shelters for hikers and climbers and are quite liberally scattered around most of the popular mountain areas. They're mostly run by mountaineering and hiking organisations. Accommodation – normally bunks squeezed into a dormitory – is usually on a first come, first served basis. In busy seasons (July and August in most areas) they can fill up quickly and you should try to book or arrive by mid-afternoon to be sure of a place. Prices per person range from nothing to 1100 ptas or so a night. Most have a bar and meals available and in many you can cook for yourself. Blankets are usually provided but you'll have to bring any further bedding yourself.

Apartments

In many places there are self-catering apartments and even larger places such as houses and villas to rent. A simple one-bedroom apartment for two or three people might cost as little as 1500 ptas a night, or a two-bedroom place for up to six people could be as little as 3000 ptas. But more often you're looking at twice that much and prices can jump in peak seasons. Apartments are most worth considering if you plan to stay several days or more, in which case there will usually be discounts from the daily rate. Tourist offices can supply lists of apartments, villas and houses for rent.

Monasteries

A rather offbeat possibility is staying in a monastery. In spite of the expropriations of the 19th century and a sometimes rough run in the 20th, plenty of orders have survived across the country. Vocations are generally not what they once were, however, and many monasteries now offer rooms to outsiders – often fairly austere monks' or nuns' cells. Generally they are single sex arrangements and the idea in some is to seek a refuge from the outside world and indulge in a little quiet contemplation. A few of these places have been listed in this guide.

ENTERTAINMENT

Simply sitting over a coffee or a glass of wine in a plaza café and watching Spanish life go on around you is often entertainment enough in itself. The innumerable fiestas that spatter the Spanish calendar provide heaps of colourful spectacle and, more often than not, a celebratory atmosphere.

Local papers often carry fairly thorough entertainment listings and Madrid, Barcelona and one or two other cities have their own what's-on magazines (see the relevant chapters for details). Some national papers such as *El País* have regional sections giving pretty good local listings. Tourist offices can always tell you about major events, and sometimes have publications listing what's on.

Discos & Clubs

Spain has some of the best nightlife in Europe; wild and *very* late nights, especially on Friday and Saturday, are an integral part of the Spanish experience. Even some small cities have very lively scenes. Most young Spaniards don't think about going out till midnight or so, though you can begin a tapas crawl at 8 or 9 pm. Bars, which come in all shapes, sizes and themes, are the main attractions until around 2 or 3 am. Some play great music, which will get you hopping before you move on to a disco, if you can afford it, till 5 or 6 am – or later! Discos can be expensive and some won't let you in wearing jeans or trainers, but they

aren't to be missed if you can manage to splurge. Techno in various guises is still the go in many discos. Spain's main contributions to dance music in recent years have been *bakalao* and *mákina*, kinds of frenzied techno.

Rock, Pop & Jazz

The home-grown Spanish rock, pop and flamenco fusion scene is large and lively (see Music in the Facts about Spain chapter). The bigger cities usually offer a good and varied choice of bands, often including foreign visitors, several nights of the week. Elsewhere gigs are mainly on weekends. Venues range from bars to clubs to theatres, stadiums and bullrings. The summer spawns hosts of festivals (see the Public Holidays & Special Events section earlier in this chapter).

Jazz has its following, with venues in most sizable cities.

Flamenco

Flamenco song, dance and music has enjoyed an upsurge in popularity in recent years, partly thanks to a wave of mainly young artists who mix it with rock, jazz, blues, rap and other idioms. Many bars and clubs – especially in flamenco's homeland, Andalucía, but also in Madrid, Barcelona, Extremadura and Murcia – stage regular flamenco nights, where you just pay for your drinks (and sometimes a small admission charge). Big-name artists also perform in theatres. Tourist offices tend to direct you towards *tablaos*, regular shows for a tourist audience with high-ish prices. Some of these are tacky and very routine; others are good. In summer Andalucian cities, towns and villages stage dozens of flamenco festivals. These are typically long-drawn-out and open-air affairs, maybe not getting going till midnight and lasting till dawn, with copious quantities of alcohol being drunk.

Flamenco fans band together in clubs called *peñas* that stage live performance nights; most peñas will admit genuinely interested visitors and the atmosphere can be most intimate and informal.

Classical Music, Dance & Theatre

For the culturally inclined, there are lots of performances, and often festivals, around the country (see Public Holidays & Special Events earlier in this chapter). Theatre is nearly all in Spanish, of course. For some background on the Spanish arts scene, see Arts in the Facts about Spain chapter.

Cinema

Cinemas abound and films are inexpensive, though foreign films are usually dubbed into Spanish. In the biggest cities a few cinemas show films in their original languages with Spanish subtitles – look for the letters 'v.o.' *(versión original)* in listings.

SPECTATOR SPORTS
Football

Fútbol (soccer) at least equals bullfighting as Spain's national sport. Around 300,000 fans attend the games in the Primera División (First Division) every weekend from September to May, with millions more following on TV. Spain suffers from little football hooliganism but Spaniards still take their favoured teams' fortunes very seriously.

Almost any game in the Primera División will be worth attending for the Spanish crowd experience even if you're not a huge fan of the game itself. But those involving the big two clubs, Real Madrid and Barcelona, have an extra passion to them. This pair has large followings throughout the country and something approaching a monopoly on the silverware: between them they have carried off the league title in all but 13 seasons since 1950. Real Madrid, thanks largely to Franco's support in the 1950s, have won Europe's major club competition, the European Cup, a record seven times. These two clubs' players and coaches are national celebrities – and their directors demand continuous success: when Real Madrid won their seventh European Cup in 1998 they promptly sacked their coach, Jupp Heynckes, because they had only finished fourth in the league.

Other leading clubs include Atlético Madrid (which won one of its occasional league titles in 1996), Athletic Bilbao, Valencia, Deportivo La Coruña, Real Zaragoza, Espanyol (of Barcelona), Real Betis (of Sevilla) and Real Sociedad of San Sebastián. A promotion and relegation system from the Segunda División allows a few minor teams their hour of glory among the big boys. Recent seasons have witnessed the odd spectacle of little CF Extremadura entertaining teams such as Barcelona and Real Madrid, whose stadiums hold three times the entire population of Extremadura's home town, Almendralejo.

League games are mostly played on Saturday and Sunday and you can pay at the gate (from about 1500 ptas) for all but the biggest matches. Games in the Copa del Rey (Spain's equivalent of the FA Cup) and matches in European competitions are held midweek at night. Watch the press (including the sports paper *Marca*) for details of upcoming fixtures.

Other Sports

Champions such as Arantxa Sánchez Vicario and Carlos Moya (tennis), Miguel Induráin (cycling) and Severiano Ballesteros and José-María Olazábal (golf) have all inspired popularity in their sports. All appear a few times a year in competitions in their home country, though Spain stages none of the really big annual international events in their sports. But golf's Ryder Cup, between Europe and the USA, took place at Valderrama, Andalucía, in 1997 – the first time it had been held in Europe outside Britain.

Bike-happy Spain stages up to three grands prix of the world motorcycle championship each year. The one at Jerez de la Frontera in May is probably the country's biggest sporting event, with around 150,000 spectators annually. Others take place at Jarama, near Madrid, and the Montmeló circuit 20km north of Barcelona. The Spanish Formula 1 motor-racing grand prix is held at Montmeló, usually in May. Spain's version of the Tour de France cycle race is the three-week Vuelta a España, usually held in September.

SHOPPING

You can find some attractive and reasonably priced handicrafts if you look in the right places. In some crafts there's wide regional variation and many products tend not to be found far from where they are made. Apart from craft shops, which abound in the producing areas, you may pick up crafts at weekly or daily markets in villages or towns and even in department stores. There are some excellent flea markets *(mercadillos)* and car boot sales *(rastros)* around the country – good for bargains.

Pottery

There are many attractive regional varieties of pottery. Products are cheap: crockery, jugs, plant pots, window boxes and tiles are likely to cost a fraction of the price of similar products at home. Islamic influence on design and colour is evident in much of the country. In Granada, the dominant colours are white splashed with green and blue, often with a pomegranate as the centrepiece of the pattern. In Córdoba the product is finer, with black, green and blue borders on white. Brighter colours are used in other parts of the country. Some excellent, more individual pieces are made in Níjar in eastern Andalucía. Many of the towns and villages around Valencia city are famous for their ceramics and pottery. There are plenty of speciality shops in the city – also a good place to buy your own paella dish.

Textiles & Clothes

Inexpensive, colourful rugs and blankets are made all over the country; try places like the Alpujarras and Níjar in Andalucía. Other textiles include lacework (from Galicia and elsewhere) and embroidery. The finest embroidery is not for sale, though! It is on religious vestments such as the ornate robes adorning the various images of the Virgin in churches and processions. Bullfighters' costumes are also elaborately embroidered; some exquisite old examples are in bullfighting museums in Ronda and Córdoba.

Ibiza city is something of a drawing card for fashion victims and a good place to buy clothes, with everything ranging from the latest and most extreme grunge statements to hippy gear straight out of Carnaby Street. Barcelona and the Costa Brava resort of Cadaqués have interesting boutiques too.

Leather

Spanish leather goods used to be quite a bargain and, though prices have gone up, you can still get good deals on leather jackets, bags, belts, shoes and boots in many places, especially Andalucía. Exquisite riding boots can be purchased in 'horsy' places like Jerez de la Frontera and El Rocío. Embossed, polychrome leather products such as poufs make a good not-too-bulky present: you can simply roll up the leather and insert the filling back at home.

Other Crafts

Gold and silver jewellery abound; some of the best is the filigree made in Córdoba. Damascene weapons (made of steel inlaid with gold, silver and copper) are still produced in Toledo. (Spain's finest gold and silverware, much of it reflecting the influx of wealth from the New World, remains in the country's splendid churches and museums.) There's some pleasing woodwork available, such as Granada's marquetry boxes and chess sets. Basketwork is produced throughout Spain but is most evident on the coasts. Esparto grass products are durable and inexpensive.

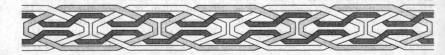

EATING & DRINKING IN SPAIN

Dunking *churros* in a big mug of *chocolate*, eating a leisurely lunch of *cochinillo*, snacking on tapas during a bar crawl or sipping on Andalucian sherry – it's not hard to see why eating and drinking is a national pastime in Spain. And it's an easy lifestyle for the traveller to adopt, whatever their budget.

FOOD

Spanish cooking is typically Mediterranean in its liberal use of olive oil, garlic, onions, tomatoes and peppers. It reflects Roman, Arabic, Jewish, New World and (in the north) French influences, but the Arabic contribution is what sets it apart in Europe. Spices like saffron and cumin, honeyed sweets and pastries, and the use of fruits and almonds with savoury dishes are all legacies of the Muslim era.

Traditional food is simple fare based on fresh ingredients with a hint of herbs and spices. But old food habits are changing fast, in part because of imported foodstuffs and convenience foods, exposure to other cuisines and the hectic pace of modern life. In all but the most rustic of kitchens, gas cookers have replaced open fires. Electric blenders are seeing off the mortar and pestle and fridges and freezers have much altered the scene.

Many typically Spanish dishes and foods are eaten countrywide, though often prepared differently in different regions. These include:

allioli – garlic mayonnaise
bacalao – salted dried cod, soaked to regain moisture before cooking
charcutería – pork products including many forms of *embutido* (sausage), some eaten cold, some cooked
chuletas and *solomillo* – chops/cutlets and sirloin, respectively, which are two of the most common cuts of pork, beef or lamb
flan – a caramel custard dessert
garbanzos – chickpeas
gazpacho – a cold, blended soup of tomatoes, peppers, onion, garlic, breadcrumbs, lemon and oil
habas – broad beans
jamón – ham
mariscos and *pescado* – seafood and fish in innumerable varieties
paella and other rice dishes
pinchitos morunos – Moroccan-style kebabs, usually made with pork
sopa de ajo – garlic soup
tortilla española – potato omelette, often served cold

The *cocido* (stew), a one-pot feast of beans, vegetables, and meat and sausage if available, was traditionally the mainstay of the Spanish diet though it's less common today. A cocido can be divided to make up a three-course meal, with the broth eaten first followed by the vegetables and lastly the meat.

The ubiquitous olive oil – the foundation of Spanish cooking

Paella

Spain's most famous dish – served throughout the country in various guises – takes its name from the wide, shallow, two-handled metal pan in which it's cooked and served. Outside restaurants, it appears mainly on Sundays and holidays. Paella is best cooked on a wood fire out of doors – what better way to feed a crowd?

Paella evolved from the rice dishes that emerged in medieval times in the Valencia area. Rice came to Spain in a big way in the 8th century with the Muslims. (The Arabic word for rice is aroz, hence the Spanish *arroz*.) With the expulsion of the Muslims in the early 17th century, rice cultivation in Spain declined and then was banned because the wetlands necessary to its growth were associated with malaria. In the late 19th century, the prohibition was lifted and land on the Ebro delta in Catalunya and in the marshlands of the Guadalquivir in Andalucía was given over to rice cultivation.

Into the paella pan went seasonal vegetables, wetland wildlife (frogs, ducks, snails, eels, partridge), seafood and saffron, if available. Tourism increased the popularity of this attractive, bright-yellow dish with titbits of chicken (instead of wild duck) and seafood and a tasty flavour resulting from the simmering rice absorbing the juices of the other ingredients.

In Valencia, paella contains green beans, white butter beans, snails, chicken and pork bites, but no seafood. In Sevilla and Cádiz, big prawns and sometimes crayfish (lobster) are added while some other ingredients are omitted. On the Costa del Sol, green peas, clams, mussels and prawns garnished with red peppers and slices of lemon are a popular combination. Saffron is expensive so today food colouring or paprika (*pimentón*) is more commonly used.

Spaniards usually eat paella at lunchtime because it's considered 'heavy'. Sometimes it's served as a tapa, or a starter. Many restaurants will only serve paella to a minimum of two people. Some require you to order it in advance, as the ingredients need to be super fresh.

This recipe was provided by Lorraine Samrt from Viveros Florena in Cómpeta, Málaga. It serves three or four people and requires a pan about 30cm in diameter. The meat, fish, seafood and vegetable content can vary. The essential ingredients are olive oil, rice, stock, and saffron or its substitute.

Paella

Ingredients
Olive oil
1 onion, chopped
3 cloves garlic, chopped
1 red pepper, chopped
1 large tomato, chopped
Approx 500g rabbit or chicken, cut roughly
125g cubed pork
1 chorizo sausage (or salami), sliced
100g peas
150g peeled prawns
250g mussels
250g clams
650ml chicken or seafood stock
250g short-grain white rice
¼ teaspoon saffron threads (or paprika or food colouring)
Salt and pepper to taste

For the garnish: lemon wedges dipped in chopped parsley, three or four unshelled medium-sized prawns (or one king prawn) per person.

Method
Several hours before cooking, put the unshelled prawns, mussels and clams in cold water with a handful of porridge oats. This flushes out the shellfish.

Fry the onions, garlic and red pepper in olive oil until soft. Add the tomatoes and simmer for five minutes. Take the mixture out of the pan and put it to one side. Now, in more olive oil, fry the rabbit/chicken and pork until they're half-cooked. Add the onion-tomato mix, chorizo slices, stock, rice and saffron. The paella now needs to cook slowly with the lid on for 20 minutes. Stir as little as possible. (Meanwhile, the shellfish need to be cooked quickly in boiling water. Take them out as soon as they open and discard any that do not open. Keep the mussel shells for garnish.) After 10 minutes, add the peeled prawns and peas to the paella.

Five minutes later, add the cooked shellfish. Five minutes more and the 20 minutes are up. Your paella is ready to garnish and serve! To garnish, you can arrange the mussel shells around the edge of the pan and the unshelled prawns overlapping in the centre. Place the lemon wedges.

For Those with a Sweet Tooth

Spain has a strong tradition of elaborate sweets, cakes and pastries, much influenced by its Islamic past. Locals eat these delectables *(dulces)* with coffee, brandy or sweet wine, especially on holidays or feast days. Some of the best dulces are made and sold at convents; others are available in *panaderías* (bakeries), *patisserías* (cake shops) and bars. Try *turrón* (almond nougat, but there are also chocolate varieties), *yemas* (candied egg yolks), marzipan, sugared almonds or pine nuts and candied fruits or some of the fancy cakes and pastries.

Seafood and meat are eaten almost everywhere. Seafood is fantastic on all coasts, particularly the Atlantic, and is cooked in 1001 ways, but doesn't usually come cheap. Freshwater fish, crayfish (lobster), eels and even the occasional lizard are also eaten.

Regional Specialities

Many of Spain's regions, especially Catalunya and the País Vasco, are extremely proud of their food and regional cuisines have flourished. Basque and Catalan food preparation is generally more elaborate than elsewhere and results in arguably the best food in Spain.

The North Catalan cuisine has strong French and Italian influences and sauces are often served with meat and fish. Pasta is also common. The Basques are really serious about eating: there are whole cooking societies (for men only) devoted to fine food. Basque cuisine, like Catalan, incorporates ingredients from the mountains and the sea and gives importance to sauces. In Cantabria and Asturias, the food reflects the cool, damp climate, with stews, apples, chestnuts, freshwater fish, seafood and cured meats predominating. Galicia is famous for its octopus, oysters, scallops, fish soups and stews and *empanadas* (pies). Lamb, game birds and freshwater fish are common fare in Navarra and Aragón. Islamic-influenced sweets such as *mazapán* (marzipan) are typical of Aragón, while the small La Rioja region is renowned for its use of hot chillies.

The Centre & East High and bleak, Castilla y León is the *zona de los asados*, the region of roasts – pork, lamb and game. Castilla-La Mancha has similar fare, with game and wheat dishes common. Extremadura has two contrasting cuisines: simple peasant foods and rich cooking harking back to the region's medieval monasteries. In Valencia

Above: The northern regions are famous for their seafood dishes

and Murcia, rice dishes, seafood, eels and abundant high-quality fruit and vegetables make for a tasty cuisine. Murcia is known for its sweet pepper salads, whole baked fish and snails.

Andalucía This large region's cuisines reflect its geographical diversity. In the sierras, hams are cured (see the boxed text 'Jamón, Jamón') and game dishes abound. On the coasts, the abundant seafood ends up in soups, is fried or, in the case of sardines, is grilled on spits over driftwood fires. Pinchitos morunos and gazpacho are true Andalucian foods. The fruit and vegetables are delicious and fresh, for the growing season here lasts all year.

Balearic Islands Mallorca has strong links with Catalunya and similar French and Italian culinary influences. Numerous invaders – Greeks, Romans, Arabs, Barbary pirates and modern-day tourists – have also left their mark. Pork and seafood take first place. Menorca was ruled by Britain for 80 years and so English gin, puddings, jams, stuffed turkey and even macaroni cheese have become a part of the local fare. Ibiza's traditional cuisine has vanished.

Typical Meals & Eating Times

Spaniards have their own timetable for eating so it's a good idea to reset your stomach clock, unless you want to eat alone or only with other tourists.

Breakfast Most Spaniards start the day with a light breakfast (*desayuno*), perhaps coffee with a *tostada* (toasted roll or slice of bread)

or *bollo* (pastry, *pasta* in Catalunya). You can put an almost infinite variety of things in or on your tostada, from olive oil (*aceite de oliva*, maybe with garlic, *ajo*) or *manteca*, pork lard, maybe coloured red with paprika, to a slice of grilled pork loin (*lomo a la plancha*) or plain old butter and jam (*mantequilla y mermelada*).

Churros con chocolate – long, deep-fried doughnuts to dip in thick hot chocolate – are a delicious, calorie-laden start to the day, unique to Spain. They're also popular after drinking expeditions; Madrid, for instance, has several late-night *chocolaterías*.

Above: Start the day with a sugar rush – churros con chocolate

Right: Chocolaterías (Xocolaterias in Catalan) as an art form

DAMIEN SIMONIS

Jamón, Jamón

JOHN NOBLE

Left: Black Iberian pigs feeding in the Sierra Morena, Sevilla Province

Facing page: Mountain-cured jamones hanging from the ceiling of a Trevélez bar

Appetising is not usually the word that springs to mind when you first set eyes on a dozen or so pigs' back legs dangling from the ceiling of a Spanish bar. But to most Spaniards there's no more mouthwatering prospect than a few thin, succulent slices of this cured *jamón* (ham). If you try it out you'll probably see why. You can eat two or three slices as a *tapa*, have it in a *bocadillo* for 300 to 400 ptas or get a *ración* for 600 to 1000 ptas.

Most of these hams are *jamón serrano* (mountain ham), which is good enough. Even better (and more expensive) is jamón ibérico, from the black Iberian breed of pig, and the best jamón ibérico is *jamón ibérico de bellota*, from Iberian pigs fed on acorns (*bellotas*). A glass of *fino* sherry is the traditional accompaniment to jamón ibérico.

Murcia, Galicia, Teruel in Aragón and Piornal in Extremadura all produce noted jamón serrano, while Guijuelo in Salamanca province has a fair ibérico. But the best jamones of all are from Montánchez in Extremadura, Trevélez in the Alpujarras south of Granada and, above all, the jamón ibérico of Jabugo in northwestern Andalucía, from free-range pigs from the Sierra Morena oak forests. The best Jabugo hams are graded from one to five *jotas* (Js) and *cinco jotas* (JJJJJ) hams are said to come from pigs that have never eaten anything but acorns.

A *tortilla* (omelette) is a good option for a more substantial breakfast, though Spaniards eat eggs at other times of the day. *Huevos fritos* are fried eggs and *huevos revueltos* are scrambled eggs; *huevos pasados por agua* will get you lightly boiled eggs; ask for *huevos cocidos* if you want hard-boiled eggs.

Jamón, Jamón

The curing process basically involves leaving the leg of the slaughtered pig in sea salt for a few days, then removing the salt (this process may be done twice) before hanging it up to mature – for between a few months to over two years, depending on the ham. Great attention has to be paid to the temperature (gradually increasing) and humidity (not too dry) during the drying process. Curing 'seals' the hams, which is why they're not covered with swarms of flies when you see them hanging in bars.

Traditionally hams were cured in cellars at home by the pig-owning family, but the business is becoming more and more industrialised. But some families still hold traditional *matanza* (slaughtering) gatherings around 11 November, the beginning of the slaughter season after the pigs have indulged in the autumn acorn harvest.

One kilogram of jamón serrano in a shop is likely to be about 2000 ptas. Ibérico can be double those prices.

Ordinary uncured cold ham, by the way, is called *jamón York*. It's dull as ditchwater after you've tasted serrano or ibérico.

DAMIEN SIMONIS

Lunch Lunch is usually a Spaniard's main meal of the day; it is eaten between about 1.30 and 4 pm and known as *comida* or *almuerzo*. It can consist of several courses including a soup and/or salad, followed by meat or fish with vegetables or a rice dish or bean stew, then a light dessert.

Menú del Día Most restaurants offer a *menú del día* (daily set menu) – the budget traveller's best friend – around 800 to 1200 ptas. You normally get a starter, a main course, dessert *(postre)*, bread and wine. Often there's a choice of two or three dishes for each course. It's normally posted up outside – if it makes no mention of drinks, dessert, bread, coffee or 'IVA incluido', your meal may cost more.

Platos Combinados The *plato combinado* is a near relative of the *menú*. It literally translates as 'combined plate' and may consist of a steak and egg with chips and salad, or fried squid with potato salad. Insipid photos of what's available can be off-putting, but more often than not a plato combinado is fine.

À la Carte You'll pay more for your meals if you order à la carte but the food will be better. The Spanish menu *(la carta)* – not *el menú*, which means the menú del día – begins with starters such as *ensaladas* (salads), *sopas* (soups) and *entremeses* (hors d'oeuvres). Entremeses can range from a mound of potato salad with olives, asparagus, anchovies and a selection of cold meats – almost a meal in itself – to simpler cold meats, slices of cheese and olives.

Later courses are often listed under headings like chicken *(pollo)*, meat *(carne)*, seafood *(mariscos)*, fish *(pescado)*, rice *(arroz)*, eggs *(huevos)* and vegetables *(verduras/legumbres)*. Meat may be subdivided into pork *(cerdo)*, beef *(ternera)* and lamb *(cordero)*.

Desserts have a low profile: ice cream *(helados)*, fruit and flan are often the only choices. There may be *arroz con leche* (cold rice pudding) or *tocino del cielo* (heavenly bacon), a type of caramel custard with a vaguely bacon-like appearance.

Dinner The evening meal *(cena)* tends to be lighter than lunch and may be eaten as late as 10 or 11 pm. But lots of people also go out for a bigger dinner in restaurants, though before about 9 pm you're unlikely to see anyone but foreigners doing this.

In-Between Times It's common (and a great idea!) to go to a bar or café for a *merienda* (snack) around 11 am and/or 7 or 8 pm. A great snack is a *bocadillo*, a white-bread roll filled with cheese or ham or salad ... You probably won't leave Spain without sampling a *bocadillo de tortilla española* or *de jamón serrano*, a roll filled with potato omelette or cured ham. Then there are tapas ... (see the boxed text 'Tapas').

Types of Eatery

Cafés & Bars Spanish life revolves around cafés and bars. The latter come in various guises, including *bodegas* (old-style wine bars), *cervecerías* (beer bars), *tascas* (bars that specialise in tapas), *tabernas* (taverns) and even *pubs*. Tapas are available in many, while some serve more substantial fare too. You will often save 10% to 20% by eating

Tapas

These saucer-sized mini-snacks are part of the Spanish way of life and come in infinite varieties. You can make a meal of *tapas*, go on to a meal afterwards or hop on to another bar to sample more tapas; a great Spanish pastime.

Tapa translates as lid. Today's snacks supposedly originated in Andalucía's sherry area in the 19th century when bar owners placed a piece of bread on top of a drink to deter flies; this developed into the custom of putting a titbit, such as olives or a piece of sausage, on a lid to cover the drink – something salty to encourage drinking. Today, tapas have become a cuisine of their own and each region and city has its specialities. They're still sometimes free, though this custom has all but disappeared in many areas. A typical tapa costs between 100 and 200 ptas (check before you order as some are a lot dearer).

Typical tapas include olives, slices of cured meats or cheese, potato salad, diced salad, bite-sized portions of fried fish, *albóndigas* (meat or fish balls), chickpeas with spinach, rabbit stew, *callos* (tripe), *gambas* (prawns) in garlic or *boquerones* (anchovies) marinated in vinegar or *rebozados* (fried in batter).

Bars often display a range of tapas on the counter or chalk a list on a board. There may even be a tapas menu. Otherwise, it seems, you're expected to know what's available and the situation *can* be rather confusing. A place that appears not to have tapas may actually specialise in them! Failing all else, you just have to ask what tapas there are, then try to recognise a few words in the long stream of verbiage that you're likely to be answered with.

A *ración* is a meal-sized serving of these snacks, a *media ración* is half a ración. When ordering, make it clear if it's a tapa you're after, not a media ración or ración, or you'll end up paying three or five times what you planned.

In the País Vasco and Asturias, tapas are often called *pinchos*.

at the bar rather than at a table, particularly if the tables are in a smart attached dining room or outside.

Restaurants Throughout Spain you'll find plenty of *restaurantes* serving good simple food at affordable prices, often featuring regional specialities. There are also some ordinary to woeful places, particularly in tourist haunts, and plenty of classy upmarket eateries too.

Cheese

Except in the north, Spain's climate and terrain are unsuitable for dairy cattle. Oil and lard, rather than butter, are used in cooking and butter is rarely spread on bread. That said, Spain does produce at least 36 varieties of *queso* (cheese). Most are fairly strong and some of the best are made from goat's or ewe's milk.

Spanish supermarkets stock a selection of local cheeses, many cheeses from other parts of Europe and also Spanish copies of cheeses such as Brie and Camembert. Spanish cheese is generally pricey, around 1500 ptas a kilo, while you can buy Edam or Gouda for as little as 1000 ptas a kilo. Spanish cheeses you might like to sample include:

Burgos – made from ewe's milk, this comes in a rindless round and is particularly delicious with honey, nuts and fruit.

Cabrales – strong Asturian cow's, goat's and sheep's-milk cheese matured in caves; it's encased in leaves and the inside is blue and creamy.

Manchego – the most famous of Spanish cheeses, it is traditionally made from ewe's milk, but now often with other milk, and cured in oil. It can be soft, fresh and mild or hard, crumbly and strong. The rind is brown/black, the inside is pale yellow.

Pasiego – made from cow's milk near Santander, this cheese has a firm, white and creamy inside.

Roncal – a hard cheese with tiny holes inside and made in Navarra's Roncal valley from ewe's milk, sometimes combined with cow's milk; the rind is brown.

A *mesón* is a simple eatery with home-style cooking, usually attached to a bar, while a *comedor* is usually a dining room at a bar or hostal – with food that is likely to be functional and cheap. A *venta* is a family-run establishment, probably once an inn, off the beaten track; the food can be delectable and cheap. A *marisquería* or *merendero* is a seafood restaurant. A *chiringuito* is a small open-air bar or kiosk, or sometimes a more substantial beachside restaurant.

Spanish law requires restaurant menu prices to include a service charge and any tip beyond that is a matter of personal choice.

Ethnic Restaurants Spain has many Chinese restaurants, generally mundane but cheap. Indian and Mexican restaurants crop up too. Italian restaurants are common and vary in quality: pizzas are mostly tasty enough and filling. There are some good Arabic restaurants in Málaga and Granada and a largely tourist-based revival of the cuisine of Al-Andalus in a few restaurants in Córdoba.

Self-Catering

Spain's *mercados* (food markets) are fun. Buy a selection of fruits, vegetables, cold meat or sausage, olives, nuts and cheese, pick up some bread from a bakery, stop in at a supermarket for a bottle of wine and head for the nearest picturesque spot. This can make a pleasant change from sitting in restaurants and you can put together a cheap, filling meal.

Only some youth hostels and just a few pensiones and hostales have facilities for cooking.

Table Talk

Here are a few basic words that can come in handy whatever kind of meal you're eating:

bill (check)	*cuenta*
breakfast	*desayuno*
change	*cambio*
cold	*frío/a*
cup	*taza*
dining room	*comedor*
dinner	*cena*
food, meal	*comida*
fork	*tenedor*
glass	*vaso or copa*
hot (temperature)	*caliente*
hot (spicy, piquant)	*picante*
ice	*hielo*
kitchen	*ocina*
knife	*cuchillo*
lunch	*almuerzo or comida*
menu	*carta*
plate	*plato*
spoon	*cuchara*
sweet	*dulce*
table	*mesa*
vegetarian	*vegetariano/a*
waiter/waitress	*camarero/a*
water	*agua*

Right: Valencia's famed oranges are a good option for self-caterers, or just a juicy snack

DAMIEN SIMONIS

Vegetarian Food

Outside the big cities and university towns, Spain can be difficult if you're a vegetarian and a real headache if you're a vegan. Vegetarian restaurants are often only open for lunch or may be tucked away in a far corner of town; these places also tend to come and go depending on demand. Some restaurants in tourist or student areas cater for vegetarians in the *menú del día*, but you can't count on it. You can, however, look forward to tasty dishes prepared in Arabic eateries in Málaga, Granada and Tarifa.

Now for more good news: Spanish fruits and vegetables are wonderfully fresh year round, so salads in any restaurant are a good bet. Red pepper salads such as *pipirrana* are common. To be on the safe side, when you order add something like '*Soy vegetariano/a, no me gusta carne/jamón/pollo/atún/huevos*' (I'm a vegetarian, I don't like meat/ham/chicken/tuna/eggs) or whatever it is you don't want in your salad. Or simply say '*Sin ...* ' (Without ...).

More generally, you need to ask '*¿Qué hay sin carne, jamón, pollo, marisco o pescado?*' (What is there without meat, ham, chicken, seafood or fish?). Check the vegetables section of the menu but remember that even dishes listed here won't necessarily come without meat unless you specify. *Alcachofas* (artichokes) and *espárragos* (asparagus) often appear on menus; they may be lightly cooked and served with mayonnaise, or tossed in oil and garlic. *Berenjenas* (aubergines) are often sliced

DRINKS

Nonalcoholic Drinks
Coffee Coffee in Spain is strong. Addicts should specify how they want their fix. A *café con leche* is about 50% coffee, 50% hot milk; ask for *grande* or *doble* if you want a large cup, *en vaso* if you want it in a glass, or *sombra* if you want lots of milk. A *café solo* is a short black; *café cortado* is a short black with a little milk.

Tea Spaniards prefer coffee. Tea in most cafés and bars is invariably weak. Ask for milk to be separate *(leche aparte)*, otherwise, you'll end up with a cup of lukewarm milky water with a tea bag thrown in. Most places also have camomile tea *(té de manzanilla)*. *Teterías* (Islamic-style tearooms) are fashionable in some cities; they serve all manner of teas, including herbal concoctions *(infusiones)*. Their bills usually end up hefty (you pay for the ambience – soft cushions, floaty music).

Vegetarian Food

thinly, dipped in batter and quickly fried – good as a side dish or a tapa. A full serve is usually plenty for two people.

A good vegetarian dish is *pisto*, similar to ratatouille, a fry-up of zucchinis (courgettes), green peppers, onions and potatoes. *Menestra* is another vegetarian dish – of artichokes, chard, peas and green beans. *Garbanzos con espinacas* (chick-peas with spinach) is a filling and tasty stew. *Setas* (wild mushrooms) often turn up on menus; usually they're cooked in olive oil and garlic, but are better in a sauce *(salsa)*. *Escalivada* is a Catalan cold dish of aubergines, peppers and onions in an oil-and-garlic sauce. *Pimientos rellenos* (stuffed peppers) generally contain meat or prawns. Tofu and seitán, a miso-like vegetable protein, usually only crop up in vegetarian restaurants.

If you eat eggs, *tortillas* (pictured left) or *huevos revueltos* are good stand-bys; you can order them with asparagus, artichokes or other vegetables. A *cocido* (stew), though it may include plenty of beans, will more often than not include bits of meat or contain meat stock. The same goes for soups, although gazpacho is a safe bet. Occasionally a meat and fish-free *empanada* (pie) will turn up. And a *bocadillo vegetal* (salad sandwich) is filling.

If you get fed up, your best bet is to cater for yourself.

Chocolate Spaniards brought chocolate back from Mexico and adopted it enthusiastically. As a drink, it's served thick; sometimes it even appears among postres on menus. Generally it's a breakfast drink consumed with churros (see Food earlier in this section).

Soft Drinks Orange juice *(zumo de naranja)* is the main freshly squeezed juice available, but expensive at around 250 ptas a glass. Boxed juices come in all varieties in shops and are good and cheap.

Refrescos (cool drinks) include the usual international brands of soft drinks, local brands such as Kas and expensive *granizado* (iced fruit crush).

Clear, cold water from a public fountain or tap is a Spanish favourite, but check that it's *potable*. For tap water in restaurants, ask for *agua de grifo*. Bottled water *(agua mineral)* comes in innumerable brands, either fizzy *(con gas)* or still *(sin gas)*. A 1.5L bottle of still water costs between 40 and 75 ptas in a supermarket.

A *batido* is a flavoured milk drink or milkshake.

Horchata (*orxata* in Catalan), made from the juice of *chufa* (tiger nuts), sugar and water, tastes like soya milk with a hint of cinnamon. You'll come across it both fresh and bottled: Chufi is a delicious brand.

Alcoholic Drinks

Wine Spain is a wine-drinking country and so wine *(vino)* accompanies many a meal. Spanish wine is strong because of the sunny climate. It can be white *(blanco)*, red *(tinto)* or rosé *(rosado)*. Wine remains cheap though there is no shortage of expensive wines. A 500 ptas bottle of wine from a supermarket or wine merchant will be better than average. The same money in a restaurant will get you an average drop. Cheap *vino de mesa* (table wine) sells for less than 200 ptas a litre in shops.

Regional Wine Specialities

Wine is made everywhere in Spain, with La Rioja, Catalunya, Castilla-La Mancha, and the Jerez de la Frontera area in Andalucía producing the country's best (Jerez wine is sherry). However, with wine production thriving and experimentation rife, competition is fierce and new wines are constantly entering the scene.

For ordinary drinking, some of the cheaper reds from La Rioja or even Valdepeñas (Castilla-La Mancha) are generally OK, as are Catalunya's *cavas* (sparkling wines like champagne) and still whites, such as Penedès. Rosé is cheap; those from Navarra, Rueda (Castilla y León) and Utiel-Requena (Valencia) are good.

Galicia's best wines include white Albariños from the Rías Baixas and red or white Ribeiros. In the **País Vasco**, a sharp, white wine known as *txacoli* is popular. In **Aragón** the Somontano area near Huesca is into high-tech wine production and comes up with some good whites. **Catalunya's** best wines come from Penedès (cava and fruity whites) and Priorato (reds).

The **Rioja** DOC (*Denominación de Origen Calificada* – see Wine) region includes areas of Navarra and the País Vasco bordering its heartland in La Rioja. The region is best known for its reds – the current trend is towards production of mature wines rather than those for the cheaper end of the market. **Navarra** is an upcoming wine producer with lots of experimentation happening.

In **Castilla y León**, the Ribera del Duero region produces excellent reds that rival those of Rioja, while the Rueda area was

You can order wine by the glass *(copa)* in bars and restaurants: the *vino de la casa* (house wine) may come from a barrel or jug at 125 ptas, sometimes less, a glass.

Spain regulates its wine fairly carefully so you can judge something of its quality from the label. The letters DOC stand for *denominación de origen calificada* and refer to wine areas that have maintained consistent high quality over a very long period. Rioja is the only DOC at present, though Jerez may join it. DO, *denominación de origen*, is one step down from DOC. There are 50-odd DO areas around Spain. A DOC or DO label tells you that the wine has been produced to certain supervised standards by serious wine-growers – though each DOC and DO covers a wide range of wines of varying quality (usually indicated by the price).

Regional Wine Specialities

famous for its whites until challenged by developments in Galicia. Now rosé is fast overtaking whites in Rueda. Toro, near Salamanca, produces some powerful reds.

Extensive **Castilla-La Mancha** produces 50% of all wine made in Spain. It has a reputation for cheap and (if you're lucky) cheerful wine, but this is fast changing with new wines hitting the scene. Its La Mancha and Valdepeñas DOs (*Denominación de Origen* – also see Wine) offer the best ranges of budget-priced wines in the country.

Valencia and **Murcia** have traditionally produced bulk wine and, more recently, concentrated grape juice for export. However, there are some good-value wines being produced in the Utiel-Requena area of Valencia (whites and rosés), and in Murcia's Jumilla (reds) and Yecla (reds, whites and rosés) areas. **Extremadura** mainly produces wine for local consumption, grape juice or distilled liquor.

Wine production in Spain began in **Andalucía** when the Phoenicians founded Cádiz around 1100 BC and introduced vine cultivation. The region is famous for sherry, a fortified wine produced by a special ageing process, mostly in the Jerez de la Frontera area (see the boxed text 'Sherry' in the Andalucía chapter). Málaga dessert wines made from the muscatel grape have been fashionable and, though their popularity has declined, they are served from the barrel in some of the city's bars.

Other categories of wine, in descending order, are: *denominación de origen provisional* (DOp); *vino de la tierra*; *vino comarcal*; and *vino de mesa*.

Vino joven is wine made for immediate drinking, while *vino de crianza* has to be stored for certain minimum periods: a red needs two full calendar years with a minimum of six months in oak; and a white or rosé needs one calendar year. *Reserva* wines require three years storage for reds and two years for whites and rosés. *Gran reserva* wines are particularly good vintages that must have spent at least two calendar years in storage and three in the bottle. They're mostly reds.

Beer The most common way to order a beer *(cerveza)* is to ask for a *caña*, which is a small draught beer. *Corto* and, in the País Vasco, *zurrito* are other names for this. A larger beer (about 300ml) is called a *tubo* (which comes in a straight glass) or in Catalunya a *jarra*, which has a handle. All these words apply to draught beer *(cerveza de barril* or *cerveza de presión)*; if you just ask for a cerveza you may well get bottled beer, which can be more expensive. A small bottle of beer is called a *botellín* or a *quinto*; a bigger one is a *tercio* or a *mediana*. Estrella de Galicia is the best beer we have found in Spain. San Miguel, Cruzcampo and Victoria are decent brands.

A *clara* is a shandy, a beer with a dash of lemonade.

Above: The traditional 15 August treading of the first grapes at Cómpeta, a noted sweet-wine-making village in Málaga province

Other Drinks *Sangría* is a wine and fruit punch sometimes laced with brandy. It's refreshing going down but can leave you with a sore head. You'll see jugs of it on tables in restaurants but it also comes ready-mixed in bottles in shops at around 300 ptas for 1.5L. *Tinto de verano* is a mix of wine and Casera, a brand of lemonade or sweet, bubbly water. Cider *(sidra)* is produced and largely consumed in Asturias and the País Vasco.

Spanish brandy *(coñac)* is popular and cheap. In bars, you'll notice locals starting the day with a coffee and a brandy, or a glass of *anís* (aniseed liqueur). Popular brandies include Centenario, Magno, 103 and Soberano. Spanish-produced spirits are generally much cheaper than imports. Larios gin made in Málaga is an example.

Spain produces a huge range of liqueurs *(licores)*. *Aguardiente* is a colourless grape-based liqueur. *Pacharán* is a red liqueur made with aniseed and sloes, the fruit of the blackthorn.

Getting There & Away

Spain is one of Europe's top holiday destinations and is well linked to other European countries by air, rail and road. Regular car ferries and hydrofoils run to Morocco.

From elsewhere in Europe flying is the simplest option. Never assume that the cheapest way is by land (or sea). By flying you often lose nothing in price and save a lot of time and hassle – unless you want to enjoy the journey to Spain as much as your trip inside the country.

Some good direct flight deals are also available from North America. Those coming from Australia and New Zealand have fewer choices and should watch out for deals including free internal European flights (see the Australia section under Air).

Insurance

See the Visas & Documents and Health sections in the Facts for the Visitor chapter for hints on travel insurance, something you should always consider.

AIR

Always reconfirm your onward flight or return bookings by the specified time: at least 72 hours before departure on intercontinental flights (on many European flights it is no longer strictly necessary to reconfirm). Otherwise you risk missing your flight because it was rescheduled or you've been classified as a 'no-show'.

Airports & Airlines

The main gateway to Spain is Madrid's Barajas airport, but there is no shortage of direct flights to other centres, particularly Barcelona, Málaga and Palma de Mallorca. Occasional flights, mostly charters, also fly direct to a range of other Spanish cities from centres like Paris and London.

Iberia flies to 11 Spanish cities from around the world but is generally the expensive way to go.

The high season for travel to Spain is July and August, as well as Easter and Christmas.

Buying Tickets

The plane ticket may be the single most expensive item in your budget, so check around the travel agents. Start early: some of the cheapest tickets have to be bought months in advance and popular flights sell out early. For much of the year it is possible to dig up good deals from Europe, especially with charter companies. Talk to other recent travellers, as they may be able to stop you making some of the same old mistakes. Look at the ads in newspapers and magazines (including Spanish press in your home country) and watch for special offers. Then phone around travel agents. (Airlines generally do not supply the cheapest tickets.) Find out the fare, the route, the duration of the journey and any restrictions (see the boxed text 'Air Travel Glossary'). Then decide which is best for you.

You may discover that those impossibly cheap flights are 'fully booked, but we have another one that costs a bit more ...'. Or that the flight is on an airline notorious for its poor safety and that leaves you in the world's worst airport for 14 hours midjourney. Or they claim only to have the last two seats available for your destination for all of July, which they will hold for you for two hours. Keep ringing around.

If travelling from the UK or USA you will find the cheapest flights are advertised by obscure bucket shops whose names haven't reached the telephone directory. They sell tickets at up to a 50% discount. Airlines may deny it, but many release tickets to selected bucket shops – it's better to sell tickets at a huge discount than not at all. Many such firms are honest but there are a few rogues who will take your money and disappear. If you feel suspicious, leave a deposit of 20% or so and pay the balance when you get the ticket. If they insist on cash in advance, go somewhere else. Once you have the ticket, ring the airline to confirm you are booked on the flight.

You could pay a little more and opt for the safety of a better known travel agent. Firms like STA Travel, with offices worldwide, Council Travel in the USA and UK or Travel CUTS in Canada are not going to disappear overnight and leave you clutching a receipt for a nonexistent ticket, but they do offer good prices to most destinations.

Once you have your ticket, write its number down, together with the flight number and other details, and keep the information somewhere separate. If the ticket is lost or stolen, this will help you get a replacement.

Fare Surfing

Tomorrow's traveller may never bother phoning a travel agent. Fare-booking services are expanding rapidly on the Internet. Still in its infancy (estimates of worldwide on-line travel sales were US$500 million in 1997 but may reach US$8 billion by 2002), the Web looks set to become a major travel market place.

Sabre, the US-based reservations agency that accounts for one-third of bookings worldwide (mostly through agents), launched its online Travelocity service in mid-1997. Another US site, Farefinder, trawls airline reservations systems daily looking for the latest deals. It concentrates on flights from the USA, but is bound to expand.

Some travel agents that offer fare-booking services include:

Airhitch
  www.airhitch.org
Council Travel
  www.counciltravel.com
STA Travel
  www.sta-travel.com
Travel CUTS
  www.travelcuts.com

Use the fares quoted in this book as a guide only. Quoted fares do not necessarily constitute a recommendation for the carrier.

Travellers with Special Needs

If you have special needs – you have a broken leg, are vegetarian, travelling in a wheelchair, taking the baby, terrified of flying – tell the airline so they can make arrangements. Remind them when you reconfirm and again when you check in. It may be worth ringing airlines before booking a flight to find out how they can handle your needs.

Airports and airlines can be surprisingly helpful, but they need warning. Most international airports provide escorts from check-in to plane where needed and there should be ramps, lifts and accessible toilets and phones. Aircraft toilets, however, could be a problem; travellers should discuss this with the airline and, if necessary, with their doctor.

Guide dogs for the blind often have to travel in a pressurised baggage compartment with other animals; smaller guide dogs may be admitted to the cabin. Guide dogs, like other animals, are subject to quarantine laws (six months in isolation etc) when entering or returning to countries free of rabies, such as Britain or Australia.

Deaf travellers can ask for airport and inflight announcements to be written down.

Children under two travel for 10% of the price (or free, on some airlines), as long as they don't occupy a seat. They don't get a baggage allowance. 'Skycots' should be provided if requested in advance. They take a child weighing up to 10kg. Children aged between two and 12 can usually occupy a seat for one-half to two-thirds of the full fare and get a baggage allowance. Pushchairs can often be taken as hand luggage.

Departure Tax

Airport taxes (fluctuating at around 1000 ptas for European flights, 2000 ptas to Morocco and rising to as much as 8500 ptas to the USA) are factored into tickets.

However, travel agents in Spain tend to quote fares *before* tax. A fare to New York of *64,000 ptas mas tasas* (plus tax) means a total price of around 72,500 ptas. Passport formalities are minimal.

The USA

The North Atlantic is the world's busiest long-haul air corridor and the range of flight options is bewildering. Several airlines fly 'direct' (many flights involve a stop elsewhere in Europe en route) to Spain, landing in Madrid and Barcelona. These include Iberia, BA and KLM-Royal Dutch Airlines. If your trip will not be confined to Spain, ask your travel agent if cheaper flights are available to other European cities.

The *New York Times*, *LA Times*, *Chicago Tribune* and *San Francisco Examiner* produce weekly travel sections loaded with travel agents' ads. Council Travel and STA Travel have offices nationwide. The magazine *Travel Unlimited* (PO Box 1058, Allston, Mass 02134) publishes details of cheap airfares.

Standard fares can be expensive. Discount and rock-bottom options from the USA include charter flights, stand-by and courier flights. Stand-by fares are often sold at 60% of the normal price for one-way tickets. Airhitch (☎ 212-864-2000, ☎ 800-326-2009 toll free), 2641 Broadway, 3rd floor, #100, New York, NY 10025, is a specialist. You will need to give a general idea of where and when you need to go; a few days before your departure you will be presented with a choice of two or three flights. Airhitch has several other offices in the USA, including Los Angeles (☎ 310-726-5000, ☎ 800-397-1098 toll free), as well as others in Amsterdam, Bonn, London, Paris, Prague and Rome. Contact its Madrid representative on ☎ 91 366 79 27 or check out its Spain Web site (www.collegeclub.com/~AHValencia).

Charter flights tend to be significantly cheaper than scheduled flights.

Otherwise, reliable travel agents include STA (☎ 800-777 0112) and Council Travel (☎ 800-226 8624); both have offices in major cities:

STA
(☎ 212-627-3111) 10 Downing Street (corner of 6th Ave and Bleeker St), New York, NY 10014
(☎ 310-824-1574) 920 Westwood Blvd, Los Angeles, CA 90024
(☎ 415-391-8407) 51 Grant Ave, San Francisco, CA 94108
Council Travel
(☎ 212-254-2525) 254 Green St, New York, NY 10003
(☎ 310-208-3551) 1094 Lindbrook Drive, Los Angeles, CA 90024
(☎ 415-421-3473) 530 Bush St, San Francisco, CA 94108

Another travel agent specialising in budget airfares is Discount Tickets in New York (☎ 212-391-2313).

Courier flights involve you accompanying a parcel to its destination. A New York-Madrid return on a courier flight can cost under US$300 in low season (more from the west coast).You may have to be a US resident and apply for an interview first. Most flights depart from New York.

Now Voyager (☎ 212-431-1616, suite 307, 74 Varrick St, New York, NY 10013) is a courier flight specialist. You pay an annual membership fee (around US$50), which entitles you to as many courier flights as you like. Phone after 6 pm for a recorded message detailing available flights and prices. The Denver-based Air Courier Association (☎ 303-278-8810) also does this kind of thing. You may be able to organise such flights direct with courier companies – try the Yellow Pages.

The high-tech navigator can find travel info and flights in the travel forums for users of the Internet and assorted computer information and communication services (see the boxed text 'Fare Surfing'). They are a step down the travellers' superhighway from television Teletext services.

Iberia flies nonstop between Madrid and New York, but often you can get better deals with other airlines if you are prepared to fly via other European centres.

Air Travel Glossary

Baggage Allowance This will be written on your ticket and usually includes one 20kg item to go in the hold, plus one item of hand luggage.

Bucket Shops These are unbonded travel agencies specialising in discounted airline tickets.

Bumped Just because you have a confirmed seat doesn't mean you're going to get on the plane (see Overbooking).

Cancellation Penalties If you have to cancel or change a discounted ticket, there are often heavy penalties involved; insurance can sometimes be taken out against these penalties. Some airlines impose penalties on regular tickets as well, particularly against 'no-show' passengers.

Check-In Airlines ask you to check in a certain time ahead of the flight departure (usually one to two hours on international flights). If you fail to check in on time and the flight is overbooked, the airline can cancel your booking and give your seat to somebody else.

Confirmation Having a ticket written out with the flight and date you want doesn't mean you have a seat until the agent has checked with the airline that your status is 'OK' or confirmed. Meanwhile you could just be 'on request'.

Courier Fares Businesses often need to send urgent documents or freight securely and quickly. Courier companies hire people to accompany the package through customs and, in return, offer a discount ticket which is sometimes a phenomenal bargain. In effect, what the companies do is ship their freight as your luggage on regular commercial flights. This is a legitimate operation, but there are two shortcomings – the short turnaround time of the ticket (usually not longer than a month) and the limitation on your luggage allowance. You may have to surrender all your allowance and take only carry-on luggage.

Full Fares Airlines traditionally offer 1st class (coded F), business class (coded J) and economy class (coded Y) tickets. These days there are so many promotional and discounted fares available that few passengers pay full economy fare.

ITX An ITX, or 'independent inclusive tour excursion', is often available on tickets to popular holiday destinations. Officially it's a package deal combined with hotel accommodation, but many agents will sell you one of these for the flight only and give you phoney hotel vouchers in the unlikely event that you're challenged at the airport.

Lost Tickets If you lose your airline ticket an airline will usually treat it like a travellers cheque and, after inquiries, issue you with another one. Legally, however, an airline is entitled to treat it like cash and if you lose it then it's gone forever. Take good care of your tickets.

MCO An MCO, or 'miscellaneous charge order', is a voucher that looks like an airline ticket but carries no destination or date. It can be exchanged through any International Association of Travel Agents (IATA) airline for a ticket on a specific flight. It's a useful alternative to an onward ticket in those countries that demand one, and is more flexible than an ordinary ticket if you're unsure of your route.

No-Shows No-shows are passengers who fail to show up for their flight. Full-fare passengers who fail to turn up are sometimes entitled to travel on a later flight. The rest are penalised (see Cancellation Penalties).

On Request This is an unconfirmed booking for a flight.

Air Travel Glossary

Onward Tickets An entry requirement for many countries is that you have a ticket out of the country. If you're unsure of your next move, the easiest solution is to buy the cheapest onward ticket to a neighbouring country or a ticket from a reliable airline which can later be refunded if you do not use it.

Open Jaw Tickets These are return tickets where you fly out to one place but return from another. If available, this can save you backtracking to your arrival point.

Overbooking Airlines hate to fly empty seats and since every flight has some passengers who fail to show up, airlines often book more passengers than they have seats. Usually excess passengers make up for the no-shows, but occasionally somebody gets bumped. Guess who it is most likely to be? The passengers who check in late.

Point-to-Point Tickets These are discount tickets that can be bought on some routes in return for passengers waiving their rights to a stopover.

Promotional Fares These are officially discounted fares, available from travel agencies or direct from the airline.

Reconfirmation At least 72 hours prior to departure time of an onward or return flight, you must contact the airline and 'reconfirm' that you intend to be on the flight. If you don't do this the airline can delete your name from the passenger list and you could lose your seat.

Restrictions Discounted tickets often have various restrictions on them – such as needing to be paid for in advance and incurring a penalty to be altered. Others are restrictions on the minimum and maximum period you must be away, such as a minimum of 14 days or a maximum of one year.

Round-the-World Tickets RTW tickets give you a limited period (usually a year) in which to circumnavigate the globe. You can go anywhere the carrying airlines go, as long as you don't backtrack. The number of stopovers or total number of separate flights is decided before you set off and they usually cost a bit more than a basic return flight.

Stand-by This is a discounted ticket where you only fly if there is a seat free at the last moment. Stand-by fares are usually available only on domestic routes.

Transferred Tickets Airline tickets cannot be transferred from one person to another. Travellers sometimes try to sell the return half of their ticket, but officials can ask you to prove that you are the person named on the ticket. This is less likely to happen on domestic flights, but on an international flight tickets are compared with passports.

Travel Agencies Travel agencies vary widely and you should choose one that suits your needs. Some simply handle tours, while full-services agencies handle everything from tours and tickets to car rental and hotel bookings. If all you want is a ticket at the lowest possible price, then go to an agency specialising in discounted tickets.

Travel Periods Ticket prices vary with the time of year. There is a low (off-peak) season and a high (peak) season, and often a low-shoulder season and a high-shoulder season as well. Usually the fare depends on your outward flight – if you depart in the high season and return in the low season, you pay the high-season fare.

With Iberia or Delta you are looking at US$783 to US$827 return to Madrid direct from Atlanta, Chicago, Miami or New York. The lowest fare from JFK airport (New York) to Madrid at the time of writing (shoulder season) was US$676, via Paris, with Air France. West-coast fares are usually about US$100 more than from the east coast.

Air Europa (☎ 888-238-7672 in the USA) occasionally has good deals between Madrid and New York, but at the time of writing no one airline leaving from Spain could claim to offer unbeatable value. Shoulder season flights from Madrid or Barcelona hover around the 73,000 ptas mark (taxes included). From Barcelona for example, the best offer was with Lufthansa via Frankfurt am Main. In the high season (15 June to 15 September) about the best you could hope for was 86,000 ptas return.

If you can't find a good deal, consider a cheap transatlantic hop to London and stalking the bucket shops there.

Canada

Iberia has direct flights to Madrid from Montreal three times weekly. Other major European airlines offer competitive fares to most Spanish destinations via other European capitals. Travel CUTS (☎ 800-777-0112) has offices in all major cities. Otherwise scan the travel agents' ads in the *Globe & Mail*, *Toronto Star* and *Vancouver Sun*.

For courier flights (see also the earlier USA section) originating in Canada, contact FB on Board Courier Services (☎ 604-278-1266 in Vancouver, ☎ 514-631-7925 in Toronto or Montreal). Airhitch (see the USA section) has stand-by fares to/from Montreal, Toronto and Vancouver.

Australia

STA Travel (Australia-wide fast fares on ☎ 1300 660 960) and Flight Centres International (Australia-wide ☎ 131 600) are major dealers in cheap airfares, although heavily discounted fares can often be found at your local travel agent. The Saturday editions of the Melbourne *Age* and the *Sydney*

Morning Herald have many advertisements offering cheap fares to Europe.

As a rule there are no direct flights from Australia to Spain. You will have to fly to Europe via Asia or America and change flights (and possibly airlines).

Discounted return airfares on mainstream airlines through reputable agents can be surprisingly cheap, with low-season fares around A$1800 return with Garuda Indonesia, which has cut its flights to Europe to three a week.

On some flights between Australia and cities like London, Paris and Frankfurt, a return ticket between your destination and a European capital is thrown in. Madrid and Barcelona can be choices in these deals.

For courier flights try Jupiter (☎ 02-9317 2230, 3/55 Kent Rd, Mascot, Sydney 2020).

The following are some addresses for agencies offering good-value fares:

Flight Centres International
   (☎ 03-9650 2899) Bourke Street Flight Centre, 19 Bourke St, Melbourne, Victoria 3000
   (☎ 02-9235 0166) Martin Place Flight Centre, shop 5, State Bank Centre, 52 Martin Place, Sydney, NSW 2000
   (☎ 08-9325 9222) City Flight Centre, shop 25, Cinema City Arcade, Perth, WA 6000
STA Travel
   (☎ 03-9349 2411) 222 Faraday St, Carlton, Victoria 3053
   (☎ 02-9212 1255) 855 George St, Sydney, NSW 2000,
   (☎ 08-9380 2302) 1st Floor, New Guild Building, University of Western Australia, Crawley, WA 6009

New Zealand

As with Australia, STA Travel and Flight Centres International are popular agents. The cheapest fares to Europe are generally routed through the USA, although in the case of Spain you may get a deal via Latin America. A RTW ticket may be cheaper than a normal return. Otherwise, you can fly from Auckland to pick up a connecting flight in Melbourne or Sydney. Return fares from NZ to London are around NZ$2700 out airlines such as Garuda or Malaysia Air-lines may offer cheaper deals.

Useful addresses include:

Campus Travel
(☎ 07-838 4242) Gate 1, Knighton Rd, Waikato University, Hamilton
Flight Centres International
(☎ 09-309 6171) Auckland Flight Centre, Shop 3A, National Bank Towers, 205-225 Queen St, Auckland
STA Travel & International Travellers Centre
(☎ 09-309 0458) 10 High St, Auckland

The UK & Ireland

London is one of the best centres in the world for discounted air tickets. Round the World (RTW) tickets are particularly good value and can be had for under UK£1000. Unfortunately, Spain rarely figures in such a ticket.

The weekend editions of national newspapers sometimes have info on cheap fares. In London try also the *Evening Standard*, the listings magazine *Time Out* and *TNT*, a free weekly magazine ostensibly for antipodeans. *TNT* comes out every Monday and is found in dispenser bins outside tube stations. Those with access to TV Teletext will find a host of travel agents advertising. As in North America, the Internet is another source.

Most UK travel agents are registered with the ABTA (Association of British Travel Agents). If you have paid for your flight with an ABTA-registered agent who then goes bust, the ABTA guarantees a refund or an alternative. Unregistered bucket shops are sometimes cheaper but always riskier.

The Globetrotters Club (BCM Roving, London WC1N 3XX) publishes a newsletter called *Globe* that can help in finding travelling companions.

One of the more reliable travel agencies is STA (☎ 0171-361 6161, from 22 April 2000 ☎ 020-7361 6161, for European flights). STA has branches in London, as well as on many university campuses and in Bristol, Cambridge, Leeds, Manchester (☎ 0161-834 0668) and Oxford. The main London branches are:

86 Old Brompton Rd, SW7 3LH
117 Euston Rd, NW1 2SX
38 Store St, WC1E 7BZ
Priory House, 6 Wrights Lane, W8 6TA
11 Goodge St, W1 1FE

Trailfinders (☎ 0171-937 5400, from 22 April 2000 ☎ 020-7937 5400, for European flights) is similar. Its short-haul booking centre is at 215 Kensington High St. Other offices are at 42-50 Earls Court Rd, London W8 6FT (☎ 0171-938 3366, from 22 April 2000 ☎ 020-7938 3366) and 194 Kensington High St, London W8 7RG (☎ 0171-938 3939, from 22 April 2000 ☎ 020-7938 3939). The latter offers an inoculation service and research library for customers. Trailfinders also has agencies in Birmingham, Bristol, Glasgow and Manchester.

Usit Campus (formerly known as Campus Travel) is in the same league, with the following branches in London:

(☎ 0171-730 3402, from 22 April 2000 ☎ 020-7730 3402, for European flights) 52 Grosvenor Gardens, SW1W 0AG
(☎ 0171-383 5337, from 22 April 2000 ☎ 020-7383 5337) University College of London, 25 Gordon St, WC1H 0AH
(☎ 0171-401 8666, from 22 April 2000 ☎ 020-7401 8666) South Bank University, Keyworth St, SE1 6NG

The two flag airlines linking the UK and Spain are British Airways (☎ 0345 222111, 156 Regent St, London W1R) and Spain's Iberia (☎ 0171-830 0011, from 22 April 2000 ☎ 020-7830 0011, in London, ☎ 0990 341341 rest of UK, 11 Haymarket, London SW1Y 4BP). Of the two, BA is more likely to have special deals. But BA's standard open-return ticket to Madrid costs UK£484 (UK£242 one way). You would have to be unlucky or feeling generous to pay that kind of money.

Think about where in Spain you want to end up. If you're not tied to a particular region, you may find more competitive fares to places like Málaga or Alicante than to Madrid or Barcelona.

If you are over 26 and have no student card, you will be looking at about UK£230 return with BA to Madrid for a month (fixed dates). Don't despair, the bucket shops can often get you across for less, usually on charter flights. And you can get occasional deals with airlines like BA. Try the BA Travel Shop (☎ 0171-434 4700, from 22 April 2000 ☎ 020-7434 4700), also at 156 Regent St.

Still with the main airlines, at the time of writing STA had low-season return flights with BA from Gatwick to Madrid for UK£168 (UK£128 for students and under-26s). The high-season version for people over 26 ranged up to UK£227. These were all open-return fares valid for a year.

The best option for Málaga is a charter flight, although this means a nonrefundable, fixed dates ticket. Direct Line Holidays (☎ 0181-239 8000, from 22 April 2000 ☎ 020-8239 8000) had return flights from UK£119, with a maximum 10-day stay.

Council Travel (☎ 0171-437 7767, from 22 April 2000 ☎ 020-7437 7767, 28a Poland St, London W1V 3DB), which specialises in student and under-26 fares, had low-season six-month returns for students (ISIC sufficient) to Madrid for UK£162.

Spanish Travel Services (STS; ☎ 0171-387 5337, from 22 April 2000 ☎ 020-7387 5337, 138 Eversholt St, London NW1 1BL) had charter flights from as low as UK£104 return (plus UK£14 taxes) to Madrid or Barcelona. It could do charters to Málaga from UK£109 return (including taxes). Another source of cheap flights is the Charter Flight Centre (☎ 0171-565 6755, from 22 April 2000 ☎ 020-7565 6755, 15 Gillingham St, London SW1 V1HN). Check the arrival and departure times on all these flights, as they can be inconvenient. If you miss a charter flight, you lose your money.

EasyJet (☎ 0870-6 000 000) has tickets from London's Luton airport to Barcelona and Palma de Mallorca for as little as UK£49 each way, plus UK£10 tax. It is an odd system in which prices rise as tickets are sold – the earlier you book a particular flight, the better your chances of a cheap flight. The highest fare is UK£99 each way (at which point you should look elsewhere).

You can book tickets on its Web site at www.easyjet.com. In Spain contact the company on ☎ 902-29 99 92.

Several times a year, usually around Easter and in autumn, charter companies put on four and five-day long-weekend fares to Madrid, Málaga and other destinations for silly prices: UK£49 return is not unheard of. The most fruitful destination/exit point is Málaga. If you are flying out of Málaga in winter, return flights can come in at less than 20,000 ptas. One-way bargains of 6500 ptas are possible.

In southern Spain, watch the local English-language rags for cheap flights. Otherwise, check around the budget travel agents.

Open jaws tickets are a possibility. STS had one with Debonair from Luton into Barcelona and out of Madrid, or the other way around, for UK£129 in the low season. Debonair is on ☎ 902-14 62 00 in Spain and ☎ 0541-50 03 00 in the UK.

You needn't fly from London, as many good deals are easily available from other centres in the UK.

If you're coming from Ireland, compare what is available direct and from London; getting to London first may save you money.

Fly-Drive Packages including flights and prebooked hire cars can be attractive, especially in the high season, when local car hire prices will always exceed (often double) those of prebooked cars. Travel agents and tour operators can make arrangements.

Passes Occasionally airlines run promotions offering passes for cheap airfares across Europe. At the time of writing, Lufthansa offered flight coupons in a system called YES. You buy up to 10 coupons, each worth UK£59 and valid for a one-way flight within 20 European countries, including Spain. For UK£177 you could fly London-Madrid-Berlin-London. The offer is for under-26s or students under 31 and coupons are valid for six months. Alitalia had a similar deal called Europa Pass.

Continental Europe

Air travel between Spain and other places in continental Europe is worth considering if you are pushed for time. Short hops can be expensive, but for longer journeys you can often find airfares that beat overland alternatives on cost.

France In Paris, Voyages et Découvertes (☎ 01 42 61 00 01), 21 rue Cambon, is a good place to start hunting down the best airfares, although given the city's proximity to Spain it often makes little financial sense. Sometimes good deals float around. It is possible to find return flights for around 1000FF to Madrid and as little as 900FF to Barcelona (plus airport taxes of around 200FF); a more likely fare to Barcelona is 1450FF. There are no charters to either city.

From Spain the choices are generally less attractive – at the time of writing a standard return fare from Madrid to Paris was 44,000 ptas (31,000 ptas students).

Germany Munich is a haven of bucket shops and more mainstream budget travel outlets. Council Travel (☎ 089-395 02 2), Adalbertstrasse 32, near the university, is one of the best. STA Travel (☎ 089-399 09 6), Königstrasse 49, is also good.

In Berlin, Kilroy Travel-ARTU Reisen (☎ 030-3 10 00 40) at Hardenbergstrasse 9, near Berlin Zoo, is good and has five branches around the city. In Frankfurt am Main, you could try STA Travel (☎ 069-70 30 35), Bockenheimer Landstrasse 133.

Italy The best place to look for cheap fares is CTS (Centro Turístico Studentesco), with branches countrywide. In Rome it is at Via Genova 16 (☎ 06-4 67 91).

Netherlands Amsterdam is a popular departure point. The student travel agency NBBS Reiswinkels (☎ 020-624 09 89), Rokin 38, offers reliable and reasonably low fares. Compare its prices with the bucket shops along Rokin before deciding. NBBS has branches throughout the city and in Brussels, Belgium.

Portugal Only those in a tearing hurry will consider flying between Madrid and Lisbon. Iberia and TAP do it for around 34,000 ptas return.

Canary Islands

Las Islas Canarias are so far away that mainlanders can't resist jokes about the islanders being Africans. Few visitors to mainland Spain combine their trip with another to the Canary Islands. There is certainly no financial incentive to do so, as charter flights to the Canaries from other European capitals often cost less than from mainland Spain.

From Madrid and other centres, Iberia, Spanair, Air Europa and charters fly to Santa Cruz de Tenerife, Las Palmas de Gran Canaria and, less frequently, Lanzarote and Fuerteventura. A return charter fare can be as low as 18,900 ptas. A more standard fare would be 27,900 ptas.

Scheduled fares tend to be higher. A one-year open-return ticket with Air Europa to Tenerife would cost 51,700 ptas from Madrid and 64,500 ptas from Barcelona.

Africa

There is little in the way of cheap flights to North Africa. Among the cheaper tickets available from Madrid at the time of writing was one for about 45,000 ptas return to Tangier with a maximum stay of one month. To Marrakesh was 62,000 ptas. Occasionally you stumble across better deals.

The options *from* Morocco are more limited still. One way to Madrid from Casablanca, regardless of the airline, comes to Dr 3300 (around 50,000 ptas). Iberia has four flights weekly from Madrid to Casablanca and two to Tangier.

Libya remains under a UN air embargo and Algeria is a no-go area.

Asia

Although most Asian countries are now offering fairly competitive fare deals, Bangkok, Hong Kong and Singapore are still the best places to shop around for discount tickets. From Hong Kong, a one-way fare to Europe can cost about US$660, but shop around. Bucket shops in Bangkok can get you a one-way fare for about US$460.

STA has branches in Bangkok, Hong Kong, Kuala Lumpur, Singapore and Tokyo.

LAND

If you are travelling by bus, train or car to Spain, check whether you require visas to the countries you intend to pass through. Although the following information on bus and rail passes concentrates on availability in the UK, most passes can be acquired throughout Europe.

Bus Passes

Eurolines offers a Eurolines Pass. One valid for 30/60 days costs UK£199/249 (UK£159/199 for under-26s and senior citizens) and allows unlimited travel between 21 European cities. The only Spanish cities are Barcelona and Madrid. Fares increase between mid-June and mid-September to UK£229/279 (UK£199/249) respectively. The pass is available at Eurolines offices across Europe.

Busabout, a UK-based alternative to Eurolines, is aimed at younger travellers. You buy a pass valid for up to four months travel as often as you like between cities on any one of three set routes. Or you can combine the routes, giving you a total of 36 cities across 10 countries in continental Europe (with an optional link trip between London and Paris). Barcelona, Granada, La Línea (for Gibraltar), Madrid, Salamanca, San Sebastián, Sevilla and Toledo are the Spanish stops in the southern zone route, which also includes four Portuguese cities, Paris and other French destinations. The one-zone pass costs from UK£129 (one month) to UK£145 (four months). These passes are discounted for those with international student and teacher cards – UK£119 (one month) to UK£135 (four months). An adult three-zone pass costs UK£325. In winter the number of destinations drops (at the time of writing only Barcelona, Madrid and San Sebastián were on the winter program). The London link costs an extra UK£30 (UK£15 if you get a two-zone pass; free if you get an all-zone pass).

You can buy Busabout tickets direct from the company (☎ 0181-784 2816, from 22 April 2000 ☎ 020-8784 2816) or from suppliers such as Usit Campus and STA Travel; its Web site is at www.busabout. com. The Eurobus company, which offered a similar service, went out of business in 1998.

Train Passes

Inter-Rail If you have been resident in the UK (or any other European country in the Inter-Rail network) for at least six months and plan to travel far and wide, it is worth thinking about an Inter-Rail pass. The Inter-Rail map of Europe is divided into zones; one zone consists of Spain, Portugal and Morocco. The ticket is designed for under-26s. Twenty-two days unlimited 2nd-class travel in one zone costs UK£159. Better value is the one-month ticket for two zones for UK£209 (which would get you across France too). If you think you can stand careering around virtually all of Europe, you could go for the three-zone and all-in passes for UK£229/259 (one month) respectively. The corresponding over-26 rates for all these options are: UK£229/279/309/349.

Inter-Railers must pay part of the fare on certain high-speed trains like Spain's Talgos and full fare on the AVE. Reservations also cost you 500 ptas.

Card-holders get discounts on travel in the country of residence where they purchase the ticket, as well as on a variety of other services such as ferry travel. In Britain you can buy Inter-Rail cards at the International Rail Centre (☎ 0990 848848) at London's Victoria station, and several other main-line stations.

If you only want to travel by rail inside Spain and you are under 26, consider getting a Euro<26 or ISIC card and then purchasing an ExploreRail pass once in Spain (see the Getting Around chapter for more details).

Eurail Eurail passes are the Inter-Rail equivalent for non-European residents. You are not entitled to one if your passport shows you have been in Europe continuously for six months or more. For some odd reason, over-26s pay for a 1st-class pass and under-26s get a 2nd-class pass (Eurail Youthpass). If you are only going to be travelling in Spain, you are unlikely to cover the cost of the pass. For it to be worth considering, you need to be planning a *lot* of long-distance travel in Europe: even Eurail says you need to do at least 2400km before you start to get value for money.

The standard Consecutive passes are expensive. You can get one valid for 15 days or one, two or three months. The 15-day pass costs UK£265 or UK£379 for over-26s.

There is a growing range of permutations of the Eurail pass, largely because the original idea is so costly. Flexipasses, with which the traveller is entitled to 10 or 15 days rail travel over a two-month period, cost, respectively, UK£312/447 and UK£412/589 for under/over-26s. If you are travelling in a group of two to five people and are 26 or older, Eurail Saver Pass is a slightly cheaper version of the same thing. The cost per person is UK£323. The Eurail Saver Flexipass costs UK£380/500 per person for 10/15 days.

Eurail Europass gives five, 10 or 15 days unlimited travel within a two-month period in Spain, France, Germany, Italy and Switzerland. The under-26 version costs UK£136/229/324 respectively. For older folks it's UK£217/358/497.

People generally purchase Eurail passes in their country of origin, but you can get them at London's International Rail Centre.

Freedom Pass You can also get Freedom passes (known as Euro-Domino outside the UK) for any one of 25 European countries, valid for three, five or 10 days travel over a month. For Spain, a 1st-class, 10-day pass costs UK£299. Second class is UK£249 and a youth version (for under-26s) is UK£199. This is a more attractive option than Eurail if you intend to spend a decent amount of time exploring Spain rather than rocketing all over the Continent. But again, you would need to be on trains a good amount

of the time to get full value from the pass. On balance, you are better off with an Inter-Rail card if you can get one.

For information on passes inside Spain, turn to the Getting Around chapter.

The UK

Bus If you plan to head straight into Spain from the UK, bus is the cheapest option. Eurolines (☎ 0990 143219, 52 Grosvenor Gardens, Victoria, London SW1), a few blocks away from the bus terminal itself, runs buses to Barcelona on Saturday, Monday (leaving at 11 am; connection to Alicante) and Thursday (9.30 pm). The trip takes 23 to 25 hours. The one-way and return fares are, respectively, UK£77 and UK£119 (UK£71 and UK£109 for under-26s and senior citizens). A bus goes to Madrid via San Sebastián on Friday at 10 pm, arriving 27 hours later. A second, Monday service runs from May to October and up to four extra services operate in summer, three via Paris (where you must endure an eight-hour layover). One-way and return fares are UK£77 and UK£138 (UK£69 and UK£125 for under-26s and seniors). Buses run to farther destinations, including the Costa del Sol, Santander, Santiago de Compostela and Sevilla. The single biggest disadvantage of the bus is that you can't get off along the way. Fares rise in the peak summer season.

You can also take a National Express bus (☎ 0990 808080) from the same terminal to connect with the Brittany Ferries service to Santander. The standard adult return fare is UK£130 or UK£167 in the high season. If you do want to take this route from London, you may as well take the bus-ferry ticket, as it saves you a couple of pounds. The bus runs at least once a week from April to November.

Under-26s pay 10% less on most bus services, as do seniors over 60 (over 50 on some National Express channel crossing services). Children up to age 12 generally pay half-price.

Train Your choices from London are limited by the options in Paris, where you must change trains. See under France later for more details.

If you optimise your choice of departure from London to keep waiting times for connections to a minimum, the trip by train to either Barcelona or Madrid is comparable with the bus for journey times. Obviously there are plenty of possibilities for the Paris leg via ferry and hovercraft (or with Eurostar, the Channel Tunnel train).

Trains run from Charing Cross or Victoria station to Paris (via ferry or hovercraft from Dover to Calais or Folkestone to Boulogne); Eurostar leaves from Waterloo. You arrive at the Gare du Nord, and must get to the Gare d'Austerlitz (take the RER B to St Michel and change there for the RER C to Austerlitz), Gare Montparnasse (Metro 4) or Gare de Lyon (RER B to Châtelet and then RER A for Gare de Lyon). See also under France later.

The one-way/return fares to Barcelona and Madrid are UK£97/153 and UK£112/185 (more if you take the Eurostar); tickets are valid for two months. Under-26s can get Wasteels or BIJ (Billet International de Jeunesse) tickets for UK£81/139 and UK£92/160 respectively.

There are discounts for children and seniors over 60 can get a Rail Europe Senior Railcard (valid only for trips that cross at least one border). UK citizens pay UK£5 for the card but must already have a British Rail card (UK£16). The pass entitles you to roughly 30% off standard fares.

For information, call European Rail (☎ 0171-387 0444) or, for trips involving the Eurostar leg to Paris, the International Rail Centre (☎ 0990 848848).

Car & Motorcycle Refer to the Sea section later in this chapter for details of sending your car by ferry direct to Spain or France from the UK. Another option is Eurotunnel, the Channel Tunnel car train connecting Folkestone with Calais. It runs around the clock, with up to four crossings (35 minutes) an hour in high season. You pay for the vehicle only and fares vary according to the time of day and season.

Economy return tickets cost from UK£130 to UK£220 or UK£65 to UK£100 for motorcycles. You can book in advance (☎ 0990 353535), but the service is designed to let you just roll up.

Paperwork & Preparations Proof of ownership of a private vehicle should always be carried (Vehicle Registration Document for UK-registered cars) when driving through Europe. All EU member states' driving licences (pink or pink and green) are recognised (although you are supposed to get a Spanish licence if you stay for more than a year – many foreign residents ignore this requirement). The old-style UK green licence is not accepted.

Other foreign licences are supposed to be accompanied by an International Driving Permit (although in practice, for renting cars or dealing with traffic police, your national licence will suffice). The International Driving Permit is available from automobile clubs in your country and is valid for 12 months.

Third-party motor insurance is a minimum requirement and it is compulsory to have a Green Card, an internationally recognised proof of insurance, which can be obtained from your insurer. Also ask your insurer for a European accident statement form, which can simplify matters in the event of an accident. Never sign statements you can't read or understand: insist on a translation and sign that only if it's acceptable.

A European breakdown assistance policy such as the AA Five Star Service or RAC Eurocover Motoring Assistance is a good investment. In Spain, get help from the Real Automóvil Club de España (RACE; see the Getting Around chapter).

Every vehicle travelling across an international border should display a nationality plate of its country of registration. A warning triangle (to be used in the event of a breakdown) is compulsory. Recommended accessories are a first-aid kit, a spare bulb kit and a fire extinguisher. If the car is from the UK or Ireland, remember to have the headlights adjusted for driving in continental Europe.

In the UK, get more information from the RAC (☎ 0990 722722) or the AA (☎ 0990 500600).

Rental Many people opt to get to Spain by other means, then rent a car once they arrive. Prebooking a car through a multinational agency – such as Hertz, Avis, Budget Car or Europe's largest rental agency, Europcar – before leaving home will enable you to find the best deals. Prebooked and prepaid rates are generally cheaper and it may be worth your while looking into fly-drive combinations and other programs. You simply pick up the vehicle on arrival and return it to a nominated point at the end of the rental period. Ask your travel agent for information or contact one of the major rental agencies.

Another possibility if you don't know when you want to rent is to call back home from Spain and reserve through an agent there. This way you get the benefits of booking from home (try to get hold of toll-free numbers for car-rental companies in your country).

No matter where you rent, make sure you understand what is included in the price (unlimited kilometres, tax, insurance, collision damage waiver etc) and what your liabilities are. The minimum rental age in Spain is 21 years. A credit card is usually required.

For more details of rental rates and options within Spain, see Car & Motorcycle in the Getting Around chapter.

Purchase Only residents may legally purchase vehicles in Spain (see Car & Motorcycle in the Getting Around chapter).

Otherwise, the UK is probably the best place to buy a vehicle for travelling in Europe, as second-hand prices are good. But bear in mind that you will be getting a left-hand drive car (ie steering wheel on the right). If you want a right-hand drive car and can afford to buy a new one, prices are relatively low in Belgium, the Netherlands and Luxembourg.

Camper Van A popular way of touring Europe is for three or four people to band together and buy a camper van to drive around. London is the usual embarkation point. Look at the ads in London's free *TNT* magazine. Private vendors gather daily at the Van Market on Market Rd, London N7 (near Caledonian Road tube station). Some second-hand dealers offer a 'buy-back' scheme for when you return from Europe but, if you have the time, buying and re-selling privately is more advantageous.

Motorcycle Spain, like the rest of Europe, is ideal for motorcycle touring, with every possible kind of terrain from mountain back roads to coastal highways. Motorcycles are easier to squeeze around city traffic and park and you will never need to book ahead to get a bike onto a ferry.

Anyone considering joining a motorcycle tour from the UK might want to join the International Motorcyclists Tour Club (UK£19 per annum plus UK£3 joining fee). The club has 400 members and, in addition to holidays on the Continent, runs social weekends. The present secretary, James Clegg, can be contacted on ☎ 01484-66 48 68.

France

Bus Enatcar and ALSA, among the bus companies representing Eurolines in Spain, have buses between various Spanish cities (including Barcelona, Madrid, Málaga, Oviedo and Santiago de Compostela) and Paris, with other destinations en route.

Eurolines has offices in several French cities; in Paris offices are at the bus station (☎ 01 49 72 51 51), 28 Ave du Générale de Gaulle, and at rue St Jacques 55, off Blvd St Germain, on the left bank. The one-way fare from Madrid is 11,300 ptas.

Local bus services cross the Franco-Spanish frontier at several locations. Details appear in the appropriate regional and city chapters.

Train About the only truly direct trains to Madrid and Barcelona are the *trenhotels*, expensive sleeping-car trains. The Barcelona service leaves at 8.47 pm daily and arrives between 9.13 and 9.30 am (stopping at Dijon, Figueres, Girona and Barcelona França). The standard one-way fare is 780FF. The Madrid equivalent (stopping at Poitiers, Vitoria, Burgos and Valladolid) leaves at 7.47 pm and arrives at Madrid Chamartín at 8.58 am. The fare is 809FF one way.

Otherwise, the cheapest and most convenient option to Barcelona is the 10.02 pm from Paris Austerlitz, changing at Latour-de-Carol and arriving at Barcelona Sants at 11.27 am. A reclining seat costs 485FF one way or 555FF in a 2nd-class couchette. There is an alternative train with a change at Portbou (on the coast).

For Madrid, the most convenient bet if you don't want to the take the sleeper train is the 10.58 pm from Paris Austerlitz via Irún. The 2nd-class couchette costs 781FF one way. First-class couchettes cost considerably more – the difference is four people to a compartment rather than six. Under-26s get a 25% reduction. Note also that fares rise in July and August.

There are several other possibilities. Two or three TGV trains leave Paris Montparnasse for Irún, where you change to a normal train for the onward trip to Madrid. Up to three TGVs also put you on the road to Barcelona (leaving from Paris' Gare de Lyon), with a change of train at Montpellier or Narbonne. Prices and timetables vary, so check the latest details.

Leaving Spain, the frequency of trains is similar. The trenhotel departs from Barcelona França at 8.15 pm and arrives 12 hours later at Paris. From Madrid, the trenhotel leaves at 7 pm and arrives at 8.29 am. The cheapest option on this train is in a sleeper cabin of four. The ticket from Madrid to Paris costs 17,900 ptas per person; the cheapest fare for the Barcelona trip is 16,500 ptas. Catching one of the other trains and sitting all the way, as opposed to taking a sleeper, can save you 2000 ptas from Madrid and as much as 4000 ptas from Barcelona.

A direct service also connects Montpellier with Barcelona (252FF in 2nd class) and Valencia (366FF). A couple of other slower services (with a change of train at Portbou) also make this run.

Car & Motorcycle See the earlier UK section for general information on taking your vehicle across Europe. The main crossings from France into Spain are the highways to Barcelona and San Sebastián at either end of the Pyrenees.

Portugal

Bus From Madrid three Eurolines buses a week go to Lisbon (nine hours; around 4680 ptas one way) via Salamanca, departing from Estación Sur de Autobuses at 11 pm and arriving at Avenida de Casal Ribeiro at 7 am. AutoRes also has a daily bus (5765 ptas) to Lisbon from its station on Calle de Fernández Shaw in Madrid. A weekly service connects Lisbon with Barcelona.

Other services to the Portuguese capital run from Málaga (via Sevilla and Cádiz), Benidorm (via Alicante and Badajoz) and La Coruña (via Santiago de Compostela and Tuy). There are also services to Oporto from Madrid and to the Algarve from Sevilla. Local buses cross the border from towns like Huelva (Andalucía), Badajoz (Extremadura) and Verín (Galicia).

Train A daily train makes its way from San Sebastián to Lisbon via Madrid, Salamanca and Oporto. From Madrid it takes 11 hours and costs 6900 ptas (one way in 2nd class). The train leaves Chamartín station at 10.35 pm. You can also pick up local trains from Vigo and Tuy to Oporto (see the Galicia chapter).

Car & Motorcycle Main roads run into central Portugal from Salamanca, Badajoz and Cáceres, while the highway from Sevilla via Huelva takes you to the Algarve. In the north there are plenty of minor approach roads from Galicia, but the main highway runs via Tuy across the Río Miño and down the Portuguese coast.

Andorra

Bus Regular buses connect Andorra with Barcelona and other destinations in Spain, including Madrid, and France. Turn to the Andorra chapter for details. Travellers usually needing visas for Spain might risk this route if they are travelling without a visa, as passport checks are not always made – but don't bank on it.

Other European Destinations

Bus Eurolines and other companies operate buses from Madrid, Barcelona and other major cities across France and into Germany (Frankfurt am Main ☎ 069-79 03 0, Hamburg, Munich and Düsseldorf), the Benelux countries, Italy (Madrid to Rome costs 16,875 ptas), Switzerland and on to Eastern European destinations like Prague (19,875 ptas from Madrid).

Train Direct trains link Barcelona with Geneva, Zürich, Turin and Milan at least three times a week. Reaching other destinations in Europe beyond these will require a change in these cities or in Paris.

Morocco

An ambitious plan to unite Spain and Morocco by tunnel could become reality early in the 21st century. In the meantime, you'll have to adopt a more conventional approach. Buses from several Spanish cities converge on Algeciras to make the ferry crossing to Tangier and head into Morocco. The trip to Tangier from Madrid can cost as little as 7900 ptas. See under Sea for more details on Spain-Morocco ferries.

SEA
The UK

Portsmouth-Bilbao Throughout the year P&O European Ferries (in Britain ☎ 0990 980980) operates a ferry from Portsmouth to Bilbao. As a rule there are two sailings a week and the voyage time is about 35 hours from England and 30 hours the other way. There are only two boats in January. For more details, turn to the Bilbao Getting

There & Away entry in the País Vasco, Navarra & La Rioja chapter.

Plymouth/Portsmouth-Santander

Brittany Ferries (in Britain ☎ 0990 360360) at Milbay Docks in Plymouth, operates a twice-weekly car-ferry service to Santander (24 hours travel time) from mid-March to mid-November. In the remaining months, the service drops to once a week and departs from Poole or Portsmouth (30 to 33 hours). For more details, see the Santander Getting There & Away section in the Cantabria & Asturias chapter.

Via France You can transport your car by ferry to France. Apex fares on Sally's (☎ 0990 595522) fast ferry for a car and two passengers in high season are:

from	to	return
Folkestone	Boulogne	UK£78
Dover	Calais	UK£97
	Ostende, Belgium	UK£109

For the Eurotunnel car-train service through the Channel Tunnel, see under The UK in the Land section earlier.

With your foot flat on the floor through France, you may save a little time over the direct Spain ferries. Whether or not it is cheaper depends on the French tollways you take, how much juice your vehicle burns and mechanical problems en route.

Italy

After a 15-year absence, the so-called *canguro* shipping run between Barcelona and Genova was relaunched in September 1998. See the Barcelona chapter for details.

Canary Islands

A car ferry leaves from Cádiz for Santa Cruz de Tenerife and Las Palmas de Gran Canaria every Saturday at 5 pm. It's a long and bumpy ride, arriving at Santa Cruz on Monday at 8 am and 4 pm in Las Palmas. The boat back to Spain leaves Santa Cruz at 8 am on Wednesday, calling in at Las

Palmas (noon) and Arrecife (Lanzarote; 9 pm) on the way. Unless you especially like ocean voyages or have to transport a car, you are better off flying.

One-way fares per person range from 29,250 ptas to 57,110 ptas, depending on the type of cabin.

Morocco

Trasmediterránea (☎ 902-45 46 45), Isleña de Navegación SA (Isnasa; ☎ 956 65 20 00) and a couple of Moroccan companies operate at least 14 daily roll-on, roll-off car ferries and hydrofoils between Algeciras and Tangier. The ferry takes about two hours and the hydrofoil manages it in an hour. Two daily ferries cross from Tarifa to Tangier.

At least 20 ferries and hydrofoils cross from Algeciras to the Spanish enclave of Ceuta, from where you can easily travel overland into Morocco. Travel times are 1½ hours and 40 minutes, respectively.

Six days a week, and three times daily from mid-June to the end of August, a Trasmediterránea ferry leaves Almería for Melilla, Spain's enclave in north-eastern Morocco. The trip takes up to eight hours. A similar service runs to Melilla from Málaga. Ferri Maroc (☎ 950 27 48 00) runs a slightly more expensive service, with similar frequency, from Almería to Nador, the Moroccan town neighbouring Melilla.

You could also go to Morocco via Gibraltar. Three ferries leave for Tangier each week.

For more details and fares see the Getting There & Away entries for Algeciras, Almería, Gibraltar, Málaga and Tarifa.

Warning Anyone driving from Morocco to Spain should be prepared for rigorous searches both in the enclaves (Ceuta and Melilla) and on disembarking on the mainland.

Algeria

Romeu y Compañía (☎ 96 514 15 09) runs car and passenger ferries from Alicante to Oran in Algeria. Return fares for passengers cost 27,700 ptas. A small car is 69,900 ptas

to transport. In summer ferries run almost daily, but out of season the frequency drops to one or two a week. Algeria is not an advisable destination while decapitation continues to be a common form of greeting from the country's more violent minority.

ORGANISED TOURS

A lot of companies offer tours to Spain, generally concentrating on a couple of regions for a week or two. Spanish tourist offices can provide a list of tour operators. What follows is a brief guide only to the kinds of options available.

The UK

Short Breaks & Holidays Brittany Ferries (see the earlier Sea section) is one of several companies that offer brief trips, lasting from two to seven days, in northern Spain. Such holidays can cost from UK£150 for two nights to UK£350 for five nights, which includes the ferry crossing and good accommodation.

Cresta Holidays (☎ 0161-927 7000, Tabley Court, Victoria St, Altrincham, Cheshire WA14 1EZ) offers a range of city tours, fly-drive trips and other holidays to Spain. Another Spain specialist is The Individual Travellers Spain (☎ 01798-869485, Manor Court Yard, Bignor, Pulborough RH20 1QD).

Walking Holidays Explore Worldwide (☎ 01252-34 41 61, 1 Frederick St, Aldershot, Hants GU11 1LQ) can take you trekking in the Picos de Europa in northern Spain or the Sierra Nevada near Granada, or trekking and sightseeing in Andalucía. Headwater (☎ 01606-48699, 146 London Rd, Northwich, Cheshire CW9 5HH) organises week-long walking holidays.

Cycling Holidays Bolero International Holidays does cycling holidays to the Costa Brava from UK£181 to UK£284. The holidays are designed to allow experienced cyclists to travel with less-enthusiastic pedallers. The company can be contacted through European Bike Express (☎ 01642-25 14 40, 31 Baker St, Middlesbrough,

Cleveland TS1 2LF). Discover Adventure (☎ 01722-74 11 23, 5 Netherhampton Cottage, Netherhampton Rd, Netherhampton, Salisbury SP2 8PX) does one-week, mountain-bike tours in Andalucía for UK£575 per person.

Under-35s Young party animals could opt for a tour from London to Pamplona (Navarra) in July for the running of the bulls. These trips, usually for a week and taking in a few other towns along the way, are popular. Top Deck Travel (☎ 0171-370 4555, from 22 April 2000 ☎ 020-7370 4555, 131-135 Earls Court Rd, London SW5 9RH) does such tours. Prices range from UK£169 to UK£209, depending on whether you camp or stay in a hotel.

Contiki Travel (☎ 0171-637 0802, from 22 April 2000 ☎ 020-7637 0802, c/o Royal National Hotel, Bedford Way, London WC1H 0DG) also does European tours that take in Spain.

Coach Tours Plenty of tour operators cater for a less boisterous clientele. Mundi Color Travel (☎ 0171-828 6021, from 22 April 2000 ☎ 020-7828 6021, 276 Vauxhall Bridge Rd, London SW1V 1BE) has two one-week coach tours: one of Andalucía and the other taking in Madrid and parts of Castilla as well. The all-in price hovers around UK£800, including flights, tour, accommodation and half-board, but rises in the high season.

Cruises If all you really want to do is cruise by the country, a couple of companies run trips of about two weeks. Fares start at about UK£1000.

One company is Fred. Olsen Cruise Lines (☎ 01473-29 22 22, Fred. Olsen House, White House Rd, Ipswich, Suffolk IP1 5LL). More expensive is the Holland America Line (☎ 0171-613 3300, from 22 April 2000 ☎ 020-7613 3300, 77-79 Great Eastern St, London EC2A 3HU).

The USA

A plethora of operators run tours from the USA. Spanish Heritage Tours (☎ 800-221-2250, 47 Queens Blvd, Forest Hills, NY 11375) is one of 22 agencies that comprise the Spain Tour Operators Association (STOA), which ensures at least a reasonable degree of reliability. But this is not to say that other operators are not perfectly efficient as well.

Escapade Vacations (☎ 800-942-2114, 630 Third Ave, New York, NY 10017) offers a range of tours, from coach trips staying in paradores, to more flexible 'plan-it-yourself' packages.

Alta Tours (☎ 800-338-4191, 870 Market St, suite 784, San Francisco CA 94102) organises anything from posh corporate trips to customised itineraries for student groups. Saranjan Tours (☎ 800-858-9594, 12865 NE 85th Street, #102, Kirkland WA 98033) sends people on trips to coincide with Spain's more popular fiestas.

Australia

You can organise tours of Spain through the following operators:

Ibertours Travel
    (☎ 03-9670 8388) 1st floor, 84 William St, Melbourne 3000, Victoria
Spanish Tourism Promotions
    (☎ 03-9650 7377) level 1, 178 Collins St, Melbourne 3000, Victoria
Ya'lla Tours
    (☎ 03-9510 2844) level 2, 608 St Kilda Rd, Melbourne, 3004, Victoria
    (☎ 02-9299 5210) level 5, 89 York St, Sydney 2000, NSW

WARNING

The information in this chapter is vulnerable to change: prices for international travel are volatile, routes are introduced and cancelled, schedules change, special deals come and go and visa requirements are amended. Before you part with your cash, you should get as much information as you can. This chapter is no substitute for your own research.

Getting Around

AIR

Several airlines link the major cities of Spain, but as a rule air travel within Spain is costly. The most frequent connections are between Madrid and Barcelona. Generally you are better off with buses and trains. Flights to farther-flung corners like the Islas Baleares are more useful.

Main airports are at Barcelona, Madrid, Málaga, Palma de Mallorca (Islas Baleares) and Santiago de Compostela.

Iberia, which has absorbed the once separate airlines Aviaco, Air Nostrum and Binter Mediterráneo (the latter still sports its own livery), has an extensive network covering all Spain. Call ☎ 902-40 05 00 for information. For info on Canary Islands flights, see the Getting There & Away chapter.

These airlines operate four basic types of ticket, listed in order from cheapest to dearest (the cheaper ones are not available on all routes):

Estrella
The cheapest – buy ticket at least two days ahead; return between four and 14 days later (return tickets only)
Supermini
Buy ticket at least four days ahead; spend one Saturday night in destination (return tickets only)
Reducida
Buy ticket at least three days ahead; spend at least one night in destination (return tickets only)
Flexible
No restrictions, refundable (one-way or return)

A standard one-way fare from Madrid to Barcelona ranges from 11,700 to 15,550 ptas. Be sure to ask about discounts and special rates. You get 25% off flights leaving after 11 pm (admittedly there are few of these). People under 22 or over 63 get 25% off *return* flights, another 20% off night flights and 15% off special deal minifares. The latter discount can shave as much as 50% off weekend return tickets.

Competing with Iberia and its subsidiaries are Spanair (☎ 902-13 14 15) and Air Europa (☎ 902-24 00 42). They used to be considerably cheaper, but the gap has closed in recent years.

Air Europa is the bigger of the two, with regular flights connecting Madrid, Barcelona and the Canary Islands, plus flights to internal destinations (such as Alicante, Asturias, Bilbao, Málaga, Palma de Mallorca, Salamanca, Sevilla, Valladolid, Vitoria and Zaragoza).

Six Air Europa flights connect Madrid with Barcelona daily (four on weekends). The one-way economy *(turista)* fare is 12,600 ptas. The return fare ranges from 25,100 ptas to 13,700 ptas (the latter for minimum stay of four days and maximum of 14 days).

The fare from the capital to Palma de Mallorca is 28,300 ptas return, to Santiago de Compostela is 28,000 ptas and to Málaga is 27,600 ptas. These fares can also drop drastically if you comply with certain restrictions.

The small, Melilla-based Pauknair links Melilla and Málaga to Almería, Barcelona, Madrid, Palma de Mallorca, Santander and Santiago de Compostela.

As a rule, one-way fares are more (sometimes much more) than half the tourist-class return fare. Tickets can easily be booked with nationwide travel agents such as Halcón Viajes. For youth fares, inquire at offices of TIVE (see Useful Organisations in the Facts for the Visitor chapter) in major cities around Spain.

BUS

A plethora of companies provide bus links, from local routes between villages to fast intercity connections. It is often cheaper to travel by bus than by train, particularly on long-haul runs.

Local services can get you just about anywhere, but most buses connecting villages and provincial towns are not geared to tourist needs. Even frequent weekday services can drop off to a trickle on weekends. Often just one bus daily runs between smaller places during the week and none operate on Sunday. It is usually unnecessary to make reservations; just arrive early enough to claim a seat.

On many regular runs (say, from Madrid to Toledo) the ticket you buy is for the next bus due to leave and *cannot* be used on a later bus. Advance purchase in such cases is generally not possible.

For longer trips (such as Madrid-Sevilla, or to the *costas*), and certainly in peak season, buy your ticket in advance. The main bus stations, like the Estación Sur de Autobuses in Madrid, can be a stifling sea of queues during major holidays.

In most larger towns and cities, buses leave from a single bus station *(estación de autobuses)*.

In smaller places, buses tend to operate from a set street or plaza, often unmarked. Locals will know where to go. Usually a specific bar sells tickets and has timetable information.

People under 26 should ask about discounts on long-distance trips. Occasionally a return ticket is cheaper than two singles.

Some sample one-way fares between cities include:

from	to	fare (ptas)
Madrid	Alicante	3270
	Barcelona	2940
	Córdoba	1550
	Granada	1945
	Málaga	2620
	Oviedo	3655
	San Sebastián	3685
	Santiago de Compostela	5500
	Sevilla	2730
Barcelona	Zaragoza	1640
	Sevilla	8820
Sevilla	Granada	2700

TRAIN

Generally, the mainline trains with the national rail network, RENFE (Red Nacional de los Ferrocarriles Españoles), are reliable if not always superfast.

It's always worth checking the relative merits of the bus. Trains tend to be more agreeable for long trips, but more expensive. Express buses between major cities are often faster, with more frequent departures, than the train. For information (in Spanish), call the local RENFE office, or have a look at www.renfe.es on the Internet.

Types of Train
A host of different train types coasts the narrow-gauge lines of the Spanish network. The difference is usually in the speed of the journey, the number of stops made and, as a consequence, the price. A saving of a couple of hours on a faster train can mean a big hike in the fare.

For short hops, bigger cities have a local network known as *cercanías*. From Madrid, for instance, cercanías trains cover the entire Comunidad de Madrid region and cities beyond like Toledo and Segovia.

Most long-distance *(largo recorrido)* trains have 1st and 2nd class. The cheapest and slowest of these are the *regionales*, generally all-stops jobs between provinces within one region (although a few travel between regions).

Diurnos and *estrellas* are the standard long-distance inter-regional trains. The latter is the night-time version of the former.

Faster, more comfortable and expensive are the Talgos (Tren Articulado Ligero Goicoechea Oriol). They make only major stops and have such extras as TVs in the carriages. The Talgo Pendular is a sleeker, faster version of the same thing that picks up speed by leaning into curves.

Some Talgos and other modern trains are used for limited-stop trips between major cities. These services are known as InterCity (and when they're really good as InterCity Plus!).

A classier derivative is the Talgo 200, a Talgo Pendular using the standard-guage, high-speed Tren de Alta Velocidad Español (AVE) line between Madrid and Sevilla on part of the journey to such southern destinations as Málaga and Cádiz. The trip from Madrid to Cádiz takes five hours and to Málaga is a little shorter. The most expensive way to go is to take the high-speed AVE train itself along the Madrid-Sevilla line (another line between Madrid and Barcelona, which would link up with the French TGV, is planned). Even in the cheapest class, AVE passengers have access to everything from videos and telephones to children's games and facilities for the disabled.

There are a couple of other one-off classy services, such as the Barcelona-Valencia-Alicante Euromed trains. This is basically an AVE train running on normal track – it still manages to crank up to 220km/h.

Autoexpreso and Motoexpreso wagons are sometimes attached to long-distance services for the transport, respectively, of cars and motorbikes.

A *trenhotel* is an expensive sleeping-car train. First class on these sleek trains tends to be called *gran clase* and 2nd class (which may not exist) is *turista*.

Couchettes & Sleepers

Couchettes are known as *literas* in Spain and are fold-out bunk beds (generally in compartments of six berths). Their standard price, in addition to your ticket, is 1300 ptas. The discounts listed later are also applied to literas.

If you want a sleeper, you have half a dozen choices, ranging from shared cabins to luxury singles. Prices vary according to your choice and the distance you travel.

Timetables & Reservations

Train timetables are posted at most stations. *Llegadas* (arrivals) tend to be listed on white posters and *salidas* (departures) on yellow ones. Often separate information on specific lines is also posted or you can ask at the *taquillas* (ticket windows). Timetables for specific lines are generally available free of charge at stations, but RENFE does not sell a comprehensive rail guide. In fact, no-one seems to.

On most trains you'll never need to book

ahead. If you want to be sure of a place, it may nevertheless be wise to do so. Bookings can be made at stations and RENFE offices and through many travel agents. There is usually no booking fee unless you have the ticket(s) mailed to you. Also, people with Eurail or Inter-Rail cards will be charged 500 ptas to reserve a seat.

Passes

Apart from the international passes described in the Getting There & Away chapter, several passes are available in Spain.

With the Euro<26, GO25 or ISIC student card you can get reductions on rail tickets (see Costs & Discounts after this section), or you can buy an ExploreRail card. This allows the holder unlimited travel on 2nd class trains across Spain, except the AVE and Euromed. You can also upgrade to 1st class by paying the difference. It is valid for seven, 15 or 30 days, and costs 19,000/23,000/30,000 ptas, respectively – a bargain for anyone contemplating serious rail travel in Spain.

The Tarjeta Dorada is a senior citizens' pass issued by RENFE for 500 ptas. The kind of rail discounts available are outlined later. You must be over 60 and a resident in Spain. The card entitles you to 25% off your first trip, 40% off the second and 50% of all subsequent trips.

RENFE also issues a Tarjeta Turística, a rail pass valid for three to 10 days travel in a two-month period: in 2nd class, four days cost around 23,000 ptas, while 10 days cost about 49,000 ptas.

Also see Costs & Discounts following.

Costs & Discounts

The variety of possible fares is even more astounding than the number of train types. All fares quoted should be considered a rough sample of basic 2nd-class fares on the diurnos and estrellas (the cheapest fares).

Cercanías have one fare (unless you get a season pass for a particular line). On regionales and some of the faster long-distance trains (diurnos and InterCitys) you have the easy choice of 2nd or 1st-class seats. The evening trains (estrellas) offer 1st and 2nd-class seats, couchettes and in some cases *camas* (sleeping compartments) – see Couchettes & Sleepers earlier. The ordinary Talgos are a faster and more comfortable version of the other long-distance services.

In some cases, the fare also depends on the time of day you travel. This mainly applies to major lines, such as Madrid-Barcelona, and the Talgo 200 and AVE lines. The cheapest Madrid-Barcelona train leaves, uncomfortably, at 7 am.

If you buy a return ticket you can get a 20% discount. Children under four travel free (age four to 11 get 40% off). Reductions are possible for holders of some discount passes, like the Euro<26 card, also known as Carnet Joven in Spain (20%), and Tarjeta Dorada.

On some major lines you can purchase multiple-trip Bonocity passes. These are four-journey passes (ie two each way) valid for six months and *transferable*, offering a slight reduction over normal single fares. Examples include Madrid-Zaragoza (6200 ptas), Madrid-Valencia (11,200 ptas), Barcelona-Zaragoza and Barcelona-Valencia (8000 ptas). There are several other types of commuter pass along these lines.

Some typical one-way 2nd class fares on diurno/estrella class trains include:

from	to	fare (ptas)
Madrid	Barcelona	4900
	Granada	3000
	León	3300
	Málaga	4500
	Salamanca	1625
	Santander	3900
	San Sebastián	4400
	Valencia	2840
	Zaragoza	2900
Barcelona	Granada	6200
	Pamplona	3900
	San Sebastian	4600
	Zaragoza	2900
León	Santiago de Compostela	3300
San Sebastián	Vitoria	1400

Talgo 200 With the Talgo 200 the story becomes more complex. Firstly there are two classes: *turista* and the more luxurious *preferente*. Then there are two fare types for each class: *valle* and *llano*. The latter is the more expensive during busier times. The cheapest one-way fare from Madrid to Málaga is 6800 ptas. Finally, you need to see if any discounts apply. The return ticket discounts are 20% and 25% respectively. Holders of Carnet Joven and Tarjeta Dorada passes get a 25% discount (Monday to Thursday, this rises to 30% for one-way trips and 40% for return tickets).

The various recognised international rail passes, such as Eurail, Europass, Euro-Domino etc (see the Getting There & Away chapter for more information) may be used for heavily discounted, but not free, travel on Talgo 200 trains – 85% off in turista and 65% off in preferente.

Finally, a multiple commuter ticket, the Bono 200, entitles you to five return trips between Madrid and Málaga (80,000 ptas in preferente; 54,400 ptas in turista) in a three-month period.

The Barcelona-Valencia Euromed service also offers preferente and turista options.

AVE The AVE is complicated further by the existence of a third, ultra-luxury class *(club)* – to which the two fare bands also apply. The Madrid-Sevilla trip can be done in as little as 2¼ hours with no stops. Similar discounts apply to the AVE as to the Talgo 200 (but not the Monday to Thursday discounts), although holders of Inter-Rail passes pay full fare. You can also buy an open return ticket valid for six months.

You have the right to request a full refund on your AVE ticket if you arrive more than five minutes late. The cheapest one-way fare to Sevilla from Madrid is 8100 ptas.

Fines

If you board a train without a ticket, the inspector will sell you a one-way ticket on the train – but for double the price. If your destination is farther than 100km away, you pay double the fare for the first 100km.

Private Railways

Several private railway lines operate, mostly in northern Spain. The Ferrocarriles de Vía Estrecha (FEVE) company runs trains from O Ferrol in Galicia to Gijón and Oviedo in Asturias, and from there to Bilbao in the País Vasco via Santander in Cantabria.

The Eusko Trenbideak (ET/FV) line in the País Vasco complements RENFE services with lines serving northern towns and linking Bilbao, San Sebastián, Irún and Hendaye (France).

International rail passes *cannot* be used for free travel or discounts on these lines.

CAR & MOTORCYCLE

If bringing your own car, remember to have your insurance and other papers in order (see the Getting There & Away chapter).

Road Rules

In built-up areas the speed limit is 50km/h, which rises to 100km/h on major roads and up to 120km/h on *autovías* (toll-free dual-carriage highways) and *autopistas* (tolled dual-lane highways). Cars towing caravans are restricted to a maximum speed of 80km/h. The minimum driving age is 18.

Motorcyclists must use headlights at all times and wear a crash helmet if riding a bike of 125cc or more. The minimum age for riding bikes and scooters under 75cc is 16 (no licence is required).

Spanish truck drivers often have the courtesy to turn on their right indicator to show that the way ahead of them is clear for overtaking (and the left one if it is not and you are attempting this manoeuvre). This does not absolve you from exercising the usual caution, but can be a great help.

Vehicles already in roundabouts have right of way.

The blood-alcohol limit is 0.05% (as of October 1998) and breath-testing is carried out on occasion. Fines ranging up to 100,000 ptas are imposed if you are caught driving under the influence. If fitted, rear seat belts must be worn. Fines for many traffic offences range from 50,000 to 100,000 ptas.

Nonresident foreigners can be fined up to 50,000 ptas on the spot – the minor compensation is that they get 20% off normal fines if they settle immediately. You can contest the fine in writing (and in English) within 10 days, but don't hold your breath for a favourable result.

Road Atlases

Several road atlases are available, including the *Mapa Oficial de Carreteras*, put out by the Ministry of Public Works, Transport & Environment for 1900 ptas. This even comes in a CD-ROM version! One of the best atlases on the market, and available in and outside Spain, is the *Michelin Motoring Atlas – Spain & Portugal*. In Spain it's called *Michelin Atlas de Carreteras y Turístico – España Portugal* and costs 2575 ptas. It is for the most part faithfully accurate.

Both atlases include maps of all the main towns and cities. You can find them at most decent bookshops and some petrol stations in Spain.

Road Assistance

The Real Automóvil Club de España's head office (RACE; ☎ 91 447 32 00) is at Calle de José Abascal 10 in Madrid. For its 24-hour, countrywide emergency breakdown assistance, call ☎ 900-11 81 18. This service is available to members of foreign motoring organisations such as the RAC and AA.

City Driving & Parking

Driving in the bigger Spanish centres can be nerve-racking at the start. Road rules and traffic lights are generally respected, but the pace and jostling take a little getting used to.

Parking can be difficult. Where possible, avoid leaving luggage and valuables in unattended vehicles. Sevilla has a particularly bad reputation for robbery from cars. If you must leave luggage in vehicles, you should probably use paid car parks (around 200 ptas per hour). Most bigger cities operate a restricted parking system and, although

Los Toros de Osborne

As you roam the highways of Spain, every now and then you'll observe the silhouette of a truly gigantic black bull on the horizon up ahead, looking your way. When you get closer to the creature, you realise it's only two-dimensional, made of metal and held up by bits of scaffolding. But what's it for?

Well, it's not a silent homage to bullfighting erected by the local folk. Nor is it a sign that you're entering a notable bull-breeding area. It's a sherry and brandy advert for the Osborne company of El Puerto de Santa María, Andalucía. And in recent years the *toros de Osborne* have been raising almost as much passion as bullfighting itself.

At the last count there were 93 of them, looming beside roads all over the country. Why doesn't Osborne put its name on the bulls if it wants to advertise, you might ask? It did, and in big letters, from 1957, when the first bull was erected on the Madrid-Burgos road, until 1988. The bulls, which each weigh 50 tonnes and at one time numbered 500, grew into a much-loved national symbol. Then in 1988 a new law banned advertising hoardings beside main roads, to prevent drivers being distracted. Osborne left the bulls standing but removed its name, which seemed to pacify the authorities – until 1994, when word got about that the law was going to be enforced strictly, meaning no more bulls. This provoked an enormous outcry, with intellectuals writing to the newspapers about the national heritage, the government of Andalucía talking about declaring the bulls protected monuments and the El Puerto de Santa María council threatening to take the matter to the supreme court.

The bulls still stand.

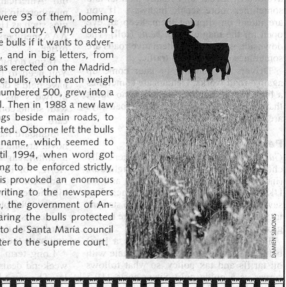

DAMIEN SIMONIS

many locals ignore the fines, you risk your car being towed away if you double-park or leave your vehicle in a designated no-parking zone. Recovering the vehicle can cost 10,000 ptas.

Tollways & Road Works

Spain, fortunately, is not yet 'blessed' with too many tollways, most of which are located in the north. Keep in mind if you are driving into Spain from France that the A-7 from the French border to Barcelona via Girona (Gerona), which continues south to Murcia, and the A-8 from Irún to Bilbao are

both tollways – and quite expensive. Some stretches along the autopistas are toll-free.

You can pay tolls with cash or with many credit/debit cards, which you swipe in machines at the tollgate. The tolls are fairly hefty. For example, Bilbao to Zaragoza costs 4620 ptas and La Jonquera to Alicante is 8155 ptas.

Other tollways include: the A-1 from Burgos to Miranda de Ebro (1125 ptas); the A-2, which connects the A-7 with Zaragoza (2305 ptas); the A-4 from Sevilla to Cádiz (1320 ptas); the A-6, a stretch of motorway along the Madrid route to La Coruña that starts at Villalba and cuts out in Adanero (1055 ptas); the A-9 that links La Coruña to Vigo (1465 ptas); the A-15 from Pamplona to Tudela (1465 ptas); the A-16 from Barcelona to Sitges (645 ptas); the A-19 from Barcelona to Palafolls (435 ptas); the A-66 from Oviedo to León (1265 ptas); and the A-8 from Bilbao to the French border (1940 ptas).

In some cases, tollways can easily be avoided in favour of virtually parallel and sometimes more scenic highways. If you are intent on slipping them, keep an eye open for the magic word: *peaje* (toll). The downside is that these alternative roads are sometimes clogged with traffic.

Drivers will sooner or later come up against road works. Detours are sometimes a little rough, but you are left in no doubt that the more mediocre of Spain's roadways are being improved.

Petrol

Gasolina in Spain is pricey, but generally cheaper than in its major EU neighbours (including France, Germany, Italy and the UK). About 30 companies, including several foreign operators, run petrol stations in Spain, but the two biggest are the home-grown Repsol and Cepsa.

Prices vary (up to four pesetas a litre) between service stations and fluctuate with oil tariffs and tax policy, so what follows serves as a guide only. Super costs 119.5 ptas a litre and the increasingly popular diesel (or *gasóleo)* is 90.9 ptas/litre. Lead-free *(sin plomo*; 95 octane) costs 113.9 ptas a litre and a 98 octane variant (also lead free) that goes by various names is up to 125.9 ptas a litre.

The fluctuations may become greater as a new law liberalising petrol prices takes effect. At any rate, the price trend over the past two years has been a slow upward drift.

Petrol is about 10% cheaper in Gibraltar than in Spain and 15% cheaper in Andorra. It's also cheap in Spain's tax-free enclaves of Ceuta and Melilla in North Africa.

You can pay with major credit cards at many service stations.

Rental

All the major international car-rental companies are represented throughout Spain and there are some local operators too.

Car hire is generally expensive, and it is worth organising prebooked car rental before arriving in Spain, for example in a fly-drive deal (see the UK section under Land in the Getting There & Away chapter). One US reader suggested taking out American Automobile Association membership before leaving home: companies such as Hertz often have discounts for AAA members booking a car through a US office.

If you do hire after arriving, shop around. You need to be at least 21 years old and have held a driving licence for a minimum of two years. It is easier, and obligatory with some companies, to pay with a credit card.

Standard rates with the bigger firms can hover around 5000 to 7000 ptas per day for a small car with unlimited kilometres. Hertz, for instance, will give you a Fiat Punto for 6900 ptas per day with unlimited kilometres. On top of this you need to calculate 1900 ptas a day in collision damage waiver, as well as 950 ptas a day in theft and third-party insurance. Add 16% IVA and you have the total daily cost.

Long-term rental and special long weekend deals can bring the price down a lot. The same Fiat Punto could cost as little as 12,500 ptas for five days plus insurance, waiver, IVA etc.

In the coastal areas most frequented by foreign tourists – basically, that means at Málaga airport, the Costa del Sol, Nerja and the Almería resorts – you can usually pick up a small car from a local agency for 16,000 to 20,000 ptas a week all inclusive, depending on the season. Car rental in the Islas Baleares is also markedly cheaper than on the mainland.

Renting motorcycles and mopeds on the mainland is expensive and outlets are few and far between. In the Islas Baleares it's a different story, where a small motor scooter can cost as little as 1400 ptas a day.

Purchase

Only people legally resident in Spain may buy vehicles there. One way around this is to have a friend who is a resident put the ownership papers in their name.

Car-hunters need a reasonable knowledge of Spanish to get through paperwork and understand dealers' patter. Trawling around showrooms or looking through classifieds can turn up second-hand Seats and Renaults (4 or 5) in good condition from around 300,000 ptas. The annual cost of third-party insurance, with theft and fire cover and national breakdown assistance, comes in at between 40,000 and 50,000 ptas.

Vehicles of five years and older must be submitted for roadworthiness checks, known as Inspección Técnica de Vehículos (ITV). If you pass you get a sticker for two years. Check that this has been done when buying: the test costs about 4000 ptas.

You can get your hands on second-hand 50cc *motos* (scooters) for anything from 40,000 to 100,000 ptas.

BICYCLE

Bicycle rental is not common in Spain, although it is more so in the case of mountain bikes *(bici todo terreno)*. If you plan to bring your own bike, check with the airline about any hidden costs. It will have to be disassembled and packed for the journey.

You should travel light on a cycle tour, but bring tools and some spare parts, including a puncture repair kit and a spare inner tube. Panniers are essential to balance your possessions on either side of the bike frame. A bike helmet is a good idea, as are a solid bike lock and chain to prevent theft.

One organisation that can help you plan your bike tour is the Cyclists' Touring Club (CTC; ☎ 01483-417217, Cotterell House, 69 Meadrow, Godalming, Surrey GU7 3HS, UK). It can supply information to members on cycling conditions, itineraries and cheap insurance. Membership costs UK£25 per annum or UK£12.50 for people aged under 18.

If you get tired of pedalling and want to put your feet up on a train, it is possible to take your bike on the train, but the conditions are restrictive. You have to be travelling overnight in a sleeper or *litera* (couchette) to have the (dismantled) bike accepted as normal luggage. Otherwise, it can only be sent separately as a parcel.

The European Bike Express is a bus service that enables cyclists to travel with their machines. It runs in summer from north-eastern England to Spain, with pick-up/drop-off points en route. The one-way/return fare is UK£99/160 (£150 return for CTC members). Phone ☎ 01642-251440 in England for details. See Activities in the Facts for the Visitor chapter for one or two hints on mountain biking in Spain.

Books

If you read Spanish, you may find some of the locally produced cycling guides of use. There are many to choose from. Libros Penthalon publishes a series of cycling and hiking books on many areas called the Colección El Búho Viajero. They generally come with maps and route planning tips that shouldn't require too deep a knowledge of the language.

HITCHING

Hitching is never entirely safe and we don't recommend it. Travellers who decide to hitch should understand that they are taking a small but potentially serious risk. You'll also need plenty of patience and common sense. Women should avoid hitching alone, and even men should consider the safer alternative of hitching in pairs.

Hitching is illegal on autopistas and autovías and difficult on major highways. You can try to pick up lifts before the tollbooths on tollways. Otherwise you need to choose a spot where cars can safely stop before highway slipways, or use minor roads. The going can be slow on the latter, as the traffic is often light. On the plus side, vehicles can stop easily and their drivers may be more inclined to do so than those screaming up and down the fast lanes. Overall, Spain is *not* a hitchhiker's paradise. Veterans of the road have particular trouble in the south, where drivers seem most suspicious.

There is little point in trying to hitch from city centres. Take local transport to town exits and carry a sign with your destination in Spanish. There are one or two organisations that organise car pooling – a kind of organised hitching service for which you pay a contribution to petrol and often a small fee. This can work out well for long-distance trips.

BOAT

Ferries and hydrofoils link the mainland ('La Península' to Spaniards) with the Islas Baleares and with Spain's North African enclaves of Ceuta and Melilla. Turn to the Sea section of the Getting There & Away chapter and the appropriate Getting There & Away entries throughout this guide for details.

LOCAL TRANSPORT

In most Spanish cities you will not need to use the local public transport much, as accommodation, attractions and mainline bus and train stations are generally within fairly comfortable walking distance. Where this is not the case, local buses connect bus and train stations with city centres.

Bus

The bus networks in larger cities can be complicated and, with some exceptions, are probably best avoided. In Madrid and

Barcelona the underground rail systems are an easier option and in most other cities you can cover most of the ground on foot.

Metro

Known as el metro, Madrid's and Barcelona's extensive underground rail networks make getting around easy if your feet are protesting.

Taxi

By European standards, taxis are fairly cheap. Flag fall and fares vary between cities, and you pay extra for luggage and airport pick-up. For more details, see the appropriate city Getting Around entries.

ORGANISED TOURS

If you want to travel around Spain in an organised tour, arrange it through travel agents in your own country (see the Getting There & Away chapter).

Guided coach tours can be organised in Spain. Pullmantur, which operates through local travel agents, offers tours ranging from two days in Toledo from Madrid to 12-day trips through Andalucía and Morocco or 14-day journeys through Andalucía, Portugal and Galicia.

Guided tours of the major cities are an option but, with a few exceptions, not especially good value.

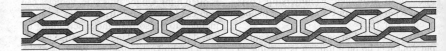

Madrid

There is little point in portraying Madrid as something it is not. It is not one of Europe's awe-inspiringly beautiful cities. It is not even particularly old and much of what may have constituted its historical legacy has over the centuries been all too quickly sacrificed to make way for the new. Madrid is a modern city, a product of the 20th and 19th centuries, and the expanses of its outer dormitory suburbs and peripheral high-rise apartment jungles are an oppressive introduction for anyone driving in for the first time.

Seen from the air, this city of 2.9 million (the surrounding region, known as the Comunidad de Madrid, counts a further two million) appears to rise out of nothing upon an unforgivingly dry plateau some 700m above sea level.

Madrid may lack the historical richness and sophistication of Rome or Paris and, moving closer to home, the physical beauty of Barcelona, but it oozes a life and character that, given the opportunity to work its magic (it doesn't take long), cannot leave you indifferent.

Leaving aside the art galleries, the splendour of the Plaza Mayor and Palacio Real, and the elegance of the Parque del Buen Retiro, the essence of Madrid is in the life pulsing through its streets. In no other European capital will you find the city centre so thronged so late into the night as here, especially on weekends. Everyone seems to stay out late, as though some unwritten law forbad sleeping before dawn. In this sense it is a city more to be lived than seen. This can work out fine, as Madrid also happens to make an ideal base for plenty of day trips. Toledo, Segovia, El Escorial, Ávila, Aranjuez and the Sierra de Guadarrama – just to name some – are all within easy striking distance.

HISTORY

Few historians place much credence in claims that a Roman settlement called

HIGHLIGHTS

- *Churros y chocolate* at Chocolatería San Ginés after a night (and early morning) out in the bars of Santa Ana & Huertas
- Bargain-hunting in El Rastro flea market
- A Sunday morning stroll in the Parque del Buen Retiro
- Summertime *cañas* and magnificent views to the Sierra de Guadarrama at Las Vistillas
- The big three art galleries: the Prado, the Reina Sofía and the Thyssen-Bornemisza
- A chicken-and-cider lunch at Casa Mingo
- Coffee and a paper on Plaza Mayor

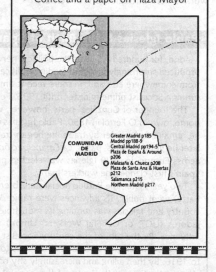

COMUNIDAD DE MADRID

Greater Madrid p185
Madrid pp188-9
Central Madrid pp194-5
Plaza de España & Around p206
Malasaña & Chueca p208
Plaza de Santa Ana & Huertas p212
Salamanca p215
Northern Madrid p217

Mantua (not to be confused with the Italian version) once stood on the banks of the Río Manzanares. The first concrete references to Madrid emerge around the 10th century.

Then it was the Muslim centre of Magerit, ceded to Alfonso VI in 1083. Surrounded by cities of far greater importance, such as Toledo, Segovia and Valladolid, Madrid was little more than a fortified village when Felipe II decided in 1561 to make it the permanent capital of the Spanish empire. The monarch conceived the city, then dominated by a stout *alcázar*, or Muslim-era fortress, as the future administrative centre, the hub from which the spokes of power would reach out to the furthest corners of the empire. He was driven by another consideration. Toledo was a more obvious choice for the capital, but its role as seat of the Church in Spain was incentive enough for Spain's temporal ruler to seek less claustrophobic lodgings.

Valladolid briefly assumed the role of capital in 1601, but the aberration lasted only five years. Madrid attracted not only civil servants: writers such as Cervantes, Lope de Vega and Calderón all lived and worked here through the 17th century.

The arrival of Carlos III in the 18th century was good news for noses (he himself was blessed with an impressive honker). He not only cleaned up the city (it had a reputation for being among the filthiest in Europe), but also completed the new Palacio Real, inaugurated the botanical gardens and carried out numerous other public works. Known as 'Madrid's best mayor', he was an enlightened ruler who did much to foster the intellectual life of the city. But he ran into trouble when his unpopular Italian minister, Squillace, declared long capes illegal in an attempt to reduce crime. Squillace argued that, now that the street cleaning had been improved, the capes were no longer necessary for keeping muck off other garments. The *madrileños* would have none of it and after long riots the measure was repealed.

Calamity befell Madrid with invasion by Napoleon. On 2 May 1808, a motley band of madrileños rose up in vain against the oc-

Pablo Iglesias & the Birth of Spanish Socialism

Madrid, for hundreds of years the political nerve centre of Spain and its one-time empire, has produced surprisingly few of its leading political figures. Kings and queens were almost always from somewhere else and, in more recent times, Franco came from Galicia, while the long-running Socialist prime minister until 1996, Felipe González, is from Andalucía.

The founder of González' party, however, was a local boy. Well, almost. Born in Franco's home town of O Ferrol in 1850, Pablo Iglesias was brought to Madrid in his infancy and there he remained. A printer by trade, he began trade-union activities at the age of 20. One year later he got a workers' paper, *La Emancipación*, off the ground. With the rise of Marxist ideas across Europe, in 1879 Iglesias was elected president of a new association that constituted Spain's first clandestine workers' party.

Two years later, the Partido Socialista Obrero Español (PSOE, or Spanish Socialist Workers' Party) went public. Its advances were rapid. Within seven years it had branches across the country and Iglesias was running its mouthpiece, *El Socialista*. The Unión General de Trabajadores (UGT, or General Workers' Union) was organised thereafter, with strong PSOE influence. By the turn of the century Socialist MPs were winning seats in local government.

Iglesias himself was elected several times to the Cortes, or national parliament, from 1910 to 1916. By then ailing and increasingly shy of the limelight, Iglesias had become a working-class myth. Even in the wake of the general strike called in 1917 by the UGT, which was suppressed without any ceremony, Iglesias was left in peace. He remained president of the PSOE and UGT, albeit in a largely honorary fashion, until his death in 1925.

cupation, which lasted, with some interruptions, until May 1813.

As Joseph Bonaparte marched out, Fernando VII waltzed back in, marking the restoration of the Bourbon family to the throne. But the country's problems were far from over. The turbulence of the Carlist wars followed and political uncertainty remained the rule well into the 20th century. In 1931 the Second Republic was proclaimed in Madrid. Franco's troops first attempted, and failed, to take Madrid in 1936. The subsequent siege and slow, grinding advance of his Nationalist forces lasted until the civil war ended in 1939.

ORIENTATION

One of the most striking aspects of Madrid's layout is the absence of water. The pathetic dribble that constitutes the Río Manzanares doesn't flow through the city centre like the Thames, Seine or Tiber – indeed, it barely flows at all – and most visitors to Madrid leave blissfully unaware that there is a 'river' here.

Madrid is also surprisingly compact. The main north-south artery, Paseo de la Castellana (which becomes Paseo de los Recoletos and Paseo del Prado at its southern end), lies in a shallow depression and connects the city's two main train stations, Chamartín and Atocha.

The area around the southern portion of this promenade captures the interest of out-of-towners. The core of the city's oldest quarters is squeezed in between Paseo del Prado in the east and the Palacio Real to the west. Roughly halfway between them is the Puerta del Sol, once a city gate but long since the point from which distances to all corners of the country are measured.

The majestic Plaza Mayor lies a short stroll west of the Puerta del Sol, surrounded by a warren of captivating back streets. East of Sol, the old *barrios* are a happening, dynamic mix of seemingly endless restaurants, bars and cafés. The tangle of lanes spills southward into the equally fascinating working-class barrio of Lavapiés. This is perhaps one of the last quarters with a real

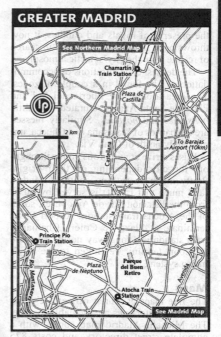

GREATER MADRID

See Northern Madrid Map

Chamartín
Train Station

Plaza de
Castilla

To Barajas
Airport (10km)

0   1   2 km

Castellana

Príncipe Pío
Train Station

Paseo de la

Plaza
de Neptuno

Parque
del Buen
Retiro

Río Manzanares

Atocha Train
Station

Paz

la

de

Avenida

See Madrid Map

feeling of local community, where the people, a mix of *gatos* (true madrileños), *gitanos* (Roma people, formerly known as Gypsies) and migrants (many from North Africa and the Middle East), live cheek by jowl. In the heat of the long summer nights, families jostle with revellers for space in the streets in a voluble but good-natured competition to fill the air with an energy rarely wasted on sleep – except in the hot, languid afternoons of the siesta. Moving westward to the area around Calle de Toledo you enter a slightly more polished version of Lavapiés, La Latina. On the way northwards to the Palacio Real it in turn feeds into one of the oldest parts of the city, once known as the *morería*, or Moorish quarter.

Madrid's great art galleries – the must-sees on everyone's list – are clustered about the Paseo del Prado. Not far from the gallery of the same name spreads out one of the city's green lungs, the elegant Parque del Buen Retiro ('El Retiro' for short). Once the preserve of royals and dandies, it now throws open its gates to all those in search of respite from the city's hectic atmosphere.

The densest concentrations of accommodation can be found in a couple of zones. The area around the Puerta del Sol and Plaza de Santa Ana is saturated with little *pensiones* and *hostales*. Similarly blessed are the barrios of Malasaña and Chueca, immediately north of Gran Vía.

Buses arrive at numerous points throughout the city, depending on their origin. Pretty much everything south of Madrid (and much that is not) is served by buses from the Estación Sur de Autobuses, south of the Atocha train station. Airport buses terminate at Plaza de Colón. Chamartín train station is a long way north. All these transport termini are linked to the city's metro system.

Maps

The free maps at tourist offices are sufficient, but better ones are available for sale. The Michelin Madrid map comes with a complete street directory and costs 825 ptas. A far more comprehensive option is the Almax *Atlas de Madrid*, a book that covers the city in minute detail and includes the rest of the Comunidad de Madrid too. Only long-termers, however, are likely to want to shell out 3040 ptas for it.

INFORMATION
Tourist Offices

The main tourist office (Oficina de Turismo; ☎ 91 429 49 51) is at Calle del Duque de Medinaceli 2 (map: Central). It is open Monday to Friday from 9 am to 7 pm and Saturday from 9 am to 1 pm. The office at Aeropuerto de Barajas (Barajas airport; ☎ 91 305 86 56) is open Monday to Friday from 8 am to 8 pm and Saturday from 9 am to 1 pm. The one at Chamartín train station (☎ 91 315 99 76) keeps the same hours.

Another Oficina de Turismo (☎ 91 364 18 76), Ronda de Toledo 1, is in the Centro Comercial de la Puerta de Toledo (map:

Central). It is open Monday to Friday from 9 am to 7.30 pm and Saturday from 9.30 am to 1.30 pm.

The Patronato Municipal de Turismo (☎ 91 588 29 06), Plaza Mayor 3, specialises in the city. It is open Monday to Friday from 10 am to 8 pm and Saturday from 10 am to 2 pm (map: Central).

The city's general information line (dealing with everything from public transport to shows) is on ☎ 010.

Foreign Consulates

For foreign embassies and consulates in Madrid, see the Embassies & Consulates section in the Facts for the Visitor chapter.

Money

There is no shortage of banks across central Madrid; most have ATMs that accept a wide range of plastic. When changing cash or cheques, always ask about commission.

Finding Your Way in Madrid

Where necessary in this chapter, the information about places and sights includes a reference to the map on which you will find them (and sometimes a reference to the nearest metro station), eg Centro de Arte Reina Sofía, Calle de Santa Isabel 52 (metro: Atocha, map: Central). The references use the following abbreviations, and the maps appear on the pages listed.

Abbreviation	Map	Page(s)
Madrid	Madrid	188-9
Central	Central Madrid	194-5
España	Plaza de España & Around	206
Mal & Ch	Malasaña & Chueca	208
Ana & Hue	Plaza de Santa Ana & Huertas	212
Sal	Salamanca	215
North	Northern Madrid	217

This can vary from bank to bank, but not greatly.

Exchange booths abound. Don't be fooled by all the 'No Commission' signs: the exchange rates are often inferior to official bank rates. A rare exception is Cambios Uno, Calle de Alcalá 20 (map: Central), which generally offers sporting rates. It's open daily from 9.30 am to 8 pm. The moral is: shop around.

Some of these places act as agents for Western Union and MoneyGram. See Money in the Facts for the Visitor chapter for more on how these work. MoneyGram has a booth on Plaza de España (map: España), as well as at Atocha and Chamartín train stations.

American Express (24 hours ☎ 91 527 03 03, ☎ 900-99 44 26 for replacing lost travellers cheques) is at Plaza de las Cortes 2. It's open Monday to Friday from 9 am to 5.30 pm and Saturday from 9 am to noon.

Post

The main *correos* (post office) is in the ornate Palacio de Comunicaciones on Plaza de la Cibeles (map: Central). The postcode for poste restante is 28080. You can buy stamps Monday to Friday from 8 am to 10 pm and Saturday from 8.30 am to 8.30 pm. To send big parcels, head for Puerta N on the southern side of the post office – they even offer a reasonably priced packing service. The parcel section is open Monday to Friday from 8 am to 9.30 pm and Saturday from 8.30 am to 2 pm.

Telephone

The two main Telefónica offices (*locutorios*) are open daily from 9.30 am to midnight. They have telephone cabins, telex services and phone directories for the whole country. One is at Paseo de los Recoletos 37-41 (metro: Colón, map: Mal & Ch). The other is at Gran Vía 30 (metro: Callao or Gran Vía, map: Central).

Private phone companies specialising in cut-rate overseas calls are beginning to appear in Madrid. One is Sol Telecom, Puerta del Sol 6 (map: Ana & Hue). It is open daily from 8 am to 11 pm and claims to undercut Telefónica by up to 60%. Compare rates before committing yourself.

Email & Internet Access

Those needing a net fix can head to La Casa de Internet, Calle de Luchana 20 (metro: Bilbao, map: Mal & Ch). You pay 500 ptas per half-hour online. Another option is El Argonauta Virtual, Calle de Gaztambide 9 (map: España). Or you could try the Connection Room (☎ 91 399 34 39), Calle de Cea Bermúdez 66, which is open daily from 8 am to midnight (map: Madrid). One hour online costs 700 ptas. Laser Coffee Shop, Calle del Rosario 21 (map: Central), is not too far from Plaza Mayor and Net Café is handy for Malasaña at Calle de San Bernardo 81 (map: Mal & Ch).

Travel Agencies

Madrid is not the ideal place for bargain-basement flights. That said, it is possible to get reasonable deals to major destinations and in some cases – such as London – steals.

One agency with a reputation for getting the best available deals is Viajes Zeppelin (☎ 91 542 51 54), Plaza de Santo Domingo 2 (metro: Santo Domingo, map: Central). Zeppelin also has offices at Calle de la Infanta Mercedes 62 (☎ 91 571 12 62; map: North) and Calle de la Hermosilla 92 (☎ 91 431 40 36; map: Madrid).

One of the country's biggest agencies is Halcón. Don't expect dirt cheap arrangements, but it is reliable and has offices all over Madrid.

Students and young people can try looking around several other agencies. Juventus Viajes (☎ 91 308 55 56), Calle de Fernando VI (map: Mal & Ch); Intercambio 66 (☎ 91 449 79 99), Calle de Fernández de los Ríos 95 (map: Madrid); and Cadimar Viajes (☎ 91 542 59 05), on the corner of Calle de San Leonardo de Dios and Plaza de España (map: España), are all worth looking at. Another good one is Unlimited (☎ 91 531 10 00), Plaza del Callao 3 (map: Central).

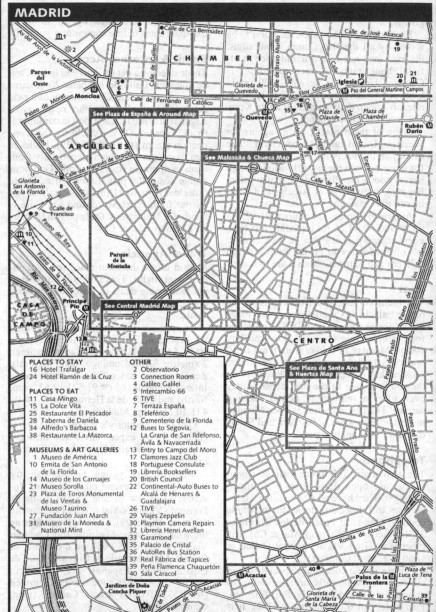

MADRID

PLACES TO STAY
16 Hotel Trafalgar
24 Hotel Ramón de la Cruz

PLACES TO EAT
11 Casa Mingo
15 La Dolce Vita
25 Restaurante El Pescador
28 Taberna de Daniela
34 Alfredo's Barbacoa
38 Restaurante La Mazorca

MUSEUMS & ART GALLERIES
1 Museo de América
10 Ermita de San Antonio
   de la Florida
14 Museo de los Carruajes
21 Museo Sorolla
23 Plaza de Toros Monumental
   de las Ventas &
   Museo Taurino
27 Fundación Juan March
31 Museo de la Moneda &
   National Mint

OTHER
2 Observatorio
3 Connection Room
4 Galileo Galilei
5 Intercambio 66
6 TIVE
7 Terraza España
8 Teleférico
9 Cementerio de la Florida
12 Buses to Segovia,
   La Granja de San Ildefonso,
   Ávila & Navacerrada
13 Entry to Campo del Moro
17 Clamores Jazz Club
18 Portuguese Consulate
19 Librería Booksellers
20 British Council
22 Continental-Auto Buses to
   Alcalá de Henares &
   Guadalajara
26 TIVE
29 Viajes Zeppelin
30 Playmon Camera Repairs
32 Librería Henri Avellan
33 Garamond
35 Palacio de Cristal
36 AutoRes Bus Station
37 Real Fábrica de Tapices
39 Peña Flamenca Chaquetón
40 Sala Caracol

Also if you are a student or under 26, visit the youth travel offices of TIVE. TIVE has a branch at Calle de José Ortega y Gasset 71 (☎ 91 347 77 78), in the offices of the Instituto de la Juventud (map: Madrid), and another at Calle de Fernando El Católico 88 (☎ 91 543 74 12; map: Central). They open Monday to Friday from 9 am to 1 pm.

Lastly, always keep an eye out for ads for charter offers.

Student & Youth Information

You can get information on youth and student affairs, youth cards for travel discounts and HI cards at the Consejería de Educación y Cultura (☎ 91 580 42 16), Calle de Alcalá 32 (map: Central).

Gay & Lesbian Information

The Colectivo de Gais y Lesbianas de Madrid (Cogam; ☎ /fax 91 532 45 17) has an information office and social centre (Urania's Café) at Calle de Fuencarral 37. Its info line (☎ 91 523 00 70) is open daily from 5 to 9 pm. Nexus (☎ 91 522 45 17) can help with AIDS counselling.

Madrid's gay & lesbian pride march is held on the last Saturday in June.

Books, Periodicals & Bookshops

Among the plethora of guides to Madrid, several stand out. *Time Out* produces a city guide along the lines of its London listings magazine. Although not strong on the sights, it offers exhaustive information on eating and nightlife.

If you plan on hanging around, invest in *Todo Madrid*, a weighty tome dealing with everything from traditional *tabernas* to where to get a cheap haircut.

The whimsical reader might search out *Madrid – A Travellers' Companion*, edited by Hugh Thomas (author of *The Spanish Civil War*). Everyone from the Duke of Wellington to Hemingway has something to say in this delightful stroll through the city's life and history. George Semler's *Madrid Walks* is another useful companion.

The free English-language monthly *In Madrid* has local listings and a mix of articles on the city and general themes. You can find it in several bars across Madrid (including Finnegan's; see Entertainment later). Another periodical to look out for is the free monthly *The Broadsheet*.

La Casa del Libro, Gran Vía 29-31 (map: Central), has a broad selection of books on all subjects and a respectable section with books in English, French and other languages.

For English-language books, you could also try either Librería Turner, Calle de Zurbano 10 (map: Mal & Ch), or Librería Booksellers, Calle de José Abascal 48 (map: Madrid).

There are a couple of specialist French bookshops: Librería Henri Avellan, Calle del Duque de Sesto 5 (map: Madrid), and El Bosque, Calle de Añastro 19 (map: North). For German-speakers, there's Lesen, Calle de Serrano 222, and Librería Alemana, Calle del Príncipe de Vergara 205 (map: North). Those in need of Italian books can head for the Librería Italiana, Calle de Modesto Lafuente 47 (map: North).

Librería de Mujeres, Calle de San Cristóbal 17 (map: Central), is a women's bookshop and well-known feminist meeting place.

On Cuesta de Claudio Moyano, along the southern edge of the botanic gardens, a row of 30-odd bookstalls bursts with a cornucopia of second-hand books, mostly in Spanish. For a more conventional selection, Librería Carmelo Blázquez at Calle de Alfonso XII 66, 1st floor, is Madrid's largest second-hand bookshop.

About the best shop in Madrid for hiking and walking literature and maps is La Tienda Verde, Calle de Maudes 38 (map: North). The owners have another shop at No 23 dedicated more to general travel and ecology.

At Calle de Gravina 11 on Plaza de Chueca (map: Mal & Ch) is a gay bookshop, Berkana. It's a good place for info on the gay scene.

Libraries

One of the most venerable old libraries in Madrid is in the Ateneo de Madrid, Calle del Prado 21 (map: Ana & Hue). It is worth poking your head in here just to admire the study rooms of another age and the hall lined with portraits of important personages – also of another age.

Otherwise look for public libraries under Bibliotecas Públicas in the Páginas Amarillas (Yellow Pages). You could also try the various cultural centres or subject libraries at the Universidad Complutense.

Film & Photography

You can have film developed all over the city. Photo Express at Gran Vía 84 (map: España), right on Plaza de España, is reliable.

A reputable place for camera repairs is Playmon (☎ 91 573 57 25; map: Madrid), Calle de Jorge Juan 133.

For second-hand camera equipment of all sorts, head for Fotocasión (☎ 91 467 64 91), Calle de Carlos Arniches 22 (map: Central), near El Rastro.

Cultural Centres

If you're yearning for a whiff of home, a first port of call should be the foreign cultural centres. They all have libraries and organise film nights and other activities.

France
 Institut Français (☎ 91 308 49 50), Calle del Marqués de la Ensenada 12 (map: Mal & Ch)
 Alliance Française (☎ 91 435 15 32), Calle de Velázquez 94 (map: Sal)
Germany
 Goethe Institut (☎ 91 319 39 44), Calle de Zurbarán 21 (map: Mal & Ch)
Italy
 Istituto Italiano di Cultura (☎ 91 547 52 04), Calle Mayor 86 (map: Central)
UK
 British Council (☎ 91 337 35 00), Paseo del General Martínez Campos 31 (map: Madrid)
USA
 Washington Irving Center (☎ 91 564 55 15), Paseo de la Castellana 52 (map: Sal)

Laundry

Well-placed coin-operated laundrettes in central Madrid include: Lavandería Alba, Calle del Barco 26 (map: Mal & Ch); Lavomatique on Calle de Cervantes (map:

España), open Monday to Friday from 9 am to 8 pm and Saturday from 10 am to 2 pm; Lavandería España on Calle del Infante (map: España); and in the north, Lavandería Automática, Calle de la Infanta Mercedes 88 (map: North).

Lost Property

The Negociado de Objetos Perdidos (☎ 91 588 43 46), Plaza de Legazpi 7 (metro: Legazpi), is open from 9 am to 2 pm.

Medical Services

If you have medical problems pop into the nearest Insalud clinic – often marked 'Centro de Salud'. Make sure you have all your insurance details with you (including your E-111 if you are an EU citizen). A handy clinic in the city centre is at Calle de las Navas de Tolosa 10 (map: Central), which is also the city's main public AIDS information centre. You can also get help at the Anglo-American Medical Unit (☎ 91 435 18 23), Calle del Conde de Aranda 1 (metro: Retiro, map: Mal & Ch). Staff speak Spanish and English.

At least one pharmacy is open 24 hours a day in each district of Madrid. They operate on a rota and details appear daily in *El País* and other papers. Alternatively, you could dial ☎ 098 to find out where the nearest one is.

Emergency

The general EU-standard emergency number is ☎ 112. In police emergency you can call the Policía Nacional on ☎ 091 or the Guardia Civil on ☎ 062.

There are six first-aid stations (*urgencias*) scattered around Madrid to help with medical emergencies (open 24 hours). Among them are Centro (☎ 91 521 00 25), Calle de las Navas de Tolosa 10 (see Medical Services earlier); Retiro (☎ 91 420 03 56), Calle del Gobernador 39 (map: Central); and Tetuán (☎ 91 579 12 23), Calle de Bravo Murillo 357 (map: North).

For an ambulance call the Cruz Roja on ☎ 522 22 22 or Insalud on ☎ 061.

Help Line

There is an English-language help line for those with the blues or who simply have a request for information. Dial ☎ 91 559 13 93 from 7 to 11 pm.

Dangers & Annoyances

Pickpockets are rife in the more touristy parts of Madrid and on some metro lines, and of course foreigners are the prime targets. The usual precautions are required (see Dangers & Annoyances in the Facts for the Visitor chapter).

Parts of the Parque del Oeste are given over to prostitution by night and not ideal for a late-evening stroll. Paseo de Camoens y Valero and Paseo de Ruperto Chapi are where most of the tricks are done. The Casa de Campo is also swarming with ladies of the night, pimps and junkies.

The area around Calle de la Luna, near Gran Vía, is similar. Most of the time you will have no problems, but it is as well to be aware of what you are walking into.

The area behind the Templo de Debod is a popular summertime cruising patch. In El Retiro the same activity is conducted in the south-western corner around La Chopera. This may not appeal to all tastes.

WALKING TOUR

What follows aims to suggest a general route through 'essential Madrid'. If you plan to spend time in any of the monuments and museums, or prefer simply meandering at will and stopping in at the many enticing bars and cafés, you will need several days to do justice to such a circuit.

Unless you want to head for the big art galleries first, the most fitting place to begin exploring Madrid is the **Puerta del Sol**, the official centre of Madrid (map: Central).

Walk up Calle de Preciados and take the second street on the left, which will bring you out on to Plaza de las Descalzas. Look at the **baroque doorway** in the Caja de Madrid building – it was built for King Felipe V in 1733 and faces the **Convento de las Descalzas Reales**.

Moving south down Calle de San Martín you come to the **Iglesia de San Ginés**, one of Madrid's oldest churches. Behind it is the wonderful **Chocolatería de San Ginés**, generally open from 7 to 10 pm and 1 to 7 am.

Continue down to and cross Calle Mayor and then walk onto Madrid's most famous square, **Plaza Mayor**. After a coffee on the plaza, head west along Calle Mayor until you come to the historic **Plaza de la Villa**, with Madrid's 17th century *ayuntamiento* (town hall). On the same square stand the 16th century **Casa de Cisneros** and the Gothic-*mudéjar* **Torre de los Lujanes**, part of the casa of the same name and one of the city's oldest buildings, dating from the Middle Ages.

Take the street down the left side of the Casa de Cisneros, cross the road at the end, go down the stairs and follow the cobbled Calle del Cordón out onto Calle de Segovia. Almost directly in front of you is the mudéjar tower of the **Iglesia de San Pedro**. Proceeding down Costanilla de San Pedro you reach the **Iglesia de San Andrés**.

From here you cross Plaza de la Puerta de Moros and head south-west to the **Basílica de San Francisco El Grande**, or you can head east past the market along Plaza de la Cebada – once a popular spot for public executions – to head into the Sunday flea market of **El Rastro**.

Otherwise, head west into the tangle of lanes that forms what was once the **morería** and emerge on Calle de Bailén and the wonderful *terrazas* of Las Vistillas – great for drinking in the views.

Follow the viaduct north to the **Catedral de Nuestra Señora de la Almudena**, the **Palacio Real** (royal palace) and Plaza de Oriente, with its statues, fountains and hedge mazes. The far eastern side of the plaza is closed off by the **Teatro Real**.

At its northern end, Calle de Bailén runs into **Plaza de España** (map: España). Nearby, you could visit the **Museo de Cerralbo**, the **Templo de Debod** and, close to the Río Manzanares, the **Ermita de San Antonio de Florida** (map: Madrid), which contains a masterpiece by Goya. If you were to continue north past the square you would pass through the barrio de Argüelles (map: Central), with some pleasant summer terrazas, and on towards the main centre of Madrid's Universidad Complutense.

The eastern flank of Plaza de España marks the beginning of **Gran Vía**. This Haussmannesque boulevard was slammed through the tumbledown slums north of Sol in 1911.

At the eastern end of Gran Vía, note the superb dome of the **Metropolis Building** (map: Central). Continue east along Calle de Alcalá until you reach **Plaza de la Cibeles**, Madrid's favourite roundabout.

Head north (left) up the tree-lined promenade of Paseo de los Recoletos (map: Mal & Ch). On the left you'll pass some of the city's best-known cafés, including Gran Café de Gijón, Café-Restaurante El Espejo and El Gran Pabellón del Espejo. On your right is the enormous **Biblioteca Nacional** (National Library) and, a little farther on, a statue of Columbus in Plaza de Colón.

From here walk around the back of the National Library, where the **Museo Arqueológico Nacional** is housed. Southwards along Calle de Serrano is Plaza de la Independencia, in the middle of which stands the **Puerta de Alcalá**. The gate was begun at Plaza de la Cibeles to celebrate the arrival of Carlos III in Madrid in 1769, completed in 1778 and later moved as the city grew.

Turn right and then left at Plaza de la Cibeles (map: Central) to head south down Paseo del Prado, an extension of the city's main tree-lined boulevard, and you'll soon reach the art gallery with which it shares its name. On the other side of the boulevard, the **Museo Thyssen-Bornemisza** is, along with the **Prado**, a must.

The area around and north of the Prado is laced with museums, while stretching out behind it to the east are the wonderful gardens of the **Parque del Buen Retiro**. Immediately south of the Prado is the **Real Jardín Botánico**. Looking onto the manic multilane roundabout that is Plaza del Emperador Carlos V are the city's main train station, **Atocha**, and the third in Madrid's big league of art galleries, the **Centro de Arte Reina Sofía**.

Head a few blocks north along Paseo del Prado again and west up Calle de las Huertas (through the tiny Plaza de Platería Martínez). The **Convento de las Trinitarias** (closed to the public; map: Ana & Hue), which backs onto this street, is where Cervantes lies buried. Turn right up Costanilla de las Trinitarias and continue along Calle de San Agustín until you come to Calle de Cervantes, then turn left. On your right you will pass the **Casa de Lope de Vega** at No 11. If the '*abierto*' ('open') sign is up, just knock and enter.

A left turn at the end of Calle de Cervantes into Calle de León will bring you back onto Calle de las Huertas, which you may have already noticed is one of Madrid's happening streets. Anywhere along here or up on Plaza de Santa Ana will make a great place to take a load off at the end of this gruelling tour! For specific tips, consult the Entertainment section.

MUSEO DEL PRADO

Built towards the end of the 18th century in the Prado (meadow) de los Jerónimos, the Palacio de Villanueva was originally conceived as a house of science, incorporating a natural history museum and laboratories. Events overtook the noble enterprise and during the Napoleonic occupation the building was converted ignominiously into cavalry barracks.

Perhaps inspired by the ideas of the French Revolution and Napoleon's short-lived administration, King Fernando VII resolved in 1814 to create a museum to put on public display a representative chunk of the country's artistic wealth. Five years later it opened with 311 Spanish paintings. Of the more than 7000 works in the Prado collection today, fewer than half are on view at any given time.

Since 1819, the museum (metro: Banco de España or Atocha, map: Central) has undergone numerous changes, but has rarely received the financial attention it deserves.

CENTRAL MADRID

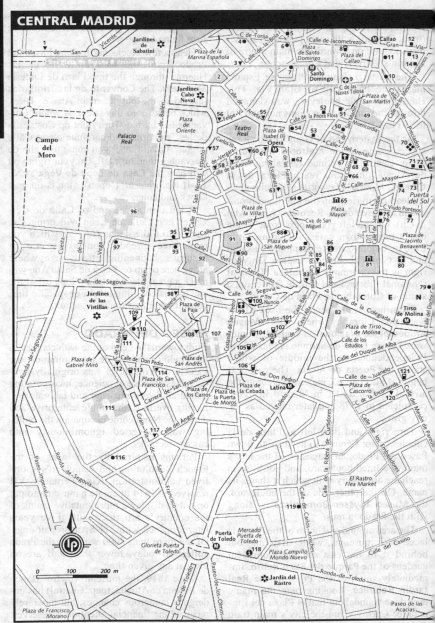

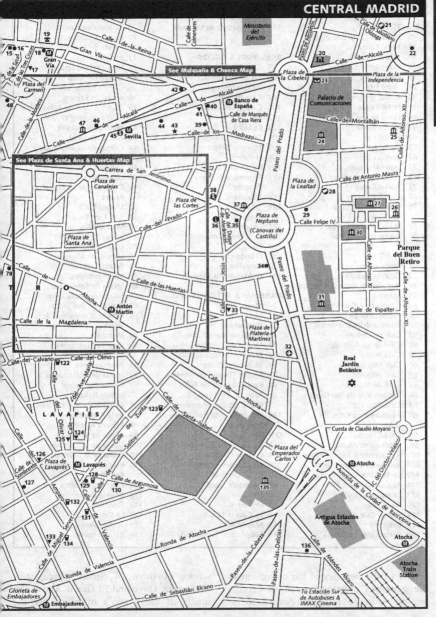

MADRID

CENTRAL MADRID

MADRID

CENTRAL MADRID

PLACES TO STAY
5 Hotel de Santo Domingo
12 Hotel California
13 Hostal Andorra
14 Hotel Regente
15 Hotel Arosa
29 Hotel Ritz
34 Hostal Sudamericano
35 Hotel Palace
46 Hotel Regina
51 Hostal Roma
52 Hostal Paz
53 Hostal Ivor
62 Pensión Luz
71 Hotel Moderno
72 Hostal Cosmopólitan
73 Hostal Riesco
74 Hostal Ruano
76 Hostal Santa Cruz & Hostal Cruz Sol
77 Hostal María del Mar
87 Hostal La Macarena

PLACES TO EAT
1 Prada a Tope
3 Taberna La Bola
17 Restaurante Integral Artemisa
33 Maceira
41 Círculo de Bellas Artes
55 Restaurante La Paella Real
56 Taberna del Alabardero
57 Café de Oriente
58 Café de los Austrias
59 Casa Marta
60 Café Vergara
61 Café del Real
63 Café de Madrid
66 Chocolatería de San Ginés
83 Casa Paco
85 Restaurante Sobrino de Botín
94 Casa Ciriaco
98 Restaurante Alamillo
101 Restaurante Julián de Tolosa
108 Restaurante Gure-Etxea
112 La Tasquita
114 Taquería de Birrä (II)
117 La Burbuja Que Ríe
120 Manhattan
124 Nuevo Café Barbieri
125 Babilonia
126 Restaurante La Pampa

130 El Granadero de Lavapiés
133 Beirut

BARS, PUBS & DISCOS
8 Calentito
68 Teatro Joy Eslava
69 Palacio Gaviria
84 Casa Antonio
100 Café del Nuncio
102 La Chata
103 La Soleá
104 Taberna Almendro 13
105 Taberna Tempranillo
106 El Viajero
109 Bar Ventorrillo
111 Champañería María Pandora
113 Travesía
121 Taberna de Antonio Sánchez
122 Candela
123 La Taberna Encantada
128 Eucalipto
131 El Boquerón
132 PakesTeis
134 La Mancha de Madrid

MUSEUMS & ART GALLERIES
24 Museo Naval
25 Museo de Artes Decorativos
26 Casón del Buen Retiro
27 Museo del Ejército
30 Real Academia Española
31 Museo del Prado
37 Museo Thyssen-Bornemisza
47 Real Academia de Bellas Artes de San Fernando
65 Real Casa de la Panadería
135 Centro de Arte Reina Sofía

OTHER
2 Convento de la Encarnación
4 Café de Chinitas
6 Localidades La Alicantina
7 Viajes Zeppelin
9 Centro de Salud
10 FNAC
11 Unlimited
16 La Casa del Libro
18 Madrid Rock
19 Telephones (Telefónica)

20 Palacio de Linares
21 French Embassy
22 Puerta de Alcalá
23 Main Correos
28 New Zealand Embassy
32 Centro de Salud
36 Oficina de Turismo
38 American Express
39 Teatro & Cine de Bellas Artes
40 RENFE Booking Office
42 Metropolis Building
43 Policía Nacional
44 Consejería de Educación y Cultura
45 Cambios Uno
48 Localidades Galicia
49 Convento de las Descalzas Reales
50 Madrid Rock
54 Real Cinema
64 Madrid Rock
67 Iglesia de San Ginés
70 El Corte Inglés
75 Librería de Mujeres
78 Teatro Calderón
79 Multicines Ideal
80 Iglesia de Santa Cruz
81 Palacio de Santa Cruz
82 Basílica de San Isidro
86 Patronato Municipal de Turismo
88 Mercado
89 Casa de los Lujanes
90 Casa de Cisneros
91 Ayuntamiento
92 Iglesia del Sacramento
93 Capitanía General
95 Istituto Italiano
96 Catedral de Nuestra Señora de la Almudena
97 Muralla Árabe
99 Iglesia de San Pedro
107 Iglesia de San Andrés
110 Corral de la Morería
115 Basílica de San Francisco el Grande
116 Laser Coffee Shop
118 Oficina de Turismo
119 Fotocasión
127 La Corrala
129 Teatro Olimpia
136 Karacol Sports

One of the beauties of the collection is the generous coverage given to certain masters. Strings of rooms are devoted to the works of three of Spain's greatest – Velázquez, Goya and El Greco. These elements of the Prado's offerings are the cream, but there is plenty of good stuff by a range of Flemish and Italian painters, as well as artists of other nationalities. The Prado demands more than one visit.

Parts of the collection are moved about as improvements and maintenance of the museum are carried out.

Velázquez

Of this 17th century old master's works, *Las Meninas* is what most people come to see, and rightly so. Executed in 1656, it is more properly known as *La Familia de Felipe IV*. It depicts Velázquez himself on the left and, in the centre, the Infanta Margarita. There is more to it than that, though: the artist in fact depicts himself depicting the king and queen, whose images appear, according to some experts, in mirrors behind Velázquez. His mastery of light and colour are never more apparent than here. It takes pride of place in room 12, the focal point of the Velázquez collection on the 1st floor.

The bulk of Velázquez' works are in rooms 11 to 15. Among some of his outstanding portraits are *La Infanta Doña Margarita de Austria* (who stars in *Las Meninas*) and *Baltasar Carlos a Caballo*. *Cristo Crucificado* manages to convey the agony of the Crucifixion with great dignity. *La Rendición de Breda* (The Surrender of Breda) is another classic.

El Greco

Domenikos Theotokopoulos, 58 years Velázquez' senior, is also represented on the 1st floor, in rooms 9B and 10B. The long, slender figures characteristic of this singular Cretan artist, who lived and worked in Toledo, are hard to mistake. Particularly striking are *La Crucifixión* and *San Andrés y San Francisco*, finished towards the end of the 16th century.

Goya

Francisco José de Goya y Lucientes is the most extensively represented of the Spanish masters in the Prado. Late to reach the heights of his grandeur, Goya, more than anyone, captured the extremes of hope and

misery his country experienced before, during and after the Napoleonic invasion. In room 36 hang probably his best-known and most intriguing oils, *La Maja Vestida* and *La Maja Desnuda*, portraits of an unknown woman, which are identical save for the lack of clothing in the latter. Other portraits are located in rooms 34 to 38.

The horrors of war had a profound effect on Goya's view of the world. *El Dos de Mayo* and, still more dramatically, *El Tres de Mayo*, bring to life the 1808 anti-French revolt and subsequent execution of insurgents in Madrid. They're in room 39.

The Goya exhibit continues on the ground floor in rooms 66 and 67, which house his *Pinturas Negras* (Black Paintings), so-called because of the dark browns and black that dominate. Among the most disturbing of these works is *Saturno Devorando a Su Hijo* (Saturn Devouring One of His Children).

Other Spanish Artists

After these greats, the remaining members of the Spanish contingent come in looking a little insipid. There are nonetheless some fine works by other figures of the 17th century, such as Bartolomé Esteban Murillo, Francisco de Zurbarán, Alonso Cano and José de Ribera.

Flemish Artists

The 17th century works are the backbone of the collection and, while for most visitors the Spanish contribution is paramount, there is a wealth of Flemish art.

The pick of the work of Hieronymus Bosch (c1450-1516) lives in room 57A on the ground floor. While *The Garden of Earthly Delights* is no doubt the star attraction of this fantastical painter's collection, all reward inspection. The closer you look, the harder it is to escape the feeling that he must have been doing some extraordinary drugs.

Peter Paul Rubens (1577-1640) gets a big run here. His works are distributed across several rooms from No 60 to 63A. He is joined by Anton van Dyck, Jacob Jordaens, David Teniers and others of the same epoch.

Italian Artists

The Italians haven't been left out either. They fully occupy rooms 2 to 10A, and count among their number Sandro Botticelli (1445-1510), Andrea Mantegna (1431-1506), Raphael (1483-1520), Tintoretto (1518-94) and, especially, Titian (Tiziano Vecelli; 1487-1576).

Elsewhere (in rooms 18A and 41, respectively) there are some works by Tiepolo (1692-1770) and Caravaggio (1571-1610).

Dutch & German Artists

Apart from a Rembrandt (Protestant Holland) and a few samples of Dürer and Carlos III's court painter, Anton Rafael Mengs (1728-79), there is not much to speak of from Germany or independent Holland. Mengs' stuff is mostly portraits, particularly of his boss, Carlos III (with the nose; room 17A).

French Artists

Nicolas Poussin (1594-1665), an important French painter of the 17th century, dominates room 15A. There is precious little else from France, but in room 16A you can see a few contributions from Louis Michel Van Loo (1707-71) and Jean-Antoine Watteau (1684-1721).

Casón del Buen Retiro

A short walk east of the Prado, the one-time ballroom of the now nonexistent Palacio del Buen Retiro houses a selection of lesser-known 19th century works. Artists include Joaquín Sorolla, Aureliano de Beruete and Vicente López. The latter's portrait of Goya hangs here. The facility was closed for renovation at the time of writing.

Entry

The Prado is open Tuesday to Saturday from 9 am to 7 pm. On Sunday and holidays it closes at 2 pm. You can enter the Prado by either the northern Puerta de Goya or the southern Puerta de Murillo. The latter leads you into the ground floor, while you can

access the ground and 1st floors from the former.

One ticket covers the Prado and Casón del Buen Retiro (500 ptas, half-price for students). Entry is free on Sunday and Saturday afternoon (from 2.30 to 7 pm), as well as on selected national holidays. See the boxed text 'Museum & Gallery Admission' for other possible tickets.

Guides & Information

There is little free printed information. The hand-out map guides you to the main schools and major artists. In rooms 9B, 12, 32 and 61 you'll find decent brochures (100 ptas each) on, respectively, El Greco, Velázquez, Goya and the Flemish artists.

MUSEO THYSSEN-BORNEMISZA

This is one of the most wide-ranging private assemblies of mostly European art in the world. It has been accumulated over two generations by the Thyssen-Bornemiszas, a family of German-Hungarian magnates. Spain managed to acquire the prestigious collection when it offered to overhaul the neoclassical Palacio de Villahermosa specifically to house most of it. Some 800 works have hung here since 1993, with a further 80 at the Monestir de Pedralbes (Barcelona). The museum is at Paseo del Prado 8 (metro: Banco de España, map: Central).

The exhibition is spread out over three floors, so you could do worse than follow the museum pamphlet's advice and start on the 2nd floor (there is a lift) and work your way down chronologically from 13th and 14th century religious art to the avant-garde and pop art on the ground floor. The eclectic nature of the collection is such that many artists of a great number of epochs and schools are represented – if only by one or two pieces.

Second Floor

The first four rooms are dedicated to medieval art, with a series of remarkable Italian triptychs and paintings to get the ball rolling. They include some by Duccio Buoninsegna, who led the Sienese school into a gentle break from Byzantine forms in the late 13th and early 14th centuries.

Room 5 contains, among others, some works by Italy's Piero della Francesca (1410-92) and a *Henry VIII* by Holbein the Younger (1497-1543). Some of the jewellery Henry VIII commissioned Holbein to design is on display in room 6 (the long Galería Villahermosa). In room 7 are some exemplary works by the brothers Gentile (1429-1507) and Giovanni Bellini (1430-1516), who together with their father, Jacopo (1400-70), launched the Venetian Renaissance in painting. Titian also pops up here, although you'll see more of his later in room 11. Rooms 8, 9 and 10 are given over to German and Dutch 16th century masters. Among them are a few works by Cranach (1472-1553).

Room 11 is dedicated above all to Titian and Tintoretto, although El Greco contributes a few pieces, including an *Asunción*. Caravaggio dominates the next room, but Spain gets a look in with some works by José de Ribera (El Españoleto), himself influenced by Caravaggio. Look out for the fine views of Venice by Canaletto (1697-1768), accompanied by some of the best works of Francesco Guardi (1712-93), in room 17. Rubens leads the way in the last rooms on this floor, which are devoted to 17th century Dutch and Flemish masters.

First Floor

The Dutch theme continues on the next floor, with interiors and landscapes. They are followed by a room (27) devoted to a still-life series; in room 28 you'll find a Gainsborough (1727-88) – one of the few British works in the collection. Next comes a representative look at North American art of the 19th century, including pieces by John Singer Sargent (1856-1925) and James Whistler (1834-1903).

All the great impressionist and post-impressionist names get a mention in rooms 32 and 33, with works by Pissarro, Renoir, Sisley, Monet and Manet. They are followed by Toulouse-Lautrec, Cézanne, Degas, Gauguin and Van Gogh. The rest of the floor is dedicated to various movements in expressionist painting. In room 35 you'll find canvases by Egon Schiele, Henri Matisse, Edvard Munch and Oskar Kokoschka.

Ground Floor

Here you move into the 20th century, from cubism through to pop art. In room 44 you'll see a nice mix of Picasso, Juan Gris

Museum & Gallery Admission

You can take advantage of several options to reduce the cost of entry to Madrid's museums and galleries. In the case of the three big art galleries – the Prado (standard admission charge 500 ptas), Centro de Arte Reina Sofía (500 ptas) and Museo Thyssen-Bornemisza (700 ptas), you can get a Paseo del Arte ticket for 1050 ptas for all three, valid year round. Better still for one-off visitors, admission to the first two is free on Saturday afternoon and Sunday.

A year's ticket for unlimited visits to either the Prado or the Reina Sofía costs 4000 ptas. A yearly ticket to both and a series of nine other museums throughout the country is 6000 ptas.

Many other galleries, museums and other sights have free entry at least one day a week. In a few cases this is restricted to EU citizens, but others may be able to sneak through too. Saturday afternoon, Sunday and Wednesday are the most common free times.

Most, but not all, museums and monuments shut on Monday. Just about everything is closed on Sunday afternoon. In July and August some close parts of their displays for want of staff, most of whom take annual leave around this time. A few minor museums even close entirely through August.

and Georges Braque. More Picasso beyond cubism follows in the next room, accompanied by works of Marc Chagall, Max Ernst, Kandinsky and Joan Miró. In room 46 the leap is made back across the Atlantic, with Jackson Pollock and Willem de Kooning (a Dutchman who moved to the USA in 1926) the stars. Lucien Freud (Sigmund's grandson and Berlin-born) and Francis Bacon represent the UK in room 47.

Entry

The gallery is open Tuesday to Sunday from 10 am to 7 pm (700 ptas, students 400 ptas). Separate temporary exhibitions generally cost more.

CENTRO DE ARTE REINA SOFÍA

Adapted from the remains of an 18th century hospital, the Centro de Arte Reina Sofía, Calle de Santa Isabel 52 (metro: Atocha, map: Central), is home to the best Madrid has to offer in modern art, principally spanning the beginning of the 20th century into the 1960s.

The permanent collection is on the 1st floor, while the two floors above are used for temporary exhibits. You'll find a café and excellent art bookshop on the ground floor.

The star attraction for most visitors is Picasso's *Guernica*. Don't just rush straight for it, though, as there is plenty of other good material.

Room 4 is dedicated to cubism, with a couple of Picassos. Dalí has a *naturaleza muerte* (still life) here, but the best work is a series of 10 pieces by Juan Gris, executed between 1913 and the 1920s. In room 6 you can see work by Miró in his surrealist phase of the 1920s – enormously different from what he was doing in the 1970s (see room 13).

The star of the show, *Guernica*, fully dominates room 7, surrounded by a plethora of preparatory sketches. Already associated with the Republicans when the civil war broke out in 1936, Picasso was commissioned by Madrid to do the painting for the Paris Exposition Universelle in

1937. Picasso incorporated features of others of his works into this, an eloquent condemnation of the horrors of war – more precisely, of the German bombing of Gernika (Guernica), in the País Vasco, in April of the same year. It has been surrounded by controversy from the beginning and was at the time viewed by many as a work more of propaganda than of art. The 3.5m by 7.8m painting subsequently migrated to the USA and only returned to Spain in 1981, to languish in the Casón del Buen Retiro until its transfer to the Reina Sofía. Calls to have it moved to the País Vasco continue unabated.

There are some nice Dalís in room 8, including a portrait of the film maker Luis Buñuel (1924). Dalí continues into the next room with such surrealist extravaganzas as *El Gran Masturbador* (1929). Room 17 has a few Picassos and a Francis Bacon.

Entry

The gallery is open Monday to Saturday from 10 am to 9 pm (except Tuesday, when it is closed) and Sunday from 10 am to 2.30 pm (500 ptas, half-price for students).

HABSBURG MADRID

Spain under Carlos I and Felipe II reached the apogee of imperial greatness, its possessions spreading from Vienna to the Low Countries, from Sevilla to the Americas. Felipe's immediate Habsburg successors were largely responsible for expressing that glory in the centre of Madrid. All the places under this heading are on the Central Madrid map.

Puerta del Sol

Once the site of a city gate, the Puerta del Sol is Madrid's most central point. On the southern side a small plaque marks Km 0, from where distances along the country's highways are measured.

The semicircular junction owes much of its present appearance to the Bourbon king Carlos III, whose statue (the nose is unmistakable) stands proudly in the middle. Just to the north of Carlos, the statue of a bear nuzzling a *madroño* (strawberry tree, so-called because its fruit looks something like a strawberry) is not only the city's symbol but also a favourite meeting place for locals, as is the clock tower on the southern side. The square was the central stage for the popular rising against Napoleon's troops on 2 May 1808. On New Year's Eve, people thronging the square wait impatiently for the clock to strike 12, and at each gong swallow a grape.

Plaza Mayor

The heart of imperial Madrid beats in the 17th century Plaza Mayor, a stroll west of Puerta del Sol. Designed in 1619 and built in typical Herrerian style, of which the slate spires are the most obvious expression, it was long a popular stage for royal festivities and *autos de fe*.

On a sunny day the plaza's cafés do a roaring trade, with some 500 busy tables groaning under the weight of the rather expensive drinks. In the middle stands an

Madrileños often meet at this statue on Puerta del Sol

equestrian statue of Felipe III, who ordered construction of the square. The colourful frescoes on the **Real Casa de la Panadería**, so-called for the bakery housed here in the 16th century, were painted in 1992. Just off the south-eastern corner of the square is the baroque edifice housing the Ministerio de Asuntos Exteriores, formerly the court prison.

South of the square, Calle de Toledo is no longer the main road to Madrid's one-time competitor for the title of national capital. It's an interesting boulevard though and you might want to have a quick look at the **Basílica de San Isidro**, long the city's principal church until Nuestra Señora de la Almudena was completed. The Instituto de San Isidro next door once went by the name of Colegio Imperial, in which from the 16th century many of the country's leading figures were schooled.

At this point the road forks. Calle de Toledo leads down to the triumphal arch at the Puerta de Toledo and beyond to the 18th century bridge of the same name across the Río Manzanares. The left fork, Calle de los Estudios, leads into the heart of El Rastro, the crowded Sunday flea market (see Shopping later).

Iglesia de San Ginés

Between Calle Mayor and Calle del Arenal, directly north of Plaza Mayor, San Ginés is one of Madrid's oldest churches: it has been here in one form or another since the 14th century. It houses some fine paintings, including El Greco's *Cleansing of the Temple*, but it is only open for services.

Plaza de la Villa

Back on Calle Mayor and heading west, you pass the central market in Plaza de San Miguel before entering Plaza de la Villa.

The 17th century **ayuntamiento** on the western side of the square is a typical Habsburg edifice with Herrerian slate-tile spires. Leaning more to the Gothic on the opposite side of the square is the **Casa de los Lujanes**, whose brickwork tower is said to have been 'home' to the imprisoned French

El Dos de Mayo

In early 1808, the French army marched into Madrid amid much confusion in the wake of the voluntary and cowardly abdication of Carlos IV and Fernando VII. General Tomás de Morla, who had armed the citizenry to help defend the city, soon found he could not control his unruly forces, which were quickly overwhelmed by Napoleon's troopers. Morla's decision to surrender probably saved the city from the wholesale destruction promised by the French emperor in the event of continued resistance.

But the madrileños were not to be so easily pacified. In the last days of April, men began to converge on Madrid from the neighbouring countryside. Pamphlets exhorting the populace to revolt were circulated and tension grew. On the morning of 2 May, the blood-letting began, with isolated troops coming under attack from armed townspeople, starting around the Palacio Real. The French commander Murat soon had units camped outside the city move in. The 'mob', as he saw them, was concentrated at various points throughout the city, but those in the centre, at the Puerta del Sol, have gone down in history as a symbol of Spanish patriotism. Murat sent in Polish infantry and Mameluke cavalry – a fearsome unit brought to Europe from Egypt for precisely this kind of situation.

The motley band of madrileños gathered in the Puerta del Sol fought with whatever came to hand – rifles, knives, bricks. As the Mamelukes charged into the crowds, sabres cutting into the rebels, local women joined in the fight, stabbing at the Mamelukes' horses and bombarding them with household items from the houses above. As the imperial forces gained the upper hand, the rebels were pushed into Calle Mayor, where some commandeered houses to subject the troops to a bloody crossfire.

All was in vain. By the end of the day the streets, here and elsewhere in the city, had been cleared. Some of the rebels were rounded up to be shot the next day, and road blocks around the city cut off all chance of escape.

Goya immortalised the events of this day and the shootings of the following day in his grim paintings, *El Dos de Mayo* and *El Tres de Mayo*, which now hang in the Prado. And *el dos de mayo* (2 May) went into the annals of Spanish history as the quintessence of the country's patriotic fervour. It also marked the beginning of the Guerra de la Independencia (War of Independence), which to the British, who ultimately tipped the balance and forced Napoleon out of Spain five years later, came to be known simply as the Peninsular War.

---

monarch François I after his capture in the Battle of Pavia. The **Casa de Cisneros**, built in 1537 by the cardinal's nephew, is plateresque in inspiration. A block south looms the 18th century baroque remake of the **Iglesia del Sacramento**.

Convento de las Descalzas Reales

Halfway between Calle del Arenal and Plaza del Callao, the grim walls of this one-time palace serve as a mighty buttress to protect the otherworldly interior from the modern-day chaos outside.

Doña Juana, daughter of Carlos I and mother of Portugal's ill-fated Dom Sebastian, commandeered the palace for conversion into a convent in the 16th century. She was followed by the Descalzas Reales (the Barefooted Royals), a group of illustrious women who became Franciscan nuns. A maximum of 33 nuns can live here, perhaps because Christ is said to have been 33 when he died. The 26 nuns in residence still live according to the rules of the closed order.

The compulsory guided tour (in Spanish) takes you up a gaudily frescoed grand stairway to the upper level of the cloister. The vault was painted by Claudio Coello and at the top of the stairs is a portrait of Felipe II and family members on the royal balcony.

You then pass several of the convent's 33 chapels. The first contains a remarkable carved figure of a dead Christ recumbent. This is paraded in a moving Good Friday procession every year. At the end of the passage you are led into the antechoir and then the choir stalls themselves, where Doña Juana is buried and a *Virgen la Dolorosa* by Pedro de la Mena is seated in one of the 33 oak stalls.

The former sleeping quarters of the nuns house a museum with some of the most extraordinary tapestries you are likely to see. Woven in the 17th century in Brussels, they include four based on drawings by Rubens. Four or five artisans could take as long as a year to weave a square metre of premium-quality tapestry, so imagine how many years must have gone into these! While on the subject of impressive numbers, Spain and the Vatican were the biggest patrons of the tapestry business; Spain alone is said to have collected four million of them.

The convent is open Tuesday to Saturday from 10.30 am to 12.30 pm and again (except Friday) from 4 to 5.30 pm. On Sunday and holidays it is open from 11 am to 1.30 pm (650 ptas, students 250 ptas, free on Wednesday for EU citizens).

Convento de la Encarnación

You could also drop into this less well-known monastery. Founded by Empress Margarita de Austria, it is still inhabited by nuns of the Augustine order (Agustinas Recoletas). Inside you'll find a copious art collection, mostly from the 17th century, and a host of gold and silver reliquaries. The most famous of these contains the blood of San Pantaleón, which purportedly liquefies every year on 28 June.

On Plaza de la Encarnación just north of the Teatro Real (metro: Ópera), it is open on Wednesday and Saturday from 10.30 am to 12.30 pm and 4 to 5.30 pm and Sunday and holidays from 11 am to 1.30 pm (425 ptas, students 225 ptas, free on Wednesday for EU citizens).

PALACIO REAL, LA LATINA & LAVAPIÉS
Palacio Real

When the Alcázar, the oft-altered forerunner of the Palacio Real, burned down in 1734, few mourned its demise. Felipe V took the opportunity to indulge in a little architectural magnificence, planning to build a palace that would dwarf all its European counterparts. The result, which Felipe did not live to see completed, is the Palacio Real, a colossus with some 2800 rooms – of which you are allowed to visit around 50. Carlos III was the first monarch to move in, but the present king is only rarely in residence. It is occasionally closed for state ceremonies of pomp and circumstance.

The **Farmacia Real** is the first set of rooms you strike after buying your tickets at the southern end of the patio known as the Plaza de Armas (or Plaza de la Armería). The pharmacy is an endless parade of medicine jars and stills for mixing royal concoctions. Westwards across the plaza is the **Armería Real** (Royal Armoury), a shiny collection of weapons and armour, mostly dating to the 16th and 17th centuries. The full suits of armour, such as those of Felipe III, are among the most striking items on show.

Access to the apartments lies at the northern end of the Plaza de Armas. The main stairway is a grand statement of imperial power leading first to the Halberdiers' rooms and eventually to the Salón del Trono (throne room). The latter is sumptuous to the point of making you giddy, its crimson velvet wall coverings complemented by a Tiepolo ceiling. Shortly after you'll encounter the Salón de Gasparini, with its exquisite stucco ceiling and embroidered silks covering the walls. The Sala de Porcelana is a heady flourish, with myriad pieces from the one-time Retiro porcelain factory screwed into the walls. The themes change as you progress, with the grand Comedor de Gala (gala dining room) marking a distinct break.

The **Biblioteca Real** (Royal Library) has been closed since the late 1980s. Only students with appropriate permission may enter.

The palace is open Monday to Saturday from 9.30 am to 5.30 pm and Sunday and holidays from 9 am to 2 pm (850 ptas, students 350 ptas, free on Wednesday for EU citizens – bring your passport). If you're lucky, you may catch the fanciful changing of the guard in full 18th century parade dress. This is supposed to occur on the first Wednesday of every month between the palace and the Catedral de Nuestra Señora de la Almudena. However, it appears that more often than not the day is changed or the ceremony doesn't take place at all.

Jardines de Sabatini
Several entrances allow access to this somewhat neglected, French-inspired garden on the northern flank of the Palacio.

Campo del Moro
Much more inspired are the wonderful gardens of the Campo del Moro, so-called because a Muslim army drew up here beneath the walls of Madrid in 1090 in the hope of retaking the town. The only entrance to the gardens is on the western side, from Paseo de la Virgen del Puerto. The gate closes at 8 pm.

Acquired by Felipe II, the partly English-style gardens, as they are now, were not laid out until 1844, with alterations in 1890. The fountain known as Fuente de las Conchas, between the visitors' entrance and the palacio, was designed by Ventura Rodríguez. Inside the grounds is the Museo de los Carruajes (map: Madrid), in which royal carriages could be seen until it was closed for restoration.

Plaza de Oriente
Eastwards across Calle de Bailén from the palace is the majestic Plaza de Oriente, once

partly occupied by dependencies of the Alcázar and given its present form under French occupation in the early 1800s. The square is dominated by an equestrian statue of Felipe IV and littered with 44 statues of monarchs, many of which had been destined to adorn the Palacio Real until it was found they were too heavy. Backing on to the eastern side of the square is the city's premier, and unhappiest, opera house, the **Teatro Real**. Built in 1850, it has been burned down, blown up in the civil war and shut several times for restoration. It finally reopened in October 1997 after nine years of restoration that cost a staggering 21 million pesetas.

Catedral de Nuestra Señora de la Almudena
South of the Palacio Real, this stark and cavernous church, Madrid's cathedral, was completed in mid-1992 after more than 110 years of construction.

Muralla Árabe
Behind the cathedral apse and down Cuesta de la Vega is a short stretch of the so-called Arab Wall, the city wall built by Madrid's early medieval Muslim rulers. Open-air theatre performances are held here in summer.

Viaduct & Calle de Segovia
The leafy area around and beneath the southern end of the viaduct that crosses over Calle de Segovia is an ideal spot to take a break from the hubbub (see Terrazas in the Entertainment section). It is also a popular spot for suicides. Head down to the busy Calle de Segovia, once a trickling tributary of the Manzanares, and cross to the southern side. Just east of the viaduct on a characterless apartment block (No 21) wall is one of the oldest coats-of-arms of the city. The site once belonged to Madrid's ayuntamiento. Calle de Segovia itself runs west between parks to a nine-arched bridge of the same name, built in 1584.

Climb up the other side and you reach Calle de la Morería. The area running from here south to the Basílica de San Francisco el Grande and south-east to the Iglesia de San Andrés was the heart of the **morería**. Strain the imagination a little and the maze of winding and hilly lanes even now retains a whiff of the North African medina. Across Calle de Bailén, the terrazas of Las Vistillas offer one of the best vantage points in Madrid for a drink, with views to the Sierra de Guadarrama. During the civil war Las Vistillas was heavily bombarded by Nationalist troops from the Casa de Campo, who in turn were shelled from a Republican bunker here.

Basílica de San Francisco el Grande

Completed under the guidance of the 18th century Sicilian architect Francesco Sabatini, the basilica has some outstanding features, including frescoed cupolas and chapel ceilings by Francisco Bayeu.

Iglesia de San Andrés

The decoration inside the dome of this church is rather unusual and worth a look if it is open. It was otherwise pretty much gutted during the civil war. As much for this reason as any it, like a good many of Madrid's churches, looks its best when lit up at night as a backdrop for the local café life.

Barrio de Lavapiés

With the exception of **La Corrala**, an intriguing traditional tenement block built around a central courtyard, which functions even now as a makeshift stage for (mainly summertime) theatre, there are no specific sights in this lively quarter. La Corrala is at Calle de Mesón de Paredes 65, opposite the ruins of a church. The real attraction of Lavapiés is the gritty feel of one of the city's last true barrios.

PLAZA DE ESPAÑA & AROUND

A curiously unprepossessing square given its grand title, Plaza de España is flanked to the east by the Edificio de España, reminiscent of some of the bigger efforts of Soviet

monumentalism, and to the north by the rather ugly Torre de Madrid. Taking centre stage in the square itself is a statue of Cervantes. At the writer's feet is a bronze of his most famous characters, Don Quixote and Sancho Panza. All the places listed in this section, unless otherwise marked, are on the Plaza de España map.

Museo de Cerralbo

You could walk past this noble mansion and barely notice it among the bustle in the tight, narrow streets just west of Plaza de España. Inside is a haven of 19th century opulence. The 17th Marqués de Cerralbo – politician, poet and archaeologist – was also an inveterate collector. You can see the results of his efforts in what were once his Madrid lodgings, at Calle de Ventura Rodríguez 17. The upper floor boasts a gala dining hall and a grand ballroom. The mansion is jammed with the fruits of the collector's eclectic meanderings – from religious paintings to Oriental pieces to suits of armour and clocks. Occasionally there's a gem, like El Greco's *Éxtasis de San Francisco*. The museum is open Tuesday to Saturday from 9.30 am to 2.30 pm and Sunday from 10.30 am to 1.30 pm (400 ptas).

Templo de Debod

Looking out of place in the Jardines del Paseo del Pintor Rosales, this 4th century BC Egyptian temple was saved from the rising waters of Lake Nasser, formed by the Aswan High Dam, and sent block by block to Spain in 1970.

The temple is open Tuesday to Friday from 10.45 am to 3.45 pm and 4.15 to 6.15 pm, and weekends from 10 am to 2 pm (300 ptas, free on Wednesday and Sunday).

Ermita de San Antonio de la Florida

Among the finest works produced by Goya are in this small hermitage, aka the Panteón de Goya, about a 10 minute walk north from the Campo del Moro (metro: Príncipe Pío, map: Madrid). You'll find two small chapels. In the southern one the ceiling and

MADRID

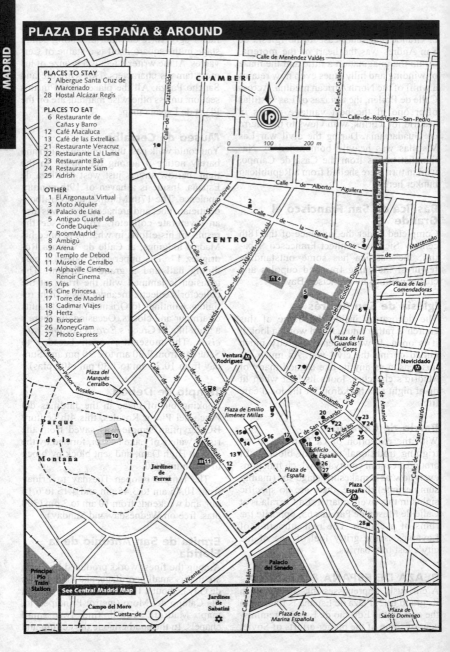

PLAZA DE ESPAÑA & AROUND

PLACES TO STAY
2 Albergue Santa Cruz de Marcenado
28 Hostal Alcázar Regis

PLACES TO EAT
6 Restaurante de Cañas y Barro
12 Café Macaluca
13 Café de las Extrellàs
21 Restaurante Veracruz
22 Restaurante La Llama
23 Restaurante Bali
24 Restaurante Siam
25 Adrish

OTHER
1 El Argonauta Virtual
3 Moto Alquiler
4 Palacio de Liria
5 Antiguo Cuartel del Conde Duque
7 RoomMadrid
8 Ambigú
9 Arena
10 Templo de Debod
11 Museo de Cerralbo
14 Alphaville Cinema, Renoir Cinema
15 Vips
16 Cine Princesa
17 Torre de Madrid
18 Cadimar Viajes
19 Hertz
20 Europcar
26 MoneyGram
27 Photo Express

dome are covered in frescoes by the master (restored in 1993). Those on the dome depict the miracle of St Anthony, who is calling on a young man to rise from the grave and absolve his father, unjustly accused of his murder. Around them swarms a typical Madrid crowd. Usually in this kind of scene the angels and cherubs appear in the cupola, above all terrestrial activity. But Goya places the human above the divine.

The painter is buried in front of the altar. His remains were transferred in 1919 from Burdeos, where he died.

The chapel is open Tuesday to Friday from 10 am to 2 pm and 4 to 8 pm and weekends from 10 am to 2 pm (300 ptas, free on Wednesday and Sunday).

Just across the road is one of Madrid's great eating institutions – the chicken and cider house, Casa Mingo (see Places to Eat later).

Across the train tracks on Calle de Francisco is the **Cementerio de la Florida** (map: Madrid), where 43 rebels executed by Napoleon's troops lie buried; they were killed on the nearby Montaña del Príncipe Pío in the pre-dawn of 3 May 1808 after the Dos de Mayo rising. The event was immortalised by Goya and a plaque was placed here in 1981. The forlorn cemetery, established in 1796, is generally closed.

Antiguo Cuartel del Conde Duque & Palacio de Liria

Over Calle de la Princesa, on the western edge of the Malasaña district (see Malasaña & Chueca later in this chapter), is the grand barracks known as the Antiguo Cuartel del Conde Duque. This has a day job housing government archives and as an occasional art exposition centre and now and then does a night gig as a music venue. Virtually next door, the 18th century Palacio de Liria, rebuilt after a fire in 1936 and surrounded by an enviably green oasis, retains an impressive collection of art, period furniture and *objets d'art*. To organise a visit, send a formal request with your personal details (Palacio de Liria, Atención Don

Miguel, Calle de la Princesa 20, 28008 Madrid). Most mortals content themselves with staring through the gates into the grounds.

Gran Vía

Gran Vía arches off eastwards from Plaza de España. It is a chokingly busy boulevard with more energy than elegance, although it gains some of the latter in the approach to Calle de Alcalá.

From luxury hotels to cheap hostales, pinball parlours and dark old cinemas to jewellery stores and high fashion to fast food and sex shops to banks, Gran Vía has it all. It's a good place to take the city's pulse. Behind the grand façades lie some of the tackier scenes of madrileño life.

MALASAÑA & CHUECA

Just north of Gran Vía is one of Madrid's sleaziest red-light zones, populated by an interesting, if not entirely savoury, collection of pimps, junkies and wasted-looking hookers. This warren of long, narrow streets intersected by even squeezier lanes is known officially as the Barrio de Universidad, but more generally as Malasaña. For the purposes of this guide, that definition extends some blocks west across Calle de San Bernardo into the area bounded by Gran Vía, Calle de la Princesa and Calle de Alberto Aguilera. Chueca is a small area around the square and metro stop of the same name.

Long one of Madrid's slummiest areas, the heart of Malasaña retains a sense of decay, but mostly in a delightful sort of way. Away from the seedy red-light zone around Calle de la Luna, it is for the most part a lively haven of bars, restaurants and other drinking dens.

It is also laced with contrasts. The northeastern corner is dominated by the Palacio de Justicia, the country's supreme law courts. Calle de Génova, which forms part of its northern boundary, is home to the headquarters of Spain's ruling Partido Popular. To the south-east, Malasaña butts against the walls of the national army

MADRID

MALASAÑA & CHUECA

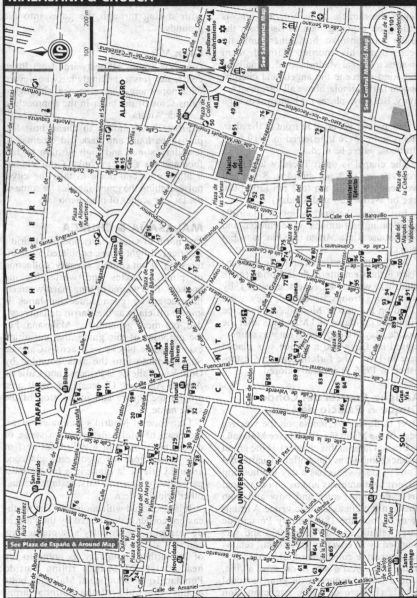

See Plaza de España & Around Map

See Salamanca Map

See Central Madrid Map

MALASAÑA & CHUECA

PLACES TO STAY
17 Hostal Senegal
19 Hostal Sil & Hostal
     Serranos
57 Hostal Medieval
61 Hostal Besaya
62 Hostal El Pinar
65 Hostal Lamalonga
66 Hotel Los Condes
82 Hostal Odesa
83 Hostal Palacios
84 Hostal Ginebra
87 Hotel Laris
88 Hostal Margarita
91 Hostal Delfina

PLACES TO EAT
5   Café Comercial
6   Casa Pablo
8   Café Isadora
21 Restaurante Sandos
24 Taquería de Birrà
26 Restaurante La Granja
27 Pizzeria Mastropiero
28 Tetería de la Abuela
30 Café Manuela
32 Crêperie Ma Bretagne
37 Trattoria Nabucco
40 Casa Manolo
42 Hard Rock Café
53 El Mentidero de la Villa
56 Café La Sastrería
70 Restaurante Dame Noire
76 Café-Restaurante
     El Espejo
79 Gran Café de Gijón
80 Restaurante Momo
81 Chocolatería Madrid

86 Bar-Restaurante Cuchifrito
93 Restaurante La Barraca
94 Restaurante Robata
95 Restaurante La Carreta
98 Restaurante Extremadura

BARS, PUBS & DISCOS
4   Vinos
9   Café del Foro
10 Corripio
11 Patatus
16 Cervecería de Santa
     Bárbara
18 Pachá
20 La Vía Lactea
22 Café Magerit
23 Café Moderno
25 Only You
29 Madrid Jazz
31 Swing
33 Triskel
52 Finnegan's
54 New Leather
58 The Quiet Man
59 Bodega de la Ardosa
64 Morocco
71 Cruising
72 Acuarela Café; Truco
73 Sierra Ángel
75 Rimmel
85 Ya'sta!
89 Del Diego Bar
90 Museo Chicote
92 Cock Bar
96 Bar La Carmencita
97 El Corazón Negro
99 Libertad 8
100 Star's Dance Café

OTHER
1   German Embassy
2   Goethe Institut
3   La Casa de Internet
7   Net Café
12 Tunisian Embassy
13 UK Embassy
14 Librería Turner
15 International House
34 Museo Municipal
35 Museo Romántico
36 Vaiven
38 Sociedad General de Autores
     y Editores
39 Juventus Viajes
41 Torres de Colón
43 Centro Cultural de la Villa &
     Café de la Villa
44 Monumento al Descu-
     brimiento
45 Airport Bus
46 Monumento a Colón
47 Biblioteca Nacional & Museo
     del Libro
48 Museo de Cera
49 Telephones (Telefónica)
50 UK Consulate
51 Institut Français
55 Iglesia de San Antón
60 Teatro Alfil
63 Avis
67 Teatro Lara
68 Lavandería Alba
69 Cogam & Urania's Café
74 Berkana
77 Museo Arqueológico Nacional
78 Anglo-American Medical Unit
101 Puerta de Alcalá

headquarters. On its western edge are the Antiguo Cuartel del Conde Duque and the Palacio de Liria (see Plaza de España & Around).

All the places listed in this section, unless otherwise marked, are on the Malasaña and Chueca map.

Museo Municipal

The main attraction here is the restored baroque entrance, originally raised in 1673 by Pedro de Ribera. Inside you'll find assorted paintings (including some Goyas and Bayeus), sculptures, period furniture, scale models, silver, porcelain and the like. All of it leans to portraying aspects of Madrid life and history.

At Calle de Fuencarral 78 (metro: Tribunal), the museum is open Tuesday to Friday from 9.30 am to 8 pm and weekends from 10 am to 2 pm (300 ptas, free on Wednesday and Sunday).

Museo Romántico

For mainly Spanish 19th century painting, along with period furniture and other curios, try this museum at Calle de San Mateo 13. It's just east of the Museo Municipal and in a lovely, if dishevelled, 18th century mansion. It is open Tuesday to Saturday from 9 am to 3 pm and Sunday and holidays from 10 am to 1.45 pm (400 ptas).

Sociedad General de Autores y Editores

A couple of blocks east of the Museo Romántico on Calle de Pelayo, this joyously self-indulgent ode to *modernisme* looks akin to a huge ice-cream cake half-melted by the summer sun. It is one of a kind in Madrid.

PLAZA DE COLÓN TO THE PRADO

The modern Plaza de Colón (metro: Colón, cercanías: Recoletos, map: Mal & Ch), with the almost surreal Torres de Colón on its western side, is at first glance a rather uninspired affair. Its physical aspect, although softened by the fountains of the Centro Cultural de la Villa, is certainly nothing to write home about. The statue of Colón (Columbus) seems neglected and the **Monumento al Descubrimiento** (Monument to the Discovery – of America, that is), for all its cleverness, does not leave a lasting impression. It was cobbled together in the 1970s.

Still, the area is a cultural nerve centre. The Centro Cultural plays host to theatrical and musical events and just south of the square looms the Biblioteca Nacional and two museums. These can be looked upon as the beginning of museum row – the walk from Colón to the Prado is laced with them.

Biblioteca Nacional & Museo del Libro

Perhaps one of the most outstanding of the many grand edifices erected in the 19th century on the avenues of Madrid, the Biblioteca Nacional was commissioned by Isabel II in 1865 and completed in 1892.

Some of the library's collections have been imaginatively arranged among displays recounting the history of writing and the storage of knowledge. The Museo del

St Valentine's Bones

Nobody much thinks about poor old St Valentine on what in Spain is called 'Lovers' Day' (El Día de los Enamorados), 14 February. This 3rd century bishop and academic was born in Terni, Italy, and according to the legend had quite a thing about young people. Apparently he was so enchanted by the blossoming of young love that he'd help to write love letters, hand out flowers to young newlyweds and even send a little money to struggling lovers in difficult financial circumstances. Whether for this or some other reason, Bishop Valentine was not popular with the Roman administration – and Christianity had yet to become Rome's official faith. So the authorities had Valentine arrested and executed on 14 February 269 AD. Make of all that what you will.

Valentine seems then to have disappeared from sight and mind until the 18th century, when his bones, along with those said to belong to hundreds of other saints, were dug up during excavations in Rome. Since the Eternal City had insufficient churches to each host one of these venerable skeletons, the Church decided to send some of them on a trip to other good Catholic countries. And so it was that St Valentine's bits landed in the crypt of the Iglesia de San Antón (more properly known as San Antonio Abad) in central Madrid. In 1986 it was decided to put this skull-and-crossbones arrangement on public view in the church proper, at Calle de Hortaleza 65, just north of Chueca metro station (map: Mal & Ch). The church is open for services and an hour before for confession.

Libro is a worthwhile stop for any bibliophile yearning to see a variety of Arabic texts, illuminated manuscripts, centuries-old books of the Torah and still more. If your Spanish is up to it, the displays come to life with interactive video commentaries.

The museum is open Tuesday to Saturday from 10 am to 9 pm and Sunday from 10 am to 2 pm (free).

Museo Arqueológico Nacional

Out the back of the same building, at Calle de Serrano 13, the portentous entrance to this museum of archaeology may seem just a little too heavy for your liking. Inside you will find a delightfully varied collection spanning everything from prehistory to the Iberian tribes, imperial Rome, Visigothic Spain, the Muslim conquest and specimens of Romanesque, Gothic and mudéjar handiwork. There is a lot in here and those passing through Madrid more than once while touring Spain could well benefit from repeated visits.

The basement contains displays on prehistoric man, the Neolithic age and on to the Iron Age. Modest collections from ancient Egypt, Etruscan civilisation in Italy, classical Greece and southern Italy under imperial Rome can also be seen. There's also some Spanish specialities: ancient civilisation in the Balearic and Canary islands.

The ground floor is the most interesting. Sculpted figures such as the *Dama de Ibiza* and *Dama de Elche* reveal a flourishing artistic tradition implanted among the Iberian tribes – and no doubt influenced by contact with Greek, Phoenician and Carthaginian civilisation. The latter bust continues, a century after it was found near the Valencian town, to attract controversy over its authenticity.

The arrival of imperial Rome brought predictable changes. Some of the mosaics here are splendid, particularly the incomplete *Triumph of Bacchus* in room 22. The display on Visigothic Spain, and especially material from Toledo, marks a clear break, but only previous experience with Muslim Spain (eg the great cities of Andalucía) or other Muslim countries can prepare you for the wonders of Muslim art. The arches taken from Zaragoza's Aljafería are a centrepiece.

The influences of pure Islamic precepts persist in the later mudéjar style of pre-Christianised Spain, which stands in remarkable contrast with Romanesque and later Gothic developments – all of which can be easily appreciated by soaking up the best of this eclectic collection.

Outside, stairs lead down to a partial copy of the cave paintings of Altamira (Cantabria), which will be as close to the paintings as many people get.

The museum is open Tuesday to Saturday from 9.30 am to 8.30 pm and Sunday from 9.30 am to 2 pm (500 ptas, students half-price, free for everyone on Sunday and from 2.30 pm on Saturday).

Museo de Cera

This is a rather pathetic version of a wax museum. Still, 450 characters have been captured in the sticky stuff – you'll need a good dose of imagination to recognise some of them.

Next to Colón metro station, it is open daily from 10 am to 2.30 pm and 4.30 to 8.30 pm (900 ptas).

Palacio de Linares

Walk southwards down Paseo de los Recoletos and you reach this 19th century pleasure dome (metro: Banco de España, map: Central), built in 1873 and a worthy member of the line-up of grand façades on Plaza de la Cibeles. Its innards are notable particularly for the copious decoration in Carrara marble.

It is open on Tuesday, Thursday and Friday from 9.30 to 11.30 am and weekends and holidays from 10 am to 1.30 pm (300 ptas).

Plaza de la Cibeles

The fountain of the Cybele is one of Madrid's most beautiful. Since it was erected in 1780, this assessment has remained much the same. Carlos III thought it so nice that he wanted to have it moved to the gardens of the Granja de San Ildefonso, on the road to Segovia, but the madrileños were so incensed that he was persuaded by leading figures of the day to let it be. The goddess Cybele had Atalanta

PLAZA DE SANTA ANA & HUERTAS

and Hippomenes, recently paired off thanks to the intervention of Aphrodite, converted into lions and shackled to her chariot for having profaned her temple. They had been put up to this by Aphrodite, irritated by the apparent ingratitude of the newlyweds for her good work.

The building you are least likely to miss on the square is the sickly-sweet Palacio de Comunicaciones – newcomers find it hard to accept that this is only the central correos.

Museo Naval

A block south, maritime-history freaks may find some interest among the charts, instruments and other seafaring paraphernalia here. Juan de la Cosa's 'seagoing map of the Indies' was supposedly the first to depict the New World. It is open Tuesday to Sunday from 10 am to 2 pm (free).

Museo de Artes Decorativos

At Calle de Montalbán 12, this museum is full of sumptuous period furniture, ceram-

PLAZA DE SANTA ANA & HUERTAS

PLACES TO STAY
4 Hostal Aguilar, Hostal León & Hostal Mondragón
10 Hostal Esmeralda
13 Hostal Tineo & Hostal Gibert
23 Hotel Inglés
29 Pensión Poza
33 Hotel Villa Real
39 Hostal San Isidro
40 Hostal Carreras & Hostal Villar
41 Hostal Lucense & Hostal Prado
45 Hostal Santa Ana
47 Hostal Sardinero
49 Hostal Dulcinea
50 Hostal Gonzalo & Hostal Cervantes
57 Gran Hotel Reina Victoria
60 Hostal Persal
62 Hostal Vetusta
65 Hostal Castro & Hostal San Antonio
67 Hostal Casanova
69 Hostal López
72 Hostal Matute
73 Hostal Castilla I & Hostal Martín

PLACES TO EAT
2 Restaurante Al Natural
6 Café del Príncipe
7 Lhardy

8 Museo del Jamón
14 Antigua Pastelería del Pozo
19 Mesón La Caserola
20 Restaurante Donzoko
21 Restaurante Integral Artemisa
25 La Oreja de Oro; Taberna Alhambra
26 La Casa del Abuelo
27 La Trucha
38 La Trucha II
42 Las Bravas
66 Restaurante Pasadero
70 El Café de Sherazade
71 Restaurante La Biotika
78 Restaurante La Sanabresa
81 Champagnería Gala

BARS, PUBS & DISCOS
3 Stella
5 Bar Cuatro Calles
11 La Fontana de Oro
15 La Cartuja
16 Suristán
17 El Trébol
18 Cuevas de Sésamo
22 La Venencia
28 La Creación
30 El Norte
31 Cardamomo
32 No Se Lo Digas A Nadie
35 Carbones
36 Los Gabrieles

37 Viva Madrid
43 Torero
44 Villa Rosa
48 Casa Pueblo
54 Cervecería Alemana
55 La Moderna
56 Bar Hawaiano
58 Bar Matador
59 España Cañí
61 Café Central
63 Casa Alberto
64 Café Populart
79 La Taberna Celta
80 El Parnaso

OTHER
1 Teatro de la Zarzuela
9 Telephones (Sol Telecom)
12 Bullfight & Football Ticket Offices
24 Teatro de la Comedia
34 Ateneo de Madrid
46 Teatro Español
51 Casa de Lope de Vega
52 Lavomatique
53 Lavandería España & Damasco Salón de Te
68 Convento de las Trinitarias
74 Casa Patas
75 Taberna Las Rejas
76 Cine Doré & Filmoteca Nacional
77 Teatro Monumental

ics, carpets, tapestries and the like spanning the 15th to 19th centuries. It is open Tuesday to Friday from 9.30 am to 3 pm and weekends and holidays from 10 am to 2 pm (400 ptas, students half-price).

Museo del Ejército

Filled with weapons, flags, uniforms and other remnants of Spanish military glory, the army museum is housed in what was the Salón de Reinos del Buen Retiro, part of the former Palacio del Retiro, at Calle de Méndez Núñez 1 (metro: Retiro). An interesting room with portraits of Franco is devoted to the glorious Nationalist campaign in the civil war, while the Sala Árabe (decorated Alhambra-style) contains vari-

ous curios including the sword of Boabdil, the last Muslim ruler of Granada, who signed the surrender in 1492 that marked the end of the Reconquista. The museum is open Tuesday to Sunday from 10 am to 2 pm (100 ptas, free on the weekend).

Plaza de Neptuno

Officially known as Plaza de Cánovas del Castillo, the next roundabout south of Cibeles is commanded by an 18th century sculpture of the sea god, by Juan Pascual de Mena. It is a haughty focal point, flanked not only by the Thyssen-Bornemisza gallery and the Prado, but also by the city's famous competitors in the hotel business, the Ritz and the Palace. A block east on Calle de Felipe IV is the custodian of the Spanish language, the Academia Española de la Lengua.

Parque del Buen Retiro

After a heavy round of the art galleries, a stroll in Madrid's loveliest public gardens (map: Madrid) might be the best way to end the day. The gardens are at their busiest on weekends, when street performers appear.

Once the preserve of kings, queens and their intimates, the park is now open to all. You can hire boats to paddle about on the artificial lake *(estanque)*, watched over by a statue of Alfonso XII. Weekend buskers and tarot readers ply their trade around the same lake, while art and photo exhibitions take place at one of a couple of places, especially the Palacio de Exposiciones. Puppet shows for the kids are a summertime feature (look for Tiritilandia, or Puppet Land). At the southern end of the park near the rose gardens (La Rosaleda), a statue of El Ángel Caído (the fallen angel, ie Lucifer) brings a slightly sinister note to the place. The southwestern end of the park is a popular cruising haunt for gay young bloods.

Real Jardín Botánico

Ask most madrileños about the city's botanic gardens (map: Central) and they won't know what you are talking about. All the worse for them, as the Real Jardín Botánico is a refuge more beautiful than El Retiro, although not nearly as extensive. Created in 1755 under Fernando VI at El Huerto de Migas Calientes, the 8 hectare gardens were transferred to their present location under Carlos III. They are open daily from 10 am to 8 pm (200 ptas).

Antigua Estación de Atocha

The old train station at Atocha has become something of a botanical sight in itself. From here the high-speed AVE leaves for Sevilla and the interior of the old terminal has been converted into a tropical garden – certainly a pleasant departure or arrival point. Virtually across the road is the Centro de Arte Reina Sofía (see earlier).

Real Fábrica de Tapices

Founded in the 18th century to provide the royal family and other bigwigs with tapestries befitting their grandeur, this workshop is still producing such works today. You can see the work in progress or just admire the products, which also include carpets. For years, unfortunately, it has been on the edge of bankruptcy and a dark cloud hangs over its future. Have a look while you can; it's at Calle de Fuenterrabía 2 (metro: Menéndez Pelayo, map: Madrid) and is open Monday to Friday from 9 am to 12.30 pm (shut in August).

THE PRADO TO SOL

The main reason for heading into the area known to locals as Huertas, roughly contained in the triangle west of Paseo del Prado and between Calle de Atocha and Carrera de San Jerónimo, is to eat and drink. It is a smaller, brighter and perhaps more touristy version of Malasaña.

Mention has already been made, in the Walking Tour section, of Cervantes' burial place and the **Casa de Lope de Vega**. The latter, at Calle de Cervantes 11 (metro: Antón Martín), should be open Tuesday to Friday from 9.30 am to 2 pm and Saturday from 10 am to 1.30 pm (200 ptas). The playwright lived here for 25 years until his death in 1635 and the place is filled with memorabilia related to his life and times.

A block to the north along Calle de León is the **Ateneo de Madrid** (see Libraries in the Information section earlier). On Calle de San Jerónimo are **Las Cortes**, the 19th century lower house of the national parliament, and its modern extension.

If you need another art injection, try the **Real Academia de Bellas Artes de San Fernando**. This fusty old institution at Calle de Alcalá 13 (map: Central) was founded in the 18th century by Fernando VI as a centre to train promising artists. Little seems to have changed since then. The 1st floor is mainly devoted to a mix of 16th to 19th century paintings. Among the stodgy portraits are some items of interest, including a couple of self-portraits by Goya and a series

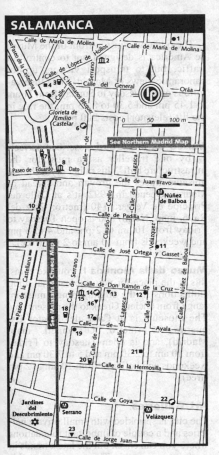

SALAMANCA

SALAMANCA

PLACES TO STAY
4 Hotel Emperatriz
21 Hostal Don Diego

PLACES TO EAT
13 Casa Julián
16 Restaurante Oter
23 Thai Gardens

EMBASSIES
6 US Embassy
14 Irish Embassy
22 Canadian Embassy

OTHER
1 Iberia
2 Museo Lázaro Galdiano
3 St Andrew's Pub
5 Washington Irving Center
7 Boulevard 37
8 Museo de la Escultura Abstracta
9 Alliance Française
10 Bolero
11 Vips
12 Mallorca
15 Fundación de Caixa
17 Max 63
18 Terraza de Serrano
19 Marks & Spencer
20 Teatriz

of full-length portraits of white-cloaked friars by Zurbarán. It is open Tuesday to Friday from 9 am to 7 pm and the rest of the week from 10 am to 2 pm (300 ptas).

SALAMANCA & AROUND

Madrid's most chichi quarter, the Salamanca area to the north-east of the city centre, is lined with elegant apartments and smart department stores. The snappy dressers wandering the grid-pattern boulevards around here seem to be on a different planet

from the people of inner-city districts like Lavapiés. Apart from shopping, you can take in a little culture.

Museo Sorolla

If you liked Sorolla's paintings in the Casón del Buen Retiro, don't miss this museum. In the artist's former residence, it contains the most comprehensive collection of his work in Spain, mostly the sunny Valencian beach scenes for which he is best known. It's set amid cool gardens at Paseo del General Martínez Campos 37 (metro: Rubén Darío, map: Madrid) and is open Monday to Saturday from 10 am to 3 pm and Sunday and holidays from 10 am to 2 pm (400 ptas, free on Sunday, students 200 ptas).

Museo Lázaro Galdiano

A surprisingly rich former private collection awaits you in this museum at Calle de

Serrano 122 (metro: República Argentina, map: Sal). Aside from some fine works by artists like Van Eyck, Bosch, Zurbarán, Ribera, Goya, Gainsborough, Constable and others, this is a rather odd-ball assembly of all sorts of collectables. The ceilings were all painted according to their room's function. The exception is room 14, where the artist created a collage from some of Goya's more famous works, including *La Maja* and the frescoes of the Ermita de San Antonio de la Florida, in honour of the genius. It's open Tuesday to Sunday from 10 am to 2 pm (400 ptas).

Museo de la Escultura Abstracta

This interesting open-air collection of 17 abstracts includes works by Chillida, Miró, Sempere and Toledo's Alberto Sánchez. The sculptures are under the overpass where Paseo de Eduardo Dato crosses Paseo de la Castellana (metro: Rubén Darío, map: Sal). All but one are on the eastern side of Paseo de la Castellana.

OUTSIDE THE CENTRE
Museums

Madrid seems to have more museums and art galleries than the Costa del Sol has high-rise apartments. The following are a sample.

Museo de América For centuries Spanish vessels plied the Atlantic between the mother country and the newly won colonies in Latin America. Most carried gold one way and adventurers the other, but the odd curio from the indigenous cultures found its way back.

The two levels show off a representative display of ceramics, statuary, jewellery and instruments of hunting, fishing and war, along with some of the paraphernalia of the colonisers. The Colombian gold collection, dating as far back as the 2nd century AD, and a couple of shrunken heads are eye-catching.

At Avenida de los Reyes Católicos 6 (metro: Moncloa, map: Madrid), it is open Tuesday to Saturday from 10 am to 3 pm and closes half an hour earlier on Sunday

and holidays (500 ptas, free on Sunday, students half-price).

The odd tower just in front of the Museo de América is designed not to control air traffic, but to transport visitors up for panoramic views of Madrid. The **Observatorio** is open Tuesday to Sunday from 11 am to 1.45 pm and 5.30 to 8.45 pm; the ride in the lift (elevator) costs 200 ptas.

Museo de la Ciudad Described perfectly by one traveller as 'a must for the infrastructure buff', this rather dry technical museum traces the growth and spread of Madrid. Opened in 1992, it's at Calle del Príncipe de Vergara 140 (metro: Cruz del Rayo, map: North) and is open Tuesday to Friday from 10 am to 2 pm and 4 to 8 pm and weekends from 10 am to 2 pm (free).

Museo de la Moneda If you like coins, this is the place for you: the national mint. Collections in the slightly dingy museum range from ancient Greek to the present day. The museum is at Calle del Doctor Esquerdo 36 (metro: O'Donnell, map: Madrid), and is open Tuesday to Friday from 10 am to 2.30 pm and 5 to 7.30 pm and weekends and holidays from 10 am to 2 pm (free).

Art Galleries

The city is sprinkled with small private galleries and a couple of important foundations where you can check out the latest trends in contemporary work. There are many exhibition spaces, so the best advice is to keep an eye on newspapers and gig guides such as the *Guía del Ocio*.

Among the most important is the **Fundación Juan March**, Calle de Castelló 77 (metro: Núñez de Balboa, map: Madrid). The foundation has its own collection and is responsible for organising some of the better temporary exhibits each year. The **Fundación La Caixa** is another busy bee, putting on regular contemporary art exhibits. It's at Calle de Serrano 60 (map: Sal).

NORTHERN MADRID

0   250   500 m

PLACES TO EAT
4 China Crown &
   Viajes Zeppelin
5 Restaurante Sulú
7 Asador La Tahona

EMBASSIES & CONSULATES
1 Netherlands Embassy
9 Moroccan Embassy
11 Moroccan Consulate
20 Australian Embassy

OTHER
2 Centro de Salud
3 Lavandería Automática
6 Maes
8 Irish Rover
10 Librería Alemana
12 Auditorio Nacional de
   Música
13 Museo de la Ciudad
14 Kangarú Australian Bar;
   Tex-Mex
15 French Consulate
16 Renoir Cinema
17 La Tienda Verde
18 Continental-Auto
   Bus Station
19 Librería Italiana
21 Escuela Oficial de
   Idiomas

MADRID

Parque del Oeste

Spread out between the university and Moncloa metro station (map: Madrid), this is a tranquil and, in parts, quite beautiful park for a wander or shady laze in the heat of the day.

By night it undergoes a transformation, as the city's transsexual prostitute population and their clients come out to play. Part of the beat is reserved for female streetwalkers too. Most of the activity takes place in cars, which become remarkably numerous as the night wears on. Although you are unlikely to be bothered – police keep an eye out for anything more untoward than the routinely untoward – the area is not the ideal choice for a late-evening family stroll.

Casa de Campo

This huge and rather unkempt semiwilderness stretching west of the Río Manzanares undergoes similar metamorphoses. It was in regal hands until 1931, when its 1200 hectares were thrown open to the people.

By day cyclists and walkers eager for something resembling nature, but with no time or desire to leave Madrid, clog the byways and low roads that crisscross the park. There are also tennis courts and Madrid's most central swimming pool (see Swimming later) as well as an amusement park for the kids (see Entertainment later).

Madrid's **zoo**, also in the park, contains some 3000 animals and a respectable aquarium (metro: Batán). It is open Monday to Friday from 10.30 am to 8.30 pm and on weekends to 9 pm. On a different animal note, the Andalucian-style ranch known as Batán is used to house the bulls destined to do bloody battle in the Fiestas de San Isidro (see Special Events). Finally, the none-too-exciting **teleférico** (cable car) from Paseo del Pintor Rosales (on the corner of Calle del Marqués de Urquijo; map: Madrid) ends at a high point in the middle of the park. It starts operating at 11 am (noon outside April to September) and continues until 10 pm; it runs from 1 April to 30 September, as well as weekends and holidays through the rest of the year (360 ptas one way, 515 ptas return).

Many people just come to sip a drink by the small artificial lake (metro: Lago).

As night sets in, the scene takes on other hues. The occasional junkie, prostitute or pimp you may have espied in the area around the lake during the day turns into something of an avalanche. As the girls (and on occasion the boys who want to be girls) jockey for position, not a few punters keep their places around the lakeside *chiringuitos* (open-air bar or kiosk) as though nothing out of the ordinary was happening. The traffic in the middle of the night here is akin to rush hour in the city centre!

SWIMMING

There are outdoor municipal pools in several locations around the city, open from June to September. During the rest of the year several municipal indoor pools open their doors. There are also various private pools.

About the handiest location is the Instituto Municipal de Deportes in the Casa de Campo (metro: Lago). From June to September it is open daily from 10 am to 8 pm. During the rest of the year, the indoor pool is open Monday to Friday from 11 am to 6 pm. Entry costs 500 ptas or you can buy a *bono*, good for 20 visits, for 7500 ptas.

LANGUAGE COURSES

The Universidad Complutense offers a range of language and culture courses throughout the year. Contact the Secretaria de los Cursos para Extranjeros (☎ 91 394 53 25, fax 91 394 52 98), Facultad de Filología (Edificio A), Universidad Complutense, Ciudad Universitaria, 28040 Madrid.

You could also sign up at the overworked and chaotic Escuela Oficial de Idiomas (☎ 91 533 00 88, ☎ 91 554 99 77), Calle de Jesús Maestro s/n (map: North). It offers courses in Spanish for foreigners (Español para Extranjeros) at most levels.

Many of the language schools aimed at teaching locals English and other foreign tongues also run courses in Spanish for foreign visitors.

The Battle of Madrid

When Franco's Nationalists rose in revolt in July 1936, the army planned a lightning assault on the capital. General Mola quickly moved several thousand troops south from Pamplona and east from Valladolid, with the aim of crossing the Somosierra and other passes and descending rapidly on Madrid before the Republicans could get organised. They never made it over the passes, which were held tenaciously by Republican militia who knew their loss would mean the loss of Madrid.

With Mola stopped in his tracks, the element of surprise was lost, but soon the capital faced a new threat as Franco's columns advanced rapidly from Seville through Extremadura and halted in the Casa de Campo, at the western gates of the city. In November the government fled to Valencia, but Madrid was not abandoned. A medley of Spanish Republican forces of all political persuasions was joined by Soviet advisers and the International Brigades. The latter would bear the brunt of Franco's assaults directed at the university part of town. Although these attacks met with some success – at the cost of a great many lives – the Nationalists never made it much beyond the barrio of Argüelles.

As fortunes seesawed and then declined for the Republicans, Madrid remained out of Nationalist hands. Fighting continued on the Madrid front but, even when communist forces clashed with other Republicans in early 1939, the Nationalists failed to move. Of course, by that time they did not really need to. The writing was on the wall and the Republicans' days were numbered. As their forces in the centre crumbled and Franco's columns advancing from Toledo and on to Guadalajara linked up, the few commanders who had not already fled surrendered Madrid on 27 March. Four days later the war was over.

WORK

About the most common source of work for foreigners in Madrid is teaching their native language. You can start your job search at the cultural centre of your country, but there is a sea of language schools around Madrid.

For English-speakers, the top choices are the British Council (see Cultural Centres earlier) and International House (☎ 91 310 13 14), Calle de Zurbano 8 (map: Mal & Ch).

ORGANISED TOURS
Central Circuit

You can pick up a special Madrid Vision bus around the centre of Madrid up to 10 times a day. There are only three on Sundays and holidays. A full round trip costs 1700 ptas and you can board the bus at any of 14 clearly marked stops. Taped commentaries in four languages, including English, are available, and the bus stops at several major monuments, including the Prado and near Plaza Mayor. If you buy the 2200 ptas ticket, you can use the buses all day to get around (2900 ptas buys you the same right for two days running); frankly, you're better off investing in 10-trip metro tickets.

Descubre Madrid

The Patronato Municipal de Turismo has chosen 80 itineraries around the capital. Tours are conducted in Spanish and you can pick up calendars detailing when and where the walks are held at any branch of the Caja de Madrid bank, which co-sponsors the Descubre Madrid program.

Paseos por el Madrid de los Austrias

The Patronato Municipal de Turismo organises Saturday morning walks around the centre of old Madrid (500 ptas). They start at 10 am (English) and noon (Spanish).

Meet outside the Patronato office at Plaza Mayor 3 half an hour before.

Other Tours
Several companies organise city tours. These range from half-day jaunts around Madrid for a costly 5100 ptas through to an evening of flamenco flouncing with a meal for up to 12,700 ptas. Most central Madrid travel agents can fill you in on the details.

SPECIAL EVENTS
Fiestas de San Isidro
Madrid's single greatest *fiesta* celebrates the city's patron saint, San Isidro, in the third week of May. It kicks off with the *pregón*, a speech delivered by the mayor, on the Friday or Saturday in the middle of the month and goes on for a week. There are free music performances around the city and the country's most prestigious *feria*, or bullfight season, at the huge Plaza de Toros Monumental de las Ventas – the feria lasts for a month. Compulsive aficionados of bullfighting may want to take a peek at the Museo Taurino out the back of the bullring; it's usually open on weekdays from 9.30 am to 2.30 pm.

Other Fiestas
The Malasaña district, which can be busy enough at any time, has its biggest party on 2 May, which follows a national holiday on 1 May (Labour Day). For obvious reasons, the celebrations centre on Plaza del Dos de Mayo.

The Fiesta de San Juan is held in the Parque del Buen Retiro over the seven days leading up to 24 June.

The few locals who haven't left town in the second week of August will be celebrating the consecutive festivals of San Cayetano (Lavapiés), San Lorenzo (La Latina) and La Paloma (around Calle de Calatrava in La Latina). In the last week of September the Fiesta de Otoño (autumn festival) is held in Chamartín; this is about the only time you'd be tempted to hang around here and *not* get a train out.

Dyed in the Wool
Especially around the Fiesta de San Isidro, the *chulapos* and *manolas* of Madrid come out of the woodwork. The gents dress in their traditional short jackets and berets and the women in *mantones de Manila*, and put their best feet forward in a lively *chotis*.

What is all this? The mantón de Manila is an embroidered silk shawl, which few people now wear, except during fiestas. The chotis is a traditional working-class dance not unlike a polka. One of the most common versions involves a quick three-step to the left, the same to the right, and is topped off with a brisk twirl. Only a small portion of the really *castizo* (true-blue) madrileños bother with this any more, but those who do so do it with a certain pride.

The chulapo – or dyed-in-the-wool, born-and-bred *madrileño* – is now more commonly known as a *chulo*. Now this is a word to beware of. It generally implies a degree of bravado and even arrogance of character, although in the eyes of madrileños this is no bad thing. But to many people the word bears quite negative qualities – brash, showy. The word can also mean 'pimp', so you'd want to be sure of your company and context before bandying it around too much. The fast-talking, hard-living, Madrid version of James Dean is also typecast as a *macarra*, which at its worst also means a spiv.

These breezy types, especially the kind you'd come across in the inner working-class barrios like Lavapiés, were also once generally referred to as *manolos* (Manolo is a common first name). So it stands to reason that their girls should be known as manolas! To complete the picture, full-blooded madrileños are also known to the rest of Spain as *gatos*, or cats – a nice image to reflect their city savvy.

September is a big month for local fiestas in several barrios of Madrid and towns around the capital.

Halfway through September, the Partido Comunista de España (Spanish Communist Party) holds its yearly fund-raiser in the Casa de Campo. The Fiesta del PCE lasts a weekend and is a mixed bag of regional food pavilions, rock concerts and political soapboxing.

PLACES TO STAY

Madrid is crawling with pensiones, hostales and hotels, so there should rarely be trouble finding a place to stay. If you arrive by air and catch the airport bus to Plaza de Colón, you'll find an accommodation service and, often, touts offering rooms.

Prices quoted below should be seen as indicative only. Proprietors often modify them at whim and have their own scale according to the size of individual rooms, length of intended stay etc.

PLACES TO STAY – BUDGET
Camping & Youth Hostels

There is one camping ground within striking distances of central Madrid. To reach *Camping Osuna* (☎ 91 741 05 10), on Avenida de Logroño near the airport, take metro No 5 to Canillejas (the end of the line), from where it's about 500m away. It charges 630 ptas per person, car and tent.

There are two HI youth hostels in Madrid. The *Albergue Richard Schirrman* (☎ 91 463 56 99) is in the Casa de Campo (metro: El Lago, bus No 33 from Plaza Ópera). B&B in a room of four costs 950 ptas (under 26) or 1300 ptas.

The *Albergue Santa Cruz de Marcenado* (☎ 91 547 45 32, Calle de Santa Cruz de Marcenado 28) has rooms for four, six and eight people (metro: Argüelles, map: España, bus Nos 1, 61 and Circular). B&B costs the same as in the other hostel. This is one of the few Spanish hostels in HI's International Booking Network.

An HI membership card is necessary for both hostels. You can obtain one at the hostels or in central Madrid at the offices of the Consejería de Educación y Cultura (☎ 91 580 42 16, Calle de Alcalá 32). The youth hostel section is on the 1st floor and is open Monday to Friday from 9 am to 2 pm. Or you could try the TIVE offices (see Travel Agencies earlier).

Other Accommodation – Atocha to Plaza de Santa Ana

Atocha train station is close to the city centre, so it is worth making the effort to walk up Calle de Atocha towards Plaza de Santa Ana if you arrive here. All the places listed are on the Plaza de Santa Ana & Huertas map.

Roughly halfway between the station and Santa Ana, *Hostal López* (☎ 91 429 43 49, Calle de las Huertas 54) is a good choice. Singles/doubles start at 2600/4000 ptas without own bath or 3800/4800 ptas with. It's on a quiet part of an otherwise lively street.

There are a few places along the noisy Calle de Atocha itself and, if you can't be bothered tramping around and looking, you could do worse than *Hostal Castilla I* (☎ 91 429 00 95) at No 43. Small, spotless rooms with private bath and TV are 4000/5000 ptas.

Hostal Casanova (☎ 91 429 56 91, Calle de Lope de Vega 8) has simple rooms at 2000/3100 ptas. *Hostal Castro* (☎ 91 429 51 47, Calle de León 13) is an attractive place with good, clean rooms at 2300/4000 ptas with own bath. *Hostal San Antonio* (☎ 91 429 51 37), one floor up, also has reasonable rooms with private bath and TV for 3000/4000 ptas.

Hostal Gonzalo (☎ 91 429 27 14, Calle de Cervantes 34) is in sparkling nick. Rooms with private shower and TV are 4000/5200 ptas. You can get a few hundred pesetas off if you stay at least three days. If that doesn't satisfy, *Hostal Cervantes* (☎ 91 429 27 45) on the 2nd floor is OK but more expensive, with rooms costing up to 4500/6000 ptas. *Hostal Dulcinea* (☎ 91 429 41 71) at No 19 has well-maintained, if simply furnished, rooms and is often full. Rooms cost 3800/4800 ptas.

MADRID

Hostal Persal (☎ 91 369 46 43, Plaza del Ángel 12) is a good but rather pricey choice where comfortable rooms with bath, TV and phone cost 5300/7500 ptas.

Hostal Carreras (☎ 91 522 00 36, Calle del Príncipe 18) is a decent if unexciting choice where rooms with washbasin start at 2000/3500 ptas. If you want your own shower, it's 500 ptas more, or 1000 ptas more for a full private bathroom. In the same building, *Hostal Villar (☎ 91 531 66 09)* is in much the same category.

A classier option at No 17 is *Hostal San Isidro (☎ 91 429 15 91)*. It has clean rooms with private bathroom, TV and phone for 4000/5500 ptas.

Hostal Matute (☎ 91 429 55 85, Plaza de Matute 11) has spacious singles/doubles for 2500/4700 ptas without own bath and 3500/5400 ptas with. *Hostal Vetusta (☎ 91 429 64 04, Calle de las Huertas 3)* has admittedly small, but cute, rooms with own shower starting at 2000/3500 ptas; try for one looking onto the street.

Hostal Santa Ana (☎ 91 521 30 58) at No 1, right on the square, has average rooms with shower for 2500/3500 ptas.

Hostal Lucense (☎ 91 522 48 88, Calle de Núñez de Arce 15) and *Pensión Poza (☎ 91 232 20 65)* at No 9 are owned by the same people (who used to live in Australia). Small and in some cases windowless rooms start at around 1000 ptas per person, but you can get better ones for 1500/2600 ptas. A hot shower costs 200 ptas extra. In the same building as the Lucense, *Hostal Prado (☎ 91 521 30 73)* on the 2nd floor offers rooms of a similar quality from 1800/3200 ptas.

North of Plaza de Santa Ana, *Hostal Mondragón (☎ 91 429 68 16, Carrera de San Jerónimo 32)* is pretty good value at 2000/2800 ptas for a biggish room without own bathroom. There are at least four other places in the same building. Of these, the *Hostal León (☎ 91 429 67 78)* is not bad and has heating. It charges 1800/3000 ptas, although some doubles are 4000 ptas. Another acceptable option in this building is *Hostal Aguilar (☎ 91 429 36 61)*, which

charges from 3500/5500 ptas for rooms with private bathroom.

Hostal Sardinero (☎ 91 429 57 56, Calle del Prado 16) is a good choice. Rooms with bath and satellite TV come in at 4000/6000 ptas.

Other Accommodation – Around Puerta del Sol

Hostal Tineo (☎ 91 521 49 43, Calle de la Victoria 6) charges a standard 2500/3500 ptas for singles/doubles with washbasin only (map: Ana & Hue). They cost up to 4000/5500 ptas for rooms with private bathroom. In the same building, *Hostal Gibert (☎ 91 522 42 14)* has rooms without bath for the same price, or doubles with private bath for 4000 ptas.

A pretty decent place is the *Hostal Esmeralda (☎ 91 521 00 77, Calle de la Victoria 1)*. Bright, clean rooms with private bath, TV and phone cost 4200/5500 ptas (map: Ana & Hue).

If you don't mind the traffic, *Hostal Cosmopólitan (☎ 91 522 66 51, Puerta del Sol 9, 3rd floor)* has basic singles/doubles from 1600/3000 ptas (map: Central).

A much better deal is *Hostal Riesco (☎ 91 522 26 92, Calle del Correo 2)*, which has comfortable rooms looking right onto Puerta del Sol (map: Central). Singles/doubles with shower cost 3200/4300 ptas or 3600/5000 ptas with full bathroom.

Hostal Ruano (☎ 91 532 15 63, Calle Mayor 1) has no-frills rooms for 2000/3200 ptas (map: Central).

South-west of Puerta del Sol towards Plaza Mayor, *Hostal Santa Cruz (☎ 91 522 24 41, Plaza de Santa Cruz 6)* is in a prime location (map: Central). Rooms here start from about 3400/4800 ptas. A cheaper option in the same building is *Hostal Cruz Sol (☎ 91 532 71 97)*. Rooms start from 2000/2700 ptas without private bath. Doubles with bath cost 4000 ptas.

Hostal María del Mar (☎ 91 531 90 64) on Calle del Marqués Viudo de Pontejos has similarly basic rooms starting at 2000/2800 ptas (map: Central).

Other Accommodation – Plaza Mayor

Hostal La Macarena (☎ 91 365 92 21, Cava de San Miguel 8) has good rooms with private bath, TV and phone but at 4500/6500 ptas you pay mainly for the position.

Other Accommodation – Around Ópera

All the places listed are on the Central Madrid map.

Pensión Luz (☎ 91 542 07 59, Calle de las Fuentes 10) is a friendly place with decent little rooms at 2500/3700 ptas.

Calle del Arenal is a good hunting ground, although it's a noisy thoroughfare. *Hostal Ivor (☎ 91 547 10 54)* at No 24 has rooms with private bath and TV for 3800/5500 ptas.

Just by the Convento de las Descalzas Reales is *Hostal Roma (☎ 91 531 19 06, Travesía de Trujillos 1)*, a reliable place with singles/doubles starting at 3500/4600 ptas with own shower or 4600/5500 ptas with full bathroom.

Hostal Paz (☎ 91 547 30 47, Calle de la Priora Flora 4) looks horrible from the outside, but the cheap rooms inside are reasonable value at 2400/4200 ptas without private bath, or a few hundred pesetas more with bath.

Other Accommodation – Paseo del Prado

If you want to be a stone's throw from El Prado, you have a couple of choices on the grand boulevard. *Hostal Sudamericano (☎ 91 429 25 64)* at No 12 is not a bad one, with singles/doubles starting at 2500/4800 ptas (map: Central).

Other Accommodation – Around Gran Vía & Malasaña

Gran Vía is laden with accommodation, but it's a noisy area. At the cheaper end of the scale you could try *Hostal Alcázar Regis (☎ 91 547 93 17)* at No 61 (map: España). Singles/doubles cost 2500/4500 ptas. Across the road and up the hill a little,

Hostal Lamalonga (☎ 91 547 26 31) at No 56 is reliable (map: Mal & Ch). Rooms with private bath start at 3800/5200 ptas. *Hostal Margarita (☎ 91 547 35 49)* at No 50 charges 3700/4750 ptas for rooms; they all have a shower, but the singles don't have their own loo.

The stylish *Hostal Besaya (☎ 91 541 32 07, Calle de San Bernardo 13)* has good rooms costing up to 4500/6200 ptas with private bath (map: Mal & Ch).

Hostal Romero (☎ 91 522 19 36, Calle de la Estrella 5) is OK and charges 2800 ptas for simple, small doubles. Singles are hard to come by (map: Mal & Ch).

Hostal El Pinar (☎ 91 547 32 82, Calle de Isabel la Católica 19) has reasonable rooms for 2300/3800 ptas (map: Mal & Ch). The communal bathroom is outside.

Hostal Andorra (☎ 91 531 66 03, Gran Vía 33) is on the 7th floor but has fine rooms with private bath, TV and phone for 4500/6400 ptas (map: Central).

Calle de Fuencarral is choked with hostales and pensiones, especially at the Gran Vía end. *Hostal Ginebra (☎ 91 532 10 35)* at No 17 is a fine choice not far from Gran Vía. All rooms have TV and phone; singles with shower start at 3600 ptas, while doubles with full bathroom cost 4800 ptas. At No 25, *Hostal Palacios (☎ 91 531 10 58)* is a safe choice with singles/doubles from 2400/3500 ptas. Rooms with private bath cost 3300/4500 ptas.

Hostal Medieval (☎ 91 522 25 49, Calle de Fuencarral 46) has spacious and bright singles/doubles with shower for 3000/4000 ptas (map: Mal & Ch). Doubles with full private bathroom cost 5500 ptas. *Hostal Serranos (☎ 91 448 89 87, Calle de Fuencarral 95)* is spick and span; rooms with bath and TV are 3000/5000 ptas. In the same building and a floor up, *Hostal Sil (☎ 91 448 89 72)* has equally good rooms and charges 2500 for singles without bath and 1000 ptas for those with. Doubles with bath start at 5000 ptas.

Hostal Odesa (☎ 91 521 03 38, Calle de Hortaleza 38) has relatively straightforward rooms for 2500/4500 ptas – the doubles have a private bath and TV (map: Mal & Ch). This place caters for a primarily gay clientele.

Hostal Delfina (☎ 91 522 64 23, Gran Vía 12) is up on the 4th floor, putting some distance between you and the traffic noise. Singles/doubles with private bath start at 3500/5000 ptas.

Hostal Senegal (☎ 91 319 07 71, Plaza de Santa Bárbara 8) is in a pretty spot and has decent rooms with private bath for 4500/5800 ptas (map: Mal & Ch).

PLACES TO STAY – MID-RANGE
Around Plaza de Santa Ana & Sol

For a hint of faded elegance, the *Hotel Inglés (☎ 91 429 65 51, fax 91 420 24 23, Calle de Echegaray 8)* is OK at 7700/10,800 ptas plus IVA (map: Ana & Hue). *Hotel Moderno (☎ 91 531 09 00, fax 91 531 35 50, Calle del Arenal 2)*, just off Puerta del Sol, has comfortable enough rooms for 8500/11,000 ptas plus IVA, but you are really paying for the position more than anything else (map: Central).

A better but more expensive option is *Hotel Regina (☎ /fax 91 521 47 25, Calle de Alcalá 19)*. Singles/doubles with private bath, phone and TV are 9200/12,400 ptas plus IVA (map: Central).

Around Gran Vía

Hotel Regente (☎ 91 521 29 41, Calle de los Mesoneros Romanos 9) has decent mid-range rooms with private bath, TV, air-con and telephone for 5500/9100 ptas plus IVA (map: Central).

Hotel Laris (☎ 91 521 46 80, Calle del Barco 3) is slightly cheaper at 5000/7900 ptas (map: Mal & Ch).

Hotel Los Condes (☎ 91 521 54 55, fax 91 521 78 82, Calle de los Libreros 7) is a comfortable, modern option with rooms starting at 7500/10,500 ptas plus IVA (map: Mal & Ch).

Hotel California (☎ 91 522 47 03, fax 91 531 61 01, Gran Vía 38) is a smart choice, with attractive rooms going for 7200/9500 ptas plus IVA (map: Central).

Salamanca & North

Those wanting to mix in the smarter parts of town could try the *Hostal Don Diego (☎ 91 435 07 60, Calle de Velázquez 45)* for size (map: Sal). It has comfortable singles/doubles with private bath, TV, minibar and phone for 7276/9630 ptas.

In the Chamberí area north of Malasaña, another perfectly good mid-range possibility is *Hotel Trafalgar (☎ 91 445 62 00, fax 91 446 64 56, Calle de Trafalgar 35)*. It's in a quiet part of town but close to several metro stops and a short stroll from the Malasaña area (map: Madrid). It charges up to 7900/13,200 ptas plus IVA.

Hotel Ramón de la Cruz (☎ 91 401 72 00, Calle de Don Ramón de la Cruz 94) has good, comfortable rooms for 6500/8990 ptas plus IVA (map: Madrid).

PLACES TO STAY – TOP END

There is no shortage of bland, four and five-star hotels with all the mod cons scattered across Madrid, particularly along the main drags like Paseo de la Castellana. An attractive alternative to these and just off the Castellana is *Hotel Emperatriz (☎ 91 563 80 88, fax 91 563 98 04, Calle de López de Hoyos 4)*. Its tranquil singles/doubles generally cost 22,000/26,500 ptas plus IVA (map: Sal).

A solid, popular choice is the *Hotel de Santo Domingo (☎ 91 547 98 00, fax 91 547 59 95, Plaza de Santo Domingo 13)*. Rooms here are fine and cost a more down-to-earth 13,750/19,350 ptas plus IVA in the high season and about 3000 ptas cheaper on weekends (map: Central).

One of the better addresses in Madrid and a good choice in terms of price is *Hotel Arosa (☎ 91 532 16 00, fax 91 531 31 27, Calle de la Salud 21)*, just off Gran Vía (map: Central). It has charming rooms and comes highly recommended. Rooms start at 12,500/19,500 ptas plus IVA.

Hotel Villa Real (☎ 91 420 37 67, fax 91 420 25 47, Plaza de las Cortes 10) is right by the parliament and provides rooms with all the accoutrements you might need for

Tiles at Villa Rosa, Plaza de Santa Ana, Madrid

Farmacia in Malasaña, Madrid

DAMIEN SIMONIS

Antigua Huevería, Malasaña, Madrid

DAMIEN SIMONIS

MADRID METRO

HORARIO: De 6:00 A 1:30.

- Estación de Cercanías
- Estación de RENFE
- Aparcamiento
- Próximas Inauguraciones

Herrera Oria 9
Fuencarral 10
Campo de las Naciones 8
Mar de Cristal 8 4
Barrio del Pilar
Begoña
Ventilla
Valdeacederas
Chamartín
Tetuán
Estrecho
Pío XII
Canillas
Plaza de Castilla 1
Cuzco
Colombia
Esperanza
Alvarado
Santiago Bernabéu
Concha Espina
Arturo Soria
Canillejas 5
Guzmán el Bueno
Cuatro Caminos
Nuevos Ministerios 6
República Argentina
Avda. de la Paz
Metropolitano
Alfonso XIII
Torre Arias
Ciudad Universitaria
Ríos Rosas
Cruz del Rayo
Prosperidad
Parque de las Avenidas
Cartagena
Barrio de la Concepción
Suanzes
Ciudad Lineal
Las Musas 7
Gregorio Marañón
Avda. de América
Diego de León
Moncloa
Quevedo
Iglesia
Pueblo Nuevo
Ascao
Argüelles 4
San Bernardo
Bilbao
Rubén Darío
Ventas 2
El Carmen
Quintana
García Noblejas
Simancas
San Blas
Ventura Rodríguez
Noviciado
Núñez de Balboa
Lista
Manuel Becerra
Plaza de España
Tribunal
Colón
Serrano
Goya
Príncipe Pío
Santo Domingo
A.Martínez
Chueca
Velázquez
Príncipe de Vergara
O'Donnell
Lago
Gran Vía
Callao
Retiro
Ibiza
Batán
Puerta del Ángel
Alto de Extremadura
Opera
Sevilla
Banco de España
Sol
S-inz de Baranda
Estrella
Vinateros
La Latina
Tirso de Molina
Artilleros
Lucero
Puerta de Toledo
Antón Martín
Campamento
Lavapiés
Atocha
Pavones 9
Laguna
Embajadores
Acacias
Pirámides
Atocha RENFE
Menéndez Pelayo
Conde de Casal
Marqués de Vadillo
Palos de la Frontera
Empalme
Carpetana
Urgel
Pacífico
Puente de Vallecas
Nueva Numancia
Aluche 10 5
Oporto
Delicias
Portazgo
Buenos Aires
Alto del Arenal
Carabanchel
Vista Alegre
Opañel
Plaza Elíptica
Usera
Legazpi 6
Méndez Álvaro
Miguel Hernández 1

Metro

DAMIEN SIMONIS

Modernisme in Madrid – the Sociedad General de Autores y Editores building on Calle de Pelayo

26,400/33,000 ptas plus IVA (map: Ana & Hue).

Among those with a touch of charm is the *Gran Hotel Reina Victoria (☎ 91 531 45 00, fax 91 522 03 07, Plaza de Santa Ana 14).* The location is great (if noisy for all the nocturnal activity) and good rooms will set you back 20,000/25,000 ptas plus IVA (map: Ana & Hue).

Heading to the top of the league is one of Madrid's old classics, the refurbished *Hotel Palace (☎ 91 360 80 00, fax 91 429 82 66, Plaza de las Cortes 7),* where elegant suites come in at 44,000/51,000 ptas plus IVA in the high season. Not far away is its old rival, the *Hotel Ritz (☎ 91 521 28 57, fax 91 532 87 76, Plaza de la Lealtad 5).* At 53,000/65,000 ptas plus IVA, this is Madrid's priciest location. It was a favourite of Mata Hari. Both are on the Central Madrid map.

PLACES TO STAY – LONG-TERM ACCOMMODATION

For longer stays in Madrid, you can usually make a deal in the pensiones and smaller hostales to include meals, laundry and so on.

For flatshares and rental, check the notice boards at cultural institutes, university campuses and the Escuela Oficial de Idiomas, as well as in the *Segundamano* magazine. Another possible source is RoomMadrid (☎ 91 548 03 35, Calle del Conde Duque 7). You fill in a form and are matched with potential flatshares.

Finding a room in shared flats is not too difficult, but look around, as you can be offered some pretty dismal mouse holes for big money. With luck and persistence you can find good-quality rooms in central locations for around 35,000 ptas a month. Your bills will include electricity (*luz*), water, gas (most places use bottled butane gas, which sells for around 1000 ptas per orange *bombona*), phone and *comunidad*. The latter is a fixed bimonthly charge for building maintenance, sometimes included in the rent.

PLACES TO EAT

Madrid is riddled with restaurants, snack bars and fast-food outlets, so rumbling tummies need not suffer long. Madrid is also one of the few Spanish cities to have a fair sprinkling of non-Spanish options.

Generally, people eat lunch (*comida* or *almuerzo*) between 2 and 4 pm. Arrive any later and you run the risk of finding the kitchen closed. Dinner *(cena)* is a little more flexible, but most people start to munch between 10 and 11 pm.

Because the line dividing bar and restaurant is often blurred, some of the places included in the Entertainment section under Bars & Pubs also serve food. They have been listed as bars because the food can be regarded as an adjunct to the drink.

Asking a madrileño where to find a 'tapas bar' may cause a moment of perplexity. In one sense there is no such thing, since virtually all bars will serve up some kind of *tapa* with a drink. True, in some cases the bar staff must be prompted and in others the tapa is nothing to write home about. It is equally true that certain places have a justly good reputation for fine bar snacks.

Restaurants

Around Sol & Plaza Mayor Plaza Mayor and the immediate area offer plenty of possibilities, but a good number are tourist traps, serving up average food at not-so-average prices. A few places, however, are worth looking for; they are shown on the Central Madrid map.

Calle de la Cava de San Miguel and Calle de los Cuchilleros are packed with *mesones* that are not bad for a little tapas-hopping, although rather touristy. In an altogether different mould is *Restaurante Sobrino de Botín (Calle de los Cuchilleros 17),* where the set *menú* costs 4165 ptas. It's popular with those who can afford it and the place featured in Pérez Galdós' novel *Fortunata y Jacinta.*

Casa Paco (Plaza de la Puerta Cerrada 11) is a classic spot to enjoy madrileño cooking at reasonable prices. More of an institution is *Casa Ciriaco (Calle Mayor 84),* a bar and restaurant with loads of character. It was founded in 1917 in a building previously popular with would-be assassins: one threw a bomb from a balcony at Alfonso XIII as he passed by with his queen, Victoria Eugenia, on their wedding day in 1906. The attack failed, but 24 people died. On the subject of eating, the set meal costs 2300 ptas.

Casa Marta (Calle de Santa Clara 10) has a nice, intimate atmosphere and is moderately priced with mains for around 1000 ptas.

If it's paella your heart desires, the best advice is to head for Valencia. Failing that, you could try the *Restaurante La Paella Real (Calle de Arrieta 2)*. This place does a whole range of rice-based dishes from 1500 ptas a head. It's not cheap, but halfway decent paella never is in Madrid.

The *Taberna del Alabardero (Calle de Felipe V 6)* is fine for a splurge – expect little change per person from 5000 ptas. Or just try a few tapas at the bar.

La Latina The places listed are on the Central Madrid map.

Restaurante Julián de Tolosa, where Calle del Almendro runs into Calle de la Cava Baja, has a pleasingly simple brick-and-timber décor and a limited menu. If you feel like a *chuletón* (huge chop) for two for 4600 ptas, this is for you.

Restaurante Gure-Etxea (Plaza de la Paja 12) is a fine Basque place and typically expensive. The *menú de degustación*, which allows you to sample a range of excellent Basque dishes, costs 3650 ptas a head. Not as well known, but extremely good and also serving a range of Basque dishes with style, is *Restaurante Alamillo* on Plaza del Alamillo.

La Tasquita, on the corner of Plaza de Gabriel Miró and Travesía de Vistillas, is an enchanting little spot serving no-nonsense Spanish cuisine at mid-range prices.

An excellent Asturian place opened up recently in Latina. *La Burbuja Que Ríe* (the 'laughing bubble'!; *Calle del Ángel 16*) serves up a tempting array of hearty dishes (try the *setas con almejas* – mushrooms and

clams) that you can wash down with cider (metro: Puerta de Toledo).

Plaza de Santa Ana, Huertas & Atocha Aside from the bars, the area around Plaza de Santa Ana is also busy with eating options. In and around Calle de la Cruz, Calle de Espóz y Mina and Calle de la Victoria is a cluster of restaurants and bars, many specialising in seafood with a more or less legitimate *gallego* (Galician) touch; these places are on the Plaza de Santa Ana & Huertas map, unless otherwise noted.

Better than any of them, however, is the newly opened *Maceira (Calle de Jesús 7)*, away from the main tourist hubbub. Splash your *pulpo a la gallega* (Galician-style octopus) down with a crisp white Ribeiro.

In *La Casa del Abuelo (Calle de la Victoria 14)*, on a back street south-east of Puerta del Sol, you can sip a *chato* (small glass) of the heavy, sweet El Abuelo red wine, made in Toledo province, while munching on heavenly king prawns, grilled or with garlic. Across the road are two other good tapas options: at No 4, *La Oreja de Oro* and, next door, the recently spiffed-up, Andalucian-style *Taberna Alhambra*. After these, duck around the corner to *Las Bravas* on Callejón de Álvarez Gato for a *caña* (beer in a glass) and the best *patatas bravas* (spicy fried potatoes) in town. The antics of the bar staff are enough to merit a pit stop and the distorting mirrors are a minor Madrid landmark.

La Trucha (Calle de Núñez de Arce 6) is one of Madrid's great bars for tapas. It's just off Plaza de Santa Ana, and there's another nearby at Calle de Manuel Fernández y González 3. You could eat your fill at the bar or sit down in the restaurant.

Something of an institution is the *Museo del Jamón*. Walk in to one of these places and you'll understand the name. Huge clumps of every conceivable type of ham dangle all over the place. You can eat plates and plates of ham – the Spaniards' single most favoured source of nutrition. There's one on Calle de la Victoria, just east of Sol.

The unassuming *Mesón La Casolera* *(Calle de Echegaray 3)* is a popular hangout with madrileños. Ask for a *fritura*, a mixed platter of deep-fried seafood.

If it's just plain cheap food you want, *Restaurante Pasadero (Calle de Lope de Vega 9)* has a solid set lunch *menú* for 1100 ptas. Cheaper still and good is *Restaurante La Sanabresa (Calle del Amor de Dios 12)*.

Lhardy (Carrera de San Jerónimo 8) has been serving up gourmet tapas since 1839. As befits its long history of attracting an illustrious local clientele, the prices are not exactly rock bottom. You can also get takeaway.

In the pleasant enclosed garden of the *Champagnería Gala (Calle de Moratín 22)* you can enjoy paella and follow the food with some celebratory *cava* (the Spanish equivalent of champagne). The Catalan influence is clear from the set *menú del día* (starting with *pa amb tomáquet* – bread with tomato, garlic and olive oil smeared on) for 1795 ptas.

International Cuisine One of Madrid's popular Japanese places is the *Restaurante Donzoko (Calle de Echegaray 3)*.

Vegetarian Vegetarians generally do not have an easy time of it Spain, but Madrid offers a few safe ports. *Restaurante La Biotika (Calle del Amor de Dios 3)* is a reliable favourite. Much of the food is vegan.

Restaurante Integral Artemisa (Calle de Ventura de la Vega 4) is excellent. A full meal can cost from 1500 ptas to 2000 ptas and there is another branch off Gran Vía at Calle de las Tres Cruces 4 (map: Central).

Restaurante Al Natural (Calle de Zorrilla 11) is another good place and also offers a nonvegetarian menu (map: Ana & Hue).

Near Atocha train station, *Restaurante La Mazorca (Paseo de la Infanta Isabel 21)* has mains for up to 900 ptas (map: Madrid).

Lavapiés These places are on the Central Madrid map, unless otherwise noted.

Manhattan (Calle de la Encomienda 5) is a busy, no-frills establishment that fills up

quickly at lunchtime for the 800 ptas set *menú*.

International Cuisine The Argentine *Restaurante La Pampa (Calle del Amparo 61)* is good for grilled meats.

The Middle Eastern and North African eateries and *salones de té* popping up around Lavapiés are fun. They are often simple, with tasty Arab food and, often on weekends, a little belly dancing. *Babilonia*, just off Plaza de Lavapiés on Calle del Ave María (just opposite the Nuevo Café Barbieri) is a perfect example. *Beirut (Calle de Miguel Servet 12)* is a highly congenial Lebanese spot, where a full set meal will cost 900 ptas.

Vegetarian You can pick up some good vegetarian food and a couple of nonvegetarian dishes at *El Granadero de Lavapiés (Calle de Argumosa 10)*.

Gran Vía, Malasaña & Chueca Plunge into the labyrinth of narrow streets and alleyways north off Gran Vía – you won't need to go far to satisfy your taste buds. They are on the Malasaña & Chueca map, unless otherwise noted.

For excellent *extremeño* food, make for the *Restaurante Extremadura (Calle de la Libertad 13)*. An excellent meal with wine can come to around 3000 ptas per person. There is a more modern and less enticing branch at No 31, but on a busy night you could wait for a table in a trio of pleasant bars around No 13.

A simple, down-market eating house is the *Bar-Restaurante Cuchifrito (Calle de Valverde 9)*, where the set *menú* is 900 ptas.

For a cheap pizza and beer out of doors, *Restaurante Sandos (Plaza del Dos de Mayo 8)* is fine. Better still is the crowded *Pizzería Mastropiero (Calle de San Vicente Ferrer 34)* on the corner of Calle del Dos de Mayo, a justifiably popular Argentine-run joint where you can get pizza by the slice. They also do a *tarta de chocolate con dulce de leche* (a thick caramel sauce) to die for.

Casa Pablo, also known as *La Glorieta* *(Calle de Manuela Malasaña 37)*, is a polished place with a solid reputation for good, modestly priced food. The set *menú* is excellent value at 1050 ptas. The fried anchovies are the best in Madrid.

One of the better places for paella is *Restaurante de Cañas y Barro (Calle de Amaniel 23)*. Expect to pay around 2000 ptas a head for the paella alone (map: España).

Tucked away at Calle de Santo Tomé 6 is one of Madrid's quality secrets, *El Mentidero de la Villa*. A pleasing selection of imaginative Spanish nouvelle cuisine is served up in intimate surroundings. You'll get little change from 5000 ptas. Also not far from the main law courts is a mid-range lunch spot, *Casa Manolo (Calle de Orellana 17)*, popular with lawyer types for its good 1500 ptas set lunch *menú*.

About the same prices can be expected at *Restaurante La Barraca (Calle de la Reina 29)*, which does a fair paella for around 2000 ptas.

Restaurante Momo (Calle de Augusto Figueroa 41) has an above-average set evening *menú* for 1500 ptas, including wine. The cuisine tends to be inventive, steering well clear of standard Spanish stuff.

Taberna La Bola (Calle de la Bola 5) has been stirring up a storm with its traditional *cocido a la madrileña* (Madrid-style stew) since 1880. The atmosphere reflects the years, making this a worthwhile once-off in spite of the prices (map: Central).

A great place for dessert or stomach-lining after a round or two of drinks, especially for the sweet teeth among us, is the *Chocolatería Madrid (Calle de Barbieri 15)*, off Plaza de Chueca.

Later in the evening, there's nothing better for soaking up alcohol than a crêpe at the *Crêpérie Ma Bretagne (Calle de San Vicente Ferrer 9)*.

International Cuisine For mouth-watering steak tartare and other French temptations, head for *Restaurante Dame Noire (Calle de Pérez Galdós 3)*.

Trattoria Nabucco (Calle de la Hortaleza 108) is a pleasant pseudo-Italian alternative with modestly priced pasta dishes that are tasty enough although not overly authentic. For the real thing try *La Dolce Vita (Calle de Cardenal Cisneros 5)*. The desserts are sublime. Count on paying about 3000 ptas per person (map: Madrid).

Restaurante Robata (Calle de la Reina 31) is reputedly one of Madrid's best Japanese eating houses. You'll end up spending about 3000 ptas a head.

One Argentine-Uruguayan rep is the *Restaurante La Carreta (Calle de Barbieri 10)*. After you've filled up on loads of South American-style meat, you are well placed to drink on into the night in the surrounding Chueca area.

Good Mexican food and excellent margaritas can be had at the *Taquería de Birrä*. There is one at Plaza de las Comendadoras 2 with a lovely summertime terraza. Otherwise, head for the branch at Calle de Don Pedro 11, just off Calle de Bailén near the Palacio Real (map: Central).

Vegetarian Restaurante La Granja on Calle de San Andrés (just off Plaza del Dos de Mayo) has a set vegetarian lunch for 900 ptas.

Río Manzanares Area Head down past the Príncipe Pío train station towards the Río Manzanares and turn northwards. At Paseo de la Florida 2 (map: Madrid) is a great old place for chicken and cider. A full roast chook, salad and bottle of cider – plenty for two – at *Casa Mingo* will cost less than 2000 ptas. They've been pouring cider here since 1888.

Prada a Tope (Cuesta de San Vicente 32) is another atmospheric place (map: Central). Señor Prada, from the El Bierzo region in north-western Castilla y León, doesn't often make an appearance here any more, but the food from his home region is as good as ever. Specialities include *cecina* (a kind of beef jerky), *empanada* and various *chorizos*.

Around Plaza de España *Restaurante Veracruz (Calle de San Leonardo de Dios 5)* has a set *menú* (including a bottle of wine) for 900 ptas (map: España). It is topped off by wonderful home-made desserts – try the *tarta de queso* and *mousse de limón* (cheesecake and lemon mousse). Manuel García López has been welcoming locals here since 1961.

International Cuisine The *Adrish (Calle de San Bernardino 1)* is about Madrid's best attempt at Indian and does pretty convincing dishes, so expect to pay a minimum of 2000 ptas per person.

Restaurante La Llama (Calle de San Leonardo de Dios 3) is a pleasant little Peruvian restaurant where a full meal generally comes in at just under 2000 ptas a head (map: España).

Restaurante Bali (Calle de San Bernardino 6) is Madrid's only Indonesian restaurant. The authentic cooking is a welcome alternative to Iberian fare. A good meal should come in at 5000 ptas or less for two.

The Thai *Restaurante Siam*, next door to the Bali and run by the same woman, is not as good as its neighbour, although the food is quite all right. The menú de degustación for 3000 ptas includes a cross-section of dishes.

Salamanca, Goya & Beyond A great little lunch stop just north of El Retiro is *Alfredo's Barbacoa (Calle de Lagasca 5)*. On the menu are lightly spiced spare ribs for about 1000 ptas and some good steaks (map: Madrid).

For midday tapas, the *Taberna de Daniela (Calle del General Pardiñas 2)* is one of the best-known places in the snootier Goya barrio (metro: Goya, map: Madrid). The tile décor is great, but service can be patchy and you're probably better off at the bar.

Casa Julián (Calle de Don Ramón de la Cruz 10) specialises in grilled meats and, for this part of town, is a no-nonsense and atmospheric place (map: Sal). Grilled meat

of various red varieties is 1500 ptas a person.

Restaurante Oter (Calle de Claudio Coello 73), around the corner, is a rather up-market spot for Navarran cuisine (map: Sal). You'll get little change from 5000 ptas.

You can dig into a limited variety of roast meats at the sumptuous-looking *Asador La Tahona (Calle del Capitán Haya 21)*. A full meal will cost you around 3000 ptas with wine (map: North).

International Cuisine If it's Chinese you're after, *China Crown (Calle de la Infanta Mercedes 620)* has the best reputation in town (metro: Tetuán, map: North).

Every city's got one. The *Hard Rock Café* on the Paseo de la Castellana side of Plaza de Colón serves up American-style club sandwiches, nachos and cocktails (map: Mal & Ch). It's lively and the food is generally good value; helpings are of the American jumbo persuasion. You can eat well for 2000 ptas or even less.

Madrid's top Thai alternative is the lavish *Thai Gardens* at Calle de Jorge Juan 5 (map: Sal). Here the menú de degustación costs 4100 ptas.

For the city's only shot at Filipino cuisine, try *Restaurante Sulú (Paseo de la Castellana 172)*. For 2300 ptas a menú de degustación (comprising eight dishes) should satisfy anyone (metro: Cuzco, map: North).

Pastry Shops
Central Madrid is riddled with pastry shops. A particularly good one is the *Antigua Pastelería del Pozo (Calle del Pozo 8)*, near the Puerta del Sol. In operation since 1830 (and for 20 years before that as a bread bakery), it is the city's oldest dealer in tooth-rotting items.

Cafés
There is no shortage of places to get a drink in Madrid – some areas are wall-to-wall bars. A feature of many that can take a little getting used to is the habit of dropping all

rubbish – from napkins and uneaten bits of tapas to cigarette ash and coffee dregs – onto the floor by the bar. At one point or another it all gets swept out and there is some logic to it. If one or two people do it, you have to sweep it up, so you may as well let everyone do it! At tables or outside on the terrazas the habit does not apply.

Unlike, say, in Italy, the price difference between drinking at the bar and at a table is not so rigidly enforced, but in some places the price of sitting down may be quite high. Table prices on the terrazas, especially in summer, are always higher than bar prices.

The neat Anglo-Saxon division between cafés (for coffee or tea and scones) and pubs or bars (for getting plastered) is a feature absent from the madrileño approach to drinking in society. Nevertheless, some bars are fairly evidently *not* intended for a leisurely *café con leche* and a read of the paper; these are dealt with under Entertainment. Others clearly do lean this way. Following are some suggestions for the latter.

Around Plaza Mayor These places are on the Central Madrid map.

Café del Real on Plaza de Isabel II is an atmospheric place with a touch of elegance. It gets busy at night but also makes a fine spot for breakfast; head for the low-ceilinged upstairs section.

Just up the cobbled lane next to it is another brilliantly positioned spot for a coffee, *Café de Madrid (Calle del Mesón de Paños 10)*. There are sometimes photo and art exhibitions here too, in case you're seeking more stimulus. Stay away in summer, as it's like being in a hothouse.

Up Calle de Vergara to Plaza de Ramales is a series of fine cafés. *Café Vergara (Calle de Vergara 1)* is good and the rather stiff *Café de los Austrias*, on the corner of the same street and Plaza de Ramales, seems as imperial as its name suggests.

Café de Oriente, on the corner of Plaza de Oriente and Calle de San Nicholás Lepanto, feels like a set out of Mitteleuropa – it's well worth stopping by.

From Colón to the Prado These places are on the Malasaña & Chueca map, unless otherwise noted.

Along Paseo de los Recoletos, just near Plaza de Colón, *Cafe-Restaurante El Espejo* doubles as one of Madrid's most elegant cafés. You could also sit in the turn-of-the-century style *Pabellón del Espejo* outside. Despite appearances, it was only opened in 1990. Both are a little expensive and the latter also forms the nucleus of one of Madrid's more expensive summer terrazas.

Just down the road is the equally graceful *Gran Café de Gijón (Paseo de los Recoletos 21)*.

If you're strolling around here but want something a little more down-to-earth, *Café de la Villa*, in the cultural centre of the same name on Plaza de Colón, is a cheery den for arty types .

Another wonderful old place with chandeliers and an atmosphere belonging to another era is the café at the *Círculo de Bellas Artes*, Calle de Alcalá 42 (map: Central). You have to buy a temporary club membership (100 ptas) to drink in here, but it's worth it.

Malasaña These places are on the Malasaña & Chueca map.

Café Comercial on Glorieta de Bilbao is an old Madrid café with a good whiff of its castizo (true-blue) past. The odd foreigner stops in, but it's just far enough off the usual tourist trail to be reasonably genuine.

Café Manuela (Calle de San Vicente Ferrer 29) lies on that borderline between café and bar. It is a young, hip place with a vaguely alternative flavour. *Café Isadora (Calle del Divino Pastor 14)* is great for chatting away the early evening over a coffee.

An enchanting teahouse with a hint of the 1960s is the *Tetería de la Abuela (Calle del Espíritu Santo 19)*. Along with the great range of teas you can indulge in scrummy crêpes.

For a somewhat camp but pleasant ambience, and a great cup of coffee and

10

cheesecake, try *Café La Sastrería (Calle de Hortaleza 74)*. In keeping with the tailor theme, the black-clad waiters wear measuring tapes for ties.

Huertas & Lavapiés Calle de las Huertas has a string of cafés and bars to choose from. On Plaza de Canalejas, you'll strike a fine, old madrileño bar, the *Café del Príncipe* (Ana & Hue). It does good food if you're peckish and the people-watching is an attraction in itself.

A wonderful old place, once the haunt of the artistic and hopefully artistic, *Nuevo Café Barbieri (Calle del Ave María 45)* even provides newspapers to browse through while you sip your cortado (metro: Lavapiés, map: Central).

If you'd prefer tea, there are several *teterías* in the Granada fashion dotted about the place. The *Damasco Salón de Te* on Calle del Infante (map: Ana & Hue) and *El Café de Sherazade (Calle de Santa María 18)* are equally good (map: Ana & Hue).

Around Plaza de España A few steps away from several of Madrid's better cinemas, off Plaza de España, is the perfectly appropriate *Café de las Extrellas (Calle de Martín de los Heros 5)*. It attracts a film-going crowd and is plastered with portrait photos of screen greats (map: España). A block away, at *Café Macaluca (Calle de Juan Álvarez Mendizábal 4)*, you can nosh up on fabulous crêpes and cheesecake, washed down with one of any number of teas and infusions (map: Ana & Hue).

Self-Catering

The *mercado* on Plaza de San Miguel is the main fresh produce market just off Plaza Mayor (map: Central). Self-caterers can also try Marks & Spencer's food department for foodstuffs generally unavailable in Spanish shops. The food departments in the Corte Inglés stores are also good.

ENTERTAINMENT

What Madrid may lack in grand sights, it makes up for in the life of its bars and night-clubs, its cinemas, theatres and cafés. Madrileños take their enjoyment seriously and there is every opportunity to join them.

The busiest time of year on Madrid's calendar – from theatre to rock concerts – runs from late September to early December in the Fiesta de Otoño.

You'll want to get some tips. *El País* has a daily listings section *(cartelera)* that is good for cinema and theatre. Original-language films and where they are shown are clearly indicated (look for movies in *versión original*, or *v.o. subtitulada*). Also listed are museums, galleries, music venues and the like. *El Mundo* publishes a weekly magazine insert, *Metropoli*, packed with info.

The weekly entertainment bible is, however, the *Guía del Ocio*, available at newsstands for 125 ptas.

You can generally get tickets for plays, concerts and other performances at the theatre concerned, but there are centralised ticketing offices too. Quite a few lottery ticket booths also sell tickets for theatre, football and bullfights. Try the Localidades La Alicantina on Plaza de Santo Domingo (map: Central) or Localidades Galicia (☎ 91 531 27 32) on Plaza del Carmen 1 (map: Central).

For many bands and popular music acts you can often get tickets at the Madrid Rock record store, at Gran Vía 25, Calle Mayor 38 (map: Central) and Calle de San Martín 3 (map: Central). You can only pay for tickets in cash. The FNAC store on Calle de Preciados also sells tickets to major concerts and not only those in Madrid. Again, you can only pay cash. See the Central Madrid map for all these. Otherwise, telephone booking is becoming increasingly popular. The Caixa de Catalunya operates the Tel-Entrada system, which covers many shows of all kinds. You call ☎ 902-38 33 33, pay for tickets by credit card and pick them up at the theatre before the show starts.

Pubs & Bars

Things have calmed down a little since the heyday of the *movida* in the years after Franco's death, but Madrid can still easily boast a breadth and depth of nightlife without compare anywhere else in Europe. Where else will you see bumper-to-bumper traffic at four in the morning? What follows is little more than a taste.

Plaza de Santa Ana & Huertas Plaza de Santa Ana is lined with interesting bars. The atmosphere in these places is a slight cut above the average, as is the price of your caña. They are on the Plaza de Santa Ana & Huertas map.

The *Cervecería Alemana* is a century-old meeting place, but any of the bars along here makes for a pleasant watering stop, especially when you can sit outside in the warmer months. In summer, *Bar Hawaiano* sets up a terraza in the middle of the square. *La Moderna* has been going since 1994 and attracts a mixed, 30-something and buzzy crowd.

La Fontana de Oro (Calle de la Victoria 2) is one of several good Irish-style pubs you'll find scattered about central Madrid, although it has rather a longer history than most. Before occupation of the city by Napoleon's troops early in the last century, it was a hotbed of political dissent, as wine and antigovernment talk flowed freely. It's still popular, with plenty of seating downstairs and standing room at street level.

La Creación (Calle de Núñez de Arce 14) is a cool place to hang out for beer, cider or vermouth. The food is not so hot though.

Although it gets hellishly crowded at weekends, you should at least poke your head into *Viva Madrid (Calle de Manuel Fernández y González 7)*. The tiled décor and heavy timber ceilings make a distinctive setting for drinks earlier in the evening. Equally beautiful, but even more cheekily expensive, is *Los Gabrieles (Calle de Echegaray 17)*, just a few steps away. If tiles are your thing, another good choice is *España Cañí (Plaza del Ángel 14)*, west off Plaza de Santa Ana. The staff do a nice sangría.

To step into a time warp, slip into *La Venencia (Calle de Echegaray 7)* for a sherry. This place is the real thing: it looks as though nothing has been done to clean it in

many a long year. Ill-lit and perfect place to sample one of sherry – from the almost s lado to the rather biting *fino* at No 10 you can indulge in of rums at *El Norte*.

A place done up to look almost as old, with a dimly lit elegance, music of a similar cocktails, is *Casa Pueblo (Ca*

At *Cardamomo (Calle de* there's flamenco and relate though nothing live. Virtua 1 corner on Calle de Manue 1 González, *Carbones* is bus about 4 am and features a go mainstream music on the juk

Cuevas de Sésamo (Calle is a wonderful old cellar bar t in sangría. The walls are aphorisms and the air is heav

Calle de la Cruz is also fu with discos and music place you could pop into *El Tréb* serves a mean pizza to go w and is open late. *Bar Matado* Torero disco, is a popular s drinks before crossing the r dance action (see the Discos Nightclubs section later).

A modern spot that's not ba up into the evening is the *Calles* on Plaza de Canalejas

Casa Alberto (Calle de las was founded in 1827 in a bu Cervantes did a spot of writi old place for vermouth on tap also get a meal.

Café Populart (Calle de las often has music, generally ja For more jazz with your d *Central* on Plaza del Ángel is choice.

Just beyond the hubbub of *Parnaso (Calle de Moratín* but engaging bar. The area aro jammed with an odd assortme tive paraphernalia, while out get the feeling you're sitting tramcar.

Nearby is a quite different atmosphere and crowd, at *La Taberna Celta (Calle de los Desamparados 3)*, one of the city's Gaelic collection.

Around Plaza Mayor & the Palacio Real Although there is no shortage of standard little bars in this area, few stand out. One exception is *Casa Antonio (Calle de Latrones 10)*, just south of Plaza Mayor, which is a wonderful old Madrid watering hole with loads of character and vermouth on tap.

Farther to the south-west things get promising again. Calle de la Cava Baja in particular is full of taverns and eating houses. *La Chata* at No 24 has a spectacular tiled frontage and is nice for a quick caña or two. Don't spend all your time here though. *Taberna Tempranillo* at No 38 has plenty of character and many bottles of different Spanish wine that you'll be encouraged to sample.

A less touristy place along similar lines to Casa Antonio is *Taborin Almendro 13 (Calle del Almendro 13)*, basically a sherry pub that shuts at midnight.

Just by the summertime terrazas of Las Vistillas (see Terrazas later) is a handful of intriguing places. The gaudily coloured *Travesía (Travesía de las Vistillas 8)* attracts a diverse crowd with its cocktails and South American music.

Café del Nuncio on Travesía del Nuncio is a wonderful bar that straggles up a stairway passage from Calle de Segovia. You can drink in the several cosy levels inside or, better still in summer, hang about at the outdoor tables – a delightful spot for a civilised early-evening tipple.

The *Champañería María Pandora (Plaza de Gabriel Miró 1)* is deliciously pretentious – a place to sip your drinks while poring over the books.

Around Lavapiés This barrio is one of the last worker-gitano quarters in central Madrid. While the bars are often *cutre* (basic, spit-and-sawdust style), they brim with a raw energy.

The *Taberna de Antonio Sánchez (Calle de Mesón de Paredes 13)* is an old-time drinking place with a slightly conspiratorial air; it serves beer, wine and snacks, and that's about it.

An excellent place for cañas and seafood *pinchos* (snacks) is *El Boquerón (Calle de Valencia 14)*, which has a rough-around-the-edges feel and is popular with people in the barrio. Round the corner you can hang out in *La Mancha de Madrid* on Calle de Miguel Servet, which attracts a colourful array of local tipplers earlier in the evening.

PakesTeis (Calle del Amparo 81) was opened years ago by a sound technician for rock bands. The name is a corruption of '*para que estéis*', which means, roughly, 'so you can hang out' and is at the same time a loose rendition of the English 'backstage'. The place has a no-nonsense rock feel and there are often impromptu sessions in the basement.

Just around the corner from the Teatro Olimpia is *Eucalipto (Calle de Argumosa 4)*, something of a local hub and a great place for daiquiris.

Gran Vía, Malasaña & Chueca Along with the Santa Ana and Huertas area, the web of streets and lanes stretching northwards off Gran Vía is Madrid's other great party paradise, with more bars, pubs, dance places and general drinking potential than you can shake a stick at. The atmosphere of the area is decidedly different, no doubt shaped by the low-life element that is an essential part of it. Whores, pimps, dealers and a general mix of down-and-outs mix with revellers of all types, ages and sexual persuasions. In particular, damsels of the night haunt Calle de la Ballesta (lined with escort bars and the like), Calle de la Luna and the immediate area. These places are on the Malasaña & Chueca map.

Cervecería de Santa Bárbara at No 8 on the plaza of the same name (metro: Alonso Martínez), is a classic old Madrid drinking house and is generally packed early in the night. It is a popular meeting place and as good as any to kick off a night in Malasaña.

It also has great seafood tapas. If you really want to get basic, the place marked *Vinos* at Calle de Sagasta 2 is for you; it serves wine and various cheeses. Around the corner you can get an Asturian cider and a tapa of empanada for 185 ptas at *Corripio (Calle de Fuencarral 102)*. Two doors down at No 98, *Patatus* is popular with a young crowd for early-evening beers and saucy potatoes.

The *Bodega de la Ardosa (Calle de Colón 13)* is a wonderful, dimly lit bar where you can sip on a vermouth drawn from the barrel. If it really must be a Guinness, step around the corner to *The Quiet Man (Calle de Valverde 44)*.

On the Irish theme, *Finnegan's (Plaza de las Salesas 9)* has become an obligatory stop for aficionados of the dark fluids. Calle de San Vicente Ferrer has a fair quota of bars, and on the corner of Corradera Alta de San Pablo is *Triskel*, yet another jolly Irish joint.

La Vía Láctea (Calle de Velarde 18) is a bright, thumping sort of place with a young, *macarra* crowd. There is plenty of mainstream music playing and a good drinking atmosphere.

In *Café del Foro (Calle de San Andrés 38)* the décor of traditional Madrid shopfronts surrounds an intimate stage where you can often hear good live music.

For one of the best *mojitos* (a delicious and popular Cuban rum-based concoction) in the area, pop into the *Café Magerit (Calle del Divino Pastor 21)*. For another version of the same tipple, try *Café Isadora* (see Cafés under Places to Eat earlier).

Plaza del Dos de Mayo can seem like a scene from a young alcoholic Ben Hur, with madrileños careering around in all directions clutching large cups and bottles of various beverages. Just off the square is a great little leap back into the Sixties, *Only You* (Calle del Dos de Mayo 6). It has a mixed age clientele and fun atmosphere.

Up on Plaza de las Comendadoras, the lightly Art Deco *Café Moderno* is a cosy place in winter, especially if you're there on a Thursday night for the belly dancing!

Calle de Campoamor and its continuation, Calle de Pelayo, running parallel to Calle de Hortaleza, are lined with an assortment of places. Heading from north to south they start off as mainly noisy rock bars for the young 'uns and gradually give over to a string of gay bars. At the bottom end of the street you are in the Chueca area, the heart of Madrid's gay nightlife (metro: Chueca).

Acuarela Café (Calle de Gravina 10) is a quiet place for an intimate drink in more of a gay arty atmosphere. Right next door on the corner with the square is *Truco*, one of the city's few predominantly lesbian bars. *Rimmel (Calle de Luis de Góngora 4)* and *Cruising (Calle de Pérez Galdós 5)* are among the more popular gay haunts. The *New Leather* bar *(Calle de Pelayo 42)* is just one of the many gay bars towards the southern end of this street.

This does not mean that all Chueca's bars are exclusively gay; everyone can enjoy this pleasingly seedy district. Watch out for the wonderful, gloomy old wine bar, the *Sierra Ángel (Calle de Gravina 11)*, overlooking Plaza de Chueca.

Heading towards Gran Vía, *Libertad 8 (Calle de la Libertad 8)* was a favoured haunt of the Left around the time of Franco's demise. It still gets an animated crowd to see singer-songwriters or sit in on the odd poetry reading. Another pleasant place with tiled walls and a cosy feel is *Bar La Carmencita* at No 16.

El Corazón Negro (Calle de Colmenares 5), a meeting place for cinema people and hopefuls, looks as though it's been trashed, but it has a grungy atmosphere worth wallowing in. The Art Deco *Del Diego Bar (Calle de la Reina 12)* does a great Cuba libre.

Star's Dance Café (Calle del Marqués del Valdeiglesias 5) is a bright new place where you can eat, drink and even be merry – it bills itself as the only *café* in Madrid where you dance in the late evening. A beer costs 250 ptas until midnight, after that it's double the price.

Museo Chicote (Gran Vía 12) is another Art Deco special (founded in 1931) and long the haunt of Madrid's chic and well connected. It used to be directly connected with *Cock Bar (Calle de la Reina 16)*, which once served as a discreet salon for a higher class of prostitution. The ladies in question have gone, but this popular bar retains plenty of atmosphere – even if the name is a little startling.

Around Plaza de Santo Domingo & Ópera

The streets around this square tend to be home to tacky 'clubs' and tawdry strip joints, but you can find a few curios worth an hour or two of your drinking time. One of the better ones is *Calentito* (map: Central), a lively salsa bar with transvestites in skimpy attire shaking their bits for you on the bar *(Calle de Jacometrezo 15)*.

Around Plaza de España

A good spot for cocktails after the movies is *Ambigú 16 (Calle de Martín de los Heros 16)*. They do a mean *caipirinha* (a Brazilian cocktail) and have all sorts of wonderful hard stuff, including Colombian rum. This is the best of a few bars along this street (map: España).

Salamanca, Cuatro Caminos & North

Teatriz (Calle de la Hermosilla 15) is a chichi hangout with a difference (map: Sal). The former Teatro Beatriz has an eerily lit bar right on the stage. Drinks are for heavily lined wallets only.

Garamond (Calle de Claudio Coello 10) has the air of a medieval parador for an expensive drink (map: Madrid). There's usually some kind of show or open buffet. It's definitely for the jacket-and-tie yuppie brigade.

Playing to a younger crowd is *Terraza de Serrano (Calle de Serrano 41)*. This cavernous drinking mall heaves with one of the greatest concentrations of adolescent hormones in the entire city (map: Sal).

Moving north, Avenida del Brasil hosts half a dozen bars that keep a faithful crowd more than occupied until around 6 am. The best is the immense and immensely popular *Irish Rover* at No 7 (map: North). At the northern end of the same street, *Maes* is an uninspiring looking place that happens to serve a wide variety of imported beers.

East of the Paseo de la Castellana there's another small strip of bars on Calle de Joaquín Costa (metro: Plaza de la República Argentina, map: North). The *Kangarú Australian Bar* at No 27 occasionally sells Coopers beer, but that's about as Australian as it gets. It vies for custom with *Tex-Mex* next door (owned by the same people) and a few others, good for the early stages of the evening before heading to Avenida del Brasil.

St Andrew's Pub (Calle de los Hermanos Bécquer 5) is a quirky departure from the standard Madrid drinking trough (map: Sal; look for the stag's head over the entrance). It's a fine old dark-wood pub in the best cigar-smoking style. Sink into a studded red leather couch of the old-boys' club variety on a Saturday night to take in the live accordion music.

Discos, Dancing & Nightclubs

On weekends in particular, it is quite possible to continue the 'night' well into the day. In some discos a 9 or 10 am finish is the norm.

Malasaña

These places are on the Malasaña & Chueca map.

Morocco (Calle del Marqués de Leganés 7), although some say it has passed its peak, is still a popular stop on the Madrid dance circuit, usually swinging into gear from about 1 am.

Ya'sta! (Calle de Valverde 10) is another place that doesn't swing into action until the early morning (about 6 am). It has a reputation as a meat market, but is a lot of good sweaty dance fun.

Pachá (Calle de Barceló 11) is an old favourite that seems to come and go. It is open until 5 am and entry can cost up to 2000 ptas (including first drink).

Around Plaza de España

Arena (Calle de la Princesa 1) offers music for all tastes – funky, house, techno and acid jazz – until 6.30 am from Wednesday to Sunday (map: España).

Plaza de Santa Ana, Sol & Latina

These places are on the Plaza de Santa Ana & Huertas map, unless otherwise noted.

Villa Rosa (Plaza de Santa Ana 15) is as remarkable for its décor as anything else, but from about 1 am is a mellow place for a drink and some shaking of stuff on the small dance floor. The tile decoration outside (pictures of Sevilla, Granada and Córdoba) and within, as well as the vaguely *artesonado*-style ceiling, make it a unique spot.

On Calle de la Cruz are a couple of dance spaces. You may well have to queue if you have no passes or fliers for them. *Torero* at No 26 has two floors, featuring Spanish music upstairs and international tunes downstairs. The bouncers can be a real pain, so you could opt for the distinctly tacky *La Cartuja* at No 10.

No Se Lo Digas A Nadie (Calle de Ventura de la Vega 7) is a popular dance spot open until 3 am. The real hardcore night owls can later make their way to *Stella (Calle de Arlabán 7)*, open until about 10 am on weekends.

El Viajero (Plaza de la Cebada 15) is good for acid jazz, trip hop and funk (map: Central).

Palacio Gaviria (Calle del Arenal 9) is indeed palatial (map: Central). It's divided into a series of old-style salons to meet most middle-of-the-road tastes, from waltzes to mainstream disco blah, with a couple of small corners scattered about for a quiet drink or snog. The place gets going about 2 am and entrance can cost up to 2000 ptas. A beer is 900 ptas and a mixed drink is 1500 ptas.

Just next door is one of Madrid's premier nightspots, *Teatro Joy Eslava* (☎ 91 366 37 33 for reservations, Calle del Arenal 11). Admission is 2000 ptas on weekends.

Terrazas

Many of the places listed earlier have terrazas – tables set up on the footpath or plaza – most of which spring up like mushrooms in the summer. The season is from about April to October and the bars that run them pay for a specific extra licence to operate.

Probably the best located one is *Bar Ventorrillo* on Corral de la Morería, just by the Jardines de las Vistillas. This is a wonderful spot to relax and drink in the views of the Sierra de Guadarrama, especially around sunset. During the Fiestas de San Isidro bands play in the gardens.

Some of the terrazas, such as those that emerge along Paseo de la Castellana and Paseo de los Recoletos, are something of a haunt for *la gente guapa* (the beautiful people) – those who want to be seen spending serious money for their libations. A perfect case in point is *Bolero (Paseo de la Castellana 33)*, where a modest beer costs 600 ptas (map: Sal). *Boulevard 37* at No 37 is largely the domain of better-off university students (map: Sal). For a more staid beginning to the evening, *El Espejo (Paseo de los Recoletos 31)* is hard to beat for elegance (see also Places to Eat).

Less pretentious and considerably more pleasant are the terrazas that set up in Argüelles – more specifically, on Paseo del Pintor Rosales. With parkland on one side and considerably less traffic than on Paseo de la Castellana, these places also exercise a little more control over their prices. *Terraza España* (map: Madrid) is one of several.

Madrid's squares make perfect locations for outdoor drinking. Several of the bars on Plaza de Santa Ana operate terrazas, as does *Café de Oriente* on Plaza de Oriente (map: Central); see Places to Eat. Bars spread summertime liquid satisfaction across such squares as Plaza del Dos de Mayo and Plaza de las Comendadoras, both in the Malasaña area, as well as Plaza del Conde Barajas (just south off Plaza Mayor) and around Plaza de los Carros.

Flamenco

There are several *tablaos* or flamenco performance spots in central Madrid, but most are designed for the tourist crowd. They generally feature dinner and flamenco performances of an indifferent quality, much avoided by locals. They all feature in entertainment guides. The best of this poor lot appears to be *Café de Chinitas* (☎ *91 559 51 35, Calle de Torija 7)*. You will almost certainly need to book ahead (map: Central). Another is *Corral de la Morería* (☎ *91 365 84 46, Calle de la Morería 17)*.

To get a feel for the more genuine article, you have several options. You can try the handful of peñas flamencas, or bars where flamenco music is often played, although not necessarily live.

For some, *La Soleá (Calle de la Cava Baja 27)* is the last real flamenco bar in Madrid, where aficionados enjoy performers who know it all (map: Central). At *Candela (Calle del Olmo 3)* the gitanos practise their music and dance out the back (and you probably won't be allowed to watch), but the bar is charged with an Andalucian flamenco atmosphere (map: Central). Occasionally you'll get lucky and witness impromptu jam sessions. Another fun little place is *Taberna Las Rejas (Calle de la Magdalena 34)*, which often has flamenco performances from 10 pm to midnight (map: Ana & Hue).

Casa Patas (Calle de Cañizares 10) is a little more organised and hosts recognised masters of flamenco guitar, song and dance (map: Ana & Hue). The *Peña Flamenca Chaquetón (Calle de las Canarias 39)* is another such place (map: Madrid).

Teatro Lara (☎ 91 521 05 52, Calle de la Corredera Baja de San Pablo 15) also sometimes puts on flamenco performances (map: Mal & Ch).

Not infrequently the bigger names play to packed houses in various of Madrid's theatres; check the papers.

Classical Music & Opera

The city's grandest stage, the *Teatro Real* (☎ *91 516 06 06, bookings through the Caja de Madrid bank on* ☎ *902-488 488)*, finally reopened in 1997. Only the great and the good could see anything in the 1998 season but, as the euphoria wears off, it might actually be possible to see a performance of opera or ballet. Tickets can range from 1000

ptas for a spot so far away you need a telescope to around 20,000 ptas.

The *Auditorio Nacional de Música* (☎ *91 337 01 40, Calle del Príncipe de Vergara 146)* is the main venue for classical music (metro: Cruz de Rayo, map: North). On a smaller scale, the *Fundación Juan March* (☎ *91 435 42 40, Calle de Castelló 77)* holds regular Sunday concerts (metro: Núñez de Balboa, map: Madrid).

If you can't get into the Teatro Real, the *Teatro Calderón* (☎ *91 369 14 34, Calle de Atocha 18)* plays second fiddle for opera (map: Central). The *Teatro de la Zarzuela* (☎ *91 524 54 00, Calle de Jovellanos 4)* is the place for that very Spanish genre of classical dance and music, the *zarzuela* (metro: Banco de España, map: Ana & Hue).

For other musical and operatic performances, the Centro Cultural de la Villa and the *Teatro Monumental* (☎ *91 429 81 19, Calle de Atocha 65)* are the main venues to look out for (map: Ana & Hue).

Other Live Music

Bands don't usually appear on stage before 10 pm and often wait until midnight. You can dance at some of these venues.

One of Madrid's better-known jazz haunts is *Clamores Jazz Club (Calle de Alburquerque 14)*. It is generally open all week (metro: Bilbao, map: Madrid). Usually there is no cover charge, and the place gets quite a good selection of acts. You can also catch the occasional jazz performance at *Café Central* and *Populart*, two bars listed earlier.

Galileo Galilei (Calle de Galileo 100) attracts a mix of Hispanic dance groups and vocalists (map: Madrid).

Latin American rhythms have quite a hold of Madrid nightlife. A good place to indulge in salsas, merengues and other Latin grooves is *Vaiven (Travesía de San Mateo 1)*. There is no cover charge, but a beer costs about 600 ptas (metro: Chueca, map: Mal & Ch).

Suristán (Calle de la Cruz 7) gets in a wide variety of acts, from Cuban to African (map: Ana & Hue). Music usually kicks off at 11.30 pm and there is sometimes a cover charge of up to 1000 ptas (including a drink).

Swing (Calle de San Vicente Ferrer 23), in the heart of Malasaña, always has some kind of performance, from longtime cantautores like Javier Krahe through to Friday pop and soul nights and Caribbean music (metro: Tribunal, map: Mal & Ch). Entry hovers around 1000 ptas (including one drink).

Madrid Jazz on the corner of Calle de San Vicente Ferrer and Calle de San Andrés (map: Mal & Ch) can get extremely packed, but occasionally features some decent live music, which more often than not has nothing to do with jazz. *La Taberna Encantada (Calle de Salitre 2)* gets a similar range of acts (map: Central).

Sala Caracol (Calle de Bernardino Obregón 18) is a venue designed to accommodate bigger acts, Spanish and foreign (metro: Embajadores, map: Madrid).

Cinemas

The standard cinema ticket costs around 700 ptas, but many cinemas have at least one day set aside as the *día del espectador* (viewer's day) for cut-price tickets (usually about 200 ptas off).

One of the best concentrations of cinemas for v.o. films is on and around Calle de Martín de los Heros and Calle de la Princesa (metro: Plaza de España, map: España). The *Renoir*, *Alphaville* and *Princesa* cinema complexes around here all screen such movies.

The *Cine Doré*, which houses the Filmoteca Nacional, is a wonderful old cinema that shows classics past and present, all in the original language. It's at Calle de Santa Isabel 3 in Lavapiés (metro: Antón Martín, map: Ana & Hue) and has a cheap restaurant attached. If you're in Madrid for any length of time, consider getting a bono for cut-price tickets.

You can also see subtitled movies at the *Multicines Ideal* complex on Calle del Doctor Cortezo (map: Central), the *Renoir* at Calle de Raimundo Fernández Villaverde

10 (metro: Cuatro Caminos, map: North) or *Real Cinema* at Plaza de Isabel II (map: Central).

The huge-screen *Cine Imax* is in the Parque Enrique Tierno Galván at Camino de Meneses s/n, south of Atocha station (metro: Méndez Álvaro). For this 3D cinema experience you pay from 850 to 1300 ptas, depending on what is showing.

Theatre

Autumn is a busy season for theatre after the torpor of summer. Although the theatre, music and dance scene is not as diverse or of as high a quality as in some other European capitals, there is plenty happening and a plethora of venues large and small, of which the following are a representative selection.

The beautiful old *Teatro de la Comedia (☎ 91 521 49 31, Calle del Príncipe 14)* is home to the Compañía Nacional de Teatro Clásico and often stages gems of classic Spanish and European theatre (map: Ana & Hue). The *Teatro de Bellas Artes (☎ 91 532 44 38, Calle del Marqués de Casa Riera 2)* also leans towards the classics (map: Central).

At the *Centro Cultural de la Villa (☎ 91 575 60 80)*, under the waterfall at Plaza de Colón, you can see anything from classical music concerts to comic theatre, opera and quality flamenco (map: Mal & Ch).

Teatro Alfil (☎ 91 521 58 27, Calle del Pez 10) is a good little alternative theatre (map: Mal & Ch). Another venue to keep an eye on is the *Teatro Olimpia (☎ 91 527 46 22)*, right by the metro on Plaza de Lavapiés (map: Central).

Major Concerts

Several venues are used for major concerts, whether of Spanish groups or international acts. A common one is the Plaza de Toros Monumental de Ventas (metro: Ventas, map: Madrid), Madrid's main bullring. Others include the former Cuartel del Conde Duque, near Plaza de España, and the Teatro Monumental (metro: Antón Martín, map: Ana & Hue).

Amusement Parks

Travellers with kids on the leash can let them loose at the Parque de Atracciones, in the Casa de Campo area west of the city centre (metro: Batán). From May to mid-September it is open daily, except on some Mondays. Opening times vary considerably (usually from noon until midnight or later, but generally from 6 pm in late July and August). In winter it tends to open on the weekend and on holidays only, from noon to 7 pm. The cheapest ticket (575 ptas) allows you entry alone. An unlimited all-rides stamp on your hand costs 2200 ptas for adults and 1225 ptas for children. Single-ride tickets are available too (most rides cost adults two such tickets).

SPECTATOR SPORTS
Football

Even if soccer (as it is known to some) doesn't interest you, a good match in Spain provides an insight into an essential side of Spanish leisure. Tickets can be bought on the day at the stadiums, starting at around 1500 ptas, although the big fixtures are often sold out. This is especially so if the two local teams, Real Madrid and Atlético de Madrid, clash or when either meets the enemies from Barcelona.

You can also get tickets in advance from the grounds or from ticket offices (more expensive) at Calle de la Victoria, near Puerta del Sol. Another option is to book them through the Servi-Caixa (☎ 902-33 22 11).

Real Madrid's home ground is the Estadio Santiago Bernabéu (☎ 91 344 00 52; metro: Santiago Bernabéu, map: North), while Atlético is based at the Estadio Vicente Calderón (☎ 91 366 47 07), south-west of the centre at Calle de la Virgen del Puerto (metro: Pirámides).

Bullfighting

In spite of the Hemingway-inspired fame of the Pamplona fiesta, connoisseurs would rather get a front seat in Madrid's huge Plaza de Toros Monumental de Las Ventas (☎ 91 356 22 00), Calle de Alcalá 237 (metro: Ventas, map: Madrid), for a good

fight. The ring is the biggest in the bull-fighting world. The best fiesta begins in mid-May, marking the holiday for Madrid's patron saint, San Isidro Labrador (see also Special Events), and lasts well into June. It is the most important bullfight season in the world, making or breaking *toreros* and bull breeders alike. Otherwise, *corridas* are organised regularly on weekends over the summer. Madrid has a second, smaller bull-ring near the Vista Alegre metro station.

Tickets (*entradas*) start at under 2000 ptas for a basic seat in the sun (*sol*) and rise steadily from there. A more comfortable position in the shade (*sombra*) can come in at anything from 3000 to 7000 ptas, depending on where the seat is in the ring.

You can purchase tickets at the rings, from the ticket offices on Calle de la Victoria (the same offices as for football tickets) or other places selling theatre tickets and the like (see Tickets under Entertainment earlier in this chapter). It is wise to buy tickets in advance, although you may be able to get basic seating in the sun on the day. Scalpers also operate outside the rings and ticket offices. During the San Isidro feria booking is mandatory. Ringside seats in the shade have been known to go for as much as two million pesetas!

SHOPPING

On Sunday morning, the Embajadores area of Madrid seems to contain half the city's population as all and sundry converge on El Rastro, the flea market. Starting from Plaza de Cascorro, its main axes are Calle de Ribeira de Curtidores and Calle de los Embajadores (map: Central). A good deal of what's on sale is rubbish, but the atmosphere alone is worth the effort, and you can find interesting items. There are a good many junk and antique stores sprinkled about and more contemporary shops in the Mercado Puerta de Toledo, just west of the Rastro area.

Calle del Prado is a good place to look for a higher class of furniture and other antique items.

Those looking to do some shopping in a more chichi environment should head for Calle de Serrano, the city's premier shopping street, in Salamanca. Of interest to those hanging around Madrid for the long haul is Marks & Spencer, whose food department carries all sorts of goodies otherwise unavailable in Madrid. Also well worth exploring is Calle del Almirante, just east of Plaza de Chueca, considered the city's best fashion showcase.

Madrid's, and indeed Spain's, best-known department store chain is El Corte Inglés. There's one located just off the Puerta del Sol on Calle de Preciados (map: Central).

For specialist purchases you need to look elsewhere. Hunt around along Calle Mayor, especially towards its western end, for guitars and other instruments. For leather try the shops along Gran Vía, or Calle de Fuencarral for shoes.

There are plenty of kitsch souvenirs of Madrid sold around Plaza Mayor and Sol, along Gran Vía or around the Prado. A popular item is a bullfighting poster with your name inscribed as lead torero.

If you're looking for nice gifts of quality Spanish wines and foodstuffs, there are quite a few shops in the Salamanca area. Mallorca, Calle de Velázquez 59 (map: Sal), is a good one. Smaller but also worth a look is Max 63 at Calle de Claudio Coello 64 (map: Sal).

CDs and cassettes are not especially cheap in Spain but, if you're looking for local music difficult to find at home, try the music sections of El Corte Inglés or FNAC, on Calle de Preciados. Madrid Rock (see Tickets under Entertainment for addresses) probably has the broadest general music selection and competitive prices.

For late-night munchies and other emergencies, there is a sprinkling of stores across central Madrid. Vips is the most widespread (a few have been marked on the maps). Others include 7-Eleven and Bob's, each of which have several branches and

remain open when everything else but the discos have shut their doors.

If you want a more comprehensive guide to Madrid shopping, ask the tourist office for its *Guía de Compras* booklet.

GETTING THERE & AWAY
Air
Regular and charter flights from all over the world arrive at Madrid's Aeropuerto de Barajas (☎ 91 305 83 43), 13km north-east of the city. There is a left-luggage centre (*consigna*; ☎ 91 305 61 12) outside the international arrivals hall. It is open daily from 7 am to midnight. You will find several banks with ATMs, a post office, tourist information, hotel booking stand, and general information office. Buses and taxis link the airport with the centre of Madrid.

Internal flights are not particularly good value unless you are in a burning hurry. Nor is Madrid exactly the budget air fare capital of Europe. That said, bargain flights to popular destinations such as London, New York and the Canary Islands can be found.

For hints on good travel agents, see Information earlier. See the Air sections in the Getting There & Away and Getting Around chapters for more information on flights and air fares.

Most airlines have representatives at the airport, as well as in Madrid itself. They include:

Aerolíneas Argentinas
 (☎ 91 564 18 50) Calle de María Molina 40
Air France
 (☎ 91 330 04 40) Torre de España, Plaza de España 18
American Airlines
 (☎ 91 597 20 68, ☎ 901-10 00 01) Calle de Pedro Teixeira 8
British Airways
 (☎ 91 577 69 59) Calle de Serrano 60
Delta Air Lines
 (☎ 91 577 06 50) Calle de Goya 8
Iberia
 (☎ 91 587 75 36, bookings ☎ 902-40 05 00 bookings) Calle de Velázquez 130 (map: Sal)
Lufthansa Airlines
 (☎ 902-22 01 01) Aeropuerto de Barajas

Qantas Airways
(☎ 91 542 15 72) Calle de la Princesa 1
Singapore Airlines
(☎ 91 563 80 01) Calle de Pinar 7
Thai Airways International
(☎ 91 411 64 11) Calle del Príncipe de Vergara 185

Bus

There are as many as eight *estación de autobuses* (bus stations) dotted about Madrid with companies servicing different parts of the country. The tourist offices can provide detailed information on where you need to go for your destination.

The Estación Sur de Autobuses on Calle de Méndez Álvaro (metro: Méndez Álvaro), is the city's principal bus station just south of the M-30 ring road. It serves most destinations to the south and many in other parts of the country. Most bus companies have a ticket office here, even if their buses depart from elsewhere. You can get information on ☎ 91 468 42 00.

The station is big and operates a *consigna* (left luggage), open from 6.30 am to midnight. There are cafés, shops, exchange booths, a bank, police and direct access to the No 6 metro line and cercanías trains to Atocha and Chamartín train stations.

Of the companies operating from other points around the city, some useful ones include:

AutoRes
Calle de Fernández Shaw 1 (☎ 91 551 72 00, bookings ☎ 902-19 29 39; map: Madrid). It operates buses to Extremadura, western Castilla y León (eg Tordesillas, Salamanca and Zamora) and Valencia via eastern Castilla-La Mancha (eg Cuenca). The nearest metro station is Conde de Casal.
Continental-Auto
Calle de Alenza 20 (☎ 91 533 04 00; map: North). This company runs buses north to Burgos, Logroño, Navarra, the País Vasco, Santander and Soria. It also runs buses to Toledo from the Estación Sur and to Alcalá de Henares and Guadalajara from Avenida de América 34 (metro: Cartagena, map: Madrid). There is a Granada service from the Calle de Alenza station.

Herranz
Its buses to San Lorenzo de El Escorial leave from the Intercambiador de Autobuses, a bus station below ground level at the Moncloa metro station on Calle de la Princesa (☎ 91 890 41 00; map: Madrid). The buses leave from platform 3.
La Sepulvedana
Paseo de la Florida 11 (☎ 91 530 48 00; metro: Príncipe Pío, map: Madrid). It operates buses to La Granja de San Ildefonso, Navacerrada and San Rafael (near Cercedilla). Buses for Talavera de la Reina also depart from here.
La Veloz
Avenida del Mediterráneo 49 (☎ 91 409 76 02; map: Madrid). Has regular buses to Chinchón. The nearest metro station is Conde de Casal.

Some sample one-way fares include (in some cases competing companies offer different prices – always check):

destination	fare (ptas)
Alicante	3270
Barcelona	2940
Córdoba	1530
Granada	1935
Lisbon (Portugal)	4680
Málaga	2620
Oviedo	3655
Santiago de Compostela	5500
Sevilla	2730
Tangier (Morocco)	7900

Train

Trains use two main stations. The more important of them is Atocha station (map: Madrid) south of the city centre. It serves all of southern Spain and many destinations around Madrid. Some northbound services also depart from here and head via Chamartín (map: North), the other station in the north of the city. This is smaller and generally serves destinations north of Madrid, although the rule is not a cast-iron one. Some services to Granada, Algecíras and so forth start in Chamartín, and don't even necessarily stop at Atocha on the way through. Be sure when getting a ticket that you find out which station the train leaves from.

International services to France and Portugal start in Chamartín and do *not* pass through Atocha.

The Príncipe Pío station serves three cercanías lines only.

The main RENFE booking office (☎ 91 328 90 20), Calle de Alcalá 44, is open Monday to Friday from 9.30 am to 8 pm.

For more details and sample fares see Train in the Getting Around chapter.

Car & Motorcycle

Madrid is surrounded by two ring-road systems, the innermost M-30 and newer M-40 (eventually a third, the M-50, will form the outer ring). Madrid, like Paris, is a hub from which spokes head out in all directions; these can be clogged at rush hour (around 8 to 10 am, 2 pm, 4 to 5 pm and 8 to 9 pm). Sunday night, especially on the highways from the south, can also be bad. If you intend to hitch, get well out of town first.

Rental The big-name car rental agencies have offices all over Madrid. Avis, Budget, Europcar, Hertz and Atesa/EuroDollar have booths at the airport. Some addresses include:

Atesa/EuroDollar
  (☎ 91 393 72 32) Aeropuerto de Barajas
Avis
  (☎ 91 547 20 48) Gran Vía (map: Mal & Ch)
Budget
  (☎ 91 393 72 16) Aeropuerto de Barajas
Europcar
  (☎ 91 541 88 92) Calle de San Leonardo 8 (map: España)
Hertz
  (reservations ☎ 900-10 01 11) Edificio de España, Plaza de España (map: España); also on the concourse outside Atocha station

You can rent motorbikes from Moto Alquiler (☎ 91 542 06 57; map: España), Calle del Conde Duque 13, but it's a pricey business. Rates start at 4500 ptas plus 16% IVA per day for a 49cc Vespino. Rental is from 8 am to 8 pm and you have to leave a refundable

deposit of 45,000 ptas. Something like a Yamaha 650 will cost you 16,000 ptas a day plus tax and the deposit is 150,000 ptas.

Bicycle

Karacol Sport (☎ 91 539 96 33), Calle de Tortosa 8, rents out mountain bikes (map: Central). The best offer is a weekend for 4000 ptas from Friday to Monday. There's a refundable deposit of 5000 ptas and you need to leave an original document (passport, driving licence or the like).

GETTING AROUND

Madrid is well served by a decent underground rail system (metro) and an extensive bus service. In addition, you can get from the north to the south of the city quickly by using short-range regional trains (cercanías) between the Atocha and Chamartín train stations. Taxis are also a viable option.

To/From the Airport

Barajas airport is linked to the city centre by a special bus leaving from an underground station in Plaza de Colón (metro: Serrano). You can also pick it up at a stop next to the Avenida de América metro station. Using a combination of this stop and the metro you can dodge much of the city-centre traffic. The fare is 380 ptas and buses leave every 12 to 15 minutes. Allow about half an hour in average traffic conditions.

A taxi from the centre will cost you about 2000 ptas, depending on traffic and how much luggage you have.

Those in a real hurry can use the Aero-CITY service (☎ 91 571 96 96), which will take you 'door-to-door' from central Madrid to the airport and vice versa. Depending on how many passengers book this minibus, the fare can range from 600 ptas to 1300 ptas a person. It operates 24 hours.

Bus

An extensive bus system operates throughout Madrid and outlying suburbs. Unless you buy season passes, you can get tickets on the bus or at most tobacconists (*estancos*). A single ride costs 130 ptas, or a

Metrobus ticket of 10 rides is 670 ptas; the latter entitles you to use the buses and metro, and you can share tickets.

Monthly or season passes *(abonos)* only make sense if you are staying for the long term and using local transport frequently. You need to get an ID card *(carnet)* from metro stations or tobacconists. Take a passport-sized photo and your passport or public transport photocard. A monthly ticket for central Madrid (Zona A) costs 4225 ptas and is valid for unlimited travel on bus, metro and cercanías.

Twenty night bus lines *(búhos)* operate from midnight to 6 am. They run from Puerta del Sol and Plaza de la Cibeles.

Information booths can be found at Puerta del Sol, Plaza de Callao and Plaza de la Cibeles. Or call ☎ 91 409 99 00. Route maps are available from the tourist offices.

Metro

The metro (☎ 91 552 59 09) is a fast, efficient and safe way to navigate Madrid and generally easier than coming to grips with bus routes. It operates from about 6.30 am to 1.30 am and you can buy tickets from booths or machines. Fares are the same as for buses. This book contains a colour map of the entire metro system.

If you've been to London, you'll notice an odd point of convergence: people take their queuing to the right on escalators surprisingly seriously here!

Cercanías

The short-range regional trains go as far afield as Toledo, Segovia, El Escorial and so on. They also serve some of the outer Madrid suburbs and the rest of the Comunidad de Madrid, and are handy for making a quick north-south hop between Atocha and Chamartín main-line train stations (with stops at Nuevos Ministerios and in front of the Biblioteca Nacional on Paseo de los Recoletos only). A direct link between Chamartín, Atocha and Príncipe Pío stations, the so-called Pasillo Verde (Green Corridor) is also handy. Metro tickets are no good on these lines, even if travelling between Atocha and Chamartín. A cercanías ticket between these stations costs 130 ptas.

Car & Motorcycle

As Latin cities go, Madrid is not the most hair-raising to drive in, although there is a fair amount of horn-honking, nippy manoeuvring, sloppy lane recognition and general 'madness' to get used to. Avoid peak hours, when the whole city heaves to the masses struggling to and from work. From about 2 to 4 pm the streets are dead. Once in the city, search for a car park or, if you are not fazed by the likelihood of getting a fine, the nearest likely looking parking space. Driving from sight to sight within Madrid is pointless.

Most of central Madrid is governed by the Operación de Regulación de Aparcamiento (ORA) parking system. This means that, apart from designated loading zones, no-parking areas and the like, all parking positions that appear legitimate are only so for people with yearly permits, or coupons obtainable from tobacconists. Some 300 parking officers stick about 12,000 fines on cars without permits every day. However, action is taken only on about 2500 and fines are rarely paid. Few locals bother buying the permits or coupons any more. The authorities are at a loss what to do about central Madrid's parking congestion – double-parking is as common as the wheel itself – so you can get away with quite a lot. However, if you park in a designated no-parking area, you risk being towed. Double parking is also risky in this way if you intend to wander far from your vehicle. Should your car disappear, call the Grúa Municipal (city towing service) on ☎ 91 345 00 50. Getting it back costs around 10,000 ptas.

If you wish to play it safe, there are plenty of parking stations across the city, starting at about 200 ptas an hour and a little less for each subsequent hour.

For details on vehicle rental, see Getting There & Away earlier and the Getting Around chapter.

Taxi

By European standards, taxis are inexpensive and well regulated. You can pick up a cab at ranks throughout town or simply flag one down. Flag fall is 170 ptas and you should make sure the driver turns the meter on. The fare from Barajas airport to Plaza de Colón should be around 2000 ptas, while the trip from Chamartín train station to the same square will be about 1000 ptas. There are several supplementary charges, usually posted up inside the taxi. They include 350 ptas for going to the airport, 150 ptas for running to rail or bus stations, 150 ptas between 11 pm and 6 am and also on public holidays, as well as 50 ptas for each piece of luggage. You can call a cab on ☎ 91 445 90 08 or ☎ 91 547 82 00.

Warning

If you have a rental car in Madrid, take extra care. Groups of delinquents are known to zero in on them occasionally, puncturing a tyre and then robbing the driver when they act to change it. This is reportedly a particular problem on the road from the airport to the centre of town.

Comunidad de Madrid

Covering about 8000 sq km, the region around Madrid boasts two million people. Sealed off to the north and west by the Sierra de Guadarrama, it can be considered part of what was once known as Castilla la Nueva (New Castile).

The capital continues to spread into the comunidad, converting former villages into drab suburbs or simply creating new ones. Through that growing urban sprawl radiate highways to the rest of the country, passing a handful of interesting places within easy one-day striking distance.

To the south lie Aranjuez and Chinchón. The former is the site of one of the royal palaces Madrid's rulers created for themselves; Chinchón is a charming village centred on a classic old Castilian plaza.

Heading east towards Guadalajara, the old university town of Alcalá de Henares is a quick train ride away. A slower journey by train (but fast enough by car on the road to Ávila) is the royal residence town of El Escorial. Nearby is the more dubious monument to Franco, the Valle de los Caídos. Both lie in the Sierra de Guadarrama, the low mountain range that runs south-west to north-east, marking the length of the Comunidad's border with Castilla y León. Farther north there is plenty of scope for walking – and in winter, with luck, a bit of low-grade skiing.

SAN LORENZO DE EL ESCORIAL & AROUND

Sheltering against a protective wall of the Sierra de Guadarrama, the majestic palace-and-monastery complex of San Lorenzo de El Escorial serves today for ordinary *madrileños* as a focal point for escape from the pressure-cooker atmosphere of the capital, just as it did for kings and sycophants of old. At just over 1000m above sea level, and protected from the worst of the winter's icy northern winds, the site enjoys a mild and exceptionally healthy climate.

Highlights

- Spending a day at the splendid El Escorial
- Long lunch of suckling pig at Mesón Cuevas del Vino in Chinchón
- A ride on the Strawberry Train (Tren de la Fresa) to Aranjuez
- Walks – or even a little skiing – in the Sierra de Guadarrama

Monasterio de San Lorenzo de El Escorial p247

MADRID

Kings and princes have a habit, before important battles, of promising rather extravagant offerings to God, the angels, saints and anyone else who'll listen, in return for help in defeating their foes. Felipe II was no exception before the Battle of St Quentin against the French on St Lawrence's day, 10 August 1557. Felipe's victory was decisive, and in thanks he ordered the construction in the saint's name of the San Lorenzo complex, above the hamlet of El Escorial. A huge monastery,

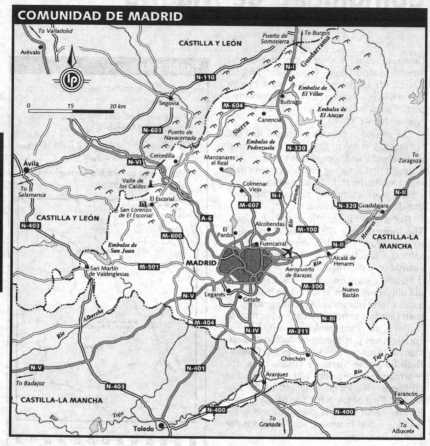

COMUNIDAD DE MADRID

royal palace and mausoleum for Felipe's parents, Carlos I and Isabel, were raised under the watchful eye of the architect Juan de Herrera. The austere style reflects Felipe's own severe outlook and desire not to be distracted by over-ornamentation. To the academics, El Escorial is a key to understanding developments in Spanish architecture over the subsequent two centuries.

The palace-monastery soon became an important intellectual centre, with a bur-geoning library and art collection and even a laboratory where scientists could dabble in alchemy. Felipe II died in El Escorial on 13 September 1598. Various additions were made in the following centuries. In 1854 the monks of the Hieronymite order, who had occupied the monastery from the beginning, were obliged to leave, to be replaced 30 years later by Augustinians.

The tourist office (☎ 91 890 15 54) is at Calle de Floridablanca 10 It is open Monday to Friday from 10 am to 2 pm and

3 to 4.45 pm and Saturday from 10 am to 1.45 pm.

The Monastery

The main entrance lies on the western side. Above the gateway a statue of St Lawrence stands watch, holding a symbolic gridiron, the instrument of his martyrdom (he was roasted alive on one). Indeed, the shape of the monastery complex recalls the same object. You enter the **Patio de los Reyes**, which houses the statues of the six kings of Judah. Directly ahead lies the sombre **basílica**. As you enter, look up to the unusual flat vaulting below the choir stalls before the main body of the church. Once inside, turn left to view Benvenuto Cellini's white Carrara marble statue of Christ crucified, carved in 1576.

The marble and bronze reredos behind the high altar is rich in decoration, largely the work of Italian artists. Leone and Pompei Leoni are among them, and they also did the bronze statue groups on either side of the altar. On the left are Carlos I and family; to the right are Felipe II, three of his wives and his eldest son, Prince Don Carlos.

When you exit the church, follow the signs to the ticket office *(taquilla)*. You will have little choice about the order in which you visit the monastery and palace quarters; just follow the arrows.

You first head downstairs in the northeastern corner of the complex, the general area of the Palacio de los Austrias, to inspect the **Museo de Arquitectura** and, subsequently, the **Museo de Pintura**. The former covers (in Spanish) the story of how the complex was built, while the latter contains a range of Italian, Spanish and Flemish art from the 16th and 17th centuries.

COMUNIDAD DE MADRID

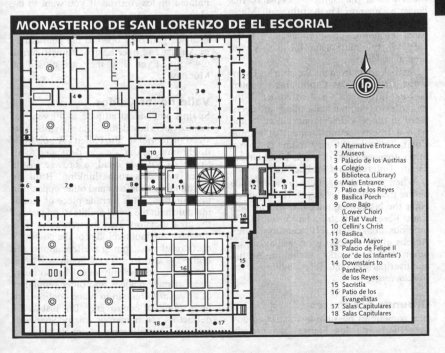

MONASTERIO DE SAN LORENZO DE EL ESCORIAL

1 Alternative Entrance
2 Museos
3 Palacio de los Austrias
4 Colegio
5 Biblioteca (Library)
6 Main Entrance
7 Patio de los Reyes
8 Basílica Porch
9 Coro Bajo
   (Lower Choir)
   & Flat Vault
10 Cellini's Christ
11 Basílica
12 Capilla Mayor
13 Palacio de Felipe II
   (or 'de los Infantes')
14 Downstairs to
   Panteón
   de los Reyes
15 Sacristía
16 Patio de los
   Evangelistas
17 Salas Capitulares
18 Salas Capitulares

At this point you are obliged to head upstairs again into a gallery around the eastern protuberance of the complex known as the Palacio de Felipe II. These apartments are richly decorated with all manner of paintings, maps and exquisite woodcarvings (some of the doorways and furniture are particularly fine).

From here you descend to the 17th century **Panteón de los Reyes**, where almost all Spain's monarchs since Carlos I lie interred with their spouses. The royal corpses lie in gilded marble coffins of subdued baroque magnificence. It appears there is not a lot of room left to add to their number.

Backtracking a little, you find yourself in the **Panteón de los Infantes**, whose nine vaults were built in the 19th century. Here lie buried *infantes* (the second-born of monarchs), princes and childless queens. Don Juan de Austria (better known to Anglo-Saxons as Don John of Austria), victor over the Turks at the Battle of Lepanto, lies beneath a memorial in the fifth vault. Maria Teresa de Austria is buried in the third vault. Most intriguing – tasteless even? – is the carousel-style mausoleum for princes who died as toddlers.

Stairs lead up from the Patio de los Evangelistas to the **Salas Capitulares** (chapter-houses) in the south-eastern corner of the monastery. Their vaulted ceilings are decorated in the so-called Pompeian style and with a free-wheeling element of trompe l'oeil. These bright, airy rooms contain a minor treasure chest of works by El Greco, Titian, Tintoretto and José de Ribera.

When you emerge, return to the entrance before the Patio de los Reyes. Here you can enter the **biblioteca**, once one of Europe's finest libraries and still a haven for 40,000 precious books. The 11th century Codex Aureus of the Gospels is on display, as are other valuable works, including Arabic manuscripts and Santa Teresa's *Libro de las Fundaciones*.

Grounds & Annexes

It is sometimes possible to wander around the **Huerta de los Frailes**, the orderly gardens just south of the monastery. In the **Jardín del Príncipe** that leads down to the town of El Escorial (and the train station) is the **Casita del Príncipe**, built under Carlos III for his heir.

Following Paseo de Carlos III (the Ávila road) out of town, you pass on the left the entrance to La Herrería, in the grounds of which stands La Silla de Felipe – a seat, carved of stone, from which Felipe observed construction of his monastery. Farther on is the **Casita de Arriba**, another 18th century neoclassical gem from the hands of Juan de Villanueva, who was responsible for the Casita del Príncipe.

Opening Times & Tickets

San Lorenzo is open Tuesday to Sunday from 10 am to 6 pm (to 5 pm from October to March; 900 ptas, students 450 ptas). Only the basilica is free. The price includes a guided tour of the *panteones* and the Palacio de los Austrias if you want to tag along.

The Casita de Arriba and Casita del Príncipe generally open to the public only in August and over Easter, from 10 am to 6.45 pm. Even then they are closed on Monday.

Valle de los Caídos

Spain's ambivalent attitude to 40 years of Francoism is best demonstrated in this oversized memorial to 'the Fallen'. An optimist might imagine the site was dedicated to all Spain's civil war dead; a browse inside quickly dispels such thinking. Built by prison labour – leftists and other opposition undesirables – it is a crude piece of monumentalism in the awful architectural taste of the great dictators. This concrete colossus is the most flagrant reminder of the country's dictatorial past, but travellers along the highways and byways of Spain will soon notice it is not the only one. That so many street names, plaques and other reminders of *el caudillo* remain in place continues to be a source of controversy. But just as his detractors are numerous, many Spaniards feel the Generalísimo was not all bad.

The turn-off and ticket booth is 9km north of El Escorial. It's another 6km drive to the shrine – you are not supposed to stop en route. There is something spooky about the subterranean basilica and little, artistically, to recommend it. By the altar lies Franco himself. Also buried here is 'José Antonio'. Before the civil war, the dashing José Antonio Primo de Rivera, son of the 1920s dictator Miguel Primo de Rivera, led the Falange, the party that later formed the fascist political component of Franco's Nationalist movement. Executed in Alicante by the Republicans in late 1936, he became a martyr figure for the Nationalists.

You can also drive up to the base of the enormous cross above the basilica, or catch a cable car (funicular). The views are splendid.

The site is open daily (except Monday) from 10 am to 6 pm (650 ptas). The funicular operates from 10.30 am to 2.10 pm and 4 to 5.40 pm. About the only way there, if you don't have a vehicle, is to get the daily Herranz bus from El Escorial.

Places to Stay & Eat

There is no need to stay in El Escorial, although it's a pleasant enough overnight stop.

You'll find a couple of youth hostels within about 1km of San Lorenzo. *Albergue El Escorial* (☎ 91 890 59 24) is at Calle de la Residencia 14 and *Albergue Santa María Buen Aire* (☎ 91 890 36 40) at Finca la Herrería. The latter also offers camping. B&B in dorms costs 950 ptas for HI members under 26 and 1300 ptas for older folk.

Otherwise, the cheapest place to stay is *Hostal Vasco* (☎ 91 890 16 19) on Plaza de Santiago. It has comfy doubles for 4700 ptas.

A few places line Calle de Juan de Toledo, the road for El Valle de los Caídos. The best value is *Hostal Cristina* (☎ 91 890 19 61) at No 6, which charges about 5000/6200 ptas.

Calle de Floridablanca is flanked by a trio of expensive upper mid-level places, and the top establishment is *Hotel Victoria Palace* (☎ 91 890 15 11, fax 91 890 12 48,

Calle de Juan de Toledo 4). Doubles cost 9200/11,300 ptas plus IVA.

The eating is not the greatest in San Lorenzo de El Escorial. With no permanent local clientele to please, most places have a rather slack attitude to quality but an all-too-keen eye for your pesetas. Keep away from the places along Calle de Floridablanca, which are generally a tourist rip-off. *Restaurante El Candil (Calle de Reina Victoria 16)* does a good *menú del día*. It's especially pleasant when they set up tables outside overlooking the lower half of the square.

Getting There & Away

Bus The Herranz bus company runs up to 30 services a day from the Intercambiador de Autobuses at the Moncloa metro station in Madrid to San Lorenzo de El Escorial (380 ptas one way). Only about 10 run on Sunday and holidays. The same company (office on Calle de la Reina Victoria) runs a bus to El Valle de los Caídos at 3.30 pm from El Escorial, returning at 5.30 pm (220 ptas). This bus does not run on Monday.

Train Up to 20 sluggish *cercanías* trains (line C-8a) serve El Escorial from Atocha station (via Chamartín) in Madrid (430 ptas, 370 ptas on weekdays). Seven of these go on to Ávila. The station is in the town of El Escorial itself, quite a hike from San Lorenzo and its hamlet. You can walk (about 2km uphill) or catch a local bus linking the two.

Car & Motorcycle From Madrid take the A-6 and follow the exits. From El Escorial, the M-505 winds its way across the low western ranges of the Sierra de Guadarrama to Ávila – a pretty drive with wonderful views back across San Lorenzo de Escorial shortly before you top the rise.

SOUTH OF MADRID
Aranjuez

A refreshing patch of green in sun-drenched central Spain, Aranjuez continues to play its centuries-old role as a haven from the capital, 48km to the north. The difference is that it's no longer a royal playground – the privilege has been extended to all and sundry. The area is an important breeding ground for butterflies – so important that engineers had to skirt round it when they built the N-IV *autovía*!

Information The tourist office (☎ 91 891 04 27), Plaza de San Antonio 9, is open Monday to Friday from 10 am to 2.30 pm. The postcode for Aranjuez is 28039.

Palacio Real When Felipe II built his summer palace here on the lush banks of the Tajo in the 16th century, there had already been a country residence on the site for 200 years. What was in Felipe's day a modest 20-room affair, later destroyed by fire, was to become under his successors the 18th century excess that stands today. With more than 300 rooms and inspired by Versailles (an ever-popular model with European monarchs), it is filled with a cornucopia of ornamentation. Of all the rulers who spent time here, Carlos III and Isabel II left the greatest mark.

Carlos III had a new portrait done of himself every year (one hangs in an apartment here) but, unwilling to waste time posing for each painting, he had court painters copy the first one each year! He took a keener interest in interior decorating. The Sala de Porcelana (Porcelain Room) is extravagant, its walls covered in hand-crafted porcelain figures (more than vaguely reminiscent of a similar chamber in Madrid's Palacio Real). It took two years to complete the decoration. The Sala Fumadora is almost as remarkable – a florid imitation of an Alhambra interior, with Arabic inscriptions in stucco and an intricate stalactite ceiling carved in wood.

After touring the palace, a stroll in the gardens makes for a relaxing antidote. The English elms that predominate are a reminder that the gardens are more than just a happy accident. The Jardín de la Isla, right by the palace and forming a tranquil island in a bend in the Tajo, is nice, but the more

extensive **Jardín del Príncipe** along the Chinchón road is more appealing.

Within its shady perimeter you'll find two other man-made attractions. The **Casa de Marinos** contains royal pleasure boats from days gone by. Farther away, towards Chinchón, is the **Casa del Labrador**, a tasteless royal jewellery box crammed to the rafters with gold, silver, silk and some second-rate art. Built for Carlos IV in 1805, it is the final Versailles touch, an attempt to emulate the Petit Trianon.

Entry The Palacio Real is open Tuesday to Sunday from 10 am to 7 pm (an hour less in winter; 500 ptas, free for EU citizens on Wednesday). Entry to the Casa del Labrador costs 425 ptas and the Casa de Marinos is 425 ptas (or 700 ptas for both). The gardens (the palace ticket covers all the gardens) are open from 8 am to 8.30 pm in summer (6.30 pm in winter).

Places to Stay & Eat There is little temptation to stay in Aranjuez but you have six hotels and a camping ground to choose from. *Camping Soto del Castillo* (☎ 91 891 13 95) lies between the N-IV and the Río Tajo. It is open from March to October.

The cheapest of the hotels is *Hostal Rusiñol* (☎ 91 891 01 55, Calle de San Antonio 76), a couple of blocks from the tourist office and with singles/doubles for 1850/2900 ptas. Doubles with private bathroom cost 4800 ptas. On the food front, many restaurants are cheekily expensive. *Casa Pablo (Calle de Almíbar 42)* does good Castilian food. A full meal will cost about 1500 ptas. *La Rana Verde (Calle de la Reina 1)*, on the Tajo, is the town's best-known restaurant, and a full meal will set you back by at least 2500 ptas.

Getting There & Away Frequent cercanías trains (line C-3) connect with Madrid's Atocha station (40 minutes; 395 ptas), and occasional trains go to Toledo. The AISA bus company has up to 17 daily services (390 ptas) from Estación Sur de

Autobuses in Madrid. Empresa Samar also has a few. Two buses run daily to Chinchón.

Tren de la Fresa A delightful option from April to October is the Strawberry Train. This day excursion sees you seated aboard a restored steam train with attendants in period dress serving up free – you guessed it – strawberries. The 3100 ptas (1900 ptas for children under 12) price tag includes the return trip from Atocha station, a bus transfer to the centre of Aranjuez and admission to monuments. Information and timetables are available at Atocha. Disappointment can set in when the steam engine has to be replaced by a boring old diesel locomotive.

Chinchón

Home of a well-known brew of *anís*, the aniseed-based heart-starter favoured by not a few Spaniards, Chinchón is an agreeable little settlement 50km south-east of Madrid. The focal point is the *plaza mayor*, ringed by centuries-old two and three-tiered balconies, most of which now accommodate dining madrileños. The plaza also doubles as a bullring. Just north of the plaza lies the 16th century Iglesia de la Asunción, containing an *Asunción* attributed to Goya. A few steps south of the square on Calle del Generalísimo is a former 18th century Augustinian monastery. It now serves as a **parador** (☎ 91 894 08 36). A couple of kilometres south of the centre you can see castle ruins – for a long time you could taste the Chinchón anís in a couple of distilleries here, but they are closed. Others operate on the eastern edge of town. If you want to buy a bottle, head for the Alcoholera de Chinchón on Plaza Mayor.

For Semana Santa Chinchón converts itself into a setting for lavish Easter processions, to the extent that Roman soldiers end up outnumbering the Guardia Civil.

Hostal Chinchón (☎ 91 893 53 98, Calle de José Antonio 12) is a pleasant place with an internal patio just off Plaza Mayor. Singles/doubles with own bath and TV cost 4000/6000 ptas plus IVA.

You can scout around the several restaurants right on Plaza Mayor, or head away

from the centre. A special but pricey option is the **Mesón Cuevas del Vino** (☎ 91 894 02 06, Calle de Benito Hortelano 13). This cavernous bodega, lined with huge wine barrels and popular with weekenders from Madrid, serves great Castilian food, but you won't get away for less than 3000 ptas per person.

Buses regularly run between Chinchón and Madrid (No 337 from Calle del Conde de Casal). There are two a day to Aranjuez.

ALCALÁ DE HENARES

A little way north of the Roman town of Complutum (of which nothing remains) and 35km east of Madrid on the N-II to Zaragoza, Alcalá de Henares entered a period of greatness when Cardinal Cisneros founded a university here in 1486. Now centred on a much-restored Renaissance building in the centre of what is virtually a satellite of Madrid, the university was long one of the country's main seats of learning. In 1836, however, Alcalá was dealt a blow with the transfer of the Universidad Complutense to the capital. The rot was only arrested with the reopening of the university in 1977. The town is also dear to the hearts of Spaniards as the birthplace of the country's literary figurehead, Miguel de Cervantes Saavedra.

A tourist office (☎ 91 889 26 94) is just off Plaza de Cervantes, the town's main square, at Callejón de Santa María 1. It is open daily from 10 am to 2 pm and 4 to 6.30 pm.

You can wander through parts of the **universidad** any time, but to visit properly you need to turn up between 11 am and 2 pm or 4 and 5 pm (Sunday at 4, 5 and 6 pm) for a guided tour. The ornate entrance, facing Plaza de San Diego, is in the plateresque style. Of particular interest inside are the Paraninfo (auditorium), with a fine *mudéjar* ceiling, and the Capilla de San Ildefonso, to the right of the main university entrance. The latter contains the tomb of Cardinal Cisneros. The visits cost 250 ptas.

Predictably, Cervantes' birthplace has been 'found' – at Calle Mayor 48, on the corner of Calle de la Imagen. A relatively new building, the **Museo Casa Natal de Miguel de Cervantes** is filled with period furniture and bits and pieces relating to the life of Don Quijote's creator. It is open Tuesday to Friday from 10.15 am to 1.45 pm and 4.15 to 6.45 pm and weekends from 10.15 am to 1.45 pm. Calle Mayor is a pleasant, arcaded boulevard.

There is no need to stay here, but *Hostal Jacinto* (☎ *91 889 14 32, Paseo de la Estación 2*) is handy for the train and charges 2000/3600 ptas for singles/doubles with shower. If you want something classier and closer to the centre, *Hotel El Bedel* (☎ *91 889 37 00, Plaza de San Diego 6*) has beautifully maintained singles/doubles for 7900/11,500 ptas plus IVA.

The *Hostería del Estudiante* is an expensive but charming restaurant backing onto the Paraninfo in the main university building.

The easiest way to get to Alcalá is by one of the frequent cercanías trains shuttling between Madrid (Chamartín) and Guadalajara. The fare is 320 ptas.

SOUTH OF ALCALÁ

Those with cars might be tempted by a quick excursion to **Nuevo Baztán**, 21km south. In the early 18th century, José Benito Churriguera was instructed to lay out a village and design its main buildings in an early Spanish attempt at town planning. It's virtually a ghost town now, and Churriguera's church and neighbouring palace are in poor shape. He did the *retablos* inside the church, which is usually closed.

You might also consider heading east along the M-219 via Olmeda de las Fuentes to cross over the regional border with Guadalajara province. Here you are near La Alcarria and its principal town Pastrana (see the Castilla-La Mancha chapter).

Empresa Argabus (☎ *91 433 91 49*) runs buses (No 261) to and from Calle del Conde de Casal in Madrid (three a day on weekdays, two on Saturday and one on Sunday). The same company also has a daily bus to Alcalá de Henares at 7 am and from Alcalá (Calle de Luis Vives) at 3.15 pm.

SIERRA DE GUADARRAMA

The hills of the Sierra de Guadarrama form a getaway for madrileños but are little frequented by foreigners. Longer-term visitors to the capital may care to explore it, popping into the odd *pueblo* and doing a little walking to relieve the big-city stress.

Colmenar Viejo

There's little to see in this town of 25,000 people, virtually a satellite of Madrid. But if you are in Madrid in the first days of February, get up here to witness the colourful Vaquilla, a fiesta with pagan origins dating back to the 13th century and vaguely reminiscent of some Chinese festivals. A highly ornamental 'heifer' is made to be pranced about the town before being 'slaughtered' by '*toreros*' dressed in Andalucian style. Dropped during the Franco years, it is an increasingly popular festival.

Manzanares El Real

Not far from Colmenar Viejo, before the granite mountain backdrop of La Pedriza, lies the charming little 15th century Castillo de los Mendoza in the town of Manzanares El Real. The castle is open Tuesday to Sunday from 10 am to 2 pm and 4 to 7 pm (10 am to 5 pm in winter; 300 ptas).

Several trails lead into the nearby Pedriza park, one of which brings you to freshwater pools. Rock climbers have a wealth of options, with 1500 climbing routes scattered throughout the park. For advice, try the Federación Madrileña de Montaña (☎ 91 593 80 74), Calle de Apodaca 16, in Madrid. Also check out the park's visitors centre.

Hostal El Tranco (☎ *91 853 00 63, Calle del Tranco 4*) has good singles/doubles for 5500/7700 ptas. When times are slow they may well halve these rates. Buses run to Manzanares from Plaza de Castilla in Madrid.

Cercedilla

The mountain town of Cercedilla and the area surrounding it are popular with hikers and mountain bikers. Several trails are marked out through the Sierra, the main one known as the Cuerda Larga or Cuerda Castellana. This is a forest track that takes in 55 peaks between the Puerto de So-mosierra in the north and Puerto de la Cruz Verde in the south-west. It would take days to complete, but shorter walks include day excursions up the Valle de la Fuenfría and a climb up Monte de Siete Picos.

Mountain bikers could take their bikes up on the local train to Puerto de los Cotos (a lovely ride in itself), scoot across to the Bola del Mundo (in good winters the top end of Guadarrama's best ski piste) and pedal downhill to Cercedilla.

You can get information at the Centro de Información Valle de la Fuenfría (☎ 91 852 22 13), a couple of kilometres from Cercedilla train station.

Group hikes, mountain bike rides or rock-climbing trips can be organised through the Puerto de Navacerrada ski-lift and sports operator, Deporte y Montaña, by calling ☎ 91 852 33 02. Alternatively approach its reps at Gran Vía 42 (☎ 91 594 30 34) in Madrid.

Accommodation is scarce, so you are best tackling this as a day trip from Madrid. Otherwise, be prepared to camp along the trail if you are doing the Cuerda Larga.

Northern Guadarrama

If you want to avoid the crowds around Cercedilla, try for quieter walking farther north. One possibility is a 10km plateau trail that connects Canencia with Garganta de los Montes (Valle de Lozoya). You're looking at about three hours hiking each way. Continental Auto has buses from Plaza de Castilla in Madrid to Canencia (685 ptas). You could stay at *Hostal Colorines* (*☎ 91 868 74 71, Calle Real 110*) in Canencia. It has doubles only for 5000 ptas.

Skiing in the Guadarrama

Skiing 60km from Madrid? Not the first image that springs to mind when one contemplates the idea of central Spain, but when the snow falls you can shoot down the pistes of Navacerrada and Cotos, just on the

border with Segovia province. Snowless years are common and the available pistes not extensive, but it's a popular business with madrileños on the weekend, when the area should be avoided. Navacerrada is the main centre and there are 13km of mostly easy – and frustratingly short – runs. The best is the Bola del Mundo. A daily ski-lift pass costs 3400 ptas.

You're not likely to want to stay, especially as the place is not fully equipped as a resort. There are a few hotels in the town of Navacerrada and also at the Puerto de Navacerrada if you really want to hang around more than a day.

You can reach Navacerrada by train from Cercedilla or bus from Madrid (station at Paseo de la Florida 11). If you're driving, note that available parking is generally full by 9 am on weekends with good snow.

NORTH OF MADRID
Palacio Real de El Pardo

Just north of Madrid is the nearest of several regal escape hatches. This one ended up as Franco's favoured residence, although the present building served Felipe II in the same fashion as far back as 1558. Carlos III used to rotate between El Pardo, El Escorial, Aranjuez and La Granja de San Ildefonso, assigning a season to each and pursuing his passion for hunting. Of the art displayed inside, the several hundred tapestries stand out, particularly those based on cartoons by Goya.

About 500m from the palace is the **Casita del Príncipe**, an elaborate 'cottage' built for Carlos IV in 1786, while he was still heir apparent. At the time of writing it was closed for restoration.

The palace is open Monday to Saturday from 10.30 am to 6 pm and Sunday and holidays from 10 am to 1.40 pm. Admission, which also covers the Casita del Príncipe, is 650 ptas (students 250 ptas).

An outing to El Pardo could be neatly combined with a lunch stop. You'll find plenty of busy restaurants around Plaza del Caudillo (just to remind you of the great man).

Who Do You Think You're Kidding, Mr Marshall?

In the unassuming village of Guadalix de la Sierra, 7km west of the Burgos highway and 50km north of central Madrid, are set some of the most memorable scenes of the 1952 classic movie *Bienvenido Mr Marshall*, directed by Luis García Berlanga. Guadalix starred as the archetypal Spanish pueblo with the name Villar del Río and whitewashed in the Andalucian manner. The townspeople gathered on the great day to greet progress and the Americans, who simply drove straight through town without stopping. A *caña* in Bar La Central on Plaza Mayor is worthwhile: the walls sport photos from the days when the filming was done. The square looked rather different then – half-real and half-movie set.

If Berlanga cast a sympathetic eye on the sufferings of the poor towns of 1950s Spain, Guadalix still has plenty of problems. With a population of 4000, the penniless town cannot afford to repair streets and the sewerage system, and the dairy business from which it survived is now in deep crisis, unable to absorb the blows dealt by EU agriculture quotas.

The palace and grounds are on the Carretera de El Pardo, about 15km north-west of central Madrid. Bus No 601 (135 ptas) leaves every 10 minutes from a stop on Paseo de Moret (metro: Moncloa) in Madrid.

Alcobendas

At Alcobendas, 17km north of Madrid along the N-I to Burgos, the only thing of interest is the Museo Interactivo de la Ciencia Acciona, in the Parque de Andalucía. Although not the greatest interactive museum in the world, this could be a good one for the kids. It was closed for refurbishment at the time of writing. Bus Nos 151, 152, 153, 154 and 157 go to Alcobendas from Plaza de Castilla.

Buitrago & the Valle de Lozoya

About 15km short of the Puerto de Somosierra rise the picturesque walls of Buitrago, surrounded by a pretty reservoir. The Iglesia de Santa María del Castillo was built in 1321, but largely destroyed in 1936. Now restored, it displays mudéjar and Romanesque elements. There is a modest castle and you can walk along part of the walls. The Museo Picasso contains autographed bits and pieces given by the artist to his barber, who lived here. You could stay, if need be, at *Hostal Madrid París* (☎ 91 868 11 26, Avenida de Madrid 23), which has singles/doubles for 2000/3500 ptas. The *Cervecería Plaza* offers a huge range of seafood. Regular buses run between Buitrago and Plaza de Castilla in Madrid.

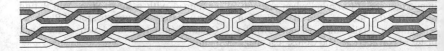

Castilla y León

Roughly taking in the territories of the former kingdom of León and Castilla la Vieja (Old Castile), this vast region offers a string of more or less important cities dotted across often desolate plains. Among the 'musts' are Salamanca, León, Segovia, Ávila and Burgos.

As if to confirm the adage that the exception proves the rule, however, fringe areas provide an enormous contrast to the monotony of 'deep Castilla'. The Leonese side of the Picos de Europa mountains (see the Cantabria & Asturias chapter for details), the Sierra de la Peña de Francia (near Extremadura), the Sierra de Gredos (bordering Castilla-La Mancha) and the Sanabria area (just short of Galicia) are some of the more obvious such exceptions. Searing summer heat and bitter winter cold further characterise the tendency to extremes in this old heartland of Spain.

For this guide, the region has been roughly divided into four zones, with some of the routes described radiating away from a theoretical starting point of Madrid.

As with most of central Spain, centuries of poverty have left their mark on the area's cuisine. The nippy winter climate and local peasant produce have favoured the development of a variety of meat dishes, and Spaniards readily recognise the region as the best to hunt out roast everything, with *cochinillo* (suckling pig) a particular speciality, above all in Segovia. C*ordero asado* (roast lamb*)* and *cabrito* (kid) are also reliable favourites. The better wines are produced along the Río Duero; Vega Sicilia is probably the best-known wine label of the region.

Highlights

- The golden hues of Spain's best plateresque architecture in the busy university city of Salamanca
- Exploring Las Médulas, the weird landscape left behind by Roman gold-miners
- Visiting the Alcázar of Segovia
- Tucking into a massive roast in the town of Sepúlveda
- Tracking down the pick of the castles, from Peñafiel to Coco
- Quiet contemplation in the monastery of Santo Domingo de Silos
- Relaxing around the pretty Lago di Sanabria

The South-West

Starting from Madrid and passing through El Escorial, an obvious route suggests itself across the most southerly tract of Castilla y León, taking in the towns of Ávila, Salamanca and Ciudad Rodrigo, from where the road continues west into Portugal. Along the way, you could detour to the Sierra de Gredos for some mountain walks and the timeless villages of the Sierra de la Peña de Francia, 40km east of Ciudad Rodrigo.

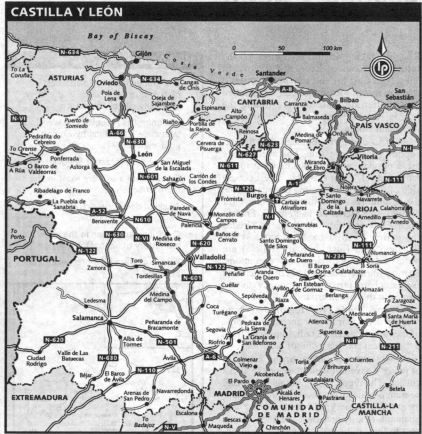

CASTILLA Y LEÓN

ÁVILA

Huddled behind hefty walls at an altitude of 1130m, Ávila must be one of the chilliest cities in Spain. Known for its long and bitter winters, it is a remarkable sight for the visitor and particularly pleasant in summer.

Although Ávila is not as captivating as Toledo or even Segovia, day-trippers from Madrid should nonetheless arrive early or consider staying overnight to do the city justice.

History

According to myth, one of Hercules' sons founded Ávila. The more prosaic truth, however, gives the honour to obscure Iberian tribes, who were soon assimilated into Celtic society and later largely Romanised and Christianised. For almost 300 years, Ávila changed hands regularly between Muslims and Christians, until the fall of Toledo to Alfonso VI in 1085.

In the following centuries, 'Ávila of the Knights' became an important commercial

The 15th century Castillo de los Mendoza in Mazanares El Real (Comunidad de Madrid)

The windmills of Castilla-La Mancha

DAMIEN SIMONIS

Sleepy Ciudad Rodrigo, (Castilla y León)

MARK DAFFEY

Walt Disney liked the Alcázar at Segovia so much, he re-created it in California (Castilla y León)

INGRID RUDDIS

centre. Its well-established noble class was not averse to a skirmish in the wars with the Muslims or, later, in the imperial escapades in Flanders and South America. The edict issued in 1492 expelling all Jews from Spain, followed a century later by moves to get rid of the *moriscos* (christianised Muslims), robbed the city of much of its lifeblood. Meanwhile, Fray Tomás de Torquemada was busy at the end of the 15th century organising the most brutal phase of the Spanish Inquisition. He ended his days in Ávila. Decades later, Santa Teresa began her difficult mystical journey and the unwelcome campaign to reform the Carmelites in the same city. By the time Teresa died in 1582, Ávila's golden days were over, as indeed were those of most of Castilla, and the city has only recently begun to shake off the deep slumber of neglect that ensued.

Orientation

The old centre is enclosed by a rough quadrangle of robust walls at the western end of town, with the cathedral butting into the walls at their eastern extremity. The RENFE train station is about a 10 minute walk north-east of the cathedral, while the *estación de autobuses* (bus station) is a little closer, just off Avenida de Madrid. Several *hostales* (budget hotels) cluster around the cathedral, and a few others are near the train station.

The tourist office, post office, telephones and banks are all near the cathedral.

Information

Tourist Offices The helpful tourist office (☎ 920 21 13 87), Plaza de la Catedral 4, is open Monday to Friday from 10 am to 2 pm and 5 to 8 pm, Saturday from 9 am to 2.30 pm and 4.30 to 8.30 pm, and Sunday from 11 am to 2 pm and 4.30 to 8.30 pm. A municipal tourist information kiosk (☎ 920 35 71 26) also operates just outside the Puerta de San Vicente.

Money Several banks in the centre of the old town have user-friendly ATMs.

Post & Communications The *correos* (post office) and Telefónica phone office are nearly next to one another, just in from the Puerta de los Leales. The latter is open Monday to Saturday from 9 am to 2 pm and 5 to 10 pm (it closes an hour earlier on Saturday). Ávila's postcode is 05080.

Medical Services & Emergency The local number for the police is ☎ 920 25 10 00. In a medical emergency, call the Cruz Roja on ☎ 920 22 22 22.

Catedral

The double vocation of Ávila's cathedral is symbolised in its menacing granite apse, which forms the central bulwark in the eastern wall of the town, the most open to attack and hence the most heavily fortified.

Around the western side, the main façade betrays the Romanesque origins of what is essentially the earliest Gothic church in Spain. It also betrays some unhappy 18th century meddling in the main portal. The 13th century northern entrance was transferred to its present position in the 15th century. Inside, the red and white limestone employed in the columns stands out.

Worth inspecting are the fine walnut choir stalls, while the Capilla Mayor boasts a retablo mainly carried out by Pedro de Berruguete in the mid-15th century. Behind the main altar lies buried a 15th century bishop and intellectual called El Tostado (The Toasted One). The Museo Catedralicio contains the usual collection of religious art, including an El Greco and a huge monstrance by Juan de Arfe, grandson of the great monstrance-maker Enrique de Arfe. The cathedral is open daily from 8.30 am to 2 pm and 4 to 7 pm, but the museum is open later and closes a little earlier (250 ptas).

Basílica de San Vicente

Lying outside the great fortified gate of the same name, the Romanesque basilica is striking in its subdued elegance. A series of largely Gothic modifications in sober granite contrast with the warm sandstone of the Romanesque original. Work started in

ÁVILA

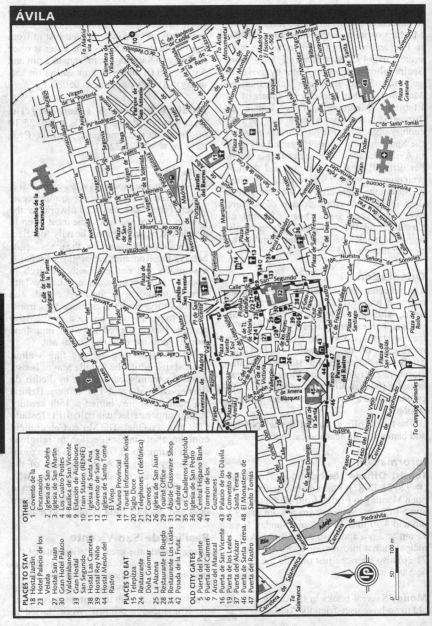

the 11th century, supposedly on the site where three martyrs, Vicente and his sisters, were slaughtered by the Romans in the early 4th century. Their sepulchre is a nice piece of Romanesque work. The church is open daily from 10 am to 2 pm and 4 to 8 pm (50 ptas). The Jardín de San Vicente across the road was, by the way, once the Roman cemetery.

El Monasterio de Santo Tomás

A grandiose combination of monastery and royal residence put up in haste by the Reyes Católicos (Catholic Monarchs), Fernando and Isabel, in 1482, this is formed by three interconnecting cloisters and the church. The first and smallest of the cloisters is in the so-called Tuscan style and is the simplest of the three. The church and second cloister (Claustro del Silencio) are Gothic, while the Claustro de los Reyes, where the royal family often resided in summer, is halfway between Gothic and Renaissance in style.

From the Claustro del Silencio you can climb up to the fine choir stalls in the adjacent church. In the grand tomb in the transept lies Don Juan, son of the Catholic Monarchs, while the retablo by Pedro de Berruguete behind him depicts scenes from the life of St Thomas Aquinas. It is thought the Inquisitor Torquemada is buried in the sacristy. The monastery complex, about half a kilometre south-east of the cathedral in the new town, is open from 8 am to 1.30 pm and 4 to 8 pm (50 ptas).

In Santa Teresa's Footsteps

Santa Teresa, the 16th century mystic and ascetic, has left her mark all over the city. Born in 1515, she joined the Carmelites 20 years later. Shaken by a vision of hell in 1560 and supported by several spiritual directors, she undertook to reform the Carmelites, an arduous task that led her to found convents of the Carmelitas Descalzas across Spain. She also coopted San Juan de la Cruz (St John of the Cross) to begin a similar reform in the masculine order, a task that earned him several stints incarcerated by the mainstream Carmelites and a good

portion of his life in fear of persecution. Santa Teresa's writings were first published in 1588 and proved enormously popular, perhaps partly for their earthy style.

The **Convento de Santa Teresa** was built over the saint's birthplace in 1636. One of the church's chapels shows what is said to have been the saint's little playground. In the tiny museum next door (through the souvenir shop) are a few bits of memorabilia and relics, including Teresa's ring finger (which supposedly spent the Franco years by the *generalísimo's* bedside) and bone fragments of San Juan de la Cruz. The museum is open from 9.30 am to 1.30 pm and 3.30 to 7.30 pm.

Nearby, the **Iglesia de San Juan** on Plaza de la Victoria contains the baptismal font in which Teresa was baptised. A five minute walk east of the cathedral is the **Convento de San José** (also known as Convento de las Madres), the first convent Teresa founded (1562). Its museum is replete with Teresian memorabilia and is open daily from 10 am to 2 pm and 4 to 7 pm (shorter hours in winter; 50 ptas). North of the city walls, the **Convento de la Encarnación** is where Santa Teresa fully took on the monastic life and launched her movement. A Renaissance complex modified in the 18th century, the convent contains further mementos of her life.

City Walls

With its eight monumental gates and 88 towers, Ávila's *muralla* (city wall) is one of the best preserved medieval defensive perimeters in the world. Raised between the 11th and 12th centuries on the remains of earlier efforts by the Muslims and Romans, the wall has been much restored and modified with various Gothic and Renaissance touches. The most impressive gates, the Puerta de San Vicente and Puerta del Alcázar, are flanked by towers more than 20m high and stand either side of the cathedral's apse, which forms the central defensive point of the eastern wall.

You can walk along the top of the walls from Puerta del Alcázar to Puerta del

Rastro and enjoy the fabulous view (from 10.30 am to 2.30 pm only in the off season, but from 11 am to 1.30 pm and 5 to 7.30 pm from April to September). Tickets (100 ptas) can be bought in the tourist office or at the green kiosk by the Puerta del Alcázar.

Churches & Mansions

Ávila is besprinkled with churches of interest. The small disused Romanesque Iglesia de Santo Tomé El Viejo on Plaza de Italia was built in the 12th century. Built a little later and since subjected to several less than fortunate alterations is the Iglesia de San Pedro on Plaza de Santa Teresa. North of the old city is the Iglesia de San Andrés, which was built in the 11th century and the oldest church in Ávila. Most churches are open daily from about 10 am to 2 pm and 4 to 7 pm.

The city also has its fair share of noble mansions, some of which now serve as upper-end hotels. The Palacio de los Velada and Palacio de los Valderrábano, on Plaza de la Catedral, fall into this category. The Palacio de los Dávila, near the Puerta del Rastro, belonged to one of the city's most illustrious fighting noble families. In the Palacio de los Deanes, on Plaza de Nalvillos, you'll find the Museo Provincial, with mainly archaeological displays from the region. The museum is open Tuesday to Saturday from 11 am to 2 pm and 5 to 7.30 pm and Sunday from 11 am to 2 pm only (200 ptas).

Los Cuatro Postes

Just north-west of the city on the road to Salamanca, this spot not only affords fine views of Ávila's walls, but also marks the place where Santa Teresa and her brother were caught by their uncle as they tried to run away from home. They were hoping to achieve martyrdom at the hands of the Moorish infidels.

Organised Tours

Guided tours of the town in Spanish are organised, usually at the weekend, by Ávila Monumental (☎ 920 25 19 21), Travesia de las Cinco Villas 4. The tourist office can tell you the latest program.

Special Events

Ávila's principal festival (15 October) takes place, not surprisingly, in memory of Santa Teresa. The early-morning Good Friday procession of *pasos* (sculpted figures depicting the passion of Christ) is equally noteworthy. Easter in general is marked by a stream of solemn marches and other events beginning on Holy Thursday.

DAMIEN SIMONIS

You can walk along the Romanesque walls that enclose Ávila's old centre

Places to Stay – Budget

Camping The nearest camping ground is *Camping Sonsoles* (☎ 920 25 63 36), a couple of kilometres south of town on the N-403 to Toledo. It is open from June to September. Rates are 300 ptas per person, car and tent.

Hostales & Hotels Among the cheaper places near the cathedral, *Hostal Las Cancelas* (☎ 920 21 22 49, Calle de la Cruz Vieja 6) has simple singles/doubles for 2500/3500 ptas. *Hostal Jardín* (☎ 920 21 10 74, Calle de San Segundo 38) is a fairly scruffy place with rooms starting at 2600/3600 ptas (up to 3500/4600 ptas with private bath). A good choice is the *Hostal San Juan* (☎ 920 21 31 98, Calle de los Comuneros de Castilla 3). Rooms with telephone and TV cost 3700/6400 ptas. Better still is the *Hostal Mesón del Rastro* (☎ 920 21 12 18, Plaza del Rastro 1). Full of character and with a good restaurant, it has rooms starting at 3400/4100 ptas. *Hostal Rey Niño* (☎ 920 21 14 04, Plaza de José Tomé 1) has adequate rooms for up to 3500/5600 ptas.

Places to Stay – Mid-Range

Just outside the Puerta de los Leales, the *Gran Hostal San Segundo* (☎ 920 25 26 90, Calle de San Segundo 28) is heading into the more expensive bracket, with decent rooms costing 4500/6000 ptas in the low season and an exaggerated 6000/8000 ptas from June to October.

Places to Stay – Top End

Top of the tree is the *Gran Hotel Palacio Valderrábanos* (☎ 920 21 10 23, fax 920 25 16 91, Plaza de la Catedral 9) in the Palacio de los Valderrábanos, where rooms cost 9000/14,000 ptas plus IVA. In a similar price league is the elegant *Hotel Palacio de los Velada* (☎ 920 25 51 00, fax 920 25 49 00), across the square at No 10; it's a grand hotel which is part of the Meliá chain.

Places to Eat

For a cheap, decent pizza in a hurry, you could do worse than *Telepizza*, on the corner of Avenida de Portugal and Calle de San Segundo. *Restaurante Los Leales (Plaza de Italia 4)* has a solid set *menú* for 1000 ptas. *La Alacena* is a cosy little place where a full meal can cost less than 2000 ptas.

A good moderately priced choice is the *Hostal Mesón del Rastro (Plaza del Rastro 1)*. The 1500 ptas set meal is good value and the *comedor* (dining room), with its dark wood beams and wrought-iron work, exudes Castilian charm. It does a tasty *ternera del Valle de Amblés*, a hearty beef dish typical of the region.

Also good and with alfresco dining is the *Posada de la Fruta (Plaza de Pedro Dávila 8)*. *Restaurante El Ruedo (Calle de Enrique Larreta 7)* is an unassuming place but offers a good, if pricey, set meal for 1600 ptas.

Restaurante Doña Guiomar (Calle de Tomás Luis de Victoria 3) has a touch of class and main meals that won't come in under 2000 ptas. The special kids' meal *(menú niños)* costs 900 ptas. Don't miss the local sweet tooth speciality – *yemas*, a scrummy, sticky business made of egg yolk and sugar.

Entertainment

Ávila is not exactly the most happening town in Spain, but *Siglo Doce*, just inside the Puerta de los Leales, is not a bad little café where you can also get a bite to eat. Otherwise, Plaza de la Victoria and Plaza de Santa Teresa are the places to look for bars, tapas and front-row people-watching seats. Later in the evening, you'll find some *marcha* (action) along Calle de Vallespín and west to the Puerta del Puente. *Los Caballeros* disco on the corner of Plaza de Italia and Calle de San Miguel is one dancing possibility.

Shopping

If you are interested in glassware, pop into *Ábside*, Calle de Alemania 1. There is a glass-blowing factory in Ávila and this shop sells some nice wares.

Getting There & Away

Bus Buses are OK for nearby and out-of-the-way destinations, but main cities are more easily reached by train. A bus leaves at 3.15 pm (from Monday to Friday) for Arenas de San Pedro in the Sierra de Gredos. It's an all-stops job and costs 210 ptas. A daily bus leaves for Valladolid at 7.30 am (no services on Sunday), and there are two to four buses daily for Madrid and Salamanca.

Train Up to 17 trains daily run to Madrid, mostly to Chamartín (up to two hours; 835 ptas). Plenty also head west to Salamanca and cost the same. At least a couple of trains daily head for cities such as Bilbao, Santander and Málaga.

Car & Motorcycle From Madrid, you need to get onto the N-VI. You can follow this or the parallel A-6 tollway as far as Villacastín, where you need to bear south-west along the N-110. You could also take the M-505 (which later becomes the C-505) via El Escorial, which branches off the N-VI just before Las Rozas.

Toros de Guisando

A curiosity just inside Castilla y León's boundary with the Comunidad de Madrid is the so-called Toros de Guisando (*not* the Guisando in the Sierra de Gredos), a good 70km east of Arenas de San Pedro. Four weather-beaten animal statues lined up behind a wall on a narrow country lane off the N-403 between Ávila and Toledo are said to have stood there since pre-Roman times. One theory claims they mark a border between Celtic tribes. At this spot, or perhaps in what remains of a monastery halfway up the hill west of the road, Isabel (as in Fernando and Isabel, the Catholic Monarchs) was supposedly sworn in as heir to the Castilian throne on 19 September 1468.

Getting Around

Local bus No 1 (red line; 75 ptas) runs past the RENFE train station to Plaza de la Catedral.

SIERRA DE GREDOS

Taking over where the Sierra de Guadarrama outside Madrid trails off, the Sierra de Gredos is a mighty mountain chain dividing the two Castiles – in modern terms, Castilla y León and Castilla-La Mancha to its south. The chain spreads across into Extremadura.

Arenas de San Pedro

This straggly town is surrounded by an assortment of villages that lend access to the mountains. You will almost definitely pass through here, but may not want to stay. It's a popular summer escape for sun-stunned Castilians and *madrileños*, where the new overshadows the old. Still, right on the Río Arenal squats the stout 15th century **Castillo de la Triste Condesa** and close by is the sober 14th century Gothic **Iglesia de Nuestra Señora de la Asunción**. A few minutes south, a **medieval bridge** still provides a secure river crossing, while the northern end of town is dominated by the neoclassical **Palacio del Infante Don Luis de Borbón** – a gilded cage for Carlos III's imprisoned brother.

Of the half-dozen places to stay, three are gathered near the castle and old centre. *Hostal El Castillo* (☎ 920 37 00 91, Carretera de Candeleda 2) has spartan singles/doubles for 1500/2500 ptas. *Pensión Yeka* (☎ 920 37 21 87), next door, has some decent rooms with private bathroom for 2500/4000 ptas. The *Hostería Los Galayos* (☎ 920 37 13 79, Plaza de Condestable Dávalos 2) offers solid if unexciting food and also has some cheap rooms.

At least four buses run daily from Madrid. One daily heads south for Talavera de la Reina. Most of the surrounding towns are connected at least once daily by bus to Arenas. Buses from Madrid and Ávila to Candeleda also pass through here.

El Hornillo, El Arenal & Guisando

Pleasant enough but showing signs of the money that has gone into filling them with holiday homes, these villages make possible starting points for walks into the Gredos. A bus for the first two leaves Arenas at 12.15 pm on weekdays. A separate one serves Guisando.

Of the two places to stay at El Arenal, the **Hostal Isabel** (☎ 920 37 51 48) on Calle de las Angustias has comfortable rooms with toilet for 2300/3300 ptas. There are a couple of places at Guisando too. All three towns are within a 10km radius north or northwest of Arenas and are far more attractively placed in the sierra.

Hikes in the Sierra de Gredos

The most popular walks in the area are best undertaken in June or September – midsummer is stifling. Most walkers with limited time aim for the Laguna Grande, in the shadow of the sierra's highest peak, Almanzor (2592m), and continue westwards to the Circo de Cinco Lagos. Possible starting points include El Hornillo and Guisando. Coming from the northern side of the range, a road also leads south from Hoyos del Espino to the Plataforma, the jumping-off point for the lakes. If you're walking from Guisando or El Hornillo, reckon on the better part of a day to come up the steep granite slopes and reach the Plataforma.

From here a well-defined trail heads south-west to the Laguna Grande de Gredos, where there is a *refugio* (shelter), which is often full, and good camping. A couple of hours farther west along Alfonso XIII's specially laid hunting track, the Cinco Lagos are spread out before you. The descent is a little wearying but worthwhile. From there you can head back whence you came (you could try hitching a lift north to Hoyos del Espino from the Plataforma). If you are too late to make a bus out of Hoyos, there are three places to stay. An alternative exit is north along the Garganta (gorge) del Pinar towards the town of Navalperal de Tormes.

Readers of Spanish who are planning serious exploration of the area should get hold of *Gredos*, by Miguel A Vidal & Carlos Frías, which contains 37 suggested walks and information on activities like rock climbing. It's available in Arenas.

Along the Northern Flank of the Sierra de Gredos

Following the southern flank of the mountain chain, the C-501 offers a pretty drive from Arenas towards Candeleda and on into Extremadura's La Vera valley.

Within Castilla y León, the northern flank is, if anything, a more picturesque proposition. From Arenas, the N-502 climbs high to the Puerto del Pico and heads on to Ávila. However, you can turn west about 5km after the pass on a route that, followed almost directly westward, would take you to the Peña de Francia and on to Portugal via Ciudad Rodrigo.

The **Parador de Gredos** (☎ 920 34 80 48), a few kilometres east of Navarredonda de Gredos, has front-row rooms overlooking the mountains for 9000/11,500 ptas in the high season. The more modest **Hostal Almanzor** (☎ 920 34 80 10), just short of the same town, is a reasonable but pricey alternative with singles/doubles for 5000/6200 ptas.

El Barco de Ávila, on a crossroads with the N-110 between Ávila and Plasencia, has a proud if ruinous castle. Another 30km west, **Béjar** is somewhat more interesting, its old quarters lined up at the western end of a high ridge, partly walled. Most eyecatching is the 16th century Palacio Ducal, just west of Plaza Mayor and now serving as a college. There's plenty of accommodation in Béjar, including the **Hostal Casa Pavón** (☎ 923 40 28 61, Plaza Mayor 3). It has rooms for 2000/3500 ptas. Buses run frequently to Salamanca and various other destinations, including Madrid and Plasencia. See later in this chapter for information on the Peña de Francia and Ciudad Rodrigo.

CASTILLA Y LEÓN

SALAMANCA

The rich copper hues of Salamanca's great university and churches are without equal in Spain. Although a shadow of its medieval self, the university has regained a degree of prestige in the past decades, particularly with its language programs. A compact and busy student town, Salamanca attracts many young people from abroad who elect to carry out their Spanish studies here.

As long ago as 220 BC, Celtiberian Salamanca found itself besieged by Hannibal.

Later, under Roman rule, it was an important staging post along the Via Lata (Ruta de la Plata, or Silver Route, from the mines in northern Spain to the south), and it changed hands repeatedly for four centuries after the Muslim invasion of Spain.

Possibly the greatest turning point in the city's history was the founding of the university in 1218. It became the equal of Oxford and Bologna, and by the end of the 15th century was the focal point of some of the richest artistic activity in the country, in

part due to the generous patronage of Queen Isabel of Castilla. In few other places will you witness the virtuosity in plateresque and Renaissance work that is on hand in Salamanca.

The city followed the rest of Castilla into decline in the 17th century, aggravated by the Napoleonic invasion (la francesada) at the beginning of the 19th century. The city suffered considerable damage before and during the Battle of Los Arapiles in 1812 between Marmont and Wellington.

Orientation

The old centre is compact and easily negotiated on foot. It lies north of the Río Tormes and at its heart lies Spain's grandest plaza mayor (main plaza). A fair range of accommodation can be found between Plaza Mayor and the river, an area that encompasses most of the university buildings. The train and bus stations are about equidistant from the centre, the former to the north-east and the latter to the north-west. If

the 20 or so minutes walk from either doesn't appeal, buses connect both to the centre.

Maps The tourist office hand-out maps are OK, but the best is that contained in the bimonthly hand-out En Salamanca.

Information

Tourist Offices The Oficina Municipal de Turismo (☎ 923 21 83 42) at Plaza Mayor 14 concentrates on the city and is open daily from 9 am to 2 pm and 4.30 to 6.30 pm. For the remainder of the province, go to the tourist office (☎ 923 26 85 71) in the Casa de las Conchas, Calle de la Compañía 2. It's open Monday to Friday from 10 am to 2 pm and 5 to 8 pm and Saturday from 10 am to 2 pm. Offices also open at the train and bus stations in summer.

Money There is no shortage of banks around the centre. American Express is represented

SALAMANCA

PLACES TO STAY
6	Pensión Cantábrico
11	Hotel Las Torres
18	Pensión Robles
20	Hostal Orly
23	Hotel El Toboso
25	Le Petit Hotel
31	Pensión Los Ángeles; Campus Cibermático
37	Gran Hotel
40	Pensión Lisboa
43	Pensión Las Vegas
44	Hostal Tormes
45	Hostal La Perla Salamantina
49	Hostal Laguna
52	Pensión Estefanía
65	Pensión Peña de Francia
67	Pensión Feli

PLACES TO EAT
21	Restaurante El Candil Viejo
24	Restaurante Llamas
27	Restaurante El Clavel
33	Mesón Cervantes
34	Mesón El Botón Charro
42	El Patio Chico

56	Restaurante El Trigal
57	Café El Ave Turuta

OTHER
1	Hospital Santísima Trinidad
2	TIVE Travel Agency
3	Iglesia de San Juan de Barbados
4	Teatro de la Caja
5	Pasada
7	Torre del Aire
8	Correos
9	Policía Nacional
10	O'Neill's Irish Pub
12	Morgana
13	Casa de las Muertes
14	Convento de las Úrsulas
15	Colegio de Arzobispo Fonseca
16	Palacio de Monterrey
17	Cum Laude
19	Museo Taurino
22	Tío Vivo
26	Iglesia de San Julián
28	Mercado Central
29	Viages Salamanca

30	Telephones (Locutorio)
32	Oficina Municipal de Turismo
35	Iglesia de San Cristóbal
36	Potemkin
38	Iglesia de San Martín
39	MusicArte Café
41	Café El Corrillo
46	Bar Bennys
47	El Gran Café Moderno
48	Palacium
50	Torre del Clavero
51	Taberna La Rayuela
53	Casa de las Conchas; Tourist Office
54	Real Clerecía de San Marcos
55	Palacio de Congresos
58	Museo de Salamanca
59	Patio de las Escuelas Menores
60	Universidad Civil
61	Catedral Nueva
62	Convento de las Dueñas
63	Convento de Las Claras
64	Convento de San Esteban
66	Catedral Vieja
68	Casa Lis

by Viajes Salamanca (☎ 923 26 77 31), Plaza Mayor 11.

Post & Communications You'll find the main correos at Gran Vía 25 and a *locutorio* (telephone office) on Plaza Mayor. The latter is open daily from 8.30 am to 11.30 pm. The postcode is 37080. For email, try Campus Cibermático (☎ 923 27 11 31), Plaza Mayor 10.

Travel Agencies TIVE (☎ 923 26 77 31), Paseo de las Carmelitas 83, can help with student travel.

Medical Services A couple of hospitals are close to the centre. You could try the Hospital Clínico Universitario (☎ 923 29 11 00), Paseo de San Vicente 58-182, or Hospital Santísima Trinidad, north-west of the town's centre.

Emergency There is a *Policía Nacional comisaría* (police station) at Ronda de Sancti Spiritus 8. In a medical emergency, call ambulances at the Cruz Roja (☎ 923 22 22 22), Plaza de San Benito s/n.

Plaza Mayor

Built between 1729 and 1755, Salamanca's grand square is considered Spain's most engaging central plaza. Designed by Alberto Churriguera, it is a remarkably harmonious and controlled display of baroque. Bullfights were held here well into the 19th century and the medallions placed around the plaza bear the busts of sundry famous figures, including the regularly defaced one of a certain Generalísimo Franco. He's the one at the top (northern) end of the eastern flank.

Just off the square, on Plaza del Corrillo, the 12th century **Iglesia de San Martín** lies wedged into a huddle of houses. It is one of several nice examples of Romanesque religious architecture dotted about the city.

Catedrales

The tower of the late Gothic **Catedral Nueva** lords over the centre of Salamanca,

its *churrigueresque* dome visible from almost every angle. It is, however, the magnificent Renaissance doorways, particularly the Puerta del Nacimiento on the western face, that stand out as one of several miracles worked in the city's sandstone façades. Inside, the most notable feature is the highly elaborate baroque choir stalls. The cathedral is open from 9 am to 2 pm and 4 to 8 pm daily from April to September (from 9 am to 1 pm and 4 to 6 pm daily in the other months).

The Catedral Nueva was raised abutting its largely Romanesque predecessor, which is predictably known as the **Catedral Vieja**. Begun as early as 1120, this church is a bit of a hybrid, with some elements of Gothic. The unusual ribbed cupola (Torre del Gallo) betrays a Byzantine influence, while the *retablo mayor* (main altarpiece) in the apse of the capilla mayor is a sumptuous work depicting scenes from the life of Christ and the Virgin Mary, topped by a representation of the Final Judgment. The cloister was largely ruined in the 1755 Lisbon earthquake, but in the Capilla de San Bartolomé you can still admire one of Europe's oldest organs. The Catedral Vieja is open daily from 10 am to 1.30 pm and 4 to 7.30 pm (300 ptas, students 200 ptas).

Universidad Civil & Around

Little can prepare you for the visual feast of the entrance façade to Salamanca's university. Founded initially as the Estudio General in 1218, the university came into being in 1254 and reached the peak of its renown in the 15th and 16th centuries. These were heady times fosr Spain, fully 'reconquered' from the Muslims in 1492 and bent on expansion in the Americas. The university's façade, more a tapestry in sandstone, bursts with images of mythical heroes, religious scenes and coats of arms, and is dominated in the centre by busts of Fernando and Isabel (encircled by an inscription in Greek).

Among the small lecture rooms arranged around the courtyard inside the building, the Aula de Fray Luis de León (named after the celebrated 16th century theologian and writer who taught here and whose statue stands in the Patio de las Escuelas outside) is perhaps the most interesting, conserving the original benches and lectern from Fray Luis' day. Arrested by the Inquisition for having translated the *Song of Solomon* into Spanish, the sardonic theologian returned to his class after five years in jail and resumed lecturing with the words, 'As I was saying yesterday ... '.

Upstairs, the university library boasts fine Late Gothic features and a beautiful *techumbre* (carved wooden ceiling). Some 2800 ancient manuscripts lie in the custody of this, one of the oldest university libraries in Europe. The university can be visited Monday to Friday from 9.30 am to 1.30 pm and 4 to 7.30 pm (7 pm on Saturday) and Sunday and holidays from 10 am to 1.30 pm (300 ptas, students half-price) and include entrance to the Museo de la Universidad (see the next section).

Patio de las Escuelas Menores Head out of the university and walk over to the south-western corner of the little square, off which opens the cloister of the Escuelas Menores. In among the arches lies the **Museo de la Universidad**, where you can see the zodiacal ceiling that once graced the university's chapel, along with a fairly standard collection of clerical art. It has the same opening hours as the university. Check out the Sala de Exposiciones, where you can admire two techumbres – one clearly *mudéjar* and the other with Renaissance Italian influences.

Museo de Salamanca Also known as the Museo de Bellas Artes, this modest gallery is as interesting for the building (notable are the little patio and the techumbre ceiling in *sala* 1) as its contents. It is open Tuesday to Saturday from 9.30 am to 1.30 pm and 4 to 7.30 pm and Sunday and holidays from 10 am to 1.30 pm (200 ptas, students half-price).

Real Clericía de San Marcos Seat of the Universidad Pontificia and formerly a Jesuit college and seminary, this building across Plaza de San Isidro from the university is no longer open to visitors except for the monumental baroque cloister – and that only in the half-hour before Mass, for which times are normally posted.

Casa de las Conchas Across the road is one of the most distinctive buildings in Salamanca, named after the scallop shells carved across its façades. Its owner, Dr Rodrigo Maldonado de Talavera, was a doctor at the court of Isabel and a member of the Order of Santiago, whose symbol is the shell.

Convento de San Esteban & Around

Standing proud in the south-eastern corner of the old city, the façade of this monastery's church is in effect a huge retablo in stone, with the stoning of San Esteban (St Stephen) its central motif. Inside, the centrepiece is also a retablo – this time an ornate masterpiece by José Churriguera.

Frog Spotting

A compulsory task facing all visitors to the Universidad Civil in Salamanca is to search out the frog sculpted on to the façade. Once pointed out, it is easily enough seen, but you can expend considerable time in vain searching otherwise. Why bother? Well, they say that those who detect it without outside help can be assured of good luck and even marriage (if you consider that good luck) within a year. Some hopeful students see an assured examinations victory in it. If you believe all this, stop reading now. If you do want help, look at the busts of Fernando and Isabel. From there, swing your gaze to the largest column on the extreme right of the façade. Slightly above the level of the busts are sculpted a series of skulls, atop the leftmost of which sits our little amphibious friend.

Through the Gothic-Renaissance cloister you can climb upstairs to the church's choir stalls. The monastery is open daily from 9 am to 1 pm and 4 to 6 pm. Entry to the cloister costs 200 ptas.

Convento de las Dueñas Easily the most beautiful cloister in the city is the irregular, pentagonal one that graces this convent of Dominican nuns, who still make and sell a range of traditional pastries. The convent is open daily from 10.30 am to 1 pm and 4.30 to 5.30 pm (200 ptas).

Torre del Clavero If you walk north a couple of blocks along Gran Vía, you will notice this defensive tower a block away to your left. It is a 15th century octagonal fortress on a square base adorned with smaller cylindrical towers. You can then turn right for the Convento de Las Claras.

Convento de Las Claras The best part of a visit to this convent, which started life as a Romanesque building but has been rebuilt on several occasions, is the chance to climb to inspect at close quarters the 14th and 15th century mudéjar *artesonado* ceilings, hidden from view for almost three centuries by the lower ceiling erected in the 18th century. You can only visit this part of the convent with a guide, and will get more out of it if you understand Spanish. It is open Monday to Friday from 9.30 am to 1.40 pm and 4 to 6.40 pm and weekends from 9 am to 2.40 pm (closed on holidays; 200 ptas).

Colegio del Arzobispo Fonseca & Around

A short stroll west of Plaza Mayor brings you to another series of Salamantine monuments. Also known as the Colegio de los Irlandeses (Irish College), this one was built in the 16th century in a sober plateresque style. Of particular note are the main entrance and courtyard. You can visit daily from 10 am to 2 pm and 4 to 6 pm. The antique clock collection is open Tuesday to Friday from 5 to 7 pm and weekends and holidays from 11 am to 2 pm (100 ptas).

Convento de las Úrsulas Nearby, this late Gothic nunnery was founded by Archbishop Alonso de Fonseca in 1516 and now contains his magnificent marble tomb, sculpted by Diego de Siloé. The nunnery is open daily from 10 am to 1 pm and 4.30 to 7 pm (100 ptas).

Palacio de Monterrey A 16th century holiday home of the Duques de Alba, the palace is a seminal piece of Spanish Renaissance architecture. The dukes pop in every now and then, and visitors are not permitted inside.

Other Museums

Casa Lis Fans of Art Nouveau and Art Deco will probably get a kick out of the gallery devoted to both in this *modernista* house on Calle de Gibraltar, built in 1905. It is open Tuesday to Friday from 11 am to 2 pm and 5 to 9 pm (4 to 7 pm in winter) and weekends and holidays from 10 am to 9 pm (11 am to 8 pm in winter; 300 ptas, students 200 ptas).

Museo Taurino Salamanca province is bull-breeding territory, one of the more important sources of *toros* (bulls) for the country. Those interested can learn a little more at this museum, just north of Plaza Mayor. It is open Tuesday to Saturday from 6 to 9 pm (also from noon to 2 pm on weekends; 200 ptas).

Language Courses

Salamanca is popular with foreigners wanting to learn the lingo. Most go to the university, although there is a plethora of private *colegios* that run language courses. For information contact Cursos Intensivos de Lengua y Cultura Españolas (☎ 923 21 83 16, fax 923 26 24 56), Universidad Pontificia de Salamanca, Calle de la Compañía 5, 37080 Salamanca.

Places to Stay – Budget

Camping There are four camping grounds around Salamanca, all outside town. The best is *Camping Regio (☎ 923 13 88 88),*

4km out of Salamanca along the N-501 to Madrid. It is open all year and charges 425 ptas per person, tent, car and for electricity.

Pensiones & Hostales It is hard to beat a room in one of the little places on Plaza Mayor, provided you can snag a room looking onto the square. *Pensión Los Ángeles* (☎ 923 21 81 66) at No 10 has rather basic singles/doubles with washbasin for 1500/2800 ptas plus IVA. *Pensión Robles* (☎ 923 21 31 97) at No 20 has perfectly adequate rooms for 2200/3300 ptas. The quadruple overlooking the square can be had for the price of a double.

Hostal La Perla Salamantina (☎ 923 21 76 56, Calle de Sánchez Barbero 7) charges 2100/4500 ptas for bright and clean singles/doubles with bath.

Calle de Meléndez has a few places. *Pensión Lisboa* (☎ 923 21 43 33) at No 1 offers small rooms starting at 1700 ptas for singles and ranging upwards to 3500 ptas for doubles with private bath. Mildly better value is the *Pensión Las Vegas* (☎ 923 21 87 49) at No 13, where clean doubles without bath cost 2400 ptas and singles without facilities are 1300 ptas.

Pensión Estefanía (☎ 923 21 73 72, Calle de Jesús 3-5) has simple but decent singles/doubles starting at 1750/3000 ptas. More awkwardly placed but a possibility if the others are filling up is the *Hostal Peña de Francia* (☎ 923 21 66 87, Calle de San Pablo 96), which charges 2700/3700 ptas for rooms with bath and a little less for those without.

Hostal Tormes (☎ 923 21 96 83, Rúa Mayor 20) is OK if a touch drab. The most expensive rooms go for 3500/4800 ptas and have private bath. Down the road from the main university building is the *Pensión Feli* (☎ 923 21 60 10, Calle de los Libreros 58). It has cheerful rooms for 2400/3400 ptas without bath. There are several pensiones by the train station, and about halfway between the station and the centre you could stop at the *Pensión Cantábrico* (☎ 923 26 29 81, Calle del Pozo Hilera 7),

which only has doubles with washbasin for 2400 ptas.

Places to Stay – Mid-Range
Hostal Laguna (☎ 923 21 87 06, Calle del Consuelo 19) has rooms with and without own bath ranging from 3300 to 4300 ptas in the high season. The more expensive *Le Petit Hotel* (☎ 923 26 55 67, Cuesta Sanctispíritus 39) has small but tidy rooms with phone and TV for 3900/6000 plus IVA.

Hostal Orly (☎ 923 21 61 25, Calle del Pozo Amarillo 5-7) offers reasonable if unexciting rooms with private bath, TV, telephone and heating for 4000/5000 ptas plus IVA. A much better deal if you can afford the extra cost is the *Hotel El Toboso* (☎ 923 27 14 62, Calle del Clavel 7). The attractive timber and tile reception is no front, and the rooms with private bath, TV and telephone are worth the 4500/6300 ptas charged. *Hotel Las Torres* (☎ 923 21 21 00, Calle de Concejo 4) has comfortable rooms with all mod cons for 9750/13,000 ptas plus IVA.

Places to Stay – Top End
The *Gran Hotel* (☎ 923 21 35 00, fax 923 21 35 01, Plaza del Poeta Iglesias 5) is the city's most expensive and, as the name suggests, grandest place to stay. Rooms cost 15,000/19,500 ptas plus IVA. Otherwise you could try the *Parador de Salamanca* (☎ 923 26 87 00, fax 923 21 54 38), south of the river. It is a modern place with a swimming pool and singles/doubles costing 11,200/14,000 ptas plus IVA.

Places to Eat
While in Salamanca, get your teeth into the local speciality, *chanfaina*, a rice dish with various meats in a spicy sauce (the closest thing to a Spanish curry).

El Patio Chico (Calle de Meléndez 13) is a lively place to sit around for beers and filling tapas for around 400 ptas a throw and has a set *menú* for 1300 ptas.

At Calle de los Libreros 24, you can get a respectable set meal for a mere 800 ptas at *Café El Ave Turuta*. Vegetarians should head for *Restaurante El Trigal* at No 20.

There are a couple of other reasonably priced eateries on the same street.

Right on Plaza Mayor near the tourist office, the *Mesón Cervantes*, with attractive upstairs dining, serves good-quality set lunches for 1500 ptas. *Restaurante Llamas (Calle del Clavel 9)* is a basic place where a tasty set lunch is about 1200 ptas. For a walk on the expensive side, try *Restaurante El Clavel* at No 6. You're looking at about 4000 ptas a head for a full meal.

Restaurante El Candil Viejo (Calle de Ventura Ruiz Aguilera 10) is another popular stop but, at around 2000 ptas for mains, is pricey. Not far off is the much recommended *Mesón El Botón Charro (Calle de Hovohambre 6)*. The set lunch costs 3000 ptas and average mains around 2000 ptas. Try the *escalopines de solomillo al oporto* (fillet in a port wine sauce).

Entertainment
The bimonthly *En Salamanca* booklet contains information on bars, cultural events, theatre and the like.

Cafés & Bars If you don't mind paying 250 ptas for your coffee, it is hard to beat sipping your way through the morning at a café on Plaza Mayor. A few steps outside the grand square, *MusicArte Café (Plaza del Corrillo 22)* is a hip place for coffee (at half that price) and cake.

Taberna La Rayuela (Rúa Mayor 19) is popular early in the evening and, when not too crowded, is pleasantly low-lit and intimate. *Café El Corrillo (Calle de Meléndez 8)* is great for a beer and live jazz. A drink in *Tío Vivo (Calle de Clavel 3)* is nearly obligatory, if only to experience the peculiar décor, which ranges from carousel horses to old cinema cameras and other oddball antiquities.

O'Neill's Irish Pub (Calle de Zamora 14) is a busy Irish pub (funny about that). Nearby is *Pasada (Plaza de San Boal s/n)*, where hidden behind a massive set of doors is the best-stocked bar in the city.

A good area to look for marcha lies just east of the Mercado Central. Calle de San Justo, Calle de Varillas and Calle del Consuelo in particular are loaded with bars. One place is *Bar Bennys (Calle del Consuelo 20)*.

Later in the night you can head for *Potemkin*, a block north on Calle del Consuelo, for live music. *Cum Laude (Calle del Prior 7)* is a favourite of Salamanca's young trendsetters.

Gran Vía is another good hunting ground for some entertainment. *El Gran Café Moderno* at No 75 or 77 (depending on which sign you believe) is a Salamanca classic. Across the road, *Palacium* at No 68 is a loud haunt for the juvenile; the bar next door is more laid-back.

Discos To dance away the wee hours on a weekend, try *Morgana*, a disco on the corner of Cuesta del Carmen and Calle de Iscar Peira.

Theatre The *Teatro de la Caja (Plaza de Santa Teresa)* is a frequent scene for concerts and theatre of all sorts.

Getting There & Away
Bus The estación de autobuses is northwest of the town centre on Avenida de Filiberto Villalobos. AutoRes has frequent services for 1690 ptas (2210 ptas express) to Madrid. About six buses also serve Valladolid.

Plenty of buses go to Alba de Tormes (180 ptas) and there is at least one daily, Monday to Saturday, to La Alberca (365 ptas). Regular buses run to Ciudad Rodrigo (715 ptas) and there are services also to Béjar, Ledesma and throughout the province.

The ALSA company runs buses as far afield as Galicia, Asturias, Cantabria and Cádiz.

Train At least four trains leave daily for Madrid's Chamartín station (3½ hours; 1450 ptas) via Ávila (1¼ hours; 835 ptas). The Lisbon train leaves at 4.55 am.

Car & Motorcycle The N-501 leads east to Madrid via Ávila and west to Portugal via Ciudad Rodrigo, while the N-630 heads north to Zamora. For the Sierra de la Peña de Francia, take the C-512.

Getting Around
Bus No 4 runs past the estación de autobuses and round the old town perimeter to Gran Vía. From the train station, the best bet is a No 1, which heads down Calle de Azafranal. Going the other way, it can be picked up along Gran Vía.

AROUND SALAMANCA
Ledesma & Embalse de Almendra
Following the Río Tormes north-west, you reach the small town of Ledesma, a grey, partly walled settlement. A medieval bridge still spans the river, and there are a few churches of minor interest, including the Gothic Iglesia de Santa María la Mayor on Plaza Mayor. You can also see remains of the castle of the Duques de Alburquerque.

A couple of buses serve the town each day from Salamanca, and if you get stuck there are a couple of pensiones. If you have transport, you might want to keep trailing the river, which feeds the Embalse de Almendra, a huge reservoir not far short of the Portuguese border.

Alba de Tormes
The resting place of Santa Teresa, Alba de Tormes is a mildly interesting and easily accomplished half-day excursion from Salamanca. Apart from the stout and highly visible **Torreón**, which is all that remains of what was the castle of the Duques de Alba, people come to visit the remains of Santa Teresa, buried in the Convento de las Carmelitas she founded in 1570. There are plenty of buses from Salamanca.

CIUDAD RODRIGO
Less than 30km from the Portuguese frontier, Ciudad Rodrigo is a sleepy but attractive walled town and a pleasant final stop on the way out of Spain. From the time the Romans left after several centuries of occupation, little is known of the city until

Count Rodrigo González arrived in the 12th century to refound the settlement as Civitas Roderici. It has always been something of a front-line city with Portugal, but never did Ciudad Rodrigo suffer as much as under siege during the Peninsular War against Napoleon. The city fell in 1811, but a year later Wellington turned the tide and dislodged the French.

Information
The tourist office (☎ 923 46 05 61), Plaza de las Amayuelas 5, is open Monday to Friday from 9.30 am to 2 pm and 4 to 7 pm and Saturday from 9.30 am to 2 pm. The correos is at Calle de Dámaso Ledesma 12. The postcode is 37500.

Things to See
The **catedral**, begun in 1165, is without doubt the city's outstanding sight. The

Life moves slowly in Ciudad Rodrigo

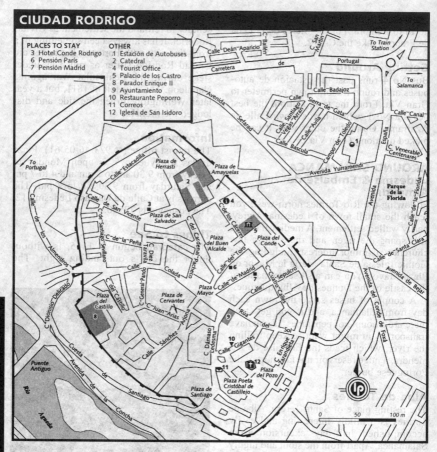

CIUDAD RODRIGO

PLACES TO STAY
3　Hotel Conde Rodrigo
6　Pensión París
7　Pensión Madrid

OTHER
1　Estación de Autobuses
2　Catedral
4　Tourist Office
5　Palacio de los Castro
8　Parador Enrique II
9　Ayuntamiento
10　Restaurante Peporro
11　Correos
12　Iglesia de San Isidoro

Puerta de las Cadenas, giving onto Plaza de San Salvador, with its Gothic reliefs of Old Testament figures, is impressive. More striking, though, is the elegant Pórtico del Perdón. Some of the great windows inside are jewels of Romanesque design, while the cloister is part Romanesque, part Gothic.

The town is liberally strewn with interesting minor palaces, mansions and churches. Among the latter is the **Iglesia de San Isidoro**, with Romanesque-mudéjar elements. Pay a visit to the **correos** to admire the artesonado ceilings. The 1st-floor gallery of the **ayuntamiento** (town hall) is a good spot to photograph Plaza Mayor. The 16th century **Palacio de los Castro**, on Plaza del Conde, boasts one of the town's most engaging plateresque façades. You can climb up onto the city walls and follow their length around the town.

Special Events

Carnaval in February is a unique time to be in Ciudad Rodrigo. Apart from the outlandish fancy dress and festivities, you can witness (or join in) a colourful *encierro* (running of the bulls) and *capeas* (amateur bullfights). It is one of the earliest events in the Spanish bullfighting calendar.

Places to Stay & Eat

There is a pair of adequate pensiones in the heart of the old town. *Pensión Madrid* (☎ 923 46 24 67, Calle de Madrid 20) has doubles with washbasin for 3500 ptas; the rooms are let out for 2000 ptas to lone travellers. *Pensión París* (☎ 923 46 13 72, Calle del Toro 10) offers fairly basic singles/doubles for 1700/3500 ptas. There are a good dozen cheap to mid-range places in the new part of town too.

For a minor splurge, try out the venerable *Hotel Conde Rodrigo* (☎ 923 46 14 08, fax 923 46 14 08, Plaza de San Salvador 9). Tastefully appointed rooms go for 5500/6800 ptas in the high season. For sheer luxury in a castle, head for the *Parador Enrique II* (☎ 923 46 01 50, fax 923 46 04 04, Plaza del Castillo), where singles/doubles will set you back 11,000/14,500 ptas.

For a tasty set *menú*, try the *Restaurante Peporro* (Calle de los Gigantes 5).

Getting There & Away

At least 10 buses daily run to Salamanca (755 ptas). There are no direct buses into the Sierra de la Peña de Francia – you need to return to Salamanca. A daily train to Lisbon passes through at 6 am.

SIERRA DE LA PEÑA DE FRANCIA

A northern extension of Extremadura's Las Hurdes, this compact mountain range could not be more different from the plains around Ciudad Rodrigo, only 40km west. Here a sprinkling of introspective villages seem even today caught in a time warp, protected, even cut off, by the cool of this craggy, grey-green oasis.

However, what may seem a quaint reminder of the idyllic good old days was until not so long ago one of the most god-forsaken parts of Spain. It was ridden with malaria until the turn of the century, and things hadn't improved much in 1932 when Buñuel came to film the locals' 'lifestyle' for *Las Hurdes – Terre Sans Pain*, the first part of which was shot here. Scenes include a competition among young townsmen about to be wed. This involved riding on donkey-back down the main street and attempting to rip the head off a live chicken strung up for the purpose across the road. When King Alfonso XIII visited in June 1922, the only milk available for his coffee was human! Touched by this abject misery, he was supposedly responsible for the introduction of the area's first cows (malaria hadn't been greatly conducive to raising them before).

La Alberca & Around

Easily the most extraordinary of the towns here, La Alberca is a claustrophobic huddle of gloomy alleys fronted by higgledy-piggledy houses built of heavy stone, wood beams and plaster – some a couple of centuries old. Tourism has arrived, but many of the townspeople still seem to live in the traditional way: donkeys remain a not-uncommon mode of transport. In winter the dark, dimly lit bars and cafés around Plaza Mayor are a cosy retreat from the season's rigours. It is the logical choice of base for the area, with half a dozen places to stay.

About a kilometre out of town on the road south, *Hospedaje Las Eras* (☎ 923 41 51 13) offers simple singles/doubles for 2200/3500 ptas. Right by the entrance to town are a couple of mid-range hotels and the comfortable *Hostal La Alberca* (☎ 923 41 52 37, Plaza del Padre Arsenio), which offers modern rooms with *en suite* bathroom for 3300/4500 ptas in high season.

If you have a vehicle, or time and a hitching thumb, the surrounding villages are more authentically caught up in the past. **Mogarraz**, to the east, and **Miranda del Castañar**, farther east again, are among the more intriguing.

Valle de las Batuecas

The drive south into Extremadura is spectacular. After you crest the Puerto del Portillo, an infinite phalanx of lower mountain ranges stretches south before you. A series of switchback roads quickly descends towards the Río Alagón in Extremadura.

About 10km down is a small Carmelite monastery (tourist visits not desired), past which rushes a babbling brook that you can follow on foot up into the surrounding hills. About a two hour walk brings you to some caves with rock carvings. It rains a lot here, so be warned: a sudden downpour could make your descent to the monastery difficult to say the least.

Those without transport could try renting a mountain bike at the Hospedaje Las Eras in La Alberca. If you're interested in horse riding, contact Caballos Peña de Francia (☎ 923 45 40 98), Carretera de la Alberca s/n, just outside the town of the same name.

Peña de Francia

Head north from La Alberca along the SA-202 and you soon strike the turn-off to the highest peak in the area, the Peña de Francia (1732m), from which you have sweeping views east to the Sierra de Gredos, south into Extremadura and west to Portugal.

The Central Plateau

With Valladolid, the regional capital, in its geographical heart, the central plateau of Castilla y León is dotted with towns and cities of varying interest. Excepting Segovia and Zamora, few cry out for an overnight stay, which places a premium on mobility. Great sweeps of barren rural plains, wrinkled by often less-than-breathtaking sierras, provide further incentive to move fast, although there are exceptions to the rule: the approaches to Galicia around the Lago de Sanabria and some of the hill country around Segovia provide a welcome contrast. What follows is an arbitrarily traced route supposing a starting point in Segovia, just across from the Comunidad de Madrid.

To make the most of what there is to see, especially if time is limited, a vehicle to chew up distance is a handy asset. That said, it is feasible to follow much of this or a similar route with public transport. Where it becomes especially tricky is with small villages. Castilla y León is liberally sprinkled with castillos, *ermitas* (hermitages or chapels), monasteries and great churches. It is astonishing just how frequently they pop up on distant horizons as you barrel down an autovía -- this is when independent transport comes into its own.

SEGOVIA

To some, the ridge-top city of Segovia resembles a warship ploughing through the sea of Castilla, the base of its prow formed by the confluence of the Río Eresma and Río Clamores. The town has a surprising array of monuments, and those contemplating visiting Segovia as a day trip from Madrid will have a full program if they are to do it justice. The lofty city walls and Roman aqueduct largely protect the city from any incursion by the characterless modern urban tangle below it to the southeast and set it apart from many other cities across Castilla y León, flat and besieged by new development.

History

The Celtic settlement of Segobriga was occupied by the Romans in 80 BC and rose to some importance in the imperial network. As Christian Spain recovered from the initial shock of the Muslim attack, Segovia became something of a front-line city until the invaders were definitively evicted in 1085. The Muslims left behind them a flourishing wool and textile industry, which only began to decline in the mid-16th century. A favourite residence of Castilla's roaming royalty, the city backed Isabel and saw her proclaimed queen in the Iglesia de San Miguel in 1474. In 1520, the rebellious Comuneros found unequivocal support in Segovia, led by Juan Bravo. From then on it was all downhill for the town until the 1960s, when tourism and the introduction of some light industry helped it pull itself up by the bootstraps.

Orientation

The old town of Segovia is strung out along a ridge, rising in the east and peaking in the fanciful towers of the Alcázar to the west. If you arrive by train or bus, the local bus will take you to Plaza Mayor, the heart of the city. Drivers will reach the same square by following the 'Centro Ciudad' signs. The cathedral, tourist office, several hotels and plenty of restaurants and bars are all on or handily close to Plaza Mayor. The main road leading downhill from Plaza Mayor to the *acueducto* (aqueduct) and the new town is a pedestrian thoroughfare that changes name several times along the way (Calle de Isabel la Católica, Calle de Juan Bravo and Calle de Cervantes); locals know the length of it simply as Calle Real.

Information

Tourist Offices The main tourist office (☎ 921 43 03 34), Plaza Mayor 10, has a decent free map and accommodation list. It's open Monday to Friday from 10 am to 2 pm and 5 to 8 pm, Saturday from 10 am to 2 pm and 4.30 to 8.30 pm, and Sunday from 11 am to 2 pm and 4.30 to 8.30 pm. There is a municipal tourist office (☎ 921 44 03 02) at Plaza del Azoguejo 1.

Money There are plenty of banks with exchange facilities on or near the so-called Calle Real. Many have ATMs and some, like the Caja de Ahorros de Segovia at Calle Juan Bravo 2, have machines for exchanging foreign cash.

Post & Communications The main correos is at Plaza de los Huertos 5. The postcode is 40080. The main Telefónica locutorio is on the same square and open daily from 10 am to 2 pm and 5 to 10 pm.

Medical Services & Emergency If you need the police, call ☎ 091. Otherwise, the Policía Nacional are on the corner of Paseo Ezequiel González and the Carretera de Ávila, in the new part of town. For an ambulance, call the Cruz Roja (☎ 921 43 01 00) or ☎ 061. The Hospital General (☎ 921 43 63 63) is about 1.5km south-west of the acueducto on the Ávila highway.

Things to See

There are three key sights not to be missed in Segovia and a warren of others worth investigation for the less time-conscious. In the first category are the acueducto, cathedral and Alcázar. Student discounts are available on entry to some sights.

Acueducto & Around The 894m granite block bridge you see today, made up of 163 arches, is the most extraordinary element of the engineering effort that went into the once 15km Roman aqueduct raised here in the 1st century AD. It measures up to 28m high, and not a drop of mortar was used to hold the thing together – just good old Roman know-how. For almost 2000 years it has withstood the elements, but the modern civilisation that so prizes such antiques is on the verge of toppling it. Pollution and heavy traffic have so weakened the structure that it might just collapse like a house of cards. A delicate billion-peseta restoration program is aimed at preventing this but, until the flow of traffic on its eastern side is permanently diverted, the single main cause of the problem will remain unresolved. For the best view of the structure, climb the steps onto the old town walls.

While at this end of town, you could inspect a few churches. The **Iglesia de San Millán** stands off Avenida de Fernández Ladreda in what looks like an abandoned building site. It is a worn example of the Romanesque typical of Segovia, with porticoes and a mudéjar bell tower. A couple of other late Romanesque churches around here are the **Iglesia de San Justo** and the **Iglesia de San Clemente**.

To the Catedral From the Plaza de Azoguejo beside the acueducto, Calle Real climbs into the innards of Segovia. About a quarter of the way up to Plaza

SEGOVIA

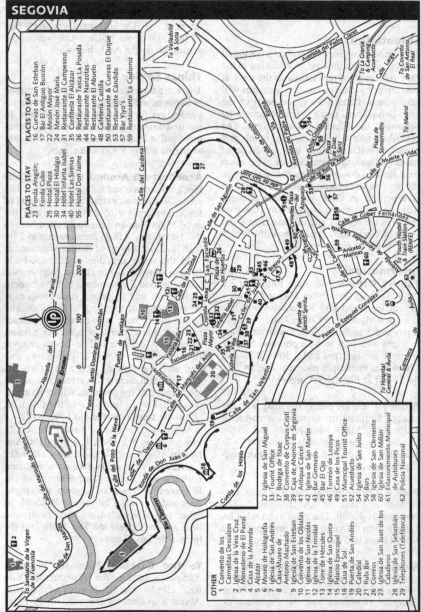

Mayor, you strike the **Casa de los Picos** on the right, a Renaissance mansion named for the diamond-shaped bosses that cover its walls. A little farther you reach one of the most captivating little squares in Segovia, **Plaza de San Martín**. It is presided over by a statue of Juan Bravo, a 15th century mansion and the 14th century **Torreón de Lozoya**, which is used for exhibitions.

The *pièce de résistance* is, however, the Romanesque **Iglesia de San Martín**, with the Segovian touch of mudéjar tower and arched gallery. The interior boasts a Flemish Gothic chapel. Next door is the former *cárcel* (prison). Shortly before Plaza Mayor, the Convento de Corpus Cristi is in the middle of the old *judería* (Jewish quarter) and used to be a synagogue, of interest if only for the fact that there are so few historic synagogues left in Spain.

The shady **Plaza Mayor** is the nerve centre of old Segovia, lined by an eclectic assortment of buildings, arcades and cafés. The **Iglesia de San Miguel**, where Isabel was crowned Queen of Castilla, recedes humbly into the background before the splendour of the cathedral across the square.

Catedral Completed in 1577, 50 years after its Romanesque predecessor had burned to the ground in the revolt of the Comuneros, the cathedral is a last, powerful expression of Gothic art in Spain. A seemingly never-ending restoration job has kept the south-western side covered in scaffolding.

The austere interior contains an imposing choir in the centre and is ringed by 20-odd chapels. Of these, the Capilla del Cristo del Consuelo houses a magnificent Romanesque doorway preserved from the original church. Through here you can get to the Gothic cloister and the rooms of the Museo Catedralicio, with a varied collection of predominantly religious art. The cathedral's museum and cloister are open daily from 9.30 am to 7 pm (9 am to 6 pm in winter; 250 ptas).

Around the Catedral The obvious way to the Alcázar is down Calle de Daoiz. About halfway along you pass yet another Romanesque church, the **Iglesia de San Andrés**. Virtually next door at No 9, suffering children might perk up in the **Museo de Holografía**, open Tuesday to Sunday from 10.30 am to 2.30 pm and 4.30 to 8.30 pm (200 ptas).

Before getting this far, you could turn right down Calle de los Desemparados for the **Casa-Museo de Antonio Machado** at No 5. It is open Tuesday to Sunday from 4 to 7 pm (to 6 pm in autumn and winter). Machado, one of Spain's pre-eminent 20th century poets, lived in this house from 1919 to 1932 and the poet's furnishings and some personal possessions are featured here. A few paces farther down the road rises the six-level tower of the 13th century Romanesque **Iglesia de San Esteban**. The scenic way around to the Alcázar along Ronda de Don Juan II passes the **Casa de Sol**, at Calle de Socorro 11. This former abattoir now houses the Museo de Segovia, but only ever displays limited exhibits. It is open Tuesday to Saturday from 10 am to 2 pm and 5 to 7 pm and Sunday from 10 am to 2 pm.

Alcázar Walt Disney liked it so much he made one in California. Blessed with unrestricted views right around, the site of Segovia's Alcázar has been fortified since Roman days. It takes its name from the Arabic *al-qasr* (castle) and was rebuilt and expanded in the 13th and 14th centuries. Felipe II added the touch of the slate witch's hats, but the whole lot burned down in 1862 and was subsequently painstakingly rebuilt, albeit as an over-the-top version of the original.

The techumbre, or ceiling in the form of an inverted ship, in the Sala de la Galera, is a remarkable reconstruction of the original, while the grand Sala de los Reyes, crowned with an intricate frieze depicting 52 monarchs and another superb ceiling, is also the work of restorers' hands. Before you leave, climb the Torre de Juan II for the magnificent views. The Alcázar is open daily from 10 am to 7 pm (6 pm in winter; 375 ptas).

Churches & Convents The rich smorgasbord of religious buildings to be discovered in Segovia goes well beyond what has been cited so far.

A string of them stretches across the luxuriant valley of the Río Eresma to the north of the city – a pleasant area for a wander in the shadow of the walls, and a favourite with local picnickers.

The most interesting of Segovia's churches – and the best-preserved of its kind in Europe – is the twelve-sided **Iglesia de la Vera Cruz**, just outside the town in the valley facing the Alcázar. It was built in the 13th century by the legendary Knights Templar on the pattern of the church of the Holy Sepulchre in Jerusalem, and long housed what was said to be a piece of the *Vera Cruz* (True Cross), now in the nearby village church of Zamarramala (and can only be viewed at Easter). In the middle of the circular nave is a curious two-storey chamber where the knights stood vigil over the holy relic. The adjacent bell tower, which has great views from the top, was closed for restoration at the time of writing. The church is open Tuesday to Sunday from 10.30 am to 1.30 pm and 3.30 to 7 pm (to 6 pm in autumn and winter; 200 ptas).

Nearby, San Juan de la Cruz is buried in the **Convento de los Carmelitas Descalzos**. The **Monasterio de El Parral** is open Monday to Saturday from 10 am to 12.30 pm

---

Juan Bravo & the Comuneros

The ascension of Carlos I to the throne in 1516, uniting under his sceptre Spain and Austria, was not at all a welcome sign to many a Castilian noble family. It soon became clear that the newcomer's absolutist ways were bad news for local overlords unimpressed by the wave of foreigners suddenly entering key positions of power. When Carlos I left for the Netherlands in May 1520, confirming the fears of many that from here on Spanish interests would be subordinated to the needs of the Holy Roman Empire, the core Castilian cities, including Segovia, Toledo, Salamanca, León and Burgos, rose up in revolt. Thus began the *Guerra de las Comunidades* (War of the Communities).

In Segovia, Juan Bravo became one of the main leaders of the movement, which in July of 1520 assumed the powers of state for itself. Although often depicted as a popular uprising, it was more about maintaining local privilege in the face of central, absolute and, to top it all, foreign control.

Segovia was soon under siege, but although Juan de Padilla, marching from Toledo, was unable to help, Bravo managed to keep the Royalists out. The Royalists then sacked Medina del Campo, which served only to push the undecided into the rebel Comunero camp. By September, the Comuneros seemed to have the backing of the queen, Juana la Loca, and the Royalists were in deep trouble. They pulled out all stops, declaring that they would prohibit the outflow of Spanish cash and halt the nomination of non-Spaniards to positions of power.

By this time the rebel camp was coming asunder, with the moderates beginning to back-pedal. In the following months, although the Comuneros won several indecisive battles, the Royalists gained the upper hand after taking Tordesillas (where Queen Juana la Loca was confined). Finally, Padilla was defeated at the Battle of Villalar on 23 April 1521. He, Juan Bravo and other leaders of the revolt were promptly rounded up and executed. Toledo, under Padilla's wife María Pacheco, held out for a while, but soon had to throw in the towel. Absolute imperial rule had arrived in Spain.

and 4 to 6.30 pm (10 to 11.30 am on Sunday). Ring the bell to get in and be shown part of the cloister and church, the latter a proud Gothic-mudéjar structure, even if the façade was never finished. On Sunday at noon you can listen in on a Gregorian chant Mass. On the other side of the city, just off Avenida de Padre Claret (which becomes the N-601), the **Convento de San Antonio El Real** is also worth a look, although it's a bit of a hike. Once the summer residence of Enrique IV, it includes a Gothic-mudéjar church with a splendid artesonado ceiling. The convent is open weekdays from 4 to 6 pm (300 ptas).

Special Events
Segovians are on the whole a sober lot, but they do let their hair down for the Fiestas de San Juan y San Pedro, which is celebrated on 24-29 June with parades, concerts and bullfights.

Places to Stay – Budget
Camping & Hostel The nearest camping ground to the city, *Camping Acueducto* (☎ 921 42 50 00), is about 2km south-east of town. Take bus No 2 from Plaza Mayor to where the road to La Granja forks with Avenida de Juan Carlos I. From here you can walk, following the CN-601. It is open from April to September and charges 400 ptas per person, tent and car.

The youth hostel, the *Albergue de la Juventud Emperador Teodosio* (☎ 921 44 10 47), is only open in July and August. It's a fair way out of town (although handy for the train station) at Avenida del Conde de Sepúlveda s/n. A bed costs 900 ptas for under-26s and 1300 ptas for other travellers.

Fondas & Hostales A box seat over Segovia's main square, *Fonda Aragón* (☎ 921 46 09 14, Plaza Mayor 4), on the 1st floor, has rambling doubles/triples for 2000/2600 ptas. There is no central heating and a shower costs 200 ptas – if there's hot water. Upstairs, *Fonda Cubo* (☎ 921 46 09 17) is in much the same category and has singles/doubles for 1100/2200.

Hostal Plaza (☎ 921 46 03 03, Calle del Cronista Lecea 11) offers a range of rooms starting at 2800/4000 ptas without private bath.

If you don't mind being farther away from the centre, about the best deal is the spick-and-span *Hostal Don Jaime* (☎ 921 44 47 87, Calle de Ochoa Ondategui 8). Singles/doubles with TV cost 3000/5400 ptas.

Places to Stay – Mid-Range & Top End
In the centre, *Hostal El Hidalgo* (☎ 921 46 35 29, Calle de José Canalejas 3-5) has rooms for 4500/5970 ptas.

Climbing the scale somewhat, *Hotel Las Sirenas* (☎ 921 46 26 63, fax 921 46 26 57, Calle de Juan Bravo 30) has reasonable rooms with TV and telephone for 5500/8500 ptas plus IVA. Top of the tree and in a prime location just off Plaza Mayor, *Hotel Infanta Isabel* (☎ 921 46 13 00, fax 921 46 22 17, Calle de Isabel la Católica 1) has all the comforts you require at 7000/10,900 ptas plus IVA.

Places to Eat
Segovians seem obsessed with roasts. Every second restaurant proudly boasts its *horno de asar* (roasts) and they say that 'pork has 40 flavours – all of them good'. Here the speciality is *cochinillo asado* (roast suckling pig, and there isn't a restaurant, no matter how unlikely, that won't do its best to serve it up). This and *judiones de la Granja* (a bean dish) are the two big culinary offerings. The town's dessert is a heavy, sweet affair made with *ponche*, a popular Spanish spirit, and hence known as *ponche segoviano*.

Snacks & Breakfast The obvious place to sit down for a morning coffee and pastry is Plaza Mayor, lined with expensive cafés. If you're not troubled by views, you could head for *Bar El Antiguo Buscón* (Calle del Marqués del Arco 32). A breakfast of juice, coffee and toast will cost 400 ptas.

An excellent place to pick up a pastry for breakfast, or some ponche segoviano, is the

CASTILLA Y LEÓN

Confitería El Alcázar (Plaza Mayor 10).
The *Cafetería Castilla (Calle de Juan Bravo 56)* is a popular spot with locals and good for baguettes with various fillings – glorified but good bocadillos. They cost around 400 ptas, depending on the fillings. *Bar Yiyo's (Calle del Doctor Sánchez 3)* has hamburgers and the like and also one of the cheapest set lunches you're likely to find in Segovia (1000 ptas).

Lunch & Dinner A widely respected favourite with Segovians is *Mesón José María (Calle del Cronista Lecea 11)*, where mains are about 1500 to 2000 ptas. A set meal featuring cochinillo will cost you 2500 ptas.

Restaurante Narizotas (Plaza de Medina del Campo 1) is ideal if only for its location – especially in summer when you're able to eat outside. You can eat well for about 2500 ptas. The nearby *Restaurante El Abuelo (Calle de la Alhóndiga 9)* has a rough-around-the-edges feel and serves solid meals for comparatively moderate prices. *Restaurante Tasca La Posada (Calle de la Judería Vieja 5)* offers various set meals for lunch, including the predictable cochinillo and judiones for 2200 ptas a head. North off Plaza Mayor, *Cuevas de San Esteban (Calle de Valdeláguila 15)* – you can also enter from Calle de los Escuderos – serves a double role as eatery and decent bar.

More pricey is *Mesón Mayor (Plaza Mayor 3)*, which is popular and recommended for traditional dishes. Ducking into another lane off Plaza Mayor, *Restaurante El Campesino (Calle de la Infanta Isabel 12)* is an equally well-known and reliable place.

At *Restaurante La Codorniz (Calle de Aniceto Marinas 1)* you can expect to pay about 2500 ptas for a good main meal. *Restaurante El Duque*, a short way up Calle de Cervantes from the acueducto, has been going since 1895 and is Segovia's oldest dining establishment. For less formality, try its *Cuevas*, in the same building but entered at Calle de Santa Engracia 10.

This is a snug place for a drink, and you can have anything on the restaurant menu as well. For a full meal you'll be lucky to get much change from 4000 ptas. In the same price bracket and another old Segovian favourite is *Restaurante Cándido (Plaza del Azoguejo 3)*.

Entertainment
Cafés & Bars In summer, *Bar Gimnasio* and *Bar El Ojo* spread out over Plaza de San Martín – a pleasant spot for coffee and an alternative to the cafés lining Plaza Mayor (the obvious choice for drinking and people-watching).

For those quirky enough to like the fast-disappearing spit-and-sawdust wine bars of old, *Rubi (Calle de los Escuderos 4)* is the place to go. The single best street for atmospheric bars and snacking is Calle de la Infanta Isabel.

You'll also find a few decent watering holes on Calle de la Judería Vieja. The *Restaurante Tasca La Posada* (see Places to Eat) can get quite lively, and *Bodega de Isaac (Puerta del Sol 1)* is a cosy retreat. For a few discos, try Calle de los Escuderos. Or there is a small but loud collection of young people's bars along Calle de Ruiz de Alda, under the arches of the acueducto – the thumping music must do it a world of good ...

Getting There & Away
Bus The Estacionamiento Municipal de Autobuses (☎ 921 42 77 07) is just off Paseo de Ezequiel González, near the junction with Avenida de Fernández Ladreda. There are up to 16 departures daily to Madrid (Paseo de la Florida 11). Regular buses also link Segovia with La Granja, Valladolid and Cuéllar. AutoRes has up to four daily services to Salamanca (1340 ptas) and there is one to Ávila. Sepúlveda, Pedraza and Coca are also served by bus. On Sunday many services do not operate at all.

Train Up to nine trains run daily to Madrid (Chamartín and Atocha), but they are pretty slow.

Car & Motorcycle Of the two main roads down to the N-IV, which links Madrid and Galicia, the N-603 is the prettier. The alternative N-110 cuts south-west across to Ávila and north-east to the main Madrid-Burgos highway.

Getting Around

Bus No 3 runs between Plaza Mayor and the train station (passing the estación de autobuses on the way). Apart from this, walking is probably the best way to get about, although it can involve some steep climbs if you intend to explore places like the Iglesia de la Vera Cruz.

AROUND SEGOVIA
La Granja de San Ildefonso

It is not hard to see why the Bourbon king Felipe V chose this site, nestling in the western foothills of the Sierra de Guadarrama 12km east of Segovia, to create his version of Versailles, the palace of his French grandfather Louis XIV, the Sun King. In 1720 French architects and gardeners, with some Italian help, began laying out the elaborate gardens. El Real Sitio de la Granja de San Ildefonso remained a favourite summer residence with Spanish royalty for the next couple of centuries – and is now a popular weekend destination for stressed madrileños.

La Granja's centrepiece is the garden's 28 fountains. Some of them are switched on from about 5 pm on Wednesday, Saturday and Sunday (subject to change). The gardens open from 10 am to 9 pm daily and entry is free except when the fountains are on, when you have to purchase a 325 ptas ticket. The 300-room Palacio Real, badly damaged by fire in 1918 and subsequently restored, is impressive but perhaps the lesser of La Granja's jewels. You can visit about half of the palace, including its Museo de Tapices (tapestry museum). Between June 1 and September 30 the palace is open daily from 10 am to 6 pm. The rest of the year it is open from 10 am to 1.30 pm and 3 to 5 pm (650 ptas, students 250 ptas).

Around the palace sprang up a busy village that today caters mostly to the passing tourist trade. There are several bars, restaurants and hotels in the area around Plaza de los Dolores, the central square. The cheapest place to stay is the *Pensión Pozo de la Nieve* (☎ 921 47 05 98, Calle de los Baños 4), with adequate rooms (bathroom outside) for 2200/3500 ptas. For a bite to eat, you might try *Restaurante Zaca (Calle de los Embajadores 6)*.

A CASTLE TRAIL
Pedraza de la Sierra

This walled village about 35km north-east of Segovia is quite a captivating place, but more an open-air museum than a living community. During the week it is quite dead, but the considerable number of restaurants and bars come to life with the arrival of weekend swarms from Madrid and Segovia.

At the far end stands a lonely **castillo**, open on the weekend. At the opposite end of town, by the only town gate, is the 14th century prison, which can also be visited on the weekend. The uneven, porticoed Plaza Mayor has a particular charm.

Turégano

About 30km north of Segovia, Turégano is dominated by a unique 15th century castle-church complex built by the then archbishop of Segovia, Juan Arias Dávila, who decided to make a personal fortress of the town. The castle walls are built around the façade of the Iglesia de San Miguel.

Coca

A typically dusty, inward-looking Castilian village, Coca is presided over by a **castillo** that is a virtuoso piece of Gothic-mudéjar architecture and made entirely of brick. It was built in 1453 by the powerful Fonseca family and is surrounded by a deep moat. The beautiful exterior was once matched by an equally breathtaking Renaissance interior, which was nearly stripped of its ornamentation in the 19th century. Now belonging to a forestry school, the castillo has

The sumptuous Coca castle, like many across Spain, was not built with warfare in mind

uncertain visiting hours, although it merits the effort just to see the exterior. Guided visits are possible on weekdays from 10.30 am to 1.30 pm and 4.30 to 6 pm or weekends and holidays from 11 am to 1.30 pm and 4.30 to 7 pm. If there's no-one about, try calling ☎ 921 58 63 59 or ☎ 921 58 66 47.

The town is just over 50km north-west of Segovia and about 60km south of Valladolid. Up to three buses daily run between Segovia and Coca.

Cuéllar

Located 60km north of Segovia on the CL-601 to Valladolid, Cuéllar is yet another dusty Castilian settlement, where the harsh summer light seems even more blinding than usual. Perhaps that impression is in part due to the whitish grey stone of its massive 15th century castillo-cum-palace, which is what makes the place interesting. It can only be visited on the weekend, from 11 am to 2 pm and 4 to 7 pm. Six buses run daily from Valladolid to Cuéllar.

VALLADOLID

Once the de facto capital of imperial Spain and a flourishing centre of the Spanish Renaissance, Valladolid is now a modern giant in which hints of former greatness are parsimoniously scattered about. With a population of some 350,000 (more than double that of 1950), Valladolid has known a rapid and unlovely expansion, buttressed by heavy industry and its position as a transport crossroads. The isolated splendours that remain of the old city repay exploration; early birds could stretch a point and make a day trip of it from Madrid.

History

Little more than a hamlet in the early Middle Ages, Valladolid had become a major centre of commerce, education and art by the time Fernando of Aragón and Isabel of Castilla discreetly contracted matrimony here in 1469. As Spain's greatest-ever ruling duo, they carried Valladolid to the heights of its splendour. Its university was one of the most dynamic on the peninsula and things only got better under Carlos I, who based the Consejo Real here and so made Valladolid the seat of imperial government. A sad and unrewarded Christopher Columbus (Cristóbal Colón to the Spaniards) ended his days here in 1506 – about as far from the sea as he could get! The seeds of Valladolid's decline were sown here too, with the birth of Felipe II in 1527. Thirty-three years later he chose to make Madrid the capital, to the displeasure not only of Valladolid but also of several other contenders too (such as Toledo).

Orientation

The centre of Valladolid lies east of the Río Pisuerga. At its southern edge are the Estación del Norte (trains) and the nearby estación de autobuses. From here it's about

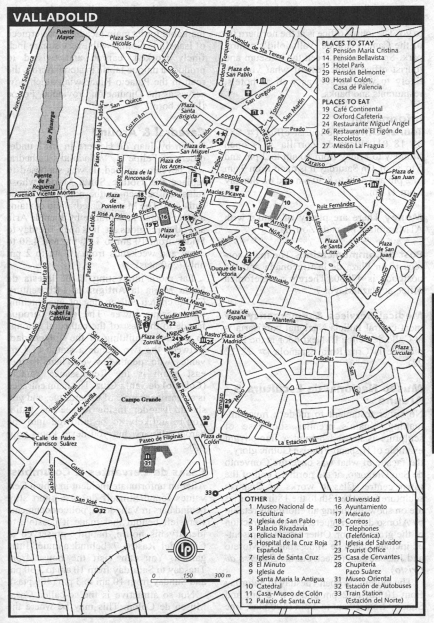

VALLADOLID

PLACES TO STAY
6 Pensión María Cristina
14 Pensión Bellavista
15 Hotel París
29 Pensión Belmonte
30 Hostal Colón;
   Casa de Palencia

PLACES TO EAT
19 Café Continental
22 Oxford Cafetería
24 Restaurante Miguel Ángel
26 Restaurante El Figón de
   Recoletos
27 Mesón La Fragua

OTHER
1 Museo Nacional de
   Escultura
2 Iglesia de San Pablo
3 Palacio Rivadavia
4 Policía Nacional
5 Hospital de la Cruz Roja
   Española
7 Iglesia de Santa Cruz
8 El Minuto
9 Iglesia de
   Santa María la Antigua
10 Catedral
11 Casa-Museo de Colón
12 Palacio de Santa Cruz
13 Universidad
16 Ayuntamiento
17 Mercado
18 Correos
20 Telephones
   (Telefónica)
21 Iglesia del Salvador
23 Tourist Office
25 Casa de Cervantes
28 Chupitería
   Paco Suárez
31 Museo Oriental
32 Estación de Autobuses
33 Train Station
   (Estación del Norte)

CASTILLA Y LEÓN

0   150   300 m

a 2.5km walk to the Museo Nacional de Escultura, as far north as you're likely to want to go. The tourist office is at the northern tip of the Campo Grande, Valladolid's central park. Spread out between the museum and tourist office is the rest of what you are likely to want to see, as well as hotels, restaurants and banks.

Information

Tourist Office The tourist office (☎ 983 35 18 01), Plaza de Zorrilla 3, is open Monday to Friday from 10 am to 2 pm and 5 to 8 pm. On Saturday it is open from 9 am to 2 pm and 4.30 to 8.30 pm and on Sunday from 11 am.

Money There are plenty of banks with ATMs around Plaza de Zorrilla.

Post & Communications The main correos is on Plaza de la Rinconada and the postcode is 47080. There's a Telefónica office at Plaza Mayor 7.

Medical Services & Emergency The most central Policía Nacional comisaría is at Calle de Felipe II. Next door is the Hospital de la Cruz Roja Española (☎ 22 22 22).

Museo Nacional de Escultura & Around

No sober testament to modern museum-making, Spain's premier showcase of sculpture is housed behind a flamboyant example of Hispano-Flemish Gothic glory – the façade of what was once the Convento de San Gregorio, at the northern end of the town centre. Classic works of Spanish sculpture from the 13th to the 18th centuries are on show, including an enormous retablo by Alonso de Berreguete, the star attraction of the ground floor. Other artists represented include Diego de Siloé, Juan de Moreto and Juan de Juni (check out his *Entierro de Cristo*).

The museum is open Tuesday to Saturday from 10 am to 2 pm and 4 to 6 pm and Sunday from 10 am to 2 pm (400 ptas, free on the weekend). Virtually next door to the museum, the **Iglesia de San Pablo** is remarkable for its main façade, a masterpiece of Isabelline Gothic with every square inch finely worked, carved and twisted to produce a unique fabric in stone. Across the road in the Palacio Rivadavia, which now serves as the Diputación Provincial, Felipe II was born.

Catedral & Around

Begun by Juan de Herrera in 1582 under orders of Felipe II, Valladolid's cathedral was never completed. It was supposed to replace the Gothic Santa María, whose ruins can be seen on the north side of the cathedral. The Museo Catedralicio contains a processional monstrance by Juan de Arfe and other religious art. It is open Tuesday to Friday from 10 am to 1.30 pm and 4.30 to 7 pm and weekends from 10 am to 2 pm only (250 ptas).

Far more interesting is the **Iglesia de Santa María la Antigua**, a 14th century Gothic church with an elegant, eye-catching Romanesque tower. The grand baroque façade to the east of the cathedral belongs to the main building of the **universidad**. Between the two stands a statue of Cervantes, who spent a few years here. Farther east again is the Renaissance **Palacio (Colegio) de Santa Cruz**. The main entrance is an early example of plateresque, and you should wander inside to see the patio. You're unlikely to be allowed into the baroque library, but you never know your luck.

Casas de Cervantes & Columbus

After an unfortunate incident in which Cervantes found himself doing a short stint behind bars in Valladolid, police documents were left behind that made it possible to identify his house, happily preserved at Calle del Rastro 7 behind a quiet little garden. You can visit the house from Tuesday to Saturday from 10 am to 3.30 pm and Sunday from 10 am to 3 pm (400 ptas).

Not so attractive is the so-called Casa-Museo de Colón. This may be where the ultimately hapless Genoese explorer lived and ended his days, but there remains not a trace of the house. The museum contains a motley collection of indigenous American art (Aztec, Incan and Mayan) and a few documents and other mementoes. It is open Monday to Friday from 10 am to 2 pm and 4 to 6 pm (5 to 7 pm in summer; free).

Special Events
Good Friday is the peak of the frenetic Easter week celebrations, with great processions and some intense partying.

Places to Stay
Near Estación del Norte If you need to doss down near the train station, there are several possibilities. *Pensión Belmonte (☎ 983 30 01 79, Calle Gamazo 27)* has basic singles/doubles for 1600/3200 ptas. A step up is *Hostal Colón (☎ 983 30 40 44, Acera de Recoletos 12)*, with rooms starting at 2300/3900 ptas.

City Centre Hostelries of all descriptions are spread across the city centre. In the shadow of the cathedral, *Pensión Bellavista (☎ 983 20 81 33, Calle de Núñez de Arce 1)* has rock-bottom digs for 2000/2800 ptas. A more salubrious option is *Pensión María Cristina (☎ 983 35 69 02, Plaza de los Arces 3)*, with rooms for 3000/4000 ptas. A good choice is *Hotel París (☎ 983 37 06 25, Calle de la Especería 2)*. Rooms with all the trimmings cost 5600/7600 ptas plus IVA.

Places to Eat
Plaza Mayor is a good place to seek out your morning coffee haunt. *Café Continental*, on the corner of Calle de Jesús, is especially good – they give you a free orange juice with your sticky bun.

Oxford Cafetería (Calle de Claudio Moyano 4) is a pleasant spot for breakfast, snacks or even a full meal. For cheap but filling tucker, you could stop in at *Casa de Palencia*, in the same building as the Hostal Colón, Acera de Recoletos 22, which does a set *menú* for 950 ptas. *Restaurante El*

Figón de Recoletos (Calle de Mantilla 2A) is one of the town's top restaurants and prices reflect this – you'll get little change from 4000 ptas. Also good and a little cheaper is *Restaurante Miguel Ángel* on the corner of Calle de Mantilla and Calle de M Escobar. There are a few others around here. *Mesón La Fragua*, on the western side of Campo Grande at Paseo de Zorrilla 10, has fine food, with mains coming in at around 1500 to 2000 ptas.

Entertainment
Cafés & Bars An excellent and popular bar-café is *El Minuto (Calle de Macías Picavea 15)*. There are a few other bars for late-night drinking on the same street. For a younger, louder scene, Calle de Padre Francisco Suárez, just west of the bottom end of Campo Grande, remains the main centre of late-night drinking action. The *Chupitería Paco Suárez* is one of many favourites here.

Getting There & Away
Air There is one flight daily on weekdays to Paris and another to Barcelona. Otherwise the odd charter flight serves Palma de Mallorca and Tenerife (Canary Islands). The airport is 12km west of town and there is no bus.

Bus There are regular buses to Madrid (Estación Sur), about a dozen to Palencia and about the same to Zamora via Tordesillas. Others run to Bilbao, Burgos, Barcelona (two daily), Logroño, Zaragoza, Segovia (five daily) and Salamanca.

Train Up to eight trains daily run between Valladolid and Madrid (Chamartín and most also to Atocha). The 2nd class one-way standard fare is 1455 ptas and the trip takes 2¾ hours. A similar number run to León (two hours). A few head north to Burgos, Vitoria and Santander. All but the Madrid-bound trains pass through Palencia.

Car & Motorcycle The N-620 motorway passes Valladolid en route from Burgos to

Torquemada & the Inquisition

There is hardly a more notorious body in the history of the Catholic Church than the Spanish Inquisition, and its most infamous member was undoubtedly Fray Tomás de Torquemada (1420-1498).

Dostoevsky immortalised him as the articulate Grand Inquisitor who puts Jesus himself on trial in *Crime and Punishment* and Monty Python created a memorable parody of the religious zealot in their Flying Circus.

Torquemada may have been articulate, but he was no comedian: in the 15 years he was Inquisitor General of the Castilian Inquisition he ran some 100,000 trials and sent about 2000 people to burn at the stake.

Born in Valladolid of well-placed Jewish *conversos* (converts to Christianity), Torquemada was deeply affected by the Spanish cult of *sangre limpia* (pure blood), the racist doctrine that inevitably accompanied the 800 year struggle to rid Spain of non-Christian peoples. Since Spain had the largest Jewish population in medieval Europe and conversion and intermarriage were commonplace, few could claim to have sangre limpia. The Spanish nobility in particular were nevertheless obsessed with the concept, and many – including Torquemada himself – went to extremes to disguise their lineage.

He joined the Dominicans, and the ruthless administration of the affairs of the Inquisition were undoubtedly the result of his efforts. Fray Tomás first came to the attention of Fernando and Isabel in 1479, when the middle-aged monk was appointed the queen's personal confessor.

Four years later he was nominated by Pope Sixtus IV to head the Castilian Inquisition, and he immediately took to his duties with relish. He devised a series of guidelines for rooting out conversos and other heretics, including his favourite targets, the *marranos*, Jews who only pretended to convert but continued to practice Judaism in private.

If someone wore fancy clothes on a Saturday, they were Jews. If a home was cleaned on a Friday night and candles lit earlier than usual, the household was Jewish. If someone ate unleavened bread and began their meal with celery and lettuce during Holy Week, they were Jews. If they said prayers facing a wall and bowed back and forth while doing so, they were Jews.

Tordesillas, where it picks up with the N-VI between Madrid and La Coruña. The N-601 heads north-west to León and south to hit the N-VI and A-6 west of Segovia.

Getting Around

Local bus Nos 2 and 10 pass the train and bus stations on their way in to Plaza de España, while No 19 passes the stations and terminates in Plaza de Zorrilla.

AROUND VALLADOLID
Medina de Rioseco & Around

Much ignored, Medina de Rioseco seems ensconced in a different century. From Plaza Mayor, the old Calle de Lázaro Alonso winds up a slope past the bulky but unattractive 16th century Iglesia de Santa Cruz. Turn off for the Iglesia de Santa María de la Mediavilla, a grandiose Is-

Torquemada & the Inquisition

If convicted, the lightest punishment dished out by Torquemada and his cronies was the confiscation of the victim's property, a convenient fund-raiser for the war of Reconquista against the Muslims. The condemned were then paraded through town wearing the *sambenito*, a yellow shirt emblazoned with crosses that was short enough to expose their genitals. They were marched to the doors of the local church, where they were then flogged (a punishment suffered by Juan Sánchez de Cepeda, grandfather of Saint Teresa of Avilá). And that was the fate of the lucky ones.

If you were unlucky, you underwent unimaginable tortures (see the section on Santillana del Mar in the Cantabria & Asturias chapter) before going through an *auto-da-fé*, a public burning at the stake. Those that recanted and kissed the cross were garrotted before the fire was set, while those that recanted only were burnt quickly with dry wood. If you stayed firm and didn't recant, the wood used for the fire was green and slow-burning, prolonging your misery.

Torquemada's career reached its apogee (or nadir) in 1490, when he presided over the La Guardia show trial, where eight Jews and conversos were accused of crucifying a Christian child and participating in the so-called 'blood libel', where Jews were supposed to sacrifice a Christian child to appease a vengeful God (a common – and unfounded – fear among medieval Catholics).

Although no victim was ever identified and no body ever discovered, the hapless innocents were condemned to death and duly executed. Seizing on the mass publicity around the trial, Torquemada pushed the Catholic Monarchs to issue an edict expelling all Jews from Spain. Two prominent Jews sought to halt the madness and offered Fernando and Isabel 30,000 ducats to let them stay.

Strapped for cash, they were tempted to accept but Torquemada convinced them otherwise, saying 'Judas sold his Master for thirty ducats. You would sell Him for thirty thousand ... Take him and sell Him, but do not let it be said that I have had any share in this transaction'. Two years later, on March 31, 1492, Fernando and Isabel issued their Edict of Expulsion, and all Jews were forced to leave within two months on pain of death. Torquemada had accomplished his goal.

The following year, he retired to the monastery of Santo Tomás in Avilá, from where he continued to administer the affairs of the Inquisition. In his final years he became obsessed with the fear that he might be poisoned, and refused to eat anything without having a unicorn's horn nearby as an antidote. Nobody got to him, however, and he died in his sleep in 1498.

abelline Gothic work with a pleasing baroque belfry. Down the hill, the Iglesia de Santiago is worth visiting for its pretty but neglected plateresque portal. Neglected is the word – some of Medina de Rioseco looks as though an earthquake just hit – but the place is interesting.

Hostal Duque de Osuna (☎ 983 70 01 79, Avenida de Castilviejo 16), not far from the end of Calle de Lázaro Alonso, in the modern part of town, has singles/doubles from 2000/3000 ptas without bath.

Restaurante Pasos (Calle de Lázaro Alonso 44), has loads of atmosphere and a set meal for 1600 ptas. *The Irish River*, another example of the Irish bar invasion, is just opposite. At least two buses connecting Valladolid, 40km to the south-east, and León call in here.

Urueña For an off-the-beaten-track diversion, head 20km south-west from Medina de Rioseco down the C-519 and take the turn-off south-east for Urueña (signposted). Judging by its powerful walls, this minuscule backwater must once have been an important place. Now you can stare out from the stout defences across the endless patchwork plains of the Tierra de Campos and wonder at glories past. Urueña is equally accessible from Tordesillas and Toro on the road to Zamora – by car, that is.

PALENCIA

As sluggish as the Río Carrión that struggles through it, Palencia has little to divert you apart from the Gothic cathedral. Known to the Romans as Pallantia and later an important Visigothic centre, Palencia reached its zenith, as did so many other Castilian towns, in the Middle Ages, only to decay rapidly after the 15th century.

Orientation & Information

The bus and train stations are adjacent in the north-eastern corner of the town centre.

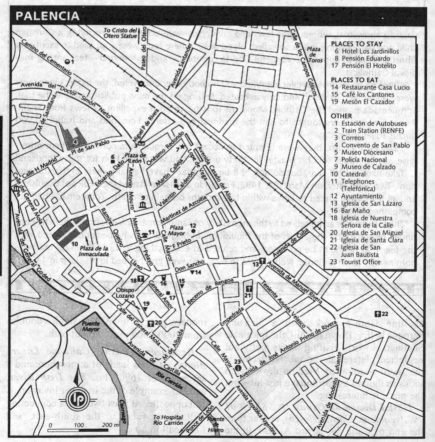

PALENCIA

PLACES TO STAY
6 Hotel Los Jardinillos
8 Pensión Eduardo
17 Pensión El Hotelito

PLACES TO EAT
14 Restaurante Casa Lucio
15 Café los Cantones
19 Mesón El Cazador

OTHER
1 Estación de Autobuses
2 Train Station (RENFE)
3 Correos
4 Convento de San Pablo
5 Museo Diocesano
7 Policía Nacional
9 Museo de Calzado
10 Catedral
11 Telephones
   (Telefónica)
12 Ayuntamiento
13 Iglesia de San Lázaro
16 Bar Maño
18 Iglesia de Nuestra
   Señora de la Calle
20 Iglesia de San Miguel
21 Iglesia de Santa Clara
22 Iglesia de San
   Juan Bautista
23 Tourist Office

From nearby Plaza de León, Calle Mayor forms the main north-south axis through Palencia, part of it pedestrianised. Several hotels lie near or just off it, as do most of the offices, banks etc that you may need.

The tourist office (☎ 979 74 00 68), Calle Mayor 105, is open Monday to Friday from 10 am to 2 pm and 5 to 8 pm, and for slightly different hours on the weekend.

There are several banks along the same street, while the correos is on Plaza de León. The postcode is 34080. You'll find a Telefónica office on the corner of Calle del Patio de Castaño and Calle de Menéndez Pelayo.

Catedral

Of the cathedral's otherwise austere exterior, the ornate Puerta del Obispo (Bishop's Door) is the most striking element, but you really need to get inside the church and, unfortunately, pay for a guided tour in Spanish to appreciate its riches.

The screen behind the choir stalls, or *trascoro*, is a masterpiece of bas-relief attributed to Gil de Siloé; it is considered the most beautiful trascoro in Spain. The plateresque stairwell leads down beneath the choir stalls to the crypt, actually remnants of the original Visigothic church and a later Romanesque replacement. The crypt is known as the Cueva de San Antolín because King Wamba supposedly had the French martyr's remains moved here from Narbonne.

In the Museo Catedralicio, you'll see some fine Flemish tapestries and a *San Sebastián* by El Greco. On the tour, the guide lights up various corners of the cathedral and takes you to the partly restored cloister. The cathedral is open Monday to Saturday from 10 am to 1.30 pm and 4 to 6.30 pm; the tour starts every hour or so in the sacristy (300 ptas).

Other Attractions

Of the half-dozen or so other churches around town, it is worth seeking out the Iglesia de San Pablo, in the convent of the same name near the estación de autobuses,

and the Iglesia de San Miguel. The former bears a Renaissance façade and in its Capilla Mayor you can see an enormous plateresque retablo. San Miguel stands out for its tall Gothic tower and, according to the legend, El Cid was betrothed to his Doña Jimena here. Just outside town, the 20m-high Cristo del Otero statue was erected in 1930 and dominates, Rio-style, the surrounding plains.

Places to Stay & Eat

Pensión Eduardo (☎ 979 74 29 48, Calle de Valentín Calderón 5) has OK singles/doubles for 2000/3000 ptas. Better still is *Pensión El Hotelito* (☎ 979 74 69 13, Calle del General Amor 5). The better doubles with private bath cost 3500 ptas. For a little more class, try *Hotel Los Jardinillos* (☎ 979 75 00 22, Calle de Eduardo Dato 2), with rooms at 4300/6400 ptas.

The *Mesón El Cazador* (Calle del Obispo Lozano 7) is a cosy little restaurant with a set meal for 1000 ptas. *Restaurante Casa Lucio* (Calle de Don Sancho s/n) is a more elegant alternative, with a varied menu and main meals costing around 1000 to 1400 ptas. There are also several restaurants on Plaza Mayor. For drinks and tapas, *Café Los Cantones* (Calle Mayor 43) is a pleasant spot. *Bar Maño* (Calle del General Franco 5) is an atmospheric old place.

Getting There & Away

Buses and trains run frequently to Valladolid and other main cities. Two buses daily go to Aguilar de Campóo via Frómista. One goes to Sahagún and several head for Paredes de Nava.

From Palencia roads fan out in a northerly arc. The N-611 heads up into Cantabria, the N-620 peels off east to Burgos and the N-610 heads west to pick up the N-601 from Valladolid to León – all of them worthy objectives.

AROUND PALENCIA
Baños de Cerrato

A couple of kilometres west of the belching industrial rail junction of Venta de Baños lies Spain's oldest church, the 7th century **Basílica de San Juan**, in Baños de Cerrato. Built by the Visigoths and modified many times since, it has a pleasing simplicity. Get a train from Palencia to Venta de Baños, then walk.

Paredes de Nava

The eminent 16th century sculptor Alonso Berruguete was born in Paredes in 1488. His father Pedro was himself an artist of some distinction, having worked in Ávila and Toledo and studied in Urbino, Italy. Paredes counts no less than four major churches, mostly in great disrepair. The exception is the eclectic **Iglesia de Santa Eulalia**, built in the 13th century and continually fiddled with for the following 300 years. Its museum contains some important artworks, including several pieces by the Berruguetes senior and junior. Several daily buses run to Palencia, about 25km southeast, and there are a couple of *fondas* (inns) if you need to stay.

Frómista

The exceptional Romanesque **Iglesia de San Martín** is the main reason for calling in here. Long left to decay, it was faithfully restored towards the end of the last century and the exterior is lined with a menagerie of human and zoomorphic figures. Inside, the capitals are also richly decorated. You can enter from 10 am to 2 pm and 4 to 7 pm.

Pensión Marisa (☎ 979 81 00 23, Plaza de Obispo Almaraz 2) offers good clean rooms for 2200/3300 ptas. It also provides meals.

There are two buses daily from Palencia and another from Burgos. The Palencia-Santander rail line also passes through Frómista. On the way up you'll notice a couple of castles, one at Fuentes de Valdepero (9km out of Palencia) and the other at Monzón de Campos (4km farther on).

From Frómista you can veer off westwards and follow the Camino de Santiago, or pursue the N-611 farther north into Cantabria via Aguilar de Campóo (see the following Montaña Palentina section).

MONTAÑA PALENTINA

The hills straddling the northern fringe of the province of Palencia are collectively known as the Montaña Palentina and are an attractive and little-visited foretaste of the massive Cordillera Cantábrica that divides Castilla from Spain's northern Atlantic regions.

Aguilar de Campóo

The squat form of Aguilar de Campóo's medieval castillo stands watch over this quiet northern town, the historic heartland of Spanish biscuit production. You'll smell the biscuits if you approach from the east. Set a few kilometres east of a big dam and about 15km short of the regional boundary with Cantabria, the town makes a pleasant base for exploring the region, which is dotted with Romanesque churches and cool hilly countryside, presaging the beauty of the Cordillera Cantábrica to the north.

Tourist, post and telephone offices are all on or just off the elongated Plaza de España, which is capped at its eastern end by the majestic **Colegiata de San Miguel**, a 14th century Gothic church with a fine Romanesque entrance and small museum. Downhill from the castillo is the graceful Romanesque **Ermita de Santa Cecilia** and just outside town on the road to Cervera de Pisuerga is the **Monasterio de Santa María la Real**, where the 13th century cloister is a masterpiece.

You'll find plenty of accommodation, including a few places right on Plaza de España. *Hostal Siglo XX* (☎ 979 12 29 00) at No 11 has perfectly good singles/doubles from 2000/3500 ptas. The square is swarming with cafés and bars and a couple of restaurants.

Regular buses link Aguilar de Campóo with Palencia and at least one bus daily goes to Burgos and Santander.

Romanesque Circuit

The area around Aguilar is studded with little villages and churches of interest. One circuit for those with their own transport takes you south along the N-611 towards Palencia. At

Olleros de Pisuerga is a little church carved into rock, while, farther south on a back road, the Benedictine **Monasterio de Santa María de Mave** has an interesting 13th century Romanesque church. The prize in this area lies to the south-west, along the P-222. The **Monasterio de San Andrés de Arroyo** is an outstanding Romanesque gem, especially its cloister (one side of which was later restyled in a mixture of plateresque and Gothic).

The C-627 highway heading to **Cervera de Pisuerga** is lined with still more little churches dating from as far back as the 12th century. Cervera de Pisuerga itself is dominated by an imposing Late Gothic church, the Iglesia de Santa María del Castillo. There are several places to stay, including the homy ***Hostal Cervera (☎ 979 87 02 34, Plaza Mayor 16)***, with singles/doubles going for 3000/5000 ptas. From Cervera you could complete the circle and return to Aguilar. Alternatively, a narrow mountain road winds west along the so-called *ruta de los pantanos* (dams route), describing an arc to Guardo, just short of the provincial frontier with León. The N-621 north from Cervera is a lovely road into Cantabria and to the southern face of the Picos de Europa (see the Cantabria & Asturias chapter).

THE ROAD TO ZAMORA

Castilla is at its least flattering around Valladolid and the road to Zamora is no exception. But while you won't want to hang around for the parched, featureless countryside, there are several worthwhile stops en route.

Tordesillas

Commanding a rise on the northern flank of the Río Duero, this originally Roman town became part of the front line between the Christians and Muslims after the latter had been thrown back from the north in the 9th century.

There is a tourist office in Las Casas del Tratado, near the Iglesia de San Antolín. It is open Wednesday to Saturday from 10.30 am to 2 pm and 5 to 8 pm and Sunday and holidays from 10 am to 2 pm.

Convento de Santa Clara Much of the history of Tordesillas has been dominated by this mudéjar-style convent, still home to 14 Franciscan nuns living in almost total isolation from the outside world. What started as a palace for Alfonso was later turned into a convent by Pedro I. It is commonly held that the mad queen Juana la Loca was locked up here for many years before her death in 1555. She was in fact buried here for 19 years before her body was exhumed and transferred to Granada (as she had wished). Her place of confinement, a nearby castle, no longer exists. Juana was shunted aside after her husband Felipe I died in 1506, although she officially remained queen and negotiated with the Comuneros during their uprising (see the boxed text 'Juan Bravo & the Comuneros').

The guided tour takes in some remarkable rooms, including a wonderful mudéjar

---

The Treaty of Tordesillas

Only two years after Columbus had sailed the ocean blue, Spain's Catholic Monarchs sat down with Portugal at the negotiating table in Tordesillas to hammer out a treaty regulating who got what in the New World. The Spanish-born Borgia pope, Alexander VI, had earlier simply pronounced that everything west of the Azores Islands belonged to Spain, something Lisbon considered slightly lopsided. The Tordesillas deal pushed the limiting line 370 leagues (a little less than 1800km) further west, after which Portugal claimed Brazil. The French monarch, François I, asked himself whether this rather pompous division of the planet (a separate treaty dividing up Africa was also signed) was part of some secret clause in Adam's last will and testament. Later on, Spain and Portugal began to recognise that more than one demarcation line for America, or at least the southern half of it, was required, and they thrashed it all out again in the Treaty of Zaragoza in 1529.

patio left over from the palace, and the church, whose stunning ceiling, or techumbre, is a masterpiece of woodwork. The convent is open Tuesday to Saturday from 10 am to 1 pm and 3.30 to 6.30 pm, and on Sunday and holidays from 10.30 am to 1.30 pm and 3.30 to 5.30 pm. Hours are slightly shorter from October to March. Entry to the convent is 425 ptas, and a separate guided tour of the Arab baths is 225 ptas.

Around Town The deconsecrated Gothic **Iglesia de San Antolín** houses a religious art museum, open Tuesday to Saturday from 10.30 am to 2 pm and 4 to 6 pm and Sunday from 10 am to 2 pm (250 ptas).

The heart of town is formed by the pretty, arcaded Plaza Mayor, whose deep yellow paintwork contrasts with dark brown woodwork and black *rejas* (grilles).

Places to Stay & Eat All of Tordesillas' hotels, many of which are expensive, are on or near the highways to Madrid, Valladolid and Salamanca. One characterless but quiet, clean place is the *Hostal Bastida (☎ 983 77 08 42, Avenida de Valladolid 38)*. You can get rooms for 2000 ptas per person and it's handy for buses. Nearby, *Hotel Los Toreros (☎ 983 77 19 00)* has comfier rooms with TV and private bath for 4500/6500 ptas plus IVA.

Bar Ruski on Calle Garabato, off Calle de Santa María, is a cheap and cheerful place to eat. The cafés on Plaza Mayor are great for a morning coffee.

Getting There & Away Buses for Valladolid and Zamora leave regularly from Avenida de Valladolid, near Calle de Santa María.

Medina del Campo

A mostly morose stop 25km south of Tordesillas, Medina del Campo does have one or two redeeming features, the best of which is the dignified mudéjar **Castillo de la Mota**, just outside town across the railway line to Madrid. Inside, there isn't much to see and it's closed for restoration anyway. In town,

make for the huge rambling Plaza Mayor de la Hispanidad (Plaza de España). Queen Isabel dictated her last will and testament in the **Palacio Real**, an unassuming edifice on the western side of the square.

You won't have any problems finding somewhere to stay and there are plenty of restaurants, especially near Plaza Mayor. Calle de Ángel Molina is loaded with bars. Buses run from various points around the town, but for most destinations you're better off with trains. More than 20 daily run to Madrid and there is regular service to Salamanca, Valladolid and Ávila.

Toro

The drama of Toro's position north of the Río Duero, a 37km sprint west of Tordesillas, only becomes clear when you get into the centre of this higgledy-piggledy place. Coming from Zamora, the wandering English writer Laurie Lee was quite unprepared for the 'ancient, eroded, red-walled town spread along the top of a huge flat boulder', which, to his surprise, 'half-ruined though it certainly was – was ... buzzing with life'. His account, from *As I Walked Out One Midsummer Morning*, would not be totally out of place today.

Having seen the whole historical parade – Celts, Romans, Visigoths, Muslims et al – Toro reached the height of its glory between the 13th and the 16th centuries. Fernando and Isabel cemented their primacy in Christian Spain at the Battle of Toro in 1476.

The tourist office (☎ 980 69 18 62) is in the ayuntamiento building on Plaza de España.

Partly inspired by the Catedral Vieja in Salamanca, the **Catedral de Santa María Mayor** boasts a fine Romanesque doorway in the northern façade and the even more magnificent Romanesque-Gothic Pórtico de la Majestad, which is being restored. The church is open from 11 am to 1.15 pm and 5 to 7.30 pm. From behind the cathedral you have a superb view south across fields to the Romanesque bridge over the Duero. The nearby 10th century Alcázar conserves its walls and seven towers.

The 13th century Romanesque-mudéjar **Iglesia de San Lorenzo el Real**, north-west of the Alcázar, is worth a look. South-west of town, the **Monasterio Sancti Spiritus** features a fine Renaissance cloister and the striking alabaster tomb of Beatriz de Portugal, wife of Juan I. It is open from 9.30 am to 2 pm and 4 to 7 pm and has a small museum too.

Most of the accommodation is out of town, but there is an adequate fonda, *Pensión Castilla (☎ 980 69 03 81, Plaza de España 19)*. It has rooms for 1400/2600 ptas. For more style, go for the *Hotel Juan II (☎ 980 69 03 00, Paseo Espolón 1)*, near the cathedral. Singles/doubles start at 3500/5000 ptas. There are plenty of little places to eat around Plaza de España.

Forget the train – the station is 2km downhill and few trains stop here anyway. Regular buses to Zamora and Valladolid leave from near the junction of Avenida de Carlos Pinilla and Calle de la Corredera, while Madrid buses leave from the edge of town at Calle de Santa Catalina de Roncesvalles. All these services stop in at Toro en route from bigger centres.

There are two direct services to Salamanca on weekdays.

ZAMORA

Another fortress town on the northern bank of the natural defensive line of the Río Duero, Zamora is far enough away from other major Castilian cities not to figure highly on travellers' itineraries. It's a middle-ranking town which in the past 30 years has slowly expanded as the surrounding rural area empties its labour force into the city. The already subdued *casco antiguo* (old town) in the western half of the city gets quieter and quieter as the people move into the growing modern *barrios* (suburbs) to the east.

History

Roman Ocelum Durii was a significant way station along the Ruta de la Plata (Silver Route) from Astorga to southern Spain. The Romans were replaced by the Visigoths, who in turn collapsed before the Muslim invasion. Zamora was twice laid to waste by the Muslims and it was not until the 11th century that the Christians began serious reconstruction. By the 12th and 13th centuries, when a fever of church-building formed the architectural core of what you see today, Zamora had reached its zenith as a commercial centre.

Orientation

The bus and train stations are a good half-hour walk roughly north-east of the town centre, from where it's another 15 minutes south-west to the cathedral and the heart of the casco antiguo. Accommodation is spread out roughly between Plaza Mayor and Calle Alfonso IX, which marks the eastern boundary of the city centre.

Information

The tourist office (☎ 980 53 18 45), Calle de Santa Clara 20, is open Monday to Friday from 10 am to 2 pm and 5 to 8 pm and Saturday from 9.30 am to 2.30 pm.

The correos is at Calle de Santa Clara 15. The postcode is 49080. There are plenty of banks on and around Plaza de Castilla y León.

Catedral

Crowning medieval Zamora's highest point, the largely Romanesque cathedral is an odd mix. Most of it was built in the late 12th century and its most notable aberration is the Byzantine dome (recalling Salamanca's Catedral Vieja). The choir stalls are a masterpiece of early Renaissance artistry. The bulk of the chapels were added from the 15th century on, some showing a markedly Gothic flourish.

Through the 17th century cloister you can reach the Museo Catedralicio. The museum has mainly religious treasures, but the star attraction, for tapestry-lovers at any rate, is the so-called Tapices Negros (black tapestries). The museum is open Tuesday to Saturday from 11 am to 2 pm and 5 to 8 pm (4 to 6 pm in winter) and Sunday and holidays from 11 am to 2 pm (250 ptas).

ZAMORA

PLACES TO STAY
8 Hostal Siglo XX
10 Pensión Balborraz
12 Hostal La Reina
14 Parador Condes de
    Alba y Aliste
23 Hostería
    Real de Zamora

PLACES TO EAT
13 Restaurante El Lagar

OTHER
1 Plaza de Toros
2 Turisnautic
3 Tourist Office
4 Correos
5 Plaza de la Constitución
6 Policía Nacional
7 Seminario
9 La Cueva del Jazz
11 Iglesia de San Juan de
    Puerta Nueva
15 Diputación Provincial
16 Iglesia de
    Santa María La Nueva
17 Museo de
    Semana Santa
18 Castillo
19 Catedral
20 Palacio Episcopal
21 Iglesia de San Pedro y
    San Ildefonso
22 Iglesia de la Magdalena

In the grounds outside stands what's left of the city's **castillo** and is where the city walls are best preserved.

Museo de Semana Santa

About 1km north-east along the northern perimeter of the old town, this museum's main attraction is the *pasos*, statues dating mostly from the beginning of this century and depicting the Passion of Christ. They are hauled out every Easter for Zamora's colourful processions. The museum is open Monday to Saturday from 10 am to 2 pm and 4 to 8 pm (to 7 pm in winter) and Sunday and holidays from 10 am to 2 pm (250 ptas). Across the road, the Iglesia de Santa María La Nueva retains some elements of the 12th century Romanesque original.

Churches

Zamora is dotted with churches built in the 12th century, but in most cases they have been much altered. Among those retaining some of their Romanesque charm are the

Iglesia de San Pedro y San Ildefonso (with Gothic touches), **Iglesia de la Magdalena** (be sure to see the southern doorway, considered the city's best) and **Iglesia de San Juan de Puerta Nueva**. They open from 10 am to 1 pm and 5 to 8 pm, and are closed on Monday.

Canoeing
Groups interested in canoeing along the Río Duero might like to approach Turisnautic (☎ 980 51 10 53), Calle de la Amargura 2.

Special Events
Easter is a good time to be in Zamora, with many processions, some involving the unique pasos, taking place through most of Semana Santa (Holy Week).

Places to Stay & Eat
Hostal Siglo XX (☎ 980 53 29 08, Plaza del Seminario 1) is in a pleasant, quiet spot and has simple singles/doubles for 1950/3500 ptas. *Pensión Balborraz* (☎ 51 55 19, Calle de Balborraz 25-29) offers more spacious rooms for 1500/3000 ptas. More attractive than either is the *Hostal La Reina* (☎ 980 53 39 39, Calle de la Reina 1), with doubles for 2500 ptas with washbasin only, 3600 ptas with private bath. Those requiring a little more style could try the *Hostería Real de Zamora* (☎ 980 53 45 45, fax 980 53 45 22, Cuesta de Pizarro 7), which starts at 7250/9475 ptas plus IVA for rooms with TV and all mod cons (including breakfast). The pick of the crop is the *Parador Condes de Alba y Aliste* (☎ 980 51 44 97, fax 980 53 00 63, Plaza Viriato 5), where princely rooms start at 13,000 ptas.

Restaurante El Lagar on Calle del Sacramento is an inviting place to try some *cabrito* (kid meat).

Entertainment
For a relaxing coffee or beer and a bit of people-watching, the cafés on Plaza Mayor are fine. If it's late-night drinking you're after, head off the square down the narrow Calle de los Herreros, which is jammed

with pubs and bars. A little more sedate is *La Cueva del Jazz (Cuesta del Piñedo 5)*.

Getting There & Away
Bus The estación de autobuses is a good half-hour's walk from the centre and there are no local buses. Still, bus is generally the best way to get to Zamora. Regular services link it with Salamanca (475 ptas; 13 daily), Valladolid (seven daily), Benavente (eight daily), León (five daily) and Madrid (3¼ hours; six daily). A couple of buses run to places as far away as Santiago de Compostela and Sevilla, as well as into Portugal.

Train The train station is just down the hill from the estación de autobuses. There are up to six trains daily to Madrid (Chamartín). A couple of these go via Ávila and one goes on to Zaragoza and Barcelona. Two trains head for Galicia (Vigo, Pontevedra and La Coruña).

Car & Motorcycle See the following Beyond Zamora section for routes out of Zamora.

AROUND ZAMORA
North to León
The N-630 heads directly north from Zamora to León. There is little to hold you up on the way, but in **Benavente** a *parador* (luxury hotel) has been built around the impressive Torre del Caracol, a squat 15th century castle tower. About 30km before, just south of the village of Granja de Moreruela, lie the ramshackle ruins of a 12th century **monastery** in a perfect state of bucolic abandon, 4km down a track west of the highway.

From Benavente you could skew west along the N-525 for La Puebla de Sanabria and on to Galicia (see the To Galicia section later), or keep bearing north for León or north-west towards Astorga and on to pick up the Camino de Santiago at Villafranca del Bierzo (see the Camino de Santiago special section later in this book for more information). Major roads also run east to

Palencia and Valladolid. Buses run to Benavente and on to León from Zamora.

To Portugal

Even if Portugal is not on your itinerary, if you have a vehicle it is worth considering heading west to the fascinating northern Portuguese town of Bragança.

To Galicia

An alternative route to Galicia runs northwest from Zamora between the Sierra de la Culebra and Sierra de la Cabrera.

La Puebla de Sanabria Here a captivating little web of medieval alleyways unfolds around the 15th century castle, built with an eye to nearby Portugal by the fourth Conde de Benavente. You can enter the castle at will and wander around the walls.

There are several hotels at the foot of the old town. *Hostal Galicia (☎ 980 62 01 06, Calle de las Ánimas 22)* has basic singles for 1800 ptas, while the nearby *Hotel Victoria (☎ 980 62 00 12, Csalle del Arrabal 29)* has doubles for 5300 ptas. *Cervecería Veti*, just off Plaza Mayor near the castle, has cheap tapas and wine.

By car you can follow the N-525 west from La Puebla over the Portilla de la Canda on the way to Verín, in Galicia. From there you could swing northwards to Orense or push on for the Rías Bajas on the Atlantic. There are buses between La Puebla and Benavente.

León & the North-West

Once the centre of Christian Spain, León now stands like a sentinel at the rim of the great Castilian heartland. The last major city on the Camino de Santiago before it climbs west into the sierras that separate Castilla from Galicia, León is also the final staging post on the road north towards the Cordillera Cantábrica and Asturias – a lush, green idyll worlds away from these sundrenched expanses. For all that, even before

you cross into Galicia, Asturias or Cantabria, you can feel the coming changes in climate, landscape, language and people. And even the Picos de Europa mountains (see the Cantabria & Asturias chapter) spill over here into Castilla y León's most northerly reaches.

LEÓN

For a couple of centuries León was the flourishing capital of the expanding Christian kingdom of Asturias and León, and the city retains a powerful hold over its visitors. In possession of the two jewels of Spanish Romanesque and Gothic creativity, the city is also liberally sprinkled with less exalted reminders of its glory days and blessed with a bustling city centre, itself a successful marriage of medieval inheritance and thoughtful modern town planning.

History

In 70 AD a Roman legion made camp at a place where later the city of León would rise. The imperial troops were based here to control the gold mines of Las Médulas, farther west. A residual settlement muddled along until the Asturian King Ordoño II decided to move his capital here from Oviedo in the 10th century. Later sacked by Al-Mansour, León was nevertheless maintained by Alfonso V as the capital of his growing kingdom, a role it continued to play until the union with Castilla in 1230. It was in this period that the city reached its zenith. Centuries of decline followed, but mining brought León back to life in the 19th century.

In this respect, the city has more in common with its Asturian neighbours across the Cordillera to the north than with its Castilian sister cities to the south and east. During the Second Republic León's workers joined their Asturian comrades in the bloody, and ultimately futile, October revolt of 1934.

Orientation

The train and bus stations lie on the western bank of the Río Bernesga, while the heart of the city is concentrated on the eastern side. Cross the river at the bridge nearest the train station and head east along Avenida de Ordoño II. From the river to the cathedral it's about a kilometre, with Plaza de Santo Domingo marking the halfway point. There are plenty of banks, hotels and pensiones on or off this axis and a good number of the restaurants and bars are within a short walking distance of the cathedral.

Information

Tourist Office The tourist office (☎ 987 23 70 82), Plaza de la Regla 3 (opposite the cathedral), is open Monday to Friday from 10 am to 2 pm and 5 to 8 pm, on Saturday from 9 am to 2.30 pm and 4.30 to 8.30 pm and Sunday from 11 am to 2 pm and 4.30 to 8.30 pm.

Money There are a number of banks along Avenida de Ordoño II. La Caixa, at No 11, has a 24-hour ATM.

Post & Communications The correos is on Avenida de la Independencia, just off Plaza de San Francisco. Central León's postcode is 24080. There is a Telefónica phone office at Calle del Burgo Nuevo 15. It is open Monday to Friday from 9 am to 2.30 pm and 4 to 11 pm and Saturday from 10 am to 2 pm and 4 to 9 pm.

Travel Agencies TIVE (☎ 987 20 09 51), Calle del Arquitecto Torbado 4, can help with student travel information and low-priced tickets.

Medical Services & Emergency In emergencies, call the police on ☎ 091 – there is a Policía Nacional comisaría on Calle de Villa de Benavente. For an ambulance call either ☎ 987 24 24 24 or ☎ 987 23 23 23. All-night pharmacy rotas are listed in the local paper, *Diario de León*.

Walking Tour

If you started from the busy traffic circus of Plaza de Santo Domingo and headed east into Plaza de San Marcelo, you would see the Renaissance-era palace that now houses the town **ayuntamiento**. A few paces farther north along the latter plaza stands Antoni Gaudí's contribution to León's skyline, the rather subdued neo-Gothic **Casa de Botines**.

Next up as you enter Calle del Generalísimo Franco is another Renaissance block, the **Palacio de los Guzmanes**, whose best features are the façade and patio. Another few hundred metres bring you to the **catedral**, from where you could venture north-west to the equally unmissable **Real Basílica de San Isidoro**. A 15 minute walk west leads to the **Hostal San Marcos**, or you can backtrack from the basilica to Calle del Generalísimo Franco. This serves as a jumping-off point for the medieval heart of León.

It's fun just to wander the streets, but worth making a conscious effort to see is the 17th century **Plaza Mayor**. Sealed off on three sides by shady porticoes and curiously devoid of cafés, it only comes alive on Saturday, market day. Another captivating square is **Plaza de Santa María del Camino**, a broad, uneven cobblestone expanse whose most outstanding features are the Romanesque **Iglesia de Santa María del Mercado** and an extremely photogenic old house and bar. From mid-June to mid-September, official walking tours are organised around the centre of León, usually twice daily (500 ptas). On weekends, evening tours are also a possibility. Ask at the tourist office for details.

Catedral

Whether spotlit by night or bathed in the glorious northern sunshine, what is one of Spain's greatest masterpieces of Gothic fancy exudes an almost luminous quality. People aren't the cathedral's only admirers, for day and night, good weather or bad, every possible pinnacle doubles as a perch for a member of León's numerous stork populace.

The main western façade is both magnificent and something of a flop. There's no doubting the quality of the sculpture and craftwork in among the pointed arches – the Last Judgment in the

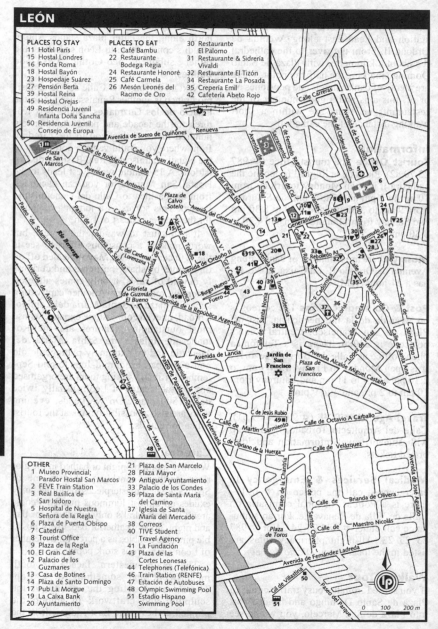

LEÓN

PLACES TO STAY
11 Hotel París
15 Hostal Londres
16 Fonda Roma
18 Hostal Bayón
23 Hospedaje Suárez
27 Pensión Berta
39 Hostal Reina
45 Hostal Orejas
49 Residencia Juvenil
     Infanta Doña Sancha
50 Residencia Juvenil
     Consejo de Europa

PLACES TO EAT
4 Café Bambú
22 Restaurante
     Bodega Regia
24 Restaurante Honoré
25 Café Carmela
26 Mesón Leonés del
     Racimo de Oro

30 Restaurante
     El Palomo
31 Restaurante & Sidrería
     Vivaldi
32 Restaurante El Tizón
34 Restaurante La Posada
35 Crepería Emil
42 Cafetería Abeto Rojo

OTHER
1 Museo Provincial;
    Parador Hostal San Marcos
2 FEVE Train Station
3 Real Basílica de
    San Isidoro
5 Hospital de Nuestra
    Señora de la Regla
6 Plaza de Puerta Obispo
7 Catedral
8 Tourist Office
9 Plaza de la Regla
10 El Gran Café
12 Palacio de los
     Guzmanes
13 Casa de Botines
14 Plaza de Santo Domingo
17 Pub La Morgue
19 La Caixa Bank
20 Ayuntamiento
21 Plaza de San Marcelo
28 Plaza Mayor
29 Antiguo Ayuntamiento
33 Palacio de los Condes
36 Plaza de Santa María
     del Camino
37 Iglesia de Santa
     María del Mercado
38 Correos
40 TIVE Student
     Travel Agency
41 La Fundación
43 Plaza de las
     Cortes Leonesas
44 Telephones (Telefónica)
46 Train Station (RENFE)
47 Estación de Autobuses
48 Olympic Swimming Pool
51 Estadio Hispano
     Swimming Pool

0   100   200 m

tympanum (the semi-circle above the main entrance) is particularly evocative. The problem is, the stone is of poor quality and will pose a challenge to those called on to preserve the grandeur of the church.

And grand it is. Inside, three naves lead to the transept, from which five naves pass on to the apse. You'll only notice this, though, if you tear your eyes from the extraordinary stained-glass windows, French in inspiration and mostly executed from the 13th to the 16th centuries. Aside from the three huge rose windows, there are some 30 grand kaleidoscopic windows around the main body of the church, and numerous smaller ones.

Adjoining the church proper is an unusually florid cloister, off which a series of rooms display what remains of the cathedral's riches, mostly religious art ranging from early Romanesque through to the baroque. A good deal of the cathedral's once exceptional wealth in gold and silver was melted down to finance the good fight against Napoleon in the Peninsular War. The cathedral and its museum are open Monday to Saturday from 9.30 am to 1 pm and 4 to 6.30 pm and Sunday morning. Entry to the museum and cloister costs 450 ptas. Or you can visit the cloister and part of the museum for 250 ptas. The bad news is that the guided tour of the museum and cloister (in Spanish) is unavoidable: the guides open and close each room as they go.

Real Basílica de San Isidoro

A step back further in history, San Isidoro is as seminal a work of Romanesque as the cathedral is a gem of Gothic. The right-hand entrance (Puerta del Perdón) has been attributed to Maestro Mateo, the genius of the cathedral at Santiago de Compostela.

You first enter what was initially a portico in front of the original main entrance to the basilica. The entrance was later sealed off and the portico became a burial place for early Leonese and Castilian royalty, later known as the **Panteón Real**. More than 40 kings, queens, princes and counts were buried here – you can see a roll posted up next to the former church entrance. Napoleon's troops sacked San Isidoro in the early 19th century, leaving behind them only about five sarcophagi. What they couldn't take remains today as one of the greatest treasures of Romanesque art in Spain, if not all Europe.

The frescoes that cover the vaults and arches of the Panteón represent the cream of 12th century art, depicting a range of Biblical scenes, among them the Annunciation, to the right of the former church entrance; King Herod's slaughter of the innocent infants; and the Last Supper, on the main central vault. One vault back is a particularly striking representation of Christ Pantocrator. Also worth noting is the medieval agricultural calendar inside an arch to the left of the church entrance. The heavily restored Romanesque wall of the otherwise Hispano-Flemish Gothic main cloister was originally the external wall of the church. Much of the gold and jewellery held as part of the church treasures was stolen by Napoleon's troops. What remains can be seen in the rooms constituting the basilica's museum.

The museum is open daily from 10 am to 1.30 pm and 4 to 6.30 pm (300 ptas). In July and August the timetable is 9 am to 2 pm and 3 to 8 pm. On Sunday it is open only for the morning session. The church remains open night and day by historical royal edict. Entry to the Panteón and other parts of the museum entails joining a guided tour.

Hostal de San Marcos

Back in the 12th century, the Knights of Santiago took up residence at this pilgrimage way station, but the bulk of what stands today was remodelled in the 16th century and the façade is largely plateresque. It is now getting some much needed restorative treatment. Behind lie the church, Museo Provincial (to the right) and the former monastery, now one of the country's better parador hotels. The museum is housed in the *sala capitular* (chapterhouse) and boasts an admirable artesonado ceiling. From the museum, given over mostly to archaeology, you pass into the cloister.

It has to be said that you can wander into the cloister from the foyer of the parador, although strictly speaking you're not supposed to. To observe the artesonado ceiling, you could enter the parador and look through the glass doors immediately to the right. The museum is open Monday to Saturday from 10 am to 2 pm and 5 to 8.30 pm (or 4.30 to 8 pm from October to April) and Sunday from 10 am to 2 pm (200 ptas).

Special Events

Although not known for the splendour of its fiestas, León does stir for Semana Santa and, more so, from 21 to 30 June for the Fiestas de San Juan y San Pedro.

Places to Stay

Hostels León's two youth hostels are open only in July and August and are fairly uninspiring buildings. The *Residencia Juvenil Consejo de Europa (☎ 987 20 02 06, Paseo del Parque 2)* and the *Residencia Juvenil Infanta Doña Sancha (☎ 987 20 34 14, Calle de la Corredera 2)* offer beds for 850 ptas for HI members under 26 or 1200 ptas for older members.

Hotels *Pensión Berta (☎ 987 25 70 39, Plaza Mayor 8)* has basic singles/doubles for 1800/3000 ptas. The position is unbeatable. *Hospedaje Suárez (☎ 987 25 42 88, Calle del Generalísimo Franco 7)* has similar rooms for 1700/3000 ptas, if you can get in. *Hostal Bayón (☎ 987 23 14 46, Calle del Alcázar de Toledo 6)* is run by a friendly woman who keeps clean rooms for 2700/3500 ptas. The *Fonda Roma (☎ 987 22 46 63, Avenida de Roma 4)* has dirt cheap rooms at 1100/1700 ptas.

At *Hotel Reina (☎ 987 20 52 12, Calle de Puerta de la Reina 2)* you can get rooms with basin for 1870/3300 ptas or with private bath for 4500/4700 ptas. *Hostal Orejas (☎ 987 25 29 09, Calle de Villafranca 8)* is a pretty good deal. Singles/ doubles with TV and telephone cost 2900/ 5000 ptas.

Also with TV and more spacious rooms is *Hostal Londres (☎ 987 22 22 74, Avenida de Roma 1)*. It has doubles only, which start at 5000 ptas.

A much better deal is *Hotel París (☎ 987 23 86 00, fax 987 27 15 72, Calle del Generalísimo Franco 20)*. It is actually two hotels, one with basic singles/doubles for 3500/5500 ptas, and another next door, with rooms starting at 5600/7500 ptas. *Parador Hostal San Marcos (☎ 987 23 73 00, fax 987 23 34 58, Plaza de San Marcos 7)* has rooms fit for royalty at 21,500 ptas plus IVA.

Places to Eat

There is any number of places to try out for breakfast, but *Cafetería Abeto Rojo (Calle de Burgo Nuevo 26)* has a decent deal. Coffee, juice and toast costs 275 ptas at the bar until midday.

At the end of the day, *Café Bambú*, behind the cathedral on Avenida de los Cubos, is a sedate vantage point for gazing on the floodlit apse of the cathedral.

The lifeblood of León's nocturnal activity flows most thickly through the aptly dubbed Barrio Húmedo (Wet Quarter), a heavy concentration of bars and restaurants packed into the crowded tangle of lanes leading south off Calle del Generalísimo Franco. Plaza de San Martín, for instance, is a particularly pleasant part of the centre for food and drinks. *Restaurante El Tizón* at No 1 is good for wine and meat dishes, and offers an abundant set meal for 1600 ptas. There are a few decent pizzerias and bars on the same square.

Restaurante Honoré (Calle de los Serradores 4) has a good-value set lunch for 950 ptas, while *Café Carmela (Calle de Caño Badillo 7)* has an inviting and relaxed atmosphere for snacks and coffee. *Mesón Leonés del Racimo de Oro* at No 2 is a long-established restaurant and reputable place where mains cost around 1600 ptas. In a similar price league, *Restaurante Bodega Regia (Calle del General Mola 5)* is a good spot for outdoor eating in summer.

Restaurante La Posada (Calle de la Rúa 31) is another popular *leonés* restaurant.

Restaurante El Palomo, on the tiny Calle de la Escalerilla off Plaza Mayor, is a quality establishment with a set lunch for 1300 ptas. Next door is the **Restaurante & Sidrería Vivaldi**, also popular, and one of the few places in León where you can get an Asturian cider.

For dessert, you might like to try *Crepería Emil (Calle de la Misericordia 8)*, with a pretty good imitation of the French original.

Entertainment

Bars Away from the traditional Barrio Húmedo area, a series of streets heading north of Calle del Generalísimo Franco is lined with bars to suit most tastes. *El Gran Café* on Calle de Cervantes is a classy and popular spot for a drink, but there are plenty of other possibilities along this street, Calle de Fernando Regueral and Calle del Sacramento.

Discos There are a few possibilities for dancing until dawn. Friday nights are the best for this sort of thing at *Pub La Morgue*, a noisy place for the young *bakalao* (techno) scene on the corner of Avenida de Roma and Calle del Cardenal Lorenzana. A more mixed crowd and music can be found until 6 am at *La Fundación*, just off Burgo Nuevo. It is one of a couple of discos and bars in the same area.

Getting There & Away

Bus Empresa Fernández has as many as eight buses to Madrid daily. The trip takes 4½ hours. Frequent buses also run to Astorga. Other destinations include Bilbao, Oviedo, Salamanca, Valladolid and Zamora.

Train Up to 10 trains daily leave for Madrid. Plenty of trains head west to Astorga, north to Oviedo and Gijón, and south to Valladolid. There are three to Barcelona and up to five to La Coruña and other destinations in Galicia.

FEVE trains run only as far as Guardo on this private line which links León with the País Vasco. These trains leave from a separate station at the northern end of the city centre.

Car & Motorcycle The N-630 heads north to Oviedo, although the A-66 tollway parallel to the west is faster. The N-630 also continues south to Sevilla via Salamanca. For Galicia take the N-120. The N-601 heads south-east for Valladolid.

EAST OF LEÓN
Iglesia de San Miguel de Escalada

In simplicity often lies a potent beauty – this restored and somewhat out-of-place treasure is a fine demonstration of the thought. Originally built in 930 by refugee monks from Córdoba, it displays the horseshoe arch typical of Muslim-inspired architecture but not often seen so far north in Spain. The graceful exterior porch is balanced by the impressive marble columns within. It is open Tuesday to Saturday from 10 am to 2 pm and 4 to 7 pm and Sunday from 10 am to 3 pm (free).

You really need your own vehicle, as there is no nearby accommodation and the two buses from León seem timed to render a visit impossible.

Sahagún & Around

An unremarkable place today, Sahagún was once home to one of Spain's more powerful abbeys, so much so that angry locals took to sacking the place towards the end of the Middle Ages. Virtually nothing remains today. Testimony to the strong Mozarabic community that once lived here are the two charming Romanesque-mudéjar churches, San Tirso next to the remains of the abbey and San Lorenzo, just north of Plaza Mayor. The former (open Tuesday to Saturday from 10.30 am to 1.30 pm and 4 to 7 pm, and on Sunday morning) was built in the 12th century and the latter 100 years later. Both have unusually fat bell towers laced with arches. San Lorenzo only opens its doors for Mass on Sunday. Near San Tirso, Benedictine nuns have a small museum containing a monstrous monstrance by Enrique de Arfe (he and his son Antonio and grandson Juan seem to have left them scattered all over Spain), but more often than not the place is closed and there's not a nun to be seen.

There are a few *hostales* scattered about town, and a few eateries where you can get a bite. The occasional bus comes through from León, and one from Valladolid, but you're better off with a train along the León-Palencia-Valladolid line.

WEST OF LEÓN

From León the old pilgrim road gradually climbs over the Montes de León and beyond into El Bierzo country – an area that displays greater similarities with Galicia than with Castilla. Finally, after Villafranca del Bierzo and one last rest, the real ascent into the Galician highlands begins.

On the way the town of Astorga, with its grand cathedral, Roman remains and splash of Gaudí, is an obvious place to call in. Farther on, Ponferrada's castle and the former Roman gold mines of Las Médulas are also worth detours before resting up in Villafranca and moving on to Galicia.

Astorga

It was the Romans who put Asturica Augusta on the map, at the head of the Ruta de la Plata. The traffic in precious metals under the Romans gave way to pilgrim traffic in the Middle Ages, and by the 15th century the town had reached its apogee. The cathedral was raised at this time, and the busy town was liberally sprinkled with hospices for pilgrims on the Camino de Santiago. Astorga's 3rd century walls were also rebuilt then but it was not until the 19th century that the cathedral acquired its distinctive neo-Gothic neighbour, Gaudí's Palacio Episcopal.

Astorga lies in a zone known as the Maragatería. Many claim the Maragatos, who with their mule trains dedicated themselves almost exclusively to the carrying trade, were descendants of the first Berbers to enter Spain in the Muslim armies of the 8th century. Local historians dismiss such assertions as pure fantasy.

Orientation & Information Astorga's old centre is compact and simple to navigate. The cathedral and Palacio Episcopal huddle together in the north-western corner of the casco antiguo, and the tourist office (☎ 987 61 68 38) lies between the two on Plaza de Eduardo de Castro. The office is open Monday to Saturday from 10 am to 2 pm and 4 to 6 pm and Sunday from 11 am to 2 pm.

Catedral & Palacio Episcopal Work on the cathedral, begun in 1471 on the site of its Romanesque predecessor, proceeded in stop-start fashion over three centuries. This led to a predictable mix of styles, with the lavishly worked plateresque main façade standing in stark contrast to the more severe Flemish Gothic elements exemplified in the apse area. Inside, the 16th century retablo behind the main altar monopolises the visitor's gaze. The museum attached to the cathedral has a varied collection of the usual religious art, documents and curios.

It was Gaudí's flair that gave Astorga its unique skyline and in some respects the more conventional cathedral seems to fade before the Catalan's extravagance. Built for the local bishop from the end of the 19th century, the Palacio Episcopal (or Palacio de Gaudí) has a typically eccentric exterior, but is bereft of interior detail. Inside, the Museo de los Caminos has Roman artefacts and religious art.

The cathedral and the Palacio Episcopal are open in summer from 10 am to 2 pm and 4 to 8 pm. The cathedral closes on Sunday, except during August. Note that entry to the Palacio Episcopal and the Museo de la Catedral each cost 250 ptas, or you can pay 400 ptas for both – you must ask specifically for the combined ticket.

Museo del Chocolate Astorga was once the capital of Spanish chocolate production, and this small private collection of old chocolate-making implements, advertising and the like could be one for the children. At Calle de José María Goy 5, the museum is open daily from noon to 2 pm and 6 to 8 pm. You can leave a small donation for upkeep.

Roman Ruins Those interested in the city's Roman origins can join a free guided tour from the tourist office (once or twice daily) to visit the Roman walls (rebuilt in medieval times), the ancient *ergastula* (prison), in the basement of the 17th century ayuntamiento, and several other minor excavation sites.

Special Events The last week of August is the most exciting time to be in Astorga,

when the city celebrates the Festividad de Santa Marta with fireworks, dances and bullfights.

Places to Stay Try, if possible, to get a room in the town itself. *Pensión García* (☎ 987 61 60 46, Bajada Postigo 5) has simple rooms for 2000/3000 ptas. Much better is the *Pensión La Peseta* (☎ 987 61 72 75, Plaza de San Bartolomé 3) but it costs 5000/7100 ptas. The pick of the crop is the *Hotel Gaudí* (☎ 987 61 50 40, Calle de Eduardo de Castro 6), with doubles for 9500 ptas plus IVA (less out of the high season).

Places to Eat *Pensión García* has a solid restaurant, while the kitchen at *Pensión La Peseta* is known well beyond the limits of Astorga. For tapas, *Restaurante La Paloma* (Calle de Pío Gullón 16) is good. Another

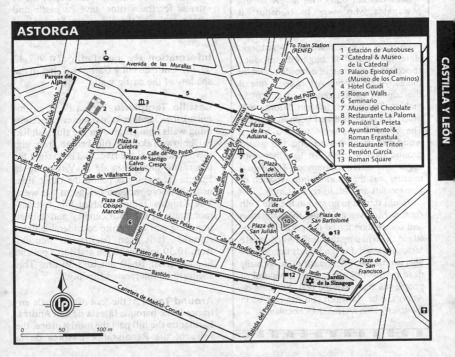

ASTORGA

1 Estación de Autobuses
2 Catedral & Museo de la Catedral
3 Palacio Episcopal (Museo de los Caminos)
4 Hotel Gaudí
5 Roman Walls
6 Seminario
7 Museo del Chocolate
8 Restaurante La Paloma
9 Pensión La Peseta
10 Ayuntamiento & Roman Ergastula
11 Restaurante Tritón
12 Pensión García
13 Roman Square

CASTILLA Y LEÓN

pleasant little place is **Restaurante Triton** (*Plaza de San Julián*). At the **Hotel Gaudí**, you can dine in elegance with a set lunch for 1500 ptas.

Getting There & Away By far the most convenient way in and out of Astorga is by bus – the station is nearly across the road from the cathedral. There are regular buses

The First Chocolatiers

Hernán Cortés, they say, first sipped a bitter chocolate drink in the palace of Moctezuma back in the 16th century. It was a while before the idea started to get around that it tasted much better if mixed with sugar, and by that stage the odd new beverage had begun to spread across Europe. When the first loads landed in Spain's Galician ports, not a few of the Maragatos who were to transport it around the country saw some business potential and were quick to introduce it in the main town of their home turf – Astorga. Here the townsfolk began to produce chocolate in commercial quantities, and by the early 17th century Astorga was one of the country's main centres of chocolate making. The process used in Astorga was much the same as it had been in Mexico. The cocoa beans were toasted over a wood fire, hand-peeled and the grains ground over a small fire together with sugar and often cinnamon. The liquid mixture was then poured into wooden or zinc moulds and left to cool – simple.

Things started to go sour in the late 19th century, however, as greater mechanisation and competition forced the price of chocolate in Spain to drop drastically. As chocolate factories closed, foreign brands flooded the Spanish market. The industry was virtually dead by the 1950s, although a handful of people still churn out the real *chocolate de Astorga*, a bar of which you can pick up in the town's little Museo del Chocolate.

to León and Ponferrada. If you do arrive by train, the station is a couple of kilometres north of town.

Around Astorga

Whatever you make of the stories surrounding the Maragatos, the 5km detour to **Castrillo de los Polvazares**, one of their villages, is a pleasant diversion. The hamlet is built of a vivid orange stone, made all the more striking by the brilliant green paint job on the doors and window frames. In late July the place livens up with the Fiestas de la Magdalena.

Ponferrada

Named after an iron bridge (*pons ferrata*) built in 1092, Ponferrada is definitely not one of the region's more enticing towns. Despite a long history, the arrival of the steel industry in the early 20th century and the resultant urban sprawl have left little of interest for the visitor, save its castle and what remains of the old centre. Stay only if you have no other choice.

Information The tourist office (☎ 987 42 42 36), Calle de Gil y Carrasco 4, lies in the shadow of the castle walls.

Castillo Templario The castle is an unmistakable landmark, its somewhat crumbling walls rising high over the sluggish Río Sil below. Take the old bridge from the town centre over the river and head right for the castle and Plaza de la Virgen de la Encina. The entry is round the other side, near the more modern bridge to the west. The Knights Templar raised this fortress-monastery in the 13th century and it is an imposing edifice despite considerable deterioration. It is open Tuesday to Saturday from 10.30 am to 1.30 pm and 4 to 7 pm and Sunday from 10.30 am to 1.30 pm. This seems to be interpreted flexibly.

Around Town At the foot of the castle entrance is the baroque **Iglesia de San Andrés**. Farther up the hill past the tourist office, the spire of the Renaissance **Basílica de la**

Virgen de la Encina dominates the square of the same name. Otherwise there is precious little of old Ponferrada. Following Calle del Reloj to the gateway that gives the street its name, you enter Plaza del Ayuntamiento – a grave disappointment. The only building of any significance is the baroque **casa consistorial** (council building), which was covered in scaffolding at the time of writing.

Places to Stay Ponferrada is not the nicest place to stay (Astorga is preferable). If you must, finding accommodation should be no problem. There are a few hostales near the train station if you need to make a quick getaway. Otherwise, *Pensión Mondelo* (☎ 987 41 14 84, *Calle de Flores Osorio*) is the only option in the old part of town, just off Calle del Reloj. It has basic rooms for 1700/2800 ptas.

In the new town, *Hostal San Miguel* (☎ 987 41 10 47, *Calle de Luciana Fernández 2*) is a comfortable option fairly close to the old centre, but only has doubles. The rooms (with TV and telephone) cost 4000 ptas.

Places to Eat *Mesón Mosteiro (Calle del Reloj 10)* does cheap set meals and is about the only place where you'll get a full meal in the old town. *Mesón El Quijote (Calle de Gregoria Campillo 3)*, just across the river in the new town, is also OK, and there is a pair of cheap places on Calle Matachana, an alley a couple of blocks farther away from the river.

Getting There & Away The estación de autobuses is awkwardly located at the northern end of town (local bus No 3 runs into the centre and to Plaza del Ayuntamiento). ALSA has five daily buses from Ponferrada to Madrid. Heading west, there are buses to most main Galician cities, with six to Lugo and five to Santiago de Compostela. ALSA also has a couple of buses to Bilbao. Regular buses run through Ponferrada between Villafranca del Bierzo and León (via Astorga).

The train station is on the west side of the centre. Eight trains daily run to León via Astorga, and four or five eastwards into Galicia. Two trains run daily to Madrid and three to Barcelona.

Around Ponferrada

A unique excursion, but one most easily done with your own transport (a daily bus runs from Ponferrada to Carucedo) would take you to the ancient Roman gold mines at **Las Médulas**.

You can drive beyond Las Médulas village (4km south of Carucedo and the N-536 highway, about 20km south-west of Ponferrada) into the heart of the former quarries, from where several trails weave away among chestnut patches and weird orange formations left behind by the miners. The Romans honeycombed the area with canals and tunnels through which they pumped water to break up the rock and free from it the gold they wanted. The result is a singularly unnatural natural phenomenon.

About 15km along the N-536 from Ponferrada to Carucedo (for Las Médulas), you'll notice the ruins of the **Castillo de Cornatel**, another Templar fortress high up on a precipice.

Eastern Castilla y León

BURGOS

A mighty chilly place in winter, with a distinctly northern European feel, Burgos makes the ideal location for Spain's greatest Gothic cathedral. The massive church entirely dominates the elegant old town centre, and houses here are characterised by the glassed-in balconies or *galerías* more readily associated with seaside towns in Galicia. On the eastern and western limits of the town are a couple of admirable monasteries.

History

Like so many Castilian towns, Burgos started life as a strategic fortress – in 884, most historians believe – facing off both the Muslims and the rival kingdom of Navarra. Around it was grouped a series of little villages, or *burgos*, which eventually would melt together to form the basis of a new city. Centuries later, Burgos was thriving as a way station on the Camino de Santiago and as a trading centre between the interior and the northern ports. Until well into the 17th century, the city's wealth came in from wool exports, mostly through Bilbao, which in turn sold Burgos much needed iron. Franco made Burgos his 'capital' during the civil war, and the industrial development he encouraged here in the 1950s and 60s brought a degree of prosperity to the city.

Orientation

The heart of old Burgos, dominated by the cathedral, is ensconced between the Río Arlanzón and the hill to the north-west that still bears remnants of the town's old castle. South of the river, in the newer half of town, you'll find the bus and train stations. The former is handily placed for some budget hotels and a quick walk from the cathedral. You'll find a couple of tourist offices on the north bank, one right by the cathedral.

Information

Tourist Offices The main regional tourist office (☎ 947 20 31 25), at Plaza Alonso Martínez 7, has good information on the city and province of Burgos in particular. It is open Monday to Friday from 10 am to 2 pm and 5 to 7 pm and Saturday from 10 am to 2 pm. There's another booth (☎ 947 27 94 32) at Calle de la Asunción de Nuestra Señora 3, open daily from 10.30 am to 2 pm and 4 to 8 pm (morning only on Sunday).

Money There are banks all over central Burgos. Citibank has a branch on Plaza del Rey Fernando, near the cathedral.

Post & Communications The main correos is on Plaza del Conde de Castro. The postcode is 09080. You'll find a Telefónica locutorio on Calle de San Lesmes. It is open

daily from 9.30 am to 3 pm, and Monday to Friday again from 5.30 to 11 pm.

Medical Services & Emergency The Policía Nacional headquarters is on Avenida de Castilla y León. The Hospital General Yagüe (☎ 947 28 18 00) is on Avenida del Cid Campeador.

Old Quarter

If you wander out of the estación de autobuses and north to cross the Río Arlanzón at the Puente de Santa María, you find yourself with the pleasant garden-like Paseo del Espolón off to the right, beyond which a great statue of El Cid looks as if about to set off in hot pursuit of some recalcitrant Muslims.

Directly ahead is the massive Arco de Santa María, which once formed part of the 14th century walls. It now hosts temporary exhibitions and a minor museum. Pass through and you find yourself confronted by the city's symbol, the cathedral.

Catedral

It is difficult to imagine that on the site of this Gothic giant there once stood a modest Romanesque church. Work on its replacement began in 1221, and within 40 years the bulk of it was finished, a dizzying masterpiece in the French Gothic style. The twin towers, which went up in the 15th century, each represent 84m of richly decorated fantasy. Probably the most impressive of the entrances is the Puerta del Sarmental, on the south flank.

Of the chapels inside, the Capilla del Condestable is a remarkable late 15th century production bridging Gothic and plateresque styles. It, like great swathes of the cathedral at the time of writing, was off limits as restoration work is carried out. The sculptures at this end of the church behind the high altar are a highlight, as is the Escalera Dorada (gilded stairway) on the north side, the handiwork of Diego de Siloé.

Beneath the star-vaulted central dome lies the tomb of El Cid, while the most intriguing chapel is probably the Capilla del

BURGOS

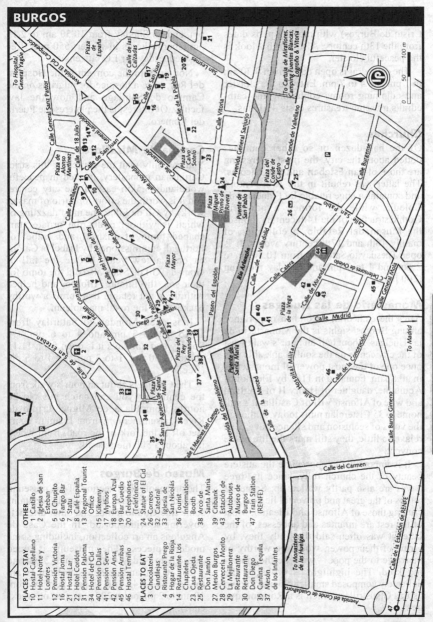

PLACES TO STAY
10 Hostal Castellano
11 Hotel Norte y Londres
12 Pensión Victoria
16 Hostal Joma
17 Hostal Lar
22 Hotel Cordón
31 Pensión Paloma
34 Hotel del Cid
40 Pensión Dallas
41 Pensión Seve
42 Pensión Ansa
45 Pensión Arribas
46 Hostal Temiño

PLACES TO EAT
3 Chocolatería Candilejas
4 Ristorante Prego
9 Hogar de la Rioja
14 Restaurante Los Chapiteles
23 Casa Ojeda
25 Restaurante Don Jamón
27 Mesón Burgos
28 Cervecería Morito
29 La Mejillonera
30 Restaurante Don Diego
35 Cantina Tequila
37 Mesón de los Infantes

OTHER
1 Castillo
2 Iglesia de San Esteban
5 El Chupito
6 Tango Bar
7 Statu
8 Café España
13 Regional Tourist Office
15 Kilkenny
18 Mythos
19 Europa Azul
20 Bar Guedio
21 Telephones (Telefónica)
24 Statue of El Cid
26 Correos
32 Catedral
33 Iglesia de San Nicolás
36 Tourist Information Booth
38 Arco de Santa María
39 Citibank
43 Estación de Autobuses
44 Museo de Burgos
47 Train Station (RENFE)

Santísimo Cristo, in the south-west corner. The leather-covered Christ (known as the Cristo de Burgos) with moving parts dates from the 13th century. Also worth a look is the peaceful cloister.

The cathedral is open daily from 9.30 am to 1 pm and 4 to 7 pm. Entry to the cloister and adjoining rooms containing the cathedral's museum treasures costs 400 ptas.

Churches

Of the half-dozen or so other churches dotted about the city, the most interesting are those of **San Esteban** and **San Nicolás**. The latter was rebuilt in the 15th century and contains a huge retablo by Francisco de Colonia, while the former, a powerful Gothic structure of the 14th century, houses the **Museo del Retablo**, a collection of mainly 16th and 17th century works. It is open Tuesday to Saturday from 10.30 am to 2 pm and 4 to 7 pm and Sunday morning (200 ptas).

Monasterio de las Huelgas

After the cathedral, second in importance among Burgos' sights is the Monasterio de las Huelgas. About half an hour's walk west of the city centre on the south bank, this was once one of the most powerful monasteries in all Spain. Founded in 1187 by Eleanor of Aquitaine, daughter of Henry II of England and wife of Alfonso VIII of Castilla, it's still home to 35 Cistercian nuns today. Although the vows of seclusion and silence have been relaxed a little, they still mark the life of the convent.

It is impossible to appreciate the austere beauty of the church fully, since its three naves are also partly walled up. Some 32 tombs of the great and powerful lie here, including those of Alfonso and Eleanor. Most of the rest are infantes and abbesses; of the latter it was often said that only they, by virtue of their power, would be worthy of marriage to the pope – were he the marrying kind. The highlight is probably the delicately composed smaller cloister known as Las Claustrillas, which is a Romanesque gem.

The monastery is open Tuesday to Saturday from 10.30 am to 1.15 pm and 4 to 5.45 pm, and on Sunday from 10.30 am to 2.15 pm (shorter hours in winter; 650 ptas, free on Wednesday for EU citizens).

Not far from the convent is the **Hospital del Rey**, once a hospice for pilgrims on the Camino de Santiago and now the law faculty. Of interest is the plateresque Puerta del Romero.

Cartuja de Miraflores

You can only visit the church of this strict Carthusian monastery, located in peaceful woodlands 3.5km east of the city centre. But it is worth the effort for a trio of master works by Gil de Siloé, the most dazzling of which is without doubt the ornate star-shaped tomb of Juan II and Isabel of Portugal, commissioned by Isabel la Católica only a few years before the fall of Granada. Gil de Siloé also did the tomb for their son, the Infante Alfonso, and helped with the giant retablo that forms a worthy backdrop to the royal mausoleum.

It is open Monday to Saturday from 10.15 am to 3 pm and 4 to 6 pm. On Sunday and holidays it is open from 11.15 am to 12.30 pm, 1 to 3 pm and 4 to 6 pm (free).

The Cartuja is about an hour's walk from the centre, or you can catch bus No 26 hourly from Plaza de Miguel Primo de Rivera in summer *only* from 11 am to 9 pm. Get off at the fork in the road, from where it's about a 500 metre walk.

Museo de Burgos

The archaeological section of the museum, housed in the Casa de Miranda, contains some fine Gothic tombs and other artefacts covering a wide period. In the Casa de Ángulo is an art collection, including some modern pieces. The museum is open Tuesday to Friday from 10 am to 2 pm and 4 to 7.30 pm, and on Saturday from 10 am to 2 pm and 4.45 to 8.15 pm (Sunday from 10 am to 2 pm only; 200 ptas, free on weekends).

Special Events

Burgos' big fiestas take place in the last days of June and the first two weeks of July to celebrate the Festividad de San Pedro y San Pablo (Feast of Saints Peter and Paul). There are bullfights, pilgrimages and much merry-making, particularly on the first Sunday of July, the Día de las Peñas. Other feast days include the Festividad de San Lesmes, for the city's patron saint, on 30 January and Las Marzas, celebrated on the first Sunday of March, a veritable 'rites of spring' fiesta.

Places to Stay – Budget

Camping & Hostels The nearest camping ground, *Camping Fuentes Blancas* (☎ 947 48 60 16), is about 4km from the centre on the same road as the Cartuja de Miraflores. Bus No 26 leaves hourly from Plaza de Miguel Primo de Rivera in summer *only* from 11 am to 9 pm.

The *Albergue de la Juventud Gil de Siloé* (☎ 947 22 03 62) is inconveniently located well east of the town centre on Avenida del General Vigón and is only open from July to mid-August.

Convent Women who fancy a stint with the Cistercian nuns in the Monasterio de las Huelgas can stay for up to eight days, paying a voluntary contribution. Call ☎ 947 20 16 30.

Pensiones & Hostales There's a fair sprinkling of down-market places on both banks of the river. Virtually around the corner from the bus station and dirt cheap is *Pensión Arribas* (☎ 947 26 62 92, Calle de los Defensores de Oviedo 6), with simple singles/doubles for 1600/2800 ptas. The rooms at *Pensión Ansa* (☎ 947 20 47 67, Calle de Miranda 9), opposite the bus station, are nicer at 3000/4200 ptas, but some of the singles are tiny.

Plaza de la Vega is not a bad position, right by the river. There are a couple of places here. *Pensión Seve* (☎ 947 26 81 05) at No 8 and *Pensión Dallas* (☎ 947 20 54 57) at No 6 both have rooms with views for

about 2300/3900 ptas. The latter is marginally better (and slightly cheaper).

If you're looking for modern conveniences, you could do worse than the *Hostal Temiño* (☎ 947 20 80 35, Calle de la Concepción 14), with comfortable if uninspiring doubles ranging from 3500 to 4750 ptas. Single occupancy of the same rooms is cheaper.

Moving into the old centre, you also have a few budget possibilities. *Pensión Victoria* (☎ 947 20 15 42, Calle de San Juan 3) has OK singles/doubles with washbasin for 2600/3600 ptas. *Pensión Paloma* (☎ 947 27 65 74, Calle de la Paloma 39) has doubles starting at 2400 ptas, but you should be able to negotiate a lower rate for single occupancy. Any closer to the cathedral and you'd be in the belfry. *Hostal Joma* (☎ 947 20 33 50, Calle de San Juan 26) is basic but in the heart of the action. Rooms go for 1700/2900 ptas. Heading up the scale and farther from the centre, *Hostal Lar* (☎ 947 20 96 55, Calle de Cardenal Benlloch 1) offers singles/doubles with private bath for 3500/6100 ptas. *Hostal Castellano* (☎ 947 20 50 40, Calle de Lain Calvo 48) only seems to want to rent out doubles at 4000 ptas, but they are decent enough.

Places to Stay – Mid-Range

Hotel Norte y Londres (☎ 947 26 41 25, Plaza de Alonso Martínez 10) is in a rather charming old building. Comfy rooms with private bath, TV and telephone cost 5700/9000 ptas in the high season plus IVA.

If you can spare a little more dough, you can make an enormous leap in quality by staying at the *Hotel Cordón* (☎ 947 26 50 00, fax 947 20 02 69, Calle de la Puebla 6), where fine rooms cost 7000/12,000 ptas in the high season plus IVA.

Places to Stay – Top End

One of the city's best establishments is the *Hotel del Cid* (☎ 947 20 87 15, fax 947 26 94 60, Plaza de Santa María 8), where good rooms cost 8000/14,500 ptas plus IVA. Or, if you want to head over the top, make for the *Landa Palace* (☎ *947 20 63 43, fax 947 26 46 76*), on the N-I to Madrid, a few kilometres out of town, where you'll shell out a fantastic 14,000/33,000 ptas plus IVA in the high season.

Places to Eat

A good place for tapas and a beer is the *Restaurante Don Jamón* on Plaza del Conde de Castro. In the heart of the old town, try around Calle de la Paloma. *La Mejillonera Restaurante* at No 33 specialises in seafood snacks, while *Mesón Burgos (Calle de la Sombrerería 8)* is a simple, homely place where you can eat a filling meal for around 1200 ptas. For more beer and good *patatas bravas* (spicy fried potato), the *Cervecería Morito*, just opposite, is popular with locals.

Nearer the cathedral, *Restaurante Don Diego (Calle de Diego Porcelos 7)* has a hearty set *menú* for 950 ptas. *Hogar de la Rioja (Calle de Lain Calvo 37)* has a higher standard and more varied menu, and a full meal will cost you about 2000 ptas. Try the *escalopines de ave al oporto* (sliced chicken in port wine sauce).

Leaning a little more to the tourist trade, but solid nonetheless, is the *Mesón de los Infantes* on Calle del Corral de los Infantes, where again you won't get much change from 2000 ptas. For a change, eat Mexican at *Cantina Tequila (Calle de Santa Agueda 10)*. It has a set meal for 1500 ptas. Better still, the Italian cooking is the genuine article at *Ristorante Prego (Calle del Huerto del Rey 4)*. There is a set meal for 1700 ptas as well as scrummy pizzas.

A Burgos institution is *Casa Ojeda (Calle de la Victoria 5)*, with a fine old upstairs terrace looking across Plaza de Calvo Sotelo. Or you can just snack at the bar downstairs. Another upmarket eating house is the *Restaurante Los Chapiteles (Calle del General Santocildes 7)*. You won't get much change from 3000 ptas.

For dessert, head for *Chocolatería Candilejas (Calle de Fernán González 36)*, where you can get sticky buns, churros or milk shakes (*batidos*).

Entertainment

Cafés Burgos has a few pleasant little cafés to hang around in, one of the better ones being *Café España (Calle de Lain Calvo 12)*.

Bars & Discos If you want a night on the tiles, ease into it in the bars along Calle de San Juan. Among popular haunts along this drag are *Mythos* at No 31, *Bar Guedio* at No 30 and *Europa Azul* at No 32. Or for a Guinness try *Kilkenny* at No 23.

From here the *marcha* migrates to the area around Calle del Huerto del Rey, locally known as *las Llanas*. The area is fairly crammed with noisy music bars to suit many tastes, including *Statu*, *Tango Bar* and *El Chupito*, all on Calle del Huerto del Rey.

There are few decent discos in Burgos, but the last stage of the pub-crawl scene is the Bernardos area, around Calle de las Calzadas, where you'll find more than your fill of alcohol and loud music.

Getting There & Away

From Burgos, roads stretch off west towards León or Palencia, south to Madrid and along several axes into Cantabria, the País Vasco and east into La Rioja.

Bus The estación de autobuses is at Calle de Miranda 3. Continental-Auto runs up to 11 buses daily to Madrid, more on Fridays. Tickets cost 1970 ptas. The same company also services Santander. Regular buses also go to San Sebastián (1825 ptas), Vitoria (940 ptas), Bilbao, Pamplona, Logroño and Zaragoza via Soria. There are also services to most towns in Burgos province, and international buses to destinations as far-flung as London and Agadir (Morocco).

Train As a rule the trains are more expensive than the bus. Main routes include north-south runs from Irún and Bilbao to Madrid and on to Alicante. From east to west, other trains run through Burgos from Barcelona to Salamanca or into Galicia.

Car & Motorcycle For Madrid, take the N-I directly south. The N-234 branches off south-east to Soria and on to Zaragoza and ultimately Barcelona. The N-623 north leads to Santander, while the A-1 autopista goes most of the way to Vitoria and hooks up with the A-68 to Bilbao. The latter two are both tollways.

AROUND BURGOS

The country south-east of Burgos offers some welcome relief from the bleak plains immediately south and to the west.

Quintanilla de las Viñas

If you take the Soria road (N-234) out of Burgos, a worthwhile stop some 35km out is the 7th century Ermita de Santa María de Lara. This modest Visigothic hermitage preserves some fine bas-reliefs around its external walls, one of the better examples of Visigothic religious art to survive in Spain. It is supposedly open Wednesday to Sunday from 9.30 am to 2 pm and 5 to 8 pm in summer (9 am to 4 pm in winter), but you might have to track down the guardian in the village of Quintanilla de las Viñas.

Covarrubias

This pretty hamlet struggles to digest the tourist influx in summer and on the weekend. Spread along the banks of the Río Arlanza, it is made up of a cluster of attractive wood-beam houses with porticoes fronting onto a network of little squares. More solid is the squat 10th century **Torre de Doña Urraca**, towering over the remains of Covarrubias' medieval walls. A little farther along the river, the Late Gothic **Colegiata de San Cosme y Damián** rises up. Its cloisters are of the same era, and inside you can also see the stone tomb of Fernán González, founder of Castilla in the 10th century. The Colegiata is open on Sunday and other holidays from 10.30 am to 2 pm and 4 to 7 pm (200 ptas). It closes altogether on Tuesday, and visits of at least four people can be organised on other days by agreement with the parish priest (inquire at No 3 on the same square).

Covarrubias is a charming spot to stay. *Casa Galín* (☎ 947 40 30 15, Plaza de Doña Urraca 4) has comfortable doubles with private bathroom that go for 3600 ptas, or half for single occupancy. There are a few cheaper rooms without their own bath. The nearby and fancier *Hotel Arlanza* (☎ 947 40 30 25, Plaza Mayor 11) charges 5500/8800 ptas in the high season. Autobuses Arceredillo runs two buses from Burgos to Covarrubias on weekdays, and one on Saturday. A road leads west to Lerma and east to hook up with the Burgos-Soria highway.

Santo Domingo de Silos

This is the monastery whose monks made the pop charts a couple of years ago, in Britain and elsewhere, with recordings of Gregorian chants. It appears probable that, as long ago as the 7th century, the Visigoths had a religious centre here, but it is not until the arrival of Santo Domingo (St Dominic) in 1040 that a surer light penetrates the swirling mists of our Dark Age ignorance. He began construction of the Benedictine abbey, still inhabited by 26 Benedictine monks today (after a period of disuse in the wake of the great confiscation of church property in the 19th century).

The jewel is the cloister, a treasure chest of some of the most remarkable and varied Romanesque art in all Spain. As you proceed around the courtyard, you are confronted with a rich series of sculptures depicting everything from lions to Harpies, intermingled with occasional floral and geometrical motifs betraying the never distant influence of Islamic art in Spain.

More important still are the pieces executed on the corner pillars, representing episodes from the life of Christ. At least two masters, anonymous as was so often the case with medieval craftsmen, were responsible for this work, and the dividing line can be divined from comparing the style of the pillars. The first master raised columns that widen in the middle while those of the second, who probably worked into the early 12th century, do not.

CASTILLA Y LEÓN

The galleries are covered by mudéjar artesonado ceilings from the 14th century. In the north-east corner sits a 13th century image of the Virgin Mary carved in stone, and nearby is the original burial spot of Santo Domingo.

The guide you will compulsorily have at your side will also show you inside the 17th century *botica*, or pharmacy. You may also be shown around other annexes making up the museum – with the predictable collection of religious artworks, Flemish tapestries and the odd medieval sarcophagus. The 18th century church is considerably less interesting, and much of the monastery is off limits to visitors.

The visitable parts are open Tuesday to Sunday from 10 am to 1 pm and 4.30 to 6 pm (250 ptas, extra 150 ptas for photography). Monday and holidays it is open only for the evening session.

Men can rent a heated room here for 2000 ptas with meals included, but it's a popular thing to do and you'll need to book well ahead. Call the Padre Hospedero between 11 am and 1 pm on ☎ 947 38 07 68. You can stay for a period of three to 10 days.

Those just passing through have a choice of at least five spots. The cheapest is *Hostal Cruces* (☎ 947 39 00 64, Plaza Mayor 2), with decent singles/doubles for 2500/4000 ptas. Rooms come with private bath. There are two other dearer hotels on the same square. *Hotel Arco de San Juan* (☎ 947 39 00 74, Pradera de San Juan 1) is nearby and has good rooms with TV and *en suite* bathroom for 3000/6000 ptas.

Autobuses Arceredillo runs two buses from Burgos to Santo Domingo de Silos on weekdays and one on Saturday.

Desfiladero de Yecla

A couple of kilometres down the back road (BU-911) to Caleruega from Santo Domingo, the spectacular Desfiladero de Yecla, a magnificent gorge, opens up. It is easily visited thanks to the installation of a walkway. There is a small office in Santo Domingo de Silos, nearly opposite Hostal Cruces, where you can get information on the gorge.

ROUTES NORTH OF BURGOS

Most people heading north from Burgos do just that – belt up the highway until they reach Cantabria, the Picos de Europa mountains or the País Vasco. Brits in particular, heading for the UK ferry from Santander, tend to pass through without stopping to look around. Although at least a bus daily serves most towns from Burgos on weekdays, getting around these parts is laborious without your own transport.

Valle de Sedano & North

The N-623 highway carves a pretty trail from Burgos, particularly between the mountain passes of Portillo de Fresno and Puerto de Carrales. About 15km north of the Portillo de Fresno, a side road takes you through a series of intriguing villages in the Valle de Sedano. The town of the same name has a fine 17th century church, but more interesting is the little Romanesque one above Moradillo de Sedano; the sculpted main doorway is outstanding.

Plenty of villages flank the highway on the way north, but **Orbaneja del Castillo** is the area's best-kept secret. Take the turn-off for Escalada and follow the bumpy road until you reach the waterfall. Park where you can and climb up beside the waterfall to the village, completely hidden from below. A dramatic backdrop of strange rock walls lends this charming spot a uniquely enchanting air. It is perfect for lunch, with two places to choose from. *El Arroyo* serves fine *menús* for 1500 ptas per person.

SOUTH TO THE RÍO DUERO

The road south from Burgos to Madrid crosses some particularly bleak Castilian country, and most people chew up kilometres as fast as their motors can carry them. Still, there are some worthwhile places to check out off the motorway, and at Aranda de Duero you could convert your north-south flight into a riverside excursion from east to west along the Río Duero, the third-longest and second-biggest river in the Iberian Peninsula.

Lerma

An ancient settlement, Lerma hit the big time in the first years of the 17th century, when Grand Duke Don Francisco de Rojas y Sandoval launched an ambitious project to create another El Escorial. He clearly failed, but the cobbled streets of the old town retain a degree of charm today.

Pass through the **Arco de la Cárcel** (prison gate) off the main road to Burgos and you climb up the long Calle del General Mola to the enormous Plaza Mayor. This is fronted by the sober **Palacio Ducal**, notable inside for its courtyards. To the right off the square is the Dominican nuns' **Convento de San Blas**. Heading downhill from Plaza Mayor at the opposite end from the palace, there opens up a pretty *pasadizo-mirador*, a passageway and viewpoint over the Río Arlanza, whose arches connect with the 17th century Convento de Santa Teresa on Plaza de Santa Clara.

Pension Martín (☎ 947 17 00 28, Calle del General Mola 23) has cheap, simple singles/doubles for 1500/3000 ptas. For more comfort, *Hostal Docar* (☎ 947 17 10 73, Calle de Santa Teresa de Jesús 18) charges 4000/6100 ptas for rooms with private bathroom. The *Mesón del Duque*, just off Plaza Mayor, is not a bad choice of restaurant.

There are regular buses from Burgos, and some buses coming north from Aranda de Duero or Madrid also stop here, as do trains running between Madrid and Burgos.

Aranda de Duero

The main attraction in this crossroads town is the main portal of the Late Gothic **Iglesia de Santa María**. This remarkably rich sculptural flourish was executed in the 15th and 16th centuries and incorporates scenes ranging from the Three Kings at Bethlehem to the death of Christ. The nearby earlier Gothic **Iglesia de San Juan** is also worth a look.

There's precious little to keep you here overnight, but should you choose to stay, there are a quite a few accommodation possibilities. Closest to the old part of town is the *Pensión Sole* (☎ 947 50 06 07), with singles/doubles going for 3500/5500 ptas without bath. For classic Castilian cooking – roast lamb – several reasonable restaurants compete for trade on and around Plaza del Arco Isilla. Look for the 'Asador' signs.

Buses connect Aranda with most major cities in Castilla y León and some beyond. About four buses daily serve Madrid (Estación Sur), and about seven head north to Burgos. Soria, Almazán and El Burgo de Osma are connected to the east, as are Peñafiel and Valladolid to the west and Segovia to the south-west.

One daily regional train stops here en route from Madrid to Burgos. A couple of more expensive Talgos connecting the País Vasco with Alicante also call in. Aranda is right on the N-I for Burgos or Madrid, or you can branch off east or west on the N-122 to follow the Río Duero.

Peñaranda de Duero

About 20km east of Aranda on the C-111, the village of Peñaranda de Duero is a much more interesting stop. It was a Celtic fortress village in origin, and it is the central plaza mayor that encompasses its surviving riches. The **Palacio de los Zúñiga y Avellaneda** is a grand Renaissance palace with a fine plateresque entrance and artesonado ceilings inside. The 16th century Iglesia de Santa Ana is also impressive. For superb views of the village and surrounding country, take a walk up to the medieval castle ruins.

Hotel Señorío de Vélez (☎ 947 55 22 01, Plaza de los Duques de Alba 1) is right in the heart of town and charges 4000/6500 ptas for singles/doubles.

If you are driving around this area and have time to kill, there are modest Roman ruins at **Clunia**, about 15km north-east, and an interesting monastery at **Vid**, just 7km south on the N-122 between Aranda and Soria.

Sepúlveda

Its houses staggered along a ridge carved out by the gorge of the Río Duratón,

Sepúlveda is one of many weekend escape hatches for stifled madrileños, but retains a little more life of its own than places such as nearby Pedraza, which tend to be virtual ghost towns from Monday to Friday. Nevertheless, you'll be about the only stranger in town during the week. The town, known under the Romans as Septempublicam, lies about 50km south of Aranda de Duero, west of the N-I.

The warm ochre tones of Sepúlveda's public buildings, fronting the central Plaza de España, are an enviable setting for a hot Sunday roast; the town is considered one of the best in Spain for roast lamb. The ayuntamiento houses a tourist office and backs onto what remains of the old castle. High above it all rises impassive the 11th century **Iglesia del Salvador**, considered the prototype of this variant of Castilian Romanesque, marked by the single arched portico. It is open on the third Sunday of every month.

Hostal Postigo (☎ *921 54 01 72, Calle del Conde Sepúlveda 22),* just off Plaza de España, charges 4000/6500 ptas for singles/doubles. There are several restaurants around Plaza de España, including ***Restaurante Filka*** at No 4. Here, as in the others, a huge dish with a quarter of a lamb (more than enough for two people) well roasted in a wood-fired oven will cost about 3500 ptas.

At least two buses link Sepúlveda daily with Madrid, one via the N-I highway, the other via the Puerto de Navacerrada, southeast of Segovia. There is at least one bus daily to Segovia from Monday to Saturday, and another east to Riaza.

Parque Natural del Hoz del Duratón

A good chunk of land north-west of Sepúlveda has been constituted as a natural park. The centrepiece is the Hoz del Duratón (Duratón gorge), in particular where it widens out behind the dam just south of Burgomillodo. A dirt track leads 5km west from the hamlet of Villaseca to the **Ermita de San Frutos**. In ruins now, the

hermitage was founded in the 7th century by San Frutos and his brother and sister, San Valentín and Santa Engracia. They lie buried in a tiny chapel nearby. This is a magic place, overlooking one of the many serpentine bends in the gorge. Come in the middle of the afternoon and you'll be accompanied by squadrons of buzzards and eagles. Stay away at the weekend though, as a surprising number of people crowd in, pretty much wrecking the atmosphere. Some people take kayaks up to Burgomillodo to launch themselves down the waters of the canyon.

Duratón

About 6km east of Sepúlveda, just outside the village of Duratón, the **Iglesia de Nuestra Señora de la Anunciación** is a fine example of Romanesque church-building in rural Castilla.

Castilnovo

Some 12km south of Sepúlveda, this rather cute little castle has more the air of a private conceit by some moneyed eccentric. Originally built in the 14th century and largely mudéjar, it has undergone a lot of alterations. It's open Monday to Friday from 10 am to 2 pm and weekends from 10 am to 1 pm and 5 to 7 pm (400 ptas); a half-hour guided tour is obligatory.

WEST ALONG THE RÍO DUERO
Peñafiel

Riding high above the medieval Castilian stronghold of Peñafiel stands what must be about the longest and narrowest castle in Spain. Its crenellated walls and towers stretch over 200m, and were raised and modified over 400 years from the 11th century. The sight of it in the distance alone is worth the effort of getting here. It's open Tuesday to Sunday from 11 am to 2 pm and 4 to 7 pm (6 pm in winter; 200 ptas).

In the town itself, the Iglesia de San Pablo is a curious mix of mudéjar, Gothic and plateresque decoration. The Plaza del Coso is another oddity, an ample square contained by the wooden balconies and houses that front onto it. It is still used for bullfights today. The Río Duratón winds its way through town to join the Río Duero just to the north.

Right in the centre is the *Hostal Chicopa* (☎ *983 88 07 82, Plaza de España 2)*, with basic rooms for 3000/3700 ptas. Just off the square is the small, pedestrianised town centre, and on Calle de José Antonio Girón de Velasco you'll find several bars and the *Restaurante El Bodegón* at No 14, where you can dig into a moderately priced meal. Four or five buses a day run to Valladolid.

EAST ALONG THE RÍO DUERO

From Aranda, you can follow the Río Duero east towards Almazán, or take the N-122 direct for Soria, Castilla y León's easternmost provincial capital. Both routes are dotted with curious little *pueblos* (villages) and plenty of worthwhile detours. Apart from what is mentioned below, it is worth heading off on your own tangent down the rural byways. Some of the hamlets you encounter in this area really give the impression that time has stopped still for centuries.

San Esteban de Gormaz

This dusty little town contains a couple of little Romanesque gems hidden away in its centre, the 11th century churches of San Miguel and Del Rivero. Both sport the porticoed side galleries that characterise the Romanesque style of the Segovia and Burgos areas, and indeed San Miguel is thought by some to have served as a model for other churches. There are three places to stay here if you need to.

El Burgo de Osma

Some 12km east of San Esteban de Gormaz and veering away from the Duero, this is a real surprise packet. Once important enough to host its own university, El Burgo de Osma is an elegant if somewhat run-down little old town, dominated by a quite remarkable cathedral. Nearby lies the partly excavated Celtiberian castro of Uxama, the area's first settlement.

Begun in the 12th century as an essentially Romanesque building, the cathedral was continued in a Gothic key and finally topped with a weighty baroque tower. Apart from the 16th century main retablo and some interesting odds and ends in the museum rooms around the cloister, the jewel in the crown is the so-called **Beato de Osma**, a precious 11th century codex (manuscript) that can be seen in the sacristy. The cathedral and museum are open from 10.30 am to 1 pm and 4 to 6 pm, although from November to February they only open on Sunday and holidays. Entry to the museum and cloister costs 250 ptas.

From Plaza de San Pedro, where the cathedral stands, Calle Mayor, its portico borne by an uneven phalanx of stone and wooden pillars, leads into Plaza Mayor. This is fronted by the 18th century ayuntamiento and the more sumptuous Hospital de San Agustín, now a cultural centre.

Outside the main approach to the town is the 16th century Renaissance former university. If you exit El Burgo from near Plaza de San Pedro, take a left for the village of Osma and high up on a hill you'll see the ruins of the Castillo de Osma.

Of the half-dozen places to stay, *Pensión El Arco* (☎ *975 36 04 62, Calle del General Álvarez de Castro 3)* is about the closest to the centre, with simple rooms for 2800 ptas. In summer, they rise to 5000 ptas. At that price you're much better off at *Hostal La Perdiz* (☎ *975 34 03 09, Calle de la Universidad 33)*, where singles/doubles with TV cost 3500/6000 ptas. The discerning traveller with dosh will go for the *Hotel Il Virrey* (☎ *975 34 13 11, fax 975 34 08 55, Calle Mayor 2-4)*. Charming, comfortable rooms go for 8000/12,000 ptas in the high season.

Apart from a couple of the hotels, the restaurant choices are limited. For simple, solid meals, try *Mesón Luis (Calle de la Universidad 2)*. From early February to March, Spaniards from as far off as Madrid flock here at the weekend to 'pig out', as it were. A pig is ritually slaughtered in the morning and then diners at the Hotel Il

Virrey indulge in an all-you-can eat food-athon, eating all the pork they can fit in. At 5500 ptas a head it's not the cheapest feed you'll ever have, but the experience is quite unique.

Buses link El Burgo with Soria and places as far afield as Valladolid. Minor roads lead south to Berlanga de Duero and north to the Cañón del Río Lobos (see later in this chapter).

Gormaz

Some 14km south of El Burgo you can rejoin the Río Duero at the virtual ghost town of Gormaz. The great castle with 21 towers was built by the Muslims in the 10th century and altered in the 13th century. Its ruins still convey enormous dignity and the views alone justify the effort of getting here. There's nowhere to stay in Gormaz, but in nearby Quintanas de Gormaz you'll find the delightful *Casa Grande de Gormaz* (☎ 975 34 09 82). This grand old house has seven rooms, which at their most expensive cost 5500/7000 ptas.

Berlanga de Duero

Another 15km or so east, Berlanga is lorded over by a powerful but ruinous castle. Down below, the Colegiata de Santa María del Mercado is a fine Late Gothic church, with the star-shaped vaulting inside perhaps its most pleasing aspect. The area around the pretty plaza mayor, with the occasional Renaissance house, is equally charming. Outside the old town centre on a desolate open plot is the Picota – to which petty criminals were tied in the good old days. The *Hotel Fray Tomás* (☎ 975 34 30 33, Calle Real 16) has comfortable but overpriced rooms for 4000/ 6500 ptas.

Beyond Berlanga de Duero

About 8km south-east of the town stands the **Ermita de San Baudelio**. The simple exterior belies a remarkable 11th century Mozarabic interior – a real gem. A great pillar in the centre of the only nave opens up at the top like a palm tree to create horseshoe arches. Some invaluable Mozarabic

wall paintings and 12th century Romanesque frescoes have been preserved. It is open Wednesday to Saturday from 10.30 am to 2 pm and 4 to 7 pm and Sunday and holidays from 10.30 am to 2 pm. Another 17km south, **Rello** still retains much of its medieval defensive walls.

To push on to Almazán you can retrace your steps and pick up the C-116 highway. More adventurously, you could follow the C-101 from Baraona or strike out down the back roads for Medinaceli to the south-east, or to Atienza and eventually Sigüenza in the province of Guadalajara to the south (see the Castilla-La Mancha chapter).

Calatañazor

As you round a tight bend in the road, the grave stone walls and odd modest turret of this one-time Muslim fort (the name comes from the Arabic *Qala'at an-Nassur*, 'the vulture's citadel') present a timeless face. Climb the uneven cobbled street through the town gate, and you step back hundreds of years into a mournful medieval village.

Virtually empty and little cared for, some of the old ochre adobe and stone houses look ready to tumble into one another. The only building that seems to be holding its own is the Iglesia de Santa María del Castillo, with a small museum and Romanesque façade. Look up to the rooftops too; many of the houses are equipped with strange-looking conical chimneys. Believe it or not, scenes for the movie *Doctor Zhivago* were shot here. Lying along a minor road off the N-122 to Soria, the village is certainly an original place to hang out.

Cañón del Río Lobos

Some 15km north of El Burgo de Osma, the Parque Natural del Río Lobos not only presents some rather bizarre rockscapes, but is home to vultures and various other birds of prey. Just outside the park is an information centre, and about 4km in from the road, along the tiny river, stands the Romanesque Ermita de San Bartolomé. You can hike deeper into the park but free camping is forbidden.

If you want to stay in the area, the best choice is El Burgo de Osma, although there are several hostales in the drab village of San Leonardo de Yagüe to the north of the park. *Camping Cañón del Río Lobos* (☎ 975 36 35 65), near Ucero, is open from June to the end of August.

To Madrid

For those wanting to maintain a vaguely southerly trajectory from this part of Castilla y León, the N-110 winds south-west from San Esteban de Gormaz to join up with the N-I highway between Madrid and Burgos just short of the Puerto de Somosierra mountain pass. Along the way, stop in at Ayllón and Riaza.

Ayllón This village lies about 50km south-west of El Burgo de Osma and bathes in the same orange glow that characterises El Burgo's townscape. You enter by a medieval archway and immediately are confronted on the right by the ornate façade of a late 15th century noble family's mansion in Isabelline style. The uneven, porticoed Plaza Mayor is capped at one end by the Romanesque Iglesia de San Miguel (being restored), and nearby stands the Renaissance-era Iglesia de Santa María la Mayor. Turn right behind this and follow the narrow street for about half a kilometre and you will come to the extensive remains of another Romanesque church, now oddly incorporated into a rambling private residence. There are two *hostales* should you get stuck.

A side road leads 44km northwards from here to Aranda de Duero. Along the way you can't miss the rather brooding walled town of Maderuelo, perched on a ridge overlooking the Linares dam.

Riaza About 20km south of Ayllón, Riaza's main claim to fame is its charming old circular plaza mayor. The sandy arena in the centre is still used for bullfights. If you want to stay, about the cheapest place is the *Hostal Las Robles* (☎ 921 55 00 54), where singles/doubles cost 1500/2200 ptas. Bull fans might like to eat at the *Restaurante Matimore* on Plaza Mayor. It is a mini-museum for bullfight posters, and the walls also support four rather large stuffed bulls' heads.

Six kilometres away is the local ski resort of La Pinilla. It's nothing superb, but if there have been good falls and you happen to have your skis handy ...

SORIA

A rather diminutive provincial capital, Soria cannot boast of the great towering cathedrals or soaring citadels emblematic of many other Castilian capitals. For all that, it does have a pleasant enough old centre and a few monuments worth a glance. Try to stay away in winter, as the city is rather chilly.

Although possibly populated before Roman times, Soria only appears in the history books with the arrival of the Muslims.

Until the crowns of Castilla and Aragón were united at the end of the 15th century, Soria was a hive of commercial and political activity, straddling the frontier territory between Old Castilla, Aragón and Navarra. From the 16th century on, however, it lost importance and, with the expulsion of the Jews, much of its business drive. It has never really recovered.

Information

Tourist Office The tourist office (☎ 975 21 20 52) on Plaza de Ramón y Cajal is open Monday to Saturday from 10 am to 2 pm and 4 to 7 pm; on Sunday it's open from from 10 am to 2 pm. However, these hours can vary somewhat between summer and winter.

Money There are several banks in the centre near the tourist office.

Post & Communications You'll find the main correos on Calle El Espolón and a small locutorio on Calle de la Aduana Vieja. The postcode is 42080.

Medical Services & Emergency In a medical emergency you can try the Cruz Roja (☎ 975 21 26 36) on Calle de Santo

Domingo de Silos. You can call an ambulance on ☎ 975 22 11 03 or ☎ 975 22 15 54.

Casco Viejo & Around

The modern centre of Soria is uninspiring to say the least, so head for the *casco viejo* (old town centre) first to get a bit of a tonic. Although there's not an awful lot to it, the few narrow streets around Plaza Mayor have some character, and the square is fronted by the attractive Renaissance-era **ayuntamiento** and **Iglesia de Santa María la Mayor**, which has a Romanesque façade.

Overlooking the town a block north is the majestic ochre **Palacio de los Condes Gomara**. Raised in the late 16th century, it is with little doubt the most impressive piece of secular architecture in the city.

Farther north again, on Calle de Santo Tomé, is Soria's most beautiful church, the Romanesque **Iglesia de Santo Domingo**, replete with blind arches and exquisite sculptures. Among other worthwhile churches is the **Iglesia de San Juan de Rabanera**, built in the 12th century and restored early in the present one. Hints of Gothic and even Byzantine art gleam through the mainly Romanesque hue of this building. Heading east towards the Río Duero you pass the **Concatedral de San Pedro**. Its incomplete Romanesque cloister is its best feature.

To the south-east of the centre, past the cemetery where the wife of the great early 20th century poet Antonio Machado lies buried, you can climb up to the remains of Soria's **castle**.

Museo Numantino

Prehistory buffs with a passable knowledge of Spanish should enjoy this well-organised museum dedicated to finds from ancient

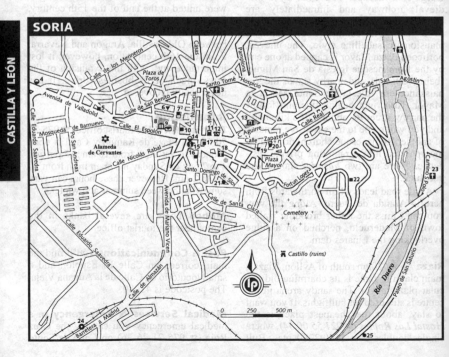

sites across the province of Soria, especially Numancia (see the Around Soria section later in this chapter for more). Starting with bones of mammoths found south of Soria in what appears to have been a prehistoric hunting ground and swamp, the displays go through important Celtiberian settlements and their Roman successors. Ceramics, tools, jewellery – the standard stuff of archaeological collections – are accompanied by detailed explanations of the historical developments in various major settlements.

It is open Tuesday to Saturday from 10 am to 2 pm and 5 to 9 pm. On Sunday and holidays it is open from 10 am to 2 pm (250 ptas).

Beside the Río Duero

With little doubt the most striking of Soria's sights is the 12th century **Monasterio de San Juan de Duero**, just over the bridge and to the left (north). What most catches the eye is the now open porticoes of what was the cloister. Each side displays a different style, underlining the unique mix of Romanesque and Oriental ideas fused together by mudéjar artists. It is open Tuesday to Saturday from 10 am to 2 pm and 4 to 7 pm. On Sunday and holidays it is open from 10 am to 2 pm.

A walk south for a couple of kilometres takes you first past the 13th century church of the former Templar **Monasterio de San Polo**, and then the baroque **Ermita de San Saturio**, its odd-looking octagonal chapel built over the cave where Soria's patron saint spent a good portion of his life.

Special Events

Since the 13th century, the 12 *barrios* (districts) of Soria have celebrated with some fervour the Fiestas de San Juan y de la Madre de Dios in the second half of June. The main events occur on Jueves (Thursday) La Saca, when each of the barrios presents a bull to be fought the next day. The day following the fight some of the meat is auctioned, after which dancing and general carousing go on into the wee hours of Sunday. Hangovers and all, the *cuadrillas* or 'teams' representing the 12 districts parade in all their finery and stage folk dances and the like. If you can find a room, this is the time to be in Soria.

Places to Stay

There are several cheap possibilities in the centre of Soria. *Pensión Sol* (☎ 975 22 72 02, Calle Ferial 8) has simple but adequate rooms for 1600/3000 ptas. In much the same league is *Pensión Casa David* (☎ 975 22 00 33, Calle del Campo 6). It charges a bit more (1800/3600 ptas) and has a decent little restaurant. In an older building behind the tourist office is the *Pensión Carlos* (☎ 975 21 15 55), which charges the same as the Sol, although in the off season you might score a single for 1200 ptas.

SORIA

PLACES TO STAY
5	Hostal Viena
7	Pensión Casa David
10	Pensión Sol
16	Hostal Alvi
17	Pensión Carlos
22	Parador Antonio Machado

PLACES TO EAT
6	Restaurante Casa Garrido
19	Mesón Castellano

OTHER
1	Monasterio de San Juan de Duero
2	Concatedral de San Pedro
3	Iglesia de Santo Domingo
4	Estación de Autobuses
8	Museo Numantino
9	Correos
11	Lázaro Pérez
12	Telephones (Locutorio)
13	Palacio de los Condes Gomara
14	Local Bus to Train Station
15	Tourist Office
18	Iglesia de San Juan de Rabanera
20	Café Hispano
21	Cruz Roja
23	Monasterio de San Polo
24	Train Station (RENFE)
25	Ermita de San Saturio

CASTILLA Y LEÓN

Although it looks austere from the outside, the *Hostal Viena* (☎ *975 22 21 09, Calle de García Solier 5)* comes with some recommendations. Rooms have TV, telephone and air-conditioning. Singles/doubles with their own bathroom cost 2100/5500 ptas in the high season.

Closer to the centre is the *Hostal Alvi* (☎ *975 22 81 12, Calle de Alberca 2)*, with reasonable rooms for 4000/6200 ptas in the high season. Top of the range is the modern *Parador Antonio Machado* (☎ *975 21 34 45, fax 975 21 28 49)* in the Parque del Castillo. Room rates cost up to 9500/13,500 ptas.

Places to Eat

On the western edge of the old centre you'll find several bars and restaurants on Plaza de Ramón Benito Aceña. Three more are lined up on Plaza Mayor, including the reasonable *Mesón Castellano*, where you can eat well for around 1500 ptas. Up behind the correos, the *Restaurante Casa Garrido* is a cosy spot, all dark wood and solid, meaty Castilian cooking.

Entertainment

The spit-and-sawdust crowd should look in at the *Lázaro Pérez* wine bar *(Calle del Collado 52)*. It's a bit male-dominated though. For something more genteel, head for the *Café Hispano*, on Plaza San Gil just north off Plaza Mayor.

No Spanish city is complete without its zone of noisy bars and discos. In this case the bulk of them are concentrated in the area north-west of the Alameda park and Avenida de Valladolid.

Getting There & Away

The estación de autobuses (☎ 975 22 51 60) is about a 15 minute walk from the centre on the road to Valladolid. There are regular services to Almazán, Logroño, Madrid, Valladolid and a host of small towns. Trains leave from the station (☎ 975 22 28 67) south-west of the centre (local buses connect with Plaza de Ramón y Cajal). Trains run north to Pamplona and beyond and connect with the main Madrid-

Barcelona line at Torralba. Roads in all directions head from Soria like spokes on a wheel, with straightforward routes to Burgos, Logroño, Valladolid, Madrid, Zaragoza and Teruel.

AROUND SORIA
Numancia

The mainly Roman ruins left today at Numancia, 8km north of Soria, suggest little of the long history of this city. Inhabited as early as the Bronze Age, Numancia would much later prove one of the most resistant cities to Roman rule. Several attempts by the Romans to take control of it were frustrated until finally Scipio, who had crushed Carthage, managed to starve the city into submission in 134 BC. Under Roman rule, Numancia was an important stop on the road from Caesaraugustus (Zaragoza) to Asturica (Astorga). Ceramics unearthed here have revealed an advanced artistic tradition among not only the Romanised inhabitants of the city, but also their Celtiberian forebears. The site is open Tuesday to Saturday, from 10 am to 3.30 pm and 4 to 6 pm (4 to 7 pm in April, May, September and October, and 5 to 9 pm in July and August). On Sunday and holidays it is open from 10 am to 2 pm (250 ptas).

Sierra de Urbión

Some of the most surprisingly green and unspoilt country in Castilla y León lies to the north-west of Soria. The Sierra de Urbión stretches north into La Rioja and is a popular weekend excursion destination with the people of Soria. The focal point is the Laguna Negra, 18km north of the pretty village of Vinuesa. The glacial lake lies still like a mirror at the base of brooding rock walls. The road is not in great shape, but the objective is well worth the battering to your shock absorbers (there are no buses). It's possible to hike to the Laguna de Urbión in La Rioja, or to the summit of the Pico de Urbión, above the village of Duruelo de la Sierra, and then on to a series of other tiny glacial lakes.

In **Vinuesa**, a good base for the area, there are two hostales. The *Hostal Urbión* (☎ *975 37 84 94*) has singles/doubles for 2500/3500 ptas (or doubles with private bath for 4000 ptas) and a popular, if somewhat pricey, restaurant. Alternatively you could try for a room at the *Casa del Cura* (☎ *975 27 04 64, Calle de la Estación*) in Herreros, a hamlet just off the N-234 highway to the south-east of Vinuesa. The nearest camping ground to the Laguna is *Camping El Cobijo* (☎ *975 37 83 31*). It is open from March to mid-October.

SOUTH OF SORIA
Almazán

Three of this small town's massive gates remain to testify to a past more illustrious than the present in this quiet backwater. It frequently changed hands between the Muslims and Christians, and for a short three months was chosen by Fernando and Isabel as their residence.

On Plaza Mayor you can see the Romanesque **Iglesia de San Miguel**, with a slightly jarring octagonal cupola-cum-bell tower. It seems usually to be closed. The prettiest face of the **Palacio de los Condes de Altamira** is actually the loggia looking out over the river, which can be seen only when approaching the town from the river side. If you want to stay, *Hostal El Arco* (☎ *975 31 02 28, Calle de San Andrés 5-7*) is by one of the three city gates. *Restaurante Puerto Rico (Calle de los Caballeros 12)* is a good cheap restaurant in the old town. There are frequent bus and train connections with Soria, 35km north.

Medinaceli

Entering Medinaceli along a slip road just north of the N-II motorway, you find a modern one-horse town. The old Medinaceli is actually draped along a high, windswept ridge 3km to the north. Its most incongruously placed landmark is a 2nd century **triumphal arch**, all that remains of the Roman settlement. Little is left to remind you of Medinaceli's Muslim occupiers; its empty streets are redolent

more of the noble families that lived clustered around the La Cerda family, pretenders to the Castilian crown, after the town fell to the Reconquista in 1124. The Plaza Mayor has a dilapidated grandeur, but the town as a whole has a distinctly ghostly feel.

There is a Centro de Iniciativa y Turismo at Plaza Mayor 16, in the old town, for information. The *Hostal Medinaceli* (☎ *975 32 61 30*) has singles/doubles for 3000/4800 ptas and the newer *Hostería El Mirador* (☎ *975 32 62 64*) offers rooms for 3000/4000 ptas (add IVA to both). You'll find several more hostales in the new town. There are a few restaurants, including those in the hotels, but arguably the town's best known is *Las Llaves (Plaza Mayor 14)*.

The odd bus leaves for Guadalajara and Madrid from in front of the ayuntamiento in the new town and the occasional slow train calls in on the Madrid-Zaragoza line. There is no transport between the old and new towns – it's quite a hike.

Santa María de la Huerta

This dusty, insignificant village off the N-II and just short of the Aragonese frontier, contains a jewel in the form of a Cistercian monastery founded in 1162. Monks lived here until 1835, when the monastery was expropriated. The order was allowed to return in 1930 and 18 Cistercians now live here. Before entering the monastery, you will see ahead of you the impressive 12th century façade of the church with its rose window (now being restored).

Inside the monastery, you pass through two cloisters, the second of which is by far the more beautiful. Known as the Claustro de los Caballeros, it is Spanish Gothic in style, although the medallions on the 2nd floor bearing coats of arms and assorted illustrious busts, such as that of Christopher Columbus, are a successful plateresque touch. Off this cloister is the *refectorio*, or grand dining hall. Built in the 13th century, it is remarkable, especially for the absence of columns to support the vault. The monastery is open daily from 9 am to 12.45 pm and 3 to 6.30 pm (300 ptas).

Pensión Santa María *(☎ 975 32 72 18)*, at the turn-off to the monastery, is a basic place with singles/doubles for 1700/3000 ptas. A couple of kilometres east, near the slip road onto the N-II, is the ***Hotel Santa***

María de Huerta *(☎ 975 32 70 11)*, with bed and breakfast for 8000/12,500 ptas plus IVA.

A couple of buses connect the village with Almazán and Soria, and slow trains on the Madrid-Zaragoza line stop in.

Castilla-La Mancha

The autonomous community of Castilla-La Mancha is a post-Franco creation with Toledo as its capital. It covers roughly what was known as Castilla la Nueva (New Castile), the territory south from Toledo that was added to the Corona de Castilla (Castilian Crown) as the Reconquista progressed through the Middle Ages. The boundaries of the region's five provinces are those drawn up in 1833, when La Mancha – the harsh, dry southern plateau that served as a frontline buffer zone against the last of Spain's Muslim rulers after the Battle of Las Navas de Tolosa in 1212 – ceased to exist as an administrative unit. Embodied by its literary hero Don Quixote, La Mancha (which comes from an Arabic expression meaning 'dry, waterless land') has nevertheless remained very much alive in the Spanish imagination.

With the exception of Toledo, little of this region – one of the country's biggest – is seen by the millions of foreigners who pour into Spain each year. The empty expanses alone are quite unique in Western Europe, reminiscent of some of the more monotonous stretches of rural Australia or the south-western USA. Many people end up crossing Castilla-La Mancha from Madrid or Toledo en route to somewhere else. Those with limited time are probably right to skip the bulk of this dispiriting, hot land of treeless plains and glum, bald hills. A closer look, however, reveals a wide smattering of pretty villages, medieval castles and, on occasion, some surprisingly varied and fertile landscape. The absence of busloads of camera-clicking tour groups presents an opportunity to see some of Spain as it really is. Given the distances involved, however, having your own vehicle is a significant asset.

The regional tourist board puts out a series of pamphlets laying out theme-oriented driving routes in the region. These in-depth tours describe every last village,

HIGHLIGHTS

- The medieval splendour of the imperial city of Toledo, particularly during the Corpus Christi festivities

- Coffee on Almagro's fine Plaza Mayor, and perhaps some theatre at the unique El Corral de Comedias

- Tilting at windmills around Consuegra

- Relaxing by the river beneath Alcalá del Júcar's cascade of houses

- Washing down a good meal of game with some Valdepeñas wine

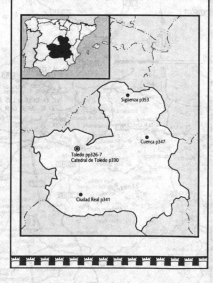

Sigüenza p353

Cuenca p347

Toledo pp326-7
Catedral de Toledo p330

Ciudad Real p341

castle, ruin, and scenic overlook in Castilla-La Mancha, while a companion set of city guides contains information on festivals, arts and cuisine as well. They are available in English and worth picking up at any tourist office.

The cuisine of Castilla-La Mancha, like that of much of Spain, is firmly based in peasant tradition. In and around Toledo, where *la caza* (hunting) has long been a big contributor to the local table, venison and partridge figure largely. The plains are hot but not unproductive.

The strong *queso manchego* (La Manchan goat and/or sheep cheese) is sold everywhere and appreciated by gourmets. Among the odder manchego dishes are *migas*, basically fried breadcrumbs mixed with garlic and other ingredients. They are better than they sound.

Traditionally, La Mancha has been given over to intense wine production. Next to olive groves, the grapevine is one of the most common agricultural sights across the country.

Quality always came second to quantity, but with EU quotas forcing drastic cutbacks, growers are now concentrating more on producing a good drop. Although not Spain's greatest wines, the products from the La Mancha and Valdepeñas areas are DO wines.

CASTILLA-LA MANCHA

Toledo

They still call it La Ciudad Imperial – and for a while Toledo indeed looked set to become the heart of a united Spain. The Iberian Peninsula's Rome and something of an army town, this remarkable medieval city bristles with monumental splendour.

By the time El Greco arrived here from Italy in 1577, Toledo's chances of becoming the permanent capital had all but evaporated. Sixteen years earlier, Felipe II had moved the court to the relatively undistinguished location of Madrid, a site that, unlike the claustrophobic Toledo, lent itself to rapid expansion in all directions as might befit a great empire. Toledo's city elders were slow to realise that, partly owing to an earlier revolt against Carlos I, they had missed the boat, and until the end of the century the city continued to enjoy one of its greatest moments of economic and artistic development. When the penny finally dropped, artists, nobles, courtesans and sycophants left in droves, leaving Toledo to sink slowly into provincial disrepair.

Like a creaky museum, spruced up but not without problems, *la ciudad de la tres culturas* (the city of the three cultures) has survived as a unique centre where Romans and Visigoths once ruled, and for a time Jews, Muslims and Christians – and all those who converted from one religion to another – lived in comparative harmony. The artistic legacy is a complex cross-breeding of European and Oriental values that can be seen elsewhere in Spain, but rarely with the intensity found here.

The seat of the head of the Catholic church in Spain for most of its Christian history, Toledo exerts a strange and sometimes dark fascination over people who stay around long enough to get over the initial monument shock and summer crowds. To see the city in the gloomy depths of winter, shrouded in fog and even more introverted than usual, is in some ways to get a truer measure of its character.

Toledo's twisting lanes and blind alleys, the extraordinarily decorated internal patios hidden by grim façades looking onto steep, cobbled streets and its sheer architectural diversity make it worthy of more attention than most visitors give it. Travellers who have passed through Damascus, Cairo or Fés will recognise the labyrinth of the *medina*, but in none of those cities will they also be confronted by the Gothic grandeur of a cathedral or the grim composure of Toledo's oft-remodelled Alcázar.

The sad part of Toledo's story is taking place almost unnoticed. People are abandoning the old city for the characterless but comfortable new suburbs sprawled out beneath it, leaving behind only public servants, students and the rent-protected elderly. If this continues, the shops and businesses will also decline, leaving only a motley collection of souvenir stalls and eateries to satisfy summer tourist crowds. The old city appears destined to become an empty open-air museum – a place without soul.

History

Its strategic position made ancient Toletum an important way station in the days of Rome's domination of the Iberian Peninsula. In the 6th century, long after Rome had ceased to have any influence on the affairs of Hispania, the Visigothic king Atanagild moved the site of his capital from Sevilla to Toletum. At once, the city also became the religious heart of the Visigothic kingdom, with no less than 18 councils held here to deal with problems such as the conversion of the Visigoths to Catholicism, the faith of the majority of the subjugated Hispano-Roman populace. But Toledo also became the scene of endless feuds between Visigothic nobles which so weakened their state that when the Muslims crossed the Strait of Gibraltar in 711 they had little problem in taking Toledo on their lightning-fast march north.

Toledo was the main city of central Muslim Spain. After the collapse of the caliphate in Córdoba in 1031 it became the capital of a vast and independent Arab *taifa* (kingdom). For the following 50 years the

TOLEDO

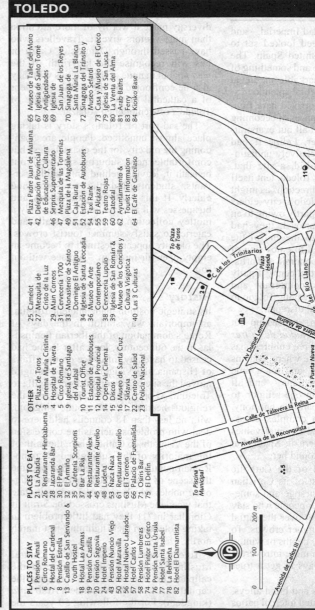

PLACES TO STAY
1 Pensión Amalí
6 Circo Romano
7 Hostal del Cardenal
8 Pensión Estrella
13 Castillo de San Servando &
   Youth Hostel
18 Hostal Las Armas
19 Pensión Castilla
20 Pensión Segovia
24 Hotel Imperio
43 Pensión Nuncio Viejo
50 Hotel Maravilla
56 Hostal Nuevo Labrador
57 Hotel Carlos V
58 Pensión Lumbreras
74 Hotel Pintor El Greco
76 Pensión Santa Úrsula
77 Hotel Santa Isabel
78 La Belviseña
82 Hotel El Diamantista

PLACES TO EAT
21 La Abadía
26 Restaurante Hierbabuena
28 Jacaranda Bar
30 El Patio
32 El Amiño
35 Cafetería Scorpions
37 Bar La Ría
44 Restaurante Alex
45 Restaurante Aurelio
48 Ludería
53 Naca Naca
61 Restaurante Aurelio
63 El Torreón
66 Palacio de Fuensalida
71 Osiris Bar
75 El Delfín

OTHER
2 Plaza de Toros
3 Cinema María Cristina
4 Hospital de Tavera
5 Circo Romano
9 Iglesia de Santiago
   del Arrabal
10 Tourist Office
11 Estación de Autobuses
12 Hospital Provincial
14 Open-Air Cinema
15 Discos
16 Museo de Santa Cruz
17 Sildavia
22 Centro de Salud
23 Policía Nacional
25 Camelot
27 Mezquita de
   Cristo de la Luz
29 Main Correos
31 Cervecería 1700
33 Monasterio de Santo
   Domingo El Antiguo
34 Iglesia de Santa Leocadia
36 Museo de Arte
   Contemporáneo
38 Cervecería Lupulo
39 Iglesia de San Román &
   Museo de los Concilios y
   Cultura Visigótica
40 Las 3 Culturas
41 Plaza Padre Juan de Mariana
42 Delegación Provincial
   de Educación y Cultura
46 Serpix Supermercado
47 Mezquita de las Tornerías
49 Plaza de la Magdalena
51 Caja Rural
52 Estación de Autobuses
54 Taxi Rank
55 El Alcázar
59 Iglesia de San Lucas
60 Catedral
62 Ayuntamiento &
   Tourist Information
64 El Café de Garcilaso
65 Museo de Taller del Moro
67 Iglesia de Santo Tomé
68 Antigüedades
69 Iglesia de
   San Juan de los Reyes
70 Sinagoga de
   Santa María La Blanca
72 Sinagoga del Tránsito y
   Museo Sefardí
73 Casa y Museo de El Greco
79 Iglesia de San Lucas
80 La Venta del Alma
81 Arab Baths
83 Ferry
84 Kiosko Base

To Train Station (130m)

Puente de Azarquiel

To Plaza de Toros

Plaza Honda

C. de los Trinitarios

Calle del Río Llano

Paseo del Miradero

Plaza del Solar

Carretera de Madrid

Av Duque Lerma

Puerta Nueva de Bisagra

Calle Real del Arrabal

Puerta del Sol

Calle de Talavera la Reina

Avenida de la Reconquista

Paseo de Recaredo

To Piscina Municipal

Paseo del Cristo de la Vega

Paseo del Circo Romano

Avenida de Carlos III

0   100   200 m

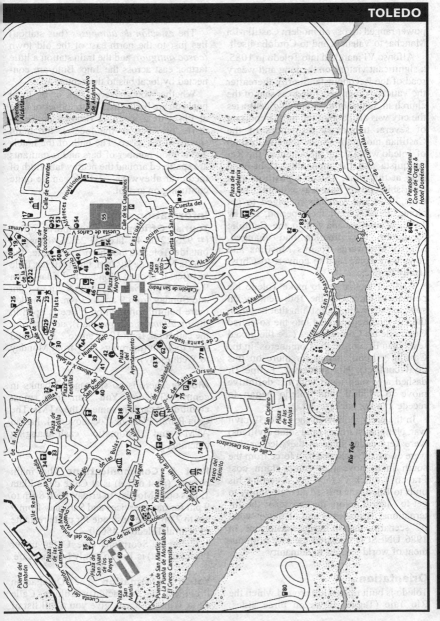

TOLEDO

CASTILLA-LA MANCHA

city was unrivalled as a centre of learning and arts in Spain, and for a brief time its power ranged across all modern Castilla-La Mancha, to Valencia and to Córdoba itself.

Alfonso VI marched into Toledo in 1085, a significant victory on the long and weary road of the Reconquista. Shortly thereafter the Vatican recognised Toledo as seat of the church in Spain. In the following centuries the city was also one of the most important of several temporary residences of the Castilian monarchy. Since the Archbishop of Toledo was a vocal proponent of the Reconquista and the monarchs' right-hand man at this time, Toledo's position as a flourishing power base was assured. Christians, Jews and Muslims managed to get along tolerably well for a period, but by 1492, when Granada fell to the Catholic Monarchs, the situation had changed. Shortly afterwards Spain's Muslims and Jews were compelled to convert to Christianity or flee.

Carlos I looked set to make Toledo his permanent capital in the 16th century, in spite of the revolt against him that began in the city and degenerated into the so-called Guerra de las Comunidades (see the boxed text 'Juan Bravo and the Comuneros' in the Castilla y León chapter for more on this civil conflict). His successor, Felipe II, dashed any such ideas with his definitive move to Madrid, and Toledo began to recede into the background.

In the early months of the 1936-39 civil war, Nationalist troops (and some civilians) were kept under siege in the Alcázar, but were eventually relieved by a force from the south in a move that some claim cost Franco a quick victory. By diverting his units to Toledo, he missed an opportunity to get to Madrid before the arrival of the International Brigades – one of those 'what if?' scenarios that so intrigue historians. In 1986 UNESCO declared the city a monument of world interest to humanity.

Orientation

Toledo is built upon a hill around which the Río Tajo (Tagus) flows on three sides;

modern suburbs spread beyond the river and walls of the old town.

The *estación de autobuses* (bus station) lies just to the north-east of the old town *(casco antiguo)*, and the train station a little farther east across the Tajo. Both are connected by local bus to the centre.

Whether you arrive on foot or by local bus, you are bound to turn up sooner or later at Plaza de Zocodover (known as Zocodover or Zoco to the locals), the main square of the casco. The bulk of the hotels and a good number of bars and restaurants are spattered around the nearby labyrinth of medieval alleyways – which can be quite confusing on arrival.

Information

Tourist Offices The main tourist office (☎ 925 22 08 43, fax 925 25 26 48) is just outside Toledo's northern main gate, the Puerta Nueva de Bisagra, though it has little to offer. It is open Monday to Friday from 9 am to 6 pm, Saturday from 9 am to 7 pm and Sunday from 9 am to 3 pm. A smaller, more helpful information office is open in the *ayuntamiento* (town hall), across from the cathedral, from 10.30 am to 2.30 pm and 4.30 to 7 pm (mornings only from Monday to Wednesday).

Money There is no shortage of banks in central Toledo. You can use most credit/debit cards in some of the ATMs. The Caja Rural, Plaza de Zocodover 14, has an ATM and automatic cash-changing machine.

Post & Communications The main *correos* (post office) is at Calle de la Plata 1. It is open Monday to Friday from 8 am to 9 pm for most services and Saturday from 9 am to 2 pm. The postcode for poste restante in central Toledo is 45080.

Cafetería Scorpions (see Cafés under Places to Eat) is Toledo's only Internet café.

Youth Information The Delegación Provincial de Educación y Cultura, Calle de la Trinidad 8, can give you a full list of youth hostels, university residences and camp sites throughout Castilla-La Mancha. It is open Monday to Friday from 9 am to 2 pm.

Books Apart from the usual tourist books, Spanish readers wanting a quality guide and account of the city should consider *Rutas de Toledo* (4000 ptas), published by Electa and available all over town.

Medical Services & Emergency There is a Policía Nacional *comisaría* in the old city on Plaza de la Ropería. For an ambulance or urgent medical help, the Cruz Roja (Red Cross) is on ☎ 925 22 22 22. You'll find a Centro de Salud (health centre; ☎ 925 21 50 54) at Calle de la Sillería 2. Duty night pharmacies change daily on a rotational basis; the week's *farmacias de guardia* are posted up in most pharmacies.

Things to See

Take the time to wander and soak up some of the most distinctive architectural combinations in Spain. The Arab influence on all you see, from church bell towers to arches in city gates, is a singular expression of Spain's mixed heritage, one that also passes through the Gothic of the cathedral to the more restrained monumentalism of the work of architects Juan de Herrera and Alonso Covarrubias.

In summer, many of Toledo's museums tend to open for about an hour longer than the times cited. Some offer student reductions, usually meaning half-price.

Zocodover From 1465 until the 1960s, Zocodover was the scene of El Martes, the city's Tuesday market and successor to the Arab *souq ad-dawab* (livestock market) from which the square derives its name. The market is now held downhill from the Museo de Santa Cruz, but Zocodover remains the casco's focal point. Apart from the market, it was here that *toledanos* for centuries enjoyed their bullfights or crowded to witness *autos de fe* carried out by the Inquisition. You can see the house of

the 16th century Inquisitor Alfonso Castellón (with the Doric doorway) on nearby Plaza de Agustín, just up from the Pensión Segovia.

The architect Juan de Herrera, who built El Escorial, wanted to convert the square into a grand Castilian plaza mayor in the late 16th century, but he was blocked by church interests. The eastern façade is all he managed to erect along the line of the former Arab city wall, punctuated by the gate now known as the Arco de la Sangre. The southern flank, into which a McDonald's has planted itself, dates from the 17th century.

Toledo's forbidding façades often hide sumptuous houses, so it is worth keeping your eye open for unexpected glimpses of internal courtyards. Calle de la Sillería has a couple of nice examples. Look for No 6 and No 3; the former's patio is adorned with an elegant fountain, while the latter is considered one of the most beautiful houses in Toledo.

Alcázar Just south off Zocodover, at the highest point in the city, looms Toledo's most recognisable edifice, the Alcázar. It is possible the Romans fortified it first. Abd ar-Rahman III raised a fortress *(al-qasr)* here in the 10th century and it was altered after the Christians retook the town in the following century. Covarrubias and Herrera rebuilt it as a royal residence for Carlos I, but the court moved to Madrid and it became a white elephant, eventually winding up as the Academia de la Infantería (now on the opposite bank of the Tajo).

The Alcázar was largely destroyed during the Republican siege of Franco's forces in 1936, but Franco had it rebuilt and turned into a military museum, a fascinating memorial to the siege and, by extension, the fascist dictator – an eloquent expression of Spain's ambiguous approach to its past. You can visit the shot-up room where Colonel (later General) Moscardó refused to surrender despite threats by the 'reds' to kill his captured son, whom he told by phone to 'get ready to die' (he was shot some time

330 Castilla-La Mancha – Toledo

later). Moscardó's words can be heard on crackling tape in half a dozen languages. And in case anyone feels left out, the words hang framed on the walls in just about every tongue imaginable from Ukrainian to Korean.

It is open from 10 am to 1.30 pm and 4 to 5.30 pm, but is closed on Monday (125 ptas).

Museo de Santa Cruz Just outside what were once the Arab city walls along Zocodover, this museum on Calle de Cervantes started life as a hospital in the early 16th century. Apart from several El Grecos (look for the *Asunción de la Virgen*), the museum contains a mixed bag of largely religious objects, including 15th century tapestries, furnishings, war standards from the Battle of Lepanto in 1571, medieval documents and other odds and ends. Built in a mix of Gothic and Spanish Renaissance styles on a Greek-cross floor plan, the former hospital is flanked by a pleasant cloister. It is open from 10 am to 6.30 pm (2 pm on Sunday), sometimes closing for lunch (200 ptas, free on Saturday afternoon and Sunday).

Catedral From the earliest days of the Visigothic occupation of the ancient Roman Toletum, the modern site of the cathedral has been the centre of worship in the city. In 646, Toledo's archbishop was first recognised as the primate of the Catholic Church in Spain. Three centuries of Muslim rule saw the Visigoths' basilica converted into Toledo's central mosque. Alfonso VI promised, in the instruments of surrender signed by Christians and Muslims in 1085, that the mosque would be preserved as a place of worship for Toledo's considerable Muslim population. Predictably enough, the promise was broken and the mosque destroyed to make way for a cathedral. The construction of a new house of worship began in the 13th century and proceeded slowly over the following centuries. Essentially a Gothic structure, the cathedral nonetheless is a hotchpotch of styles re-

flecting the mixed history of the city. *Mudéjar* elements are plain to see in the interior decoration and the Spanish Renaissance makes itself felt in various chapels that line the church naves. Behind the main altar lies a masterpiece of *churrigueresque* baroque, the Transparente. A lavish 18th century embellishment, it also serves to remedy the lack of light in the cathedral.

Entering through the **Puerta de los Leones** at the side, you are immediately in the cathedral's main nave. The centre is dominated by the highly unusual **coro** (choir stalls), a feast of sculpture and carved wooden stalls. The lower tier was carved in the 15th century in late Gothic style and depicts the conquest of Granada, while the upper, Renaissance level features images of saints and apostles, many by Alonso de Berruguete.

Opposite is the **Capilla Mayor**, too small to accommodate the choir stalls as originally planned, but an extraordinary work of art dating back to 1498. A lengthy restoration is due to be completed in mid-1999. This altar

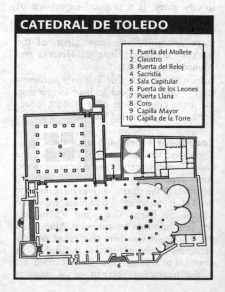

CATEDRAL DE TOLEDO

1 Puerta del Mollete
2 Claustro
3 Puerta del Reloj
4 Sacristía
5 Sala Capitular
6 Puerta de los Leones
7 Puerta Llana
8 Coro
9 Capilla Mayor
10 Capilla de la Torre

serves in part as a mausoleum for Cardinal Mendoza (prelate and adviser to Fernando and Isabel) and several kings. The masterpiece is the *retablo* in Flemish Gothic style, depicting scenes from the life of Christ and culminating with a *Calvario* and an *Asunción de la Virgen*. The oldest of the magnificent stained glass is in the rose window above the Puerta del Reloj.

All the chapels and rooms off the main church body are worth visiting. Among the 'don't misses' are the **Capilla de la Torre**, in the north-western corner, and the **sacristía**. The latter contains what amounts to a small gallery of El Greco (for more on whom, see below), while the former houses what must be one of the most extraordinary monstrances in existence, the Custodia de Arfe, by the celebrated 16th century goldsmith Enrique de Arfe. With 18kg of pure gold and 183kg of silver, this 16th century conceit bristles with some 260 statuettes. Its big day is the feast of Corpus Christi (see Special Events), when it is paraded around the streets of Toledo on a special vehicle that prevents it tipping over in spite of the medieval ups and downs.

The **sala capitular** (chapterhouse) boasts a remarkable *artesonado* ceiling in the so-called Cisneros style, Renaissance murals depicting the life of Christ and the Virgin Mary, and other artworks.

The cathedral's cool and pretty cloister is entered through the **Puerta del Mollete** facing the square under the Arco del Palacio that links the cathedral to the Palacio Arzobispal (Archbishop's Palace). For centuries the city's destitute would line up at this entrance for daily bread distribution.

The cathedral is open to visitors daily from 10.30 am to 1 pm and 3.30 to 6 pm (7 pm in summer). Tickets (500 ptas; no student discount) can be bought at a souvenir shop across the street from the main (side) entrance.

El Greco Trail Hordes of tourists pile down Toledo's narrow streets searching out the paintings of El Greco. First stop is the **Iglesia de Santo Tomé** on Plaza del Conde, which contains his masterpiece, *El Entierro del Conde de Orgaz* (The Burial of the Count of Orgaz). When the count, a 14th century benefactor of the church, was buried in 1322, Sts Augustine and Stephen supposedly descended from heaven to attend the funeral. El Greco's work depicts the miracle and features some of his chums in the lower, terrestrial part of the painting. The church, in the south-west of the town, is open from 10 am to 6.45 pm (150 ptas).

Afterwards you can follow the tourist stream past rows of souvenir shops to the **Casa y Museo de El Greco** on Calle de Samuel Leví. This was set up as a museum by a noble chap, Don Benigno de Vega-Inclán, in 1910, but it is unlikely that El Greco actually ever lived here. Inside you will find *Vista y Plano de Toledo* and about 20 of the Cretan's minor works. The museum also has a small collection of minor works of the 17th century Toledo, Madrid and Sevilla schools. It's open from 10 am to 2 pm and 4 to 6 pm but closed Sunday evening and Monday (400 ptas, students 200 ptas).

If you want to develop your own El Greco trail, other places in Toledo where you can see his works include the Museo de Santa Cruz, the sacristía of the cathedral, the Monasterio de Santo Domingo El Antiguo and the Hospital de Tavera.

Jewish Quarter Toledo still considers itself the 'city of the three cultures'. Near El Greco's supposed house is what was once the *judería* or Jewish quarter. 'Once' because, as a huge plaque in the cathedral proudly proclaims, the bulk of Toledo's Jews, like those elsewhere in Spain, were expelled in 1492. In prior centuries, Toledo's Jews worshipped in 11 synagogues.

Of the two synagogues that survive, the **Sinagoga del Tránsito** on Calle de los Reyes Católicos is the most interesting. Built in 1355 by special permission of Pedro I (construction of synagogues was by then prohibited in Christian Spain), its main prayer hall has been expertly restored. The

El Greco in Toledo

DAMIEN SIMONIS

El Greco, but as the subject and not the creator of art

After a long apprenticeship in Crete, where he was born in 1541, Domenikos Theotokopoulos moved to Venice in 1567 to be schooled as a Renaissance artist. He learned to extract the maximum effect from few colours, concentrating the observer's interest in the faces of his portraits and leaving the rest in relative obscurity, a characteristic that remained one of his hallmarks. From 1572 he learned from the mannerists of Rome and the work left behind by Michelangelo.

He came to Toledo in 1577 hoping to get a job decorating El Escorial. Things didn't quite work out, and Felipe II rejected him as a court artist. In Toledo, itself recently knocked back as permanent seat of the royal court, the man who came to be known simply as El Greco felt sufficiently at home to hang around, painting in a style different from anything local artists were producing. He even managed to cultivate a healthy clientele and command good prices. His rather high opinion of himself and his work, however, did not endear him to all and sundry. He had to do without the patronage of the cathedral administrators, the first of many clients to haul him to court for his obscenely high fees.

El Greco liked the high life, and with things going well in the last decade of the 16th century, he took rooms in a mansion on the Paseo del Tránsito, where he often hired musicians to accompany his meals. As Toledo's fortunes declined, so did El Greco's personal finances, and although the works of his final years are among his best, he often found himself unable to pay the rent. He died in 1614, leaving his works scattered about the city, where many have remained to this day.

---

mudéjar decoration – yet another reminder of the unique cultural mix of the city – is particularly striking. Academics are still puzzling over the full meaning of the Hebrew inscriptions that line the walls, but less attention seems to have been paid to those in Arabic in the ceiling. From 1492 until 1877 it was variously used as a priory, hermitage and military barracks. The modern **Museo Sefardí** it now houses affords insights into the history of Jewish culture in Spain. The complex is open from 10 am to 1.45 pm and 4 to 5.45 pm, except Sunday morning and Monday (400 ptas, free on Saturday afternoon and Sunday).

Jewish Quarter Toledo still considers

A short way north along Calle de los Reyes Católicos, the **Sinagoga de Santa María La Blanca** is characterised by the horseshoe arches that delineate the five naves – classic Almohad architecture. Opening times are from 10 am to 1.45 pm and 3.30 to 6.45 pm (150 ptas).

San Juan de los Reyes A little farther north lies one of the city's most visible sights. The Franciscan monastery and church was founded by Fernando and Isabel to demonstrate the power of the crown over the nobles and the supremacy of the Catholic faith in Spain – for how else could you interpret the decision to erect such an edifice in the heart of the Jewish *barrio*? The rulers had planned to be buried here but, when they took Granada in 1492, they opted for the brilliance of the southern city's Muslim palace.

Begun by the Breton architect Juan Güas in 1477, San Juan de los Reyes was finished only in 1606. Throughout the church and two-storey cloister the coat of arms of Fernando and Isabel (or in other words of the united Spain) dominates, and the chains of Christian prisoners liberated in Granada hang from the walls. The prevalent late Flemish-Gothic style is tarted up with lavish Isabelline ornament and counterbalanced by unmistakable mudéjar decoration, especially in the cloister, where typical geometric and vegetal designs stand out. The church and cloister are open daily from 10 am to 1.45 pm and 3.30 to 6.45 pm (150 ptas).

Muslim Toledo Although many of Toledo's great buildings betray the influence of its medieval Muslim conquerors, expressed in the mudéjar style adopted in churches, synagogues, city gates and other edifices, little that is specifically Muslim remains.

On the northern slopes of town you'll find the **Mezquita de Cristo de la Luz**, a modest mosque built at the turn of the millennium that suffered the usual fate of being converted to a church – as the religious frescoes make clear. The narrow, steep Calle del Cristo de la Luz continues past the mosque and its charming gardens, and under a gate the Muslims knew as Bab al-Mardum (also the original name of the mosque). Here, the city wall marked the boundary between the Muslim medina proper and Ar-Rabal, the 'outer suburbs'. Entry to the mosque is free, but only when the guardian is around (forget it from about 1 to 4 pm). If you can't see the guardian, try calling at No 11.

The remnants of another modest mosque, the **Mezquita de las Tornerías**, in the street of the same name, now house an arts and crafts display.

Museums Around the corner from the Iglesia de Santo Tomé and the adjoining 15th century Palacio de los Condes de Fuensalida is the 14th century **Taller del Moro** on Calle del Taller del Moro. Formerly part of a noble family's residence, it now houses a modest museum with a small collection of mudéjar decorative items, ceramics, wood architraves and stucco work. It is open from 10 am to 2 pm and 4 to 6.30 pm, but is closed on Mondays, and Sunday afternoon (100 ptas).

The **Museo de Arte Contemporáneo**, housed in the restored 16th century mudéjar Casa de las Cadenas, in the lane of the same name, is home to a modest collection of Spanish modern art, including a couple of pieces by Joan Miró and some turn of the century Toledo landscapes by Aureliano de Bcructe. Opening hours and entry are as for the Taller del Moro.

The Iglesia de San Román, an impressive hybrid of mudéjar and Renaissance styles, houses the **Museo de los Concilios y Cultura Visigótica**. The documents, jewellery and other items are perhaps less interesting than the building itself, located up Calle de San Román from Plaza del Padre Juan de Mariana. Opening hours and entry are as above.

Farther north, below Plaza de Padilla, the **Monasterio de Santo Domingo El Antiguo** is one of the oldest convents in Toledo, dating from the 11th century. It houses some of El Greco's early commissions (most are copies) and an eclectic display of religious artefacts. It's open from 11 am to 1.30 pm and 4 to 7 pm (100 ptas).

Outside the city walls on the road to Madrid, the one-time **Hospital de Tavera**, built in 1541, contains an interesting art collection, including some of El Greco's last works. It is open daily from 10.30 am to 1.30 pm and 3.30 to 6 pm (500 ptas).

Around the City Walls Large portions of the old city walls remain intact, and for many people the first sight of old Toledo is the hefty turrets of the 16th century **Puerta Nueva de Bisagra**, emblazoned with

Carlos I's coat of arms and as imposing now as they must have appeared to visitors approaching from Madrid down the Camino Real de Castilla.

Just outside the Puerta Nueva de Bisagra is a shaded park with outdoor cafés. Down the hill to the west is another park in which fragments of the former **Circo Romano**, or Roman Circus remain. They aren't impressive really, but you can see the elliptical outline.

You can follow the walls around to the west until you reach the solid **Puerta del Cambrón** (Buckthorn Gate), also known as Puerta de los Judíos (Jews' Gate) for its proximity to the judería. A short walk from here past Iglesia de San Juan de los Reyes brings you down to one of the two remaining medieval bridges in Toledo – the **Puente de San Martín**, several times rebuilt and altered since its initial construction in the 14th century.

From here a path continues on along the river, a nice shady walk in the summer heat. At the southern tip of the casco, you'll find (if you poke around) the remnants of what was once **Arab baths** and cloth-dyeing tubs. The site is not marked: follow the path off

the Carreras de San Sebastián road westward from near the Hotel El Diamantista.

Outside the City For more fresh air and some of the best views of the city, head over the Puente de Alcántara to the south bank of the **Río Tajo**. Alternatively, you can get the tiny cable-ferry (if it's running) from near the Hotel El Diamantista, in the south end of the casco, and hike up the opposite bank. Scattered about this hinterland are the *cigarrales*, country estates of wealthy toledanos.

Swimming
Midsummer in Toledo is scorching, and several pools open in the hot months. The best is the Piscina Municipal on the roundabout at the northern end of Avenida de la Reconquista (take bus No 1 from Zocodover or walk).

Special Events
The feast of Corpus Christi falls on the Thursday of the ninth week after Easter and is by far the most extraordinary event on Toledo's religious calendar. Several days of festivities culminate in a procession in which the massive Custodia de Arfe (see Catedral earlier) is paraded around the city. It is preceded on the Thursday by hundreds of people marching in traditional dress in the name of countless religious fraternities *(cofradías)* and other groups, as well as the army (the troops always get a big hand in this traditionally military town).

Easter is also marked by several days of solemn processions by masked members of cofradías. In the key days of Holy Week some of these processions take place around midnight.

The Feast of the Assumption is 15 August. On this day of the Sagrario de la Virgen, you can drink of the cathedral's well water. The water is held by many to have miraculous qualities; the queues for a swig from an earthenware *botijo* can be equally astonishing.

Places to Stay
Camping & Youth Hostel There are two convenient camp sites, the closest of which

---

Bitter Tears & Peaceful Strolls

Most day-trippers to Toledo follow a well-defined and restricted route through the city, and it is quite easy to flee the crowds by diving off into less explored barrios. The medieval labyrinth that spreads south of the cathedral and the Alcázar was, and to an extent remains, a largely working-class district, and reading the various explanatory plaques in the streets (unfortunately, in Spanish only) adds flavour to an otherwise uncluttered stroll. The waters of the Pozo Amargo (Bitter Well), in the centre of this area, are said to have gone bad after a young Jewish woman's Christian lover was murdered by her father, for in her grief she spent much of the remainder of her life crying tears of bitterness into the well.

is **Circo Romano** (☎ *925 22 04 42, Avenida de Carlos III 19)*; it charges 590 ptas per person, tent and car. Better and marginally cheaper, but more awkward for those without their own vehicle, is **El Greco** (☎ *925 22 00 90)*. It's a couple of kilometres south-west of town, on the road to La Puebla de Montalbán, and has good views of Toledo from the pool.

The **HI youth hostel** (☎ *925 22 45 54)* is exceptionally well located in the Castillo de San Servando, a castle that started life as a Visigothic monastery and later belonged to the Knights Templar. B&B costs 1100 ptas (under 26) or 1350 ptas per person. A membership card is necessary.

Pensiones, Hostales & Hotels – Old City The fair range of accommodation is offset by the number of people looking for a bed, especially from about Easter to September, so arrive early. Lower-end places generally skimp on heating in winter and have only communal showers. Some of the mid-range and top-end hotels have discount rooms in January and February.

Toledo's cheapest place lies in the maze of alleys directly south of the Alcázar, an area little visited by tourists which retains the air of the medieval working-class quarter it once was. **La Belviseña** (☎ *925 22 00 67, Cuesta del Can 5)* is a basic affair at 1200 ptas per person, plus 100 ptas for a shower. The **Pensión Virgen de la Estrella** (☎ *925 25 31 34, Calle Real del Arrabal 18)*, just inside the Puerta Nueva de Bisagra, is in the same class and has rooms for 1600 ptas per person.

Farther into the tangle of the casco is the simple, pleasant **Pensión Segovia** (☎ *925 21 11 24, Calle de Recoletos 2)*. It has spotless doubles ranging in price from 2100 to 2500 ptas, with a slight reduction for single occupancy. Around the corner is the cheerful **Pensión Castilla** (☎ *925 25 63 18)*, with tiny rooms at 2200/3900 ptas plus IVA, some with bath. Virtually on Zocodover, **Hostal Las Armas** (☎ *925 22 16 68, Calle de las Armas 7)* is several hundred years old

and retains a run-down flavour. Rooms cost 2200/3400 ptas plus IVA.

Near the Alcázar, **Pensión Lumbreras** (☎ *925 22 15 71, Calle de Juan Labrador 9)* has reasonable singles/doubles/triples around a pleasant courtyard for 1700/3000/4200 ptas, and the **Hostal Nuevo Labrador**, (☎ *925 22 26 20)* has rooms for 3210/6420 ptas plus IVA. The **Pensión Nuncio Viejo** (☎ *925 22 81 78, Calle del Nuncio Viejo 19)*, on the other side of the cathedral, is pretty, but its doubles are unexceptional at 3000 ptas, or 3300 ptas with own bathroom.

Moving up the scale, **Pensión Santa Úrsula** (☎ *925 21 09 63, Calle de Santa Úrsula 14)* has decent doubles with bathroom for 5500 ptas. The **Hotel Santa Isabel** (☎ *925 25 31 36, Calle de Santa Isabel 24)* has been recommended by readers. Rooms cost 3673/5720 ptas plus IVA.

The **Hotel Maravilla** (☎ *925 22 83 17, Plaza de Barrio Rey 7)* is in a quiet spot off Zocodover. Rooms with private bath cost 4000/6500 ptas plus IVA. Nearby is the pleasant **Hotel Imperio** (☎ *925 22 76 50, Calle de las Cadenas 7)* charging 4250/6200 ptas plus IVA. For about the same you can be down on the river in the gracious **Hotel El Diamantista** (☎ *925 25 14 27, Plaza de Retama 5)*.

Pricier is the **Hotel Pintor El Greco** (☎ *925 21 42 50, fax 925 21 58 19, Calle de Alamillos del Tránsito 13)*. Singles/doubles cost 10,960/13,700 ptas plus IVA. **Hostal del Cardenal** (☎ *925 22 49 00, fax 925 22 29 91, Paseo de Recaredo 24)* sits in a beautiful garden just down from Puerta Nueva de Bisagra and has a popular restaurant. Singles/doubles are good value at 7300/11,800 ptas plus IVA, less in low season. **Hotel Carlos V** (☎ *925 22 21 00, fax 925 22 21 05, Calle de Trastámara 1)* has rooms for 8870/12,980 ptas plus IVA.

Pensiones, Hostales & Hotels – Outside the Old City If all else fails, there is a cluster of places near the Plaza de Toros, a five minute walk north along the Carretera de Madrid from Puerta Nueva de Bisagra. The most amenable of these is probably the **Pensión Amalí** (☎ *925 22 70 18, Calle de Alonso Berruguete 1*) with doubles at 4100 ptas.

On the southern bank of the Tajo and boasting magic views of the city is Toledo's premier establishment, the **Parador Nacional Conde de Orgaz** (☎ *925 22 18 50, fax 22 51 66*). Rooms cost 18,500 plus IVA. Without a car it's awkward to reach, although bus No 7 from Zocodover goes close.

Places to Eat

There is occasionally a mediocre **produce market** on Plaza Mayor where you can buy your own supplies. The **Serprix supermarket** at Calle del Comercio 4 is central.

The cuisine of Toledo and indeed the whole region is based on simple peasant fare. Partridge, cooked in a variety of fashions, is probably the premier dish and particularly representative of Toledo. *Carcamusa*, a meat dish, is also typical, as is *cuchifritos*, a kind of potpourri of lamb, tomato and egg cooked in white wine with saffron.

Restaurants Toledo is predictably full of restaurants, many serving up average food for not-so-average prices.

For excellent bocadillos – great after a round of the bars – it is hard to beat *Ñaca Ñaca* on Zocodover (skip McDonald's across the road!). If you just want to pick at a pâté and cheese platter over a beer, try the **Jacaranda Bar** (*Callejón de los Dos Codos 1*). It's a cosy place and you could eat the equivalent of a full meal for about 1200 ptas. **Ludeña** (*Plaza de la Magdalena 13*) is an excellent little place for a full meal (set lunch for 1200 ptas) or simply a beer and tapas.

Among the cheap lunch spots, **El Delfín**, opposite the Museo de Taller del Moro, has a set *menú* for 900 ptas. For outdoor dining, the **Osiris Bar** on the shady Plaza de Barrio Nuevo is a decent choice, with set lunches from 1400 ptas. Other outdoor options include the slightly pricier **Restaurante Alex** on Plaza del Amador de los Ríos, or **El**

Patio (*Plaza de Vicente 4*), which sits in a lovely courtyard.

Palacio de Fuensalida (*Plaza del Conde 2*), in the palace of the same name and near the Iglesia de Santo Tomé, serves paella under vaulted ceilings. For slow service but good food (including a selection of pizzas), the family-run **El Armiño** (*Calle de las Tendillas 8*) is solid.

La Abadía (*Plaza de San Nicolás 3*), as well as being a popular bar, offers excellent downstairs dining with typical Toledan dishes such as *perdiz estofada* (stewed partridge). The set lunch *menú*, at about 1800 ptas, is reliable.

For Toledo's best seafood, **Bar La Ría** (*Callejón de los Bodegones 6*) is hard to beat. The place, allegedly run by Galicians, has a wide menu – problem is, it's popular and tiny. A good meal will cost about 2000 ptas a head. Have a shot at the *mariscada*, a cold and hot seafood platter.

Among the best known of Toledo's more expensive restaurants is **Restaurante Aurelio** (*Calle de la Sinagoga 1*). You will eat very well for about 5000 ptas a head. There is an extension across the road at No 6 and the proprietors have another restaurant at Plaza del Ayuntamiento 4. Better still is the **Restaurante Hierbabuena** (*Callejón de San José 17*). The food is expensive but imaginatively classy – a considerable step up from the usual traditional fare.

Cafés The cafés on Zocodover are pleasant for a morning coffee or lunchtime beer over a paper, but the prices reflect the predominantly tourist clientele – that is, you pay double the usual.

Near the cathedral, **El Torreón** (*at Plaza del Consistorio 3*) is a nice stop for coffee or lunch.

Cafetería Scorpions (*Calle del Pintor Matías Moreno 10*) is a trendier place to while away a Sunday afternoon. It has board games too and is Toledo's only Internet café.

Just outside Toledo is a charming old roadside hostelry – **La Venta del Alma** (*Carretera de Piedrabuena 25*). Cross the

Puente de San Martín and turn left up the hill – it's a couple of hundred metres up on your left.

For splendid views of the city, head out of town. Where the Carretera de Circunvalación (the ring road on the south bank of the Tajo) forks for the parador there is a small roadside drink stop, the *Kiosko Base*. Or you could enjoy still more sweeping views and more expensive drinks from the *parador* itself. Farther up again, *Hotel Doménico* has a beer terrace with views – about the only place you'll get a breeze in the stifling midsummer months.

Entertainment

Bars & Discos Toledo is not known for outstanding nightlife, but there are enough watering holes and noisy discos bursting with the city's young student population to keep you happy for a couple of days.

Start on a sedate note at *1700*, a pleasant cervecería on Plaza de las Tendillas. A couple of places serve a variety of Spanish and foreign beers – a decent one is *Lupulo*, just off Calle de Alfonso XII. Another is *La Abadía*. In the streets around here, particularly Calle de los Alfileritos and Calle de la Sillería, are many of the old city's busier, student-oriented bars. *Camelot (Calle del Cristo de la Luz 10)* is a standard late-night watering hole. Calle del Ángel also has a throng of lively places.

At *Sildavia (Calle de Santa Fe 12)* go downstairs and ask for your favourite cocktail in a *porrón*, the glass version of a wine pouch – stained shirts are inevitable.

For more old-fashioned dancing and a decidedly more refined atmosphere, *El Café de Garcilaso (Calle de Rojas 5)* is a unique spot that doesn't get moving until quite late. Back in the early 1970s it was about the only place young toledanos could let their hair down – and was much disapproved of by the Church.

Most of the young people finish the night in one of the discos down by the Miradero (a terrace overlooking the northern end of town), on the road from Zocodover to Puerta Nueva de Bisagra.

Theatre & Cinema *Teatro Rojas (☎ 925 22 39 70)* on Plaza Mayor often has an interesting program of theatre and dance, sometimes with prestigious Spanish and foreign companies. Tuesday nights are reserved for film cycles, often foreign pictures in the original language. Check for weekend kids' matinees. Otherwise there is the *María Cristina cinema complex (Calle del Marqués de Mendigorría 10)* near the Plaza de Toros. In summer an open-air cinema functions at the Miradero.

Spectator Sports

Bullfighting aficionados can occasionally indulge their whims at the Plaza de Toros (built in 1866) on the road to Madrid. Quality *corridas* are more the exception than the rule.

Shopping

For centuries, Toledo was renowned for the excellence of its swords. Few people need such weapons these days, but toledanos keep forging them, along with all sorts of other metalwork. Sword sheaths, lighters and other objects bearing damascene *(damasquinado)* decoration (a fine encrustation of gold and/or silver in Arab artistic tradition) can make decent souvenirs. Another Arab bequest is the art of ceramics, which the whole region churns out in all imaginable forms. Toledo is bursting with stores selling this stuff, so shop around.

Among all the souvenir shops it is possible to find a few places of a more original bent and higher quality. The Antigüedades shop at Calle de los Reyes Católicos 8, near the Sinagoga de Santa María La Blanca, has good antiques – among them a lot of Jewish religious items – and attractive lithographs. For hand-painted copies of mainly medieval art on solid wood bases, peek into Las 3 Culturas, Calle de San Román 3.

Toledo is also famed for its marzipan *(mazapán)*, which city merchants flog to all and sundry. There is good and bad. The Santo Tomé brand is reputable. You could also try El Convento, made by Dominican nuns at the Monasterio de Jesús y María.

Take bus No 4 from Zocodover along Avenida de Europa to Buenavista. At the second roundabout, turn right up the hill, and the new monastery is to your left after another roundabout. When you enter you'll see a kind of antique rotating dumb waiter. The nuns don't want to see or be seen, so hit the buzzer and tell them what you want, then put your money in the dumb waiter and they rotate the marzipan out.

Getting There & Away

For most major destinations, you will need to backtrack to Madrid (or at least as far as Aranjuez).

Bus Galiano Continental buses run every half-hour between Madrid (Estación Sur) and Toledo's estación de autobuses (☎ 925 21 58 50) from about 6 am to 10 pm (to 11.30 pm on Sunday and holidays). Direct buses (50 minutes) run roughly every hour; the remainder call at all *pueblos*. The fare is 580 ptas. Other companies run to most surrounding towns and villages, such as Orgaz, Alcázar de San Juan and La Puebla de Montalbán. The Aisa bus company has a service to Cuenca at 5.30 pm from Monday to Friday, and daily buses to Albacete at 3 pm and Ciudad Real at 3.30 pm.

Train Built in 1920 in neomudéjar style, Toledo's train station (☎ 925 22 12 72) is a pretty introduction to the city. Although the *cercanías* operating to Madrid (Atocha) via Aranjuez are more pleasant than the bus, there are only ten of them per day (the first at 9 am, the last at 9.00 pm). From Madrid, the first leaves at 7.20 am and the last at 8.43 pm; a one-way ticket costs 630 ptas.

Car & Motorcycle The N-401 connects Toledo with Madrid. Heading south, you can take the same road to Ciudad Real, from where it becomes the N-420 to Córdoba. If you want the N-IV Autovía de Andalucía, the main motorway running south from Madrid to Córdoba and Sevilla, take the N-400 for Aranjuez. The N-403 heads

north-west for Ávila and continues as the N-501 for Salamanca.

Getting Around

You won't want wheels to explore the nooks and crannies of Toledo's casco, but buses circulate through it and connect with outlying suburbs. Handy ones run between Zocodover and the train station (Nos 5 and 6) or the estación de autobuses (No 5).

There is a taxi rank just up from Zocodover in the shadow of the Alcázar, and another at the estación de autobuses. Or you can call one on ☎ 925 25 50 50.

Parking is possible, but not easy. Car parks charge around 150 ptas an hour.

AROUND TOLEDO
Carranque

Since its discovery in 1983, archaeologists have been excavating what they believe to be the foundations of a late 4th century Roman basilica, which would make it the oldest in Spain. The remains of a 12th century monastery with some valuable mosaics are also undergoing excavation and study. Work is expected to keep archaeologists busy until 2000, after which the site will be opened to the public. Check with the tourist office in Toledo. Carranque is just off the N-401 highway some 35km north of Toledo.

Castles

Castilla-La Mancha is littered with castles in varying states of upkeep. Some are readily accessible by public transport, while others are near impossible to get to without your own wheels. The following is a selection of castles within striking distance of Toledo.

Orgaz About 40km south of Toledo on the N-401 to Ciudad Real, this cheery village boasts a modest 15th century *castillo*. It's in good nick but only open every second Wednesday from April to November. According to a rather enigmatic plaque, El Cid's wife, Doña Jimena, 'played here'. The leafy Plaza Mayor is flanked by attractive buildings with heavy wood-beam arcades and an 18th century church built by Alberto Churriguera. Buses run fairly regularly from Toledo.

If you have a vehicle, a more interesting way of reaching Orgaz is via the C-400 road. About 20km out of Toledo, the ruined Arab castle of **Almonacid de Toledo** rises up directly in front of you. Some legends suggest El Cid lived here, but the lonely ruins have long been abandoned. A few kilometres farther down the road is another, smaller castle, in the centre of the village of **Mascaraque**.

Castillo de Montalbán Standing majestically over the Río Torcón valley some 30km south-west of Toledo, this hulking ruin is believed to have been erected by 12th century Knights Templar. Its isolated setting leaves much to the imagination. Officially it's open from May to January only, but there's little to stop you wandering around at any time. Unfortunately, you'll need a vehicle to get here. Take the C-401 from Toledo to the C-403 junction and turn right toward La Pueblo de Montalbán. Ten kilometres up you'll see signs pointing to the castle.

Escalona This town sports a castle ruin of Arab origin, prettily located on the banks of the Río Alberche. If you're mobile it's worth stopping for and is located 52km north-west of Toledo on the N-403.

The West

TALAVERA DE LA REINA

Scene of a key battle between Wellington and the French in 1809, and overrun by the Muslim Almoravid dynasty seven centuries earlier, Talavera betrays little evidence of its long and varied history. Though the town was the birthplace of Fernando de Rojas, whose *Celestina* (published in 1499) is judged by some as Europe's first great novel, the only evidence of artistic activity of any sort today lies in the ubiquitous ceramics for which the town has long been justly famed. A fine example of their use is the façade of the recently restored **Teatro Victoria**, just off Plaza del Padre Juan de Mariana. Within the old city walls is the **Museo Ruiz de Luna**, which houses a good collection of ceramic plates, jugs and even an impressive tiled altar, much of which dates from the 16th and 17th centuries. The museum is in a beautifully restored convent at Calle de San Agustín el Viejo s/n, and is open from 10 am to 2 pm and 4 to 6.30 pm, but closed Sunday afternoon and Monday (100 ptas). To make your own purchases, follow the road leading north to the N-V motorway, which is lined with ceramics factories and shops.

There is no particular reason to stay, but you'll find a few *hostales* around if you need them. *Hostal Edan (☎ 925 80 69 89, Paseo de Extremadura 24)* has singles/doubles for 2500/5000 ptas.

The estación de autobuses is in the town centre. Regular buses between Madrid and Badajoz stop here and 10 daily go to Toledo (90km east; 715 ptas). You can also reach Mérida, Cáceres, Plasencia, and Guadalupe (twice daily). Talavera is on the Madrid-Lisbon train line, not one of Spain's fastest.

AROUND TALAVERA DE LA REINA

More pleasant than Talavera is the village of **Oropesa**, 34km west along the N-V. Its 14th century **castle** (open daily except Monday from 10 am to 2 pm and 4 to 8 pm; entry 200 ptas) looks north across the plains to the Sierra de Gredos and also hosts a *parador (☎ 925 43 00 00)* which has comfortable doubles for 15,000 ptas plus IVA.

Another 13km south, **El Puente del Arzobispo** is another well-known ceramics centre. There are plenty of places where you can inspect the town's wares. The bridge after which the town is named was built in the 14th century.

MONTES DE TOLEDO

Beginning as the low foothills that lie south of Toledo astride the road to Ciudad Real, the Montes de Toledo rise westwards towards Extremadura. Exploring the Montes takes you into the heart of some of the most sparsely populated country of Spain's interior. You can't get much farther away from the tourist routes, but you could make a slow trip through the mountains on the way from Toledo to Guadalupe (or vice-versa). Most towns are served by the occasional bus – often no more than one a day on weekdays – from Toledo.

If you have a vehicle, the most straight-forward route is the C-401, which skirts the northern slopes of the Montes. Eleven kilometres short of Navahermosa, a trail leads south to the **Embalse de Torcón**, a popular lakeshore picnic spot.

Beyond Navahermosa you have several options for branching south. Some of the more heavily wooded areas offer unexpectedly charming vistas, and apart from the odd tiny pueblo, you will hardly see a soul. One longish route that gives a taste of the area would see you dropping south off the C-401 at Los Navalmorales. Take the TO-752 toward Los Navalucillos, a few kilometres after which is a peaceful *bar* right on the banks of the lively little Río Pusa. From here you keep heading south past run-down little villages until you hit a T-junction. Turning right (west) you wind 35km to the northern reaches of the huge Embalse de Cijara, part of a chain of reservoirs fed by the Río Guadiana. After the tiny village of Cijara, swing north towards Puerto Rey, a mountain pass from where you can branch off west along a back road to the C-401 and the last curvy stretch towards Guadalupe (see the Extremadura chapter).

Yet another alternative is to head for the **San Pablo de los Montes** area. You can take the TO-781 via Argés south of Toledo, and onward via Las Ventas con Peña Aguilera (renowned for its venison). San Pablo de los Montes is an average hill town, but a 10km drive farther south and over the mountaintop brings you to **Baños de Robledillo**, with thermal springs. *Balnearios Baños de Robledillo* (☎ *925 41 53 00*) has beds for 1500 ptas per person, *en suite* doubles for 2300

ptas, and a restaurant. For 900 ptas you can soak in the curative waters.

The South

CIUDAD REAL

Just 110km down the road from the Imperial City of Toledo lies its royal counterpart, Ciudad Real. Founded by Castilian King Alfonso X in 1255 to check the power of the Knights of Calatrava, who were based in nearby Almagro, Ciudad Real quickly became an important provincial capital, although only finally eclipsing Almagro in the 18th century. Little remains today of the old city, and you'd not be missing much by following the ring road around it and continuing on your way.

Information
The Oficina de Información Turística (☎ 926 21 29 25), Avenida de Alarcos 31, is open Monday to Friday from 9 am to 2 pm. It has a reasonable stock of information on the province. The main correos is on Plaza de la Constitución. The postcode for poste restante is 13080.

Things to See
Coming from the north, you enter Ciudad Real by the **Puerta de Toledo**, a 14th century defensive gate built in mudéjar style by Alfonso XI.

Inside the largely modern city, the pick of the crop is the **Museo Provincial**, Calle del Prado 4, which offers a reasonable display of archaeological finds dating from Palaeolithic times, along with a collection of artworks, mostly provincial, covering the past four centuries. It is open from 10 am to 2 pm daily (except Monday) and 5 to 8 pm from Tuesday to Saturday (free).

Of the few churches to be seen, the most striking is the 14th century Gothic **Iglesia de San Pedro**.

Places to Stay & Eat
Accommodation is a little sad, so try not to be caught in Ciudad Real. Just outside the

southern end of the city centre is a pair of undistinguished places. Cheapest and most spartan is the *Pensión Villa Oriente (☎ 926 25 42 77, Carretera de Valdepeñas 12)* with rooms for 1200/2200 ptas (communal bathroom). The *Pensión Escudero (☎ 926 25 23 09, Calle de Galicia 48)* has rooms starting at 2400/3600 ptas with shared bathroom. Bus No 5 from the train station runs past these. If you've got a bit more cash to spare, the four-star *Hotel Santa Cecilia (☎ 926 22 85 45, Calle de Tinte 3)* is a steal at 7500 ptas (plus IVA) per room.

For all your food and drinking requirements, head for Avenida del Torreón del Alcázar and the parallel Calle de los Hidalgos. The former is lined with cafés and restaurants, such as *El Torreón* at No 7, which specialises in game from the region, and *El Barco* at No 11, more of a bar with a sailing theme (in this part of the country?)

and decent seafood. In Calle de los Hidalgos you can snack well on tapas while imbibing *cañas* in the string of bars. Otherwise, the *Restaurante Villa Real (Calle de las Postas 12)* does *platos combinados* from 650 ptas.

Getting There & Away

Bus The estación de autobuses is south of the town centre, off Ronda de Ciruela. There's a bus to Toledo at 8 am, another to Córdoba at 11 am and five a day to Madrid. Most surrounding towns can be reached by bus.

Train The bulk of trains linking Madrid with Andalucía, including the high-speed AVE to Sevilla, call in at Ciudad Real (☎ 926 22 02 02; the station is east of the town centre). Trains also head east to Albacete, Valencia and Alicante, as well as to Badajoz in Extremadura. Local bus Nos 5 and 2 run to the station from Plaza del Pilar in the centre.

CIUDAD REAL PROVINCE
Almagro

It may have come second in the struggle for local supremacy with Ciudad Real, but Almagro has retained a charm long lost in its competitor. De facto medieval capital of what even today is still known as the Campo de Calatrava, Almagro underwent a unique face-lift in the 16th century after the arrival of several German families, including the Fuggers of Augsburg, bankers to Spain's Carlos I. It is largely to them and their successors that Almagro's porticoed **Plaza Mayor** owes its present distinctive appearance.

At No 18 you'll find **El Corral de Comedias**, a 17th century theatre still often used, especially for the annual Festival Internacional de Teatro Clásico in July. It is open from Tuesday to Friday from 10 am to 2 pm and 5 to 8 pm (shorter hours on the weekend; closed on Monday); buy tickets (400 ptas) at the small Museo del Teatro (same hours) across the square. A smattering of churches, convents and public

CIUDAD REAL

PLACE TO STAY
12 Hotel Santa Cecilia

PLACES TO EAT
6 Restaurante Villa Real
10 El Torreón
11 El Barco

OTHER
1 Puerta de Toledo
2 Main Correos
3 Museo Provincial
4 Plaza Mayor
5 Ayuntamiento
7 Oficina de Información Turística
8 Plaza del Pilar
9 Iglesia de San Pedro
13 Estación de Autobuses
14 Parque de Gasset

The Battle of Alarcos

On 19 July 1195, the greatest of all the Almohad rulers, Yacoub Al-Mansour (the Victorious), drew his forces up near the settlement of Alarcos, about 5km southwest of Ciudad Real, to face the Castilian army of Alfonso VIII. Unwilling to wait for the arrival of reinforcements marching from the north, Alfonso decided to unleash his cavalry at the Muslim forces, recently arrived from Morocco to restore Muslim control over Spain. Alfonso's horsemen crushed Al-Mansour's vanguard but quickly found themselves surrounded. A promising start thus turned into a rout.

According to the Almohad chronicler Ibn Idari: 'Allah granted us victory and the defeated Christians turned their backs and abandoned their swords. The tyrant's camp was sacked and swept as in a harvest with the Christians' deaths – said to be around 30,000 ... Alfonso, the enemy of God, escaped to Toledo ...'. Some say only 300 soldiers survived the disaster.

A Christian observer saw Alfonso's role a little differently: 'The noble king advanced and, plunging in amongst the enemy, felled with manliness many Moors ... but as his men realised that Spain was in imminent danger, pulled him from the battle. He later arrived in Toledo with a few soldiers, aggrieved by the great misfortune.'

Al-Mansour never really capitalised on his victory, and 17 years later it was made irrelevant by the crushing Christian victory in the Battle of Las Navas de Tolosa. Today there is little to see at the battleground except a chapel dedicated to Our Lady of Alarcos.

Almagro is preferable to Ciudad Real for an overnight stop. *Fonda Peña* (☎ 926 86 03 17, Calle de Emilio Piñuela 10), just north of Plaza Mayor, is a good, clean deal at 1300/2300 ptas for singles/doubles. The *Hospedería Convento de la Asunción de Calatrava* (☎ 926 88 20 87, Calle de Ejido de Calatrava s/n) has doubles for 3500 ptas with shower or 4000 ptas with full bath. Nearby, *Hotel Don Diego* (☎ 925 86 12 87, Calle de Bolaños 1) charges 4280/6490 ptas plus IVA for singles/doubles (more in the high season).

If you want to do it in a little more style, the *parador* (☎ 926 86 01 00), in a former convent on Ronda de San Francisco, has rooms for 14,000/17,500 ptas plus IVA.

There are several cafés and bars on Plaza Mayor; the *Restaurante Airén* at No 41 has tables on the square.

Two trains a day go to Madrid and three or four to Ciudad Real and Jaén. You can also get to Alicante and Barcelona, both in the morning. Buses run from near the Hotel Don Diego to Ciudad Real, but there are none on Sunday.

Castillo de Calatrava

About 30km south of Almagro, the brooding walls of the castle-and-monastery complex of Calatrava La Nueva (signposted as Castillo de Calatrava) command magnificent views across the sierra of the same name. Once a forward base of the medieval order of knights that long controlled this frontier area of La Mancha during the Reconquista, the complex is open from Tuesday to Sunday from 10 am to 2 pm and 4 to 7 pm (closed to 8 pm in summer; 300 ptas). Even if closed it merits a visit for the site alone. From Calzada de Calatrava, it's 7km south along the CR-504 and is accessible only with your own vehicle.

Parque Nacional de Las Tablas de Daimiel

You get used to a steady diet of olive-studded red plains and forbidding plateaus while traversing much of southern Castilla-

buildings around the town make Almagro a pleasant spot for a little exploration. The Oficina de Turismo de Almagro (☎ 926 86 07 17) is two streets south of Plaza Mayor at Calle de Bernardas 2.

La Mancha, but a couple of exceptions prove the rule.

The reedy lakes of Las Tablas, 11km north of Daimiel, are no great inspiration, but an early morning stroll here in spring or autumn can be profitable for the birdwatcher. The park's information centre is open daily from 8 am to dusk. There is no public transport to the park, and years of near drought have taken their toll. Fortunately, heavy rains in late 1995 and a subsequent deal to transfer water from the Río Tajo arrested the slow but steady decline.

Parque Natural de las Lagunas de Ruidera

A more unexpectedly green patch in the middle of parched Castilla-La Mancha is the Parque Natural de las Lagunas de Ruidera. Surrounding a series of small lakes, with the odd waterfall and diverse bird life, it is a favoured summer retreat for hot and bothered Castilians. There is an HI youth hostel on the Laguna Colgada, the *Albergue Juvenil Alonso Quijano (☎ 967 21 50 12 for reservations)*. Beds go for 1000 ptas if you're under 26, and meals are available. You need a membership card. Among several other options farther around the lakes is the *Hostal El Molino (☎ 926 69 90 73)*, which has doubles for 2500 ptas, or 3000 ptas with own bath. There are a few camping grounds too. The tourist office in the town of Ruidera has local maps.

You really need wheels to get into and around the park. The town of Ruidera and the lakes are about halfway between Ciudad Real and Albacete on the N-430 highway, and buses connect with Albacete.

Valdepeñas

The people of Castilla-La Mancha usually drink their own local wines but make an exception for the fruit of the Valdepeñas area's vines, which finds its way round not only the region, but the whole country. For those weary of long, dusty drives between the odd castle and provincial pueblos, a spot of wine tasting in one of this town's several *bodegas* might be just the ticket. The best

are north of town on the road to Madrid. If that's not your scene, don't bother stopping in this surprisingly large and uninviting place.

Villanueva de los Infantes

About 30km east of Valdepeñas along the C-415 road to Alcaraz (see the Sierra de Alcaraz section later) lies Villanueva de los Infantes, the fruit of a repopulation campaign in La Mancha as the Muslims fell back into Andalucía after the Battle of Las Navas de Tolosa in 1212. Like Almagro, the town's **plaza mayor** offers its most pleasing aspect, although the deep ochre-coloured buildings and heavy wooden balconies are altogether in a different style. On the square stands the **Iglesia de San Andrés**, with two doors and a pulpit in plateresque style. The 16th century poet Francisco Gómez Quevedo y Villegas was buried here. Like Almagro, Villanueva is studded with old nobles' houses and rewards a bit of a wander. You could do worse than stay a night in the *Hostal Imperio (☎ 926 36 00 77, Calle de las Monjas Franciscanas 14)*, where rooms are 2500/5000 ptas. Buses head west to Ciudad Real.

SOUTH-EAST TO ALBACETE

The highways leading south-east from Madrid to Albacete and on into Valencia take you through arguably some of the most depressing examples of Spanish countryside. The shrivelled, treeless expanses of La Mancha soon weary all but the most enthusiastic lovers of scorched earth. If you're heading to the Valencian *costas* from Madrid, about all you can do is scream down the road as fast as your wheels will carry you. Offerings along the way are sparse, but there are a few potential stops to break the journey.

Windmills & More Castles

Consuegra Following the C-400 out of Toledo (see Around Toledo earlier) the first stop of interest beyond Mora is Consuegra, set in classic La Mancha country. The tumbledown village huddles below a hill topped by a 13th century castillo that once belonged to the Knights of Malta. Fans of Don Quixote will be delighted to know that the castle is flanked by a dozen restored windmills. The site is well chosen: it gets quite blowy. There's a tourist office (☎ 925 47 57 31) in the Bolero mill (they all have names) open from 9 am to 2 pm and 3.30 to 6 pm (from 10.30 am on weekends) and the guy there can open up some of the mills for you. You can see at least one in action during the annual Fiesta de la Rosa del Azafrán, held on the last weekend of October.

The only place to stay is the *Hotel Las Provincias* (☎ 925 48 03 00), not a great option, out on the Toledo-Alcázar de San Juan highway. Singles/doubles cost 3500/6000 ptas. If you haven't got wheels to get away on, there are up to eight daily buses between Consuegra and Toledo (three on weekends) and a couple to Madrid.

Campo de la Criptana & Around Don Quixote thought he might do battle here, mistaking for enemies the windmills that are the only interesting feature in this otherwise dispiriting place. The Infotur tourist office (☎ 926 56 22 31) in the Poyatos mill is open from 10 am to 2 pm and 4 to 7 pm (5 to 8 pm in summer). There are a few small hotels in town, including the *Fonda Los Molinos* (☎ 926 56 02 90, *Calle de la Soledad 1)* with acceptable rooms for 1500 ptas per person (250 ptas extra for a shower).

The odd train and regional bus calls in, but options are greater from **Alcázar de San Juan**, 7km west of Campo de la Criptana (about five buses a day run between the two). In fact, if you're travelling around this area without your own wheels, you could wind up in Alcázar, a major rail junction. Apart from the 18th century Iglesia de Santa María (it is thought Cervantes was baptised here) in the square of the same name, and the nearby Torreón (tower) de Don Juan de Austria, there is nothing to draw you to Alcázar but its transport options. If you get stuck, the *Hostal Numancia* (☎ 926 54 11 47, *Avenida de*

Criptana 11), near the station, has decent rooms for 2000/3800 ptas. Trains leave for destinations throughout the country, including Albacete, Barcelona, Cádiz, Ciudad Real, Madrid, Málaga and Sevilla. Occasional buses serve Belmonte, Cuenca and Toledo.

The windmill-obsessed can see still more at **Mota del Cuervo**, 29km north-east of Campo de la Criptana, at the junction with the N-301.

Belmonte About 25km north-east of Mota del Cuervo is one of the better preserved Castilian castles. Set on a low knoll above the village of the same name, the 15th century Castillo de Belmonte, with its six round towers, was for a while home to France's Empress Eugénie after her husband Napoleon III lost the French throne in 1871. It's open Tuesday to Sunday from 10 am to 1 pm and 4.30 pm to sunset (300 ptas); there's not an awful lot to see inside. Also worth a visit, if you can find the curate, is the Iglesia Colegial de San Bartolomé, or **Colegiata**, with an impressive retablo. If you need to stay, *La Muralla* (☎ 967 17 10 45) is clean and cheap at 1500/3000 ptas, or the *Palacio Buenavista Hospedería* (☎ 967 18 75 80), near the church, is lovely and charges 5880/6950 ptas plus IVA.

ALBACETE

Named after its location (*al-basit*, in Arabic, refers to the plains), this dull provincial city expanded rapidly after malarial swamps were drained in the 19th century – too late to create anything of great interest. At best, it may serve as a transport junction for people wandering about this part of the country.

If you do get stuck between connections, wander toward the centre and down Paseo de la Libertad, which soon becomes Calle de Tesifonte Gallego. A few streets down and off to the right you'll find the **catedral**, appealing enough with its four Ionic columns. Otherwise, you could kill an hour or two in the leafy Parque de Abelardo

Tilting at Life

Time and again as you march across the glum stretches of La Mancha you are reminded by roadside plaques and signs that you are in the territory of Don Quixote (Don Quijote to the Spaniards). The potty and idealistic *manchego* knight, or rather his creator, Miguel de Cervantes, could not have chosen a more challenging territory for his character's search for a new individualism, unfettered by the rigidity of 16th century Spanish society.

But Cervantes, however well he may have known La Mancha, sensibly spent most of his years elsewhere, painting his life on a much vaster canvas than he allows his hapless but tenacious hero. A brief look at Cervantes' CV reveals an equally tenacious and perhaps even more accident-filled existence. Having passed his younger years between Valladolid, Salamanca, Madrid and Sevilla, the 19-year-old writer and soon-to-be adventurer fled to Italy in 1568 to escape a prison sentence for assault. Three years later he was wounded at the Battle of Lepanto. In 1573 he participated in the seizure of Tunis, and in 1575 he hopped on a galley for Spain from Naples. It seems natural that Cervantes, ever in trouble, should have been on board the boat that was separated from the convoy and taken by corsairs. Sold as a slave in Algiers, he only managed to escape, after four failed attempts, in 1580. After trying unsuccessfully to get passage to America, he married and almost settled down in Sevilla. Vexation was never far from Cervantes' door, however, and in 1602 he ended up in chains for his involvement in a bank's collapse. He did time again a few years later under an unproved charge of murder, and subsequently moved to Madrid, where in the years until his death in 1616 he wrote the bulk of his work, of which *El Ingenioso Hidalgo Don Quijote de la Mancha* was the jewel in his literary crown.

Sánchez, farther down Calle de Tesifonte Gallego, and the **Museo Provincial** therein.

The tourist office (☎ 967 58 05 22), at Calle del Tinte 2 south of the cathedral, is open Monday to Friday from 10 am to 2 pm and 4.30 to 6.30 pm, Saturday from 10 am to 6 pm, and Sunday until 3 pm, and does its best to promote the place.

There is a ton of accommodation in all categories if you end up needing to stay here. The *Aparicio* (☎ 967 21 78 90, Calle de los Zapateros 20) in the centre has simple rooms for 1300/2500 ptas.

A good thing to do in Albacete is leave. The estación de autobuses, next to the train station, is at the north-eastern end of town. Enatcar buses serve Madrid, Barcelona, Alicante, Valencia and Seville. There's a bus to Toledo at 5.30 am and to Cuenca at 6 am and 3 pm (nothing to either on Sunday). Buses run to most destinations in the province, including Chinchilla de Monte Aragón, Alcaraz and other villages in the Sierra, Ruidera and Almansa.

Trains serve Alicante, Ciudad Real, Madrid, Toledo via Aranjuez, and Valencia.

AROUND ALBACETE

There are several interesting little places scattered around Albacete, and at its more distant margins the scenery changes quite unexpectedly for the better.

Two local castles that Albacete's tourist office pushes hard are located just off the N-430 motorway toward Valencia. First is the restored fortress in **Chinchilla de Monte Aragón**, a whitewashed village with a pretty square, served by bus from Albacete. About 60km farther on, a square-turreted **castle** built by the Muslims stands high above the town of **Almansa**.

Río Júcar

Cutting a deep, tree-filled gorge to the north-east of Albacete, the Río Júcar makes for a pleasant back-road drive. About halfway along the east-west route, **Alcalá del Júcar** is impossible to miss – its 15th century castle tower is an unmistakable landmark. The village houses are piled crazily one above the other up the steep bank of the Júcar; the foot of the town is a wonderful place to admire this while having a drink or even a swim in the pool. There is a camping ground and a few cheap pensions, plus the pleasant *Hostal Rambla* (☎ *967 47 40 64, Paseo de los Robles 2)* with doubles for 5000 ptas and a terrace restaurant.

Sierra de Alcaraz

Stretching across the southern strip of Albacete province, the cool, green peaks of the Sierra de Alcaraz are laced with small, intensively farmed plots, dotted with villages and are a great escape from the dusty plains around Albacete. The Río Mundo begins its life as a waterfall near Riópar, and **Alcaraz** is itself an attractive little place with a pretty plaza mayor. You can follow a circuit passing through or past Alcaraz, Vianos, Riópar, Ayna, and Bogarra. Donkey-mounted shepherds still watch over their small flocks of sheep in the remoter corners of this low mountain territory. The odd bus gets to some of these towns, but you really would be better off

with a vehicle – and some good hiking boots. There are a few *hostales* in the area, including Alcaraz and Vianos.

The North-East

CUENCA

Castilla-La Mancha's most interesting town after Toledo offers relief from the parched countryside typical of most of the region. Spreading north and east of the city, the Serranía de Cuenca is a heavily wooded and fertile zone of low mountains and green fields. With a vehicle you could explore the city and the local region in two or three days.

History

Although it was probably inhabited before Roman times, nothing much is known of Cuenca until the period of Muslim occupation. Fortified by one Ismail bin Dilnun early in the 11th century, the city became a flourishing textile centre. The Christians took their time about conquering the place, and it fell only in 1177 to Alfonso VIII. The city continued to prosper in the following centuries, but the malaise that crippled much of the interior of Spain from the 16th century led to a decline from which Cuenca only began to recover this century.

Orientation

Cuenca is relatively small, its old centre a narrow rise high up at the northern end of the city between the river gorges of the Júcar and Huécar. The train and bus stations are virtually opposite each other near the centre of the new town, and a 10-minute walk from the foot of the casco antiguo. It's a long climb to Plaza Mayor, the main square in the casco. Most of the hotels and offices are in the new part of town.

Information

Tourist Office The Infotur office (☎ 969 23 21 19) at Calle de Alfonso VIII 2, just before the arches of Plaza Mayor, is especially helpful. It is open from 9.30 am to 2 pm and 4 to 6 pm.

Money There are plenty of banks in the new town, especially around Calle de la Carretería.

Post & Communications The main correos is on the corner of Calle del Parque de San Julián and Calle del Dr Fleming; the postcode for central Cuenca is 16080. The main Telefónica phone office is at Calle de Cervantes 2.

Medical Services & Emergency If you need the police in a hurry, call ☎ 091. In a medical emergency, call ☎ 969 23 01 31 for

the Cruz Roja. The Hospital de la Virgen (☎ 969 22 42 11) is off Avenida de la Cruz Roja at the north-western edge of the new town.

Catedral

Everyone seems to agree that the western façade of this Gothic cathedral is an unfortunately tasteless aberration. The initial errors were committed in the 1600s and compounded by restoration early this century. Built on the site of a mosque, the

CUENCA

PLACES TO STAY
3 Hotel Leonora de Aquitania
4 Parador
5 Posada de San José
25 Pensión Tintes
26 Posada de San Julián
29 Hostal Avenida
31 Pensión Central
33 Hotel Figón de Pedro
34 Pensiónes Marin & Adela

PLACES TO EAT
6 Bar Dulcinea
7 Restaurante San Nicolás
11 Bar La Tinaja
13 Mesón Casas Colgadas

OTHER
1 Castillo Walls
2 Iglesia de San Pedro
8 Plaza San Nicolás
9 Iglesia de San Miguel
10 Catedral & Palacio Episcopal
12 Museo Diocesano
14 Casas Colgadas & Museo de Arte Abstracto Español
15 Museo de Cuenca
16 Ayuntamiento
17 Infotur Tourist Office
18 Teatro Auditorio
19 Iglesia de la Santa Cruz
20 Torre de Mangana
21 Iglesia de San Felipe
22 Iglesia Plaza de El Salvador
23 Discos
24 Main Correos
27 Supermercado
28 La Caixa Bank
30 Deutsche Bank
32 Telephones (Telefónica)
35 Local Bus Nos 1 and 2 Plaza Mayor
36 Plaza de Toros
37 Train Station (RENFE)
38 Discos & Pubs
39 Estación de Autobuses

nave dates back as far as the early 13th century, although other elements such as the apse were constructed in the mid-15th century. The modern stained glass windows add cheery colour to an otherwise drab interior. There is a small **Museo de la Catedral** inside, open from 11 am to 2 pm and 4 to 6 pm, but the cathedral itself tends to open earlier in the morning.

Casas Colgadas

Possibly the most striking element of the medieval city is these so-called 'hanging houses', some of which jut out precariously over the steep defile of the Huécar. This is economical use of restricted living space! A couple of much-restored examples, characterised by layers of wooden balconies, now contain a posh restaurant and an art museum (see the next section).

Museums

All the museums are closed on Sunday afternoon and Monday. Depending on your taste in art, the star of the Cuenca line-up may be the **Museo de Arte Abstracto Español**. The setting, one of the casas colgadas, sports a fine artesonado coffered ceiling, and the artists represented include Chillida, Millares, Sempere and Zobel. Initially a private initiative of Fernando Zobel to unite works by fellow artists of the 1950s Generación Abstracta, it now includes works up to the present day. The museum is open from 11 am to 2 pm and 4 to 6 pm, and to 8 pm on Saturday (300 ptas).

Virtually opposite each other on Calle del Obispo Valero are the **Museo de Cuenca** (at No 12) and the **Museo Diocesano**. The former has a reasonable archaeological collection from the Cuenca area, ranging from prehistory through the Romanisation of this part of classical Hispania and on up to the 12th century. Of the religious art and artefacts in the latter, the 14th century Byzantine diptych is the jewel in the crown. How such a piece ended up in Cuenca, no-one seems to know. Each museum charges entry. Their opening hours are 11 am to 2 pm and 4 to 6 pm, but both are closed on Sunday afternoon and Monday (200 ptas each).

Muslim Cuenca

Down the hill from the casco antiguo along Calle de Alfonso VIII, you'll notice the **Torre de Mangana** off to the west, all that remains of a fortress built by Cuenca's Muslim rulers.

Places to Stay

Camping There are several camping grounds in the area around Cuenca. The relatively new *Camping Cuenca (☎ 969 23 16 56)* is 8km out of town on the road towards the Ciudad Encantada.

Pensiones & Hotels – Casco Antiguo

There is not a lot in the old part of town. Up at the top of the casco is the clean and simple *Pensión La Tabanqueta (☎ 969 21 12 90, Calle de Trabuco 13)* charging 2000 ptas per person. Ask for a room with views of the Júcar gorge. Bus No 2 from the stations comes all the way up here. Just beyond the cathedral, *Posada de San José (☎ 969 21 13 00, Ronda de Julián Romero 4)* is a lovely 16th century residence with doubles for 8900 ptas plus IVA. The only other possibility in the casco antiguo is the *Hotel Leonora de Aquitania (☎ 969 23 10 00, Calle de San Pedro 60)*, a classy place but with less character than the others. Singles/doubles cost 6500/8900 ptas plus IVA, but rooms are 1500 ptas more on weekends and from June to October.

Pensiones & Hotels – New Town

Cuenca's new part of town is littered with places to stay. The *Pensión Tintes (☎ 969 21 23 98, Calle de los Tintes 7)* has basic rooms for about 1500 ptas a head in summer. It is just outside the old town, as is the *Posada de San Julián (☎ 969 21 17 04, Calle de las Torres 1)*, a cavernous old place with doubles for 3000 ptas (3800 ptas with own bathroom).

A spartan sort of a place is the *Pensión Central (☎ 969 21 15 11, Calle del Doctor Chirino 9)*, with rooms for 1390/2550 ptas.

There are two no-frills pensiones in the same building at Calle de Ramón y Cajal 53, a short walk from the train station. *Pensión Adela* (☎ 969 22 25 33) has rooms for 1250 ptas per person, plus 200 ptas for showers. The *Pensión Marín* (☎ 969 22 19 78) upstairs is marginally better value at about the same price.

The *Hostal Avenida* (☎ 969 21 43 43, Calle de la Carretería 25) has basic singles for 1800 ptas and doubles with bath for 3500 ptas (more in summer). A decent low to mid-range place is the *Hotel Figón de Pedro* (☎ 969 22 45 11, Calle de Cervantes 13) with rooms for 3700/5000 ptas plus IVA, also costing slightly more in summer.

Parador The top of the tree is the *parador* (☎ 969 23 23 20) in the converted Dominican Convento de San Pablo on the southern bank of the Río Huécar. Rooms cost 14,000/17,500 ptas plus IVA. A footbridge connects the parador with the old town across the Huécar gorge.

Places to Eat

Restaurants There are several restaurants scattered around Plaza Mayor in the heart of the casco – easily the nicest part of town to eat in. The city's star is the rather expensive *Mesón Casas Colgadas (Calle de los Canónigos 3)* next to the Museo de Arte Abstracto Español. It is a wonderful location, but you won't get away for much less than 3000 ptas. Another decent establishment for solid manchego food is the *Restaurante San Nicolás (Calle de San Pedro 15)*. A full meal will come in at around 5000 ptas for two.

If you're not fussed about eating in the casco, your choices expand down the hill. The *Pensión Tintes* (see Places to Stay) has a pleasant dining room with a set meal for 1500 ptas.

Cafés The cafés on Plaza Mayor are perfect for a relaxing drink and people-watching. *Bar La Tinaja (Calle del Obispo Valero 4)* is a good one. *Bar Dulcinea (Calle de San Pedro 10)* is a pleasant and popular place for a drink.

Entertainment

Bars & Discos You can join the young set that crowds together along Calle de San Miguel for loads of noisy evening *copas* (drinks). There are a couple of bars here, but many of the locals just bring their own.

If you're looking for a bit more excitement, you'll find some discos across the road from the train station, and a few others on the slightly less tacky Calle del Doctor Galindez.

Shopping

You might want to pick up a special bottle of the local firewater, Resoli, made in the shape of the Casas Colgadas – an unusual souvenir idea.

Getting There & Away

Local bus Nos 1 and 2 for Plaza Mayor leave from near the train station.

Bus Up to nine daily runs (two express) with AutoRes serve Madrid (2½ hours; 1305 ptas or 1600 for the express). Other companies run buses to Valencia (up to three a day; 1300 ptas) and Albacete (up to two a day), and one to Barcelona (nine hours; 4170 ptas) via Teruel. This last one leaves at 9.30 am. There is a bus a day to Aranjuez, Beteta and Belmonte (3 pm, Monday to Saturday), and a 5.30 am to Toledo.

Train Cuenca lies on a line connecting Madrid to Valencia. Five trains a day go to Madrid (Atocha). They take 2½ hours and a 2nd-class ticket costs 1355 ptas. Four go to Valencia (3¼ hours; 1490 ptas).

Car & Motorcycle From Madrid, the quickest route to Cuenca is the N-III, turning east onto the N-400 at Tarancón.

SERRANÍA DE CUENCA

The rivers Júcar and Huécar flow through Cuenca from the high hinterland to the north-east of the city known as the Serranía de Cuenca. If you have transport (there are no buses), the area is worth a day of exploration.

From Cuenca, take the CM-2105 (formerly CU-921) about 30km to the so-called **Ciudad Encantada**, or Enchanted City. Extremely popular with locals, this series of rocks eroded into some quite fantastical shapes have been lent equally outlandish names by human observers. Still, it is possible to see a boat on its keel, a dog and a Roman bridge if you let your imagination carry you away. The site is open daily from 10 am to sunset (200 ptas). There is a *hostal* opposite the entrance with a restaurant and bar.

You could head back to the CM-2105 and proceed east. The country is pleasant, dotted by a couple of sleepy villages and the clear blue lake of the **Embalse de la Toba**. About 6km on from Huélamo, a turn-off to the right leads across the Montes Universales to Albarracín (see the Aragón chapter) – a perfect place to end the day's drive and stay overnight.

Alternatively, the CM-2105 swings north to the **Nacimiento del Río Cuervo**, a pretty enough spot with a couple of small waterfalls where the Río Cuervo rises. From here you could loop around towards **Beteta** and the gorge of the same name, or cross the provincial frontier into Guadalajara to make for the pleasant if unspectacular **Parque Natural del Alto Tajo**. To the west lies La Alcarria, about which see the Guadalajara section below.

AROUND CUENCA
Alarcón
One hundred kilometres or so south of Cuenca is the triangle-based Muslim castle at Alarcón, which has been converted into a *parador (☎ 969 33 03 15)*, with rooms for 19,000 ptas plus IVA.

Segóbriga
These marvellous Roman-era ruins may date from as far back as the 5th century BC. Visigoths then added their own touches to what had become a small but wealthy trade centre. The best-preserved structures are a Roman theatre and amphitheatre, and other remains include the outlines of a Visigothic basilica and a section of the aqueduct, which helped keep the city green in what is otherwise quite a barren desert. It appears you can explore the ruins at any time.

The site is near Saelices, 2km south of the N-III motorway between Madrid and Albacete. From Cuenca, drive west 55km on the N-400, then turn south on the C-202.

GUADALAJARA
Founded as Roman Arriaca and today a grubby provincial capital, Guadalajara (from the Arabic *wad al-hijaara*, or 'stony river') was in its medieval Muslim heyday the principal city of a large swathe of northern Spain under the green banner of Islam. At that stage, Madrid was no more than a military observation point. In 1085, however, the Castilian king Alfonso VI finally took Guadalajara as the Reconquista moved ponderously south. Under the Mendoza family, the city experienced its most prosperous era from the 14th to the 17th centuries, but from then on it was repeatedly sacked during the War of the Spanish Succession, the Napoleonic occupation and the Spanish Civil War.

Little remains of the city's glory days, but the much-restored **Palacio de los Duques del Infantado**, where the Mendoza family held court, is worth visiting. Its striking façade is a fine example of Gothic-mudéjar work. The heavily ornamental patio is equally admirable. The local art museum is housed here too, for what that's worth. It is open Tuesday to Saturday from 10 am to 2 pm and 4.15 to 7 pm, and morning only on Sunday (200 ptas).

The tourist office (☎ 949 22 06 98) is at Plaza de los Caídos 6, opposite the palacio. It is open daily from 10 am to 2 pm and 4 to 7.30 pm (morning only on Sunday).

Guadalajara is a simple day trip from Madrid, but you can stay if need be. A cheap, no-frills possibility is the *Hostal Venecia (☎ 949 21 13 52, Calle del Doctor*

Benito Hernando 12). Rooms cost 1600/3000 ptas. The *Restaurante Miguel Ángel* on Calle de Alfonso López de Haro, just off Calle Mayor, has a pleasant atmosphere, and offers set meals at 2500 ptas.

The estación de autobuses is on Calle del Dos de Mayo, a short walk from the palacio. About 20 buses daily connect Guadalajara with Madrid (Avenida de América) and charge 475 ptas one way. Buses from Madrid stop here en route to Zaragoza (three a day), Soria (at least one a day) and Teruel (one a day). Sigüenza, Pastrana and Brihuega get two connections daily on weekdays, one on Saturday and none on Sunday.

The train station is 2km out of town. Regular cercanías go to Madrid (Atocha and Chamartín) from about 5 am to 11.30 pm. Up to eight regional trains go to Sigüenza, beyond which occasional trains go on to Soria and Zaragoza.

LA ALCARRIA & BEYOND

The N-320 south-east from Guadalajara (it soon becomes the C-200) takes you towards the so-called **Mar de Castilla**, a collection of lakes formed by dams built in the late 1950s, in an area known as La Alcarria. Hardly a touristic goal of the first order, it was nevertheless immortalised in an enchantingly simple account of a walking trip made there in 1946 by Camilo José Cela, *Viaje a La Alcarria*.

Pastrana

Of the many pueblos Cela called in at, Pastrana is the most worthwhile for a brief stop. Forty-two kilometres south of Guadalajara along the C-200, it is a quiet medieval town. The area closest to the main road, Albaicín, was once populated mainly by *moriscos*, converts from Islam to Christianity. Passing through here you arrive at Plaza de la Hora, an airy and somewhat uncared-for square fronted by the impressive and equally unloved Palacio Ducal, where the one-eyed Princess of Eboli, Ana Mendoza de la Cerda, was confined in 1581 for a love

affair with Spanish King Felipe II's secretary. She died here 10 years later.

Proceed from the square along the main street and you soon reach the massive, gloomy **Iglesia de Nuestra Señora de la Asunción**. Inside is a small museum containing jewels and other personal effects of the Princess of Eboli. There are also some interesting 15th century Portuguese tapestries. Entry is 300 ptas, if the person with the keys is around.

You can stay and eat at the *Hostal Moratín* (☎ 949 37 06 28), a decent place on Calle de Moratín, just in from the main highway. Singles without bath cost 1800 ptas, and doubles with private bath 3800 ptas. A bus leaves early in the morning for Madrid, and two a day (on weekdays) go to Guadalajara.

Around Pastrana

Some 20km north-east of Pastrana is the area's main reservoir, the **Embalse de Entrepeñas**, where you can swim. You could push north on the C-204 to **Cifuentes**, with its 14th century castle, and on to the N-II, which you take for a few kilometres before branching off north again for Sigüenza.

There are other alternatives. From Guadalajara you could follow the motorway north-east and turn off at **Torija**, which has a rather impressive, if empty, castle. Take the C-201 for La Alcarria's second town after Pastrana, **Brihuega**, a leafy village that preserves stretches of its medieval walls. The drive east along the Río Tajuña is one of the more pleasant in this part of Castilla-La Mancha. The road forms a T-junction with the N-204, from where you can head north for Sigüenza or south to the great lake of the Embalse de Entrepeñas (see earlier in this section).

Yet another possibility from La Alcarria is to head east from the lake towards the **Parque Natural del Alto Tajo**, which also makes for some unexpectedly pretty drives. Combined with the Serranía de Cuenca (see under Cuenca earlier) farther south and east, the area is a popular weekend escape hatch for *madrileños* fleeing their hectic city lives.

SIGÜENZA

This tranquil medieval town, built on a low hill cradled by the Río Henares and a slender tributary, disguises a less peaceful past. Fighting here during the civil war was heavy and it was a long while before most, but not all, of the scars of the conflict could be removed.

Originally a Celtiberian settlement, Segontia became an important Roman and, later, Visigothic military outpost. The arrival of the Muslims in the 8th century changed the town's strategic situation, putting it in the front-line provinces facing the Christians. In fact Sigüenza remained in Muslim hands for considerably longer than towns farther to the south-west such as Guadalajara and Toledo (which fell in 1085), resisting until the 1120s. It was occupied by the Aragonese and later ceded to the Castilians, who turned Sigüenza and its hinterland into a vast church property. The bishops remained complete masters, material and spiritual, of the town and land until the end of the 18th century. About this time things began to go downhill, as Sigüenza found itself repeatedly in the way of advancing armies, from the War of the Spanish Succession until the civil war.

Information

The Infotur tourist office is in the Ermita del Humilladero (☎ 949 39 32 51), open weekdays from 10 am to 2 pm and 4.30 to 7 pm and weekends from 9 am to 2.30 pm and 4.30 to 7 pm. The correos is on Calle de la Villa Viciosa and is open only until 2.30 pm on weekdays (1 pm on Saturday). The postcode is 19250. There are several banks (some with ATMs) where you can change money on and near Calle del Cardenal Mendoza. In a medical emergency call the Cruz Roja on ☎ 949 22 22 22.

Catedral

The heart of the old town is made up of the combination of the cobbled Plaza Mayor and Plaza del Obispo Don Bernardo. Rising up on their northern flank is the centrepiece of the city, the completely oversized cathedral. It was begun as a Romanesque structure in 1130, and work continued for four centuries as the church was expanded and adorned. The largely Gothic result is laced with elements of other styles, from Renaissance through plateresque to mudéjar. The church was heavily damaged during the civil war and subsequently restored.

You can wander about the nave for no charge, or for 300 ptas you can be guided around the church's chapels, sacristy and neglected Gothic cloister. First up you will probably be shown the **capilla mayor**, a chapel containing the reclining marble statue of El Doncel, aka Don Martín Vázquez de Arce, who died fighting the Muslims in the final stages of the Reconquista. Of particular beauty is the **Sacristía de las Cabezas**, whose ceiling is covered with hundreds of heads sculpted by Covarrubias. His intention was to represent all humanity, and his characters, Christian and Muslim, range from knights to knaves. The **Capilla del Espíritu Santo** boasts a doorway combining plateresque, mudéjar and Gothic styles. Inside you'll see a remarkable dome and an *Anunciación* by El Greco. The cathedral can be visited daily from 11 am to 1.30 pm and 4 to 7 pm.

Museo Diocesano

Across the square from the cathedral, this museum houses a fairly extensive collection of religious art from Sigüenza and the surrounding area, including a series of mainly 15th century retablos. The museum is open weekdays from noon to 2 pm, and 4 to 5 pm, and weekends from 11 am to 2 pm and 5 to 7 pm (200 ptas).

Alcazaba

Calle Mayor heads south up the hill from the cathedral to what was once the archbishops' castle, originally built by the Muslims and still known as the Alcazaba. There has probably been some kind of fort here since pre-Roman times, but what you see today is the much-restored residence

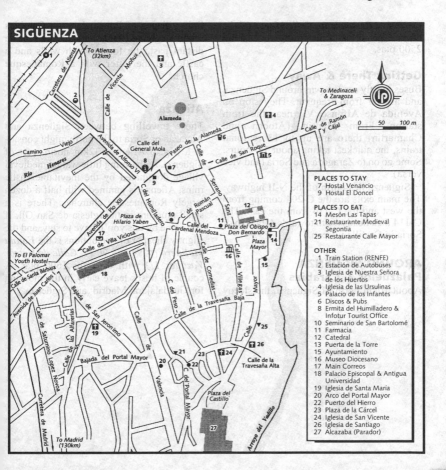

SIGÜENZA

To Atienza (32km)

To Medinaceli & Zaragoza

To El Palomar Youth Hostel

To Madrid (130km)

Alameda

Río Henares

Plaza de Hilario Yaben

Plaza del Obispo Don Bernardo

Plaza Mayor

Plaza del Castillo

Calle de la Travesaña Alta

0   50   100 m

PLACES TO STAY
7 Hostal Venancio
9 Hostal El Doncel

PLACES TO EAT
14 Mesón Las Tapas
21 Restaurante Medieval Segontia
25 Restaurante Calle Mayor

OTHER
1 Train Station (RENFE)
2 Estación de Autobuses
3 Iglesia de Nuestra Señora de los Huertos
4 Iglesia de las Ursulinas
5 Palacio de los Infantes
6 Discos & Pubs
8 Ermita del Humilladero & Infotur Tourist Office
10 Seminario de San Bartolomé
11 Farmacia
12 Catedral
13 Puerta de la Torre
15 Ayuntamiento
16 Museo Diocesano
17 Main Correos
18 Palacio Episcopal & Antigua Universidad
19 Iglesia de Santa María
20 Arco del Portal Mayor
22 Puerto del Hierro
23 Plaza de la Cárcel
24 Iglesia de San Vicente
26 Iglesia de Santiago
27 Alcazaba (Parador)

erected by the archbishops. It now functions as a parador (see Places to Stay & Eat).

Places to Stay & Eat

There is a handful of accommodation possibilities in Sigüenza. *El Palomar* youth hostel (☎ 949 39 12 99, Calle de Santa Bárbara) is nominally open from 1 July to 30 September, but call ahead to make sure. B&B is 1100 ptas (under 26) or 1500 ptas.

Hostal Venancio (☎ 949 39 03 47, Calle de San Roque 1) has simple singles/doubles

without bathroom for 2200/33000 ptas. *Hostal El Doncel* (☎ 949 39 10 90, Calle del General Mola 1) across the road, has rooms with shower, TV and telephone starting at 3800/5200 ptas plus IVA. A real treat, the *parador* (☎ 949 39 01 00) has doubles for 13,500 ptas plus IVA.

For snack food, the *Mesón Las Tapas (Plaza Mayor 1)* is a good spot. The *Restaurante Medieval Segontia (Calle del Portal Mayor 2)* offers solid meals, including a set *menú* for 1200 ptas, while the more expensive *Restaurante Calle Mayor (Calle Mayor 21)* offers fine dining for around 2500 ptas.

Getting There & Away

Buses mostly serve towns around Sigüenza, and are far from frequent. They stop on Avenida de Alfonso VI, near the train station. From Madrid (Atocha and Chamartín) there are up to 13 regional trains, the quickest taking about 1½ hours. Some go on to Zaragoza and Soria (and vice versa).

Sigüenza lies north of the N-II highway. The main exits are the C-204 coming from the west and the C-114 from the east. The C-114 then heads north towards Almazán or Soria in Castilla y León.

AROUND SIGÜENZA
Palazuelos & Carabias

About 10km north of Sigüenza, the sleepy little villages of Palazuelos and Carabias retain neglected remnants of their more distant past, the former with walls and a castle and the latter with a Romanesque church.

Atienza

Those travelling between Sigüenza and Almazán or Soria to the north might consider a trip to Atienza, 32km north-west of Sigüenza. A charming little walled medieval village dominated by the inevitable castle ruins, Atienza is jammed with half a dozen largely Romanesque churches. There is a small museum in the Iglesia de San Gil. If you come by bus you'll have to stay, and the slightly cheaper of two options is the *Fonda Molinero (☎ 949 39 90 17, Calle de Héctor Vázquez 11)* with beds for 1600 ptas. A couple of buses leave early in the morning for Guadalajara, Madrid and Sigüenza.

Barcelona

Some say Barcelona is the most southern city of northern Europe. The city has earnt this description not only through its nearness to France, but also by its industrious (and industrial) character, densely packed urban centre and obeisance to cool and chic – not exactly the fiesta-and-siesta image of more southerly Spanish regions.

Actually, Barcelona shares the good and bad of the south *and* north. It's probably Spain's most cosmopolitan and stylish city, and certainly one of its richest. But with 1.5 million people in the city proper (four million if you include its satellite towns), it has its hard side: wealth and poverty face each other daily on its streets.

Barcelona is the capital of a region, Catalunya (Cataluña in Castilian), that has its own language, distinct character and turbulent history. In many ways it thinks of itself as a separate country. This gives the city a rather self-absorbed aspect that sits oddly with the openness you'd expect of a major Mediterranean port.

Set on a plain rising gently from the sea to a range of wooded hills, Barcelona enjoys fine vistas, lovely and unusual parks and a fascinating medieval core dotted with pearls of Gothic construction. Beyond this core is perhaps some of the world's most bizarre architecture: the surreal modernist spectacles capped by Antoni Gaudí's La Sagrada Família church.

Barcelona has great nightlife, some superb restaurants and top-class museums. It has been breaking ground in art, architecture and style for at least a century, from the turn-of-the-century *modernista* architects led by Gaudí to the adventurous redevelopments on the waterfront and Montjuïc hill brought to life by the 1992 Olympics; and from Pablo Picasso and Joan Miró, whose spirits still haunt the city, to the weird postmodern concoctions of contemporary artists and nightclub designers.

HIGHLIGHTS

- Rambling along La Rambla, Spain's most famous street
- Exploring the Barri Gòtic, a classic medieval quarter
- The Museu Picasso, Spain's best collection of this major modern artist's work
- La Sagrada Família, Spain's most original 'work-in-progress'
- A day on Montjuïc, the hill of parks, museums and stadiums which hosted the 1992 Olympics
- A first-class Catalan meal at *Can Solé*
- An absinthe or two in *Bar Marsella*
- *Cava* (Catalan champagne) at *El Xampanyet*
- Dancing the night away at stylish *Otto Zutz*
- Following the *modernista* trail of architecture

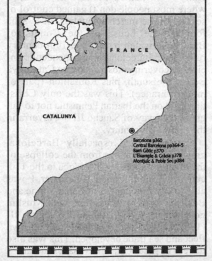

CATALUNYA

Barcelona p360
Central Barcelona pp364-5
Barri Gòtic p370
L'Eixample & Gràcia p378
Montjuïc & Poble Sec p384

HISTORY

Barcelona and Catalunya have a history that for long periods was distinct from the rest of Spain; this is largely responsible for their independent-mindedness today.

Early Barcelona

Barcelona was probably founded by the Carthaginians in about 230 BC, taking the surname of Hamilcar Barca, Hannibal's father. Roman Barcelona covered an area within today's Barri Gòtic and was overshadowed by Tarraco (Tarragona), 90km to the south-west. Under the Visigoths, and then under the Muslims who took it in 713 AD, Barcelona remained a modest place.

The Counts of Barcelona

Frankish armies soon pushed the Muslims back from present-day France and set up a buffer zone along the south of the Pyrenees known as the Frankish March, which included Barcelona. Indeed the Catalan language's closest relative is said to be the *langue d'oc*, the old tongue of southern France.

As the Frankish empire fractured in the 9th century, one Guifré el Pilós (Wilfrid the Hairy – so named because he had hair where most people don't) gained control of several of the march's counties. In 878 he founded the house of the Counts of Barcelona, which by the late 10th century ruled, from Barcelona, an independent principality covering most of modern Catalunya except the south, plus Roussillon (part of modern France). This was the only Christian state on the Iberian Peninsula not to fall under the sway of Sancho III of Navarra in the early 11th century.

Catalunya, and especially Barcelona, grew rich on pickings from the collapse of the Muslim caliphate of Córdoba in the 11th century. Count Ramon Berenguer I was able to buy the counties of Carcassonne and Béziers, north of Roussillon, with Muslim gold bounty. Under Ramon Berenguer III (1082-1131) Catalunya launched its own fleet and sea trade developed. This was also the era of great Catalan Romanesque art.

The Golden Age

In 1137 Ramon Berenguer IV was betrothed to Petronilla, heiress of Catalunya's western neighbour Aragón, creating a joint state and setting the scene for Catalunya's golden age. He took southern Catalunya from the Muslims in the 1140s and his successors styled themselves as the Monarchs of Aragón.

Meanwhile, Castilla was laying sole claim to the reconquest of Muslim territory in the south – a claim recognised by Aragón's Alfonso II in 1179. Suffering reverses in France too, Catalunya turned to the Mediterranean. Jaume I (1213-76) took the Islas Baleares and the Valencia region from the Muslims in the 1230s. Barcelona finally grew too big for its Roman walls and Jaume I built new walls enclosing an area 10 times larger.

Jaume I's son Pere II conquered Sicily in 1282. Then followed a spectacular expansion of Catalunya's Mediterranean trade-based empire, albeit hampered at home by divisions in the ruling family, the odd war with Castilla and trouble with the aristocracy in Aragón. Malta (1283), Athens (1310), Corsica (1323), Sardinia (1324) and Naples (1423), as well as several ports in North Africa, all fell, for varying periods, under Catalan dominance.

Catalunya's Corts, or parliament, first met under Jaume I. Committees formed by the Corts in 1289 to control taxes were the origin of the Generalitat, a council with powers over law and order, public spending and the armed forces. It functioned until the 18th century.

Decline & Castilian Domination

Like many empires, Catalunya's came to exhaust its homeland. Sea wars with Genoa, resistance in Sardinia, the rise of the Ottoman empire and the loss of the gold trade all drained the coffers. The Black Death and famines killed about half of Catalunya's population in the 14th century.

After Martí I, the last of Guifré el Pilós' dynasty, died heirless in 1410, a special council elected Fernando de Antequera, a

Castilian prince, to the Aragonese throne. This was engineered by the nobility in Aragón, who saw a chance to reduce Catalan influence over their affairs. Fernando and his successors were soon at daggers drawn with their Catalan subjects, who felt that they were being exploited for Castilian interests. A rebellion against King Joan II that began in 1462 ended in a siege in 1473 that devastated Barcelona.

Joan II's son, Fernando, succeeded to the Aragonese throne in 1479 and married Isabel, queen of Castilla, uniting Spain's two most powerful monarchies. Catalunya effectively became part of the Castilian state, but was excluded from the exploitation of the Americas that brought such riches to 16th century Castilla.

Disaffection led to revolts, the last during the War of the Spanish Succession (1702-13), in which Catalunya sided with Britain and Austria against Felipe V, the French Bourbon contender for the Spanish throne. But Catalunya ended up fighting alone and Barcelona fell in 1714 after a 14-month siege. Felipe V abolished the Generalitat, built a huge fort, the Ciutadella, to watch over Barcelona and banned the writing and teaching of Catalan.

Economic Growth & the Renaixença

The late 18th and 19th centuries finally brought new economic development. From 1778 Catalunya was permitted to trade with America, boosting shipping and launching an industrial revolution – Spain's first – based on American cotton. Wine, cork and iron industries also developed. So did working-class poverty, overcrowding, disease and unrest. To ease the crush, Barcelona's medieval walls were demolished in 1854 and in 1869 work began on l'Eixample, an extension of the city beyond Plaça de Catalunya, which was then its limit. The flourishing bourgeoisie paid for lavish, ostentatious buildings, many of them in the unique, Art Nouveau-influenced modernista style, whose leading exponent was Antoni Gaudí.

Modernisme was the most visible aspect of the Catalan Renaixença (Renaissance): a movement for the revival of Catalan language and culture in the late 19th century. By the turn of the century Barcelona was also Spain's hotbed of avant-garde art, with close links to Paris.

The Renaixença's political sibling was Catalanism, a new-found Catalan nationalism intensified by Spain's loss of Cuba in 1898. Many Catalans had prospered in Cuba, so the loss – blamed on Madrid's incompetence – brought a new wave of poverty.

Mayhem

Neither the Renaixença nor Catalanism cut much ice with Barcelona's exploited workers, whose numbers were rising fast. The city's population grew from 115,000 in 1800 to more than 500,000 by 1900 and over one million by 1930.

The decades around the turn of the 20th century were ones of wild mayhem in Barcelona, which became a swirling vortex of anarchists, Republicans, bourgeois regionalists, gangsters, police terrorists, political gunmen called *pistoleros* and meddling by Madrid.

Anarchists were reckoned to be behind the Semana Trágica (Tragic Week) in 1909 when, following a military call-up for a Spanish campaign in Morocco, mobs wrecked 70 religious buildings and workers were shot on the streets.

In the post-WWI slump, unionism took hold, led by the anarchist CNT, which embraced as many as 80% of the city's workers. During a wave of strikes in 1919-20, employers hired assassins to eliminate union leaders.

Catalan Nationalism Rampant

Within days of the formation of Spain's Second Republic in 1931, Catalan nationalists led by Francesc Macià and Lluís Companys proclaimed Catalunya a republic within an imaginary 'Iberian Federation'. Madrid pressured them into accepting a unitary Spanish state, but Catalunya got a new regional government, with the old title of Generalitat.

After the leftist Popular Front won the February 1936 Spanish general election, Catalunya gained, for a brief time, genuine autonomy.

The Civil War

On 17 July an army uprising in Morocco began the Spanish Civil War. Barcelona's army garrison failed to take the city for Franco and for nearly a year Barcelona was run by revolutionary anarchists and the POUM (Partido Obrero de Unificación Marxista, or Workers' Marxist Unification Party) Trotskyist militia, with Lluís Companys president only in name.

The revolutionary atmosphere waned as, under Soviet influence, the Catalan communist party PSUC grew increasingly powerful. After three days of street fighting between anarchists and the PSUC during May 1937, in which at least 1500 people were killed, the anarchists asked for a cease-fire. They and the POUM were soon disarmed.

But the Republican effort across Spain remained tainted by infighting, killing any chances they might have had of defeating Franco. Barcelona fell to the Nationalists on 25 January 1939 and the war ended on 1 April.

Modern-day Catalanism

Catalunya (Cataluña) is engaged in an ongoing struggle for more autonomy within Spain, but full independence is a dream dreamt only by a few. The pro-independence party Esquerra Republicana de Catalunya (ERC; Republican Left of Catalonia) has won only 8% to 10% of the vote in recent elections. ERC is avowedly nonviolent and there's no Catalan equivalent of the Basque ETA terrorist movement. But there's still a deep antipathy among many Catalans to the Spanish state and its influence over Catalunya. A survey in 1995 found that 38% of people in Catalunya considered themselves either more Catalan than Spanish, or not Spanish at all.

Catalans remain strongly aware of their region's historic rivalry with Castilla and are infused with the sense that Catalunya enjoyed its golden ages when it was independent or under minimal Castilian influence. They like to think of themselves as more civilised and worldly than other Spaniards. These notions have probably been reinforced since the 1940s by the arrival of around two million people from poorer parts of Spain, chiefly Andalucía, seeking work. The rest of Spain looks on Catalans (whom they sometimes disparagingly refer to as *polacos*, or Poles) as somewhere between irritatingly quirky and provocatively arrogant.

The cliché is that Catalans are harder working, more sober and more commercially minded than other Spaniards. They certainly seem to be less addicted to noise, colour and flamboyance – compare the sedate Catalan national dance, the *sardana*, with Andalucian flamenco – although Catalan *festes* (fiestas) can still be riotous.

Because of immigration from other parts of Spain, today probably less than half the almost four million people in Barcelona and its satellite towns speak Catalan, although the figure is around two-thirds in Catalunya as a whole and nearly everyone claims to understand it.

Everyone in Barcelona *does* speak Spanish; French is fairly widely understood and English less so. Although you'll find all street names, and many signs and menus, in Catalan, you'll have no greater language difficulty here than anywhere else in Spain. If you know some Spanish and/or French you can make sense of much written Catalan (see the Language section at the back of the book for some useful words and phrases, and the boxed text 'Catalan Cuisine' in the Catalunya chapter for help with Catalan menus).

The Franco Era

Franco banned public use of Catalan and by the 1950s opposition had turned to peaceful mass protests and strikes. In 1960 an audience at the city's Palau de la Música Catalana sang a banned Catalan anthem in front of Franco. The ringleaders included a young Catholic banker, Jordi Pujol, who spent two years in jail as a result. Pujol was to become Catalunya's president in the post-Franco era.

The big social change under Franco was the flood of immigrants from poorer parts of Spain, chiefly Andalucía, attracted by economic growth in Catalunya. Some 750,000 came to Barcelona in the 1950s and 1960s, and almost as many to the rest of Catalunya. Many lived in appalling conditions.

After Franco

The 1978 Spanish constitution bowed to Catalan nationalism by creating the autonomous community of Catalunya, with Barcelona as its capital. The Generalitat, its parliament, has wide powers over matters like agriculture, education, health, industry, tourism and trade. Education is now nearly all in Catalan, and a new bilingualism law passed in 1998 aims to increase use of the language at all levels.

Jordi Pujol's moderate nationalist Convergència i Unió (CiU) coalition has controlled the Generalitat since the first elections in 1980, although the CiU lost its overall majority in 1995. The CiU does not want full independence from Spain but constantly seeks to strengthen Catalan autonomy. On broader issues, CiU is right of centre. Barcelona itself has favoured the Partit Socialista de Catalunya (PSC), which is aligned with the national PSOE (Partido Socialista Obrero Español, or Spanish Socialist Worker Party).

The 1992 Olympics spurred a burst of public works, bringing new life to areas like Montjuïc, where the major events were held, and the once-shabby waterfront, which is now strung with promenades, beaches, marinas, restaurants, leisure facilities and new housing. The Olympics also focused world attention on Barcelona's prosperity and cultural, entertainment and tourist attractions, making the city something of a household name.

ORIENTATION

Barcelona's coastline runs roughly from north-east to south-west, with many streets are parallel or perpendicular to it.

La Rambla & Plaça de Catalunya

The focal axis is La Rambla, a 1.25km boulevard running north-west and slightly uphill from Port Vell (Old Harbour) to Plaça de Catalunya. The latter marks the boundary between the old centre, the Ciutat Vella and the more recent parts farther inland.

Montjuïc & Tibidabo

Two good landmarks for orientation are the hills of Montjuïc and Tibidabo. Montjuïc, the lower of the two, begins about 700m south-west of the bottom (south-eastern end) of La Rambla. Tibidabo, with its landmark TV tower and golden Christ statue, is 6km north-west of the top (north-western

---

Finding Your Way in Barcelona

Where necessary in this chapter, the information about places and sights includes a reference to the map on which you will find them (and sometimes a reference to the nearest metro station), eg Escola Oficial d'Idiomes de Barcelona, Avinguda de les Drassanes s/n (metro: Drassanes, map: Central). The references use the following abbreviations and the maps appear on the pages listed.

end) of La Rambla. It's the high point of the range of wooded hills forming a backdrop to the city.

Ciutat Vella

The Ciutat Vella (Old City), a warren of narrow streets, centuries-old buildings and a lot of budget and mid-range accommodation, spreads either side of La Rambla. Its heart is the lower half of the section east of La Rambla, called the Barri Gòtic (Gothic quarter). West of La Rambla is El Raval,

whose lower half is the seedy Barri Xinès (Chinese quarter, a strange expression meaning red-light zone).

The Ciutat Vella continues north-east of the Barri Gòtic, across Via Laietana, to the area called La Ribera, east of which lies the pretty Parc de la Ciutadella.

Waterfront

Port Vell has an excellent modern aquarium and two marinas. At its north-eastern end is La Barceloneta, the old sailors' quarter,

from where beaches and a pedestrian promenade stretch 1km north-east to the Port Olímpic, a harbour built for the Olympics and now surrounded by lively bars and restaurants.

L'Eixample

Plaça de Catalunya at the top of La Rambla marks the beginning of l'Eixample (el Ensanche in Spanish, meaning 'the Enlargement'), the grid of straight streets into which Barcelona grew in the 19th century. This is where you'll find most of Barcelona's modernista architecture – including La Sagrada Família – as well as its glossiest shops and many expensive hotels.

The main avenues are Passeig de Gràcia and Rambla de Catalunya, running parallel to the north-west from Plaça de Catalunya.

Gràcia

Beyond l'Eixample you're in the suburbs, some of which have plenty of character as they began life as villages outside the city. Gràcia, beyond the wide Avinguda Diagonal on the northern edge of central l'Eixample, is a net of narrow streets and small squares with a varied population and can be a lively place to spend a Friday or Saturday night. Just north of Gràcia is Gaudí's Parc Güell.

BARCELONA

PLACES TO STAY		
7	Alberg Mare de Déu de	
	Montserrat	
43	Alberg Studio	
52	Alberg Pere Tarrès	
70	Hotel Roma	
71	Hostal Sofia	
77	Hostal Sans	

PLACES TO EAT	
2	Mirablau Terrazza

TRAIN STATIONS	
1	Peu del Funicular
5	Avinguda de Tibidabo
16	Sagrera
18	Clot
33	El Putxet
34	Pàdua
35	Sant Gervasi
38	Muntaner
40	La Bonanova
41	Les Tres Torres
42	Sarrià
44	Reina Elisenda
67	Estació de França
72	Estació Sants
83	Gornal
84	Ildefons Cerdà

METRO STATIONS	
6	Penitents
8	Vallcarca
10	Alfons X
12	Guinardó

13	Camp de l'Arpa	
14	Sagrera	
15	Navas	
19	Clot	
21	Hospital de Sant Pau	
23	Monumental	
26	Glòries	
27	Poblenou	
28	Llacuna	
30	Marina	
32	Lesseps	
57	Maria Cristina	
61	Palau Reial	
64	Les Corts	
65	Plaça del Centre	
66	Entença	
74	Sants-Estació	
75	Hostafrancs	
76	Plaça de Sants	
78	Mercat Nou	
79	Badalè	
80	Collblanc	
81	Torrassa	
82	Santa Eulàlia	

OTHER	
3	Tibidabo Funicular Lower Station
4	Mirablau
9	Casa Museu Gaudí
11	Hospital de Sant Pau
17	Savannah
20	Hospital Creu Roja
22	Temple Expiatori de la Sagrada Família

24	Plaça de Braus Monumental
25	Els Encants Flea Market
29	Zeleste
31	Estació del Nord Bus Station
36	Institute of North American Studies
37	Luz de Gaz; La Antilla Cosmopolita
39	British Council
45	US Consulate
46	Museu-Monastir de Pedralbes
47	Sarrià Stadium
48	International House Language School
49	UK Consulate
50	Filmoteca
51	Vanguard Rentacar
53	Ronicar
54	Irish Consulate
55	Netherlands Consulate
56	Japanese Consulate
58	Finca Güell Gate
59	Palau Reial de Pedralbes (Museu de Ceràmica & Museu de les Arts Decoratives)
60	Jardins del Palau Reial
62	Camp Nou & Museu del Futbol Club Barcelona
63	Cinema Renoir-Les Corts
68	Estació Marítima N-1
69	Usit Unlimited
73	Estació d'Autobusos de Sants

Main Transport Terminals

The airport is 14km south-west of the city centre at El Prat de Llobregat. The main terminus for domestic trains is Estació Sants (metro: Sants-Estació, map: Barcelona), 2.5km west of La Rambla, on the western fringe of l'Eixample. International trains usually terminate at Estació de França, 1km east of La Rambla, near Barceloneta metro station (map: Barcelona). The main bus station, Estació del Nord (metro: Arc de Triomf, map: Barcelona), is 1.5km northeast of La Rambla.

Maps

Tourist offices hand out free city and transport maps which are OK, but better is the Michelin *Barcelona* map (825 ptas), which comes with a comprehensive street index.

INFORMATION
Tourist Offices

The main tourist office is the Centre d'Informació Turisme de Barcelona (☎ 93 304 31 35) at Plaça de Catalunya 17-S (actually underground; map: L'Eixample); it concentrates on the city. It is open daily from 9 am to 9 pm. Staff also sell the Barcelona Card, which entitles the holder to discounts on many sights, transport and some shops and restaurants. It costs 2500 ptas (24 hours), 3000 ptas (48 hours) or 3500 ptas (72 hours).

The regional tourism office (☎ 93 238 40 00) is in the Palau Robert, Passeig de Gràcia 107 (map: L'Eixample). It is open Monday to Saturday from 10 am to 7 pm and Sunday from 10 am to 2 pm. In the *ajuntament* (town hall) on Plaça de Sant Jaume is another information office with similar hours but more information on Catalunya.

Turisme de Barcelona in Estació Sants (map: Barcelona) covers Barcelona only. It's open Monday to Friday from 8 am to 8 pm and weekends and holidays from 8 am to 2 pm (8 am to 8 pm daily in summer). There's also a tourist office (☎ 93 478 05 65) in the EU airport arrivals hall, open Monday to Saturday from 9.30 am to 8 pm and Sunday from 9.30 am to 3 pm (about a

half-hour later in summer; map: Barcelona). It has information on all Catalunya. Another office (☎ 93 478 47 04) at the international arrivals hall is open Monday to Saturday from 9.30 am to 3 pm (map: Barcelona).

In summer up to 20 temporary information booths are placed at handy points around the city and usually are open from 9 am to 9 pm. Also in this period, tourist officers in red jackets roam strategic parts of the city to help out forlorn foreigners.

For accommodation information, you can phone ☎ 93 304 32 32 or check out www.barcelona-on-line.es on the Internet.

Foreign Consulates

Most of the consulates in Barcelona are open Monday to Friday from 9 or 10 am to 1 or 2 pm. For a list of foreign consulates in Barcelona, see the Embassies & Consulates section in the Facts for the Visitor chapter.

Money

Barcelona abounds with banks, many with ATMs, including several around Plaça de Catalunya and more on La Rambla and on Plaça de Sant Jaume in the Barri Gòtic.

The exchange offices you see along La Rambla and elsewhere are open for longer hours than banks but generally offer poorer rates.

American Express (☎ 93 415 23 71 or ☎ 93 217 00 70, fax 93 217 19 50) at Passeig de Gràcia 101 (the entrance is on Carrer del Rosselló; map: L'Eixample) has a currency exchange desk with good rates and a machine giving cash on American Express cards. The office is open Monday to Friday from 9.30 am to 6 pm and Saturday from 10 am to noon. There's another branch on La Rambla dels Capuxtins 74 (map: Gòtic).

Post & Communications

The main *correos* (post office; ☎ 93 318 38 31) is on Plaça d'Antoni López (map: Central), opposite the north-eastern end of Port Vell. It's open for stamp sales, poste restante (window No 36) and information

Monday to Saturday from 8 am to 10 pm (to 8 pm Saturday). The postcode for poste restante is 08080.

The post office also has a public fax service, as do many shops and offices around the city.

Another useful post office is at Carrer d'Aragó 282 (map: L'Eixample), just off Passeig de Gràcia and open Monday to Friday from 8.30 am to 9 pm and Saturday from 9 am to 2 pm.

American Express (see Money) holds mail for American Express card and travellers cheque holders.

There are telephone and fax offices at Estació Sants (open daily, except Sunday, from 8.30 am to 9 pm) and Estació del Nord.

You can use the Internet for 600 ptas a half-hour (or 800 ptas an hour for students) upstairs at El Café de Internet (☎ 93 412 19 15), Gran Via de les Corts Catalanes 656 (L'Eixample); also see Places to Eat. Other options include Café Insòlit (☎ 93 225 81 78) in the waterfront Maremàgnum shopping complex (map: Central) and the self-service Internet kiosk at Estació Sants (map: Barcelona).

Travel Agencies

The youth travel agent Usit Unlimited (☎ 93 423 33 60, ☎ 93 426 57 00) at Carrer de Rocafort 116-122 (metro Rocafort, map: Barcelona) acts as Catalunya's version of TIVE, the Spanish youth travel organisation, and sells youth tickets and student air, train and bus tickets. It has another branch (☎ 902-32 52 75) at Ronda de l'Universitat 16 (map: L'Eixample). Viajes Wasteels at Catalunya metro station (map: L'Eixample) has similar youth and student airfares and other discounted tickets.

Halcón Viatges is a reliable chain of travel agents which sometimes has good deals. Its branch at Carrer de Pau Claris 108 (☎ 93 412 44 11; map: L'Eixample) is one of 25 around town.

Press & Bookshops

Many newsstands, especially on La Rambla, carry a wide range of foreign newspapers. Here's a selection of Barcelona's many good bookshops:

Barri Gòtic & El Raval

These places are on the Barri Gòtic map.

Cómplices (Carrer de Cervantes 2)
  gay and lesbian books
Documenta (Carrer del Cardenal Casañas 4)
  novels in English and French, maps
Próleg (Carrer de la Dagueria 13)
  women's bookshop
Quera (Carrer de Petritxol 2)
  specialist in maps and guides, including hiking and trekking
Salas Llibreteria (Carrer de la Uniò 3)
  new and used books in several languages

L'Eixample

These places are on the L'Eixample & Gràcia map, unless otherwise noted.

Altaïr (Carrer de Balmes 71)
  great travel bookshop with maps, guides and travel literature
BCN (Carrer d'Aragó 277)
  literature and travel guides in English, some French literature, good for dictionaries
Come In (Carrer de Provença 203)
  specialist in English-teaching books, also plenty of novels and books on Spain, in English and French
Laie (Carrer de Pau Claris 85)
  novels and books on architecture, art and film in Catalan, English, French and Spanish
Librería Francesa (Passeig de Gràcia 91)
  lots of novels and guidebooks in Catalan, English, French and Spanish
The English Bookshop (Carrer d'Entença 63; map: Montjuïc)
  a good range of literature, teaching material and children's books

Gràcia

Bookstore (Carrer de la Granja 13; map: L'Eixample)
  second-hand English-language books

For some recommended books on Barcelona, see the Books section in the Facts for the Visitor chapter.

Cultural Centres

There are English-language libraries at the British Council (☎ 93 209 63 88) at Carrer d'Amigó 83 (map: Barcelona) as well as the Institute for North American Studies

BARCELONA

(☎ 93 200 75 51) at Via Augusta 123 (map: Barcelona). The Institut Français de Barcelona (☎ 93 209 59 11) at Carrer de Moià 8 (metro: Diagonal, map: L'Eixample) puts on films, concerts and exhibitions.

Gay & Lesbian Information
Casal Lambda (☎ 93 412 72 72) at Carrer Ample 5 (map: Gòtic) is a gay and lesbian social, cultural and information centre. Coordinadora Gai-Lesbiana (☎ 93 309 79 97, fax 93 309 78 40, cogailes@pangea.org), Carrer de Buenaventura Muñoz 4 (map: Central), is the city's main coordinating body for gay and lesbian groups. Some of the latter, such as Grup de Lesbianes Feministes, can be found at Ca la Dona (☎ 93 412 71 61), Carrer de Casp 38 (map: L'Eixample).

Photography
There are plenty of places to have films developed. FotoK, Ronda de l'Universitat 7 (map: L'Eixample), is fairly reliable.

Laundry
Lavandería Tigre at Carrer d'En Rauric 20 (map: Gòtic) will wash, dry and fold 3kg in a couple of hours for 820 ptas (1265 ptas for 7kg). Doing it yourself costs 495 ptas and 745 ptas respectively to wash, plus extra to dry. It's open daily, except Sunday, from 8 am to 6.30 pm.

Lost & Found
The city's main *objetos perdidos* (lost and found) office is on ☎ 93 402 31 61. If you leave anything in a taxi, you can call ☎ 93 223 40 02 to see if it's been handed in.

Medical Services
Hospitals with emergency services include the Hospital Creu Roja (☎ 93 433 15 51), Carrer del Dos de Maig 301 (metro: Hospital de Sant Pau, map: Barcelona), and Hospital de Sant Pau (☎ 93 291 90 00), Carrer de Sant Antoni Maria Claret 167 (metro: Hospital de Sant Pau, map: Barcelona).

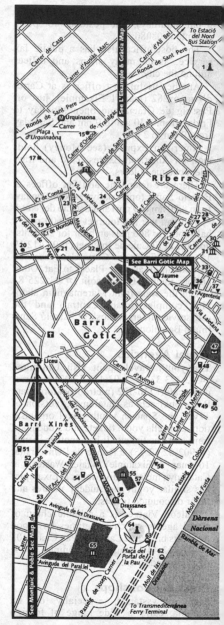

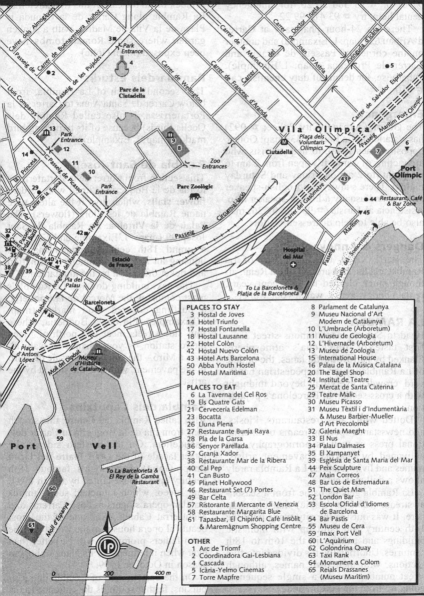

PLACES TO STAY
3 Hostal de Joves
14 Hotel Triunfo
17 Hostal Fontanella
18 Hostal Lausanne
22 Hotel Colón
42 Hotel Nuevo Colòn
43 Hotel Arts Barcelona
50 Abba Youth Hostel
56 Hostal Marítima

PLACES TO EAT
6 La Taverna del Cel Ros
19 Els Quatre Gats
21 Cervecería Edelman
23 Bocatta
26 Lluna Plena
27 Restaurante Bunja Raya
28 Pla de la Garsa
36 Senyor Parellada
37 Granja Xador
38 Restaurante Mar de la Ribera
40 Cal Pep
41 Can Busto
45 Planet Hollywood
49 Bar Celta
57 Ristorante Il Mercante di Venezia
58 Restaurante Margarita Blue
61 Tapasbar, El Chipirón, Café Insòlit
   & Maremàgnum Shopping Centre

OTHER
1 Arc de Triomf
2 Coordinadora Gai-Lesbiana
4 Cascada
5 Icària-Yelmo Cinemas
7 Torre Mapfre

8 Parlament de Catalunya
9 Museu Nacional d'Art
   Modern de Catalunya
10 L'Umbracle (Arboretum)
11 Museu de Geologia
12 L'Hivernacle (Arboretum)
13 Museu de Zoologia
15 International House
16 Palau de la Música Catalana
20 The Bagel Shop
24 Institut de Teatre
25 Mercat de Santa Caterina
29 Teatre Malic
30 Museu Picasso
31 Museu Tèxtil i d'Indumentària
   & Museu Barbier-Mueller
   d'Art Precolombí
32 Galeria Maeght
33 El Nus
34 Palau Dalmases
35 El Xampanyet
39 Església de Santa Maria del Mar
44 Peix Sculpture
47 Main Correos
48 Bar Los de Extremadura
51 The Quiet Man
52 London Bar
53 Escola Oficial d'Idiomes
   de Barcelona
54 Bar Pastis
55 Museu de Cera
59 Imax Port Vell
60 L'Aquàrium
62 Golondrina Quay
63 Taxi Rank
64 Monument a Colom
65 Reials Drassanes
   (Museu Marítim)

For an ambulance, call ☎ 061, ☎ 93 329 97 01 or ☎ 93 300 20 20; for emergency dental help, try ☎ 93 415 99 22.

There's a 24-hour pharmacy at Carrer d'Aribau 62 (map: L'Eixample) and another on the corner of Passeig de Gràcia and Carrer de Provença (map: L'Eixample). Otherwise, for details of duty chemists call ☎ 010.

Emergency

The Guàrdia Urbana (City Police; ☎ 092) has a station at La Rambla 43 (map: Gòtic), opposite Plaça Reial, to help tourists who are victims of crime. It's open from 7 am to midnight (to 2 am on Friday and Saturday nights). There's always an English-speaker on duty and usually a French-speaker also. Asistencia al Turista (☎ 93 482 05 26) may also be able to help distressed visitors.

Dangers & Annoyances

The Barri Xinès, the lower end of La Rambla and the area around Plaça Reial, although much cleaned up in recent years, remain dodgy areas – watch your wallets.

LA RAMBLA

Head to Spain's most famous street for a first taste of Barcelona's atmosphere. Flanked by narrow traffic lanes, the middle of La Rambla is a broad, pedestrian boulevard, crowded every day beyond midnight with a cross-section of Barcelona's population.

Dotted with cafés, restaurants, kiosks, and newsstands sporting reams of international press as well as pornography, and enlivened by buskers, pavement artists, mimes and living statues, La Rambla rarely allows a dull moment.

La Rambla gets its name from a seasonal stream (*raml* in Arabic) that once ran here. It was outside the city walls until the 14th century and built up with monastic buildings and palaces in the 16th to 18th centuries. Unofficially, it's divided into five sections, with their own names, although street numbers are in a single sequence, going up from the bottom end.

Rambla de Canaletes

A block off to the east of this first stretch of La Rambla along Carrer de la Canuda is Plaça de la Vila de Madrid, with a sunken garden where some **Roman tombs** have been exposed (map: Gòtic).

Rambla dels Estudis

This second stretch of La Rambla, from below Carrer de Santa Anna to Carrer de la Portaferrissa, is also called Rambla dels Ocells (birds) because of its twittering **bird market** (map: L'Eixample)

Rambla de Sant Josep

This section from Carrer de la Portaferrissa to Pla de la Boqueria is lined with verdant **flower stalls**, which give it the alternative name Rambla de les Flors (flowers). The **Palau de la Virreina**, La Rambla de Sant Josep 99 (maps: L'Eixample and Gòtic), is a grand 18th century rococo mansion housing an arts-entertainment information and ticket office run by the ajuntament.

The next building down is La Rambla's most colourful: the **Mercat de la Boqueria**, a bustling covered food market (map: L'Eixample). Pla de la Boqueria, where four side streets meet just north of Liceu metro station, is your chance to walk all over a Miró – the colourful **Mosaïc de Miró** in the pavement, with one tile signed by the artist.

Rambla dels Caputxins

Also called Rambla del Centre, this stretch runs from Pla de la Boqueria to Carrer dels Escudellers. On the western side is the intact façade of the **Gran Teatre del Liceu** (map: Gòtic), Barcelona's famous 19th century opera house gutted by fire in 1994. The Liceu, which launched such famous Catalan opera singers as José Carreras and Montserrat Caballé, was one of the most beautiful opera houses in the world and the town fathers promise it will be better than ever when it reopens for its inaugural opera season in October 1999.

On the eastern side of Rambla dels Caputxins, farther south, is the entrance to the large Plaça Reial (see the Barri Gòtic section). Just below the plaça, La Rambla becomes seedier, with a few strip clubs and peep shows reflecting the surrounding streets' former status as Barcelona's chief red-light area.

Rambla de Santa Mònica

This final stretch of La Rambla widens out to approach the Columbus monument overlooking Port Vell. On the eastern side, at the end of narrow Passatge de la Banca, is the **Museu de Cera** (Wax Museum; map: Central), which has tableaux of a *gitano* cave, a bullring medical room and a hall of horror, as well as wax figures of Cleopatra, Franco etc; it's not bad as wax museums go. It's open Monday to Friday from 10 am to 2 pm and 4 to 8 pm; weekends and holidays from 4.30 to 8.30 pm (900 ptas). In September it is open daily from 10 am to 8 pm.

Monument a Colom

The bottom of La Rambla, and the harbour beyond it, are supervised by the tall Columbus monument, built in the 1880s (map: Central). You can ascend by lift (250 ptas) daily from 10 am to 7.30 pm, except for a 1.30 to 3.30 pm break from Monday to Friday.

Museu Marítim

West of the Monument a Colom on Avinguda de les Drassanes stand the **Reials Drassanes** (Royal Shipyards; map: Central), a rare work of nonreligious Gothic architecture. They now house the Museu Marítim, which, together with its setting, forms a fascinating tribute to the seaborne contacts that have shaped Barcelona's history.

The shipyards, first built in the 13th century, gained their present form (a series of long bays divided by stone arches) a century later. Extensions in the 17th century made them big enough to accommodate the building of 30 galleys. In their shipbuilding days (up to the 18th century) the sea came right up to them.

Inside is an impressive array of boats, models, maps, paintings and more, with sections including the port and city of Barcelona, the Reials Drassanes themselves, ships' figureheads, Columbus and Magellan, and 16th century galleys (the full-scale replica of Don Juan of Austria's royal galley from the battle of Lepanto is a highlight).

The museum is open Tuesday to Saturday from 10 am to 6 pm and Sunday from 10 am to 2 pm (800 ptas).

BARRI GÒTIC

Barcelona's 'Gothic quarter', east of La Rambla, is a classic medieval warren of narrow, winding streets, quaint little plazas and wonderful structures from the city's golden age. It also has most of the city's best budget accommodation and plenty of good bars, cafés and restaurants. Few of its great buildings date from after the early 15th century – the decline Barcelona went into at that time curtailed grand projects for several centuries.

The Barri Gòtic stretches from La Rambla in the west to Via Laietana in the east and roughly from Carrer de la Portaferrissa in the north to Carrer de la Mercè in the south. Carrer de Ferran and Carrer de Jaume I, cutting across the middle, form a kind of halfway line: these streets and those to their north tend to be strung with chic

Barcelona Museums

Every Barcelona museum has its own concoction of opening days and hours, sometimes with seasonal variations. Many have a range of prices too, with students and pensioners often paying half-price and under-16s getting in for free. Some are free to everyone on the first Sunday of the month and/or half-price on nonholiday Wednesdays. Where only one price is given in this chapter, that's the normal full adult price.

little shops and feel 100% safe, while those to their south become darker and, below Carrer de Ferran, seedier – although they still contain several good and perfectly respectable places to eat, drink and stay.

All the places listed are on the Barri Gòtic map unless otherwise noted.

Plaça de Sant Jaume

This square at the eastern end of Carrer de Ferran has been Barcelona's political hub on and off since the 15th century and is a good place to start exploration. Facing each other across it are the Palau de la Generalitat (the seat of Catalunya's government) on the northern side and the ajuntament (city hall) on the southern. Both have fine Gothic interiors, which, unfortunately, the general public can only enter at limited times.

The **Palau de la Generalitat**, founded in the early 15th century to house Catalunya's parliament, is open only on 23 April, the Dia de Sant Jordi (St George, Catalunya's patron saint), when it's decked out with roses and very crowded, and 24 September (Festes de la Mercè). At any time, however, you can admire the original Gothic main entrance on Carrer del Bisbe Irurita.

It's a similar story with the **ajuntament**. Most of the time the original, now disused, Gothic entrance on Carrer de la Ciutat is the only feature of note. But on Saturday and Sunday from 10 am to 2 pm you can take your passport and ask permission to see the Saló de Cent, a fine arched hall created in the 14th century for the medieval city council, the Consell de Cent (but since remodelled).

Catedral & Around

You can reach Barcelona's cathedral, its most magnificent Gothic structure, by following Carrer del Bisbe Irurita north-west from Plaça de Sant Jaume. The narrow old streets around the cathedral are beautifully traffic-free and dotted with buskers playing classical guitar or Catalan folk songs.

At the northern end of Carrer del Bisbe Irurita poke your head into the courtyards of the 16th century **Casa de l'Ardiaca**

(archdeacon's house) and the 13th century **Palau Episcopal** (bishop's palace). On the outside of both buildings at the very end of Carrer del Bisbe Irurita you can make out the bottom parts of the rounded **Roman towers** that guarded a Roman gate here. The lower part of the Casa de l'Ardiaca's north-western wall was part of the **Roman walls**.

The best view of the cathedral is from Pla de la Seu beneath its main **north-west façade**. Unlike most of the building, which dates from between 1298 and 1460, this façade was not created till the 1870s, although it is closely based on a 1408 design, itself more intricate and pointy than the rest of the cathedral.

The interior is a broad, soaringly high space divided into a central nave and two aisles by lines of elegant, thin pillars. Unlike many much-visited cathedrals, this one maintains a truly serene atmosphere, which at its height is hushed worshippers gather for evening Mass. The cathedral was one of the few churches in Barcelona spared by the anarchists in the civil war, so its ornamentation, never over-lavish, is intact.

In the first chapel on the right from the north-western entrance, the main Crucifixion figure above the altar is the **Sant Crist de Lepant**, said to have been carried on the prow of the Spanish flagship at the battle of Lepanto. Farther along this same wall, past the south-west transept, are raised the wooden **coffins of Count Ramon Berenguer I and Almodis**, his wife, the founders of the 11th century Romanesque predecessor of the present cathedral.

The **crypt** beneath the main altar contains the tomb of Santa Eulàlia, one of Barcelona's patron saints and a good Christian lass of the 4th century who suffered terrible tortures and death at the hands of the pagan Romans. Her alabaster sarcophagus was carved by an Italian in 1327.

You can visit the cathedral's **roof** and **tower** by *ascensor* (lift), which rises every half-hour from 10.30 am to 12.30 pm and 4.30 to 6.30 pm from the Capella de les Animes del Purgatori near the north-east transept. Tickets (200 ptas) are sold in the *coro* (choir), the enclosed section in the middle of the nave.

From the south-west transept, exit to the lovely **claustre** (cloister), with its trees, fountains and flock of geese (there have been geese here for centuries). One of the cloister chapels commemorates 930 priests, monks and nuns martyred in the civil war. The interior of the cathedral is open from 8.30 am to 1.30 pm and 4 to 7.30 pm (5 to 7.30 pm on weekends).

Opposite the south-eastern end of the cathedral, narrow Carrer del Paradís leads back down towards Plaça de Sant Jaume. Inside No 10 are four columns of Barcelona's main **Temple Romà d'Augustí** (Roman Temple of Augustus), built for emperor worship in the 1st century AD. You can visit Monday to Saturday from 10 am to 2 pm and 4 to 8 pm and Sunday from 10 am to 2 pm (free).

Plaça del Rei & Around

Just a stone's throw east of the cathedral, Plaça del Rei is the former courtyard of the Palau Reial Major, the palace of the counts of Barcelona and monarchs of Aragón.

Museu d'Història de la Ciutat Most of the tall, centuries-old buildings surrounding the Plaça del Rei are now open to visitors as the City History Museum. This is one of Barcelona's most fascinating non-art museums, combining large sections of the palace with a subterranean walk through Roman and Visigothic Barcelona.

The entrance to the museum is through the **Casa Padellàs** on Carrer del Veguer just south of Plaça del Rei. Casa Padellàs, built for a 15th century noble family, has a court-yard typical of Barcelona's Gothic mansions, with an outdoor staircase up to the 1st floor. Today the staircase leads to a restored Roman tower and a section of Roman wall. Below ground is a remarkable walk through excavated **Roman and Visigothic Barcelona** – complete with sections of Roman street, Roman baths, remains of a Visigothic basilica and a Visigothic baptismal pool. The route extends underneath

the cathedral, where there are traces of the earlier Romanesque structure. You emerge from this part of the museum on Plaça del Rei.

A fan-shaped stairway in the northern corner of Plaça del Rei leads up to the Saló del Tinell, on the left, and the Capella Reial de Santa Àgata on the right. The **Saló del Tinell** was the royal palace's throne hall, a masterpiece of strong, unfussy Catalan Gothic, built in the mid-14th century with wide, rounded arches holding up a wooden roof. The **Capella Reial de Santa Àgata**, also from the 14th century, whose spindly bell tower rises from the north-eastern side of Plaça del Rei, was the palace's chapel. It's plain inside except for its 15th century altarpiece, painted wood roof and relatively recent stained glass. Follow the staircases up inside either of its side walls and you'll come out on the multi-tiered **Mirador del Rei Martí** (Lookout Tower of King Martin), built in 1555. The tower dominates Plaça del Rei and affords excellent views over the city.

The museum is open Tuesday to Saturday from 10 am to 2 pm and 4 to 8 pm and Sunday from 10 am to 2 pm (500 ptas, free on first Wednesday of the month and Wednesday afternoon).

Palau del Lloctinent The south-western side of Plaça del Rei is taken up by the Palau del Lloctinent (viceroy's palace), built in the 1550s as the residence of the Spanish viceroy of Catalunya.

Museu Frederic Marès A short distance down Carrer dels Comtes is the Museu Frederic Marès, in another part of the Palau Reial Major. Marès was a rich 20th century Catalan sculptor, traveller and obsessive collector. He specialised in medieval Spanish sculpture, huge quantities of which are displayed on the ground and 1st floors, including some lovely coloured wood sculptures of the Crucifixion and the Virgin. The top two floors, known as Museu Senti-mental, hold a mind-boggling array of other Marès knick-knacks, from toy soldiers and cribs to scissors and tarot cards. The museum is open Tuesday to Saturday from 10 am to 5 pm and Sunday and holidays from 10 am to 2 pm. The museum was closed at the time of writing.

Roman Walls

From Plaça del Rei it's worth a little detour to see the two best surviving stretches of Barcelona's Roman walls. One is on the south-western side of Plaça de Berenguer Gran, with the Capella Reial de Santa Àgata

atop them. The other is a little farther south, by the northern end of Carrer del Sots-tinent Navarro. They date from the 3rd and 4th centuries, when the Romans rebuilt their walls after the first attacks by Germanic tribes from the north.

Plaça de Sant Josep Oriol & Around

This small plaza not far off La Rambla is the prettiest in the Barri Gòtic. Its bars and cafés attract buskers and artists and make it

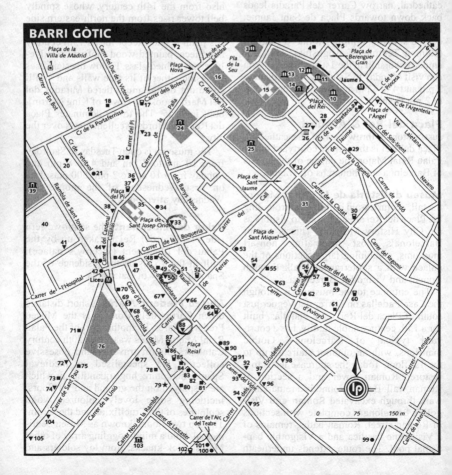

BARRI GÒTIC

a lively place to hang out for a while. It's surrounded by some of the Barri Gòtic's quaintest little streets, many of them dotted with other appealing cafés, restaurants and shops. The plaza is dominated by the **Església de Santa Maria del Pi**, a Gothic church built in the 14th to 16th centuries, open daily from 8.30 am to 1 pm and 4.30 to 9 pm. The beautiful rose window above its entrance on Plaça del Pi is claimed to be the world's biggest. The inside of the church was gutted by fire in 1936 and most of the stained glass is modern. The third chapel on the left is dedicated to Sant Josep Oriol, with a map showing spots in the church where he was supposed to have worked numerous miracles.

The area between Carrer dels Banys Nous and Plaça de Sant Jaume is known as the Call and was Barcelona's **Jewish quarter** – and centre of learning – from at least the 11th century until anti-Semitism saw Jews expelled from it in 1424.

Plaça Reial & Around

Just south of Carrer de Ferran, near its La Rambla end, is Plaça Reial, a large, traffic-free plaza surrounded by eateries, bars, nightspots and budget places to stay. The plaza's 19th century neoclassical architecture looks as if it would be at home in some elegant quarter of Paris, but before its 1980s cleanup this area had a fearsome reputation for poverty, crime and drugs. Indeed the whole area between Carrer d'Avinyò and La Rambla was once a red-light zone and a notorious den of lowlife.

The plaza still has a restless atmosphere, with respectable tourists, ragged buskers and down-and-outs coming face to face. Don't be put off, but watch your bags and pockets. The lampposts by the central fountain are Antoni Gaudí's first known works.

This southern half of the Barri Gòtic is imbued with the memory of Picasso, who lived as a teenager with his family on Carrer de la Mercè, had his first studio on Carrer de la Plata and was a regular visitor to a brothel at Carrer d'Avinyò 27, which may have inspired his famous 1907 painting *Les Demoiselles d'Avignon*.

EL RAVAL

West of La Rambla, the Ciutat Vella spreads to Ronda de Sant Antoni, Ronda de Sant Pau and Avinguda del Paral.lel, which together trace the line of Barcelona's 14th century walls. Known as El Raval, the area contains one of the city's most dispiriting slums, the seedy red-light zone and drug-abusers' haunt of the Barri Xinès. Take care in this area.

Museu d'Art Contemporani & Around

More upbeat is the Plaça dels Àngels in the north of El Raval (map: L'Eixample). Here the vast, white Museu d'Art Contemporani de Barcelona (MACBA) opened in 1995. Artists include Joan Miró, Antoni Tàpies, Paul Klee and Alexander Calder. Opening hours are Monday to Friday (closed Tuesday) from noon to 8 pm, Saturday from 10 am to 8 pm and Sunday and holidays from 10 am to 3 pm (700 ptas, 350 ptas on non-holiday Wednesdays).

On Carrer de Montalegre behind the museum is the **Centre de Cultura Contem-**porània de Barcelona, a complex of auditoriums and exhibition and conference halls created in the early 1990s from an 18th century hospice. The big courtyard, with a vast glass wall on one side, is spectacular. Exhibitions are held here regularly.

Antic Hospital de la Santa Creu

Two blocks south of Plaça dels Àngels is an architectural masterpiece from another age (map: Montjuïc). Founded in the early 15th century as the city's main hospital, the Antic Hospital de la Santa Creu today houses the Biblioteca de Catalunya (Catalunya's national library) and the Institut d'Estudis Catalans. You can walk through its beautiful courtyards, stretching between Carrer del Carme and Carrer de l'Hospital and surrounded by stone buildings from the 15th, 17th and 19th centuries.

Palau Güell

A few steps off La Rambla at Carrer Nou de la Rambla 3-5 (map: Gòtic), the Palau Güell is the only Gaudí house completely open to the public in Barcelona and one of the few modernista buildings in the Ciutat Vella. Gaudí built it in the late 1880s for his most important patron, the industrialist Eusebi Güell, as a guest wing and social annexe to Güell's main mansion on La Rambla. The Palau Güell lacks some of Gaudí's later playfulness but is still a characteristic riot of styles – Art Nouveau, Gothic, Islamic – and materials. After the civil war it was in police hands and political prisoners were tortured in its basement.

Features to look out for include the carved wooden ceilings and fireplace, the stonework, the use of mirrors, stained glass and wrought iron, and the main hall with its dome reaching right up to the roof. There's little colour until you come out on the roof with its spectacularly tiled and fantastically shaped chimney pots. The Palau Güell is open Monday to Saturday from 10 am to 2 pm and 4 to 8 pm (400 ptas, students 200 ptas). This is also where to pick up Ruta del Modernisme tickets, which allow you to see others of Gaudí's efforts around the city.

Picasso, who hated Gaudí's work, began his Blue Period in 1902 in a studio across the street at Carrer Nou de la Rambla 6.

Museu de l'Eròtica

Barcelona seems to pride itself as something of a pleasure centre and in here you can observe how people have been doing it since ancient times: lots of Kamasutra and flickering porn flicks from the 1920s. It's at La Rambla 96 (map: Gòtic) and is open daily from 10 to 10 pm (975 ptas).

LA RIBERA

La Ribera is the area of the Ciutat Vella north-east of the Barri Gòtic, from which it's divided by noisy Via Laietana, which was driven through this part of the city in 1907. La Ribera has intriguing, narrow streets, some major sights and good bars and restaurants, and lacks the seedy character of some parts of the Barri Gòtic.

All of the following are on the Central Barcelona map.

Palau de la Música Catalana

This concert hall at Carrer de Sant Pere més alt 11 is one of the high points of modernista architecture. It's not exactly a symphony, more a series of crescendos in tile, brick, sculptured stone and stained glass. Built between 1905 and 1908 by Lluís Domènech i Montaner for the Orfeó Català musical society, with the help of some of the best Catalan artisans of the time, it was conceived as a temple for the Catalan Renaixença.

You can see some of its splendours – such as the main façade with its mosaics, floral capitals and sculpture cluster representing Catalan popular music – from the outside and glimpse lovely tiled pillars inside the ticket office entrance on Carrer de Sant Francesc de Paula. But the best is the richly colourful auditorium upstairs, with its ceiling of blue and gold stained glass and, above a bust of Beethoven, a towering sculpture of Wagner's Valkyries (Wagner was No 1 in the Renaixença charts). To see this, you need to attend a concert, book yourself on one of the regular free building tours (☎ 93 268 10 00) or get the Ruta del Modernisme ticket from Palau Güell (see Organised Tours later in this chapter).

Museu Picasso

Barcelona's most visited museum, the Museu Picasso, occupies three of the many fine medieval stone mansions on narrow Carrer de Montcada. The street was cut through the southern part of La Ribera in the 12th century as an approach to the port, then farther east than it is today. The mansions belonged to nobles and merchants who grew rich off Mediterranean trade.

The Museu Picasso, at No 15-19, is at its best with the artist's Barcelona periods. It shows clearly how the young Picasso learned to handle a whole spectrum of subjects, styles and treatments before developing his own forms of expression.

On the 1st floor are ceramics and 1890s paintings from Barcelona, Madrid and Málaga. The 2nd floor starts with work of 1900-4 from Barcelona and Paris, with more impressionist-influenced paintings such as *Waiting* and Blue Period canvases like *The Defenceless*. There's also the haunting *Portrait of Senyora Canals* (1905) from the following Pink Period.

Among the later works, all done in Cannes in 1957, are a complex technical series *(Las Meninas)*. These consist, for the most part, of studies on Diego Velázquez's masterpiece of the same name (which hangs in the Prado in Madrid), but also include eight appealing treatments of *Pichones* (Pigeons).

The museum is open Tuesday to Saturday from 10 am to 8 pm, and Sunday from 10 am to 3 pm (600 ptas, 250 ptas on non-holiday Wednesdays and free on the first Sunday of each month). There are additional charges for special exhibitions.

Museu Tèxtil i d'Indumentària

This Textile and Costume Museum is in the 14th century Palau dels Marquesos de Lió at Carrer de Montcada 12. Its 4000 items range from 4th century Coptic textiles to 20th century local embroidery. The highlight is the big collection of clothing from the 16th century to the 1930s. Its hours are Tuesday to Saturday from 10 am to 5 pm and Sunday and holidays from 10 am to 2 pm (400 ptas, 700 ptas including the Museu Barbier-Mueller d'Art Precolombí next door). There's a nice café in the old courtyard.

Museu Barbier-Mueller d'Art Precolombí

Occupying the Palau Nadal at No 14, this museum holds one of the most prestigious collections of pre-Colombian art in the world. The artefacts from South American 'primitive' cultures come from the collections of the Swiss businessman Josef Mueller (who died in 1977) and his son-in-law Jean-Paul Barbier, who directs the Musée Barbier-Mueller in Geneva. It is open Tuesday to Saturday from 10 am to 8 pm and Sunday from 10 am to 3 pm (500 ptas, 700 ptas including the Museu Tèxtil i d'Indumentària).

Along Carrer de Montcada

Several other mansions on the street are now commercial art galleries where you're welcome to browse (they often stage exhibitions). The biggest is the **Galeria Maeght** at No 25 in the 16th century Palau dels Cervelló.

Barcelona has dozens of other art galleries, by the way; you'll find listings in *Guia del Ocio* (see Entertainment later in this chapter).

Església de Santa Maria del Mar

Carrer de Montcada opens at its southeastern end into **Passeig del Born**, a plaza where jousting tournaments took place in the Middle Ages and which was Barcelona's main square from the 13th to 18th centuries. At the south-western end of Passeig del Born stands one of Barcelona's finest Gothic churches, Santa Maria del Mar. Built in the 14th century, Santa Maria was lacking in superfluous decoration even

before anarchists gutted it in 1909 and 1936. This only serves to highlight its fine proportions, purity of line and sense of space. There's a beautifully slim arcade in the apse and some lovely 15th to 18th century stained glass. The church is open daily from 9 am to 1.30 pm and 4.30 to 8 pm.

PARC DE LA CIUTADELLA

East of La Ribera and north of La Barceloneta, Parc de la Ciutadella is perfect if you just need a bit of space and greenery, but also has some more specific attractions, all of which are on the Central Barcelona map.

After the War of the Spanish Succession, Felipe V built a huge fort (La Ciutadella) to keep watch over Barcelona. It became a much loathed symbol of everything Catalans hated about Madrid and was later used as a political prison. Only in 1869 did the government allow its demolition. The site was turned into a park and used as the main site for the Universal Exhibition of 1888. It's open daily from 8 am to 8 pm (to 9 pm from April to September). Arc de Triomf and Barceloneta, both about half a kilometre away, are the nearest metro stations.

The single most impressive thing in the park is the monumental **Cascada** near the Passeig de les Pujades entrance, created in 1875-81 by Josep Fontsère with the help of the young Gaudí. It's a dramatic combination of classical statuary, rugged rocks, greenery and thundering water.

South-east of here, in the fort's former arsenal, are the **Museu Nacional d'Art Modern de Catalunya** and the **Parlament de Catalunya**, where the Generalitat meets. The art gallery, despite its title, is devoted to Catalan art from the mid-19th century to the 1920s, the era of modernisme and its classicist antithesis, Noucentism (literally '19th-centuryism'). Look for the works by the two leading lights of modernista art, Ramon Casas and Santiago Rusiñol, especially Casas' drawings of the habitués of Els Quatre Gats and Rusiñol's landscapes. The museum is open Tuesday to Sunday from 10 am to 7 pm (300 ptas, students 200 ptas).

The southern end of the park is occupied by a large **Parc Zoològic** (zoo), which is best known for its albino gorilla called Copito de Nieve (Snowflake), who was orphaned by poachers in Africa in the 1960s. It's open daily from 10 am to 7 pm (1400 ptas).

Along the Passeig de Picasso side of the park are several buildings constructed for, or just before, the Universal Exhibition. These include two arboretums, the specialised Museu de Geologia and the **Museu de Zoologia** or Castell dels Tres Dragons (open Tuesday to Sunday from 10 am to 2 pm; 300 ptas). The contents of this museum are less interesting than the building itself, by Lluís Domènech i Montaner, who put medieval castle trimmings on a pioneering steel frame.

North-west of the park along Passeig de Lluís Companys is the imposing modernista **Arc de Triomf**, with unusual, almost Islamic-style brickwork. It was designed by Josep Vilaseca as an entrance to the Universal Exhibition.

PORT VELL

Barcelona's old port at the bottom of La Rambla, once such an eyesore that it caused public protests, has been transformed since the 1980s into an attractive and people-friendly environment with some excellent leisure developments.

All the places listed are on the Central Barcelona map.

For a view of the harbour from the water, you can take a **Golondrina** excursion boat (☎ 93 442 31 06) from Moll de les Drassanes in front of the Monument a Colom. A 35 minute trip to the breakwater *(rompeolas)* and lighthouse *(faro)* on the seaward side of the harbour is 465 ptas; an 80 minute trip to Port Olímpic is 1250 ptas (less for under-19s). This latter trip is on a glass-bottomed catamaran. The number of departures depends largely on the season and demand. Breakwater trips normally leave at least hourly in the daytime, while

Port Olímpic trips go at least three times daily. North-east from the Golondrina quay stretches the palm-lined promenade **Moll de la Fusta**.

At the centre of the redeveloped harbour is the **Moll d'Espanya**, a former wharf linked to Moll de la Fusta by a wave-shaped footbridge, the **Rambla de Mar**, which rotates to let boats enter the marina behind it. At the end of Moll d'Espanya is the glossy Maremàgnum shopping and eating complex, but the major attraction is **L'Aquàrium** (☎ 93 221 74 74) behind it – an ultra-modern aquarium that opened in 1995. It's claimed to be Europe's biggest aquarium and to have the world's best Mediterranean collection. A highlight is the 80m-long shark tunnel. Entry is a steep 1400 ptas (950 ptas for four to 12-year-olds and pensioners). It's open daily from 9.30 am to 9 pm (until 11 pm in July and August). Beyond L'Aquàrium is the IMAX Port Vell big-screen cinema.

The **cable car** *(telefèric* or *funicular aereo)* strung across the harbour to Montjuïc provides another view of the city. You can get tickets at Miramar (Montjuïc), the Torre de Jaume I and the Torre de Sant Sebastià (in Barceloneta). A return ticket from Miramar to Sant Sebastià will cost 1200 ptas. A return between the central Torre de Jaume I and either Miramar or Torre de Sant Sebastià is 1000 ptas, while a one-way on either run is 800 ptas. The cable car operates daily from midday to 7 pm.

LA BARCELONETA & PORT OLÍMPIC

It used to be said that Barcelona had 'turned its back on the sea', but an ambitious Olympics-inspired redevelopment program has returned a long stretch of coast northeast of Port Vell to life.

All the places listed are on the Central Barcelona map.

La Barceloneta, at the north-eastern end of Port Vell, is an old sailors' quarter now mostly composed of dreary five or six-storey apartment blocks. It's known for its seafood restaurants, although some of the most characteristic ones were knocked down in the redevelopment. In the Palau de Mar building facing the harbour is the new **Museu d'Història de Catalunya** (History of Catalunya Museum), a 4500 million peseta (US$35 million) affair opened in 1996. It's an almost Disneyesque sort of place, incorporating lots of technological wizardry, with audiovisuals and interactive information points galore. Nearly all the labelling is in Catalan, but you can request a returnable explanatory booklet in several languages, including English. Covering the region's prehistory and history to 1980, the museum has re-creations including a Roman house and a civil war air-raid shelter. The museum is open Tuesday to Thursday from 10 am to 7 pm, Friday and Saturday from 10 am to 8 pm and Sunday and holidays from 10 am to 2.30 pm (500 ptas).

Barcelona's fishing fleet ties up along the Moll del Rellotge, south of the museum. On La Barceloneta's seaward side are the first of Barcelona's **beaches**, once dirty and unused but now cleaned up and popular on summer weekends. **Passeig Marítim**, a 1.25km promenade from La Barceloneta to Port Olímpic (through an area formerly full of railway sidings and warehouses) is pleasant.

Port Olímpic was built for the Olympic sailing events and is now surrounded by bars and restaurants. An eye-catcher on the approach from La Barceloneta is the giant copper *Peix* (Fish) sculpture by Frank Gehry, one of a series of modern sculptures dotted around this part of town. The area behind Port Olímpic – dominated by Barcelona's two tallest skyscrapers, the luxury Hotel Arts Barcelona and the Torre Mapfre office block – is the Vila Olímpica, the living quarters for the Olympic participants, now mostly sold off as expensive apartments. To the north-east are more beaches.

L'EIXAMPLE

L'Eixample (the Enlargement), stretching 1 to 1.5km north, east and west of Plaça de

Catalunya, was Barcelona's 19th century answer to overcrowding in the confines of the medieval city.

Work on l'Eixample began in 1869, following a design by the architect Ildefons Cerdà, who specified a grid of wide streets with plazas formed by their cut-off corners. Cerdà also planned numerous green spaces but these didn't survive the intense demand for Eixample real estate.

L'Eixample has been inhabited from the start by the city's middle classes, many of whom still think that it's the best thing about Barcelona. Along its grid of straight streets are the majority of the city's most expensive shops and hotels, plus a range of eateries and several nightspots. The main sightseeing objective is modernista architecture, the best of which – apart from La Sagrada Família – is clustered on or near l'Eixample's main avenue, Passeig de Gràcia.

All these places are on the L'Eixample & Gràcia map.

Manzana de la Discordia

The so-called 'Block of Discord' on the western side of Passeig de Gràcia, between Carrer del Consell de Cent and Carrer d'Aragó, gets its name from three houses remodelled in a highly contrasting manner between 1898 and 1906 – one by each of

---

Manzana de la Discordia

Despite the Catalanisation of most Barcelona names in recent decades, the Manzana de la Discordia has kept its Spanish name to preserve a pun on *manzana*, which means both '[city] block' and 'apple'. According to Greek myth, the original Apple of Discord was tossed on to Mt Olympus by Eris (Discord) with orders that it be given to the most beautiful goddess, sparking jealousies that helped start the Trojan War. The pun won't transfer into Catalan, in which block is *illa* and apple is *poma*.

the three leading modernista architects. You can't normally go inside any of the rooms, but the concierges will sometimes let you peep into the hallways and up the stairs.

At No 35, on the corner of Carrer del Consell de Cent, is **Casa Lleo Morera**, Domènech i Montaner's contribution, with Art Nouveau carving outside and a bright, flower-tiled lobby. The chief glories – mosaics, stained glass and sculpture – are in the Patronat de Turisme offices upstairs. You can go up and get a glimpse of them in working hours, or wait for a, slightly more, extended tour of this floor on the hour.

The Modernistas

A mosaic-roofed fantasy near the entrance to Parc Güell, Barcelona, Catalunya

BETHUNE CARMICHAEL

Most visitors to Barcelona will have heard of Antoni Gaudí ('gow-DEE'), whose La Sagrada Família church is one of the city's major drawing cards. But Gaudí (1852-1926) was just one, albeit the most spectacular, of a generation of inventive architects who left their mark on Barcelona between 1880 and 1910. These were the *modernistas*, or Catalan modernists.

Modernisme is usually described as a version of Art Nouveau, from which it certainly derived its taste for sinuous, flowing lines and decorative artisanry. Art Nouveau also inspired modernisme's adventurous combinations of materials like tile, glass, brick, and iron and steel (which provide the unseen frames of many buildings). But Barcelona's modernistas used an astonishing variety of other styles too: Gothic and Islamic, Renaissance and Romanesque, and Byzantine. Some of their buildings look like fairy-tale castles. They were trying to create a specifically Catalan architecture, often looking back to Catalunya's medieval golden age for inspiration.

It's significant that the two other leading modernista architects, the tongue-twisting Lluís Domènech i Montaner (1850-1923) and Josep Puig i Cadafalch (1867-1957), were also prominent in the Catalan nationalist political movement. Gaudí too was a Catalan nationalist, although he turned increasingly to spiritual concerns as he grew older.

L'Eixample, where most of Barcelona's new building was happening at the time, is home to many of the modernista creations. Others in the city include Gaudí's Palau Güell and Parc Güell; Domènech i Montaner's Palau de la Música Catalana, Castell dels Tres Dragons and Hotel España restaurant; and Puig i Cadafalch's Els Quatre Gats. There are many, many more.

Nor was modernisme confined to architecture: you can explore its painting and drawing side at the Museu Nacional d'Art Modern de Catalunya.

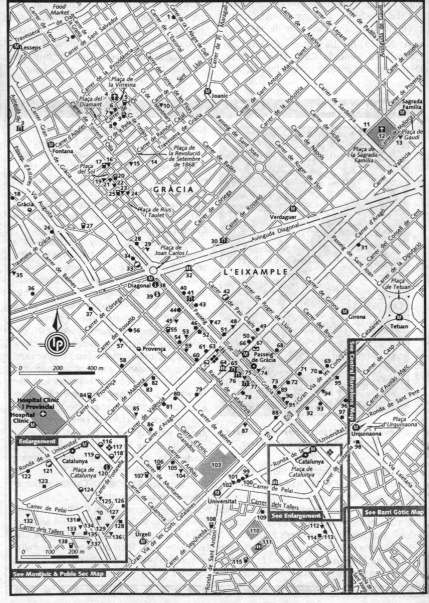

L'EIXAMPLE & GRÀCIA

L'EIXAMPLE & GRÀCIA

PLACES TO STAY
46 Comtes (Condes) de Barcelona Hotel
51 Hotel Majestic
52 Comtes de Barcelona Hotel
60 Hotel Regente
70 Hostal Palacios
72 St Moritz Hotel
73 Hostal Oliva
82 Hotel Balmes
88 Hotel Avenida Palace
92 Hotel Gran Via
95 Hotel Ritz Husa Palace
97 Hostal Goya
98 Hostal Fontanella
109 Hotel Mesòn de Castilla
114 Le Meridien
123 Hotel Ducs de Bergara
126 Pensiòn Estal
128 Hotel Nouvel
130 Hotel Continental
131 Pensiòn Noya & Restaurant Nuria
135 Hotel Lloret

PLACES TO EAT
6 Cal Majó
7 Casa de Pizzas
10 Taverna El Glop
11 La Baguetina Catalana
13 La Casa del Jamón
15 El Tastavins
16 Equinox Sol
19 Tetería Jazmín
21 Botiga del Sol
22 Aroma
23 Mario Pizza
24 Bar Candanchu
29 La Miel
35 Pastafiore
45 Pastafiore & Pans & Company
47 Centro Asturiano
48 FresCo
50 L'Hostal de Rita
53 Lizarran
57 La Gran Tasca
59 Bocatta
63 Cafè Torino
74 Cerveseria Tapa Tapa
75 Pans & Company
85 Bar Ariño 2

87 Pans & Company
90 Ba-Ba-Reeba
91 Quasi Queviures (Qu Qu)
94 El Café de Internet
99 Pans & Company
102 Bar Estudiantil
104 La Flauta
112 Viena
125 Hard Rock Cafe
127 Self-Naturista
129 Bocatta
132 Xaica Pizzeria
133 Restaurant Tallers
134 Pastafiore
136 Santa Ana
137 Pans & Company

OTHER
1 KGB
2 Bookstore
3 Casa Vicenç
4 Església de Sant Josep
5 Café La Virreina
8 Cinema Verdi
9 Café Salambó
12 Temple Expiatori de la Sagrada Família
14 Mercat
17 Café del Sol
18 Otto Zutz
20 El Dorado
25 Bar Chivito de Oro
26 Cinema Arkadín
27 Café de la Calle
28 Martin's
30 Casa de les Punxes (Casa Torrades)
31 Hertz
32 Palau Quadras (Museu de la Música)
33 German Consulate
34 Cinema Casablanca
36 Institut Français de Barcelona
37 Velvet
38 Palau Robert (Regional Tourist Office)
39 American Express
40 Vinçon
41 La Pedrera (Casa Milà)
42 Swedish Consulate
43 24-Hour Pharmacy

44 Librería Francesa
49 Cinema Capsa
54 Cinema Alexis
55 La Bodegueta
56 Nick Havanna
58 Come In Bookshop
61 Camper
62 Boulevard Rosa
64 Fundació Antoni Tàpies
65 Casa Batlló
66 BCN Bookshop
67 Correos
68 Europcar Rentacar
69 Pullmantur
71 Halcón Viajes
76 Casa Amatller
77 Casa Morera
78 Natura Selection
79 Avis
80 Altaïr Bookshop
81 CR
83 Planet Music
84 La Fira
86 24-Hour Pharmacy
89 Iberia
93 Laie Bookshop
96 Ca la Dona
100 FotoK
101 Julià Tours & Rentacar
103 Universitat de Barcelona
105 Satanassa
106 Este Bar
107 Punto BCN
108 Metro Disco
110 Centre de Cultura Contemporània de Barcelona
111 Museu d'Art Contemporàni de Barcelona (MACBA)
113 Simago Supermarket
115 Casa Almirall
116 T1 Tombus and Tibibùs
117 El Corte Inglés
118 Bus Turistic (South Circuit)
119 A1 Aerobùs
120 Centre d'Informació Turisme de Barcelona
121 French Consulate
122 Usit Unlimited
124 Bus Turistic (North Circuit)
138 L'Ovella Negra

Casa Amatller at No 41, by Puig i Cadafalch, combines Gothic window frames with a stepped gable reminiscent of Amsterdam. The pillared entrance hall and the staircase lit by stained glass are like the inside of some romantic castle.

Casa Batlló, next door at No 43, is one of Barcelona's gems. Of course it's by Gaudí. The façade, sprinkled with bits of blue, mauve and green tile and studded with wave-shaped window frames and balconies, rises to an uneven blue-tiled roof with a solitary tower. Although the roof may represent Sant Jordi and the dragon, the whole building's effect is, if anything, that of an underwater castle. In the lobby and on the stairs are more curves and white and light-blue tiles.

Fundació Antoni Tàpies

Round the corner from the Manzana de la Discordia, at Carrer d'Aragó 255, this is both a pioneering modernista building of the early 1880s and the major collection of a leading 20th century Catalan artist. The building, designed by Domènech i Montaner, combines a brick-covered iron frame with Islamic-inspired decoration. Antoni Tàpies, whose experimental art has often carried political messages (he opposed Francoism in the 1960s and 70s) launched the *fundació* in 1984 to promote contemporary art, donating a large collection of his own work. Plans are afoot to broaden the collection.

The fundació is open Tuesday to Sunday from 11 am to 8 pm (500 ptas, students 300 ptas, pensioners and under-12s free).

La Pedrera (Casa Milà)

Back on Passeig de Gràcia, 450m up at No 92, is another Gaudí masterpiece, built between 1905 and 1910 as a combined apartment and office block. Formally called the Casa Milà after the businessman who commissioned it, it's better known as La Pedrera (the quarry) because of its uneven grey-stone façade, which ripples round the corner of Carrer de Provença. The wave effect is emphasised by elaborate wrought-iron balconies.

The Fundació Caixa Catalunya office (☎ 93 484 59 95) has opened the place up to visitors, organising it as the Espai Gaudí (Gaudí Space) and guiding visitors through the building and up on to the roof, with its giant chimney pots looking like multi-coloured medieval knights. Gaudí wanted to put a tall statue of the Virgin up here too: when the Milà family said no, fearing it might make the building a target for anarchists, Gaudí resigned from the project in disgust. It is open daily from 10 am to 8 pm (500 ptas, students 300 ptas). Guided visits take place at 6 pm (11 am on weekends and holidays).

You can also visit La Pedrera on the Ruta del Modernisme ticket. The Caixa Catalunya organises its own tours of other Gaudí landmarks – for more on both options, see Organised Tours later in the chapter.

Palau Quadras & Casa de les Punxes

Within a few blocks north and east of La Pedrera are two of Puig i Cadafalch's major buildings. The nearer is the Palau del Baró de Quadras at Avinguda Diagonal 373, created between 1902 and 1904 with detailed neo-Gothic carvings on the façade and fine stained glass. It houses the Museu de la Música, with a collection of international instruments from the 16th century to the present. It's open Tuesday to Sunday from 10 am to 2 pm (Wednesday until 8 pm; 300 ptas).

The Casa Terrades is on the other side of Avinguda Diagonal, 1½ blocks east at No 420. This apartment block of 1903-5, like a castle in a fairy tale, is better known as the Casa de les Punxes (House of the Spikes) because of its pointed turrets.

La Sagrada Família

If you only have time for one sightseeing outing in Barcelona, this should probably be it. La Sagrada Família inspires awe by its sheer verticality and, in the true manner of the great medieval cathedrals it emulates, it's still not half-built, after more than 100 years. If it's ever finished, the topmost tower will be more than half as high again as those standing today.

The Temple Expiatori de la Sagrada Família (Expiatory Temple of the Holy Family) was the project to which Antoni Gaudí dedicated his life. It stands in the east

Gaudí & La Sagrada Família

The idea for La Sagrada Família came from Josep Maria Bocabella, a rich publisher who was worried about the growth of revolutionary ideas in Barcelona and set up a religious society dedicated to Sant Josep, patron saint of workers and the family. Construction of the society's church (it's not a cathedral) began in 1882 under Francesc de Villar, who planned a relatively conventional neogothic structure. Villar fell out with Bocabella and was replaced, in 1883, by the 31-year-old Antoni Gaudí.

Gaudí, born into an artisan family in Reus, southern Catalunya, and trained as a metalsmith, was already a successful *modernista* architect. Up to 1909 he worked on other projects in Barcelona and elsewhere as well as La Sagrada Família. After that he devoted himself entirely to La Sagrada Família, attending to every detail and becoming increasingly single-minded, spiritual, ascetic and unkempt. When he was run over by a tram on Gran Via de les Corts Catalanes in 1926, he had been living in a workshop at La Sagrada Família. His clothes were held together by pins and at first no-one recognised him. He died in hospital three days later.

As he worked on La Sagrada Família, Gaudí evolved steadily grander and more original ideas for it. He stuck to the basic Gothic cross-shaped ground plan with an apse, but eventually devised a temple 95m long and 60m wide, able to seat 13,000 people and with a central tower 170m high and 17 others of 100m or more. With his characteristic dislike for straight lines (there were none in nature, he said), Gaudí gave his towers swelling outlines inspired by the weird peaks of the holy mountain Montserrat outside Barcelona, and encrusted them with a tangle of sculpture that seems an outgrowth of the stone.

At Gaudí's death only the crypt, the apse walls, one portal and one tower had been finished. Three more towers were added by 1930 – completing the north-eastern (Nativity) façade – but in 1936 anarchists burned and smashed everything they could in La Sagrada Família, including the workshops, models and plans. Work restarted in the 1950s using restored models and photographs of drawings, with only limited guidance on how Gaudí had thought of solving the huge technical problems of the building. Today the south-western (Passion) façade, with four more towers, isn't very far off completion, and the nave, started in 1978, is coming along nicely.

Constant controversy has dogged the building program. There are those who say the quality of the new work and its materials – concrete instead of stone for the new towers – are inferior to the earlier parts; others who say that in the absence of detailed plans, the shell should have been left as a kind of monument to Gaudí; and yet others who simply oppose the spending of large amounts of money on a new church (although the funding is all private). The chief architect, Jordi Bonet, and his supporters, aside from their desire to see Gaudí's mighty vision made real, argue that their task is a sacred one – that it's not just any old building, but a church intended, as its 'Temple Expiatori' title indicates, to atone for sin and appeal for God's mercy on Catalunya.

Four of La Sagrada Família's towering spires

DAMIEN SIMONIS

of l'Eixample (metro: Sagrada Família) and is open to visitors daily – April to the end of August from 9 am to 8 pm; March, September and October from 9 am to 7 pm; and November to February from 9 am to 6 pm. The entry charge of 800 ptas for everybody (the money goes towards the building program) includes a good museum in the crypt.

What you're visiting is a building site, but the completed sections and the museum can be explored at leisure. A couple of times a day 50-minute guided tours are offered (500 ptas).

The entrance is by the south-western façade fronting Carrer de Sardenya and Plaça de la Sagrada Família. Inside is a bookstall where you should invest 500 ptas in the *Official Guide* if you want a detailed account of the church's sculpture and symbolism. To get your bearings, you need to realise that this façade, and the opposite one facing Plaça de Gaudí, each with four skyscraping towers, are at the *sides* of the church. The main façade, as yet unbuilt, will be at the south-eastern end, on Carrer de Mallorca. The 170m central tower will be above the crossing, halfway between the two existing façades.

Nativity Façade This, the north-eastern façade, is the building's artistic pinnacle, mostly done under Gaudí's personal supervision and much of it with his own hands. You can climb high up inside some of the four towers by a combination of lifts (when they're working) and narrow spiral staircases, a vertiginous experience. The towers are destined to hold tubular bells capable of playing complex music at great volume. Their upper parts are decorated with mosaics spelling out '*Sanctus, Sanctus, Sanctus, Hosanna in Excelsis, Amen, Alleluia*'. When asked why he lavished so much care on the tops of the spires, which no-one would see from close up, Gaudí answered: 'The angels will see them'.

Beneath the towers is a tall, three-part portal on the theme of Christ's birth and childhood. It seems to lean outward as you stand beneath looking up. Gaudí used real people and animals as models for many of the sculptures.

The three sections of the portal represent, from left to right, Hope, Charity and Faith. Among the forest of sculpture on the Charity portal, you can make out, low down, the manger surrounded by an ox, an ass, the shepherds and kings, with angel musicians above. Directly above the blue stained-glass window is the Archangel Gabriel's Annunciation to Mary. At the top is a green cypress tree, a symbolic refuge in a storm for the white doves of peace dotted over it.

Lower sculptures on the Hope portal show the Flight into Egypt and the Massacre of the Innocents, with Jesus and Joseph in their carpenters' workshop just above. Sculpture on the Faith portal includes, in the centre of the lower group, the child Jesus explaining the Scriptures to the temple priests.

Interior The apse wall at the north-western end of the church was the first part to be finished (in 1894). From the altar steps you can look down the nave at work in progress, with the walls and columns near completion and the roofs begun. The main Glory Façade on the south-eastern end will, like the north-eastern and south-western façades, be crowned by four towers – the total number representing the 12 apostles. Further symbolism will make the building a microcosm of the Christian church, with Christ represented by the massive central tower above the transept.

Passion Façade This south-western façade, on the theme of Christ's last days and death, has been built since the 1950s with, like the Nativity Façade, four needling towers and a big, sculpture-bedecked portal. The sculptor, Josep Subirachs, has not attempted to imitate Gaudí's work but has produced strong images of his own. The sculptures, on three levels, are in an S-shaped sequence starting with the Last

Supper at bottom left and ending with Christ's burial at top right.

Museu Gaudí Open at the same times as the church, the museum includes interesting material on Gaudí's life and other work, as well as models, photos and other material on La Sagrada Família.

GRÀCIA

Gràcia is the area north of the middle of l'Eixample (map: L'Eixample). Once a separate village, then in the 19th century an industrial barrio famous for its republican and liberal ideas, it became fashionable among radical and bohemian types in the 1960s and 1970s. Although now more sedate and gentrified, it retains much of its style of 20 years ago, with a mixed-class population. Gràcia's interest lies in the atmosphere of its narrow streets, small plazas and the bars and restaurants on them. An evening or night-time wander is the best way to savour these. Diagonal and Fontana are the nearest metro stations to central Gràcia.

The liveliest plazas are **Plaça del Sol**, **Plaça de Rius i Taulet** with its clock tower, and **Plaça de la Virreina** with the 17th century Església de Sant Josep. Three blocks east of Plaça de Rius i Taulet there's a big covered **market**. West of Gràcia's main street, Carrer Gran de Gràcia, there's an early Gaudí house, the turreted, vaguely *mudéjar* **Casa Vicenç** at Carrer de les Carolines 22.

MONTJUÏC

Montjuïc, the hill overlooking the city centre from the south-west, is home to some of Barcelona's best museums and leisure attractions, some fine parks and the main group of 1992 Olympics sites. It's well worth a day or two of your time.

The name Montjuïc (Jewish Mountain) indicates there was once a Jewish settlement here. Before Montjuïc began to be turned into parks in the 1890s, its woodlands had long provided food-growing and breathing space for the people of the cramped Ciutat Vella. Montjuïc also has a darker history: its castle was used by the Madrid government to bombard the city after political disturbances in 1842 and as a political prison right up to the Franco era. The first main burst of building on Montjuïc came in the 1920s, when it was chosen as the stage for Barcelona's 1929 World Exhibition. The Estadi Olímpic, the Poble Espanyol and some museums all date from this time. Montjuïc got a face-lift and more new buildings for the 1992 Olympics.

Abundant roads and paths, with occasional escalators, plus buses and even a chair lift allow you to visit Montjuïc's sights in any order you choose. The five main attractions – the Poble Espanyol, the Museu Nacional d'Art de Catalunya, the Estadi Olímpic, the Fundació Joan Miró and the views from the castle – would make for a full day's sightseeing.

DAMIEN SIMONIS

Passion façade of La Sagrada Família, sculpted by Josep Subirachs

All of the places listed are on the Mont-juïc & Poble Sec map

Getting There & Away

You could walk from the Ciutat Vella (the foot of La Rambla is 700m from the eastern end of Montjuïc).

More comfortable is bus No 61, which runs every 15 to 30 minutes until 8.30 pm (later on Sunday and holidays) from Avinguda de la Reina Maria Cristina, just off Plaça d'Espanya at the northern foot of the hill (metro: Espanya). This goes to the Estació Parc Montjuïc funicular and chairlift station via the Poble Espanyol, the Estadi Olímpic and the Fundació Joan Miró. The Bus Turístic (see Getting Around) also makes several stops on Montjuïc.

Another way of saving your legs is the funicular railway from Paral.lel metro station to Estació Parc Montjuïc (215 ptas one way, 375 ptas return). From mid-June to mid-September, this goes daily from 11 am to 10 pm; from mid-March to mid-June

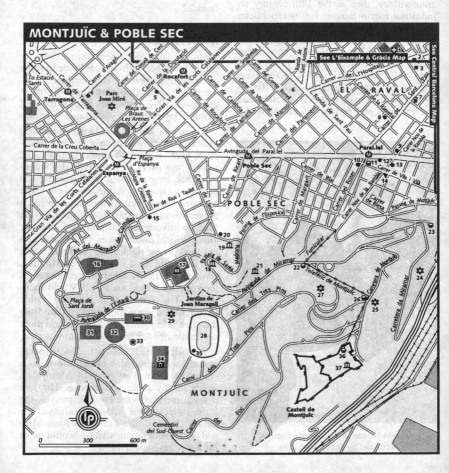

MONTJUÏC & POBLE SEC

and mid-September to the end of October (and during the Christmas holiday period), daily from 10.45 am to 8 pm; and the rest of the year, only on Saturday, Sunday and holidays from 10.45 am to 8 pm.

From Estació Parc Montjuïc, the Telefèric de Montjuïc chair lift will carry you yet higher, to an upper entrance of the former Parc d'Atraccions (Mirador stop) and then the castle (Castell stop) for 425 ptas one way (adults) and 625 ptas return. From mid-June to the end of September, this operates daily from 11.30 am to 9.30 pm; in October and the Christmas and Semana Santa periods, daily from 11 am to 2.45 pm and 4 to 7.30 pm; and the rest of the year, only on Saturday, Sunday and holidays from 11 am to 2.45 pm and 4 to 7.30 pm.

Another option is the *funicular aereo*, or cable car, that runs between Miramar and Sant Sebastià (Barceloneta). See Port Vell earlier in the chapter.

Around Plaça d'Espanya

The approach to Montjuïc from Plaça d'Espanya gives you the full benefit of the landscaping on the hill's northern side and allows Montjuïc to unfold for you from the bottom up. On Plaça d'Espanya's northern side is the big **Plaça de Braus Les Arenes** bullring, built in 1900 but no longer used

for bullfights. The Beatles played here in 1966. Behind the bullring is the **Parc Joan Miró**, created in the 1980s – worth a quick detour mainly for Miró's giant, highly phallic sculpture *Dona i Ocell* (Woman and Bird) in the north-western corner.

Fountains & Museu Nacional d'Art de Catalunya

Avinguda de la Reina Maria Cristina, lined with modern exhibition and congress halls, leads from Plaça d'Espanya towards Montjuïc. On the hill ahead of you is the Palau Nacional de Montjuïc and stretching up a series of terraces below it are Montjuïc's fountains, starting with the biggest, La Font Màgica. These come most alive with a lights-and-music show on summer evenings; the show lasts for about 15 minutes and is held from late June to late September on Thursday, Friday and Saturday, every half-hour from 10 to 11.30 pm.

The **Palau Nacional**, built in the 1920s for displays in the World Exhibition, houses the Museu Nacional d'Art de Catalunya. The museum's Romanesque section consists mainly of 11th and 12th century murals, woodcarvings and altar frontals (painted, low-relief wooden panels that were forerunners of the elaborate *retablos* adorning later churches). These works,

MONTJUÏC & POBLE SEC

gathered from decaying country churches in northern Catalunya early in the 20th century, constitute probably Europe's greatest collection of Romanesque art. The museum's other main section is devoted to Gothic art, but is less interesting. As you enter the museum, it's well worth forking out 100 ptas on a guide booklet in your own language, as the museum's labelling is mostly in Catalan.

Highlights to look for include the murals from the church of Sant Pere in La Seu d'Urgell, and the bright, rather modern-looking altar frontals from La Seu d'Urgell and Ix, in hall No 1; the murals from the church of Sant Joan de Boí, displayed in a space re-creating the shape of the church they came from (hall No 2); and the murals from the church of Sant Climent de Taüll, which rank among the masterworks of all Romanesque art, in hall No 5. You can also see a collection of Spanish paintings ranging from the Renaissance to the baroque.

The museum is open Tuesday to Saturday from 10 am to 7 pm (Thursday to 9 pm) and Sunday and holidays from 10 am to 2.30 pm (closed Monday and on 1 January, 1 May and 25 December). Entry is 600 ptas (500 ptas if you only want to see the Romanesque section).

Poble Espanyol

This 'Spanish Village' in the north-west of Montjuïc, 10 minutes walk from Plaça d'Espanya or the Museu Nacional d'Art, is both a tacky tourist trap and an intriguing scrapbook of Spanish architecture. Built for the Spanish crafts section of the 1929 exhibition, it's composed of plazas and streets lined with surprisingly good copies of typical buildings from all the country's regions.

You enter via Avinguda del Marquès de Comillas, beneath a towered medieval gate from Ávila. Inside, to the right, is an information office with free maps. Straight ahead from the gates is a *plaza mayor*, or town square, surrounded with mainly Castilian and Aragonese buildings. Elsewhere you'll find an Andalucian *barrio*, a

Basque street, Galician and Catalan quarters and even, at the eastern end, a Dominican monastery. The buildings house dozens of mid-range to expensive restaurants, cafés, bars, craft shops and workshops, and a few souvenir shops.

The Poble Espanyol is open from 9 am daily (Monday to 8 pm, Tuesday to Thursday to 2 am, Friday and Saturday to 4 am and Sunday to midnight). Entry is 950 ptas (or 1200 ptas combined entry with Galería Olímpica – see later). Students and children aged from seven to 14 pay 525 ptas. After 9 pm daily, except Friday and Saturday, it's free; at night, the restaurants, bars and discos become a lively corner of Barcelona nightlife.

Museu Etnològic & Museu d'Arqueologia

Down the hill east of the Museu Nacional d'Art, these museums are worth a visit if their subjects interest you, although neither is very excitingly presented and most explanatory material is in Catalan.

The Museu Etnològic on Passeig de Santa Madrona has extensive displays covering a range of cultures from other continents and puts on some interesting temporary exhibitions; it's open Tuesday to Sunday from 10 am to 3 pm (Tuesday and Thursday to 7 pm, except in summer; 300 ptas).

The Museu d'Arqueologia, at the corner of Passeig de Santa Madrona and Passeig de l'Exposició, covers Catalunya and related cultures elsewhere in Spain. Items range from copies of pre-Neanderthal skulls to lovely Carthaginian necklaces and jewel-studded Visigothic crosses. There's good material on the Islas Baleares (rooms X to XIV) and Empúries, or Emporion, the classical city on the Costa Brava (rooms XV and XVI). Hours are Tuesday to Saturday from 9.30 am to 7 pm and Sunday from 10 am to 2.30 pm (200 ptas, free on Sunday).

Anella Olímpica

The 'Olympic Ring' is the group of sports installations where the main events of the 1992 Olympics were held, on the ridge above the Museu Nacional d'Art. Westernmost is the **Institut Nacional d'Educació Física de Catalunya** (INEFC), a kind of sports university, designed by the best-known contemporary Catalan architect, Ricardo Bofill. Past a circular arena, the Plaça d'Europa, with the **Torre Calatrava** telephone tower behind it, is the **Piscines Bernat Picornell** building, where the swimming and diving events were held; it's now open to the public (see the Swimming & Gym section later in the chapter).

Next comes a pleasant little park, the Jardí d'Aclimatació, followed by the **Estadi Olímpic**, the main stadium of the games. It's open daily from 10 am to 6 pm (free); enter at the northern end. If you saw some of the Olympics on TV, the 65,000 capacity stadium may seem surprisingly small. So may the Olympic flame-holder rising at the northern end, into which a long-range archer spectacularly deposited a flaming arrow in the opening ceremony. The stadium was opened in 1929 but completely restored for 1992. At the southern end of the stadium (enter from the outside) is the **Galería Olímpica**, which has an exhibition, including videos, on the 1992 games; it's open Tuesday to Saturday from 10 am to 2 pm and 4 to 6 pm (to 8 pm in summer) and Sunday and holidays from 10 am to 2 pm (390 ptas).

West of the stadium is the **Palau Sant Jordi**, a 17,000-capacity indoor sports, concert and exhibition hall opened in 1990 and designed by the Japanese architect Arata Isozaki.

Cementiri del Sud-Ouest

On the hill south of the Anella Olímpica you can see the top of a huge cemetery, the Cementiri del Sud-Ouest or Cementiri Nou, which extends right down the southern side of the hill. Opened in 1883, it's an odd combination of elaborate architect-designed tombs for rich families and small niches for the rest. It contains the graves of numerous Catalan artists and politicians.

Joan Miró

Miró was born and grew up in the Barri Gòtic and lived a third of his life in Barcelona. A shy man, he practised and studied art from childhood but had no natural ability for lifelike drawing, being more attracted to art lacking perspective. He was deeply drawn to the Catalan countryside and coast, and divided his time from 1919 to the early 1930s between winters in Paris and summers at his family's farmhouse at Mont-roig on the southern Catalan coast. In Paris he mixed with Picasso, Hemingway, Joyce & co and made his own mark, after several years of struggle, with an exhibition in 1925. In the early 1930s he went through an artistic crisis, temporarily rejecting painting in favour of collage and other techniques.

By the 1940s Miró's characteristic style had emerged: arrangements of lines and symbolic figures in primary colours, with shapes reduced to their essence. Among his most important images are women, birds (the link between earth and the heavens), stars (the unattainable heavenly world, source of imagination) and a sort of net entrapping all these levels of the cosmos. In the 1960s and 1970s Miró devoted more time to sculpture and textiles. From 1956 he lived on Mallorca, home of his wife Pilar Juncosa.

An anti-Francoist, Miró had a stormy relationship with Barcelona after the civil war, but in the early 1970s he set up the Fundació Joan Miró for display of his own work and promotion of avant-garde art. He was supported in the project by two close Barcelona friends, the art patron and hat-shop owner Joan Prats, to whom Miró had given many paintings in exchange for hats, and the architect Josep Lluís Sert. Sert designed the building, which is notable for its abundant natural light.

Fundació Joan Miró

Barcelona's gallery for the greatest Catalan artist of the 20th century, Joan Miró (1893-1983), is 400m east of and downhill from the Estadi Olímpic.

Miró gave 379 paintings, sculptures and textile works, and almost 5000 drawings, to the collection, but only a selection of these is displayed at one time. The displays tend to concentrate on Miró's more settled last 20 years, but there are some important exceptions. The ground-floor Sala Joan Prats shows the younger Miró moving away, under surrealist influence, from his *relative* realism, then starting to work toward his own recognisable style. This section also includes the 1939-44 Barcelona Series of tortured lithographs, Miró's comment on the Spanish Civil War.

The Sala Pilar Juncosa, upstairs, also displays works from the 1930s and 1940s. Another interesting section is devoted to the 'Miró Papers', which include many preparatory drawings and sketches, some on bits of newspaper or cigarette packets. 'A Joan Miró' is a collection of work by other contemporary artists, donated in tribute to Miró.

The fundació also has a contemporary art library open to the public, a good specialist art bookshop and a café, and stages exhibitions and recitals of contemporary art and music. It's open Tuesday to Saturday from 10 am to 7 pm (Thursday to 9.30 pm) and Sunday and holidays from 10 am to 2.30 pm (700 ptas, students 400 ptas).

Castell de Montjuïc & Around

The south-east of Montjuïc is dominated by the big Parc d'Atraccions funfair (now closed) and the Castell de Montjuïc on the hill top above it. Near the bottom of the Parc d'Atraccions are the Estació Parc Montjuïc funicular/telefèric station, the big open-air Piscina Municipal de Montjuïc (see Swimming & Gym) and the ornamental **Jardins de Mossén Cinto**.

From the **Jardins del Mirador** opposite the Mirador telefèric station there are fine views over the port of Barcelona.

The Castell de Montjuïc dates in its present form from the late 17th and 18th centuries. For most of its existence it has been used to watch over the city and as a political prison and execution ground. Anarchists were executed here around the turn of the century, fascists during the civil war and Republicans after it – most notoriously, Lluís Companys in 1940. It was finally given by the army to the city in 1960. The castle is surrounded by a network of ditches and walls. Its **Museu Militar** has a section on Catalan military history, plus old weapons, uniforms, maps, castle models etc (open daily, except Monday, from 9.30 am to 8 pm; 200 ptas). Best of all are the excellent views from the castle area of the port and city below.

Towards the foot of this part of Montjuïc, above the thundering traffic of the main road to Tarragona, the **Jardins de Costa i Llobera** have a good collection of tropical and desert plants; they're open from 10 am to sunset.

PARC GÜELL

North of Gràcia and about 4km from Plaça de Catalunya, Parc Güell (map: Barcelona) is where Gaudí turned his hand to landscape gardening. It's a strange, enchanting place and is where his passion for natural forms really took flight, to the point where the artificial almost seems more natural than the natural.

Parc Güell originated in 1900, when Count Eusebi Güell bought a tree-covered hill side (then outside Barcelona) and hired Gaudí to create a miniature garden-city of houses for the wealthy in landscaped grounds. The project was a commercial flop and was abandoned in 1914, but not before Gaudí had created 3km of roads and walks, steps and a plaza in his inimitable manner, plus the two gatehouses. In 1922 the city bought the estate for use as a public park.

The simplest way to Parc Güell is to take the metro to Lesseps, then walk 10 to 15 minutes: follow the signs north-east along Travessera de Dalt then left up Carrer de Larrard, which brings you out almost at the park's two Hansel and Gretel-style gatehouses on Carrer d'Olot. The park is open daily from 9 am: June to September to 9 pm, April, May and October to 8 pm, March and November to 7 pm and other months to 6 pm (free). It's extremely popular and its quaint nooks and crannies are irresistible to photographers – who on busy days have trouble keeping out of each other's pictures.

The steps up from the entrance, guarded by a mosaic dragon/lizard, lead to the **Sala Hipóstila**, a forest of 84 stone columns (some of them leaning), intended as a market. To the left from here curves a gallery whose twisted stonework columns and roof give the effect of a cloister beneath tree roots, a motif repeated in several places in the park. On top of the Sala Hipóstila is a broad open space whose centrepiece is the **Banc de Trenadis**, a tiled bench curving sinuously round its entire perimeter.

The spired house to the right is the **Casa Museu Gaudí**, where Gaudí lived for most of his last years (1906-26). It contains furniture by Gaudí and other memorabilia and is open April to August daily from 10 am to 8 pm; during the rest of the year it's open Sunday to Friday from 10 am to 2 pm and 4 to 6 pm (300 ptas).

Much of the park is still wooded but full of pathways. The best views are from the cross-topped **Turo del Calvari** in the southwestern corner.

TIBIDABO

Tibidabo (542m) is the highest hill in the wooded range that forms the backdrop to Barcelona. It's a good place for some fresh air (it's often a few degrees cooler than in the city) and, if the air's clear, views over the city and inland as far as Montserrat. Tibidabo gets its name from the devil, who, trying to tempt Christ, took him to a high place and said, in the Latin version: '*Haec omnia tibi dabo si cadens adoraberis me*' ('All this I will give you if you will fall down and worship me').

All of the places listed are on the Barcelona map.

Getting There & Away

This is half the fun if you go the traditional way. First get an FGC suburban train to Avinguda de Tibidabo from Catalunya station on Plaça de Catalunya – a 10 minute ride for 140 ptas. Outside Avinguda de Tibidabo station, hop on the *tramvia blau*, Barcelona's last surviving tram line, which runs between fancy turn-of-the-century mansions to Plaça del Doctor Andreu for 225 ptas (350 ptas return). The tram runs daily in summer and on Saturday, Sunday and holidays the rest of the year; it leaves every 15 or 30 minutes from 10 am to 9.30 pm. On other days a bus (140 ptas) serves the route at similar times. From Plaça del Doctor Andreu the Tibidabo funicular railway climbs through the woods to Plaça de Tibidabo at the top of the hill for 300 ptas (400 ptas return); it leaves every 15 to 30 minutes from 7.15 am to 9.45 pm daily. If you're feeling active, you can walk up or down through the woods instead. The funicular only operates when the Parc d'Atraccions is open.

The cheaper alternative is bus No T2, the 'Tibibús', from Plaça de Catalunya to Plaça de Tibidabo (225 ptas). This runs on Saturday, Sunday and holidays year round; it leaves every 30 minutes from 10.30 am. From late June to early September it runs Monday to Friday too; it leaves every hour from 10.30 am. The last bus down leaves Tibidabo 30 minutes after the Parc d'Atraccions closes.

Temple del Sagrat Cor

The Church of the Sacred Heart, looming above the top funicular station, is meant to be Barcelona's answer to Paris' Sacré Coeur. It's certainly equally visible and even more vilified by aesthetes. It's actually two churches, one on top of the other. The top one is surmounted by a giant Christ and has a lift to the roof (100 ptas). Visiting times to the church are 8 am to 7 pm daily.

Parc d'Atraccions

The reason most Barcelonese come up to Tibidabo (☎ 93 211 79 42) is for some thrills in this funfair, which is also close to the top funicular station. Entry is 700 ptas plus extra for each ride, or 2400 ptas with access to all rides – including seven minutes in the Hotel Krueger, an *hospedaje* of horrors inhabited by actors playing out their Dracula, Hannibal Lecter and other fantasies. The funfair's opening times change with the season, so check with a tourist office. In summer it's usually open daily until late at night; in winter it may open only on Saturday, Sunday and holidays from about noon to 7 pm.

Torre de Collserola

From the top of the funicular it's a few minutes walk west to the 288m Torre de Collserola telecommunications tower, built in 1990-92. The external glass lift to the visitors' observation area, 115m up, was as hair-raising as anything at the Parc d'Atraccions. From the top they say that you can see for 70km on a clear day. It reopened in the summer of 1998 for the first time in many years and it was not clear how long this might last (call ☎ 93 406 93 54 for info). At the time of writing it was open Wednesday to Friday from 11 am to 2.30 pm and 3.30 to 8 pm and weekends from 11 am to 8 pm (500 ptas).

CAMP NOU

Hard on the heels of the Museu Picasso, as one of Barcelona's most visited museums, comes the Museu del Futbol Club Barcelona at the club's giant Camp Nou stadium, 3.5km west of Plaça de Catalunya (metro: Collblanc, map: Barcelona). Barça, as it's known, is one of Europe's top football (soccer) clubs, having carried off the Spanish championship a couple of dozen times and the European Cup more than once. Barça has also been described as Catalunya's unarmed army: the club was banned for a while in the 1920s because the Spanish government feared its potential for focusing Catalan nationalism and today its annual matches with Real Madrid act as a modern safety-valve for the age-old rivalry between Catalunya and Castilla. The many

world greats who have worn Barça's blue and red stripes include Johann Cruyff and Diego Maradona.

Camp Nou, built in the 1950s and enlarged for the 1982 World Cup, is one of the world's biggest stadiums, holding 120,000 people, and the club has a world record membership of over 100,000. Soccer fans who can't get to a game (see Entertainment) should find the museum, on the Carrer d'Aristides Maillol side of the stadium, worthwhile. The best bits are the photo section, the goal videos and the visit to seats high up overlooking the pitch. It's open Monday to Saturday (Tuesday to Saturday from October to March) from 10 am to 1 pm and 3 to 6.30 pm (475 ptas).

PEDRALBES

This is a wealthy residential area north of Camp Nou.

Palau Reial

Right by Palau Reial metro station, across Avinguda Diagonal from the main campus of the Universitat de Barcelona (map: Barcelona), is the entrance to the Jardins del Palau Reial, a verdant park open daily. In the park is the Palau Reial de Pedralbes, an early 20th century building that has served as a residence for Gaudí's patron Eusebi Güell, king Alfonso XIII, the president of Catalunya and General Franco. Today it houses the Museu de Ceràmica, with a good collection of Spanish ceramics from the 13th to 19th centuries including work by Picasso and Miró, and the Museu de les Arts Decoratives. Both museums are open Tuesday to Sunday from 10 am to 3 pm (500 ptas for both).

Over by Avinguda de Pedralbes are the Gaudí-designed stables and porter's lodge for the Finca Güell, as the Güell estate here was called. They were done in the mid-1880s, when Gaudí was strongly impressed by Islamic architecture. They can only be visited as part of a tour, although there is nothing to stop you admiring Gaudí's wrought-iron dragon gate from the outside.

Museu-Monestir de Pedralbes

This lovely old convent building, now a museum of monastic life also housing part of the famous Thyssen-Bornemisza art collection, stands at the top of Avinguda de Pedralbes, 700m from Finca Güell (map: Barcelona). Probably the easiest way here is to get the suburban FCG train to Reina Elisenda (the end of the line) and then either walk or pick up one of the buses running along Passeig de la Reina Elisenda (such as Nos 22, 64 and 75).

The convent, founded in 1326, still houses a community of nuns who inhabit separate closed quarters. The museum entrance is on Plaça del Monestir, a lovely quiet corner of Barcelona. Opening hours are Tuesday to Sunday from 10 am to 2 pm (700 ptas, 400 ptas for either the monastery *or* the Thyssen-Bornemisza collection).

The architectural highlight is the large, elegant, three-storey **cloister**, a jewel of Catalan Gothic architecture built in the early 14th century. Off this is the **Capella de Sant Miquel** with fine 14th century murals, plus a restored refectory, a kitchen and a reconstruction of the old infirmary – all giving a good idea of old convent life.

The **Col.lecció Thyssen-Bornemisza**, also here, is part of a fabulous art collection acquired by Spain in 1993. Most of the collection has gone to the Museo Thyssen-Bornemisza in Madrid; what's here is mainly religious work by European masters including Rubens, Titian and Velázquez.

SWIMMING

The Olympic pool on Montjuïc, the Piscines Bernat Picornell (☎ 93 423 40 41; map: Montjuïc), is open to the public daily from 7 am (until midnight Monday to Friday, 9 pm Saturday), except Sunday (from 7.30 am to 2.30 pm). Entry is 1200 ptas and includes use of the good gym inside. From June to late September entry to the outdoor pool alone costs 650 ptas.

LANGUAGE COURSES

Some of the best-value Spanish courses are offered by the Universitat de Barcelona,

which runs intensive courses (40 hours tuition over periods ranging from two weeks to a month, costing 45,000 ptas) all year. Longer Spanish courses, and courses in Catalan, are also available. For more information you can ask at the university's Informació office at Gran Via de les Corts Catalanes 585 (metro: Universitat, map: L'Eixample), open Monday to Friday from 9 am to 1 pm and 4 to 8 pm. For Spanish, contact its Instituto de Estudios Hispánicos (☎ 93 403 55 19, fax 93 403 54 33), while for Catalan, try the Servei de Llengua Catalana (☎ 93 403 54 77, fax 93 403 54 78); both are in the same building as Informació.

The university-run Escola Oficial d'Idiomes de Barcelona (☎ 93 329 24 58, fax 93 441 48 33) at Avinguda de les Drassanes s/n (metro: Drassanes, map: Central) is another place offering economical, 80 hour summer Spanish courses, as well as longer part-time courses in Spanish and Catalan.

International House (☎ 93 268 45 11, fax 93 268 02 39, spanish@bcn.ihes.com) is at Carrer de Trafalgar 14 (map: Central). Intensive courses start at 48,000 ptas a week. It has another branch (☎ 93 202 26 00) at Avinguda Diagonal 612 (map: Barcelona) and can organise accommodation with families or in pensiones.

The CIAJ youth information service at Carrer de Ferran 32 (map: Gòtic), open Monday to Friday from 10 am to 2 pm and 4 to 8 pm, and the British Council at Carrer d'Amigó 83 (map: Barcelona) have information on courses. Ads for courses and private tuition are posted on the noticeboard at the above-mentioned university building, Come In bookshop at Carrer de Provença 203 (map: Barcelona) and the British Council. Also advertised at Come In are some jobs for English teachers.

ORGANISED TOURS
Gaudí

If you want to approach the work of Gaudí and the modernistas in a systematic fashion, a couple of options present themselves.

The Agència del Paisatge Urbà (Urban Landscapes Agency; ☎ 93 488 01 39) offers four tours (of eight buildings including the Palau Güell, La Sagrada Família, Manzana de la Discordia and Palau de la Música Catalana), plus gives you written description of 50 modernista buildings throughout the city (there is also a map *Ruta del Modernisme*, which you can pick up free at the tourist office). Of the three buildings making up the Manzana de la Discordia, you see inside Casa Lleo Morera only. The whole lot costs 1600 ptas and you get the ticket (valid for a month) at the Palau Güell.

The Centre Cultural Caixa Catalunya (☎ 93 484 89 09) organises two four-hour Gaudí tours. The first covers his work in Barcelona, including the Casa Batlló (but not inside), La Sagrada Família and Parc Güell (departures from La Pedrera at 9 am and 3 pm). The second covers the Finca Güell at Pedralbes (see earlier in this chapter) and the Colònia Güell at Santa Coloma de Cervelló (outside Barcelona), which was intended as a kind of Utopian working families' colony. Its main interest lies in the crypt of the unfinished church (departures from La Pedrera at 9 pm). Tickets cost 5000 ptas and places are limited.

Other Tours

The Bus Turístic (see the Getting Around section later in this chapter) is better value than conventional tours for getting around the sights. But if you want a guided trip, Julià Tours (☎ 93 317 64 54) at Ronda de la Universitat 5 (metro: Universitat, map: L'Eixample) and Pullmantur (☎ 93 318 02 41) at Gran Via de les Corts Catalanes 635 (metro: Girona, map: L'Eixample) both do daily city tours by coach, plus out-of-town trips to Montserrat, Vilafranca del Penedès, the Costa Brava and Andorra. Their city tours are about 4000 ptas for a half-day, 10,000 ptas a full day.

A walking tour (950 ptas) of the Ciutat Vella on Saturday mornings departs from the Centre d'Informació Turisme de Barcelona on Plaça de Catalunya (English at 10 am; Spanish and Catalan at noon). A similar tour for 1½ hours (1000 ptas) starts at Plaça de l'Àngel – look for the guide in the yellow

BCN T-shirt. Tours in English go daily, except Monday, at 10.30 am and 4 pm.

For other guide services and tailor-made options, get in touch with the Barcelona Guide Bureau (☎ 93 310 77 78, fax 93 268 22 11).

SPECIAL EVENTS

Barcelona's main festivals include:

24 April
: *Dia de Sant Jordi* – the day of Catalunya's patron saint and also the Day of the Book: men give women a rose, women give men a book, publishers launch new titles; La Rambla and Plaça de Sant Jaume (where the Generalitat building is open to the public) are filled with book and flower stalls

23 June
: *Verbena de Sant Joan* – midsummer celebrations with bonfires, even in the squares of l'Eixample, and fireworks (a big display on Montjuïc)

28 June
: *Dia per l'Alliberament Lesbià i Gai* – gay and lesbian festival and parade

Late June to August
: *Grec arts festival* – music, dance, theatre at many locations

Around 15 August
: *Festa Major de Gràcia* – big local festival in Gràcia; decorated streets, dancing, music

11 September
: *La Diada* – Catalunya's national day, marking the fall of Barcelona in 1714, and a holiday in Barcelona

Around 24 September
: *Festes de la Mercè* – the city's major festival; several days of merrymaking including concerts, dancing, a swimming race across the harbour, *castellers* (human castle builders), a firework display synchronised with the Montjuïc fountains, dances of giants on the Saturday and *correfocs*, a parade of firework-spitting dragons and devils from all over Catalunya, on the Sunday

Late October to late November
: *Festival Internacional de Jazz de Barcelona* – jazz and blues around the city

PLACES TO STAY – BUDGET
Camping

The nearest camp site is the large **Cala Gogó** (☎ */fax 93 379 46 00, Carretera de la*

Platja s/n), 9km south-west of the centre at El Prat de Llobregat, near the airport (map: Barcelona). It's open from February to November and charges 1900 ptas per site plus 580 ptas per person. You can get there by bus No 65 from Plaça d'Espanya, or by suburban train from Plaça de Catalunya to El Prat, then a 'Prat Playa' bus.

There are some better – but still vast – sites a few kilometres farther out to the south-west on the coastal C-246 road, the Autovía de Castelldefels *(not the A-16 autopista* heading for Sitges, and *not* the C-245 through central Viladecans and Gavà). All are reachable by bus No L95 from the corner of Ronda de la Universitat and Rambla de Catalunya. They include (with prices for a car, a tent and two adults):

Albatros
  (☎ 93 633 06 95, Carretera C-246, Km 15), Gavà; open May to September; 3100 ptas
El Toro Bravo
  (☎ 93 637 34 62, Carretera C-246, Km 11), Viladecans; open all year; a tad shabby; 2800 ptas
Filipinas
  (☎ 93 658 28 95, Carretera C-246, Km 12), Viladecans; open all year; one of the best value for money; 2800 ptas
La Ballena Alegre
  (☎ /fax 93 658 05 04, Carretera C-246, Km 12.4), Viladecans; open Easter to end September; also good; 3800 ptas
La Tortuga Ligera
  (☎ 93 633 06 42, Avenida Europa 69), Gavà; open all year except December; 2750 ptas

Eleven kilometres north-east of the city there's *Camping Masnou (☎ 93 555 15 03, Carretera N-II, Km 639.8)*, open all year at El Masnou. It's 200m from El Masnou train station (reached by suburban trains from Catalunya station on Plaça de Catalunya) and charges 2560 ptas for a car, tent and two adults (map: Barcelona).

Youth Hostels

Barcelona has four HI hostels and several non-HI hostels. All require you to rent sheets (150 to 350 ptas) if you don't have a sleeping bag or sheets, and some lock their gates in the early hours and so aren't suitable if you plan to party on late. Except at the Kabul, which doesn't take bookings, it's advisable to call ahead in summer.

The non-HI *Youth Hostel Kabul (☎ 93 318 51 90, fax 93 301 40 34, Plaça Reial 17)* is a rough-and-ready place but does have, as its leaflets say, a 'great party atmosphere' and no curfew (map: Gòtic). If sleep is a priority, you're better off somewhere else. The price is 1700 ptas, plus a 1000 ptas key deposit. Security is not great but safes are available for valuables. There's room for about 150 people in bare and basic bunk rooms holding up to 10 each (keep an eye on your belongings). There's a small restaurant and washing machines. During July and August you should get there by 10 am to get a place.

The biggest and most comfortable hostel is the 183-place *Alberg Mare de Déu de Montserrat (☎ 93 210 51 51, fax 93 210 07 98, Passeig Mare de Déu del Coll 41-51)*, 4km north of the centre. It's a 10 minute walk from Vallcarca metro or a 20 minute ride from Plaça de Catalunya on bus No 28 (the last bus leaves at 1.30 am) which stops almost outside the gate (map: Barcelona). The main building is a former private mansion with a wonderful mudéjar-style lobby. Most rooms sleep six and a hostel card is needed. If you're under 25 or have an ISIC or FIYTO card, B&B is 1700 ptas; otherwise it's 2275 ptas. The hostel is in HI's IBN. You can also book through the central booking service of Catalunya's official youth hostels organisation, the Xarxa d'Albergs de Joventut (☎ 93 483 83 63, fax 93 483 83 50). Note: the other Barcelona hostels, even the HI ones, are not in the Xarxa.

Alberg Juvenil Palau (☎ 93 412 50 80, Carrer del Palau 6) has a friendly atmosphere and just 40 places in separate-sex bunk rooms (metro: Liceu, map: Gòtic). Cost is 1300 ptas, including breakfast. There's a kitchen and a good common-cum-eating room.

Hostal de Joves (☎ 93 300 31 04, Passeig de les Pujades 29) faces the northern end of Parc de la Ciutadella, a few minutes walk from the Estació de França and Arc de Triomf metro station (map: Central). It has 68 bunk places in small dorms, and a kitchen with a sociable dining area. The price, 1500 ptas including breakfast, is the same for all. The hostel closes at 2 am on Friday and Saturday night and 1 am other nights.

Abba Youth Hostel (☎ 93 319 45 45, Passeig de Colom 9) has beds in a separate-sex dorm arrangement for 1300 ptas including breakfast. It's handy for the Barri Gòtic and waterfront, but not so much for the metro (map: Central).

Alberg Pere Tarrès (☎ 93 410 23 09, fax 93 419 62 68, Carrer de Numància 149), 1km north of Estació Sants and 600m from the Les Corts and Maria Cristina metro stations, has 90 places in bare dorms with four to eight bunks. B&B costs from 1500 to 2000 ptas, depending on your age and whether or not you have a hostel card (map: Barcelona). The building has been renovated and is in good nick, with a courtyard and cooking and washing facilities. The gates are shut from 10 am to 4 pm and 11.30 pm to 8.30 am (they're opened briefly to let guests in at 2 am).

The small and distant *Alberg Studio (☎ 93 205 09 61, fax 93 205 09 00, Carrer de la Duquessa d'Orleans 58)*, 4km northwest of Plaça de Catalunya, is open only from 1 July to 30 September, and has about 40 places (map: Barcelona). It stays open 24 hours and charges 1500 ptas. Suburban trains run to nearby Reina Elisenda station from Catalunya station.

Hostales, Pensiones & Hotels

Finding a room should be easy from mid-September to early July (although Easter can be tricky). In the busier periods it's worth ringing ahead to book at the smaller places. Many of these places adjust prices according to demand and, if you intend to stay several days, some may make a small reduction (it's worth asking). Some charge 100 to 350 ptas extra for a shower if you don't have a room with one. Many places have three or four-bed rooms that are little

dearer than a double. Bathrooms in these places are generally shared.

The prices below are for high season. The more expensive places can drop prices considerably in the off season, while the smaller pensiones hardly vary in price at all.

La Rambla Little *Pensión Noya (☎ 93 301 48 31, Rambla de Canaletes 133)*, at the top of La Rambla, above Restaurante Nuria, has 15 smallish but clean rooms at 2200/4500 ptas for singles/doubles in the high season. Front rooms overlooking La Rambla can be noisy (metro: Catalunya, map: L'Eixample).

Down near the bottom of La Rambla at No 4, the friendly *Hostal Marítima (☎ 93 302 31 52)* is a time-honoured backpackers' lodging with a dozen worn but adequate rooms. You pay a flat 2000 ptas per person. The entrance is on Passatge de la Banca leading to the Museo de la Cera (metro: Drassanes, map: Central).

Barri Gòtic This central, atmospheric area has many of the better bottom-end places. A few of those listed below are not strictly speaking in the Barri Gòtic but within a couple of minutes walk of it.

All are on the Barri Gòtic map unless otherwise stated.

Pensión Estal (☎ 93 302 26 18, Carrer de Santa Anna 27) is a friendly place on a quiet street with a mixed bag of rooms going for 2500/4000 ptas with shared bathroom. Some of the doubles have balconies and bath (5500 ptas) but singles tend to be dingy interior jobs (metro: Catalunya, map: L'Eixample).

Hostal Lausanne (☎ 93 302 11 39, Avinguda del Portal de l'Àngel 24) is a friendly, helpful place with good security. Its popularity has seen prices sneaking up, but on balance it remains a good place. Clean rooms without bath 3500/4900 ptas. The doubles with private bath are overpriced at 8900 ptas (metro: Catalunya, map: Central).

Hostal Fontanella (☎ /fax 93 317 59 43, Via Laietana 71) is a friendly, immaculately cared-for place, with 10 rooms costing 2900/5000 ptas or 4200/6600 ptas with bathroom (metro: Urquinaona, map: Central).

Pensión-Hostal Fina (☎ *93 317 97 87, Carrer de la Portaferrissa 11)*, on another quiet street, has 28 plain, clean rooms for 2750/3750 ptas, or 4750 ptas for a double with private bath (metro: Catalunya or Liceu, map: Gòtic). *Hostal-Residencia Rembrandt* (☎/*fax 93 318 10 11)* at No 23 has good rooms at 2700/4000 ptas, or 3000/5000 ptas with shower. Doubles with full private bathroom cost 5500 ptas.

Hostal Paris (☎/*fax 93 301 37 85, Carrer del Cardenal Casañas 4)* has 42 mostly large rooms for 3000/4000 ptas, or 4000/5800 ptas with private bathroom. Prices can go down a couple of hundred pesetas at quiet times. There's a TV room (metro: Liceu).

Hostal Galerias Maldà (☎ *93 317 30 02)*, upstairs in the arcade by Carrer del Pi 5, is a rambling family house with 21 rooms, some of them really big. It's one of the cheapest places in town, charging 1500/3000 ptas, and has one great little single set aside in a kind of tower for 1000 ptas (metro: Liceu).

Pensión Dalí (☎/*fax 93 318 55 80, Carrer de la Boqueria 12)* has doubles with own loo and shower costing up to 4800 ptas; those without cost 3700 ptas. There are large sitting and TV rooms (metro: Liceu). *Pensión Europa* (☎ *93 318 76 20)* at No 18 has some rather small and bare singles for 2000 ptas and better doubles with own bath for 4800 ptas. There's a big sitting room with TV, too.

Pensión Bienestar (☎ *93 318 72 83, Carrer d'En Quintana 3)* has clean, ordinary rooms, charging 1300/2400 or 1500/2600 ptas depending on size (metro: Liceu).

Hostal Layetana (☎ *93 319 20 12, Plaça de Ramon Berenguer El Gran 2)* is friendly and well kept, with 20 good-sized rooms at 2200/3500 ptas, or 4900 ptas for doubles with bathroom (metro: Jaume I).

Pensió Colom 3 (☎ *93 318 06 31, Carrer de Colom 3)*, virtually on Plaça Reial, has

converted itself into an unofficial basic youth hostel with dorm beds for 1400 ptas. There's a few pool tables (metro: Liceu). A couple of doors up, *Pension Villanueva* (☎ *91 301 50 84, Plaça Reial 2)* is cheap and quiet, but involves a bit of a climb up three flights of stairs. At their most expensive, doubles with own bathroom are 4500 ptas.

Hostal Levante (☎ *93 317 95 65, Baixada de Sant Miquel 2)* is a large, clean hostal, popular among travellers, which charges up to 2500/4000 ptas, or 5000 ptas for doubles with private bath (metro: Liceu).

Casa Huéspedes Mari-Luz (☎ *93 317 34 63, Carrer del Palau 4)* has friendly management, a sociable atmosphere, and room for 52 people in doubles and dorms (metro: Liceu or Jaume I). The dorms are a little oppressive, but the doubles are fine and cost 3800 ptas (double bed) and 4800 ptas (two beds).

Pensión Alamar (☎ *93 302 50 12, Carrer de la Comtessa de Sobradiel 1)* has 13 rooms, some with balcony, for 1700/3500 ptas. It's cheap and basic, but you can use the kitchen and washing machine, too (metro: Liceu).

El Raval *Hotel Peninsular* (☎ *93 302 31 38, Carrer de Sant Pau 34)* is a bit of an oasis on the fringe of the Barri Xinès. Once part of a convent, it has a plant-draped atrium extending the full height and most of the length of the hotel. The 80 rooms are clean and spacious; they cost 5000/6300 ptas in high season, with continental breakfast included (metro: Liceu, map: Gòtic).

Hostal Residencia Opera (☎ *93 318 82 01, Carrer de Sant Pau 20)* is a bit tatty but it's worth trying if other places are full. Rooms are 2500/4000 ptas, or 3000/5000 ptas with private bath (metro: Liceu, map: Gòtic).

Hostal La Terrassa (☎ *93 302 51 74, Carrer de Junta de Comerç 11)* is another big hostal, with basic but well-kept rooms costing 2100/3600 without own shower and 3200/4200 ptas with (metro: Liceu, map: Montjuïc).

La Ribera *Pensión Lourdes (☎ 93 319 33 72, Carrer de la Princesa 14)* has about 20 clean rooms for 1900/3000 ptas (metro: Jaume I, map: Gòtic).

Hostal Nuevo Colón (☎ 93 319 50 77, Avinguda del Marquès de l'Argentera 19), opposite Estació de França, has cheerful rooms for 2800/4000 ptas, or 4000/5500 ptas with private bath (metro: Barceloneta, map: Central).

L'Eixample There are only a few cheapies in this upmarket part of town north of Plaça de Catalunya.

Hostal Goya (☎ 93 302 25 65, Carrer de Pau Claris 74) has just 12 nice, good-sized rooms at 2600/3800 ptas (loners can get a double for 2800 ptas) or 3700/4400 ptas with shower and loo (metro: Urquinaona, map: L'Eixample).

Hostal Palacios (☎ 93 301 30 79, Gran Via de les Corts Catalanes 629 bis) has 25 decent rooms. Singles without bath cost 2900 ptas. The few singles with shower are 4000 ptas and doubles with the whole shebang are 5620 ptas (metro: Catalunya or Urquinaona, map: L'Eixample).

Hostal Oliva (☎ 93 488 01 62, Passeig de Gràcia 32, 4th floor) is a friendly little place, clean and well kept. Some of the varied rooms are refurbished and modern, while others are older but still fine. Singles/doubles are 3100/5700 ptas and doubles with private bath are 6700 ptas (metro: Passeig de Gràcia, map: L'Eixample).

Near Estació Sants *Hostal Sofia (☎ 93 419 50 40, Avinguda de Roma 1-3)* is just across the square in front of the station. The 12 sparkling clean rooms cost 3000/5500 ptas, or 6500 ptas for doubles with private bathroom (metro: Sants-Estació, map: Barcelona).

Hostal Sans (☎ 93 331 37 00, Carrer de Antoni de Capmany 82), a five minute walk south-west of the station, is a modern place with rooms for 2200/3200 ptas, or 4200/4900 ptas with private bathroom (metro: Plaça de Sants, map: Barcelona).

PLACES TO STAY – MID-RANGE
Hotels
All rooms in this range have attached bathrooms.

La Rambla *Hotel Continental (☎ 93 301 25 70, fax 93 302 73 60, Rambla de Canaletes 138)* has 35 pleasant, well-decorated rooms, all with cable TV, microwave, fridge, safe and fan. Room rates with good breakfast start at 6900/9000 ptas in summer and rise for doubles with Rambla views. (metro: Catalunya, map: L'Eixample). It seems OK to us, but some readers have reported being disappointed.

Hotel Lloret (☎ 93 317 33 66, fax 93 301 92 83, Rambla de Canaletes 125) has 50 varied rooms; some are worn and not very big (metro: Catalunya, map: L'Eixample). All have air-con and TV and cost 5200/7800 ptas (a little less in the off season).

Hotel Internacional (☎ 93 302 25 66, fax 93 317 61 90, La Rambla 78-80) on Pla de la Boqueria has 60 simple, clean rooms with TV at 6530/12,840 ptas (the doubles are, frankly, over-priced). There's a breakfast room and bar with a balcony over La Rambla (metro: Liceu, map: Gòtic).

Hotel Oriente (☎ 93 302 25 58, fax 93 412 38 19, La Rambla 47) is famous for its modernista design and has a fine sky-lit restaurant and other public rooms, but the staff can be offhand. The bedrooms are slightly past their prime but still comfortable, with tiled floors and bathrooms, safes and TV. Singles/doubles are 7000/12,000 ptas plus IVA (metro: Liceu, map: Gòtic).

Hotel Cuatro Naciones (☎ 93 317 36 24, fax 93 302 69 85, La Rambla 40) has adequate rooms for 6420/8025 ptas. It was built in 1849 and was once – a long time ago – Barcelona's top hotel (metro: Liceu, map: Gòtic).

Barri Gòtic *Hotel Roma Reial (☎ 93 302 03 66, Plaça Reial 11)* has decent rooms, all with private bath, at 4800/6800 ptas in high season (map: Gòtic).

Hotel Nouvel (☎ 93 301 82 74, fax 93 301 83 70, Carrer de Santa Anna 18-20) has elegant modernista touches and good air-con rooms with satellite TV for 10,300/15,750 ptas plus IVA, including breakfast (metro: Catalunya, map: L'Eixample).

Hotel Suizo (☎ 93 315 04 61, fax 93 310 40 81, Plaça de l'Àngel 12) was recently modernised and has a restaurant and snack bar. Rooms, comfortable if unspectacular, are about 11,000/14,000 ptas plus IVA (metro: Jaume I, map: Gòtic).

El Raval *Hotel Mesón de Castilla* (☎ 93 318 21 82, fax 93 412 40 20, Carrer de Valldonzella 5) has some lovely modernista touches – stained glass and murals in its public rooms, Gaudíesque window mouldings. Its 56 good, quaintly decorated rooms with breakfast cost 9800/12,600 ptas plus IVA. There's easy parking too (metro: Universitat, map: L'Eixample).

Hotel San Agustín (☎ 93 318 16 58, fax 93 317 29 28, Plaça de Sant Agustí 3) is a modern place on a quiet square, with rooms for 8500/12,500 ptas plus IVA, including breakfast. All rooms have air-con and satellite TV (metro: Liceu, map: Montjuïc).

Hotel España (☎ 93 318 17 58, fax 93 317 11 34, Carrer de Sant Pau 9-11) is famous for its two marvellous dining rooms designed by the modernista architect Lluís Domènech i Montaner: one with big sea-life murals by Ramon Casas, the other with floral tiling and a wood-beamed roof. The 60-plus comfortable rooms are 5400/10,300 ptas including breakfast (metro: Liceu, map: Gòtic).

Near Parc de la Ciutadella *Hotel Triunfo* (☎ 93 315 08 60, Passeig de Picasso 22) is not a bad bet and good for price, especially if you can get a room with views across to the park. Rooms cost 5500/8500 ptas (metro: Jaume, map: Central).

L'Eixample A fine choice for a bit of old-fashioned style is *Hotel Gran Via* (☎ 93 318 19 00, fax 93 318 99 97, Gran Via de les Corts Catalanes 642), with 53 good-sized rooms at 9000/12,000 ptas plus IVA and a big, elegant lounge opening onto a roof terrace. Breakfast is available for 700 ptas (metro: Catalunya, map: L'Eixample).

Near Estació Sants *Hotel Roma* (☎ 93 410 66 33, Avinguda de Roma 31) is a comfortable, upper mid-range option, handy for the train station. Rooms will cost you 10,200/15,300 ptas in the high season (metro: Entença, map: Barcelona).

PLACES TO STAY – TOP END
You can get top-end quality at mid-range prices in Barcelona by taking advantage of some price cuts for double rooms – 50% or even more – at these hotels' off-peak times, when business travellers are absent.

Hotels
La Rambla The top hotel on La Rambla is the elegant *Le Meridien* (☎ 93 318 62 00, fax 93 301 77 76) at No 111. Its top-floor presidential suite is where the likes of Michael Jackson, Madonna and Julio Iglesias stay. Normal singles/doubles are 26,000/32,000 ptas plus IVA (metro: Catalunya or Liceu, map: L'Eixample).

Barri Gòtic *Hotel Colón* (☎ 93 301 14 04, fax 93 317 29 15, Avinguda de la Catedral 7) is a good choice for its location facing the cathedral. The 146 comfortable and elegant rooms are 15,500/23,000 ptas plus IVA. There's a restaurant and piano bar (metro: Jaume I, map: Central).

L'Eixample All of these places are on the L'Eixample & Gràcia map.

Hotel Balmes (☎ 93 451 19 14, fax 93 451 00 49, Carrer de Mallorca 216) is a good, modern hotel with white bricks much in evidence in the interior. Average-sized rooms with air-con, nice tiled bathrooms and satellite TV are comparatively good value at 12,600/16,500 ptas plus IVA. There's garage parking, a coffee shop, a garden with bar and swimming pool, and a restaurant (metro: Passeig de Gràcia).

The renovated *Hotel Regente* (☎ 93 487 59 89, fax 93 487 32 27, Rambla de Catalunya 76) is probably a more attractive deal. Rooms with air-con and satellite TV come in at 14,900/17,500 ptas plus IVA. The rooms feature wood panelling and have a nice feel (metro: Passeig de Gràcia).

The *St Moritz Hotel* (☎ 93 412 15 00, fax 93 412 12 36, Carrer de la Diputació 262 bis) is another upmarket hotel with 92 rooms at 16,900/19,900 ptas plus IVA. It has a restaurant and pleasant terrace bar (metro: Catalunya or Passeig de Gràcia).

The *Hotel Majestic* (☎ 93 488 17 17, fax 93 488 18 80, Passeig de Gràcia 70) is a sprawling, comfortable place with a nice line in modern art on the walls and a rooftop swimming pool. The 300-plus rooms, all with air-con and satellite TV, cost from 13,500/15,000 ptas to 19,000/22,000 ptas (including breakfast) plus IVA (metro: Passeig de Gràcia).

The *Comtes* (or *Condes*) *de Barcelona Hotel* (☎ 93 488 22 00, fax 93 488 06 14, Passeig de Gràcia 73-75) is one of Barcelona's best hotels. It has two separate buildings facing each other across Carrer de Mallorca. The older one occupies the Casa Enric Batlló, built in the 1890s but now stylishly modernised. The soundproofed rooms have marble bathrooms and air-con. A double can be had for 20,500 ptas plus IVA and the same room for use as a single is 1000 ptas less (metro: Passeig de Gràcia).

The *Hotel Ritz*, aka *Husa Palace* (☎ 93 318 52 00, fax 93 318 01 48, Gran Via de les Corts Catalanes 668), is the top choice for old-fashioned elegance, luxury, individuality and first-class service. It has been going since 1919. Rooms are 28,500/32,000 ptas. Other rooms with tiled step-down 'Roman baths' cost almost double and suites can be more than 200,000 ptas. Add IVA to all prices (metro: Urquinaona).

A less expensive choice for old-fashioned elegance is *Hotel Avenida Palace* (☎ 93 301 96 00, fax 93 318 12 34, Gran Via de les Corts Catalanes 605). The doubles are fine at 24,000 ptas plus IVA, but single occupation is a measly 2000 ptas less (metro: Catalunya).

Alternatively, if you can cough up 20,900 ptas for a double, consider the recently re-furbished *Hotel Ducs de Bergara* (☎ 93 317 34 42, Carrer de Bergara 11). The building is a fine modernista piece with an 18th century artesonado ceiling and some nice Art Deco touches.

Port Olímpic Barcelona's most fashionable, if rather impersonal, lodgings is the *Hotel Arts Barcelona* (☎ 93 221 10 00, fax 93 221 10 70, Carrer de la Marina 19-21) in one of the two sky-high towers that dominate the Port Olímpic. It has over 450 rooms and charges up to 40,000 ptas plus IVA for a double (metro: Ciutadella; map: Central).

PLACES TO STAY – RENTAL ACCOMMODATION

The Universitat de Barcelona at Gran Via de les Corts Catalanes 585 (metro: Universitat, map: L'Eixample), the Usit Unlimited youth and student travel agency at Carrer de Rocafort 116-122 (metro: Rocafort, map: Barcelona) and the British Council at Carrer d'Amigó 83 (near Muntaner suburban train station, map: Barcelona) all have notice boards advertising flat shares and rooms to let.

Otherwise check out *Primeramà*, the weekly classifieds paper. The last few pages of the *Suplement Immobiliària* (real estate supplement) carry ads for share accommodation under 'Lloguer/Hostes i vivendes a compartir'. Most of the ads tend to be in Spanish rather than Catalan. Rooms can come as cheap as 25,000 ptas a month, but for something halfway decent not too far from the centre you're looking at a minimum of 35,000 ptas. You need to add bills (gas, electricity, water, phone and *comunidad*, building maintenance charges).

PLACES TO EAT

Barcelona is packed with good places to eat. Menus may be in Catalan or Spanish, or both; some places have foreign-language menus too. Specifically Catalan food tends to be a bit expensive in Barcelona, but you won't regret having at least one Catalan meal while you're here (see the boxed text

'Catalan Cuisine' in the Catalunya chapter for a rundown on some typical dishes and words you'll encounter on Catalan menus).

Barcelona folk usually eat lunch between about 2 and 4 pm and don't start a dinner out until 9 or 10 pm. Most restaurants stop serving between 11 pm and midnight. Many have a weekly closing day and some stay shut throughout August, when natives abandon the city in droves. Telephone numbers are given for places where it may be worth booking ahead.

La Rambla

All of the following are on the L'Eixample & Gràcia map unless otherwise stated.

Restaurant Nuria (Rambla de Canaletes 133), just down from Plaça de Catalunya, is a big, busy place doing pasta from 500 ptas, and fish and meat courses from 700 ptas. There's a three-course *menú del día* for 1100 ptas.

Viena (Rambla dels Estudis 115) is a popular café with stools round a central counter and good *barretas* (baguettes) for 300 to 500 ptas.

Cafè de l'Òpera (La Rambla 74), opposite the Liceu opera house, is La Rambla's most interesting café, with elegant 1920s décor (map: Gòtic). It gets busy at night (see Bars), but is quieter for morning coffee and croissants. There are also *bocadillos*, from 350 ptas, and tapas.

Barri Gòtic

This area is peppered with good eateries, some of them excellent value. All of the following are on the Barri Gòtic map unless otherwise stated.

Restaurants *Santa Ana (Carrer de Santa Anna 8)* is a bright, friendly place with quick service. Pizzas and sizable *platos combinados* are 700 to 900 ptas, while baguettes are 300 to 400 ptas (all plus IVA).

Self-Naturista at No 13 is a popular self-service vegetarian place with a four-course lunch *menú* for 810 ptas (map: L'Eixample).

Just in off La Rambla is *The Bagel Shop (Carrer de la Canuda 25)*, the only place in

Cool Cats of the 1900s

Els Quatre Gats was opened in 1897 by four Barcelonese who had spent time in Paris artistic circles: the modernista artists Ramon Casas and Santiago Rusiñol, and their friends Miquel Utrillo and Pere Romeu who, among other things, were deeply interested in shadow puppetry. Romeu, the manager, was a colourful character equally devoted to cabaret and cycling.

The name Els Quatre Gats is Catalan for 'the four cats', and alludes both to the café's four founders and to Le Chat Noir, an artistic café in Montmartre, Paris. Idiomatically, it means 'a handful of people, a minority' – no doubt how its avant-garde clientele saw themselves. Situated in the first Barcelona creation of the modernista architect Josep Puig i Cadafalch, Els Quatre Gats quickly became an influential meeting, drinking and cavorting place of young artists, writers, actors, musicians and their circles.

It published its own magazine and staged exhibitions, recitals and, of course, shadow puppet shows. Picasso's first exhibition was here in 1900, and included drawings of many of the customers. Els Quatre Gats closed in 1903. Later it was used as an art gallery, before its present incarnation as a restaurant.

town where your lox and cream cheese bagel will be the genuine article (map: Central).

Els Quatre Gats (☎ 93 302 41 40, Carrer de Montsió 3 bis) is the famous turn-of-the-century artists' hang-out (see the boxed text 'Cool Cats of the 1900s'), now a fairly expensive restaurant (map: Central). It was restored a few years ago to its original appearance, with reproductions of its old customers' portraits of each other, including one of Ramon Casas swinging on a chandelier. Starters/snacks such as *esqueixada* (salad of shredded salted cod with tomato, red pepper, onion, white beans, olives, olive oil and vinegar) or *escalivada* (red peppers and aubergines) *amb torrada* are close to 1000 ptas and main fish and meat dishes from 1100 to 2700 ptas – but you can stick to a drink if you just want to sample the atmosphere.

Cervecería Edelman (Avinguda del Portal de l'Àngel 6) is a bright, friendly bar-cum-restaurant with platos combinados from around 500 ptas, and good, crisp, filled baguettes called *bocadillos en xapata*.

A Basque favourite is *Irati (Carrer del Cardenal Cassanyes 17)*. The set *menú* is 1500 ptas, or you can enjoy the great tapas and a *zurrito* of beer, or six (map: Gòtic). A couple of doors down is the psychedelic *Juicy Jones*, where a vegetarian set *menú* costs 975 ptas or you can just sip on their juices.

Can Culleretes (Carrer d'En Quintana 5) is Barcelona's oldest restaurant, founded in 1786. It's still going strong, with old-fashioned décor and good Catalan food. A three-course *menú* including half a bottle of wine will cost around 2000 ptas.

Les Quatre Barres (Carrer d'En Quintana 6) serves up more excellent Catalan food; it'll cost 3000 or 4000 ptas for a meal with drinks.

Mesón Jesús (Carrer dels Cecs de la Boqueria 4), between Plaça de Sant Josep Oriol and Carrer de la Boqueria, is a cosy little place with a homey ambience, doing a good 1250 ptas three-course *menú* including a drink.

El Gran Café (Carrer d'Avinyò 9) is classier, with modernista décor and good Catalan-French food. À la carte main dishes are 1200 to 3000 ptas, but there's an entire lunch *menú* for the same price.

El Gallo Kiriko at No 19 is an inexpensive Pakistani restaurant. A good tandoori chicken with chips or salad, or couscous with chicken, beef or vegetables, is just 450 ptas. Curries with rice are 600 ptas.

Little *Bar-Restaurant Cervantes (Carrer de Cervantes 7)* does a good three-course lunch *menú* with plenty of choice, plus a drink, for 900 ptas. The basic *Cal Kiko* on the corner of Carrer de Cervantes and Carrer del Palau does a four-course *menú* for 725 ptas.

Les Quinze Nits (☎ 93 317 30 75, Plaça Reial 6) is a stylish bistro-like restaurant on the borderline between smart and casual, with a long menu of good Catalan and Spanish dishes at reasonable prices. Three courses with wine and coffee typically come to about 2500 ptas. This place has such a reputation that long queues can often be seen outside.

Facing each other across Carrer del Vidre off the southern end of Plaça Reial are two cheap, busy little places: *Restaurante Senshe Tawakal*, which serves lentils and vegetables or chicken and chips for 450 ptas and couscous for 550 ptas, and *Restaurante Rincón de Ríos Baixas*, with economical daily dishes such as paella for 500 ptas. Both stay open until 2 or 3 am.

La Fonda Escudellers on the corner of Carrer dels Escudellers and Passatge dels Escudellers is run by the same people as Les Quinze Nits on Plaça Reial, and has similar menu, prices, hours, ambience and standards.

Bar Comercio, across Carrer dels Escudellers from La Fonda, is a much plainer affair but will give you a decent feed: salads are from 300 to 400 ptas, mussels are 475 ptas and chicken or rabbit is 500 to 550 ptas.

Los Caracoles, a block along at No 14, is one of Barcelona's best-known restaurants – although more so now among tourists than among the celebrities whose photos adorn it. It's still good and lively, and offers a big choice of seafood, fish, rice and meat; a typical full meal is 3000 or 4000 ptas, although you could get away with less. Try the snails.

The best Italian food in town can be had at *Ristorante Il Mercante di Venezia (Carrer de Josep Anselm Clavé)*, where a set *menú* cost 1180 ptas (map: Central). *Margarita Blue (Carrer Ample 6)* does imaginative versions of Mexican food and doubles as a bar.

Pastry Shops & Coffee Bars Tempting pastry and/or chocolate shops, often combined with coffee bars, abound all over the Barri Gòtic. There's a special concentration along Carrer and Baixada de la Llibreteria, north-east of Plaça de Sant Jaume: among the least resistible pastry-chocolate places are *Santa Clara (Carrer de la Llibreteria 21)* and *La Colmena* on the corner of Baixada de la Llibreteria and Plaça de l'Àngel. Two places with particularly good coffee in this area are the *Bon Mercat* on the corner of Baixada de la Llibreteria and Carrer de la Freneria and *Il Caffè di Roma* on Plaça de l'Àngel.

Xocolateria La Xicra (Plaça de Sant Josep Oriol 2) has great cakes, various coffees, teas and hot chocolate (*xocolata*; 230 ptas) so thick it's listed under *postres* (desserts) on the menu. Two other good places nearby to sit down for a coffee and croissant are *Granja La Pallaresa (Carrer de Petritxol 11)* and *Croissanterie del Pi (Carrer del Pi 14)*.

Tapas Bars Down on Carrer de la Mercè and nearby streets near the bottom end of the Barri Gòtic is a cluster of old-fashioned tapas bars that can get very lively, especially on weekend evenings. *Bar Celta (Carrer de la Mercè 16)* is a good one, specialising in seafood (map: Central). Be careful – accumulating tapas and raciones can be an expensive exercise at any of these places. At Bar Celta, tapas of *sepia* (cuttlefish) and *patatas bravas*, with a beer, come to around 800 ptas.

Takeaway Felafel & Kebabs *Disco-Bar Real* on the corner of Plaça Reial and Carrer de Colom has a takeaway counter doing good felafel for 250 ptas. *Buen Bocado (Carrer dels Escudellers 31)* has felafel for 300 ptas and shawarma for 400 ptas. It's open evenings only, until 2 am. Another, nameless, *felafel and kebab takeaway* on Escudellers, just east of Carrer dels Obradors, charges 50 ptas less for each.

El Raval

Xaica Pizzeria (Carrer de Jovellanos 7) does good-sized pizzas for one person for 550 to 825 ptas and a three-course *menú* for 995 ptas (map: L'Eixample).

Restaurant Tallers (Carrer dels Tallers 6) is a clean, modest place with an adequate four-course lunch *menú* for 850 ptas (map: L'Eixample).

Bar Restaurante Romesco (Carrer de l'Arc de Sant Agustí), just off Carrer de Sant Pau, is a no-frills, almost hole-in-the-wall joint serving up good portions of home-style cooking at great prices, such as chicken and chips for 400 ptas, or squid, cuttlefish or baby octopus dishes for 500 to 700 ptas (map: Gòtic).

Restaurante Els Tres Bots (Carrer de Sant Pau 42) is grungy but cheap, with a *menú* for 875 ptas (map: Gòtic). Along the same street at No 31, *Restaurante Pollo Rico* has a downstairs bar where you can get a quarter chicken, an omelette or a veal steak, with chips, bread and wine, from 500 ptas, and a more salubrious but only slightly more expensive upstairs restaurant.

Kashmir Restaurant Tandoori at No 39 does tasty curries and biryanis from around 800 ptas (map: Gòtic).

Poble Sec

Restaurant Elche (☎ 93 441 30 89, Carrer de Vila i Vilà 71) does some of Barcelona's best paella. Several varieties are on offer, mostly costing around 1400 to 1700 ptas per person for a minimum of two people (map: Montjuïc).

La Ribera

All of the following are on the Central Barcelona map unless otherwise stated.

Comme-Bio, aka *La Botiga (Via Laietana 28)*, is a modern, chemical-additive-free vegetarian restaurant and wholefood shop, with a good four-course *menú* for 1125 ptas that includes a help-yourself salad bar (map: Gòtic). Many à la carte dishes, including pizzas and spinach and Roquefort crêpes, are around 900 ptas, or there are tofu and *seitán* (vegetable protein) dishes for 1210 to 1475 ptas.

Lluna Plena (Carrer de Montcada 2) is a brick-walled, cellar-style place with good Catalan and Spanish food, open Tuesday to Saturday. It's packed for its four-course 1050 ptas lunch *menú* and often in the evenings, too. À la carte you could go for escalivada or esqueixada (around 450 ptas), followed by a quarter-chicken (300 ptas) or rabbit *a la brasa* (500 ptas).

Nearby, *Pla de la Garsa (Carrer dels Assaonadors 13)* is an old-style Catalan restaurant with attractive tiles, lamps and paintings. The 1350 ptas *menú* gives you three courses plus good wine and cheese.

A couple of doors back, at No 9, *Restaurante Bunja Raya* makes a nice change with Malaysian and Indonesian cooking. There's a set *menú* for 1795 ptas.

For a bit of a splurge on superb, mainly Catalan and French, cooking you can't do much better than the informally chic *Senyor Parellada (☎ 93 310 50 94, Carrer de l'Argenteria 37)*. You should book for dinner. Mains start at 1800 ptas. You might start with mushroom and fish crêpes or monkfish soup, followed by duck breast with cherry vinegar, and round it off with a *crema Catalana* (a cream custard with a crisp burnt sugar coating) or *mel i mató* (honey and fresh cream cheese).

Granja Xador (Carrer de l'Argenteria 61-3), around the corner from Santa Maria del Mar, is a bright, modern place with a big choice of platos combinados costing from 575 to 775 ptas.

Restaurante Mar de la Ribera on Carrer dels Sombrerers right by Santa Maria del Mar does a decent three-course *menú* for 1000 ptas, including half a bottle of wine. It's a pleasant place with ceramics and paintings on the walls.

There are several more little restaurants on and around Passeig del Born and Plaça de les Olles east of Santa Maria del Mar, among them the cheap and speedy *Can Busto (Carrer de Rera Palau 3)*, with a three-course *menú* for 900 ptas and many individual dishes from 400 ptas. *Cal Pep*

(☎ 93 310 79 61, Plaça de les Olles 8), across the way, has great tapas and a small dining room with good seafood; a three-course Catalan meal with drinks will be around 3500 ptas.

Port Vell & La Barceloneta

All of the following are on the Central Barcelona map.

In the Maremàgnum building on the Moll d'Espanya, a couple of popular waterside eateries are *Tapasbar* and *El Chipirón*. Both specialise in seafood. Several fast-food places lurk around here too.

Restaurant Set (7) Portes (☎ 93 319 30 33, Passeig d'Isabel II 14) is a classic Barcelona restaurant, founded in 1836. The atmosphere is old-fashioned with wood panelling, tiles, mirrors and plaques naming some of the famous – such as Orson Welles – who have eaten here. Paella (1400 to 2300 ptas) is the speciality but there's other fish, seafood and meat at similar prices. It's near-essential to book.

La Barceloneta has some good seafood restaurants. Many, such as *El Rey de la Gamba*, are on Passeig de Joan de Borbó facing Port Vell. Most main dishes here (it's at No 46) are 1000 to 2000 ptas plus IVA.

For a real treat (and splurge) make for *Can Solé (Carrer de Sant Carles 4)*. The food is superb, the desserts to die for and the service little short of amazing – when you're halfway through your fish, they remove it and discretely strip away all the bones for you. You can fill up on a salad and first course of paella alone (1450 ptas). Expect to pay about 5000 ptas for a full four courses, wine and coffee.

Port Olímpic

All of the following are on the Central Barcelona map.

The harbour here is lined on two sides by dozens of restaurants and tapas bars, which are extremely popular in spring and summer. None is cheap but some are good. The northern side is less expensive than the eastern and one of the more economical places is *La Taverna del Cel Ros*, which has a three-course *menú* for 975 ptas plus IVA. The irritating thing with most of the restaurants here is the touting by bored waiters in slack periods.

Just west of the Port Olímpic, beneath the giant copper *Peix* sculpture, is *Planet Hollywood*, one of a chain part-owned by Arnold Schwarzenegger and Sylvester Stallone. Here you can eat pasta and pizza as well as burgers and Tex-Mex (900 to 1500 ptas for most things) and admire the décor of Hollywood costumes, props and stills. The cyborg used in *Terminator 2: Judgement Day* revolves revoltingly in a glass cylinder at the restaurant's upper entrance.

L'Eixample

This is another area with loads of places to eat. A good place to start an Eixample visit is the 9th-floor cafeteria at *El Corte Inglés* department store on Plaça de Catalunya (map: L'Eixample). It's reasonably priced and has tremendous views.

All of the following are on the L'Eixample & Gràcia map.

Restaurants *Bar Estudiantil* on Plaça de la Universitat does economical platos combinados eg chicken, chips and *berenjena* (aubergine), or *botifarra* (beans and red pepper), each for around 600 ptas.

El Café de Internet (Gran Via de les Corts Catalanes 656) has a double bill of food and the Internet: before, during or after your meal or snack, you can use an Internet terminal upstairs for 600 ptas a half-hour. Downstairs, there's a lunch *menú* for 950 or 1050 ptas, or you can just go for a bocadillo and coffee.

The restaurant of the classy *Hotel Ritz* (☎ *93 318 52 00, Gran Via de les Corts Catalanes 668)* has particularly good seafood; the daily *menú* is 3350 ptas.

L'Hostal de Rita, on Carrer d'Aragó a block east of Passeig de Gràcia, is an excellent mid-range restaurant. The 950 ptas four-course lunch *menú* is a good deal. A la carte mains are 700 to 1000 ptas.

FrescCo (Carrer de València 263), half a block east of Passeig de Gràcia, packs 'em

in with its all-you-can-eat buffet of salads, soups, pizza, pasta, fruit, ice cream and drinks for 975 ptas.

Around the corner is a great little place, the *Centro Asturianò (Passeig de Gràcia 78)*. This club is tucked away up on the first floor and occasionally opens its doors to the lunchtime rabble for the 1150 ptas *menú*. The open-air interior patio is a wonderful spot to eat, but you can deal with inclement weather inside too.

Bar Ariño 2 (Carrer d'Aribau 82) is one of the more economical eateries in l'Eixample. The three-course *menú* (eg macaroni or soup, a meat dish and dessert) is 800 ptas.

La Gran Tasca (Carrer de Balmes 129 bis) is a big, bright restaurant-cum-tapas bar, busy in the evening with people heading for a night out. Tapas are 275 ptas-plus, while main dishes, like a quarter-chicken or rabbit, or meat brochete, cost from 500 to 600 ptas.

There's one in every city and for portions as big as your head the *Hard Rock Cafe (Plaça de Catalunya 21)*, may well be the place for you.

Cafés & Tapas Bars A number of glossy but informal tapas places congregate near the bottom end of Passeig de Gràcia. At No 24 is *Quasi Queviures (Qu Qu)*, with a big choice from sausages and hams to pâtés and smoked fish. Many tapas are over 400 ptas but portions are decent. Similar, but less Catalan, is *Ba-Ba-Reeba* at No 28, which also serves baguettes. *Cerveseria Tapa Tapa* at No 44, on the corner of Carrer del Consell de Cent, is another big, bright place with a great range of tapas from 250 ptas.

Lizarran (Carrer de Mallora 257) is a lively spot with excellent tapas. It gets particularly busy at night.

La Flauta (Carrer d'Aribau 23) is well known for its tasty baguettes with a range of cheese, ham and sausage fillings.

For an excellent coffee on Passeig de Gràcia pop into *Cafè Torino* at No 59, on the corner of Carrer de València; it's a neat, friendly place, popular with a mildly chic, young clientele.

Around La Sagrada Família

This area is not a great culinary cubby hole. But if starvation strikes during your visit, *La Baguetina Catalana* on the corner of Carrer de Provença and Carrer de Sardenya does good baguettes for 300 to 400 ptas, while *La Casa del Jamón* on the corner of Carrer de Mallorca and Carrer de la Marina has an appetising range of tapas and raciones (map: L'Eixample).

Gràcia

All of the following are on the L'Eixample & Gràcia map.

La Miel (Carrer de Bonavista 2) is popular for its good *crepas* (pancakes) from 450 to 700 ptas.

Bar Candanchu (Plaça de Rius i Taulet 9) has a restaurant with many platos combinados and *paella* for 1100 ptas. *Mario Pizza* on the same square does pizzas for from 700 to 900 ptas.

Equinox Sol (Plaça del Sol 14) does a good trade in felafel for 300 ptas and shawarma for 375 ptas, as well as baba-ghanug, hummus and shish kebabs at similar prices. Don't be put off by the bright, plastic décor. You can stock up on wholefoods in *La Botiga del Sol* on Carrer de Maspons on the corner of Plaça del Sol, then take a few steps west on Maspons to sip tea and herbal infusions in a youthful, Granada-like ambience at *Teteria Jazmín*.

El Tastavins (Carrer de Ramon i Cajal 12) does good home-style cooking in a bright, neat environment. Starters, such as spinach with Roquefort, cost mainly from 600 to 1000 ptas and there's have a *menú* for 850 ptas.

Taverna El Glop (Carrer de Sant Lluís 24) is a rustic but classy – and busy – spot specialising in *torrades*, grilled meats and salads. A meal with drinks costs 2500 to 3000 ptas.

Two inexpensive small restaurants just off Plaça de la Virreina are *Cal Majó (Carrer de l'Or 21)* and *Casa de Pizzas* at No 19. Cal Majó's dishes of the day will probably include such Catalan specialities as escalivada, *fricandó* (pork and vegetable

stew) and *mandonguilles amb sipia* (meatballs with cuttlefish) for 800 to 1000 ptas.

Aroma on the corner of Travessera de Gràcia and Carrer de Xiquets specialises in coffees and teas from around the world. You can drink in (with snacks) or take away.

Tibidabo

Plaça del Doctor Andreu at the foot of the Tibidabo funicular is a good place to stop on your way to or from Tibidabo (map: Barcelona). The best views are from the *Mirablau Terrazza*, an open-air café by the tramvia blau stop, and the *Mirablau* bar next door. There's a line of more expensive restaurants across the street.

Restaurants

There are a few good local restaurant chains where you can get a quick, decent snack or meal with minimum effort. A few of the branches are listed below.

Bocatta – Hot and cold baguettes with a big range of fillings, mostly 300 to 400 ptas; at La Rambla 89; Carrer de Santa Anna 11, Plaça de Sant Jaume and on the corner of Carrer de Comtal and Carrer d'en Amargós (all Barri Gòtic or nearby); Rambla de Catalunya between Carrer de Mallorca and Carrer de València (l'Eixample); most branches are open daily from 8 am to midnight.

Pans & Company – Similar fare and prices to Bocatta; at La Rambla 123; Carrer de Ferran 14, and on Carrer dels Arcs off Plaça Nova (both Barri Gòtic); Ronda de la Universitat 7, Passeig de Gràcia 39, Rambla de Catalunya 13 and Carrer de Provença 278 (all l'Eixample)

Pastafiore – Pizza and pasta: a half-pizza *(media)* is 395 to 575 ptas but you'll need a whole one *(entera)* for 550 to 865 ptas if you're hungry; pasta is around 475 to 675 ptas but tends to be less appetising; at Rambla de Canaletes 125 and Carrer de Provença 278 (all l'Eixample); and Travessera de Gràcia 60 (Gràcia)

Self-Catering

There's great fresh food of all types at the *Mercat de la Boqueria* on La Rambla, open Monday to Saturday from 8 am to 8 pm (map: Gòtic). In La Ribera, *Mercat de Santa Caterina* is open Monday to Saturday from 7 am to 2 pm (map: Central). In

Gràcia there's a big, covered *food market* on the corner of Travessera de Gràcia and Carrer de la Mare de Déu dels Desemparats (map: L'Eixample).

Simago, near the northern end of La Rambla, is a convenient central supermarket (map: L'Eixample).

ENTERTAINMENT

Barcelona's entertainment bible is the weekly Spanish-language magazine *Guía del Ocio* (125 ptas), which comes out on Thursday and lists almost everything that's on in the way of music, film, exhibitions, theatre and more. You can pick it up at most newsstands. An alternative is *La Agenda de Barcelona* (225 ptas).

Bars

Whole books have been written on Barcelona's bars, which run the gamut from wood-panelled wine cellars to bright waterfront places and trendy haunts sporting gimmicky modern design ('designer bars'). Each is its own different scene – some very local, some full of foreigners, some favoured by students, others by the well-dressed middle classes. Some play great music, others are places for a quiet talk. Most are at their liveliest from about 11 pm to 2 or 3 am, especially from Thursday to Saturday, as people meet for the beginning of a night out. Here are a few places to start.

La Rambla *Cafè de l'Òpera (La Rambla 74)*, opposite the Liceu opera house, is the busiest and classiest place on the strip (map: Gòtic).

Barri Gòtic All of the following are on the Barri Gòtic map.

Bar del Pi on Plaça de Sant Josep Oriol is a little local bar with a mixed local clientele and lots of character. You can drink outside on one of the Barri Gòtic's nicest little plazas.

For a low-key drink early in the evening, *La Pineda (Carrer del Pi 16)* is a happy haunt with great hams seemingly dripping off the ceiling.

Glaciar, in a corner of Plaça Reial, gets busy with a young crowd of foreigners and locals in the evening and stays open till 2 or 3 am (beer: 300 ptas). The more basic *Bar Reixas* in the opposite corner of the square is also popular. You can also get cheap drinks at *Restaurante Senshe Tawakal*.

Tiny *Bar Malpaso* on Carrer d'En Rauric, just off Plaça Reial, is packed at night with a young, casual crowd and plays great Latin and African music. Another hip, low-lit place with a more varied clientele is *Schilling (Carrer de Ferran 23)*. Mixed drinks are about 700 ptas at both.

Bar L'Ascensor (Carrer de Bellafila 3), off Carrer de la Ciutat east of the ajuntament, is a cosy little place with good taped music and a young clientele. The entrance, as the name might suggest, is a demounted lift.

El Raval This area still has a number of old harbour-style bars – dark, wood-panelled and bare except for the odd mirror and vast arrays of bottles behind the bar. These tend to be bohemian hang-outs rather than dens of real lowlife now, but are still atmospheric places to drink. One not to miss is *Bar Marsella (Carrer de Sant Pau 65)*, which specialises in absinthe (*absenta* in Catalan), a beverage hard to find because of its supposed toxic qualities. Your glass of absinthe (400 ptas) comes with a lump of sugar, a fork and a little bottle of mineral water (100 ptas). Hold the sugar on the fork, over your glass, and drip the water onto the sugar so that it dissolves into the absinthe, which turns opaque yellow. The result should be a warm glow within yourself and a mellow atmosphere in the bar. The Marsella is open from 6 pm to about 2 am nightly (map: Montjuïc).

Nearby is *The Quiet Man (Carrer del Marquès de Barberà 11)*, a relaxed Irish pub which attracts both locals and foreigners (500 ptas for a pint of Guinness). There's live music some nights (map: Central).

Another good place is *Casa Almirall (Carrer de Joaquín Costa 33)*, which has been there since the 1860s; it's both dark and intriguing, with modernista décor and a mixed clientele (map: L'Eixample). Little *Bar Pastís (Carrer de Santa Mònica 4)* is a tiny old bar with a French cabaret theme (lots of Piaf in the background). It's been going on and off since the end of WWII (map: Central).

L'Ovella Negra (Carrer de Sitges 5), aka The Black Sheep, is a noisy, fun, barn-like tavern with a young crowd and pool and *fútbol* games (map: L'Eixample).

If by 2.30 am all these places have shut their doors, you still need a drink and you don't want a disco, your best bet (except on Sunday) is the *London Bar (Carrer Nou de la Rambla 36)*, which sometimes has live music and is open until about 5 am (bottled beer: 450 ptas; map: Central).

La Ribera The following are all on the Central Barcelona map.

El Xampanyet (Carrer de Montcada 22) is the city's best-known *cava* bar – a small, cosy place with nice tiled walls and good tapas as well as cava, which is around 500 ptas for a typical bottle but also available by the glass.

Next door at No 20, the baroque magnificence of the *Palau Dalmases* is matched only by the luxurious plushness inside. You almost feel you should don a powdered wig to sip on your cocktails and on some nights you'll have classical music playing in the background. The snag is cost: a glass of wine will cost 1000 ptas! Come for the music and masked opera performance on Thursday night and your 2500 ptas will get you the show and one drink.

El Nus (Carrer dels Mirallers 5) is a small, dim and chic bar in the narrow, old streets near the Església de Santa Maria del Mar and is decked out with pictures of its Maharishi-lookalike owner. It's good for a quiet drink after dinner.

People in need of an early morning heart starter (or pre-sleep hair of the dog) can call in at *Bar Los de Extremadura (Carrer Ample 51)*, which has little to recommend it except that it is open for a tipple from about 6 am.

Port Olímpic Just wander round the harbour here and take your pick of the many bright and busy spots, all with open-air tables out front; some have good music inside too. Problem is, the area is a little artificial and touristy (map: Central).

L'Eixample *La Bodegueta (Rambla de Catalunya 100)* is a classic wine cellar. Bottles and barrels line the walls, and stools surround marble tables (map: L'Eixample).

La Fira (Carrer de Provença 171), or The Fair, is a designer bar with a difference. You enter through a hall of distorting mirrors, and inside everything is fairground paraphernalia. It sounds corny but the atmosphere is fun (map: L'Eixample).

Gràcia All of the following are on the L'Eixample & Gràcia map.

Café del Sol and *Eldorado* are the lively bars on Plaça del Sol. The former has a vaguely Bohemian crowd, tapas and tables outside too. The main bar on Plaça de Rius i Taulet is *Bar Chirito de Oro*.

Café Salambó (Carrer de Torrijos 51) is a gentle kind of designer bar, imitating some village bars with benches at low tables, and has an upper level with pool tables. It's a favourite of writers, being owned by Carme Balcells, literary agent of Gabriel García Márquez, Milan Kundera and others who have spent time in Barcelona. There's food too – 1150 ptas for a three-course *menú*.

A bit farther up the hill, there are several bars and cafés with potential around the corner of Carrer de Torrijos and Carrer de la Perla. A block north, *Café La Virreina* on Plaça de la Virreina is a relaxed place with a mixed-ages crowd, 1970s rock music, cheap hot bocadillos and tables outside.

Montjuïc The Poble Espanyol has several bars that get lively. The most original is *Torres de Ávila* inside the tall entrance towers themselves. Created by the top Barcelona designer Javier Mariscal, it has several levels and all sorts of surreal touches, including an egg-shaped room and glass lifts that you fear will shoot you through the roof. It's open from 10 pm to 4 am (map: Montjuïc).

Gay & Lesbian Bars Two of the best gay bars are *Punto BCN (Carrer de Muntaner 63-65)* and *Este Bar (Carrer del Consell de Cent 257)* round the corner. Both are relaxed places where people meet and talk before maybe moving on to a disco (map: L'Eixample). Punto BCN has pool tables, too. *Café de la Calle (Carrer de Vic 11)* is a cosy meeting place for lesbians and gay men (map: L'Eixample).

Live Music
There's a good choice most nights of the week. Most places with live music also have bars (a beer is usually between 300 and 600 ptas); many also have dance space, with the bands playing before or between disco sessions, for which you won't have to pay any extra. Starting times are rarely before 10 pm, more often midnight or 1 am. Normal entry charges range from nothing to 1500 ptas or so – the higher prices usually include a drink or two. You may pay more for visiting 'name' bands. Really big touring bands often play in the Palau Sant Jordi on Montjuïc.

For what's on, look in *Guía del Ocio*'s 'Música' section and check posters and leaflets in places like Glaciar bar on Plaça Reial. Here are some of the most dependable places, both for music and liveliness:

Barri Gòtic
All of the following are on the Barri Gòtic map.

Barcelona Pipa Club (Plaça Reial 3)
   jazz Thursday to Saturday around midnight (usually 1000 ptas plus drinks); open from 10 pm (ring the bell to get in) to 2 or 3 am; it's like someone's flat inside

Harlem Jazz Club (Carrer de la Comtessa de Sobradiel 8)
   music from around 11 pm to 2 am nightly except Monday; often jazz, but also some rock and Latin (entry free, a drink compulsory)

Jamboree (Plaça Reial 17)
   varied jazz and funk nightly, usually at 9 pm and midnight (1000 to 1800 ptas, usually including first drink); disco later

Sala Tarantos
   next door to the Jamboree; class flamenco some nights, most often Friday and Saturday at midnight (around 1500 ptas)

Poble Sec
Club Apolo (Carrer Nou de la Rambla 113)
   world music – chiefly African, Latin and Spanish – several nights a week around 10.30 pm (2000 ptas for big names), followed by live salsa or, on Friday and Saturday, a disco (map: Montjuïc)

Port Vell
This area has several bars and discos open in the Maremàgnum complex until the wee hours (map: Central)

Western Gràcia/Avinguda Diagonal
   all within a few blocks of Avinguda Diagonal; the nearest stations are Diagonal (metro), Hospital Clínic (metro) and Gràcia (FGC suburban train)

La Antilla Cosmopolita (Carrer de Muntaner 244)
   full of Latin Americans and Caribbeans dancing salsa (normally 1500 ptas); live bands at 12.30 am or later several nights a week (map: Barcelona)

Luz de Gas (Carrer de Muntaner 246)
   live soul, country, salsa, rock, jazz or pop most nights at midnight or 1 am; usually 1500 ptas (map: Barcelona)

La Boîte (Avinguda Diagonal 477)
   jazz or blues – sometimes jams – several nights a week at midnight (1200 to 2500 ptas); disco later (map: Barcelona)

Other Areas
Savannah (Carrer de la Muntanya 16)
   in the El Clot area (metro: Clot, map: Barcelona); has rock or punk bands a few nights a week, often around 10.30 pm (usually 1000 to 1300 ptas); disco later (map: Barcelona)

Zeleste (Carrer dels Almogàvers 122)
   in Poble Nou (metro: Marina, map: Barcelona); this huge club was converted from a warehouse, regularly hosting visiting rock and pop bands – as does its smaller neighbour, *Zeleste 2 (Carrer de Pamplona 88)*, round the corner; name bands are usually on around 10 pm, for 1500 to 2500 ptas

Discos

Barcelona's discos come alive from about 2 or 3 to 5 or 6 am, and are best on Friday and Saturday. Some have live bands, often starting at midnight or so to fill the place up a bit before the real action. (Places where the bands are likely to be an attraction in their own right are listed in the Live Music section.) Disco cover charges range from nothing to as much as 3000 ptas: they depend partly on how busy the place is and whether the bouncers like the look of you (which puts women at an advantage). If you go early, you'll often get in cheaper. Drinks are expensive, of course: anything up to 800 ptas for a beer. Some discos are fairly smart and won't let you in in sneakers or runners.

Guía del Ocio lists many discos in its 'Tarde & Noche' section. Where's hot (or should we say cool?) changes as fast as it does everywhere, but these will give you a start:

Barri Gòtic & Ramblas

All of the following are on the Barri Gòtic map.

Jamboree (Plaça Reial 17)
from around 1.30 am, after the nightly jazz (see Live Music); a lively disco with two spaces: one for Latin rhythms, one for rock; open till 5 am or so; entry from nothing to 1500 ptas

Karma (Plaça Reial 10)
youngish, studenty basement place with good music; open from around 11 pm to 4 am; usually 1000 ptas including a drink

Moog (Carrer del Arc del Teatre 3)
another good disco – upstairs Latin and dance hits from as far back as the 70s; downstairs strobe lights and techno; open until about 7 am on weekends; entry is 1000 ptas (as are the mixed drinks!)

Poble Sec

Club Apolo (Carrer Nou de la Rambla 113)
ethnic-funk-house-soul-R&B disco Friday and Saturday at 1.30 am, live salsa Wednesday and Thursday at 12.30 am, following main live band (see Live Music); 1000 ptas including a drink but free if you stay on after the main band (map: Montjuïc)

L'Eixample

All of the following are on the L'Eixample & Gràcia map.

CR (Carrer de València 234)
relaxed bar-cum-disco with standard disco music and a mixed-ages, fairly clean-living crowd; entry free, beer 350 ptas

Nick Havanna (Carrer del Rosselló 208)
big 1980s 'designer bar' with a video bank at one end of the dance space and glass-backed urinals flushed by veritable cascades of water; open nightly from 11 pm to 4 or 5 am, often with bands or salsa-merengue classes at midnight; free entry, beer 650 ptas

Satanassa (Carrer d'Aribau 27)
'anti-design' haunt of androgynous people of both sexes (with a notable gay leaning), with gaudy erotic murals; open from about 11 pm to 4 or 5 am; free entry

Velvet (Carrer de Balmes 161)
smallish designer bar and disco inspired by the film *Blue Velvet*, with 1960s music; busy with a fairly straight crowd; free entry, beer around 500 ptas

Western Gràcia/Avinguda Diagonal

La Antilla Cosmopolita (Carrer de Muntaner 244)
salsa scene, popular with Latin Americans and Caribbeans, often live bands on late; usually 1500 ptas including a drink (map: Barcelona)

La Boîte (Avinguda Diagonal 477)
disco after the nightly jazz or blues (see Live Music); entry 1200 to 2500 ptas, beer 600 ptas (map: Barcelona)

Otto Zutz (Carrer de Lincoln 15)
west of Via Augusta, this is for beautiful people (the bouncers will decide how beautiful you are) and those who favour black in their dress sense; often bands at midnight with no cover – you can stay after the band finishes without paying; beer 800 ptas (map: L'Eixample)

Other Areas

Mirablau (Plaça del Doctor Andreu)
at the foot of the Tibidabo funicular, this is a bar with great views and a small disco floor; open daily from 11 am until 4.30 or 5 am; entry free, beer around 450 ptas (map: Barcelona)

Savannah (Carrer de la Muntanya 16)
good dance music nightly from 8 pm, Sunday until midnight, Tuesday to Thursday to 3 am and Friday and Saturday to 5 am (closed Monday; map: Barcelona)

Zeleste (Carrer dels Almogàvers 122)
vast ex-warehouse on several levels including huge dance space and a long, quiet bar with waiter service; best from around 2.30 to 5 am, Friday and Saturday nights (map: Barcelona)

Late-Night Venues

KGB (Carrer de ca l'Alegre de Dalt 55)
hard rock warehouse-type scene; open from 10 pm to 4.30 am, then again from about 5.30 to 8 am for tireless all-nighters (map: L'Eixample)

Gay & Lesbian Venues

Metro (Carrer de Sepúlveda 185) and *Martin's (Passeig de Gràcia 130)*
the two top gay and lesbian discos; Metro, near Plaça de la Universitat, attracts some lesbians and heteros as well as gay men (it's packed for its regular Monday-night cabarets); Martin's is gay men only; both are open from midnight to 5 am and also have 'dark rooms' (map: L'Eixample)

Classical Music, Theatre & Dance

There's plenty to choose from in these fields too. *Guía del Ocio* has ample listings. The monthly *Informatiu Musical* leaflet has the best classical music listings: you can pick it up at tourist offices and the Palau de la Virreina arts info office at La Rambla de Sant Josep 99, which also sells tickets for many events.

Although Barcelona's great opera house, the Gran Teatre del Liceu, is still out of action (following a fire in 1994), there's still opera at places such as the *Teatre Malic (Carrer de la Fusina 3)*, both in La Ribera (map: Central).

The chief venue for classical and choral music is the *Palau de la Música Catalana (Carrer de Sant Pere més alt 11)* in La Ribera, which has a busy and wide-ranging program (map: Central). Attending a concert here is also a way to see the gorgeous interior of this modernista building (see the earlier La Ribera section). The *Palau Sant Jordi* on Montjuïc hill is used for bigger concerts (map: Montjuïc). The *Mercat de les Flors (Carrer de Lleida 59)*, at the foot of Montjuïc, is an important venue for dance and drama as well as music

(map: Montjuïc). The *Teatre Victòria (Avinguda del Paral.lel 67-69)* often stages ballet and contemporary dance (map: Montjuïc).

Theatre is nearly all in Catalan or Spanish (*Guía del Ocio* specifies which). More meaningful to the average visitor than straight drama might be Barcelona's music hall-cabaret scene, a tradition dating from the turn of the century and still alive and well at theatres on and near Avinguda del Paral.lel (map: Montjuïc) like the *Arnau (Avinguda del Paral.lel 60)*, the *Llantiol (Carrer de la Riereta 7)* and *El Molino (Carrer de Vila i Vilà 99)*.

The easiest way to get hold of tickets for most theatres is through the Caixa Catalunya's Tel-Entrada service on ☎ 902-10 12 12. You can also book at www.telentrada.com on the Internet.

Sardana

The *sardana*, Catalunya's national dance, is danced every week – except sometimes in August – on Pla de la Seu in front of the cathedral at 6.30 pm on Saturday and noon on Sunday, and on Plaça de Sant Jaume at 6 pm on Sunday. These are not shows for tourists, but ordinary Catalans doing something they enjoy and expressing their Catalanity. The dancers join hands to form ever-widening circles, placing their bags or coats in the centre. The dance is intricate but, in true Catalan style, not flamboyant. The steps and the accompanying brass and reed music are rather sedate, at times jolly, at times melancholy, rising to occasional crescendos, then quietening down again.

Flamenco

Barcelona is not a major centre of this sultry Andalucian dance, but a few somewhat tacky *tablaos* are scattered about. If this is the only way you can see it, perhaps it's better than nothing. For more on the subject, see the Arts section of the Facts about Spain chapter. You could try *El Tablao de Carmen* (☎ 93 325 68 95) at Carrer dels Arcs in the Poble Espanyol or the *Cordobés* (☎ 93 317 66 53, La Rambla 35), which is on the Barri Gòtic map. Book ahead.

Cinema

Foreign films shown with subtitles and original soundtrack, rather than dubbed, are marked 'v.o.' *(versión original)* in movie listings. There's *Icària-Yelmo (Carrer de Salvador Espriu 61)*, on the Central Barcelona map; *Maldà (Carrer del Pi 5)* on the Barri Gòtic map; and *Alexis (Rambla de Catalunya 90), Arkadín (Travessera de Gràcia 103), Capsa (Carrer de Pau Claris 134), Casablanca (Passeig de Gràcia 115)* and *Verdi (Carrer de Verdi 32)* on the L'Eixample & Gràcia map. In the Les Corts district (map: Barcelona) are the *Filmoteca (Avinguda de Sarrià 33)* and *Renoir-Les Corts (Carrer de Eugeni d'Ors 12)*. A ticket is usually 600 to 750 ptas but most cinemas have a weekly *día del espectador* (viewer's day; often Monday), when they charge 400 to 600 ptas.

Amusement Centres

Apart from the fun parks already mentioned (see the Tibidabo section earlier), there is an indoor amusement parlour at the Centre Comercial New Park, Rambla de Sant Josep 88-94 (map: Gòtic).

SPECTATOR SPORTS
Football

Barcelona football club has not only one of Europe's best teams but also one of its best stadiums, the 120,000 capacity Camp Nou in the west of the city (metro: Collblanc, map: Barcelona). Games here against any opposition good enough to fire up the home team and the crowd are quite an occasion. Check the daily press for upcoming games. Tickets, available at the stadium and through some banks, cost from around 3000 to 8000 ptas; the cheapest are in the one small standing section, a long, long way above the pitch. For more information call ☎ 93 496 36 00. See the earlier Camp Nou section for more on the club.

The city's other club, Espanyol, based at the Estadi Olímpic on Montjuïc (map: Montjuïc), traditionally plays a quiet second fiddle (in the top division) to Barça, although lately they have been improving their game.

Bullfighting

Bullfighting to the death is not a favourite Catalan pastime, but there are some fights on summer Sunday afternoons at the Plaça Monumental, on the corner of Gran Via de les Corts Catalanes and Carrer de la Marina (metro: Monumental, map: Barcelona).

SHOPPING

Barcelona's obsession with style is, needless to say, reflected in its shops. There are enough chic – and expensive – little boutiques and trendy shoe shops to keep the fashion-conscious happy (or worried) for weeks. The best hunting areas are Passeig de Gràcia and the streets to its west (including the Bulevard Rosa arcade just north of Carrer d'Aragó) and Barri Gòtic streets such as Carrer de la Portaferrissa, Carrer de la Boqueria, Carrer del Call, Carrer de la Llibreteria and Carrer de Ferran, and around Plaça de Sant Josep Oriol. Also in these areas you'll find some interesting shops specialising in Latin American, African and other crafts.

The famous red and blue stripes of Barcelona football club attract big home crowds

The best single place to look for anything you need is the El Corte Inglés department store on Plaça de Catalunya (map: L'Eixample): nine floors of everything, open Monday to Saturday from 10 am to 9.30 pm. Here's a small sample of other shops that caught our eye:

Shoes

There's a gaggle of relatively economical shoe shops on Avinguda del Portal de l'Àngel, off Plaça de Catalunya (map: L'Eixample). Camper at Carrer de València 249 just off Passeig de Gràcia has a good range of Doc Marten-type boots, mostly around 10,000 ptas a pair (map: L'Eixample).

Music

Planet Music at Carrer de Mallorca 214 near Carrer d'Enric Granados, in l'Eixample, has vast selections of all types of music (map: L'Eixample). Several small shops specialise in indie and other niche music on Carrer de Sitges and nearby on Carrer dels Tallers (El Raval).

Design

Vinçon, next door to La Pedrera at Passeig de Gràcia 96 (map: L'Eixample), has the slickest designs in furniture and household goods, both local and imported.

Clothes & Fabrics

Jeanne Weis, Carrer d'En Rauric 8 north of Carrer de Ferran (map: Gòtic), is a tiny shop with some nice lines in African printed fabrics, cushions and shirts.

Crafts & Antiques

Carrer dels Banys Nous in the Barri Gòtic is lined with antique shops. Casa Miranda at No 15 has woven baskets of all shapes and sizes.

Natura Selection at Carrer del Consell de Cent 304 between Passeig de Gràcia and Rambla de Catalunya (map: L'Eixample) has a big stock of ethnic bags (leather and cloth), jewellery, pots, drums, carvings, glass, baskets, tablecloths, rugs and more.

Condoms

Barcelona even has an exotic condom shop on one of the prettiest squares of the Barri Gòtic: La Condoneria at Plaça de Sant Josep Oriol 3 (map: Gòtic). Here you can purchase condoms of every colour and shape you could dream of (and some you never could).

Markets

The large Els Encants flea market is held every Monday, Wednesday, Friday and Saturday from 8 am to 6 pm (8 pm in summer) next to Plaça de les Glòries Catalanes (metro: Glòries, map: Barcelona). In the Barri Gòtic, there's a craft market on Plaça de Sant Josep Oriol on Thursday and Friday, an antiques market on Plaça Nova on Thursday and a collectors' coin market on Plaça Reial on Sunday morning. On the western edge of El Raval (map: Montjuïc), the Mercat de Sant Antoni dedicates Sunday morning to old maps, stamps, books and cards.

GETTING THERE & AWAY

See the Travel Agencies section earlier in this chapter for some agents offering cheap airfares and youth and student train and bus tickets.

Air

The airport (☎ 93 478 50 00) is 14km southwest of the centre at El Prat de Llobregat (map: Barcelona). Barcelona is a big international and domestic destination, with direct flights from North America as well as many European cities.

Unfortunately it's not the greatest discount city. Coming from the UK you can snag flights as cheap as UK£100 with EasyJet (conditions apply). Otherwise, Debonair (☎ 902-14 62 00) is about as cheap as it gets, with 38,000 ptas return in high season. To New York you are looking at up to 86,000 ptas return in high season – often routed through another European capital.

Tickets can be bought at almost any travel agency. Iberia (☎ 902-40 05 00) is at

Passeig de Gràcia 30; Spanair (24 hours ☎ 902-13 14 15) and Air Europa (☎ 93 298 33 28) are at the airport. Other airline numbers include Air France (☎ 93 379 74 63), Lufthansa (☎ 93 379 37 66), TWA (☎ 93 379 51 12), Alitalia (☎ 93 379 25 62), KLM-Royal Dutch Airlines (☎ 93 379 54 58) and British Airways (☎ 93 379 44 68).

Bus

The main intercity *estació d'autobusos* (bus station) is the modern Estació del Nord at Carrer d'Alí Bei 80, 1.5km north-east of La Rambla and 1½ blocks from the Arc de Triomf metro (map: Barcelona). Its information desk (☎ 93 265 65 08) is open daily from 7 am to 9 pm. You'll also find a luggage *consigna* out by the platforms, a currency exchange office (with poor rates), a La Caixa ATM and a telephone and fax office.

A few services – most importantly some international buses and the few buses to Montserrat – use Estació d'Autobusos de Sants beside Estació Sants train station (map: Barcelona).

International The main services are run by Eurolines/Julià Via (☎ 93 490 40 00) from Estació d'Autobusos de Sants, and by Eurolines/Linebús and Starbus (both ☎ 93 265 07 00) from Estació del Nord. Services include:

London
    Eurolines/Julià Via or Eurolines/Linebús (24 hours; 13,450 ptas; three to five times weekly)
Marseille
    Eurolines/Julià Via (11½ hours; 6700 ptas; daily, except Sunday)
Milan
    Eurolines/Julià Via (17½ hours; 11,875 ptas; three to six times weekly)
Paris
    Eurolines/Julià Via or Eurolines/Linebús (15 hours; 11,450 ptas; daily except Sunday)

Eurolines/Julià Via also has services at least three times weekly to Amsterdam, Brussels, Florence, Geneva, Montpellier, Nice, Perpignan, Rome, Toulouse, Venice and

Zürich, and twice a week to several cities in Morocco.

Domestic There are buses to most large Spanish cities. A plethora of bus companies operate to different parts of the country, although many come under the umbrella of Enatcar. You can also get schedule information on ☎ 93 265 65 08.

Departures from Estació del Nord include the following, with journey time and fare (where frequencies vary, the lowest figure is usually for Sunday):

Almería
    13½ hours; 7045 ptas; two daily
Burgos
    eight hours; 4960 ptas; two to four daily
Granada
    13 to 15 hours; 7830 ptas; four daily
Madrid
    seven or eight hours; 2940 ptas; up to 16 daily
Salamanca
    11½ hours; 6425 ptas; three daily
Sevilla
    16 hours; 8820 ptas; one daily
Valencia
    4½ hours; 2900 ptas; five to 10 daily
Vigo
    15 hours; 6710 ptas; two daily
Zaragoza
    4½ hours; 1640 ptas; nine daily

For buses to other places in Catalunya, see the relevant sections in the Catalunya chapter.

Train

The two main stations are Estació Sants, on Plaça dels Països Catalans, 2.5km west of La Rambla (metro: Sants-Estació); and Estació de França on Avinguda del Marquès de l'Argentera, 1km east of La Rambla (metro: Barceloneta, map: Barcelona).

All trains within Spain (except some Barcelona suburban services) use Estació Sants. Some, but by no means all, trains to/from France or beyond use Estació de França. A few stop at both.

Other useful stations for long-distance and regional trains are Catalunya on Plaça de Catalunya (metro: Catalunya, map:

L'Eixample) and Passeig de Gràcia, on the corner of Passeig de Gràcia and Carrer d'Aragó, 700m north of Plaça de Catalunya (metro: Passeig de Gràcia, map: L'Eixample).

Information & Tickets It's advisable to book at least a day or two ahead for most long-distance trains, domestic or international. There's a RENFE information and booking office in Passeig de Gràcia station, open daily from 7 am to 10 pm (9 pm on Sunday). At Estació Sants, the Informació Largo Recorrido windows give information on all, except suburban, trains. The station has consigna lockers open from 5.30 am to 10 pm (400 or 600 ptas for 24 hours), a tourist information office, a telephone and fax office, a hotel reservations office, currency exchange offices open from 8 am to 10 pm daily, and ATMs.

Estació de França has a train information office and consigna lockers (600 ptas for 24 hours).

For information on international trains you can call ☎ 93 490 11 22; for domestic trains call ☎ 93 490 02 02.

International Direct trains from Estació de França include those to Paris (12 hours), Zürich (13 hours) and Milan (12¾ hours), all overnight. The Paris train is daily; the others are either daily or three times weekly, depending on the season. These trains meet connections for numerous other cities. The cheapest beds to Paris, Zürich and Milan cost respectively 27,800, 30,000 and 29,000 ptas. You can get seats on the latter two for 22,400 and 22,000 ptas respectively. Otherwise you can get a couchette in a cabin of four for 16,500 ptas to Paris.

From Estació Sants there are two daily trains to Perpignan (three hours) and Montpellier (4½ hours). Montpellier is 5305/8370 ptas in 2nd/1st class.

You can also reach a variety of destinations, in some cases several times a day, by changing trains just across the French border at Cerbère (opposite Portbou) or Latour-de-Carol (opposite Puigcerdà), or at

Montpellier. From Estació Sants there are 6 to 10 trains a day to Cerbère (2½ hours) and one to three to Latour-de-Carol (3½ hours). This way, Paris is nine to 16 hours from Barcelona for around 12,800 ptas in 2nd-class seats, Amsterdam up to 23 hours (from 22,000 ptas), Venice 17¼ to 22¼ hours (from 13,500 ptas), Florence 16½ to 22 hours (from 12,685 ptas) and Rome 18½ to 23 hours (from 14,280 ptas).

Domestic There are trains to most large Spanish cities, with the usual huge range of train types and fares. Most services depart from Estació Sants (some also stopping at Estació de França and/or Passeig de Gràcia). For sample fares, see the Getting Around chapter.

Euromed The AVE train on normal tracks connects Barcelona with Valencia (3 hours) five times a day, and twice a day with Alicante (4¾ hours). The respective turista/preferente fares are 4600/6500 ptas to Valencia and 6300/8800 ptas to Alicante.

Barcelona & Catalunya Services For suburban trains around Barcelona, see Getting Around in this chapter and relevant destination sections. Regional trains within Catalunya all go from Estació Sants; some also stop at Catalunya or Passeig de Gràcia. See the destination sections for more detail.

Car & Motorcycle

Autopistas head out of Barcelona in most directions you'd want to go, including the A-19 to the southern Costa Brava; the A-16 to Sitges; the A-18 to Manresa (with a turn-off for Montserrat); and the A-7 north to Girona, Figueres and France, and south to Tarragona and Valencia (turn off along the A-2 for Lleida, Zaragoza and Madrid). All these have tolls (over 1500 ptas to La Jonquera near the French border, for instance) but the toll-free alternatives, such as the N-II north to Girona, Figueres and France, and west to Lleida and beyond, or the N-340 to Tarragona, tend to be busy and slow.

Rental If you haven't organised a rental car from abroad, local firms such as Julià Car, Ronicar and Vanguard are generally cheaper than the big international names. From these a typical small car like a Ford Fiesta or Renault Twingo, with minimum compulsory insurance, should cost around 2500 ptas a day plus 25 ptas a kilometre, plus IVA. For unlimited kilometres, they're around 20,000 ptas for three days or 35,000 ptas a week, plus IVA. Special low weekend rates (from Friday lunchtime or afternoon to Monday morning) are worth looking into. Rental firms (which are all on the L' Eixample & Gràcia map unless otherwise stated) include:

Avis
   (☎ 93 487 87 45) Carrer d'Aragó 235, l'Eixample
Europcar
   (☎ 93 488 23 98) Carrer del Consell de Cent 363, l'Eixample
Hertz
   (☎ 93 217 32 48) Carrer d'Aragó 382-384, l'Eixample
Julià Car
   (☎ 93 317 64 54) Ronda de la Universitat 5, l'Eixample
Ronicar
   (☎ 93 405 09 51) Carrer d'Europa 34-36, Les Corts (map: Barcelona)
Vanguard
   (☎ 93 439 38 80) Carrer de Londres 31, l'Eixample (map: Barcelona)

Vanguard also rents out motorcycles. If you want something decent for touring outside Barcelona, you'll be looking at around 12,000 ptas a day (plus 7% IVA).

Boat

Islas Baleares Passenger and vehicular ferries to the Islas Baleares, operated by the Trasmediterránea line, dock near the new Trasmediterránea office near the Moll de Barcelona wharf in Port Vell (map: Central). Information and tickets are available from Trasmediterránea (☎ 93 295 90 00,

fax 93 295 91 34) there, or from travel agents. Also, in 1998 a new highspeed ferry, Buquebús (☎ 902-41 42 42), began operations.

For information on schedules and fares, see the introductory Getting There & Away section in the Islas Baleares chapter.

Italy The Italian company Grimaldi is doing the so-called *canguro* shipping run between Barcelona and Genova (17 hours), which has been re-established after a 15-year break. Its vessel, the *Fantastic*, can carry 1900 passengers, 760 cars and a hefty goods load.

Three weekly trips from Moll de Ponent, Barcelona, are planned: Tuesday and Thursday at 10 pm and Sunday at 3 am. From Genova, departures are on Monday, Wednesday and Friday.

An airline-style seat is 8300 one way and a car is 12,700 to 14,300 ptas, depending on size. Luxury suites cost 25,100 ptas for two. Book tickets with any travel agent.

GETTING AROUND

The metro is the easiest way of getting around and reaches most places you're likely to visit (although not the airport). For a few trips you need buses or FGC suburban trains. The main tourist office on Plaça de Catalunya gives out the comprehensive *Guia d'Autobusos Urbans de Barcelona*, with a metro map and all bus routes. For public transport information you can call ☎ 010 or ☎ 93 412 00 00, or ☎ 93 205 15 15 for suburban trains only. For info on disabled facilities call ☎ 93 412 44 44.

Targetas

Targetas are multiple-trip city transport tickets, offering worthwhile savings. They are sold at most city-centre metro stations. Targeta T-1 (775 ptas) gives you 10 rides on the metro, buses or suburban (FGC) trains; Targeta T-2 (760 ptas) gives 10 rides on the metro or suburban trains; and Targeta T-DIA (575 ptas) gives unlimited metro, bus or suburban train travel in one day. A plethora of other options exists, including monthly passes for unlimited use of all public transport at 3810 ptas (you need to get a Targetren ID card, available at the Centre d'Atenció al Client in the Plaça de Catalunya and Plaça d'Espanya stations), Targeta T-50/30 (for 50 trips within 30 days) and discounted tickets/passes for pensioners and students.

If you only want to use buses and the metro (and not the FGC suburban trains), the three and five-day Abonament tickets are good value at 1300/2000 ptas.

If you take the Aerobús from the airport, you can get an all-in ticket for the bus and unlimited use of Barcelona's buses and metro for three days (1800 ptas) or five days (2300 ptas).

Fines
The fine for being caught without a ticket on public transport is 5000 ptas.

To/From the Airport
Rodalies trains run from the airport to Estació Sants and Catalunya station on Plaça de Catalunya every 30 minutes from 6.10 am to 10.40 pm daily. It's 16 minutes to Sants, 21 minutes to Catalunya, 305 ptas to either place (350 ptas on weekends and holidays). Departures from Sants to the airport are from 5.45 am to 10.15 pm; from Catalunya they're five minutes earlier.

The A1 Aerobús bus service runs from the airport to Plaça de Catalunya and Estació Sants Monday to Friday every 15 minutes from 6 am to 11 pm, and Saturday, Sunday and holidays every 30 minutes from 6.45 am to 10.45 pm. Departures from Plaça de Catalunya are Monday to Friday from 5.30 am to 10 pm, Saturday, Sunday and holidays from 6 am to 10 pm. The trip is about 40 minutes – depending on traffic – for 475 ptas.

Cheaper suburban buses (Buses EA and EN) leave every 80 minutes for Plaça d'Espanya and cost 140 ptas. They take about 50 minutes.

A taxi to/from the centre, a half-hour ride, is about 2500 ptas.

Bus
Buses run along most city routes every few minutes from 5 or 6 am to 10 or 11 pm. Many routes pass through Plaça de Catalunya and/or Plaça de la Universitat. After 11 pm, a reduced network of yellow *nitbusos* (night buses) runs until 3 to 5 am. All nitbus routes pass through Plaça de Catalunya and most run every 30 to 45 minutes. A single fare on any bus is 140 ptas.

Bus Turístic This bus service covers two circuits (24 stops) linking virtually all the major tourist sights. Tourist offices and many hotels have leaflets explaining the system, or you can call ☎ 93 423 18 00. Tickets, available on the bus, are 1700 ptas for one day's unlimited rides, or 2300 ptas for two consecutive days. Service is about every 20 minutes from 9 am to 9.30 pm. Tickets entitle you to discounts of up to 300 ptas on entry fees and tickets to more than 20 sights along the route, as well as shopping discounts and a meal at KFC and Pizza Hut (oh great!). The discounts don't *have* to be used on the day(s) you use the bus.

Tombbus The T1 Tombbus has been thought out for shoppers and runs regularly from Plaça de Catalunya up to Avinguda Diagonal, along which it proceeds west to Plaça de Pius XII, where it turns around again. On the way you pass such landmarks as El Corte Inglés (several of them), Bulevard Rosa, FNAC and Marks & Spencer. Tickets are 160 ptas per trip.

Train
FGC suburban trains are useful for reaching some places within the city as well as some outside it. Most run Monday to Thursday from 5 am to 11 pm and Friday to Sunday from 5 am to 1 am. Rides within the city are 130 ptas. The main city-centre stations for these trains, all with metro stations on the spot, are Catalunya (on Plaça de Catalunya), Passeig de Gràcia, Espanya (on Plaça d'Espanya), Arc de Triomf and Estació Sants. See sections that refer to

suburban destinations for detail on services. They're operated by Ferrocarrils de la Generalitat de Catalunya (FGC), not by the national network, RENFE.

Metro

The metro has five lines, numbered and colour-coded, and is efficient and easy to use. A single ride is 140 ptas and tickets are easily available from machines at most stations. At interchange stations, you just need to work out which line and which direction you want. The metro runs Monday to Thursday from 5 am to 11 pm, Friday and Saturday from 5 am to 2 am and Sunday from 6 am to midnight. See the colour metro map.

Car & Motorcycle

An effective one-way system makes traffic flow fairly smoothly, but you'll often find yourself flowing the way you don't want to go – unless you happen to have an adept navigator and the Michelin

Barcelona map (see Orientation earlier in this chapter), which shows one-way streets. Parking can also be tricky and expensive if you choose a parking garage. It's better to leave your car alone while you're here and use Barcelona's public transport.

Taxi

Taxis are black and yellow and cost 295 ptas plus meter charges. These work out to about 100 ptas per kilometre (slightly more from 10 pm to 6 am weekdays and all day Saturday, Sunday and holidays). A further 300 ptas is added for all trips to/from the airport, and 100 ptas for luggage bigger than 55cm by 35cm by 35cm. The trip from Estació Sants to Plaça de Catalunya, about 3km, is about 700 ptas. You can call a taxi on ☎ 93 225 00 00, ☎ 93 481 10 85 or ☎ 93 490 22 22 (☎ 93 358 11 11 for wheelchair-adapted taxis). General information on taxis is available on ☎ 010 and ☎ 93 428 10 85.

The elaborate world of modernisme in Barcelona (clockwise from top): Palau Quadras, Palau de la Música Catalana and La Sagrada Família

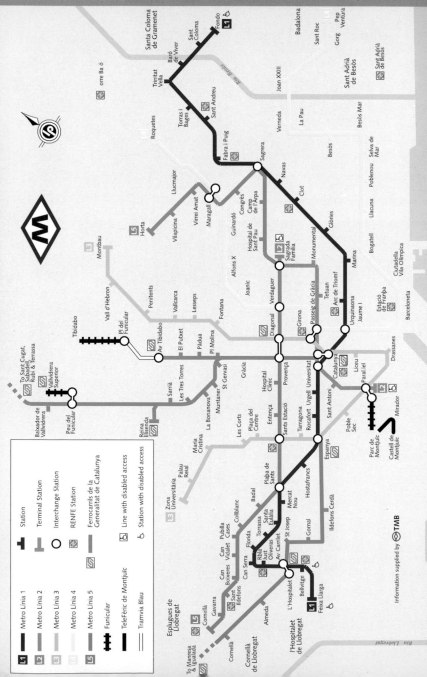

BARCELONA METRO

Catalunya (Cataluña)

North, south and west of Barcelona spreads a land of such diversity that, although its farthest-flung corner is no more than 200km (six hours by bus) from Barcelona, you could spend weeks exploring it and still feel that you'd barely begun. The Costa Brava, for all its dreary concrete pockets of mass tourism, still has the wild beauty that brought visitors there in the first place and in many places remains little touched by the tour operators. Inland, the Pyrenees rise to mighty 3000m peaks from a series of green and often remote valleys, dotted with villages that retain a palpable air of the Middle Ages. These mountains provide some magnificent walking and good skiing.

Excitement runs thinner in the flatter far west and south, but even here there's enough to keep you happily exploring for a few days, from the wetlands of the Ebro delta to the historic cities of Tarragona and Lleida. Throughout Catalunya (Catalonia in English) the sense of difference from the rest of Spain is intense, not only in the use of the Catalan language (although everyone speaks Castilian too) but also in the unusual festivals, the cuisine and constant reminders of the region's unique history. Among the latter, the wealth of superb Romanesque and Gothic buildings speak with greatest eloquence of Catalunya's distinct past. It doesn't take long to understand why so many people here think of themselves as Catalans first, and as Spaniards, if at all, a distant second.

Accommodation

Room and camping ground prices in this chapter are for the high season – July and August, plus around January to March in ski resorts – when it's often advisable to ring ahead to ensure a room. Most establishments charge around 10% or 20% less at other times; some of the more expensive places drop rates by almost half in the off season.

Highlights

- Exploring the coves and beaches near Palafrugell or Begur

- Cadaqués, a magical Costa Brava village haunted by the memory of Salvador Dalí

- Sunrise or sunset at beautiful Cap de Creus, the easternmost point of mainland Spain

- The Teatre-Museu Dalí in Figueres, a voyage through one of the 20th century's strangest minds

- Riding the Cremallera narrow-gauge railway up to the Vall de Núria

- Walking in the Parc Nacional d'Aigüestortes i Estany de Sant Maurici

- A visit to the weird, rock-pillar mountain of Montserrat

- A night or two on the town at Sitges, Spain's most outrageous resort

CATALUNYA

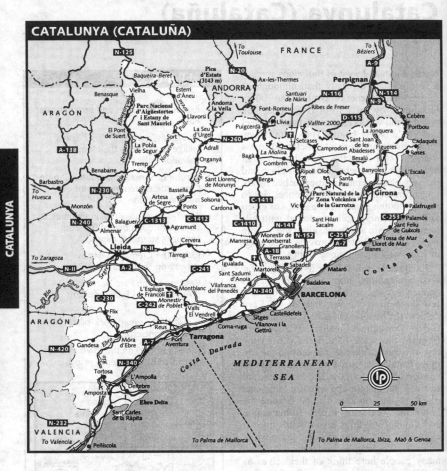

CATALUNYA (CATALUÑA)

Catalunya has a wide network of *cases de pagès*, the local name for *casas rurales*, which often provide economical and good accommodation in country areas.

Youth Hostels The 24 member hostels of Catalunya's official youth hostel network, the Xarxa d'Albergs de Joventut, all share a central booking service (☎ 93 483 83 63, fax 93 483 83 50) at the Oficina de Turisme Juvenil, Carrer de Rocafort 116-122, Barcelona. Nearly all hostels in Catalunya outside Barcelona are Xarxa (and REAJ/HI) hostels.

At Xarxa hostels you need an HI card. With a few minor exceptions, all have the same price structure: if you're under 25 or have an ISIC or FIYTO card, B&B is 1475 ptas in the low season and 1700 ptas in the high season; otherwise it's 1950 ptas low season, 2275 ptas high season. There's no cheaper rate for bed without breakfast. High and low seasons vary from hostel to hostel and are specified where hostels are mentioned in this chapter. The Christmas and Semana Santa holidays and all long weekends are high season everywhere. If you don't have a sleeping bag or sheets, hostels charge 350 ptas for sheet hire.

Getting Around
A good network of RENFE *trens regionals* (regional trains) fans out across Catalunya from Barcelona. There are three types of tren regional: a Catalunya Exprés is the fastest, with limited stops and 1st as well as 2nd class carriages; a Delta stops more often and is 2nd class only; and a plain Regional, also 2nd class only, stops everywhere. Catalunya Exprés fares are about 15% higher than the others.

The Portbou, Lleida and Tarragona lines are also served by RENFE long-distance trains, with fares around twice those on trens regionals.

For some places closer to Barcelona, such as Montserrat, Sant Sadurní d'Anoia and Sitges, the best services are often *rodalies*, the Catalan version of *cercanías*. Fares are a little higher on weekends on these trains.

Places off the railways are served by buses, often including direct services from Barcelona. In general there are more buses in summer than winter, and more from Monday to Friday than at the weekend and on holidays. On some routes fares go up by around 15% at the weekend and on holidays.

Costa Brava

The Costa Brava, stretching from Blanes, 60km north-east of Barcelona, to the French border, ranks with the Costa Blanca and Costa del Sol as one of Spain's three great holiday '*costas*'. Don't let that put you off. It has its share of awful concrete development, English breakfasts and *Konditoreien*, but as the name 'Rugged Coast' suggests, it also offers some spectacular stretches strung with picturesque headlands, inlets and waters of unbelievably inviting shades of blue.

Nestling in the hilly country – green and covered in umbrella pine in the south, barer and browner in the north – are a number of attractive old, country towns. A little farther inland are the bigger towns of Girona (Gerona in Castilian), with a sizable medieval centre, and Figueres (Figueras), famous for its bizarre Teatre-Museu Dalí, the foremost of a series of sites associated with the eccentric surrealist artist Salvador Dalí.

The Costa Brava does get packed in the second half of July and August – you should ring ahead to avoid a lengthy room search in many places. June and September are a pleasant couple of degrees cooler than July and August, while May and October are nicely warm. Sea temperatures hold up well through September, too.

Diving
The ruggedness of the Costa Brava continues under the sea to provide some of the best diving in Spain. Approved tourist diving centres with certified instructors operate at a dozen or more places. The Illes Medes off L'Estartit are a group of protected islets with probably the most diverse sea life along the Spanish coast. Other top diving spots include the Illes Formigues, rocky islets off the coast between Palamós and Calella de Palafrugell with waters down to 45m, and Els Ullastres, three underwater hills off Llafranc with some sheer walls and depths to 54m.

Getting There & Away
Direct buses from Barcelona go to most towns on and near the Costa Brava. The railway between Barcelona and the coastal border town of Portbou runs inland most of the way, through Girona and Figueres. From Girona and Figueres there are fairly good bus services to the coast.

In summer, you could take an alternative approach to the southern Costa Brava from Barcelona by a combination of suburban rodalia train and boat (see Getting There & Away in the Tossa de Mar section).

Catalan Cuisine

Catalans love their food, and with good reason, for it nudges Basque cuisine for the title of Spain's best. Its variety and originality stem mainly from Catalunya's geographical diversity, which is the source of fresh, quality seafood, meat, poultry, game, fruit and vegetables. These can come in unusual and delicious combinations: meat with seafood (a genre known as *mar i muntanya*, 'sea and mountain'), poultry with fruit, fish with nuts. You'll probably eat more truly Catalan food away from Barcelona, where it tends to be expensive.

The essence of Catalan food lies in its sauces for meat and fish. These sauces may not be mentioned on menus as they're so ubiquitous. There are five main types: *sofregit*, of fried onion, tomato and garlic; *samfaina*, sofregit plus red pepper and aubergine or zucchini (courgette); *picada*, based on ground almonds, usually with garlic, parsley, pine or hazel nuts, and sometimes breadcrumbs; *allioli*, garlic pounded with olive oil, often with egg yolk added to make a mayonnaise; and *romesco*, an almond, tomato, olive oil, garlic and vinegar sauce, also used as a salad dressing.

Catalans find it hard to understand why other people put mere butter on bread when *pa amb tomáquet*, bread slices rubbed with tomato, olive oil and garlic, is so easy. They eat it with almost everything and prefer their *entrepans* (bocadillos) this way, too.

And some old standbys you may have come to rely on elsewhere in Spain are here too, only with different names. Try asking locals why a *sandwich mixto* (humble toasted cheese and ham sandwich) is known in Catalunya as a *bikini*. And try asking for a bikini outside Catalunya!

Most main courses are meat or fish with a sauce and potatoes. There are some good stews too. You can wash it all down with good Catalan wine, including *cava*, the inexpensive local version of champagne. Here are some typical dishes:

Starters

amanida Catalana – Catalan salad; almost any mix of lettuce, olives, tomatoes, hard-boiled eggs, onion, chicory, celery, green pepper and garlic, with fish, ham or sausage, dressed with mayonnaise or vinaigrette

calçots amb romesco – calçots, a type of long onion, are delicious as a starter with romesco sauce

escalivada – red peppers and aubergines (sometimes with onions and tomatoes), grilled, peeled, sliced and served lukewarm dressed with olive oil, salt and garlic

esqueixada – salad of shredded salted cod *(bacallà)* with tomato, red pepper, onion, white beans, olives, olive oil and vinegar

Main Dishes

arròs a la cassola or *arròs a la Catalana* – Catalan paella, cooked in an earthenware pot, without saffron

botifarra amb mongetes – pork sausage with fried white beans

cargols – snails; a religion in parts of Catalunya; popular stewed with rabbit *(conill)* and chilli

escudella – a meat, sausage and vegetable stew whose liquid, mixed with noodles or rice, is served as a soup, followed by the rest as a main course known as *carn d'olla*

fricandó – a pork and vegetable stew

mandonguilles amb sipia – meatballs with cuttlefish, a subtly flavoured *mar i muntanya* combination

pollastre amb escamerlans – chicken with shrimps, another amphibious event

sarsuela (zarzuela) – a Barcelona invention of mixed seafood cooked in sofregit with various seasonings

Catalan Cuisine

Desserts
crema Catalana – a cream custard with a crisp burnt sugar coating
mel i mató – honey and fresh cream cheese, simple but delicious

Other good things to look out for include duck *(ànec)*, goose *(oca)* and *canalons* (Catalan cannelloni). *Fideuas* (noodles) are usually served with tomato and meat/sausage or fish sauces. Wild mushrooms are a Catalan passion – people disappear into the forests in autumn to pick them. There are many, many types; the large succulent *rovellons* are a favourite. Here are more words (with, where they differ, their Spanish equivalents) to help you with Catalan-only menus:

Catalan	Spanish	English
ametller	almendra	almond
anyell	cordero	lamb
bou	carne de vaca	beef
caldereta		a seafood stew
carxofe	alcachofa	artichoke
castanya	castaña	chestnut
ceba	cebolla	onion
costella	chuleta	cutlet
cranc	cangrejo	crab
entrepan		bocadillo
farcit	relleno	stuffed
formatge	queso	cheese
fregit	frito	fried
fuet		salami-type sausage
gelat	helado	ice cream
llagosta	langosta	lobster
llenties	lentejas	lentils
llet	leche	milk
llonganissa	longaniza	pork sausage
oli	aceite	oil
orxata	horchata	almond drink
ostra		oyster
ous	huevos	eggs
pastis	pastel	cake
pebre	pimienta	pepper
peix	pescado	fish
pernil de la comarca		country-cured ham
pops	pulpo	octopus
rap	rape	monkfish
suquet		seafood stew
torrada	tostada	open toasted sandwich
truita	trucha	trout
truita	tortilla	omelette
xai	cordero	lamb

CATALUNYA

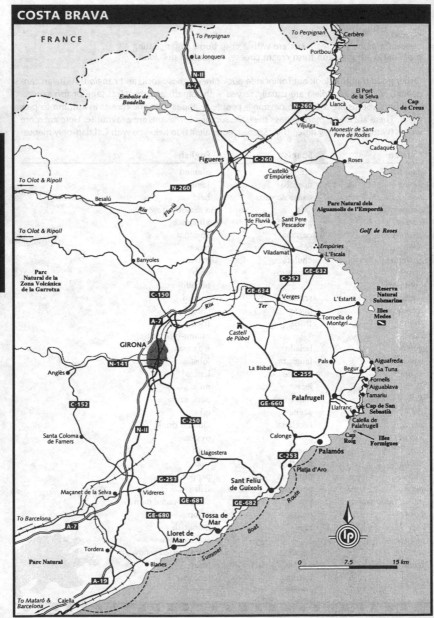

The A-7 *autopista* and the toll-free N-II highway both run from Barcelona via Girona and Figueres to the French border a few kilometres north of La Jonquera. The A-19 autopista follows the N-II up the coast as far as Blanes. Other roads run up the coast and inland to Girona and Figueres.

TOSSA DE MAR

Curving round a boat-speckled bay guarded by a headland crowned with medieval defensive walls and towers, Tossa de Mar is a white village of crooked, narrow streets onto which tourism has tacked a larger, modern extension of straighter, wider ones. In July and August it's hard to reach the water's edge without tripping over oily limbs, but it is heaven compared with its bigger neighbour 12km to the south-east, Lloret de Mar – a real concrete and neon jungle of Piccadilly pubs, *Bierkeller* and soccer chants.

Tossa was one of the first places on the Costa Brava to attract foreign visitors – a small colony of artists and writers gravitated towards here in the 1930s. The French painter Marc Chagall spent the summer of 1934 in Tossa and dubbed it the 'Blue Paradise'.

Orientation & Information

The *estació d'autobusos* (bus station) is beside the GE-682 road where it leaves Tossa for Lloret de Mar. It fronts onto a roundabout with the unmistakably Catalan name Plaça de les Nacions sense Estat (Stateless Nations' Plaza). Almost next door, at Avinguda del Pelegrí 25, is the tourist office (☎ 972 34 01 08), open June to August, Monday to Saturday from 9 am to 9 pm and Sunday 10 am to 1 pm; in other months it is open for fewer hours and is closed on Sunday. The main beach, Platja Gran, and the older part of town, are a 10 minute walk to the south-east.

You'll find banks, many with ATMs, along streets like Avinguda de la Costa Brava and around Plaça d'Espanya. The *correos* (post office) is on Carrer de Maria Auxiliadora, one block east of Avinguda del Pelegrí. The postcode is 17320.

The police station (☎ 972 34 01 35) is in the *ajuntament* (town hall) at Carrer de l'Església 4 in the old town. The Centre Mèdic Tossa (☎ 972 34 14 48, Carrer de Sant Sebastià 2) is a private-practice medical clinic. The state clinic is the Ambulatori (☎ 972 34 18 28) in the Casa del Mar at Avinguda de Catalunya s/n, about 1km north-west of the old town. It has emergency and ambulance services.

Old Tossa

The **walls and towers** on the pine-dotted headland, Mont Guardí, at the end of the main beach, were built in the 12th to 14th centuries. The area they girdle is known as the **Vila Vella** (old town). You can walk up on Mont Guardí, where there are also vestiges of a castle, and a *far* (lighthouse), at any time of the day or night.

In the lower part of the Vila Vella is the interesting **Museu Municipal** in the 14th and 15th century Palau del Batlle, open Tuesday to Sunday from 10 am to 1 pm and 3 to 6 pm (200 ptas). In the museum are mosaics and other finds from a Roman villa off Avinguda del Pelegrí, and Tossa-related art including *El Violinista* by Chagall. Behind the musician in question, a Tossa window opens on to a landscape of Chagall's Belarus birthplace. A new art gallery to exhibit some 400 minor works by Salvador Dalí, including lithographs and etchings, is being planned. The Californian collector Dmitry Piterman is behind the effort.

The so-called **Vila Nova** (new town) is actually the part of the old town that stands outside, north of the walled Vila Vella. Much of its tangle of lanes dates from the 18th century. The real new town stretches a lot farther north, north-west and north-east.

Beaches & Coves

The main town beach, **Platja Gran**, tends to be busy. Farther along the same bay are the little **Platja del Reig** and **Platja Mar Menuda** at the end of Avinguda de Sant Ramon Penyafort, which tends to be less

CATALUNYA

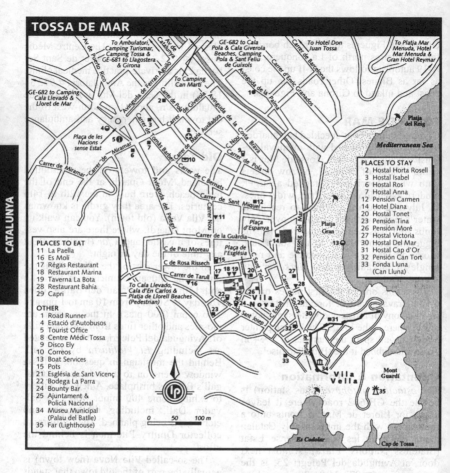

TOSSA DE MAR

PLACES TO STAY
2 Hostal Horta Rosell
3 Hostal Isabel
6 Hostal Ros
7 Hostal Anna
12 Pensión Carmen
14 Hotel Diana
20 Pensión Tonet
23 Pensión Tina
26 Pensión Moré
27 Hostal Victoria
30 Hostal Del Mar
31 Hostal Cap d'Or
32 Pensión Can Tort
33 Fonda La Mar
     (Can Lluna)

PLACES TO EAT
11 La Paella
16 Es Molí
17 Régas Restaurant
18 Restaurant Marina
19 Taverna La Bota
28 Restaurant Bahía
29 Capri

OTHER
1 Road Runner
4 Estació d'Autobusos
5 Tourist Office
8 Centre Médic Tossa
9 Disco Ely
10 Correos
13 Boat Services
15 Pots
21 Església de Sant Vicenç
22 Bodega La Parra
24 Bounty Bar
25 Ajuntament &
    Policía Nacional
34 Museu Municipal
    (Palau del Batlle)
35 Far (Lighthouse)

crowded. The coasts north-east and south-west of Tossa have rocky coves, some with small beaches (sometimes sandy, more often stony). You can walk cross-country from Tossa to the small **Cala Llevado** and **Cala d'En Carlos** beaches, 3km south-west, or the longer **Platja de Llorell** (3.5km), or drive down to Platja de Llorell from the GE-682. To the north-east, you can walk down from the GE-682 to small beaches like **Cala Pola** (4km), **Cala Giverola** (5km), **Cala Salions** (8km) and **Platja Vallpregona**

(11km). In summer, glass-bottomed boats run about hourly to some of these north-eastern beaches from Platja Gran, calling in at a few sea caves (about 1000 ptas return).

Places to Stay

Tossa has over 80 hotels, *hostales* and *pensiones*. You'll find plenty of them open from Semana Santa to October, but only a handful outside those months. Some of the best-value places get booked up weeks, even months, ahead for high summer.

Places to Stay – Budget

Camping There are five camping grounds around Tossa, each holding between 800 and 1700 people, but you're unlikely to find any of them open between mid-October and Semana Santa. Nearest to town, and one of the cheapest, is *Camping Can Martí* (☎ 972 34 08 51) on Rambla Pau Casals, 1km back from the beach. Two adults with a car and tent pay 2775 ptas. *Camping Turismar* (☎ 972 34 04 63) and *Camping Tossa* (☎ 972 34 05 47) are respectively about 1 and 2.5km farther out, on the GE-681. *Camping Pola* (☎ 972 34 10 50), 4km out on the GE-682, is well sited in a shady valley that leads to a picturesque cove. *Camping Cala Llevadó* (☎ 972 34 03 14) is 3km out on the GE-682 to Lloret de Mar.

Pensiones & Hostales In July and August it's easier to find rooms in the streets just down from the tourist office and bus station than in the older part of town or on the seafront. Even so, you might want to start looking in the more atmospheric older area. One of the cheapest places here is *Pensión Moré* (☎ 972 34 03 39, Carrer de Sant Elm 9) has good-sized singles/doubles for 1300/2600 ptas; bathrooms are shared. *Fonda Lluna* (☎ 972 34 03 65, Carrer de la Roqueta 20), also called *Can Lluna*, is good value at 1900/3800 ptas for small rooms with private bath, and breakfast included.

Pensión Can Tort (☎ 972 34 11 85) on the corner of Carrer del Portal and Carrer dels Pescadors has sizable doubles with breakfast for 4900 ptas with bath, or 4300 ptas without. It's open from April to the end of October. *Pensión Tina* (☎ 972 34 01 44, Carrer dels Tapers 4) has doubles with bath and breakfast for 4000 ptas (open April to September). *Hostal Tonet* (☎ /fax 972 34 02 37) on Plaça de l'Església, where doubles with bath cost up to 4900 ptas plus IVA, is open all year.

A dozen or so pensiones and hostales lie scattered about within three blocks of the tourist office – most close from November to April. *Hotel Ros* (☎ 972 34 02 11, Avin-guda del Pelegrí 27), right by the tourist office, has good rooms with bath for 2500/3900 ptas. Comparable places include *Hostal Isabel* (☎ 972 34 03 36, Carrer de Sant Vicenç 3); *Hostal Anna* (☎ 972 34 06 44, Carrer de Tomàs Barber s/n); and *Hostal Horta Rosell* (☎ 972 34 04 32, Carrer de Pola 29).

A few blocks towards the old town, *Pensión Carmen* (☎ 972 34 05 26, Carrer de Sant Miquel 8), with signs also saying *Pensión Pepi* and, for good measure, *Pensión Carmen-Pepi*, has decent doubles only, with shower, for 4000 ptas (5000 ptas from mid-July to the end of August).

A decent beachfront hostal is *Hostal Del Mar* (☎ 972 34 00 80, Passeig del Mar s/n) with rooms for about 2500/4000 ptas.

Places to Stay – Mid-Range & Top End

On the beachfront, *Hostal Victòria* (☎ 972 34 01 66, Passeig del Mar s/n) is plain but adequate and charges 3200 ptas per person including breakfast. In high summer, *media pensión* (half-board) is obligatory and costs 5685 ptas per person.

The more attractive, *Hostal Cap d'Or* (☎ /fax 972 34 00 81, Passeig de la Vila Vella 1), right in front of the old town walls, charges 3875/7500 ptas.

Hotel Diana (☎ 972 34 18 86, fax 972 34 11 03, Plaça d'Espanya 6) is a relaxed, small-scale, older hotel fronting Platja Gran. It has a Gaudí fireplace in the lounge and offers doubles costing 11,200 ptas with sea views or 10,100 ptas looking onto the square.

On Platja Mar Menuda, the 40-room *Hotel Mar Menuda* (☎ 972 34 10 00, fax 972 34 00 87) has high standards of comfort and service at 11,800 ptas for doubles with breakfast plus IVA. From mid-July to mid-August it offers *pensión completa* (full board) only at 10,000 ptas per person (plus IVA). *Hotel Don Juan Tossa* (☎ 972 34 07 62, Carrer de Barcelona 22) charges 7500 ptas per person in July and August.

The 166-room *Gran Hotel Reymar* (☎ 972 34 00 00, fax 972 34 15 04) on Mar

Menuda beach is the top place in town, with doubles at 25,800 ptas plus IVA in July and August. It's closed from November to April.

Places to Eat

Tossa has a lot of bland, overpriced eateries. The al fresco restaurants lining Carrer del Portal are nicely sited and do some good fish and seafood, but are expensive for what you get.

On the beachfront Passeig de Mar, the *Capri* serves up some of the better value food, offering a bit of almost everything – salads from 600 ptas, pizzas, pasta, meat or seafood from around 950 ptas. *Restaurant Bahía (Passeig de Mar 19)* does some of Tossa's best food, with a set *menú del día* for 1885 ptas.

On Carrer de Tarull, beside the church in the old town, *Restaurant Marina* at No 6 offers a fairly good *menú* for 1250 ptas and also does some economical specials such as chicken, chips, salad and beer for 500 ptas. *Taverna La Bota* next door has a simpler *menú* for 975 ptas. At No 12, *Règas Restaurant* offers Indian cooking as well as some local standard dishes. The Indian mains are 1000 ptas or less.

Es Molí at No 3, farther up the same street, serves up classier local cooking, including good prawns and *fideuas*, and has a tranquil, shady garden patio. There are *menús* for 2500 ptas and a gourmet version for 4500 ptas.

La Paella (Carrer Nou 12) is one of the cheaper places in town, with a *menú* for 950 ptas, or sandwiches from 300 ptas.

Entertainment

The old town's lively bars, some with music, are along and near Carrer de Sant Josep. *Bodega La Parra* at No 26 is one that manages to maintain an old-fashioned wine-cellar atmosphere. *Bounty Bar (Carrer de l'Església 6)*, around the corner, is a lively little watering hole where they line up shots for 200 ptas each. *Pots*, on the corner of Carrer Nou and Carrer de Rosa Rissech, is a big barn of a place that certainly grabs attention. *Disco Ely* off

Avinguda de la Costa Brava is the in place to carry on at later.

Getting There & Away

Bus SARFA runs to/from Barcelona's Estació del Nord up to 10 times daily. The trip takes 1¼ hours and costs 985 ptas.

There are fairly frequent buses to/from Lloret de Mar (150 ptas): in summer they go every 30 minutes from 8.45 am to 8.45 pm.

In July and August one all-stops bus leaves for Sant Feliu de Guíxols daily at 10.40 am, returning at 7 pm. From Sant Feliu there are SARFA buses to Girona, Palafrugell, Torroella de Montgrí and L'Escala (most several times daily). In June, July or August you can also reach Sant Feliu by one of the six daily boats from Tossa (see later).

Two or three buses daily run direct between Tossa and Girona in July and August; otherwise there's one daily on school days. Year round there are more frequent connections to Girona from Lloret de Mar.

Car & Motorcycle From Barcelona, the 440 ptas of tolls on the A-19 autopista, which takes you almost to Blanes, save a weary trudge on the toll-free N-II. To the north, the 23km stretch of the GE-682 to Sant Feliu de Guíxols is a great drive, winding its way up, down and around picturesque bays. On this road Rose Macaulay, author of *Fabled Shore* (1950), 'met only one mule cart, laden with pine boughs, and two very polite *guardias civiles*'.

Boat In June, July and August two boat services offer a scenic way of reaching Tossa, or of taking an outing from it. Crucetours (☎ 972 37 26 96 or ☎ 909 76 60 91) and Viajes Marítimos (☎ 908 93 64 76) run several times a day between Blanes, Lloret de Mar and Tossa (one to 1½ hours), with stops at a few in-between points. A few of the services continue to/from Calella, 12km south of Blanes (*not* Calella de Palafrugell farther north), and/or Palamós, north of

Tossa, again with intermediate stops (including Sant Feliu de Guíxols). You could catch one of the frequent suburban rodalia trains from Barcelona's Catalunya station to Calella or Blanes, then transfer to the boat. A return boat ticket to Tossa is 1675 ptas from Calella (with Crucetours), or 1200 ptas from Sant Feliu de Guíxols. In many places the boats simply pull up at the beach (in Tossa, at Platja Gran) and tickets are sold at a booth there.

Getting Around

Road Runner (☎ 972 34 05 03) on Avinguda de la Palma rents out mopeds for 3900 ptas a day, scooters for 4900 ptas, mountain bikes for 2000 ptas and other bikes for 1100 ptas.

PALAFRUGELL & AROUND

The 21km reach of coast from Sant Feliu de Guíxols to Palamós is unattractively built up all the way, but north of Palamós begins one of the most beautiful stretches of the Costa Brava. The town of Palafrugell, 5km inland, is the main access point for a cluster of attractive beach spots.

East of Palafrugell are Calella de Palafrugell, Llafranc and Tamariu, once fishing villages squeezed into small bays and now three of the Costa Brava's most charming, low-key and low-rise little resorts. Even in July and August they remain relatively laid-back, although accommodation is on the expensive side (Palafrugell itself has some cheaper rooms). Begur, 7km north-east of Palafrugell, is a slightly shabby village of 2700 souls, with a cluster of less developed beaches nearby.

Palafrugell

Palafrugell, a pleasant enough town of 17,000, is the main transport, shopping and service hub for the area.

Orientation & Information The C-255 Palamós-Girona road passes through the western side of Palafrugell, a 10 minute walk from the central square, Plaça Nova. The tourist office (☎ 972 30 02 28) is at Carrer del Carrilet 2 beside the C-255. It's open Monday to Saturday from at least 10 am to 1 pm and 5 to 7 pm and Sunday and holidays from 10 am to 1 pm. In July and August, it's open Monday to Saturday from 9 am to 9 pm.

The SARFA estació d'autobusos is at Carrer de Torres Jonama 73-79, five minutes walk from the tourist office and 10 minutes from Plaça Nova. Banks, many with ATMs, and telephones and shops cluster on and around Plaça Nova. The correos is at Carrer de Torres Jonama 16. The postcode is 17200. The local police (☎ 092 or ☎ 972 61 31 01) are in the ajuntament at Carrer de Cervantes 4, two blocks south of Plaça Nova.

Museu del Suro The Museu del Suro, dedicated to the important local cork industry, is one block east of Carrer de Pi i Margall at Carrer de la Tarongeta 31. It's open Tuesday to Saturday from 5 to 9 pm and in summer also from 10 am to 1 pm (and Sunday from 10.30 am to 1.30 pm).

Places to Stay *Fonda L'Estrella* (☎ 972 30 00 05, Carrer de les Quatre Cases 13-17), 1½ blocks west of Plaça Nova, is a pleasant, cool, old-fashioned house where singles/doubles with shared bathrooms are 2400/4000 ptas. It's closed from October to March.

Two blocks in the opposite direction from the plaça, *Residència Familiar* (☎ 972 30 00 43, Carrer de Sant Sebastià 29) is ordinary but good and clean with rooms at 2000/4000 ptas. It closes between mid-November and mid-March. The good *Hostal Plaja* (☎ 972 61 08 28) across the street at No 34 has a nice courtyard, and rooms with bath for 2700/5000 ptas. It's open all year.

Getting There & Away SARFA (☎ 972 30 06 23) runs buses to/from Barcelona's Estació del Nord (two hours; 1500 to 1705 ptas) seven to 12 times daily and to/from Girona (one hour; 520 ptas) up to 15 times daily. SARFA also has a few daily services north to Begur, Torroella de Montgrí, L'Escala and Figueres (1½ hours), and in July and August only two daily buses to Lloret de Mar and Tossa de Mar (two hours).

Calella de Palafrugell

The southernmost of the three Palafrugell resorts, Calella is also the most spread out. Its low buildings are strung Aegean-style around a bay of rocky points and small beaches, with a few fishing boats still hauled up on the sand. The tourist office (☎ 972 61 44 75), down near the seafront at Carrer de les Voltes 6, is open from April to September, Monday to Saturday from 10 am to 1 pm and 5 to 8 pm and Sunday and holidays from 10 am to 1 pm.

Things to See & Do Apart from plonking on one of the beaches, you can stroll along nice coastal footpaths north-east to Llafranc (20 or 30 minutes), or south to Platja del Golfet beach close to Cap Roig (about 40 minutes). Atop Cap Roig, the **Jardí Botànic de Cap Roig** is a beautiful garden of 1200 Mediterranean species, set around the early 20th century castle/palace of Nikolai Voevalsky, a tsarist colonel who fled the Russian Revolution. The garden is open daily, from 8 am to 8 pm in summer and 9 am to 6 pm in winter (300 ptas).

Special Events Calella stages probably the Costa Brava's biggest summer *cantada de havaneres* sing-song. Havaneres are strangely melancholy songs from the Caribbean that became popular among Costa Brava sailors in the 19th century, when Catalunya maintained busy links with Cuba. Havaneres are traditionally accompanied by the drinking of *cremat*, a rum, coffee, sugar, lemon and cinnamon concoction that you set alight briefly before quaffing. Traditionally, Calella's cantada is held in August.

Places to Stay & Eat *Camping Moby Dick* (☎ 972 61 43 07, *Carrer de la Costa Verde 16-28*), in the village, has room for

470 people. *La Siesta Camping* (☎ 972 61 51 16) has a shady site by the Palafrugell road 1.25km back from the beach, with space for 2000. Both open from April to September. Moby Dick charges 2140 ptas plus IVA for two adults, a tent and a car; at La Siesta it's 3005 ptas plus IVA.

Hostería del Plancton (☎ 972 61 50 81, *Carrer de Codina 12*) – follow the signs to Església de Sant Pere – has the best-value rooms in any of three Palafrugell resorts. Unfortunately it's only open from June to September. Good, clean little rooms, some with balconies and all sharing bathrooms, are 2100 ptas per person (1750 ptas in low season).

Hotel Batlle (☎ 972 61 59 05, *Carrer de les Voltes 2*), just back from the beach, has doubles with bathroom and breakfast for 9500 to 10,500 ptas, depending on the view.

Restaurant Tragamar on the beach offers mains from 900 to 1350 ptas. *La Clova* (*Carrer de Codina 6*), a friendly and sometimes lively bar at near the Hostería del Plancton, has platos combinados from 575 ptas and a *menú* for 900 ptas.

Getting There & Away Buses from the SARFA station in Palafrugell run to La Siesta Camping, then Calella, then Llafranc, then back to La Siesta and Palafrugell, a return trip of 30 minutes (140 ptas). They go every half-hour or so from 7.40 am to 8.30 pm in July and August; the rest of the year, the service is progressively reduced to three or four buses a day from November to February.

Llafranc

Barely 2km north-east of Calella de Palafrugell and now merging with it along the roads back from the rocky coast between them, Llafranc has a smaller bay but a longer stretch of sand, is a bit more fashionable and lively, and gets more crowded. The tourist office (☎ 972 30 50 08), a kiosk on Carrer de Roger de Llúria just back from the western end of the beach, is open June to September, the same hours as Calella de Palafrugell's office.

Things to See & Do From the **Far de Sant Sebastià** lighthouse and **Ermita de Sant Sebastià** hermitage, up on Cap de Sant Sebastià, the cape to the east of the town, there are tremendous views in both directions along the coast. It's a 30 or 40 minute walk up: head up the steps from the harbour, then follow the road up to the right. You can walk on to Tamariu, too, but check with the tourist office about the most scenic of the several routes available.

Places to Stay & Eat *Camping Kim's* (☎ 972 61 67 75) is in a pine wood on Camí de la Font d'en Xeco, about 750m back from the beach. It's open from April to September and charges 2950 ptas, plus IVA, for two adults, a tent and a car.

Residencia Montaña (☎ 972 30 04 04, *Carrer de Cesàrea 2*), off Plaça del Promontori, is not a bad deal if you don't mind taking half-board (5350 ptas, or 6650 ptas from late July to mid-August). Prices drop to 3200/4300 ptas for B&B in the low season. *Pensió Celimar* (☎ 972 30 13 74, *Carrer de Carudo 12*), also off Plaça del Promontori, is more modern, stays open all year and has doubles with private bath for 6000 ptas plus IVA.

La Pasta at the western end of Passeig de Cipsela is popular for its pizzas and salads from 700 ptas. About 50m in from the beach, *Restaurante Bahía (Plaça del Promontori 8)* has a variety of main courses ranging from 800 ptas to 1800 ptas.

Getting There & Away See the Calella de Palafrugell section for information on bus services. The Llafranc stop is on Carrer de la Sirena, up the hill on the Calella side of town.

Tamariu

Three or four kilometres north up the coast from Llafranc as the crow flies, and nearly twice as far by road, Tamariu is smaller and attracts a quieter, more select Catalan crowd. Its beach has some of the cleanest waters on Spain's Mediterranean coast. The tourist office (☎ 972 62 01 93), in the middle of the village on Carrer de la Riera, is open the same months and hours as Llafranc's office.

Places to Stay & Eat *Camping Tamariu* (☎ 972 62 04 22), about 1km back from the beach on Carrer de la Riera, is open from May to September and charges 2300 ptas plus IVA for two adults, a tent and a car.

Hotel Sol d'Or (☎ 972 30 04 24, *Carrer de la Riera 18*), 500m nearer to the beach, is open from June to September. Doubles with private bath are 5850 ptas plus IVA. *Hotel Tamariu* (☎ 972 62 00 31, *Passeig del Mar 2*) is right on the beach and has doubles for up to 8400 ptas (closed October to mid-May) and a good but expensive Catalan restaurant, with few main dishes under 1500 ptas. The beachfront is lined with seafood eateries – *Restaurant Royal* is one of the best.

Getting There & Away SARFA buses from Palafrugell run to Tamariu (15 minutes; 140 ptas) three or four times daily, from mid-June to mid-September only.

A rough road will take you on to Aiguablava (see Beaches near Begur later).

Begur

The **castell**, dating from the 10th century, on a rock above the village, is still pretty much in the state in which it was left by Spanish troops who wrecked it in 1810 to impede the advance of Napoleon's army. Dotted around the village are half a dozen towers built for defence against 16th and 17th century pirates. There's a tourist office (☎ 972 62 40 20) on Plaça de l'Església, in the ajuntament facing the church.

Places to Stay The pine-shaded *Camping Begur* (☎ 972 62 32 01), open from April to September, is about 2km south on the road from Palafrugell. *Hotel Rosa* (☎ 972 62 30 15, *Carrer de Forgas i Puig 6*), a few steps towards the castle from the church, has nice rooms with bath; singles/doubles with buffet breakfast are

CATALUNYA

4300/9800 ptas (3700/7300 ptas in June and September).

Getting There & Away SARFA (☎ 972 62 24 26) at Plaça de Forgas 6 runs three daily buses to Barcelona's Estació del Nord (2¼ hours) via Palafrugell. On weekdays one SARFA bus runs to Girona.

Beaches near Begur

You can reach a series of smallish beaches, on an enticing stretch of coast, by turning east off the Palafrugell road 2km south of the centre of Begur. About 2km down is a turning to the black sand beach of **Platja Fonda** (1km). Half a kilometre farther on is the turning to **Fornells** (1km), a small village on one of the most picturesque bays of the whole Costa Brava, with a marina, beach and incredibly blue waters.

The large but friendly *Hotel Aiguablava* *(☎ 972 62 20 58, fax 972 62 21 12)* overlooking most of this has doubles for 13,000 ptas plus IVA (closed mid-November to mid-February). *Hotel Bonaigua (☎ 972 62 20 50, fax 972 62 20 54)*, back up the street a little, charges 10,000 ptas plus IVA (closed October to March). Back up at the Fornells turning, *Restaurant Ondina (☎ 972 62 20 52)*, open April to October, has four rooms at 7500 ptas a double, plus IVA.

One kilometre on from the Fornells turning is **Aiguablava**, with a slightly bigger and busier beach, and the *Parador Nacional de la Costa Brava (☎ 972 62 21 62)* enjoying lovely views back across the Fornells bay. Doubles start at 19,500 ptas plus IVA.

Another road from Begur leads a couple of kilometres east to **Aiguafreda**, a beach on a lovely cove backed by pine-covered hills, and, a bit farther south, the slightly more built-up **Sa Tuna** beach. If you fancy staying, try *Hostal Sa Rascassa (☎ 972 62 42 47)* at Aiguafreda.

Getting There & Away A Bus Platges (beach bus) service runs from Plaça de Forgas in Begur between late June and mid-September.

CASTELL DE PÚBOL

The Castell de Púbol at La Pera, just south of the C-255 and 22km north-west of Palafrugell, forms the southernmost point of north-east Catalunya's 'Salvador Dalí triangle', whose other elements include the Teatre-Museu Dalí in Figueres and the Cadaqués area where the artist spent much of his life.

Dalí bought the Gothic and Renaissance castle – which includes a 14th century church – in 1968 and gave it to his wife, Gala, who lived here without him until her death. Local lore has it that the notoriously promiscuous Gala was still sending for young village men almost right up to the time she died in 1982, aged 88. On her death, Dalí himself moved into Púbol, but abandoned it after the fire, which nearly burnt him to a crisp in 1984, to live out his last years at Figueres.

The castle was done up by Dalí in his inimitable style, with lions' heads staring from the tops of cupboards, statues of elephants with giraffes' legs in the garden and a stuffed giraffe staring at Gala's tomb in the crypt. The strength of the artist's passion for Gala is shown by motifs and reminders of her all over the castle. A visit is in effect a tour of the couple's tortured relationship. The blue bedroom in which Dalí nearly burnt to death now has a bright red fire extinguisher standing ready in the corner. There are many other sumptuous beds in other rooms. In the garage is the blue Cadillac in which Dalí took Gala for a last drive round the estate – after she died.

It is open from March to October only. From July to the end of September the hours are from 10.30 am to 8 pm daily. For the remaining months it opened daily but Monday from 10.30 am to 5.30 pm (600 ptas). SARFA buses between Palafrugell and Girona run along the C-255.

GIRONA

Northern Catalunya's largest city, Girona (Gerona in Castilian, population 75,000) sits in a valley 36km inland from Palafrugell. Its impressive medieval centre, climbing a hill above the Riu Onyar, makes it well worth a visit.

The Roman town of Gerunda lay on the Via Augusta, the highway from Rome to Cádiz (Carrer de la Força in Girona's old town follows part of the line of the Via Augusta). Taken from the Muslims by the Franks in 797, Girona became capital of one of Catalunya's most important counties, falling under the sway of Barcelona in the late 9th century. Its wealth in medieval times produced many fine Romanesque and Gothic buildings, which have survived repeated attacks and sieges down the centuries.

Orientation

The narrow streets of the old town climb above the eastern bank of the Riu Onyar and are easy to explore on foot. Several road and foot bridges link it to the new town across the river. The train station is 1km to the south-west, on Plaça d'Espanya off Carrer de Barcelona, with the estació d'autobusos behind it on Carrer de Rafael Masó i Valentí.

Information

The tourist office (☎ 972 22 65 75) is towards the southern end of the old town, at Rambla de la Llibertat 1. It's open Monday to Friday from 8 am to 8 pm, Saturday from 8 am to 2 pm and 4 to 8 pm and Sunday from 9 am to 2 pm.

There are branches of La Caixa bank, with ATMs, on Carrer dels Abeuradors off Rambla de la Llibertat and on Carrer Nou just across the Riu Onyar. The main correos is at Avinguda de Ramon Folch 2, also across the river. The postcode is 17080. You can connect to the Internet at Ciberxuxes at Carrer del Carme 55.

The Policía Nacional *comisaría* (☎ 091), Carrer de Sant Pau 2, is at the north end of the old town; the Policía Municipal (☎ 972 41 90 92) are at Carrer de Bernat Bacià 4. The Hospital de Santa Caterina (☎ 972 18 26 00) is at Plaça de l'Hospital 5, also west of the river.

Two good bookshops in the old town for maps and local guides are Les Voltes on Plaça del Vi and Geli at Carrer de la Argenteria 18.

Catedral

The fine baroque façade of the cathedral stands at the head of a majestic flight of steps rising from Plaça de la Catedral. Most of the building, however, is much older than its façade. Repeatedly rebuilt and altered down the centuries, it has Europe's widest Gothic nave (23m). The cathedral's museum, through the door marked 'Claustre Tresor', contains the masterly Romanesque *Tapís de la Creació* (Tapestry of the Creation) and a Mozarabic illuminated *Beatus* manuscript from 975. The 400 ptas fee for the museum also admits you to the beautiful 12th century Romanesque cloister, whose 112 stone columns have some fine, although rather weathered, carving. From the cloister you can see the 13th century Torre de Carlemany bell tower, also Romanesque.

Museu d'Art

Next door to the cathedral, in the 12th to 16th century Palau Episcopal, the art museum's collection ranges from Romanesque woodcarvings through to early 20th century painting. It's open Tuesday to Saturday from 10 am to 6 pm (to 7 pm in summer), Sunday and holidays from 10 am to 2 pm. Entry is 200 ptas.

Església de Sant Feliu

Girona's second great church, in part unflatteringly disguised by scaffolding at the time of writing, stands downhill from the cathedral. The 17th century main façade, with its landmark single tower, is on Plaça de Sant Feliu, but the entrance is round the side. Put 100 ptas in the slot inside the door to light up the interior. The nave has 13th century Romanesque arches but 14th to 16th century Gothic upper levels. In the northernmost of the chapels at the far (western) end of the church there's a masterly Catalan Gothic

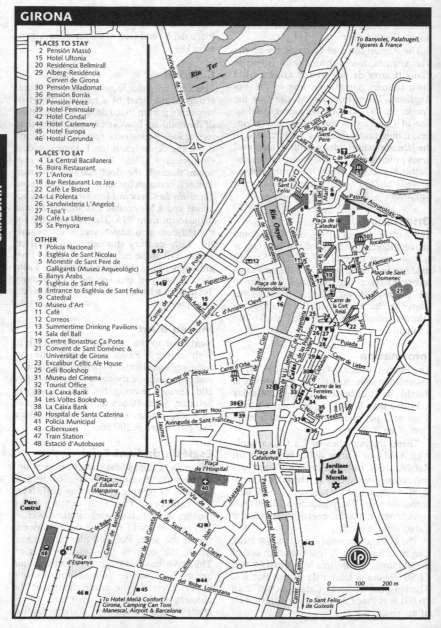

GIRONA

PLACES TO STAY
2 Pensión Massó
15 Hotel Ultonia
20 Residéncia Bellmirall
29 Alberg-Residéncia
   Cerveri de Girona
30 Pensión Viladomat
36 Pensión Borràs
37 Pensión Pérez
39 Hotel Peninsular
42 Hotel Condal
44 Hotel Carlemany
45 Hotel Europa
46 Hostal Gerunda

PLACES TO EAT
4 La Central Bacallanera
16 Boira Restaurant
17 L'Anfora
18 Bar Restaurant Los Jara
22 Café Le Bistrot
24 La Polenta
26 Sandwixteria L'Angelot
27 Tapa't
28 Café La Llibreria
35 Sa Penyora

OTHER
1 Policia Nacional
3 Església de Sant Nicolau
5 Monestir de Sant Pere de
   Galligants (Museu Arqueològic)
6 Banys Àrabs
7 Església de Sant Feliu
8 Entrance to Església de Sant Feliu
9 Catedral
10 Museu d'Art
11 Café
12 Correos
13 Summertime Drinking Pavilions
18 Sala del Ball
19 Centre Bonastruc Ça Porta
21 Convent de Sant Doménec &
   Universitat de Girona
23 Excalibur Celtic Ale House
25 Geli Bookshop
31 Museu del Cinema
32 Tourist Office
33 La Caixa Bank
34 Les Voltes Bookshop
38 La Caixa Bank
40 Hospital de Santa Caterina
41 Policia Municipal
43 Ciberxuxes
47 Train Station
48 Estació d'Autobusos

sculpture, Aloi de Montbrai's alabaster *Crist Jacent* (Recumbent Christ).

Banys Àrabs

The 'Arab baths' on Carrer de Ferran Catòlic are, although modelled on earlier Muslim and Roman bathhouses, actually a 12th century Christian affair in Romanesque style. They're the only public baths yet discovered from medieval Christian Spain, where, in reaction to the Muslim obsession with water and cleanliness, washing almost came to be regarded as ungodly. The baths contain a changing room, the *apodyterium*, followed by the *frigidarium* and *tepidarium*, with respectively cold and warm water, and the *caldarium*, a kind of sauna. Opening hours are Tuesday to Saturday from 10 am to 7 pm (summer only) and Sunday and holidays from 10 am to 2 pm; the rest of the year it's open daily from 10 am to 2 pm (200 ptas).

Passeig Arqueològic

Across the street from the Banys Àrabs, steps lead up into lovely gardens that follow the city walls up to the 18th century Portal de Sant Cristòfol gate, from which you can walk back down to the cathedral.

Monestir de Sant Pere de Galligants

Down across the little Riu Galligants, this 11th and 12th century Romanesque monastery has another lovely cloister with some marvellous animal and monster carvings on the capitals of its pillars. The monastery houses Girona's **Museu Arqueològic** (archaeology museum), whose exhibits range from prehistoric to medieval times and includes Roman mosaics and medieval Jewish tombstones. Opening hours are Tuesday to Saturday from 10.30 am to 1.30 pm and 4 to 7 pm (winter from 10 am to 2 pm and 4 to 6 pm) and Sunday and holidays from 10 am to 2 pm (200 ptas).

Església de Sant Nicolau

This pretty little Lombard-style 12th century Romanesque church in front of the Monestir de Sant Pere de Galligants is unusual in having an octagonal tower, and three apses laid out in a trefoil plan.

Catalan Romanesque Architecture

Catalunya, through its contacts with southern France and northern Italy, was the first part of Spain affected by the wave of Romanesque architecture and art that rippled across Western Europe from about the 10th century. A blend of ancient Roman traditions and Carolingian experimentation, the Romanesque style was at first disseminated chiefly by master builders from Byzantine-influenced Lombardy in northern Italy.

Typical features of the simple early Romanesque churches were massive masonry to support barrel vaults; tall, square bell towers; aisles separated by lines of pillars joined by semicircular arches; semicircular arches round doors and windows; semicircular apses; and blind arcades and pilasters on outside walls.

From the end of the 11th century stonemasons began to deck Catalan churches with increasing amounts of sculpture (notably on the capitals of columns), and bigger churches started to appear, with up to five aisles and apses, transepts and some fine cloisters.

Catalunya has over 2000 surviving Romanesque buildings. They're much more numerous in what's known as Catalunya Vella (Old Catalunya) – roughly north of a line from Sitges to Tremp – which was taken from the Muslims in the 9th century, than in the southern Catalunya Nova (New Catalunya), which remained in Muslim hands till the mid-12th century.

The Call

Until 1492, Girona was home to Catalunya's second most important medieval Jewish community (after Barcelona), and its Jewish quarter, the Call, centred on Carrer de la Força. For an idea of medieval Jewish life and culture here, visit the **Centre Bonastruc Ça Porta**, entered from a narrow alley off the upper side of Carrer de la Força. Named after Jewish Girona's most illustrious figure, a 13th century Cabbalist philosopher and mystic, the centre – a warren of rooms and stairways around a courtyard – has exhibitions and a café and is a focus for studies of Jewish Spain. It's open Monday to Saturday from 10 am to 8 pm and Sunday and holidays from 10 am to 2 pm (200 ptas).

Passeig de la Muralla

You can walk along a good length of the top of the city walls, the Passeig de la Muralla, from Plaça de Josep Ferrater i Mora, just south of the Universitat de Girona building at the top of the old town, down to Plaça del General Marvà near Plaça de Catalunya. This southern part of the old town dates from the 13th century onwards – a bit younger than the more northerly area centred on the cathedral, where the Roman and early medieval towns stood.

Museu del Cinema

In 1998 Spain's first cinema museum opened its doors in the Casa de les Aigües and has proven one of the town's biggest hits. The Col.lecció Tomàs Mallol includes not only has displays tracing the history of cinema, but a parade of hands-on items for indulging in shadow games, optical illusions and the like – great for kids. The museum is open daily, except Monday, from 10 am to 8 pm (6 pm from October to May; 400 ptas).

Places to Stay – Budget

The nearest camping ground is *Camping Can Toni Manescal* (☎ 972 47 61 17, *Fornells de la Selva*), 7km south of Girona. It only holds 140 people but is open all year.

Girona has a good modern youth hostel, the *Alberg-Residència Cerverí de Girona* (☎ 972 21 80 30, *Carrer dels Ciutadans 9*), which is well placed in the old town. It's only available from July to September. High-season rates are charged all year.

There are several pensiones and hostales in the old town. In July and August the better ones fill up quickly. *Pensión Pérez* (☎ 972 22 40 08, *Plaça de Bell.lloc 4*) has .a gloomy entrance stairway but clean, adequate singles/doubles for 1600/2800 ptas. The owners have another cheap place with the same phone number, the *Pensión Borràs* round the corner at Travessera d'Auriga 6.

Pensión Massó (☎ 972 20 71 75, *Plaça de Sant Pere 12*) has rooms with shared baths for 2900 ptas a double; the sign just says '*Habitacions*'.

One of the nicest cheaper places in the old town is *Pensión Viladomat* (☎ 972 20 31 76, *Carrer dels Ciutadans 5*). Comfortable singles/doubles without own bath are 2000/4000 ptas, and there are a few doubles with private bath for 6000 ptas.

The fairly modern *Hotel Peninsular* (☎ 972 20 38 00, *Carrer Nou 3*), just west of the Riu Onyar, has 68 rooms at 2200/3250 ptas with shared bath, or 3950/6000 ptas with private bath, all plus IVA. *Hostal Gerunda* (☎ 972 20 22 85, *Carrer de Barcelona 34*), near the train station, has doubles with private bath for 3600 ptas.

Places to Stay – Mid-Range & Top End

The attractive little *Residència Bellmirall* (☎ 972 20 40 09, *Carrer de Bellmirall 3*) is in a lovely medieval building with singles/doubles for 4540/7200 ptas, or 4800/7800 ptas with shower and toilet, including breakfast.

Everything else in this price range is in the new town west of the Riu Onyar. *Hotel Condal* (☎ 972 20 44 62, *Carrer de Joan Maragall 10*) and *Hotel Europa* (☎ 972 20 27 50, *Carrer de Julí Garreta 21*) both have doubles for from 5000 to 6000 ptas. *Hotel Ultònia* (☎ 972 20 38 50, *Gran Via de*

Jaume I 22) is ugly on the outside but has well-equipped double at 9900 ptas plus IVA.

Top of the tree are the modern *Hotel Melià Confort Girona (☎ 972 40 05 00, Carrer de Barcelona 112)*, where a double costs 13,800 ptas plus IVA, and *Hotel Carlemany (☎ 972 21 12 12)* on Plaça de Miquel Santaló, with doubles for 15,470 ptas plus IVA.

Places to Eat

The cafés under the arcades on Rambla de la Llibertat and nearby Plaça del Vi are good places to soak up a bit of atmosphere. Several of those on Rambla de la Llibertat offer decent paella for 850 ptas or more.

The bright *Sandwitxeria L'Angelot (Carrer de la Cort Reial 3)* is popular for its pancakes and salads from 475 ptas. Across the street, *Tapa't* has a great range of tapas from 225 ptas. You can tuck into some vegetarian goodies at *La Polenta (Carrer de la Cort Reial 6)*, where mains range from 600 to 1000 ptas. Another veggie option is *Sa Penyora (Carrer Nou del Teatre)*, with a *menú* for 1500 ptas.

Cafè Le Bistrot on Pujada de Sant Domènec, one of the most picturesque stairways in the old town, is a treat. Vaguely bohemian, it serves salads, *pizzes de pagès* (good, little bread-based pizzas) and crêpes for between 500 and 700 ptas. Also nice is the calm *Cafè La Llibreria* on Carrer de les Ferreries Velles, doing light meals such as lasagne or *escalivada* for 700 ptas or green salads for up to 500 ptas.

Bar Restaurant Los Jara (Carrer de la Força 4) and *L'Anfora* just up the hill at No 15 both have four-course *menús* for around 1500 ptas.

Plaça de la Independència in the new town is a popular munching area. The busy *Boira Restaurant* offers two *menús*: one at 1200 ptas and the other for 1950 ptas.

If you're a cod-lover, *La Central Bacallanera (Carrer de Santa Lucia 4)* might be for you. You can sup on variations of the *bacalao* theme from 750 to 1450 ptas amid a fishy blue décor.

Entertainment

Students make the nightlife here, so in summer things tend to calm down. Thursday is actually the big night, as most people head for the coast on weekends.

The old town has lots of good bars and cafés for evening *copas* along Rambla de la Llibertat and around Carrer de Carreras Peralta. A seemingly nameless *café (Carrer de les Ballesteries 23)* stays open longer than some and is a popular spot overlooking the river. If the Irish theme is your thing, try *Escalibur Celtic Ale House (Carrer de la Cort Reial)*. You can keep going to 3 am or so near the river just north of the old town, where streets such as Carrer de Palafrugell and Ronda de Pedret harbour several lively and varied music bars.

In summer, a series of drinking tents go up in the park west of the railway line – that's where the action is at that time of year. Across the road, the cyber-techno *Sala del Ball* is Girona's dance destination.

Getting There & Away

Air Girona's airport (☎ 972 18 66 00), 11km south of the centre just off the A-7 and N-II, is devoted to summer charter flights for Costa Brava tourists.

Bus Barcelona Bus (☎ 972 20 24 32) runs to/from Barcelona's Estació del Nord (1¼ hours) and Figueres (50 minutes) three to seven times daily. SARFA (☎ 972 20 17 96) runs buses to most parts of the Costa Brava. TEISA (☎ 972 20 02 75) runs eight services daily (four on Sunday) to Besalú (50 minutes) and Olot (1¼ hours; 620 ptas).

Train Girona (station ☎ 972 20 70 93) is on the railway between Barcelona, Figueres and Portbou on the French border. There are around 20 trains a day to Figueres (30 to 40 minutes; 320 to 370 ptas, 2nd class) and Barcelona (1½ hours; 765 to 880 ptas), and about 15 to Portbou and/or Cerbère (500 to 575 ptas). A few trains a day go through to Montpellier in France, or beyond.

Getting Around

There's no airport bus service. You can call a taxi on ☎ 972 20 33 77 or ☎ 972 22 23 33.

Parking in the old town is fraught, but you can leave your metal steed in several parking areas across the river.

BESALÚ

In the 10th and 11th centuries, pretty Besalú was the capital of an independent county that stretched as far west as Cerdanya, before it came under Barcelona's control in 1111.

Most picturesque of all is the view of the village across the tall, crooked 11th century **Pont Fortificat** (fortified bridge), with its two tower-gates, from the southern side of the Fluvià.

The tourist office (☎ 972 59 12 40) on the arcaded central square, Plaça de la Llibertat, is open only from June to mid-October, from 10 am to 2 pm and 4 to 7 pm daily. It hands out a decent map-brochure, sells 50 ptas tickets for the **Miqvé** (a 12th century Jewish ritual bath by the river) and does worthwhile guided visits to the Miqvé, the bridge and the Romanesque **Església de Sant Vicenç**, otherwise normally closed. Have a look at the 11th century Romanesque church of the **Monestir de Sant Pere**, with an unusual ambulatory (walkway) behind the altar, and the 12th century Romanesque **Casa Cornellà**.

Places to Stay & Eat

There are three good little places to stay. *Habitacions Venència (☎ 972 59 12 57, Carrer Major 8)* has singles/doubles for 2200/4000 ptas. *Fonda Siques (☎ 972 59 01 10, Avinguda del President Lluís Companys 6)* offers doubles with bath for 3800 ptas and 4900 ptas plus IVA; the latter were renovated a couple of years back. *Residència Marià (☎ 972 59 01 06, Plaça de la Llibertat 15)* has doubles with bathroom, TV and heating (handy in winter) for 4200 ptas.

Restaurant Can Quei, facing the Església de Sant Vicenç, has a three-course *menú* for 1200 ptas including wine. Or you can eat at a couple of places on Plaça de la Llibertat (*Residència Marià* is good), or at the *Fonda Siques*, which has good home-style food in a 1100 ptas *menú*, or at the more expensive *Restaurant Pont Vell*, by the bridge, where good Catalan mains can cost up to 1750 ptas.

Getting There & Away

The N-260 road from Figueres to Olot meets the C-160 from Girona at Besalú. See the Girona and Figueres sections for information on TEISA bus services to Besalú and on to Olot. The stop in Besalú is on the main road just west of Fonda Siques.

TORROELLA DE MONTGRÍ

On the Riu Ter about 30km north-east of Girona and 15km north of Palafrugell, the agreeable old town of Torroella de Montgrí (population 7000) is the funnel through which travellers to the coastal resort of L'Estartit must pass.

The tourist office (☎ 972 75 73 01) is at Carrer Major 1.

Things to See

About 100m south of the porticoed central square, Plaça de la Vila, in an old mansion at Carrer Major 28, the **Museu del Montgrí** will tell you about local history and archaeology, and a bit about the Illes Medes off L'Estartit. Entry is free and it's open Monday to Saturday from 10 am to 2 pm and 6 to 9 pm (5 to 7 pm from October to March) and Sunday and holidays from 11 am to 2 pm (closed Tuesday and holidays from October to March). Three blocks north of Plaça de la Vila is the **Església de Sant Genís**, which is mainly 15th century Gothic (with fine ceiling tracery) but has an 18th century baroque main façade at the western end.

Overlooking the town from the top of the 300m limestone Montgrí hills to the north, the impressive but empty **Castell de Montgrí** was built between 1294 and 1301 for King Jaume II in his efforts to bring to heel the disobedient counts of Empúries, to the north. There's no road and by foot it's a 40 minute climb from Torroella. Head north from Plaça del Lledoner along Carrer de Fàtima, at the end of which is a sign pointing you to the castle.

Places to Stay & Eat

Pensió Mitjà (☎ 972 75 80 03, Carrer de l'Església 14), open all year and a block north of Plaça de la Vila, has bare but decent singles/doubles with bath and TV for 2500/5000 ptas. They do food too.

Four blocks west of Plaça de la Vila, *Pensión Marin (☎ 972 75 87 74, Plaça de Quintana i Combis 12)* has doubles only, with shower, for 4200 ptas.

The *cafés* on Plaça de la Vila are the best place for people-watching.

Getting There & Away

AMPSA (☎ 972 75 82 33) at Plaça d'Espanya 19 (three blocks west, then two south, from Plaça de la Vila) runs buses about hourly to L'Estartit (140 ptas) and three or four daily to Girona. SARFA (☎ 972 75 90 04) at Passeig de Catalunya 61 (three blocks east, then one north, from Plaça de la Vila) has three or four daily buses to Barcelona's Estació del Nord (1¾ hours), four to Palafrugell and three or four to L'Escala and Figueres (1¼ hours).

VERGES

About 15km east of Girona, this town has little to offer, but if you happen to be in the area on Holy Thursday (Easter) make an effort to see the rather macabre evening procession, the *Dansa de la Mort*. People dressed up as skeletons dance the Dance of Death through the streets in a festivity that seems to have little to do with the Last Supper! The fun usually starts about 10 pm. Girona-Torroella buses pass through here.

L'ESTARTIT & THE ILLES MEDES

L'Estartit, 6km east of Torroella de Montgrí, has a long, wide beach of fine sand but nothing over any other Costa Brava package resort – except for the Illes Medes (Islas Medes). The group of rocky islets barely 1km offshore are home to some

of the most abundant marine life on Spain's Mediterranean coast.

The main road in from Torroella de Montgrí is called Avinguda de Grècia as it approaches the beach; the beachfront road is Passeig Marítim, at the northern end of which is the tourist office (☎ 972 75 19 10).

Illes Medes

The shores and waters around these seven islets, an offshore continuation of the limestone Montgrí hills, have been protected since 1985 as a Reserva Natural Submarina (underwater natural reserve), which has brought a proliferation in their marine life and made them Spain's most popular goal for snorkellers and divers. Some 1345 vegetable and animal species have been identified here. There's a big bird population too; one of the Mediterranean's biggest colonies of yellow-legged gulls (8000 pairs) breeds here between March and May.

A series of kiosks by the harbour at the northern end of L'Estartit beach offer snorkelling and glass-bottomed boat trips to the islands. Other glass-bottomed trips go to a series of caves along the coast to the north, or combine these with the Medes. A two-hour snorkelling trip to the Illes Medes costs about 1400 ptas including equipment. Trips go frequently every day from June to September and, depending on demand, in April, May and October.

Diving

The range of depths (down to 50m), and the number of underwater cavities and tunnels around the Illes Medes contribute much to their attraction. On and around rocks near the surface are colourful algae and sponges as well as octopuses, crabs and some large and small fish. Below 10 or 15m, cavities and caves harbour lobsters, scorpion fish and large conger eels and groupers. Some groupers and perch may feed from the hand. If you get down to the sea floor you may see angler fish, thornback rays or marbled electric rays.

At least half a dozen outfits in L'Estartit can take you out scuba diving, at the Medes or off the mainland coast – the tourist office has lists of them. It's worth shopping around before taking the plunge. If you're already a qualified diver, a single two hour trip usually costs between 2500 and 4000 ptas per person. If you need to rent all the gear, the extra cost will be somewhere between 2000 and 3500 ptas. Night dives are possible too. If you're a novice, you can do a one-day introductory course for around 7000 ptas or a full, five day PADI Open Water Diver course for 50,000 to 60,000 ptas.

Places to Stay

Apart from the eight camping grounds in and around the town (none are open from November to March), budget accommodation doesn't really exist unless you're on a package.

Some of the better options are opposite the harbour at the northern end of the beach. *Hostal La Sirena (☎ 972 75 07 22, Passeig Marítim 19)* charges 3500/7000 ptas for rooms with balcony and a little less without. It is open from April to October. *Pensión Xumetra (☎ 972 75 85 96, Carrer de Les Illes 55)* nearby has no sea view and charges around 3200/4000 ptas plus IVA with bath. *Hotel Les Illes (☎ 972 75 12 39)*, next door at the same address and open March to November, has rooms with bath for 3640 ptas per person with breakfast.

Places to Eat

The northern end of Passeig Marítim, by the roundabout, is swarming with eateries, as is its immediate vicinity. These places are all pretty similar, presenting a mix of Spanish fare and straightforward chicken-and-chips-style meals. Among the fancier restaurants, *La Gaviota (Passeig Marítim 92)* has good fish and seafood. Expect to pay around 3000 ptas per person.

Getting There & Around

AMPSA buses to Torroella de Montgrí (about one hourly) and Girona (three or four daily) go from Passeig Marítim, 150m south of the tourist office. SARFA runs to Barcelona three or four times daily.

L'ESCALA & EMPÚRIES

L'Escala, on the coast 11km north of Torroella de Montgrí, is a pleasant medium-sized resort on the southern shore of the Golf de Roses. It's close to the ancient town of Empúries (Ampurias in Castilian) and, a few kilometres farther north, the wetlands of the Parc Natural dels Aiguamolls de l'Empordà.

Orientation & Information

If you arrive by SARFA bus, you'll alight on L'Escala's Plaça de les Escoles, where you'll find the tourist office (☎ 972 77 06 03) at No 1. The tourist office's summer hours are Monday to Saturday from 9 am to 8.30 pm and Sunday 10 am to 1 pm. Empúries is one kilometre round the coast to the north-west of the town centre.

Empúries

Empúries was probably the first, and certainly one of most important, Greek colonies on the Iberian Peninsula. Early Greek traders, pushing on from a trading post at Masilia (modern Marseille in France), set up a new post around 600 BC at what's now the village of Sant Martí d'Empúries, then an island. Soon afterwards they founded a mainland colony nearby, which forms part of the site you visit today. The colony came to be called Emporion (literally 'market') and remained an important trading centre, and conduit of Greek culture to the Iberians, for centuries.

Empúries was also the place where, in 218 BC, Roman legions landed in Spain to cut off Hannibal's supply lines in the Second Punic War. About 195 BC they set up a military camp and by 100 BC had added a town. A century later it had merged with the Greek one. Emporiae, as the place was then known, was abandoned in the late 3rd century AD, after raids by Germanic tribes. Later, an early Christian basilica and cemetery stood on the site of the Greek town, before the whole place, after over a millennium of use, disappeared altogether, to be rediscovered by archaeologists at the turn of the 20th century.

Many of the ancient stones now laid bare don't rise more than knee-high. You need a little imagination – and perhaps the aid of a taped commentary (600 ptas from the ticket office) – to make the most of it.

The Site In spring and summer the site is open from 10 am to 8 pm, with a pedestrian entrance from the seafront promenade in front of the ruins; just follow the coast from L'Escala to reach it. At other times the opening hours are from 10 am to 6 pm and the only way in is the vehicle approach from the Figueres road, about 1km from central L'Escala. Entry is 400 ptas.

The Greek town lies in the lower part of the site, closer to the shore. Main points of interest include the thick southern defensive walls; the site of the Asklepion, a shrine to the god of medicine, with a copy of his statue found here; and the Agora (town square), with remnants of the early Christian basilica and the Greek Stoa (market complex), beside it.

A small museum (the Museu d'Arqueologia in Barcelona has a bigger and better Empúries collection) separates the Greek town from the larger Roman town on the upper part of the site. Highlights of the Roman town include the mosaic floors of a 1st century BC house; the Forum; and the strong 1st century BC walls, said to have been built by Julius Caesar. Outside the walls is an oval amphitheatre.

A string of brown sand beaches stretches along in front of the site. On one stands a Greek stone jetty.

Places to Stay

Camping The nearest camping ground to the centre of L'Escala is the small *Camping La Escala* (☎ 972 77 00 84, Camí d'Ample 21), about 700m south of La Platja, charging 2950 ptas plus IVA for two adults with a car and tent. It is open from April to September. There are four other sites 2 to 4km east of the centre in the Riells and Montgó

areas of town and a further half-dozen or so along or near the beach within a few kilometres north of Empúries.

Youth Hostel The *Alberg d'Empúries* (☎ 972 77 12 00, Les Coves 41) is just south of the Empúries ruins. It has room for 68 people, in dorms of six or more. High-season rates are charged from April to September.

Hostales, Pensiones & Hotels A good bet, although often booked up in high season, is *Hostal Mediterrà/Mediterráneo* (☎ 972 77 00 28, Carrer de Riera 22-24), a block west of Carrer del Pintor Joan Massanet. Singles/doubles with shower cost 1800/3550 ptas in summer. Equally good is *Pensió Torrent* (☎ 972 77 02 78) at No 28, with rooms at 1900/3800 ptas. Singles are hard to come by in summer.

A step up in quality is *Hostal El Roser* (☎ 972 77 02 19, Carrer de l'Església 7), on the first street on the right as you go down Carrer de Santa Màxima from Plaça de les Escoles. Good-sized modern rooms with TV and bath are 3200/4700 ptas plus IVA; there are also some slightly cheaper older rooms in an annexe next door. In high season media pensión costs 4200 ptas per person.

On Passeig de Lluís Albert, 10 minutes walk east along the seafront from La Platja, *Hotel Voramar* (☎ 972 77 01 08) at No 2 has rooms for 4375/8750 ptas plus IVA and *Hotel Bonaire* (☎ 972 77 32 33) at No 4 has for 5158/10,117 plus IVA for B&B.

Places to Eat

L'Escala is famous for its *anchoas* (anchovies) and good fresh local fish, both of which are likely to crop up on *menús*.

The seafront restaurants are mostly expensive but, if your wallet is fat enough, try *Els Pescadors* on Port d'En Perris, the next bay west from La Platja (five minutes walk), which does superb baked and grilled seafood, *suquet* (seafood stew) and rice dishes. You will pay from 3000 to 4000 ptas a head unless you opt for the *menú* at

1680 ptas. *L'Olla* and *Volanti*, also on Port d'En Perris, both do pizzas for 700 to 950 ptas.

Just in from Port d'En Perris, **Restaurant El Gotin** *(Carrer de Puig Sureda 16)* offers a fair *menú* for 900 ptas. **Bar La Cala**, between La Platja and Port d'En Perris, has tables set up amid the rocks on the point.

Some of the hostales have good restaurants. **Hostal Poch** will do you a *menú* with paella starring as main course for 995 ptas.

Getting There & Away

SARFA has one bus from Barcelona (via Palafrugell) on weekdays (1½ hours), rising to three on Sunday. Five a day run to Figueres (50 minutes) and two to Girona (one hour).

PARC NATURAL DELS AIGUAMOLLS DE L'EMPORDÀ

This natural park preserves the remnants of marshes that once covered the whole coastal plain of the Golf de Roses, an important site for migrating birds. Birdwatchers have spotted over 100 species a day in the March-May and August-October migration periods, which bring big increases in the numbers of wading birds and even the occasional flamingo, glossy ibis, spoonbill or rare black stork. There are usually enough birds around to make a visit worthwhile at any time of year.

The best place to head for is the El Cortalet information centre (☎ 972 45 42 22), 1km off the Sant Pere Pescador-Castelló d'Empúries road. Marked paths lead to a 2km stretch of beach and a number of hides *(aguaits)* where you can view saltwater marshes and their bird life. The paths are always open, but morning and evening are the best times for watching birds (and mosquitoes!).

The nearest places to El Cortalet that you can reach by bus are Sant Pere Pescador, 6km south (served by four or five SARFA buses daily from L'Escala and Figueres), and Castelló d'Empúries, 4km north.

CASTELLÓ D'EMPÚRIES

This old town of 4000 people was the capital of Empúries, a medieval Catalan county that maintained a large degree of independence up to the 14th century. At the heart of the narrow streets in the old part of town you'll find Plaça dels Homes, with a tourist office (☎ 972 15 62 33) in a 14th century building.

The finest monument is the **Església de Santa Maria** on Plaça de Jacint Verdaguer, a large 13th and 14th century Gothic church with a fine Romanesque bell tower remaining from an earlier church on the site.

Places to Stay & Eat

Hotel Canet (☎ *972 25 03 40, fax 972 25 06 07, Plaça del Joc de la Pilota 2)*, a modernised 17th century mansion in the centre, has elegant singles/doubles with bath and breakfast for 4500/7500 ptas and a swimming pool in an interior courtyard. Its restaurant is reasonably priced.

In the newer part of town to the south there are three decent places close together on and just off Carrer de Santa Clara, with rooms for around 3000/5500 ptas: the modern **Hotel Empòrium** (☎ *972 25 05 93)* next to the bus stop, **Hostal Ca L'Anton** *(☎ 972 25 05 09)* and **Pensió/Fonda Serratosa** *(☎ 972 25 05 08)*. All have restaurants with *menús* ranging from 1000 to 1500 ptas.

Just off Castelló's southern bypass, **Hotel Allioli** *(☎ 972 25 03 20)* in the Urbanització Castell Nou is an attractively modernised old farmstead with a pool, garden, a fine array of Jabugo hams in the bar and simple but comfortable wood-beamed rooms with bath; it charges 7500/12,500 ptas plus IVA in July-August, but little more than half that for most of the rest of the year.

Getting There & Away

SARFA runs up to 15 buses a day to Figueres, as few as three to Cadaqués (50 minutes), three daily to/from Girona (45 minutes) and up to four to Barcelona's Estació del Nord (1½ hours).

CADAQUÉS & AROUND

If you have time for only one stop on the Costa Brava, you can hardly do better than Cadaqués. Little more than a whitewashed village round a rocky bay, it and the surrounding area have a special magic – a fusion of wind, sea, light and rock – that isn't dissipated even by the throngs of mildly fashionable summer visitors.

A portion of that magic owes itself to Salvador Dalí, who spent family holidays in Cadaqués in his youth and lived much of his later life at nearby Port Lligat. The empty moonscapes, odd-shaped rocks and barren shorelines that litter Dalí's paintings weren't just a product of his fertile imagination. They're strewn all round the Cadaqués area in what Dalí termed a 'grandiose geological delirium'.

The country here is drier than farther south. The sparseness continues to dramatic Cap de Creus, 8km north-east of Cadaqués, lending itself to some coastscapes of almost (if you'll permit us, Sr Dalí) surreal beauty.

Thanks to Dalí and other artists, Cadaqués pulled in an artistic, offbeat and celebrity crowd for decades. One visit by the poet Paul Éluard and his Russian wife Gala in 1929 caused an earthquake in Dalí's life: he broke with his family, ran off to Paris with Gala (who was to become his lifelong obsession and, later, his wife) and joined the surrealist movement. In the 1950s, after Dalí's success in the USA, the crowd he attracted was more jet-setting – Walt Disney, the Duke of Windsor and Greek ship-owner Stavros Niarchos. In the 1970s Mick Jagger and Gabriel García Márquez turned up. Today the crowd is neither so creative nor so famous – and a lot bigger – but Cadaqués' atmosphere remains.

Information

The tourist office (☎ 972 25 83 15) is at Carrer del Cotxe 2. The Policia Local (☎ 972 15 93 43) are a few steps behind the tourist office, on Carrer del Vigilant. There's a hospital (☎ 972 25 88 07) on Carrer de Guillem Bruguera, just west of the church.

The Town

Cadaqués is perfect for wandering, either around the town or along the coast. The 16th and 17th century **Església de Santa Maria**, with a gilded baroque *retablo*, is the focus of the older part with its narrow hilly streets.

Two art museums worth visiting are the **Centre d'Art Perrot-Moore** off Carrer del Vigilant, founded by Dalí's secretary and focusing on Dalí and Picasso. It is open daily from 10.30 am to 1.30 pm and 4 to 8 pm (800 ptas). The **Museu de Cadaqués**, Carrer de Narcís Monturiol 15, includes Dalí among other local artists. It is open daily from 11 am to 1.30 pm and 3 to 8 pm (600 ptas).

Beaches

Cadaqués' main beach, and several others along the nearby coasts, are small, with more pebbles than sand, but their picturesqueness and beautifully blue waters make up for that. Overlooking Platja Llaner on the southern side of the bay is Dalí's parents' holiday home; out the front is a statue by Josep Subirachs dedicated to Federico García Lorca, in memory of his 1920s stay.

Port Lligat

Port Lligat, a 1.25km walk from Cadaqués, is a tiny settlement around another lovely bay, with fishing boats pulled up on its beach. The **Casa Museu Dalí** here began as a fisherman's hut and was steadily altered and enlarged by Dalí, who lived here, apart from a dozen or so years abroad during and around the Spanish Civil War, from 1930 to 1982. It's the house with a lot of little white chimney pots and two egg-shaped towers, overlooking the western end of the beach.

Visits must be booked (☎ 972 25 80 63) and you are allowed a grand total of about 30 minutes inside as you are guided through. From mid-March to 1 November the house is open daily, except Monday,

CATALUNYA

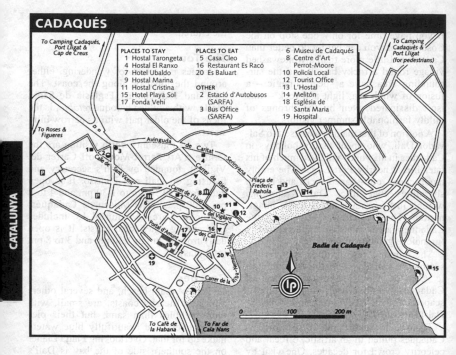

CADAQUÉS

To Camping Cadaqués,
Port Lligat &
Cap de Creus

To Roses &
Figueres

To Camping
Cadaqués &
Port Lligat
(for pedestrians)

PLACES TO STAY
1 Hostal Tarongeta
4 Hostal El Ranxo
7 Hotel Ubaldo
9 Hostal Marina
11 Hostal Cristina
15 Hotel Playa Sol
17 Fonda Vehí

PLACES TO EAT
5 Casa Cleo
16 Restaurant Es Racó
20 Es Baluart

OTHER
2 Estació d'Autobusos
(SARFA)
3 Bus Office
(SARFA)

6 Museu de Cadaqués
8 Centre d'Art
Perrot-Moore
10 Policía Local
12 Tourist Office
13 L'Hostal
14 Melitón
18 Església de
Santa Maria
19 Hospital

Avinguda de Caritat

Plaça de
Frederic
Rahola

Badia de Cadaqués

To Café de
la Habana

To Far de
Cala Nans

0   100   200 m

---

from 10.30 am to 6 pm. From mid-June to mid-September the hours are extended until 9 pm daily.

Cap de Creus

Eight kilometres north-east of Cadaqués by road, Cap de Creus (Cabo de Creus in Castilian) is the most easterly point of the Spanish mainland and a place of sublime, rugged beauty. With a steep, rocky coastline indented by dozens of lovely, turquoise-watered coves, it's an especially wonderful place to be at dawn or sunset. Atop the cape stand a lighthouse and a single good, mid-priced restaurant.

Hiking

There are infinite possibilities: out along the promontory between Cadaqués and Port Lligat; to Port Lligat and beyond; along the southern side of the Cadaqués bay to the Far

de Cala Nans lighthouse; or over the hills south of Cadaqués to the coast east of Roses. For a full day's outing you could walk to the Monestir de Sant Pere de Rodes and back, possibly via El Port de la Selva (see the Cadaqués to the French Border section later in this chapter); the Cadaqués tourist office can give you directions.

Places to Stay

Camping Cadaqués (☎ 972 25 81 26), about 1km from central Cadaqués on the road to Port Lligat, has room for about 500 people and can get crowded. Two adults with a tent and car pay 2880 ptas plus IVA. It is open from Semana Santa to September.

Fonda Vehí (☎ 972 25 84 70, Carrer de l'Església 5), near the church, has rooms with shared baths for 2000/3700 ptas, but it's only open in summer and tends to be booked up for July and August.

Hostal Cristina (☎ 972 25 81 38, Carrer de Riera s/n) has doubles only – they cost 4000 ptas or 5000 ptas with private bath. *Hostal Marina* (☎ 972 25 81 99, Carrer de Frederic Rahola 2) is probably a better bet, with singles/doubles at 3000 ptas per person, all with private bath.

Hotel Ubaldo (☎ 972 25 81 25, Carrer de la Unió 13), towards the back of the old part of town, has good doubles with bath, some with balcony, for 6900 ptas plus IVA. The singles, at 4500 ptas plus IVA, are not so hot. *Hostal El Ranxo* (☎ 972 25 80 05, Avinguda de Caritat Serinyana s/n) may have a room when others don't. Pleasant doubles with bath are 7000 ptas.

Hotel Playa Sol (☎ 972 25 81 00, fax 972 25 80 54, Platja Pianc 3) on the eastern side of the bay has singles for 9900 ptas and doubles for up to 17,500 ptas, plus IVA. Rooms have air-con, satellite TV and bath. There's a nice pool area too.

In Port Lligat, *Residencia/Aparthotel Calina* (☎ 972 25 88 51), near the small beach, has a range of pleasant modern rooms and one-room apartments from 8100 to 10,350 ptas a double. Its mid-priced restaurant opens on to a pool area. It's closed from November to February. *Hotel Port Lligat* (☎ 972 25 81 62), just back up the hill, has doubles from 10,600 ptas.

Places to Eat

The eastern part of the central beachfront is lined with spots proffering uninspired *menús* for 900 to 1200 ptas, or pizzas for 700 or 800 ptas. *Restaurant Es Racó*, (Carrer del Dr Callis 3) does a fine *fideuá* for 1250 ptas per person. Its balcony (400 ptas surcharge) overlooking the western half of the beach catches some breeze. *Fonda Vehí's* 2nd-floor restaurant does three-course *menús* for 1100 to 1300 ptas plus IVA.

Es Baluart (Carrer de Riba Nemesi Llorens 2) is several steps up in quality (and cost). A good full Catalan and/or seafood meal costs around 3000 ptas. If you feel less financially empowered, there's also a *menú* for 1450 ptas.

For a change from local fare, the Swedish-run *Casa Cleo*, a block behind the Centre d'Art Perrot-Moore, offers a variety of refreshing dishes. Count on leaving about 3500 ptas poorer.

Entertainment

L'Hostal, facing the beachfront *passeig* has live music on many nights. Press clippings posted outside proclaim that one night in the 1970s Dalí called it the 'lugar más bonito del mundo' ('the most beautiful place in earth'). The beachfront *Melitón* bar has a fine *terraza* but with prices to match. *Cafè de la Habana* can get lively, too.

Getting There & Away

SARFA (☎ 972 25 87 13) has buses to Castelló d'Empúries and Figueres (one hour) up to eight times daily (three in winter), to Girona (1½ hours) three times daily (one in winter) and to Barcelona (2¼ hours) two to five times daily.

CADAQUÉS TO THE FRENCH BORDER

If you want to prolong the journey to France, **El Port de la Selva**, **Llançà** and the border town **Portbou** are pleasant enough minor beach resorts-cum-fishing towns, all with a range of accommodation.

A more spectacular stop is the **Monestir de Sant Pere de Rodes**, a classic piece of Romanesque architecture looming 500m up in the hills south-west of El Port de la Selva, with great views. Founded in the 8th century, it later became the most powerful monastery between Figueres and Perpignan in France. The great triple-naved, barrel-vaulted basilica is flanked by the fine square Torre de Sant Miquel bell tower and a two-level cloister. The monastery (300 ptas, students 150 ptas) is open daily (closed Monday) and in July and August the hours are 10 am to 7 pm, while during the rest of the year it's open from 10 am to 1.30 pm and 3 to 5.30 pm (closed Monday).

CATALUNYA

CATALUNYA

Getting There & Away

The monastery is on a back road over the hills between Vilajuïga, 8km to its west, and El Port de la Selva, 5km north-east. Each town is served by three or four SARFA buses from Figueres daily, but there are no buses to the monastery. Vilajuïga is also on the railway between Figueres and Portbou.

FIGUERES

Twelve kilometres inland from the Golf de Roses, Figueres (Figueras in Castilian) is a humdrum town (some might say a dive) of 35,000 people with a single attraction: Salvador Dalí. In the 1960s and 70s Dalí created here, the town of his birth, the extraordinary Teatre-Museu Dalí. Whatever your feelings about old Salvador, this is worth every minute you spend on it.

Orientation

From the bus and train stations, on Plaça de l'Estació, it's a 10 minute walk north-west to the central boulevard, the Rambla. The Teatre-Museu Dalí is 200m north of the Rambla, with most of the sleeping and eating options concentrated within a few blocks of it.

Information

The tourist office (☎ 972 50 31 55) on Plaça del Sol is open Monday to Saturday from 9 am to 8 pm. In summer information kiosks also set up outside the bus station and the Teatre-Museu Dalí.

There's no shortage of banks or ATMs in the central area. American Express is at Viajes Figueres (☎ 972 50 91 00, Carrer de Peralada 28).

The correos is behind the tourist office on Plaça del Sol. The postcode is 17600. Cafè Virtual (☎ 972 67 51 90, cafevirtual@ sol10.es) at Plaça del Sol 10 has email and Internet facilities.

The police are on Carrer de Pep Ventura. A Creu Roja (Red Cross; ☎ 972 50 17 99) post is at Carrer de Santa Llogaia 67 and there's a hospital on Ronda del Rector Aroles.

Teatre-Museu Dalí

Salvador Dalí was born in Figueres in 1904 and went to school here. Although his career took him for spells to Madrid, Barcelona, Paris and the USA, he remained true to his roots and lived well over half his adult life at Port Lligat, near Cadaqués on the coast east of Figueres. Between 1961 and 1974 Dalí converted Figueres' former municipal theatre, ruined by a fire at the end of the civil war in 1939, into the Teatre-Museu Dalí. 'Theatre-museum' is an apt label for this multidimensional trip through one of the most fertile (or disturbed) imaginations of the 20th century, full of surprises, tricks and illusions, and containing a substantial portion of his life's work. 'The museum should not be considered as a museum, it is a gigantic surrealist object, everything in it is coherent, there is nothing which escapes my net of understandings,' explained its creator with characteristic modesty.

Even outside, the building aims to surprise, from the collection of bizarre sculptures outside the entrance on Plaça de Gala i Salvador Dalí to the pink wall along Pujada del Castell, topped by a row of Dalí's trademark egg shapes and what appear to be female gymnast sculptures.

Inside, the ground floor (level 1) includes a semicircular garden area on the site of the original theatre stalls. In its centre is a classic piece of weirdness called *Taxi Plujós* (Rainy Taxi), composed of an early Cadillac – said to have belonged to Al Capone – and a pile of tractor tyres, both surmounted by statues, with a fishing boat balanced precariously above the tyres. Put a coin in the slot and water washes all over the inside of the car. The Sala de Peixateries (Fish Shop Room) off here holds a collection of Dalí oils including the famous *Autoretrat tou amb tall de bacon fregit* (Self-Portrait with Fried Bacon) and *Retrat de Picasso*. Beneath the former stage of the theatre is the crypt, with Dalí's plain tomb.

The stage area (level 2), topped by a glass geodesic dome, was conceived as Dalí's

Dalí – the Last Decades

Salvador Dalí's life, itself never short on the surreal, seemed to tip over the edge during the time the Figueres theatre-museum was getting under way.

Having won huge success in the USA in the 1940s (and earned the anagram Avida Dollars) Dalí returned to his roots. In 1948 he came with Gala, the lover to whom he was obsessively devoted and who was the subject of many of his paintings, to live at Port Lligat near Cadaqués. In 1958 Dalí and Gala were married in a secret Catholic ceremony.

By the late 1960s, according to Colm Toíbín's *Homage to Barcelona* (1990), the couple had 'a whole court of helpers, hangers-on, advisers, secretaries and sexual performers'. Dalí bought the Castell de Púbol near Girona and in 1970 gave it to Gala, who was now enjoying a string of young lovers. He masochistically contracted never to visit the castle unless she summoned him, which she rarely did (although she phoned daily).

In 1975 Dalí, ever a glutton for outrage, sent the dying Franco a telegram of congratulations on the execution of five prisoners, a gesture which provoked widespread disgust and for which many people never forgave him. Subsequently, he became increasingly depressed and inaccessible; a prisoner himself, some say, of Gala and/or the 'minders' enriching themselves at his expense.

On Gala's death in 1982, Dalí moved into Púbol himself, but he almost died in a fire two years later. Frail and malnourished, he retired to the Torre Galatea, a tower adjoining the theatre-museum at Figueres (and now part of it), hardly ever leaving his room before he died in 1989. His tomb is part of the theatre-museum.

Sistine Chapel. The large egg-head-breasts-rocks-trees backdrop was part of a ballet set, one of Dalí's many ventures into the performing arts. If proof were needed of Dalí's acute sense of the absurd, *Gala mirando el Mar Mediterráneo* (Gala looking at the Mediterranean Sea) would be it. The work appears from the other end of the room, with the help of coin-operated viewfinders, to be a portrait of Abraham Lincoln. Off this room is the Sala del Tresor, where paintings such as *La panera del pa* (The Breadbasket) show that Dalí was a master draughtsman, too.

One floor up (level 3) you come across the Sala de Mae West, a living room whose components, viewed from the right spot, make up a portrait of Ms West: a sofa for her lips, twin fireplaces for nostrils, impressionist paintings of Paris for eyes. On the top floor (level 5) is a room containing works by other artists from Dalí's own collection, including El Greco's *Sant Pau* (St Paul).

From July to September the museum is open from 9 am to 7.15 pm daily and for most of this period there are night sessions from 10 pm to 12.30 am. Queues are long on summer mornings. From October to

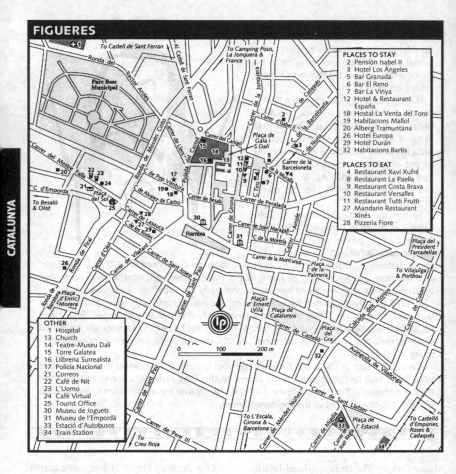

FIGUERES

PLACES TO STAY
2   Pensión Isabel II
3   Hotel Los Ángeles
5   Bar Granada
6   Bar El Reno
7   Bar La Vinya
12 Hotel & Restaurant España
18 Hostal La Venta del Toro
19 Habitacions Mallol
20 Alberg Tramuntana
26 Hotel Europa
29 Hotel Durán
32 Habitacions Bartis

PLACES TO EAT
4   Restaurant Xavi Xufré
8   Restaurant La Paella
9   Restaurant Costa Brava
10 Restaurant Versalles
11 Restaurant Tutti Frutti
27 Mandarin Restaurant Xinés
28 Pizzeria Fiore

OTHER
1   Hospital
13 Church
14 Teatre-Museu Dalí
15 Torre Galatea
16 Llibreria Surrealista
17 Policía Nacional
21 Correos
22 Café de Nit
23 L'Uomo
24 Café Virtual
25 Tourist Office
30 Museu de Joguets
31 Museu de l'Empordà
33 Estació d'Autobusos
34 Train Station

June it's open from 10.30 am to 5.15 pm daily (closed Mondays until the end of May, on 1 January and 25 December). Entry is 1000 ptas (800 ptas October to May) and 1200 ptas for the summer night sessions.

Other Things to See & Do

The **Museu de l'Empordà** at Rambla 2 combines Greek, Roman and medieval archaeological finds with a sizable collection of art, mainly by Catalan artists but there's also some works lent by the Prado in

Madrid. It is open from Tuesday to Saturday from 11 am to 1 pm and 3 to 7 pm and Sunday from 11 am to 1.30 pm (300 ptas).

At Rambla 10, the **Museu de Joguets**, Spain's only toy museum, was due to reopen by early 1999 after expansion works. It has more than 3500 Catalunya and Valencia-made toys from the pre-Barbie 19th and early 20th centuries.

The large 18th century **Castell de Sant Ferran** stands on a low hill 1km north-west of the centre. Built in 1750, it saw almost no action in the following centuries. After abandoning Barcelona, Spain's Republican government held its final meeting of the civil war on 1 February 1939 in the dungeons. Until 1997 it was owned by the army. It is open daily from 10.30 am to 2 pm (until 7 pm from June to September; 350 ptas).

The tourist office organises free guided tours of Figueres (minimum of eight participants), mostly in Spanish and Catalan but occasionally in English and French.

Places to Stay – Budget

Camping Pous (☎ *972 67 54 96)*, north of the centre on the N-II towards La Jonquera, is small and charges 2000 ptas for site, car and two adults. It closes in December. Don't sleep in the Parc Bosc Municipal: people have been attacked there at night.

The *Alberg Tramuntana* youth hostel (☎ *972 50 12 13, Carrer d'Anicet de Pagès 2)* is two blocks west of the tourist office. It holds only 56 people (in dorms of four to 24) but is open nearly all year; high-season rates are charged from July to September. It is one of the few hostels for which you can book through the IBN system.

Habitacions Bartis (☎ *972 50 14 73, Carrer de Méndez Núñez 2)*, on the way into the centre from the bus and train stations, has adequate singles/doubles for 1500/2500 ptas plus IVA.

Bar La Vinya (☎ *972 50 00 49, Carrer de Tins 18)*, three short blocks east of the Teatre-Museu Dalí, has bare rooms up the street on Carrer de la Muralla for 1200/2400 ptas. *Bar Granada* and *Bar El Reno*, also on Carrer de la Muralla, have rooms.

Much better is the almost elegant *Hotel España* (☎ *972 50 08 69, Carrer de la Jonquera 26)*, which has decent rooms for up to 4000/6600 ptas with shower, and a few cheaper ones without.

Pensión Isabel II (☎ *972 50 47 35, Carrer de Isabel II 16)* has reasonable rooms with bath for 2000/3800 ptas. *Hostal La Venta del Toro* (☎ *972 51 05 10, Carrer de Pep Ventura 5)* has bare but adequate doubles for 2700 ptas, or one with own shower for 3000 ptas. *Habitacions Mallol* (☎ *972 50 22 83)*, along the street at No 9, charges 1850/3200 ptas.

Places to Stay – Mid-Range

Hotel Los Ángeles (☎ *972 51 06 61, Carrer de Barceloneta 10)* is good value with roomy singles/doubles for 3980/6770 ptas plus IVA. *Hotel Europa* (☎ *972 50 07 44, Ronda Firal 37)* is another respectable mid-range hotel. Rooms with bath are 3250/5600 ptas plus IVA. *Hotel Durán* (☎ *972 50 12 50, fax 972 50 26 09, Carrer de Lasauca 5)*, just off the top end of the Rambla, has a bit more style. Comfortable, homy singles/doubles are 6200/8900 ptas plus IVA.

Places to Eat

Carrer de La Jonquera, just down the steps east of the Teatre-Museu Dalí, is lined with restaurants, among them *Restaurant España*, *Restaurant Tutti Frutti*, *Restaurant Versalles* and *Restaurant Costa Brava*, offering reasonable three-course *menús* for 700 to 900 ptas. *Restaurant La Paella*, two short blocks east on Carrer de Tins, does one for 950 ptas.

A quality leap upwards is *Restaurant Xavi Xufré (Carrer de la Muralla 7)* where you can get a bog standard *menú* for 1000 ptas, or try the gastronomic version for 2300 ptas.

For food of a different nationality, *Mandarin Restaurant Xinès (Carrer de Lasauca 11)* has a Chinese *menú* for 900 ptas, and *Pizzeria Fiore* across the street at No 16 does pizzas for 510 to 850 ptas.

The excellent restaurant of the *Hotel Durán (Carrer de Lasauca 5)* is a big step up, serving Catalan and Spanish specialities like *suquet de peix* (baked fresh fish) and *muslo de pato con nabos* (duck leg and turnips). You won't get much change from 3500 ptas for a full meal.

Entertainment

Two of the grooviest café-bars in town are right next to one another on Carrer del Mestre Falla – *Café de Nit* and *L'Uomo*.

CATALUNYA

Getting There & Away

Bus Barcelona Bus (☎ 972 50 50 29) runs to Girona (50 minutes) seven times a day, and on to Barcelona six times a day (2¼ hours).

SARFA serves Castelló d'Empúries 10 to 20 times daily and Cadaqués (one hour) up to eight times daily. TEISA runs to Besalú and Olot two or three times daily.

Train Figueres is on the railway between Barcelona, Girona and Portbou on the French border, and there are regular connections to Girona (30 to 40 minutes; 320 to 370 ptas in 2nd class), Barcelona and the French border.

The Pyrenees

The Pyrenees in Catalunya aren't as high as those in neighbouring Aragón, but still throw up some awesomely beautiful mountains and valleys.

If you have time to sample only one area of the Catalan Pyrenees, make for the Parc Nacional d'Aigüestortes i Estany de Sant Maurici, a jewel-like area of lakes and dramatic peaks in the north-west. Aside from the natural beauty of the mountains and valleys and the obvious attractions of walking, skiing and other activities, the Catalan Pyrenees and their foothills also have a rich cultural heritage, notably many lovely Romanesque churches and monasteries, often tucked away in surprisingly remote valleys. These are mainly the product of a time of prosperity and optimism in these regions in the 11th and 12th centuries, after Catalunya had broken ties with France in 988 and as the Muslim threat from the south receded. The distant past also remains alive in the distinctly medieval atmosphere of some of the mountain towns and villages, and in the region's rich folklore.

Skiing

Baqueira-Beret in the Vall d'Aran is one of Spain's biggest and best ski resorts. La Molina near Puigcerdà is also good, and

there are several other smaller ones, plus a number of Nordic skiing centres.

Trekking

The Pyrenees provide magnificent walking and trekking areas and this chapter suggests numerous routes, ranging from strolls of a couple of hours to day hikes that can be strung together into treks of several days. Nearly all of these can be done without camping gear, with nights spent in villages or *refugis*, mountain refuges that offer basic dormitory accommodation and often meals. If you're relying on a refuge, however, you should try to reserve places or at least establish that it's not going to be full. Contact numbers are given for most mentioned in this chapter and tourist offices can often tell

---

Walking in the Pyrenees

The best season for walking in the high Pyrenees is from late June to early September. Earlier than that, snow can make things difficult, and avalanches are possible. Later, the weather can turn poor. It can get very hot even at high altitudes in high summer, but nowhere in the Pyrenees is the weather reliable; even in July and August you can get plenty of rainy days and cloud – and cold at high altitude.

The Pyrenees are to be respected and anyone heading into the hills should be suitably fit, experienced and properly equipped for any conditions. This book suggests a number of walks, of varying length and toughness, but it is *not* a trekking or walking guide. The same can be said of other mountain areas covered in the course of the book.

For detailed route descriptions and advice on equipment and preparation, consult other sources such as those mentioned under Maps (under Planning), Books and Activities in the Facts for the Visitor chapter. Local advice from tourist offices, park rangers, mountain refuges and other walkers is also invaluable.

egants parade in Barcelona's biggest festival, the Cavalcada, Festes de la Mercè

Music, dancing and merrymaking in the Festes de la Mercè in Barcelona

you whether a booking is needed. Nearly all the refuges mentioned in this chapter are run by two Catalan alpine clubs based in Barcelona, the Federació d'Entitats Excursionistes de Catalunya (FEEC; ☎ 93 412 07 77), and the Centre Excursionista de Catalunya (CEC; ☎ 93 315 23 11). A night in a refuge costs up to 1200 ptas. Normally FEEC refuges allow you to cook, CEC ones don't. Moderately priced meals are often available.

The coast-to-coast GR-11 long-distance footpath traverses the entire Pyrenees from Cap de Creus on the Costa Brava to Hondarribia on the Bay of Biscay. Its route across Catalunya goes by way of La Jonquera, Albanyà, Beget, Setcases in the upper Ter valley, the Vall de Núria, Planoles, Puigcerdà, Andorra, south of Catalunya's highest peak, Estats (3143m), over to the Parc Nacional d'Aigüestortes i Estany de Sant Maurici, then on to the southern flank of the Vall d'Aran and into Aragón.

Other Activities

The Riu Noguera Pallaresa around Llavorsí and Sort has some of Spain's most exciting white water and is a centre not just for **rafting**, **canoeing** and **hydrospeed** (watertobogganing) but for several other adventure sports too.

You can go **horse riding** almost anywhere – there are *hípicas* (riding stables) all over the place. Mountain bikes are, by Spanish standards, relatively easy to rent in the Pyrenees area. Another sport that's taking off here is **parapenting**, a cross between hang-gliding and parachuting. And of course there's boundless scope for **climbing** – Pedraforca in the Serra del Cadí offers some of the most exciting ascents.

OLOT

Olot is only 450m above sea level and the hills around it are little more than pimples, but the pimples are the volcanoes of the Parc Natural de la Zona Volcànica de la Garrotxa. Admittedly they're extinct or dormant volcanoes, but one erupted as re-

cently as 11,500 years ago. Olot, if not the world's prettiest place, is an obvious base for the natural park.

Orientation

At the heart of town is a small grid of old streets centred on Plaça Major, with the parish church, the Església de Sant Esteve, three blocks west of the plaça. The main road through the centre, Carrer del Bisbe Lorenzana (bus station at No 20), runs east-west three blocks south of Plaça Major.

Information

The best town map is given out by the Patronat Municipal de Turisme (☎ 972 26 01 41) at Carrer del Bisbe Lorenzana 15 opposite the bus station. It's open Monday to Friday from 9 am to 3 pm and 5 to 7 pm, Saturday from 10 am to 1 pm and 5 to 7 pm and Sunday from 11 am to 2 pm.

The Casal dels Volcans (☎ 972 26 62 02) concentrates on information about the Parc Natural de la Zona Volcànica de la Garrotxa. It's in the Jardí Botànic on Avinguda de Santa Coloma de Farners, 1km southwest of Plaça de Clarà. Its hours are Monday to Saturday from 9 am (10 am on Saturday) to 2 pm and 4 to 6 pm (5 to 7 pm from July to September) and Sunday from 10 am to 2 pm.

Things to See

The **Museu Comarcal de la Garrotxa**, at Carrer de l'Hospici 8, covers Olot's growth as an early textile centre and includes a collection of local 19th century art. It's open from 11 am to 2 pm and 4 to 7 pm (closed Tuesday, Sunday and holiday afternoons).

The **Jardí Botànic**, a botanical garden of Olot area flora, contains the interesting **Museu dels Volcans**, covering local flora and fauna as well as volcanoes and earthquakes.

Four **volcanoes** stand sentry on the fringes of Olot. Head for Volcà Montsacopa, 500m north of the centre, or Volcà La Garrinada, 1km north-east of the centre. Both have paths climbing to their craters.

An International Language

As a result of Catalunya's role in the Reconquista in the middle ages, the Catalan language (*català*) is also the first language of most people in the Balearic Islands and nearly half those in Valencia, areas that were taken from the Muslims by Catalunya in the 13th century.

Catalan is also spoken in a narrow strip of Aragón bordering Catalunya – and in the French district of Roussillon, a wedge spreading east from Andorra to the Mediterranean, including the city of Perpignan (Perpinyà in Catalan). Roussillon was ruled from Barcelona for most of the Middle Ages until the Treaty of the Pyrenees in 1659, which set the current French-Spanish border. Farther afield, the residents of the town of Alghero in Sardinia (L'Alguer in Catalan) speaks Catalan too, a remnant of Catalunya's medieval empire. And so, back in the Pyrenees, do the people of Andorra, always closely connected with Catalunya. Much to Catalans' delight, Andorra's recent entry to the United Nations has meant that Catalan is now heard there too.

Like all languages, Catalan has its dialects. The main distinction is between western and eastern Catalan; the former is used in Andorra, western and far southern Catalunya and the Catalan-speaking parts of Aragón and Valencia, the latter in the rest of the Catalan world. Expert ears go on to subdivide these into a total of 12 sub-dialects! Valencians prefer to call their sub-dialect *valencià* rather than *català*, while in the Balearic Islands you may hear of languages called *mallorquí*, *menorquí* and *eivissenc* – actually the Catalan sub-dialects used in Mallorca, Menorca and Ibiza, respectively.

The 'language question' has plagued relations between Barcelona and Madrid for some years now. In 1998, after much heated debate, Catalunya passed the Ley de la Lengua, which seeks to enshrine the use of the language in all official activities and promote its use in everyday life. Castellano speakers fear it is an attempt to marginalise them, and Jordi Pujol's enemies on the right and left have used every opportunity to take him to task on the issue. A simple fact of life is that Catalan is hard to do without if you want to work anywhere in the public sector or in business in Catalunya.

The issue is just as vexing elsewhere. Catalanists in the Balearic Islands fear that the language is being swamped by the waves of foreign tourists and mainlanders, whose lingua franca (where there is one!) is Spanish. In Valencia, with a higher non-Catalan speaking population than Catalunya, the authorities have tried to steer a middle course: when Catalan and Valencian officials meet (and relations between the two *comunidades* could be better) it is not unusual to hear the former chatting in Catalan and the latter replying in Spanish!

Places to Stay & Eat

Camping Les Tries (☎ 972 26 24 05, *Avinguda de Pere Badosa s/n)*, on the eastern edge of town, is open from Semana Santa to October; it charges 2200 ptas for two people with a car and tent. The *Torre Malagrida* youth hostel *(☎ 972 26 42 00, Passeig de Barcelona 15)* is an unusual early 20th century modernist building. The high season, price-wise, is March to September.

Hostal Stop (☎ 972 26 10 48, *Carrer de Sant Pere Màrtir 29)*, 500m west of Plaça Major, has adequate doubles for 2600 ptas. The central *Hostal Residència Garrotxa* (☎ 972 26 16 12, *Plaça de la Mora 3)* offers bare but big singles/doubles with private shower for 1600/3500 ptas plus IVA. *Pensión Narmar* (☎ 972 26 98 07) on Plaça Major has good, modern rooms starting at 3200/4500 ptas.

Aparthotel Perla D'Olot (☎ 972 26 23 26, fax 972 27 04 74, Avinguda de Santa Coloma de Farners 97) has 30 rooms with own kitchen, bathroom and TV for 6100 ptas a double, plus IVA.

Pensión Narmar runs a restaurant with main dishes (which include trout and chicken) from 650 ptas and a *menú* for 1100 ptas. Across the plaça, *La Plaça dels Gegants* is a haven for vegetarians, with dishes ranging from 300 to 800 ptas.

Getting There & Away

Bus TEISA (☎ 972 26 01 96) runs buses to: Barcelona two to four times a day (two hours; 1775 ptas); Girona via Besalú eight times daily (1¼ hours; 620 ptas; four on Sunday); Figueres via Besalú three times daily (one hour); Ripoll three or four times daily (one hour; 455 ptas), most via Sant Joan de les Abadesses; and Camprodon once or twice daily (45 minutes).

Car & Motorcycle The easiest approach from Barcelona is by the A-7 and C-152. The N-260 runs west to Ripoll and east to Besalú and Figueres, passing Olot on a northerly ring road.

PARC NATURAL DE LA ZONA VOLCÀNICA DE LA GARROTXA

The natural park surrounds Olot on all sides but the most interesting area is between Olot and the village of Santa Pau, 10km south-east.

Volcanic eruptions began here about 350,000 years ago and the most recent one, at Volcà del Croscat, happened 11,500 years ago. In the park are about 30 volcanic cones, up to 160m high and 1.5km wide. Together with the lush vegetation, a result of fertile soils and a damp climate, these create a landscape of unusual beauty. Between the woods are crop fields, a few hamlets and scattered old stone farmhouses.

Information

The main information office for the park is the Casal dels Volcans in Olot. There are two others: the Centre d'Informació Can

Serra (☎ 972 19 50 74), beside the GE-524 Olot-Banyoles road, 4.5km from the middle of Olot; and the Centre d'Informació Can Vayreda (☎ 972 68 03 49) on Plaça Major in Santa Pau.

Santa Pau

The old part of the village, perched picturesquely on a rocky outcrop, contains a porticoed plaza, the Romanesque Església de Santa Maria, and a locked-up baronial castle.

Castellfollit de la Roca

This village on the N-260 8km north-east of Olot stands atop a crag composed of several layers of petrified lava – most easily viewed from the road north of the village.

Hiking

The heart of the park encompasses the Fageda d'en Jordà beech wood and two of the biggest volcanoes, Volcà de Santa Margarida and Volcà del Croscat; all are included in the marked walking route No 1, an 11km, four hour circuit from Can Serra. Moving east from the beech wood to the Volcà de Santa Margarida, you pass the little 11th century Romanesque Església de Sant Miquel de Sacot. You then ascend 100m to the 330m wide crater of Santa Margarida, containing a small Romanesque hermitage. From Santa Margarida you head north across the GE-524 and around the Volcà del Croscat, part of which has been quarried, enabling you to see its lava strata. At least three other well-marked routes allow you to roam the park with ease.

Places to Stay & Eat

Just off the GE-524 and close to the most interesting parts of the natural park are two pleasant, small country camping grounds, which are open all year: *Camping La Fageda* (☎ 972 26 38 58), 4km from the middle of Olot, and *Camping Lava* (☎ 972 68 03 58), 7km out. *Restaurant Can Xel*, about halfway between the two on the GE-524, does meals. Wild camping is banned throughout the Garrotxa district, which stretches from east of Besalú to west of Olot, and from the French border to south of Sant Feliu de Pallerols.

In Santa Pau, there are 10 quaint old rooms with own bath at *Bar-Restaurant Cal Sastre (☎ 972 68 00 49, Cases Noves 1)* on Placeta dels Balls in the old part of the village. Doubles start at around 7000 ptas.

RIPOLL

Ripoll, 30km from Olot in the next valley west, is a shabby industrial town of 12,000 people. But it can claim, with some justice, to be the birthplace of Catalunya. At its heart, in the Monestir de Santa Maria, is one of the finest pieces of Romanesque art in Spain.

Back in the 9th century Ripoll was the power base from which the local strongman, Guifré el Pilós (Wilfred the Hairy), succeeded in uniting several counties of the Frankish March along the southern side of the Pyrenees. Guifré went on to become the first Count of Barcelona. In 879, to encourage repopulation of the Pyrenees valleys, he founded the Monestir de Santa Maria, the most powerful monastery of medieval Catalunya.

Orientation & Information

The tourist office (☎ 972 70 23 51) is on Plaça del Abat Oliba, by the Ribes de Freser-Sant Joan de les Abadesses road, which runs through the north of town. It's open from 10 am to 1 pm and 5 to 7 pm. The Monestir de Santa Maria is virtually next door.

Monestir de Santa Maria

Following its founding in 879, the monastery grew rapidly richer, bigger and more influential. From the mid-10th to mid-11th centuries, under famous abbots such as Arnulf and Oliba, it was Catalunya's spiritual and cultural heart. A great five-naved basilica was built, and adorned in about 1100 with a stone portal that ranks among the high points of Romanesque art. The decline began in the 12th century, when Poblet replaced Ripoll as the burial place of

Catalan royalty. The monks were evicted during 19th century anticlerical reforms and two fires left the basilica in ruins by 1885, after which it was restored in rather gloomy imitation of its former glory. The most interesting feature inside now is the restored tomb of Guifré el Pilós.

You can visit the basilica and its great portal, now protected from atmospheric decay by a wall of glass, daily from 8 am to 1 pm and 3 to 8 pm (free). A chart near the portal (in Catalan) helps to interpret the feast of sculpture: a medieval vision of the universe, from God the Creator, in the centre at the top, to the month-by-month scenes of daily rural life on the innermost pillars.

Down a few steps to the right of the doorway is the monastery's beautiful *claustre* (cloister) open daily from 10 am to 1 pm and 3 to 7 pm (100 ptas). It's a two-storey affair, created in the 12th to 15th centuries.

Museu Etnogràfic de Ripoll

Next door to the Monestir de Santa Maria, this museum, housed in part of the medieval Església de Sant Pere, covers local crafts, industries and religious art (300 ptas).

Places to Stay & Eat

The friendly *Hostal Paula (☎ 972 70 00 11, Carrer de Berenguer 8)* is barely a stone's throw from the Monestir de Santa Maria. Its 11 rooms, modernised with sparkling bathrooms, are 4500/6000 ptas plus IVA for a double/triple. Closer to the train and bus stations, *Hostal La Trobada (☎ 972 70 23 53, Passeig de Honorat Vilamanyà 4)* has good rooms at up to 7500 ptas a double.

Reasonable cafés near the Monestir de Santa Maria include *Bar El Punt*, across the road on Plaça Ajuntament, where you can tuck into an array of tapas from 200 to 400 ptas – three or four of them make a decent light lunch. *Hostal Paula* has a restaurant offering a stocky *menú* for 1000 ptas.

Getting There & Away

The bus and train stations are almost side by side on Carrer del Progrés, 600m south-east of the centre. Connections with Barcelona,

Ribes de Freser and Puigcerdà are all much better by train than bus. About 12 trains a day run to Barcelona (two hours), nine to Ribes de Freser (20 minutes) and six to Puigcerdà (1¼ hours).

VALL ALTO DEL TER

From Ripoll, this upper part of the Riu Ter valley reaches north-east to the pleasant small towns of Sant Joan de les Abadesses and Camprodon (950m), then north-west to the modest Vallter 2000 ski centre (2150m) just below the French border. The area is a more pleasant overnight stop than Ripoll and from the upper reaches there are some excellent hikes west to the Vall de Núria.

The C-151 road leaves the Ter valley at Camprodon to head over the 1513m Collado d'Ares pass into France.

Information

Sant Joan de les Abadesses has one tourist office (☎ 972 72 05 99) and Camprodon has two (☎ 972 74 09 36, ☎ 972 74 00 10). Salvat bookshop at Carrer del Beat Miró 8 in Sant Joan stocks Editorial Alpina map-guides and other guidebooks.

Things to See

Worth a look in Sant Joan de les Abadesses are the restored 12th century **bridge** over the Ter, and the **Museu del Monestir** on Plaça de l'Abadessa. This monastery, another Guifré el Pilós foundation, began life as a nunnery but the nuns were expelled in 1017 for alleged licentious conduct. Its elegant 12th century church contains the marvellous *Santíssim Misteri*, a 13th century polychrome woodcarving of the descent from the cross, composed of seven life-size figures. It's open daily from at least 11 am to 2 pm and, except Monday to Friday from November to mid-March, 4 to 6 pm (200 ptas).

Skiing

Lying at 2150m in an impressive mountain bowl about a kilometre from the French border, **Vallter 2000** is the easternmost Pyrenean ski resort and snow can be unreli-

able (☎ 972 13 60 75). It has 12 pistes of all grades, eight lifts and a ski school. A day's lift pass is about 3100 ptas. You can rent gear at the resort or in Setcases or Camprodon.

In summer, the Telecadira Jordi Pujol chair lift is open from late July to early

The Legend of Comte Arnau

Sant Joan de les Abadesses is one of many places in the country north of Ripoll associated in perhaps the strangest of Pyrenean legends: that of Comte Arnau, the wicked medieval Count of Mataplana, who cheated his workers of their due payments of wheat and had more than his quota of lust for local womanhood. The insatiable count, it seems, came by tunnel to Sant Joan from Campdevànol, 10km west, for covert trysts with the abbess and other nuns. When the abbess, his favourite, died, her pious replacement barred him from the convent, but, thanks to help from the devil, he still got in – and carried on.

Eventually, Arnau fell in love with a local lass, whose only refuge was the nunnery at Sant Joan. Arnau forced his way into the convent to find his beloved dead, from fear and misery, it's surmised. Her corpse, however, revived just long enough to give the count a good ticking-off for his misdeeds. Overcome by remorse, Arnau retired to the Serra de Mogrony, where, condemned to eternal misery for his sins, his tortured soul still wanders, returning on thundery nights (and, some say, under a full moon) to the convent: a horrific vision on horseback with a pack of balefully howling dogs.

If you visit Sant Joan or other villages in the region in summer, you might be lucky enough to catch one of the occasional re-enactments of bits of the Arnau legend. Or you can look at his supposed residence, the Castell de Mataplana, at Gombrèn, about 11km north-west of Ripoll on the GE-401.

September from 11 am to 4 pm. It rises to the Cafeteria Les Marmotes at 2535m, from where on a good day there are magnificent views.

Hiking

The fit and well equipped can undertake excellent full-day hikes west from the topmost part of the Ter valley to the Vall de Núria, 10 to 12km away as the crow flies. Get the Editorial Alpina *Puigmal* map-guide.

One route takes you through Tregurà de Dalt (1400m) north-west over the Coll dels Tres Pics pass (2400m), down to the FEEC's small Coma de Vaca refuge (closed) at the top of the steep Gorges del Freser valley, then north-west up to the Coll de Torreneules (2585m), and down to the Vall de Núria (1970m). Shorter walks down in the valley or higher up are also possible.

Places to Stay & Eat

There are many accommodation options, including camping grounds near Sant Joan and Camprodon and the good *Camping Conca de Ter* (☎ 972 74 06 29) at Vilallonga de Ter, 5km north-west of Camprodon; it is open all year, charging 2645 ptas plus IVA for two adults with a car and tent.

Hostal Janpere (☎ 972 72 00 77, Carrer del Mestre Andreu 3) has good rooms with private bath costing 3000 ptas per person.

Camprodon is a popular base for walkers and skiers. *Can Ganansi* (☎ 972 74 01 34, Carrer de Josep Morera 9), 100m south of the central Plaça d'Espanya, has doubles with bath and TV for 4400 ptas, which includes lunch or dinner. *Can Juan (Carrer d'Isaac Albèniz 10)* is a cheerful spot where mains cost from 1100 to 2000 ptas. *Restaurant Núria* on Plaça d'Espanya has good Catalan country cooking, with a three-course *menú* for 1250 ptas.

North-west up the valley from Camprodon, the villages of Vilallonga de Ter, Tregurà de Dalt (5km up a steep side road, 12km from Camprodon) and Setcases (11km) have at least one pensión or hostal each. Setcases has half a dozen.

Getting There & Away

Güell i Güell runs around seven buses daily from Ripoll to Sant Joan de les Abadesses and Camprodon. The only daily bus north-west from Camprodon, as far as Setcases, leaves in the early afternoon and returns soon after. TEISA runs a couple of buses daily from Olot to Sant Joan de les Abadesses and Camprodon.

VALL DE NÚRIA & RIBES DE FRESER

Around 700 AD, the story goes, Sant Gil (St Giles) came from Nîmes to live in a cave in an isolated mountain valley 26km north of Ripoll, preaching the Gospel to shepherds. Before he left four years later, apparently fleeing Visigothic persecution, Sant Gil hurriedly hid away a wooden Virgin and child image he had carved, a cross, his cooking pot and the bell he had used to summon the shepherds. They stayed hidden until 1079, when an ox miraculously led some shepherds to the spot. The statuette, the Mare de Déu de Núria, became the patron of Pyrenean shepherds and Núria's future was assured. The first historical mention of a shrine here was made in 1162.

Sant Gil would recoil in shock if he came back today. The large, grey sanctuary complex squatting at the heart of the valley is an eyesore and the crowds would make anyone with hermitic leanings run a mile. But Núria remains almost pristine, a wide, green, mountain-ringed bowl which is the starting point for numerous fine walks. Getting there is fun too, either on foot up the Gorges de Núria – the green, rocky valley of the thundering Riu Núria – or by the little 'Cremallera' railway from Ribes de Freser, which rises over 1000m on its 12km journey up the same valley.

Bring warm clothes as the high altitude can bring quite a temperature drop.

Orientation

Unless you're hiking to Núria across the mountains, you must approach from the small town of Ribes de Freser, on the N-152 14km north of Ripoll. The Cremallera starts at Ribes-Enllaç station, just off the N-152 at the southern end of Ribes, and makes two stops on the way to Núria: at Ribes-Vila station, near the north end of Ribes after 1km, and at the village of Queralbs (1200m) after 6km. There's a road from Ribes to Queralbs, but from there on it's the Cremallera or your feet.

Information

Núria's tourist office (☎ 972 73 20 20), open daily from 8 am to 9 pm, is in the Núria station of the Cremallera, beside the sanctuary.

Ribes de Freser's main tourist office (☎ 972 72 77 28) is at Plaça de l'Ajuntament 3.

Santuari de Núria

The large 19th and 20th century building dominating the valley contains a hotel, restaurants and exhibition halls as well as the *santuari* itself, which holds the sacred *símbols de Núria*. The santuari is open daily from 9 am to 8 pm. The Mare de Déu de Núria sits behind a glass screen above the altar and is in the Romanesque style of the 12th century, so either Sant Gil was centuries ahead of his time or this isn't his work! Steps lead up to the bell, cross and cooking pot (all dating back to at least the 15th century). To have a prayer answered, put your head in the pot and ring the bell while you say it.

Hiking & Skiing

Get Editorial Alpina's *Puigmal* map-guide before you come to Núria if you plan on some walking. If you want to walk up to Núria, you can avoid the first unexciting 6km from Ribes de Freser by taking the Cremallera (or road) to Queralbs, saving your energies for the steepest and most spectacular part of the approach – about three hours up the good (and sometimes busy) track climbing the Gorges de Núria. Or take the Cremallera up and walk down!

From the Vall de Núria (where you're advised to fill in a route sheet at the information office before heading off), you can

cap several 2700 to 2900m peaks on the main Pyrenees ridge in about 2½ to three hours walking each.

In winter Núria is a small-scale ski resort with 10 short runs.

Places to Stay & Eat

Wild camping is banned in the whole Ribes de Freser-Núria area.

Núria There's a cheap and basic *zona d'acampada* (camping area with limited facilities) behind the sanctuary. Space is limited (bookings ☎ 972 73 20 20).

The *Alberg Pic de l'Àliga* youth hostel (☎ 972 73 20 48) is up at the top of the cable car *(telecabina)* on the east side of the valley. It has 138 places in dorms of four to 14. High-season prices (plus a 100 ptas surcharge) apply all year except April, June, October and November. The cable car runs daily from 9 am to 8.15 pm and also on Friday and Saturday from 9.30 to 10 pm.

The *Hotel Vall de Núria* (☎ 972 73 20 00) in the sanctuary building has 65 comfortable singles/doubles with bath and TV ranging from about 4500/5600 ptas (from Monday to Friday most of the year) to 8100/12,300 ptas in August. It also lets out some apartments. In the sanctuary building, the *Autoservei* self-service cafeteria and the *Bar Finistrelles* both have starters in the 450 ptas region and main courses for around 800 ptas. The hotel restaurant has a *menú* for 2200 ptas. A shop in the sanctuary building sells food.

Ribes de Freser *Fonda Vilalta* (☎ 972 72 70 95, Carrer de Cerdanya 6) has a variety of basic but clean doubles at 3000, 4000 (views and shower) or 5000 ptas (views and full private bathroom). Three lower mid-range hotels, with doubles at 6000 to 7000 ptas, are on Carrer de Sant Quintí.

Getting There & Away

Transports Mir runs between Ripoll and Ribes de Freser, with two or three buses a day Monday to Friday and one on Saturday.

About six RENFE trains a day run to Ribes-Enllaç from Ripoll (20 minutes), and Barcelona (2¼ hours).

The Cremallera (☎ 972 73 20 20), a narrow-gauge electric-powered cog-wheel railway operating since 1931, runs from Ribes-Enllaç to Núria and back six to 12 times a day depending on the season. Some services connect with RENFE trains at Ribes-Enllaç.

The Cremallera ride is about 45 minutes one way and all trains stop at Ribes-Vila and Queralbs. It's a spectacular trip, particularly after Queralbs as the train winds up the Gorges de Núria. The one-way/return fare from Ribes to Núria is 1375/2200 ptas.

PUIGCERDÀ

Just a couple of kilometres from the French border, Puigcerdà (pronounced 'puh-cher-DA'; population 6000) is not much more than a way station, but it's a jolly little one, particularly in summer and the ski season. A dozen Spanish, Andorran and French ski resorts lie within 45km.

At a height of 1200m, Puigcerdà is capital of the district of Cerdanya which, with French Cerdagne across the border, occupies a low-lying basin between higher reaches of the Pyrenees to the east and west. Cerdanya and Cerdagne, once a single Catalan county, were divided by the Treaty of the Pyrenees in 1659 but still have a lot in common. It's in areas like this that you have the strongest sense of being neither in Spain nor in France, but in Catalunya.

Orientation & Information

Puigcerdà stands on a small hill, with the train station at the foot of its south-western side. A few minutes climb up some flights of steps takes you to Plaça de l'Ajuntament, off which is the tourist office (☎ 972 88 05 42) at Carrer de Querol 1. You'll find plenty of banks on the main plaças. The correos is at Avinguda del Coronel Molera 11 and the postcode is 17520. The Guàrdia Urbana (municipal police; ☎ 972 88 19 72) are in the ajuntament on Plaça de l'Ajuntament.

The Hospital de Puigcerdà (☎ 972 88 01 50) is central at Plaça de Santa Maria 1.

Things to See

Despite being seriously damaged in the civil war, the town centre retains a relaxed and old-fashioned air. Of the 17th century Església de Santa Maria, only the tower remains; the rest fell victim to the civil war. The 13th century Gothic Església de Sant Domènec on Passeig del 10 d'Abril was also wrecked in the war, but was rebuilt. It contains 14th century Gothic murals which somehow survived. The Estany (lake) in the north of town, created back in 1380 for irrigation, is surrounded by turn-of-the-century summer houses built by wealthy Barcelona families.

Places to Stay

Camping Stel (☎ 972 88 23 61) on the Llívia road is open all year and charges 3180 ptas plus IVA for two adults with a car and tent.

Right outside the train station, Hostal Estación (☎ 972 88 03 50, Plaça de l'Estació 2) has plain but adequate rooms for 2500/4600 ptas, or 2700/5400 ptas with private bath, all plus IVA, and a handy café downstairs.

Up in town, the friendly Hostal Alfonso (☎ 972 88 02 46, Carrer d'Espanya 5) is a bit better at 2000/4000 ptas for large singles/doubles with bath. Hostal La Muntanya (☎ 972 88 02 02, Avinguda del Coronel Molera 1) is also good and charges the same amount. Hostal Núria (☎ 972 88 17 56, Plaça de Cabrinetty 18) has nice doubles with bath and balcony for 5500 ptas.

Hotel Maria Victoria (☎ 972 88 03 00 or ☎ 972 88 17 56, Carrer de Querol 9) has some fine views, with rooms starting at 3500/6500 ptas (including breakfast). Hotel Del Lago (☎ 972 88 10 00, Avinguda del Dr Piguillem s/n), near the Estany, has old-fashioned style and a nice garden for 10,000 ptas a double plus IVA.

Top of tree is Hotel Avet Blau (☎ 972 88 25 52, Plaça de Santa Maria 14). It is a fine old mansion overlooking the centre of the village; comfortable doubles cost 11,000 ptas plus IVA.

Places to Eat

One of the best-value places is *El Niu (Carrer Alfons I 15)*, where the 1175 ptas *menú* appears to be just two courses but is actually three (one of which is usually trout) with wine thrown in, too.

If you want cheap snacks, try the *Creperia* on the corner of Carrer Major and Carrer dels Escoles Pies, which has tapas and savoury crêpes from 250 ptas to 450 ptas, as well as pizza for up to 800 ptas.

At *Granja Fran Ros (Plaça dels Herois 8)* you can get platos combinados for around 700 ptas, chicken and chips for 550 ptas or a green salad for 275 ptas. *Restaurant Kennedy* at No 2, with tables on the square, is popular and has a good three-course *menú* with wine for 1450 ptas (plus IVA). *Restaurante Casa Clemente (Avinguda del Dr Piguillem 6)* has a *menú* for the same price. At *Restaurant La Tieta* on Carrer dels Ferrers you can choose between pizza for about 900 ptas or a *menú* for 1500 ptas. It's an intimate, cavernous place.

Getting There & Away

Bus Alsina Graells runs two daily buses (one at weekends) to Barcelona (three hours) via the 5km Túnel del Cadí; three to La Seu d'Urgell (one hour); and one to Lleida (four hours). They stop at the train station. The tourist office has timetables.

The quickest way to Andorra is by train to Latour-de-Carol, then by bus, a journey of 2¼ to 2¾ hours. See the Andorra chapter for information on the bus connections. You can also reach Andorra la Vella by changing buses in La Seu d'Urgell.

Train About six trains a day run to Ribes de Freser, Ripoll and Barcelona (3¼ hours;

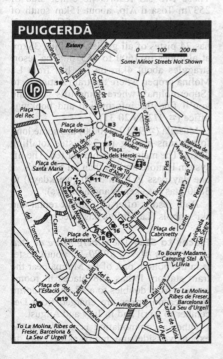

PUIGCERDÀ

PLACES TO STAY
1 Hotel Del Lago
3 Hostal La Muntanya
9 Hostal Alfonso
11 Hotel Avet Blau
14 Hotel Maria Victoria
16 Hostal Núria
19 Hostal Estació

PLACES TO EAT
2 Restaurant Casa Clemente
5 Restaurant La Tieta
6 Restaurant Kennedy
7 Granja Fran Ros
10 El Niu
15 Creperia

OTHER
4 Correos
8 Església de Sant Domènec
12 Tower of Església de Santa Maria
13 Hospital de Puigcerdà
17 Tourist Office
18 Guàrdia Urbana
20 Train Station

1085 ptas). Five in each direction make the seven-minute hop over the border to Latour-de-Carol in France. These connect at Latour-de-Carol with trains from Toulouse or Paris, and with the narrow-gauge Train Jaune down the Têt valley to Perpignan. Puigcerdà station (☎ 972 88 01 65) has details on the French trains.

Car & Motorcycle From Barcelona, the A-18 autopista feeds into the C-1411, which approaches Puigcerdà through the Túnel del Cadí. Bicycles are not allowed in the tunnel, which is a tollway.

The N-152 from Ribes de Freser climbs west along the northern flank of the Rigard valley, with the pine-covered Serra de Mogrony rising to the south, to the 1800m Collado de Toses pass, then winds down to Puigcerdà.

The main crossing into France is at Bourg-Madame, immediately east of Puigcerdà, from where roads head to Perpignan and Toulouse.

AROUND PUIGCERDÀ
Llívia
Six kilometres east of Puigcerdà across flat farmland, the little town of Llívia is a piece of Spain in France. Under the 1659 Treaty of the Pyrenees Spain ceded 33 villages to France, but Llívia was a 'town' and so, together with the 13 sq km of its municipality, remained a Spanish possession.

The interest of Llívia's tiny medieval nucleus, near the top of the town, centres on the **Museu Municipal** at Carrer dels Forns 4 and the 15th century Gothic **Església de Nostra Senyora dels Àngels** just above the museum. There's a tourist office (☎ 972 89 63 13) in the museum and both museum and church open Tuesday to Saturday (and Monday in July and August) from 10 am to 1 pm and 3 to 6 pm and summer Sundays from 10 am to 2 pm. The museum (150 ptas) is in what's claimed to be Europe's oldest pharmacy, the Farmacia Esteva, which was founded in 1415. The church contains an 18th century baroque retablo and a processional cross given to Llívia by Carlos I. From the

church you can walk up to the ruined **Castell de Llívia**, where, during the short-lived period of Islamic dominion in the Pyrenees, the Muslim governor Manussa enjoyed a secret dalliance with Lampègia, daughter of the Duke of Aquitaine (or so legend has it).

You can stay here if you want and dine on the balconies of the *Restaurant Can Ventura (Plaça Major 1)*, a ramshackle building dating to 1791.

At the time of writing, one Alsina Graells bus a day connected Puigcerdà train station with Llívia. Otherwise, it's not a long walk, and the road is flat and quiet. You only cross about 2km of France before entering the Llívia enclave and, apart from an abandoned border post just past Camping Stel and a couple of French road signs, you'd hardly know you'd left Spain.

La Molina & Masella
These two ski resorts lie either side of 2537m Tosa d'Alp, about 15km south of Puigcerdà. La Molina is one of Catalunya's biggest popular ski centres. Altogether it has 24 pistes of all grades, totalling 38km, at altitudes of 1600 to 2537m. The resort straggles about 4km up the hill from La Molina proper, where the train station is, to 'Supermolina', where some lifts start and you'll find the information and bookings office (☎ 972 89 20 31).

Masella (☎ 972 14 40 00) has some long forest runs among its 34 pistes totalling 48km. The majority are blue or red. The lift system is more limited than La Molina's. A one day pass is from 3300 (weekdays) to 3800 ptas (weekends and holidays).

Both resorts offer equipment rental and ski schools (La Molina has three).

Places to Stay The *Alberg Mare de Déu de les Neus (☎ 972 89 20 12)* youth hostel is in the bottom part of La Molina near the train station. It has 148 places in rooms ranging from doubles to a 38-person dorm. High-season prices are charged from December to April and in July and August.

Other accommodation is mostly on the expensive side and many skiers stay in

Puigcerdà or even farther afield. *Hostal 4 Vents* (☎ *972 89 20 97, Pista Standard s/n)*, about halfway up the hill to Supermolina, has doubles from 6000 to 8000 ptas, some with bath. *Hotel Solineu* (☎ *972 14 50 16)* in Supermolina is a bit cheaper. If you're coming for more than a day's skiing, you're probably best booking a package through the La Molina booking centre. A two day weekend deal including accommodation, lift pass and some meals costs from 12,000 ptas per person.

Getting There & Away La Molina is on the Barcelona-Ribes de Freser-Puigcerdà railway, with about six trains a day each way. In the ski season there's a bus service from Puigcerdà. Most people come by car; the easiest route from Barcelona is by the A-18 autopista and the C-1411 through the Túnel del Cadí. Roads also wind down to La Molina and Masella from the N-152 west of the Collado de Toses.

SERRA DEL CADÍ

The N-260 runs west along the wide Riu Segre valley from Puigcerdà to La Seu d'Urgell, with the Pyrenees climbing away northward towards Andorra, and one of the finest pre-Pyrenees ranges, the Serra del Cadí, rising steep and high along the southern side. Although this face of the Cadí – rocky and fissured by ravines known as *canales* – looks daunting enough, the range's most spectacular peak is Pedraforca (2497m), a southern offshoot with probably the best rock climbing in Catalunya. Pedraforca and the main Cadí range also offer some excellent mountain hiking for those suitably equipped and experienced. Together with the dramatic scenery, attractive villages and some unpaved roads in among the hills that are passable for non-4WD vehicles in dry conditions, the area is well worth some of your time.

Orientation

The area around Pedraforca is most easily reached from the C-1411, along the B-400, which heads west 1.5km south of Guardio-

la de Berguedà. Pedraforca looms mightily into view about halfway to the village of Saldes, which sits 1215m high at its foot, 15km from the C-1411. The main Cadí range runs east to west about 5km north of Saldes. The Refugi Lluís Estasen (see Places to Stay & Eat) is under the northern face of Pedraforca 2.5km north-west of Saldes. You can reach it by footpath from Saldes or by a partly paved road that turns north off the B-400 about 1km west of Saldes. Park at the Mirador de Gresolet, from where it's a 10 minute walk up to the refuge.

Information

The Parc Natural del Cadí-Moixeró's main Centre d'Informació (☎ 93 824 41 51) is in Bagà, a village on the C-1411 4km north of Guardiola de Berguedà. Open Monday to Friday from 9 am to 1.30 pm, Saturday from 10 am to 2 pm and 4 to 6.30 pm and Sunday and holidays from 10 am to 2 pm, the office is a mite inconveniently placed at Carrer de la Vinya 1, on the Gisclareny road on the western edge of Bagà. Some information on the park is also available from the tourist offices at the service area at the northern end of the Túnel del Cadí (☎ 973 51 02 33), in Bellver de Cerdanya (☎ 973 51 00 16), in Tuixén (☎ 973 37 00 30) and in La Seu d'Urgell (☎ 973 35 00 10).

In Saldes, the Centre d'Informació Massís del Pedraforca (☎ 93 825 80 05), open daily from 11 am to 2 pm and 5 to 7 pm, has information on the Saldes and Pedraforca area only.

Editorial Alpina's *Serra del Cadí – Pedraforca* map-guide covers the Saldes-Tuixén route, Pedraforca, the main Cadí range and its northern slopes. For areas east of Saldes you will need *Moixeró – Tosa d'Alp*, while for the Segre valley you require *Cerdanya*.

Hiking

Pedraforca The name means 'Stone Fork' and the approach from the east makes clear why. The two separate rocky peaks, the northern Pollegó Superior (2497m) and

PUIGCERDÀ & SERRA DEL CADÍ AREA

southern Pollegó Inferior (2400m), are divided by a saddle called L'Enforcadura. The northern face, rising near-vertically for 600m, has some classic rock climbs; the southern has a wall that sends alpinists into raptures.

Pedraforca is also quite possible for walkers, but certainly exhilarating. From Refugi Lluís Estasen you can reach the Pollegó Superior summit in about three strenuous hours – either southwards from the refuge, then up the middle of the fork

from the south-eastern side (a path from Saldes joins this route); or westwards up to the Collada del Verdet, then south and east to the summit. The latter route has some hairy precipices and requires a good head for heights, but is classed as a walk rather than a climb. However it's not suitable for coming down: you must use the first route.

Other Hikes Hikers can ascend Comabona (2530m), towards the eastern end of the main Cadí ridge, in about four or five hours from the Refugi Lluís Estasen. Puig de la Canal del Cristall (2563m) and Puig de la Canal Baridana (2647m, the highest in the range) are longer walks that may require a night in the hills.

There are various routes of one to two days right across the Cadí, from Saldes, the Refugi de Lluís Estasen or Gósol, to the Segre valley. If you want to overnight in the mountains, the FEEC's small *Refugi Prat d'Aguiló*, at 2037m on the northern slopes, has room for 20 and a kitchen.

Gósol

The B-400 continues paved from Saldes to the pretty stone village of Gósol, 12km farther west. Pedraforca looks slightly less daunting from here. The original Gósol (the Vila Vella), which dated back to at least the 9th century, is now abandoned on the hill south of the present village and worth a look. Picasso spent some of 1906 painting in Gósol and the village has a museum just off the *plaça major* with a section devoted to him.

Tuixén & Beyond

An unpaved road west from Gósol climbs the 1625m Coll de Josa pass then descends past the picturesque hamlet of Josa del Cadí to Tuixén (1206m), another attractive village on a small hill. From Tuixén, scenic paved roads lead north to La Seu d'Urgell (36km) and south to Sant Llorenç de Morunys (28km), which is on a beautiful cross-country road from Berga to Organyà.

Places to Stay & Eat

Saldes & Around There are at least four camping grounds along the B-400 between the C-1411 and Saldes, some open year round. In Saldes, *Can Manuel (☎ 93 825 80 41)* on the plaza has singles/doubles from 1000/2000 to 1250/2500 ptas and economical food. *Fonda Carinyena (☎ 93 822 70 25)* near the church is cheap too. Saldes has a couple of food stores.

The FEEC's *Refugi Lluís Estasen (☎ 93 822 00 79)* near the Mirador de Gresolet (see Orientation) is open year round with

100 places, meals and a warden in summer, and about 30 places in winter. When the refuge is full you can sleep outside, but not in a tent.

Gósol *Hostal Cal Francisco (☎ 973 37 00 75)*, by the road at the eastern end of the village, has singles/doubles for 2200/4400 ptas. The smaller *Hostal Can Triuet (☎ 973 37 00 72, Plaça Major 4)*, in the centre, requires you to take at least half-board (3900 ptas per person).

Tuixén The friendly *Can Farragetes (☎ 973 37 00 34, Carrer del Coll 7)* nearby has doubles with bath for 3000 ptas and food in the bar. There are a couple of other places nearby. The small *Camping Molí de Fòrnols (☎ 973 37 00 21)*, open all year, is about 4km north of Tuixén, down by the Riu de la Vansa off the La Seu d'Urgell road.

Elsewhere There are pensiones and/or hostales in Bagà, Guardiola de Berguedà and Sant Llorenç de Morunys and at Martinet in the Segre valley.

Getting There & Around

Berga, Guardiola de Berguedà and Bagà are all on the Alsina Graells bus routes from Barcelona to Puigcerdà and La Seu d'Urgell via the Túnel del Cadí. There's a bus between Guardiola de Berguedà and Ripoll once or twice daily, Monday to Saturday.

Getting to Saldes, Gósol or Tuixén basically requires your own transport or an itchy hitching thumb. This is feasible along the B-400 as far as Saldes or Gósol in July or August, or on the weekend during the other summer months, but there won't be much traffic at other times.

For a taxi you can call ☎ 973 37 00 65 (Gósol) or ☎ 93 822 71 30 (Guardiola de Berguedà).

LA SEU D'URGELL

The lively valley town of La Seu d'Urgell (pronounced 'la SE-u dur-ZHEY'), with a population of 10,400, is Spain's gateway to

Andorra, 10km north. It's a pleasant place to spend a night, with a fine medieval cathedral. The Castilian version of its name is Seo de Urgel.

When the Franks evicted the Muslims from this part of the Pyrenees in the early 9th century, they made La Seu the seat of a bishopric and capital of the counts of Urgell. It has been an important market and cathedral town since the 11th century and has also played a key role in the history of Andorra (see the Andorra chapter).

Orientation & Information

The main axis runs north-south under the names Avinguda de les Valls d'Andorra, Avinguda de Pau Claris, Carrer de Sant Ot and Passeig de Joan Brudieu, with the old part of town to its east.

The tourist office (☎ 972 35 15 11) is at the northern entrance to town, at Avinguda de les Valls d'Andorra 33. It is open Monday to Saturday from 9 am to 2 pm and 4 to 7 pm and Sunday and holidays from 10 am to 2 pm. The staff can give you pamphlets describing walking and horse-riding itineraries in the area. The postcode is 25700.

The Policia Municipal (☎ 972 35 04 26) are in the Casa de la Ciutat (Town Hall) at Plaça dels Oms 1. There's a hospital (☎ 972 35 00 50) at the southern end of Passeig de Joan Brudieu.

Llibreria Ribera de Antich on Carrer de Sant Ot is a good source of maps and local guides.

Catedral de Santa Maria & Museu Diocesà

Looming on the southern side of Plaça dels Oms, the 12th century *seu* (cathedral) is one of Catalunya's outstanding Romanesque buildings despite various remodellings over the centuries. It is one of more than a hundred Romanesque churches lining what has come to be known as the Ruta Románica from Perpignan (France) to the Urgell district.

The fine western façade, through which you enter, is decorated in typical Lombard style. At the time of writing it was hidden by restorers' scaffolding. The inside is dark and plain but still impressive, with five apses, some murals in the south transept, and a 13th century Virgin and child sculpture in the central apse. The cathedral is open daily from 9.30 am to 1 pm and Monday to Saturday from 4 to 6 pm.

From inside the cathedral you can enter the good Museu Diocesà. This encompasses the cathedral cloister and the 12th century Romanesque Església de Sant Miquel, as well as some good medieval Pyrenees church murals, sculptures and altarpieces and a rare 10th century Mozarabic *Beatus* (illustrated manuscript of the Apocalypse). From June to September the museum is open daily from 10 am to 1 pm and (except Sunday and holidays) from 4 to 7 pm. In other months it's open only from noon to 1 pm (11 am to 1 pm on weekends and holidays)! Entry is 300 ptas.

Places to Stay

Camping En Valira (☎ 972 35 10 35) in the north of town on Avinguda del Valira has room for 1200 people at 2100 ptas for two adults with a car and tent. It's open all year.

The modern *Alberg La Valira* youth hostel (☎ 972 35 38 97, Carrer de Joaquim Viola Lafuerza 57), 800m west of the centre, has spacious public areas and 100 places in eight-bunk dorms. The high season is May to August. There's little other cheap accommodation.

By contrast there are lots of good lower mid-range hotels. *Hotel Avenida* (☎ 972 35 01 04, Avinguda de Pau Claris 18) is a good bet, with bright singles/doubles for up to 3300/6500 ptas plus IVA. On a fairly quiet street, *Residència Duc d'Urgell* (☎ 972 35 21 95, Carrer de Josep de Zulueta 43) has nice modern rooms with TV and bath for 3500/5500 ptas. *Hotel Andria* (☎ 972 35 03 00, Passeig de Joan Brudieu 24) has sizable rooms with a certain antiquated charm, but overpriced (for loners at least) at 7300/7800 ptas with bath. The bigger 56-room *Hotel Nice* (☎ 972 35 21 00, Avinguda de Pau Claris 4-6) is a better deal, with smart rooms for 4500/7000 ptas.

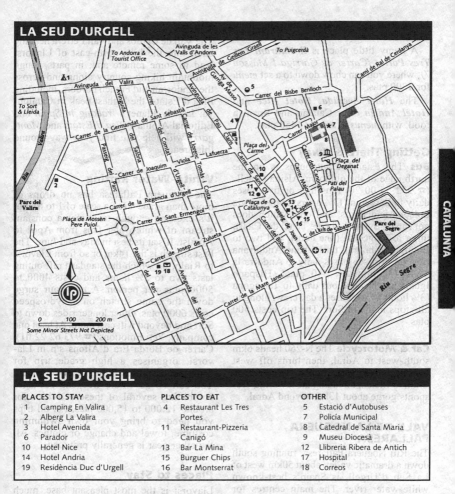

LA SEU D'URGELL

PLACES TO STAY		PLACES TO EAT		OTHER	
1	Camping En Valira	4	Restaurant Les Tres	5	Estació d'Autobuses
2	Alberg La Valira		Portes	7	Policía Municipal
3	Hotel Avenida	11	Restaurant-Pizzeria	8	Catedral de Santa Maria
6	Parador		Canigó	9	Museu Diocesà
10	Hotel Nice	13	Bar La Mina	12	Llibreria Ribera de Antich
14	Hotel Andria	15	Burguer Chips	17	Hospital
19	Residència Duc d'Urgell	16	Bar Montserrat	18	Correos

La Seu's **Parador** (☎ 972 35 20 00, *Carrer de Sant Domènec s/n*), built around the restored cloister of the 14th century Sant Domènec convent, is suitably luxurious with doubles at 15,000 ptas plus IVA.

Places to Eat

Bar La Mina (*Passeig de Joan Brudieu 24*) does good pizzas for 725 ptas and a range of mains for 750 ptas to 1500 ptas. Its outside tables are a fine place to watch the world go by. **Restaurant-Pizzeria Canigó** (*Carrer de Sant Ot 3*) has a reasonable four-course lunch *menú* for 900 ptas, pizzas, pasta and salads for 500 to 900 ptas and à la carte Catalan dishes for 600 to 1400 ptas.

On Carrer de Fra Andreu Capella, **Burguer Chips** has reasonably priced salads and platos combinados from 450 ptas (quarter-chicken, chips and salad) to 775 ptas, and **Bar**

Montserrat does platos combinados from 575 to 900 ptas.

A homy little place is *Restaurant Les Tres Portes (Carrer de Garriga I Massou 7)*, where you can chow down to a set *menú* for 1300 ptas.

The *Hotel Avenida*, *Hotel Nice* and *Hotel Andria* offer Catalan and Spanish food, with *menús* at around 1450 ptas.

Getting There & Away

Bus The estació d'autobusos is on the north edge of the old town. Alsina Graells (☎ 972 35 00 20) runs four or five buses daily to Barcelona (3½ hours; two each via Solsona and Ponts, and one, which does not run on Sunday, via the Túnel del Cadí); three to Puigcerdà (one hour); and two to Lleida (2½ hours). La Hispano Andorrana runs up to seven buses daily to Andorra la Vella (30 minutes; 340 ptas). Hispano Igualadina has one bus daily to Tarragona (3¼ hours). Two buses a day crawl along in all-stops mode to Sort. The trip costs 500 ptas.

Car & Motorcycle The N-260 heads 6km south-west to Adral, then turns off west over the hills to Sort. The C-1313 carries on south to Lleida, threading the towering Tresponts gorge about 13km beyond Adral.

VALL DE LA NOGUERA PALLARESA

The Riu Noguera Pallaresa, running south down a dramatic valley about 50km west of La Seu d'Urgell, is Spain's best-known white-water river. The main centres for white-water sports are the town of Sort and the villages of Rialp and Llavorsí, upstream. You'll find firms to take you rafting, hydrospeeding, canoeing, kayaking – or, when you feel like getting out of the river, canyoning, trekking, climbing, mountain biking, horse riding or *ponting* (involving dangling by a rope from bridges).

The tourist office (☎ 973 62 10 02) in Sort is at Avinguda dels Comtes del Pallars 21.

Hiking

The Vall de Cardós and Vall Ferrera heading back into the hills north-east of Llavorsí lead to some remote and, in parts, tough mountain hiking country along and across the Andorran and French borders, including Pica d'Estats, the highest peak in Catalunya. Lonely Planet's *Walking in Spain* and Editorial Alpina's *Pica d'Estats* and *Montgarri* will help you find your way around this area.

White-Water Rafting

The Noguera Pallaresa has no drops of more than grade 4 (on a scale of 1 to 6), but it's exciting enough to attract a constant stream of white-water fans from April to August. It's at its best in May and June. The best stretch is the 14km or so from Llavorsí to Rialp, on which the standard raft outing lasts two to 2½ hours and costs 4000 to 5000 ptas per person. A two-hour surge down the same stretch on a hydrospeed costs 6000 ptas. Other longer rides down to Sort and beyond will cost more. At least one company, Yeti Emotions (☎ 973 62 22 01), Carrer de Borda Era d'Alfons s/n in Llavorsí, organises a high grade trip for experienced rafters only higher upstream. You can do adventure weekend packages combining several of these activities for around 12,000 to 15,000 ptas. For all trips you need to bring your own swimming costume, towel and change of clothes. All the other gear is generally provided.

Places to Stay

Llavorsí is the most pleasant base, much more of a mountain village than Rialp or Sort. *Camping Riberies (☎ 973 62 21 51)* has a good riverside site and charges 450 ptas per person, per tent and per car, but is open from mid-June to mid-September. *Camping Aigües Braves (☎ 973 62 21 51)*, about 1km north by the river, is slightly dearer. *Hostal de Rey (☎ 973 62 20 11)*, *Hostal La Noguera (☎ 973 62 20 12)* and *Hotel Lamoga (☎ 973 62 20 06)* all overlook the river. They charge 4000, 5080 and

6900 ptas, respectively, for doubles with bath.

Getting There & Away

Alsina Graells runs one daily bus (at 7.30 am) from Barcelona to Sort, Rialp, Llavorsí (5½ hours) and Esterri d'Àneu. From June to October it continues to the Vall d'Aran. The return bus leaves Llavorsí at 1.55 pm. Alsina Graells also has a daily bus (except on Sunday) between Lleida and Esterri d'Àneu via Sort, Rialp and Llavorsí.

PARC NACIONAL D'AIGÜESTORTES I ESTANY DE SANT MAURICI & AROUND

Catalunya's only national park extends 20km cast to west and only 9km from north to south, but packs in more beauty than most areas 100 times its size. The product of glacial action over two million years, it's essentially two east-west valleys at 1600 to 2000m altitude lined by jagged 2600 to 2900m peaks of granite and slate. Against this backdrop, pine and fir forests and open bush and grassland – bedecked with wild flowers in spring and early summer – combine with some 200 *estanys* (small lakes) and countless streams and waterfalls to create a wilderness of rare splendour.

The national park (whose boundaries were extended in 1996 and cover 14,119ha) lies at the core of a wider wilderness area whose outer limit is known as the *zona perifèrica* and includes some magnificent high country to the north and south. The total area covered is 40,852 ha and is monitored by park rangers, who ensure that activities permitted between the two boundaries do not adversely affect the area (see also Park Rules later).

Although the park's main valleys are easily accessible and there are numerous marked walking routes, off the main trails it's not hard to lose your way, and the peaks themselves are mainly for mountaineers only. The whole park is normally under snow from December to April.

Chamois are relatively abundant. In summer they prefer to stick to high altitudes, but you may spot some lower down when they feed in the early morning and evening. Deer are more common at lower altitudes. Spectacular birds include the capercaillie and golden eagle.

Apart from its natural wonders, the region also contains a cluster of Catalunya's most charming Romanesque churches, in the Boí and Taüll area south-west of the park.

Orientation

Approaches One main approach to the park is from the village of Espot (1320m), 4km east of its eastern boundary. An 8km paved road leads west up to Espot from the C-147 road 12km north of Llavorsí (see the Vall de la Noguera Pallaresa section).

The other main approach – and in summer the easier one if you're dependent on buses (see Getting There & Away) – is from the L-500, which heads north-east off the N-230 Lleida-Vielha road 2km north of El Pont de Suert. From this turning it's 15km to the turning for Boí (1km east), then a farther 1.5km to the turning for the park, which begins 4km east.

Walkers can also enter the park by passes from the Vall Fosca to the south and the Vall d'Aran to the north.

The Park The two main valleys are those of the Riu Escrita in the east and the Riu de Sant Nicolau in the west. The Escrita flows out of the park's largest lake, the 1km-long Estany de Sant Maurici. The Sant Nicolau's main source is Estany Llong, 4km west of Estany de Sant Maurici across the 2423m Portarró d'Espot pass. Three kilometres downstream from Estany Llong, the Sant Nicolau runs through a particularly beautiful stretch known as Aigüestortes (Twisted Waters).

Apart from the valley openings at the eastern and western ends, virtually the whole perimeter of the park is mountain crests, with numerous spurs of almost equal height reaching in towards the centre. One of these, from the south, ends in the twin peaks Els Encantats (2746m and 2733m),

CATALUNYA

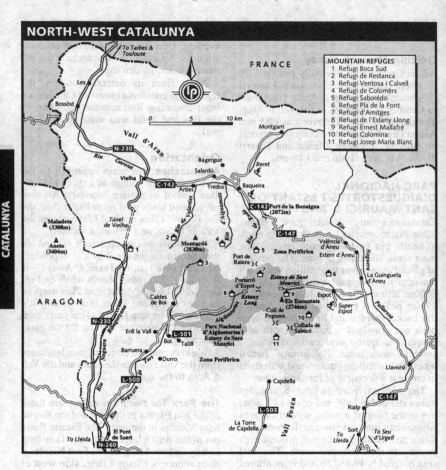

NORTH-WEST CATALUNYA

FRANCE

MOUNTAIN REFUGES
1 Refugi Boca Sud
2 Refugi de Restanca
3 Refugi Ventosa i Calvell
4 Refugi de Colomèrs
5 Refugi Saboredo
6 Refugi Pla de la Font
7 Refugi d'Amitges
8 Refugi de l'Estany Llong
9 Refugi Ernest Mallafré
10 Refugi Colomina
11 Refugi Josep Maria Blanc

towering over Estany de Sant Maurici, a scene so photographed that it has almost become the park's emblem.

Maps & Guides Editorial Alpina's map-guides are adequate, although they don't show every single trail. *Sant Maurici – Els Encantats* covers the eastern half of the park and its approaches; *Vall de Boí* covers the western half and its approaches; *Montsent de Pallars* covers the Vall Fosca; and *Vall d'Aran*, naturally, covers the Vall

d'Aran. The help of guides can be enlisted at the Espot and Boí information offices.

Information

Tourist Offices National park information offices in Espot (☎ 973 62 40 36) and Boí (☎ 973 69 61 89) are open daily from 9 am to 1 pm and 3.30 to 7 pm. The tourist office (☎ 973 69 40 00) in Barruera, on the L-500 10km up from the N-230, is a good source of information on the area around the western side of the park. It's open Monday to Saturday (closed on holidays) from 10 am to 2 pm and 4 to 7 pm. There are other tourist offices south of the park in El Pont de Suert (☎ 973 69 06 40), La Torre de Capdella (☎ 973 66 30 01) and La Pobla de Segur (☎ 973 68 02 57).

Money Boí has a Caixa de Catalunya ATM just up the road from the Pensió Pey. In Espot and Barruera are branches of La Caixa bank.

Park Rules Private vehicles cannot enter the park. From Espot, they can go to the park entrance; on the western side they must stop about 2.5km short of the park on the approach from the L-500. Jeep-taxis, however, offer easy transport into the park from Espot and Boí (see Getting Around).

Wild camping is not allowed in the park, nor are swimming or other 'aquatic activities' in the lakes and rivers. Hunting, fishing, mushroom picking and just about every other kind of potentially harmful activity are banned. Between the limit of the park core and that of the zona perifèrica, most such activities are allowed, but subject to control (to avoid such problems as overfishing). Indeed the weird shape of the park's western end is due to the protests of locals who wanted several important lakes kept open to them for fishing.

Romanesque Churches

The Vall de Boí south-west of the park is dotted with some of Catalunya's loveliest little Romanesque churches. Two of the finest are at Taüll, 3km east of Boí. **Sant Climent de Taüll** at the entrance to the village, with its slender six-storey bell tower, is a gem, not only for its elegant, simple lines but also for the art that graced its interior until the works were transferred to museums in the 20th century. The central apse contains a copy of a famous 1123 mural which resides in Barcelona's Museu Nacional d'Art de Catalunya. At its centre is a Pantocrator whose rich Mozarabic-influenced colours, and expressive but superhuman features, have become a virtual

emblem of Catalan Romanesque art. Other art from this church has found its way to museums as far away as Boston, USA! The church is supposedly open daily from 10.30 am to 2 pm and 4 to 8 pm – but don't count on it (as your friendly LP author discovered this time around!).

Santa Maria de Taüll, up in the old village centre with a five-storey tower, is also well represented in the Barcelona museum, but lacks the *in situ* copies that add to the interest of Sant Climent. However, it's another elegant building and the only one of this group of churches (apart from Sant Climent) that's open (so they say) daily.

Other Romanesque churches in the area are at Boí, Barruera, Durro, Erill la Vall, Cardet and Coll. Erill la Vall's has a slender six-storey tower to rival Sant Climent's. All of these, however, can only be entered on (free) guided tours at fixed hours two or three times a week; the tourist office in Barruera has the timetable.

Trekking

The park is crisscrossed by plenty of paths, ranging from well marked to unmarked,

The Romanesque Sant Climent de Taüll was once home to magnificent works of art

CATALUNYA

JOHN NOBLE

enabling you to pick routes and circuits to suit yourself.

East-West Traverse You can walk right across the park in one day. The full Espot to Boí (or vice-versa) hike is about 25km and takes nine hours, but you can shorten this by using jeep-taxis to/from Estany de Sant Maurici and/or Aigüestortes. Espot (1300m) to Estany de Sant Maurici (1900m) is 8km (two hours). A path then climbs to the Portarró d'Espot pass (2423m), where there are fine views over both of the park's main valleys. From the pass you descend to Estany Llong and Aigüestortes (1820m; about 3½ hours from Estany de Sant Maurici). Then you have around 3.5km to the park entrance, 4km to the L-500 and 2.5km south to Boí (1260m) – a total of about three hours.

Shorter Treks Numerous good walks of three to five hours return will take you up into spectacular side valleys from Estany de Sant Maurici or Aigüestortes.

From the eastern end of Estany de Sant Maurici, one path heads south 2.5km up the beautiful Monastero valley to Estany Monastero (2171m), passing Els Encantats on the left. Another goes 3km north-west up by Estany de Ratero to Estany Gran d'Amitges (2350m). From Planell Gran (1850m), 1km up the Sant Nicolau valley from Aigüestortes, a path climbs 2.5km south-east to Estany Gran de Dellui (2370m). You can descend to Estany Llong (3km) – about four hours from Aigüestortes to Estany Llong.

A good walk of three to four hours one way from Espot goes south-west up the Peguera valley to the Refugi Josep Maria Blanc (2350m) by Estany Tort. A marked turning to the right just out of Espot on the road up to the small ski resort of Super Espot points the way. This walk is the first half of the route to the Refugi Colomina (see Other Traverses).

Other Traverses Serious hikers and trekkers have many options for extended trips in and out of the park. Several of these are detailed in Lonely Planet's *Walking in Spain*.

One of the most attractive areas to head to or from is the lake-rich basin south of the middle part of the park. The Refugi Colomina here is about four hours from the Refugi Josep Maria Blanc via the 2630m Collada de Saburó pass, or about seven hours from Estany de Sant Maurici by the more difficult Coll de Peguera (2726m). You can reach the Refugi Colomina from the south by a half-day walk up from the village of Capdella at the head of the Vall Fosca, 20km north off the N-260 La Pobla de Segur-El Pont de Suert road. (Capdella, sometimes spelt Cabdella, is not to be confused with La Torre de Capdella, which is 8km farther south.) From July to September you can shorten the walk by taking a cable car from the Sallente reservoir to Estany Gento.

The most obvious route between the park and the Vall d'Aran to the north is via Estany de Ratera and the Port de Ratera pass (2530m) over to the Refugi de Colomers (2125m), in a fine lake-strung valley – a not-too-long day from Estany de Sant Maurici. From the Refugi de Colomers it's about 10.5km down the Vall de l'Aiguamotx, mostly by a partly paved road, to Tredòs. A slightly longer alternative, diverging at Port de Ratera, is via the Refugi de Saborèdo (2310m) and the Ruda valley (east of the Aiguamotx). There are also good, more westerly routes using the Refugi Ventosa i Calvell at the head of Vall de Boí and the Refugi de la Restanca on the Aran side. See the Vall d'Aran section.

Places to Stay

Camping At Espot the small *Camping Solau* (open all year; ☎ 973 62 40 68) is at the top of the village and *Camping Vorapark* (☎ 973 62 41 08), 1km up towards the park entrance, is open from April to October. Two bigger camping grounds below the village have summer-only seasons. At Taüll, *Camping Taüll* (☎ 973 69 61 74) is open all year. There are three camping grounds on the L-500 between El Pont de Suert and Boí. All charge around 525 ptas per person, per tent and per car.

Mountain Refuges Five refuges in the park and six more inside the zona perifèrica provide accommodation for hikers. In general they tend to be staffed from early or mid-June to September, and for some weeks in the first half of the year for skiers. At other times several of them leave a section open where you can stay overnight; if you are unsure call ahead or ask at the park info offices.

In the Park You don't usually need to book for these except in August. The Espot park office can contact the Mallafré, Amitges and JM Blanc refuges for you to check on availability.

Refugi Ernest Mallafré (☎ 973 25 01 18), sometimes called *Refugi Sant Maurici*, near the eastern end of Estany de Sant Maurici (1885m), is run by the FEEC and has 24 places, with meals available. *Refugi d'Amitges* (☎ 973 25 00 07) at Estany Gran d'Amitges (2380m) in the north of the park is run by the CEC and has 66 places. Meals are available.

Refugi de l'Estany Llong (☎ 929 37 46 52 for reservations) near Estany Llong (2000m) is run by the national park, with 40 places and a kitchen. *Refugi Josep Maria Blanc* (☎ 93 423 23 45 for reservations) near Estany Tort (2350m) is run by the CEC, with 40 places and meals available when staffed.

In the north-west of the park, the CEC's *Refugi Ventosa i Calvell* (☎ 93 450 09 66) has 80 places.

Zona Perifèrica Refugi Colomina (☎ 973 68 10 42 for reservations), south of the park by Estany de Colomina (2395m), is run by the FEEC and has 40 places, and meals available, when staffed.

Refugi Colomèrs (☎ 973 64 05 92), north of the park in the lovely Circ de Colomèrs (2130m), is run by the FEEC, with 40 places, and meals available when staffed.

Refugi Saborèdo (☎ 93 329 97 36), north of the park in the lake-strewn Circ de Saborèdo (2310m), is run by the FEEC and has 21 places.

The FEEC's *Refugi de la Restanca* (☎ 908 03 65 59) has 80 places.

Hostales & Hotels The villages of Espot, Boí and Taüll have a range of accommodation options.

Espot The following places are all near the centre of this small village. The friendly, family-run *Residència Felip* (☎ 973 62 40 93) has clean singles/doubles, with shared bathrooms, for 2000/4000 ptas (3000/5000 ptas in July and August) including breakfast. *Casa La Palmira* (☎ 973 62 40 72) has rooms with bath for 2300/4600 ptas. *Hotel Roya* (☎ 973 62 40 40) has rooms with shower or bath for 4200/6100 ptas. The big *Hotel Saurat* (☎ 973 62 41 62) has doubles for 7800 ptas plus IVA.

Boí Hostal Fondevila (☎ 973 69 60 11), on the right as you enter the village, and *Pensió Pey* (☎ 973 69 60 36), on the small village square, have doubles for 6500 ptas plus IVA.

Cases de pagès have cheaper rooms with shared baths. To find *Casa Cosan* (☎ 973 69 60 18) and its nice garden, head down into the village from the square, bear right and ask. The seven rooms are 1700 ptas per person. *Casa Guasch* (☎ 973 69 60 42) charges 2000 ptas per person; take the lane along the right side of the Pensió Pey, then fork right down the hill.

Taüll Although 3km uphill from Boí, Taüll is more picturesque and a nicer place to stay. *Restaurant Sant Climent* (☎ 973 69 60 52), on the road into the village from Sant Climent church, is a new stone building with rooms for 1500/3000 ptas, or 2000/4000 ptas with private bath.

Casa Chep (or Xep; ☎ 973 69 60 54), up in the village on Plaça de Santa Maria, has rooms for 1600/3200 ptas, and a kitchen is available. *Casa Llovet* (☎ 973 69 60 32), an atmospheric old four-storey stone house on Plaça de Franc, charges 1500 ptas per person. Follow Carrer de l'Església up from the Santa Maria church to find it.

Elsewhere There are hostales and/or cases de pagès in Barruera, El Pont de Suert, Capdella and La Torre de Capdella.

Places to Eat

Espot has a couple of supermarkets and Boí one small one. Espot's best-value meals seem to be at **Restaurante Ivan**, up the lane past Casa Palmira, then down to the left. They have snacks and a Catalan *menú* for 1300 ptas. **Casa La Palmira's** restaurant is also popular. Another good option is **Restaurant Juquim**, on the main square. Its *menú* is varied and costs 1250 ptas.

In Boí, **Pensió Pey** does set *menús* for 1600 ptas or bocadillos from as little as 375 ptas. In Barruera, **Hostal Noray** does a good *menú* for 1300 ptas. Right opposite the Sant Climent church in Taüll, **Restaurant Mallador** is set in a tumbledown house with a leafy garden – a perfect place for lunch.

Getting There & Away

Bus La Pobla de Segur, a staging post on some approaches, can be reached by bus from Barcelona (twice daily) and by bus or train from Lleida. For further information you can ring tourist offices or the Alsina Graells bus company (in La Pobla de Segur, ☎ 973 68 03 36).

Espot Daily Alsina Graells buses from Barcelona, Lleida and La Pobla de Segur to Esterri d'Àneu (and in summer to the Vall d'Aran) will stop at the Espot turning on the C-147, from where you have an 8km uphill walk (or hitch) to Espot.

Boí From June to mid-September, an Alsina Graells bus from La Pobla de Segur and El Pont de Suert stops daily at Barruera and the Boí turn-off *(el Cruce de Boí)* on the L-500. The rest of the year it runs on Friday only. At the time of writing the bus left La Pobla de Segur at 9.30 am and El Pont de Suert at

11.15 am. The southbound return bus stops at the Boí turn-off about 2 pm. Both buses connect at El Pont de Suert with Alsina Graells buses from Lleida. You can also get from Boí to Vielha, or vice versa, in one day with a change at El Pont de Suert.

Capdella Alsina Graells runs a daily bus on weekdays between La Pobla de Segur and Capdella. The service is often cut during holiday periods like Easter. The trip is about one hour.

Taxi For a taxi in Boí call ☎ 973 69 60 15 or ☎ 973 69 60 36.

Getting Around

Once you've got close to the park, the easy way of getting inside it is by jeep-taxi from Espot or Boí. Fleets of these things, whose drivers congregate loudly in local bars in their off-duty moments, run a more or less continuous shuttle service between Espot and Estany de Sant Maurici, and between Boí and Aigüestortes, saving you, respectively, 8 and 10km of walking. The one-way fare for either trip is 550 ptas per person and the services run from outside the park information offices in Espot and Boí (from July to September from 8 am to 7 pm, other months from 9 am to 6 pm; in July or August you may have to queue).

VALL D'ARAN

This lush green valley, Catalunya's northernmost outpost, is almost entirely surrounded by spectacular 2000m-plus mountains. Its only natural opening is northwards to France, to which it gives its river, the Riu Garona (Garonne), flowing down to Bordeaux. Thanks to this geography, Aran's native language is not Catalan but Aranese *(aranés)*, a dialect of Occitan or the *langue d'oc*, the old Romance language of southern France (still spoken in some areas there). Most Aranese, however, can switch equally happily into Catalan, Castilian or French.

Despite this northward orientation, Aran has been tied politically to Catalunya since

1175, when Alfonso II took it under his protection to forestall the designs of rival counts on both sides of the Pyrenees. In 1312, following one of many French takeover bids, the Aranese voted by popular referendum to stay with Catalunya – perhaps because in practice this meant a large degree of independence. The major hiccup came with a Napoleonic occupation from 1810 to 1815.

For all its intriguing past, however, the Vall d'Aran is in danger of being overrun by tourism, which since the opening of the Baqueira-Beret ski resort in 1964 has replaced farming and herding as the economic mainstay. A valley that 30 years ago probably was still a pocket of scattered stone villages centred on quaint, pointy-towered Romanesque churches is being swamped by ski-apartment development. That said, most of the villages retain an old-fashioned core and from Aran's pretty side valleys hikers can continue over the mountains in any direction, notably southwards to the Parc Nacional d'Aigüestortes i Estany de Sant Maurici.

The Vall d'Aran (population about 7000) is some 35km long and is considered to have three parts: Naut Aran (Upper Aran), the eastern part, aligned east-west; Mijaran (Middle Aran) around Vielha; and Baish Aran (Lower Aran), where the Garona flows north-east to France. Despite Baqueira-Beret, Naut Aran is still the most attractive area, and the pleasant village of Salardú is a base for some of the best outings. Four bears live in the valley too, closely monitored by satellite but otherwise unlikely to be sighted.

Editorial Alpina's *Vall d'Aran* is a useful aid here.

Hikes & Treks

One nice shortish walk, if you have a vehicle to get to Beret (some 8km north up a hairpin road from Baqueira), is the 5km from Beret along the headwaters of the Riu Noguera Pallaresa to the abandoned village of Montgarri, with a 16th century shrine.

More spectacular routes head south up into the mountains on the northern fringes

of the Pa... Na...
Estany de S...
three can all...
and end at mou...
want to linger o...
tional park.

From the village...
of and below Salar...
valley of the Riu d'A... ...an get
a car about 8km up, ...vel of about
1850m. From there it's a 2.5km walk up to the Refugi de Colomers at 2125m, set in a beautiful lake-strewn bowl. From the refuge there are easy marked circuit walks of two and four hours.

Or from Tredòs you could head south-east up the valley of the Riu de Ruda to the Refugi Saborèdo, some 12km up at 2310m, in another fine lake-dotted cirque. This route is motorable about two-thirds of the way.

If you happen to stop at Arties, call in at the *Hotel Valarties* (☎ 973 64 43 64). Set in a house that is a heterodox mix of local building tradition and tarty avant-garde, it houses a restaurant known to skiers and hikers for miles around. You can stay too if you want, although it's a touch expensive with doubles ranging up to 8700 ptas in high season.

From Arties, 3km west of Salardú, it's 8km up the Riu de Valarties valley to the Refugi de la Restanca. It's drivable for about the first 4.5km; from there you must walk the steeper part, about 3.5km, up to the refuge at 2000m. From the refuge you can walk for about one hour south-west up to the lake Estany de Mar, amid extremely rugged scenery at 2250m, or spend a day climbing and descending 2830m Montardó (to the east), with magnificent views.

The Refugi de Colomers and Refugi de la Restanca are a short day's walk from each other, on the GR-11. From Restanca the GR-11 heads about five hours west to the *Refugi Boca Sud* (☎ 973 64 28 90), near the southern end of the Túnel de Vielha. From there it's two days (with a night's camping) past the Maladeta massif over to Benasque in Aragón.

e & Away

from Lleida and El Pont de eaches Aran through the 5.25km el de Vielha (built in the 1940s and showing its age), then heads north from Vielha to the French border at Eth Pont de Rei. Continuing as the French N-125, it reaches the Toulouse-Pau road at Montréjeau, 46km from the border.

From the Vall de la Noguera Pallaresa, the C-147 crosses the 2072m Port de la Bonaigua pass – which may be closed in winter – into Nautaran, where it becomes the C-142, meeting the N-230 at Vielha.

Two Alsina Graells buses daily run between Barcelona and Vielha via Lleida and El Pont de Suert. The leg from Lleida, where there is usually a half-hour layover, takes three hours. From June to October a daily Alsina Graells bus connects Barcelona and Vielha via La Pobla de Segur, Llavorsí, the Espot turning on the C-147, Port de la Bonaigua and Salardú (the total journey time is about seven hours). At the time of writing the southbound departure from Vielha was at 11.44 am.

A local bus service connects Vielha with Baqueira, Eth Pont de Rei and intervening villages from four (weekends) to 10 times a day.

Vielha

Vielha is Aran's junction town, at an altitude of 975m. The Aranese spelling of its name is more common than the Catalan and Castilian version, Viella.

Orientation The Alsina Graells bus stop and ticket office are by the roundabout in the west of town where the N-230 meets the C-142. The centre is south-east of the roundabout along the C-142, which is at first called Avenguda de Castièro, then, from the central square Plaça dera Glèisa onward, Avenguda deth Pas d'Arró.

Information The Vall d'Aran's main tourist office (☎ 973 64 01 10, Carrèr de Sarriulèra 5) is open daily from at least 10 am to 1 pm and 4.30 to 7.30 pm. There are

banks along Avenguda de Castièro and Avenguda deth Pas d'Arró. The correos is at Carrèr de Sarriulèra 4. The postcode is 25530. The Mossos d'Esquadra (Catalunya regional police; ☎ 973 64 20 44) are 1km south-east of town along Avenguda deth Pas d'Arró. There's a hospital (☎ 973 64 00 66) on Carrèr deth Espitau off Avenguda deth Pas d'Arró.

Things to See The small old quarter is around Plaça dera Glèisa and across the little Riu Nere just west of the square. The **Glèisa de Sant Miquèu** church on Plaça déra Glèisa is a mix of 12th to 18th century styles, with a 13th century main portal. It contains some notable medieval artwork, especially the 12th century *Crist de Mijaran*, an almost life-sized wooden bust thought to have been part of a Descent from the Cross group. The **Musèu dera Val d'Aran** at Carrèr Major 11 tells the interesting tale of Aran's history up to the present. It's open Tuesday to Friday from 5 to 8 pm, Saturday from 10 am to 1 pm and 5 to 8 pm, and Sunday from 10 am to 1 pm (200 ptas).

Places to Stay For some of the cheaper places, head down Passeg dera Llibertat, north off Avenguda de Castièro just west of Plaça dera Glèisa. *Hostal El Ciervo (☎ 973 64 01 65, Plaça de Sant Orenç 3)*, just off Passeig déra Llibertat, has ageing but adequate singles/doubles for 1500/3000 ptas, or 2500/5000 ptas with private bath. On Camin Reiau, a north-east extension of Passeg dera Llibertat, *Pensión Puig (☎ 973 64 00 31)* at No 6, with no sign except a 'P', has doubles for just 1400 ptas; *Casa Vicenta (☎ 973 64 08 19)* at No 7 is much better at 4600 ptas for doubles with bath and breakfast.

For a bit more comfort, *Hotel Urogallo (☎ 973 64 00 00, Avenguda del Castièro 7)*, *Hotel Arán (☎ 973 64 00 50)* at No 5 and *Hotel Riu Nere (☎ 973 64 01 51, Carrèr Major 1)* all have doubles with bath ranging from around 5000 to 11,000 ptas depending on the season.

VIELHA

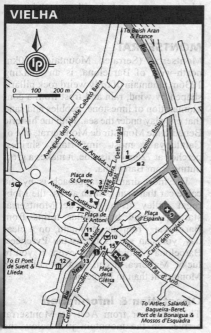

VIELHA

PLACES TO STAY
1	Casa Vicenta
2	Pensión Puig
4	Hostal El Ciervo
6	Hotel Urogallo
7	Hotel Arán
11	Hotel Riu Nere

PLACES TO EAT
3	El Curné
8	Bar Espres
13	Restaurant All i Oli
15	Sidreria Eth Plaça

OTHER
5	Alsina Graells Bus Stop
9	Hospital
10	Correos
12	Musèu dera Val d'Aran
14	Tourist Office
16	Glèisa de Sant Miquèu

Places to Eat *Sidreria Eth Plaça* has pleasant outside tables on Plaça dera Glèisa and good-value platos combinados (meat or squid with salad, chips and two eggs) from 850 ptas – also *torrades* for 500 ptas.

An unassuming little place is *Bar Espres* on Passeg dera Llibertat, where they will sell you Aranese products or whip you up a quick tapa or two to try the wares.

El Curné on Plaça de Sant Orenç is a cosy little bar and restaurant in a charming old house where mains are from 900 ptas to 1200 ptas.

Restaurant All i Oli (Carrèr Major 9) is one of the costlier places in town with a *menú* for 2100 ptas. Anyone for snails?

Salardú

Nine kilometres east of Vielha and 1270m up, Salardú's little nucleus of old houses and narrow streets has largely resisted the temptation to sprawl. If you come in May, June, October or November, however, you'll find only a few hotels open. The tourist office (☎ 973 64 57 26) is by the car park near the middle of the village. In the apse of the village's 12th and 13th century church you can admire the 13th century *Crist de Salardú* crucifixion carving.

Places to Stay & Eat *Xalet-Refugi Juli Soler Santaló (☎ 973 64 50 16)*, just above the main road towards the east end of the village, has dormitory places for 900 ptas and bunk rooms at 1700 ptas a person, plus a kitchen and cafeteria. The large *Alberg Era Garona* youth hostel (☎ 973 64 52 71) nearby has room for 180 people, at 100 ptas more than the normal Catalunya rates; the high season is December to April and July and August. In the centre, *Refugi Rosta* (☎ 973 64 53 08, fax 973 64 58 14, Plaça Major 1) is a 18th century place full of character and with dormitory bunks for 1925 ptas a person and double rooms for 4600 ptas in July and August or 5600 ptas in the ski season (prices include breakfast). It's closed at most other times. There's a great wood-panelled bar, where you can eat sausage, pâté or crêpes for 500 to 750 ptas, and a good dining room.

Pensión Montaña (☎ *973 64 41 08, Carrèr Major 4)* has doubles for 3200 ptas. **Residència Aiguamòg** (☎ *973 64 54 96, Carrèr de Sant Andreu 14)*, near the centre, has quaint singles/doubles with bath for up to 3000/6000 ptas. **Hotel Deth Pais** (☎ *973 64 58 36)* has nice pine-panelled rooms with bath for 4600 ptas plus IVA, single or double. There are five more-expensive places.

Baqueira-Beret

Baqueira (Vaquèira in Aranese), 3km east of Salardú, and Beret, 8km north of Baqueira, form Catalunya's premier ski resort, favoured by the Spanish royal family, no less! Its good lift system gives access to over 40 varied pistes totalling over 70km (more than any other Spanish resort), amid fine scenery at between 1500 and 2510m, and there's a big ski school. A one-day lift pass is 4200 ptas.

In summer the Bosque and Mirador chair lifts open from some time in July to some time in September to carry you from Baqueira almost to the top of 2500m Cap de Baqueira for around 1600 ptas. There's nowhere cheap to stay in Baqueira, and nowhere at all at Beret. Many skiers stay down the valley in Salardú, Arties or Vielha. Information on packages is available from Baqueira-Beret's Central de Reservas (☎ 973 64 44 55, fax 973 64 44 88), Apartado 60, 25530 Vielha. The cheapest five day, room-only apartment packages range from around 18,000 to 30,000 ptas per person depending on dates.

West of Barcelona

The mountain and monastery of Montserrat and the Penedès wine-growing area are both within day-trip distance of Barcelona. From Montserrat you could continue north to the Pyrenees, and from Vilafranca del Penedès you can reach the coast to the south. From either place you could head on west to Lleida, a transport hub with enough history to detain you briefly, and Aragón.

MONTSERRAT

Montserrat (Serrated Mountain), 50km north-west of Barcelona, is an amazing 1236m mountain of truly weird rock pillars, shaped by wind, rain and frost from a conglomeration of limestone, pebbles and sand that once lay under the sea. With the historic Benedictine Monestir de Montserrat, one of Catalunya's most important shrines, perched at 725m on its side, it makes a great outing from Barcelona.

The most dramatic approach is by the cable car that swings high across the Llobregat valley from Aeri de Montserrat station, served by regular trains from Barcelona. From the mountain, on a clear day, you can see as far as the Pyrenees, Barcelona's Tibidabo and even, if you're lucky, Mallorca. It can be a lot colder on Montserrat than in Barcelona.

Orientation & Information

The cable car from Aeri de Montserrat arrives on the mountain just below the monastery. Just above the cable-car station is a road. To the left is the information office (☎ 93 835 02 51), open daily from 9 am to 6 pm, with a good free leaflet-map on the mountain and monastery. Past here, a minor road doubles back up to the left to the lower station of the Funicular de Sant Joan. The main road curves round and up to the right, passing the blocks of cel.les (see Places to Stay & Eat) to enter Plaça de Santa Maria at the centre of the monastery complex.

Monestir de Montserrat

The monastery was founded in 1025 to commemorate a 'vision' of the Virgin on the mountain. Wrecked by Napoleon's troops in 1811, then abandoned as a result of anti-clerical legislation in the 1830s, it was rebuilt from 1858. Today there is a community of about 80 monks. Pilgrims come from far and wide to venerate La Moreneta (the Black Virgin), a 12th century Romanesque wooden sculpture of Mary with the infant Jesus which has been Catalunya's official patron since 1881.

The two-part **Museu de Montserrat** on Plaça de Santa Maria has an excellent collection ranging from an Egyptian mummy and Gothic retablos to art by El Greco, Monet, Degas and Picasso. It's open weekdays from 10 am to 6 pm (weekends and holidays from 9.30 am to 6.30 pm) for 500 ptas (students 300 ptas).

From Plaça de Santa Maria you enter the courtyard of the 16th century **basilica**, the monastery's church. The basilica's façade, with its carvings of Christ and the Apostles, dates from 1900-1 despite its 16th century plateresque style. Daily from 8 to 10.30 am and noon to 6.30 pm (and weekends from 7.30 to 8.30 pm), you can file past the image of the **Black Virgin**, high above the basilica's main altar: follow the signs to the Cambril de la Mare de Déu, to the right of the main basilica entrance.

The **Montserrat Boys' Choir** or Escolania, reckoned to be Europe's oldest music school, sings in the basilica every day at 1 and 7 pm, except in July. The church fills up quickly, so try to arrive early. It is a rare treat, as the choir does not perform often outside Montserrat – five concerts a year and a world tour every two.

On your way out have a look in the room across the courtyard from the basilica entrance, filled with gifts and thank-you messages to the Montserrat Virgin from people who give her the credit for all manner of happy events. The souvenirs range from plaster casts to wedding dresses.

The Mountain

You can explore the mountain above the monastery on a web of paths leading to some of the peaks and to 13 empty and rather dilapidated hermitages. The **Funicular de Sant Joan** (550/875 ptas one way/return) will carry you up the first 250m from the monastery. If you prefer to walk, the road past the funicular's bottom station will lead you up and round to its top station in about one hour (3km).

From the Sant Joan top station, it's a 20 minute stroll (signposted) to the **Sant Joan hermitage**, with fine westward views. More exciting is the hour's walk north-west along a path marked with occasional blobs of yellow paint to Montserrat's highest peak, **Sant Jeroni**, from which there's an awesome sheer drop on the northern side. The walk takes you across the upper part of the mountain, with a close-up experience of some of the weird rock pillars. Many have been given names: on your way to Sant Jeroni look over to the right for La Prenyada (the pregnant woman), La Mòmia (the mummy), L'Elefant (the elephant), the phallic Cavall Bernat and El Cap de Mort (the death's-head).

Organised Tours

You can purchase an Avui Montserrat (information ☎ 93 490 40 00) ticket for 3850 ptas (4000 ptas on weekends). This includes

The statue of the Black Virgin attracts pilgrims to Montserrat from far afield

CATALUNYA

museum entry, return bus ride from Sants bus station in Barcelona, breakfast and lunch.

Places to Stay & Eat

If you want to stay over, there are several options at the monastery; all can be contacted on ☎ 93 835 02 01. A small camping ground 300m along the road past the lower Sant Joan funicular station is open from Semana Santa to October. The cheapest rooms are in the *Cel.les de Montserrat*, three blocks of simple apartments for two to 10 people. A two person apartment costs from 3900 ptas to 5350 ptas in high season. Overlooking Plaça de Santa Maria are the *Hotel El Monestir*, with singles/doubles in high season from 3290/6015 ptas; and the comfortable *Hotel Abat Cisneros*, with rooms from 6520/10,755 ptas in high season.

The *Snack Bar* near the top cable-car station has platos combinados from 875 ptas and bocadillos from about 350 ptas. *Bar de la Plaça* in the Abat Oliva cel.les building has similar prices. *Cafeteria Self-Service* near the car park has great views but is dearer. *Hotel Abat Cisneros* has a four-course *menú* for 2700 ptas.

Getting There & Away

Bus There's a daily bus with the Julià company to the monastery from Estació d'Autobusos de Sants in Barcelona at 9 am (plus 8 am in July and August) for a return fare of 1300 ptas. It returns at 5 pm.

Train & Cable Car Trains run from Plaça d'Espanya station in Barcelona to Aeri de Montserrat five to 10 times a day (peak frequency are summer weekdays) – a 1½ hour ride. Return tickets for 1770 ptas include the cable car between Aeri de Montserrat and the monastery. The cable car goes about every 15 minutes, Monday to Saturday from 10 am to 1.45 pm and 3 to 6.35 pm and Sunday and holidays from 10 am to 6.15 pm.

From Aeri de Montserrat, trains continue north to Manresa, from which there are three trains daily west to Lleida and one or two Alsina Graells buses daily north to Berga, Guardiola de Berguedà, Puigcerdà and (except on Sunday) La Seu d'Urgell.

Car & Motorcycle Probably the most straightforward route from Barcelona is by Avinguda Diagonal, Via Augusta, the Túnel de Vallvidrera and the E-9. Turn on to the BP-1213 just past Terrassa and follow it 18km north-west to the C-1411. Then head a couple of kilometres south on this road to Monistrol de Montserrat, from which a road snakes about 7km up the mountain to the monastery.

SANT SADURNÍ D'ANOIA & VILAFRANCA DEL PENEDÈS

Some of Spain's best wines come from the area centred on these towns. Sant Sadurní d'Anoia, a half-hour train ride west of Barcelona, is the capital of *cava*, Spanish 'champagne'. Vilafranca del Penedès, 12km down the track, is the heart of the Penedès DO, which produces noteworthy light, still whites. Visitors are welcome at numerous wineries; there'll often be a free glass or two included in the tour, and plenty more for sale, but if you fancy a full-scale tasting you should ring ahead.

Sant Sadurní d'Anoia

A hundred or so wineries around Sant Sadurní produce 140 million bottles of cava a year – something like 85% of the entire national output. Cava is made by the same method as French champagne. Freixenet (☎ 93 891 70 00), the best-known cava company, is based right next to the train station at Carrer de Joan Sala 2. Free tours are given Monday to Thursday at 9, 10 and 11.30 am and 3.30 and 5 pm; in December there's also tours on Friday morning, Saturday and Sunday. Codorníu (☎ 93 818 32 32) is at Can Codorníu, at the entry to the town by road from Barcelona. Manuel Raventós, head of this firm back in 1872, was the first Spaniard successfully to produce sparkling wine by the champagne method. The Codorníu headquarters, a modernist building, is open for free visits Monday to Friday from 9 am to 5 pm and weekends from 9 am to 1 pm.

Vilafranca del Penedès

Vilafranca is larger than Sant Sadurní and much more interesting. The helpful tourist office (☎ 93 892 03 58) on Plaça de la Vila is open Tuesday to Friday from 9 am to 1 pm and 4 to 7 pm and Saturday from 10 am to 1 pm. In summer it also is open on Saturday from 5 to 8 pm and Sunday from 10 am to 1 pm. A block north, the mainly Gothic **Basílica de Santa Maria** faces the combined **Museu de Vilafranca** and **Museu del Vi** (Wine Museum) across Plaça de Jaume I. The museum, a fine Gothic building, covers local archaeology, art, geology and bird life, and also has an excellent section on wine, at the end of which you're treated to a free copa. It's open Tuesday to Saturday from 10 am to 2 pm and 4 to 7 pm (9 am to 9 pm in summer) and Sunday and holidays from 10 am to 2 pm (400 ptas). A statue on Plaça de Jaume I pays tribute to Vilafranca's famous *castellers*, who do their thing during Vilafranca's lively *festa major* (main annual festival) at the end of August.

Vilafranca's premier winery is Torres (☎ 93 817 74 87), 3km north-west of the town centre on the BP-2121 road near Pacs del Penedès. The Torres family revolutionised Spanish wine-making back in the 1960s by introducing new temperature-controlled, stainless-steel technology and French grape varieties that helped produce much lighter wines than the traditional heavy Spanish plonk. Torres is open for visits Monday to Friday from 9 am to noon and 3 to 5 pm and weekends from 9 am to 1 pm. Most other Penedès wineries are, like Torres, out of town.

Getting There & Away

Up to three rodalies trains an hour run from Barcelona Sants to Sant Sadurní and Vilafranca. By car, take the A-2, then the A-7. From Sitges, both places are a short drive inland, or a longer train journey involving a change at Coma-ruga.

LLEIDA

Western Catalunya is flat and drab, but if you're not in a hurry Lleida (Lérida), Catalunya's second city with 144,000 people, is a likeable place with a long, varied history. It's also the starting point of several routes towards the Pyrenees.

Orientation

The centre spreads around the southern side of a hill dominated by the old cathedral, La Seu Vella, with Carrer del Carme, Carrer de Sant Joan, Plaça de Sant Joan and Carrer Major forming a mainly pedestrianised axis from north-east to south-west. The train station is at the north-eastern end of Rambla de Ferran, with the estació d'autobusos 1.25km away on Carrer de Saracíbar, off Avinguda de Madrid.

Information

The tourist office (☎ 973 27 09 97) is at Avinguda de Madrid 36. The main correos is on Rambla de Ferran (postcode 25080). If you're heading for the Pyrenees, Caselles at Carrer Major 46 and Ramon Fregola at Carrer de Sant Joan 18 stock maps and guidebooks.

La Seu Vella

Lleida's 'old cathedral' towers above all else in position and grandeur. It stands within a *recinte* (compound) of defensive walls erected between the 12th and 19th centuries. The main entrance to the recinte (open daily from 8 am to 9 pm; free) is from Carrer de Monterey on its western side, but during the cathedral's opening hours you can use the *ascensor* (lift) from above Plaça de Sant Joan. The cathedral was built in sandy-coloured stone in the 13th to 15th centuries on the site of a former mosque (Lleida was under Muslim control from 719 to 1149). It's a masterpiece of the Transitional style, although it only recently recovered from 241 years use as a barracks which began as Felipe V's punishment for the city's opposition in the War of the Spanish Succession. A 70m octagonal bell tower rises at the south-western end from

Of Giants, Dragons & Human Castles

DAMIEN SIMONIS

The Castellers de Barcelona making a 'quatre de vuit'

As befits a people of such independent traditions, Catalans get up to all sorts of unusual tricks at *festa* time.

Fire and fireworks play a big part in many Spanish festivals, but Catalunya adds a special twist with the *correfoc* (fire-running), in which devil and dragon figures run through the streets spitting fireworks at the crowds. (Wear protective clothes if you intend to get close!) Correfocs are often part of the *festa major* – a town or village's main annual festival. Many of these are in July or August. Also usually part of the festa major fun are the *sardana* (Catalunya's national round-dance), all sorts of costumed local dances, and *gegants*, splendidly attired and lifelike 5m high giants who parade through the streets or dance in the squares to the sound of old-fashioned instruments. Giants usually come in male-female pairs: a medieval king and queen, a Muslim sultan and a Christian princess. Almost every town and village has its own – sometimes just one pair, sometimes five or six. They're usually accompanied by an entourage of grotesque 'dwarfs' (otherwise known as *capgrossos*, or bigheads).

On La Nit de Sant Joan, 23 June, big bonfires burn at crossroads and on town squares in a combined midsummer and St John's Eve celebration. Fireworks go on all night. But Catalunya's supreme fire festival is the Patum in the otherwise unexceptional Pyrenean foothill town of Berga. An evening of dancing and firework-spitting angels, devils, mule-like monsters,

---

the cloister, whose windows have exceptionally fine Gothic tracery. The spacious but rather austere interior, used as stables and dormitories during the military occupation, has a forest of slender columns with carved capitals. The cathedral is open Tuesday to Saturday from 10 am to 1.30 pm and 3 to 5.30 pm (4 to 7.30 pm from June to September) and Sunday and holidays from 10 am to 1.30 pm (400 ptas).

Above the cathedral are remains of the Islamic fortress and residence of the Muslim governors, known as the Castell del Rei.

Carrer Major & Around

A 13th century Gothic mansion, **La Paeria** has housed the city government almost since its inception. The 18th century neoclassical **Seu Nova** on Plaça de la Catedral was built when La Seu Vella was turned into barracks.

Opposite is the **Hospital de Santa Maria**, with a Gothic courtyard. It now houses the **Museu Arqueològic**, which includes Iberian and Roman finds from the Lleida region; it's open Tuesday to Saturday from noon to 2 pm and 5.30 to 8.30 pm.

Of Giants, Dragons & Human Castles

dwarfs, giants and men covered in grass culminates in a kind of mass frenzy of fire and smoke that has been likened to a medieval vision of hell. The 'real' Patum happens on Corpus Christi (the Thursday following the eighth Sunday after Easter Sunday) although there are watered-down versions on the next two or three days.

An activity demanding rather more calm and order, but still emotive, is the building of *castells*, human castles. This tradition is strongest in southern and central Catalunya: Valls, Vilafranca del Penedès and Terrassa have three of the most famous groups of *castellers*. The golden age was the 1880s, when castells of *tres de nou* and *quatre de nou* ('three of nine' and 'four of nine', ie nine storeys of three people and nine storeys of four people) were achieved.

There are all sorts of permutations in the construction of the castell: those built without a *pinya*, *folre* or *manilles* – extra rings of support for the first, second and third storeys – are particularly tricky and termed *net* (clean). A completed castell is signalled by the child at the top (the *anxeneta*) raising their arm – a cue for tumultuous applause and cheering from the onlookers. A castell that manages to dismantle itself without collapsing is *descarregat*. Especially difficult is a *pilar*, a tower of one person per storey. The best pilar ever done was eight storeys, a *pilar de vuit*.

Since the 1980s the practice has experienced a revival, which is threatening to break all-time records for degrees of difficulty. Building castells is a sort of sport and competitions are held, often at festes majors. Festivals where you can expect to see castellers include: Vilafranca del Penedès, at the end of August; Tarragona, in the last week of September; El Vendrell, around 16 October; and Valls, on the first Sunday after 21 October.

A castell is completed by a child at the top

Carrer dels Caballers and Carrer de la Palma climb from Carrer Major up through the old part of town. The **Antic Convent del Roser** at Carrer dels Caballers 15, with an unusual three-storey cloister, houses the **Museu d'Art Jaume Morera** and its collection of work by Lleida-associated artists.

Places to Stay

Camping Les Basses (☎ 973 23 59 54) at Km 5 on the N-240 to Huesca charges 575 ptas per person, per tent and per car. Lleida's youth hostel, *Alberg Sant Anastasi*

(☎ 973 26 60 99, Rambla d'Aragó 11), has room for 120 and no high season, but it's used as a student residence from mid-September to June, so you may have trouble getting in then.

The friendly *Hostal Mundial* (☎ 973 24 27 00, Plaça de Sant Joan 4), with an entrance on Carrer Major, is hard to beat, with its range of worthy rooms costing from 1500/2700 ptas to 1600/3200 ptas with private bath.

Convenient for the train station are *Hotel La Canonja* (☎ 973 23 80 14, Carrer del

CATALUNYA

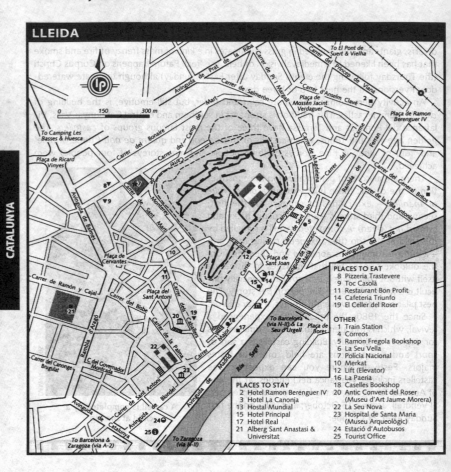

LLEIDA

0 150 300 m

To El Pont de Suert & Vielha

To Camping Les Basses & Huesca

Plaça de Ricard Vinyes

Plaça de Mossèn Jacint Verdaguer

Plaça de Ramon Berenguer IV

Plaça de Cervantes

Plaça de Ramón y Cajal

Plaça de Sant Antoni

Plaça de Sant Joan

Plaça de Bores

To Barcelona (via N-II) & La Seu d'Urgell

To Barcelona & Zaragoza (via A-2)

To Zaragoza (via N-II)

PLACES TO EAT
8 Pizzeria Trastevere
9 Toc Casolà
11 Restaurant Bon Profit
14 Cafeteria Triunfo
19 El Celler del Roser

OTHER
1 Train Station
4 Correos
5 Ramon Fregola Bookshop
6 La Seu Vella
7 Policía Nacional
10 Merkat
12 Lift (Elevator)
16 La Paeria
18 Caselles Bookshop
20 Antic Convent del Roser (Museu d'Art Jaume Morera)
22 La Seu Nova
23 Hospital de Santa Maria (Museu Arqueològic)
24 Estació d'Autobusos
25 Tourist Office

PLACES TO STAY
2 Hotel Ramon Berenguer IV
3 Hotel La Canonja
13 Hostal Mundial
15 Hotel Principal
17 Hotel Real
21 Alberg Sant Anastasi & Universitat

General Britos 21) and *Hotel Ramon Berenguer IV* (☎ 973 23 73 45, *Plaça de Ramon Berenguer IV 3)*. Doubles without and with bath are 4000 ptas and 5000 to 5500 ptas, respectively.

If you're looking for a bit more style, two good central options are the *Hotel Principal* (☎ 973 23 08 00, *Plaça de la Paeria 8)* on Carrer Major, with doubles for 6500 ptas, and the modern *Hotel Real* (☎ 973 23 94 05, *Avinguda de Blondel 22)*, charging 8200 ptas.

Places to Eat

Despite the many pleasant cafés around Plaça de Sant Joan and elsewhere, the downtown options for an actual meal are limited, especially in the evening. *Cafeteria Triunfo* on Carrer Major, just off Plaça de Sant Joan, has a set *menú* for 950 ptas.

The cheapest food deal in town is *Restaurant Bon Profit* on Carrer dels Caballers. The area is home to many black and North African migrants, and the eatery serves up all sorts of mains, including couscous, from 500 ptas.

Lleida is Catalunya's snail-eating capital. So many *cargols* are swallowed during the annual Aplec del Cargol snail feast, held on a Sunday in early May, that some of them have to be imported. *El Celler del Roser (Carrer del Caballers 24)* serves the slithering things *a la llauna* (baked on tin over hot coals), as well as other Catalan fare.

A less central hunting ground is the area around Plaça de Ricard Vinyes, north-west of La Seu Vella, where you'll find good places like *Pizzeria Trastevere (Carrer del Camp de Mart 27)* with pasta and pizzas from 780 ptas, and *Toc Casolà*, down the street, which serves meaty main dishes from 750 ptas and salads for two at 1300 ptas. This area is also the heart of Lleida's nightlife.

Getting There & Away

Bus Daily services by Alsina Graells (☎ 973 27 14 70) include up to 13 buses to Barcelona (2¼ to 2¾ hours); two to El Pont de Suert and Vielha (2¾ hours); one (except Sunday) to La Pobla de Segur, Sort, Llavorsí and Esterri d'Àneu (three hours); two to La Seu d'Urgell (2½ hours); and one to Puigcerdà (four hours). Other buses go to Tarragona (six daily), and westward to Zaragoza (four or five daily from Monday to Saturday, but only one on Sunday) and Barbastro and Huesca (four daily).

Train Lleida (station ☎ 973 22 02 02) is on the main Barcelona-Zaragoza-Madrid line. Up to 21 trains daily run to Barcelona, most taking about two hours, although some dawdle for four. Second-class fares range from 1220 ptas upwards. There are up to 12 daily trains to Zaragoza (1¾ hours) and up to five to Madrid. Other direct services run to Tarragona (1¼ hours; from 630 ptas; 10 daily), La Pobla de Segur (two hours; four daily), Valencia, San Sebastián and as far afield as Galicia, Andalucía and Cerbère (France).

Car & Motorcycle The quickest routes to Barcelona, Tarragona and Zaragoza are by the A-2, but you can avoid tolls by taking the N-II to Zaragoza or Barcelona or the N-240 to Tarragona. The main northward roads are the C-1313 to La Seu d'Urgell, the N-230 to Vielha and the N-240 to Barbastro and Huesca.

CONCA DE BARBERÀ

This hilly green back country district comes as a refreshing surprise in the otherwise drab flatlands of south-western Catalunya. Vineyards and woods succeed one another across green rolling hills, studded by occasional medieval villages and monasteries.

Monestir de Poblet

The jewel in the crown in the Conca de Barberà is doubtless this imposing fortified monastery. It was founded by Cistercian monks from southern France in 1151.

The walls of this abbey devoted to Santa Maria, as much as a defensive measure, also symbolised the monks' isolation of themselves from the vanities of the outside world. Within the triple line of walls stand out several magnificent buildings. But before you even get inside you must pass between the powerful towers flanking the Porta Reial. Inside, the Gothic **Capilla de Sant Jordi** is also known as 'la dorada', because bronze panels on the chapel were made over with gold to impress the visiting emperor Felipe II in 1564. In the **Palau del Rei Martí**, the most captivating element are the exquisitely crafted Gothic windows. The oldest part of this sprawling abbey is the **cloister**, a Transitional work showing clearly enough its Romanesque origins.

Without doubt, it is the haughty **iglesia** that most impresses itself on the memory. Begun in 1161, it is the largest Cistercian church in Spain. The high altar is presided over by a magnificent alabaster retablo.

The monastery is open daily from 10 am to 12.30 pm and 3 to 6 pm (5.30 pm in winter; 500 ptas, students 300 ptas). Hourlong guided tours (in Catalan and/or Spanish) start every 15 to 30 minutes.

Over Easter and the summer months you can stay across the road from the monastery at the cheerful *Hostal Fonoll*

(☎ 977 87 03 33). Singles/doubles start at 1995/2750 ptas without own bathroom, or 3900/5000 ptas with.

Of six Vibasa buses (☎ 902 10 13 63) from Tarragona to Montblanc and L'Espluga de Francolí, three also stop at the monastery. Regular trains from Barcelona to Tarragona via Reus (line Ca4) stop at Montblanc and L'Espluga de Francolí, a 40 minute walk to the monastery.

Around Monestir de Poblet

It is worth spending time exploring the vicinity. **L'Espluga de Francolí**, 2.5km away from the monastery along a pleasant tree-lined country road that makes walking tempting, is a bright little town with several small hotels.

More interesting still is **Montblanc**, 8km away. Still surrounded by medieval battlements, this one-time royal residence is jammed with medieval jewels, including a Gothic royal mansion and a couple of churches from the same era, as well as some vestiges of its Romanesque origins. The winding cross-country drive to **Prades** also takes you through lovely country.

If monasteries are your thing, the less imposing **Monestir de Santes Creus**, east of Montblanc, and **Vallbona de les Monges**, to the north, are also worth searching out.

Southern Catalunya

Sitges, 35km south-west of Barcelona, is the wildest resort on the Catalan coast. From there to the Valencian border stretches the Costa Daurada (Golden Coast), a series of far less exciting resorts along a mainly flat coast varied only by the delta of the Río Ebro, which protrudes 20km out into the Mediterranean Sea. Along the way, however, are the old Roman capital of Tarragona and the modern extravaganza of Port Aventura – Spain's answer to EuroDisney.

SITGES

Sitges attracts everyone from jet-setters to young travellers, honeymooners to week-ending families, Barcelona night owls to an international gay crowd. The beach is long and sandy, the nightlife thumps till breakfast and there are lots of groovy boutiques if you need to spruce up your wardrobe. In winter Sitges can be dead, but it wakes up with a vengeance for *carnaval*, when the gay crowd puts on an outrageous show.

Sitges has been fashionable in one way or another since the 1890s, when it became an avant-garde art world hang-out. It has been Spain's most anti-conventional, anything-goes resort since the 1960s. One thing it isn't, though, is cheap.

Orientation

The main landmark is the Església de Sant Bartomeu i Santa Tecla parish church, atop a small rocky elevation that separates the 2km long main beach, to the south-west, from the smaller, quieter Platja de Sant Sebastià to the north-east. The old part of town climbs gently inland from the church area, with the train station some 500m back, at the top of Avinguda de Artur Carbonell.

Information

The tourist office (☎ 93 811 76 30, Carrer de Sínia Morera 1) is open daily in July and August from 9 am to 9 pm; in other months, it's open Monday to Friday from 9 am to 2 pm and 4 to 6.30 pm (Saturday from 10 am to 1 pm). You can pick up a free map of gay-oriented bars, hotels, restaurants and shops, the *Plano Gay de Sitges*, at several spots around town including Parrots Pub on Plaça de la Industria.

There are several banks and ATMs on and around Plaça del Cap de Vila in the old town. The correos is on Plaça d'Espanya. The postcode is 08870. The Policia Local (☎ 93 811 76 25) are on Plaça d'Ajuntament behind the parish church. The Hospital Sant Joan (☎ 93 894 00 03) is on Carrer del Hospital in the upper part of town above the railway.

Museums

The **Museu Cau Ferrat** on Carrer de Fonollar was built in the 1890s as a house-

SITGES

PLACES TO STAY
1   Camping El Rocá
5   Hostal Julián
6   Hostal Residència
    Internacional
7   Romàntic Hotel
8   Park Hotel
12 Hostal Mariàngel
16 Hotel Madison Bahía
17 Hostal Parelladas
23 Hotel Lido
25 Hotel Capri
27 Hostal Rivamar
29 Hostal Bonaire
30 Hotel Celimar

PLACES TO EAT
9   La Granja de Sitges
10 Restaurant La Viña
14 Los Vikingos
15 La Oca
18 Eguzki
20 La Torreta
21 Rugantino
22 Restaurant Miami
26 Hotel La Santa Maria
28 Restaurante El Velero

OTHER
2   Hospital Sant Joan
3   Train Station
4   Tourist Office
11 Museu Romàntic
13 Correos
19 Trailer Disco
24 Parrots Pub
31 Policia Local
32 Museu Cau Ferrat
33 Museu Maricel del Mar
34 Església de Sant
    Bartomeu i Santa Tecla

cum-studio by Santiago Rusiñol, a co-founder of Els Quatre Gats in Barcelona, and the man who attracted the art world to Sitges. In 1894 Rusiñol reawakened the world to the then unfashionable work of El Greco by parading two of the Cretan's canvases in from Sitges railway station to Cau Ferrat. These are now on show in the museum along with the remainder of Rusiñol's large art and crafts collection, which includes paintings by the likes of Picasso, Ramon Casas and Rusiñol himself.

Next door is the **Museu Maricel del Mar**, with art and artisanry from the Middle Ages to the 20th century. The museum is part of the Palau Maricel, a stylistic fantasy built around 1910 by Miquel Utrillo. The **Museu Romàntic** at Carrer de Sant Gaudenci 1 recreates the lifestyle of a 19th century Catalan landowning family and contains a collection of several hundred antique dolls.

From late June to early September all three museums are open Tuesday to Sunday from 10 am to 9 pm; at other times, they're open Tuesday to Sunday from 9.30 am to 2 pm, plus Tuesday from 4 to 6 pm and Sunday from 4 to 8 pm (200 ptas each museum).

Beaches

The main beach is divided by a series of breakwaters into sections with different names. A pedestrian promenade runs its whole length. In high summer, especially on the weekend, the end nearest the parish church gets jam-packed. Crowds thin out slightly towards the south-west end. Sitges also has two nude beaches – one exclusively gay – about 20 minutes walk beyond the Hotel Terramar at the far end of the main beach. To reach them, you have to walk along the coast past a sewage plant, over a hill and along the railway a bit.

Special Events

Carnaval in Sitges is a week-long riot of the extravagant, ambiguous and exhibitionist, capped by an extravagant gay parade on the last night. June sees the Sitges International Theatre Festival, with a strong experimental leaning. Sitges' festa major in late August features a huge firework show on the 23rd. Early October is the time for Sitges' International Fantasy Film Festival.

Places to Stay

Sitges has over 50 hotels and hostales, but many close from around October to April, then are full in July and August. If you haven't booked ahead, it's not a bad idea, especially if you arrive late in the day, to ask the tourist office to ring around for you.

Camping *Camping El Rocà (☎ 93 894 00 43, Avinguda de Ronda s/n)* is in the upper part of town north of the railway, 1km from the beach. It has room for 600 people and charges 630 ptas per adult, per car and per tent. It's open from April to September. *Camping El Garrofer (☎ 93 894 17 80)* and *Camping Sitges (☎ 93 894 10 80)* are out of town off the C-246.

Hostales Two friendly places popular with travellers, both on the central Carrer de les Parellades, are *Hostal Mariàngel (☎ 93 894 13 57)* at No 78 and *Hostal Parelladas (☎ 93 894 08 01)* at No 11. The Mariàngel has rooms from 2000/3750 ptas to 3000/5000 ptas (with shower). The Parelladas has singles without own shower for 2400 ptas and doubles with private bathroom for 5000 ptas.

Hostal Julià (☎ 93 894 03 06, Avinguda de Artur Carbonell 2), near the train station and tourist office, has garish wallpaper but good-sized rooms, with shared baths, for 3300/5000 ptas. Close by, *Hostal Residència Internacional (☎ 93 894 26 90, Carrer de Sant Francesc 52)* has eight sizable and clean doubles for 5000 ptas (6000 ptas with private shower).

One place open all year is *Hostal Bonaire (☎ 93 894 53 26, Carrer de Bonaire 31)*, where doubles are 4000 ptas with washbasin or 5500 ptas with bathroom. *Hostal Mogar (☎ 93 811 00 09, Carrer de Bonaire 2)* has similar prices. *Hostal Rivamar (☎ 93 894 34 08, Passeig de la Ribera 46)* is right on the seafront. Doubles with bathroom, if you're lucky enough to get one, are 7000 ptas plus IVA.

Hotels *Hotel Lido (☎ 93 894 48 48, Carrer de Bonaire 26)*, a popular gay haunt, has good doubles with bathroom for 6500 ptas plus IVA.

Hotel Madison Bahía (☎ 93 894 00 12, Carrer de les Parellades 31-33) has friendly management and singles/doubles with bath at 7800/8900 ptas. All 25 rooms have exterior windows. The *Park Hotel (☎ 93 894 02 50, Carrer de Jesús 12-14)* is a slight step up with doubles at 11,000 ptas plus IVA.

The *Romàntic Hotel (☎ 93 894 83 75, Carrer de Sant Isidre 33)* comprises three adjoining 19th century villas, sensuously restored in period style, with a leafy dining courtyard. It's popular with gay visitors, although not exclusively so. There are about 60 rooms with shower starting from 7300/10,100 ptas.

On the seafront near the parish church, *Hotel Celimar (☎ 93 811 01 70, Passeig de la Ribera 20)* has rooms for 9750 to 16,950 ptas plus IVA. *Hotel Capri (☎ 93 811 02 67, Avinguda de Sofía 13-15)* is a good family-run place with doubles at 14,500 ptas plus IVA.

Places to Eat

You'll be lucky to find a *menú* for less than 1200 ptas. The self-service *Los Vikingos (Carrer del Marques de Montroig 7-9)* in the thick of the action, does tolerable pasta, pizza and seafood from 725 ptas. *La Oca*, round the corner on Carrer de les Parellades, is popular for its pizzas from 585 ptas and grilled chicken at 340 ptas for a quarter-bird. *Hotel La Santa Maria (Passeig de la Ribera 52)* has a vast Catalan and Spanish restaurant, partly open-air, with starters like *xató* (a local fish salad in piquant dressing), escalivada and *esqueixada*, and a full range of meat and fish mains, all from around 1000 ptas. *Restaurante El Velero* along the street is a classier fish and seafood joint with most mains at 1500 ptas or more.

Carrer de Sant Pau has a string of good restaurants including the Basque *Eguzki* at No 3, which has good tapas and a mixed menu of seafood and meat mains from 800 to 1600 ptas. *Restaurant Miami* at No 11 has a decent four-course *menú* for 1300 ptas.

La Granja de Sitges (Plaça del Cap de Vila) is a lively tapas spot. *Restaurant La Viña (Carrer de Sant Francesc 11)* also has a range of generous tapas starting at around 400 ptas.

A calmer area to eat is over on Platja de Sant Sebastià, where *Rugantino* does pizza, pasta, and meat and vegetarian dishes from 850 ptas, and the classy *La Torreta* deals mainly in seafood, from 1600 to 2200 ptas a main course.

Entertainment

Much of Sitges' nightlife happens on one short pedestrian strip packed with humanity right through the night in summer: Carrer del 1er de Maig, Plaça de la Industria and Carrer del Marques de Montroig, all in a short line off the seafront Passeig de la Ribera. Carrer del 1er de Maig – or Calle del Pecado (Sin Street) – vibrates to the volume of 10 or so disco-bars all trying to outdo each other in decibels. They start to fill at about midnight. Plaça de la Industria and Carrer del Marques de Montroig have the bars and cafés where people sit, drink and watch other people. All you have to do is cruise along, see what takes your fancy and try not to bust your budget. If you're in need of a change of location, head round the corner to Carrer de les Parellades, Carrer de Bonaire or Carrer de Sant Pere, where there's more of much the same. Carrer de Sant Bonaventura has a string of gay bars, mostly behind closed doors. *Trailer* (Carrer del Àngel Vidal 36) is a popular gay disco.

Getting There & Away

Four rodalies trains an hour, from about 6 am to 10 pm, run from Barcelona Sants to Sitges, taking 30 minutes and charging 305 ptas (350 ptas on weekends). Several trains a day leave Sitges for Tarragona (one hour), where you can change for Port Aventura, Valencia and beyond.

The best road from Barcelona is the A-16 tollway. In Sitges itself, the traffic usually makes it quicker to walk than drive.

TARRAGONA

Tarragona was first occupied by the Romans, who called it Tarraco, in 218 BC. In 27 BC Augustus made it capital of his new Tarraconensis province (which comprised pretty much modern Spain) and stayed here till 25 BC while directing campaigns in Cantabria and Asturias. Tarragona was abandoned when the Muslims arrived in 714 AD, but reborn as the seat of a Christian archbishopric in 1089. Today, with 111,000 people, it's a mainly modern city, but its rich Roman remains and fine medieval cathedral make it an absorbing place.

Tarraco, An Archaeological Guide by Xavier Aquilué and others will help you unravel Tarragona's ancient history and complicated archaeology; one place selling it is the Museu Arqueològic.

Orientation

The main street is Rambla Nova, which runs roughly north-west from a cliff-top overlooking the Mediterranean. A couple of blocks to the east, and parallel, is Rambla Vella, which marks the beginning of the old town and, incidentally, follows the line of the Via Augusta, the Roman road from Rome to Cádiz.

The train station is half a kilometre south-west of Rambla Nova, near the seafront, and the estació d'autobusos is about 2km inland, on Plaça Imperial de Tàrraco.

Information

The main tourist office (☎ 977 24 50 64, at Carrer Major 39) is open Monday to Friday from 10 am to 2 pm and 4.30 to 7 pm and weekends and holidays from 10 am to 2 pm (and extra hours from July to September). There's also a Catalunya regional tourist office (☎ 977 23 34 15, Carrer de Fortuny 4) and a couple of info booths scattered about the old town that open on weekends and in summer.

Several countries have consulates in Tarragona. The main correos (postcode 43080) is on Plaça Corsini.

The Guàrdia Urbana (municipal police; ☎ 092 or ☎ 977 24 03 45) are at Carrer de Pare Palau 7. There's a hospital (☎ 977 23 27 14) on Passeig de Torroja.

Catedral

Sitting grandly at the top of the old town, Tarragona's cathedral is a treasure house deserving 1½ hours or more if you're to do it justice. Built between 1171 and 1331 on the site of a Roman temple, it combines Romanesque and Gothic features, as typified by the main façade on Pla de la Seu. The entrance is by the cloister on the north-western side of the building. At our last check the cathedral was open for tourist visits from Monday to Friday for hours that vary with the season but always include from 10 am to 1 pm and (except from mid-November to mid-March) 3 to 6 pm. The 300 ptas charge includes a detailed booklet.

The cloister has Gothic vaulting and Romanesque carved capitals, one of which shows rats conducting what they imagine to be a cat's funeral, until the cat comes back to life! Rooms off the cloister house the Museu Diocesà, with an extensive collection extending from Roman hairpins to some lovely 12th to 14th century polychrome woodcarvings of a breastfeeding Virgin.

The interior of the cathedral, over 100m long, is Romanesque at the north-eastern end and Gothic at the south-west. The aisles are lined with 14th to 19th century chapels and hung with 16th and 17th century tapestries from Brussels. The arm of St Thecla, Tarragona's patron saint, is normally kept in the Capella de Santa Tecla on the south-eastern side. The choir in the centre of the nave has 15th century carved walnut stalls. The marble main altar was carved in the 13th century with scenes from the life of St Thecla.

Museu d'Història de Tarragona

This museum comprises four separate Roman sites around the city. A single 475 ptas ticket (students free) is good for all four, along with the modest Museu d'Art Modern, Carrer de Santa Anna 8, and the 14th century noble mansion now serving as the Museu Casa Castelarnau, Carrer dels Cavallers 14.

A good one to start with is the Museu de la Romanitat on Plaça del Rei, which includes part of the vaults of the Roman circus, where chariot races were held. The circus, 300m long, stretched from here to beyond Plaça de la Font. Close to the beach is the well-preserved Amfiteatre, where gladiators battled each other, or wild animals, to the death. In its arena are the remains of 6th and 12th century churches built to commemorate the martyrdom of the Christian bishop Fructuosus and two deacons, burnt alive here in 259.

By Carrer de Lleida are remains of a forum. The north-western half of this site was occupied by a judicial basilica (where legal disputes were settled), from which the rest of the forum stretched downhill to the

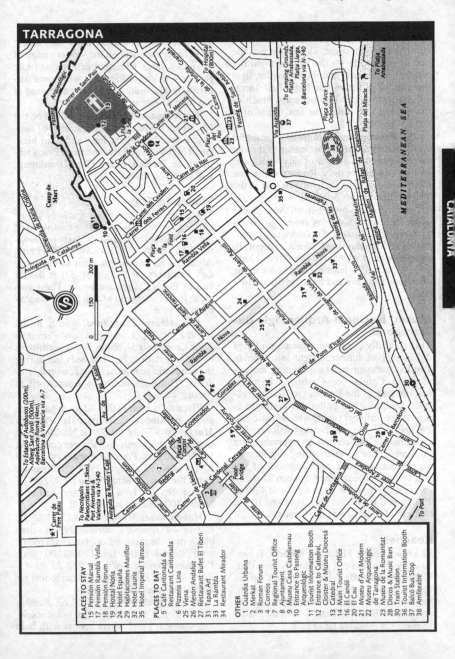

TARRAGONA

PLACES TO STAY
15 Pensión Marsal
17 Pensión Rambla Vella
18 Pensión Forum
19 Hostal Noria
24 Hotel España
29 Habitaciones Mariflor
32 Hotel Lauria
35 Hotel Imperial Tarraco

PLACES TO EAT
5 Café Cantonada &
  Restaurant Cantonada
6 Pizzeria Lina
25 Viena
26 Mesón Andaluz
27 Restaurant Bufet El Tiberi
31 Tapas Art
33 La Rambla
34 Restaurant Mirador

OTHER
1 Guàrdia Urbana
2 Merkat
3 Roman Forum
4 Correos
7 Regional Tourist Office
8 Ajuntament
9 Museu Casa Castelarnau
10 Entrance to Passeig
   Arqueològic
11 Tourist Information Booth
12 Entrance to Catedral,
   Cloister & Museu Diocesà
13 Catedral
14 Main Tourist Office
16 El Candil
20 El Cau
21 Museu d'Art Modern
22 Museu Arqueològic
   de Tarragona
23 Museu de la Romanitat
28 Discos & Music Bars
30 Train Station
36 Tourist Information Booth
37 Balcó Bus Stop
38 Amfiteatre

south-west. Linked to the site by a foot-bridge is another excavated area with a stretch of Roman street. This forum was the hub of public life for the Roman town but was less important, and much smaller, than the provincial forum, the hub of all Tarraconensis province. This occupied much of the existing old town, but few traces of it are visible now.

The **Passeig Arqueològic** is a peaceful walk round part of the perimeter of the old town between two lines of city walls; the inner ones are mainly Roman while the outer ones were put up by the British in the War of the Spanish Succession.

From June to September, all these places open Tuesday to Saturday from 9 or 10 am to 8 pm (the Passeig Arqueològic to midnight) and Sunday from 10 am to 2 pm. In other months, they tend to open from 10 am to 1.30 pm and at least for two hours in the afternoon (Sunday and holidays 10 am to 2 pm).

Museu Nacional Arqueològic de Tarragona

This carefully presented museum on Plaça del Rei gives further insight into Roman Tarraco, although most explanatory material is in Catalan or Castilian. Exhibits include part of the Roman city walls, frescoes, sculpture and pottery. A highlight is the large, almost complete *Mosaic de Peixos de la Pineda* showing fish and sea creatures. In the section on everyday arts you can admire ancient fertility aids including an outsize stone penis, symbol of the god Priapus. The museum is open Tuesday to Saturday from 10 am to 1 pm and 4.30 to 7 pm and Sunday and holidays from 10 am to 2 pm (100 ptas, free on Tuesday).

Beaches

The town beach, **Platja del Miracle**, is reasonably clean but can get terribly crowded. **Platja Arrabassada**, 1km north-east across the headland, is longer, and **Platja Llarga**, beginning 2km farther out, stretches for about 3km. Bus Nos 1 and 9 from the Balcó stop on Via Augusta go to both.

Other Attractions

The **Necròpolis Paleocristians** on Passeig de la Independència on the western edge of town is a large Christian cemetery of late Roman and Visigothic times with some surprisingly elaborate tombs. It was closed at the time of research.

The **Aqüeducte Romà**, 4km inland on the N-240 Lleida road, is a fine stretch of two-tiered aqueduct 217m long and 27m high. Bus No 5 to Sant Salvador from Plaça Imperial de Tàrraco, every 10 to 20 minutes, will take you there.

Places to Stay

There are eight camping grounds on or close to the beach within 11km north-east of the city along the N-340. Nearest is *Camping Tàrraco* (☎ 977 23 99 89) behind Platja Arrabassada, but others, such as *Camping Las Palmeras* (☎ 977 20 80 81) at the far end of Platja Llarga, are better. These two close from October to March but others stay open all year.

The *Alberg Sant Jordi* youth hostel (☎ 977 24 01 95, Avinguda del President Lluís Companys 5), about 300m north-west of the bus station, has 192 beds but during the academic year most are taken up by students. The high season is from April to August.

Plaça de la Font in the old town has three good pensiones. Cheapest is *Pensión Marsal* (☎ 977 22 40 69) at No 26. Basic singles/doubles with own shower come in at 1650/3300 ptas. *Pensión Forum* (☎ 977 23 17 18) at No 37 charges 2500/4500 ptas for much the same. *Hostal Noria* (☎ 977 23 87 17) at No 53 is a bit better value at 2600/4300 ptas but is often full.

Habitaciones Mariflor (☎ 977 23 82 31, Carrer del General Contreras 29), in a drab block near the train station, has clean rooms with shared baths for 1700/3300 ptas. *Pensión Rambla Vella* (☎ 977 23 81 15, Rambla Vella 31) has small, clean rooms for 2200/4000 ptas with shower.

Hotel España (☎ 977 23 27 12, Rambla Nova 49) is a well-positioned, but unexciting, one-star hotel where rooms with bath cost 3300/6000 ptas plus IVA. The three star *Hotel Lauria* (☎ 977 23 67 12) at No 20 is a worthwhile splurge at 5500/10,000 ptas plus IVA, with a good location and a pool. *Hotel Imperial Tàrraco* (☎ 977 23 30 40), at No 2, is the best in town, with a great position overlooking the Med and rooms for 13,200/17,800 ptas plus IVA. Several of the better hotels offer big discounts on Friday, Saturday and Sunday nights.

Places to Eat

The *Pensión Marsal* has a respectable four-course lunch or dinner *menú* for just 700 ptas. For Catalan food, head for the stylish *Restaurant Bufet El Tiberi (Carrer de Martí d'Ardenya 5)*, which offers an all-you-can-eat buffet for about 1400 ptas per person. Nearby *Mesón Andaluz (Carrer de Pons d'Icart 3)* is a backstreet local favourite (upstairs), with a good three-course *menú* for 1100 ptas. *Café Cantonada (Carrer de Fortuny 23)* has a lunch *menú* for 900 ptas; next door, *Restaurant Cantonada* has pizzas and pasta from around 600 ptas.

A popular little place is *Pizzeria Lina (Carrer de Fortuny 8)*, which has a set *menú* for 775 ptas. It serves pizza, couscous and a ragbag of other dishes.

Several good spots line Rambla Nova. *Viena* at No 50 has croissants and a vast range of entrepans from 250 ptas. *Tapas Art* at No 26 has good tapas from 200 ptas. *La Rambla* at No 10 has a set *menú* for 1500 ptas or you can eat à la carte for around 3000 ptas. Across the road, *Restaurant Mirador* has a swankier set *menú* for 2500 ptas.

Entertainment

El Candil (Plaça de la Font 13) is a popular, relaxed bar-café with a student clientele. *El Cau*, in a Roman circus vault on Carrer de Trinquet Vell, is similar, but with music. *Café Cantonada (Carrer de Fortuny 23)*, with its pool table, is nice for a drink or two. A few louder music bars and discos cluster on Carrer de la Pau del Protectorat near the train station.

Getting There & Away

Lying on main routes south from Barcelona, Tarragona is well connected. Train is the easiest way to Barcelona.

Bus Services run to Barcelona (1¾ hours; 780 ptas; 10 buses Monday to Friday, one or two on the weekend), Valencia (3½ hours; nine daily); Lleida (two hours) and Zaragoza (2¾ hours; up to six daily); La Seu d'Urgell (3¼ hours); and Andorra la Vella (one daily). Other buses run daily to Madrid, Alicante, Pamplona, the main Andalucian cities and the north coast.

Train About 20 regional and long-distance trains a day run to/from Barcelona's Passeig de Gràcia station (one to 1½ hours; the cheapest fare is 630 ptas in 2nd class). Around eight stop at Sitges (one hour from Tarragona). Twelve trains run daily to Valencia (three to 3½ hours; 2030 ptas in 2nd class) and at least eight a day to Lleida (one to 1½ hours) and Zaragoza (three to 3½ hours). To Madrid, there are four trains each day – two via Valencia in seven hours and two via Zaragoza in six hours – with fares starting at 4400 ptas.

Boat In summer Trasmediterránea (☎ 977 22 55 06) runs a 'Fast Ferry' service to Palma de Mallorca, taking just 3¾ hours one way, four days a week. Passenger fare is 7000 ptas and a car is 18,000 ptas.

PORT AVENTURA

Port Aventura (☎ 902 20 22 20), which opened in 1995 7km west of Tarragona, near Salou, is Spain's biggest and best funfair-adventure park. In mid-1998 a new wave of investment which would convert the park into the biggest in all Europe was announced.

If you have 4100 ptas to spare (3100 ptas for children aged five to 12), it makes an amusing day out, especially if you have ankle-biters in tow. It only is open from Semana Santa to October. Apart from hair-raising experiences like the Dragon Khan, claimed to be Europe's biggest roller coaster (with eight loops and speeds up to 110km/h), and the Tifon, which simulates a tropical typhoon, there are gentler rides and areas especially for children. Port Aventura also has a hectic street life that includes Wild West shoot-outs, Polynesian dance troupes and theatres with Chinese acrobats. The park is divided into five theme areas: China, a Mediterranean fishing village, the American Far West, Polynesia and ancient Mexico.

Port Aventura is open daily during its season from 10 am to 8 pm (to midnight from around mid-June to mid-September). Night tickets, valid from 7 pm, are 2500 ptas.

Trains run to Port Aventura's own station, about 1km walk from the site, several times a day from Tarragona and Barcelona (1200 ptas return). By road, take exit 35 from the A-7, or the N-340 from Tarragona. Parking is 500 ptas. One option is to stay in nearby Salou, from where the park is a 10 minute walk away.

TORTOSA

Home to Iberian tribes two thousand years ago, Tortosa has seen them all come and go: Greeks, Romans, Visigoths and Muslims. The town was on the northern front line between Christian and Muslim Spain for four centuries.

The tourist office (☎ 977 51 08 22, Avinguda de la Generalitat) is open Tuesday to Saturday from 10 am to 2 pm and 4 to 8 pm and Sunday from 10 am to 2 pm.

The old town, concentrated in the west end of the city north of the Ebro, is watched over by the imposing **Castell de la Suda**, in whose grounds is now a fine *parador* (☎ 977 44 44 50). The Gothic **Catedral** (or Seu) dates to 1347 and contains a pleasant cloister. Other attractions include the **Palau Episcopal** and the lovely **Jardins del Príncep**, perfect for a stroll.

About the cheapest place to stay is *Hostal Virginia* (☎ 977 44 41 86, *Avinguda de la Generalitat 133)*, where singles/doubles with bath cost up to 2500/3500 ptas.

The train and bus stations are opposite each other on Ronda dels Docs. There are regular connections with Tarragona and Vinarós (Valencia), and occasional buses into the Ebro Delta area.

EBRO DELTA

The delta of the Río Ebro (Delta de l'Ebre in Catalan), formed by silt brought down by the river, sticks 20km out into the Mediterranean near Catalunya's southern border. Dotted with reedy lagoons and fringed by dune-backed beaches, this flat and exposed wetland is northern Spain's most important water-bird habitat. The October-November migration season sees the peak bird population, with an average of 53,000 ducks and 15,000 coots, but they're also numerous in winter and spring. Ten per cent of all water birds wintering on the Iberian Peninsula do so here.

Nearly half the delta's 320 sq km are given over to rice-growing. Some 77 sq km, mostly along the coasts and around the lagoons, form the Parc Natural Delta de l'Ebre.

Orientation

The delta is a seaward-pointing arrowhead of land with the Ebro flowing eastwards across its middle. The town of Deltebre straggles about 5km along the north bank of the river at the centre of the delta. Deltebre's western half is called Jesús i Maria and the eastern half La Cava. Facing Deltebre on the southern bank is Sant Jaume d'Enveja. Roads crisscross the delta to Deltebre and beyond from the towns of L'Ampolla, Amposta and Sant Carles de la Ràpita, all on the N-340. Three ferries *(transbordadors)*, running from early morning till nightfall, link Deltebre to Sant Jaume d'Enveja. They charge 40 ptas per pedestrian and 200 ptas for a car with two people.

Information

There is a tourist office (Centre d'Informació; ☎ 977 48 96 79) at Carrer de Martí Buera 22, Deltebre. Adjoining is an Eco-museu which has some examples of delta environments and an aquarium-terrarium of delta species.

There's another information office, with a bird museum, at Casa de Fusta, by L'Encanyissada lagoon about 10km south-west of Deltebre. Other offices are in Sant Carles de la Ràpita, Amposta and L'Ampolla.

Things to See & Do

A good way to explore the delta is by bicycle and you can rent one for about 1000 ptas a day at several places in Deltebre. Early morning and evening are the best times for birdwatching, and good areas include L'Encanyissada and La Tancada lagoons and Punta de la Banya, all in the southern part of the delta. L'Encanyissada has two observation towers and La Tancada one. La Tancada and Punta de la Banya are generally the best places to see the greater flamingoes, the delta's most spectacular birds. Punta de la Banya is joined to the delta by a 5km sandspit with the wide, long and sandy Platja de l'Eucaliptus beach at its north end.

The Garriga (☎ 977 48 91 22) and Olmos (☎ 977 48 04 73 or ☎ 977 48 05 48) companies run daily tourist boat trips from Deltebre to the mouths of the Ebro and the Illa de Buda at the delta's tip. Trips last 1½ hours and cost 500 ptas a person. They go daily, but the frequency depends on the season: in summer both companies do several trips a day.

Places to Stay

Camping Mediterrani Blau (☎ 977 47 90 46, Platja de l'Eucaliptus) is open from April to September with room for 240 people in a small eucalyptus grove, charging 450 ptas plus IVA per adult, per car

and per tent. It has a restaurant. There are two more camping grounds, open all year, at Riumar, 10km east of Deltebre.

Habitacions Cal d'Àngela (☎ 977 48 07 62, Carrer de Pompeu Fabra 4), Jesús i Maria, has technically closed, but if you can't find a room elsewhere, will give you a basic single for 1500 ptas. It's a short walk from the tourist office. *Restaurant Can Salat* (☎ 977 48 02 28, Carrer de Ramon i Cajal 14) in the centre of La Cava has a few adequate singles/doubles for 1500/3000 ptas, or 1700/3400 ptas with private bathroom. The *Delta Hotel* (☎ 977 48 00 46, Avinguda del Canal, Camí de la Illeta s/n), on the northern edge of Deltebre by the road to Riumar, has nice modern singles/doubles costing up to 5100/8200 plus IVA and a good restaurant.

The most pleasant places to eat are out by Riumar and the mouth of the river. *Restaurante Galach*, by the Llacuna Garxal (the end of the road as it were), does Ebro specialities, which include *anguilas* (eels), *angules* (baby eels), and shellfish.

There are several places to stay in Sant Carles de la Ràpita, a pleasant fishing town with a marina.

Getting There & Away

The delta is easiest to get to and around with your own wheels, but it is possible to reach it by bus or a train-bus combination.

Autocars Hife runs to Jesús i Maria and La Cava from Tortosa (one hour) five times daily (twice on Saturday, Sunday and holidays), and from Amposta (30 minutes) once or twice daily.

Andorra

The Catalan-speaking principality of Andorra (population 65,000), whose mountainous territory comprises only 464 sq km, nestles in the Pyrenees between Catalunya and France. Although it *is* tiny, this political anomaly contains some of the most dramatic scenery and best skiing in the Pyrenees. And in summer there's plenty of good walking in the higher, more remote parts of the principality, away from the overdevelopment of Andorra's valley towns. There's relatively little of historical interest other than a handful of Romanesque churches and a few simple but elegant stone bridges.

Facts about Andorra

HISTORY

By tradition, Andorra's independence is credited to Charlemagne, who captured the region from the Muslims in 803. His son, Louis I (the Pious), presented the area's inhabitants with a charter of liberties. The earliest known document concerning Andorra is an order of 843 by Charlemagne's grandson, Charles II, granting the Valls d'Andorra (Valleys of Andorra) to Sunifred, Count of Urgell, whose base was La Seu d'Urgell, Catalunya. From the counts, Andorra later passed to the bishops of Urgell, also based in La Seu. In 1278 and 1288, following a succession dispute between the bishops and the French counts of Foix to the north, Andorra's first constitutional documents, the Pareatges, established a system of shared sovereignty between the bishops and the counts. This feudal setup created a peculiar political equilibrium that saved Andorra from being swallowed up by its powerful neighbours despite recurrent tension between the co-princes down the centuries.

Highlights

- Andorra la Vella's quaint Casa de la Vall, parliament of one of the world's smallest nations
- Skiing at Ordino-Arcalís
- Walking in the valleys and mountains of north-western Andorra
- A ride over the spectacular Port d'Envalira, the highest pass in the Pyrenees

Since the 1950s Andorra has developed as a centre for skiing and duty-free shopping – the latter business grew out of the smuggling of French goods to Spain during the Spanish Civil War and Spanish goods to France in WWII (Andorra remained neutral in both). These activities have brought not only wealth, foreign workers and eight million visitors a year, but also some unsightly development and heavy traffic for several kilometres either side of the capital, Andorra la Vella.

GEOGRAPHY

Andorra consists of a group of valleys and their surrounding mountains in the midst of the Pyrenees. It measures 25km from north to south at its maximum and 29km from east to west. Most of its 40 or so towns and hamlets – some with just a few dozen people – are in the valleys. The main river, the Riu Gran Valira, is formed near the capital, Andorra la Vella, by the confluence of the Valira d'Orient and the Valira del Nord.

Pic de Coma Pedrosa (2942m) in western Andorra is the highest mountain. The lowest point, on the Spanish frontier at La Farga de Moles, is 838m above sea level. Andorra's mountain peaks remain snow-capped until early July or later.

GOVERNMENT & POLITICS

For seven centuries Andorra was a 'co-princedom', with its sovereignty vested in two 'princes': the French president, who inherited the job from France's pre-Revolutionary kings (who had taken it over from the counts of Foix), and the bishop of La Seu d'Urgell.

Then in March 1993, 75% of the 9123 native Andorrans who were eligible to vote (less than one-sixth of the population) voted in a referendum to establish Andorra as an independent, democratic 'parliamentary co-princedom'. The new constitution placed full sovereignty in the hands of the Andorran people, although the co-princes continue to function as joint heads with much reduced powers.

The country's elected parliament, the Consell General (General Council), took over from the Consell de la Terra (Land Council), which had run the show since 1419. The Consell General's 28 members – four from each of the seven parishes – are elected for four-year terms. The Consell meets three or four times a year and is chaired by two presiding officers called *síndics*. It appoints a *cap de govern* (prime minister), who chooses ministers whose programs have to be approved by the Consell. The liberal Marc Forné has been cap de govern since 1994, although

rumours began to spread (and were vigorously denied) in mid-1998 that his party was looking for a replacement.

Women were given the vote in 1970, and all Andorran citizens over 18 can now vote. Andorra is a member of the United Nations, but not of the EU.

Andorra is divided into seven parishes *(parròquies)*. Six of them have existed since at least the 9th century. The seventh, Escaldes-Engordany, was created in 1978 by dividing the parish of Andorra la Vella.

ECONOMY

The Andorran economy is based on cheap shopping, tourism and banking. The most important components of the agricultural sector, which makes up only 1.2% of total economic activity, are tobacco growing and cattle raising.

POPULATION & PEOPLE

Only about a quarter of Andorra's 65,000 inhabitants, almost two-thirds of whom live in Andorra la Vella and its suburbs, are Andorran nationals. The rest are Spaniards (about 30,000), Portuguese (5000), French (5000) and others. Until the 1950s Andorra's population was only 6000 or so.

LANGUAGE

The official language is Catalan, but nearly everyone speaks Spanish too. Local lore has it that everyone speaks Catalan, Spanish and French, but there are plenty of people who only know 10 words of French, and some Spanish residents who speak little Catalan. Few people speak English. See the Language Guide at the back of the book for Catalan pronunciation and handy phrases.

Facts for the Visitor

TOURIST OFFICES

There are two tourist offices in Andorra la Vella and several others around the country (see Information in the sections of this

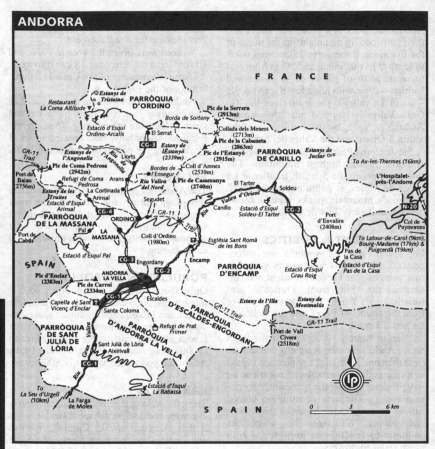

ANDORRA

(map labels)

FRANCE

PARRÒQUIA D'ORDINO

Restaurant La Coma Altitude
Estanys de Tristaina
Estació d'Esquí Ordino-Arcalís
El Serrat
Borda de Sorteny
Pic de la Serrera (2913m)
Collada dels Meners (2713m)
Pic de la Cabaneta (2863m)
Estany de l'Estanyó (2339m)
Pic de l'Estanyó (2915m)
Estanys de Juclar

GR-11 Trail
Estanys de l'Angonella
Pic de Coma Pedrosa (2942m)
Refugi de Coma Pedrosa
Port de Baiau (2756m)
Riu de l'Angonella
Llorts
Bordes de l'Ensegur
Coll d'Arenes (2539m)
Pic de Casamanya (2740m)
To Ax-les-Thermes (16km)
L'Hospitalet-près-l'Andorre

PARRÒQUIA DE CANILLO

Arans
La Cortinada
Arinsal
Estació d'Esquí Arinsal
Riu Valira del Nord
Segudet
ORDINO
GR-11
Riu
Canillo
El Tarter
Soldeu
Valira d'Orient
Estació d'Esquí Soldeu-El Tarter
N-20
Port d'Envalira (2408m)
Col de Puymorens

PARRÒQUIA DE LA MASSANA

Pal
LA MASSANA
Coll d'Ordino (1980m)
Església Sant Romà de les Bons
Pas de la Casa
Estació d'Esquí Pas de la Casa

Port de Cabús
Estació d'Esquí Pal
SPAIN
Engordany
Encamp
PARRÒQUIA D'ENCAMP
Estació d'Esquí Grau Roig
To Latour-de-Carol (9km), Bourg-Madame (17km) & Puigcerdà (19km)

Pic d'Enclar (2383m)
Pic de Carroi (2334m)
ANDORRA LA VELLA
CG-2
Escaldes
GR-11 Trail
PARRÒQUIA D'ESCALDES-ENGORDANY
Estany de l'Illa
Estany de Montmalús
GR-11 Trail

Capella de Sant Vicenç d'Enclar
Santa Coloma
PARRÒQUIA D'ANDORRA LA VELLA
Refugi de Prat Primer
Port de Vall Civera (2518m)

PARRÒQUIA DE SANT JULIÀ DE LÒRIA
Riu Gran Valira
Sant Julià de Lòria
Aixirivall
CG-1

To La Seu d'Urgell (10km)
La Farga de Moles
Estació d'Esquí La Rabassa

SPAIN

0   3   6 km

---

chapter). Andorra's tourist offices or tourism representatives abroad include the following:

Belgium
(☎ 02-502 12 11, fax 02-513 39 34)
10 Rue de la Montagne, 1000 Brussels
France
(☎ 01 42 61 50 55, fax 01 42 61 41 91)
26 Ave de l'Opéra, 75001 Paris
Germany
(☎ 030-415 49 14) Finsterwalder Strasse 28, 13435 Berlin

Spain
(☎ 91 431 74 53) Calle del Alcalá 73, 28009 Madrid
(☎ 93 200 07 87) Carrer de Marià Cubí 159, 08021 Barcelona
UK
(☎ 0181-874 48 06; from 22 April 2000 ☎ 020-8874 4806) 63 Westover Road, London SW18 2RF
USA
(☎ 708-674 30 91) 6899 N Knox Avenue, Lincolnwood, IL 60646

VISAS & DOCUMENTS

Visas are not necessary; the authorities figure that if Spain or France let you in, that's good enough for them. But you must carry your passport or national identity card.

EMBASSIES & CONSULATES

Andorra does not have any diplomatic legations abroad, but Spain and France maintain embassies in Andorra la Vella. See the Embassies & Consulates section in the Facts for the Visitor chapter.

CUSTOMS

Duty-free allowances, per adult, for goods entering Spain or France from Andorra include: 5L of still wine; either 1.5L of spirits of 22% or higher alcohol content, or three litres of lighter spirits or sparkling wine; 300 cigarettes; 4kg of cheese; and 525 ecus (about 81,000 ptas) worth of industrial products such as electronic goods, clothes and jewellery. For more information, ask a tourist office for the leaflet *Franquícies dels Viatgers*. Checks for smugglers are rigorous on the Spanish border.

MONEY

Andorra, which has no currency of its own, uses the peseta and the French franc (FF). Except in Pas de la Casa on the French border, prices are usually noted in pesetas. The exchange rate for francs in shops and restaurants is seldom in your favour.

Exchange Rates

Australia	A$1	=	98 ptas	=	3.47FF
Canada	C$1	=	92 ptas	=	3.60FF
euro	1€	=	167 ptas	=	6.59FF
France	1FF	=	25 ptas		
Germany	DM1	=	85 ptas	=	3.36FF
Japan	¥100	=	121 ptas	=	4.80FF
Morocco	Dr1	=	15 ptas	=	0.61FF
New Zealand	NZ$1	=	74 ptas	=	2.91FF
Portugal	P100$00	=	83 ptas	=	3.06FF
Spain			100 ptas	=	3.94FF
UK	UK£1	=	238 ptas	=	9.37FF
USA	US$1	=	141 ptas	=	5.56FF

POST & COMMUNICATIONS
Post

Andorra has no post office of its own; letters mailed to destinations within the country are free. France and Spain each operate a separate postal system with their own Andorran stamps. Those by La Poste (France) are in francs while the Spanish ones are in pesetas. They are valid only for items posted within Andorra and are necessary only for international mail. Regular French and Spanish stamps cannot be used.

International postal rates are the same as those of the issuing country, with the French tariffs a little higher. International mail (except letters to Spain) is better routed through the French postal system. There are two kinds of postboxes, but if you use the wrong one your letter will be transferred.

Letters to Andorra la Vella marked 'Poste Restante' are sent to the town's French post office. There's a charge of about 3FF for each letter you pick up. American Express card or travellers' cheque holders can also receive mail via the American Express agent in Andorra la Vella. The best way to get a letter to Andorra (except from Spain) is to address it to 'Principauté d'Andorre via FRANCE'.

Telephone

International Andorra's country code is ☎ 376. To call Spain from Andorra, dial ☎ 00-34 followed by the local number. To call France, dial ☎ 00-33 (☎ 00-33-1 for the Paris area), then the local number.

Directory assistance (☎ 111) has operators who speak Catalan, Spanish and French. To Spain and France, telephone rates are 50% cheaper between 10 pm and 8 am and all day on Sunday and holidays. Reverse-charge (collect) calling is not available in Andorra. A three-minute call to the USA at normal rates costs 330 ptas.

Public Telephones Public telephones take pesetas (francs in Pas de la Casa) or an Andorran *teletarja*, which operates like the *tarjeta telefónica* in Spain (see Post &

ANDORRA

Communications in the Facts for the Visitor chapter). Telephone cards worth 50 and 100 units are sold at post offices, tourist offices, tobacconists and some other shops for 500 ptas and 900 ptas. One unit is good for a local call of about three minutes.

MEDIA

There are two radio stations in Andorra: the government-run Ràdio Nacional Andorra (RNA), which broadcasts on 94.2 MHz and 91.4 MHz on FM, and the private Ràdio Valira (93.3 MHz and 98.9 MHz FM). You can see Spanish and French TV, along with the local ATV station.

The principality's main Catalan daily paper is the conservative *Diari d'Andorra*.

TIME

Andorra, like Spain, is two hours ahead of GMT/UTC from the last Sunday in March to the last Sunday in October, and one hour ahead at other times.

ELECTRICITY

The electric current is either 220V or 125V, both at 50 Hz.

HEALTH

Visitors must pay for all medical care in Andorra.

USEFUL ORGANISATIONS

For information on weather and snow conditions in winter, call ☎ 84 88 52 (Spanish), ☎ 84 88 53 (French) or ☎ 84 88 51 (Catalan). Ring ☎ 84 88 84 for information about road conditions in Spanish, French and Catalan.

DANGERS & ANNOYANCES

The country's minimal legislation to protect the consumer is often not enforced, so that hotels and petrol stations sometimes neglect to post their prices, and restaurants are free to refuse to serve tap water with meals. The road system is underdeveloped, leading to long traffic jams. Emergency telephone numbers include:

Police	☎ 110
Medical emergency	☎ 116
Fire or ambulance	☎ 118
Mountain rescue service	☎ 112
Car assistance & towing	☎ 86 99 86

BUSINESS HOURS & PUBLIC HOLIDAYS

Shops in Andorra la Vella are open daily from 9.30 am to 1 pm and 3.30 to 8 pm, except (in most cases) Sunday afternoon, 1 January, Good Friday, 8 September (a national holiday) and 25 December.

ACTIVITIES
Skiing

Downhill Andorra, with five downhill ski resorts *(estaciós d'esquí)*, has the best inexpensive skiing and snowboarding in the Pyrenees. For more information contact one of the capital's two tourist offices or Ski Andorra (☎ 86 43 89, fax 86 59 10) at Avinguda de Carlemany 65 in Escaldes.

The biggest, best and most expensive are the linked resorts of Pas de la Casa-Grau Roig and Soldeu-El Tarter, in the east. Arinsal, Pal and Ordino-Arcalís are in the north-west.

The skiing is good for beginners and intermediates, but has little for experts. The season normally lasts from December to April, depending on snow conditions, which in the past decade have not been reliable (all the resorts have snow making machines). Ski schools operate at all the resorts – the biggest are at Soldeu-El Tarter and Pas de la Casa-Grau Roig.

Prices for lift passes, ski school and, often, accommodation rise in the high seasons: weekends; the early (around 6 and 8) December Spanish long weekend; 23 December to 7 January; 10 February to early March; and Semana Santa. Low and high-season lift pass prices are given for individual resorts later. You can also get a five-day pass for all resorts for 14,150 ptas (low season) or 16,950 ptas (high season). Ski school costs from 3400 to 3725 ptas an hour for individual tuition, 2800 to 3000 ptas for three hours of group classes, or 9600 to 11,475 ptas for 15 hours of group classes.

The hire of ski gear doesn't vary in cost much from resort to resort. It's around 1600 ptas a day for skis, poles and boots. Snowboards go for up to 3000 ptas a day.

Ski Touring You can choose from many variations of a circular ski trip, or shorter ones. With 26 mountain shelters you shouldn't need a tent. However, an all-seasons sleeping bag is essential, and an ice axe, food and a camping stove (some huts lack cooking facilities). One of the popular routes, taking about six days, starts in Aixirivall, just east of Sant Julià de Lòria in southern Andorra, and goes anticlockwise around the country to the Pal ski station. This should only be attempted by experienced ski tourers.

There's also a cross-country skiing centre at La Rabassa in the south, with 15km of marked forest trails.

Hiking

The tranquillity of Andorra's unspoiled back country begins only a few hundred metres from the bazaar-like bustle of the towns. The north-west has especially good hiking. More than 50 lakes lie hidden among the soaring mountains.

The best season for hiking is June to September, when temperatures climb well into the 20°Cs, although they drop to around 10°C at night. June can be wet.

The GR-11 trail that traverses the Spanish Pyrenees from the Mediterranean to the Atlantic, crosses Andorra from the Port de Vall Civera pass (2518m) in the south-east to the Port de Baiau pass (2756m) in the north-west.

Hikers can sleep for free in more than 20 mountain refuges *(refugis)* dotted around the high country. A 1:25,000 government *mapa topogràfic* of the country costs 1200 ptas in bookshops and some tourist offices. The country is also covered in 19 *Valls d'Andorra* sheets at 1:10,000 (375 ptas

each), which you can get at Papereria Sol, Avinguda de Meritxell 28, Andorra la Vella.

Tourist offices give out a useful booklet (*Sport Activities* in English), with 52 recommended walks of 15 minutes to eight hours duration and 17 mountain bike routes.

ACCOMMODATION

Almost all of Andorra's hotels stay open year round. They are fullest in July and August and from December to March – when some places put prices up a bit – but since turnover is high (except in winter, most people just stay to do a bit of shopping), rooms are almost always available in the morning.

There are no youth hostels in Andorra. The 26 refugis – mountain huts used by shepherds and hikers (one room for each) – do not require reservations, and all except one are unstaffed and free. Most have bunks, fireplaces, drinkable water but no cooking facilities. Tourist offices have maps indicating their location.

Tourist offices can provide information on apartments and chalets *(xalets)* available for short-term rental.

SHOPPING

With low customs duties and taxes, Andorra is famous for cheap electronic goods, photographic equipment, shoes, clothing, perfume, petrol and, above all, alcohol, cigarettes and French dairy products. Shops selling these goods cluster in Andorra la Vella and suburbs, Encamp, Pas de la Casa and near the Spanish border. Visitors from Spain and France come for the shopping, although potential savings are no longer what they were. Shopping around and bargaining down to the '*precio último*', the final price, you'll pay about 20% or 30% less than in Spain or France.

If you're after particular photographic or electronic equipment, you can probably find it. But if you don't know what you want, Andorra is not such a great place to shop since most places sell a bit of everything, and salespeople know little about the merchandise.

ANDORRA

Some shops add a surcharge if you pay by credit card. If you're buying something that comes with a warranty, make sure the store fills in the card and rubber stamps it. Some warranties are valid only in the country of purchase, so read the fine print. Beware of confusion, unintentional or otherwise, that may result from going between pesetas, francs and your home currency.

Getting There & Away

The only way into Andorra – unless you trek across the mountains – is by road. One of the two roads in comes from La Seu d'Urgell in Spain, 20km south of Andorra la Vella. The other enters Andorra at Pas de la Casa on the eastern border with France, then crosses the spectacular 2408m-high Port d'Envalira (the highest pass in the Pyrenees, occasionally closed by snow in winter) en route to Andorra la Vella. It's approached along the French N-22 from the N-20 Bourg-Madame–Toulouse road, which begins just across the French-Spanish border from Puigcerdà. Both routes have bus services.

Petrol is about 15% cheaper than in Spain and 25% cheaper than in France. There are a number of petrol stations near the borders.

The nearest major airports are at Barcelona (225km south), Toulouse, France (180km north) and Perpignan, France (166km east). All three cities are linked to Andorra by bus or train-bus combinations.

Schedules of some of the following buses are subject to changes. Check with the municipal tourist office in Andorra la Vella.

BUS & TRAIN
Spain
La Hispano Andorrana (☎ 82 13 72) runs five or more buses daily between La Seu d'Urgell and Plaça de Guillemó in Andorra la Vella (30 minutes; 340 ptas).

Alsina Graells (☎ 82 73 79) runs five or six buses a day between Barcelona's Estació

del Nord and Andorra la Vella's *estació d'autobusos* (bus station) on Carrer de Bonaventura Riberaygua (four hours; 2505 ptas). Viatges Relax, the American Express agent in Andorra la Vella (see Money in that section) runs minibuses to Barcelona airport for 4000 ptas a person, one way. Departures from the airport are at 1 and 5 pm, and from Andorra la Vella at 5 and 8 am. They leave from in front of the Spanish embassy in Andorra la Vella. Tickets must be purchased in advance at Viatges Relax.

Samar/Andor-Inter (☎ 82 62 89 in Andorra, ☎ 91 468 41 90 in Madrid) has buses to Zaragoza (2300 ptas) and Madrid (4700 ptas) three times a week; Hispano Igualadina runs buses to Tarragona (four hours; 1800 ptas) once daily. Andor-Inter/Nort-Bus (☎ 82 62 89) operates services to various cities in Galicia and Portugal.

An interesting alternative approach is by train from Barcelona, Ripoll, Ribes de Freser or Puigcerdà to Latour-de-Carol in France. The 9.18 am train from Barcelona Sants (12.35 pm from Puigcerdà) connects with the 1 pm bus from Latour-de-Carol to Andorra la Vella – a total journey from Barcelona of 5½ hours for about 2500 ptas. An additional evening bus from July to late September connects with the 3.16 pm train from Barcelona Sants (6.17 pm from Puigcerdà). In the reverse direction the connections don't work so well, and you're better off getting a direct bus to Barcelona or La Seu d'Urgell (from where there are three connections to Puigcerdà). See also the Puigcerdà section of the Catalunya chapter and the France section below.

France
Samar/Andor-Inter (☎ 82 62 89 in Andorra, ☎ 61 58 14 53 in Toulouse) runs a bus on Saturday morning from Andorra la Vella's estació d'autobusos (bus station) in Toulouse, taking four hours for 2600 ptas. It returns on Sunday morning.

Otherwise you can take a train from Toulouse to one of three French stations near

Andorra from which there are buses to Plaça de Guillemó in Andorra la Vella via Pas de la Casa. The three stations are Ax-les-Thermes (1½ to 1¾ hours from Toulouse), L'Hospitalet-près-l'Andorre (L'Hospitalet, 2¼ to 2¾ hours) and Latour-de- Carol (2½ to 3¼ hours). This station is actually close to Entveig, while the town of Latour-de-Carol is 2km away!

From Latour-de-Carol station, Autos Pujol Huguet (☎ 82 13 72) runs a daily bus to Andorra la Vella, leaving at 1 pm and arriving at 2.40 pm (1125 ptas). The other way, it leaves at 7.15 pm and arrives at 9.40 am. This allows you to connect with several trains to Toulouse and Barcelona, as well as local buses running to Font-Romeu (a good French ski resort), Perpignan (three daily), L'Hospitalet and Ax-les-Thermes (where train connections deeper into France multiply).

Should you get to Latour-de-Carol and miss the 1 pm bus for Andorra la Vella, you could get the 3.32 pm bus to L'Hospitalet (½ hour), from where there are two or three daily buses with La Hispano Andorrana (☎ 82 13 72 in Andorra) to Andorra la Vella (two hours; 925 ptas). One leaves at 5.20 pm or 6.05 pm. Otherwise, there's another at 7.35 am the next day. On Saturdays there are as many as five buses to Pas de la Casa, and you can head on through to Andorra la Vella.

If you're picking up a bus mid-route – at Soldeu for instance – get to the stop in good time, as they sometimes go through earlier than scheduled.

Getting Around

BUS

Cooperativa Interurbana (☎ 82 04 12) runs eight bus lines along the three main roads from Andorra la Vella, and Autobus Parroquial de La Massana i d'Ordino operates a few services from La Massana. See individual destination sections for details; the municipal tourist office in Andorra la Vella has current timetables.

CAR & MOTORCYCLE

Andorra has four main roads. The CG1 (CG stands for Carretera General) runs 10km from Andorra la Vella via Sant Julià de Lòria to the Spanish border, from where it's a further 10km to La Seu d'Urgell. The CG2 runs 33km from Andorra la Vella to Escaldes, Encamp, Canillo, Soldeu, Port d'Envalira – which has something in common with the road from Kashmir to Ladakh – and Pas de la Casa on the French border. The CG3 heads north from the capital via La Massana, Ordino and Llorts to the Ordino-Arcalís ski area. The CG4 branches west off the CG3 at La Massana up to the Pal ski area.

The speed limit in populated areas is 40km/h. With all the traffic and twists and turns, it's almost impossible to reach the inter-hamlet speed limit of 90km/h. Using a seat belt is not compulsory, but motorcycle helmets are.

The biggest problems are Andorra la Vella's horrendous traffic jams and the vigilant parking police. If you do not buy one of the coupons available from machines everywhere and place it on the dashboard, you will be fined for sure.

Andorra la Vella

Andorra la Vella (Vella, literally 'old', is pronounced 'VEY-yah'), the capital of the principality and its largest town (population 22,000), lies on the Riu Gran Valira in a valley just over 1000m above sea level, surrounded by mountains of up to 2400m. The town is almost entirely for retailing duty-free electronics and luxury goods. With the mountains, constant din of jackhammers and 'mall' architecture, you could almost be in Hong Kong, were it not for the snow-capped peaks and the lack of noodle shops!

Orientation

Andorra la Vella is strung out along one main street, whose name changes from Avinguda del Príncep Benlloch to Avinguda de Meritxell at Plaça de Rebés. The little Barri Antic (historic quarter) stretches from

ANDORRA

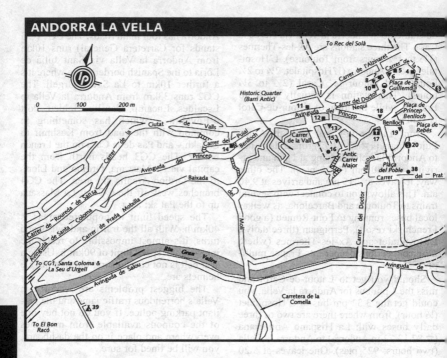

ANDORRA LA VELLA

the Església de Sant Esteve to Plaçeta del Puial. The town merges with the once separate villages of Escaldes and Engordany to the east and Santa Coloma to the south-west.

Information

Tourist Offices The helpful municipal tourist office (Oficina d'Informació i Turisme, ☎ 82 71 17) on Plaça de la Rotonda is open daily from 9 am to 1 pm and 4 to 8 pm (7 pm on Sunday). In July and August, it's open from 9 am to 9 pm (7 pm on Sunday). The office has maps, all sorts of brochures, stamps and telephone cards.

The national tourist office (Sindicat d'Iniciativa Oficina de Turisme; ☎ 82 02 14) is at Carrer del Doctor Vilanova s/n just down from Plaça de Rebés. It is open Monday to Saturday from 10 am (9 am from July to September) to 1 pm and 3 to 7 pm and Sunday morning.

There's a tourist information kiosk (☎ 82 09 63) on Plaça dels Co-Prínceps, about one kilometre east of the STA telephone office in Escaldes.

Money Banks are open Monday to Friday from 9 am to 1 pm and 3 to 5 pm (some stay open through lunch) and Saturday from 9 am to noon. Very few charge a commission, but rates vary. Avinguda de Meritxell and Avinguda del Príncep Benlloch in the town centre are lined with banks and ATMs. Crèdit Andorrà, next to the river at Avinguda de Meritxell 80, has a 24-hour banknote exchange machine that accepts 15 currencies.

American Express (☎ 82 20 44, fax 82 70 55) is represented by Viatges Relax, a travel agency at Carrer de Mossén Tremosa 2. It is open Monday to Friday from 9 am to 1 pm and 3.30 to 7 pm. The office cannot change

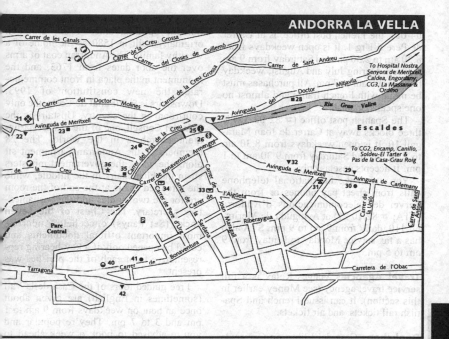

ANDORRA LA VELLA

ANDORRA LA VELLA

PLACES TO STAY
4 Hotel Florida
5 Residència Benazet
7 Hostal del Sol
10 Hotel Les Arcades
11 Hôtel Pyrénées
12 Pensió La Rosa
14 Habitacions Baró
23 Hotel Costa &
   Restaurant Martí
28 Hotel Residència Albert
35 Novotel Andorra
39 Càmping Valira

PLACES TO EAT
6 El Timbaler del Bruch
8 Restaurant La Cantina

13 Restaurant Can Benet
15 Restaurant Ca La Conxita
18 Papanico
19 Pans & Company
22 KFC & Pizza Hut
27 Pizzeria La Mossegada
29 McDonald's
32 Pans & Company
42 McDonald's

OTHER
1 French Embassy
2 French Consulate
3 Viatges Relax/
  American Express
9 Plaça de Guillemó Bus Stop
16 Casa de la Vall

17 Església de Sant Esteve
20 National Tourist Office
21 Pyrénées Department
   Store
24 Casa del Llibre
25 Municipal Tourist Office
26 Crèdit Andorrà
30 Papereria Sol
31 Telephones (STA)
33 Correos (Spanish Post Office)
34 La Poste (French Post Office)
36 Servei de Policía
37 Spanish Embassy
38 Public Lift to
   Plaça del Poble
40 Estació d'Autobusos
41 Llibreria Francesa

money (you have to go to a bank for that), but it can reissue a lost or stolen American Express card, provide a reimbursement for lost or stolen travellers' cheques, and sell travellers cheques against card-holders' personal cheques.

Post & Communications La Poste (☎ 82 04 08), the French post office, is at Carrer de Pere d'Urg 1. It is open weekdays from 8.30 am to 2.30 pm and Saturday from 9 am to noon. During July and August, weekday hours are 9 am to 7 pm. All purchases must be made with French francs and almost no one speaks Spanish.

The Spanish post office (☎ 82 02 57) is three blocks away at Carrer de Joan Maragall 10. It is open weekdays from 8.30 am to 2.30 pm and Saturday from 9.30 am to 1 pm. It accepts pesetas only.

You can make international telephone calls from street pay phones or from the Servei de Telecomunicacions d'Andorra (STA; ☎ 82 10 21) at Avinguda de Meritxell 110, daily from 9 am to 9 pm. STA also has a fax service Monday to Friday from 9 am to 5 pm.

Travel Agencies Viatges Relax is a full service travel agency (see Money earlier in this section). It can issue French and Spanish rail tickets, and air tickets.

Bookshops Casa del Llibre on Carrer de Fiter Rossell has a good selection of books, some in English. For French, try the Llibreria Francesa, Carrer de Bonaventura Riberaygua 42.

Medical Services & Emergency The modern Hospital Nostra Senyora de Meritxell (☎ 87 10 00) is at Avinguda de Fiter i Rossell 1-13 in Engordany, about 1.5km east of Plaça de Guillemó.

The main police station (*servei de policia/despatx central*; ☎ 82 12 22) is at Carrer del Prat de la Creu 16.

Barri Antic

The Barri Antic was the heart of Andorra la Vella when the principality's capital was little more than a village. The narrow cobblestoned streets around the Casa de la Vall are lined with stone houses.

Casa de la Vall The pride of the Barri Antic is Casa de la Vall (House of the Valley), which has served as Andorra's parliament building since 1702, although originally built in 1580 as the home of a wealthy family. The Andorran coat of arms over the door dates from 1763, and the monument in the plaça in front commemorates the new constitution of 1993. Downstairs is **El Tribunal de Corts**, the only courtroom in the country. Upstairs is the **Sala del Consell**, one of the cosiest parliament chambers in the world. The 28 members of the Andorran parliament sit along the walls, the government ministers sit in the blue chairs in the middle, while the three red chairs at the end of the room are for the two síndics and the parliamentary secretary. The **Chest of the Seven Locks** (Set Panys) once held Andorra's most important official documents and could be opened only if a key-bearing representative from each of the parishes was present.

Free guided tours of the Casa de la Vall (sometimes in English) are given about once an hour on weekdays from 9 am to 1 pm and 3 to 7 pm. They're popular and you're advised to book a week ahead to ensure a place, but individuals can sometimes join a group at the last minute.

Església de Sant Esteve The parish church is at the edge of the Barri Antic across the street from Plaça del Príncep Benlloch. It dates from the 11th century, but apart from the Romanesque apse has been largely modernised. The paintings date from as far back as the 13th century.

Plaça del Poble

This large public square just south of Plaça de Rebés occupies the roof of the Edifici Administratiu Govern d'Andorra, a modern government office building at Carrer del Prat de la Creu 64. It affords good views and is a popular local gathering place, especially in the evening. The lift in the south-east corner whisks you down to the car park at Carrer del Prat de la Creu 54-58.

Caldea

In Escaldes, what looks like a large, futuristic cathedral is actually the Caldea spa complex (☎ 80 09 99), a fine place for a spot of soothing relaxation after exertions in the mountains. Fed by hot springs, the complex centres on a 600 sq m lagoon kept at a constant 32°C. A series of other pools, plus Turkish baths, saunas, jacuzzis and hydromassage are all included in the three-hour entrance ticket for 2500 ptas. Caldea is at Parc de la Mola 10, just east of Avinguda de Fiter i Rossell, about a 2km walk from Plaça de Guillemó. It is open daily from 10 am to 11 pm (last entry at 9 pm).

Places to Stay – Budget

Camping *Camping Valira* (☎ 82 23 84), open all year at the southern edge of town on Avinguda de Salou, charges 525 ptas per person, tent and car. There's a small indoor swimming pool. *Camping Riberaygua* (☎ 82 66 99) and *Camping Santa Coloma* (☎ 82 88 99), both in Santa Coloma about 2.5km south-west of Plaça de Guillemó, are also open all year, with similar prices.

Pensiones, Hostales & Hotels The helpful, 15 room *Residència Benazet* (☎ 82 06 98, Carrer de la Llacuna 21, 1st floor), just off Plaça de Guillemó, has large, serviceable rooms with washbasin for up to four people at 1300 ptas a person. Bathrooms are shared. Nearby, *Hotel Les Arcades* (☎ 82 13 55, Plaça de Guillemó 5) has singles/doubles with shower, TV and toilet from 2000/3000 to 3000/5000 ptas depending on the season. On the same square at No 3, *Hostal del Sol* (☎ 82 37 01) is not as good but is centrally placed. Rooms cost 2000/3500 ptas with bath.

In the Barri Antic, *Pensió La Rosa* (☎ 82 18 10, Antic Carrer Major 18) has nondescript rooms for 1700/3000 ptas. *Habitacions Baró* (☎ 82 14 84, Carrer del Puial 21) is one of the cheapest places, charging 1300/2400 ptas in the off season. It's worth ringing first as sometimes it's unattended.

Hotel Costa (☎ 82 14 39, Avinguda de Meritxell 44) has basic but clean rooms for

1600/3000 ptas. *Hotel Residència Albert* (☎ 82 01 56, Avinguda del Doctor Mitjavila 16), east of the centre, has rooms with shower for 1500/3000 ptas.

Places to Stay – Mid-Range & Top End

The 74 room *Hotel Pyrénées* (☎ 86 00 06, fax 82 02 65, Avinguda del Príncep Benlloch 20) is only one block from Casa de la Vall. It has a tennis court and a swimming pool behind it. Singles/doubles cost from 5000/8000 to 5750/9300 ptas. Ask for a room away from the street if you want a good night's sleep.

The delightful *Hotel Florida* (☎ 82 01 05, fax 86 19 25, Carrer de la Llacuna 15), one block from Plaça de Guillemó, has modern rooms for 6300/9600 ptas (including breakfast).

The *Novotel Andorra* (☎ 86 11 16, fax 86 11 20, Carrer del Prat de la Creu s/n) is devoid of character but has all the mod cons you could hope for. Rooms start at 10,800/13,750 ptas.

Places to Eat

The big supermarket on the 2nd floor of the *Pyrénées* department store *(Avinguda de Meritxell 21)* is open Monday to Saturday from 9.30 am to 8 pm and Sunday to 7 pm.

Restaurants *El Timbaler del Bruch* on Plaça de Guillemó is a good spot for breakfast or a light meal at any time of day. Excellent *torrades* (open toasted sandwiches), with generous toppings, cost from 375 ptas. On the same square at No 4, *Restaurant La Cantina* is a friendly place where you can expect to get huge servings. An *amanida variada* (mixed salad) as an entrée is almost big enough to make you forget about the main course. Mains start at about 800 ptas.

In the Barri Antic, *Restaurant Ca La Conxita* (Placeta de Monjó 3) is a busy little family business where you can see the staff preparing your hearty meal. You can eat well for around 2500 ptas. Virtually around the corner, *Restaurant Can Benet*

ANDORRA

(Carrer Major 9) is a little more pricey but also delightful.

The restaurant of the *Hotel Pyrénées* (see Places to Stay) serves Catalan, French and Spanish dishes amid sparkling chandeliers and two-tone tablecloths. *Platos combinados* go from 575 ptas to 1200 ptas.

Restaurant Martí (☎ 82 43 84, Avinguda de Meritxell 44), upstairs, has an ordinary *menú* for 1100 ptas, a better one for 1425 ptas and platos combinados from 590 ptas.

The best place for real Catalan cooking is the upmarket *El Bon Racó (Avinguda de Salou 86)* in Santa Coloma, about a kilometre west of Camping Valira. Meat – especially *xai* (lamb) – roasted in an open hearth is the speciality, but you might also try *escudella*, a Catalan stew of chicken, sausage and vegetables. Expect to part with close to 3000 ptas for a full meal with wine.

Fast Food & Snacks *Papanico* on Avinguda del Príncep Benlloch has tasty *tapas* from 245 ptas to 395 ptas.

Pans & Company at Plaça de Rebés 2 and Avinguda de Meritxell 91 is good for hot and cold baguettes with a range of fillings for 350 to 500 ptas.

Pizzeria La Mossegada (Avinguda del Doctor Mitjavila 3) overlooks the river. Pizzas cost between 750 and 875 ptas, or there are burgers and grilled meat dishes from 850 to 1150 ptas.

If you find that all the corporate products on sale in Andorra la Vella make you crave multinational food, *McDonald's*, on Avinguda de Tarragona (with a drive-through section), opposite the bus station and at Avinguda de Meritxell 105, are open weekdays to 11 pm and to 1 am on the weekend. Or there's *KFC* and *Pizza Hut* together at Avinguda de Meritxell 26.

Entertainment

Cultural events sometimes take place at Plaça del Poble, where you'll find Andorra la Vella's theatre and its music academy. Contact the tourist office for details of festivals, dance performances etc. For the handful of discos and the like scattered about town, buy a copy of the *Guia de l'Oci* (175 ptas).

Shopping

Most of Andorra la Vella's duty-free shops are strung along the eastern part of Avinguda del Príncep Benlloch, the length of Avinguda de Meritxell and into its continuation, Avinguda de Carlemany in Escaldes.

Getting There & Around

Buses to La Seu d'Urgell, France and all destinations within Andorra leave from Plaça de Guillemó. Buses to other places in Spain use the estació d'autobusos on Carrer de Bonaventura Riberaygua, south of the river. For details of Spain and France services, see the introductory Getting There & Away section; for services within Andorra, see the relevant destination sections.

Call ☎ 82 70 00 to order a taxi in Andorra la Vella.

AROUND ANDORRA LA VELLA
Església de Santa Coloma

The Church of Santa Coloma, mentioned in documents from the 9th century, is Andorra's oldest, but its pre-Romanesque form has been modified over the centuries. The four-storey, almost round bell tower was built in the 12th century, apparently in two stages. All the church's 12th century Romanesque murals, except one entitled *Agnus Dei* (Lamb of God), were taken to a museum in Berlin for conservation in the 1930s and are still there. The church is 2.5km south-west of Plaça de Guillemó along the road to La Seu d'Urgell.

Hiking

The **Rec del Solà** (altitude 1100m) is an almost flat, 2.5km path which follows a small irrigation canal running along the hillside just north of Andorra la Vella. Another walk heads south-eastwards from Carretera de la Comella up to the **Refugi de Prat Primer** mountain refuge (2250m), where you can stay overnight. The walk up will take you about three hours from Andorra la Vella.

From Carrer dels Barrers in Santa Coloma, a path leads north-west up the hill to the **Capella de Sant Vicenç d'Enclar** (20 minutes), the site of an important castle before the Pareatges of the 13th century, which banned castles in Andorra. As well as the view, you'll see a recently reconstructed church, a cemetery, several silos and some ruins. A trail continues up the valley to **Bony de la Pica** (2405m) on the Spanish border, from which you can follow the crest north-east to **Pic d'Enclar** (2383m) and **Pic de Carroi** (2334m), which overlooks Santa Coloma from the north – a day's walk there and back.

North-Western Andorra

La Massana, 6km north of Andorra la Vella, is the gateway to the ski centres of Arinsal and Pal. From La Massana the CG3 continues north into the mountainous Parròquia d'Ordino, arguably the country's most beautiful parish, with slate and fieldstone farmhouses, gushing streams and picturesque stone bridges. It has plenty of fine walks and, in winter, skiing at the Ordino-Arcalís ski area.

LA MASSANA

The town of La Massana (population 2164; altitude 1252m) is much less attractive than its smaller neighbours a few kilometres north but it has a number of hotels and some good restaurants.

The tourist office (☎ 83 56 93) is on Plaça de la Caseta d'Informació, on La Massana's main street, the CG3.

Places to Stay

La Massana is a little too brash and noisy and not close enough to either the skiing or hiking action to make a great base. It can be a backup if the places farther into the mountains are full.

Camping Santa Catarina (☎ 83 50 65) is in a grassy field next to a rushing stream, at the proprietors' home just outside La Massana by the CG3. It is open from late June to mid-September. Charges are 375 ptas per person and 300 ptas per tent and per car. Buses to Ordino stop a bit down the hill from the camping ground opposite the Hotel Les Costes de Giberga.

Hotel Palanques (☎ 83 50 07) on the corner of the CG3 and Carrer Major has doubles from about 2500 ptas to 3250 ptas.

Places to Eat

You can get a pizza for 900 ptas at *Pizzeria Vesuvio* on the main road just north of Hotel La Massana. A better stop is *Restaurant Cal Cristobal*, a block west of the main road on the corner of Carrer de Josep Rossell and Carrer de l'Església. It has a hearty set grill *menú* for 1500 ptas.

Two of Andorra's better restaurants, *La Borda de l'Avi* and *La Borda Raubert*, are a couple of kilometres north of La Massana on the road to Arinsal. Both are 'country-style' places with open hearths and have lots of grills, Andorran specialities and good wine selections.

Getting There & Away

Buses from Andorra la Vella to La Massana (110 ptas) run daily about twice an hour from 7 am to 9 pm. The same buses continue to Ordino.

ESTACIONS D'ESQUÍ ARINSAL & PAL

Arinsal (☎ 83 58 22, fax 83 62 42), 5km north-west of La Massana, has good skiing and snowboarding for beginners and intermediates, and a lively après-ski scene. Pal (☎ 83 62 36, fax 83 59 04), 9km from La Massana, has gentler slopes that make it ideal for families.

Skiing

Arinsal has 13 lifts, 28km of pistes and a vertical drop of 1010m. Lift passes cost 2600/3150 ptas a day in the low/high season. For three days it's 6475/7850 ptas.

Pal has 12 lifts, 30km of pistes and a vertical drop of 578m. Lift passes cost 2700/

ANDORRA

3400 ptas for a day in the low/high season. For three days it's 6725/8500 ptas.

Hiking

From the bottom of the Arinsal ski slopes, a trail leads north-west then west to a 2260m-high lake called **Estany de les Truites**. The walk up takes around 1½ hours. The *Refugi de Coma Pedrosa*, Andorra's only staffed mountain refuge, is just above the lake. Cost per night is 1000 ptas, and meals are available (dinner 1700 ptas). The refuge is normally open from June to late September, but you should confirm this with a tourist office or by ringing the Spanish number ☎ 908-14 55 17 (from Andorra ☎ 00-34-08-14 55 17). From the lake, it's about a further 3½ hours to the highest point in Andorra, **Pic de Coma Pedrosa** (2942m).

Other Activities

From June to mid-September, chair lifts open at Pal and Arinsal and mountain bikes are available at Pal for around 2800 ptas a day. Horse riding costs 1700 ptas an hour.

Places to Stay

The large *Camping Xixerella* (☎ 83 66 13) between Pal and Arinsal is open all year and has an outdoor swimming pool. Charges are 450 ptas each per adult, tent and car.

In Arinsal the basic *Hostal Pobladó* (☎ 83 51 22) is cheap, with rooms costing 1800 ptas per person. One of the more popular upmarket places is *Hotel Solana* (☎ 83 51 27, fax 83 73 95), which has large rooms with bath and toilet for 5500/8000 ptas. There's no accommodation at Pal.

Entertainment

A late-night bar in Arinsal that's popular with English skiers and occasionally has live music is *Quo Vadis*. *Pub Solana* at the Hotel Solana is for dancing.

Getting There & Away

Buses leave Andorra la Vella for Arinsal (185 ptas) via La Massana at 9.30 am and 1

and 6 pm. The last one back from Arinsal is at 3 pm. In the ski season there are seven buses daily from La Massana to the Arinsal ski slopes and four to Pal.

ORDINO

Ordino (1304m), with a population of about 1000, is large as local villages go, but despite recent development (holiday homes and English-speaking residents abound), it remains peaceful and Andorran in character, with most building still in stone.

Orientation & Information

The tourist office (☎ 83 69 63), on the CG3, is open Monday to Saturday from 9 am to 1 pm and 3 to 7 pm and on Sunday from 9 am to noon. The Banc Agrícol i Comercial d'Andorra, with an ATM, is opposite the tourist office.

Museu d'Areny i Plandolit

The ancestral home of one of Andorra's great families, the Areny Plandolits, built in 1633 and modified in the mid-19th century, is now a museum (☎ 83 69 08). The family's most illustrious member was Don Guillem, síndic and leader of the political reform movement of the 1860s. The house has furnished rooms (the library and dining room are particularly fine) and is of typically rugged Andorran design. Half-hour guided visits cost 200 ptas. It is open Tuesday to Saturday from 9.30 am to 1.30 pm and 3 to 6.30 pm and Sunday morning.

Hiking

From the hamlet of Segudet, just east of Ordino, a path goes up through fir woods to the **Coll d'Ordino** (1980m), about 1½ hours from Ordino. **Pic de Casamanya** (2740m) where you can enjoy expansive panoramas is about two hours walk north from Coll d'Ordino.

Places to Stay & Eat

Just off Plaça Major, in the alley behind the Crèdit Andorrà bank, is *Hotel Quim* (☎ 83 50 13). Doubles with shower cost up to 4500 ptas. More expensive is *Hotel*

Santa Bàrbara de la Vall d'Ordino (☎ *83 71 00*) on Plaça Major, which has singles/doubles for as much as 7000/8500 ptas.

Restaurant Ricard on Plaça Major has mainly Catalan dishes for 1700 ptas. *Restaurant Armengol*, nearby, has a less imaginative *menú* for 1500 ptas.

Getting There & Away
The bus from Andorra la Vella (130 ptas) runs daily about every 30 minutes from 7 am to 9 pm.

LLORTS
The tiny mountain hamlet of Llorts (1413m), on the CG3 6km north of Ordino, has traditional architecture set amid tobacco fields and a near pristine mountain setting. Only 100 people live here.

Hiking
A trail leads west from the village up the Riu de l'Angonella valley to a group of lakes, the **Estanys de l'Angonella**, at about 2300m. Count on three hours to get there.

From slightly north of the even smaller settlement of El Serrat (1600m), about 3km up the CG3 from Llorts, a secondary road leads 4km east to the Borda de Sorteny mountain refuge (1969m). From there, a trail goes south-east to **Estany de l'Estanyó** lake (2339m). Another heads east up to the Collada dels Meners pass (2713m; about 1½ hours), from which you can go north to **Pic de la Serrera** (2913m; 30 minutes) or a couple of hours south and west via **Pic de la Cabaneta** (2863m) to **Pic de l'Estanyó** (2915m), Andorra's second highest peak. In about eight hours from Borda de Sorteny you could bag all three peaks and continue via the Coll d'Arenes pass (2539m) and Pic de Casamanya to the Coll d'Ordino (see Ordino earlier in this chapter), enjoying great views along the way.

From Arans (1385m), a village 2km south of Llorts, a trail goes north-eastward to **Bordes de l'Ensegur** (2180m), where there is an old shepherd's hut.

The tiny, partly Romanesque **Església de Sant Martí** in La Cortinada, 1km south of

Arans, has 12th century frescoes in remarkably good condition.

Places to Stay
Some 200m north of Llorts, *Camping Els Pardassos* (☎ *85 00 22*), one of the most beautiful camping grounds in Andorra, is surrounded by forested mountains and has its own spring. Open from mid-June to mid-September, it costs 300 ptas per person, per tent and per car. Bring your own provisions.

Hotel Vilaró (☎ *85 02 25*), 200m south of the village limits, has singles/doubles with washbasin and bidet for 2100/3925 ptas. It is open all year. Up at El Serrat, the *Hotel Subirà* (☎ *85 00 37*) has fabulous views of the valley and surrounding mountains. It is open all year, with rooms at 4500/6000 ptas.

Getting There & Away
Buses to Llorts and El Serrat (225 ptas) leave Andorra la Vella at 1 and 8.30 pm. Downward buses leave El Serrat at 7.45 am and 2.45 pm. In summer a few minibuses a day from Ordino to the Estació d'Esquí Ordino-Arcalís go through Llorts and El Serrat.

ESTACIÓ D'ESQUÍ ORDINO-ARCALÍS
The Ordino-Arcalís ski area (☎ 85 01 21, fax 83 92 25) is in Andorra's far north-western corner. The slopes are mostly good for beginners and intermediates, although experts can have some fun on a mogul run, and there are good prospects for ski touring. A number of the rugged peaks in this beautiful area reach 2800m.

The closest accommodation is at El Serrat and Llorts. There are also more hotels, as well as banks and post offices, in Ordino.

Orientation & Information
Lifts start from three car parks along the road. Restaurant La Coma Altitude at the end of the paved road near the uppermost car park at an altitude of 2200m is a useful landmark. The Telecadira La Coma chair lift rises opposite it.

ANDORRA

Skiing

In winter, Ordino-Arcalís has enough snow and a decent selection of runs, but it can be cold and windy. There are 12 lifts (mostly drag lifts) covering 24km of pistes at altitudes between 1940m and 2600m. A lift ticket costs 2700/6725 ptas for one/three days in the low season, or 3400/8425 ptas in the high season.

Helitransfer For 7000 ptas you can be whisked across to the Pas de la Casa and Grau Roig skifields in a helicopter, using the lift pass you have bought for Ordino-Arcalís.

Hiking

The trail behind the Restaurant La Coma Altitude leads eastwards across the hill, then north and over the ridge to a group of beautiful mountain lakes called **Estanys de Tristaina**. The walk to the first lake takes about 30 minutes.

In summer, you can also start walking from the 2700m top of Telecadira La Coma chair lift, which operates daily from late June to early September from 10 am to 6 pm. Summer fees are 450/780 ptas one way/return.

Other Activities

The souvenir kiosk opposite the Telecadira La Coma's lower station rents mountain bikes from late June to early September (daily from 10 am to 6 pm; closed Monday in June and July). It charges up to 3200 ptas for a full day.

Places to Eat

Restaurant La Coma Altitude is open from December to early May with both snacks and a full menu. From late June to early September, it's open daily from 10 am to 6 pm (closed Monday in June and July).

Getting There & Away

In the ski season there are five shuttle buses a day between Arinsal, La Massana and the first car park. There are also four minibuses daily from Ordino to the ski station, passing through Llorts and El Serrat, some of which operate in summer too.

Eastern Andorra

The best skiing in Andorra is here, at Soldeu-El Tarter and Pas de la Casa-Grau Roig.

ENCAMP

The town of Encamp (altitude 1266m) has one of the few museums in Andorra: the **Museu Nacional de l'Automòbil** (National Automobile Museum, ☎ 83 22 66). At Avinguda del Príncep Episcopal 64, it has about 100 cars dating from 1898 to 1950 as well as 50 antique motorcycles and 100 bicycles. It is open Tuesday to Saturday from 9.30 am to 1.30 pm and 3 to 6 pm and Sunday from 10 am to 2 pm. Visits are by guided tour only (300 ptas).

Most of the **Església Sant Romà de les Bons**, about a kilometre north of Encamp, dates from the 12th century. The Romanesque frescoes in the apse are reproductions of the originals, which are in the Museu Nacional d'Art de Catalunya in Barcelona.

Buses run from Andorra la Vella to Encamp (110 ptas) every 20 or 30 minutes from 7 am to 9.30 pm.

ESTACIÓ D'ESQUÍ SOLDEU-EL TARTER

The Soldeu-El Tarter ski area (☎ 85 11 51, fax 85 13 37) is 19km north-east of Andorra la Vella, midway between the town of Canillo, which has a splendid Romanesque church (Sant Joan de Caselles) dating from the 11th century, and Port d'Envalira. Soldeu and El Tarter, both popular with British and French skiers, are separate villages 2km apart, but their ski lift systems interconnect. The Crèdit Andorrà bank just up the road from the Soldeu bus stop has an ATM.

Skiing

The 21 lifts, which are mostly tow lines, connect 62km of runs with a vertical drop of 850m. The skiing is similar to that at Pas de la Casa except that the black runs into the villages are steeper and more picturesque. Soldeu, higher than El Tarter at 1826m, has the bulk of the accommodation and facilities.

There are plenty of shops renting ski equipment from about 1600 ptas a day (snowboard and boots about 2500 ptas). Lift tickets for a half-day/day/three days cost 2200/3200/7800 ptas in the low season, 2700/3700/8850 ptas in the high season.

Other Activities
From mid-July to the end of August, chair lifts operate up to 2400m (1000 ptas return or 2100 ptas for a day pass). Mountain bikes, which can be taken aboard and ridden down, are rented here.

Places to Stay & Eat
Most of the accommodation and restaurants are along the main road, the CG2. In Soldeu, *Hotel Soldeu Maistre (☎ 85 10 35)* is not bad for the price with doubles for 2850 ptas. *Residència Supervalira (☎ 85 10 82, fax 85 10 62)* has better rooms costing up to 5250 ptas for a double – it is 2km up the road from Soldeu towards Pas de la Casa. A more upmarket place to stay is the popular *Sport Hotel (☎ 85 10 51, fax 85 15 93)*, which has singles/doubles for 7500/10,000 ptas.

Snack-Bar Bonell on the way down to the Soldeu ski lifts has reasonable platos combinados from 750 ptas, and pizzas. The restaurant at the *Hotel Soldeu* has tasty *menús* for 1200 or 1500 ptas. *Restaurant Espiolets* on the Soldeu ski slopes, open from December to April, has also been recommended.

Entertainment
The night scene at Soldeu-El Tarter gets hopping in winter. *Hardrock Soldeu* is a popular bar and *Piccadilly Pub* by the Sport Hotel is a typically British pub that occasionally has bands. *Capital Discoteca*, across the road from the Crèdit Andorrà bank, is a busy dance hangout.

Getting There & Away
Buses run from Andorra la Vella to El Tarter and Soldeu (340 ptas; 40 minutes) hourly from 9 am to 8 pm. Both places are also on the routes of buses between Andorra la Vella and the French railheads of Ax-les-Thermes, Latour-de-Carol and L'Hospitalet (see the introductory Getting There & Away earlier in this chapter). You can check bus times at the Soldeu post office.

ESTACIÓ D'ESQUÍ PAS DE LA CASA-GRAU ROIG
Pas de la Casa and Grau Roig are linked ski stations either side of the Port d'Envalira pass, boasting the highest skiing in Andorra at 2050m and 2600m, with the country's most reliable snow conditions. Grau Roig, with just one hotel, is on the west side of the col, 2km south of the CG2; Pas de la Casa, on the French border, is a large, unattractive village with numerous shops catering to French visitors.

Information
Pas de la Casa's tourist office (☎ 85 52 92) is across the road from the Andorran customs station. You'll find banks and a post office here.

Skiing
The combined ski area (☎ 85 56 92) has a network of 29 lifts and 87km of pistes. The skiing and snowboarding are well suited to beginners and intermediates. Ski touring is also possible. Several ski rental shops hire complete ski equipment for around 1600 ptas and snowboards for around 2500 ptas a day. Lift tickets are 2350/3400/8125 ptas for a half-day/day/seven days in low season, and 2725/3900/9375 ptas in high season.

Places to Stay & Eat
There is plenty of accommodation in Pas de la Casa, most of it with a wide seasonal price range. One of the least expensive places is *Hotel Llac Negre (☎ 85 51 98, fax 85 51 37, Carrer de Sant Jordi 43)*. Its basic rooms go from 3000/4000 to 5000/6250

ANDORRA

ptas. A reasonable mid-range place is *Hotel Les 4 Estacions (☎ 85 53 29, Avinguda d'Encamp 9)*, with rooms ranging up to 5750 ptas, single or double. At the top end, *Hotel Residència Envalira (☎ 85 50 95, fax 85 53 71, Carrer de Bearn 8)* has rooms for up to 7100/10,200 ptas.

Many people stay for a week or longer in Pas de la Casa on a full or half-board basis at their hotel. A popular place for breakfast is the bar at *Hotel Els Cims (Carrer Major 4-6)*. At the top end, the *Restaurant Marseillais (Carrer de Bearn 10)* has à la carte meals for about 1800 ptas. Around at Grau

Roig, you can get a cheap bite at *Restaurant Snack Tito's* at the base of the ski lifts.

Getting There & Away

From Andorra la Vella, there is one bus a day at 9 am to Pas de la Casa (590 ptas). It returns at 11.30 am. In winter there are an extra three buses daily to/from Andorra la Vella and Soldeu-El Tarter. Pas de la Casa is also on the bus routes between Andorra la Vella and the French railheads of Ax-les-Thermes, L'Hospitalet and Latour-de-Carol (see the introductory Getting There & Away earlier in this chapter).

Aragón

Little explored by foreign tourists and sparsely populated, Aragón is flanked by several worlds: France, Catalunya, the Basque territory of Navarra and the north-eastern reaches of Spain's Castilian heartland.

Aragón's northern strip, taking in some of the best of the Spanish Pyrenees, offers a wealth of walking and skiing that could easily extend to the French side of the frontier. Along the valleys and down into the lower pre-Pyrenees hills is a surprising mix of canyons, pretty villages, lonely castles and venerable monasteries.

The bigger cities are not among the country's most enticing, but lovers of monuments are in for a treat in places like Teruel and Zaragoza, where you can admire samples of a striking version of *mudéjar* architecture.

Central Aragón consists mainly of a forlorn series of treeless depressions and high plateaus. It was the scene of some of the nastiest fighting in the civil war, and the two sides could hardly have chosen a more comfortless place to do combat. However, you then come up against the mysterious mountain region of El Maestrazgo in the south, peppered with isolated and picturesque villages.

Various local culinary specialities are much touted, however there is little to differentiate average Aragonese cooking from the efforts of its Castilian neighbours. *Ternasco* (lamb's ribs) is a standard local dish, while ham shavings make an occasional appearance as the millionth variation on the Spanish pig theme.

Though overshadowed by the fame of neighbouring La Rioja and Navarra in the wine production game, Aragón doesn't produce a bad drop. Of the four areas at work, wines from the Cariñena zone just south of Zaragoza are among the best.

Although Aragón gave its name to one of the Iberian Peninsula's great medieval

Highlights

- Skiing in the Pyrenees (Candanchú, Astún, Panticosa and El Formigal)
- Summertime hiking in the Parque Nacional de Ordesa y Monte Perdido in the Pyrenees
- Eating and drinking in El Tubo, the heart of Zaragoza
- Villages of stone houses in the Valles de Ansó and Hecho
- The *mudéjar* towers of Teruel
- The brick-red medieval town of Albarracín
- Getting off the beaten track in the hill *pueblos* of El Maestrazgo

kingdoms, the so-called Crown of Aragón was actually dominated by Catalunya, with which Aragón itself united in the 12th century. Territories ranging from Valencia and the Balearic Islands to Sardinia and

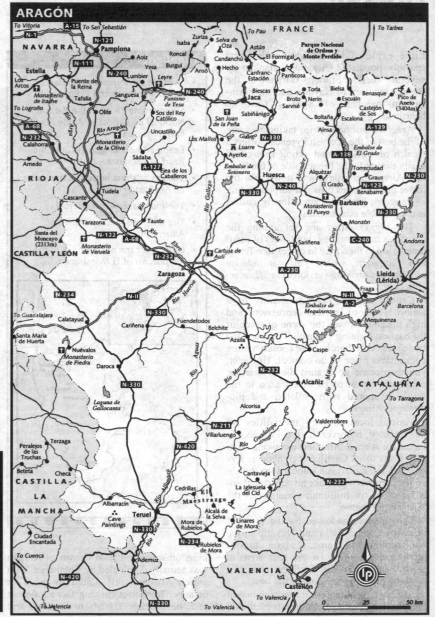

ARAGÓN

To Vitoria
N-1
A-15
To San Sebastián

FRANCE

To Tarbes

To Pau

NAVARRA

N-121

Pamplona

Aoiz

Yesa

Lumbier

N-240

N-111

Estella

Los Arcos

Puente de la Reina

Tafalla

Monasterio de Iraphe

To Logroño

A-68

N-232

Calahorra

Amedo

RIOJA

Sanguesa

Olite

Sos del Rey Católico

Uncastillo

Sádaba

Ejea de los Caballeros

A-127

Monasterio de la Oliva

Río Aragón

Pantano de Yesa

Leyre

N-240

Isaba

Zuriza

Selva de Oza

Roncal

Burgui

Ansó

Hecho

Candanchú

Astún

El Formigal

Canfranc-Estación

Panticosa

Biescas

Jaca

Broto

Nerín

Sarvisé

San Juan de la Peña

Sabiñánigo

Los Mallos

Loarre

Ayerbe

Embalse de Sotonera

Río Gállego

N-330

Parque Nacional de Ordesa y Monte Perdido

Torla

Bielsa

Escuain

Boltaña

Ainsa

Benasque

Pico de Aneto (3404m)

Castejón de Sos

Escalona

A-139

Embalse de El Grado

A-138

Torreciudad

Alquézar

El Grado

Graus

N-230

N-123

Barbastro

Benabarre

Monasterio El Pueyo

Monzón

C-240

N-230

To Andorra

Río Cinca

Río Ésera

Río Alcanadre

Huesca

N-240

N-330

Río Gállego

Río Alcanadre

Santa del Moncayo (2313m)

Tarazona

Monasterio de Veruela

CASTILLA Y LEÓN

Cascante

Tudela

Tauste

N-122

A-68

Río Arba

Río

Ebro

N-232

Zaragoza

Cartuja de Aula

Sariñena

A-230

Río Huerva

N-234

N-II

To Guadalajara

Calatayud

Cariñena

N-330

Fuendetodos

Belchite

Azaila

Río Aguas

Río Martín

N-232

Alcañiz

CATALUNYA

To Tarragona

Santa Maria de Huerta

Nuévalos

Monasterio de Piedra

Daroca

Laguna de Gallocanta

Alcorisa

Caspe

Río Guadalope

N-211

Villarluengo

Río

N-420

Cantavieja

La Iglesuela del Cid

Valderrobres

N-232

Río Maestrazgo

Fraga

N-II

A-2

To Barcelona

Embalse de Mequinenza

Mequinenza

To Lleida (Lérida)

Peralejos de las Truchas

Terzaga

Beteta

Checa

CASTILLA-LA MANCHA

Albarracín

Cave Paintings

Teruel

N-330

El Maestrazgo

Cedrillas

Alcalá de la Selva

Mora de Rubielos

Linares de Mora

Ciudad Encantada

To Cuenca

Ademuz

N-420

Rubielos de Mora

N-234

Río Alfambra

Río Turia

VALENCIA

Castellón

To Valencia

To Valencia

N-330

0   25   50 km

LP

Sicily were conquered in the name of Aragón, but this was actually the work of the more commercially minded and cosmopolitan Catalan half of the joint kingdom. The feudal nobility of Aragón proper took some revenge on the Catalans in 1412, when they engineered the election of a Castilian, Fernando of Antequera, to the vacant throne. This set the scene for the union of Aragón and Castilla later in the century under their respective monarchs Fernando and Isabel, which effectively gave birth to what we know as Spain.

Get a copy of the *Guía de Servicios Turísticos de Aragón*, published by the Aragonese tourism department. It contains complete lists of hotels, camping grounds, *casas rurales*, mountain refuges and other information.

Skiing
Aragón is well endowed with ski resorts, mainly along the Pyrenees in the north. The tourist offices in Zaragoza, Huesca and Jack have plenty of information but you are generally better off arranging a package rather than turning up under your own steam. The downhill version is the most popular, but cross-country skiing is gaining a higher profile.

Walking
The mountains are, if anything, more popular in summer than in winter, with innumerable options for walking – anything from gentle rambles of a few hours to long-distance hikes taking up to a week. A network of long-distance trails (Grandes Recorridos, or GRs) are marked throughout the northern strip of Aragón and overlap into neighbouring regions and France. The GR-11 pretty much follows the mountain line just south of France, beginning on the coast of Catalunya and heading west to Navarra and the coast of the País Vasco, but there are plenty of others.

The optimum time to lace up your hiking boots is from late June to early September. Even then the weather can be unpredictable, so serious hikers need to come prepared for most contingencies. Mid-July to mid-August is the peak summer holiday period in Spain, when the more popular parks and hiking routes can become very crowded.

The Federación Española de Montañismo (☎ 91 445 13 82) in Madrid can be contacted for guidance on routes, refuges and specialist equipment shops. Or you can try the Federación Aragonesa de Montañismo in Zaragoza (☎ 976 23 63 55). Editorial Alpina publishes a series of maps of the entire Aragonese Pyrenees at a scale of 1:40,000 and 1:25,000. It comes with booklets that outline walking routes. This series of red (in some cases orange) booklets generally cost from 450 to 650 ptas.

Walkers should see the boxed text 'Walking in the Pyrenees' in the Catalunya chapter.

Adventure Sports
Rock climbing, paragliding and white-water rafting, plus mountain biking and horseback riding, are all options in Aragón, mainly in the Pyrenees. We've provided a few tips and tourist offices have more information on local firms that organise these activities.

Central Aragón

ZARAGOZA
With more than 600,000 inhabitants, Zaragoza (Saragossa) is like an outsized section of an otherwise thinly populated Aragón, which has some 1.2 million people. Long an important crossroads on one of Spain's most important waterways, it is today a centre of industry, producing iron, steel, chemicals, plastics, canned food and electrical goods.

The lively old centre (which somehow doesn't feel so old) is definitely worth a day or two's exploration, if only to sample the atmosphere in the bars and restaurants.

On a bad day it can get blowy, and locals call the north wind that seems to tear right through you 'El Cierzo'. Fortunately, it is not a permanent phenomenon, so Zaragoza has avoided that unfortunate sobriquet of 'the Windy City'.

ARAGÓN

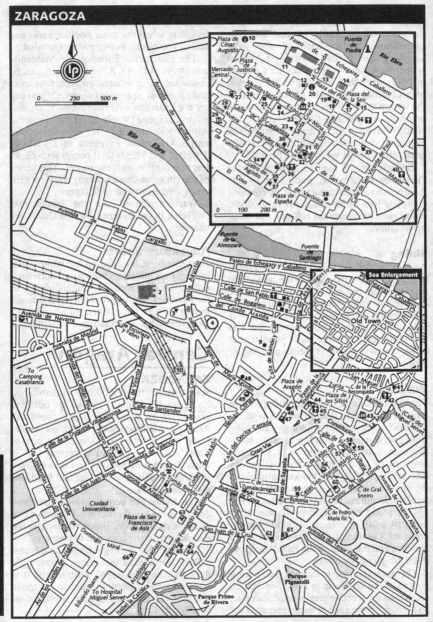

ZARAGOZA

ZARAGOZA

PLACES TO STAY		57	Risko Mar	27	Bar Corto Maltés
6	Posada de las Almas;	58	Restaurante El Mangrullo	29	Museo de Pablo Gargallo
	Hotel San Blas	59	Churrasco	30	Café El Prior
12	Hotel Las Torres	62	Los Borrachos	31	Chastón
17	Hotel Via Romana	63	Café Universal	36	Iglesia de San Gil
18	Hostal Ambos Mundos	64	Casa Tena	38	Roman Theatre
19	Hostal Plaza	65	Casa Martín	39	Lesbianas y Gays de
24	Fonda Satué				Aragón
25	Fonda Manifestación	**OTHER**		40	Iglesia de Santa María
32	Pensión Rex	1	Cinco Villas Buses		Magdalena
33	Fonda Peña	2	Aljafería	42	Iglesia de San Miguel
46	Pensión Canfranc	4	Plaza de Toros	43	Museo de Zaragoza
51	Albergue de la Juventud	5	Iglesia de San Pablo	44	Correos
	Baltasar Gracián & TIVE	7	Casa Perdiguer	45	Iglesia de Santa Engracia
55	Pensión La Dama	8	Oasis	47	Airport Bus
		9	Sphinx	48	Museo Pablo Serrano
PLACES TO EAT		10	Torreón de la Zuda &	49	Agreda Bus Company
3	Restaurante Casa Emilio		Regional Tourist Office	50	El Portillo Train Station
22	Casa Juanico	11	Basílica de Nuestra Señora		(RENFE)
23	Café Praga; Café Gaudí		del Pilar	52	Phone & Fax Office
26	Café de Orfeo	13	Ayuntamiento		(Loctel)
28	Crêpêrie Flor	14	La Lonja	53	Mambo
34	Pascualillo	15	Roman Forum	56	Therpasa Buses
35	Jamaica Coffee Shop	16	La Seo	60	Lavandería Casa
37	Casa Lac	20	Oficina Municipal de Turismo	61	American Express
41	Restaurante la Retama	21	Palacio de los Pardo &	66	Policía Local
54	Restaurante La Alcarabea		Museo Camón Aznar	67	KWM

History

Although inhabited beforehand, this Ebro town gained importance when refounded by the Romans as Caesaraugusta (hence the modern corruption of its name). As many as 25,000 people came to live in the prosperous city, which in 380 AD played host to a synod of the Christian church. From 714 it remained in the hands of the Muslim invaders for four centuries, falling to the Aragonese king Alfonso el Batallador in 1118.

Centuries later, as Napoleon's troops marched all over the country, Zaragoza put up unusually stiff resistance under siege, although it was finally compelled to capitulate in 1809. Its growth late in the 19th century as an industrial city made it a centre of militant trade unionism, but in 1936 the Republicans had no time to organise themselves and Zaragoza was quickly put under Nationalist control. The country's main military academy was set up here under General Franco in 1928.

Orientation

The core of old Zaragoza lies on the southern bank of the Río Ebro, the outline of its former walls marked by Avenida de César Augusto and El Coso. Much of what there is to see and a good choice of hotels, restaurants and bars lie within the old city limits. To the south, several great avenues stretch into the city that has grown up over the past hundred years, capped by the extensive Parque Primo de Rivera. The train station is about a 15 minute walk west of the old centre, and many regional and national buses depart from a station halfway between the two.

In the old centre, Plaza del Pilar, a kind of open arcade dominated by Zaragoza's great basilica, gives way to a labyrinth of lanes and alleys, the heart of which is known as El Tubo.

ARAGON

Information

Tourist Office The main regional tourist office (☎ 976 39 35 37) is in the Torreón de la Zuda, Glorieta Pío XII, at the western end of Plaza del Pilar. It is open Monday to Friday from 8 am to 3 pm and 4 to 6 pm and Saturday from 10 am to 1 pm. For information on the city alone, try the Oficina Municipal de Turismo (☎ 976 20 12 00) across from the basilica. It is open Monday to Saturday from 9.30 am to 1.30 pm and 4.30 to 7.30 pm and Sunday from 10 am to 2 pm. A summer tourist office is open at El Portillo train station.

Money Banks abound all over the city, most with ATMs that accept a wide range of foreign credit cards.

American Express (☎ 976 38 39 11), officially at Paseo de Sagasta 47, is actually in the Turopa travel agency around the corner on Camino de las Torres.

Post & Communications The main *correos* (post office) is at Paseo de la Independencia 33. The postcode for central Zaragoza and poste restante is 50080. Telefónica has no telephone office, but the private Loctel company at Calle de Tomás Bretón 26 offers a telephone and fax service.

Travel Agencies Students and young people can get international student ID cards and discount travel advice at the TIVE office at Calle de Franco y Lopez 4, in the youth hostel complex.

Gay & Lesbian Information Small but picking up steam, Lesbianas y Gays de Aragón has an info centre and bar at Calle de Juan de Aragón 6 (☎ 976 39 55 77), open Monday to Friday from 7 to 10 pm. See Entertainment for gay nightspots.

Laundry Lavandería Casa at Calle de Pedro Maria Ric 37 does your wash and dry for 900 to 1000 ptas per load.

Medical Services Hospital Miguel Servet (☎ 976 35 57 00) is on Paseo de Isabel la Católica, south of the centre.

Emergency The Policía Local is based at Calle de Domingo Miral. Call ☎ 092 in case of emergency and ☎ 976 35 85 00 for an ambulance. It's a long shot, but if you have lost something, you might try ☎ 976 55 91 76, at the Policía Local headquarters.

Basílica de Nuestra Señora del Pilar

One day while preaching in Spain, Santiago (St James) is supposed to have beheld a vision of the Virgin Mary, descended from the heavens atop a marble pillar. This she left behind and around it was built a chapel. At least that's the story of the *pilar* around which was later built the overwhelming baroque edifice on Plaza del Pilar. Designed in 1681 by Francisco de Herrera, the building was later altered by Ventura Rodríguez and José Ramírez. The towers were not completed until the early 20th century. The main dome is accompanied by 10 smaller ones, all decorated with tiles of blue, green, yellow and white.

The Capilla Santa, the oval chapel in which the supposed pilar is enshrined, is a sumptuous pink marble structure at the eastern end of the church. The paintings in the cupola above it were carried out by Antonio González Velázquez. Goya also worked here, his most important contribution being the painting inside the cupola above the Capilla de San Joaquín.

A small portion of the supposed pilar is accessible at the rear of the Capilla Santa, and for centuries pilgrims have come to kiss and touch it.

The single greatest piece of fine art is the alabaster high altar piece by Damián Forment, actually done in the early 16th century, well before the present church was started.

In the northern flank is the **Museo Pilarista**, which has a small collection of jewellery, 'capes of the Virgin' and a planning model of the chapel built for the holy pillar.

The basilica is open daily from 5.45 am to 9.30 pm (8.30 pm in winter). The museum is open daily from 9 am to 2 pm and 4 to 6 pm (150 ptas).

Plaza del Pilar

Roman Forum The unassuming trapezoid at the eastern end of Plaza del Pilar is in fact the modern entrance to ancient Caesaraugusta's forum, well below the present city's ground level. Apart from the sparse remains of the Roman wall at the western end of the square and traces of the theatre, this is the most substantial reminder of the empire's presence here.

What you see underground are the remains of shops, porticoes, the great *cloaca* (sewerage system) built in Tiberius' time, and a limited collection of artefacts. Perhaps most interesting are sections of lead pipes used to channel water to the city's populace – they look much like modern piping and are a reminder of the Romans' genius for engineering. All of this dates from between the 1st century BC and the 1st century AD. A well done 'cyclorama' show of slides, music and commentary, presented on the hour in Spanish, breathes life into the old crockery.

The forum is open Tuesday to Saturday from 10 am to 2 pm and 5 to 8 pm (mornings only on Sunday; 400 ptas, students half-price).

La Seo Once the main church in Zaragoza and built over the site of what had been the central mosque, the Catedral de San Salvador, known as La Seo, is a smorgasbord of styles. From its 12th century Romanesque apse to its 16th century Late Gothic additions, there's a bit of everything.

Circle around this brooding building to view the north-western façade, an Aragonese mudéjar masterpiece combining classic dark brickwork and ceramic decoration. The main colours are a restrained mix of greens, blues and white deployed in a series of eye-pleasing geometrical patterns. Opposite this extraordinary façade lies the low and, in comparison, humble Palacio Arzobispal, or seat of the archbishop.

There are several admirable works inside the cathedral, but it has been closed for some time while excavation and restoration work are carried out.

La Lonja The fairly plain building between the Palacio Arzobispal and the *ayuntamiento* (town hall) was built in the mid-16th century in the Renaissance style and is now only open for exhibitions.

Torreón de la Zuda This is all that remains of the Muslim governors' palace, at the western end of the square. The tower was modified in the 15th century.

Mercado Central The central market, off the western corner of Plaza del Pilar, is a good example of late *modernista* architecture – and a great place to stock up on picnic supplies.

Aljafería

For all the changes it has undergone, the Aljafería remains the greatest Muslim era edifice outside Andalucía. Built as a pleasure dome for Zaragoza's Muslim rulers, it was never intended as a serious defensive installation. From the 12th century, Zaragoza's Christian rulers made alterations, and in 1486 the Inquisition moved in to the main square tower, the Torre del Trovador. At the end of the 15th century, Fernando and Isabel tacked on the new palace. From then it was used as a hospital and barracks, at the same time being allowed to decay. From the late 1940s serious restoration was carried out and in 1987 the Aragonese parliament *(Cortes)* established itself here. Restoration continues today.

Once you pass through the main gate, cross the courtyard into a second, known as Santa Isabel's courtyard. Here you are confronted to the north and south by the opulence and geometric mastery of Muslim architecture, with its arches like fine lacework. Opening off the northern porch is the small oratory. A magnificent horseshoe-arched doorway leads inside, where you

ARAGÓN

find the *mihrab*, or prayer niche indicating the direction of Mecca. The finely chiselled floral motifs, inscriptions in Arabic from the Qur'an and pleasingly simple inner side of the cupola are impressive examples of high Muslim art.

As though by way of a riposte, the Catholic Monarchs' new palace, upstairs, also has treasures, especially the *artesonado* ceilings – beautiful mudéjar work that took much of its original inspiration from Oriental sources.

The Aljafería is open Monday to Saturday from 10 am to 2 pm and 4 to 8 pm (4.30 to 6.30 pm in winter) and Sunday from 10 am to 2 pm (free).

Churches

Apart from the two great houses of worship that dominate Plaza del Pilar, several minor churches dotted in and around the centre are also worth a quick look. The **Iglesia de Santa María Magdalena**, at the eastern end of Calle Mayor, is remarkable for its mudéjar tower. The **Iglesia de San Pablo**, too, boasts an impressive mudéjar tower and a retablo by Damián Forment. Much the same story applies to the **Iglesia de San Miguel**. The tower of the **Iglesia de San Gil** underwent something of a baroque transformation, but remains largely faithful to its 14th century mudéjar origins. In the newer part of town, the **Iglesia de Santa Engracia** is notable for its intricately carved entrance.

Museums

Museo de Zaragoza The archaeology and fine arts section is the main part of this museum on Plaza de los Sitios. On display are artefacts from prehistoric to Muslim times and an important collection of Gothic art, as well as contributions from Damián Forment and Goya (including a self-portrait). There is also an Ethnology section in the Parque de Primo de Rivera, south of Paseo de Fernando el Católico. Both sections are open Tuesday to Saturday from 9 am to 2 pm and Sunday from 10 am to 2 pm (200 ptas, free for EU citizens).

Museo Camón Aznar Housed in the Palacio de los Pardo, this eclectic collection of Spanish art from the 15th to the 20th centuries is spread out over the three storeys of the Renaissance mansion at Calle de Espoz y Mina 23. It is open Tuesday to Friday from 9 am to 2.15 pm, Saturday from 10 am to 2 pm and Sunday from 11 am to 2 pm (50 ptas).

Museo de Pablo Gargallo This is a representative display of bronze sculptures by Pablo Gargallo, possibly Aragón's most gifted artistic son after Goya. The works, mostly done in the first decades of this century, are housed in a mid-17th century mansion. It is open Tuesday to Saturday from 10 am to 2 pm and 5 to 9 pm (mornings only on Sunday; free).

Museo Pablo Serrano Modern art fans might examine this collection of works by yet another Aragonese, Pablo Serrano, who died in 1985. Expressive sculptures in bronze are his forte. The museum at Paseo de María Agustín 20 is open Tuesday to Saturday from 10 am to 2 pm and 6 to 9 pm (5 to 8 pm in winter) and Sunday from 10 am to 2 pm (free).

Modernisme

As well as the Mercado Central, Paseo de Sagasta is a good place to scout for samples of Zaragoza's remaining late modernista architecture, particularly street numbers 11, 13, 19, 40 and 76.

Organised Tours

The Oficina Municipal de Turismo organises free tours (in Spanish) on Sunday at 11 am of some of the sights of the old town.

Special Events

The Fiesta de San Valero, the day of the city's patron saint, is celebrated in rather muted fashion throughout the province on 29 January. The big treat is the *roscón*, a rich cake loaded with cream in the shape of a doughnut – a super huge one is placed in Plaza del Pilar if the weather permits.

In the last days of February, Zaragoza joins most other cities throughout Spain to celebrate *carnaval*. But the city's big event is the Fiestas del Pilar, a week of celebrations around 12 October.

In November, the city hosts an international jazz festival.

Places to Stay – Budget

Camping & Hostel The city's only camping ground, *Camping Casablanca (☎ 976 75 38 70)* is a few kilometres out of town to the south-west, off the Autovía de Madrid towards Valldefierro. It's not cheap, at 600 ptas per person, tent site and car.

The *Albergue de la Juventud Baltasar Gracián (☎ 976 55 13 87, Calle de Franco y López 4)* is open all year to members only. Beds cost 1425 ptas, or 1025 ptas for under-26s.

Fondas, Hostales & Pensiones Zaragoza is full to bursting with *fondas*, *hostales* and hotels of most categories. Many of the cheap places are true dumps, so look out.

A good choice in the heart of El Tubo is *Fonda Peña (☎ 976 29 90 89, Calle de Cinegio 3)*, with rooms for 1200/1800 ptas. There is a decent little *comedor* here, too.

Another reasonable cheapie is the *Fonda Manifestación (☎ 976 29 58 21, Calle de la Manifestación 36)*, with singles/doubles for 1500/3000 ptas. Just down the street is *Fonda Satué (☎ 976 39 07 09, Calle de Espoz y Mina 4)*, with doubles for 2600 ptas. There's also the quite decent *Pensión Rex (☎ 976 39 26 33, Calle de Méndez Núñez 31)*, with prices ranging from 1820 ptas for a single without bath to 4280 ptas for an *en suite* double.

If you want to be right on Plaza del Pilar and have the opportunity of views of the basilica, try *Hostal Plaza (☎ 976 29 48 30)* at No 14. It has quite reasonable singles/doubles for 3000/3900 ptas. *Hostal Ambos Mundos (☎ 976 29 97 04)*, at No 16, is a little more tatty, but also has fairly good rooms for 2300/4500 ptas with bath.

There are a couple of inexpensive, good value pensiones in the new part of town – perhaps worth the extra walk. *Pensión La Dama (☎ 976 22 39 99, Calle del Doctor Casas 20)* has clean rooms with outside shower for 1700/2600 ptas (slightly more in high summer). *Pensión Canfranc (☎ 976 22 46 95, Calle de Canfranc 8)* is on a pretty street just off Paseo de la Independencia and has doubles for 2800 ptas.

Places to Stay – Mid-Range

The *Posada de las Almas (☎ 976 43 97 00, Calle de San Pablo 22)* has been going since 1705 and has an atmospheric restaurant. The rooms are good but few have any of the character you might have expected. Singles/doubles cost up to 4100/7100 ptas. The same people run the marginally cheaper *Hotel San Blas* across the road.

A comfortable, if also fairly characterless, option for views of the basilica is the *Hotel Las Torres (☎ 976 39 42 50, fax 976 39 42 54)*, with singles/doubles from 4500/7000 ptas plus IVA. The latter are fine, but the former can be pokey. Not all rooms come with views.

Places to Stay – Top End

Hotel Vía Romana (☎ 976 39 82 15, fax 976 29 05 11, Calle de Don Jaime I 54-56) is not the most expensive hotel in Zaragoza, but it is a comfortable place overlooking Plaza del Pilar. Singles/doubles cost from 6500/8000 ptas plus IVA.

Places to Eat

There are several zones to look for restaurants. For the cheaper end of the scale, El Tubo, in the heart of the old town, is the place to start. In the new town, the area around Calle de Francisco Vitoria is also good and there's a clutch of mid-range spots on Plaza de San Francisco de Asís.

In the heart of El Tubo, *Pascualillo (Calle de la Libertad 5)* has good set *menú* for under 1000 ptas. More upmarket with a touch of fading class is *Casa Lac (Calle de los Mártires 12)*, which has been going nonstop since it received its licence in 1825.

ARAGÓN

Casa Juanico (Calle de la Santa Cruz 21) is a popular old style tapas bar with a comedor out the back. The solid set *menú* costs 1500 ptas. A great dessert of crêpes can be had in the *Crêperie Flor*, just off Plaza de San Felipe.

Outside this area but in a similar vein is the *Restaurante Casa Emilio (Avenida de Madrid 5)*, a simple sort of place with low-priced, home-cooked meals; it'll win no cuisine medals, but it serves wholesome stuff and you'll find no tourists about.

Casa Martín (Plaza de San Francisco de Asís 9) is a bright place. Set *menús* cost from 1300 to 3000 ptas. Try the *pastel de puerros y gambas* (leek and prawn pie) as a starter. *Casa Tena* at No 16 has mains for 1000 to 1500 ptas.

Risko Mar (Calle de Francisco Vitoria 16) is one of the city's best-known fish restaurants, but it's pricey. An excellent set meal for two will cost 5000 ptas. Across the road, you could try *Restaurante El Mangrullo* at No 17 for Argentine food. Main dishes go for about 1000 to 1500 ptas. Next door, *Churrasco* feels a bit like a tavern. It offers a wide variety of meat and fish dishes, which will cost you up to 3000 ptas a head. *Los Borrachos (Paseo de Sagasta 64)* is a Zaragozan institution, and it ain't cheap.

For vegetarian food, try *Restaurante La Alcarabea (Calle de Zumalacárregui 23)*, which has a student menu for 650 ptas, but keeps unpredictable hours. Another veggie place is *Restaurante la Retama*, just outside the old town on the corner of Calle de la Reconquista and Plaza de San Miguel.

Cafés In keeping with its profile as a burgeoning metropolis, Zaragoza is blessed with some particularly pleasing and elegant cafés, as well as a number of real dives which you'll have no trouble finding.

In the old town, the *Jamaica Coffee Shop (Calle de Don Jaime I 5)* offers a variety of black brews in a comfy setting.

Café de Orfeo (Calle de Santa Isabel 3) is an old-fashioned café-bar. *Café Praga* on Plaza de la Santa Cruz is bare, blue and trendy, while *Café Gaudí* next door lives up to its name. Both sprawl out onto the plaza in the warm months.

Café Universal (Paseo de Fernando el Católico 32) is a long-standing Zaragozan institution. You almost feel as though you should dress up to be there.

Entertainment

Bars Drinking is as serious a business in Zaragoza as in any other big Spanish city and there are several zones to explore. One is the area around the university, with a fairly young student crowd. Closer to where most travellers are likely to hang out, El Tubo, or the adjacent Mercado Central area, has no shortage of options. The streets around Calle del Doctor Cerrada and Calle de San Miguel are also lively. Keep an eye out for *sidra*, powerful cider that some places occasionally stock.

Bar Corto Maltés (Calle del Temple 23) is one of a string of rather cool places on a lane near the Mercado Central. All the barmen seem to sport the '*corto maltés*' – the cut of the sideburns in the theme picture. In El Tubo itself, *Chastón (Plaza de Ariño 4)* is a relaxing little jazz club.

Nightclubs & Discos *Oasis (Calle de Boggiero 28)* was founded in 1909 as a concert hall and underwent various transformations until it became Oasis in 1942. It hosts lots of variety shows.

For drinks and casual dancing, *Café El Prior* on Calle de Contamina is a good place to start.

KWM (Paseo de Fernando El Católico 70) is a popular mainstream disco open until about 5 am. *Mambo (Calle de San Antonio Maria Claret 54)*, close by, has reggae-salsa-meringue nights in the heart of the student district.

Torreluna (Calle de Miguel Servet 193) is a favourite, built inside a severe-looking old mansion out of town. Catch bus No 38 from Plaza de España (and a taxi back!).

Gay nightspots include *Sphinx* on Calle de Ramón y Cajal.

Spectator Sports

Zaragoza is a particularly active bullfighting town, with regular spectacles held in the Plaza de Toros.

Shopping

Shops in and around El Tubo sell the usual kitsch as well as ceramics from various parts of Aragón. For something a little different, wine lovers should drop in at Casa Perdiguer, Calle de San Pablo 39, purveyors of fine wines in bottles and huge wooden vats.

A good flea market, El Rastro, takes place on Sunday morning by the Plaza de Toros.

Getting There & Away

Air Zaragoza is linked by air to Madrid, Barcelona and, for some reason, Jerez. There is also the occasional direct flight to London and Paris.

Bus A dozen or so companies serve Zaragoza, with offices all over the city – there is no central station. The Agreda company operates buses to most major Spanish cities from Paseo de María Agustín 7. The one-way trip to Madrid costs 1750 ptas and to Barcelona is 1640 ptas. La Oscense also operates from here to Huesca and Jaca. The tourist office has a full list of bus company addresses and destinations. Check other destinations in this chapter for relevant addresses.

Train All trains use the shiny El Portillo station. Zaragoza is an important junction and there are connections to most destinations. Up to 14 serve Madrid (3000 to 3700 ptas) daily and a similar number run to Barcelona (3000 ptas). Trains travel as far afield as Galicia, Valencia and even Cádiz. Closer to home, the trip south to Teruel costs 1355 ptas, as does the voyage to Jaca (via Huesca; 675 ptas).

Car & Motorcycle Zaragoza is on a major junction. The A-2 *autopista* hooks up with the A-7 for Barcelona and the N-II heads

south-west for Madrid. The N-330 will take you north to Huesca and the Pyrenees and south towards Teruel. The A-68 heads north-west through Navarra and La Rioja to Bilbao.

Getting Around

To/From the Airport Ebrobus (☎ 976 32 40 09) runs buses from Plaza de Aragón to link with flights. They leave up to five times daily.

Bus Bus No 22 links the El Portillo train station to Plaza de España, which is served by almost all routes.

AROUND ZARAGOZA

The pickings are slim in the immediate vicinity, but the farther you get away, particularly to the south and south-east, the more little gems you'll run into. Most of the following places can be reached by bus, but having your own transport is ideal.

Cartuja de Auli

This Carthusian monastery about 10km north of Zaragoza contains a series of frescoes by Goya depicting the lives of Christ and the Virgin Mary. The frescoes had suffered badly since the monastery was suppressed early in the 19th century, but have been lovingly repainted. Restoration work continues on the rest of the monastery, so check with the tourist office in Zaragoza to make sure it's open. Until now only men have been allowed in, but women in Zaragoza recently ran a campaign to have access available to both sexes; the current restorations will provide a separate entrance for women. The occasional Agreda bus goes past the monastery.

Muel & Cariñena

Wine fans heading south for Teruel could do worse than pass through Cariñena country – home of the best viticultural industry you'll find in Aragón. Along the way, peek into the chapel in Muel, 19km before Cariñena, which sports paintings by Goya.

ARAGÓN

Lest We Forget

In the summer of 1937, Republican forces fought a savage battle with Franco's troops for control of the small town of Belchite. By the time they had finished, the elegant houses along the Calle Mayor, along with the town's two churches, mostly built of the narrow bricks typical of *mudéjar* architecture, had been thoroughly blasted. The Torre del Reloj (clock tower) was left leaning precariously, the clock face blown away. In March of the following year Nationalist forces marched back in as the seesaw war in this heavily fought-over part of Spain moved back in Franco's favour. By now the town's populace lived in a labyrinth of wreckage, struggling to keep life going in the midst of disaster. The Franco government judged the town too far gone to be rebuilt, and decided to build it afresh next door. That plan was not completed until 1954 – a long wait for people living in such misery. Today, it is an eerie experience to wander past the shell-shocked buildings down silent streets, where for a time life and death led a tragic coexistence.

There isn't much to see in Cariñena's old core, so head to one of the many *bodegas* on the main road into town. If you decide to linger, the *Hostal Iliturgis* (☎ 976 62 04 92, Plaza de Ramón y Cajal 1) has comfortable singles/doubles for 1800/3800 ptas. Three daily trains on the Zaragoza-Teruel line stop here, and a couple of Agreda buses leave from Zaragoza's Avenida de Valencia 20.

Fuendetodos

Some of the biggest start small, especially in the case of Francisco Goya y Lucientes, who was born in this insignificant Aragonese hamlet in 1746. His house stayed in the family until the beginning of the 20th century, when the artist Ignacio Zuloaga found and bought it. Partly destroyed during the civil war, the humble three-storey abode has been restored. Down the road, the **Museo del Grabado de Goya** contains an impressive collection of the painter's etchings and is well worth a visit. Entry to both is Tuesday to Sunday from 11 am to 2 pm and 4 to 7 pm (the combined ticket costs 300 ptas). The Samar Buil company runs daily buses to Zaragoza (Calle de Borau 13).

Belchite

This town, or rather the twin towns that constitute Belchite, must be one of the most eloquent reminders of the destruction wrought in the civil war. The ruins of the old town, replaced by a new village next door, have been left standing as a silent memorial. A few kilometres west stands the strangely neglected 18th century **Santuario de Nuestra Señora del Pueyo**.

Azaila

Those with vehicles may wish to continue east on the A-221 to inspect the remains of a hill-top Celtic-Roman *castro*, 1km outside of Azaila. The streets and a water channel are clearly laid out, and the views seem limitless.

Along the Río Ebro

Dams have created a large reservoir of the Río Ebro for miles before and after **Caspe**. This hill-top town was also heavily damaged during the civil war, as the 13th century Colegiata church in the centre still shows. Caspe is known to lovers of Spanish history for the Compromiso de Caspe (Caspe Compromise), signed in 1412 to settle the Aragonese succession by putting a Castilian from the Trastámara house on Aragón's throne. There's a camping ground on the dam 14km to the north-east.

A bit farther on is **Mequinenza**, dominated by a medieval castle that saw action in the War of the Spanish Succession and as late as 1938 during the civil war. Virtually destroyed then, it was later rebuilt.

EAST OF ZARAGOZA

The often disconsolate plains that stretch east of Zaragoza, sliced by waves of bare plateaus, are for all their Spartan appearance not entirely empty of interest, and a couple of short stops along the way to or from Catalunya suggest themselves.

Monasterio de Sigena

Lying in a quiet clearing off the A-131 Fraga-Sariñena road, this monastery was first raised in the 12th century and for 800 years occupied by the Order of St John of Jerusalem. Since 1985 the order has been replaced by a handful of nuns living under a vow of silence. It's not open to the public, but you can catch a glimpse of the Romanesque church with its graceful arches.

Fraga

The old core of this town makes for an intriguing stroll. Its centrepiece is the much-remodelled 12th century **Iglesia de San Pedro**, seemingly growing out of the steeply sloping streets. *Cobertizos*, the galleries that allow passage between houses above the streets, cast deep shadows over the dishevelled maze below. Head uphill from the church for views across the *casco histórico*, the wide Río Cinca valley and the chain of parched hills to the west.

Hostal Flavia (☎ 974 47 15 40, Paseo de Barrón 13) is on the downhill edge of the old town and has basic rooms for 1300/2500 ptas. Calle Mayor links this square with Plaza de San Pedro. It serves food too, and some of the town's more happening *bars* are on the same square – which may prove a little noisy.

The *estación de autobuses* (bus station) is just on the west bank of the river on Avenida de Aragón. Up to 10 daily head east to Lleida (Lérida), three to Zaragoza and two to Huesca. Some take roundabout routes and there is hardly a bus to anywhere on Sunday.

TARAZONA

West of Zaragoza on the N-122, Tarazona is a remarkable reminder of the Muslim occupation and is often likened to Toledo. This is overdoing it, although the town may resemble Toledo of 20 years ago – its dimly lit serpentine streets see few tourists and the crumbling old town has a way to go in providing restaurants and entertainment.

Turiaso, as the town was then known, was the scene of a famous victory by a small band of imperial Roman soldiers over a far greater Celtiberian army. Later it was a Visigothic bishopric before being taken by the Muslims. By 1118 it was again in Christian hands.

Information

The tourist office (☎ 976 64 00 74) in an outside corner of the cathedral is open weekdays from 9 am to 1.30 pm and 4.30 to 7 pm and weekends from 10 am to 2 pm and 4 to 7 pm.

Things to See

The **catedral**, closed for restoration, is a mixed bag of Romanesque, Gothic, mudéjar and Renaissance. The mudéjar cloisters are particularly pretty, while the prime oddity is a brick dome, fashioned by Juan Botero.

Nearby, the old **Plaza de Toros** is an original bullring. The octagonal ring is made up of 32 houses and was built at the end of the 18th century as a private housing initiative – with entertainment thrown in.

The rest of Tarazona's sights are within the twisting cobbled ways of the medieval 'high part' of the town, on the other side of the Río Queiles (really just a ditch). From all around you can see the slender mudéjar tower of the **Iglesia de Santa María Magdalena**. The **Palacio Episcopal** opposite was a Muslim fortified palace. Farther north on Plaza de España is the richly decorated 16th century ayuntamiento, among whose reliefs is supposedly one of Hercules.

Places to Stay & Eat

You can stay in one of three places. The cheapest is the *Hostal María Cristina (☎ 976 64 00 84, Carretera de Castilla 3)*, which looks like it's been going for a century but is quite OK. Rates are 1500 ptas per person, plus an extra 300 ptas for a hot shower.

On the opposite way out of town is the *Hotel Brujas de Becquer* (☎ 976 64 04 04, *Carretera de Zaragoza s/n*), with rooms for 4000/5700 ptas (slightly more in summer).

Borgia by Another Name

About 25km east of Tarazona, you pass through a small town with yet another castle. 'So what?', you might think. After all, there's hardly a town in central Spain that doesn't have a castle. True, but this is a *pueblo* with a difference. Borja is not only at the centre of one of Aragón's four main wine-growing districts, but it is also the ancestral stamping ground of one of the most notorious families in Italian history! Borja, written in Italian, comes out as Borgia – the crumbly castle of Borja was once home to the colourful crew of that name.

Rodrigo Borgia, as Alexander VI, became Rome's most talked-about pope in history – a wheeler-dealer philanderer who was nothing if not irreligious. And his offspring (he did little to hide his paternity), Cesare and Lucrezia, have had bad press ever since they romped across the world stage in the first half of the 16th century. Cesare probably deserved his reputation as a vicious and cynical murderer, prepared to do anything to fulfil his grandiose plans for secular rule over much of Italy. Whether or not Lucrezia was the husband-poisoner she was made out to be is less certain; nor is it clear whether the rumours that she had an incestuous relationship with her father the pope are true.

The little old town of Borja had long been forgotten and picked up not a ray of reflected 'glory'. For Rodrigo's ancestors had moved to the more salubrious climes of Valencia in the early 14th century. One can only guess at what the upright citizens of 15th and 16th century Borja made of their one-time neighbours' doings.

Hotel Ituri Asso (☎ 976 64 31 96, *Calle de la Virgen del Río 3*), right on the river, has good rooms with bath, TV and phone for 5000/8000 ptas plus IVA. Both hotels have decent restaurants, or you could try the ternasco at *El Galeón*, just off centre at Avenida de la Paz 1.

Getting There & Away

Therpasa buses run regularly between Soria and Zaragoza (Calle del General Sueria 22-24) from its station on Avenida de Navarra. For Pamplona and the Monasterio de Veruela you need to go to a different stop on Carrera de Zaragoza. Both streets branch off Plaza de San Francisco in the centre.

AROUND TARAZONA

The fortified walls of the **Monasterio de Veruela** are more reminiscent of a Castilian castle than a monastery, yet from its founding in the 12th century that's what it was. Starting in the hands of Carthusians, it was long inhabited by Jesuits. It now belongs to Zaragoza's provincial government. The cold Gothic church is flanked by a charming cloister, whose lower Gothic level is counterbalanced by a Renaissance upper gallery. Inside the complex is a small wine museum, but you'll have to buy a bottle in the restaurant as it doesn't offer free samples. It is open Tuesday to Saturday from 10 am to 2 pm and 4 to 7 pm (10 am to 1 pm and 3 to 6 pm in winter; 200 ptas). Several buses come here from Tarazona.

If you have a car and time, go for a spin in the nearby **Parque Natural de la Dehesa del Moncayo**.

Pyrenees & the North

As you leave behind the multiple *sierras* and parched depression of Zaragoza province to head north, a hint of green tinges the landscape. Although the town of Huesca lies in a basin, the first of the hilly ranges preceding the Pyrenees are not far off.

The Aragonese section of the Pyrenees is among the most rewarding on the Spanish side of the French border, with half a dozen decent ski resorts and some good walking and trekking, especially in the eastern Parque Nacional de Ordesa y Monte Perdido. There are many ways to approach the area, with several main routes clawing up through the valleys and some crossing into France.

A few things are worth bearing in mind when you reach the Pyrenees. Maintenance on walking tracks seems haphazard at best. Some designated paths are in good shape. Others marked on maps are little more than goat trails; even stretches of main routes are often impossible to make out. We refer to some mountain refuges in what follows, but there are others. They are basic and generally overpriced. They are also often fully booked by clubs well in advance, so go prepared to camp.

HUESCA

Known to the Romans as Osca and to its Muslim masters of nearly four centuries as Washka, Huesca today is a quiet place. The surprisingly interesting medieval centre has that down-at-heel feel of many Aragonese towns. This has its charm and renders Huesca a reasonable starting point for exploring the north.

As in many centres across Spain at the end of the 15th century, the decision to expel the Jews and the subsequent dispersal of the Muslims and *moriscos* (christianised Muslims) struck a blow from which the flourishing trading town never recovered. During the civil war it was under siege by Republican forces for a long time, but never taken.

Orientation & Information

Huesca is seated on a slight rise, to the north-east of which flows the modest Río Isuela. The estación de autobuses is just off Plaza de Navarra in the heart of town and a short walk from the old town and tourist office. The train station is a few hundred metres farther south.

The helpful tourist office (☎ 974 29 21 00) is in the ayuntamiento and is open daily from 11 am to 1 pm and 4 to 6 pm, but mornings only on weekends.

There are plenty of banks in the centre. Banesto and Banco Santander on Plaza de Navarra have ATMs.

The correos is on the corner of Calle del Coso Alto and Calle de Moya. Send poste restante mail to Huesca 22080. The main police station (☎ 091) is on Plaza de Luis Buñuel. For an ambulance, call ☎ 974 22 92 92.

Plaza de la Catedral & Around

At the heart of the *casco antiguo*, this pleasant leafy square is presided over by a venerable Gothic **catedral**, unusually bare inside. The main portal belongs to an earlier 13th century church, and is topped by typically Aragonese eaves *(aleros)*. Next door is the **Museo Diocesano**, with a collection of religious art. It is open Monday to Saturday from 10 am to 1 pm. The 16th century ayuntamiento across the square is another Aragonese gem. A little way north, the octagonal Museo Provincial was once the Palacio de los Reyes de Aragón (Palace of the Kings of Aragón). Its contents include local archaeological finds and *bellas artes*, including works by Goya. After lengthy renovations, it should be open by the time you read this.

Iglesia de San Pedro El Viejo

Directly south of Plaza de la Catedral is Huesca's masterpiece, an understated 12th century Romanesque wonder. Begun in 1134, the church was not finished until well into the following century. The cloister in particular is worth a close look. The bell tower is a graceful, six-sided addition.

Parque Municipal de Miguel Servet

The newer part of town has few saving graces apart from this well-manicured, shady park.

HUESCA

PLACES TO STAY
6   Hotel Pedro I de Aragón
8   Pensión Augusto
10 Hostal El Centro
12 Hostal San Marcos;
    Restaurante El Molinero

OTHER
1   Policía Nacional
2   Museo Provincial
3   Museo Diocesano
4   Catedral
5   Ayuntamiento & Tourist Office
5   Rincón Musical
9   Iglesia de San Pedro El Viejo
11 Restaurante Os Danzantes
13 Correos
14 Estación de Autobuses
15 Banco Santander;
    Banesto (ATMs)
16 Train Station (RENFE)

Places to Stay & Eat

You'll find a camping ground called *San Jorge* south of town off the Zaragoza road.

All the following tend to raise prices in August. *Pensión Augusto* (☎ *974 22 00 79, Calle de Aínsa 16*) has adequate singles/doubles from 1500/2500 ptas. *Hostal El Centro* (☎ *974 22 68 23, Calle de Sancho Ramírez 3*) has pleasant rooms with shower and TV for 2900/4200 ptas. *Hostal San Marcos* (☎ *974 22 29 31, Calle de San*

Orencio 10) has good rooms for 4000/5775 ptas and *Hotel Pedro I de Aragón* (☎ *974 22 03 00, fax 974 22 00 94, Calle del Parque 34*) is upmarket and has rooms for 8900/11,000 ptas plus IVA.

Restaurante Os Danzantes (*Calle de Sancho Ramírez 18*) is an understated place that does a set evening meal for 1500 ptas; try the rabbit and mushrooms. Classier is *Restaurante El Molinero*, below Hostal San Marcos. You won't get much change from 3000 ptas a head.

For late-night drinking, Calle de San Lorenzo and the surrounding area are loaded with **bars**. Or you could try *Rincón Musical (Calle de San Jorge 29)* for live music.

Getting There & Away

Bus The estación de autobuses is at Calle del Parque 3, just back from Plaza de Navarra. Twelve buses run to Zaragoza (Paseo de María Agustín 7) daily (about an hour), four to Lleida (Lérida; two hours) and Jaca (one hour), two to Pamplona (about three hours) and four to Barcelona (2½ hours). Eight leave for Barbastro and other destinations with at least one daily service include Fraga, Benasque, Biescas and Panticosa (for skiing).

Train The RENFE train station is a couple of blocks farther south of the estación de autobuses and is of little use except to get to Zaragoza (four trains daily). One daily train connects with Madrid.

Car & Motorcycle The N-330 passes Huesca on the way from Zaragoza to Jaca and France. The N-240 heads south-east to Lleida (Lérida) in Catalunya.

NORTH OF HUESCA
Castillo de Loarre

Rambling and haughty on its rocky perch just south of the Sierra de Loarre, the **castillo** was perfectly placed as a lookout for Muslim raiders bolting across the wheat plains to the south. It was put up in the 11th century by Sancho VII of Navarra and is uncannily reminiscent of crusader castles in the Holy Land.

Built in and around the living rock, the labyrinthine string of dungeons, tunnels and towers has been left in a state of partial restoration, giving it a suitably untamed feeling. You can climb two of the towers for magnificent views and get to the Romanesque church's crypt via trapdoors before the altar. It is open daily, except Monday, from 10 am to 1.30 pm and 4 to 7 pm (free).

A couple of buses run to Loarre from Huesca. That's the easy part. It's then a long 5km walk or hitch to the castle. There is nowhere to stay in Loarre or Ayerbe, 7km away on the Huesca-Pamplona road.

Los Mallos

After a boring patch along the Huesca-Pamplona road, you unexpectedly round into a pretty stretch along the Río Gallego as you push north of Ayerbe. On the eastern bank, bizarre rock formations known as Los Mallos (or 'mallets') rise up – they would not look out of place in the Grand Canyon. For a closer look, head for **Riglos**, something more easily said than done without your own vehicle.

EAST OF HUESCA
Alquézar

Drivers who love back roads veer northward off the N-240 heading east from Huesca and follow the narrow A-1229 to the picturesque village of Alquézar. As well as the inevitable castle, the 16th century church is worth a look and the tiny square is an inviting space to relax and sip a soothing *caña*. Places to stay include the charming *Casa Jabonero (☎ 974 31 83 99)*, with doubles starting as low as 2000 ptas. *Pensión Narbona (☎ 974 31 80 78)* is a touch dearer and has a lovely terrace restaurant. There is a camping ground about 4km away, down on the Río Ena.

If you're heading north, follow the road through Colunga up to Aínsa, a fantastic drive through pre-Pyrenean canyons.

Monasterio El Pueyo

Six kilometres short of Barbastro on the main highway from Huesca, the hill-top Monasterio El Pueyo commands unlimited vistas in all directions. For that alone it is worth a stop if you're motorised, but there's also a quaint chapel. In July 1936, 20 monks were shot here by Republican militia.

Barbastro

An ancient town already well established in Roman times, Barbastro spent some 350

ARAGÓN

years as one of Muslim Spain's most northerly outposts. Today it's a grimy spot, although the area around Plaza del Mercado is enticing and the 16th century cathedral has a high altar partly done by the Renaissance master Damián Forment.

In time, the town's greatest claim to fame may lie in more recent history. Opus Dei fans may know that the organisation's founder, Josemaría Escrivá de Balaguer (1902-75), who is now well on the way to being canonised, grew up at Plaza del Mercado 11.

There are about 10 places to stay. *La Sombra* (☎ 974 31 10 64, *Calle de Argensola 9*) has simple rooms from as low as 850 ptas per person. *Fonda San Ramón* (☎ 974 31 02 50, *Calle de San Ramón 28*) wins the ragged glory award, and has singles from 1600 ptas and doubles with bathroom for 3500 ptas. It is also one of the better restaurants in town. *La Brasería* (*Plaza del Mercado 9*) has tables on the square and a good set *menú* for 1100 ptas.

Buses run to Barcelona (four daily), Lleida (Lérida; four), Huesca (up to seven), Benasque (up to two), Monzón (six), Fraga (one), Aínsa and Boltaña (one).

Monzón

Enemies riding against this town must have been fazed by the impregnable walls of the Templar castle that stands proudly over the jumble of Monzón. Once there was a Celtiberian settlement here, but it was the Muslims who built Monzón's first great fortress, taken by Sancho Ramírez in 1089. The Knights Templar took it over in 1143, and used it mostly as a convent and centre of education. Later, after the order of knights fell, the fortress decayed under the effect of several sieges over the 16th to 19th centuries. Part of the castle is being restored, as is the 12th century town church, the **Colegiata de Santa María del Romeral**, below. The castle is open daily from 11.30 am to 1 pm and 3 to 5 pm (100 ptas).

There are a number of scruffy pensiones across from the train station. Towards the centre, *Hotel Vianetto* (☎ 974 40 19 00,

Avenida de Lérida 25) is Monzón's premier choice with rooms from 3600/5900 ptas plus IVA and a good restaurant.

Buses connect with Barbastro and Huesca, as well as Fraga to the south, and numerous trains bound for Barcelona and Zaragoza pull in here.

Torreciudad

North-east of Barbastro, above the grand **Embalse de El Grado** (El Grado reservoir), is the spiritual heart of modern Catholicism's most controversial movement, Opus Dei. A religious complex of questionable artistic taste, the **Santuario de Torreciudad** was opened for business in 1975, the year of the death of Opus' founder, Josemaría Escrivá.

Much ink has been spilled on Opus Dei, most of it in vitriolic attack or in defence of what is a highly conservative and secretive body. With nearly 80,000 followers worldwide, this prelature responsible to the pope alone has fewer than 1000 clergy. The text by which Opus members lead their spiritual lives is the 999 aphorisms of Escrivá's *El Camino* (The Way). Enthusiastic members indulge in medieval mortification of the flesh and several people who have left the order have kicked up a stink about Opus' doings. Elitist, it attracts high-flying professionals and encourages them to continue their careers rather than become clerics – making them useful contributors to the Opus coffers, said to be substantial. Beatified in 1992 (with unusual haste), Escrivá may soon become a saint, giving Opus Dei (Latin for 'the work of God') a credibility boost that would undoubtedly further frustrate the critics.

The site is accessible daily from 9 am to 8.30 pm, but the *santuario* building itself is open from 10 am to 2 pm and 4 to 8.30 pm. Buses from Huesca or Barbastro run to El Grado. You have to get a taxi or make your own way from there.

BENASQUE & THE NORTH-EAST

Even in midsummer the peaks of this extreme north-eastern corner of Aragón can be covered in a blanket of snow and ice. Climbers have a choice of peaks to attack, while walkers can join the long-distance GR-11 trail – just one of several hiking options. Hostales and camping grounds abound, and they don't come more beautifully situated.

Benabarre to France

The easternmost corner of the Aragonese Pyrenees is easily reached from Huesca or from Lleida (Lérida) in Catalunya. Most directly, the route from Huesca takes you east via Barbastro (see earlier in this section) and on towards Graus and Benabarre. Benabarre makes a pleasant stop if you are following the highly picturesque river route to France up the Río Noguera Ribagorçana (N-230). A couple of reservoirs, the **Embalse de Escales** and the **Embalse de Baserca**, are among the highlights along this way.

Graus to Benasque

To get to the Reserva Nacional de Benasque, you would follow the A-139 up the Río Ésera from Graus. The drive is hairraising as you pass through the narrow defile of the Congosto de Ventamillo to reach **Castejón de Sos**. There is little to note about this village, but the location is pleasant and offers a wealth of accommodation if you have trouble farther north. Five *hostales*, with singles/doubles at around 2000/3000 ptas and rising according to type of room and season, are supplemented by the refuge-style **Albergue Pájaro Loco** (☎ *974 55 35 16*) and a *camping ground*. You'll also find shops and banks here.

A nice drive eastwards brings you to the N-230 to France, while the A-139 north proceeds to Benasque.

Benasque

In this happening nerve centre of the Valle de Benasque, the typical grey-stone and ragged slate tile roofs of old Benasque (known locally as Benás) have been swamped by new construction, mostly in keeping with the style of the area. Walkers and climbers in summer and skiers in winter flock here for weekend nightlife. It makes a convenient if unprepossessing base for the area.

The Els Ibons shop on Calle Mayor, next door to the Pensión Barrabés, sells books and maps dealing with the Benasque area. Vit's shop on Plaza Mayor rents out crampons and other climbing equipment, as well as mountain bikes. A couple of shops on Avenida de los Tilos, such as Casa de Montaña opposite the Hotel Ciria, offer trekking and other guide services.

Accommodation is offered by more than a dozen places. One of the better budget choices is *Pensión Barrabés* (☎ *974 55 16 54, Calle Mayor 5*) with singles/doubles starting at 1500/2500 ptas in the off season. Another cheap deal is *Pensión Solana* (☎ *974 55 10 19, Plaza Mayor 5*). Rooms cost up to 5500 ptas for a double with bath. *Hotel Ciria* (☎ *974 55 16 12*), down the street, has good rooms from 5500 ptas plus IVA (9275 ptas plus IVA during skiing and hiking seasons).

There are several camping grounds outside town on the road north of Benasque. Of these *Camping Aneto* (☎ *974 55 11 41*) is closest (about 2km away) and open all year, while *Senarta* a few kilometres north is utterly bucolic.

A number of places in town serve pizzas for around 1000 ptas. A fun place to hang out is *Pepe & Company*, across the road from Pensión Barrabés. It has pizzas, Spanish food, snacks and ice creams.

One or two buses run daily (except Sunday) to Benasque from Huesca, via Barbastro.

Around Benasque

Cerler Six kilometres east of Benasque lies Aragón's easternmost ski resort, based on the Pico de Cerler (2409m). On offer are 26 varied runs totalling 34km, and there are ski hire outlets in the town. With only two midrange hotels here, you're better off staying in Benasque.

Hiking & Climbing The broad valley in which Benasque nestles is green and pretty, with steep rocky peaks rising suddenly on three sides. This makes for good hiking, and there are plenty of walks from town of four hours or less (one way). One exacting piste sets out from Hospital de Benasque (about 15km north-east of Benasque) for the French frontier. The trail heads north-east and upwards to the Peña Blanca and from there winds steeply to the Portillón de Benasque on the frontier. This should take fit walkers about 2½ hours. Another three to 3½ hours north would take you past the Boums del Port (lakes) to the French town of Bagnères-de-Luchon.

The GR-11 runs across this area. From Benasque head about 3.5km north along the surfaced road to the Puente de Cuera. You could cross the river and follow the piste north along the Río Ésera, and then drop east along the Ballibierna valley. The wide trail as far as the *Refugio de Pescadores* involves about 2½ hours walking. There it narrows on its long way into Catalunya, and the new *Refugio de Llauset* is about five hours on from here – check with the tourist office to make sure it's open.

Alternatively, heading west from Puente de Cuera, make first for the *Refugio de Estós* (open all year), about a three hour walk. Another five or so hours brings you to Viadós (sometimes written Biadós), where a *refuge may* be open. Call ahead (☎ 974 50 80 82) to be sure. This is a good base for ascents of the **Pico de Posets** (3371m), or could be an intermediate stop along the GR-11, which continues west to Bielsa and beyond into the eastern reaches of the Parque Nacional de Ordesa y Monte Perdido. **Bielsa** itself is a good place to recharge batteries, with several *hotels* and *hostales*.

Experienced climbers will find the challenge of the glacial **Macizo de la Maladeta** hard to resist. This forbidding line of icy peaks, culminating in the **Pico de Aneto** (3404m), is the highest in the entire Pyrenees system and still contains glaciers suspended from the higher crests. From the Refugio de la Renclusa (which can be reached in a car by following the Río

Ésera), you can tackle Aneto in a minimum of five hours. You'll need crampons, ropes and ice axes. The massif offers other peaks to explore as well, including Pico de la Maladeta (3308m) and the Cresta del Medio (3355m). Get hold of the Editorial Alpina map and guide entitled *Maladeta Aneto*, but bear in mind that they are not completely accurate.

PARQUE NACIONAL DE ORDESA Y MONTE PERDIDO

First created in 1918 as El Parque Nacional del Valle de Ordesa, then greatly expanded in 1982 to encompass the area around Monte Perdido, this national park contains some of the most varied scenery, and diverse animal and plant life, in the Pyrenees. Its most striking feature is the deep gorges cut by streams falling into the Río Arazas and Río Vellos. This creates a tiered effect of lush green forest huddled beneath jagged cliffs, all capped by smooth, bare rock.

Bears were nearly wiped out by hunting earlier this century, but two females and a male from Slovenia were recently set free on the French side of the mountains east of the park. You're hardly likely to see these, nor the odd fox or wild boar that still lives here, but you may run across chamois *(rebeco)* in the upper reaches. In the skies fly the rare and ugly *quebrantahuesos* (lammergeier, also referred to as the 'bearded vulture') and the more common golden eagle. Otters and various newts frolic in the rivers. In the thick forests along the waters sprout birches, boxwoods, willows, firs and ashes, and black pines shimmy up the steep cliffs at impossible angles. Edelweiss and other wild flowers add colour.

From mid-1995, a ceiling was placed on the number of visitors allowed into this park – 1500 at any one time – in an attempt to reduce damage. The easiest way to enter the park is from Torla, which is easily approached from Jaca and Huesca via Biescas, or from Barbastro via Aínsa.

Approaches to the Park

Aínsa The wide cobblestoned plaza of this attractive hill-top settlement draws a disconcerting number of tour buses each day; this is no surprise though, as it is one of the prettiest towns in the area.

The wonderfully helpful tourist office (☎ 974 50 07 67), Avenida Pirenaica 1, is open April to October from 10 am to 2 pm and 4.30 to 8 pm. Across the street, Aguas Blancas (☎ 974 90 05 83) rents out rafting and climbing equipment and organises expeditions.

Just back from the eastern corner of the square rises the town **colegiata**, a restored Romanesque church, with a pleasing little cloister and a belfry you can climb. The latter served as part of the town defences during the civil war when the whole area suffered heavy damage. The western end of town is dominated by the remains of defensive walls, where you can now park your car.

The best place to stay is just across the road from the east door of the church (☎ 974 50 07 50); look for the 'Habitaciones' sign Spotless rooms cost 3500/5000 ptas for single/double rooms in high season.

Otherwise, there is a hive of *hostales* and *pensiones* at the foot of the town, and a *camping ground* 1km north. If you feel like splashing out on food, *Restaurante Bodegas del Sobrarbe* is recommended. It's just off Plaza Mayor, and a meal will cost about 3000 ptas per person.

One bus daily runs between Barbastro and Boltaña, passing Aínsa on the way. It leaves Boltaña at 6.45 am and Barbastro at 7.45 pm.

Aínsa to Torla First stop on the N-260 from Aínsa to Torla is the pretty stone village of **Boltaña**. Once a Celtic settlement, it has a church and many houses which date from the 16th century. Unfortunately, the old town is being engulfed by the new town. The tourist office (☎ 974 50 20 43) on the main road is open all year round. *Fondu Alegría (☎ 974 50 21 83, Avenida de Ordesa 20)* is the cheapest deal here at 2000/3000 ptas for singles/doubles.

From Boltaña the road winds up the Valle de Solana towards **Broto** and the valley of the same name. Along the way you'll pass **Sarvisé**, and 2km south-west of Broto is the village of **Oto**; all are pleasant. Broto has several accommodation options. The cheapest at 4000 ptas is *Hostal Español (☎ 974 48 60 07, Avenida de Ordesa 20)*. In Sarvisé, try the cosy *Casa Frauca (☎ 974 48 61 82)*, on the main road. It has a variety of rooms starting at 3500 ptas for a double (no bath). In Oto, there are two *casas rurales* along Calle de la Peña, both charging 3500 ptas for doubles.

From Broto, it's a few serpentine kilometres north to **Torla**, the last hamlet on the way in to the Parque Nacional de Ordesa y Monte Perdido. A bus runs Monday to Saturday from Aínsa to Torla.

Aínsa to Torla via Escalona A more dramatic route suggests itself for people with wheels. From Aínsa head 11km north to Escalona and turn west along the HU-631, a minor road that links up with Sarvisé. The road passes the nearly deserted villages of Buerba and Vió, shortly after which you get spectacular views over the Garganta de Añisclo gorge (see later). There is a small *albergue (☎ 974 48 90 10)* in Nerín and two more small places in Fanlo, the last town before Sarvisé.

Sabiñánigo to Torla Those approaching Torla from Jaca will pass through the tawdry town of Sabiñánigo. You'll need to change buses here, but it's possible you'll only get as far as **Biescas** in the same day. Biescas is not a bad little spot to get stuck, and *Pensión Las Heras (☎ 974 48 50 27, Calle de Agustina de Aragón 35)* is the cheapest place for a bed with singles/doubles starting at 2000/3000 ptas. There is also a *camping ground*.

Torla The location remains enchanting, but holiday boom building is increasingly obscuring this stone village's charm. There is

ARAGÓN

an information office for the national park (summer only). If you need to use an ATM, or to change money, do it here. You can also ferret out Editorial Alpina maps of the park area (650 ptas).

With so many places to stay, getting a bed for the night is tricky only in the monster season of July-August, when booking well ahead is mandatory. There are four camping grounds in and around Torla.

Refugio L'Atalaya (☎ 974 48 60 22), in the town itself, has dormitory beds for 1000 ptas, or half-board 2800 ptas. The nearby *Refugio Lucien Briet* (☎ 974 48 62 21) has the same deal. Otherwise, all hotels charge similar rates. *Hostal Alto Aragón* (☎ 974 48 61 72, Calle de Capuvita 11) has doubles in season at 5200 ptas. The same people run the slightly dearer *Hotel Ballarín* (☎ 974 48 61 55) across the street. It also has a good restaurant with a 1300 ptas set meal. *Hotel Villa de Torla* (☎ 974 48 61 56, Plaza Nueva 1) is a touch classier, with singles/doubles at 4500/6500 ptas plus IVA. You can stock up on supplies in supermarkets seven days a week.

A bus daily connects Torla with Aínsa, and another with Sabiñánigo.

Information

Eight kilometres north-east of Torla the road ends in a car park marking the entrance to the national park. You will find a restaurant and souvenir shop here. A few kilometres before this, the visitors centre *(centro de visitantes)* has interactive displays on flora and fauna in the area and sells trail maps. It is open daily from 9 am to 1 pm and 3.30 to 7 pm (shorter hours in winter).

The range of walking possibilities in and beyond the park is great enough to keep walkers of most levels well occupied for days. Indeed, the first walk may be from Torla itself to the park proper, as there are no buses. A path leads across the Río Ara from the Hostal Bella Vista (on the main road in Torla) northwards for a few kilometres before hitting the GR-11 long-distance path, and then east along the Río Arazas.

Those planning to walk into France should have their passports with them.

Circo de Soaso

Once in the park, one of the easier walks leads 7km east along the gorge of the Valle de Ordesa to the Circo de Soaso, a rocky balcony whose centrepiece is the Cascada de la Cola del Caballo waterfall. Follow the signs for '*cascada*' and '*gradas*' through the beech woods. Along the way you pass the little stone Refugio de Pastores, and several charming waterfalls along the north bank of the Río Arazas. Most hikers return along the south bank on the Senda de los Cazadores (hunters' trail). From this side you get a better impression of the grandeur of the north side of the gorge. The whole circuit takes about seven hours.

Monte Perdido

Fitter trekkers, having climbed by a series of steep switchbacks to the top of the Circo de Soaso, strike out north for the *Refugio de Góriz* (☎ 974 34 12 01). This refuge is open all year and makes an ideal base for attempting the ascent of Monte Perdido, although the facilities are nothing great. You'll need climbing gear to bag the peak, one of the highest in the Pyrenees (3355m).

Circo de Cotatuero

Another interesting walk veers north from the gorge shortly after leaving the car park. Follow the signs for Cotatuero and after a couple of hours and a fairly steep hike you reach another impressive waterfall. The sturdy hearted may climb the wall of the Circo by the series of iron pegs installed back in 1881. From here you are about 2½ hours march from La Brecha de Rolando – a gap in the mountainous wall forming the frontier with France.

To France via Valle de Bujaruelo

A long but rewarding route into France starts about 3km north of Torla, where the GR-11 trail forks north from the asphalt road. The GR-11 describes a 6km arc along the Valle de Bujaruelo to San Nicolás de

PARQUE NACIONAL DE ORDESA Y MONTE PERDIDO

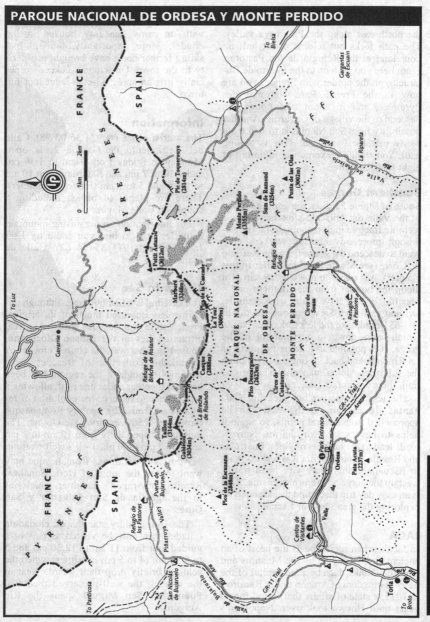

Bujaruelo, where there is a *camping ground*. From there it's a three hour hike to the north-east along the Piñarroya valley. The path forks but rejoins about half an hour later at the Refugio de los Pastores. From here you push on to the Puerto de Bujaruelo, on the border with France. You are now in the French Parc National des Pyrénées, and in about two hours can descend to the village of Gavarnie. Another possibility from San Nicolás is to strike out westwards for Panticosa. This is a long haul. You should reckon on a minimum of eight hours walking.

Southern Gorges

South of Monte Perdido, the gaping wound of the **Valle del Añiscolo** stretches away, a tectonic fracture in the mountain fabric. Although more adventurous walkers may want to descend the gorge from the Refugio de Góriz (see Monte Perdido earlier in this chapter), it is easier to make a day trip of it along the bottom from the southern end – feasible if you have your own vehicle. Driving east from Sarvisé along the minor HU-631 road, take the left fork after Nerín, which leads down to an opening in the gorge. It is possible to hike as far north as La Ripareta and back in one day. Although the Editorial Alpina map only shows one trail, there are in fact two.

The less spectacular but pleasing **Gargantas de Escuain** to the east can be approached from several points, so again it helps to have your own chariot. Narrow roads lead to the hamlets of Tella, Puértolas and Revilla. From Revilla it is a short walk to Escuain, from where you head north-west up the gorge and return at leisure. This is an easy day trip that could be extended by exploring the area south of Escuain.

JACA

In Jaca's urban sprawl beats the heart of an ancient city. Occupied by the Muslims and later the Franks, Jaca became capital of the nascent kingdom of Aragón under Ramiro I in 1035, a state of affairs that lasted for 60 years until Huesca took over. Napoleon's troopers moved in for five years in 1809. The military continues to play a role here, with an army academy housed in the citadel. More importantly, tourism and skiing farther north have brought prosperity to the town. On winter weekends especially it is an aprés ski-cum-lager lout fun town.

Information

The tourist office (☎ 974 36 00 98), Calle del Regimiento de Galicia 2, is open Monday to Friday from 9 am to 1.30 pm and 4.30 to 7 pm and Saturday from 10 am to 1 pm and 5 to 7 pm (longer in summer). There are plenty of banks, including a couple on Calle Mayor.

For information on organising mountain activities and ski hire you could try Eski Jaca 2000 (☎ 974 35 54 62), Calle de Francia 31.

Things to See

The **catedral** is a fine building, although tinkering has obscured much of its original French-style Romanesque grace. The real attraction lies in the **Museo Diocesano**, housed in what was the church cloister. A remarkable collection of frescoes, from churches throughout the region, has been brought together under one roof, allowing a rare chance to observe the evolution of religious art from 12th century Romanesque through to 15th century Late Gothic. The museum is open daily from 10 am to 2 pm and 4 to 7 pm (300 ptas) – it's well worth it.

Addicts of all things Romanesque may want to see the tomb of Doña Sánchez, Ramiro I of Aragón's daughter, which lies in the **Iglesia de San Salvador y San Ginés**.

The 16th century star shaped **ciudadela** (citadel) can only be visited as part of a guided tour from 11 am to 12.30 pm and 5 to 6.30 pm (4 to 5 pm in winter), when the soldiers briefly drop their guard. West of the citadel, the well-preserved medieval **Puente de San Miguel** spans the Río Aragón.

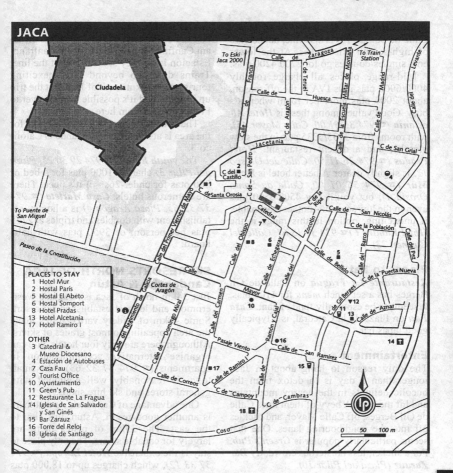

JACA

Ciudadela

To Eski
Jaca 2000

To Train
Station

To Puente de
San Miguel

Paseo de la Constitución

PLACES TO STAY
1 Hotel Mur
2 Hostal París
5 Hostal El Abeto
6 Hostal Somport
8 Hotel Pradas
13 Hotel Alcetania
17 Hotel Ramiro I

OTHER
3 Catedral &
  Museo Diocesano
4 Estación de Autobuses
7 Casa Fau
9 Tourist Office
10 Ayuntamiento
11 Green's Pub
12 Restaurante La Fragua
14 Iglesia de San Salvador
  y San Ginés
15 Bar Zarauz
16 Torre del Reloj
18 Iglesia de Santiago

0   50   100 m

Special Events

Jaca puts on its party outfit for the week-long Fiesta de Santa Orosia, the town's patron saint, which starts on 23 June. If you want to see medieval jousts, visit on the first Friday of May, when Jaca celebrates a famous victory over Muslims in 760.

Places to Stay

There are few cheap options in Jaca, and the place can fill up in peak periods, particularly summer, Easter and holiday weekends.

Camping Peña Oroel (☎ 974 36 02 15), a few kilometres out on the road to Sabiñánigo, is open for Easter and from mid-June to mid-September.

In town, *Hostal París* (☎ 974 36 10 20, *Plaza de San Pedro 5*) is one of the few places suitable for a low budget. Singles/doubles with shower start at 2100/3600 ptas plus IVA. *Hostal Somport* (☎ 974 36 34 10, *Calle de Echegaray 11*) is a clean and reliable place. Rooms cost 3000/4500 ptas, plus or minus 500 ptas depending on the season. *Hostal El Abeto (☎ 974 36 16 42, Calle de Bellido 15)* is also fine, but beware of high-season price hikes. At the lower end, singles/doubles go for 2700/4200 ptas.

Mid-range places all charge roughly 4000/6000 ptas plus IVA in the off season, about 2000 ptas more per room when it's busy. Good value among these is *Hotel Alcetania (☎ 974 35 61 00, Calle Mayor 45)*, with rooms from 3135/5335 ptas in the slow months, and a decent restaurant. *Hotel Pradas (☎ 974 36 11 50, Calle del Obispo 12)* is slightly dearer. A better hotel is *Hotel Mur (☎ 974 36 01 00, Calle de Santa Orosia 1)*, but you'll pay 4500/6500 ptas even in the low season. Another reasonable, if unexciting, option in this range is the *Hotel Ramiro I (☎ 974 36 13 67, Calle del Carmen 23)*.

Places to Eat
Restaurante La Fragua on Calle de Gil Berges has a set lunch *menú* for 1100 ptas. It seems to be especially fond of ham. *Casa Fau* on Plaza de la Catedral, is a typically good tapas bar.

Entertainment
The only reason to hang about in Jaca longer than a day is to detox from the bucolic delights in the nearby mountains and hit the bars. A bevy of them lines Calle de Gil Berges, off Calle Mayor, and trickles off into the neighbouring lanes. One that seems particularly popular is *Green's Pub*. For a slicker, less boisterous crowd, try *Bar Zarauz (Plaza del Pilar 10)*.

Getting There & Away
Bus is the best way to get around and the estación de autobuses is fairly handy at Avenida Jacetania. There are four to five buses to Huesca (745 ptas) and Sabiñánigo (180 ptas), three daily to Zaragoza (1450 ptas) and one late afternoon service to Pamplona (855 ptas). Up to five daily head up the valley to the ski slopes at Astún and two daily wind up to El Formigal. The RENFE station is about a half-hour walk north-east of the centre of town.

CANFRANC-ESTACIÓN
Not to be confused with the even less pleasant Canfranc-Pueblo to the south, Canfranc-Estación is, as they say, the end of the line. Trains don't go beyond this unexciting tourist stop, 25km north of Jaca, but the trip up is pretty and it's possible to cross over to France by bus from here.

The tourist office (☎ 974 37 31 41) for the area is at Avenida de Fernando el Católico 3.

The *youth hostel (☎ 974 29 30 25, Plaza del Pilar 3)* charges 1000 ptas for a bed or 800 ptas for under-26s – if it's open. There are numerous hotels. *Casa Marieta (☎ 974 37 33 65, Plaza Aragón 4)* is a homey establishment with doubles and triples at 2775 ptas per person, or 3950 ptas with half-board.

SKI RESORTS NORTH OF JACA
Candanchú & Astún
Just 34km north of Jaca is Aragón's westernmost and longest established ski resort. Some 40km of widely varied pistes make the area appealing to most grades of skiers. Although there are only four hotels, you can organise alternative accommodation in apartments (☎ 974 37 32 63). The small town is reasonably well equipped with general stores and ski hire shops.

One advantage of Candanchú is that there is another good resort, Astún, just 3km to the east. The 33km of pistes there are largely for capable skiers. The only place to stay is the expensive *Hotel Europa (☎ 974 37 33 12)*, which charges up to 18,000 ptas per double.

Panticosa & El Formigal
The comparatively small Panticosa ski resort has a bigger counterpart about 10km farther north, El Formigal. The runs at Panticosa aren't too distressing and the long, pretty Mazarranuala is a must for everyone. Cross-country skiing is also an option in the area.

El Formigal, a regular host for ski competitions, is a livelier place with far more extensive infrastructure than Panticosa.

Tunnel Vision

Candanchú is just inside Spain's border with France and is reached along a steep, winding road loaded with switchbacks and plenty of great views. But if you're just passing through (so to speak), you'll soon be steered through the new Somport Tunnel, scheduled to open in 2000. This controversial project caused an outcry from ecologists, who claim that construction of the 9km tunnel will adversely affect the last remaining bears *(osos pardos)* living in the Pyrenees (estimates range from as few as two on the Spanish side to 15 on both sides of the border), as well as various species of eagles and other birds. The expected cost is over 200,000 million pesetas and opponents to the effort say the average time-saving for vehicles will be only 16 minutes.

Here you have the full range of facilities, including restaurants, bars, discos, saunas, at your disposal as well as 50km of ski runs. To book accommodation anywhere in this area (highly recommended), call the Asociación Turística Valle de Tena (☎ 974 49 01 96).

WEST OF JACA

San Juan de la Peña

A much recommended excursion from Jaca, but difficult to undertake without independent transport, is to the mountain eyrie of one of Aragón's more memorable monasteries, San Juan de la Peña. The first 11km you could cover by Jaca-Pamplona bus, getting off at the turn-off for **Santa Cruz de la Seros** (4km), a quaint tumbledown village gathered in under the skirts of its sparsely decorated Romanesque parish church. The snug and cosy *Hostelería Santa Cruz (☎ 974 36 19 75)* has beds for 1500 ptas per person and good food. It also organises worthwhile day trips in the area.

From here you can walk up a marked path to San Juan de la Peña (about 50 minutes), or follow the circuitous road if you have a vehicle. The views from vantage points higher up on this road are magnificent, taking in the Pyrenees to the north and several peaks to the east and west.

You suddenly come upon the original monastery, sheltering below an overhanging lip of rock in a bend in the road. Established in the 9th century, it has suffered all that history could throw at it, sacked and rebuilt repeatedly until Napoleon's troops ransacked it in 1809. It is said to have once held the Holy Grail (now in Valencia) and the lower level of the monastery, with its Mozarabic church, is thought to have been built in the 10th century. The Romanesque cloister has, in a loose sense, the existing rock for a roof. It is open Tuesday to Sunday from 10 am to 1.30 pm and 4 to 7 pm.

A couple of kilometres farther up, and set in a lush meadow, is the more recent baroque monastery.

Valle de Hecho

Less spectacular than the territory farther to the east, the Valle de Hecho nonetheless boasts some charming old stone villages and culminates, at its northern end, in the beautiful Selva de Oza.

A bus leaves Jaca weekdays only at 6.30 pm for Hecho, returning at 6.45 am. There are no buses farther up the valley.

Hecho The biggest village in the valley, Hecho (Echo) is a surprising warren of silent stone houses and winding lanes. Unlikely though it may seem, it was briefly the seat of the Kingdom of Aragón in the 9th century. The only 'sight' is the **Museo Etnológico**, which has displays characteristic of rural life in the area. It's near the church.

You could not do better than stay at *Pensión Casa Blasquico (☎ 974 37 50 07, Plaza de la Fuente 1)*, almost totally obscured by exotic flora. The charming rustic lodgings rest above a highly proclaimed restaurant. Rooms cost 2500/3500 ptas. If it's full, there are two other bland *hostales* and a *hotel* to choose from.

Siresa A couple of kilometres up the road to the north, Siresa is another hamlet typical of the region and is dominated by the formidable Iglesia de San Pedro. *Fonda Pirineos (☎ 974 37 51 13)* on Plaza Mayor is the cheaper of two places, where basic singles/doubles without bathroom go for 2000/3000 ptas. A few kilometres north on the road to the Selva de Oza, the colourful *Hospedería Usón (☎ 974 37 53 58)* lies in splendid isolation with fine rooms equipped with TV for 4000/5500 ptas in the high season, 1000 ptas cheaper at other times.

Selva de Oza The main attraction of the valley lies at the top end. From Siresa the road follows Río Aragón Subordán another 12km and ends at the sprawling but beautifully located *Camping Selva de Oza (☎ 974 37 51 68)*, open June to September. The GR-11 trail passes a few kilometres north of the camping ground, and at least half a dozen mountain peaks are in an arc to the north and east for strenuous day assaults.

Valle de Ansó

As with the Valle de Hecho, the main interest for walkers only begins at the northern end of the valley, but the village of Ansó is an enticing stop on the way up.

The bus from Jaca to Hecho continues to Ansó (arriving at 8.10 pm and returning at 6 am). There are no buses farther up the valley. The Editorial Alpina map entitled *Ansó-Echo* is very useful for this area.

Ansó The rough-hewn stone houses here repeat the pretty picture of Hecho, but on a smaller scale. Like its bigger brother in the next valley, it could make an ideal base for exploring the region, especially if you have the freedom of movement your own transport can provide.

The *Posada Magoria (☎ 974 37 00 49)* is a superb country cottage – the rooms even have old porcelain hand basins. Singles/doubles cost 3000/4600 ptas and downstairs

you can savour the delights of good vegetarian cooking.

Four other *hostales* also compete for trade, all with restaurants. *Bar Zurizo* is a great old drinking establishment with a wide selection of beers, tapas and local cider.

Zuriza Walkers head north 15km from Ansó to Zuriza, basically little more than a camping ground and glorified refugio. *Camping Zuriza (☎ 974 37 01 96)* is popular, so you should book ahead if you plan to stay there in peak periods and weekends. If you don't want to camp, there is also a handful of double rooms starting at 4000 ptas. A rough but drivable track leads 5km farther north to the *Refugio Linza (☎ 974 37 01 12)*, open all year and with a bar.

The GR-11 long-distance walking route passes right through Zuriza. You could follow it west to Isaba (Navarra), which takes at least six hours. Eastwards, the path meanders on via the Selva de Oza (see earlier) to Candanchú. This involves at least 10 hours legwork. A couple of peaks on the border with France – Sobarcal (2249m) and Petrechema (2360m) – attract a lot of attention. Both can be done as day excursions from the Linza refuge, or even from Zuriza but that is a trickier ascent than the former.

Walks of varying duration and difficulty abound, as do opportunities for rock climbing and caving.

NORTH-WESTERN ARAGÓN
Sos del Rey Católico & the Cinco Villas

Just inside the border with Navarra and about 150km north-west of Zaragoza, or 85km west of Jaca, Sos del Rey Católico takes its name from a son of whom any town would be proud: Fernando II of Aragón, born here in 1452. He married Isabel I of Castilla and together, as Los Reyes Católicos (the Catholic Monarchs), they finished off the Reconquista and united all Spain. The old medieval town, which could do with a little loving care, is a fascinating little spider's web of twisting, cobbled lanes and claustrophobic houses atop a hill on the northern rim of the Aragonese wheat plains.

The Castillo de la Peña Feliciano forms the crown on the hill top and the Gothic Iglesia de San Estéban below it is worth a peek. Fernando is said to have been born in one of several mansions scattered about the centre, the Palacio de Sada. Apart from the expensive *parador*, the only place to stay is the *Fonda Fernandina* (☎ *976 88 81 20*), which has basic singles/doubles for 2000/3300 ptas.

If you have a car, a little travelled back route (A-1601) connects Sos with the N-240 east of the Embalse de Yesa. Urriés is a crumbling, near abandoned village that invites exploration. If you really want abandoned, push on 14km east of Urriés to a ghost town, where the only signs of life are in the recently reopened pilgrim *Albergue Ruesta*. It is not even marked on most maps.

A zigzagging route south from Sos towards Zaragoza takes you through the remaining four of the Cinco Villas, which were declared towns *(villas)* by Felipe V of Spain in the 18th century. A minor road bearing south-east leads to Uncastillo, little touched by the passage of time and dominated by the Gothic tower of the mainly Romanesque Iglesia de Santa María. Follow the Río Riguel 16km south-west into the plains and you reach Sádaba, which has a 13th century castle and remains of a synagogue. From Sádaba the A-127 proceeds south to Ejea de los Caballeros, by far the largest of the Cinco Villas and once a walled town. If you need to stay, there are four hotels. From here the road drops another 26km south to Tauste, about 50km short of Zaragoza to the south-east and sporting a mudéjar church. *Hostal Casa Pepe* (☎ *976 85 58 32, Calle de Santa Clara 7)* has singles/doubles for 2600/4000 ptas.

Cinco Villas buses run daily from Avenida de Navarra 81 in Zaragoza to all these towns.

The South

Although vast sweeps of the country immediately south of Zaragoza are dreary plains or bald, uninviting ridges, there are several exceptions. Teruel, the capital of Aragón's southernmost province of the same name, is a storage house of some of the best examples of mudéjar work you will find anywhere and the nearby town of Albarracín is a medieval Muslim treat. To the east of Teruel stretch the uplands of El Maestrazgo, a rugged and sparsely populated mountain area where dry fields and valleys alternate with hostile gorges and at times snowbound slopes.

Calatayud

There are only a few points of interest in this busy, dusty town, just off the N-II motorway connecting Zaragoza with Madrid. Head for the maze of narrow streets in the old town and search out the Iglesia de Santa María, with a fine plateresque portal and mudéjar bell tower. The Iglesia de San Pedro's tower on Rua de Eduardo Dato looks as though it's about to topple into the street – which would upset the storks which nest on it! The castle ruins above the town are extensive, but not among the country's best.

Should you have to stay, there are several cheap and basic places in the centre to choose from, such as *Pensión La Perla* (☎ *976 88 13 40, Calle de San Antón 17)* with singles/doubles for 1600/2850 ptas. *Hotel Calatayud* (☎ *976 88 13 23)*, on the road to Zaragoza at the north-eastern edge of town, has quality doubles ranging from 7050 to 8850 ptas plus IVA. There are regular buses from the estación de autobuses, hidden in a building on Calle de Ramón y Cajal in the centre of town, to Zaragoza (Calle de Almagro 18), and three daily to Madrid. Trains go the same way.

Monasterio de Piedra

Set in the soothing park of the same name, the one-time Cistercian Monasterio de Piedra tends a little to the Disneyesque.

Founded in 1194 and moved to its present site in 1218, the monastery was abandoned in the 1830s. Now in private hands and partly restored to house a posh hotel, much of it remains a shell. The park around it, with its waterfalls and caves, is pleasant, but the whole experience reeks of the artificial. It's not cheap either – 950 ptas to see both the monastery and park, or 800 ptas for the park and 300 ptas for the monastery alone. The monastery is open for (generally guided) visits from 10 am to 1.30 pm and 3 to 7 pm. The park is open until dusk.

There are a few hostales in nearby Nuévalos and on the way there. The *Hostal San Sebastián* (☎ 976 87 04 96), about 3km from the monastery on the way to Nuévalos, has decent rooms for 2000 ptas per person. Singles/doubles at the *hotel* in the monastery (☎ 976 84 90 11, fax 976 84 90 54) start at 9000/10,500 ptas plus IVA.

One or two daily buses run between Nuévalos and Calatayud, but nothing to the monastery. In summer, the Automovil Zaragoza company runs direct buses to the monastery from its office in Calle de Almagro 18, Zaragoza. Otherwise, it runs a couple on weekends.

Daroca

An attractive possibility for an overnight stop, Daroca lies low in a valley near the junction of highways N-234 and N-330. The N-234 runs south to Teruel while the latter climbs north to Zaragoza. On the hills to either side of town rise the crumbling remnants of the once extensive city walls. Some of the original 114 towers have been restored, but most have disappeared. Calle Mayor, the main street, is marked at either end by monumental gates. About midway along it and up to the right (when looking south towards the lower gate) lies the main square, Plaza de España, dominated by the Iglesia Colegiata de Santa María. Restructured in the 16th century, it is largely a Renaissance building, although the bell tower is mudéjar. Its Museo de los Sagrados Corporales contains a modest display of religious art.

The best place to stay is the *Pensión El Ruejo* (☎ 976 80 11 90 or ☎ 976 80 09 62, Calle Mayor 88). It has singles/doubles with no bath for 2000/4000 ptas and 3000/5600 ptas with. Just outside the northern entrance to town is the *Hostal Legido* (☎ 976 80 01 90), with functional rooms for 3600/6400 ptas plus IVA.

Buses stop outside the Mesón Felix, Calle Mayor 104. There are at least three daily to Zaragoza (Agreda Automovil company at Avenida de Valencia 20) and five to Teruel. An early morning service goes to Calatayud.

TERUEL

A compact provincial capital of 30,000, Teruel contains a handful of some of the most ornate and striking mudéjar monuments in the country. Its hill-top casco merits a few hours of your time at least. Teruel makes a decent stopover if you are travelling between Zaragoza and Valencia, or indeed for those making their way eastwards to the coast from Cuenca.

History

Although the region has been inhabited since prehistoric times, the town of Teruel only became significant under the Muslims. Retaken by the Christians in 1171, the city was an operational base for Jaume I of Aragón in his campaign to wrest Valencia from Muslim hands.

Orientation & Information

They say there are no distances in Teruel – you can get around easily on foot. The train station is downhill to the west of the town, and the estación de autobuses is to the east. From either it is a short walk into the centre. There's a cluster of hostales close to the cathedral in the northern, older half of town.

The tourist office (☎ 978 60 22 79) is at Calle de Tomás Nogués 1 and is open Monday and Saturday from 9 am to 1.30 pm and 5 to 7.30 pm and Tuesday to Friday from 8 am to 2 pm and 5 to 7.30 pm.

The correos is on Calle de Yagüe de Salas and the postcode is 44080.

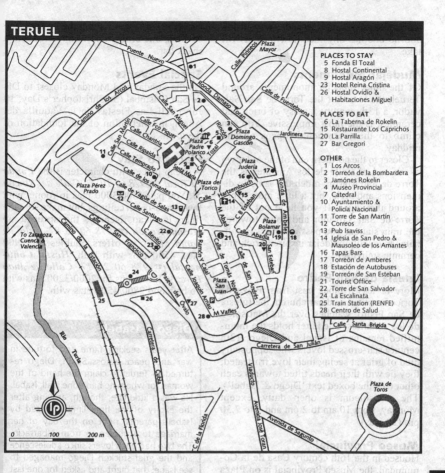

TERUEL

PLACES TO STAY
5 Fonda El Tozal
8 Hostal Continental
9 Hostal Aragón
23 Hotel Reina Cristina
26 Hostal Ovidio &
   Habitaciones Miguel

PLACES TO EAT
6 La Taberna de Rokelin
15 Restaurante Los Caprichos
20 La Parrilla
27 Bar Gregori

OTHER
1 Los Arcos
2 Torreón de la Bombarda
3 Jamónes Rokelin
4 Museo Provincial
7 Catedral
10 Ayuntamiento &
   Policía Nacional
11 Torre de San Martín
12 Correos
13 Pub Isaviss
14 Iglesia de San Pedro &
   Mausoleo de los Amantes
16 Tapas Bars
17 Torreón de Amberes
18 Estación de Autobuses
19 Torreón de San Esteban
21 Tourist Office
22 Torre de San Salvador
24 La Escalinata
25 Train Station (RENFE)
28 Centro de Salud

If you need an ambulance, call the Cruz Roja on ☎ 978 60 22 22. The Hospital General Obispo Polanco (☎ 978 64 66 00) is at Calle de Ruiz Jarabo 7. There is a small Centro de Salud on Calle Joaquin Arnau.

There are plenty of banks around Plaza Torico. The local police can be found in the basement of the ayuntamiento.

Catedral

Viewed from outside, the cathedral is like a brick wedding cake, decorated with bright-

ly coloured ceramic tiles – a rich example of the mudéjar imagination at work. First begun in 1176, work continued on the church until it was raised to cathedral status in the 16th century. The bell tower is its most appealing feature, but then beautiful bell towers are a hallmark of Teruel. It was erected in the 12th and 13th centuries and the mainly mudéjar style is tinged with a little Romanesque.

With that enticement, you'll probably have to satisfy yourself with the exterior, as

ARAGÓN

a complete restoration is under way inside and no one has any idea how long it will take.

Mudéjar Monuments

Of the other mudéjar monuments around Teruel, the tower of the Torre de San Salvador, a 13th century fantasy of brick and ceramics, is the most impressive. You can climb to the top when it opens around midday.

Closer to the northern end of the old town at the end of Calle de los Amantes is the Torre de San Martín, much the same in dimensions and style, but a little more worn around the edges. If you head out of the Torre de San Salvador and down towards the train station, you pass down La Escalinata, an equally mudéjar inspired brick and ceramic staircase.

Iglesia de San Pedro

More or less a block east from Plaza de Torico, another mudéjar church, the Iglesia de San Pedro, watches over the **Mausoleo de los Amantes**. The latter holds the mummified remains of Isabel and Diego, 13th century star-crossed lovers who supposedly died of grief at seeing their love frustrated; they lie with their heads tilted towards each other (see the boxed text 'Diego & Isabel'). The mausoleum is open daily, except Monday, from 10 am to 2 pm and 5 to 7.30 pm (50 ptas).

Museo Provincial

Housed in the 16th century Casa de la Comunidad, the Museo Provincial is on Plaza Padre Polanco. The building is Teruel's best example of Aragonese Renaissance and was completely restored in the 1970s and 80s. It contains mainly archaeological exhibits. It is open Tuesday to Friday from 10 am to 2 pm and 4 to 7 pm, but mornings only on weekends (free).

Los Arcos & Walls

At the northern end of the town stands an aqueduct built in 1533 and known as Los Arcos (the arches). Little remains of the city's medieval walls, but a couple of turrets

(torreóns) still stand along the eastern side of town, one of them now converted into a snack bar.

Special Events

On the Sunday and Monday closest to Día de San Cristóbal (St Christopher's Day; 10 July) fall Las Fiestas de la Vaquilla del Ángel, in celebration of the foundation of the town.

Places to Stay

A cheap place with character is the *Fonda El Tozal* (☎ 978 60 10 22, Calle del Rincón 5). You pay 1500/3000 ptas in rooms with low, wood-beam ceilings, but make sure the linen is clean. Nearby, the spruced up *Hostal Aragón* (☎ 978 60 13 87, Calle de Santa María 4) offers doubles for 2900 ptas, 4500 ptas with bath. *Hostal Continental* (☎ 978 60 23 17, Calle de Juan Pérez 9) has rooms for 2000/3200 ptas with no bath and 2800/4500 ptas with.

Diego & Isabel

After years seeking fame and fortune in war and peace across Spain, Diego returned to Teruel to claim the hand of the woman for whom he had done it all, Isabel. He was a little late, though, arriving after the expiry of the time limit imposed by Isabel's parents, right on the day of her marriage to a nobleman from Albarracín. The two had been lovers since adolescence and the grief-stricken Diego managed to see Isabel that night and asked for one last kiss. His request refused, he promptly expired at her feet. At his funeral in the Iglesia de San Pedro the following day, Isabel, still in her wedding finery, stepped forward to give Diego the kiss he had pined for, and she, too, promptly died. So astounded were the townspeople that they decided to bury the two lovers together in the church where Isabel had died. The bodies, it is said, were later transferred to what is now their mausoleum.

Near the train station are a couple of simple but acceptable options. **Hostal Ovidio** (☎ *978 60 28 66, Calle de la Estación 6*) has singles/doubles with no bath for 1600/3000 ptas. On the 2nd floor of the same building, **Habitaciones Miguel** (☎ *978 60 04 31*) has four rooms for 2000/3000 ptas.

Close to the Torre de San Salvador is the **Hotel Reina Cristina** (☎ *978 60 68 60, Paseo del Óvalo 1*), the most expensive place in town at 10,500/15,950 ptas plus IVA.

Places to Eat

Spain is pretty obsessed with all things porcine, and Teruel is no exception, going to great lengths to promote its local version of *jamón*. *Virutas de jamón* (ham shavings) is one form in which it arrives at your table.

One of the best places to try the local favourite is **La Taberna de Rokelin** (*Calle de Tozal 33*), a narrow bar with a beautiful rack of smoked pig hocks. It is linked to a shop called **Jamónes Rokelin** just up the street, which has an impressive selection of smoked meats, sausages and cheeses. Load up here for a week's worth of picnics.

Bar Gregori (*Paseo del Óvalo 6*) is a popular spot for tapas and raciones. There are a couple of tapas bars on Plaza de la Judería too.

La Parrilla (*Calle de San Estéban 2*) is a good place to get a hearty meal in Teruel's bar zone. A brighter, more genteel place is the **Restaurante Los Caprichos**, a block behind the Iglesia de San Pedro on Calle de Hartzembusch.

Entertainment

Most of the late-night excitement takes place in the bars of Calle de San Estéban and the immediate area. The spacious bar underneath Fonda El Tozal is active and has live music some nights. For a more relaxed drink or coffee, **Pub Isaviss** is at the lower end of Plaza del Torico.

Getting There & Away

Bus Services depart from the bright new bus terminal on Ronda de Ambeles for many destinations. There is frequent service to Zaragoza and Valencia, one or two daily to Cuenca and Madrid (2330 ptas) and one daily to Alcañiz, Ademuz, and Barcelona (this last at 8.30 am).

Train Teruel is about equidistant from Zaragoza and Valencia on the train line linking the two. There are three services daily, and the trip in either direction can take up to three hours.

Car & Motorcycle The main road north to Zaragoza is the N-330. It changes in Teruel to the N-234 and continues south-east to Sagunto on the Valencian coast and thence to Valencia itself.

RINCÓN DE ADEMUZ

A picturesque drive south from Teruel along the N-330 leads towards the so-called Rincón de Ademuz – the 'Ademuz corner'. This will soon be overshadowed by a faster (and presumably safer!) highway nearing completion but, if you've got the time, the rough and winding N-330 is a joy. The road follows the heavily cultivated green valley of the Río Turia, closed in by arid, tabletop mountains, and gradually dips into a narrow ravine as far as Villel, where it opens up again before entering an enclave of Valencia province.

The Rincón's main town is **Ademuz**, a steep and unremarkable little place, beyond which the road winds its way south through two small villages – Casas Altas (High Houses) and Casas Bajas (Low Houses) – that appear not to have changed much in centuries. The road continues to trail the deepening gorge of the Alto Turia before crossing into Castilla-La Mancha in quite spectacular fashion. At Santa Cruz de Moya the road forks. You can take the scenic but slow C-234 into Valencia or follow the faster N-330 around the long way to Valencia city via Requena.

Back at Ademuz, a secondary road (the N-420) cuts west towards Cuenca (see the Castilla-La Mancha chapter), skirting the southern hills of the Serranía de Cuenca.

ARAGÓN

If you need to stay in this area, try the large *Hostal Casa Domingo* (☎ 978 78 20 30, *Avenida Valencia 1)* in Ademuz. Decent rooms cost 2350/3725 ptas. There is also a pensión in Torre Baja a few kilometres north.

A bus leaves Ademuz daily for Teruel at 8 am and one or two per day go to Valencia. Buses stop in Ademuz outside the Hostal Casa Domingo.

ALBARRACÍN

The crenellated walls overshadowing the brick-red medieval town of Albarracín dramatically announce the hillside town's presence before you arrive. For four years from 1009 it was the seat of the tiny Islamic statelet of Ibn Razin, and subsequently an independent Christian kingdom under the Azagra family, sandwiched between Castilla and Aragón from 1170 to 1285.

The cool, narrow lanes of Albarracín even today are in the best tradition of the Arab medina and are vaguely reminiscent of Toledo – on a small scale. Centuries-old buildings lean and bulge alarmingly over some streets, but there is none of the mucky chaos of the true medina. It has been proposed as a UNESCO monument of worldwide interest.

Information

The tourist office (☎ 978 71 02 51) is in the Casa de la Sierra on Calle de la Excma Diputación Provincial, just off Plaza Mayor; it's open daily from 10 am to 2 pm and 5 to 8 pm. You'll find the correos and a couple of banks on or just off Plaza Mayor. The postcode is 44100.

Things to See

The cathedral, with its cupola typical of the Spanish Levant, has an elaborate gilded altar. The Palacio Episcopal to which it is connected houses the **Museo Diocesano**, which contains 16th century paintings, tapestries, and religious *objets d'art* from the palace's collection. It is open daily except Monday from 10.30 am to 2 pm and 4 to 6 pm (200 ptas).

Not far off lie the ruins of a castle erected by the Muslims. The city walls that climb the slopes above the city have been restored, and are imposing. Best of all, walk the lanes and enjoy the play of colour – the earthy red of the town's buildings and green of its gardens, which are particularly striking in the evening.

Places to Stay & Eat

The pleasant *Ciudad de Albarracín camping ground* is 2km out of town. Of the many hotels in town, the most cost-effective is the reasonable *Mesón del Gallo* (☎ 978 71 00 32, *Calle de los Puentes 1)* on the main road just beyond the tunnel. Rooms with TV and phone cost 2100/4200 ptas.

Possibly the most attractive deal is the *Casa de Santiago* (☎ 978 70 03 16, *Subida a las Torres 11)*. This cosy place has five charmingly appointed rooms and lies a short way off Plaza Mayor. Doubles cost 6300 ptas (7000 ptas in high season). It also has an excellent, and equally tiny, restaurant. The *Hotel Albarracín* (☎ 978 71 00 11, *Calle de Azagra s/n)* is a comfy hotel with singles/doubles for 9600/15,950 ptas plus IVA.

There are several restaurants in the streets off Plaza Mayor. *La Taberna*, on the square itself, does good raciones and tapas. The nearby *Bar Aben Razin* is an atmospheric place for a drink.

Getting There & Away

A daily bus connects the town with Teruel, 38km east. It stops near the Mesón del Gallo.

Around Albarracín

The back road leading south-east towards Bezas passes by some intriguing *pinturas rupestres* – **Neolithic cave paintings**. Those at Cocinilla del Obispo and Prado de los Toros del Navazo are of particular interest; the former have paintings of bison in good condition. The caves are all free but check at the tourist office in Albarracín first for a full rundown. There are no buses here, but the hardy could walk along a 5km trail from Albarracín.

ALBARRACÍN TO CASTILLA-LA MANCHA

For those with a vehicle, a couple of routes suggest themselves if you plan to travel via Albarracín into Castilla-La Mancha. The bumpy TE-903, west from Albarracín, forks after 7km. The way to the left leads into Cuenca province through varied and pretty countryside, joining the Río Júcar gorge about halfway.

The right fork takes you through the picturesque Reserva Nacional de los Montes Universales and into Guadalajara province. You could follow several routes, but perhaps the one that passes Checa, Terzaga and Peralejos de las Truchas across the mountains of the Serranía de Cuenca, and then down the Hoz de Beteta (Beteta Gorge) towards the Alcarria area of Cuenca and Guadalajara provinces, is the most scenic. See also the Castilla-La Mancha chapter.

EL MAESTRAZGO

The series of sierras which stretches east of Teruel across southern Aragón and into the province of Castellón de la Plana in Valencia (see also El Maestrazgo in the Valencia chapter) presents a smorgasbord of bleak rocky peaks and dramatic gorges. The highest peaks just top 2000m and among them the small pueblos seem to be left to their own devices. Unless you have a lot of time, you need your own vehicle to explore El Maestrazgo. Buses link most places, but rarely more than once daily, and forward connections are virtually impossible on the same day. What follows is a serpentine route from Teruel to Alcañiz, with a selection of interesting villages and scenic roads. Keep in mind that winter weather can be unpredictable, and roads are often twisting and rugged.

Southern Maestrazgo

One approach to the area from Teruel is the TE-800 road, which forks off the northbound N-420 a few kilometres out of the city. A 35km drive through largely inhospitable country brings you to **Cedrillas**, a dishevelled little spot with castle ruins and a mudéjar church.

Fifteen kilometres east of Cedrillas, the narrow TE-802 winds down a few hundred metres and the change in scenery is almost instant, leafy and soothing as you make your way to **Alcalá de la Selva**. In winter, this and the tranquil village of **La Virgen de la Vega**, just down the Río Valbona, are popular bases for skiers – if there is enough snow. Both have a camping ground and somewhat pricey hostales, due perhaps to the ski fields of **Valdelinares** to the east.

The next stop of note, 19km on, is **Mora de Rubielos**. Little is known about the place before the arrival of the Muslims and, for centuries after they were expelled in 1170, Mora was passed around from one noble family to another until definitively attached to the Aragonese Crown in 1365. The stout castillo and Iglesia Colegiata were built in the 15th century, suffered badly during the civil war and have since been restored.

Another 14km south-east along the A-232 is the pretty **Rubielos de Mora**. Rubielos is a tranquil patchwork of narrow lanes whose houses are all adorned with the typically small Aragonese balconies. Franco made Rubielos the headquarters of his Navarran corps in 1938. There are a few places to stay and, for those with some money to spare, the nicest is the *Hotel Portal del Carmen* (☎ *978 80 41 53, Calle de la Glorieta 2*). It has doubles for 6900 ptas (8000 ptas in the high season).

Turning back north (take the TE-811), you can head up into the hills of El Maestrazgo proper, with the Sierra de Nogueruelas to the west. Shortly before crossing one of the highest passes (Puerto de Linares at 1720m), you'll pass the dusty pueblo of **Linares de Mora**. *Pensión La Venta* (☎ *978 80 20 18, Calle de Regajo 6*) has basic doubles for 2200 ptas.

Northern Maestrazgo

From Linares de Mora the road loses altitude as it twists northwards to **La Iglesuela**

del Cid. This place is worth a quick stop to see the old ayuntamiento and the main parish church. The *Casa Amada (☎ 964 44 33 73, Calle de la Fuente Nueva 10)* has rooms for 2000/3000 ptas and a good restaurant. An early morning bus passes through here on its way to Teruel via Cantavieja. To go east, the bus from Teruel stops here in the afternoon and takes you about 15km to Villafranca del Cid, from where you can get a bus to Castellón the *following* morning.

Some 13km north-west lies **Cantavieja**, reputedly founded by Hannibal in the days when Carthage reigned supreme in Spain. In two of the Carlist wars during the 19th century it was heavily damaged. The best preserved (and partly restored) part of town is the porticoed Plaza del Ayuntamiento. The cheapest of the two places to stay here is *Pensión Julián (☎ 964 18 50 05, Calle de García Valiño 6)*, with no-frills doubles for 2000 ptas, and home-cooked meals for guests. The odd bus runs to Teruel, Alcorisa (to the north, via Villarluengo) and Morella (to the north-east, in Valencia). The latter is a destination well worth seeking out – see the El Maestrazgo section in the Valencia chapter.

West of Cantavieja, you find yourself on a particularly pretty stretch of the TE-800. The TE-804 tacks to the north from here, an attractive drive past the precariously located **Villarluengo** and, a few kilometres farther on, the weird rock formations of the **Órganos de Montoro** that form the river valley walls of the Río Guadalope. A beautifully located place to stay is the *Hostal La Trucha (☎ 978 77 30 08)*, about 10km north of Villarluengo and right on the river.

Singles/doubles cost 6500/10,000 ptas plus IVA.

Another 30km north and you hit the N-211, which connects with the main Zaragoza-Teruel road to the west, and Alcañiz to the north-east.

Alcañiz, set amid drab country plains, doesn't warrant going out of your way, although it does make a serviceable rest stop halfway between Zaragoza and the coast. Hasdrubal gave the Romans a drubbing here in 212 BC. It was later known to the Arabs as *al-kenees* (the churches), and the city's oversized castillo (now a parador) came under the control of the Knights of Calatrava in 1179, who for centuries used it as their Aragonese base. Of equally exaggerated dimensions is the Iglesia de Santa María Mayor, dwarfing all around it in Plaza de España with its huge baroque portal. Also on the square is the 14th century Lonja and adjoining ayuntamiento, which boasts a Renaissance façade.

A dozen or so hotels serve travellers' needs, including central *El Trillero (☎ 978 83 10 26, Plaza de Santo Domingo 1)*, with doubles at 3000 ptas. Buses run to Barcelona, Zaragoza, Alcorisa (for other connections), Castellón and other destinations, although in most cases only once or twice daily.

About 40km south-east of Alcañiz, **Valderrobres** is another pretty riverside pueblo in the foothills of El Maestrazgo. Again, it is the castillo and principal church that stand out, although the town's Plaza Mayor is also made appealing by its 17th century ayuntamiento. There is a handful of cheap pensiones, should you need to stay.

CAMINO DE SANTIAGO

Pilgrims' Progress

Nowadays it's not only the faithful who walk the Camino de Santiago, the way of St James pilgrim route (or, rather, routes). Many walk or cycle the Camino to Santiago de Compostela in Galicia as a simple hiking or travel exercise, staying at the ancient *hospitales*, or wayside guest houses, which mark the way.

Plenty, however, still do it in a religious context and have the option of staying overnight in pilgrims' refuges. In this case, you can apply for a letter of recommendation in your local parish or at the start of the Camino. You need to keep the letter and a record booklet (which most pilgrim refuges can provide) in which you collect date stamps as you go. Those who complete at least 100km on foot or 200km on bicycle can, on arrival in Santiago, pick up the *compostela*, a document testifying that the bearer has completed at least part of the Camino as a pilgrim (rather than as a tourist). The refuges are free, with priority going to walkers and stays generally limited to one night; it is customary to leave at least a few hundred pesetas for maintenance. The greatest distance between refuges along the route is the 23km from Ponferrada to Villafranca del Bierzo in León province.

Below: Puente de la Peregrinos, the bridge leading out of Puenta de la Reina, Navarra, which is crossed by pilgrims on the Camino de Santiago

St James the Moor-Slayer

Queen Lupa was more than a little suspicious when two Palestinian refugees landed up in her territory, near Padrón in northern Galicia, with the decomposing and headless body of a Christian martyr and requested permission to bury him. The apostle Santiago Apóstol (St James), son of Zebedee, is by tradition thought to have preached in Spain, turning up in Zaragoza at one point. Herod Agrippa had him executed on his return to Jerusalem and Santiago's followers whisked the body to Jaffa, from where they let Providence guide them on an incredible sea voyage to Spain.

The good queen sent the pair on to the nearest Roman governor, in Finisterre, who promptly incarcerated them. What state the apostle was in at this point is hard to imagine but, before the Romans had a chance to kill his disciples, they were freed by an angel and returned to Queen Lupa. Impressed by this and other exploits, she eventually converted to Christianity. Santiago was buried and a small mausoleum was erected (its remains are located beneath the *altar mayor* in the cathedral in Santiago de Compostela) to mark the spot. He was then forgotten for about 750 years until his tomb was rediscovered in 813. Things were tough for Spain's Christians in those days, with most of the country in Muslim hands.

Nevertheless, tales abound of Santiago's spirit appearing on various battlefields and cheerfully cutting down Moors left and right; he became known as Santiago Matamoros (St James the Moor-Slayer). Understandably, his figure became of prime symbolic importance in Spain and the word soon spread across Europe. By the 11th century streams of pilgrims were descending on Santiago, mostly crossing the Pyrenees at Roncesvalles and walking 687km via Pamplona, Logroño and León.

In the 12th century, the Castilian and Aragonese monarchs upgraded the Camino (Pilgrims' Way). At the same time a group of Castilian knights formed a new military order with a religious bent, the Orden de Santiago, which, apart from taking an active part in the Reconquista, also saw aiding and protecting pilgrims as part of its duty. The pilgrimage route also became an important commercial conduit across northern Spain, stimulating local trade. The route's current revival as a tourist activity is just as important for the local economy today. There is no shortage of people on the Camino in the warmer months with the telltale staff and scallop shell. The latter was a practical device for sipping water from streams while on the road.

There are plenty of guidebooks dedicated to the subject of the Camino de Santiago. A few are mentioned in the Books section of the Facts for the Visitor chapter. You can pick up several brochures and a small guidebook to the Camino in Castilla y León from most tourist offices in the region. The latter lists *albergues* (refuges) for pilgrims and other accommodation possibilities in towns right along this stretch. Some Camino destinations are covered in this section, while others are listed in the Aragón; País Vasco, Navarra & La Rioja; Cantabria & Asturias; and Galicia chapters.

The Camino Francés

The Camino Francés is what most people have in mind when they talk of the Camino de Santiago. Not everyone followed it, however. Other routes include: the Camino del Norte, which passes along the Cantabrian coast and turns inland at Ribadeo; the Camino de Fonsagrada, which crosses the Cordillera Cantábrica and passes via Lugo; the Camino Portugués, which crosses into Galicia at Tuy and heads north; and even a Camino Inglés, from La Coruña and O Ferrol (which presumably entails an initial journey by sea!). Pretty much all the albergues and information centres for pilgrims are along the Camino Francés, but signs and references to the Camino de Santiago proliferate over north-western Spain, making it a collective term for the various caminos.

The Camino Francés is intertwined with asphalted roads, meaning you can drive bits of the old route, and of course all the main towns on the route are linked by road. The camino is at its most rewarding, however, when it leaves the highway and becomes a minor back road or walkers' track.

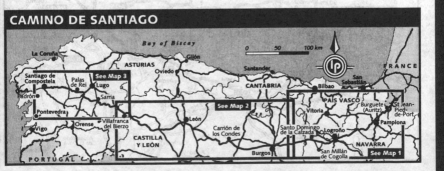

CAMINO DE SANTIAGO

Navarra to Santo Domingo de la Calzada

Navarra to Santo Domingo de la Calzada The principal route for pilgrims to Santiago de Compostela enters Navarra, and hence Spain, at the pass through the Pyrenees just north of Roncesvalles. Refer to the País Vasco, Navarra & La Rioja chapter for accommodation and general information on the places listed in this section.

The Camino makes its way through Pamplona and proceeds southwest to **Puente de la Reina** on the Río Arga. A beautiful bridge, the pilgrims' bridge, spans the river at this point, where a secondary camino from Aragón joins the main road. From Puente de la Reina the Camino de Santiago follows the way to **Logroño**. Of major interest en route are Estella (Lizarra) and, just beyond, the Monasterio de Irache. Other stops worth a look include Torres del Río and Viana. The Pamplona-Logroño stretch of the Camino is covered in the País Vasco, Navarra and La Rioja chapter in the West of Pamplona section.

Beyond Logroño (in the modern autonomous region of La Rioja), the Camino heads west to Burgos. You can take or leave Nájera, but make an effort to visit the cathedral in Santo Domingo de la Calzada and the monastery of San Millán de Cogolla (see the West of Logroño section of the País Vasco, Navarra and La Rioja chapter) before continuing the route to **Burgos** in Castilla y León. Lists of pilgrims' hostels for the Camino are available in tourist offices at Pamplona and Estella.

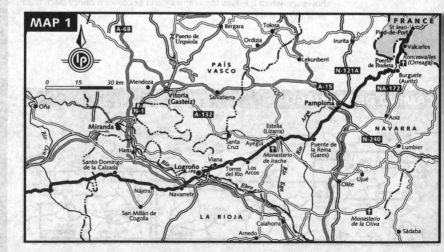

DAMIEN SIMONIS

Right: Detail, Iglesia de
San Martín, Frómista,
Castilla y León

Logroño to Astorga After leaving Logroño behind and traipsing
the length of La Rioja, the route enters Castilla y León 54km east of
Burgos at the tiny settlement of Redecilla del Campo. Refer to the
Castilla y León chapter for accommodation and general information on
the places listed in this section.

Apart from the great cities of Burgos and León, several other important towns are distributed along the 390km that the Camino covers
in Castilla y León. At Frómista, the Romanesque Iglesia de San Martín
has long been a must on the pilgrim's list of things to see, and the
churches of San Tirso and San Lorenzo in Sahagún are two more gems.
The cathedral and Palacio de Gaudí of Astorga mark a unique juxta-
position of the very best of classic religious architecture and modern
flights of fantasy.

The country across this northern strip of Castilla y León is largely
typical of Castilla, with plains of cereal crops interrupted at intervals by
low rises and winding streams. It is well protected from the capri-
ciousness of Atlantic weather by the rock barrier of the Cordillera Cantábrica, but still uncomfortably cold throughout the long, dark months
of winter. Only in its latter stages, as the *meseta* (tableland) gives way
to the mountains of Galicia, do real changes appear, setting the tone
for what awaits those determined to pursue the Camino to the end.

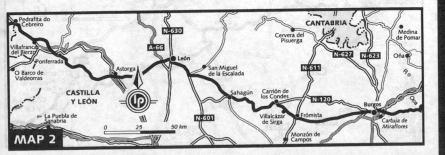

MAP 2

O Cebreiro to Santiago de Compostela Those pilgrims with true grit – the ones who didn't give up at Villafranca del Bierzo (see the Castilla y León chapter) – face the formidable task of climbing to the mountain pass of **Pedrafita do Cebreiro** (1109m), the main gateway to Galicia in the Cordillera Cantábrica mountain chain that separates the Castilian meseta from Galicia and the northern Atlantic regions.

From here it is another 5km to O Cebreiro, a tiny, wind-battered settlement of stone houses high above a patchwork of green valleys. In among the huddle of houses and a couple of *pallozas* (traditional circular, thatch-roofed houses) remains an 11th century church. O Cebreiro makes a lovely stop and, apart from a refuge for pilgrims, you can stay in the *Hospedería O Cebreiro* (☎ 982 36 71 25), next to the church. There are comfortable rooms for 3000/4000 ptas, and a great restaurant. Failing that, try *Mesón Antón* (☎ 982 15 13 36), which has a couple of nice rooms for the same price.

About 10km on, the Camino crosses its highest point in Galicia, the Alto do Poio. Another 14km brings you to sleepy **Triacastela**, near the Río Oribio. There are a couple of places to stay and eat, a bank and a post office. At this point the route forks. The main road dips south via Samos on the way to Sarriá, 23km west, while the original Camino takes you along narrow, wooded paths to the north, past small farming hamlets and the odd wayside chapel, meeting the highway at Sarriá.

If you do follow the road, a stop at **Samos** is a must. The imposing Benedictine monastery here is worth visiting, although its history is tragic. The original 6th century monastery was replaced in the 12th century by another, which in turn was destroyed by fire and rebuilt in

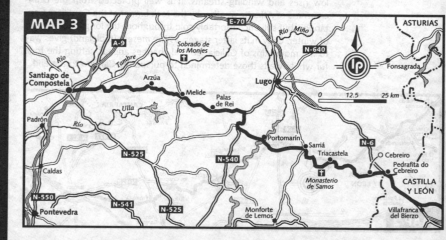

the Gothic style in the 16th century. Fire struck again in 1951, killing one person and destroying anything not made of stone. Only the 18th century church was unharmed. The place was rebuilt, and the exquisite cloister gardens must be among the most lovingly maintained in all Iberian Christendom. It is open Tuesday to Saturday from 10 am to 1.30 pm and 4 to 7 pm, and Sunday from 10 am to 2 pm only. Entry for the compulsory guided tour costs 200 ptas.

Twelve kilometres on is **Sarriá**, a town grown too big to be charming, although the older hill-top area is vaguely interesting. Sarriá is a transport junction, with regular buses north to Lugo and south to Monforte de Lemos. Along the Camino, you cannot count on much more than one or two services a day to places like Triacastela, Portomarín and O Cebreiro. Few services operate on Sunday.

Better than Sarriá as an overnight stop is **Portomarín**, in spite of the fact that the original village was flooded by the damming of the Río Miño in 1963. The 13th century Iglesia de San Nicolás, with an impressive rose window, was transferred to the new town and dominates the central square. Parts of several other buildings on the square were also salvaged from the old town. You might try for rooms at the *Posada del Camino* (☎ 982 54 50 07), just opposite San Nicolás. Rooms cost 2000/3500 ptas and the restaurant serves up a decent *empanada*.

Below: Cruceiro at Melide, the oldest in Galicia

There's little to detain you at **Palas de Rei**, the next town on the Camino, but there are several places to stay if you need them. **Melide**, 15km on, is a little nicer, and is home to the oldest *cruceiro* (14th

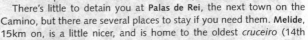

century) in Galicia; this stands outside the unassuming Gothic Iglesia de San Pedro on the main road before you reach the centre. One kilometre west of Melide is the Romanesque Iglesia de Santa María. A few kilometres before Melide, you may notice a turn-off to the village of **Furelos**. Pilgrims can pick up a stamp at the local tavern here, and the Romanesque bridge that crosses a tributary of the Río Ulla is a beauty.

If you have the time and inclination, detour north from Melide. The Cistercian monastery of **Sobrado de los Monjes** (Sobrado dos Monxes), which forms the hub of an otherwise humdrum hamlet, came close to falling into irrecoverable disrepair in the years following its expropriation in 1834. However, a small band of Cistercians returned in 1954 and much has been restored. The ornate Galician baroque façade of the church belies its comparatively austere, and mouldy, interior. The bare Claustro de los Peregrinos, the first cloister you enter in the complex, was completely rebuilt in 1972. The Claustro de los Medallones, erected in the mid-18th century to replace its 12th century Romanesque forerunner, takes its name from the 'medallions' (containing busts) that line the porticoes. Off this, the kitchen contains a huge 13th century chimney flue. Possibly the most incongruous element inside the church are the much-neglected choir stalls, jammed in here when it was decided not to lodge them in the Santiago cathedral, as originally intended. The monastery buildings are open Monday to Saturday from 10.30 am to 1 pm and 4.15 to 6.15 pm and Sunday and holidays from 12.15 to 1 pm and 4.15 to 6.15 pm (100 ptas).

Back on the Camino, there's little of interest until you crest the last hill before Santiago, **Monte do Gozo** (or Monxoi). Pilgrim groups would race to the top and the first to take in the views of the Catedral de Santiago was proclaimed king of the group. After enjoying (hence the Spanish *gozo*) this satisfaction, only a few kilometres separate weary walkers from that final personal victory.

DAMIEN SIMONIS

Left: Baroque façade of the Catedral del Apóstol, Santiago de Compostela (Galicia)

País Vasco, Navarra & La Rioja

The territories of the Basques, which take in the three provinces of the País Vasco (Basque Country) and Navarra, as well as the abutting parts of south-western France, together form a remarkable historical anomaly. Descended from a people who, according to some theories, predate even the earliest Indo-European invasions of Europe in prehistoric times, the Basques have retained a language whose origins still puzzle linguists and a sense of separateness that has been the bane of everyone from the Muslims through Charlemagne to Franco.

A mountainous, green interior, often shrouded in Atlantic mists, presents a soothing and beautiful counterpoint to the rugged coast and its cosmopolitan centres. People are drawn here for all manner of reasons: the sophisticated seaside life of San Sebastián, the surfing, the (in)famous festivities at the running of the bulls in Pamplona, and the striking countryside. The area's proximity to France is also an attraction.

Created as a separate region in 1978, La Rioja is for most people synonymous with wine. Indeed the vineyards of the Ebro valley form a kind of buffer zone between the Basque territories and the broad expanse of Castilla to the south.

Across the País Vasco and, to a lesser extent, in Navarra, the Basque names for towns are gaining the upper hand over the Castilian versions, which in many cases only pose minor variations in spelling anyway. In this guide, Basque has been favoured in all cases except for the provincial capitals, which are still better known by their Castilian names.

País Vasco

Known as Euskadi or Euskal Herri to the Basques, the País Vasco is made up of three provinces: Guipúzcoa (Gipuzkoa in the Basque language), Álava (Araba) and

Vizcaya (Bizkaia, and hence Biscay in English).

Just what to call the Basque country presents a smorgasbord of options. In Spanish, País Vasco is the common term used to denote the three provinces of what is officially the Comunidad Autónoma Vasca

PAÍS VASCO, NAVARRA & LA RIOJA

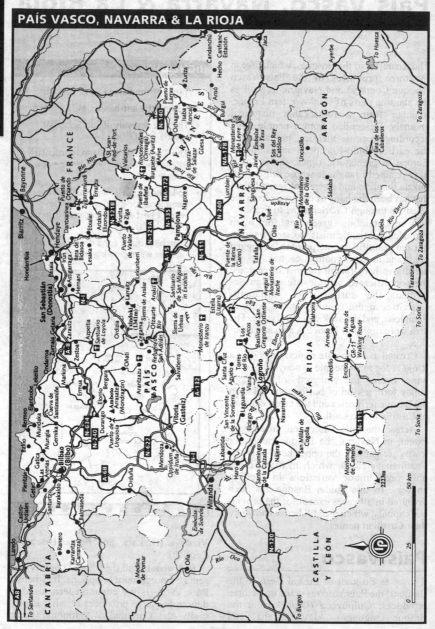

(CAV). In Basque *(euskara)*, the nationalists coined the term Euskadi at the end of the 19th century. The classic term is Euskal Herri (or Euskal Herria – the final 'a' means 'the'). Any of these terms can mean: Iparralde (the three Basque provinces in France); Navarra; Egoalde (the three provinces of the CAV); or any combination you like of the above. It all depends on who you talk to!

History

Throughout much of the Middle Ages rival warlords fought constantly for control over Basque territory, and the expanding Castilian crown only gained sovereignty with some difficulty. Neighbouring Navarra in fact constituted a separate kingdom until 1512.

Still, Navarra and the three provinces were able to extract broad autonomy arrangements, known as the *fueros*, from Madrid. These were first repealed by Napoleon at the opening of the 19th century. The new ideas of the centralised state were anathema to more conservative Basques, who tended to support the reactionary Don Carlos during the Carlist wars. The colour red was associated with the Carlists, and has since come to be emblematic of the Basque assertion of separateness.

At the close of the Second Carlist War in 1876 all provinces but Navarra were stripped of their coveted fueros, although a measure of economic autonomy remained. This of course alienated the many Basques who had sided with liberal Madrid, and by the end of the century their resentment had taken shape in the form of nascent Basque nationalism. The Basque Nationalist Party (PNV) was formed in 1894, but support was never uniform, as Navarra and the province of Álava had a considerable Castilian contingent. When the Republican government in Madrid proposed the possibility of home rule to the Basques, the regions of Navarra and Álava both declined the offer. Navarra in particular, with the bulk of its fuero rights intact, had little to gain. The remaining provinces liked the idea, and when the

Spanish Civil War broke out in 1936, they threw in their lot with the Republicans. Conservative rural Navarra and Álava sided with Franco, so of course it was Vizcaya and Guipúzcoa that paid the heaviest price for backing the wrong horse. In fact Navarra managed to retain its fuero rights in spite of Franco's penchant for ultra-centralised government.

In 1961, a small group of Basque nationalists known as ETA (Euskadi Ta Askatasuna) carried out its first terrorist attack, setting in motion a cycle of violence and repression that has continued to this day, in spite of the death of Franco and the granting of wide-ranging autonomy in the early 1980s. ETA has undergone innumerable transformations and still commands the support of as much as 15% of the Basque populace.

The public political wing, Herri Batasuna (HB), constitutes a marginal but vocal parliamentary force, but perhaps more worrying is the youth group, Jarrai, from whose ranks tomorrow's assassins are often picked. Thought to have been all but dismantled after numerous successful police operations in the early 1990s, ETA began to hit back with surprising vigour in 1994, with bomb attacks in places as far apart as San Sebastián, Madrid, Alicante and Sevilla. Towards the end of the 90s, ETA switched its targets increasingly to local politicians, usually of the conservative Partido Popular. The staggered assassinations of several *concejales* (councillors) seemingly put the terrorists even further beyond the pale. This was followed by some tough action by both Madrid and the Ertzaintza: the whole leadership of HB was jailed for seven years in December 1997 for association with known terrorists and several terrorist cells were broken up. But after a number of assassinations in early and mid-1998, ETA declared a voluntary cease-fire in September. This was met with more scepticism than relief, as many felt it to be a veiled excuse to buy time and reorganise forces in the wake of federal crackdowns.

Language

In the modern autonomous region of the País Vasco the *ikurriña* (Basque flag) flies everywhere, and a renewed sense of Basque identity has thankfully not only expressed itself in violence, but also in such areas as language. Suppressed by Franco, the idiom is being learned by a growing number of young Basques, although comparatively few people use it as the main language of everyday discourse.

You may in fact never hear a word of Basque spoken throughout your stay in the País Vasco, though there are Basque radio and TV stations. In Guipúzcoa province especially, the zeal to promote it is leading to the extinguishment of Spanish in one of its most useful forms – signs. Most street signs have both the Castilian and the Basque names, but the Castilian has often been spray-painted over! This can cause some confusion, especially if you're driving.

Bear in mind that many Castilian words are also written slightly differently in the País Vasco. *Tx* often replaces *ch*, *b* replaces *v*, and *k* takes over from the hard Castilian *c*. The letter *g* is always pronounced hard in Basque. For more information on the Basque language, turn to the Language Guide at the back of the book.

Food

Basque cuisine is generally regarded as Spain's finest. Catalans might dispute that, but if you can wangle your way into one of the private Basque gastronomic societies (traditionally all-male affairs) you'll certainly be in food heaven. They emerged mainly in San Sebastián, formed by groups of chefs cooking for each other and friends. San Sebastián is home of the greatest tapas in Spain – just entering some bars is enough to get you salivating. Apart from beer and cider, the traditional plonk of the region is a crisp, slightly tart white wine called *txacoli*.

The classics of Basque cooking are simple enough, and seafood is the staple ingredient. Famous dishes include *bacalao al pil pil* (salt cod cooked with garlic and chill-

ies), *merluza a la vasca* (hake in green sauce), *chipirones en su tinta* (cuttlefish in their own ink) and *chuletas de buey* (enormous beef chops). What has really brought the area's restaurants to grandeur is the flood of nouvelle cuisine influences that have taken hold in San Sebastián especially. Led by such chefs as Juan Mari Arzak, the Basque country's more imaginative cooks have, since the 1970s, made a name for themselves in Spain and abroad with what is commonly called the *nueva cocina vasca*, a tasty genre in constant evolution.

Sport

The Basques indulge in a rather odd assortment of sports, ranging from grass-cutting and log-chopping through to caber-tossing and tug-of-war. The most famous is *pelota vasca* (or *jai-alai* in Basque), a form of handball played on a walled court known as a *frontón*. There is also a version involving the use of a *txistera*, a kind of hand-held basket which allows the ball to be hurled with disconcerting velocity at the wall. You can often see local teams whacking away at the town frontón.

Signs in Basque

Basque words which commonly appear on signs include:

Basque	English/Spanish
ERDIALDEA	*city centre*
ERDIA	*centre*
JATETXEA	*restaurant*
KALEA	*street (calle)*
KALE NAGUSIA	*main street (calle mayor)*
KOMUNA/K	*toilet/s*
KONTUZ!	*caution/ beware!*
NEKAZAL-TURISMOA	*casa rural*
ONGI ETORRI	*welcome*
TURISMO BULEGOA	*tourist office*

The traditional game is played with the bare hand, but there are up to 20 variants of the sport, now played in one form or other all over the world. Fourteen variants are accepted at world championship level. The bare-handed version, *esku huska*, is played in several different ways, with court and ball sizes, and rules, varying. The Txistera version is the newest and the French Basques have a variant involving use of a smaller catch-hurl scoop called a *joko garbi*. The five-a-side game *rebot* is supposedly the hardest in which to score properly. Some export versions are odder still, such as *xari*, an Argentine derivation in which a string racquet is employed.

Cycling is wildly popular and drivers in the region should pay heed to entire squadrons of cyclists on the roads.

Emergency

The general telephone number for all emergency situations (police, ambulance, fire) in the País Vasco is ☎ 088. There are also local numbers, some of which are noted in this chapter.

SAN SEBASTIÁN

Forming a half-moon around the beautiful bay of La Concha, this most Basque of Basque cities is at the same time a captivating crossroads. A seaside resort surrounded by the low green hills of Guipúzcoa (Gipuzkoa), the province of which it is the capital, San Sebastián (Donostia) is a stone's throw from France.

Although at first you could be forgiven for drawing comparisons with its French Basque cousin, Biarritz, the two could not be further apart in atmosphere. Where the latter has a rather reserved quality, San Sebastián's Parte Vieja (Old Town) boasts possibly the greatest concentration of bars per square metre in Spain.

Although in many people's minds Bilbao has a bad reputation for street confrontations between the police and ETA sympathisers, San Sebastián is, if anything, worse. Bands of young Jarrai members hurling bottles and rocks at the local autonomous police (the Ertzaintza) are not an uncommon sight – although not common enough to put you off a visit.

History

Long little more than a fishing village privileged by its position on a protected bay at the mouth of the Río Urumea, San Sebastián was later the Kingdom of Navarra's principal outlet to the sea. By the 16th century, it had become a prosperous trade centre specialising first in the export of Castilian wool and other products to France, the Low Countries and England, and later benefiting from burgeoning commerce with the Americas. Disaster came with the Peninsular War, during which Anglo-Portuguese forces virtually razed the city in 1813 after wresting it from French hands. The city you see today is, hardly surprisingly, largely a product of the years following the withdrawal of Napoleon's troops from Spain.

Orientation

The heart of San Sebastián beats in the Parte Vieja, squeezed together in the narrow grid of lanes below Monte Urgull on the eastern spur of the Bahía de la Concha. This is where you'll find the greatest concentration of bars and restaurants, and many of the cheaper hotels. More hotels are scattered about the newer parts of town to the immediate south, also known as the Zona Romántica. Just across the river is the RENFE train station, while the main *estación de autobuses* (bus station) is farther south along the river.

Information

Tourist Office The Oficina Municipal de Información (☎ 943 48 11 66), Boulevard Reina Regente s/n, has comprehensive information on the city and the province of Guipúzcoa. In summer it is open Monday to Saturday from 8 am to 8 pm and Sunday from 9 am to 2 pm. Otherwise it is open from 9 am to 2 pm and 3.30 to 7 pm, but is closed on Sunday afternoon.

SAN SEBASTIÁN

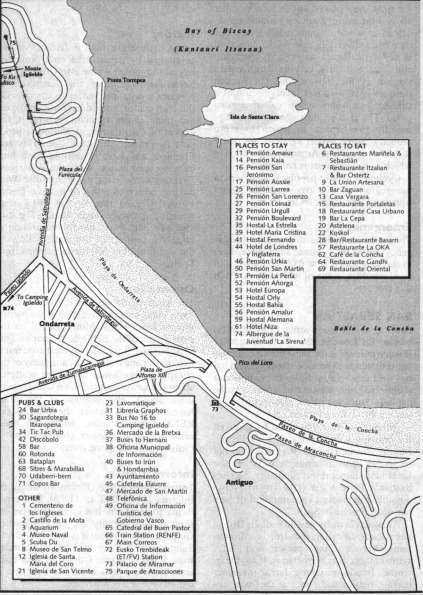

Bay of Biscay

(Kantauri Itsasoa)

Monte Igueldo

To Ku s disco

Punta Torrepea

Isla de Santa Clara

Plaza del Funicular

Avenida de Satrustegui

Paseo Igueldo

To Camping Igueldo

■74

Ondarreta

Playa de Ondarreta

Avenida de Satrustegui

Avenida de Zumalacarregui

Plaza de Alfonso XIII

Pico del Loro

Bahía de la Concha

Playa de la Concha

Paseo de la Concha

Paseo de Mraconcha

Antiguo

75

PLACES TO STAY
11 Pensión Amaiur
14 Pensión Kaia
16 Pensión San Jerónimo
17 Pensión Aussie
25 Pensión Larrea
26 Pensión San Lorenzo
27 Pensión Loinaz
29 Pensión Urgull
32 Pensión Boulevard
35 Hostal La Estrella
39 Hotel María Cristina
41 Hostal Fernando
44 Hotel de Londres y Inglaterra
46 Pensión Urkia
50 Pensión San Martín
51 Pensión La Perla
52 Pensión Añorga
53 Hotel Europa
54 Hostal Orly
55 Hostal Bahía
56 Pensión Amalur
59 Hostal Alemana
61 Hotel Niza
74 Albergue de la Juventud 'La Sirena'

PLACES TO EAT
6 Restaurantes Mariñela & Sebastián
7 Restaurante Itzalian & Bar Ostertz
9 La Unión Artesana
10 Bar Zaguan
13 Casa Vergara
15 Restaurante Portaletas
18 Restaurante Casa Urbano
19 Bar La Cepa
20 Astelena
22 Koskol
28 Bar/Restaurante Basarri
57 Restaurante La OKA
62 Café de la Concha
64 Restaurante Gandhi
69 Restaurante Oriental

PUBS & CLUBS
24 Bar Urbia
30 Sagardotegia Itxaropena
34 Tic Tac Pub
42 Discóbolo
58 Bar
60 Rotonda
63 Bataplan
68 Sitres & Marabillas
70 Udaberri-berri
71 Copos Bar

OTHER
1 Cementerio de los Ingleses
2 Castillo de la Mota
3 Aquarium
4 Museo Naval
5 Scuba Du
8 Museo de San Telmo
12 Iglesia de Santa María del Coro
21 Iglesia de San Vicente
23 Lavomatique
31 Librería Graphos
33 Bus No 16 to Camping Igueldo
36 Mercado de la Bretxa
37 Buses to Hernani
38 Oficina Municipal de Información
40 Buses to Irún & Hondarribia
43 Ayuntamiento
45 Cafetería Elaurre
47 Mercado de San Martín
48 Telefónica
49 Oficina de Información Turística del Gobierno Vasco
65 Catedral del Buen Pastor
66 Train Station (RENFE)
67 Main Correos
72 Eusko Trenbideak (ET/FV) Station
73 Palacio de Miramar
75 Parque de Atracciones

İÜ
73

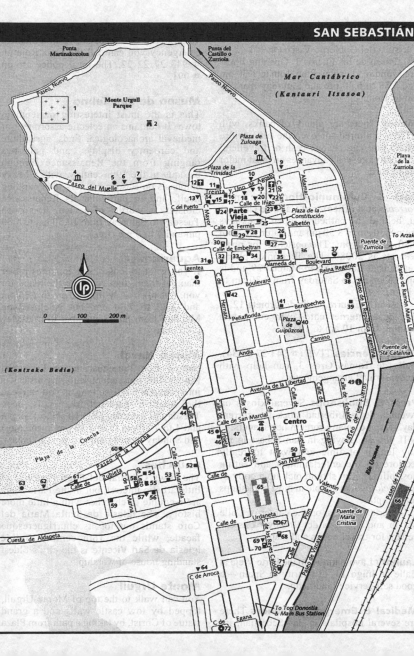

SAN SEBASTIÁN

Punta Martinakozolua

Paseo Nuevo

Punta del Castillo o Zurriola

Paseo Nuevo

Mar Cantábrico
(Kantauri Itsasoa)

Monte Urgull Parque

Playa de la Zurriola

Plaza de Zuloaga

Paseo del Muelle

Plaza de la Trinidad

Treinta y Uno de Agosto

Calle de Iñigo

C del Puerto

C Mayor

Parte Vieja

Calle de Fermín

Plaza de la Constitución

Calbetón

To Arzak

Puente de Zurriola

Calle de Embeltran

Alameda del Boulevard

Igentea

Boulevard

Reina Regente

Puente de Sta Catalina

Peñaflorida

Bengoechea

Plaza de Guipúzcoa

Camino

Andía

Avenida de la Libertad

Calle de San Marcial

Centro

Paseo de la Concha

Playa de la Concha

Zubieta

Calle de la Marina

Calle de Manterola

Calle de

San Martín

Valentín Olano

Río Urumea

Paseo de Francia

Cuesta de Aldapeta

Urdaneta

Puente de María Cristina

C de Arroca

To Top Donostia & Main Bus Station

C de

Egana

(Kontxako Badia)

0   100   200 m

For more information on the rest of the País Vasco, try the Oficina de Información Turística del Gobierno Vasco (☎ 943 42 62 82), Paseo de los Fueros 1. Opening hours are Monday to Friday from 9 am to 1.30 pm and 3.30 to 6.30 pm and Saturday from 10 am to 1 pm.

Money There are plenty of banks, with ATMs, scattered all over the city centre where you can change cash or travellers' cheques or get cash advances on most major credit cards.

Post & Communications The main *correos* (post office) is at Calle de Urdaneta, behind the cathedral, open weekdays from 8.30 am to 8.30 pm and Saturday from 9.30 am to 2 pm. The postcode for poste restante is 20080. The Telefónica phone centre is at Calle de San Marcial 29 and is open Monday to Saturday from 9.30 am to 11 pm.

Cafetería Elaurre, Calle de Urbieta 12, is the local Internet café, with computers running from 10 am to 10 pm.

Travel Agencies TIVE (☎ 943 27 69 34), Calle de Tomás Gros 3, can help with student travel arrangements.

Press & Bookshops Several kiosks on Avenida de la Libertad stock the current day's issue of many foreign newspapers.

If you are staying in San Sebastián for any length of time and want to really explore all the entertainment and eating possibilities, you should pick up a copy of *El Sabelotodo*, available in most bookshops for 595 ptas.

Librería Graphos, on the corner of Calle Mayor and Alameda del Boulevard, is excellent for travel books and maps.

Laundry Lavomatique, in the Parte Vieja at Calle de Iñigo 14, is a rarity in Spain – a good self-service laundrette.

Medical & Emergency Services There are several hospitals in San Sebastián, in-cluding the Hospital de Gipuzkoa (☎ 943 45 40 00), Alto de Zorroaga s/n. In a medical emergency you can call the Cruz Roja on ☎ 943 27 22 22. The local police are on ☎ 091.

Museo de San Telmo

This is the most interesting museum in town. It contains an eclectic assortment of medieval archaeological finds, agriculture and carpentry displays, and paintings ranging from the Renaissance through baroque to the 19th century, with a heavy emphasis on Basque painters. The building itself, and in particular its Renaissance cloister, is worthy of a visit. It is open Tuesday to Saturday from 10.30 am to 1.30 pm and 4 to 8 pm (free).

Aquarium

If you want to look at sea creatures rather than eat them, this could be the place for you. It is open daily from 10 am to 1.30 pm and 3.30 to 7.30 pm, but is closed on Monday from mid-September to mid-May (700 ptas).

Museo Naval

Not far from the aquarium, on Paseo del Muelle, this museum of seafaring history is interesting enough, so long as you can read the Spanish explanations. It is open Tuesday to Saturday from 10 am to 1.30 pm and 4 to 7.30 pm (5 to 8.30 pm in summer) and Sunday from 11 am to 2 pm (200 ptas).

Churches

The city's **Catedral del Buen Pastor** is of little artistic interest, but in the Parte Vieja are a couple of churches with a little more history. The **Iglesia de Santa María del Coro** stands out for its churrigueresque façade, while the 16th century **Gothic Iglesia de San Vicente** is the city's oldest standing house of worship.

Monte Urgull

You can walk to the top of Monte Urgull, topped by low castle walls and a grand statue of Christ, by taking a path from Plaza de Zuloaga. The views across the Bahía de la Concha and the city are wonderful.

Monte Igueldo

The views from the summit of Monte Igueldo are better still. You can save your legs by catching the funicular to the **Parque de Atracciones** (amusement park).

Beaches & Isla de Santa Clara

The Playa de la Concha and its westerly extension, the Playa de Ondarreta, are among the best city beaches in Spain, although the water can be nippy. It's placid too, shielded as it is from the open sea by the Isla de Santa Clara. You can swim out to the island, or landlubbers can hop aboard the boats that run there every half-hour in summer. The Playa de Zurriola (aka known as Playa de Gros), east of the Río Urumea, is not as clean and hence not as crowded.

Diving

The Scuba Du dive shop (☎ 943 42 24 26), Paseo del Muelle 23, runs diving courses (CMAS and PADI) and hires out gear.

Swimming

If the Atlantic is too chilly for your tootsies, you can have a swim at the Piscinas Anoeta on Paseo de Anoeta.

Special Events

Among San Sebastián's top drawing cards are the International Jazz Festival in July and the two week Festival de Cine (film festival), which has been held annually in the second half of September since 1957. There are all sorts of minor fiestas during the summer, including several rowing and sailing regattas and a surfing championship in July. Other fiestas worth watching out for are those of the Festividad de San Sebastián on January 20, and *carnaval* in mid-February.

Places to Stay – Budget

As in much of northern Spain, July and August can be trying months for searching out accommodation in San Sebastián.

Arrive early or call ahead and be aware that summer prices often rise sharply. Rates given here for singles/doubles tend to jump up about 1000/1500 ptas in peak periods, unless otherwise noted. They may also drop significantly in winter (try bargaining).

Camping & Hostel The nearest camping ground is rather a long way west of the city. *Camping Igueldo* (☎ 943 21 45 02), also called *Garoa*, is out beyond Monte Igueldo and can be reached by bus No 16 from Alameda del Boulevard.

Twenty kilometres west of San Sebastián and accessible by ET/FV train (get out at Orio, then walk 2km up the valley) is the peaceful *Ziringa* (☎ 943 13 20 79) camping ground. There's a hostel and restaurant here, too, and the managers are happy to sell bottles of their home-made cider.

Albergue de la Juventud La Sirena (☎ 943 31 02 68, Paseo de Igueldo 25) is San Sebastián's HI hostel. It charges 1550 ptas for a bunk bed and breakfast (1850 ptas if you're over 26). There is a midnight curfew during the week, extended to 2 am on weekends.

Pensiones & Hostales The old quarter is almost as replete with pensiones as it is with bars – which is great for stumbling home, but can be disturbing if you want to sleep.

La Parte Vieja Pensión Amaiur (☎ 943 42 96 54, Calle de 31 de Agosto 44) is as pretty as a picture and has rooms ranging from 2800 to 4800 ptas, although you may be able to bargain them down a little. *Pensión Urgull* (☎ 943 43 00 47, Calle de Esterlines 10) is quiet and amiable, with comfortable rooms costing 2500/3500 ptas.

There are a couple of cheapies next to one another on Calle de San Jerónimo. *Pensión Aussie* (☎ 943 42 28 74) at No 23 is indeed run by an Australian ex-patriate and has reasonable rooms for 1750 ptas per person (2000 ptas in peak season). The proprietor can help to arrange private rooms if all else fails. Rooms in *Pensión San Jerónimo*

PAÍS VASCO

(☎ 943 28 64 34) at No 25 cost around the average 2500/3500 ptas.

Pensión Larrea *(☎ 943 42 26 94, Calle de Narrika 21)* has been recommended by travellers. It is simple but pleasant and singles/doubles start at 2500/3500 ptas. Another nice place is **Hostal La Estrella** *(☎ 943 42 09 97, Plaza de Sarriegi 1)*, where prices range from 2500 ptas plus IVA for a basic single to 7000 ptas plus IVA for a good double with own shower.

Pensión San Lorenzo *(☎ 943 42 55 16, Calle de San Lorenzo 2)* has a kitchen that guests can use. Singles/doubles start at 2500/3500 ptas. **Pensión Loinaz** *(☎ 943 42 67 14)*, farther down the road at No 17, is also fine but just a little pricier.

Pensión Kaia *(☎ 943 43 13 42, Calle del Puerto 12)* has good rooms with private bath starting at 3000/4000 ptas plus IVA, all increasing to 7000 ptas plus IVA in July and August.

Just on the edge of the Parte Vieja is **Pensión Boulevard** *(☎ 943 42 94 05, Alameda del Boulevard 24)*, where singles/doubles without private bath start at 2000/3000 ptas in the off season and cost up to 5000/8000 ptas with shower in summer.

Centro The **Pensión Añorga** *(☎ 943 46 79 45, Calle de Easo 12)* has a range of rooms with or without private bath/shower. Singles/doubles are 2000/3000 ptas plus IVA.

Pensión La Perla *(☎ 943 42 81 23, Calle de Loyola 10)* has excellent rooms with private shower, and some look over the cathedral. Rooms range from 2750/3750 ptas to 3000/5000 ptas plus IVA. Keeping it in the family, **Pensión Urkia** *(☎ 943 42 44 36, Calle de Urbieta 12)* is run by the sister of La Perla's proprietor. It is just as good and charges the same prices.

Hostal Fernando *(☎ 943 42 55 75, Plaza de Guipúzcoa 2)* is not a bad spot on one of the city's more attractive squares. Simple but clean rooms cost 3500/4500 ptas.

If Calle de San Martín were a bough it would be bending under the weight of the hotels along it. Towards the eastern end at No 10, **Pensión San Martín** *(☎ 943 42 87 14)* has squeaky-clean doubles with private bath for 5900 ptas plus IVA (7200 ptas plus IVA in summer), which will be rented out for about 4000 ptas plus IVA to lone travellers.

Pensión Amalur *(☎ 943 46 08 61)* at No 43 offers functional rooms without bath for 2000/3000 ptas. There's also more-expensive rooms with their own bath.

Places to Stay – Mid-Range

Rooms in **Hostal Alemana** *(☎ 943 46 25 44, Calle de San Martin 53)* come well-equipped and you can get drinks and snacks in the salon. It's a friendly place with singles/doubles from 6000/8000 ptas plus IVA, climbing by around 2000 ptas in the hottest months.

Hotel Niza *(☎ /fax 943 42 66 63, Calle de Zubieta 56)* is a good upper mid-range hotel with rooms just off the waterfront for 6450/13,700 ptas plus IVA. **Hostal Bahía** *(☎ 943 46 92 11, Calle de San Martín 54)* is not quite as good value, but has comfortable rooms for 9900/13,400 ptas plus IVA. Next door at No 52, the **Hotel Europa** *(☎ 943 47 08 80, fax 943 47 17 30)* has rooms for up to 12,000/15,500 ptas.

Places to Stay – Top End

Hotel Orly *(☎ 943 46 32 00, fax 943 45 61 01, Plaza de Zaragoza 4)* is a modern upper-level option in the heart of the centre and a brisk walk from the beach. Smallish but well-appointed singles/doubles are 14,000/17,000 ptas plus IVA.

Hotel de Londres e Inglaterra *(☎ 943 42 69 89, fax 943 42 00 31, Calle de Zubieta 2)* overlooks the waterfront. Singles/doubles cost up to 14,000/22,300 ptas plus IVA.

The truly extravagant could throw their credit cards at the **Hotel María Cristina** *(☎ 943 42 49 00, fax 943 42 39 14, Paseo de la República Argentina 4)*, where prices soar into the stratosphere at 19,900/27,500 ptas plus IVA for the *least* expensive.

Places to Eat

In San Sebastián you will experience some of the tastiest cuisines in Spain. The choice of venues seems virtually limitless and it is here that the art of the bar snack has been refined, with tray after tray of mouth-watering goodies lining the bars. Snacking in this way is not the cheapest way to fill your stomach, but it's a lot of fun!

If you want to stock up to make your own meals, go where the locals go – the *Mercado de la Bretxa*. Another busy market in the centre is the *Mercado de San Martín* on Calle de San Marcial.

For seafood by the sea, there is a string of places down by the fishing harbour. *Restaurante Mariñela* and *Restaurante Sebastián* are side by side on Paseo del Muelle and much of a muchness. They both charge around 1300 to 2000 ptas for main courses. A little farther along you can either eat the same at *Restaurante Itzalian* or indulge in snacks and a beer at *Bar Ostertz*.

For those in a financial jam, *Bar Zaguan* (*Calle de 31 de Agosto 31*) does a set lunch for 950 ptas and *platos combinados* for as little as 650 ptas. Even better is the delicious lunch deal offered by the tiny *Koskol* (*Calle de Iñigo 5*). For 1000 ptas you get exceedingly generous portions – the *ensalada mixta* is a meal in itself, and the fried anchovies with garlic are divine.

Bar/Restaurante Basarri (*Calle de Fermín Calbetón 17*) is plain and simple but the cooking is good – worth every one of the 1400 ptas for the set meal. *Casa Vergara* (*Calle Mayor 21*) is another good little place where you dine on a set *menú* lunch for 1800 ptas.

Bar La Cepa (*Calle de 31 de Agosto 7*) is just one of many bars in the Parte Vieja that comes warmly recommended for its tapas. *Restaurante Casa Urbano* at No 17 is a more upmarket choice and an old favourite with a well-entrenched reputation for quality seafood. Mains cost around 2500 ptas. The heavy timber beams that dominate its décor help make the *Restaurante Portaletas* (*Calle del Puerto 8*) a popular place

with the locals. Meat and fish dishes cost upwards of 1400 ptas.

Plaza de la Constitución is loaded with atmosphere and a great choice of bars. *Astelena* is one of the city's grand old institutions and something of a must on your culinary and liquid odyssey through San Sebastián. It's not that the food is necessarily better than in the other places, but it goes back a long way.

One of the country's most acclaimed chefs, Juan Mari Arzak, cooks up his world-renowned Basque nouvelle cuisine at *Arzak*, east of centre at Alto de Miracruz 21. You can sample his goodies in a special menu for two for 7000 ptas.

If you're after a little variety, you could have Indian and/or Middle-Eastern at *Restaurante Gandhi* (*Calle de Arroca*), just off Plaza de Easo. A *menú de degustación* for two costs 5400 ptas, and the *menú del día* is 1500 ptas. Very good value too is the Chinese *Restaurante Oriental* (*Calle de los Reyes Católicos 6*) just south of the cathedral. They use a little more than the usual dose of imagination and even serve vaguely spicy food – in spite of the generally disapproving Spanish palate.

A fun self-service vegetarian place is *Restaurante La OKA* (*Calle de San Martín 43*).

Cafés For your morning coffee and cake, there are several promenade cafés along Alameda del Boulevard. Considerably more chic is *Café de la Concha*, overlooking the beach. For a smoky, old-style ambience, try *La Unión Artesian*, on the corner of Plaza de Zuloaga and Calle de 31 de Agosto.

Entertainment

Bars San Sebastián has two good areas for bar activity – the Parte Vieja and around Calle de los Reyes Católicos.

Parte Vieja The Parte Vieja is crawling with all sorts of bars. The area comes to life from about 8 pm virtually every day of the week, although weekends are predictably more intense. Late-night bars rock on when the tapas bars close, with Calle de la Pescadería and Calle de Fermín Calbetón being two of the busier streets. The pudgy little glasses many people drink their beer and wine from are called *zurritos* – their size allows the locals to indulge their custom of fitting in as many drinking establishments as possible in one evening.

It is difficult to single out particular bars, as they're all full of merrymakers. *Bar Urbia* on Calle del Puerto is a downstairs dance bar that attracts a mixed crowd. *Tic Tac Pub* on Calle de Embeltran is similar.

If you'd like to have a swig of Basque cider *(sidra)*, head for *Sagardotegia Itxaropena (Calle de Embeltran 16)*.

Calle de los Reyes Católicos The other easily accessible concentration of nocturnal activity is down by Calle de los Reyes Católicos, just south of the cathedral.

Just before you launch into it, have an early evening libation at the great old nameless *bar* on the corner of Calle de San Martín and Calle de Lezo.

Copos Bar, on the corner of Calle de General Prim and Calle de los Reyes Católicos, has a laid-back pub feel to it. *Udaberri-berri*, on the corner of Calle de los Reyes Católicos and Calle de Larramendi, has a cool bar upstairs and a rather hysterical Spanish music karaoke scene downstairs. If that's not loud enough, try *Sitres (Calle de Sánchez Toca 3)* for some head-banging heavy metal. *Marabillas*, next door, couldn't be further removed – a great mellow spot for a late-night snack and tipple.

Discos & Nightclubs One of the better known discos is *Ku*, a taxi ride away near the Monte Igueldo funicular. It keeps its doors open until around 3 am. Closer to the centre, *Bataplan* and *Rotonda* are both on the beach promenade. *Discóbolo* on Alameda del Boulevard is the nearest disco to the Parte Vieja.

Getting There & Away

For further information on crossing the border with France, turn to the Irún section later.

Air The city's airport (information on ☎ 943 64 12 67) is 22km out of town, near Hondarribia. There are regular flights to Madrid and occasional charters to major European capital cities.

Bus The main estación de autobuses, some 20 minutes walk south of the Parte Vieja, is basically a car park between Plaza de Pío XII and the river. Ticket offices huddle just north of it along Avenida de Sancho el Sabio and Paseo de Vizcaya.

Turytrans buses (☎ 943 46 23 60) serve many major European destinations. Enatcar (☎ 943 46 80 87) has weekday buses to Sevilla (7500 ptas) via Salamanca (3700 ptas). Vibasa (aka Irbarsa; ☎ 943 45 75 00) has three buses daily to Barcelona for 2450 ptas. Continental Auto (943 46 90 74) runs nine times daily to Madrid (3685 ptas) and seven times daily to Vitoria (930 ptas). La Roncalesa (☎ 943 46 10 64) has eight buses daily to Pamplona (750 ptas) and six to Zaragoza (2335 ptas for the fast service). The PESA (☎ 943 46 39 74) company runs half-hourly buses to Bilbao along the *autopista* from 6.30 am to 10 pm for 1060 ptas. It also sends a few buses along the coast as far as Lekeitio and has twice-daily buses to Biarritz and Bayonne in France.

Buses depart regularly for Pasaia, Irún and Hondarribia (195 ptas) from Plaza de Guipúzcoa.

Train The main RENFE train station is just across the Río Urumea on Paseo de Francia, on a line linking Paris to Madrid. There are six services daily to Madrid, taking anything from six to nine hours. The cheapest one-way ticket is 4400 ptas on a night train (200 ptas more on the slower day trains). Trains to Barcelona run a few times each day via Pamplona and Zaragoza. The cheapest one-way fare is 4600 ptas.

There is only one direct train to Paris (a 2nd-class, one-way ticket costs 11,000 ptas), but you can pick up plenty more from the French border town of Hendaye. About half a dozen trains daily run to Hendaye from San Sebastián and there are plenty to Irún, just on the Spanish side of the frontier.

There are also daily trains going as far afield as Alicante, Algeciras, Salamanca, La Coruña, Vigo, Porto (in Portugal) and Lisbon (one daily).

A second station is used by the private rail company (international passes not valid) Eusko Trenbideak (ET/FV) south of the town centre near Plaza de Centenario. Rather slow trains head west to Bilbao (change at Ermua; 800 ptas) via Durango (600 ptas). Others go east to Hendaye via Irún for 125 ptas.

Car & Motorcycle The A-8 tollway passes through San Sebastián to Bilbao on the west and into France (where it becomes the A-63) to the east. You can avoid the toll on the virtually parallel N-634. The most picturesque route west is along the minor coast roads. The main route south is the N-I, which runs to Madrid via Vitoria.

Rental Several major companies are represented by agencies in San Sebastián, including Atesa (☎ 943 46 30 13), Calle de Gregorio Ordoñez 10; Avis (☎ 943 46 15 27), Calle del Triunfo 2; Europcar (☎ 943 32 23 04) in the RENFE train station; and Hertz (☎ 943 46 10 84), Calle de Zubieta 5.

Bicycle You can rent bicycles and mountain bikes at Comet (☎ 943 42 23 51), Avenida de la Libertad 6.

EAST OF SAN SEBASTIÁN
Pasaia
Pasaia (Pasajes) is asphyxiated by a clot of highway bypasses, industry and a port, so it's unlikely Victor Hugo would want to hang around here at all now, as he did for a summer back in 1843. Still, down by the waterside two of the three constituent bits of Pasaia retain some charm. Calle de San Juan and the area immediately around the central square are lined with some pretty houses vaguely reminiscent of what one can better contemplate in Hondarribia, to the east.

Irún
A more nondescript introduction to Spain you could hardly get, so you'd best move straight on to Hondarribia or San Sebastián.

If you do find yourself obliged to stay, don't despair. Half a dozen relatively cheap places are within a stone's throw of the trains. *Pensión Los Fronterizos (☎ 943 61 92 05, Estación Kalea 7)* is a perfectly clean and decent little place with rooms for 2500/3500 ptas.

Getting There & Away To shuttle between Irún and Hendaye in France, take the half-hourly train (known as 'El Topo' – 'the mole') for 105 ptas from the ET/FV station on Paseo de Colón – look for the 'Eusko Tren' sign. Regular trains to San Sebastián also use this line, or you can take a cercanía from the RENFE station, five minutes walk to the south. Frequent buses connect Irún (there's a stop on Paseo de Colón) with San Sebastián (Plaza de Guipúzcoa) and Hondarribia.

Long-distance trains from the RENFE station trundle to Madrid, Barcelona, Alicante, Galicia and other destinations. Long-distance buses to many destinations also depart from here.

Up to 10 trains daily leave the SNCF station in Hendaye for Paris (six of them high-speed TGVs). Other trains serve Pau, Lille and Bordeaux, and there is a daily train to Rome via Ventimiglia.

Hondarribia
Hondarribia (Fuenterrabía in Castilian), founded by the Romans and the scene of several sieges throughout its history, has managed to preserve its charming old city. Although it has a character all its own, the whiff of France, lying just across the bay, is somehow also perceptible in the reserved orderliness of the place.

The tourist office (☎ 943 64 54 58), Jabier Ugarte Kalea 6, is open Monday to Friday from 9 am to 1.30 pm and 4 to 6.30 pm and Saturday from 10 am to 2 pm.

You can enter the partly intact old town walls through the Puerta de Santa María, traditionally the main gate. To the left and right as you climb Kale Nagusia are the proud houses of Hondarribia's one-time high-fliers. Past the Gothic Iglesia de Santa María de la Asunción you arrive in the expansive Plaza de Armas, dominated by a palace attributed to King Sancho Abarca de Navarra but renovated by Spain's Carlos I. Around the other sides of the plaza spreads a profusion of the engaging wood-beam houses that are a hallmark of the town. The town also has a fine beach.

Places to Stay & Eat There are about 10 places to choose from, all of them raising prices a bit in summer. The cheapest option is *Hostal Álvarez Quintero* (☎ 943 64 22 99, Beñat Etxepare Kalea 2), with singles/doubles from 3400/4600 ptas. Those with more dosh have a tempting range of options in the *casco*, starting with the homy and postcard-pretty *Hotel San Nicolas* (☎ 943 64 42 78, Plaza de Armas 2), with rooms starting at 5500/6500 ptas. At the other end of the scale is the grand *Parador El Emperador* (☎ 943 64 55 00, fax 943 64 21 53), housed in the Castillo de Carlos V. Rooms are 12,000/15,000 ptas plus IVA.

The casco has oodles of eating places, though none are particularly cheap. In the new part of town, *Bar Maitane*, just behind the tourist office, is popular with locals, has good bar snacks and serves up low-priced meals.

Getting There & Away Buses leave from near the post office for Irún, San Sebastián and occasionally across the border to Hendaye.

SOUTH OF SAN SEBASTIÁN
Cider Territory

The lush green hinterland just in from the coast, far removed from worldly San Se-bastián, has long been home to a liquid tradition most pleasing to the palate. The cider produced here is like pure apple juice, only with an alcoholic kick. The best place to look is in and around the towns of Hernani and Astigarraga. Most stay open only from January to the end of April, the season for making the cider. They then bottle the surplus and close the doors to their bars, though a few stay open as restaurants.

A well-signposted series of half a dozen sidrerías lies along a 2km winding, hilly road off the narrow highway connecting Hernani to Astigarraga (3km apart). To get to the area, take a bus from Calle de la Reina Regente in San Sebastián.

If you turn up out of season, head for *Sagardotegia Mendizabal* (☎ 943 55 57 47), the last of the above-mentioned series, or *Sagardotegia Petritegi* (☎ 943 45 71 88) in Astigarraga itself. Their restaurants get packed out on weekends, so call in advance.

Walking in the Hills

Ordizia, 30km south of San Sebastián and served by frequent buses, is the best base from which to visit the hills to the east. The popular 1½ hour walk up to the top of Monte Txindoki, one of the highest peaks (1341m) in the Sierra de Aralar, begins from the village of **Larraitz**, about 8km to the east (follow the signs for Zaldibia). A few buses make the run from Ordizia on weekends only. More ambitious walkers head for other peaks farther into the chain and even make for the Santuario de San Miguel in Excelsis – a good day's strong hiking to the south-east in Navarra.

Push on south from Ordizia to Zagama and the hamlet of **Otzaurte** just beyond, and you can pick up a stretch of the GR-12 trail heading 5km westwards to the Refugio de San Adrián and a **natural tunnel** of the same name (higher up from the refuge). This medieval pilgrim route linked the heart of Spain with the rest of Europe. Traces of an early medieval highway can still be seen on the approach to the tunnel – inside which rests a small chapel. The medieval road then emerges from the tunnel and continues southwards.

Trains serve Otzaurte from Vitoria. The refuge supposedly is open on weekends and in summer, but it's a little unreliable.

The Interior

The hills rising to the south between San Sebastián and Bilbao are dotted with several towns offering an appealing variety of architectural monuments, all settled into a luxuriant green backdrop reminiscent of Tuscany – but much more affordable. There is plenty of accommodation, with *nekazalturismoas* (agrotourism homes) spread throughout the area.

Santuario de Loyola Just outside Azpeitia (12km south of the A8 motorway) lies the portentous Santuario de Loyola, dedicated to St Ignatius, the founder of the Jesuit order. This sumptuous baroque spectacle seems out of place in its peaceful rural setting. Inside, the circular-plan basilica is laden with dark grey marble and plenty of ornament. The house where Loyola was born is conserved in one of the two great wings of the *santuario*. It is open daily from 10 am to 12.30 pm and 3.30 to 7 pm, but you can generally wander into the church any time that services are not on.

Bergara Bear south-west from Azpeitia along the Río Urola, and a delightful back road (GI-3750) winds through the hills to the rather scraggly town of Bergara. The main square and Iglesia de San Pedro retain just enough reminders of a prosperous past to merit a stop.

Oñati One of the most enticing towns in the interior of the País Vasco, Oñati is a short hop from Bergara down the GI-627. The tourist office (☎ 943 78 34 53) on Foru Enparantza is open Monday to Friday from 10 am to 1 pm and 3.30 to 7.30 pm, Saturday from 10 am to 1 pm and 4.30 to 6.30 pm and Sunday from 11 am to 2 pm and 4.30 to 6.30 pm.

A Renaissance gem is the **Universidad de Sancti Spiritus**, where for 350 years alumni were schooled in philosophy, law and medicine until its closure in 1902. The plateresque façade and courtyard are the highlights. Virtually across the road stands the **Iglesia de San Miguel**, a Late Gothic creation with its cloister built over the river. The church faces onto the main square, Foru Enparantza, with the eye-catching baroque façade of the *ayuntamiento* (town hall) on the eastern side.

You can stay at the *Hostal Echeverria* (☎ 943 78 04 60, Kalebarria Kalea 19), which has rooms for as little as 2200/3500 ptas in the off season. Stretch just a bit more, though, and you can live in rural luxury at the *Nekazalturismoa Arregi* (☎ 943 78 36 57, ☎ 943 78 08 24), 2km south of town. This splendid home is set in beautiful countryside, charges just 3500/5000 ptas for singles/doubles and has a kitchen for guests to use.

For inventive cuisine in town, try *Itturitxo Jatetxea (Atzeko Kalea 32)*. Their scrumptious set *menú* is 900 ptas for lunch and 1300 ptas for dinner.

There are frequent buses to San Sebastián, Bilbao and Vitoria.

Arantzazu About 10km south of Oñati, the modern Santuario de Arantzazu is something of a shrine for Basques, since Nuestra Señora de Arantzazu is Guipúzcoa's patron saint. Various modern artists had a hand in its design, including Eduardo Chillida, who did the entrance doors. The road up and the setting are themselves worth the effort, and the whole area lends itself to some nice walks – the Oñati tourist office can sell you a collection of route maps. That said, there are no buses go to Arantzazu from Oñati, although there is supposed to be a weekend service.

ALONG THE COAST

The coast road out of San Sebastián snakes its way past some spectacular ocean scenes, with cove after cove stretching west and verdant fields suddenly dropping away in rocky shafts to the sea. The bulk of the towns and fishing villages on the way are, with a few exceptions, an average lot – richer pickings lie farther west in Cantabria, Asturias and Galicia. Fairly regular buses from San Sebastián run as far as Lekeitio, and *agroturismos* and camping grounds are plentiful.

Getaria

If surfing is your thing, you may want to check into one of the serried ranks of hotels fronting the long beach in **Zarautz**, 23km west of San Sebastián, which hosts a round of the World Surfing Championship every September.

Otherwise, bypass this holiday haven and pull in at Getaria, a small medieval fishing settlement huddled in the shadow of El Ratón (the Mouse), the distinctive islet visible long before you enter the town. The sober mass of the 14th century Iglesia de San Salvador stands sentinel over the port, which back in 1522 saw the return of its most illustrious son, Juan Sebastián Elcano, after more than three years spent in the first successful circumnavigation of the globe. He had joined Magellan's (Magallanes to the Spaniards) expedition in 1519 – its aim to find a passage to India across the Atlantic and Pacific. Magellan and most of the fleet perished, but Elcano crawled back to Spain with just 18 other survivors.

A couple of local homes offer cheap beds, and the *Pensión Getariano Ostatua* (☎ 943 14 05 67) has singles/doubles at 4000/5300 ptas plus IVA. Getaria is a fine place for a meal, with a series of outdoor *harbourfront restaurants* all grilling up the fresh catch of the day.

Zumaia

A few kilometres farther around the coast, Zumaia has sprawled itself out to accommodate summer beach-goers aplenty. The **Playa de Izturun** beach is wedged in among cliffs while, a couple of kilometres east of the town centre, the Playa de Santiago is a more open strand. Just near the latter stands the **Museo de Zuloaga**, in the Basque artist

Zuloaga's one-time farmhouse and now containing some of his important works as well as a handful by other big names, such as Goya and El Greco. The museum is open Wednesday to Sunday from 4 to 8 pm.

Mutriku

The picturesque fishing village of Mutriku is clamped by a steep rocky vice cut into the coast, its streets winding tortuously down to a small harbour. *Restaurante Zumalage* up above the eastern end of town affords great views. You can expect to pay about 2000 ptas for lunch. Five *camping grounds* surround the town, largely because of the fine beach of **Saturrarán**, a few kilometres west.

Ondarroa

Fishing is big business in modern Ondarroa and that's about all there is to say of the place. It's not unpleasant, though, and the *Hostal Vega* (☎ 94 683 00 02, Calle de Antiguako Ama 8) has large clean rooms overlooking the water for 2600 ptas per person. There is no shortage of harbourside eateries and bars.

Inland to Markina

About 10km inland from Ondarroa, the pretty town of Markina is the home of pelota – the local frontón is known as the Universidad de la Pelota! Five kilometres south lies the birthplace of Simón Bolívar, the great early 19th century South American independence fighter. A **museum** here dedicated to his exploits is open Tuesday to Friday from 10 am to 1 pm and weekends from noon to 2 pm. In July and August it is open Tuesday to Sunday from 5 to 7 pm. Hourly buses between Ondarroa and Bilbao stop at Iruzubieta, from where it's a 2km walk.

Lekeitio

Another 12km west from Ondarroa brings you to this attractive fishing town. Of the two beaches, the one just east of the river is nicer. The harbourside is dominated by the Late Gothic **Iglesia de Santa María de la Asunción**. Unfortunately, the hostales here are not cheap and they fill up quickly in summer. Alternatively, in summer you could try *Camping Endai*, on Playa Menedexa, a few kilometres east. The waterfront and back streets of the old part of town are teeming with bars and snack joints.

Elantxobe

Sticking to the 'coast road' unfortunately does not mean hugging the cliffs, although occasionally you get some great views. The tiny hamlet of Elantxobe is worth a look, seemingly glued onto the almost perpendicular rock walls leading down to the sea. A couple of buses run from Gernika every day except Sunday.

The odd bus from Gernika also crawls up the broad Ría de Mundaka to the lovely beaches of Laga and Laida, a couple of kilometres west of Elantxobe.

Cueva de Santimamiñe

Just north of Gernika is a turn-off to the grotto of Santimamiñe. Apart from some impressive stalactites and stalagmites, you can also see prehistoric cave paintings. The obligatory guided tours (maximum 15 people per tour) start at 10 and 11.15 am, 12.30, 4.30 and 6 pm, and are very popular, so arrive early or inquire about organised trips at the Gernika tourist office. There is no public transport, although the Gernika-Lekeitio bus can drop you at Kortezubi, from where it's a 40 minute walk.

Gernika

The attraction of Gernika (Guernica) lies more in the symbolic than in any specific sights. Here, on 26 April 1937, Hitler's Condor Legion, sent to aid Franco's forces, unleashed the first-ever massive air raid against a civilian target. Almost 2000 people died in the attack, later immortalised in Picasso's nightmare vision *Guernica* (the painting is now housed in the Reina Sofía gallery in Madrid, though it may be moved here or to the new Guggenheim museum in Bilbao).

The events of that day are captured in detail in the **Gernika Museoa**, in the Foru

Plaza, which was rebuilt to its original state after the entire centre of town was demolished. This new museum is dedicated to civilian victims of war: photo displays bring to life the damage not only done here but also to cities such as Hiroshima, Warsaw, Baghdad, and Sarajevo. It is open daily from 11 am to 2 pm and 4 to 8 pm (200 ptas).

In the grounds of the **Casa de Juntas** above the plaza is the remains of the stump of the Árbol de Gernika, a tree beneath which the Basque parliament traditionally used to meet. The local government now meets inside the Casa, where a huge stained-glass window depicts historic scenes. Down the road, the **Euskal Herriko Museoa** is housed in the 18th century Palacio de Montefuerte. The museum, dedicated to Basque history and culture, is open Tuesday to Saturday from 10 am to 2 pm and 4 to 7 pm and Sunday from 10 am to 1.30 pm (free). There are pleasant gardens behind it.

Gernika is an easy day trip from Bilbao by bus or train (from Atxuri station). There are a few hotels, but frankly you are better off staying in Bilbao or pushing on northwards to Mundaka.

Mundaka

The legend of one of the world's longest left-handers still attracts surfers the world over to this unassuming little estuary town 10km north of Gernika. They may well want to track down Craig at his Billabong surf gear shop. He came to Mundaka at the beginning of the 1980s and hasn't been able to drag himself away since. The surf is at its best in September and October.

Aside from *Camping Portuondo* (☎ 94 687 63 68), there is little in the way of cheap accommodation. *Hotel El Puerto* (☎ 94 687 67 25, Portu Kalea 1) has the prettiest location overlooking the town's minute fishing port, but charges anything up to 5000/7000 ptas plus IVA in the high season. It also has a popular tapas bar spilling onto the patio. Buses and ET/FV trains connecting Bilbao with Bermeo stop here.

Bermeo

A stone's throw up the coast, the fishing port of Bermeo looks appealing at first sight, but turns out to be a rather sprawling and gritty place. Those interested in commercial fishing could poke their noses into the **Museo del Pescador** (Fishing Museum). Housed in a 16th century *casa-torre*, the style of aristocratic house typical in much of the País Vasco, it is replete with model boats and a great many hooks. The tourist office (☎ 94 618 65 43) is at Askatasun Bidea 2, on the waterfront.

There are five places to stay. Cheapest are *Pensión Talape* (☎ 94 688 16 77, Calle de Garabilla tar José 1), with singles/doubles for 3000/4000 ptas, and the *agroturismo* (☎ 94 688 23 12, Calle de Artike Auzoa 16), with doubles for 4500 ptas. If you want raucous blue-collar bars, this could be a good place to look. Buses and ET/FV trains run to Bilbao.

The coast road west from Bermeo offers some tantalising glimpses of the rugged and at times forbidding Basque coast. A few kilometres beyond Bermeo, the **Ermita de San Juan de Gaztelugatxe** juts out to sea from an odd lick of land. The minor fishing village of **Bakio**, on around the tip, has an attractive beach.

BILBAO

Bilbao (Bilbo), the capital of Vizcaya (Bizkaia) province, has a twin vocation which becomes obvious from whatever angle you approach the city. Maritime commerce and, from a later date, heavy industry have dominated the life of Bilbao since its emergence in the Middle Ages.

Today much of the industry has gone – a chimney stands in the green plain of the Parque de Extebarria as a solitary reminder of what once lay behind the city's prosperity. Shipbuilding, too, is an endangered species, but the port remains busy, and the city – easily the largest in the País Vasco – has managed to transform itself from industrial centre to financial capital of the north.

City authorities have made great efforts to thrust Bilbao boldly into the future by spearheading ambitious urban renewal projects. The recently-opened metro line, which runs all the way through the string of interlocking suburbs to Plentzia, is one, but what really draws attention is the new Museo Guggenheim, a wonder of contemporary architecture and an extraordinary gallery of modern art.

Central Bilbao's business-like and sober air is reminiscent of many a French provincial capital, its architectural face reflecting the bourgeois boom days of the mid-19th and early 20th centuries. Hang around for an evening, though, and any comparisons with stuffy French cities disappear in a whirlwind of frenzied partying in Las Siete Calles – the nucleus of the medieval *casco viejo*. Here the Spanish propensity for raucous night-long revelry is taken for a serious spin – there is nothing sober about a weekend night out in Bilbao.

History

Bilbao was granted the title of *villa* (a city statute) in 1300 and medieval *bilbaínos* went about their business in the bustle of Las Siete Calles and on the wharves of San Antón and Abando. As the boats got bigger and the business more sophisticated, the quays moved farther towards the coast and the city grew. Conquest of the Americas stimulated trade growth and by the late 19th century the area's skyscape was crimped by the slender smoke stacks of furnaces and smelters. Bilbao's golden age was fed by steelworks, shipbuilding yards and chemical plants, though the crises that have affected all of Europe's heavy industries in the past few decades have also hit Bilbao. Commerce remains buoyant, however, and the city sees itself increasingly as a centre of learning and culture, to which its two universities and several good museums attest.

Orientation

The nerve-centre of Bilbao, the Casco Viejo, lies bundled up on the right bank of the Ría de Bilbao, also sometimes known as the Río Nervión, which it becomes upriver.

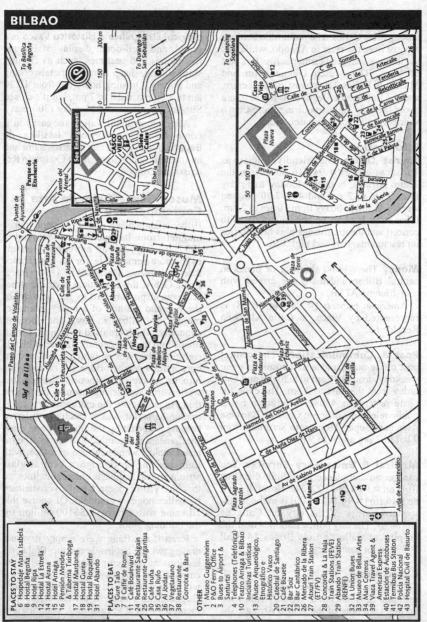

BILBAO

PLACES TO STAY
6 Hospedaje María Isabela
8 Hostal Begoña
9 Hostal Ripa
12 Hostal La Estrella
14 Hostal Arana
15 Hotel Arriaga
16 Pensión Méndez & Taberna Txiriboga
17 Hostal Gurea
18 Hostal Mardones
19 Hostal Roquefer
31 Hotel Abando

PLACES TO EAT
5 Gure Talo
7 Il Caffe de Roma
11 Café Boulevard
24 Restaurante Saibigain
25 Restaurante Gargantua
30 Café Iruña
35 Casa Rufo
36 Al Jordan
37 Vegetariano
38 Restaurante Gorrotxa & Bars

OTHER
1 Museo Guggenheim
2 P&O Ferry Office
3 Buses to Airport & Santurtzi
4 Telephones (Telefónica)
10 Teatro Arriaga & Bilbao Iniciativas Turísticas
13 Museo Arqueológico, Etnográfico e Histórico Vasco
20 Catedral de Santiago
21 Café Bizuete
22 Bar Soiz
23 Bar Cantábrico
26 Mercado de la Ribera
27 Atxuri Train Station
28 Concordia & La Naja Train Stations (FEVE) (ET/FV)
29 Abando Train Station (RENFE)
32 La Unión Buses
33 Museo de Bellas Artes
34 Main Correos
39 Viaca Travel Agent & American Express
40 Estación de Autobuses
41 Termibus Bus Station
42 Policía Nacional
43 Hospital Civil de Basurto

Many hotels, restaurants and an innumerable concentration of bars are found in among Siete Calles. The main train stations are just over the river in Abando, while bus stations are scattered farther across this part of town. The Museo Guggenheim and Museo de Bellas Artes, west of the centre, and the Basílica de Begoña, to the east, are about the only sights requiring more than a shortish walk from the casco viejo.

Information

Tourist Office The friendly Iniciativas Turísticas office (☎ 94 416 00 22), in the Teatro Arriaga, is open Monday to Friday from 9 am to 2 pm and 4 to 7.30 pm and weekends and holidays from 10 am to 2 pm. It has a free booklet, updated quarterly, with concert and theatre listings plus helpful tips on restaurants, bars and nightlife.

Money There is no shortage of banks in central Bilbao and many are armed with user-friendly ATMs.

American Express (☎ 94 444 48 58) is represented by Viaca, at Calle Alameda Recalde 68.

Post & Communications The central post office on Alameda de Urquijo is open weekdays from 8.30 am to 8.30 pm and Saturday from 9.30 am to 2 pm. The code for poste restante is 48080. Telefónica has a public telephone office at Calle de Barroeta Aldamar 7, open Monday to Saturday from 9 am to 2 pm and 4 to 9 pm.

Medical & Emergency Services You can get an ambulance by calling the Cruz Roja on ☎ 94 422 22 22. The Hospital Civil de Basurto (☎ 94 441 87 00) is in the southwestern corner of the city on Calle de Gurtubay. The city police station is near the hospital at Calle de Luis Briñas 14. Call ☎ 092 in an emergency.

Casco Viejo

The casco viejo, loaded with bars and restaurants, is in itself a 'sight'. While wandering, take note of the **Teatro Arriaga**, the arcaded Plaza Nueva, and the sooty Gothic **Catedral de Santiago**. The **Museo Arqueológico, Etnográfico e Histórico Vasco** is a proud, and well-done, display of Basque livelihoods and pastimes, such as fishing, shipbuilding, sheep farming, metalworking and pottery. Opening hours are from 10.30 am to 1.30 pm and 4 to 7 pm, but it's closed Sunday afternoon and Monday (300 ptas).

After a long uphill walk to the east you'll come to the monumental **Basílica de Begoña**, home of the city's patron saint and an interesting crossover from Gothic to Renaissance contours.

Museo Guggenheim de Arte Contemporáneo

Bilbao's showpiece and an instant tourist magnet from its opening in September 1997, the Guggenheim museum is perhaps even more remarkable for its appearance than its contents. Designed by US architect Frank Gehry, this fantastical, swirling structure was inspired in part by the anatomy of the fish and the hull of a boat – both elements of Bilbao's past and present economy, which are used to project a fresh image into the 21st century. Indeed it blends right into the river on which it sits, and incorporates a nearby bridge and railroad line into its sphere of aesthetic influence. It's well worth wandering around the entire thing to appreciate the extraordinary imagination behind it, and to catch the different colours reflected by the titanium and glass shell, meant to resemble fish scales. The interior makes wonderful use of space, with light pouring in through a central glass atrium and an emphasis on organic lines, so that the visitor doesn't feel overwhelmed by hallucinogenic grandeur. Of course this all came with a price: US$100 million for the building alone.

Even if the thing were empty it would draw gawkers, but inside is a top-flight collection of contemporary art, with an emphasis on the past 40 years. Many of the works are supplied by the New York Guggenheim's modern art riches, supplemented by local acquisitions, commissions and temporary exhibitions. A gallery on the ground floor is longer than a football pitch and contains works by Warhol and Liechtenstein, plus Richard Serra's 1996 enormous steel *Snake* – walk through it and check out the aural effects it can create. Rooms upstairs contain works such as Picasso's *Mandolin and Guitar*, a Modigliani nude, paintings by Braque, Ernst, Schiele, Kandinsky and Miró, and a fat Botero statue.

The museum is open Tuesday to Sunday from 11 am to 8 pm (700 ptas, students half-price). Guided tours in English, which provide a wonderful means of comprehending the building and some of its more bizarre contents, take place at 1 and 4 pm (at 4 pm only on weekends). Sign up 30 minutes before at the information desk. Given the museum's popularity (it saw 700,000 visitors in its first eight months), try to arrive early.

Museo de Bellas Artes

Decidedly diminished in significance by the Guggenheim, just 300m up the street, this is nevertheless a wonderful art gallery in its own right. It spans the millennium, from Gothic statuettes to 20th century pop art. Features include a selection of Flemish works by Jordaens and van Dyck, a healthy dose of El Greco, Velázquez and Goya, and recent efforts by the likes of Francis Bacon as well as several regional artists. World-class temporary exhibits are also a strong lure. The museum is open Tuesday to Saturday from 10 am to 1.30 pm and 4 to 7.30 pm and Sunday from 10 am to 2 pm (400 ptas, free on Wednesday, students half-price); you can get a 900 ptas ticket for both this and the Guggenheim.

Special Events

Carnaval, held in February, is celebrated with particular vigour, but the grandest fiesta in Bilbao begins on the first Saturday after 15 August and is known as the Aste Nagusia (Big Week). Traditional parades and music mix with a full program of cultural events over 10 days.

About 25km north of Bilbao, Getxo hosts the first of a series of week-long international jazz festivals held in the País Vasco in July (the second takes place in Vitoria and the last in San Sebastián).

Places to Stay – Budget

Camping The nearest pleasant place to camp is *Camping Sopelana* (☎ 94 676 21 20), by the beach in the town of the same name north-east of central Bilbao – it's on the metro line.

Pensiones & Hostales *Pensión Méndez* (☎ 94 16 03 64, Calle de Santa María 13) is about as central as you can get and it's cheap too, at 2000/3000 ptas for singles/doubles. Be prepared to sleep little because of all the street noise. The friendly *Hostal Roquefer* (☎ 94 415 07 55, Calle de la Lotería 2) has rooms without own bath starting at 2000/3500 ptas and doubles with for 4500 ptas.

Hostal La Estrella (☎ 94 416 40 66, Calle de María Múñoz 6) is a charming, brightly painted little place also right in the heart of the old town. Rooms without bath go for 2500/3750 ptas and those with bath are 3100/5000 ptas.

Hostal Gurea (☎ 94 416 32 99, Calle de Bidebarrieta 14) is another solid choice with singles/doubles costing 3100/3500 ptas without private bath and 3450/4150 ptas with bath. *Hostal Mardones* (☎ 94 415 3105, Calle de Jardines 4) is excellent value. Rooms are small, but have beautiful hardwood floors. Bathless singles start at 3000 ptas and *en suite* doubles cost from 6000 to 8000 ptas.

Hostal Arana (☎ 94 415 64 11, Calle de Bidebarrieta 2) is a little more expensive than your average hostal but well placed on the edge of the casco – just far enough away to ensure a quiet night's sleep. Rooms with private bath start at 4500/5800/7200 ptas plus IVA and cost about 1000 ptas less without bath.

On the other side of the river, *Hospedaje María Isabela* (☎ 94 424 8566, Calle de la Amistad 5) is characterless but cheap at

1500 ptas per person. **Hostal Begoña** (☎ 94 423 01 34), just down the street at No 2, is another reliable if unexciting option. Rooms without private bath start at 2600/3800 ptas.

Places to Stay – Mid-Range

A charming and moderately priced mid-level option is **Hotel Arriaga** (☎ 94 479 00 01, Calle de la Ribera 3) right by the theatre. Rooms here are 5500/7500 ptas plus IVA. **Hotel Ripa** (☎ 94 423 96 77, Calle de Ripa 3) just across the river is also fine but can get a little noisy. You pay 5500/8000 ptas plus IVA.

Places to Stay – Top End

Of the many upper-end hotels in town, **Hotel Abando** (☎ 94 423 62 00 Calle de Colón de Larreátegui 7) is well situated and offers doubles for 17,000 ptas plus IVA, reduced to 11,000 ptas plus IVA on the weekend.

Places to Eat

Some of Bilbao's better restaurants offer what's called a *Menú Bit*, a lunch or dinner special which allows you a taste of haute cuisine without assaulting the bank account. The tourist office's quarterly booklet includes a list of these. Otherwise, there are plenty of eating options across the centre of town. Many of Bilbao's bars, including some of those listed later under Bars, have a restaurant attached, usually out the back. To pack your own, the **Mercado de le Ribera** is a bustling riverside indoor market in the Casco Viejo, with three storeys of meat, fish, cheese and produce.

Restaurants *Restaurante Saibigain (Calle de Barrencalle Barrena 16)* is a good bar-restaurant. There is a tasty set *menú* for 2300 ptas or you can pick away at tapas at the bar beneath rows of heavy-hanging hams overhead. Good lunchtime value is the set meal at **Restaurante Gargantua** *(Calle de Barrencalle Barrena 3)* which costs from 1500 ptas.

Gure Talo *(Calle del Príncipe 1)* is an earthy place serving up good Basque food and it's popular with bilbaínos. The set lunch meal costs 950 ptas.

Vegetarians have at least two options in town, including the aptly-named *Vegetariano (Alameda de Urquijo 33)* open from 1 to 4 pm only.

For a trip to the other end of the Med, try **Al Jordan** *(Calle de Elcano 26)*. You can have a mint tea and baklava for breakfast, or an Arabic evening meal with belly dancing.

Casa Rufo (☎ 94 443 21 72, Calle Hurtado de Amézaga 5) is an extraordinary place – an intimate comedor behind a gourmet food store. Prices for the inventive Basque cooking are moderately expensive and you should call in advance to be sure of a table.

Restaurante Gorrotxa *(Alameda de Urquijo 30)* is in an arcade crammed with bars in the new part of town, so after enjoying gourmet nouvelle and traditional Basque cooking (count on at least 3000 ptas a head), you need do no more than stumble out the door to continue merry-making into the wee hours.

Cafés Bilbao is graced with a pleasing collection of fine old cafés, of which **Café Iruña**, going strong since 1903 on Calle de Colón Larreátegui, is probably the most celebrated. The décor in one half of the café has its inspiration in the Alhambra – right down to the endlessly repeated carved inscriptions in Arabic declaring 'la ilah illa Allah' – 'There is no god but Allah'.

Café Boulevard, just by the Teatro Arriaga, is equally atmospheric and, in addition to great coffee, does lunchtime platos combinados for 800 ptas. **Il Caffe de Roma** *(Calle de Navarra 6)* has a wide variety of coffee and tea in a modern earth-toned décor.

In summer, **Café Bizuete** sets up tables in the square next to the cathedral. The porticoed Plaza Nueva is another good spot for coffee and people-watching.

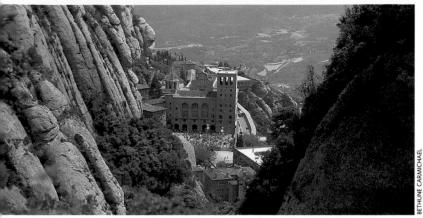

The Monestir de Montserrat, one of Catalunya's most important shrines

Summer in Catalunya, near Palafrugell

The Teatre-Museu Dalí, Figueres, is a trip through surrealist artist Salvador Dalí's imagination (Catalunya)

The 11th century Església de Sant Esteve, Andorra la Vella (Andorra)

Autumn colours in the fields in the Pyrenees (Aragón)

Entertainment

Bilbao is a good place to catch a stage show or concert, with two main theatres and its own symphony orchestra. *La Ría del Ocio* (125 ptas) is a handy weekly what's-on guide to all the bars, concerts, film and theatre in Bilbao; it's sold at newsagents.

Bars There are several areas to search out nightlife, but the most obvious is the central Siete Calles. That said, it can be extremely crowded, rowdy and adolescent. Calle de Barrencalle is probably the most concentrated scene of drinking and post-tipple lunacy in the country.

Taberna Txiriboga, next to the Pensión Méndez at Calle de Santa María 13, is a curious mix – a kind of Basque nationalist-cum-gay crowd hang out here. It has a cheap set *menú* for 900 ptas in the comedor out the back.

Bar Soiz, on the corner of Calle de la Torre and Calle de Barrencalle, is a tiny den with a weird and wonderful collection of cocktails. The nearby *Bar Cantábrico* is a popular if more straightforward watering hole.

There is a line of bars along La Ripa, between the Puente del Ayuntamiento and the Puente del Arenal, while the zone around the intersection of Calle de Licenciado Poza and Calle de Gregorio de la Revilla is a fruitful hunting ground.

Getting There & Away

Air Iberia flies from Bilbao to Madrid, Barcelona, London and Paris.

Bus Most buses use one of two main stations. Long-distance services to Madrid (3245 ptas; up to 12 daily), Barcelona (4750 ptas; four daily) and other cities depart from the estación de autobuses at Avenida de la Autonomía 17. Most other buses use the new Termibus lot in the south-western corner of town (metro: San Mamés). Turytrans and ALSA buses serve destinations along the coast to Gijón (west), and PESA has a half-hourly service to San Sebastián and other towns across the País Vasco.

Enatcar buses serve many international destinations from here. For Vitoria, go to La Union's station at Calle de Henao 29.

Train RENFE's Abando station in the city centre sends out three trains daily to Madrid (4300 ptas) and two to Barcelona (4800 ptas), Alicante and Galicia.

Next door is the rather fancy Concordia train station used by the FEVE private rail company for trains west into Cantabria and Asturias. Below it is La Naja cercanías station, where trains run to Santurtzi.

ET/FV has local Basque services from Atxuri train station, which is across the river and a short way south of Concordia. There are trains to Bermeo via Gernika and Mundaka, and others to San Sebastián (change at Ermua).

Car & Motorcycle The A-68 tollway leads directly south and is the quickest way to make for Vitoria, Burgos and Madrid. The A-8 autopista west to Santander is not a tollway, but you pay heading east to San Sebastián. In all cases there are alternative highways that, in general, are slower but more picturesque.

Boat P&O ferries leave for Portsmouth from Santurtzi, about 14km north-west of Bilbao's city centre. The voyage takes about 36 hours from England and 28 hours the other way. Service is curtailed in mid-winter. From Portsmouth, sailings are on Tuesday and Saturday at 8 pm and from Bilbao they leave Monday and Thursday at 12.30 pm.

The range of fares is bewildering, depending on season and other factors. Figure on a one-way foot passenger fare of 11,800 ptas in low season and up to 20,000 ptas in August. Return fares are from about one-third to double this amount. On top of this you must add on cabin accommodation, which runs anywhere from 7,100 to 45,800 ptas each way.

The cost of taking a vehicle up to 5m long and 1.5m high ranges from 35,000 to 65,000 ptas one way, including driver. Ask about special family, group, and return fares. Motorcycles and scooters cost from 21,200 to 35,300 ptas one way, including rider, while bicycles cost from 1600 to 2400 ptas one way.

Enquiries and reservations can be made at P&O's office (☎ 94 423 44 77), Calle de Cosme Echevarrieta 1, or by calling ☎ 0990-980980 in the UK.

Santurtzi can be reached by cercanía train from La Naja station in central Bilbao or by Bizkaibus bus from La Sendeja, near the Puente del Ayuntamiento.

Getting Around

A measure of the way in which Bilbao has merged with adjacent towns up and down the estuary is the extent of its spanking new metro line. It runs to the north coast from a number of stations on both sides of the river, and makes getting to the beaches (see later) nearest Bilbao relatively simple.

Bizkaibus operates a regular service to the airport from Calle de La Sendeja.

AROUND BILBAO
Beaches

There are better beaches farther east and west of Bilbao, but if you want something relatively close you can try **Las Arenas**, near Algorta, or the beaches farther north outside Plentzia, such as Sopelana. The left end of the Playa Salvaje, in the same area, is for nudists. The Bilbao metro runs to Algorta and Plentzia (180 ptas).

Castillo de Butrón

Walt Disney probably would have done it better. This sugary castle a few kilometres west of the village of Gatica (Gatika) and roughly 20km north-east of Bilbao was first built in the 14th century as the bastion of the Basque Butrón clan, but was recently redone. Groups of rowdy school kids romp past sickly looking wax mannequins of soldiers, prisoners and fair damsels, and the scene is completed with audiovisual tall tales and a tacky souvenir stall. If you've got kids this could be just the ticket. In summer it is open daily from 10.30 am to 8 pm and in winter from 11 am to 6.30 pm

(700 ptas). Bizkaibus buses from Bilbao run past but are irregular.

Cueva de Pozalagua

Few travellers venture into the Encartaciones, the westernmost district of Vizcaya province, but if you like caves try this array of weird and wonderful stalactites. It's just outside the village of Ranero, 7km northwest of Karrantza, and is open on weekends and holidays from 11 am to 7 pm (to 6 pm from October to May; 500 ptas). If you want to stay in the area, there are several *casas rurales* in and around Karrantza, which is served by Bilbao-Santander FEVE trains.

Durango & Elorrio

The industrial town of Durango has few drawing cards, although the massive oak portico of the Iglesia de Santa María de Uribarri is quite remarkable. The real attraction is the Duranguesado, the mountainous area around the city. The drive south to the **Puerto de Urquiola** pass is festooned with spectacular lookouts. Climbers make for the summit of Amboto (1327m), 5km east of the pass.

It seems that at one stage just about everyone in nearby Elorrio was a VIP, if the number of mansions bearing family crests is anything by which to judge. San Balentin Berrio-Otxoa Kalea in particular is loaded down with the impressive façades of past greatness. It spills onto the delightful Plaza Gernikako Arbola, dominated by the austere countenance of the 15th century Basílica de la Purísima Concepción. Opposite is the local frontón, packed in the evening for the serious business of pelota, while less sport-inclined people pass the time in neighbouring cafés.

Apart from an expensive hotel, you could try one of two local agroturismos: *Arabio-Azpikoa* (☎ 94 658 33 42, *Arabio Kalea 8*) and *Galartza Barrena* (☎ 94 658 27 07, *Zenita Kalea 1*); both have double rooms for 4000 ptas.

There are regular buses and trains from Bilbao to Durango, from where buses run every hour or so to Elorrio.

VITORIA

Capital not only of the southern Basque province of Álava (Araba) but of the entire País Vasco, Vitoria (Gasteiz) is a strange mix of sober, business-like city and ebullient student enclave. This cocktail is of course given that special Basque twist, with enough ETA posters and graffiti to remind you of its presence, and you could easily stumble across a game of pelota down at the frontón on Plaza de los Fueros.

History

Nueva Vitoria was founded in 1181 by the Navarran king Sancho VI (El Sabio) on the site of the old Basque village of Gasteiz. It later swapped hands between the Castilian and Navarran crowns. The expansion that began in the 18th century picked up pace in the 20th with the growth of industry. The city was named capital of the País Vasco in 1979.

Orientation

The old city centre is composed of narrow alleys arranged more or less as a series of concentric circles around a slight hill-top swell. A 10 minute walk south brings you to the train station, while the estación de autobuses lies a few blocks to the east of the centre. Hotels of all categories are spread out between the two, with a handful in the old city itself.

Information

Tourist Office The tourist office (☎ 945 13 13 21) in Parque de la Florida is open Monday to Thursday from 9 am to 1.30 pm and 3 to 6 pm and Friday from 9 am to 2 pm. It is open summer weekends too.

Money There is no shortage of banks with ATMs in the newer part of town between the train station and Plaza de España.

Post & Communications The main correos is on Calle de las Postas and the postcode for poste restante is 01080.

Medical & Emergency Services Hospital de Santiago (☎ 945 25 36 00) is handily

placed on Calle de la Paz. If you need an ambulance, call the Cruz Roja on ☎ 945 22 22 22. The main police station is on Calle de Olaguibel.

Things to See

Although charming enough to stroll around, Vitoria is a little short on outstanding sights. The **Iglesia de San Miguel**, overlooking Plaza de la Virgen Blanca and its monument to Wellington's victory over the French in 1813, is dedicated to the White Virgin, patron of the city. Adjoining is the porticoed Plaza de España. North of both stands the 15th century **Iglesia de San Vicente**. Of the several noble houses scattered about the old town, the Gothic-era **Casa del Cordón** and the plateresque-fronted **Palacio de Escoriaza-Esquivel** are among the more interesting.

The **Catedral de Santa María**, softened by the leafy plaza in which it stands, is closed for restoration – but you can get a glimpse of its magnificent Gothic entrance shielded inside a portico. Continue downhill to inspect **El Portalón**, a series of 16th century brick and timber houses within which are embedded a rustic bar and an appealing restaurant. The building opposite, home to the **Museo de Arqueología**, is in much the same style.

The city's oldest church is the 14th century **Iglesia de San Pedro**. A block north, the Torre de Doña Otxanda houses the town's **Museo de Ciencias Naturales** (Natural Science Museum).

South of the railway tracks runs the elegant Calle de Fray Francisco de Vitoria. Its freestanding palatial houses count among their number the **Museo de Bellas Artes**, the **Museo de Armería** (you know, suits of armour and the like) and the **Palacio de Ajuria-Enea**, residence of the *lehendakari* (head of the regional government).

Special Events

Vitorianos let their hair down for the Fiestas de la Virgen Blanca from 4 to 9 August. A jazz festival is held in July, usually just before the San Sebastián spectacle.

PAÍS VASCO

VITORIA

PLACES TO STAY
- 8 Casa de Huéspedes Antonio
- 10 Hostal Eguileta
- 18 Pension Mari
- 20 Hotel Dato

PLACES TO EAT
- 1 Cantina Mariachi
- 12 Bar El 7

OTHER
- 2 Iglesia de San Pedro
- 3 Museo de Ciencias Naturales
- 4 Taberna del Tuerto
- 5 El Portalón & Restaurante El Portalón
- 6 Museo de Arqueología
- 7 Catedral de Santa María
- 9 Palacio de Escoriaza Esquivel
- 11 Casa del Cordón
- 13 Iglesia de San Vicente
- 14 Iglesia de San Miguel
- 15 Main Correos
- 16 Polica Nacional
- 17 Estación de Autobuses
- 19 Hospital de Santiago
- 21 Tourist Office
- 22 Catedral de María Immaculada
- 23 Museo de Bellas Artes
- 24 Museo de Armería
- 25 Palacio de Ajura-Enea
- 26 Train Station (RENFE)
- 27 Baco

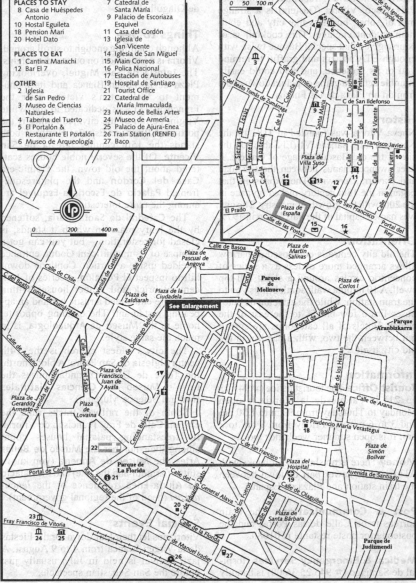

Places to Stay

There are plenty of small hostales in Vitoria. The *Casa de Huéspedes Antonio* (☎ 945 26 87 95, Calle de la Cuchillería 66) has small but comfortable singles/doubles for 1500/3000 ptas.

There are a few places on Calle de Prudencio María de Verastegui near the bus station, including the *Pensión Mari* (☎ 945 27 73 03), where clean, comfy beds are 2000/3300 ptas. Inquire around the corner at Calle de Francia 23. Rooms at *Hostal Eguileta* (☎ 945 25 17 00, Calle de Nueva Fuera 32) are of much the same standard, going for 3100/3500 ptas plus IVA.

The spick and span *Hotel Dato* (☎ 945 14 72 30, Calle de Eduardo Dato 28), with a nice location, has attractive rooms with private bath for 3990/5490 ptas.

Places to Eat

You can get tapas and menús del día at many of the bars in the old town. *Bar El 7 (Calle de la Cuchillería 3)* has a set lunch for 1100 ptas. For something quick and a little different, *Cantina Mariachi (Calle de las Cercas Bajas 17)* has budget-friendly Mexican food.

You can dine on quality Basque cuisine at *Restaurante El Portalón*, in El Portalón. There's a lunch and dinner special for 2950 ptas.

The cafés on Plaza de España are the most atmospheric for your morning coffee.

Entertainment

The centre of the old town, and in particular Calle de la Cuchillería and Calle de la Pintorería, is wall to wall bars, creating an intense, largely student, nightlife. A good late-night haunt is *Baco (Calle de los Fueros 39)*. *Taberna del Tuerto* in El Portalón has a dance floor in the rear and you can get tattoos with your drinks.

Getting There & Away

Continental-Auto has about six buses daily to Madrid (2800 ptas), and four to Barcelona (4250 ptas). Other companies have regular services to San Sebastián,

Bilbao (655 ptas), Durango, Pamplona (875 ptas), Logroño and Estella.

Six trains daily go to Madrid for 4000 ptas and one daily to Barcelona for 5000 ptas. You can also get to San Sebastián, Salamanca and Pamplona.

The N-I highway linking Madrid to San Sebastián passes by Vitoria. Take the N-240 for Bilbao.

AROUND VITORIA
Mendoza & Oppidum de Iruña

About 15km west of Vitoria (take the N-I for Burgos), the farming village of Mendoza features the Torre de los Mendoza, a castle now converted into the Museo de Heráldica, of interest for those keen to study Basque coats of arms. A few kilometres farther south, a medieval bridge at Trespuentes leads to the ancient Roman settlement of Oppidum de Iruña.

Laguardia & Around

The prettiest of the Rioja wine-growing towns is undoubtedly Laguardia, about 45km south of Vitoria along a picturesque road. The area has been inhabited since the Iron Age, and the old walled town is filled with the houses of noble families. Look for the **Iglesia de Santa María de los Reyes**, which features a rare example of a grand Gothic doorway with its polychrome colouring intact. Virtually every house in town has a basement wine cellar, and bars and *bodegas* have the local goods for as little as 50 ptas a glass. For more on the area's wines, see the Wine Region section in the La Rioja part of this chapter.

There is a choice of five places to stay, including the *Casa de Huéspedes (☎ 941 60 01 14, Calle Mayor 17)*, where comfortable beds are 2000 ptas a pop. A few slow buses connecting Vitoria and Logroño daily pass through Laguardia.

You'll find plenty of interesting little villages if you have a vehicle to tour around. Headed for Haro in La Rioja, the road west from Laguardia briefly hops the border to take in **San Vicente de la Sonsierra**, a dead sort of place whose remaining castle walls spill off their hill-top perch. There's little to disturb the bare stillness, but the views across the plains are marvellous and an impressive medieval bridge spans the Río Ebro below. Continuing on, **Labastida** straggles up a small hillside capped by the Ermita del Cristo with a fine Romanesque entrance.

To the north-east of Laguardia, you could happily disappear on back roads through the hamlets of Elvillar, Cripán, Meano, Aguilar and Santa Cruz, where you can switch north-west along the A-132 for Vitoria.

Navarra

Several Spains intersect in Navarra (Nafarroa in Basque). The fiercely independent traditions of the Basques here have their special flavour in the historical fueros, or autonomous rights long exercised by the Navarrese and resurrected today – the region is in fact officially known as the Comunidad Foral de Nafarroa.

The Navarrese are strong on symbolic points – red dominates the region's coat of arms. The Policía Foral have bright red cars, motorbikes and uniforms. In the Navarran Pyrenees everyone seems to paint doors and window frames red; when villages celebrate local fiestas, half the locals wear the traditional Basque white trousers and tops with red scarves, and red geraniums seem to be the main form of floral decoration in the ubiquitous window box.

The soft greens and bracing climate of the Navarran Pyrenees lie like a cool compress across the sunstruck brow of the south, which is all stark plains, cereal crops and vineyards, sliced up by high, forbidding sierras. Navarra is pilgrim territory – for centuries the faithful have used the pass at Roncesvalles to cross from France on their way to Santiago. Here too armies have crossed to and from Spain, but not always with success: Roland's retreating Frankish forces were harried and decimated by Basques in 778, leaving behind little but one of the great *gestes* of early medieval French literature, *La Chanson de Roland*.

Although many associate Navarra exclusively with the running of the bulls in Pamplona, the region's real charm is in its small towns, many in possession of fine monuments ranging from Romanesque to Renaissance.

If you're planning to spend any time in or near the Pyrenees of Navarra, pick up a copy of the *Guía de Alojamientos de Turismo Rural*, available from most tourist offices in Navarra, which lists all the private homes and farmsteads that rent out rooms. The standards are often higher and rates lower than in your average hostal.

PAMPLONA

Pamplona (Iruña, Iruñea), capital of the fiercely independent-minded Navarrese, is an attractive display of centuries-old middle-class wellbeing set behind the remains of its once haughty city walls. A fine cathedral is the jewel in the crown, but the footloose wanderer will get pleasure from simply meandering along narrow streets fronted by tall, elegant apartment houses.

On 6 July, all hell breaks loose as Spain's best known bull fest, the Fiesta de San Fermín (or the Sanfermines) kick-starts the city into a frenzy of drinking and mayhem. The running of the bulls *(el encierro)*, made famous by Hemingway, is accompanied by a stampede of visitors from all over the world bent on having such a good a time they are unlikely to remember much of it at all.

History

The Romans called the city Pompaelo, after its founder Pompey the Great. They were succeeded by the Visigoths and briefly by the Muslims, but by the 8th century Pamplona formed the nucleus of an independent power – the future kingdom of Navarra. It reached the height of its glory under Sancho III in the 11th century, and its position on the Camino de Santiago assured it prosperity. When Franco did his thing in 1936, Pamplona and indeed the rest of Navarra sided with the Nationalists.

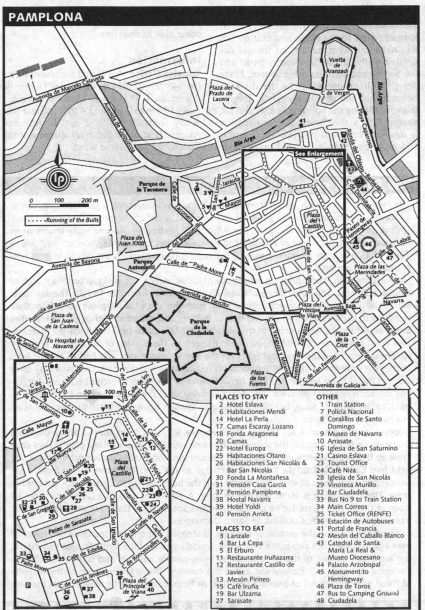

PAMPLONA

0   100   200 m

······ Running of the Bulls

0   50   100 m

PLACES TO STAY
2   Hotel Eslava
6   Habitaciones Mendi
14   Hotel La Perla
17   Camas Escaray Lozano
18   Fonda Aragonesa
20   Camas
22   Hotel Europa
25   Habitaciones Otano
26   Habitaciones San Nicolás &
      Bar San Nicolás
30   Fonda La Montañesa
31   Pensión Casa García
37   Pensión Pamplona
38   Hostal Navarra
39   Hotel Yoldi
40   Pensión Arrieta

PLACES TO EAT
3   Lanzale
4   Bar La Cepa
5   El Érburo
11   Restaurante Iruñazarra
12   Restaurante Castillo de
      Javier
13   Mesón Pirineo
15   Café Iruña
19   Bar Ulzama
27   Sarasate

OTHER
1   Train Station
7   Policía Nacional
8   Coralillos de Santo
      Domingo
9   Museo de Navarra
10   Arrasate
16   Iglesia de San Saturnino
21   Casino Eslava
23   Tourist Office
24   Café Niza
28   Iglesia de San Nicolás
29   Vinoteca Murillo
32   Bar Ciudadela
33   Bus No 9 to Train Station
34   Main Correos
35   Ticket Office (RENFE)
36   Estación de Autobuses
41   Portal de Francia
42   Mesón del Caballo Blanco
43   Catedral de Santa
      María La Real &
      Museo Diocesano
44   Palacio Arzobispal
45   Monument to
      Hemingway
46   Plaza de Toros
47   Bus to Camping Ground
48   Ciudadela

Orientation

The old city centre is extremely compact. It is marked off to the north and east by the Río Arga and what remains of the old defensive walls, and to the west by parks and the former citadel. The main square, Plaza del Castillo, roughly marks the division between old and new in the south. Everything, including the bullring, is a short walk away. Much of the cheaper accommodation is in the streets west of Plaza del Castillo and near the centrally located estación de autobuses. The train station is awkwardly placed north-west of the city centre, on the other side of the river.

Information

Tourist Office You'll find the tourist office (☎ 948 22 07 41) at Calle del Duque de Ahumada 3. It is open Monday to Friday from 10 am to 2 pm and 4 to 7 pm and Saturday from 10 am to 2 pm. In July and August it is open Saturday afternoon and Sunday as well, same times.

The Running of the Bulls

The Fiesta de San Fermín, or Sanfermines, has its origins in medieval legend. Fermín, son of a recently Christianised Roman governor of Pamplona, went off to spread the word in Gaul, ending up imprisoned and decapitated in Amiens for his trouble. No-one really knows when he became the patron saint of Navarra and Pamplona, but his feast day was set on 7 July in 1591. A 15th century wooden statue of the saint is hauled around the city in solemn procession at 10 am on 7 July.

The fiesta is an almost nonstop cacophony of music, dance, fireworks, processions and, of course, bullfights. The fights take place at 6.30 pm each day from 7 to 14 July. The day starts early – at 6.45 am bands march around town with the aim of waking everyone from their slumbers to launch them into another day of festivity and abandon. Although the festivities begin on 6 July, the first running of the bulls doesn't take place until the following morning. This is not some one-off tradition peculiar to Pamplona. The running of the bulls, or *el encierro*, always preceded the day's bullfights for the simple reason that you had to get the bulls to the ring somehow. Originally, the *toros bravos* (fighting bulls) were accompanied by *toros mansos* (quiet bulls) and herded from behind. How or when this exercise became a dangerous diversion remains unknown. Nowadays in many cities the bulls are often transported by truck to the *plaza de toros*, but plenty of smaller Spanish towns celebrate the encierro as an integral part of the fiesta.

Every morning from 7 to 14 July, the bulls are let loose from the Coralillos de Santo Domingo and charge across the square of the same name (a good vantage point). They continue up the street, veering into Calle de los Mercaderes from Plaza Consistorial and sweeping right into Calle de la Estafeta for the final charge to the ring. The brave or the foolish, depending on one's point of view, race madly with the bulls, aiming to keep close – but not too close. The total course is some 800 metres long. A little later, *vaquillas* (small cows) are let loose in the ring to chase (or be chased by) other spectators – these are *not* the bulls that have been run from the Coralillos de Santo Domingo.

The entire ethos of the *corrida*, or bullfight, is steeped not only in measuring the valour of man against beast, but also in the skill, some would say art, of the fight. To a certain extent, the same can be said of the encierro. Every year, people are hurt and sometimes killed in encierros, not only in Pamplona but across the country. This is largely because the majority of those who run are full of bravado (or drink, or both) but have little idea of what they are

Money There is no shortage of banks where you can change cash and travellers' cheques or get cash advances. There's plenty of ATMs around the city too. Note, however, that throughout the Fiesta de San Fermín the banks open during the morning only.

Post & Communications The correos is at Calle de Estella 10. The postcode for poste restante at the central correos is 31080.

Medical & Emergency Services The main police station is on Calle del General Chinchilla. The Hospital de Navarra (☎ 948 10 21 00) is on Calle de Irunlarrea. The emergency number for all services, including ambulances, is ☎ 112.

Catedral de Santa María La Real & Museo Diocesano

Pamplona's main house of worship stands on a rise just inside the city ramparts. Its single most outstanding feature is the

---

The Running of the Bulls

doing. It is difficult to recommend this activity, but plenty participate anyway. Try to run with someone experienced, and above all do not get caught near bulls that have been separated from the herd. Keep ahead of the herd and you should be all right. To increase the thrill, some runners try whacking bulls with rolled up newspapers and the like. Not a very nice thing to do and designed to get one taking a special interest in you. That kind of attention you can well live without!

To participate you must enter the course before 8 am from Plaza de Santo Domingo and take up your position. Around 8 am two rockets are fired. The first announces that the bulls have been released from the corrals. The second lets you know they are all out and running. The first truly dangerous point is where Calle de los Mercaderes leads into Calle de la Estafeta. Here many of the bulls crash into the barriers because of the sheer speed at which they attempt to take the turns, and this is where at least some bulls are likely to be separated from the herd. A bull thus separated and surrounded by charging humans is probably rather more frightened than the

people. And 300 to 400kg of frightened bull make for an unpredictable and dangerous animal. Another particularly dangerous stretch comes towards the end, where Calle de la Estafeta slopes down into the final turn to the Plaza de Toros. A third rocket goes off when all the bulls have made it to the ring, and a final one when they have been rounded up in the stalls where they will await the fight. If you want to watch a fight and fail to get tickets in advance at the ring, you'll usually find scalpers selling cheaper seats for around 1000 ptas. The whole shebang winds up at midnight on 14 July with a candlelit procession, known as the Pobre de Mí, which starts from Plaza Consistorial.

Gothic cloister in the French style. Inside the church lie buried in some splendour Carlos III of Navarra (the Noble) and his wife Doña Leonor. The museum houses mainly religious art, including some fine woodcarving dating from the 12th to the 14th centuries.

The cathedral and museum are visited as a unit and are open from 10.30 am to 1.30 pm and 4 to 7 pm, but closed Saturday afternoon and Sunday (500 ptas).

Iglesia de San Saturnino

This ornate and unusual church in the centre of town is in fact two churches in one. The 13th century chapel was doubled in size with a baroque annexation, segmenting off from its midpoint.

City Walls

The most intact section of the wall encloses the north-eastern corner of the old town, perched high above a gentle bend in the shady Río Arga. You can get up to the ramparts from behind the cathedral. Farther around to the left is the gateway known as the Portal de Francia, which was once the main entrance to Pamplona.

Museo de Navarra

This contains a mildly interesting and eclectic selection ranging from archaeological finds through to a small art collection, including a Goya. It is open Tuesday to Saturday from 10 am to 2 pm and 5 to 7 pm and Sunday and holidays from 11 am to 2 pm (200 ptas).

Ciudadela & Parks

Built and remodelled much in line with the classic schemes of Vauban, the walls and bulwarks of the grand fortified citadel, the **Ciudadela**, can barely be made out for all the grass and trees in what now constitutes a park. It's open daily from 7.30 am to 9.30 pm. Pamplona's northern flank is laced with green, and the gardens of Parque de la Taconera are nice for an evening stroll.

Places to Stay – Budget

Plenty of cheap *fondas* and pensiones lurk in Pamplona's old centre. In the first two weeks of July (Sanfermines) some places as much as triple their normal rates and it is next to impossible to get a room during the fiesta without booking ahead. Touts will often greet you at the train station or tourist office at this time, offering rooms in private houses.

Otherwise you can join the many who simply sleep in the parks. Leave your belongings in the *consigna* (left-luggage office) at the bus and train stations. People opting for the parks should be aware that they are a prime target for thieves. Expert at slitting sleeping bags and whipping out anything from inside apart from yourself, these people have been known to make off artfully with victims' watches.

Alternatively, base yourself outside Pamplona, although you may still have to put up with a night in the park if you are relying on public transport and want to be in Pamplona in good time for the early morning running of the bulls.

Camping The nearest camping ground, *Ezcaba* (☎ 948 33 03 15), is 7km north of town. It normally is open from Easter to October, but like just about everything else is full for the fiesta. Basic temporary camping facilities are set up nearby during this time. A bus service runs four times daily from just near the Plaza de Toros. Look for the Montañesa bus to Arre/Oricain.

Fondas, Pensiones & Hostales *Fonda La Montañesa* (☎ 948 22 43 80, Calle de San Gregorio 2) has basic rooms for 1500 ptas per person. A little better is *Pensión Casa García* (☎ 948 22 38 93) at No 12, with similar rates. *Camas Escaray Lozano* (☎ 948 22 78 25, Calle Nueva 24) has small but clean singles/doubles for 2000/4000 ptas and is probably the best value in this range.

If you have no luck with these, there are others in the same category, including the

Fonda Aragonesa (☎ 948 22 34 28 Calle de San Nicolás 32); *Habitaciones San Nicolás* at No 13; *Bar/Habitaciones Otano* at No 5; and a place with a sign saying *'Camas – Beds'* at Calle del Pozo Blanco 16.

Near the bus station you'll find several clean and comfortable places that all look much the same inside. Best of these is *Pensión Arrieta (☎ 948 22 84 59, Calle de Arrieta 27)*, whose lovely rooms come with TV and ceiling fans. The bathroom is down the hall and rates are 3000/4500 ptas (500 ptas more each in summer). *Pensión Pamplona (☎ 948 22 99 63, Calle de Tudela 5)* has small rooms starting at 4000/5000 ptas. Two doors down, *Hostal Navarra (☎ 948 22 51 64, Calle de Tudela 9)* offers small rooms with own bath for 4000/5140 ptas plus IVA.

Habitaciones Mendi (☎ 948 22 52 97, Calle de las Navas de Tolosa 9) is a particularly good deal. Its rooms have character and come with own loo. They cost 3000/5000 ptas.

Places to Stay – Mid-Range

Hotel Eslava (☎ 948 22 22 70, Plaza Virgen de la O 7) is a homey little place which charges 4000/8000 ptas (plus IVA) for singles/doubles with a TV, phone and bath.

With a touch of slightly faded class, the *Hotel La Perla (☎ 948 22 77 06, Plaza del Castillo 1)* has rooms for 3900/6900 plus IVA on weekends. At other times the rooms will cost you 5000/8000 ptas plus IVA.

More expensive and with less character is the *Hotel Yoldi (☎ 948 22 48 00, Avenida de San Ignacio 11)*, where weekend and summer discount rates are 6000/8000 ptas plus IVA.

Places to Stay – Top End

For a tad more elegance, the *Hotel Europa (☎ 948 22 18 00, fax 948 22 92 35, Calle de Espoz y Mina 11)* has a weekend rate of 5000/7850 ptas plus IVA for singles/ doubles, or 5750/9850 ptas plus IVA during the week.

Places to Eat

Calle de San Nicolás is densely packed with tapas bars, and *Bar Ulzama* is particularly good for snacking. The popular *Bar San Nicolás* at No 13 does a Basque set meal for 1500 ptas. When you tire of the dangling pig haunches and the bulls running to the slaughter, make for the vegetarian *Sarasate*, along here at No 23.

More options abound on Calle de San Lorenzo. *El Erburo* at No 19 has a set *menú* for 1500 ptas and *Lanzale* at No 31 has fish and meat main dishes from 900 to 1600 ptas. *Bar La Cepa* at No 2 also serves up food.

Restaurante Iruñazarra (Calle de los Mercaderes 15) offers tempting platos combinados for 1200 ptas.

The cosy, timber-laden atmosphere of the *Mesón Pirineo (Calle de la Estafeta 41)* has mains at about 900 to 1400 ptas. Around the corner, *Restaurante Castillo de Javier (Calle de Javier 2)* is the place to head for upmarket Basque cuisine.

If you need to stock up on vast amounts of good Navarran wine, the *Vinoteca Murillo*, on the corner of Calle de San Gregorio and Plaza de San Nicolás, will fill 5L containers for 690 ptas.

Entertainment

The cafés on Plaza del Castillo with their French-style awnings are a great place to start the day, or end it. *Café Iruña*, on the northern side of the square, is one of Pamplona's grand dames, an elegant spot for coffee or an apéritif. *Casino Eslava* on the opposite end is a more reservedly modern chic.

Café Niza on Calle del Duque de Ahumada appears to be in the same mould, but attracts a young and energetic crowd. *Arrasate (Calle de San Saturnino 16)* is tidy and refined.

Bar Ciudadela (Calle de la Ciudadela 3) has a great upstairs section where you can sip a beer on the little balconies in summer. Better still is the outdoor *Mesón del Caballo Blanco*, just inside the city walls north of the cathedral.

Calle de Jarauta is wall to wall with bars of the loud and late variety.

Getting There & Away

Bus Buses run from the central estación de autobuses, on Avenida de Yanguas y Miranda, to most towns throughout Navarra, but in many cases there is no service on Sunday.

Six buses run daily to Bilbao (1510 ptas), about 10 run to Vitoria (875 ptas) and up to 12 run to San Sebastián (700 ptas). Four daily go to Madrid (3140 ptas) and three to Barcelona (2090 ptas). Other destinations with regular services include Estella, Logroño, Zaragoza, Tafalla, Tudela and Soria.

Train Pamplona is on the San Sebastián-Zaragoza line, but the station is awkwardly situated north of town. If you arrive this way, catch bus No 9 to Paseo de Sarasate.

Car & Motorcycle The A-15 tollway rounds the city and links up other autopistas to Zaragoza to the south and San Sebastián to the north. Several pretty routes lead north into the Pyrenees and on to France, while the N-240 heads east into Aragón (Jaca) and the N-111 goes southwest to Logroño.

EAST OF PAMPLONA

South-east along the N-240, a handful of interesting towns and a grand monastery lying virtually on the southern rim of the Pyrenees together form a worthwhile excursion or stopover before heading on into Aragón. Buses are infrequent, however, and accommodation is pricey.

Sangüesa

The biggest town in eastern Navarra and once an important stop on the pilgrim route to Santiago de Compostela for those crossing from France via Somport, Sangüesa retains a sense of its past.

From the north, you cross the Río Aragón and immediately on the left are presented with one of the premier examples of Ro-manesque religious art in Navarra, the Iglesia de Santa María. Entry is through an exquisite 12th century portal. Simpler, but with its own charm, is the Iglesia de Santiago, which shows signs of the transition to Gothic. All sites in town must be visited by guided tour from the information office in the ayuntamiento. These start every half-hour Tuesday to Sunday from 10 am to 12.30 pm and 4 to 5.30 pm. It's 400 ptas for the whole shebang. Sangüesa is not a bad place to lay over for the night since it has more life than any of the nearby pueblos, and a sufficient assortment of minor monuments and mansions to keep you interested.

The only place to stay in town is *Pensión Las Navas* (☎ 948 87 07 00, *Calle de Alfonso el Batallador 7*), near the ayuntamiento, with singles/doubles for 2500/4200 ptas. It also has decent food. Buses run daily to Pamplona.

Javier

From Sangüesa, it's 11km north-east to Javier (or Xavier), where the patron saint of Navarra, San Francisco Xavier, was born in 1506. The town, an eminently forgettable grid of dead streets, lies downhill from Javier's *castillo*. Every March it is the object of the Javierada, when thousands of people flock to commemorate the saint. Inside the castle is a small display devoted to his life, and also a chapel decorated with macabre figures doing the dance of death.

South of the castle stands a church erected in memory of San Francisco Xavier, who is said to have been baptised in the font that is preserved here.

The two hotels have a monopoly on food and beds and are overpriced, but if you must stay, *Hotel El Mesón* (☎ 948 88 40 35) is the cheaper one at 4500/6200 ptas plus IVA. A daily bus passes through from Pamplona and Sangüesa en route for Huesca, while another heads up the Valle de Roncal.

Yesa & the Monasterio de Leyre

If you have wheels and no luck with rooms in Sangüesa, skip those in Javier and try here. There's not much to the village, but a couple of places rent out rooms, including the *Hostal El Jabalí* (☎ 948 88 40 42) on the Jaca road. Rooms start at 3000/4000 ptas.

About 5km north lies the **Monasterio de Leyre** (or Leire), set in the shadow of the Sierra de Leyre, virtually the last mountain range before the Pyrenees. A religious community was first established here in the 9th century. By the 12th century, it had become a powerful Cluniac bastion, looming large in the religious and cultural life of all Navarra and pretty much in command of all the pilgrim-route passes from France. By the time the Cistercian reform was introduced in the 13th century, the monastery was beginning to lose influence. In 1836 the monks were turfed out, and over the next 100 years local shepherds used the monastery to shelter themselves and their flocks. In 1954, when the Benedictines moved in, they found themselves confronted by the enormous task of restoration.

The early Romanesque crypt is the most fascinating part of the complex. It is a three nave structure with a low roof and its squat columns and vaguely horseshoe-shaped arches are unique to the monastery. The Romanesque cloister was destroyed after the expulsion of the Cistercians, but the 12th century main portal of the church is a fine reminder of Romanesque artistry at its most challenging and is rich in symbolism. Much of the church is, however, built in the early-Gothic style.

The monks sell recordings of themselves performing Gregorian chants. If you can make it to the 9 am Mass or 7 pm Vespers service, you can hear the real thing.

The monastery is open from 10.15 am to 1.30 pm and 3.30 to 6.30 pm (225 ptas).

Apart from the *Hospedería de Leyre* (☎ 948 88 41 00), which is a little expensive at 4800/7000 ptas plus IVA for singles/doubles, men could try getting a bed in the monastery itself – ask at the *portería* (reception).

There's an early morning bus from Yesa to Pamplona and one to Huesca. You might also be able to pick up the daily service

connecting Pamplona and the Valle de Roncal in north-east Navarra. Virtually no buses run on Sunday, and none at all from Yesa to the monastery.

WEST OF PAMPLONA

The main route west out of Pamplona winds gently south-west to Logroño following the Camino de Santiago. Dotted with a handful of charming villages and especially bursting with colour after the spring rains, it is one of the more enticing stretches for those walking the Camino. Virtually every town has a pilgrims' hostel. Buses regularly run between Pamplona and Logroño along this route.

Puente de la Reina

It is at Puente de la Reina (Gares) that pilgrims approaching from Roncesvalles to the north and Aragón to the east have for centuries joined forces to take the one main route west. Their first stop here was the late-Romanesque **Iglesia del Crucifijo**, erected by the Knights Templar and still containing one of the finest Gothic crucifixes in existence. From here, those eager to push on would walk down the narrow Calle Mayor past the **Iglesia de Santiago** and its Romanesque portal to the Río Arga. The six arched medieval **Puente de los Peregrinos** at the end of Calle Mayor remains the nicest way to cross the river and pursue the Camino.

Places to Stay & Eat Apart from the *refugio* for pilgrims (summer only), there's no really cheap accommodation. The cheapest option is *Hostal Puente* (☎ 948 34 01 46) on Plaza de los Fueros, whose singles/doubles with private bath start at 4000/6000 ptas (higher in summer). They have a few slightly cheaper rooms without private bath. Several bars in town dish up reasonable food.

Estella

The highlight on this route is the picturesque town of Estella (Lizarra), huddled on the bend of the tree-shaded Río Ega. It makes a good base for excursions in the vicinity and is certainly the best place to end up for the night.

Seat of the Carlists in the 19th century, the village of Lizarra acquired its Castilian name in 1090 when Sancho Ramírez (king of Navarra and Aragón) made it the primary reception point for the growing flood of pilgrims along the Camino.

Every year from 31 July to 8 August, Estella hosts a feria with its own running of the bulls – not nearly as hyped as Pamplona's but equally thrilling.

The extremely helpful tourist office (☎ 948 55 40 11) on Calle de San Nicolás 1 is right in among the most important monuments on the south-western bank of the river. It is open (from April to September) Monday to Friday from 10 am to 2 pm and 4 to 7 pm and weekends from 10 am to 2 pm.

Just opposite, the fortified tower of the 13th century Iglesia de San Pedro de la Rúa lords it over the town. The tourist office gives tours (200 ptas), or you can view the cloister by climbing the steps farther along the street. Next door to the tourist office is a rare example of Romanesque civil construction, the so-called Palacio de los Reyes. Across the river and overlooking the town is the Iglesia de San Miguel. Its most interesting feature is the Romanesque north door.

Places to Stay & Eat

Camping Lizarra lies on the river at the edge of town. *Fonda Izarra* (☎ 948 55 06 78, Calle de la Caldería 20) has basic doubles for 3500 ptas, and the *Pensión San Andrés* (☎ 948 55 04 48, Plaza de Santiago 58) has plain singles without bath for 1600 ptas and doubles with bath for 4000 ptas; these prices rise with the flow of pilgrims and during feria. *Hostal Cristina* (☎ 948 55 04 50, Calle de Baja Navarra 1) occupies a fine spot by the main square and charges 3500/6000 ptas plus IVA for rooms with bath (add 1000 ptas in peak season). Plaza de los Fueros is a good spot for a meal or drink at an outdoor café.

Monasterio de Irache

Just outside Ayegui, this ancient Benedictine monastery has undergone many changes over the centuries, and is now partially under restoration. Its most alluring feature is the slightly tumbledown plateresque cloister, erected in the 16th century. It is open daily from 10 am to 1.30 pm (Wednesday to Friday also from 5 to 7 pm, and weekends also from 4 to 7 pm). Virtually next door you can taste some local reds at the Bodega de Irache.

Los Arcos & Torres del Río

The only point of interest in Los Arcos is the Iglesia de Santa María and its Gothic cloister. If you need to stay, try *Hotel Mónaco* (☎ 948 64 00 00, Plaza del Coso 22), where singles/doubles are 2750/3950 ptas plus IVA.

The road on this stretch twists and turns through rolling country to Torres del Río, whose little gem is the simple 12th century Romanesque Iglesia del Santo Sepulcro.

Viana

Only about 10km short of Logroño, Viana is a quiet spot with the mansions of noble families peppered around its old centre. The Gothic Iglesia de Santa María has an outstanding Renaissance doorway.

Valle de Lana & Sierra de Aralar

This area, north of the Pamplona-Logroño road, is dotted with minor Romanesque jewels hidden away in little-visited hamlets. With the Sierra de Urbasa, the Valle de Lana marks the changeover from a Mediterranean to Atlantic geography. Interesting spots in this area include the Monasterio de Iranzu, near Abárzuza; the Basílica de San Gregorio Ostiense at Sorlada; and the town of Azuelo. The tourist office at Estella has loads of information on the zone.

Farther north again, up towards the N-130 road that sheers off the A-15 to San Sebastián, you find yourself in the Sierra de Aralar. This area is dominated by a series of mountain ridges and was much beloved by Hemingway, an avid trout fisherman. From the area's main town, Lekunberri, you can head 15km westwards for the **Santuario de San Miguel in Excelsis**, which lies in the shadow of Monte Altxueta (1343m).

THE PYRENEES

Remember that Navarra has a particularly well-organised set of casas rurales across its northern strip. These are often beautifully looked-after houses in mountain villages and are popular in peak periods – reservations are recommended, and there is a central reservations switchboard on ☎ 948 22 93 28. You can recognise the casas rurales by one of two small plaques – one has 'CR' in white on a dark green background; the more modern one, in brown, olive green and white, displays the letter 'C' and the outline of a house.

Walkers should refer to the boxed text 'Walking in the Pyrences' in the Catalunya chapter. Trekkers and skiers alike should note a couple of emergency numbers in case they get into serious trouble on the Navarran or French side of the mountains. Call ☎ 088 in Navarra or ☎ 17 in Aquitaine (France).

Valle del Baztán & Regata de Bidasoa

If you're headed for San Sebastián, the coast and/or France from Pamplona, you have several options. The quickest dash to San Sebastián can be made up the A-15, or more picturesquely along the national (N) roads that hug it.

A preferable and dawdling route would, however, see you pushing straight up north along the N-121A (keep alert for the right exit from Pamplona by car as it's a little confusing). The initial stretch is pretty enough, but there's little to stop for until you wind over the **Puerto de Velate** pass. From here you could follow the same highway along the valley known as the **Regata de Bidasoa**.

If you're in no tearing hurry, consider making a detour up the lush Valle del Baztán to the north-east. Minor roads take you past charming little villages like **Ziga**

(which has a 16th century church and, about 1km farther north, a beautiful lookout point) and **Irurita** (with another fine church) before reaching the valley's biggest town, **Elizondo**, on the N-121B. Although not the prettiest of the Baztán pueblos, this can make a convenient base for exploring the area, and there is plenty of accommodation.

Casa Jaén (☎ 948 58 04 87) is a casa rural with cute little doubles for 3700 ptas. About 10km out of town, *Casa Urruska* (☎ 948 45 21 06) is in a more tranquil, rural setting and offers singles/doubles for 1500/3000 ptas.

The estación de autobuses is on the main road and services go to Pamplona and San Sebastián up to three times daily, stopping in many of the smaller villages up and down the valley on the way.

Beyond Elizondo, a particularly lovely road climbs eastwards through the enchanting villages of **Arizkun** and **Erratzu** to the French border pass of Puerto de Izpegui. Coming the other way, this is without doubt one of the prettiest introductions to Spain from France. You'll find two *casas rurales* in Arizkun, plus six more and a *camping ground* (☎ 948 45 31 33) in Erratzu.

Back on the N-121B, turn northwards for the Puerto de Otxondo and the border crossing into France at Dantxarinea. Just before the border a minor road veers west to **Zugarramurdi**, whose main claim to fame is its caves. For centuries they have been known also as the Witches' Caves, for legends tell of a coven (or *akelarre* in Basque) held in the fields just behind them. A trail snakes around and through a huge rock tunnel (300 ptas). A few kilometres away are more caves, this time with the odd stalactite and stalagmite, at Urdazubi-Urdax.

There are two welcoming casas rurales in Zugarramurdi, and one bus daily (except Sunday) to Elizondo.

From Zugarramurdi you could now follow a tiny back road south to Mugairi (Oronoz), putting you back on the N-121A and into the Regata de Bidasoa. The first worthwhile stop from there heading north along the N-121A is a few kilometres off to

NAVARRA

the east at **Etxalar** (also spelled Echalar). The churchyard is sprinkled with traditional tombstones in the shape of small discs. A

Bewitched

1610 was a lousy year for the wicked witches and warlocks of Zugarramurdi. Fear and loathing on the part of God-fearing locals had prompted Don Juan del Valle Alvarado, Inquisitor from the Tribunal of Logroño, to make the arduous trip to this sodden corner of northern Navarra to investigate reports of rampant witchery. It appears folk from all around were only too willing to denounce anyone they could think of. 'She's a witch!' (or 'He's a warlock!') was a common cry, and no fewer than 300 luckless individuals found themselves accused. Don Juan was anxious to get home, so he picked out those he considered to be the worst offenders, about 40 in all, and carted them off to Logroño for further questioning. Of these, 18 were absolved and 12 were burned at the stake. Well, seven of them were – five had already died in the inquisitorial prison and were burned in effigy. The rest received punishments ranging from the confiscation of their property to life imprisonment.

What did these people get up to? According to the Inquisition they not only worshipped the devil as a god, but practised metamorphosis (which might have come in handy while in prison); caused wild storms in the Bay of Biscay; cast spells on fields, animals and even people; and indulged in vampirism and occasionally tucked into a good meal of corpse.

And the poor sods who had to put up with all this – did they have no remedy? To make a witch disappear, you could make a sign of the cross and hiss the word 'Jesús' at the unwelcome interlocutor. To keep the nasties out of the home, one attached to the door a cross made of two ash-tree branches, and next to it a blessed branch of laurel.

little farther north and off to the west, **Lesaka** is noted for its Iglesia de San Martín de Tours and the so-called *casherna*, a medieval tower in the village centre. Last stop before the coast is **Bera (Vera) de Bidasoa**, with an atmosphere virtually indistinguishable from that of French Pyrenees towns. Its ayuntamiento and 15th century church are impressive. All these towns have casas rurales.

To France via Roncesvalles

As you bear north-east out of Pamplona along the N-135 and ascend into the Pyrenees, the yellows, browns and olive green of lower Navarra begin to give way to a more luxuriant vegetation.

Burguete This spotless mountain village straddling the main road was a favourite getaway for Hemingway – worlds apart from its dusty counterparts farther south. There is a fair spread of accommodation, including the *Casa Vergara* (☎ 948 76 00 44), which charges 4500 ptas, and *Hostal Juandeaburre* (☎ 948 76 00 78), which is good value at 2100/3700 ptas for singles/doubles. *Camping Urrobi* (☎ 948 76 02 00), open April to October, is a few kilometres south. For a meal out, *Restaurante Tikipolit*, on the main drag, has tasty mains for around 1000 ptas. There is also a supermarket and a bank.

Roncesvalles A few kilometres farther north, Roncesvalles (Orreaga) is little more than a monastery complex sitting within a mountain pass which for centuries has been a major Pyrenees crossing point for pilgrims on the Camino de Santiago. It is said Roland and the remains of his soldiers were buried here on Charlemagne's orders. The spot is now covered by the 12th century Capilla de Sancti Spiritus. In the 13th century Gothic Real Colegiata de Santa María church, the cloister (rebuilt in the 17th century) is of interest, and more particularly the *sala capitular* off it. This contains the tomb of King Sancho VII (El Fuerte) of Navarra, the apparently 2.25m high victor in the Battle of Las Navas de Tolosa, which was fought against the Muslims in 1212. All sites are open daily from 10.30 am to 1 pm and 4 to 5.30 pm; a single ticket for all costs 425 ptas.

HI members can try the *albergue de la juventud* (☎ 948 76 00 15), housed in an 18th century hospital where pilgrims used to take respite. Of the two hotels, the highly-regarded *Hostal La Posada* (☎ 948 76 02 25) has rooms with private bath for 5100/6300 ptas. The afternoon bus (daily except Sunday) from Pamplona through Burguete terminates here.

Puerto de Ibañeta & Valcarlos From Roncesvalles, the road climbs to the Puerto de Ibañeta, the pass where Roland and his men were attacked – a modern memorial marks the spot. From here you have magnificent views across into France. The last town before the frontier is Valcarlos, a sleepy but pretty spot. Twice a year it comes to life, on Easter Sunday and 25 July, when the colourful Bolantes take over the streets with their folk dances and comic antics.

Casa Etxezuria (☎ 948 79 00 11), on the main road heading towards France, is a private house with absolutely delightful doubles for just 3800 ptas (2000 ptas for single occupancy). The owner has a couple of other places nearby. Those (with own transport) exploring the Spanish and French sides of this part of the Pyrenees might want to consider this as a base.

From Valcarlos, you'll know you've crossed the border when you pass the Campsa petrol station – it is well worth pursuing the road on to St Jean Pied-de-Port.

Into the Backblocks If little villages and quiet country roads are an attraction, there is plenty of scope for losing yourself in the area east of the main Roncesvalles road. A couple of kilometres south of Burguete, the NA-202 branches off east to Garralda. Push on to **Arive**, a charming hamlet on the crossroads of several country lanes. You could continue east to the Valle del Salazar (see

Roland's Swan Song

After an unsuccessful foray against the Muslims in northern Spain back in 778, Charlemagne decided it was time to call it a day and pull back from Zaragoza into France. His chosen route via Roncesvalles through the Pyrenees was, although one of the few viable options, not among the safest. He managed to get the bulk of his army across without great incident, but his rearguard under Roland de Bretagne was not so lucky. Caught in the gorge of Roncesvalles, he and his men were ambushed by local Basque (or Gascon) guerrillas and slaughtered to the last man.

Out of this unfortunate incident emerged one of the great medieval *gestes* (epic poems), *La Chanson de Roland*, which gave rather a different slant to the whole story. The essence of it has Roland as the unwitting victim of a nasty plot between another of Charlemagne's lieutenants, Ganelon, and the wicked Saracens. His heroism in the face of overwhelming odds is matched only by the Frankish emperor's almost divine instinct for justice, which he exacts at the expense of the Muslim Emir Baligant near Zaragoza. Ganelon is of course found out and sentenced to death. The geste is thought to have been composed about 1090, although the legend surrounding Roland's death was born shortly after the historical events. The extant version of the *La Chanson de Roland* manuscript, consisting of 3998 Anglo-Norman verses, is held in the Bodleian Library in Oxford.

the next section), go south along the Río Irati past the fine Romanesque church near Nagore, or take a loop north-east through the Bosque de Irati forest, which again would eventually bring you to the Valle del Salazar, at Ochagavía. The forest, full of elms, beeches and lime trees, is one of Europe's most extensive, inviting you to dump your vehicle and head off for a hike.

Valle del Salazar

A bus runs the length of the Salazar valley from Pamplona to Ochagavía.

The NA-178 heads north-east off the N-240 through the decaying town of **Lumbier**, only worth a stop for its medieval bridge and proximity to the gorge *(foz)* of the same name. Farther up, the NA-178 crosses paths with another beautiful gorge, the Foz de Arbayún. Just after you see the sign, swing right for the platform that affords splendid vistas. Those with binoculars will be able to see flights of eagles.

Many of the hamlets that line the road north contain some gem of medieval handiwork, and in some cases their quiet cobbled streets and little plazas are equipped with the odd bar or café. Among the candidates are **Güesa**, nearby **Igal**, **Sarriés** and particularly **Esparza de Salazar**, with its mansions, medieval bridge and restored Iglesia de San Andrés.

Ochagavía Busier than the rest of the valley, this Pyrenean town lying astride the narrow Río Zatoya sets itself quite apart from the villages farther south. Grey stone and slate are the main building materials in the old centre and the place has a sober dignity reinforced by the looming presence of the Iglesia de San Juan Evangelista.

This is a popular base for walkers and even skiers, so many local families have opened up their homes as casas rurales – there are no less than 12 of them. There is also a *camping ground (☎ 948 89 01 84)*.

A lively place for a meal or drink is *Iratxo Bar*, the first place to the left on the main drag when you arrive from the south.

Heading North The smaller of the two roads north from Ochagavía winds 24km over the Pyrenees into a dead end in the Bosque de Irati, where you can embark on some pleasant, solitary walks.

For France you take the N-140 north-east from Ochagavía into the Sierra de Abodi and cross at the Puerto de Larrau (1585m), a majestically bleak pass where you won't even realise you've crossed the frontier

north until you're already over. Four kilometres short of the border is a restaurant and bar for skiers. Day-trippers come here to ski, but there are no lifts or other facilities.

Valle del Roncal

This easternmost valley in the Navarran Pyrenees is in most respects also the region's most attractive. Its mountain territory is Navarra's most spectacular, although for skiing and alpine splendour, neighbouring Aragón has more to offer. One daily bus leaves Pamplona on weekdays at 5 pm (Saturday at 1 pm, nothing on Sunday), passing through all these towns on its way to Uztárroz. It returns early in the morning.

Burgui The gateway to this part of the Pyrenees is Burgui. Its Roman bridge over the Río Esca, combined with its huddle of stone houses, is an evocative introduction to the rural Pyrenean towns farther upstream. Nice as it is, you should really push on upriver for Roncal or Isaba. Be warned, however, that these can get crowded in summer. If you need to stay here, *Pensión El Almadiero (☎ 948 47 70 86, Calle Mayor s/n)* is kind of pricey at 5500 ptas per double.

Roncal This brooding, tightly knit village boasts a 16th century parish church, but it is the cobblestone alleyways twisting between dark stone houses that lend the village its charm.

The tourist office (☎ 948 47 51 36), on the main road towards the Isaba exit from town, can provide photocopies of walking maps. It is open Monday to Saturday, in summer only, from 10 am to 2 pm and 4.30 to 7.30 pm and Sunday from 10 am to 2 pm. There is one bank and even a ski-hire outlet here.

Although Isaba, farther north, makes a better base, you could do a lot worse than to choose one of the four casas rurales in the centre of Roncal as a place to stay. *Casa Pili (☎ 948 47 51 35)* and *Casa Txarpa (☎ 948 47 50 68)* are both traditional houses in the centre of the village and charge 3300 ptas for a double room.

Isaba The village of Isaba is another popular base for walkers and skiers, lying on the confluence of the Río Belagua and Río Uztárroz, which together flow into the Río Esca. There are a few banks with ATMs and a tourist office (☎ 948 89 32 51) open for long hours.

Among the better casas rurales are *Casa Katalingarde* (☎ 948 89 31 54) and *Casa Francisco Mayo* (☎ 948 89 31 66), both with doubles at 3300 ptas. Or there's *Camping Asolaze* (☎ 948 89 30 34) nearby.

A good restaurant is the *Tapia*, just out of the old centre on the road to Roncal. You can eat well for 1500 ptas a head or even less.

North of Isaba The *Refugio Belagua*, 19km north of Isaba, is a handy base for trekkers in summer and skiers in winter. It operates a restaurant and bar, and has some bunks to throw a sleeping bag onto. There is no bus up this way.

Uztárroz This pretty hill-top hamlet lies about 3km north-west of Isaba. There are a few casas rurales, or you could try the *Fonda Ekia* (☎ 948 89 30 20), which has doubles for 3200 ptas. The staff also organise hikes and canyoning expeditions.

Hiking

In addition to numerous local walking trails, those with more time can follow the GR-12 long-distance trail across the best Navarra has to offer. You will need a sleeping bag and even in summer you should have all-weather gear. Starting in Burguete, you head north to Roncesvalles, cross the Puerto de Ibañeta and steer eastwards to Fábrica de Orbaitzeta. You may need to head south to the town of Orbaitzeta proper to get a bed (there are three casas rurales).

The next day would take you through the Bosque de Irati to Las Casas de Irati; you can stay in the *Casa del Guarda* (a kind of warden's house) but will more likely end up free camping. The following stage sees you climbing to the bare heights of the Puerto de Larrau (ask at the restaurant-bar 4km south of the French border about bunk beds). The trail then cuts across the Sierra de Abodi and you can reach the Belagua refugio in about five hours march.

The final trek takes you to the highest mountain in Navarra, La Mesa de los Tres Reyes (2438m), from where the easiest thing to do is descend to the town of Zuriza at the top end of the Valle de Ansó, in Aragón (see the Valle de Ansó section of the Aragón chapter).

SOUTH OF PAMPLONA
Olite & Tafalla

The extensive medieval defensive complex known as the **Palacio Real**, which completely dominates the small town of Olite, was built on the site of what was originally a fortified Roman *praesidium* (garrison). The bulk of what you see today was built by Carlos III of Navarra in the early 15th century, and its centrepiece is the Gran Torre, one of a straggle of towers and annexes. In summer it is open daily from 10 am to 2 pm and 4 to 7 pm; in winter the hours are a little shorter (350 ptas).

Olite would make a nice place to spend a night if you've got money to spare. The only option for cheap beds is the house adjacent to the ayuntamiento on the main square; look for the little *Camas* sign. Otherwise, *Hotel Casa Zanito* (☎ 948 74 00 02) on Rúa Revillas and *Hotel Merindad de Olite* (☎ 948 74 07 35, *Rúa de la Judería 11)* both charge around 6000/8500 ptas plus IVA for rooms with all mod cons. There's also a *parador* (☎ 948 74 00 00, fax 74 02 01, Plaza de los Teobaldos 2) with singles/doubles beginning at 11,600/14,500 ptas plus IVA.

Buses between Olite and Pamplona stop 3km north in the rambling old city of **Tafalla**. There's little to detain you save for the dominating Iglesia de Santa María. *Pensión Arotza* (☎ 948 70 07 16, Plaza de Navarra 3) has rooms with bath, TV and phone for 3000/5000 ptas plus IVA. Head to *Sidreria Iñaki, (Calle de García Goyena 14)* for strong cider right from the barrel and good meals right from the grill.

Ujué

Just 19km east of Tafalla (there is another back road from Olite too, via San Martín de Unx, this tiny medieval village clings to the summit of a hill dominating the plains around it. The icing on the cake) as it were, is the hybrid **Iglesia de Santa María**, a fortified church of mixed Romanesque-Gothic style. Several casas rurales offer affordable beds.

Monasterio de la Oliva

Off another side road to the east of the main Pamplona-Zaragoza highway lies the quiet backwater of **Carcastillo**. Two kilometres farther on the formidable Monasterio de la Oliva was begun by the Cistercians in the 12th century. Its austere church was built during the 12th and 13th centuries and gives onto a particularly pleasing Gothic cloister.

There are two or three buses daily between Pamplona and Carcastillo.

Tudela

An ancient city that was in Muslim hands for some 400 years, Tudela's twisting street layout serves as a reminder of its Islamic past. It's well worth a wander, not least to observe the extraordinary sight of an entire colony of storks, who descend on Tudela every summer to occupy huge nests perched atop just about any high spot available. The cathedral tower itself is home to half a dozen stork families.

There is a tourist office (☎ 948 82 15 39) opposite the cathedral which is open weekdays from 9 am to 3 pm and weekends from 10 am to 2 pm.

Things to See Most people set out to explore the town from the brightly decorated Plaza de los Fueros. From here, take Calle de Yanguas y Miranda through the arch and at the next square take a right into Calle de las Carnicerías. This leads to the **catedral**, a sober 12th century Gothic structure built of stone and brick. The west door is particularly striking, its many sculpted figures looking decidedly uneasy about their participation in the Last Judgment. There are some good retablos inside, and if you're lucky you can see the beautiful Romanesque cloister attached. In 1993, traces of the central mosque that had preceded the cathedral were identified adjacent to it.

Perhaps the quirkiest of Tudela's attractions is its 13th century **bridge** over the Río Ebro. To get to it, follow Calle del Portal eastwards (downhill) from the cathedral to the Iglesia de la Magdalena and then head out the scruffy town gate (topped by the railway line). The Spaniards call a botch job a *chapuza*, and this bridge, with its arches all different shapes and sizes, seems to fit the bill perfectly. Yet seven centuries later, it still works fine! The Ebro flows mightily by, quite unperturbed by the lack of symmetry above it.

Of the other churches in Tudela, the **Iglesia de San Nicolás** still sports a fine tympanum featuring lions above one of its doors. It's at the end of Calle Rúa. Take time to wander the streets, as there are some fine old mansions, many with Aragonese-style awnings *(aleros)* jutting out from the roof; the **Palacio del Marqués de San Adrián** at Calle de Magallón 10 is an impressive example.

Places to Stay & Eat *Hostal Remigio* (☎ 948 82 08 50, *Calle de Gaztambide Carrera 2)*, just off Plaza de los Fueros, offers singles from 1850 to 3200 ptas plus IVA and doubles from 3700 to 5800 ptas plus IVA, all depending on room and season. They also have a venerable old dining room.

Getting There & Away Tudela is on the Pamplona-Zaragoza train line and buses operate from next to the train station, southeast of centre.

La Rioja

Mention the word Rioja and thoughts turn to some of the best red wines produced in Spain. The bulk of the vineyards line the Río Ebro around the town of Haro and extend into neighbouring Navarra and the Basque province of Álava (Araba). Logroño, the capital, lies on the Camino de Santiago, which constitutes the area's other main attraction, although the handful of pilgrim stops through here on the road to Burgos are not among the most awe-inspiring.

LOGROÑO

Although Logroño is an important agricultural, industrial and commercial centre, it also owes some of its wealth to its position on the Río Ebro and the Camino de Santiago. There is not a helluva lot to see, but the centre of town is really quite enjoyable and it's not a bad place for an overnight stop and a little bar-hopping.

History

It was the Muslim armies in the 8th century that gave Logroño its name. In the Middle Ages Logroño was the object of a dispute between the crowns of Castilla and Navarra, but its fortunes declined in the 18th century. By 1861, when the walls were torn down to permit expansion, things were looking up and La Rioja's agricultural riches were reflected in the prosperity of the capital.

Orientation

If you arrive at the train or estación de autobuses, south of the town centre, head up Calle del General Vara de Rey until you reach the big square known as the Espolón. The tourist office is here and the old town starts on the north side of the square. A bed, food and drink can all be easily had in the old city.

Information

Tourist Office The tourist office (☎ 941 26 06 65), in the Espolón square, is open Monday to Friday from 9 am to 2 pm. From June to October it's open Monday to Saturday from 10 am to 2 pm and 4.30 to 7.30 pm and Sunday from 10 am to 2 pm.

Post & Communications The main correos is in the old quarter on Calle de Portales. The postcode for central Logroño poste restante is 26080.

Things to See

The cathedral, the **Iglesia de Santa María Redonda**, started life as a Gothic church, a fact easily overlooked when your eyes are held by the voluptuousness of the churrigueresque towers added in the 18th century. Closer to the river and right on the pilgrims' route through the city is the predictable **Iglesia de Santiago**. Above one of the portals is a somewhat uncared for equestrian statue of the church's patron saint. Take a look at the impressive main entrance to the **Iglesia de San Bartolomé** too.

A stroll around the old town and down to the river is a pleasant diversion, or you could pop in to see the free art exhibits in the **Museo de la Rioja**.

Special Events

Try to be in Logroño for the Fiesta de San Mateo on September 21. This also doubles as a harvest festival, for which all of La Rioja comes to town to celebrate and to watch the grape-crushing ceremonies in the Espolón. Another day to watch is 11 June, when the Fiesta de San Bernabé is held.

Places to Stay

At the budget end you can choose from a few fondas in the centre, including *Fonda Bilbaína* (☎ 941 25 42 26, *Calle del Capitán Gallarza 10*). It has quite decent singles/doubles for 2000/3500 ptas. *Casa de Huéspedes Villar* (☎ 941 22 02 28, *Calle de Martínez Zaporta 7*) is really a big apartment, whose owner lets out cosy rooms for 1500 ptas per person. Up the ladder, the *Hostal La Numantina* (☎ 941 25 14 11, *Calle de Sagasta 4*) is reasonable at

3200/4700 ptas plus IVA for rooms with private bath. For even more comfort, *Hostal Marqués de Vallejo* (☎ 941 24 83 33, *Calle del Marqués de Vallejo 8*) is good value. Singles/doubles with *en suite* bath and TV are 5950/8400 ptas plus IVA.

Places to Eat

The area around Calle de San Agustín and Calle de Laurel is jammed with tapas bars and restaurants. You can get great *pinchos morunos* (the Spanish version of kebabs)

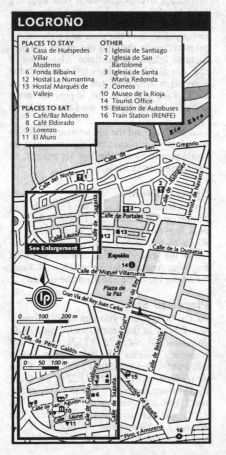

LOGROÑO

PLACES TO STAY
4 Casa de Huéspedes Villar Moderno
6 Fonda Bilbaína
12 Hostal La Numantina
13 Hostal Marqués de Vallejo

PLACES TO EAT
5 Café/Bar Moderno
8 Café Eldorado
9 Lorenzo
11 El Muro

OTHER
1 Iglesia de Santiago
2 Iglesia de San Bartolomé
3 Iglesia de Santa María Redonda
7 Correos
10 Museo de la Rioja
14 Tourist Office
15 Estación de Autobuses
16 Train Station (RENFE)

for 75 to 110 ptas a stick at *Lorenzo* on Travesío de Laurel. *El Muro* on Calle de Laurel is a cosy place for tapas or a meal – the set meal for 1300 ptas is excellent.

Café/Bar Moderno (Calle de Franco Martínez Zaporta 7) is something of a local institution, with old men playing dominoes and drinking wine amid black-and-white photos of the good old days. *Café Eldorado (Calle de Portales 80)* sometimes provides live music to accompany your beer.

Getting There & Away

Up to five buses leave daily for Burgos (835 ptas) via Santo Domingo de la Calzada (360 ptas). Six buses daily head north for Bilbao (1435 ptas), while five services daily go to Madrid (2485 ptas). Other destinations such as Vitoria, Pamplona, Haro and Calahorra are regularly served.

Logroño is connected by train to Zaragoza, and to Burgos and Vitoria. Generally, buses are cheaper and more frequent.

The A-68 tollway from Zaragoza to Bilbao skirts Logroño to the south. The N-111 heads north-east to Pamplona and south to Soria, while the N-120 reaches west for Burgos.

WINE REGION

Spain's best known wines come from La Rioja – the vine has been exploited here since Roman times. When talking wine, the name 'La Rioja' really refers to the banks of the Río Ebro. Much is in fact produced on the País Vasco side of the river, known as La Rioja Alavesa (from the southern Basque province of Álava). Reds, rosés and whites are all produced.

The bulk of the reds are designed to be aged and some of the best years include 1994, 1982 and 1964. Around Laguardia, on the Basque side, some nice drops are also made. They are fruity and soft, and can only be grown in this part of La Rioja because the area has a unique microclimate. Protected by the Sierra de Cantabria from the worst of the bitter northern cold and blessed with an ochre soil different from the red earth of the south bank, the vine produces quite a distinct result from elsewhere in the region.

Most of the wine produced in La Rioja is bought up and marketed by big concerns, but small family bodegas are reasserting themselves. Wine tasting for passing tourists is not a common phenomenon in Spain. Most bodegas reserve such activity for people in the business. Here again, things are changing a little, and some smaller bodegas will open their doors to curious passers-by.

Exploring the Rioja region will almost inevitably take you across the border into the País Vasco and La Rioja Alavesa. See Laguardia & Nearby in the País Vasco section earlier in this chapter.

Haro

The rather dusty town of Haro is considered the capital of La Rioja's wine-producing region. There's not a whole lot of interest here, although the compact old quarter leading off Plaza de la Paz has some intriguing alleyways and bars, and it makes a good enough base from which to scoot out into the vineyards. The tourist office (☎ 941 31 27 26) is downhill from Plaza de la Paz on Plaza de Florentino Rodríguez and in summer is open daily from 10 am to 2 pm and 4.30 to 7.30 pm (mornings only on Sunday and in winter).

The **Museo del Vino** (or Estación Enológica), near the bus station on Calle de Cira Anguciana, houses a detailed display on how wine is made. It is open Tuesday to Saturday from 10 am to 2 pm (300 ptas, free on Wednesday). Check at the tourist office for wineries open to the public; Bodega Muga, just after the railway bridge on the way out of town, sometimes gives guided tours. You can also pick up various bottles of local wines at shops, such as Todos los Vinos de Rioja, which certainly has many, if not all that its name claims. It's just off the main square on Calle de San Martín.

Places to Stay & Eat There are a few budget places on Calle de la Vega just off the square, such as the creaky *Hostal Aragón* (☎ 941 31 00 04) at No 9. Rooms

start at 1600/2800 ptas. Better value are the bright, clean rooms above the *Restaurante La Peña* (☎ 941 31 00 22) at No 1, which start at 2000/3000 ptas (more with bath). Some overlook Plaza de la Paz. The restaurant itself comes recommended, with a set *menú* for 1100 ptas.

For a classier meal washed down with fine Rioja wines, try *Restaurante Beethoven (Calle de Santo Tomás 10)*. Mains cost from about 1500 to 2000 ptas.

Getting There & Away Regular trains and buses connect Haro with Logroño and Vitoria, and buses additionally serve Bilbao, Santo Domingo de la Calzada and Laguardia.

WEST OF LOGROÑO

The road west from Logroño to Burgos is part of the ancient Camino de Santiago (see the Camino de Santiago special section). The route can be covered by bus.

Nájera

The main attraction of this town is the Gothic **Monasterio de Santa María la Real** and in particular its fragile-looking early 16th century cloisters. Inside the church you can see a pantheon of tombs containing the remains of kings of Castilla, León and Navarra. It is open Tuesday to Sunday from 9.30 am to 1.30 pm and 4 to 7.30 pm, closing a little earlier on Sunday and in winter (200 ptas).

San Millán de Cogolla

If you have a vehicle, hit the back roads south-west of Nájera to take in the Monasterio de San Millán de Cogolla. First built in the 10th century to house the remains of the 6th century hermit San Millán, the original Mozarabic structure has undergone many changes. They say that the 43 words scribbled into a Latin codex by a monk in the 10th century here were the first-ever Castilian words committed to paper.

In the same valley is the 16th century church complex of San Millán de Yuso, known a little optimistically as El Escorial de la Rioja.

Santo Domingo de la Calzada

The baroque bell tower of the cathedral stands tall above what little is left of this scrappy town's old centre. Back in the 11th century, a hermit later known as Santo Domingo took pity on the poor pilgrims struggling along a Roman road that had seen better days. He undertook some improvements – including a 24 span bridge.

Among notable artworks in the cathedral is a retablo done by Damián Forment in 1550, but the most curious bits of 'decoration' are the live white rooster and hen kept in a special niche and swapped for new ones every month. The tall tale is that a young German pilgrim, about to be wrongly hanged for theft whilst staying here, was saved by the intercession of Santo Domingo and survived. When told of this, the disbelieving local ruler *(corregidor)* exclaimed that the lad was about as alive as the roast chook he was about to tuck into. The hen and rooster on his plate then sprouted feathers and began to leap about the table!

Restaurante Albert's (☎ 941 34 08 27), just off Plaza de San Jerónimo Hermosilla, has a few cheap rooms and serves a hearty set meal for 1200 ptas. *Hostal Santa Teresita (☎ 941 34 07 00, Calle del General Mola 2)* has better beds for 2845/5395 ptas. The pick of the crop is the attractively presented *parador (☎ 941 34 03 00, fax 34 03 25)*, a former pilgrims' hospice where St Francis of Assisi is said to have stopped over while on pilgrimage.

Buses leave the square for Burgos (66km west) and Logroño (48km east).

SOUTH OF LOGROÑO

A couple of picturesque routes suggest themselves if you're heading south for Soria in Castilla y León. The N-111 itself, after a boring start, picks up as it follows deep canyon walls along the Río Iregua into

---

In the Footsteps of Big Feet

Dinosaurs tramped about most of Spain, but far and away their favourite stomping ground was La Rioja – long before wine was an attraction. Hikers looking for something a little different could choose to follow a route dotted with traces of this prehistoric passing trade. The section of the long-distance walking route GR-93 between the villages of Enciso,  about 10km south of the spa village of Arnedillo, and Muro de Aguas, about 15km east of Enciso, has eight fossil prints of dinosaurs along the way, signposted and with explanations posted in Spanish. In Valdecevillo, for example, you can see the footprints left by an enormous carnivorous biped. Other such fossils can be seen scattered about the area along different tracks. You'll be accompanied overhead by Leonado (griffon) vultures along the 20km route, which lies about midway between Logroño and Soria (Castilla y León). The most attractive place to stay around here is Arnedillo.

the sierras that mark Soria province off from the flatlands of central La Rioja. Several pretty villages, including Villanueva de Cameros, line the lower half of the route. About halfway to Soria you could turn west for Montenegro de Cameros and then drop south for Vinuesa and the Laguna Negra (see the Castilla y León chapter).

Calahorra

Calahorra overlooks the Río Ebro and its tributary Río Cidacos, upon which dwells a moderately interesting Gothic cathedral. To get in you'll have to ask the parish priest in the Palacio Obispal opposite. If you want a room in the heart of what used to be the medieval labyrinth, try *Fonda López (☎ 941 13 14 92, Calle de la Estrella 12)*, just off Calle Mayor.

A Route to Soria

Another good road to Soria departs from Calahorra towards Arnedo, and then follows the Río Cidacos through quite dramatic country. The small, traditional spa town of **Arnedillo**, gathered up in a fold of the valley, it is in a pretty location ideal for a night or two if you plan to do a spot of walking in the area. The road starts to climb after entering Soria province and is frequently blocked by snow in winter.

Cantabria & Asturias

For all they hold in common, the neighbouring regions of Cantabria and Asturias, stretching west across the northern Spanish seaboard from the Basque territories, throw up some striking differences.

Established as a province only late in the 18th century, Cantabria was, until after Franco's demise, merely an extension of Castilla la Vieja (Old Castile). Asturias, on the other hand, has a long history of independence and, along with Galicia, was exclusively Celtic territory before the arrival of the Romans. Asturians take pride, too, in coming from the sole patch of Spain untouched by the Muslims. Asturias, they say, is the real Spain; the rest is simply reconquered land – *tierra de la Reconquista*.

The two regions share a coastline of alternating sheer cliffs, sandy beaches and tiny protected coves. The lifestyles and history of both have been in great measure dictated by the chain-mail strip of highlands and mountains that together form the Cordillera Cantábrica. The rich green pastures reaching down from the hills to the sea could not stand in greater contrast to the standard images of a dry, sun-drenched Spain. To cross the cordillera is to taste that contrast. While to the south the broad, parched sweep of the Castilian *meseta* (tableland) is generally bathed in sunshine, to the north the verdant, undulating hills and meadows are just as likely to be shrouded in sea mist.

Cantabria

The Romans reported having a hard time dealing with the Cantabrians, a people of obscure origins who inhabited coastal and mountain areas beyond the limits of modern Cantabria. From 29 to 19 BC, the fortunes of war fluctuated, but in the end Rome carried the day and the subdued coastal tribes were absorbed into imperial Hispania.

Until the constitution of 1978 created the region of Cantabria, the area had, unlike the País Vasco to the east and Asturias to the

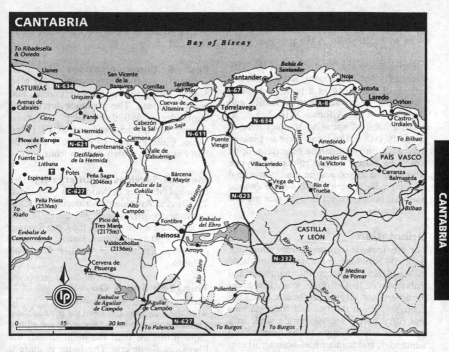

CANTABRIA

Bay of Biscay

(map of Cantabria showing towns including Santander, Torrelavega, Reinosa, Santillana del Mar, Comillas, San Vicente de la Barquera, Laredo, Potes, and roads N-634, A-67, A-8, N-611, N-621, N-623, N-627, N-232, C-627)

west, known no separate identity. Rather, it was always regarded as a coastal extension of the Castilian kingdom (later Castilla la Vieja) and as its direct gateway to what was confidently known as the Mar de Castilla (Castilian Sea).

With a few obvious exceptions, Cantabria is not over-endowed with grand monuments. Its main attractions are natural, from the eastern flank of the Picos de Europa mountains through the evergreen rural hinterland, to the rippled coastline and its sprinkling of pretty beaches and coastal towns. Santander itself boasts fine beaches and a thumping nightlife, while Santillana del Mar and Comillas to the west are among the region's prettiest towns.

SANTANDER

A bustling centre with a clanking port and shapeless suburbs reaching inland, the bulk

of modern Santander stands in somewhat drab contrast to its pretty beaches, particularly the haughty old-world elegance of El Sardinero, which is reminiscent of the French resort of Biarritz, albeit without much of the ritz.

A huge fire raged through the city in 1941, but what's left of the 'old' centre is certainly a lively source of entertainment for the palate and liver. All up, however, Santander is a good deal more staid than its resort cousin, San Sebastián. And if nightlife is low on your list of priorities, you may well want to search out smaller and prettier seaside towns farther west in Cantabria or Asturias.

History

When the Romans landed on the beaches here in 21 BC, they named the place Portus Victoriae (Victory Harbour) and indeed, within two years they had finally vanquished the Cantabrian tribes that had given them so much strife in the previous eight years.

From that time, Santander, as the city eventually became known, led a modestly successful existence as a port. Its heyday came rather late, when the royal family, and especially King Alfonso XIII, began to make a habit of spending summer here in the early 1900s. The locals were so pleased they gave him Magdalena peninsula, upon which he raised a little palace. Everyone who wanted to see and be seen converged on Santander, giving rise to a *belle époque* building boom – most in evidence around El Sardinero.

Orientation

The city spreads long and narrow along the Bahía de Santander out to the Península de la Magdalena. Between the peninsula and Cabo Menor to the north-west, Playa del Sardinero, the city's main beach, faces the open sea. From the bus and train stations and ferry port it's a 10 minute walk in a north-easterly direction to the heart of old Santander, and another half-hour stroll east to the nearest beaches. Most of the cheaper hotels, along with the majority of restaurants and bars, are in a compact area taking in the stations and the old quarter, including the pedestrianised Calle de Burgos, which has most of the shops and makes for a pleasant evening walk.

Information

Tourist Offices The Oficina Municipal de Turismo (☎ 942 36 20 54), Jardines de Pereda, is open Monday to Friday from 9.30 am to 1.30 pm and 4.30 to 7.30 pm and Saturday from 10 am to 1 pm. Another office on the north-eastern corner of Plaza de Velardo (also known as Plaza Porticada) is open Monday to Friday from 9 am to 1 pm and 4 to 7 pm.

Money There are plenty of banks, especially in the newer part of central Santander around Avenida de Calvo Sotelo. American

Express (☎ 942 31 17 00) is represented by Viajes Altair at Calle de Calderón de la Barca 11.

Post & Communications The main *correos* (post office) is on Avenida de Calvo Sotelo, facing the Jardines de Pereda, and has telephones. The postcode for central Santander is 39080. Emailers can avail themselves of the facilities at El Libro Viejo, Calle Perines 19 (just off Calle de San Fernando), which is open from 7 pm.

Medical Services & Emergency The Hospital Marqués de Valdecilla (☎ 942 20 25 20) is at Avenida de Valdecilla 25. Casualty *(urgencias)* is on ☎ 942 20 25 76. For an ambulance you can call the Cruz Roja on ☎ 942 27 30 58. The main Policía Nacional *comisaría* (station) is on the Plaza de Velardo.

Things to See & Do

Santander is rather thin on sights, so do what the locals do and head for the beaches. Those on the Bahía de Santander are a little more protected than the main strand, the Playa del Sardinero. The latter is quite a walk from the centre, so catch one of the local buses from the *ayuntamiento* (town hall). Different lines drop you at various points on and around the beach. Bus Nos 1, 2, 3, 4, 7, 8 and 9 will all get you to the general vicinity. Less crowded are the beaches across the Bahía de Santander. You can catch the launch for Somo island (350 ptas return) from the quay near the tourist office. It runs every half-hour from 7.30 am to 8 pm.

If you are stuck with a rainy day, the pickings are limited. In the centre, the **Museo de Bellas Artes** has a dusty old collection of mostly 19th century works by obscure local artists. The otherwise uninteresting **catedral** boasts a 13th century Gothic crypt. Marginally more interesting than either is the **Museo Regional de Arqueología y Prehistoria** on Calle de Casimiro Sainz. Copies and photocopies of cave paintings, such as those in Altamira,

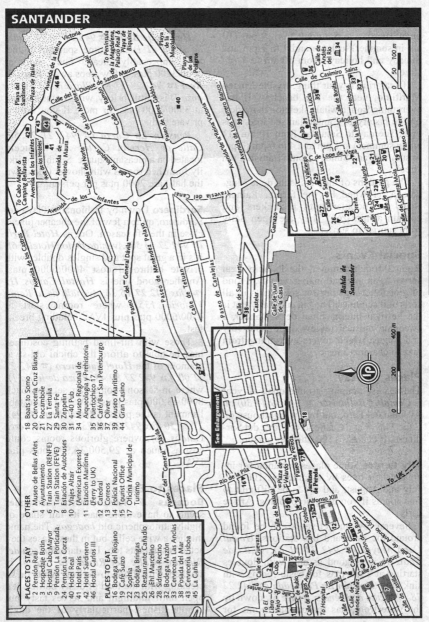

SANTANDER

PLACES TO STAY
2 Pensión Real
3 Hospedaje Botín
5 Hostal Cabo Mayor
9 Pensión La Porticada
24 Pensión La Corza
40 Hotel Real
41 Hotel París
42 Hotel Sardinero
46 Hostal Carlos III

PLACES TO EAT
16 Bodega del Riojano
19 Café Suizo
22 Sophia
23 Bodega Bringas
25 Restaurante Cañadío
26 ¡Eh! Marcelino
28 Sidrería Recino
32 Bodega Mazón
33 Cervecería Las Anclas
38 Posada del Mar
43 Cervecería Lisboa
45 La Caña

OTHER
1 Museo de Bellas Artes
4 Ayuntamiento
6 Train Station (RENFE)
7 Train Station (FEVE)
8 Estación de Autobuses
10 Viajes Altair (American Express)
11 Estación Marítima (Ferry to UK)
12 Catedral
13 Correos
14 Policía Nacional
15 Tourist Office
17 Oficina Municipal de Turismo
18 Boats to Somo
20 Cervecería Cruz Blanca
21 Rocambole
27 La Tertulia
29 Santa Fe
30 Zeppelin
31 4-40 Pub
34 Museo Regional de Arqueología y Prehistoria
35 Puertochico
36 Café/Bar San Petersburgo
37 Oliver
39 Museo Marítimo
44 Gran Casino

and a hotchpotch of ancient bric-a-brac makes up the bulk of the collection. It is open Tuesday to Saturday from 9 am (10 am in summer) to 1 pm and 4 to 7 pm and Sunday and holidays from 10 am to 1 pm (free).

If seafaring is your thing, try the **Museo Marítimo**, near the bay beaches. It has everything from a whale skeleton to models on the history of Cantabrian sea lore. It is open Tuesday to Saturday from 10 am (11 am in summer) to 1 pm and 4 to 6 pm (7 pm in summer) and Sunday from 11 am to 2 pm (free).

The **gardens** of the Península de la Magdalena, crowned by the former Palacio Real, are popular with picnickers and contain a mini-zoo. They are open daily from sunrise to sunset.

Special Events

Right through summer, the Palacio Real serves as an international university, a kind of global get-together for specialists in all sorts of disciplines. The big cultural event is the Festival Internacional de Santander, a sweeping musical review throughout July and August which covers everything from jazz to chamber music.

Places to Stay

The nearest camping ground open all year is *Camping Bellavista* (☎ 942 39 15 30) on Avenida del Faro, out by the lighthouse on Cabo Mayor at the far end of Playa del Sardinero. It charges 1500 ptas per person.

City Centre Some places in Santander increase their rates by as much as 100% in July and August, and it can be difficult to find rooms if you have no booking. Arrive early.

Several low-budget spots can be found around the train and bus stations. *Hostal Cabo Mayor* (☎ 942 21 11 81, Calle de Cádiz 1) is as good as any, with doubles starting at 2500 ptas for basic rooms with sink only. *Pensión La Porticada* (☎ 942 22 78 17, Calle de Méndez Núñez 6), down by the waterfront, has reasonable rooms for

3000/4000 ptas. Try for one overlooking the bay.

Hospedaje Botín (☎ 942 21 00 94, Calle de Isabel II 1) has some spacious rooms kept impeccably clean. They start at 2000/3200 ptas. A few steps away, *Pensión Real* (☎ 942 22 57 87, Plaza de la Esperanza 1) is a little pricey, with rooms starting at 3500/4000 ptas, or more if you want a private bath.

Pensión La Corza (☎ 942 21 29 50, Calle de Hernán Cortés 25) is nicely located on a pleasant square. Sizable, quirkily furnished rooms with shower (loo down the hall) are 2000 ptas per person.

Sardinero Down by fashionable Playa del Sardinero, quite a few of the cheaper places close in the off season. One is *Hotel París* (☎ 942 27 23 50, Avenida de los Hoteles 6). It's in a great spot and singles/doubles with private bathroom cost 4000/6000 ptas. Another good one is *Hostal Carlos III* (☎ /fax 942 27 16 16, Avenida de la Reina Victoria 135), where rooms start at 4500/6000 ptas plus IVA, including breakfast.

Those with fur-lined bathing costumes may be able to afford the chichi old-style glamour of the *Hotel Sardinero* (☎ 942 27 11 00, fax 942 27 89 43, Plaza de Italia 1), where in-season rooms can set you back 8000/13,000 ptas plus IVA. The top establishment is the palatial *Hotel Real* (☎ 942 27 25 50, fax 942 27 45 73, Paseo de Pérez Galdós 28), where glorious rooms could cost as much as 29,500/36,900 ptas plus IVA.

Places to Eat

Bodegas & Restaurants Santander seems to have more than its fair share of highly atmospheric old *bodegas*. The name implies a wine cellar but in these cases they act as restaurants too. The dark *Bodega del Riojano* (Calle del Río de la Pila 5) is stacked with floor-to-ceiling wine racks creaking with the load of dusty bottles. It's open until midnight and serves tasty but simple dishes, particularly of the day's catch. Another good one is *Bodega Mazón (Calle de Hernán Cortés 57)*, jammed with great lumbering wine vats. *Bodega Bringas*, up the street at No 47, serves excellent anchovy and pepper tapas.

If you have some spare cash and a taste for non-Spanish food, *Sophia (Calle de Lope de Vega 15)* is a fine Italian restaurant. The service is slightly eccentric, but the pasta is fresh.

On a more down-to-earth level, the tile décor makes *¡Eh! Marcelino*, on the corner of Calle de Santa Lucía and Calle de Pizarro, a welcoming place and ideal for snacking and doing the bar-fly thing. *Sidrería Recino (Calle de Santa Lucía 20)* has a set lunch for 1100 ptas and you can down a cider with such rarities as Hungarian goulash. The desserts are home-made.

If price is the main concern, one of the cheapest meals in town is the set *menú* for 800 ptas at *Cervecería Las Anclas* on Calle de Casimiro Sainz, opposite the Museo Regional de Arqueología y Prehistoria.

For a seafood blowout *Posada del Mar (Calle de Juan de la Casa 3)* has a set *menú* fish feast for 2800 ptas; the décor is suitably maritime.

One of the most innovative places in town is the *Restaurante Cañadío (Calle de Gómez Oreña 15)*. A full meal *a la carta* would leave you little change from 5000 ptas, but the more modest set lunch *menú* of 1550 ptas allows you a taste of the exquisite cooking here. Even the bar snacks are a class apart.

In El Sardinero, *La Cañía (Calle de Joaquín Costa 45)* has an excellent set *menú* for 1300 ptas.

Dessert should prove no problem if you like ice cream, as the city seems unusually well endowed with *heladerías*.

Cafés The waterside promenades brim with cafés. *Café Suizo (Paseo de Pereda 28)* is a pricey choice, but it has a great range of sandwiches and ice-cream desserts.

Down near the beach at El Sardinero, *Cervecería Lisboa* on Plaza de Italia is a bit of an institution in the town.

Entertainment

For an overview of what's happening nocturnally in town, get a copy of the *Guía Secreta de Santander*. Apart from what is listed below, check out Calle del Río de la Pila and the immediate neighbourhood – it's teeming with bars of all descriptions.

Bars An enjoyable first port of call might be the *Cervecería Cruz Blanca*, on the corner of Calle de Hernán Cortés and Calle de Lope de Vega. It has 32 different non-Spanish beers in bottles and a few more on tap.

The *Santa Fe (Calle de Valliciergo 2)* seems to be the present summertime favourite, with revellers spilling onto the street outside. A quieter bar nearby is *La Tertulia (Calle de Santa Lucía 17)*, with a range of cocktails.

Zeppelin, at the junction of Calle de Valliciergo and Paseo de Menéndez Pelayo, is just one of a half-dozen café-bars around the same junction. The heavily mood-lit *Oliver (Paseo de Menéndez Pelayo 14)* is the perfect place for a sleek late-night cocktail to mellow jazz tunes. Another place for a quiet drink is *Puertochico 17* on Calle de Santa Lucía. You'd never know it was here, as it's virtually hidden behind a garage – enter by the 'salida vehículos' sign.

The *Café/Bar San Petersburgo* on Calle de Andrés del Río is a cross between a bar and a disco.

Discos The *4-40 Pub*, on a small square off Calle de Santa Lucía, is very clearly a disco of the brash variety. Another popular late-night dance spot is *Rocambole* on Calle de Hernán Cortés.

Getting There & Away

Air The airport is about 5km east of town at Parayas. A handful of regular flights serves Madrid and Barcelona.

Bus Continental-Auto runs six buses daily to Madrid (3225 ptas) via Burgos. Frequent services run south to Reinosa and less frequently on to destinations in Castilla y

León, such as Valladolid (1265 ptas) and Salamanca (1820 ptas). Turytrans buses run along the coast as far as San Sebastián (1790 ptas) and Irún in the east and Gijón/Oviedo (1970 ptas) in the west.

Train There are two train stations. From the main RENFE station there are three weekday departures for Madrid, two on weekends. The cheapest one-way fare is 3550 ptas. More than a dozen trains serve Reinosa, five of which continue south to Valladolid.

The private FEVE line is next door. There are two trains daily to Oviedo (1650 ptas) and three to Bilbao (910 ptas). Surfers report being allowed to transport bicycles and surfboards in the guards' van.

Car & Motorcycle Heading west, take the A-67 for Torrelavega for a quick getaway. Watch for the turn-off to Santillana del Mar, an obligatory first stop on a coastal tour out of Santander. Two pretty routes take you south – the N-623 to Burgos (and from there the N-I to Madrid) or the N-611 to Palencia and Valladolid.

Boat Brittany Ferries (☎ 0990-360360 in the UK), at Milbay Docks in Plymouth, operates a twice-weekly car ferry to Santander (24 hours) from mid-March to mid-November. In the remaining months, the service drops to once a week and departs from Portsmouth (30 to 33 hours). There are five fare periods, the highest being from mid-July to mid-August (outbound), or the month of August (from Spain). The standard return fare for car and driver is UK£499 in this period, or UK£654 with one passenger. The cheapest low-season one-way foot passenger fare is UK£87. In addition you will normally be obliged to pay for some form of accommodation, or at least reserve a seat (UK£6). In Santander, tickets can be bought at the *estación marítima* (port) itself, or reservations made by calling ☎ 942 36 06 11.

AROUND SANTANDER
Dunes
About 10km west of Santander lies the most extensive stretch of dunes on Spain's northern coast. From the Isla de la Virgen del Mar, north-east of Soto de la Marina, a walk of up to 16km west to the Playa de Valdearenas is tempting, taking in the dunes and a series of attractive cliffs. You could go to the town of **Liencres** and head for the coast from there, turning east to the Isla de la Virgen del Mar. The best time to visit is summer and autumn, not only for the weather, but also to avoid disturbing the sea birds that breed in the dunes area in spring.

Puente Viesgo
The valley town of Puente Viesgo is downhill from some impressive caves, about 30km south of Santander on the N-623 highway to Burgos. Of the four caves, two can be visited, including the most spectacular, known as El Castillo. In addition to a labyrinth of stalactites and stalagmites, it contains a series of prehistoric wall paintings that, while not as breathtaking as the ones you probably have *not* seen at Altamira (see Western Cantabria), are still worth inspecting. The caves are open Tuesday to Sunday from 10 am to 1 pm and 3 to 7 pm (10 am to 3 pm in winter). Admission to El Castillo costs 225 ptas, while entry to the lesser cave known as Las Monedas is 125 ptas.

The cheapest place to stay is *Hostal La Terraza* (☎ 942 59 81 02) on the turn-off from the highway to the caves. It charges 2500/3500 ptas for singles/doubles but is only open in July and August. The alternative is the expensive *Gran Hotel* (☎ 942 59 80 61). Regular buses run to Puente Viesgo from Santander.

EASTERN CANTABRIA
The stretch of coast between Santander and the industrial city of Bilbao, 95km east, offers jaded citizens of both cities several seaside escape hatches. Some, such as Noja, are little more than beaches fronted by endless rows of holiday flats. The pick of

The Guggenheim museum, Bilbao (País Vasco)

The spa town of Arnedillo (La Rioja)

he view of Olite from the Gran Torre of the Palacio Real (Navarra)

View over the valley of the Río Nansa from east of Carmona (Cantabria)

the bunch is undoubtedly Castro Urdiales, 35km short of Bilbao.

Santoña

The fishing port of Santoña is dominated by two forts, the Fuerte de San Martín and, higher up, the Fuerte de San Carlos. You can take a pleasant walk around these or plonk yourself on the sandy Playa de San Martín.

Buses serve Santander and other towns along the coast, and a ferry links Santoña with the west end of Laredo beach.

Oriñon

One of the nicer beaches along this stretch of coast is at Oriñon, 14km east of Laredo. Popular on summer weekends, the broad sandy strip is set deep behind protective headlands, making the water calm and *comparatively* warm. In contrast, you'll find a chilly sea and some surfable waves on the windward side of the western headland. All-stops buses between Santander and Castro Urdiales can drop you near Oriñon.

Castro Urdiales

The haughty Gothic **Iglesia de Santa María de la Asunción** stands out like a beacon to the curious traveller, high above the tangle of narrow lanes that make up the medieval centre of Castro Urdiales. Equally popular with city folk from Santander and Bilbao, it makes a pleasant overnight stop. Next to the 13th century church stand the ruins of what was for centuries the town's defensive bastion, now home to a lighthouse. Take time to wander the streets of the old town too. Of the two **beaches**, the westerly Playa de Ostende is the more attractive.

Of the dozen or so places to get a bed, one of the cheapest is the *Hostal La Marina* (☎ 942 86 13 45, La Plazuela 20) – a nice if rowdy location. Singles/doubles with washbasin cost 2500/3800 ptas. There are several other small places scattered about the old centre of town, but most tend to open in the summer only.

A dependable place is *Hostal La Mar* (☎ 942 87 05 24, Calle de la Mar 27), with

bright, functional rooms for 3500/5000 ptas (a little more in the high season).

La Pizzeria di Stefano, at the western end of town on Paseo de Ostende, serves excellent thin-crust pizzas for around 1300 ptas; the menu also includes pasta. Great places to snack include *Fast Food Serman (Avenida Constitución 4)*, which does huge sandwiches. Otherwise, more traditional fare abounds in *mesones* and *tabernas* all over the old centre. *Bar La Puerta del Sol*, at the junction of Calle de la Mar and Calle de Ardigales, has a wonderful range of bar snacks.

At weekends in particular, Castro is pretty lively and you'll have no trouble finding late-night drinks in the numerous old town bars.

Eastern Valleys

Short on specific sights but rich in some of Cantabria's least spoiled rural splendour, the little-visited valleys of eastern Cantabria are great for exploring – especially for those who can get hold of a vehicle. Plenty of route combinations suggest themselves, so what follows is by way of an example only.

From Puente Viesgo (see the Around Santander section), take the S-580 southeast and make for Vega de Pas. The town is of minimal interest, but the drive is quite something. The views from the **Puerto de Braguía** pass in particular are stunning. From Vega de Pas you could continue south-east, briefly crossing into Castilla y León, before turning north again at Río de Trueba and following the Río Miera up through San Roque de Riomeira towards Santander.

Another option from Río de Trueba is to take the BU-571 road up via the Puerto de la Sía pass towards Arredondo. This road is full of switchbacks, a couple of mountain passes and isolated little farmhouses. The drive along the Río Gandara and Río Asón, farther east again, is just as rewarding. You'll find places to stay in **Arredondo** and **Ramales de la Victoria**.

SOUTHERN CANTABRIA

Wonderful views of high peaks and deep river valleys flanked by patchwork quilts of green await the traveller penetrating deeper into the Cantabrian interior. Every imaginable shade of green seems to have been employed to set this fairy-tale stage, strewn with warm stone villages and held together by a network of narrow and often poorly maintained country back roads. It is the delight of meandering about here, rather than any extraordinary monuments, that makes an excursion into this countryside so attractive. Many of the small villages have at least one *casa de labranza* (the Cantabrian equivalent of a *casa rural*) where you can stay.

Reinosa & Alto Campóo

Reinosa, the main town in southern Cantabria, is drab, with little to recommend stopping for. That said, 5km south of the city in Cervatos is one of Cantabria's finest Romanesque collegiate churches, the **Monasterio de San Pedro**. And if you're around in winter and have skis itching for a brief run, you could head 27km west to the ski 'resort' of **Alto Campóo**, which has one rather expensive hotel.

In town, the tourist office, near the bridge at Avenida del Puente de Carlos III, is open Monday to Saturday from 9.30 am to 2 pm.

If you get stuck in Reinosa (try not to), there are options for a bed. *Hostal Sema (☎ 942 75 00 47, Calle de Julióbriga 14)* is handy to the train and bus stations and has singles/doubles for 2200/3000 ptas. The part of Avenida del Puente de Carlos III between the bus station and the Río Ebro is jammed with bars, snack joints and the odd restaurant. The most atmospheric is *Pepe de los Vinos*, near the tourist office.

The train and bus stations are adjacent. Five trains run through Reinosa to Santander and Valladolid (in Castilla y León). Buses serve various destinations along the Cantabrian coast and south into Castilla y León, and several local villages, including Polientes (three daily), San Martín de Elines and Arija (along the Embalse del Ebro reservoir).

Along the Río Ebro

The Río Ebro, one of Spain's primary rivers, rises about 10km west of Reinosa, spills into the artificial lake of the Embalse del Ebro and then meanders south and east into Castilla y León. You can follow the river course along minor roads out of Reinosa.

Head first towards Arroyo on the south bank of the lake (you will pass the ruins of Roman Julióbriga). Just before Arroyo, make a right (south). You will pass the Monasterio de Montes Claros, then descend to Carabeo and finally hit a T-junction. Turn left and follow the signs for Polientes. Along the way, several small churches hewn into the rock can be visited in the pueblos of **Olleros**, **Campo de Ebro** and **Arroyuelos**. The best example, the Iglesia de Santa María de Valverde, is actually about 10km *west* of the T-junction. At **Polientes** you'll find banks, a petrol station and a couple of places to stay.

About 10km farther on, **San Martín de Elines** has a fine Romanesque church and marks the end of the line for the daily bus from Reinosa via Polientes. Those with their own transport should push on for Orbaneja del Castillo (see Routes North of Burgos in the Castilla y León chapter).

WESTERN CANTABRIA

Santillana del Mar

You could easily drive through this medieval jewel and never know what lies off the main road. Declared a national monument in 1899, it has preserved its exquisite medieval buildings and cobbled streets, but its appearance is that of an almost artificial town whose public face is entirely given over to the tourist trade. The shops hawk everything from cowbells and handmade pitchforks to Mexican sombreros and a number of workshops specialise in locally made 'Spanish-style' furniture for the more well-to-do visitors.

Jean-Paul Sartre was among the more illustrious of the town's guests to remark on Santillana, but since all the other guidebooks quote him on the subject, we won't.

Locals themselves have something to say about it: *'Santillana es la villa de las tres mentiras – no es santa, no es llana y no tiene mar '* (Santillana is the city of the three lies – it is neither holy nor flat, nor does it have a sea).

Information You'll find a small tourist information office (☎ 942 81 82 51) on Plaza de Ramón Pelayo (Plaza Mayor), along with a post and telephone office. Banks abound.

Things to See A stroll down the cobbled Calle del Cantón past solemn nobles' houses, some with magnificent coats of arms, leads you to the exquisite Romanesque **Colegiata de Santa Juliá**. The drawing card inside is the cloister, a formidable reliquary of Romanesque artisanry, with its lines of twin columns surmounted by variegated reliefs. Santa Julia, who was supposedly tortured by her husband for not wanting to renounce her faith, lies buried in the centre of the church. You can visit daily from 9.30 am to 1.30 pm and 4 to 7.30 pm (shorter hours in winter; 300 ptas). The same ticket allows you entry to the **Museo Diocesano**, housed in the Convento Regina Coeli, across the Santander highway from the rest of the old town.

A little way down the main road from the *colegiata* is the **Museo de la Inquisición**, with instruments of medieval barbarity on show that can leave the visitor feeling a little queasy. It is open daily from 10 am to 10 pm (600 ptas).

Places to Stay Three or four private houses along the main street and Plaza de las Arenas (behind the Colegiata church) have good rooms.

Casa Octavio (☎ 942 81 81 99, Plaza de las Arenas 4) has charming rooms with timber-beam ceilings for 2500/3500 ptas with own bathroom, or less without. There are a couple more such places on, and also just off, Plaza de Ramón Pelayo.

Otherwise, there must be around 20 other places of varying standards, mostly around

the park known as the Campo de Revolgo and out along the road to Santander. The latter area should be tried only if all else fails.

The three *hospedajes* on Calle de la Robleda, overlooking the park, have reliable rooms starting at around 2200/3200 ptas.

More upmarket and good value is the *Hotel Altamira (☎ 942 81 80 25, fax 942 84 01 36, Calle del Cantón 1)*. The rooms are well appointed with private bath, TV and telephone, and start at 5600/6500 ptas plus IVA in the low season. For a classier stay, head for the luxury *parador (☎ 942 81 80 00)* on Plaza de Ramón Pelayo. Doubles start at 14,000 ptas.

Places to Eat *Casa Cossío*, the nearest restaurant to the Colegiata, serves a good range of seafood. The *Restaurante Altamira*, attached to the hotel of the same name, has a reliable set lunch for 1100 ptas. There are also several snack and burger places if you want to keep it simple.

Getting There & Away Several buses call in at Santillana en route between Santander and other destinations farther west, like Comillas and San Vicente de la Barquera, but more frequent services connect the town with Torrelavega, itself easily reached by FEVE train from Santander.

Cuevas de Altamira

Lots of hot air from the yearly flood of tourists to the prehistoric caves *(cuevas)* of Altamira, 2km west of Santillana, led to the inevitable result. The extraordinary wall paintings of bison, boar and other beasts have been closed since 1977 to all but 20 visitors daily – to protect the already damaged images from the moisture caused by, well, too much breathing. You need to plan well ahead to see the famous paintings, scratched into the cave walls around 12,000 BC. You are supposed to write a year in advance to the Centro de Investigación de Altamira, Santillana del Mar 39330, Cantabria, Spain. Admission is 400 ptas (students half-price). For information call ☎ 942 81 80 05. A small museum at the caves contains the fossil of a prehistoric man. It is open Tuesday to Sunday from 9.30 am to 2.30 pm.

Comillas

Easily one of the most attractive towns west of Santander, Comillas offers the combination of a genuinely enchanting old town centre, a handful of monuments and a couple of good beaches nearby to choose from. One result is that you can all but forget about trying to find a bed here in midsummer without a reservation.

The tourist office (☎ 942 72 07 68) is at Calle de María de Piélago 2. It is open Monday to Saturday from 10 am to 1 pm and 5 to 9 pm (and 11 am to 1 pm and 5 to 8 pm on Sunday in summer).

There are several banks with ATMs around the centre.

Things to See Antoni Gaudí left few reminders of his genius beyond Catalunya but, of those that he did, his 1885 **Capricho** in Comillas is easily the most flamboyant, although modest in stature. If he reined in his imagination in Astorga and León, the opposite can be said here. The building – now an expensive restaurant – is plastered liberally with ceramic sunflower motifs on a green background.

Next door is the neo-Gothic **Capilla Panteón de los Marqueses de Comillas**, set in lovely gardens dominated by the nearby **Palacio de Sobrellano**. The latter is a majestic piece of neo-Gothic architecture conceived by Joan Martorell Montells, a Catalan modernist like Gaudí. The buildings and gardens are privately owned, so all you can do is admire them through the garden gates.

Martorell also had a hand in what was until 1968 the **Universidad Pontificia**. Lluís Doménech i Montaner, another Catalan modernist, contributed a medieval flavour to the elaborate design of the building, which stands on a rise between the Palacio de Sobrellano and the coast.

In keeping with the theme, Comillas brims with what might be unkindly seen as

a minor rash of *caprichos* (caprices), the lavish private residences of the town's well-to-do. Comillas' compact medieval centre is full of its own little pleasures. Plaza del Generalísimo Franco is its focal point, an inclining cobbled square flanked by the ayuntamiento, the Iglesia de San Cristóbal and a series of pleasing old sandstone houses with flower-bedecked timber balconies.

Places to Stay You can pitch a tent at **Camping Comillas** (☎ 942 72 00 74), a couple of minutes out of town by car on the main road to Santillana.

About the cheapest place to stay if you need a hotel double is **Pensión La Aldea** (☎ 942 72 10 46, Barrio Velecio 12), near the tourist office and with simple rooms for 4200 ptas. They won't reduce the price for lone travellers at the height of the season.

The ramshackle **Hostal Fuente Real** (☎ 942 72 01 55), in a dead-end lane just behind the Capricho de Gaudí (signposted), has beds for 2600 ptas a person. Back in the centre, **Pensión Tuco** (☎ 942 72 10 30, Calle de Antonio López 4) is a respectable place offering doubles for 3500 ptas, or 4500 ptas with private bath.

If you're in the mood to splurge, head straight for the **Casal del Castro** (☎ 942 72 00 36, fax 942 72 00 61, Calle de San Jerónimo 2). This period-furnished, 17th century mansion could compete with the better paradores. Singles/doubles with private bath, TV, telephone and breakfast cost 7800/11,300 ptas plus IVA.

The town's newest – and most expensive – hotel is the elegant **Hotel Comillas** (☎ 942 72 23 00, fax 942 72 23 39, Paseo de Solatorre 1), which has rooms with all mod cons for 9000/12,800 in high season, dropping to as low as 5500/6900 during winter.

Places to Eat For snack food, tapas and the like, **Pensión La Aldea** is a decent bet, or you could try **Bar El Galeón** across the road. You can eat well at either for around 1700 ptas. A cute little place (try for a table by the window upstairs) is the **Restaurante**

El Pirata on Calle del Marqués de Comillas. They have a set meal for 1200 ptas. Opposite the park leading to the Palacio de Sobrellano, *Restaurante Martina (Paseo de Solatorre 6)* also has good tapas. At the *Capricho de Gaudí*, you'd be lucky to get away with less than 5000 ptas a head for a full meal.

Getting There & Away Up to eight buses daily head east to Santander and Torrelavega and west to San Vicente la Barquera. The bus stop is on Paseo de Solatorre, close to the Palacio de Sobrellano park.

Around Comillas

Of several beaches around Comillas, the **Playa de Oyambre**, 5km west, is decidedly superior – so much so that the road is choked on summer weekends. Inland from the beach lie the wetlands of the small Parque Natural de Oyambre.

Farther west, the **Playa de Merón** is bigger still, a little wild and less crowded. From here you could walk westwards along the beaches to San Vicente de la Barquera. There are a few hotels on the road from Comillas to Playa de Oyambre, as well as *Camping El Rodero (☎ 942 72 20 40)*, just back from the beach and open all year.

San Vicente de la Barquera

San Vicente fell for a time under Roman control and was then occupied and expanded by Alfonso I of Asturias in the 8th century. Throughout the Middle Ages it was an important fishing port and later became a member of the so-called Cuatro Villas de la Costa – converted by Carlos III into the province of Cantabria in 1779.

Today, streams of lorries and, in summer, holiday traffic pour through the largely modern town and across the low arches of the 15th century Puente de la Maza. Towering above it all is the craggy outcrop that contains what remains of the old town. East of the estuary a string of good beaches begins.

There is a tourist office (☎ 942 71 07 97) at Avenida del Generalísimo 20 (the main

street), open in summer only, and several banks along the same street.

Apart from a few remnants of the old city walls and former *castillo*, the one outstanding monument is the largely 13th century **Iglesia de Santa María de los Angeles**. Although Gothic, it sports a pair of impressive Romanesque doorways. Inside, the reclining statue of the Inquisitor Antonio del Corro is deemed by those who know to be the best example of Renaissance funerary art in all Spain.

Aside from *Camping del Rosal*, just across the estuary on the beach, there are a handful of hotels in town. About the cheapest is *Hostal La Paz (☎ 942 71 08 97, Calle del Mercado 2)*, with singles/doubles starting at 2600/3900 ptas. A good deal is *Pensión Liébana (☎ 942 71 02 11, Calle Ronda 2)*, a block back from the main square, Plaza de José Antonio. It has doubles with own bath and TV starting at 4000 ptas. If that fails, try *Hospedaje El Nido (☎ 942 71 26 28, Calle de Carlos V)*, with doubles for 6400 ptas. Outside the high season, lone travellers can usually negotiate a reduced rate.

As for food, there is no shortage of choice. *Restaurante Maruja (Avenida del Generalísimo 22)* is a long-established posh seafood spot. A little scruffier and easier on the wallet is *Restaurante Las Redes* at No 24. Both have tables set up out the back looking over the estuary. In the town centre, *Sidrería La Brasa*, at the top of the steps leading from the square to Calle Ronda, has a 1000 ptas set *menú*.

Up to 15 buses daily run to Santander and as many as 13 go on to Bilbao. Several buses head into Asturias, reaching Arriondas, Oviedo and Ribadesella. AutobusesPalomera has a couple of services that link Santander to Potes and Fuente Dé in the Picos de Europa, via San Vicente.

Western Valleys

Generally ignored by holiday-makers concentrating their attention on the Picos de Europa farther west, the valleys of the Río Nansa and, next over to the east, the Río

Saja make a soft contrast to the craggy majesty of the Picos.

People starting from the Picos might well take the following route. A narrow, winding way snakes up high and eastwards from La Hermida, on the Río Deva. It is a beautiful drive and there is a small hospedaje in **Quintanilla**. The village of **Puentenansa** (with banks and bars) forms a crossroads. The road south follows the Río Nansa and eventually passes the man-made Laguna (a reservoir) to join the C-627 road back up to Potes (this could be done as a circuit from Potes).

Along the way, **Tudanca** (before the Laguna) is an attractive hamlet. Its distinctive houses, or *casonas*, were built by one-time migrants returned from the Americas – known as *indianos*. You can stay in the *fonda* and get a hearty meal here too. The place also acts as a general store.

To proceed east you'll have to retrace your steps to Puentenansa and take the road for Carmona. When you reach the town of Valle de Cabuérniga and the Río Saja, head south for Reinosa. The views are magnificent and the country is among the least spoiled in the region. **Bárcena Mayor**, about 9km east off the main road, is a popular spot with a couple of places to stay and great mesones where you can eat cheaply and well. Locals often hike there from Reinosa (see Southern Cantabria) on weekends. Leaving at about 7.30 am gives them ample time to enjoy the trail and arrive at Bárcena Mayor for lunch, where you should go for the local specialty, *cocido montañés* (a type of mountain stew).

Principado de Asturias

'*Ser español es un orgullo,*' the saying goes, '*ser asturiano es un título*'. If being Spanish is a matter of pride, to be called Asturian is a title, or so some of the locals will have you think.

Ever since King Pelayo warded off the Muslims in the Battle of Covadonga in 722

and laid the foundations of Christian Spain's 800 year comeback, Asturians have thought of themselves – or been seen to think of themselves – as a cut above the rest of the peninsula's inhabitants. One can only wonder if this local pride has anything to do with the fact that the region's name appears to be in the plural – a phenomenon for which no-one appears to have a convincing explanation.

Be that as it may, the Reconquista's slow southwards progress left Asturias increasingly as a backwater. As a concession, the king of Castilla y León, Juan I, made Asturias a principality in 1388 and to this day the heir to the Spanish throne holds the title of Príncipe de Asturias. Annual literary and other prizes in the prince's name to personalities of distinction are Spain's rough equivalent of the Nobel prize.

Although Oviedo and other towns have their moments, the area's real beauty lies beyond the cities. Much of the grand Picos de Europa mountain range is on Asturian territory, and coastal towns such as Llanes and Cudillero make great bases for exploring the coast's riches. For the art and architecture buff, Asturias is the land of pre-Romanesque – modest but unique leftovers of early medieval church-building and decoration.

Asturias' climate is great for growing apples – you'll never eat a better apple anywhere else in Spain. And true to the area's Celtic roots, these apples are put to good use in the production of cider *(sidra)*, which you'll see drinkers and bartenders pouring, bottle held high overhead, more or less successfully into their glasses in *sidrerías* across the region. Traditional dishes are simple, peasant fare. The best known is the *fabada asturiana*, a hearty bean dish jazzed up with bits of meat and sausage. Mountain streams teem with salmon, always a treat for fish-lovers. Another tasty dish you may come across in western Asturias is *repollo relleno de carne* – cabbage stuffed with meat.

Should you be in doubt about local emergency numbers, call ☎ 006 from anywhere in Asturias for any service.

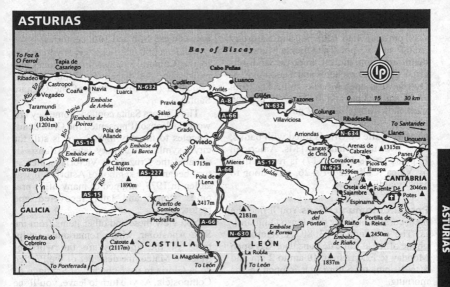

ASTURIAS

ASTURIAS

OVIEDO

Capital of Asturias and in parts a depressingly industrial city of 205,000, Oviedo nonetheless presents a remarkably cosmopolitan face. The modern part of the city centre, with its elegant parks and shopping streets, is agreeably offset by what remains of the *casco antiguo* (old town). Out in the periphery, the hum and heave of factories is a reminder that Oviedo is a key producer of textiles, pharmaceutical products, metal goods, sugar and chocolate.

History

When the Asturian king Alfonso II El Casto (the Chaste) defeated a Muslim detachment that had all but destroyed the small town of Oviedo, he was sufficiently impressed by the site to rebuild and expand it and move his court there from Cangas de Onís. By the 14th century, with the declaration of Asturias as a principality and the construction of the cathedral, Oviedo had secured its place as an important religious and administrative centre. In the 16th century the university opened its doors and in the 19th century industry began to take off. A miners'

revolt in 1934 and a nasty siege in the first months of the Spanish Civil War led to the destruction of much of the old town.

Orientation

From the main-line RENFE train station, Oviedo's main drag, Calle de Uría, leads south-east right into the old part of town. If you arrive at the main *estación de autobuses* (bus station), get yourself to the same street. Along Calle de Uría you'll pass a string of hotels, banks and shops, not to mention the Campo de San Francisco, a huge shady park with swings and the like to keep ratty kids amused. The cathedral rises up in the north-eastern corner of the old town, a mostly pedestrianised district. A good collection of restaurants, cafés and bars waits to be discovered in the narrow streets around and south of the cathedral, while the biggest concentration of traditional sidrerías lies to the north-west, just outside the historic centre.

Information

Tourist Offices The main tourist office (☎ 98 521 33 85), Plaza de Alfonso II 6, is open Monday to Friday from 9.30 am to 1.30 pm and 4 to 6.30 pm and Saturday from 9 am to 2 pm. The Oficina Municipal de Información, in the Campo de San Francisco, also has brochures and a good map of Oviedo. It is open Monday to Friday from 10.30 am to 2 pm and 4.30 to 7.30 pm and weekends from 11 am to 2 pm.

Money Calle de Uría is lined with banks, most with user-friendly ATMs. American Express (☎ 98 522 52 17) is represented by Viaca, Calle de Uría 26, next door to McDonald's.

Post & Communications You'll find the main correos on Calle de Alonso Quintanilla. The postcode is 33080. A Telefónica phone office at Calle de Foncalada 6 is open Monday to Friday from 10 am to 2 pm and 5 to 10 pm; on Saturday it is open in the morning.

Medical Services & Emergency The Policía Municipal is at Calle de Quintana 6 and there's a comisaría of the Policía Nacional on Calle del General Yagüe. In case of medical emergency, try ☎ 006, or Ambulancias Asturias on ☎ 98 523 50 25. The Hospital General de Asturias (☎ 98 523 00 00) is on Avenida de Julián Clavería about a kilometre west of the Campo de San Francisco.

Trekking Information The Federación de Montañismo del Principado de Asturias (☎/fax 98 525 23 62), Avenida de Julián Clavería s/n, has information on mountain refuges and other issues connected with activities in the Asturian part of the Picos de Europa (see that section later in this chapter).

Catedral de San Salvador

In a sense, the Gothic structure you see today forms the outer casing of a many-layered history in stone of Spanish Christianity. Its origins lie in the Cámara Santa, a chapel built in 791 by Alfonso II to house holy relics. It is now the inner sanctuary of the cathedral, which was built between the 14th and 16th centuries.

Inside, a 300 ptas ticket gives you access to the Cámara Santa, Museo Diocesano, cloister and the 9th century Cripta de Santa Leocadia (the lower half of the Cámara Santa).

The Cámara Santa contains some key artworks. Alfonso II presented the Cruz de los Angeles to the city in 808 – it is still the city's symbol. A century later, Alfonso III donated the Cruz de la Victoria, which in turn became the symbol of Asturias. It was stolen in 1977, stripped of many of its precious stones and later recovered and restored.

You view these and other items from the Sala Apostolar, whose remarkable sculptures of the apostles are the work of Maestro Mateo, the designer of the Pórtico de la Gloria in the cathedral of Santiago de Compostela. As you turn to leave, you'll see three heads sculpted out of a single block of stone above the doorway. This strikingly simple and anguished piece of work depicts, from left to right, the Virgin Mary, Christ and St John on Calvary.

The *claustro* (cloister) is pure 14th century Gothic, rare enough in Asturias, and just off it the *sala capitular* (chapterhouse) contains some well-restored Flemish Gothic choir stalls.

The Museo Diocesano houses an interesting display of ecclesiastic art. The cathedral is open Monday to Friday from 10 am to 1 pm and 4 to 7 pm and Saturday from 10 am to 1 pm and 4 to 6 pm.

Around the Catedral

Behind the cathedral is the small but interesting **Museo Arqueológico**, housed in the former Monasterio de San Vicente in the street of the same name. Artefacts from across the spectrum of Asturian history are represented here, but the Roman mosaic and rooms dedicated to pre-Romanesque art are of particular note. The museum is open Tuesday to Saturday from 10 am to 1.30 pm and 4 to 6 pm and Sunday and holidays from 11 am to 1.30 pm (free).

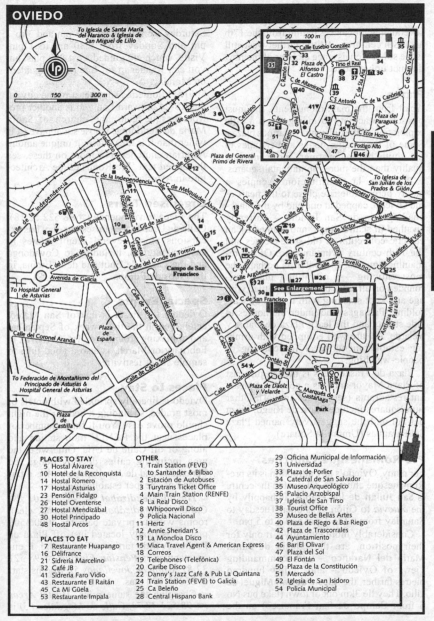

OVIEDO

To Iglesia de Santa María
del Naranco & Iglesia de
San Miguel de Lillo

0   150   300 m

0   50   100 m

To Iglesia de
San Julián de los
Prados & Gijón

See Enlargement

PLACES TO STAY
5 Hostal Álvarez
10 Hotel de la Reconquista
14 Hostal Romero
17 Hostal Asturias
23 Pensión Fidalgo
26 Hotel Oventense
27 Hostal Mendizábal
30 Hotel Principado
48 Hostal Arcos

PLACES TO EAT
7 Restaurante Huapango
16 Délifrance
21 Sidrería Marcelino
32 Café JB
41 Sidrería Faro Vidio
43 Restaurante El Raitán
45 Ca Mi Güela
53 Restaurante Impala

OTHER
1 Train Station (FEVE)
  to Santander & Bilbao
2 Estación de Autobuses
3 Turytrans Ticket Office
4 Main Train Station (RENFE)
6 La Real Disco
8 Whipoorwill Disco
9 Policía Nacional
11 Hertz
12 Annie Sheridan's
13 La Moncloa Disco
15 Viaca Travel Agent & American Express
18 Correos
19 Telephones (Telefónica)
20 Caribe Disco
22 Danny's Jazz Café & Pub La Quintana
24 Train Station (FEVE) to Galicia
25 Ca Beleño
28 Central Hispano Bank

29 Oficina Municipal de Información
31 Universidad
33 Plaza de Porlier
34 Catedral de San Salvador
35 Museo Arqueológico
36 Palacio Arzobispal
37 Iglesia de San Tirso
38 Tourist Office
39 Museo de Bellas Artes
40 Plaza de Riego & Bar Riego
42 Plaza de Trascorrales
44 Ayuntamiento
46 Bar El Olivar
47 Plaza del Sol
49 El Fontán
50 Plaza de la Constitución
51 Mercado
52 Iglesia de San Isidoro
54 Policía Municipal

Plaza de Alfonso II El Casto and neighbouring Plaza de Porlier are both fronted by several elegant palaces dating from the 17th and 18th centuries. A little farther west still is the sober Renaissance cloister of the now defunct **universidad**.

Plazas

Apart from the main monuments, the most pleasurable activity to indulge in is a little exploration of the old centre's various plazas. Some of the smaller nooks and crannies to the south have a warmer, more intimate quality than the more monumental squares.

Plaza de la Constitución occupies a barely perceptible rise close to the heart of old Oviedo, capped at one end by the blackened Iglesia de San Isidoro – currently swathed in scaffolding – and fronted by an eclectic collection of old stores, cafés and the 17th century ayuntamiento. Of the remaining squares, El Fontán is perhaps the most enticing – a crumbling plaza surrounded on all sides by houses mottled with age and kept standing with the aid of scaffolding. Passages lead under the houses to side streets and the leafy Plaza de Daoíz y Velarde. All are well equipped with drinking establishments ideal for chatting or people-watching.

Plaza de Trascorrales is hidden just east of Plaza Mayor and has a couple of pleasant restaurants (see Places to Eat). Other little squares include Plaza de Riego, Plaza del Sol and the suggestively named Plaza del Paraguas (Umbrella Square).

Pre-Romanesque Churches

For many, Oviedo's key attraction is its pre-Romanesque churches. Closest to the centre is **San Julián de los Prados**, unhappily by the *autovía* to Gijón. It is open Tuesday to Saturday from 12 to 1 pm and 4 to 5 pm.

Considerably more evocative, if only for their position, are the **Iglesia de Santa María del Naranco** – with commanding views of Oviedo – and, a few hundred metres farther, the **Iglesia de San Miguel de Lillo**. They lie 3km out of town (take bus No 6 from Campo de San Francisco) on the

slopes of Monte Naranco. The two monuments are open in summer Monday to Saturday from 9.30 am to 1 pm and 3 to 7 pm and Sunday from 9.30 am to 1 pm. Visits, which are guided, cost 200 ptas, but you can wander in for free (and unguided) on Monday.

Five kilometres south-east of the city on the AS-242 toward Langreo is another pre-Romanesque gem, the church of **Santa María de Bendones**, whose squat nave (it is wider than it is tall) makes it unique among Asturian churches. For more on these, see the boxed text 'Pre-Romanesque Architecture in Asturias'.

Organised Tours

The Viaca travel agency (☎ 98 522 52 18), Calle de Uría 26, organises one-day bus excursions along several scenic routes in eastern Asturias, including to Covadonga and the Lagos de Enol and de la Ercina, in the Picos de Europa.

Special Events

Oviedo's top fiesta is that of San Mateo, celebrated in the third week of September and climaxing around the 21st. Carnaval, in February or March, is also a good time to sample street festivities.

Places to Stay

Oviedo is liberally sprinkled with hotels of most grades, so finding a bed for the night should prove easy. You'll find a number of places near the RENFE train station and along or off Calle de Uría. Otherwise, the area including calles de Covadonga, de Foncalada and de Jovellanos also has a fair spread of cheaper establishments.

Hostal Mendizábal (☎ *98 522 01 89, Calle de Mendizábal 4)* has good, clean rooms without private bath for 2000/3500 ptas. It is neatly located just off Plaza de Porlier. A little farther off and solid, if unspectacular, is *Pensión Fidalgo (*☎ *98 521 32 87, Calle de Jovellanos 5)*. Rooms start at 2500/4000 ptas.

Charging the same price, *Hostal Arcos (*☎ *98 521 47 73, Calle de Magdalena 3)* is

Pre-Romanesque Architecture in Asturias

More or less cut off from the rest of Christian Europe by the Muslim invasion and occupation of most of Spain, the small, rough-and-tumble kingdom that emerged in the mountains of Asturias gave rise to a style of art and building distinct not only in Spain, but in all Europe.

The 30 or so buildings, mostly churches, that survive from the 150-odd years of the Asturian kingdom take some inspiration from other sources but are unique. The four in Oviedo are representative of the best pre-Romanesque you'll find. Typical of all is their straight profile – no curves and cylinders here. The semicircular arches that abound to a greater or lesser extent in all the pre-Romanesque churches are an obvious forerunner to a style that would later triumph in northern Spain and across much of Europe – Romanesque. Another precursor to the Romanesque style is the complete vaulting of the nave.

Roman and Visigothic elements *are* visible. In many cases the bases and capitals of columns, with their Corinthian or floral motifs, have simply been cannibalised from earlier structures. Another adaptation, which owes something more to developments in Muslim Spain, was the use of lattice windows. They appear purely as a design effect, since their eastern progenitors were inspired by the desire to maintain privacy from the outside world – hardly an issue in a church.

The **Iglesia de San Julián de los Prados**, in Oviedo, is the largest remaining pre-Romanesque church, and one of the oldest, built under Alfonso II. It is flanked by two porches – another very Asturian touch – and the inside was once covered with frescos. The church of **Santa María de Bendones**, just outside Oviedo, also dates from the days of Alfonso II. It is unique for its extra-wide nave, a peculiarity that is the result of the influence of the Romans, and its simple altar, one of the oldest in Spain. The **Iglesia de Santa María del Naranco** and the nearby **Iglesia de San Miguel de Lillo** stem from the reign of Ramiro I, and mark an advance in Asturian art. An outstanding feature of the decoration in the former is the *sogueado*, the sculptural motif imitating rope used in its columns. Other decoration was influenced by Byzantine and Near Eastern art. The large windows are a pointer to later Gothic solutions in church architecture. The tall, narrow Iglesia de Santa María was originally intended as a royal residence, while San Miguel is thought to have started life as Ramiro I's palace.

ideally located within stumbling distance of some of the best of central Oviedo's watering holes. *Hostal Asturias (☎ 98 521 46 95, Calle de Uría 16)* is an old-style place with loads of character. Low-season singles/doubles without private bath cost 2500/4000 ptas, while doubles with bath go for 6000 ptas. Up the road at No 36, *Hostal Romero (☎ 98 522 75 91)* charges about the same and has decent-sized rooms with TV. *Hostal Álvarez (☎ 98 525 26 73, Calle de la Independencia 14)* is run by the same people and is similar in quality and price.

Of the several more expensive options, *Hotel Oventense (☎ 98 522 08 40, Calle de San Juan 6)* is comfortable and has rooms starting at 4500/7000 ptas. Heading into luxury class is *Hotel Principado (☎ 98 521 77 92, Calle de San Francisco 6)*, with rooms starting at 10,500/15,000 ptas plus IVA. Top of the heap is the *Hotel de la Reconquista (☎ 98 524 11 00)*, in the rather opulent former Real Hospital at Calle de Gil de Jaz 16. Doubles go for up to 29,000 ptas plus IVA.

Places to Eat

Restaurants *Restaurante Impala (Calle de Cabo Noval 10)* does good Asturian food at reasonable prices. The set lunch is good value at 1000 ptas.

Restaurante El Raitán (Plaza de Trascorrales 6) is an atmospheric place where a satisfying meal will probably set you back about 2500 ptas. Next door is their rather classy version of a *chigre*, or traditional tavern. *Logos (Calle de San Francisco 10)* is a good grill restaurant with a touch of class and a set lunch for 1700 ptas.

On the Latin American front, *Restaurante Huapango (Calle del Matemático Pedrayes 16)* offers Mexican cuisine. Lunchers up on Monte Naranco should check out the *Parrilla Buenos Aires*, about a kilometre up the hill from the Iglesia de Santa María, with unbeatable views over Oviedo.

Cafés & Bars Plaza de Porlier is speckled with a nice crowd of cafés for your morning coffee. And the dark woodwork of *Café JB (Calle de Ramón y Cajal 16)* makes it a cosy alternative when the sun's not shining; ensconce yourself upstairs. The lacework of squares around the old town is loaded with cafés to suit all tastes. Plaza del Paraguas in particular can be pleasant in summer, when a couple of cafés put out tables and chairs and later in the evening a tiny unnamed *bar* fills with a lively thirty-something clientele.

For lunchtime *pinchos* (snacks) and a beer, locals tend to converge on the bars along Calle del Rosal. *Délifrance (Calle de Uría 20)* makes a welcome change from standard Spanish set *menús* at the lower end of the eating scale or the usual fast-food alternatives. For 1000 ptas you can get a decent pizza sub, salad and drink.

Most of the places along Calle de Mon are bars pure and simple, but at one or two you can get food. *Ca Mi Güela* at No 9 has a straightforward set lunch for 1000 ptas. More is said below about sidrerías, but it's worth noting that you can get a square meal in most of them, as well as tippling on fermented apples. One of the more popular ones for a feed is *Sidrería Marcelino (Calle de Santa Clara 4)*. A slightly more upmarket option is *Sidrería Faro Vidio (Calle de Cimadevilla 19)*.

Entertainment

Bars & Sidrerías If you're after no-frills drinking Asturian-style, you need to check out the sidrerías. In these places you will often see practised drinkers pouring cider into glasses from a bottle held high overhead. You may just want to have a drink yourself and skip the pouring. This is easily enough done; in most places the bartenders are happy to get themselves wet as they pour. Calle de la Gascona is a classic street lined with the old no-nonsense version, but you'll soon start turning them up all over town.

Annie Sheridan's (Calle Campoamor 4) is an Irish bar with a decent pint of Guinness. *Ca Beleño (Calle de Martínez Vigil 4)* is a well-established spot for indulging in Celtic music, whether of Asturian, Galician or Irish extraction – and those who feel the need can swig a Foster's.

If you're not interested in Celtic music, you could have a stab at *Danny's Jazz Café*, just next door to *Pub La Quintana (Calle de la Luna 9)*.

Calle de Mon is the place to seek out rowdier and later-opening bars, mainly on weekends. *Bar El Olivar* at No 14 is a slightly psychedelic joint, but if it's not your scene there's plenty of choice. Other streets to explore in the area are Calle de Altamirano and Calle de la Canóniga.

Discos Apart from some sleazy 'clubs', central Oviedo is not richly blessed with discos and all-night dance-till-you-drop places. One handy place to check out is *Caribe (Calle de Foncalada 4)*. Not far off is *La Moncloa (Calle de Covadonga 28)*. Farther into the new part of the city are *La Real (Calle de Cervantes 19)* and *Whipoorwill (Calle del Matemático Pedrayes 18)*.

Getting There & Away

Air The Aeropuerto de Asturias is 43km north-west of Oviedo, 39km east of Gijón and 15km from Avilés. There are flights with Iberia to main cities within Spain year round and the occasional flight, including summer charters, to several European destinations such as London, Paris and Brussels.

Bus The main estación de autobuses is at Plaza del General Primo de Rivera 1, but the entrance is unmarked – look for what appears to be an arcade.

The ALSA company runs buses to destinations over much of Spain, including Madrid (3530 ptas; about eight daily), Salamanca, Sevilla, Bilbao and various cities in Galicia. The same company also has an extensive network covering Asturias. Direct services charge up the motorway to Gijón (235 ptas) and Avilés (240 ptas) every few minutes from 7 am to 10.30 pm. Each trip takes about 30 minutes. Intercar has services across northern Spain from Bilbao as far as Tuy in Galicia. You can pick up international services from the same station to places as far afield as Lisbon, Paris, London and Zürich.

Of the half-dozen or so smaller companies, the most important is Turytrans, with offices at Calle de Jerónimo Ibrán 1. Its buses run to Gijón, Llanes and on to Santander (1790 ptas; seven daily) and a string of cities in the País Vasco and Navarra, including Pamplona, San Sebastián (3470 ptas; five daily) and Bilbao. More locally, the same company has buses to Arriondas (655 ptas), Cangas de Onís (670 ptas), Covadonga (800 ptas) and Lago de Enol (1000 ptas). Services to the latter two are not too reliable outside summer and can be cancelled in bad weather.

Train The best way to Gijón and Avilés is by *cercanías* trains. They run from 6 am to midnight and take 30 to 45 minutes to either destination. Eight daily RENFE trains serve León. A handful of these go on to Madrid, Barcelona and Vigo (Galicia).

Finally, there are two stations for the FEVE trains. The first, just down the road from the RENFE station, has two daily trains for Santander (1575 ptas) and Bilbao

via Gijón. For Bilbao you must change in Santander. The other station, parallel to Calle de Jovellanos, is for trains heading to O Ferrol in Galicia.

Car & Motorcycle The main north-south axis through Oviedo is the A-66. If you're going to León, the more picturesque but slower N-630 forks off to the left after 36km. The N-634 is the main choice east towards the Picos de Europa.

Rental There are about 10 car rental companies in Oviedo. Hertz (☎ 98 527 08 24) is handy to the train station, at Calle de Ventura Rodríguez 4.

Getting Around
Up to four buses daily run to the Aeropuerto de Asturias (55 minutes; 650 ptas) from the estación de autobuses, timed to coincide with departing flights; these also bring arriving passengers into town.

About the only bus you might need is the No 6 from the central park, Campo de San Francisco, to Monte Naranco (for the Iglesia de Santa María).

Radio taxis can be called by ringing ☎ 98 525 25 00.

WESTERN ASTURIAS – THE COAST
Avilés
What may have been good news on the employment front in Avilés has done nothing for the aesthetic appeal of this once small but dignified town of nobles, artisans and fishermen. The 1950s changed all that, and the now ageing steel industry has created a nightmarish landscape of factories and workers' slums. If that doesn't deter you, the much neglected old centre is worth a visit – an easy half-day trip from Oviedo or Gijón. The tourist office (☎ 98 554 43 25) is at Calle de Ruiz Gómez 21, off Plaza de España.

Old Centre Just south off Parque del Muelle on Calle de la Ferrería stands the Franciscan **Iglesia de San Nicolás**, whose

ASTURIAS

12th century Romanesque façade has been much restored. Next door is the Gothic **Capilla de las Alas**.

A few blocks west you can admire the crumbling remains of what must have been a stylish baroque structure, the **Palacio de Camposagrado**. Calle de la Ferrería is an enticing street, its porticoes lending shelter from the probable rain – nobly assisted by the range of *chigres* (old-style watering holes). The plaza is fronted by several 17th century mansions.

Cross the square and make for Calle de San Francisco, whose **Iglesia de San Nicolás de Bari** (formerly Iglesia de San Francisco) is essentially a 17th century structure, but with a hotchpotch of elements dating as far back as the 12th century.

From here, the cobbled Calle de Galiana, Avilés' most atmospheric street, stretches south-west away from the centre. The porticoed walkway on one side shelters various eateries and bars; jutting higgledy-piggledy into the street are the glassed-in balconies of centuries-old houses jammed up against each other. If you have time, visit the 12th century Romanesque **Iglesia Vieja de Sabugo**, a few blocks north-west of Parque del Muelle.

Special Events The time to be in Avilés is for carnaval in February or March. It's a frenetic four-day celebration of the end of the winter and the whole event is so big it's known by the plural: Carnavales.

Places to Stay Accommodation is scarce and, frankly, Oviedo is a much better base. If you need to stay, *Fonda El Norte (Calle de la Estación s/n)* is a cheap and cheerless dive across from the RENFE train station with singles/doubles for 2200/3500 ptas.

A better option is *Pensión Conde 2 (☎ 98 556 93 01, Calle del Doctor Graiño 1)*, which has doubles only for 3500 ptas. Those with a healthy credit card can sleep at *Hotel Luzana (☎ 98 556 58 40, Calle de la Fruta 9)*, the top establishment in the heart of town. Singles/doubles cost 8000/10,500 ptas plus IVA.

Places to Eat For food and drink, hunt around Calle de la Ferrería and Calle de Galiana. On the former you'll strike some wonderful cavernous old taverns, among them the *Chigre Gorfoli* at No 20. *Casa Alvarín*, tucked away on Calle de las Alas, just off Calle de la Ferrería, is a classic chigre where you can get simple local meals. *Entre Calles (Calle de San Francisco 14)* is a lively little bar-cum-restaurant.

The pick of the crop is *Restaurante Serrana (Calle de la Fruta 9)*, where superb and well-presented meals should not cost more than 2000 ptas a head. Or for something different, head for *Charolita Cantina Mexicana (Calle de Pablo Iglesias 9)*.

For a drink, the *Queen Maeve (Calle de la Ferrería 4)* comes close to the atmosphere of a good UK pub. Maybe it's the weather and the industry, but not a few of the sidrerías have that 'pub feeling' – only they don't close at 11 pm like pubs in the UK!

Getting There & Away The main bus company, ALSA, has its office on Calle de la Muralla, on the Parque del Muelle. Regular services leave for Oviedo, Gijón and Luarca via Cudillero. The only direct rail line to Gijón is FEVE, but services are regular. For Oviedo, get the cercanías trains from the RENFE station.

Cudillero

Cudillero is the most picturesque fishing village on the Asturian coast, and it knows it. The houses, freshly painted in varying pastel shades, cascade down to a tiny port, where half a dozen restaurants compete for custom. Despite its touristy feel, Cudillero *is* cute and pretty laid-back. The nearest beach is the **Playa de Aguilar**, a fine, sandy strand 3km east. Heading west a few kilometres, the pick is the small but pretty **Playa de San Pedro**.

The tourist office (☎ 98 559 01 18) is on Calle de Suárez Inclán, shortly before the port.

The closest camping grounds are *Camping Cudillero (☎ 98 559 06 63)*,

Playa de Aguilar, and *L'Amuravela* (☎ 98 559 09 95), El Tolombrero, open from 1 June to the middle of September. They are packed in August.

The only accommodation in town itself is the *Hotel San Pablo* (☎ 98 559 11 55, Calle de Suárez Inclán 36-38). Singles/doubles cost up to 5000/8000 ptas. About 2km back on the road towards Avilés (a hefty uphill walk) is the perfectly adequate *Hostal Álvaro* (☎ 98 559 02 04, Avenida Selgas s/n), with rooms for 4000/8000 ptas in high season.

There is no shortage of places to eat. A full meal with wine will cost you about 3000 ptas wherever you try. *Restaurante El Remo*, beside the port, and *Mesón El Pescador* (Calle de Suárez Inclán 9), up the hill, are both reliable seafood places.

Some ALSA buses on the Gijón-Ribadeo (Galicia) route stop here, as does the occasional FEVE train – the station is about 3km out of town.

To Luarca via the Coast

The road west from Cudillero is decent for about 10km, after which weekenders find themselves trapped in traffic jams most of the way to Luarca. This stretch is slowly being replaced by an autovía – to the distress of those who prefer scenery to asphalt. The pebbly **Playa de Cadavedo** is pleasant and from nearby Cabo Busto you can get some measure of the Asturian coast's wildness.

To Luarca via Salas

Instead of choosing the coast road the whole way west, a pretty alternative suggests itself in the N-634, which snakes north-west up and down lush valleys from the Asturian capital to meet the N-632 coast road about 10km east of Luarca. The most significant stop along the way is **Salas**, 45km from Oviedo. It soon becomes clear that Cardinal Fernando de Valdés Salas, founder of Oviedo's university in the 16th century, was the town's most illustrious son. His **castle** has been converted into a hotel (you can climb the tower next door). The

venerable clergyman lies buried in the nearby **Colegiata de Santa María**.

There are several pensiones in Salas, and the *Hotel Castillo de Valdés Salas* (☎ 98 583 22 22) makes an attractive place to stop, with doubles for 6200 ptas plus IVA. It's the best choice of restaurant too. There are regular buses to Oviedo.

Luarca

Larger and more dishevelled than Cudillero to the east, Luarca will appeal to lovers of seaside decay. This is one of those places that, simply because it is carved in two by a murky stream equipped with a handful of bridges, gets the tourist trade accolade as the 'Venice of ...' – in this case, of Asturias. It's certainly interesting enough and it has a couple of mediocre beaches; Venice, however, it's not.

For a better beach, head 7km east to the **Playa de Cuevas**, set back from a dramatic headland and occasionally throwing up some decent surf.

Places to Stay & Eat Those with a taste for the Middle Ages might try the ancient *Pensión El Cocinero* (☎ 98 564 01 75) on Plaza de Alfonso X. The rooms are OK and cost 2000/3000 ptas for singles/doubles. In the same price bracket is *Pensión La Moderna* (☎ 98 564 00 57, Calle del Crucero 2).

Reasonable value is *Hotel La Colmena* (☎ 98 564 02 78, Calle de Uría 2), with rooms costing 4000/6500 ptas in the high season. The most enticing place in the more expensive range is the *Hotel Báltico* (☎ 98 564 09 91) on Paseo de Muelle, overlooking the port. Doubles cost up to 10,000 ptas plus IVA. The restaurant has a wide menu.

You should first direct your search for food to the waterfront. *Mesón de la Mar*, at the end of the jetty, is a huge and popular seafood establishment, but there are other options. *Mesón El Ancla* (Paseo del Muelle 15) has tapas and cider. On the central Plaza de Alfonso X, the *Restaurante Leonés* is a reliable mid-range option.

ASTURIAS

Getting There & Away The easiest way in and out of Luarca is by bus. Regular services run along the coast to Oviedo (2¼ hours) and into Galicia (Ribadeo). The estación de autobuses is on Paseo de Gómez, near the centre. FEVE trains leave from a station a couple of kilometres out of town. There are three daily to Oviedo and two direct to O Ferrol (Galicia).

Navia

Twenty kilometres farther west you strike Navia, another busy port. Rather than hang about, cross the estuary (a modest version of Galicia's grander *rías* to the west) and take a sharp left along what becomes the Río Navia towards Coaña (see Western Asturias – Inland Routes).

Tapia de Casariego

A welcoming fishing haven along the west Asturian coast, Tapia de Casariego makes a pleasant lunch stop but little else. The best of the unspectacular beaches here is Playa de Represas, where you may be able to get a wave. Uluru (☎ 98 562 86 02) on Calle de Santa Rosa is one of several local surf shops.

The most convenient and cheapest places to stay are *Hotel La Ruta (☎ 98 562 81 38)*, on the main coast road, and *Hotel Puente de los Santos (☎ 98 562 81 55)*, just across the road. In the high season, singles/doubles are about 4000/6000 ptas in the former and up to 5000/8000 ptas in the latter.

For nutrition, try *Bar Maxin's (Calle del Arquitecto Villanil 7)*, which offers a tasty set lunch for 1000 ptas. Otherwise, *La Marina*, down by the port, is popular. If seafood delicacies are your thing, you might have the chance to eat *percebes* (a kind of barnacle), more commonly found in Galicia.

Castropol to Galicia

The majestic **Ría de Ribadeo** marks the frontier between the Principado de Asturias and Spain's north-westernmost region, Galicia. Spanning the broad mouth of this, the first of the many grand rías that slice up the length of Galicia's Atlantic coast, is the Puente de los Santos.

Just before you make the move across (or shortly after arriving from Galicia), you could detour a few kilometres down the eastern side of the Río Eo (which joins the ría here) to visit the small, whitewashed town of Castropol. *Pensión de San Vicente (☎ 98 562 30 51)* is nicely situated above the river and is a tranquil alternative to staying in Ribadeo, just inside Galicia. Singles/doubles cost 3000/5000 ptas. The road south offers itself as a little-travelled back route into Galicia (see later).

WESTERN ASTURIAS – INLAND ROUTES

Although somewhat off the beaten track and possible only if you are driving, there are some splendid inland routes into Castilla y León and Galicia that are a rewarding alternative to the more obvious coastal run or the autovía linking Oviedo and León.

Cudillero to Ponferrada & León

Pick up the AS-16 in Soto del Barco, 7km east of Cudillero. From here there are several possibilities – the most promising takes you along the placid valley of the Río Nalón and then the Río Narcea. Head southwest for Soto de los Infantes on the AS-15. The wooded hills on either side of the valley begin to acquire stature here and 8km on the dammed **Río Narcea** matches them.

Just before the misnamed Puente del Infierno (Hell's Bridge), there is a turn-off west to **Pola de Allande**, a peaceful village dominated by the lugubrious 16th century Palacio de Peñalbas. The *Hostal La Nueva Allandesa (☎ 98 580 73 12, Calle de Donato Fernández 3)* has modern singles/doubles for 4500/6500 ptas.

Back on the AS-15, the road to Cangas del Narcea passes the **Monasterio de Corias**. Cangas itself is a rather large and modern place, although not without some charm. Of the two roads south into Castilla y León, the AS-213 offers the more spectacular pass across the Cordillera, the Puerto de Leitariegos (1525m). From the pass it's about 80km to Ponferrada. Alternatively, you could take the AS-227 8km before Soto de los Infantes and travel through the southern reaches of the **Reserva Nacional de Somiedo**, a hunting reserve. Once in Castilla y León, you are about equidistant from León (south-east) and Ponferrada (south-west).

Coaña & the Río Navia

The small town of Coaña lies about 4km inland along the Río Navia. There's nothing much here, but a couple of kilometres beyond is one of the best preserved Celtic settlements, or **castros**, in northern Spain. It is open Tuesday to Sunday from 11 am to 2 pm and 4 to 7 pm in summer, but 11 am to 1.30 pm and 4 to 5 pm in winter (200 ptas).

From the castro, a poor road snakes its way high above the cobalt blue Río Navia, through classic Asturian countryside – meadows alternating with rocky precipices – to Lugo in Galicia, and on into some of the province's least visited and wildest territory, around the town of **Fonsagrada**.

Castropol to Lugo

Rather than hug the length of Galicia's coast, you could proceed south from Castropol along the wooded route via Vegadeo. Take the AS-21 for **Taramundi**, 20km on, a quiet settlement surrounded by rich meadows. You could arrange to stay at the classy *Hotel La Rectoral* (☎ *98 564 67 67, fax 98 564 67 77)*, an 18th century nobleman's house. It's a little pricey at up to 14,000 ptas a double, but there are also separate apartments for less.

EASTERN ASTURIAS – THE COAST

With the magnificent Picos de Europa rising up some 25km inland, the coast of eastern Asturias attracts a good number of Spanish holiday-makers over the summer. A string of pretty beaches and coves provides a tempting counterpoint to the mountains.

Gijón

Bigger, busier and gutsier than Oviedo, the province's largest city produces iron, steel, chemicals and oil, as well as being the main loading terminal for Asturian coal. Many of Gijón's 260,000 inhabitants think it should be the capital and some go to the trouble of buying cars in Girona (Gerona), Catalunya, to have a 'GI' number plate instead of one with 'O' (for Oviedo). As if that were not enough, Gijón in the local dialect is written Xixón anyway!

There's not an awful lot to see here, although over summer some Spaniards are attracted by the notion of being by the sea and mountains and still enjoying what a large city can offer.

Information The main tourist office (☎ 98 534 60 46) at Calle del Marqués de San Esteban 1 is open Monday to Friday from 9.30 am to 1.30 pm and 4.30 to 6.30 pm and Saturday from 9 am to 2 pm. In summer, another booth is open on Playa de San Lorenzo. The main correos is on Plaza Seis de Agosto and the postcode is 33200. There's a Telefónica office on Plaza del Carmen.

Old Gijón The ancient core of Gijón is concentrated in the headland, known as Cimadevilla, that juts out into the Bay of Biscay. Seawards, what used to be a fortified military zone has now been converted into something of a park. Wrapped around the landward side of the hill, descending to the isthmus which connects the old town with the rest of the city, is a fine web of narrow lanes, small squares and dead ends. Plaza de Jovellanos is dominated by the 16th century house of the poet and politician of the same name, now housing a modest **museum** devoted to archaeology, history of the city and some fine artworks, some by Goya and Murillo.

To the east, in front of the modern Iglesia de San Pedro, are what remain of the town's **Roman walls** and **Termas Romanas**, or baths. Built in the 1st century AD, they were only rediscovered in 1903.

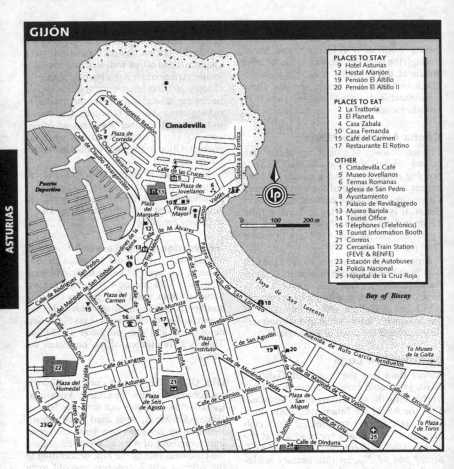

GIJÓN

PLACES TO STAY
9 Hotel Asturias
12 Hostal Manjón
19 Pensión El Altillo
20 Pensión El Altillo II

PLACES TO EAT
2 La Trattoria
3 El Planeta
4 Casa Zabala
10 Casa Fernanda
15 Café del Carmen
17 Restaurante El Rotino

OTHER
1 Cimadevilla Café
5 Museo Jovellanos
6 Termas Romanas
7 Iglesia de San Pedro
8 Ayuntamiento
11 Palacio de Revillagigedo
13 Museo Barjola
14 Tourist Office
16 Telephones (Telefónica)
18 Tourist Information Booth
21 Correos
22 Cercanías Train Station
(FEVE & RENFE)
23 Estación de Autobuses
24 Policía Nacional
25 Hospital de la Cruz Roja

Possibly the most harmonious square is **Plaza Mayor**, with porticoes on three sides and the 19th century ayuntamiento on the fourth. Just to the west, the 17th century **Palacio de Revillagigedo** – now an art gallery – is Gijón's most noticeable monument. It is open Tuesday to Saturday from 11 am to 1.30 pm and 4 to 9 pm and Sunday from noon to 2.30 pm (free).

The **Museo de la Gaita** is part of a complex of museums at the Feria de Muestras, on the Río Piles in the east of the city.

This particular museum not only displays bagpipes but has a workshop for their production and repair. It is open Tuesday to Saturday from 10 am to 1 pm and 5 to 8 pm and Sunday from 11 am to 2 pm (free).

For swimming, the **Playa de San Lorenzo** is a surprisingly good city beach, broad and clean.

Organised Tours Autocares Faro (☎ 98 538 69 79), Calle del Professor A González Muñiz 13, organises mostly one-day tours throughout Asturias. As a rule, you need to book through travel agents; they tend to cram in a lot of people.

Special Events Carnaval (February or March) is the first major excuse in the year for fancy-dress partying in the streets, although it's not as big as in Avilés. In July, Gijón hosts a cinema festival and the Festival Internacional de Música.

Places to Stay There are plenty of budget places scattered about the centre of the new town between the train station and Cimadevilla.

Closer to the Playa de San Lorenzo, *Pensión El Altillo (☎ 98 534 33 30, Calle de Capua 4)* has reasonable doubles with private bath for a maximum of 6500 ptas. Outside the high season, doubles cost 4500 ptas. The owners also have another place at No 17.

A good spot overlooking the port is *Hostal Manjón (☎ 98 535 23 78, Plaza del Marqués 1)*. Singles/doubles cost 3500/5800 ptas plus IVA. *Hotel Asturias (☎ 98 535 06 00, Plaza Mayor 12)* is one of two hotels in the heart of Cimadevilla. Comfortable rooms cost 3500/5000 ptas in the low season, but up to 7000/10,000 ptas in the high season.

Places to Eat Just off Plaza Mayor is a series of lively little sidrerías including *Casa Fernanda*, and if you venture farther in you'll find another popular group of places to eat and drink along Calle de Oscar Olavarría, such as *El Planeta*.

For a change from the local cuisine, you could head for the classy Italian restaurant *La Trattoria (Cerro de Santa Catalina 10)*. Also in the old town is the prize-winning *Casa Zabala (Calle del Campo Grande 2)*. *Café del Carmen (Calle de Pedro Menéndez 3)* offers reasonable-value set lunches for 1300 ptas.

Restaurante El Rotino (Calle de Begoña 28) is a popular, if slightly expensive, and long-standing Gijón restaurant. Mains cost upwards of 1500 ptas.

Entertainment The glassed-in *café* on the Cimadevilla headland is a great place to sip a coffee and watch the waves. If you'd rather observe human behaviour, the sidrerías already mentioned are the place to be.

On the subject of sidrerías, cafés and bars, Calle de San Bernardo and its parallel streets are teeming with them. Check out Calle de la Corrida and also Calle de los Moros. The *bars* and *clubs* that litter the waterfront streets and spill into the *barrio* known as La Calzada are good hunting grounds for late-night excitement.

Getting There & Away For most destinations, buses are the best bet. ALSA has at least 12 daily to Madrid (5½ hours), 10 to León (2½ hours), one to Tuy (Galicia) via Santiago de Compostela and one to Barcelona. Closer to home, there are frequent departures to Oviedo and Avilés. Buses to Cudillero leave regularly and three go to Ribadeo (Galicia). The estación de autobuses is on Calle de Llanes, near Plaza del Humedal.

There are two train stations. The main one (known as Cercanías) is on Plaza del Humedal. FEVE trains leave from here for Oviedo (from where you can connect to O Ferrol in Galicia) and eastwards to Santander. FEVE has direct trains to Avilés too. Regular cercanías trains run to Oviedo. A few long-distance trains also leave from here, although at night they often only depart from the Estación Norte (about half a kilometre west). All trains stop at the Estación Norte anyway, but you're better off arriving at the main station (Cercanías) wherever possible.

The A-8 motorway heads west for Avilés, with the A-68 branching south for Oviedo. Heading east, the narrow N-632 goes to Villaviciosa and Ribadesella.

Villaviciosa & Around

Apart from the Iglesia de Santa María, a 13th century late Romanesque structure, this pretty town is mostly a child of the 18th century. Avenida de García Caveda, the main street, is lined with noble houses, mostly in good condition.

The town makes a good base for church-lovers. The surrounding area is fairly sprinkled with often diminutive places of worship bearing Romanesque or even pre-Romanesque features. Many are for aficionados only, but one that should not be missed is the pre-Romanesque **Iglesia de San Salvador de Valdediós**, about 8km south along the road to Pola de Siero. It was built in 893 as part of a palace complex for Alfonso III in what Asturians dubbed 'God's Valley', but archaeologists have failed to find any remnant beyond this simple church. Next door are the Romanesque **Iglesia & Monasterio de Santa María**, of the Cistercian persuasion. From May to November they can all be visited from 11 am to 1 pm and from 4.30 to 6 pm. Outside of these months, opening times are only from 11 am to 1 pm. Another fine Romanesque church is the **Iglesia de San Juan de Amandi**, 1.5km from Villaviciosa.

Facing the open sea on the western side of the Ría de Villaviciosa is the minute port of **Tazones**, where Carlos I supposedly first landed in Spain in 1517. It is quite a popular spot and in summer gets a little crowded. The eastern side of the ría is covered by the golden sands of **Playa Rodiles**.

Places to Stay & Eat Playa Rodiles has a *camping ground*. There are several cheapish places in Villaviciosa. *Hospedaje Pedro* (☎ *98 589 00 03, Calle del Deán José Cuesta 3)* has singles/doubles for 1500/4000 ptas, while *Café del Sol* (☎ *98 589 11 30)* on Calle del Sol offers them for 2000/3300 ptas. Several upmarket options line Avenida de García Caveda, but for a real treat try *La Casona de Amandi* (☎ *98 589 01 30)*, a mid-19th century farmhouse in Amandi, 1.5km from Villaviciosa. Doubles with their original Isabelline furnishings cost up to 13,900 ptas. On the food front, head for *Casa Milagros*, next to Hospedaje El Ñeru. The *salmon a la*

ribereña (salmon in a rich sauce) is delicious.

In Tazones, the waterfront *Hotel Imperial* (☎ *98 589 71 16)* has singles/doubles for 5000/6000 ptas. Seafood is the speciality in Tazones, although the restaurants are pricey.

Getting There & Away ALSA buses along the coast call in at Villaviciosa on the way to and from Oviedo and Gijón. You can get to Lastres (145 ptas), Ribadesella (325 ptas) and Covadonga (425 ptas) by bus. In summer there are buses to Playa Rodiles. The station is behind Bar El Ancho, off Plaza de Obdulio Fernández.

Villaviciosa to Ribadesella

The only worthwhile stop along this 40km stretch is the precarious cliff-side fishing village of **Lastres**, a scruffier version of Cudillero (see Western Asturias – The Coast) with a couple of 16th century churches thrown in. Try for a room with a sea view at *Hostal Miramar* (☎ *98 585 01 20)*, Bajada al Puerto. Doubles in high season cost 5000 ptas plus IVA. A few kilometres east of Colunga and south off the N-632 is the delightful *La Cabaña del Roble* (☎ *98 585 30 10)*, near Caravia, a great *turismo rural* (rural accommodation with activities). It's often booked up weeks ahead.

Ribadesella

Unless you've booked in advance, stay away from here on the first weekend of August, when the place goes mad over the Río Sella kayak festival. Otherwise, Ribadesella is a low-key resort. Split by the river, the two halves are joined by a causeway. The westernmost half has a good, fairly clean beach, while the old town and fishing harbour are on the eastern side.

Information The tourist office (☎ 98 586 00 38) is in an *hórreo* (see the Galicia chapter for more on these traditional grain stores) just on the western side of the causeway. It is open Monday to Saturday from April to the end of September. The operating hours are 9.30 am to 1.30 pm and 4.30 to 8 pm.

Cueva de Tito Bustillo Those who missed out on Altamira can make up for it a little by visiting the Cueva de Tito Bustillo, on the beach side of Ribadesella (signposted). The **cave drawings** here, mostly depictions of animals, are roughly 12,000 years old; the best of them are in the western half (Sector Occidental). The site is open from April to September, Tuesday to Saturday from 10 am to 1 pm and 3.30 to 5.15 pm and Sunday from 10 am to 1 pm (300 ptas, free on Wednesday). There is a limit of 400 visitors daily, so turn up early in August.

Activities Ribadesella is an adventure sports centre. Turaventura (☎/fax 98 586 02 97), Calle de Manuel Caso de Villa 26, hires out bicycles for 2000 ptas daily and organises white-water canoeing on the Río Sella for 12,000 ptas for two days.

Or you could look in at the Centro de Información de Turismo Activo (CITA) at the Albergue Roberto Frassinelli youth hostel (☎/fax 98 586 13 80) on Calle de Ricardo Cangas. Here you can hire everything from mountain bikes to surfboards and kayaks. The staff also organise kayak and mountain bike trips.

Places to Stay & Eat *Camping Los Sauces* (☎ 98 586 13 12) on Carretera de San Pedro, just in off the west end of Playa de Santa Marina (the main beach), is open from mid-June to late September. Farther inland, *Camping Ribadesella* (☎ 98 585 77 21) on Calle de Sebreño, with its own pool, charges a little more and is open from Easter to the end of September.

A bed (in rooms of two or four) at the *Albergue Roberto Frassinelli* (☎ 98 586 13 80) on Calle de Ricardo Cangas costs 1500 ptas (2000 ptas in July and August). You don't need a HI card and the hostel is on the beach. Otherwise, there's not too much cheap accommodation. *Hostal Varadero*

(☎ 98 586 01 22, Gran Vía 22) has basic doubles for 3700 ptas (negotiable outside the high season). *Hostal Apolo* (☎ 98 586 04 42, Gran Vía 31) has singles/doubles for 2600/4200 ptas. A classier choice is *Hotel Covadonga* (☎ 98 586 02 22), which has rooms from about 3200/4700 ptas without private bath in the low season. In the high season, prices rise to 5500 ptas for a double without own bath and 7000 ptas with (no singles).

The Gran Vía area of the old part of town is a good place to look for a variety of cafés and places to eat. *Restaurante Rico (Calle del Infante López Muñiz 27)* has set meals for 900 ptas.

Getting There & Away Up to eight ALSA buses run to Gijón each day. If your destination is Oviedo, change at Villaviciosa. EASA buses run four times daily to Cangas de Onís, while six daily head east for Llanes. La estación de autobuses is just out of the town centre on Paseo del Cobayo. The FEVE train station is farther out on the old Carretera de Santander.

Ribadesella to Llanes
Several little beaches and coves await discovery on the way from Ribadesella to Llanes, and those with transport and time should always be ready to duck off the main road to see what's about. About 10km short of Llanes, the **Playa de San Antolín** is an open and comparatively unprotected beach where you might pick up the odd wave. More interesting for some will be the nearby Benedictine **Monasterio de San Antolín de Bedón**, founded in the 11th century. You'll be lucky to find anyone in the surrounding half-dozen houses to let you inside the Romanesque church which is its main feature. The unkempt setting makes up for it though.

Llanes
Inhabited since ancient times, Llanes was long an independent-minded town and whaling port with its own charter awarded by Alfonso IX of León in 1206. Today it is

ASTURIAS

one of northern Spain's more popular holiday destinations and, although pleasant enough, has clearly been marred by the nascent urban spread and construction work around the port. However, it is a handy base for some pretty beaches and only a few kilometres inland rise the first rocky walls of the Picos de Europa.

Information The tourist office (☎ 98 540 01 64) is in the Torre Medieval (behind Calle de Nemesio Sobrino), a ruined tower left over from the town's 13th century defences. It is open Monday to Friday from 10 am to 2 pm and 4 to 6.30 pm and Saturday from 10.30 am to 1.30 pm and 4.30 to 6.30 pm.

Things to See & Do Of the two town beaches, Playa de Toró to the east is infinitely preferable to the tiny Playa del Sablón. If you are interested in organised trips into the Picos de Europa, caving, canoeing or horse riding, see what Naturas (☎ 98 540 22 00), Calle Mayor s/n, has to offer. Another such group is Senda (☎ 98 540 26 42) on Avenida de las Llamas (just outside Llanes on the road to Cué).

Places to Stay Finding a room in July and August is next to impossible – and lone travellers will be lucky indeed to get a single.

Camping Entre Playas (☎ 98 540 08 88), just near Playa de Toró, is open from June to the end of September. *Camping Las Bárcenas* (☎ 98 540 28 87) is just shy of the eastern side of town on the main highway.

About a kilometre east of town, the *Albergue de la Portilla* (☎ 98 540 14 66) has beds (without sheets, which you can hire) for 2500 ptas, or more decent doubles for 7000 ptas. Similarly cheap but a little on the nose is the *Pensión La Guía* (☎ 98 540 25 77, Plaza de Parres Sobrino 1), which charges 2500 ptas per person. *Hospedaje del Río* (☎ 98 540 11 91, Avenida de San Pedro 3) is a good place with rooms for 4200/5300/6800 ptas.

Places to Eat A series of lively *marisquerías* (seafood eateries) along the banks of the unimpressive Río Carrocedo (down steps off the main street through the heart of the town, heading away from the port) are the obvious places to look for seafood – *raciones* (meal-sized serves of tapas) start at about 750 ptas. There are a few bars and nightclubs in the side streets too. Otherwise, the narrow Calle de Manuel Cué has some more mainstream restaurants.

Restaurante Siete Puertas on Plaza de la Magdalena is an upmarket place where you'll pay around 2000 ptas for a full meal. If it's just a cider and tapas you want, try *El Bodegón,* the big old sidrería on the same square.

Getting There & Away Buses along the coast to Ribadesella (six daily) and on to Oviedo and Gijón leave from a station about half a kilometre east of the centre. In summer there is usually a daily service to Covadonga, and one or two to Arenas de Cabrales.

The FEVE train station is a five minute walk west of the centre. Up to four trains head for Oviedo, while as few as two run to Santander.

Beaches near Llanes
The little beaches and coves on either side of Llanes form one of the most appealing coastal stretches this side of Santander.

Particularly worth noting is the long **Playa Ballota**, a few kilometres east of Llanes. It is hemmed in by green cliffs and accessible by dirt track; part of it is for nudists. About 7km to the west is the village-cum-understated holiday resort of **Barro**. Its main beach is a little bigger than the average cove and not too crowded. You can stay at *Hostal La Playa* (☎ 98 540 07 66), a friendly little place with singles/doubles for 4000/6500 ptas plus IVA.

Llanes to Cantabria
Apart from continuing your exploration of beaches (Playa de la Franca is nice and has a camping ground), there is little to hold

Picos de Europa 631

you up en route into Cantabria. The N-634 skirts the north of **Unquera**, just inside Cantabria, and through which passes the main route south from the coast into the eastern Picos de Europa. If you're headed east, push on for San Vicente de la Barquera, or even on to Comillas (see the Cantabria section).

Picos de Europa

In May 1995, the Cortes (parliament) in Madrid voted to create the biggest national park in Europe, the Parque Nacional de los Picos de Europa (647 sq km). Way back in 1918, the Marqués de Villaviciosa had established Spain's first-ever national park, the Parque Nacional de la Montaña de Covadonga – the 170 sq km precursor of the new park. Straddling three regions (Asturias, Cantabria and Castilla y León), the mountains are roughly bounded by the Río Sella to the west, the Cabrales valley (highway AS-114) to the north, and the Río Deva to the east and south.

The Picos consist of three *macizos*, or massifs. From west to east they are: the Cornión (or Occidental), Los Urrieles (or Central) and the Andara (or Oriental). The mostly limestone mountains, although not extraordinarily high (the highest peak, Torre Cerredo, is 2648m), offer plenty for walkers, climbers and cavers of all skill levels. Paragliding and white-water rafting are alternative activities and the pretty beaches along the Bay of Biscay are never far away.

As a measure of its popularity (mostly with Spaniards), the former Parque Nacional de la Montaña de Covadonga was getting 1.2 million visitors a year by 1995 – mostly in summer and at Easter.

Ecologists were chuffed by the 1995 result to enlarge the park, but opposition was fierce from some quarters, particularly inhabitants of various villages inside the park who feared they would find themselves reduced to exhibits in a reserve. With some 30 species of reptile and amphibious animal, 130 species of bird and the occa-

sional wolf and bear, the park is a rare enclave of what remains of Europe's once-teeming wildlife.

Information

The park's main tourist office is the Casa Dago (☎ 98 584 86 14), Avenida Covadonga 43, Cangas de Onís. The office has dozens of guides available for walking tours. Other information booths are in Arenas de Cabrales and Potes.

All three towns have banks (ATMs are in short supply, so remember that most banks open Monday to Friday from about 8.30 am to 2 pm) and good supermarkets.

Slow and virtually deserted in winter, the area is full to bursting in August and you should always try to call ahead, whether you are heading for a hotel or a mountain refuge.

Several operators offering everything from 4WD tours to mountain bike rental are listed throughout this section.

Ecology & Environment

One disconcerting aspect of the massive summer influx is the rubbish many people leave behind, especially by the lakes and along the Cares gorge. The opinion seems to prevail that *someone* will come and tidy it all up. It's important not to fall into this selfish habit. You transported your rubbish up here, so take it out again.

Flora & Fauna

At first glance, talking of flora in the bald, grey peaks of the Picos may seem hopeful, but of course at lower levels there is plenty. Among native trees thrive oaks, chestnuts, hazelnuts and corks.

Although the odd bear *(oso pardo)* still survives, along with dwindling packs of wolves *(lobo)*, you are highly unlikely to see either. Elsewhere in the Cordillera Cantábrica wolves are occasionally driven down towards the mountain pueblos when snow sets in, but again it is hardly a frequent occurrence. A total of perhaps 50 bears survive across the entire Cordillera Cantábrica. Mountain wildcats *(gato*

PICOS DE EUROPA

PICOS DE EUROPA

montés) are also increasingly rare. More common in the Picos is the chamois (*rebeco*), a kind of cross between antelope and mountain goat. Foxes, squirrels and wild boar abound in more heavily wooded areas, while beavers can be found in the rivers.

Lack of space prevents us from individually covering all the frog, lizard and other reptile species that inhabit the Picos.

A variety of eagles, hawks and other raptors fill the skies above the Picos, but you'd be truly lucky to catch sight of the majestic golden eagle (*águila real*) or the huge scavenging griffon vulture (*buitre leonado*).

Planning

When to Go The weather across northern Spain is similar to what you'd find in Great Britain, Ireland or Brittany; in the Picos it's notoriously changeable. You could begin a walk in brilliant sunshine, only to find yourself enveloped in a chilly pea-soup fog a few hours later. That said, the south-eastern end of the Picos is generally drier than farther north and west, as much of the moist weather coming in off the Atlantic doesn't make it right across the range.

Given that there are no guarantees of pleasant weather at any time of year, the time to avoid is August, when most of Spain is on the move and finding rooms is near impossible. July is not far behind. May, June and September are about the best times to visit – more tranquil and just as likely to be candidates for sunshine as August. In fact, most serious hikers and climbers choose September, as it tends to be the driest month – an important consideration when stuck up in the heights. Drivers should beware of bad weather. Conditions can become extremely dangerous – especially in winter, when chains are needed.

What to Bring For the walks mentioned here, you don't need special equipment. However, sun protection (hats, creams, sunglasses) is a good idea, as is a water bottle – sources of water are irregular at best. Proper walking shoes are helpful, if not absolutely necessary, and even on a sunny day you might consider taking some items of warmer clothing and even a raincoat. For any treks or climbs off established tracks, you'll need the appropriate gear and experience.

Books & Maps For more detailed information on the Picos de Europa, refer to Lonely Planet's *Walking in Spain*.

One of the better general maps of the whole Picos area is by Miguel Ángel Adrados at a scale of 1:75,000. For Spanish-readers there is a detailed accompanying walking guide. The same guy has also written a route guide for mountain bikers that includes the Picos, *Cordillera Cantábrica – Ciclo-Travesías*.

More detailed maps include the set of two published by Editorial Alpina for 500 ptas each (scale 1:25,000) and a series covering an area considerably beyond the boundaries of the Picos and put out by IGN.

Warning

The Picos de Europa are not the highest mountains in Europe, but walkers and climbers should come armed with a dose of respect. In particular, those attempting the tougher walks and climbs must bear several factors in mind: the weather is changeable, and snow, rain and fog are common problems. Higher up, few trails are marked and there is virtually no animal life or vegetation. Water sources are infrequent. Paying insufficient attention to these details has cost several lives over the years and you don't want to join the statistics.

Each sheet (1:25,000) costs 300 ptas (look for the plain blue covers). Unfortunately none is free of errors. The bookshops in Potes and Cangas de Onís are stacked with guidebooks of varying quality to the area, a couple of them in English.

Getting Around

Without your own wheels, getting around can be frustrating if you aim to taste the main delights of the Picos without hanging around long enough to crisscross them on foot.

The most frequent transport all year round links Cangas de Onís with Oviedo, Arenas de Cabrales and Ribadesella. In summer a couple of buses daily run between Arenas and Panes, as well as between Panes and Potes (and on to Fuente Dé). Up to five daily connect Covadonga with the lakes.

For the rest of the year, services drop to a trickle, sometimes not even one bus daily. In summer at least, several private operators run 4WDs between less accessible parts of the mountains.

Where you enter the Picos will largely depend on where you're coming from and what most grabs your fancy. Many visitors combine excursions into the mountains with a stay on or near the coast. Here we can do

ing in the north-west (Covadonga and the lakes) and taking in the western flank of the Picos. We then proceed east across the northern rim of the massifs, exploring trails into the mountains. From there we follow the road that descends along the east side of the Picos towards the southern approaches.

WESTERN PICOS & THE LAKES
Arriondas

Eighteen kilometres inland from Ribadesella on the N-634 highway to Oviedo, Arriondas is only interesting as the starting point for white-water excursions down the Río Sella. There is a camping ground, the *Sella (☎ 98 584 09 68)*, and a youth hostel, the *Arriondas (☎ 98 584 03 34, Calle del Barco s/n)*. The former is open for Easter and from June to September; the latter is open all year.

Canoasturs (☎ 98 584 05 72), near the camping ground, and Jaire (☎ 98 584 14 64), Calle de Juan Carlos I 7, will both send you downriver to Ribadesella. Such a trip can cost 3000 ptas, but shop around and find out what each company throws in (such as transport from and to the town you are staying in). The descent takes about four to five hours and these companies provide all the equipment.

Cangas de Onís

Good King Pelayo, after his victory at Covadonga, moved down the hill about 12km to settle the base of his nascent Asturian kingdom in Cangas in 722. Though Cangas had been inhabited since well before the Romans arrived on the scene, this was nevertheless the town's big moment in history, lasting 70 years until the capital was moved to Oviedo.

Its second boom time seems to have arrived with the latter 20th century invasion of tourists. In August especially the largely modern town is full to bursting with trekkers, campers, holiday-makers and not a few people desperately searching for a room – a common story throughout eastern Asturias in high summer.

If you do get a room, Cangas makes a reasonable base, although as usual you'll be better placed if you have a vehicle. The town itself, sitting astride the Río Sella, is a pleasant enough little spot.

Information In addition to Casa Dago (see earlier), there is a tourist kiosk (☎ 98 584 80 05) on Avenida de Covadonga. It is open only in summer, from Monday to Saturday from 10 am to 2 pm and 4 to 9 pm and Sunday from 10 am to 1 pm and 4 to 8 pm. It is surprisingly bereft of information. There is a fair smattering of banks with ATMs in Cangas; stock up on cash here.

Things to See With one outstanding exception, Cangas is bereft of historical monuments. The so-called **Puente Romano** spanning the Río Sella is almost certainly medieval, but no less impressive for all that. Not far off, the tiny **Ermita de Santa Cruz** is an entirely modern building standing on what has been a sacred site for several millennia. Walk inside and you can observe a megalithic tomb in the crypt. The first Christian church was built here in 437 AD, on the remains of a modest Roman temple.

Activities Cangas Aventura (☎ 98 584 92 61), Avenida de Covadonga s/n, offers a range of activities, including excursions to the Cares Gorge, descents of the Río Sella by canoe (3000 ptas), horse riding (3000 ptas for three hours) and rock climbing (6000 ptas). They hire out mountain bikes for 2000 ptas daily. You could also try Guías de Montaña (☎ 98 584 89 16), Calle de Emilio Laria 2, for walking and trekking information.

Places to Stay & Eat One of the best deals you'll find is *Pensión El Chofer (☎ 98 584 83 05, Calle de Emilio Laria 10)*, which has doubles only for 5000 ptas in the high season. There are a couple of nameless *pensiones* near the Puente Romano. The first *(Avenida de Castilla 1)*, on the road to Riaño, is on the 1st floor and has doubles for 3700 ptas. The other, around the corner on the main drag (look for the red '*Pensión*' sign) has doubles/triples for 4500/6600 ptas. Even if these places were willing to give their telephone numbers, they wouldn't take a booking.

If you miss out on these in the high season, you'll be looking at about 4000/6000 ptas minimum for singles/doubles in any one of several hostales. For a little more comfort, try the *Hotel Puente Romano* (☎ 98 584 93 39), about 50 metres from the bridge on the road to Oviedo, with singles/doubles for 6000/8000 ptas. Note that August is the peak month and prices drop considerably in September and even July.

Restaurante Mario (Avenida de Covadonga 19) is a good bet. Next door, *Los Arcos* has an excellent set meal for 1300 ptas.

Getting There & Away There are buses (ALSA and Turytrans) from Oviedo and a few from Gijón, as well as local connections to Ribadesella, Llanes and Arenas de Cabrales. In summer there are up to six buses to Covadonga. The main stop is nearly opposite the tourist office on Avenida de Covadonga. If you have a group, you might consider using Taxitur (☎ 98 584 87 97) to reach the lakes above Covadonga.

Covadonga

Covadonga's importance lies in what it represents rather than what it is. It was here that the Muslims were defeated in 722 by King Pelayo, who set up the Asturian kingdom considered the beginning of the Reconquista – a mere 800 year project. More recently, Covadonga was also the object of much fascist propagandist rot about Spanish unity, attracting right-wing rallies aimed at returning Spain to its Fascist past.

The place is an object of pilgrimage, for in a cave here the Virgin supposedly appeared to Pelayo's warriors before the battle. Subsequently a holy **sanctuary** *(santuario)* was built, and it still attracts crowds of faithful today. Landslides destroyed

much of the zone in the 19th century, so the little chapel and statuette of the Virgin (Nuestra Señora de Covadonga) are comparatively modern, as is the basilica. A **magic spring** is supposed to assure marriage to those who drink from its waters. Weekend and summer queues of faithful or superstitious lined up to get into the cave are matched only by the frightening parade of cars crawling past to get up to the Lago de Enol and Lago de la Ercina. Opposite the basilica is the **Tesoro de la Santina**, a museum filled with all sorts of items, mostly donations by the illustrious faithful. It is open daily from 11.30 am to 2 pm and 4 to 6 pm (50 ptas).

The *Hostal El Peregrino* (☎ 98 584 60 47) is a pleasant mid-range accommodation possibility, with views across to the santuario. The restaurant here is well overpriced and those who can should dine in Cangas or prepare their own food. There is at least one other mid-range hostal within the town boundaries and several scattered along the road to Cangas de Onís.

In summer up to six buses daily come from Cangas de Onís, and three or so from Oviedo and Gijón.

Lago de Enol & Lago de la Ercina

In summer, don't be deterred from joining the almost unbroken line of vehicles crawling up the 12 steep kilometres from Covadonga to the last remaining glacial lakes in the Picos, possibly the most overrun part of the national park. Most of the day-trippers don't make it past patting a few cows' noses near the lakes, so walking here is as pleasant as anywhere else in the Picos.

Lago de Enol is the first lake you strike. There is a *refugio* (☎ 98 584 85 76), open all year, and a *camping ground* (also ☎ 98 584 85 76) here, and there's another *camping ground* at Lago de la Ercina, farther east. When mist descends, the lakes, surrounded by the green pasture and bald rock that characterise this part of the Picos, take on an eerie appearance. In July and

take on an eerie appearance. In July and August, five EASA buses daily come up to the lakes from Covadonga.

Hikes from the Lakes Two classic and fairly easy trails begin and end at the lakes. The first leads from Lago de la Ercina south-east to the **Vega de Ario**, where there is a *refugio (for information call ☎ 98 522 79 75)* with room for 40 people (1000 ptas for a bunk bed).

The last stages around the Vega Robles are marked with splodges of yellow paint, and the reward for about 2½ hours effort is some magnificent views across the Cares gorge to the Macizo Central of the Picos.

The alternative walk takes you roughly south from Lago de Enol to the ***Refugio de Vegarronda** (information ☎ 98 584 91 54)*, and on to the **Mirador de Ordiales** (lookout point), which overlooks a 1km sheer drop down into the Valle de Angón. It's about a three hour walk – virtually a stroll along a mule track as far as the refugio, then a little more challenging on up to the mirador.

Río Sella

The road south of Cangas de Onís follows the Río Sella into one of the most extraordinary passes in Spain, if not all Europe. The Desfiladero de los Beyos road is a remarkable feat of engineering, and links Asturias directly to Castilla y León. The gorge is a dramatic demarcation line of the western extremity of the Picos.

Oseja de Sajambre Once inside the province of León you soon strike Oseja de Sajambre, an average sort of town in a highly picturesque bend of the road, with magnificent views across the gorge. *Hostal Pontón (☎ 987 74 03 16)*, on the main road, charges 3500/4500 ptas for singles/doubles. As well, you can usually find someone renting rooms privately. There are also a couple of restaurants and grocery shops in the town.

Three days a week in each direction, the Madrid-Llanes bus calls in at Oseja de Sajambre: Sunday, Tuesday and Thursday heading to Llanes via Cangas de Onís and Ribadesella; and Monday, Wednesday and Friday to Madrid via Riaño, Sahagún and Valladolid. A separate bus runs to Cangas on Monday, Wednesday and Friday (with extra services in July and August).

Soto de Sajambre For a better base for walking, you could head 6km north-east from Oseja de Sajambre to Soto de Sajambre, considerably higher up and a much prettier village by a freshwater stream. The *Hostal Peñasanta (☎ 987 74 03 26)* on Calle Principal charges 3000/4500 ptas and can organise horse-riding excursions. Here, as in Oseja de Sajambre, you can usually rent a private room.

Various walking possibilities present themselves from Soto de Sajambre, including about a five hour hike north to Amieva, accessible to most walkers, and a more difficult trail eastwards to Posada de Valdeón. The only real option is to hitch from Oseja de Sajambre to Soto de Sajambre if you don't have your own vehicle.

Embalse de Riaño The road south from Oseja de Sajambre to the beautiful Embalse de Riaño is a worthwhile drive, and the reservoir itself, with its stunning rocky backdrop, is a delight to the eyes, although there has been much controversy over its creation. In 1987 the valley was flooded and its inhabitants evacuated with paltry compensation. The town of the same name is pretty characterless as a result. The bus between Llanes and Madrid (see Oseja de Sajambre earlier) stops here, but only runs three times a week in each direction.

MACIZO CENTRAL

The star attraction of the central massif of the Picos is the gorge that divides it from Cornión, its western counterpart. The Garganta del Cares (Cares Gorge) is possibly the most popular walk in the Picos. The trail can be crowded in summer but the walk is worthwhile, and this part of the Picos has plenty of less heavily tramped walking paths and climbing challenges once you've 'done' the Cares.

You can approach the area from several directions, but for many the easiest will be to come from the north. A good base would be in or near Arenas de Cabrales, if not right up on the trailhead at Poncebos.

Cangas de Onís to Arenas de Cabrales

The AS-114 takes you east from Cangas along a road that roughly marks off the northern side of the Picos. There are several hotels, hostales and camping grounds along the way.

Carreña Some 25km along you hit this unassuming town on the Río Casaño, a few kilometres short of the more bustling Arenas de Cabrales and the confluence with the Río Cares. There are a couple of banks in Carreña, but no ATMs. For English-speaking guides to the Picos de Europa, try Spantrek (☎ 98 584 55 41) or inquire at the Hostal Casa Corro.

There are a few fairly cheap places to stay on the main road here if you have no luck farther on in Arenas. *Hostal Cabrales* (☎ 98 584 50 06) is a friendly little place with singles/doubles for 2500/4000 ptas. *Hostal Casa Ramón* (☎ 98 584 50 39) charges about the same for fairly modern, characterless rooms with bath – although in both cases lone travellers will probably pay for double occupancy in the high season. A slight step upwards is the *Hostal Casa Corro* (☎ 98 584 52 15), which charges 5500 ptas for a double with private bathroom.

Arenas de Cabrales

Another 5km east, Arenas de Cabrales (or just plain Arenas), lies at the confluence of the Río Cares and Río Casaño. The busy main road is lined with hotels, restaurants and bars, and just off it lies a quiet little tangle of tranquil squares and back lanes. Arenas makes as good a base as any for the Picos.

Information The tourist office (☎ 98 584 52 84), in a kiosk on the main road in the middle of town, is open in summer, at Easter and on long weekends. Opening hours are Tuesday to Sunday from 10 am to 2 pm and 4 to 7 pm, and the staff have quite a lot of information on activities in the area. Albergue de Cabrales (☎ 98 584 64 45) on Plaza del Castañeu organises 4WD excursions and the like. Its office is open from 8 to 10 am and 6 pm to midnight in summer. Maps of the Picos are available at newsstands. There is a correos, bank and ATM on the main street.

Places to Stay The *Pensión El Castañeu* (☎ 98 584 65 73), Barrio El Castañeu, is set on a quiet little square just back from the tourist office. Small singles without private bath cost 1900 ptas, and doubles with private bathroom are 4500 ptas. The *Pensión Casa Fermín* (☎ 98 584 65 66),

Say Cheese

The Cabrales valley, running along the northern rim of the Picos de Europa and kept fertile by regular rains coming in off the Atlantic, is home to a blue cheese much appreciated by connoisseurs. Untreated cows' milk, particularly that milked over the months of May to July, is mixed with lesser quantities of goats' and sheep's milk. It then takes up to six months for the cheese to mature in caves scattered across the valley. It is the penicillium fungus that gives the cheese its blue hue and a creamy consistency – not to mention a rather strong odour. In this case the bite is every bit as powerful as the olfactory bark, as a good Cabrales cheese tends to have considerable kick. Every August, Arenas de Cabrales hosts a 'cultural week' to celebrate cheese. Apart from the inevitable mutual back-slapping about how great the cheese is, and the predictable cheese tastings, there are exhibitions and folkloric musical performances. Similar cheeses made elsewhere in the Picos include the *picón*, produced in Treviso.

just around the corner from the tourist office, has doubles for 3400 ptas without private bath and 4000 ptas with. You can bargain for singles outside the high season. *Hotel Naranjo de Bulnes (☎ 98 584 65 19, Carretera General s/n)* is a comfortable mid-range spot with rooms for 3800/6000 ptas plus IVA.

Places to Eat The restaurant in the *Hotel Picos de Europa* has a good set meal for 1300 ptas. Otherwise, the *Pensión El Castañeu* has a modestly priced restaurant with a varied menu. You could eat well a la carta for less than 2000 ptas. A classier choice is *Casa Victoria*, across the river on the road to Poncebos.

Entertainment For drinks and a little *movida*, the *Sidrería La Palma* at the eastern end of town is one of the best places. *Disco Xana*, two doors down from the supermarket, is about the only late-night dancing alternative.

Getting There & Away There are one or two buses in the summer months between Arenas and Llanes on the coast. Otherwise, four regular buses run west to Cangas de Onís (from where you can push on to Oviedo), and two east to Panes (where you can pick up a connection for Potes and Fuente Dé). Buses stop next to the tourist office.

Garganta del Cares

Twelve kilometres of well-maintained track high above the Río Cares between Camarmeña/Poncebos and Caín constitute, perhaps unfortunately, one of the most popular walks in the Picos; in August the experience is akin to London's Oxford Street on a Saturday morning. If you do arrive with the holiday rush, try not to be put off – the walk is a spectacular excursion between two of the Picos' three massifs. If you're feeling fit (or need to get back to your car), it is possible to walk the whole 12km and back as a (somewhat tiring) day's outing.

Camarmeña A clump of houses barely distinguishable from those belonging to Poncebos up the road, Camarmeña has a fairly decent **mirador** looking out over the Cares valley and surrounding mountainscape. It's signposted and only a short stroll away.

Poncebos This straggle of buildings is exclusively dedicated to Picos tourism. The closest place to the Garganta del Cares trail for a bed is the *Hostal Garganta del Cares (☎ 98 584 50 63)*, which has doubles without private bath for 4000 ptas and others with for 4600 ptas. Next closest is the *Hotel Mirador de Cabrales (☎ 98 584 66 73)*, with rooms for 6200/7800 ptas plus IVA. *Hostal Poncebos (☎ 98 584 64 47)* has adequate rooms for 4000 ptas.

From July to September, an EASA bus runs to Oviedo Monday to Friday at 10.15 am. Another bus leaves at 6.15 pm, doing something of a grand tour to Llanes, Cangas de Onís, Oviedo and other destinations in between. Should you want to, you can get on a 4WD excursion to Caín from Poncebos. The trip takes about 2½ hours and costs 3000 ptas. Ask at the Hostal Garganta del Cares.

Hikes up the Cares By doing the walk in this direction, approaching from Poncebos, you save the best until last. The initial stages involve a steady climb upwards through the wide and mostly bare early stages of the gorge. After about 3.5km you'll reach some abandoned houses and probably a makeshift drinks stand. A little farther and you are over the highest point in the walk. Within a kilometre or so you should encounter another drinks stand (they lug the stuff up on horseback).

As you approach the regional boundary with Castilla y León, the gorge becomes narrower and its walls thick with vegetation, creating greater contrast with the alpine heights above. The last stages of the walk are possibly the prettiest, and as you descend closer to the valley floor, you pass through a series of low (and wet) tunnels to emerge at the end of the gorge among the meadows of Caín. Along the way, there are several paths – most of them on the slippery side – leading down to the river, which you can follow for stretches.

Caín If coming from the south, the trailhead is at Caín, where the rickety (and picturesque) road from Posada de Valdeón ends. You can stay at *Pensión Casa Cuevas*, which is open all year and charges 2500 ptas for basic rooms with basin. There are at least two other places to stay, plus a couple of bars and restaurants. You'll find further places to stay at the string of villages south of Caín, including Cordiñanes and Posada de Valdeón.

No buses make it up to Caín, but you can try Taxi Emiliano Martínez (☎ 987 74 26 09), based in Soto de Valdeón, if you need transport. The company operates 4WDs all over the Picos.

Sotres

A side road leads off eastwards at first, then south, from Camarmeña to Sotres, the highest village in the Picos system and the starting point for a number of popular walks. The people at Casa Cipriano arrange 4WD drives to Fuente Dé, the lakes near Covadonga and other destinations, as well as mountain-bike excursions.

Pensión La Perdiz in Sotres (☎ 98 594 50 11) charges 3000/3900 ptas for singles/ doubles with private bath (less without). The two top rooms have balconies and wonderful views. *Casa Cipriano* (☎ 98 594 50 24), across the road, is a little more expensive. There are two basic *albergues* as well, plus a couple of restaurants and a shop. You'll need your own car to get here.

Hikes around Sotres A common route takes you east to the village of **Treviso** and on to **Urdón**, on the Potes-Panes road. If the fact that this route is paved as far as Treviso reduces its attractiveness, there are options. A path winds off the Treviso trail and snakes down to **La Hermida** in the pass of the same name via the hamlet of Bejes. (If you know what you're up to, you can do it in a 4WD, although the trail is generally only feasible in summer.)

Heading west from Sotres, many walkers choose to march first to **Pandébano** (about 90 minutes) across the open meadows known as the Praderías del Tejo (again, you can actually drive on the rough track). From Pandébano it is possible to see the **Naranjo de Bulnes** (2519m), a favourite peak with climbers and one of the highest in the Picos.

It is possible to walk from Pandébano to **Vega de Urriello**, at the foot of the northwest face of the mountain, where there is a *refugio*. Otherwise, you can continue west to Bulnes (about an hour). **Bulnes** is divided into two parts, Barrio del Castillo and La Villa. All the amenities are in La Villa, including a couple of small places to stay and eat. You can also get to Bulnes by walking south-east from Poncebos (about 1¼ hours).

Once they get this close, few hikers can resist the temptation of getting even closer to El Naranjo de Bulnes, but be prepared – the trek from Bulnes is uphill virtually all the way and tough going (it is easier from Pandébano). From Sotres, another trail can be walked or driven (4WD) south to the Fuente Dé teleférico (cable car; see the Fuente Dé & the Teleférico section at the end of this chapter).

Arenas de Cabrales to Panes

Following the Río Cares eastwards to Panes, there are several alternative places to put you up for a night or two. Most of this stretch takes you through a minor but attractive gorge. A particularly pretty spot on a bend in the Cares is *Hostal Casa Julian* (☎ 98 541 57 79) in Niserias, about 15km east of Arenas. Rooms cost 4000/7500 ptas plus IVA. The restaurant does great salmon dishes. Oviedo-Panes buses call in here.

About 8km farther, you arrive in Panes, something of a minor crossroads on the east-west route from Cantabria across the northern flank of the Picos and the roughly north-south route from the coast to Potes, Fuente Dé and the south-eastern side of the massifs. It is not a pretty town, and you should avoid staying here if you can. Autobuses Palomera runs two or three services daily between Santander (Cantabria) and Potes. In Panes these buses stop outside Bar Composta. The trip to Santander takes about 2½ hours. Two EASA buses head from Panes (Bar La Cortina) to Oviedo Monday to Friday. Times are apt to change, but generally there is one each way in the morning and early evening.

EASTERN PICOS
Desfiladero de la Hermida
Things quickly improve when you leave Panes behind and head south along the Río Deva. For about 10km you remain on Asturian turf, and as the river cuts its way deeper into what quickly becomes a ravine, you cross into Cantabria and arrive at the little hamlet of **La Hermida**, which lends its name to the narrow pass. There's not much here but the bubbling stream of the Deva, the Picos looming to the west and a trio of *hostales*. A narrow, winding road off east to Puentenansa, deep inside Cantabria, makes for a pretty alternative route if you are heading away from the Picos by car or motorcycle – or indeed a fine and little-used first approach from the east (see the Western Cantabria section earlier). To the west, a 4WD track (generally only viable in summer) heads to Sotres. Panes-Potes buses stop at La Hermida.

Lebeña About 7km farther south from La Hermida, this spot warrants visiting. A couple of kilometres to the east off the N-621 main road lies the 9th century Mozarabic **Iglesia de Nuestra Señora de Lebeña**. The horseshoe arches in the bell tower are a telltale sign of the architectural style of the place – not often seen this far north in Spain. That the bell tower is separate from the main body of the church also gives it away. Inside, the floral motifs on the columns are Visigothic, while below the main retablo lies a Celtic stone engraving. A couple of wooden sculptures were stolen from the church in 1993. They say the big olive tree outside was planted 1000 years ago.

If you want to stay in this peaceful location, the **Casa de Labranza** (☎ 942 73 09 44), on the main road from Panes to Potes, charges 5200 ptas for good doubles with private bath. Out of season you can negotiate down for single occupancy.

Panes-Potes buses stop in Lebeña.

Potes
A substantial town, somewhat overrun in peak periods but with some charm in the old centre (much restored after suffering considerable damage during the civil war), Potes is a popular staging post for walkers at the south-eastern edge of the Picos. Most of its 1500 inhabitants ride on tourism's coat-tails.

Information The tourist office (☎ 942 73 07 87), Plaza de Jesús de Monasterio, is open daily in summer from 9 am to 2 pm and 4 to 7 pm. There are several banks with ATMs, and a couple of big supermarkets for stocking up on supplies before heading into the mountains.

Things to See Right in the centre of the town, the squat **Torre del Infantado** is impossible to mistake. Built as a defensive tower in the 14th century, it now houses government offices, having served for a long time as a prison. The **Iglesia de San Vicente Mártir**, built at the same time and deconsecrated in the 19th century, is a nice example of rustic Gothic architecture.

Activities Wentura (☎/fax 942 73 21 61), Calle de la Independencia 10, can help organise paragliding at Fuente Dé, horse riding, mountain-bike excursions and walks.

Places to Stay *Camping La Viorna* (☎ 942 73 20 21) is about 1km from Potes en route to Fuente Dé (take the turn-off for the Monasterio de Santo Toribio). It has its own bar and pool.

A cheap place in town with spacious rooms, some looking over the Torre del Infantado, is the *Hostal Lombraña* (☎ 942 73

05 19, Calle del Sol 2). Singles/doubles with private bath cost 2600/3500 ptas and there are slightly cheaper rooms without their own facilities.

Restaurante El Fogón de Cus on Calle del Capitán Palacios has a little pensión upstairs with small but spotless, pretty rooms. The three singles and three doubles here cost around 2800/3700 ptas. The pick of the bunch is *Casa Cayo* (☎ *942 73 01 50, Calle Cántabra 6)*, which has tiny but lovely rooms smelling of timber and in some cases overlooking the river. They start at 2800/4000 ptas. *Hostal Rafa* (☎ *942 73 09 24)*, around the corner from the correos on the main road, has attractively furnished rooms for 2000/3400 ptas. If you're looking for more class, *Hotel Picos de Valdecoro* (☎ *942 73 00 25, fax 942 73 03 15)*, which was refurbished in 1992, charges 4000/7400 ptas. It's at the entrance to town coming from Panes.

Places to Eat The *Restaurante El Fogón de Cus* has a good-value set *menú* for 1150 ptas; go for the *trucha a la plancha* (grilled trout). *Casa Cayo* has an excellent restaurant where you can eat well for about 2000 ptas a head.

Getting There & Away Up to three Palomera buses run north to Panes and on to Santander. You can get off at Panes and connect for a bus to Arenas de Cabrales, Cangas de Onís or even Oviedo. Take the earliest departure to have a hope of making a connection on the same day. In summer, two daily buses go from Potes to Fuente Dé. A bus between Santander and León passes through daily. Information and tickets can be obtained from the Hostería Peñasagra, next to the Hotel Picos de Europa.

Potes to Fuente Dé

Turieno The Liébana area, of which Potes is in a sense the 'capital', was repopulated with Christians from the meseta by Alfonso I, putting it on the front line between Muslim Spain and what little there was at this stage of its Christian opponent.

The **Monasterio de Santo Toribio de Liébana**, in the hamlet of Turieno (signposted off the road to Fuente Dé outside Potes), was built at this time, although the present austere Gothic church dates from 1256. Since the 8th century, the monastery has housed the Lignum Crucis, a purported piece of Christ's cross supposedly transported from Jerusalem by Bishop Toribio de Astorga in the 9th century. The relic was inserted in a crucifix of gold-plated silver, and according to the tradition features the hole left by the nail that passed through Christ's left hand. It remains an extraordinary magnet for the faithful.

Camping La Isla (☎ *942 73 08 96)* is just outside Turieno and 4km from Potes. There are a few small *hostales* here too. Farther up the road at Quintana, 5.5km from Potes, you could try *Camping San Pelayo* (☎ *942 73 30 87)*, which has a swimming pool. Between here and Cosgaya, about 10km closer to Fuente Dé, you will find several other possible places to bunk down, and it is possible to pitch a tent in Los Llanos.

Potes-Fuente Dé buses call in here.

Cosgaya The small town of Cosgaya, about 16km from Potes, is a nice spot in which to rest up. *Hostal Mesón Cosgaya* (☎ *942 73 30 47)* has singles/doubles without own bath for 2500/3500 ptas and doubles with bath for 4500 ptas. In a rather classier range are the two hotels *Del Oso* (☎ *942 73 30 18)*. The two-star hotel has rooms for 6400/8000 ptas in July-September, while its three-star counterpart over the road charges 7900/8900 ptas. Add IVA. Prices drop 1000 ptas on all rooms during the rest of the year. Potes-Fuente Dé buses call in here.

Espinama This is the last stop of any significance before Fuente Dé and for most people's money and taste probably makes a more appealing base if you have your own transport. You could follow a trail leading north of Espinama to reach the *Hotel Refugio de Aliva*. It's an 11km uphill hike.

PICOS DE EUROPA

There's a surprising choice of decent places to stay here, all on or just off the main road through town – you can't miss them.

Hotel Máximo (☎ 942 73 66 03) has rooms for 3300/5300 ptas and is possibly the pick of the crop; it has a good restaurant as well. *Hostal Remoña (☎ 942 73 66 05)* has doubles for 4000 ptas. One of the first places you pass on the way in from Potes is *Habitaciones Sebrango (☎ 942 73 66 15)*, which offers doubles only for 3500 ptas, or 4000 ptas with private bathroom. There are self-contained apartments for 6000 ptas, which could be good value.

Another attractive option is *Hostal Puente Deva (☎ 942 73 66 58)*, with rooms for 2700/4000 ptas. *Hostal Nevandi (☎ 942 73 66 08)* has good rooms for 3000/4500 ptas. The latter two have restaurants, as does *Hotel Máximo*.

Potes-Fuente Dé buses call in here.

Fuente Dé & the Teleférico
At 1078m, Fuente Dé lies at the foot of the stark southern wall of the Macizo Central. In four minutes the teleférico (cable car) here whisks people 762m to the top of that wall, from where walkers and climbers can make their way deeper into the central massif.

Be warned that during the peak season (especially August) you can wait for hours at the bottom before your numbered ticket comes up (numbers are called out on a PA system). Coming down again, you simply join the queue and wait – OK on a sunny summer's day, but otherwise a little unpleasant if the queue's long. Day return tickets cost a hefty 1200 ptas, and the service basically runs from 9 am until shortly before sunset (8 pm in summer).

Hiking & Climbing Walk to the *Hotel Refugio de Aliva* from the top of the teleférico, or catch one of the private 4WD shuttles that do the trip for 250 ptas per person. The refuge has its own restaurant and even a solarium, but is open only from June to September. From here, two somewhat more exacting trails descend into the

valley that separates the central massif from its eastern cousin. The first winds its way 11km south to Espinama, while the other will get you north to Sotres. On the way you pass through the hamlet of Vegas de Sotres, from where a trail departs westwards to the Naranjo de Bulnes (see under Sotres earlier in this chapter). 4WDs also cover this route if there is a demand.

Other possibilities for the well-prepared include climbing the Peña Vieja (2613m) and making your way across the massif to the Naranjo de Bulnes. This requires proper equipment and experience – Peña Vieja has the sad record of having claimed more climbers' lives than any other in the Picos. Less exacting is the trail leading north-west, passing below the Peña Vieja by marked trails to the *Cabaña Verónica Refugio* (about two hours), near the Horcados Rojos. From there hikers can proceed to the Vega de Urriello, at the base of the Naranjo de Bulnes.

Paragliding Alas Cantabria (☎ 942 73 61 25, fax 942 27 56 12), actually based in Vega de Liébana, organises beginner flights on paragliders. Prices for one/two/four days are 6000/10,000/20,000 ptas plus insurance. Beginners will be accompanied by an instructor.

Eagle Show If it looks like you'll have a long wait for the teleférico, check to see if the Montaña de las Águilas is in operation. At the time of writing, the people organising this performance by low-flying eagles, buzzards and other birds of prey were putting on a show at 1, 4 and 6.30 pm (500 ptas). It's a rare chance to see these birds, including the majestic golden eagle, trained to swoop in over the audience and pick up their reward of meat. The organisers use the money to promote rehabilitation of injured birds and increase awareness of the dangers many of these species face.

Places to Stay & Eat There is an adequate camping ground, *El Redondo*, about 100m from the Montaña de las Águilas, along with refugio-style accommodation for 20. Otherwise there are no cheap choices.

Hotel Rebeco (☎ *942 73 66 01*) has singles/doubles/triples for 4800/6800/8400 ptas plus IVA. It also has a *restaurant*. The **Parador de Fuente Dé** (☎ *942 73 00 01, fax 942 73 02 12*) is more expensive.

Apart from some overpriced tourist cafés and the hotel restaurants, you have no real dining options here either.

Getting There & Away In summer there are two buses daily between Fuente Dé and Potes.

Galicia

If the regions of Spain were identified by colour, Galicia's might well be green tinged with grey. In the same way that Andalucía wears its dazzling whitewash and Castilla-La Mancha bathes in the burnt red and dusty olive green of its sun-scorched plains, so the characteristic granite and ubiquitous slate rooftops on a verdant rural background seem symbolic of Galicia. Doubtless, the often inclement weather contributes to the impression.

Battered by the Atlantic, the wild coastline is sliced up and down its length by *rías*, a series of majestic estuaries. Separated from the *meseta* by the Cordillera Cantábrica in the east, Galicia is bounded to the south by the Portuguese border and the region's main river, the Río Miño. Frenetic deforestation has unfortunately stripped the region of its indigenous trees, mostly replaced by eucalyptus.

Inhabited since at least 3000 BC, by the Iron Age Galicia was populated by Celts living in *castros*, villages of circular stone huts surrounded by a defensive perimeter. The arrival in the 1st century BC of the Romans, who seem to have mingled tolerably well with the locals, gave the area its name: Gallaecia. The Muslim invasion barely touched Galicia, and the big event in the area's medieval history was the 'rediscovery' of the grave of Santiago Apóstol (St James the Apostle) in 813, at what would become Santiago de Compostela. The site became a rallying symbol for the Reconquista, but by the time this was completed, Galicia had become an impoverished backwater in which the centralist-minded Catholic Monarchs Fernando and Isabel had already begun to supplant the local tongue and traditions with Castilian methods and language. The first signs of the *Rexurdimento*, a reawakening of the Galician consciousness, did not surface until late in the 19th century, and then suffered a 40-year interruption during the Franco era.

HIGHLIGHTS

- Completing the Camino de Santiago walk from the French border to Santiago de Compostela
- The magnificent Catedral de Santiago de Compostela
- Some of Spain's best and most varied seafood, washed down with a crisp Ribeiro white
- Exploring the *rías* (estuaries) along the coast
- Gazing over the Atlantic from the heights of Cabo Ortegal and Cabo Finisterre
- *Pimientos de Padrón*
- Stretching out on the beaches around Cedeira
- Catching a *curro*, or round-up of wild horses
- The pretty town of Tuy, right on the Río Miño and just across a bridge from the Portuguese fortress town of Valença

Rural and still much ignored by the rest of Spain, Galicia is in many senses another country. Rather than hope for any good from the nation's centre, Galicians have traditionally looked to the sea. Fishing has long been a mainstay and the region's seamen have cast their nets far and wide, at least until now. With world fish stocks falling and international conflict over fishing rights growing, Galicia's fleet finds itself staring at an uncertain future. Much as in England's Cornwall, smuggling is an in-

tegral part of Galicia's seafaring lore, but the growth of drug-running from South America has led to fears that Galicia is becoming 'another Sicily'.

Most travellers in Galicia make a beeline for Santiago de Compostela, and no-one can blame them. This melancholy medieval city-shrine is surely one of Spain's most engaging urban centres. Beyond it, however, lies plenty more. The popular Rías Bajas and less well known Rías Altas are dotted with coves, beaches and enticing villages,

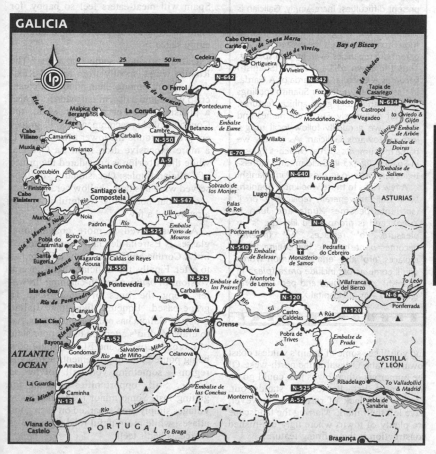

GALICIA

Travelling in Tongues

Long suppressed during the Franco years (strange, really, since Franco was born in Galicia), the Galician language (*galego* or, in Spanish, *gallego*) sounds much like a cross between Castilian Spanish and Portuguese. It is widely spoken and in recent years has been pushed as the main local language. News broadcasts are often in Galician.

Although the issue of Spanish vs Galician usage is not as politically charged as the parallel debate in Catalunya, it does present difficulties. Increasingly, Galician is used in road signs. Map and atlas publishers, however, all go their own way. A further complication is the existence of apparent discrepancies even in local spelling. Thus the town of La Guardia (Spanish) becomes A Guardia, A Guarda or A Garda. In this chapter we favour Spanish spellings for cities and other geographical features, but not exclusively. For street names and the like we generally follow local usage, leaning towards Galician. As a rule, we name monuments such as churches (*iglesia* in Spanish, *igrexa* in Galician) and monasteries *(monasterio* vs *mosteiro)* in Spanish.

A few clues to those who know Spanish: 'x' in Galician generally replaces 'g' or 'j' (so Junta becomes Xunta and Juan is Xuan), and is pronounced like the 's' in pleasure; 'o' replaces 'ue' (*puente* becomes *ponte*); while the ending 'eiro' replaces 'ero' and 'erio'. Common words you'll come across include *praza* (*plaza* in Spanish), *praia* (*playa)* and perhaps *xeral* (*general)* – as in Hospital Xeral.

When stomachs grumble in Galicia, thoughts turn to seafood. Although some may feel the quality is higher in Portugal, there is no doubt that you can eat better here than in much of the rest of Spain. And as a rule, eating out is generally cheaper in Galicia. *Pulpo* (octopus) is a staple, but there are plenty of options (see the boxed text 'Food Fare'). Even more so than in neighbouring Asturias, Galicia's biggest export has traditionally been labour, in particular to Argentina – something reflected in its modern eating habits. Nowhere else in Spain will meat-eaters feel so happy, for this is *churrasco* territory – slabs of grilled meat or ribs accompanied by a slightly tangy sauce.

Galicia produces some fine wines. The Ribeiro wines, mostly from around Ribadavia, count among their number a clean, crisp white and a decent red. Mencia is also a pleasing red. For a robust white, the Condado label is recommended – its grapes are grown around the lower Miño. Rosal is a more expensive drop from La Guardia, while the Albariño is considered the prince of Galician tipples. Occasionally you'll be served wine in small, shallow ceramic cups – cute, but potentially wasteful if you've already had a few.

Always served in more conventional glasses is Estrella de Galicia beer, brewed in La Coruña and about the best Spain has to offer. Finally, the Galicians brew several versions of *orujo*, a breath-catching firewater along the lines of *aguardiente* (a grape-based liqueur, like the Italian *grappe*). Galicia has only recently managed to draw Madrid's attention to the poor state of its road network, and EU funds are now being poured into improvements across the region – something you will not fail to notice. Still, opportunities abound for getting lost. Some minor roads and many villages simply aren't marked on even good atlases, while meaningful road signs are as scarce as hen's teeth.

and you'll see some of Spain's wildest coast towards Cabo Ortegal in the north-west. Of the numerous other towns that could go on to a must list, Pontevedra stands out. Poverty and lack of resources, however, have left their mark. Marring the landscape are plenty of towns where ugly unfinished construction is the defining feature.

Santiago de Compostela

There can be few cities in the world as beautiful as Santiago that are founded on the basis of so preposterous a story. The corpse of Santiago Apóstol, the myth relates, was transported to the far side of Spain by two disciples after his execution in Jerusalem. They landed at Padrón and, so they say, managed to bury Santiago in a spot about 20km inland.

In 813 the grave was supposedly rediscovered by a bishop following a guiding star (hence the second part of the city's name, a corruption of the Latin Campus Stellae, or Field of the Star). The saint's purported grave became a welcome rallying symbol for Christian Spain, and work began on a church above his remains. The myth gained strength in following centuries, and Santiago de Compostela became a quietly impressive city (of 90,000). It has improved with both age and the various architectural additions made after the initial wave of enthusiasm for the pilgrimage in the 12th century.

Apart from the undisputed splendour of its gold-tinged (at least when the sun's out) monuments and the charm of its medieval streets, Santiago de Compostela is lively, full of bars and, in summer especially, with a packed program of concerts, theatre and exhibitions. This, the city's beauty and a renewed interest in the Camino de Santiago (see the Camino de Santiago special section) no doubt helped Santiago de Compostela to be chosen as one of nine Cultural Capitals across Europe for 2000.

History

Although the history of Santiago de Compostela virtually begins with the story of Santiago Apóstol, the area had long been inhabited by Visigoths, Romans and Celts. In any event, Alfonso II, the Asturian king, soon turned up to have the first church erected in honour of the saintly discovery.

By 1075, when the Romanesque basilica was begun and the pilgrimage was becoming a major European phenomenon, Santiago de Compostela had already been raided on various occasions by the Normans and Muslims. The worldly Bishop Diego Gelmírez added numerous churches to the city in the 12th century, a period when homage paid to its saint brought in a flood of funding, used to build much of the present city.

The following couple of centuries were marked by internecine squabbling between rival nobles, dampened by the conclusion of the Reconquista and greater attention paid by Fernando and Isabel to internal affairs. After backing the wrong horse and siding with the Carlists in the 1830s, Santiago de Compostela slipped into the background. Only since the early 1980s has the city, as Galician capital and a rediscovered tourist target, really begun to emerge.

Orientation

Santiago's compact *casco antiguo* (old town centre) is virtually all pedestrianised. The RENFE train station is about a 15-minute walk downhill from the centre, while the estación de autobuses lies about the same distance away to the north-east. Local city buses pass both and take you as far as the main road, Rúa de Senra, running along the southern fringe of the old town. Most of the monuments, accommodation, main tourist office, banks and the like can be found in the casco, whose more important streets include Rúa Nova, Rúa do Vilar and Rúa do Franco.

Information

Tourist Offices The tourist office (☎ 981 58 40 81), Rúa do Vilar 43, is open Monday to Friday from 10 am to 2 pm and 4 to 7 pm and Saturday from 10 am to 2 pm. There is also an information kiosk on Praza de Galicia (handy if you arrive by train). It is open daily from 10 am to 2 pm and 5 to 8 pm.

Money There are banks dotted about the centre of town. A handy one is the Central Hispano at Rúa do Vilar 30-32.

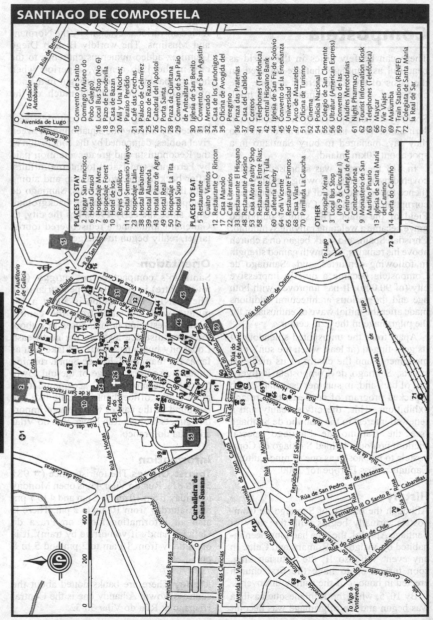

SANTIAGO DE COMPOSTELA

PLACES TO STAY
2 Hogar San Francisco
6 Hostal Girasol
7 Hospedaje Mera
8 Hospedaje Forest
10 Hotel de los
   Reyes Católicos
11 Hostal Seminario Mayor
23 Hospedaje Lalín
38 Hostal Barbantes
39 Hostal Alameda
43 Hostal Pazo de Agra
49 Hostal Real
50 Hospedaje La Tita
57 Hostal Suso

PLACES TO EAT
5 Restaurante
   Cuatro Vientos
12 Restaurante O' Rincon
17 Casa Manolo
22 Café Literanos
33 Restaurante El Hispano
48 Restaurante Asesino
53 Casa Mora Pastry Shop
58 Restaurante Entre Rías;
   Restaurante A Tulla
60 Cafetería Derby
64 Toñi Vicente
65 Restaurante Fornos
68 Casa Vilas
70 Parrillada La Gaucha

15 Convento de Santo
   Domingo (Museo do
   Pobo Galego)
16 Local Bus Stop (No 6)
18 Pazo de Fondevilla
19 Casa de Bazan
20 Mil y Una Noches;
   Paraíso Perdido
21 Café das Crechas
24 Palacio de Gelmírez
25 Pazo de Raxoi
26 Catedral del Apóstol
27 Porta Santa
28 Praza da Quintana
29 Convento de San Paio
   de Antealtares
30 Iglesia de San Benito
31 Convento de San Agustín
32 Mercado
34 Casa de los Canónigos
35 Oficina de Avogda del
   Peregrino
36 Praza das Praterías
37 Casa del Cabildo
40 Correos
41 Telephones (Telefónica)
42 Central Hispano Bank
44 Iglesia de San Fiz de Solovio
45 Convento de la Enseñanza
46 Universidad
47 Arco de Mazarelos
51 Oficina de Turismo
52 Cinema
54 Policía Nacional
55 Colegio de San Clemente
56 Ultratur (American Express)
59 Convento de las
   Madres Mercedarias
61 Night Pharmacy
62 Tourist Information Kiosk
63 Telephones (Telefónica)
66 Maycar
67 Vie Viajes
69 Makumba
71 Train Station (RENFE)
72 Colegiata de Santa María
   la Real de Sar

OTHER
1 Hospital Xeral
3 Local Bus Stop
   (No 9 & Circular I)
4 Centro Galega de Arte
   Contemporánea
9 Monasterio de San
   Martiño Pinario
13 Iglesia de Santa María
   del Camino
14 Porta do Camiño

American Express (☎ 981 58 70 00) is in the Ultratur travel agency at Avenida Figueroa 6. It is open Monday to Friday from 9.30 am to 2 pm and 4.30 to 7 pm and Saturday from 10 am to 12.30 pm.

Post & Communications The main *correos* (post office) lines Travesía de Fonseca and is open from 8.30 am to 8.30 pm. The postcode is 15700. The telephone office (Telefónica) is in the same building. It is open Monday to Friday from 8.30 am to 1.30 pm, but there are several other phone offices and plenty of pay phones scattered about town.

Oficina de Acogida del Peregrino People who have walked all or part of the Camino de Santiago as pilgrims and want the certificate to prove it can head for this 'pilgrims reception office' (☎ 981 56 24 19) in the Casa del Deán, Rúa do Vilar 1. It is open daily from 10 am to 2 pm and 4.30 to 7.30 pm.

Medical Services & Emergency The Policía Nacional *comisaría* (station) is on Avenida de Rodrigo de Padrón – call ☎ 092 in an emergency. The Hospital Xeral is north-west of the town centre on Rúa das Galerías. There is a night pharmacy where Rúa das Orfas meets Canton de Toral.

Catedral del Apóstol

Those who have chosen to trudge the Camino de Santiago will hardly be disappointed on finally entering Praza do Obradoiro to behold the lavish baroque façade of the Catedral del Apóstol's western flank. Prior to its construction in the 18th century, the less overwhelming but artistically unparalleled **Pórtico de la Gloria** (Porta da Gloria) was the first scene to greet weary pilgrims. The bulk of the Romanesque cathedral was built from 1075 to 1211. Much of the 'bunting' – the domes, statues, pyramids and endless flourishes – came later.

There is little doubt that construction of the baroque icing on the essentially Ro-

manesque cake muted the impact of the portico, which was put in place in the 12th century. But it has also been something of a blessing, protecting the sculptures of Maestro Mateo and his team from the elements. The main figure in the central archway is Christ risen, at his feet and hands the four Evangelists, and around them angels with the crown of thorns and other instruments connected with Jesus' passion. Below Christ's feet is represented Santiago, and the tradition says that below him is the figure of Maestro Mateo. Bump your head on it three times and you're supposed to acquire some of his genius; the problem is that his bust appears, if at all, on the other side, facing the altar, while the popular but mistaken head belongs to Samson. The other tradition calls for a brief prayer of thanksgiving as you place your fingers in the five holes created near Samson's head by the repetition of this very act by millions of faithful over the centuries.

The remarkably life-like figures that dominate the columns on the right side of the portico are the remaining apostles, while those to the left represent prophets of the Old Testament. Almost nothing remains of the portico's original colouring.

Approaching the *churrigueresque* **altar mayor**, you may notice an opening and stairs on the left side. Head down here to contemplate what you are assured is the tomb of Santiago. You emerge on the right side and a little farther on see another entrance with steps going up. Follow the crowds up and embrace the 13th century statue of Santiago. There was a time when pilgrims would lift a gold crown from the statue's head and put it on their own, exchanging it briefly for their own more humble hats.

With luck, you may catch one of the special masses where the greatest dispenser of incense in the world, the *botafumeiro*, is swung heftily across the length of the transept by an expert team of *tiraboleiros* using an ingenious pulley system – an unforgettable sight.

You really need to make more than one visit to cope with the cathedral's remarkable riches. To the right of the Pórtico de la Gloria is the entrance to the Museo Catedralicio. Entrance costs 400 ptas and includes a visit to the *cripta* (crypt), *tesoro* (treasury) and *claustro* (cloister). The museum is spread over several floors and has an impressive collection of religious art, including Romanesque sculptures, tapestries, a library, and not a few images of Santiago. The main item of the tesoro (in the Capilla de San Fernando, on the south side of the nave) is the 16th century silver and gold-plated processional monstrance. The cloister replaced the Romanesque original in the 16th century and is a successful mix of Late Gothic and plateresque.

The cathedral is open all day, but the museum, cloister etc are open only from 10 am to 1.30 pm and 4 to 6.30 pm (a combined ticket for all these costs 500 ptas).

Palacio de Gelmírez

On the cathedral's left flank, the Palacio de Gelmírez was built for the bishop of the same name in 1120 and subsequently altered. There is not an awful lot left to this Gothic adjunct, but worth seeking out is the Sala de Banquetes, the main dining hall. The exquisite little busts around the walls depict happy feasters and musicians, as well as the odd king and juggler. Diego Gelmírez's biggest contribution to Santiago de Compostela was to resuscitate the myth of the Battle of Clavijo. Supposedly Santiago appeared to Ramiro I and joined him in this fiesta of Moor-slaying in 844, for which the grateful king promised to dedicate the first fruits of every harvest to the saint. Few historians believe the battle ever took place, but Gelmírez turned the myth into one of the city's biggest revenue sources for centuries after his demise.

The palacio is open daily from 10 am to 1.30 pm and 4 to 7.30 pm, but is closed in the afternoon on public holidays (200 ptas).

Around the Catedral

However much the cathedral dominates the heart of Santiago de Compostela, the area around it is rich in other architectural jewels. The northern end of Praza do Obradoiro is closed off by the Renaissance Hotel de los Reyes Católicos, built by Fernando and Isabel with some of the loot from Granada to shelter the poor and infirm. It now shelters the well-off instead, as a *parador*. Fronting the western side of the square is the elegant 18th century Pazo de Raxoi, in French neoclassical style and housing the *ayuntamiento* (town hall).

A stroll around the cathedral takes you through some of the city's most inviting squares. To the south is Praza das Praterías (Silversmiths Square), the centre of which is marked by the Fuente de los Caballos (1829). Up the steps is the only original façade of the cathedral, a Romanesque masterpiece.

Following the cathedral walls you enter Praza da Quintana, split into two parts by a low staircase. The lower part, '*dos mortos*', was once a cemetery. Facing onto it is the Puerta Santa of the cathedral, opened only in Holy Years when the Feast of St James falls on a Sunday. Keep following the walls and you will reach Praza da Azabachería. Rising up on the far side is the huge Benedictine Monasterio de San Martiño Pinario. The classical façade hides a couple of extensive cloisters inside, built in the 17th century.

Behind them (and best approached from Praza de San Martiño) is the monastery's captivating church, an elaborate piece of baroque on which construction began in 1611. The church's towers were never finished, their construction apparently blocked by officials of the cathedral anxious not to see any shadows cast on its greater glory.

Beyond the Old City

Just north-east of the old city, the former Convento de Santo Domingo stands out, an impressive baroque structure that now houses the Museo do Pobo Galego. The most singular feature is the triple spiral staircase, off which lie rooms of the museum. These contain a variety of displays on different aspects of Galician life, tradition and arts, covering everything from the fishing industry through music and crafts to traditional costumes. The museum is open Monday to Saturday from 10 am to 1 pm and 4 to 7 pm (free). Facing it is the **Centro Galego de Arte Contemporánea**, open Tuesday to Saturday from 11 am to 8 pm and Sunday from 11 am to 2 pm (free). It hosts temporary exhibitions of modern art.

About 1km south down Rúa do Patio de Madres stands, in precarious fashion (it suffers a pronounced tilt), the Romanesque **Colegiata de Santa María la Real de Sar**. Part of the beautiful cloister, supposedly designed by Maestro Mateo, can still be admired, and there is a small museum containing mainly religious art and Romanesque sculpture.

Organised Tours

One-day bus tours are organised through various hotels and travel agents. They are pretty busy affairs – designed for those with more money than time – covering the Rías Bajas, Rías Altas, Vigo and Portugal, and Finisterre. The tours (5200 ptas) include lunch. Inquire at Vie Viajes (☎ 981 56 44 19), Rúa do Hórreo 44.

Special Events

July is the month to be in Santiago de Compostela. The 25th is the Feast of St James and simultaneously Galicia's 'national' day. The night before, Praza do Obradoiro comes alight with the *fogo do Apóstolo*, a spectacular fireworks display that dates to the 17th century and culminates in the *quemada de la fachada mudéjar* (literally 'burning of the mudéjar front'), a mock burning of the façade. This spectacular performance's days may be numbered, as fears are growing for the safety of the cathedral's façade. Apart from the processions and lots of people getting about in traditional costume, the town authorities organise numerous concerts, notably in Praza da Quintana, and other cultural activities.

Places to Stay

Santiago is crawling with accommodation. In the casco, half the bars advertise rooms for rent *(habitaciones)* and the number of teeny hostelries *(hospedajes)* should be reassuring. Touts frequently intercept new arrivals at the train and bus stations. All this means that you should rarely have trouble finding a place. If you can't find anything in the casco, there are plenty of options on and around Praza de Galicia, between the old town and the train station.

Places to Stay – Budget

Camping There are several camping grounds on the road to La Coruña, but none is close to the city.

Hospedajes & Hostales As you wander into the casco from the train station, a quiet option is *Hospedaje La Tita (☎ 981 58 39 81, Rúa Nova 46)*, with clean singles/doubles for 1600/3100 ptas. For the same price and a view of Praza da Quintana, head for *Hospedaje Lalín (☎ 981 58 21 23)*. The rooms are a little basic and light sleepers might find it *too* central. A quieter and cheaper alternative with better rooms – especially if you can get a top-floor double – is *Hospedaje Forest (☎ 981 57 08 11, Callejón de Don Abril Ares 7)*, with rooms starting at 1300/2400 ptas.

Hospedaje Mera (☎ 981 58 38 67, Porta da Peña 15) has decent singles/doubles/triples, some with pleasant views, for 3000/4200/5000 ptas. Virtually across the road at No 4, *Hostal Girasol (☎ 981 56 62 87)* has reliable doubles for 3500 ptas, or 4300 ptas with private bath. *Hostal Real (☎ 981 56 66 56, Rúa da Caldereería 49)* has good-sized singles/doubles without private bath for 2200/3300 ptas.

An attractive option is the *Hostal Pazo de Agra (☎ 981 58 90 45, Rúa da Caldereería 37)*. Rooms without private bath in this homy and spotless old house start at 2000/4000 ptas – a little more for private bath.

GALICIA

Galician Food Fare

Here is an introductory vocabulary to Galician food:

almejas – clams.
anguilas – small eel from the Río Miño.
caldo gallego – broth with cabbage or turnip, potato and usually a token clump of meat.
caldeirada de pescado – a hotpot of different types of fish and potato.
chinchos – various tiny fried fish.
chipirones – chopped squid cooked in its own ink.
chocos/choquitos – a variation on the squid theme.
cigalas – crayfish.
empanada/empanadilla – something like a pasty. The most common version is done with tuna and tomato and is very tasty. *Empanada a la gallega* contains *chorizo* (sausage), onion and occasionally other vegetables. *Empanadilla* is the bite-size snack version.
gambas – prawns; most commonly done *al ajillo* (with garlic) and *a la plancha* (lightly grilled).
mejillones – orange mussels, mostly bred on the odd web-like platforms you'll see all over most of the rías.
pimientos de Padrón – small green peppers cooked in loads of garlic, with the occasional seriously hot one thrown in.
pulpo a la gallega – *the* Galician dish; basically boiled octopus bits.
vieiras – scallops.
xoubas/xoubiñas – sardines.
zorza – a local equivalent of kebabs.

Inquire at Restaurante Zíngara on Rúa de Cardenal Payá. *Hostal Suso* (☎ 981 58 66 11, Rúa do Vilar 65) is popular, with rooms for 3000/4200 ptas (less in the low season).

Places to Stay – Mid-Range

At *Hostal Barbantes* (☎ 981 58 10 77, Rúa do Franco 1) you're paying for the lovely position overlooking little Praza de Fonseca. Singles/doubles/triples cost 3500/5000/6000 ptas.

Hostal Seminario Mayor (☎ 981 58 30 08, Praza da Inmaculada 5) has somewhat bare rooms but offers what some might consider a one-off experience – to stay inside the Monasterio de San Martiño Pinario. The rooms cost 3000/5000/6500 ptas plus IVA, mostly with private bath. Rooms are only available from July to September, when student lodgers are away.

Along the same lines but a step or two up in class and comfort is *Hogar San Francisco* (☎ 981 57 24 63), in the monastery of the same name, which has doubles starting at 5700/8300 ptas plus IVA.

Cheaper and in a lovely position just below the Carballeira de Santa Susana is the *Hostal Alameda* (☎ 981 58 81 00, Campo de San Clemente 32), with doubles for 4900 ptas plus IVA, or 6500 ptas with private bath.

Places to Stay – Top End

The *Hotel de los Reyes Católicos* (☎ 981 58 22 00, fax 981 59 02 87) is itself one of Santiago's prime monuments, closing off the northern flank of Praza do Obradoiro (see Things to See). In keeping with its exalted past, guests pay rather splendid prices: 26,500 ptas plus IVA for a double – but what a double!

Places to Eat

The do-it-yourself crowd should visit Santiago's majestic *mercado*, along Rúa de Santo Agostiño in the south-east of the casco.

Restaurants It's possible to eat well for less than 1200 ptas in one of several little places tucked away around town. The *Restaurante O' Rincon* (Rúa da Algalia de Arriba 21) is a tiny spot where you'll get simple but filling *raciones* for a few hundred pesetas. For a full and solid meal with wine and dessert for less than 1000 ptas, try *Restaurante Cuatro Vientos* (Rúa de Santa Cristina 19). Popular with readers of travel guides is *Casa Manolo* (Rúa Travesa 27), which has a good-value set meal for 700 ptas without drinks.

GALICIA

A couple of modestly priced places that come up with some good dishes are **Restaurante Entre Rúas** and **Restaurante A Tulla**, next to each other in the tiny square on Entrerúas, a laneway linking Rúa do Vilar and Rúa Nova. You should get away with spending around 1500 ptas and, while the latter is marginally better, the *ternera rellena* (stuffed veal) in the Entre Rúas is very tasty. Likewise the home-made flan for dessert.

For a *parrillada de pescados* (fresh fish grill), head for **Restaurante El Hispano** *(Rúa de Santo Agostiño)*, just opposite the market – you can't get much closer to the raw materials.

A long-time institution in Santiago de Compostela is **Restaurante Asesino** *(Praza da Universidade 16)*. There's no sign, and although the food is good, prices have lifted well out of the budget bracket.

A good place to have a tasty *churrasco* is **Parrillada La Gaucha** *(Rúa da Rosa 42)*, in the happening area of the new town known as El Ensanche. After your ribs you could hit the tiles in the surrounding pubs.

On a slightly pricier level, **Restaurante Fornos** *(Rúa do Hórreo 24)*, near Praza de Galicia, has a solid local reputation.

If you want to really splash out, Avenida de Rosalía de Castro is home to a couple of prime targets. **Casa Vilas** at No 88 is a staunch bastion of the best in Galician cuisine. Various characters – from Fidel Castro to Pope John Paul II – have tucked in here. You're looking at 4500 ptas a head at least. Similarly expensive is the nouvelle cuisine specialist **Toñi Vicente** at No 24.

For takeaway dessert or a daytime sweet fix, pop in to **Casa Mora** *(Rúa do Vilar 60)*.

Cafés As a general rule, a cup of coffee will not cost you more than about 150 ptas wherever you go, although close to half that price is the going rate in the simple bars. A breakfast of fruit juice, coffee and toast can be had for about 300 ptas in the smaller places. **Café Literarios** on Praza da Quintana is a laid-back place in a great location. It does a couple of decent breakfast deals.

The brasher sidewalk cafés along Rúa do Franco and Rúa do Vilar and on the main squares charge up to double this just for coffee and juice.

Virtually on the border of the old and new towns, **Cafetería Derby** *(Rúa das Orfas 29)* is one of Santiago's oldest cafés and something of an institution.

Entertainment

Try to get hold of *Compostelán*, a local monthly student news rag. It has a fairly comprehensive local listings guide covering restaurants, bars and nightlife.

Bars If you want to hear traditional Celtic music Galician-style, head for **Café das Crechas** *(Vía Sacra 3)*. Sometimes it's live, other times you'll have to make do with recordings. **Mil y Una Noches** and **Paraíso Perdido** are bars equally good for a coffee or drinks later in the evening. They are both on the tiny square of Entrealtares and the latter is one of Santiago's oldest bars.

Discos You'll possibly get a better feel for the local drinking and dancing scene if you head for the new town. Taking Praza Roxa (Red Square) as your point of reference, cafés, bars and discos fan out along the streets off and near the square. Explore Rúa de Fernando III o Santo, Rúa Nova and Rúa de Frei Rodendo Salvado. **Black** *(Avenida de Rosalía de Castro s/n)* is a popular nightclub. **Maycar** *(Rúa do Doutor Teixeiro 5)* is apparently one of the last stops on an all-night trek. For more of a Latin American touch, have a look in at **Makumba** *(Rúa de Frei Rodendo Salvado 16)*.

Concerts *Tunas* – traditionally university students dressed up in medieval garb and busking towards the end of the academic year – seem to be a year-round phenomenon in Santiago. The tradition is an old one and the music, when played well, is entertaining. The hard sell of cassettes and CDs on Praza do Obradoiro is less so.

The modern **Auditorio de Galicia**, north of the centre, hosts concerts, art exhibitions

GALICIA

Dancing to Their Own Tune

Perhaps it is in Galicia's rich tradition of folk music that the Galicians' Celtic strains come most vividly to the fore. Although the sounds and rhythms differ noticeably from those played by their cousins in Brittany, Ireland and Scotland, the links between them all are impossible to deny. Most readily recognisable is the *gaita* (Galician bagpipes), of which there are several versions. Summertime in Santiago is a good time to catch buskers playing traditional Galician tunes. There is quite an inventory of instruments at the disposal of folk musicians. In addition to the standard gaita, *tamboril* (big drum) and *violín*, there is a range of simple wood instruments, including the *pito* and *penteiro*; the *pandereita* (tambourine); *buguinas* (small ceramic trumpets); the *birrimbao* (Jew's harp); *ferriños* (triangles); *castañolas* and *tarrañolas* (both variations on castanets); and the *zanfona*, a string and key instrument vaguely along the lines of an accordion.

Possibly the best internationally known Galician traditional music group is the very polished Milladoiro. Pallamallada is a Santiago group that does a mix of instrumental and vocal pieces based on traditional popular music. A very middle-of-the-road but lively enough band is Aroda Os Quintos. In a different league altogether is Uxía, a powerful female vocalist very roughly of the Enya genre. Another, more staid chap is Amancio Prada, actually from the province of León, who does his folk interpretations in Galician and Castilian. The group Keltoi, from the Pontevedra area, does Celtic music, but it's mostly of the elevator variety.

and other cultural events, especially crammed through the summer months. The ayuntamiento also sponsors similar events

elsewhere throughout town, such as in the church of the former Convento de Santo Domingo.

Cinema There is a cinema at Rúa do Vilar 53-55, near the tourist office.

Getting There & Away

Air Lavacolla airport is 11km south-east of Santiago. There are up to six flights daily to Madrid with Iberia and Air Europa. The latter also has several flights to Barcelona, the Canary Islands and Málaga as well as international destinations.

Bus Along with La Coruña to the north, Santiago is the main bus terminus for Galicia. Castromil runs regular services to Vigo via Pontevedra, south-east to Orense and north to La Coruña. For the Costa da Morte, Transportes Finisterre runs buses to Finisterre, Malpica de Bergantiños. Enatcar has three buses to Barcelona (8½ hours). Dainco has three daily to Salamanca, two to Cádiz and one to Algeciras. International services connect La Coruña with Paris, Belgium, Holland and various destinations in Germany.

Train There are up to four trains daily to Barcelona (from La Coruña) via León and Zaragoza, and another four to Madrid (Chamartín).

Regular trains run north to La Coruña (about 1½ hours; 475 ptas for a one-way, 2nd-class ticket) and south to Vigo (about 2½ hours; 760 ptas) via Pontevedra (one hour; 490 ptas). Less frequent trains connect with Tuy, Orense, León (2750 ptas) and Zamora (2395 ptas).

Car & Motorcycle Santiago is on the A-9 tollway between La Coruña and Vigo. Parallel, slower and free is the N-550.

Getting Around

Santiago de Compostela is walkable, although it's a hike to the train and bus stations. A public bus system runs *around* the old town. Bus No 10 runs from the estación de autobuses to Praza Roxa via Praza de Galicia. You could get out at Rúa de San Roque or Praza de Galicia. The Circular I bus can drop you in the same places. Bus Nos 6 and 9 pass near the train station and go to Praza de Galicia.

La Coruña & the Rías Altas

Often more intemperate and certainly much less visited than the southern coast of Galicia (Rías Bajas), the northern coast is peppered with pleasant surprises. La Coruña is a busy and surprisingly attractive port city with decent beaches. There are plenty of smaller towns and fishing villages worth exploring too, and some of the most impressive coast in all Galicia.

LA CORUÑA

With 250,000 inhabitants, La Coruña (A Coruña) has only in recent years been overtaken by Vigo as Galicia's biggest city. It remains, however, the region's most go-ahead, outward-looking urban centre. It has a liberal-republican tradition at variance with the conservatism of the remainder of Galicia, and its port has kept it open to the rest of the world. It has also been a gateway for those outward bound – everyone from Galician emigrants to the doomed Armada.

Initially a Celtic port on the tin route to the British Isles, the site was later occupied by the Romans, who in the 2nd century AD built the lighthouse known as the Torre de Hércules. Nothing much is known of La Coruña's subsequent history until 991, when the port was put under control of the Church in Santiago.

Britain looms large on La Coruña's horizon. Felipe II embarked here for England to marry Mary Tudor in 1554, and 34 years later the ill-fated Armada also weighed anchor in La Coruña. The following year Sir Francis Drake tried to occupy the town but was seen off by María Pita, a heroine whose name lives on in the town's main square. Napoleon's troops occupied La Coruña for the first six months of 1809. Their British opponents were able to 'do a Dunkirk' and evacuate, but their commander, General Sir John Moore, died in the covering Battle of Elviña and was buried here.

Orientation

The RENFE train station and the estación de autobuses are a couple of kilometres south-west of the heart of town. La Coruña gets interesting along a fairly narrow isthmus and the large headland to its east. The old part of town *(ciudad vieja)* is huddled together in the southern tip of the headland, while the Torre de Hércules caps its northern extreme. Most offices, hotels, restaurants and bars are in the newer, predominantly 19th century part of town that fills the isthmus. Its northern side is lined with sandy beaches, while to the south lies the port.

Information

Tourist Office The tourist office (☎ 981 22 18 22) on the Dársena de la Marina is open Monday to Friday from 9 am to 2 pm and 4.30 to 6.30 pm and Saturday from 10.30 am to 1 pm.

Money The Banco Zaragozano on Calle de Durán Loriga is one of several banks with ATMs on this and nearby streets. American Express (☎ 981 22 99 72), represented by Viajes Amado, is at Calle de Compostela 1.

Post & Communications The central correos is on Avenida de la Marina and the postcode is 15080. Phone and fax offices are scattered about the town centre.

Medical Services & Emergency In a medical emergency call ☎ 061 or the Cruz Roja on ☎ 22 22 22. There's a night pharmacy on Calle Fernández Latorre, near the estación de autobuses.

Torre de Hércules

One myth says Hercules built the original lighthouse here after slaying the cruel king

GALICIA

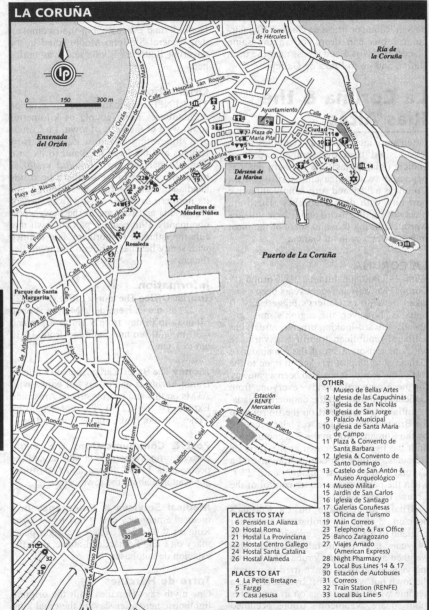

LA CORUÑA

Ensenada
del Orzán

Playa del Orzán

Playa de Riazor

Parque de Santa
Margarita

To Torre
de Hércules

Ría de
la Coruña

Paseo Marítimo

Ayuntamiento

Plaza de
María Pita

Ciudad

Vieja

Dársena de
La Marina

Jardines de
Méndez Núñez

Rosaleda

Puerto de La Coruña

Estación
RENFE
Mercancías

Estación de
Acceso al Puerto

Ronda de Nelle

0   150   300 m

OTHER
1 Museo de Bellas Artes
2 Iglesia de las Capuchinas
3 Iglesia de San Nicolás
8 Iglesia de San Jorge
9 Palacio Municipal
10 Iglesia de Santa María
  de Campo
11 Plaza & Convento de
  Santa Barbara
12 Iglesia & Convento de
  Santo Domingo
13 Castelo de San Antón &
  Museo Arqueológico
14 Museo Militar
15 Jardín de San Carlos
16 Iglesia de Santiago
17 Galerías Coruñesas
18 Oficina de Turismo
19 Main Correos
23 Telephone & Fax Office
25 Banco Zaragozano
27 Viajes Amado
  (American Express)
28 Night Pharmacy
29 Local Bus Lines 14 & 17
30 Estación de Autobuses
31 Correos
32 Train Station (RENFE)
33 Local Bus Line 5

PLACES TO STAY
6 Pensión La Alianza
20 Hostal Roma
21 Hostal La Provinciana
22 Hostal Centro Gallego
24 Hostal Santa Catalina
26 Hostal Alameda

PLACES TO EAT
4 La Petite Bretagne
5 Farggi
7 Casa Jesusa

of a tribe of giants who kept the local populace in terror. All we know is that Romans built a lighthouse here in the 2nd century. It was later used as a fort and restored in 1792. As you enter, you can see the excavated remains of the original Roman base and medieval meddling. Climb to the top for some views of the city. It is open daily from 10 am to 7 pm.

Galerías

La Coruña has been dubbed the 'city of glass', and to find out why you need to head down to waterfront Avenida de la Marina. Multistorey houses sport what could almost pass as a uniform protective layer of *galerías* or glassed-in balconies – although the effects of the inclement weather and an apparent lack of care has diminished its effect.

Ciudad Vieja

This is a compact zone that constitutes almost all of that part of La Coruña older than the middle of the 19th century, and the elegant Plaza de María Pita is the western boundary of this zone. Sealed off on three sides by porticoes, the city's flamboyant **ayuntamiento** is an unmistakable landmark. At the time of writing, the square was undergoing some heavy repairs, and access was limited to the arcades only.

The **Iglesia de Santiago**, with its three Romanesque apses backing on to the pretty little Plaza del General Azcarraga, is the city's oldest church. A short walk through the labyrinth brings you to the slightly unkempt **Jardín de San Carlos**, where General Sir John Moore lies buried. Across the street, war aficionados can look over the **Museo Militar**, which houses arms from the 18th to the 20th centuries. It is open Monday to Saturday from 10 am to 2 pm and 4 to 7 pm (Sunday from 10 am to 2 pm; free).

Castelo de San Antón

Outside the old town walls and keeping a watch over the port, this 12th century fortress was converted into a prison in the 18th century. It now houses a Museo Arqueológico made up of an eclectic collection of items ranging from Roman and Visigothic artefacts, through some rather incongruous pieces from ancient Egypt and on to items from more recent times. It is open Tuesday to Saturday from 10 am to 2 pm and 4 to 7.30 pm (Sunday from 10 am to 2.30 pm; 300 ptas).

Museo de Bellas Artes

Towards the end of 1995, a new art gallery opened in La Coruña on the site of a former Capuchin convent. In addition to works by Rubens and etchings by Goya, there is a representative collection of 16th and 17th century European paintings (taken from the museum's forerunner, virtually next door), as well as contributions from the El Prado and Reina Sofía museums in Madrid. The building is quite innovative, managing to salvage something of the atmosphere of the former convent within the bounds of a modern museum. It is open Tuesday to Sunday from 10 am to 2.30 pm (200 ptas).

Casa de las Ciencias

La Coruña's science museum and planetarium has become one of the country's most popular museums. It's in the Parque de Santa Margarita, and is open Tuesday to Saturday from 11 am to 9 pm in summer and 10 to 7 pm in winter (Sunday from 11 am to 2.30 pm).

Beaches

Aside from the protected city beaches, Playa de Riazor and Playa del Orzán, several others stretch away along the 30km sweep of coast west of the city. In summer RutaBus buses run regularly out to Barrañán, Casón and Baldaio. The last of the three is a long sandy beach.

Places to Stay

There is no shortage of lower-range hotels in La Coruña. Calle de Riego de Agua is a good spot to look, as close to the old centre and surrounded by streets with some of the best eating in La Coruña.

GALICIA

Pensión La Alianza (☎ *981 22 81 14, Calle de Riego de Agua 8)* is one of several little places on this street that would see you in the heart of the most interesting part of town. It charges 2000/3500 ptas for average singles/doubles.

Hostal Roma (☎ *981 22 80 75, Rúa Nueva 3)* is another cheapie, offering basic doubles for 2100 ptas. Virtually round the corner, *Hostal Centro Gallego* (☎ *981 22 22 36, Calle Estrella 2)* has a range of rooms starting at 1500/3000 ptas in high season.

A step up is the *Hostal La Provinciana* (☎ *981 22 04 00, Rúa Nueva 7-9)*, which has rooms for 4000/6000 ptas in the high season. In about the same category is the reliable *Hostal Santa Catalina* (☎ *981 22 66 09, Travesía de Santa Catalina 1)*.

A little farther away from the centre is the extremely pleasant *Hostal Alameda* (☎ *981 22 70 74, Calle de la Alameda 12)*. Doubles range from 4700 to 7500 ptas, depending on season and demand.

Places to Eat

The narrow lanes stretching west of Plaza de María Pita are the first place to make for in search of good food. Calle de la Franja in particular is lined with options. *Casa Jesusa* at No 8 offers a tasty set lunch usually composed of seafood (the *empanadillas* are especially good) for 1200 ptas. Calle de los Olmos and Calle Estrella are also rich hunting grounds – you'll see plenty of octopuses in the windows.

For a dessert with a difference, try the crêpes at *La Petite Bretagne (Calle de Riego de Agua 13)*. *Farggi* at No 5 (closed Sunday) is good for breakfast and sticky things.

Although you pay a little over the odds for your coffee, the cafés on Plaza de María Pita are an unbeatable choice for at least one people-watching session. Just as good is the Avenida de la Marina.

Entertainment

You'll find plenty to drink with your tapas in the central streets already mentioned. If you're more interested in drinking than eating, try one of the 50 or so watering holes crammed into the streets off Playa del Orzán. As the night wears on, Calle de Juan Florez is also worth checking out, as are many of its side streets.

Getting There & Away

Bus There are plenty of buses to most destinations throughout Galicia and several beyond. Castromil runs regular services to Vigo via Santiago de Compostela and Pontevedra. You can change at Santiago for Orense. IASA has buses to Lugo, O Ferrol and Betanzos. For destinations to the Costa da Morte area, Transportes Finisterre runs up to 30 buses daily to Carballo (510 ptas), four daily to Finisterre (1450 ptas) and two to Malpica de Bergantiños. ACP serves Betanzos (310 ptas).

Train Up to 12 trains daily head south to Vigo (1095 ptas) via Santiago de Compostela (475 ptas) and Pontevedra (970 ptas). There are three daily to Madrid (Chamartín), one of which continues to Alicante, and two to Barcelona via Zaragoza. The twice-daily train to O Ferrol (1½ hours; 475 ptas) stops at Betanzos (290 ptas).

Car & Motorcycle The A-9 is the quickest road out of La Coruña. This tollway passes east by Betanzos before heading down to Vigo via Santiago de Compostela and Pontevedra. The N-550 to Santiago is prettier but slower. For Lugo and Madrid, take the N-IV.

Getting Around

Local bus No 5 links the train station with central La Coruña, while Nos 14 and 17 go from the estación de autobuses through the centre and out to the Torre de Hércules. To avoid a long walk to the Torre de Hércules, catch No 3A from Plaza de España or Jardín de San Carlos.

RÍAS ALTAS

Although the Rías Altas and surrounding countryside are less extensive and visited less often than the Rías Bajas, in many respects they have quite an edge over their more popular counterpart. For starters, they are not nearly as populated, retaining a greater natural attraction. And when the weather is good, many beaches on this stretch are every bit as good as anything you'll find to the south. A handful of enticing little towns like medieval Betanzos and Pontedeume are handsomely accompanied by some of the most dramatic coast you will see in all Galicia – that of the Serra de la Capelada and Cabo Ortegal.

Betanzos

Just 24km east of La Coruña, Betanzos can be seen as a small-scale Toledo of the north, decidedly flavoured *a la gallega* with its multistorey houses glassed in by the classic white galerías. Re-sited here in 1219, the port of this medieval walled town was long a busy haven until eclipsed by La Coruña. Lately it has made valiant – and fairly successful – efforts to stave off the tangible effects of economic depression.

The Oficina de Información, in the same building as the Museo das Mariñas on Rúa de Emilio Romay, has a map and list of hospedajes. Several banks are located on or near the main sprawling square of the town, Praza dos Irmáns García Naveira. The correos is on Paseo de Alfonso IX, also near the square.

The Celtic settlement *(castro)* that predated the town was located in what is now Praza da Constitución, flanked notably by the neoclassical ayuntamiento and Gothic Iglesia de Santiago. More interesting is Praza de Fernán Pérez de Andrade. The Gothic churches of **Santa María do Azogue** and **San Francisco** stand opposite each other, separated by the small square. Inside the latter is the tomb of Fernán Pérez de Andrade, the noble who founded a monastery in nearby O Ferrol in the 14th century, supported by the family emblems in stone – a bear and a wild boar.

The **Museo das Mariñas** contains a lot of curios, including fragments of medieval sculpture and a display of traditional Galician costumes. It is open daily from 10 am to 1 pm and 4 to 8 pm (100 ptas).

The Fiesta de San Roque, held annually on August 16, is marked by the sending up of a huge, 'home-made' paper hot-air balloon.

Places to Stay & Eat Of the half-dozen or so places to stay, many are always full with workers on local road-building projects. A last-ditch effort for the desperate is the *Mesón Cortés (Rúa de Saavedra Meneses 4)*, just across the Ponte Vello (old bridge) from the medieval town. It has dingy singles/doubles for 1500/2500 ptas.

In the centre of town are rooms above the tapas bar in a lane just off the main square. The unnamed lane is loaded with bars and so it's a noisy option (it leads off the square between Café La Goleta and a pharmacy). Look for the *pensión* at No 17 (☎ 981 77 03 79). Singles/doubles cost 1500/2500 ptas.

Hostal Barreiro (☎ 981 77 22 59, Rúa de Argentina 6) has simple rooms for 1400/2300 ptas. Doubles with private bath are 2500 ptas. *Hotel Los Angeles (☎ 981 77 15 11, Rúa dos Anxeles 11)* charges 4700/6200/8900 plus IVA for singles/doubles/triples.

The unnamed lane referred to above is the focus of Betanzos' culinary life. *O' Pote* at No 9 and the *Mesón O' Progreso* at the end of the lane are decent. The next lane parallel has more tapas bars. The cafés on the main square are popular for breakfast. You can quench a thirst at the *Cervecería Old Inn*, just off the Praza de Domingo, which has a fair selection of Irish and German beers.

Getting There & Away The easiest way in and out of Betanzos is by bus. Regular services to and from La Coruña run from Praza dos Irmáns García Naveira. Less frequent buses head to Lugo and O Ferrol. The closest of the town's two train stations, Betanzos Cidade, is north of the old town, just across the Río Mendo. Two trains daily go to O Ferrol and La Coruña.

GALICIA

Pontedeume

Founded in 1270, this hillside feudal bastion, while scruffier than Betanzos, is an appealing stop with the advantage of having a beach close by the town's fishing port. Rúa Real, the porticoed main street, climbs past a cheerful little square (in front of the *concello*, or town hall) up to the 18th century Iglesia de Santiago. Winding down the hill from here are numerous lanes characterised by Galician galerías. Down on the waterfront, near the market, rises the **torreón** (main tower) of what was once the Palacio de Andrade, named after the local feudal lord.

Fonda Martis (☎ 981 43 06 37, Rúa Real 23) has Spartan rooms in the heart of things for 1500/2500 ptas. This street is lined with taverns and eateries. At **Bar Cañiza** at No 28 you can try a *queimada* (a kind of hot punch).

O Ferrol

For a town with rather leftist leanings, it is a small irony of history that Franco was born here in 1892. Under his rule the town was known as El Ferrol del Caudillo, and his equestrian statue still dominates Plaza de España. The house he was born in is at Calle María 136. Otherwise there is little to see in a town that has been badly hit by the decline of its shipyards in the past few decades.

If you decide to take a look at the not unpleasant town centre, head for Calle de Pardo Bajo for food and lodgings. **Hostal Aloya (☎ 981 35 12 31)** at No 28 is a reliable place to stay, with doubles for 4700 ptas in high season. Otherwise, check out some of the cheaper hospedajes on the same street. In between them is crammed a selection of restaurants and bars. **Restaurante Côté** is so good that there's two of them – at Nos 19 and 24. Oddly enough for a port town, their meat dishes are the best.

Regular buses run to Santiago de Compostela (895 ptas) via Betanzos, and to Viveiro and Vigo (1790 ptas) via Pontevedra (1495 ptas). A couple of long-distance buses from Galicia to Madrid call in here.

Two daily RENFE trains connect O Ferrol with La Coruña (310 ptas) via Betanzos, and up to four FEVE trains head east to Oviedo via Ribadeo.

Cedeira

If possible, give O Ferrol a miss and make for Cedeira, 38km up the coast and sitting on a stream that spills into the pretty Ría de Cedeira. The older nucleus of this little town fronts the river with traditional glassed-in galerías, while across two bridges on the modern side of town is a pleasant, sheltered beach. Better still, head south over to the next estuary, the Ría de Esteiro, where you'll find a still more appealing beach which is popular with free-campers. The local tourist office is at Arriba da Ponte 22 and is open Monday to Saturday from 11 am to 2 pm and 6 to 9 pm (Sunday from noon to 2 pm in summer).

There are a few **hostales** to choose from. A cheap alternative is an **unnamed place** *(Calle de los Excombatientes 2)* –look for the CH sign – which has clean singles/doubles from 1500/2500 ptas. For accommodation information, look out for the **Habitaciones El Puente** sign near the second bridge. A popular place for raciones and a beer is **Mesón Muiños Kilowato** *(Avenida a Moreno 12)*, farther along the waterfront of the old town.

Regular buses connect Cedeira with O Ferrol to the south-west and Cariño to the north-east.

Serra de la Capelada

North from Cedeira things only get better. On the road to San Andrés de Teixido, you exchange the ever-changing horizons of the rías for higher, wilder ground. The Serra de Capelada is heavily wooded and instead of milestones, the winding road is regularly marked by spectacular *miradores* (viewpoints) over some of the sheerest Atlantic coast in Europe. Windy even on a hot summer day, this territory can be downright fear-inspiring in the midst of a winter storm.

Wild horses still mingle here with cattle, and early June tends to be the main time for the *curro*, the festive rounding up and breaking in of these free-spirited animals (see the boxed text 'Galician Round-Up').

San Andrés de Teixido Along a particularly pretty stretch of coast, this hamlet is renowned as a sanctuary of relics of St Andrew. Spaniards flock to see the sanctuary and fill up a few bottles with spring water from the so-called Fuente de la Suerte (Lucky Spring). The result of this is a predictable line of kitsch tourist stalls – enough to make you wonder if there's anyone out in the surrounding fields. Don't let this put you off. Anyone with a vehicle should take this route for the views – before, in and after the village. Buses from Cedeira to Cariño occasionally stop in.

Cabo Ortegal Another 20-odd kilometres north, Cabo Ortegal is the mother of Spanish capes. Great stone shafts drop sheer into the ocean from such a height that the waves crashing onto the rocks below seem pitifully – and deceptively – benign. The cape is a few kilometres beyond the soulless fishing town of Cariño. Travellers without their own wheels can get buses to Cariño from O Ferrol, Cedeira and Ortigueira, and there are a couple of hostales around if you need one. The problem remains thumbing a ride out to the cape.

Cariño to Viveiro

From Cariño the road roughly follows the contours of the Ría de Ortigueira southwards to the Río Mera. The area is rich in water-bird life and the only town of any consequence is **Ortigueira**, a not unattractive but hardly captivating fishing town. One time when it is worth being here is during the annual Mundo Celta music festival, usually held in the first week of August.

Otherwise you'll be happier if you continue your way north-east to **O Barqueiro**, a Galician fishing village as you might imagine one. White houses capped with slate-tile roofs cascade down to a small protected port. There's little to do but watch the day's catch come in, but that's the point –

this is the real thing. There are a couple of places to stay down on the waterfront. Try *Hostal La Marina* (☎ 981 41 40 98), which has doubles only for 3000 ptas, or 4200 ptas with private bath.

Campers should push on up to **Porto de Vares (Bares)**, 2km past Vila de Vares. The place is smaller and boasts a pair of beaches (the one closer to town is more protected). *Restaurante La Marina*, with a terrace overlooking the beach, does acceptable seafood and paella. A side road leads to **Cabo Estaca de Vares** (you can't miss the windmills), Spain's most northerly point.

Beaches The coast eastwards to Viveiro is broken up by several decent beaches. It is wise to choose one at least 5km short of Viveiro, or you'll have to put up with comparatively built-up stretches.

Viveiro

Behind the grand Puerta de Carlos V (the most impressive of Viveiro's three remaining medieval gates) lies a straggle of cobbled lanes and plazas where little seems to have changed since the town was rebuilt after a fire in 1540. There is a small tourist office (☎ 982 56 04 86) inside the gate. Directly up the road past Praza Maior is the **Iglesia de Santa María do Campo**, displaying Romanesque and Gothic features. Nearby is a bad-taste reproduction of Lourdes, while to the north, the 14th century **Iglesia de San Francisco** is the most interesting of Viveiro's buildings.

Fonda Nuevo Mundo (☎ 982 56 00 25, Rúa de Teodoro de Quirós 14) is one of several modest hostelries inside the old town and is a good, clean deal. Singles/doubles cost 1700/2600 ptas – try for a room in one of the galerías. There are more hostales and a couple of camp sites on the beaches outside town, particularly at Praia de Covas.

For a decent seafood meal, try *Bar Serra* (Rúa de Antonio Bas 2). The area around Placiña da Herba presents a few appetising options. *Mesón O' Tunel* (Rúa Fernández Victorio 6) has good tapas. Alternatively, look in at **Mesón A Cepa** at No 7. For a late-night drink, Rúa Pérez das Mariñas and Rúa Almirante Chicarro are promising.

FEVE line trains call in here between Oviedo and O Ferrol, but buses along the coast are more frequent. They leave from a station just north of the Puerta de Carlos V, on the waterfront.

Mondoñedo

Compared with the natural spectacles of north-western Galicia's Atlantic coast, the offerings east of Viveiro cut a poor figure. For much of the trip towards Asturias the road lies well inland from the coastline and what beaches there are pale before their cousins farther west and east. The towns of Cervo, Sargadelos, Burela and Foz are all pretty drab and best examined from the comfort of whatever transport you happen to be in.

By contrast, a rewarding detour inland from Foz down the Río Masma brings you to Mondoñedo, first settled in the 5th century by a group of restless migrants from Brittany. An important religious centre and long a provincial capital in the old Kingdom of Galicia, Mondoñedo's slightly down-at-heel appearance in no way diminishes its interest. The tourist office (☎ 982 50 71 77) is just off Praza de España, near the impressive cathedral. Also fronting the old square is the Palacio Episcopal, next to the cathedral, and the porticoed *cantón*. The old fountain (Fonte Vella) that you can see just south of the square was built in 1548.

The **Pensión La Tropicana** (☎ 982 52 10 08, Rúa de Lodeiro Piñeiroa 8) is the closest place to the centre of town. Singles/doubles cost 2400/4000 ptas. There are several buses to Foz and Lugo.

Into Asturias

Aside from the odd mediocre beach, there is little to keep you waiting along the coast between Foz and **Ribadeo**. The best thing about this frontier town is its ría, a broad expanse and an obvious natural frontier between Galicia and Asturias. The great Puente de los Santos fords the waterway

that, in the guise of the Río Eo, continues to mark the regional frontier for some 30km south. A busy little place, Ribadeo contains nothing at all to see or do. If you get stuck, the area around the central Praza de España is awash with hotels of every conceivable category.

The Costa da Morte

On one of those not-so-frequent hot, sunny days, you could be forgiven for thinking that the tales of danger surrounding this stretch of the Atlantic seaboard – the 'Death Coast' – are greatly exaggerated. But the idyll can undergo a rapid metamorphosis when ocean mists blow in and envelop the whole region.

On the way out of La Coruña, there are a few ocean beaches such as the Playa de Barrañán and Playa de Sorrizo where you must be mindful of the currents. The Costa da Morte begins at the unassuming point of Caión. If travelling by bus, you may find yourself passing inland via Carballo, one of the costa's main transport hubs. Heading south-west along the coast from Caión towards Malpica de Bergantiños, you pass a turn-off for Buño, known for its ceramics.

MALPICA DE BERGANTIÑOS

Malpica has a sandy beach on one side and a busy port on the other. The main attraction is the liveliness of the village centre and its bars and eateries, several of which overlook the beach. Off the coast you can see the Islas Sisargas, home to various nesting bird species, mostly various types of seagull. **Hostal JB** (☎ 981 72 02 66) on Rueiro da Praia has comfortable rooms, some virtually overhanging the beach. Singles/doubles with TV and private bath start at 3500/4500 ptas. **Hostal Panchito** (☎ 981 72 30 07) on Praza de Anselmo Villar Amigo has decent rooms without the views for about the same price. For a place to eat, hunt around the various bars squeezed in just back from the beach. Buses run from La Coruña to Malpica and on to Corme.

CORME

Climb Corme's steep, winding streets from the waterfront and you'll notice how its fishing port feel gives way to that of the agricultural hinterland (known as Corme Aldea) – quite a complementary arrangement. Although most of the buildings are modern, the place has some of its old *pueblo* atmosphere and a serviceable nearby beach. If the latter does not meet your expectations, move south to **Praia Hermida**, an attractive and uncrowded ocean beach. Harder to reach without your own transport but just as pleasant is **Praia Balarés**. Perhaps not so nice is a growing side industry here, as in other Galician ports. In January 1996 an old fishing vessel was impounded with 2600kg of cocaine – the biggest haul by Spanish authorities on record.

LAXE & AROUND

If you're driving down the coast, make first for Ponteceso, a local crossroads. Nearby Laxe has a white sandy beach, but like quite a few of these fishing towns, its mostly modern buildings deprive it of character. For something a little easier on the eye, dare to penetrate the unsignposted maze of roads south of Laxe that should eventually get you to the wilder **Praia de Traba**.

CAMARIÑAS & AROUND

In essence a modern fishing village, Camariñas for some reason attracts a steady trickle of mainly Spanish tourists. The place does have something of a reputation for *encajes* (lacework) and you may see women making the stuff in strategic locations for passers-by.

Apart from the craftwork, there are really only two reasons for passing through. The first is to take a look at **Cabo Vilán**, an impressive cape 5km north-west of the town. The Atlantic storms are put to good use with the modern windmills of the Parque Eólico.

The second reason is the restaurant at *Hostal La Marina* (☎ 981 73 60 30, *Rúa de Miguel Feixoo 4)*. For about 2000 ptas you can taste some of the best value seafood you're likely to encounter in Galicia. The Valencians could learn a thing or two from their version of paella. You can stay overnight too, and add dinner to lunch, for 2100/3700 ptas for singles/doubles in high season. Transportes Finisterre buses connect Camariñas with Santiago de Compostela and La Coruña.

About 17km north of Camariñas, **Arou** is a much less visited fishing village with a couple of pleasant swimming areas – especially if you follow the track along the coast. Here you'll find *señoras* working on lace and probably get better prices than in Camariñas.

A lousy track leads off from near Arou towards **Ensenada de Trece**, a not overly-visited beach. After 10km the track passes a cemetery where 172 English cadets lie buried (they died in a shipwreck off the coast in 1890).

MUXÍA & AROUND

Getting to and from Camariñas you'll pass through Ponte do Porto, which fords the Río Grande. The coast road south for Os Muiños passes the pretty hamlet of **Cereixo** and heads down a narrow, shaded road. Along here, near Leis, you'll find one of the most inviting beaches along the Costa da Morte, **Praia do Lago**. The sand fronts the ocean and also a quiet river. There are a couple of camping grounds and at least one hostal around it.

From Os Muiños the road passes the Romanesque **Monasterio de San Xián de Moraime**, built over a Roman settlement. Muxía itself is nothing special, but once here it is worth pushing on to the **Punta da Barca**, which affords good views of the coast. The rocks in front of the baroque Santuario de Nuestra Señora de la Barca are the scene of a popular *romería* (festive pilgrimage) in September. *Hostal La Cruz* (☎ 981 74 20 84, *Avenida de Calvo Sotelo 53)* has singles/doubles for 4500/6500 ptas in the high season.

FINISTERRE

Those poking their noses about the Costa da Morte will want to make it to Galicia's version of England's Land's End, Finisterre, or Fisterra in Galician. From Vimianzo the road drops south through Corcubión, a largish, unappealing sort of place, although there are a few hostales if you need one. The tree-lined road is appealing, but the towns less so, and Sardiñeiro is hardly much better than Corcubión, only smaller. The nearby *Ruta Finisterre camping ground* (☎ 981 74 55 85) is not a bad place to stop for the night. There is a reasonable beach a couple of kilometres farther on, stretching almost to the town of Finisterre. Like most of the towns around here, this is nothing to write home about. It's another 3.5km to **Cabo Finisterre**, where Spain stops and the Atlantic begins. To the right on the way out of town is the 12th century **Iglesia de Santa María das Areas**, a mix of Romanesque, Gothic and baroque. The westernmost shelter for pilgrims en route to Santiago de Compostela once stood just opposite. The best views of the coast are to be had by climbing up the track to Monte Facho and Monte San Guillermo. The area is laced with myth and superstition, and they say childless couples used to come up here to increase their efforts to conceive.

Pensión Casa Velay (☎ 981 74 01 27), just off the main square in the older part of the town, has decent doubles without private bath for 2000 ptas (3500 ptas with facilities). The owners also run a restaurant, or you could hang around *Bar Tito* on the main square for snacks and beer.

TOWARDS THE RÍAS BAJAS

The southernmost stretch of the Costa da Morte has its moments. At **Ézaro**, 27km from Cabo Finisterre, a steep road climbs 2km to a mirador with breathtaking views over the Atlantic. **O Pindo** (El Pindo), is a cute fishing village set back on a shallow, tranquil bay. *Hospedaje La Morada* (☎ 981 85 80 70) has singles/doubles for about 2500/4000 ptas. Another 10km south and you reach the Playa de Carnota, a long,

sandy beach – usually not too crowded, and fine if the wind isn't up. For beaches farther on, see Muros later. **Carnota** town, towards the southern end of the beach, is renowned for being home to the longest *hórreo* (grain store; see the boxed text 'Of Grain Stores and Crossroads' for background) in Galicia – 34.5m long, it was built late in the 18th century.

Rías Bajas

The four great estuaries of Galicia's south, the Rías Bajas (Rias Baixas) are doubtless the grandest of all the rías that indent the length of the Galician coast, and they are justifiably well known. There are plenty of beaches and several relatively low-key resorts, and in summer good weather is a better bet here than farther north. Throw in the Islas Cíes, the lovely medieval town of Pontevedra and the more harried centre of Vigo, and you have a travelling mix that is hard to beat.

RÍA DE MUROS Y NOIA
Muros

A pleasant enough stop along the shores of this ría, Muros is perhaps not quite as wonderful as the travel literature makes out. Founded in the 10th century, it was long an important port for Santiago de Compostela. Today it lives mainly from fishing and a passing tourist trade. From the main seaside square dominated by the ayuntamiento, follow Calle Real vaguely in the direction of Santiago. Along the way are some attractive porticoes, the odd *cruceiro* (crucifix; see the boxed text 'Of Grain Stores and Crossroads'), a couple of ageing churches and an overly extravagant mercado. Apart from the pleasure of having a beer or meal on the waterfront, that's about all there is to the place, besides a couple of nice beaches west of the town.

Noia

Noia is worth visiting for its old centre, which preserves some reminders of its glory days: in particular, the main entrance and rose window of the 15th century Gothic **Catedral de San Martiño**. Nearby is the highly evocative **Casa de Costa**, whose four arches date back to at least the mid-14th century. The former **Iglesia de Santa María La Nova**, a short walk from the old centre, was built in 1327 and today, together with its cemetery, forms a unique museum of headstones and funerary art. It is open Tuesday to Friday from 11 am to 1.30 pm and 6.30 to 8 pm and weekends from 11 am to 1.30 pm.

The *Hospedaje Marico* (☎ *981 82 00 09, Rúa de Galicia s/n)*, on the road to Santiago and near the old part of town, is a good deal at 1500/2500 ptas for rooms without private bath (doubles with own bath cost 3000 ptas). For snacks and drinks, you cannot beat *Tasca Típica*, right in the Casa de Costa, with tables spilling out under the arches. Several buses call in at Noia en route from Santiago to Muros. A couple also serve Padrón.

South Shore

From Noia you could head east for Santiago or turn down along the southern shore of the ría. The main attraction of the latter option, if the weather is good, is the long series of beaches – such as Arealonga, one of the first you encounter. On a headland near **Baroña** are the remains of a Celtic castro, signposted from the roadside café. The beach nearby is for nudists.

RÍA DE AROUSA

Those hugging the coast and coming from the southern shore of the Ría de Muros y Noia will almost certainly end up in **Ribeira**, the first town of any significance on the Ría de Arousa (Ria de Arosa). A drab and drizzly fishing town, it has virtually nothing to recommend it.

If you are driving in the area, you might just want to make a detour to see the **Dolmen de Axeitos**, a well-preserved megalithic monument. It's signposted off the road between Ribeira and Xuño.

There is little to delay you on the road east. However, a few kilometres past the

Of Grain Stores & Crossroads

Away from the famous façades, Galicia is studded with a wealth of 'popular architecture' quite specific to the region. Most common of all is the *cruceiro*, a crucifix usually bearing a statue of Christ on one side and a distraught Virgin Mary on the other. The more ornate ones represent key scenes from the Bible. In both cases they are most commonly found at crossroads – where they served an orientational function for wayfarers in the days before street signs – and in churchyards. The bulk of them have been erected over the centuries by various religious orders and they are said to possess a protective power, as well as being a subliminal reminder of the religious status of the area in case anyone were in any doubt. As it happens, they frequently became the object for local cult 'worship' of particular saints.

The simple 14th century cruceiro of Melide, along the Camino de Santiago, is the oldest in existence, while the complex 19th century one at Hio (Ría de Vigo), depicting the taking down of Christ from the cross, was carved from a single block of granite and is judged by those in the know to be the most beautiful.

The other odd-looking construction you will see all over the place is the *hórreo*. Generally made of granite, and sometimes partly of wood, this rectangular structure has for centuries served as a grain store. Sitting on squat stilts, the hórreo serves to keep grain easily accessible and dry. Some, like the one in Carnota, are extremely long, generally a reflection of the owners' wealth. Your average family hórreo, nowadays more often than not used as a junk shed and clothes line, is of more modest proportions. If you end up in Asturias, you will notice (virtually as soon as you cross the border) that the Asturians have their own version, a square-based wooden affair, sometimes with a tiled roof and quite often a sort of mini-verandah all the way around.

GALICIA

rather awful town of Boiro is a wonderful place to stay and an ideal country base for exploring the area. The *Casa da Posta de Valmaior (☎ 981 86 25 48)*, Cespón Boiro, has a series of lovely rooms in a country home. Prices range from 3500 ptas for a single to 7000 ptas for a double. It is *turismo rural* at its best, and is well signposted off the N-550 between Boiro and Padrón. You'll need your own transport to get here.

Padrón

The hottest thing to come out of Padrón is peppers. That's right, *pimientos de Padrón* – shrivelled little green things that taste very good, but beware the odd *very* hot one. Franciscan friars first imported them from Mexico in the 16th century, and the whole area now grows them to meet the high demand. This town of 4000, where Santiago's corpse supposedly arrived in Galicia, is struggling valiantly to make a tourist attraction of itself, putting most effort into the Galician poet Rosalía de Castro, who died here in 1885. The Casa y Museo de Rosalía, just behind the train station, contains memorabilia and is one stop in the so-called Ruta Rosaliana that has been mapped out in various locations throughout this region. It is open Tuesday to Sunday from 9.30 am to 2 pm and 4 to 8 pm (9.30 am to 1.30 pm and 4 to 7 pm in winter).

Hostal del Jardín (☎ 981 81 09 50, Rúa de Salgado Araujo 3) is opposite the park on the road leading to the train station. Singles/doubles in high season start at 2500/3500 ptas.

Catoira

About 15km down the Río Ulla, which shortly after widens into the Ría de Arousa, stand the Torres do Oeste. These towers are the remainder of Castellum Honesti, the early medieval castle that was the key in protecting (not always successfully) Santiago de Compostela against Norman landings. On the first Sunday of every August, a Viking landing is staged here as an excuse for a boisterous fiesta.

Caldas de Reyes

An inland diversion from Villagarcía de Arousa or directly along the road between Pontevedra and Padrón, Caldas de Reyes is an old spa town and something of a curiosity. At one end of the cobbled Calle Real stands a small medieval bridge, while on the Río Umia, the two spa hotels, or *balnearios*, still function. It is worth having a peek inside *Hotel Acuña (☎ 986 54 00 10, Calle de Herrería 2)*. You can have a bath if you want to, but generally guests here are under medical supervision. The whole place exudes a mouldy 19th-century feeling. The other balneario, *Hostal Dávila (☎ 986 54 00 12, Calle de Laureano Salgado 11)*, is even more dilapidated. Just outside it is As Burgas, a small spa water fountain.

Hostal Buceta (☎ 986 54 00 31, Calle de José Salgado 34) is something of an ageing piece as well, where singles/doubles cost 2000/3000 ptas without private bath and 3000/4700 ptas with. *Taberna O' Muiño* is an old, run-down riverside bar and grill.

Isla de Arousa

Back by the water, you could drive straight past Vilanova de Arousa (although it has a few reasonable beaches) and make for Isla (Illa) de Arousa, an island connected to the mainland by a long, low bridge. The small town lives mainly from fishing and the whole place has a low-key profile. Some of the beaches facing the mainland are very pleasant and protected and have comparatively warm water.

A couple of *camping grounds* open in summer on the island and at Vilanova. The occasional bus runs between here and Pontevedra.

Cambados

Founded by the Visigoths and a victim of constant harrying by Vikings in the 9th and 10th centuries, Cambados is today a peaceful seaside town. Coming from the north you enter by the magnificent Praza de Fefiñáns. On two sides it is bordered by a grand 17th century pazo and on another by the 18th century Iglesia de San Benito.

Several appealing little streets branch off the square and nearby another pazo has been converted into a parador. There's a small tourist office on Rúa de Novedades. If you have a car, a pretty inland excursion via San Salvador de Meis will take you to the **Monasterio de Santa María de Armenteira**, founded in 1162.

Hostal Pazos Feijoo (☎ *986 54 28 10, Calle de Curros Enríquez 1*) is near the waterfront in the newer part of town. Singles/doubles cost 2500/4000 ptas. The *Parador El Albariño* (☎ *986 54 22 50, fax 986 54 20 68*) on Paseo Cervantes charges 10,000/13,500 ptas plus IVA in high season.

The otherwise unnamed *Café-Bar* on Rúa Caracol is an unpretentious place where you can get a reasonable seafood meal for about 1000 ptas. Cambados is in the heart of Albariño wine country, and Praza de Fefiñáns is swarming with bodegas and bars flogging what can be a very good drop.

Buses to Pontevedra and Santiago de Compostela leave from along the waterfront, near Hostal Pazos Feijoo.

O Grove & A Toxa

How you react to O Grove may well depend on the weather. It's a strange mix of England's Blackpool and some of Italy's Adriatic 'family' resorts. In summer you'll find little more than hotel blocks, unexciting restaurants, mediocre nightclubs, a fairground and Galicia's unpredictable climate. In winter most of the above is closed, and the weather is worse.

Still, it could make a lunch stop on your way through the area, and there are several beaches around the little peninsula of which it is a part. As for the island of A Toxa, connected to O Grove by a bridge, this onetime natural beauty spot has been irreparably spoiled by holiday-makers and builders with more money than sense. The place is crawling with 'classy' hotels and holiday apartments.

Should you want to stay, the only potential problem times are August and summer weekends. The tourist office lists 40 hotels, but there are plenty of cheap hostales and other options. *Hostal María Aguiño* (☎ *986 73 11 87, Rúa de Pablo Iglesias 26*) has decent singles/doubles for 1900/3300 ptas. Across the road at No 23, *Residencia Marisé* (☎ *986 73 08 40*) has clean singles/doubles costing 1700/2400 ptas. If hunger strikes, the restaurants around Praza da República Argentina are OK, and *Taberna O' Pescador* (*Rúa de Pablo Iglesias 9*) is a popular and reasonably priced seafood joint.

Buses run to Sanxenxo, Pontevedra, Padrón and towns in between. In summer, Cruceros Rías Bajas runs boats across to Ribeira. In addition, they sometimes organise trips around the Isla de Arousa.

RÍA DE PONTEVEDRA (NORTH SIDE)

As you swing around to the south from O Grove you strike the longest beach on offer in the Ría de Pontevedra – **La Lanzada**. There is a string of camping grounds and the odd hostal around here, but the beach is free of the resort feel. Surfers may find the odd decent wave, although it is generally better for windsurfers.

Sanxenxo & Portonovo

A long way from the holiday *costas* on the Mediterranean, this is about as close as Galicia comes to emulating them. The Praia de Silgar, the best beach Sanxenxo (Sangenjo) has to offer, is fine and sandy but crowded in summer. The town itself, however, has little to offer in the way of sights. In summer, a tourist information kiosk is open seven days a week on Rúa de Madrid from 11 am to 9 pm.

One possible diversion is to take a boat to the **Isla de Ons**, beyond the mouth of the ría. Cruceros Rías Bajas (☎ 986 73 13 43), based at Rúa Reboredo 76, O Grove, organises return trips from Sanxenxo and Portonovo from mid-July to mid-September. In Sanxenxo, buy tickets at the port, just east of the Praia de Silgar.

As far as accommodation goes, late July to early September is the most difficult period, although in practice the main problem is elevated prices. Out of high season, quite a few places have moderately priced rooms. *Hostal Cucos (☎ 986 72 01 64, Rúa de Carlos Casa 17)* is near Praia de Silgar and has singles/doubles for 2000/3500 ptas in the low season (doubles go for up to 7500 ptas in the high season). Similarly priced is the nearby *Hostal Casa Román (☎ 986 72 00 31)* at No 2. For food and drink, you're best off trekking down the road a couple of kilometres to Portonovo, where you'll find more tapas bars and seafood places than you can poke a stick at. Buses between Pontevedra and O Grove stop here.

Combarro

The road east from Sanxenxo remains fairly liberally laced with hostales and the odd camp site as you head towards Pontevedra. But nothing could stand in greater contrast to the organised amusement of Sanxenxo than the fishing village of Combarro. Although hardly insensitive to the tourist dollar, Combarro has managed to retain some degree of measure. It is best known for the string of hórreos along and near the waterfront Rúa do Mar – a tranquil spot for a leisurely lunch. A tourist office operates Monday to Saturday from 10.30 am to 1.30 pm and 6 to 9 pm.

There are at least three cheapish hostales along the main road from Pontevedra. *Hostal La Parada (☎ 986 77 01 41)* has singles/doubles for 1700/3000 ptas. You could also ask at *Café Xeito (☎ 986 77 00 39)*, about 10 metres away. With a little money you could enjoy some well-prepared tapas or a full meal at the *Restaurante Alvariñas*, on Rúa do Mar.

La Unión company runs buses by Combarro en route from Pontevedra to O Grove.

Monasterio de San Juan de Poio

Three kilometres east of Combarro and just short of Pontevedra, Poio is dominated by its grand monastery. This was long a Benedictine stronghold – the first church here

may have been built in the 7th century – but the Benedictines abandoned the site in 1835, to be replaced 55 years later by the Mercedarios (roughly translated, the Fathers of Mercy). You can visit two cloisters and the church daily from 10 am to 1.30 pm and 5 to 8.30 pm (10 am to 1 pm and 4 to 6 pm in winter). The gardens of the 16th century Claustro de las Procesiones are gathered around a baroque fountain.

PONTEVEDRA

Galicia's smallest provincial capital is perhaps its most striking. With only about 50,000 people, it has managed to preserve intact a classic medieval centre backing on to the Río Lérez – ideal for simply wandering around and poking one's nose into all sorts of nooks and crannies.

History

Known to the Romans as Ad Duos Pontes, Pontevedra reached the height of its glory in the 16th century, at which time it was the biggest city in Galicia and an important port. The *Santa María*, the flagship of Columbus' journey of discovery, was built here, and a local legend that the Genoese explorer was born in Pontevedra persists to this day. From the 17th century on, the city began to decline in the face of growing competition in the ría and the silting up of its port. The 1719 sacking of the town by the British did not help matters. In spite of it all, Pontevedra was made provincial capital in 1835 despite fierce opposition from Vigo, and tourism is proving a healthy boon.

Orientation

The historic centre, or *zona monumental* as the local authorities refer to it, is clearly confined to a circle formed by Calle del Arzobispo Malvar, Calle de Michelena, Calle de Cobián Raffignac, Calle de Padre A Carballo and the Río Lérez, itself forded by two bridges (not the original *duos pontes* of the Roman name, though they may be in the same place). The walls have gone, but the boundaries remain the same. Inside this area you'll find several hotels, all your eating and drinking needs and much of what you'll want to see. Banks and other offices lie on or near Calle de Michelena, the main drag of the newer town.

Information

Tourist Office The tourist office (☎ 986 85 08 14), Calle del General Mola 3, is open Monday to Friday from 9.30 am to 2 pm and 5 to 7 pm, Saturday from 10 am to 12.30 pm and 5 to 8 pm and Sunday from 11 am to 1.30 pm.

Money There are plenty of banks near the tourist office on Calle de Michelena. They generally open on weekdays from 8.30 am to 2 pm (Saturday until 1 pm in winter).

Post & Communications The main correos is on Calle de la Oliva and is open Monday to Friday from 8.30 am to 8.30 pm. The postcode for central Pontevedra is 36080. There is a phone office at Calle de la Oliva 26.

Medical Services & Emergency The Policía Municipal are on Praza de Indalecio Armesto. In an emergency, call them on ☎ 092. The comisaría of the Policía Nacional is at Calle de Joaquín Costa 19 (☎ 091). There is a walk-in medical clinic on Calle de la División Azul.

Zona Monumental

Starting on the south-eastern edge of the zona monumental, you can't miss the distinctive curved façade of the **Capilla de la Virgen Peregrina**, an 18th century baroque-neoclassical caprice with a distinctly Portuguese flavour. Virtually across the street lies **Praza da Ferrería** and the immediately adjoining Praza da Estrela. The former, colonnaded on one side and displaying an eclectic collection of buildings dating as far back as the 15th century, was once the scene of the town's bullfights. Set back from the square in its own gardens is the **Iglesia de San Francisco**, believed by some to have been founded personally by St

Francis of Assisi when on pilgrimage to Santiago de Compostela. What was the adjacent convent is now the local tax office.

Head down Calle de la Pasantería and you emerge in the Eirado da Leña, one of Pontevedra's most enchanting little corners, partly colonnaded and with a cruceiro in the middle. Just off it lie the main buildings of the **Museo Provincial**, two baroque palaces joined by an arch in 1943. The collection ranges from Bronze Age finds right through to the work of contemporary Galician artists. It is open Tuesday to Friday from 10 am to 2.15 pm and 5 to 8.45 pm, Saturday from 10 am to 12.30 pm and 5 to 8 pm and Sunday from 10 am to 2 pm (200 ptas). The museum is closed on Monday.

A block west of the Eirado da Leña is **Praza da Verdura**, so called because of the luxuriant trees that fill what is officially known as Praza de Indalecio Armesto. North-east of the Museo Provincial rises the baroque façade of the Jesuit **Iglesia de San Bartolomé**.

Farther to the west, the area known as **Las Cinco Calles** is a hub of Pontevedra nightlife. The tiny square where the five lanes converge is marked by a cruceiro. From here you can wander north to the Río Lérez and the bustling **mercado**. Take a look at the parador along the way – it's housed in venerable neoclassical **Pazo del Barón de Maceda**.

West up Calle de Isabel II stands the **Basílica de Santa María**, a mainly Gothic church with a whiff of plateresque and Portuguese Manueline influences. At the time of writing it was closed for restoration. On the way up is signposted the **Santuario de las Apariciones**, a chapel and lodgings where Lucía of Fatima resided and the Virgin Mary is said to have appeared to her.

New Town

The elegant Alameda and Jardines de Vicenti spread south-west of the medieval centre and together form modern Pontevedra's green lung. Alongside them are the ruins of the 15th century **Convento de**

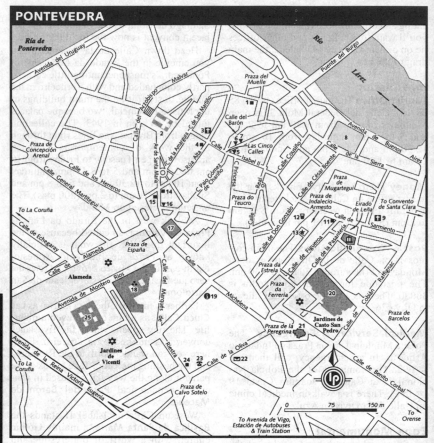

PONTEVEDRA

Santo Domingo, which also house part of the Museo Provincial's archaeological collection.

Places to Stay

There are about half a dozen places to stay in the old town. *Hospedaje Penelas (☎ 986 85 57 05, Rúa Alta 17)* has small but decent rooms for 2200/3100 ptas. *Hospedaje Margó (☎ 986 85 26 94, Calle de Riestra 4)*, just outside the old town, is nothing special, but has cheap rooms (1500/2500 ptas).

Much better located are the *Casa Alicia (☎ 986 85 70 79, Avenida de Santa María 5)* and *Casa Maruja (☎ 986 85 49 01)* over the road. The former has homy doubles for around 2700 to 3000 ptas, while the latter charges 3000/4000 ptas for spotless rooms. For those with a little dosh to fling around is the elegant and popular *Hotel Ruas (☎ 986 84 64 16, fax 986 84 64 11, Calle de Sarmiento 37)*. Singles/doubles start at 3000/5500 ptas and head up to 4500/8000 ptas plus IVA at the height of the season.

PONTEVEDRA

PLACES TO STAY
1 Parador Casa del Barón
4 Hospedaje Penelas
11 Hotel Ruas
14 Casa Maruja
15 Casa Alicia
24 Hospedaje Margó

PLACES TO EAT
5 Restaurante Agudelo
6 O' Noso Bar
7 Casa Fidel – O' Pulpeiro
16 O' Merlo

OTHER
2 Basílica de Santa María
3 Santuario de las Apariciones
8 Mercado
9 Iglesia de San Bartolomé
10 Museo Provincial
12 Bar
13 Policía Municipal
17 Ayuntamiento
18 Ruins of Convento de Santo Domingo
19 Tourist Office
20 Iglesia & Convento de San Francisco
21 Capilla de la Virgen Peregrina
22 Correos
23 Telephones (Telefónica)
25 Palacio de la Diputación

At the top of the tree is one of Spain's more appealing paradores, the *Parador Casa del Barón* (☎ 986 85 58 00, fax 986 85 51 00, Calle del Barón 19). Rooms here cost 10,200/13,200 ptas plus IVA at the height of the tourist season.

Places to Eat

The hub of Pontevedra's eating and drinking is the Cinco Calles area in the old town. Converging on Praza de Rogelio Lois, handily marked by a cruceiro, you could keep yourself well occupied here.

An unbeatable 1000 ptas *menú* is worth checking out at *O' Merlo* (Avenida de Santa María 4). At *Casa Fidel – O' Pulpeiro* (Calle de San Nicolás 7) watch out for the boiling tubs of chopped-up octopus. You can also eat cheaply at No 5, *O' Noso Bar*. Right on the little square, the newly refur-

bished *Restaurante Agudelo* is more expensive – a fine seafood meal will cost you about 2000 ptas.

Dessert is important here, and Pontevedra is known for its pastries, particularly its *tarta a las almendras*, an almond-topped cake you can find in many pastry shops around Calle de Michelena.

Entertainment

The best places for coffee and people-watching are the cafés along the squares. Praza da Ferrería probably wins on this score. For drinking of a more nocturnal kind, head first for the pocket of bars on Calle del Barón, and then, for some heftier *marcha*, up the road to Calle de Charino – you'll soon get a feel for what's right for you. There is a nameless and popular *bar* on Praza da Verdura. If it's nightclubs you're after, try Calle de Benito Corbal.

Getting There & Away

Bus The estación de autobuses is a couple of kilometres south-east of the centre on Avenida de los Alféreces Provisionales. As many as 20 buses daily head for Santiago de Compostela, some stopping in Padrón, others moving north to La Coruña. The latter follow the A-9 and are quicker. Other buses serve Vigo, Orense, Lugo and O Ferrol.

The train station is by the estación de autobuses. Pontevedra is on the Vigo-La Coruña line, and there are regular connections with those cities and Santiago de Compostela.

The A-9 motorway and N-550 lead south to Vigo and north to Santiago. For Orense, take the N-541 east.

Getting Around

Local circle line buses run from the bus and train stations to Praza de España (the *gobierno civil* building).

SOUTH OF THE RÍA DE PONTEVEDRA

Don't be put off by the road from Pontevedra to Marín. It's an ugly business that bears little resemblance to what lies beyond

GALICIA

Marín, a foul industrial port and home to the country's naval academy.

Around Hío

A few kilometres south-west of Aldán, the cluster of houses that constitutes Hío has its focal point in Galicia's most remarkable cruceiro. It was sculpted last century from a single block of stone and the great passages in Christian history, from Adam and Eve's sinful errors through to the taking down of Christ from the cross, are narrated up its length.

A couple of kilometres on are a few tranquil beaches at **Vilanova**, while south of Hío, on the Ría de Vigo, are Praia de Nerga and Praia de Barra. Part of the latter is for nudists, and although both are good they can get windy. The reward for covering 5km of mostly dirt track from Hío to **Cabo de Home** is great views of the Islas Cíes and the Atlantic.

Hío is a peaceful base. *Hostal Stop (☎ 986 32 94 75)*, near the famous cruceiro, has rooms for as little as 1200/2300 ptas in winter, but more like 3000/5000 ptas in summer. There are also rooms in Vilanova.

NORTH OF THE RÍA DE VIGO

From Hío you can head for Cangas, which passes for a resort town on the Ría de Vigo and is arguably the ría's least attractive feature. The drive along the north bank of the ría is magnificent in parts, but the surrounding area is not Galicia's best shot at beaches or rural splendour.

Cangas

A bustling but ill-ordered port town, Cangas had its big moment in history, but it was a tragic one. In 1617, a band of several thousand Saracens (possibly Algerians) landed nearby and proceeded to sack the whole area in grand style. Such was the thoroughness of the slaughter, the story goes, that quite a few women went mad and became witches – some good *(meigas)* and others bad *(brujas)*. The Inquisition took things in hand, and so a number of these witches ended up burning at the stake. There is little

of specific interest to see, although you could while away an hour or two strolling around the back streets of the port. There's a tourist information booth at the port.

Few conceivable reasons for hanging about overnight spring to mind, but if you feel some irresistible urge, head for the east end of Praia de Rodeira (about a 2km walk from the estación de autobuses and port). *Hostal Playa (☎ 986 30 36 74, Avenida de Orense 78)* has rooms for around 4000/6000 ptas in the high season.

There are few places to eat. You might try *Restaurante Casa Juan (Rúa de Hío 2)*, which does reasonable seafood tapas.

Buses run regularly from the port to Vigo, Bueu, Hío and other points along the peninsula. There are also frequent ferries to Vigo.

On to Vigo

From Cangas there is little to hold you up before you make the decision about whether to head north to Pontevedra or south to Vigo and beyond. **Moaña** has a modest Romanesque church and an hourly ferry to Vigo; otherwise the best part of the trip along this part of the ría is just that: the trip. You can see serried ranks of *bateas* – platforms that look like miniature oil rigs, where *mejillones* (mussels) are grown – and observe Vigo in the distance. If you have transport, head inland a few kilometres to the **Mirador de Cotorredondo**, a lookout commanding magic views over the Ría de Vigo, with its imposing suspension bridge, the Puente de Rande, and the Ría de Pontevedra.

If you follow the old N-550 down the east side of the ría, you could make a quick diversion east to see the well-preserved **Castillo de Soutomaior**. The N-550 proceeds directly south to Tuy and Portugal. Otherwise, stick to the coast for Vigo, which you will need to pass through in order to enjoy the southernmost stretch of Galician coast beyond the rías.

VIGO

Arriving from anywhere else in Galicia, Vigo can come as a shock. With 280,000 inhabitants, this is a big city, traffic-choked and chaotic. Its long port is protected from Atlantic disturbances by the Islas Cíes and once boasted a busy passenger terminal. These days, the farthest you'll get from Vigo by sea is Cangas. The small nucleus of tangled lanes of old Vigo exerts a fascination in a down-and-out sort of way, but overall this city comes as a disappointment given its wonderful setting.

People only started to notice Vigo in the Middle Ages as it began to overtake Bayona as a major port. Sir Francis Drake thought it sufficiently interesting to take control for a few days in 1589. In 1702 the English were back with their Dutch allies to sink a galleon fleet bearing gold from the Americas near where the Puente de Rande crosses the narrowest neck of the ría today – so near, yet so far.

Orientation

The RENFE train station is about 1.5km south-east of the town centre. Between the two you'll find plenty of accommodation, although for eating and drinking you're best off hunting around the old town centre. From the station, Rúa Urzaiz and its partly pedestrianised continuation, Rúa do Príncipe, lead you to the centre and port. The estación de autobuses is on Avenida de Madrid, south of Praza de España.

Information

Tourist Offices There are tourist offices all over town. You'll find them at Muelle de Trasatlánticos, by the Estación Marítima (port); on Praza de España; Praza da Estación (train station); and Paseo de Alfonso XII. All are open Monday to Friday from 10 am to 2 pm and 5 to 9 pm. One is open at the airport for incoming flights, and there is another at Lonja de Concello, open Monday to Friday from 9 am to 2 pm and 4.30 to 6.30 pm and Saturday from 10 am to 12.30 pm. For information by telephone, call ☎ 986 43 05 77.

Money There is no shortage of banks, mostly with ATMs, particularly around Rúa

do Príncipe. American Express (☎ 986 43 44 05), represented by Ultratur, is at Calle Cánovas del Castillo 5.

Post & Communications You'll find the main correos on Rúa da Victoria; you can make phone calls from it. The postcode is 36200.

Medical Services & Emergency Call ☎ 091 in a police emergency. There is a comisaría at Rúa de Luís Taboada 3. In a medical emergency, try ☎ 986 47 11 11. Hospital Xeral, just off Praza de España, is the nearest to the town centre.

Old Town

Praza da Constitución, lined by elegant old houses seated above arcades, marks the entrance into the casco antiguo from the bustling thoroughfares of downtown Vigo. Take Rúa dos Cesteiros north and you'll stumble upon the **Iglesia Colegiata de Santa María**, a neoclassical construction of 1816. Nearby **Praza da Pedra** hosts a sad-looking, off-the-back-of-a-boat market where the *ostreiras* (oyster catchers) hawk their slithery wares in the morning. Rúa Real is the old town's main street, on or near which you'll find a fair selection of taverns.

Parque do Castro

Directly south (and uphill) of the casco you can wander in this park for a little peace and quiet, and have a look at the castillo that formed part of the town defences built under Felipe IV.

Beaches

The best beaches within reach are the **Playa de Samil** and another farther on at Candido, south-west of Vigo. Local buses run there (see Getting Around below).

Places to Stay

Around the Train Station There is a host of hotels around the train station, not distressingly far from the centre. *Hostal Madrid* (☎ *986 22 55 23, Rúa de Alfonso XIII 63)* has a variety of rooms, with

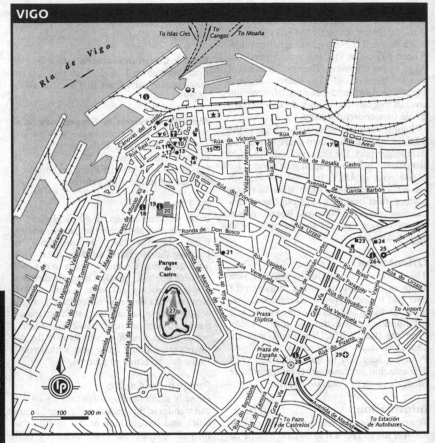

VIGO

To Islas Cíes
To Cangas
To Moaña

Ría de Vigo

Parque do Castro

0   100   200 m

doubles going for 2500 ptas with shower or 4500 ptas with full private bathroom. *Hotel Pantón* (☎ 986 22 42 70, *Rúa de Lepanto 18*) has rooms with private bathroom and TV for 2800/4800 ptas. Not too far away, *Hostal Krishna* (☎ 986 22 81 61, *Rúa de Urzaiz 57*) has modern if unspectacular rooms for 3000/4500 ptas out of season.

Around the Old Town In the heart of the old town is a sprinkling of generally run-

down and poor value *casas de huéspedes* (marked by the blue CH signs) and fondas.

Hostal Princesa (☎ 986 43 37 00, *Calle de Fermín Penzol 14*) has decent singles/ doubles with private bath, phone and TV for 2500/4000 ptas. Rooms at *Hotel El Águila* (☎ 986 43 13 98, *Rúa do Victoria 6*) start from 3000/3500 ptas and rise to 4500/5000 ptas.

Places to Eat

The winding lanes and blind alleys of old Vigo are laced with tapas bars and eateries

VIGO

PLACES TO STAY
8   Hostal El Águila
14   Hostal Princesa
22   Hostal Krishna
23   Hotel Pantón
24   Hostal Madrid

PLACES TO EAT
6   Restaurante Fay-Bistes
9   Restaurante Senen
10   Taberna Ramón
11   Patio Gallego
12   Bar Chavolas
16   Ristorante Il Tartufo

OTHER
1   Tourist Office
2   Boats to Islas Cíes, Cangas & Moaña
3   Policía Nacional
4   Praza da Pedra; Oyster Market
5   Ultratur
7   Iglesia Colegiata de Santa María
13   Praza da Constitución
15   Correos
17   74
18   Tourist Office
19   Tourist Office
20   Town Hall (Concello)
21   El Malecón
25   Train Station (RENFE)
26   Tourist Office
27   Castillo
28   Tourist Office
29   Hospital Xeral

of all descriptions – part of the fun is looking around. *Bar Chavolas (Rúa dos Cesteiros 3)* is a cheap, spit-and-sawdust place off Praza da Constitución – itself a pleasant spot for a morning cup of coffee. At No 2A is the *Taberna Ramón*, in much the same league. The *Patio Gallego* at No 7 has a decent set lunch for 1000 ptas. You'll find *Restaurante Senen (Rúa da Palma 3)* is similar. *Restaurante Fay-Bistes (Rúa Real 7)* has a set lunch for 950 ptas and good tapas.

If you want a change and have 2500 ptas to spare, *Ristorante Il Tartufo (Praza de Compostela 16)* is hard to beat for quality Italian food (the pasta is made on the premises).

Entertainment

At weekends in particular, head for Rúa Real in the old town. Here and in the surrounding lanes is a fair smattering of taverns. Otherwise, you'll find a couple of busy places on Rúa de Churruca, a small lane near the train station. For late-night dancing, *El Malecón (Rúa de Taboada Leal)*, off Rúa de Venezuela, is a Vigo favourite. Another late-night drinking place that attracts a mixed crowd is *74 (Rúa Areal 74)*. Don't bother arriving before 2.30 am. In summer, the Playa de Samil area also gets busy late at night.

Getting There & Away

Air The airport is about 10km east of town. Iberia has flights to/from Bilbao, Barcelona, Madrid and Las Palmas. In summer you can sometimes get charter flights to the UK.

Bus From the estación de autobuses, well south of town on Avenida de Madrid, you can pick up services to all the main Galician destinations, as well as long-distance ones like Madrid, Barcelona and the País Vasco.

Train There are three trains daily to Madrid, two to Barcelona (via Oviedo) and another two to Irún, on the French border. Regular services run to Santiago de Compostela (690 ptas for a 2nd-class one-way fare). Pontevedra (295 ptas), La Coruña (1235 ptas), Orense (875 ptas) are also accessible.

Car & Motorcycle The A-9 tollway to La Coruña via Pontevedra and Santiago starts here. The C-550 hugs the coast to La Guardia, the Río Miño and Portugal.

Boat There are regular ferry crossings to the Islas Cíes (see below), as well as to Cangas and Moaña. Either of the latter costs 185 ptas one way. A fast boat to Cangas costs 325 ptas. A boat runs to/from Cangas about every half-hour from 8 am to 9.30 pm.

GALICIA

Getting Around

Vigo has a fairly decent local bus system. From Porta do Sol, Nos 21, 14 and 7 run to the estación de autobuses. No 10 goes to the beach at Candido, while Nos 15, 16 and 27 pass Samil beach.

AROUND VIGO
Islas Cíes

The best beaches in the Rías Bajas aren't really in the rías at all. Rather, you need to head out for the Islas (Illas) Cíes. Of the three islands, one has been declared off limits as a national park. The other two, Isla de Monte Faro and Isla de Monte Agudo, are linked by a white sandy crescent that also forms a lagoon known as Lago dos Nenos. The little archipelago forms a 9km breakwater, protecting Vigo and its harbour from the Atlantic's fury.

You can only visit the islands from mid-June to the end of September, and numbers are strictly limited. To stay overnight you must book for the camping ground at the office in the Estación Marítima in Vigo – places are limited. You pay a 1000 ptas reservation fee for the camping voucher, and you can then organise a return boat ticket for the day you require. Without the camping voucher, you must get a same-day return ticket. Camping costs 485 ptas per person and per tent plus IVA. At the camping ground, the 1000 ptas reservation fee will be used as a credit towards your overall camping costs.

The return boat ticket costs 1700 ptas and the frequency of services depends largely on the weather. While it is also possible to get a boat to the islands from Bayona, you can only arrange camping in Vigo.

The South

THE COAST
Bayona

On 1 March 1493, the caravel *Pinta* came into view off Bayona, bearing the remarkable news that Columbus had made it to the Indies. In fact, as would later become clear, he and his band had bumped into something quite different – the Americas. In those days Bayona (Baiona) was an important trading port. Later it was eclipsed by Vigo, and its population dropped to 150 in the 17th century. Nowadays it is one of Galicia's premier summer resorts, but understated compared with its Mediterranean counterparts.

There is a tourist information booth just before the gateway to the parador and city walls. It's open daily from 10 am to 8 pm.

The mighty **walls** stretching round the pine-covered west side of town were erected between the 11th and 17th centuries. It costs 100 ptas to walk into the grounds (500 ptas to take a car in), and it's worth it. In the placid harbour, a remake of the *Pinta* serves as a small **Museo Flotante**. Heading west out of town is the unlovely 15m stone statue of the Virgen de la Roca, finished in 1930. You can climb up inside the statue (if it's open) and take in the views from the boat-shaped lookout in her hand.

For beaches, head out on the coast road to Vigo. First up is **Praia Ladeira**, but better is the **Praia América**, a couple of kilometres farther on. Most Vigo buses call in at these beaches.

At **A Ramallosa** you'll notice a wonderful old medieval bridge (often mistaken for a Roman one). There was a time when women three months pregnant came here to perform superstitious rites to assure themselves of an easy birth.

A couple of camping grounds open in summer. *Bayona Playa* (☎ 986 35 00 35) is at Sabaris on Praia Ladeira, but it's pricey – 670 ptas per person, 485 ptas per tent, 740 ptas per car.

About the cheapest place to find a room is *Hospedaje Kin* (☎ 986 35 56 95, *Rúa de Ventura Misa 29* (inquire in the café of the same name at No 53). Basic rooms start at 1800 ptas per person. Next up is the *Hostal Mesón del Burgo* (☎ 986 35 53 09, *Barrio del Burgo*), heading out of town on the road to Vigo, with rooms for 3000/4800 ptas in high season.

The cobbled lanes in the centre of town, including Rúa de José Antonio, Rúa do Conde and Rúa de Ventura Misa, are full of restaurants, tapas bars and watering holes. Try the *Freiduría Jaqueyvi (Rúa José Antonio 2)*.

Frequent buses north for Vigo and south toward La Guardia (A Guarda) leave from near the waterfront at Calle de la Carabela La Pinta. Most of the latter also go to Tuy. In summer you can get boats to the Islas Cíes (see the earlier section).

Oia

About 20km south of Bayona, a small cove giving shelter to some fishing boats is presided over by the majestic baroque façade of the **Monasterio de Santa María de Oia**. Although the present façade was erected in 1740, the monastery church dates from the 16th century, when it was remodelled.

La Guardia

A ramshackle and unlovely port, La Guardia (A Guarda, A Garda) nevertheless is in a prime position, sitting just north of where the Río Miño enters the Atlantic. There is a tourist information office on Calle de Rosalía de Castro. The treat here is to head south out of the town centre up Monte de Santa Tecla (100 ptas per person if you drive up). On the way up you can inspect a Celtic castro, where a couple of the primitive circular dwellings have been restored. Once at the top, there's a small museum with some Celtic finds. It's open Tuesday to Sunday from 11 am to 2 pm and 3.30 to 7.30 pm (free). Better than all that are the wonderful views up the Miño, across to Portugal and out over the Atlantic. A few kilometres from La Guardia you'll find a beach at **Camposancos**, just inside the heads of the Río Miño, although you'd be much better off on the other side of the river and on an ocean beach in Portugal.

Places to Stay & Eat The place to choose is *Hotel Pazo de Santa Tecla (☎ 986 61 00 02)*, up on top of the mountain. Average singles/doubles with private bath cost

3600/4650 ptas. The best feature is the view. There's also a restaurant here.

There are several undistinguished budget hotels in the town itself. *Hostal Celta (☎ 986 61 09 11, Calle de Pontevedra s/n)* has basic rooms for 2400/3500 ptas, and slightly better ones with private bath for 2800/4000 ptas. The *Hostal Martirrey (☎ 986 61 03 49, Calle de José Antonio 8)* charges up to 2700/4300 ptas in the high season. Hunt around the centre of town for tapas bars – most of what you eat will have been caught that day.

Getting There & Away ATSA has regular buses to Vigo via Bayona, and some to Tuy. In summer, buses connect La Guardia with the Camposancos beaches. There is supposed to be a ferry from Camposancos to

Galician Round-Up

The length of Galicia's Atlantic coast is dotted with pastures favoured by wild horses, particularly in the hills south and east of Bayona, but also in the north around Cabo Ortegal. Locals occasionally head out to round the horses up in what becomes a day-long fiesta or *curro*. You'll need to ask around for information about when and where they are on. At the time of writing, curros were held in the following villages, but there are bound to be others:

June
    Torroña (south of Bayona), first Sunday
    Mougas (south of Bayona), second Sunday
    Morgadanes (east of Bayona), third Sunday
    San Cibrán (east of Bayona), fourth Sunday
July
    Curota, Pobra do Caramiñal, second Sunday
August
    Galiñeiro (near Gondomar, east of Bayona), last Sunday

Caminha in Portugal (from where you can get to the first in a string of sandy ocean beaches on the way south to Viana do Castelo). At the time of writing it was to be up and running by the middle of the summer of 1998.

RÍO MIÑO
Tuy

Tuy (Tui) is a gem, a pretty old town sitting on the Río Miño. Especially popular in summer when its little bars come alive, it is ideally situated by a bridge across to Portugal's equally interesting Valença. Some of Portugal's best northern beaches are just 35km away. A fair crowd of Portuguese day-trippers fill Tuy on weekends, and Spaniards reciprocate in Valença.

Roman Tude for a short while hosted the court of the Visigothic king Witiza (702-10). Tuy was subsequently attacked several times by Spain's Muslim invaders and Norman raiders. Later still, the town found itself on the front line during various wars between Spain and Portugal.

The tourist office (☎ 986 60 17 89) on Avenida de Portugal is in a kiosk about a kilometre before the Portuguese frontier.

Things to See The brooding, fortress-like **catedral** dominates Tuy's small medieval centre. Completed in 1287, it was much altered in the 15th century and the extra stone bracing was added after the Lisbon earthquake in 1755. The main 13th century portal is opulently decorated with sculptures in a style typical of so many Galician churches. If you want to visit the claustro and Museo Catedralicio, as well as climb the Torre de Sotomayor, the ticket will cost you 250 ptas. The cathedral is open from 9.30 am to 1.30 pm and 4.30 to 9 pm. Opposite the cathedral lies the **Museo Diocesano**, with a modest archaeology collection. It is open Tuesday to Sunday from 10 am to 1.30 pm and 4.30 to 8 pm (150 ptas).

The surrounding steep, narrow lanes all afford tempting glimpses of Portugal across the Miño. They shelter a pair of cruceiros

and chapels, including **Capilla de San Telmo** (St Elmo), which contains relics of the patron saint of seamen.

Beyond the old town centre, the pleasant riverside walk around the **Convento de San Domingo** is enticing. The monastery church's baroque façade hides a largely 14th century interior.

While here, take a look at the Portuguese town of **Valença**, just across the century-old Puente Internacional. It is a charming fortress town and, with border formalities nonexistent, makes a pleasant diversion even if you don't want to go any farther into Portugal.

Places to Stay You will find a couple of simple places to stay in the centre of town – but they tend to fill up quickly in August. The pick of the bunch is the *O Cabalo Furado* (☎ 986 60 12 15, Calle de Seijas), which charges 1500 ptas per person. *Hostal Generosa* (☎ 986 60 00 55, Calle de Calvo Sotelo 37) has singles/doubles for 1900/2700 ptas. *Hostal Cruceiro do Monte* (☎ 986 60 09 53, Carretera de Bayona 23) has a good reputation and offers decent singles/doubles with private bath for 2500/3500 ptas. The *Parador de Tuy* (☎ 986 60 03 09, fax 986 60 21 63), on the road to Portugal, has rooms for 10,500/13,500 plus IVA.

Places to Eat There are several inviting places to eat in the area immediately around the cathedral. You could try the *Jamonería* on Plaza del Generalísimo or the *Pizzeria di Marco* on Calle de Seijas. The streets between the cathedral and the river are laced with great drinking establishments. A good one with views of the river is *Pub Zuriza* on Calle de Cuenca.

Getting There & Away Buses stop along the main road through town. ATSA has regular buses to Vigo and La Guardia, and you can also get to Bayona and Pontevedra from Tuy.

The train station just north of the centre is on the Vigo-Porto (Portugal) line. There are three trains daily each way. If you are headed for Portugal, you could also try getting a train from Valença to Porto (five daily).

For other destinations such as León, Bilbao, and other cities in Galicia you need to get to the train station at Guillarey (Guillarei), a few kilometres away. It would be easier to make for Vigo first.

Around Tuy

About 20km south-west of Tuy, Goyán (Goián) is special only because it has a car ferry to Vila Nova de Cerveira in Portugal every half-hour (320 ptas plus 100 ptas for each passenger). East of Tuy there's a less reliable car ferry which crosses from Salvaterra de Miño.

Ribadavia

In the heart of Ribeiro wine country, Ribadavia was once Galicia's most important Jewish settlement. Even after Their Catholic Majesties decided to expel all Jews in 1492, most managed to hang on, either converting to Christianity or fleeing temporarily to Portugal and returning after the hue and cry had died down.

There is a tourist booth on Praza Maior (☎ 988 47 12 75), open Monday to Saturday from 10 am to 3 pm and Sunday from 11 am to 3 pm.

It is a pleasure to wander around the medieval town centre, characterised by a patchwork of uneven little cobbled squares, lined with heavy stone arcades and galerías. The Barrio Judío (Jewish quarter) is signposted and the usually indifferent weather lends the area a melancholy air. Nearby Praza de García Boente is fronted by the Casa de la Inquisición. Of the several churches dotted about the town, the Romanesque Iglesia de Santiago and Iglesia de San Juan stand out. The castle remains date from the 15th century.

There's nowhere much to stay in the centre of this surprisingly big town, unless you get lucky with a cheap room at *Bar Celta (Praza da Fonte de Prata 8)*. *Hostal Vista Alegre (☎ 988 47 12 86, Avenida Rod-*

ríguez de la Fuente 14) is a possibility at 1300 ptas a head, but it is often full with road-workers. Another hostal is the *Hostal Evencio 2 (☎ 988 47 10 45, Avenida de Rodríguez Valcarcel 30)*, out of town. Singles/doubles cost 3500/5000 ptas. There are a few places around the town to eat and drink; for a tavern atmosphere, dive into the gloomy and cavernous *Bar O Xudío (Rúa de Caula 10)*, between Praza Maior and Praza da Magdaleña.

Six trains daily run to Vigo and Orense from a station just over the Río Avia. Regular buses run to Orense from a station nearby.

Ribadavia to Celanova

From Ribadavia, the road to Celanova via Cortegada is a marvel of green – mostly Ribeiro vines – and of curves. From Cortegada turn eastwards for Celanova, unless you want to proceed west into Portugal.

Celanova is a nondescript sort of place, except for the massive and tatty Benedictine Monasterio de San Salvador on Praza Maior. Though the place is now partly used as a school, you can generally wander into the two cloisters at any time. At the time of writing, you could peer through the doors into the cathedral to see what a pitiful state it's in. From the Claustro de las Procesiones (the mixed Gothic and baroque cloister), there is access to the tiny 10th century Mozarabic Oratorio de San Miguel. You can supposedly get keys for the cathedral and oratorio in the rectory.

The Interior

With the notable exception of the well-trodden Camino de Santiago, inland Galicia is much unvisited. Of its cities, Orense has a surprisingly attractive, compact centre, while Lugo's main claim to fame is its Roman walls. Away from the towns, nothing man-made can match the natural splendour of the Sil valley, which stretches from the border with Castilla y León to the Río Miño.

GALICIA

ORENSE

Orense (Ourense in Galician) may well be the first Galician city that travellers emerging from neighbouring Castilla encounter. With more than 100,000 inhabitants, the first impression is of a uniformly dissatisfying modern sprawl. Give it a chance, as buried deep in the heart of it lies a wonderful old town core bursting with life.

History

Orense was a Roman settlement of some importance. Later the Visigoths raised a cathedral here before the arrival of the Muslims, who destroyed the place in several raids. Repopulated by Sancho II in 1071, the town eventually began to take off as a trade centre. Orense's considerable Jewish population, having contributed generously to the campaign against Granada, was rewarded in 1492 with expulsion – an order the local branch of the Inquisition was particularly scrupulous in executing. Essentially an ecclesiastical town, it declined for centuries until the arrival of the railway in 1882 put it back on the map.

Orientation

The train and bus stations are a few kilometres north of the old town, to which they are linked by local buses. Enter the city over the *ponte romano*, a mostly medieval bridge constructed in place of an older Roman one, spanning the Río Miño. Head straight for the Catedral do San Martiño, around which unfolds the casco antiguo. Rúa do Capitán Eloy marks the northern boundary of this part of town, the life of which is played out on Praza Maior, Praza do Trigo, Praza dos Flores and Praza do Ferro.

Information

The tourist office (☎ 988 23 47 17), at Rúa de Curros Enríquez 1, is open Monday to Friday from 10 am to 2 pm and 4.30 to 6.30 pm. There's also a little kiosk on the corner of the same street and Rúa do San Lázaro.

There is no shortage of banks along Rúa de Curros Enríquez and its continuation, the pedestrianised Rúa do Paseo.

The correos is at Rúa do Progreso 53, and there is a telephone office just off Praza de Paz Novoa. The postcode is 32080.

There is a Policía Nacional comisaría just by the cathedral. In an emergency, call ☎ 091 or ☎ 988 38 81 00. The handiest medical clinic *(centro de salud)* is at Rúa de Juan XXIII 6-8.

Casco Antiguo

A leap of about 1000 years and a walk south into the casco antiguo brings you to Catedral do San Martiño, a rather gloomy 13th century church whose main feature is a Gothic copy of Santiago's Pórtico de la Gloria, in this case the Pórtico del Paraíso.

Around the cathedral unfolds a chain of charming little squares and alleys, inviting exploration by day or night. Praza Maior is the grandest of them, sloping away from the casco antiguo and hemmed in by arcaded walkways, above which stand out the elegant galerías of private houses and the restrained dignity of the *casa consistorial* (town hall). The Museo Arqueológico also backs on to this square, but at the time of writing was closed.

Fontes As Burgas

Since the Romans arrived on the scene, the thermal baths of Orense have been a blessing for the sick and tired, or simply those with sore feet. The steaming mineral waters gush out in fountains on Praza das Burgas, and the water is still used for heating in the surrounding houses.

Places to Stay

The choice area is around the cathedral. *Hostal Cándido* (☎ 988 22 96 07, Rúa dos Hermanos Villar 25) faces the delightful Praza do Cid, otherwise crowded with restaurants and bars. Singles/doubles cost 1700/2500 ptas. There are a few places around Praza do Alférez Provincial. The best is *Hostal Lido* (☎ 988 21 33 00, Rúa de Juan XXIII 6), with singles/doubles starting at 2000/3000 ptas, or 3200/4000 ptas with private bath and TV.

ORENSE

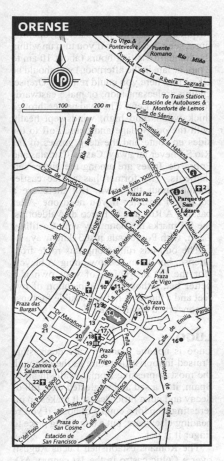

To Vigo & Pontevedra
Puente Romano
Río Miño
Avenida de la Ribeira Sagrada
To Train Station, Estación de Autobuses & Monforte de Lemos
Calle de Sáenz Díez
Avenida de la Habana
Río Barbaña
Calle del Concejo
Rúa de Juan XXIII
Calle de Erevedelo
Praza Paz Novoa
Rúa do Capitán Eloy
Rúa do Paseo
Parque do San Lázaro
San Lázaro
Calle de Dr Fleming
Progreso
Cardenal Quevedo
Rúa de Outrora
Manuel Pedro
Domingo
A Praza de Vigo
San Miguel
Rúa
Obispo
Lamas
Levanto
Paz
Praza do Ferro
Praza das Burgas
Dr Marañón
Peña Corneira
Cabeza de Peña Trevinca
Calle de Emilia Pardo
Praza do Trigo
Carretera de la Granja
To Zamora & Salamanca
C de Padre Feijoo
Prieto
C de Julio
Praza do San Cosme
C del Poio
Estación de San Francisco

0   100   200 m

ORENSE

1   Tourist Office
2   Iglesia de San Francisco
3   Tourist Information Kiosk
4   Hostal Lido
5   Telephones (Telefónica)
6   Iglesia de Santo Domingo
7   Restaurante Sanmiguel
8   Correos
9   Iglesia de Santa Eufemia
10 Hostal Cándido
11 Praza do Cid
12 Policía Nacional
13 Praza Maior
14 Catedral do San Martiño
15 Bar Cazador
16 Claustro de San Francisco
17 Praza de Magdalena
18 Iglesia de Santa María Madre
19 Museo Arqueológico
20 Casa Consistorial
21 Fontes As Burgas
22 Iglesia de la Santísima Trinidad

Getting There & Away

The estación de autobuses is well away from the town centre across the Ponte Nova and has regular services to surrounding towns. At least one bus daily heads for Verín and Portugal, and a couple head east for the towns along the Sil valley. The RENFE train station is closer to town. At least five trains daily take up to eight hours to reach Madrid. Several connect with Santiago de Compostela, Vigo and La Coruña. Local bus Nos 1, 3, 6, 12 and 15 run past both stations to the Parque do San Lázaro in the centre.

AROUND ORENSE
South to Portugal

The N-525 south of Orense crosses several low ranges on the way to the Portuguese border. The only noteworthy stop along the way is **Verín**. An average sort of place with a vaguely charming plaza mayor (in a faded sort of a way), it merits a halt for those with their own transport for the nearby Castillo de Monterrei. In a commanding position 4km away, the castle's main tower offers

Places to Eat

The streets and squares around the cathedral are bursting with places to eat. For simple, cheap Galician dishes, head for *Bar Cazador* on Rúa dos Fornos, just near the cathedral. Orense's top restaurant is the *Restaurante Sanmiguel*, at No 18 on the street of the same name. There are innumerable tapas bars, cafés, watering holes and ice-cream joints in this small area. For the latter try Praza Maior or Rúa do Coronel Ceano Vivas (Calle de Juan de Austria).

spectacular views on all sides. It is open Wednesday to Sunday from 10.30 am to 1.30 pm and 5 to 8 pm (free).

Monforte de Lemos

Inhabited before the Romans appeared and later converted into the medieval Mons Forti, this dishevelled place has made its living as Galicia's principal rail junction since 1883, when the Madrid-La Coruña line was completed. It is actually quite interesting if you should be caught between trains.

Long before you reach the town centre you'll see the **Torre del Homenaje**, the most intact part of the 13th century castle at the top of the *monte forte*. Across the river from the town centre stands the proud **Colegio de Nuestra Señora la Antigua**, which once housed a Jesuit seminary.

Should you decide to stay, head for the 16th century bridge over the Río Cabe. *Hostal Puente Romano* (☎ 982 41 11 67) on Paseo del Malecón has singles/doubles for 1800/3000 ptas. There are a few cafés and eateries around the bridge and river.

Most trains crossing Galicia call in here, and there are plenty of buses (the station is near the centre) heading north to Lugo and south-west to Orense.

RÍO SIL

Take the N-120 north-east out of Orense (the Monforte road) along the Río Miño, a pretty stretch but nothing compared to what's in store if you turn off east at Os Peares. Here the Miño meets the Río Sil, and the ensuing 15km make for a spectacular drive (or, indeed, hike) along the upper reaches of the **Gargantas del Sil** (Sil Gorges). The Orense-Monforte railway also follows the gorge for about 10km.

This road ends in a T-junction with another minor road that winds its way about 90km east before again hitting the N-120 to Castilla y León. Take a right (heading to Orense) at the T-junction and after 5km you reach the **Monasterio de San Esteban (San Estevo) de Ribas de Sil**. Some of this huge complex, with three cloisters, dates from the 10th century, although much has been stripped bare. The monastery's opening times seem haphazard; if you turn up within the standard visiting hours (about 10 am to 2 pm, or late in the afternoon) you should be OK. From here you could return to Orense, ending a pleasant loop, or make eastwards for Castilla y León. The road passes through thick woods and high, windswept heath, with the odd village and church off to the sides en route and the deep gorges of the Río Sil never far away. **Castro Caldelas** and **Pobra de Trives** are among the bigger settlements. The former has a nice castle; shame about the town. But there are a couple of hostales if you need one. After passing A Rúa and O Barco de Valdeorras, the Sil marks the boundary with Castilla y León, with Ponferrada just 31km away.

The odd bus runs along this route from Orense, but it can be slow going. A bicycle (for the fit) or vehicle of your own is a better bet, although a combination of two feet and a thumb is not impossible for those unconcerned about time.

LUGO

Lugo is not the place to cure depression. Praised in tourist literature as the city with the most impressive Roman walls in all of Spain, it is a sad and neglected city, full of decay and not a little sleaze. It makes an interesting stop for a couple of hours if you're heading elsewhere, but a tantalising place to linger it is not.

The Romans established Lucus Augusti over a Celtic castro in the 1st century AD. The walls went up two centuries later, but were not enough to keep out the Visigoths in the 5th century, or indeed the Muslims 300 years later. Until well into the 19th century the city gates were closed at night and tolls were charged to bring in goods from outside.

Orientation & Information

Whether you arrive in Lugo by train or bus (the latter is more convenient), you will end up not too far from the Roman walls. Once inside the city, there are a couple of focal points. The cathedral is near the Porta (gate) de Santiago, where you can climb up onto the city walls. Rúa Nova, the town's main street for bars, tapas and restaurants, stretches more or less east to west from near the cathedral to the Porta Nova. Be aware that the area between the cathedral and the Porta do Carmen is an unsavoury red-light zone.

The tourist office (☎ 982 23 13 61) is in an arcade at Praza Maior (Plaza de España) 27-29. There are several banks with ATMs around town. The Central Hispano and Deutsche Bank are on Praza de Santo Domingo.

The main correos is just off Praza Maior on Rúa de San Pedro and there is a phone office on Praza de Santo Domingo. Lugo's central postcode is 27080. The local number for the police is ☎ 982 21 36 40. In a medical emergency call ☎ 061 or the Cruz Roja on ☎ 982 23 16 88.

Roman Walls

More than 2km long and up to 15m high, the Roman walls enclosing Lugo are the best preserved of their kind in all of Spain, if not the world. You can climb up onto the ramparts and walk right round the town.

Catedral

Back on the ground inside the Porta de Santiago, the imposing grey edifice of the cathedral rises. It might not seem so at first glance, but it is basically a Romanesque-Gothic structure, begun in 1129 and inspired by the cathedral in Santiago de Compostela. Work went on until the 14th century, and a neoclassical layer was coated on later still. Inside, the walnut choir stalls are a baroque masterpiece. Across Praza de Santa María is the Palacio Episcopal, reconstructed in the early 1990s.

Museo Provincial

Halfway down Rúa Nova, the museum is housed in the former Convento de San Francisco. Apart from the Gothic cloister, old kitchen and refectory of the convent, the museum's religious art collection is housed on the ground floor. Considered Galicia's

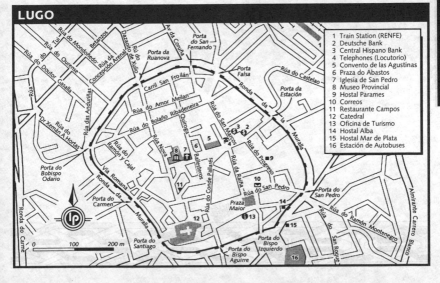

LUGO

1 Train Station (RENFE)
2 Deutsche Bank
3 Central Hispano Bank
4 Telephones (Locutorio)
5 Convento de las Agustinas
6 Praza do Abastos
7 Iglesia de San Pedro
8 Museo Provincial
9 Hostal Parames
10 Correos
11 Restaurante Campos
12 Catedral
13 Oficina de Turismo
14 Hostal Alba
15 Hostal Mar de Plata
16 Estación de Autobuses

GALICIA

best museum, the collections also include archaeological finds and works by local artists. It is open Monday to Friday from 11 am to 2 pm and 5 to 8 pm and Saturday from 10 am to 2 pm (250 ptas).

Places to Stay & Eat

Hostal Alba (☎ *982 22 60 56, Rúa de Calvo Sotelo 31)* has simple singles/doubles for 1800/3400 ptas. *Hostal Parames* (☎ *982 22 62 51, Rúa do Progreso 28)* is quite reasonable at 2200/3900 ptas for singles/doubles with private bath. Near the estación de autobuses, just outside the walls, you could try *Hostal Mar de Plata* (☎ *982 22 89 10, Ronda da Muralla 5)*. Rooms start at 2000/3000 ptas in the low season.

A decent seafood place is the *Restaurante Campos* on Rúa Armaña, where you can eat well for 2000 ptas. But before diving straight in here, take a stroll along Rúa Nova, full to bursting with tapas bars and restaurants.

Getting There & Away

Up to fours buses daily connect Lugo with destinations across northern Spain in Asturias, Cantabria and the País Vasco. Four buses also pass through Lugo from Santiago de Compostela and/or La Coruña en route to Madrid (6½ hours). Regular buses run south to Monforte de Lemos and Orense. Up to six trains daily run to La Coruña and Monforte de Lemos.

Valencia

The very name Valencia has a familiar ring, even to people who have never looked at a map of Spain ... Valencia oranges. The famed citrus. This coastal Mediterranean region is a strange mix. Long in Muslim hands, its Christian European history has been shaped as much by Catalunya as by Castilla. The flag bears the red and yellow stripes of Catalunya and many Valencianos (particularly in the hinterland) prefer to speak Catalan. For all that, Catalanist militancy has never been as strong here as in its northern neighbour. True, more and more street signs and place names now appear in Catalan – but often as not with their Castilian translations.

Valencia, the capital, is roughly halfway along the coast and famed for its exuberant nightlife and the wild Las Fallas festival.

To the north along the Costa del Azahar is a series of low-key resorts and several worthwhile attractions, including the historic town of Sagunto.

South of Valencia, the Costa Blanca is one of Spain's horror stories – the ghastly tourist developments reach their dubious pinnacle in a kind of Manhattan on Med – the infamous Benidorm. The story is not all bad. Like beachcombers with a metal detector, the patient traveller will uncover a few gems along the coast that have retained their charm – the old towns of Jávea and Altea in particular. And it is hard to argue with the beauty of many of the beaches – even if the people you rub shoulders with are splotchy Dutch, Brits and Germans. Where have all the Spaniards gone? Sounds like a song.

Inland from the coastal A-7 motorway lies another world. Mountains buckle towards the 'real Spain', that rough and ready interior of Aragón, Castilla-La Mancha and Murcia. Castles abound. The drive to Guadalest is particularly stunning. Other towns to make for include Morella and Játiva, while Elche's endless palm

HIGHLIGHTS

- The Las Fallas festival in Valencia city
- Alicante's nightlife
- Valencia city's Museo de Bellas Artes
- The medieval fortress town of Morella
- Lunch at the Mare de Déu restaurant in Sant Mateu
- Elche's palm forests and gardens
- Guadalest and the valley drive

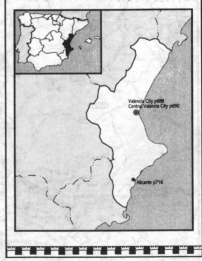

groves are a potent reminder of Valencia's Islamic heritage.

Other mementos of five centuries of Islamic settlement are the names of towns, cities and rivers. A town that begins with 'Al' (Arabic for 'the') is a give away – Alicante is a prime example. Those that begin with 'Beni' (such as Benidorm) are what remain of the one-time Muslim tribal districts of Valencia. The word means 'sons of'

685

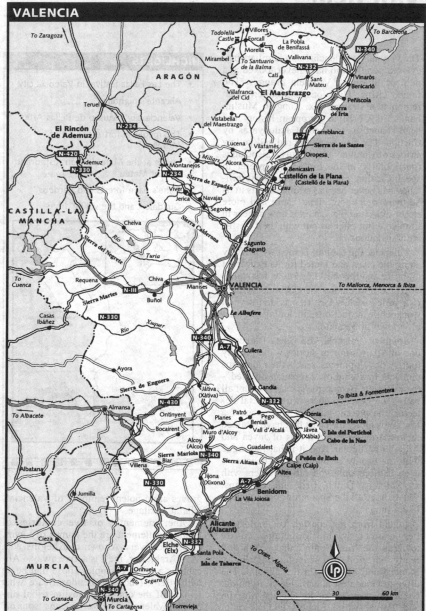

and in the Middle East and North Africa was commonly matched with a proper name to identify a tribe. And, as elsewhere in southern Spain, river and gorge names beginning with *guad* are also derived from Arabic – the word is a deformation of *wadi*, which means valley or river.

Warning

The tendency to replace old Castilian street signs with the Catalan equivalent is bound to be a source of confusion. Occasionally we use the Catalan version, but since Castilian (for the moment at any rate) remains fairly common, we have elected to stick with it in most cases.

Valencia City

Spain's third-largest city and capital of the Comunitat Valenciana, Valencia comes as a pleasant surprise. Home to *paella* and the Holy Grail, it is also blessed with great weather and the festival of Las Fallas (in March), one of the country's wildest parties.

Much of the city's appeal lies in what it isn't. It isn't particularly attractive, with the exception of the old quarter. Nor is it crammed with must see museums and world famous monuments. It certainly isn't overrun by foreign tourists.

It *is* a vibrant, friendly and chaotic city that boasts an outstanding fine arts museum and one of the most exciting nightlife scenes in Spain. So blend in, relax and enjoy Valencia for what it is (and isn't).

History

Following on the heels of Greek and Carthaginian settlers, the Romans founded Valentia on the banks of the River Turia in 138 BC and began to develop irrigation for the surrounding regions.

As Rome collapsed the Visigoths moved in, but they only lasted until the arrival of the Muslim cohorts in 711 AD. They made it a rich agricultural and industrial centre, establishing ceramics, paper, silk and leather industries.

Muslim rule was briefly interrupted by the triumphant rampage of the legendary Castilian knight, El Cid, in 1094. The Christians only definitively retook the city in 1238, when Jaime I incorporated the area into his burgeoning Catalan kingdom.

Valencia boomed in the 15th and 16th centuries, becoming one of the strongest Mediterranean trading centres. That was Valencia's (and Spain's) Golden Age. Ever since things have been rocky.

Like Catalunya, Valencia backed the wrong horse in the War of the Spanish Succession, and the Bourbon king Felipe V's retribution was swift – he abolished Valencia's *fueros*, or autonomous privileges. The Spanish Civil War proved similarly unlucky, as siding with the Republicans (and acting as seat of the Republican government from November 1936 until October 1937) did not endear the city to General Franco.

Orientation

The city centre is 4km inland from the beaches, south of a bend in the Río Turia. This once mighty river is now almost dry, and has been turned into a park and recreation area.

Plaza del Ayuntamiento marks the centre of Valencia. Surrounded by flower stalls, the plaza is home to the *ayuntamiento* (town hall), tourist office and the main post office. The Estación del Norte (the main train station) is 250m south, but the Estación Central de Autobuses, the main bus station, is almost 2km north-west on Avenida de Menéndez Pidal.

About 500m north of Plaza del Ayuntamiento is Plaza de la Reina (also known as Plaza de Zaragoza). Farther north again is Plaza de la Virgen, and between the two stands Valencia's cathedral.

West of the cathedral and north of the Mercado Central are the oldest parts of the city, the Barrio del Carmen (or 'El Carme').

Valencia's commercial and shopping districts spread around both sides of Plaza del Ayuntamiento, although the most upmarket

VALENCIA

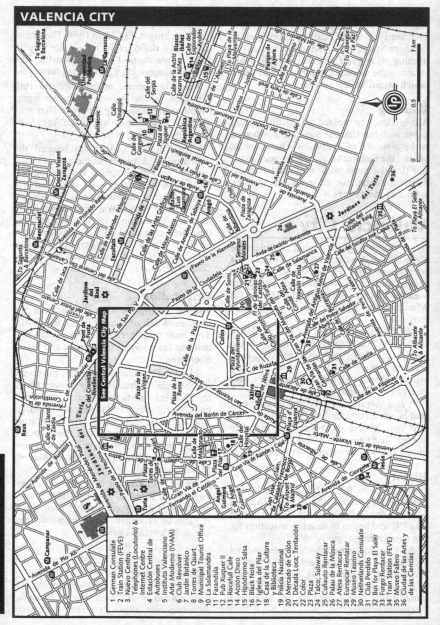

VALENCIA CITY

1 German Consulate
2 Train Station (FEVE)
3 Nuevo Centro,
   Telephones (Locutorio) &
   Internet Centre
4 Estación Central de
   Autobuses
5 Instituto Valenciano
   Arte Moderno (IVAM)
6 Club Revolver
7 Jardín Botánico
8 Torres de Quart
9 Municipal Tourist Office
10 La Salamandra
11 Farándula
12 Pub Xúquer II
13 Rocatull Café
14 Acción Disco
15 Hipódromo Salsa
16 Black Note
17 Iglesia del Pilar
18 Casa de la Cultura
    y Biblioteca
19 Policía Nacional
20 Mercado de Colón
21 Década Loca; Tentación
22 Color
23 Plaza
24 Talco; Subway
25 Cuñauto Rentacar
26 Palau de la Música
27 Atesa Rentacar
28 Europcar Rentacar
29 Museo Taurino
30 Netherlands Consulate
31 Club Perdido
32 Bus for Playa El Saler
33 Furgo Rentacar
34 Train Station (FEVE)
35 Museo Fallero
36 Ciudad de las Artes y
    de las Ciencias

shops are in the ritzy areas to the east and north-east of the plaza.

With the exception of a couple of museums and gardens, there is little of interest in Valencia's outer suburbs.

Information

Tourist Offices Valencia's municipal tourist office (☎ 96 351 04 17) on Plaza del Ayuntamiento is open weekdays from 8.30 am to 2.15 pm and 4.15 to 6.15 pm and Saturday from 9.15 am to 12.45 pm. This office specialises in city info.

Two provincial tourist offices have information on Valencia province. The one at Estación del Norte (☎ 96 352 85 73) is open weekdays from 9 am to 6.30 pm; another at Calle de la Paz 48 (☎ 96 394 22 22) is open weekdays from 10 am to 6.30 pm (Thursday to 6 pm) and Saturday from 10 am to 2 pm.

Foreign Consulates Several countries have consulates in Valencia. See the Embassies & Consulates section in the Facts for the Visitor chapter.

Money You'll find plenty of banks with ATMs around Plaza del Ayuntamiento.

Post & Communications The main *correos* (post office) is open weekdays from 8 am to 8.30 pm and Saturday from 9.30 am to 2 pm. The poste restante is on the 1st floor. The post code is 46080.

There's a *locutorio* phone office in the basement of the Nuevo Centro shopping complex on the corner of Avenida de Pío XII and Avenida de Menéndez Pidal (beside the main bus station). You can access the Internet and send email here (600 ptas per half-hour).

Bookshops The English Book Centre, Calle de Pascual y Genis 16, has a small but excellent selection of English-language novels and classics.

Laundry The best and most central laundrette is Lavandería Autoservicio 'El Mercat' at Plaza del Mercado 12. It is open

weekdays from 10 am to 2 pm and 4.30 to 8.30 pm and Saturday from 10 am to 2 pm. Another is Lavamatic, near the train station at Calle de Pelayo 11.

Medical Services In medical emergency, call ☎ 085. To find your nearest all night pharmacy, call free phone ☎ 900-16 11 61. The general hospital (☎ 96 386 29 00) is on Avenida del Cid in the west of the city.

Emergency The Policía Nacional (☎ 96 351 08 62) are at Gran Vía de Ramón y Cajal 40.

Museo de Bellas Artes

The Museo de Bellas Artes (Fine Arts Museum) ranks among the best in the country. Set in the Jardines del Real, the collection includes works by El Greco, Goya and Velázquez, and features artists from the school of Valencian impressionists including Ribalta, Sorolla, Pinazo and Espinosa.

The museum is across the river on Calle de San Pío V. You can get there on bus No 11 from Plaza del Ayuntamiento. Opening hours are Tuesday to Saturday from 9 am to 2.15 pm and 4 to 7.30 pm, and Sunday from 10 am to 2 pm (free).

Catedral

The cathedral is a microcosm of the city's architectural history: the Puerta del Palau is Romanesque; the dome, tower and Puerta de los Apóstoles are Gothic; the presbytery and main gate are baroque; and there are a couple of Renaissance chapels inside.

The cathedral's **museum** claims to be home to the **Holy Grail** (Santo Cáliz), a gold cup purportedly used by Christ during the Last Supper. The museum also contains a collection of religious icons and several works by Goya. It is open Monday to Saturday from 10 am to 1 pm and 4.30 to 6 pm (7 pm in summer).

On the south-western corner is the **Miguelete**, the cathedral's octagonal bell tower. Its 207 steps wind up a circular staircase to the top of the tower, which has great

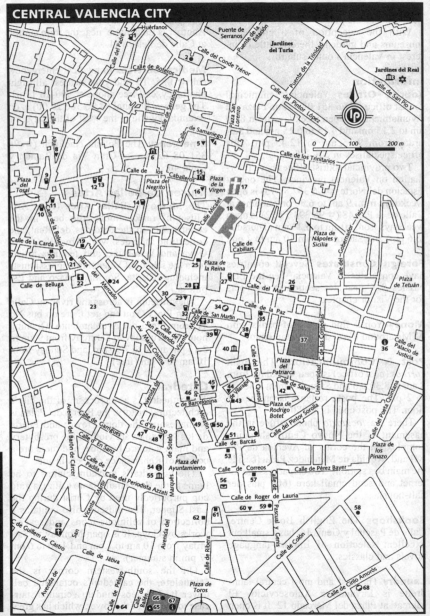

CENTRAL VALENCIA CITY

CENTRAL VALENCIA CITY

PLACES TO STAY

19	Hospedería del Pilar
20	Hostal El Rincón
25	Habitaciones CH Reina
31	Hostal El Cid
38	Hotel Inglés
42	Pensión París
43	Hotel Astoria Palace
46	Hotel Londres
50	Hostal Moratin
51	Hostal-Residencia Universal
53	Hotel Reina Victoria
57	Hotel Continental
61	Hostal Castelar
62	Hostal-Residencia Alicante

PLACES TO EAT

4	Las Cuevas
5	Café de las Horas
8	John Silver
16	Restaurante El Generalife
29	Horchatería de Santa Catalina
44	Restaurante Nuevo Don Ramón
45	Cezar's Plaza
47	Bar-Cafetería Olimpya
48	Fosters Hollywood
60	Cervecería Pema

OTHER

1	Coyote Bar
2	Torres de Serrano
3	Museo de Bellas Artes
6	Palau de Balia
7	Circus
9	El Café
10	Café Bolsería
11	Café Infanta
12	Johnny Maracas
13	Fox Congo
14	Café-Bar Negrito
15	Palau de la Generalitat
17	Real Basílica de Nuestra Señora de los Desamparados
18	Catedral; Capilla
21	Lavandería El Mercat
22	Iglesia de los Santos Juanes
23	Mercado Central (Food Market)
24	La Lonja de los Mercaderes
26	Johann Sebastian Bach
27	Finnegan's of Dublin
28	Iglesia de Santa Catalina
30	Plaza Redondo
32	Taverna Clot

33	Iglesia de San Martín
34	US Consulate
35	Iberia Office
36	Regional Tourist Office
37	Real Colegio del Patriarca
39	Cervecería Madrid
40	Palacio del Marqués de Dos Aguas & Museo Nacional de Cerámica
41	Iglesia de San Juan de la Cruz
49	Filmoteca & Teatro Rialto
52	Teatro Principal
54	Municipal Tourist Office
55	Ayuntamiento, Museo Histórico & Museo Paleontológico
56	Correos
58	Avis Rentacar
59	English Book Centre
63	Iglesia de San Agustín
64	Lavamatic
65	Estación del Norte (Train Station)
66	Train Information Office
67	Regional Tourist Office
68	French Consulate

360° views of the city rooftops and skyline. The tower is open daily from 10 am to 1 pm and 4.30 to 7 pm (100 ptas).

As it has done for the past thousand years, the **Tribunal de las Aguas** (Water Court) meets every Thursday at noon outside the cathedral's Gothic doorway, where the irrigation disputes of the local farmers are settled in Catalan.

A walk-bridge connects the cathedral with the **Real Basílica de Nuestra Señora de los Desamparados**, which houses a small collection of artworks, including a fresco by Palomino.

Right by the cathedral, a 15th century **capilla** (chapel) was reopened in mid-1998. It is thought to be the site of the crypt that served as the martyr San Vicente's prison in the 4th century, and now contains archaeological remains ranging from a Roman era mural to Islamic pottery.

Ayuntamiento

This is a palatial 18th century building, impressively floodlit by night. Inside are two small museums: the collection of the **Museo Histórico** includes a map of Valencia in 1704, paintings by Sorolla and the sword of King Jaime I (open weekdays from 9 am to 2 pm); and the **Museo Paleontológico** includes a collection of artefacts from South America (open Tuesday to Saturday from 9.15 am to 2 pm and 4.30 to 8 pm (morning session only on Sunday). Both are free.

Palacio del Marqués de Dos Aguas

This baroque palace on Calle del Poeta Querol, extensively rebuilt during the 18th century, is fronted by an extravagant façade in the *churrigueresque* style, hand-carved out of alabaster.

VALENCIA

Inside, the **Museo Nacional de Cerámica** boasts ceramics from Manises, Alcora and Paterna. Most are on view at the IVAM (see Other Museums & Galleries) while restoration work on the palace continues.

Torres de Serranos

On the (dry) banks of the Río Turia, this well preserved 14th century tower was part of the original walls around the Ciutat Vella, Valencia's old quarter.

Ciudad de las Artes y de las Ciencias

The first stage of what promises to be the city's premier attraction, **L'Hemisfèric** opened in 1998. It is the latest generation in 3-D IMAX style cinema experiences (1000 ptas).

The rest of the centre is being built around L'Hemisfèric at Calle del Arzobispo Mayoral 14 and will eventually contain a Palacio de las Artes, Museo de las Ciencias and Parque Oceanógrafico (acquarium). Bus No 15 runs past from Calle del Pintor Salvador Abril.

Other Things to See & Do

On the south-west corner of Plaza de la Reina is the early Gothic **Iglesia de Santa Catalina**. Its beautiful baroque belfry was added in the 18th century and is one of the city's best-known landmarks. Farther north on Calle de los Caballeros, the lovely **Palau de la Generalitat** is fronted by a garden of orange trees.

The small circular **Plaza Redondo** is worth a visit. Around the plaza there is an interesting collection of market stalls selling clothes, souvenirs and locally made crafts and ceramics.

Opposite the Mercado Central is **La Lonja de los Mercaderes**, Valencia's former silk exchange. This late Gothic structure has a strikingly colonnaded hall now used for exhibitions.

The **Estación del Norte** is one of Valencia's most impressive *modernista* buildings. Opened in 1917, its entrance hall is decorated with ceramic mosaics and unusual murals.

Other Museums & Galleries The Instituto Valenciano Arte Moderno (IVAM), north-west of the centre at Calle de Guillem de Castro 118, houses an impressive collection of 20th century Spanish art. Its permanent collection features the works of the abstract sculptor Julio González, and there are frequent temporary exhibits by modern artists. IVAM is open Tuesday to Sunday from 10 am to 7 pm (350 ptas, free on Sunday).

Another museum with works by El Greco, among others, is the **Real Colegio del Patriarca** on Plaza del Patriarca. It is open daily from 11 am to 1 pm (100 ptas).

The small **Museo Taurine** behind the Plaza de Toros holds an interesting collection of bullfighting memorabilia.

South-east of the centre on Plaza del Monteolivete is the **Museo Fallero**. Dedicated to Las Fallas, it houses the best floats from every festival since 1934, as well as posters and photographs.

Other places of interest include the **Centro de Artesanía de la Comunidad** (with a collection of the works of Valencian artisans) and the **Casa Museo José Benlliure** (the painter's studio, housing some of his paintings and ceramics).

Parks & Gardens

The dry bed of the Río Turia has been turned into a large park. It's a patchy collection of dusty playing fields, running paths, plantations, fountains and children's playgrounds. The best areas are east of the centre around the Palau de la Música, where pleasant lawns and paths are shaded by big old pine trees.

North of the river and the Museo de Bellas Artes are the large **Jardines del Real** (Royal Gardens), on the site of the former Royal Palace. These gardens are a lovely spot for strolling and picnics, and include a rose garden, a sculpture garden and a zoological park.

North-west of the centre and on the river opposite the main bus station, Valencia's **Jardín Botánico** is said to be Spain's first botanic gardens.

Beaches

Valencia's main city beach is the broad **Playa de la Malvarrosa**. It's not the cleanest beach in Spain, but it's OK. A string of restaurants, bars and discos line the waterfront, and especially in the warmer weather it's a lively area. Bus No 19 from Plaza del Ayuntamiento will take you there.

A better bet is to take a bus from Gran Vía de las Germanias 10km south to the **Playa El Salér**, which is backed by attractive public gardens.

Special Events

Las Fallas Valencia's Las Fallas de San José is an exuberant and anarchic blend of fireworks, music, festive bonfires and all-night partying. If you're in Spain between 12 and 19 March, don't miss it.

The *fallas* are huge papier-mâché sculptures built by teams of local artists. Each neighbourhood sponsors its own fallas, and by festival time more than 350 have been unveiled on local plazas. Reaching up to 15m in height, these colourful and grotesque effigies satirise celebrities, current affairs and local customs.

Dozens of events fill the festival week, including street parties, parades, open air concerts, bullfights and fireworks displays – some organised, some spontaneous. Valencia considers itself the pyrotechnics capital of the world, and each day at 2 pm a deafening 10-minute fireworks display is held in Plaza del Ayuntamiento. On the final night, *La Nit del Foc* (Night of Fire) each of the fallas is sent up in flames, backed by more fireworks of course.

If you haven't booked ahead, accommodation is hard to find, although rooms are rented out in private homes – check with the tourist office on Plaza del Ayuntamiento or haggle with the locals at the train and bus stations.

Other Festivals & Events Valencia celebrates Semana Santa (Holy Week) with elaborate processions. Each 14 April the Fiesta de San Vicente Ferrer sees colourful parades with bands and traditional cos-

Big *falla* destined for the flames at Valencia's Las Fallas de San José festival

INGRID RUDDIS

tumes, while on the second Sunday in May locals celebrate the feast of the Virgen de los Desamparados, patroness of the city.

The festival of Corpus Christi, held in June, was first celebrated here way back in 1355. Each 24 June on the Día de San Juan, thousands of locals spend the evening on the Playa de la Malvarrosa and take part in a traditional cleansing ceremony that involves washing your feet in the ocean, writing your bad habits on a piece of paper and then burning it in a bonfire.

The Feria de Julio, in the second week of July, features a packed program of performing arts, music contests, concerts, bullfights, fireworks and the 'battle of the flowers'.

The Trobada de Música del Mediterrani music festival is held during September and the Mostra de Valencia Cinema del

VALENCIA

Mediterrani international film festival takes place in October.

Places to Stay

A few dodgy *hostales* are around the western side of the train station, but the budget options in the Barrio del Carmen are better. They put you close to the best nightlife (and, unfortunately, the red light district).

The hostales around Plaza del Ayuntamiento tend to be more expensive – you're paying extra for the central location and better neighbourhood.

Valencia's best hotels and hostales are generally in the upmarket areas to the east and north-east of Plaza del Ayuntamiento.

Places to Stay – Budget

Camping The nearest camping ground, *Camping del Salér* (☎ 96 183 00 23), is on the coast 10km south of Valencia and is open in summer only.

Youth Hostel *Albergue La Paz* (☎ 96 369 01 52) is 3km east of the centre at Avenida del Puerto 69 – take bus No 19 from Plaza del Ayuntamiento. The hostel is open from July to mid-September and costs 900/1100 ptas for juniors/seniors.

Pensiones & Hostales There's quite a few cheap places around.

Barrio del Carmen Hospederia del Pilar (☎ 96 391 66 00, Plaza del Mercado 19) is a rambling hostal with clean singles/doubles from 1500/2800 ptas. The front rooms are the brightest but get more traffic noise.

Nearby, *Hostal El Rincón* (☎ 96 391 79 98, Calle de la Carda 11) is one of Valencia's oldest and best-known hostales. Most of its 56 rooms are small and dim with a shabby charm; nightly costs are 1500/2800 ptas. It also has three spacious renovated front rooms with modern bathrooms and soundproofed windows – excellent value at 2200/4200 ptas.

Hostal El Cid (☎ 96 392 23 23, Calle de los Cerrajeros 13) is in a narrow side street behind Plaza Redondo. It's another reasonable budget option, with 12 cosy rooms at 1600/3000 ptas, or 3200/4000 ptas for doubles with shower/bath.

Right on Plaza de la Reina (3rd floor, no lift!), *Habitaciones CH Reina* (☎ 96 392 18 92) is very basic but well placed. It's also cheap with one single at 1400 ptas and doubles at 2300 ptas.

Around Plaza del Ayuntamiento Pensión París (☎ 96 352 67 66, Calle de Salva 12, 1st and 3rd floors) is one of Valencia's best budget options. It's friendly, in a good area and has 13 freshly painted rooms with white walls, beige tiled floors and spotless bathrooms. Singles/doubles/triples cost 2000/3000/4500 ptas; doubles with shower are 3600 ptas.

Near Plaza del Ayuntamiento, *Hostal Moratín* (☎ 96 352 12 20, Calle de Moratín 15, 5th floor) is quiet, clean and secure. Singles/doubles start at 2000/3500 ptas.

Hostal-Residencia Universal (☎ 96 351 53 84, Calle de Barcas 5) is run by the same family as Pensión París (and to similar standards). It charges 2000/3000/4200 ptas (doubles with shower 3600 ptas).

South of Plaza del Ayuntamiento, *Hostal Castelar* (☎ 96 351 31 99, Calle de Ribera 1) has rooms from 2000/3800 ptas – they're not flash but the front ones have good plaza views. *Hostal-Residencia Alicante* (☎ 96 351 22 96, Calle de Ribera 8, 2nd floor) is across the road. Long, colourfully tiled hallways lead to 16 quaint, oldish rooms with showers and TVs; singles/doubles cost 3200/4500 ptas.

Places to Stay – Mid-Range

Just off Plaza del Ayuntamiento, the popular *Hotel Londres* (☎ 96 351 22 44, Calle de Barcelonina 1) has well-worn but cosy rooms with TV, phone and bathroom from 4500/7700 ptas including breakfast (less on weekends).

Hotel Continental (☎ 96 351 09 26, Calle de Correos 8), behind the post office, is a modern and friendly mid-range hotel with straightforward rooms ranging up to 6350/10,350 ptas (plus IVA).

Places to Stay – Top End

Valencia is a business centre and the big hotels struggle to fill their rooms on weekends. So they offer fantastic discounts for Friday, Saturday and/or Sunday stays – if you have money to splurge, ask the following hotels about special offers.

In the centre of town, **Hotel Reina Victoria** (☎ 96 352 04 87, Calle de Barcas 4) is a grand old four-star place. Some of the facilities are dated but the gracious old-world atmosphere more than compensates. Standard rooms are usually 12,500/20,000 ptas.

Hotel Astoria Palace (☎ 96 352 67 37, Plaza de Rodrigo Botet 5) is a classy hotel in the most upmarket part of town. The modern rooms cost from 15,900/25,700 ptas (plus IVA).

Hotel Inglés (☎ 96 351 64 26, Calle del Marqués de Dos Aguas 6) is an older three-star hotel with 63 comfortably refurbished rooms with all mod cons. Rates are from 15,000/19,000 ptas (plus IVA).

Places to Eat

Valencia is the capital of a fertile agricultural district often referred to as Spain's fruit and vegetable bowl. Apart from oranges, the surrounding countryside supplies the city with a diverse range of fresh produce.

Rice is the cornerstone of Valencian cuisine – and the basis of the most famous local dish, *paella valenciana*. Paella appears on the menu of almost every restaurant, but to avoid disappointment it's worth paying a bit more for the real McCoy. You'll encounter plenty of other rice dishes too, including *arroz a la banda* (rice and seafood cooked in a fish stock), *arroz negro* (rice with squid in its ink), *arroz al horno* (rice with pork baked in the oven) and *arroz caldos* (a soup-like version of paella). Then there's *fideuá*, a paella made with noodles instead of rice.

You could also try a glass of *horchata*, a popular local drink that originated in the nearby *pueblo* of Alboraya (5km north of the centre). It's a strange milky substance made from pressed *chufas* (tiger nuts) – an acquired taste. The **Horchatería de Santa Catalina** (Plaza de Santa Catalina 6) is a traditional horchata house.

The modernista **Mercado Central** on Plaza del Mercado is one of Europe's biggest markets.

The shiny **Bar-Cafetería Olimpya** (Calle d'En Llop 2) is great for a quick bite. It has good breakfasts, tapas and fresh salads, as well as an excellent *menú* (950 ptas).

At **Restaurante El Generalife** (Calle de los Caballeros 5) you can eat well in the pleasant upstairs dining room for 2000 ptas a head. It has a *menú* for 1100 ptas.

Café de las Horas (Calle del Conde de Almodóvar 1), a block north, is a wonderful 19th century style salon with mosaic tiled floors, wax dripping candelabras, tapestries and classical music. It serves herbal teas, coffees, sandwiches, salads and great chocky fudge cake!

Across the road is **Las Cuevas**, a subterranean eatery that specialises in tapas, bocadillos and jugs of sangría.

You'll come across good budget eateries in the Barrio del Carmen nightlife zone. One is **John Silver** (Calle Alta 8), just north of Plaza del Tosal. Named after Long John himself (his wooden leg hangs behind the bar), it's a cluttered bar with an affordable menu that includes salads, bocadillos, *bocatas* and *platos combinados*.

Fosters Hollywood, on the corner of Plaza del Ayuntamiento and Calle d'En Llop is about as Spanish as Mel Gibson, but if you need something familiar … Part of a restaurant chain, it combines a movie set décor with an Americanised menu that offers nachos, burgers and Tex-Mex.

Calle de Mossén Femádes, a pedestrian street one block south-east of Plaza del Ayuntamiento, is home to a cluster of upmarket seafood restaurants. If the high prices scare you off, head for **Cervecería Pema** at No 3. The décor is straightforward but the food, some cooked on a street-front barbecue, is tasty and reasonably priced.

VALENCIA

For a splurge, try **Restaurante Nuevo Don Ramón** *(Plaza de Rodrigo Botet 4)*. It's a stylish (and somewhat touristy) place with gingham tablecloths and matching curtains. It specialises in paella Valenciana (2500 ptas), with other main courses in the 1100 to 2200 ptas range.

Across the plaza, **Cezar's Plaza** is good for a drink or a pre-dinner snack. It's a narrow and cheerful pine panelled bar with a fine selection of tapas.

Entertainment

Fuelled by a large student population and an overdeveloped sense of competitiveness with Madrid and Barcelona, Valencia has a reputation for one of the best nightlife scenes in the country. For many visitors, Valencia's party long and hard attitude is the motivation for coming.

There are several different nocturnal zones. The trick is knowing when to be where.

The Barrio del Carmen is the scene of the grungiest and grooviest collection of bars. The other major spot is the Ciutat Universitaria, the university area 2km east of the centre. Along Avenida de Blasco Ibáñez and particularly around Plaza de Xuquer are enough bars and discos to keep you busy beyond sunrise.

Also worth checking out is the area around Plaza de Cánovas del Castillo, and the beach suburbs of Malvarrosa and El Salér, which come alive with disco fever in summer.

Valencia's best 'what's-on' guides, *Que y Donde* (150 ptas) and *Turia* (175 ptas), are available from newsstands.

Bars & Pubs Valencia is well equipped with places to enjoy a *copa* or two.

Barrio del Carmen Known locally as El Carme, this area has everything from up-market designer bars and yuppie pubs to grungy thrash-metal haunts and psychedelic punk bars.

El Carme doesn't get going until after 11 pm, and most places stay open until 2 am early in the week and until 3 or 3.30 am on Thursday, Friday and Saturday. Calle de los Caballeros is the main street and is usually crammed with people on *la marcha*. It's fairly safe, but use common sense and stick to well lit and busy streets. The area around Plaza del Carmen is dodgy.

Plaza del Tosal has some of the most sophisticated bars this side of Barcelona. **Café Bolsería** is a stylish upstairs-downstairs job that attracts a well dressed crowd of 30-somethings. On the opposite corner, **Café Infanta** is a swanky salon style bar with old stone walls covered with red velvet wall hangings and Hollywood posters. On the northern side of the plaza, the smaller **El Café** has a quiet upstairs area.

From here you can head east along Calle de los Caballeros to **Johnny Maracas** at No 39, a suave Cuban salsa bar and the perfect place to drink and dance at the same time. At No 35, **Fox Congo** has an amazing interior with its marble bar, patchwork suede benches, scrap-metal montage ceilings and glass-walled toilets.

A block south on Plaza del Negrito, **Cafe-Bar Negrito** is another popular watering hole where the crowd and the music usually spill out onto the plaza.

The bars just north of Plaza del Tosal along Calle Alta are cheaper and grungier, and most have tables out on the street. At No 8 is **John Silver** (see Places to Eat), while **Circus** at No 11 has a narrow mezzanine level from where you can watch the goings-on in the street.

Farther north the streets get darker, but there are some interesting places to discover. **Coyote Bar** *(Calle del Padre Huérfanos 14)* is a student hang-out with alternative music, pool table and an Arizona-esque décor. **Club Revolver** *(Calle de Ripalda 24)* has a rock 'n' roll attitude and psycho space-age murals on the downstairs walls.

Other Areas Finnegan's of Dublin on Plaza de la Reina is a popular meeting place for English speakers. The music and atmosphere are good and it has Guinness,

Kilkenny Speçial and Olde English cider on tap.

Taverna Clot on Plaza Redonda is good for an early evening drink and tapas.

Johann Sebastian Bach (Calle del Mar 31) is in a superb baroque mansion. It's quite a place but it was closed when we visited (but has since reopened). Be prepared for a cover charge.

The area around Plaza de Cánovas del Castillo is tamer and more upmarket than El Carme and attracts a younger crowd, many under parental supervision.

Plaza is a stylish corner bar on the plaza itself. Around the corner there's a string of places along Calle de Serrano Morales: *Década Loca* at No 7 does the retro 60s thing with hits and memories from the hippy era, while *Tentación* next door is a salsa dance bar. *Color* at No 2 is also popular. Farther south, Calle de Salamanca also has plenty of bars. *Talco* and *Subway*, both on the Calle del Conde Altea corner, are worth a look.

Live Music Plenty of places around town have live music on a spontaneous basis, especially in the Barrio del Carmen.

Cervecería Madrid (Calle de la Abadía de San Martín 10) takes you back to the jazz of the 1920s. It's an atmospheric bar with soft lighting and walls covered with the paintings of local artist Constante Gil. *Club Perdido (Calle de Suecia 17)* is another happening jazz venue. Across the river, *Black Note (Calle de Polo y Peyrolón 15)* has jazz, blues and soul sessions practically every night. Another one is *Roxy (Avenida de San Vicente Mártir 200)*, well south of the train station.

Discos A handful of discos are scattered around the centre but if you really want to experience life after 3 am in Valencia, head for the Ciutat Universitaria (600 ptas by taxi). This zone is spread for almost a kilometre along and around Avenida de Blasco Ibáñez.

Plaza de Xuquer, where students pack the bars, is the place to go early on. Those worth checking out include *La Salamandra*, *Farandula*, *Pub Xuquer II* and the *Rocafull Cafe*.

Around 3 am the stayers, with cash to splash, move on to the big discos along Blasco Ibáñez. Most discos have cover charges between 600 and 1200 ptas, although discounted passes are often available from local bars.

If you're into South American salsa and reggae, head for the funky *Hipodromo Salsa (Avenida de Blasco Ibáñez 146)*. Most of the other places, including the *Acción Disco* across the road, are dominated by *bacalao* dance music.

During summer there's a big disco scene in Malvarrosa and El Salér, concentrated along the main waterfront roads.

Theatre & Performing Arts The *Teatro Principal (☎ 96 351 00 51, Calle de Barcas 15)* is Valencia's main venue for opera and the performing arts. It's an intimate theatre with a plush red velvet interior and steeply rising stalls (tickets from 600 to 2000 ptas).

The *Palau de la Música (☎ 96 337 50 20)*, a huge glass-domed concert hall in the Jardines del Turia, hosts more than 200 concerts a year including opera, classical music and solo performances.

Cinemas On the 4th floor of the Teatro Rialto building, the *Filmoteca (for tickets ☎ 96 399 55 77, Plaza del Ayuntamiento 17)* screens classic, art-house and experimental films in their original languages (200 ptas, students 150 ptas). For other cinemas that screen films in their original language, look for those coded '*v.o. subtitulada*' in listings publications.

Getting There & Away

Air Aeropuerto de Manises (☎ 96 360 95 00) is 15km west of the centre. Regular flights connect Valencia with Madrid, Barcelona, Palma de Mallorca and Ibiza.

Bus The *estación de autobuses* (bus station; ☎ 96 349 72 22) is an inconvenient 2km north-west of the centre on Avenida de

Menéndez Pidal. Bus No 8 runs between the estación de autobuses and Plaza del Ayuntamiento.

AutoRes runs 10 to 12 buses to Madrid daily and Enatcar six to eight buses to Barcelona daily. Ubesa has regular services to Alicante, stopping in all the towns and resorts of interest. Express services do the same run, without the stops.

Train Estación del Norte (☎ 96 352 02 02), is on Calle de Játiva. Up to 10 trains daily run between Valencia and Madrid; the trip takes about four hours (or six hours via Cuenca) and costs from 2840 ptas one way. A dozen daily trains make the three to five hour haul north to Barcelona (via Tarragona), including the high-speed Euromed (see the Barcelona chapter). Seven trains head daily to Alicante.

Boat Trasmediterránea operates frequent car and passenger ferries (including high-speed 'fast ferries') from Valencia to Mallorca, Menorca and Ibiza. It has an office (☎ 96 367 39 72) at the harbourside *estación marítima*. Tickets can also be bought from any travel agency (see the Islas Baleares chapter for more details).

Getting Around

To/From the Airport A taxi into the centre should cost around 1800 ptas.

Bus Maps and timetables for the local EMT bus services (☎ 96 352 83 99) are available from the municipal tourist office. Buses on most lines run from 5.30 am to 11 pm, with nocturnal services continuing on seven services until about 1.30 am.

Points of interest outside the city centre can generally be reached by bus, most of which depart from Plaza del Ayuntamiento. Bus No 19 goes to Valencia's beach, Malvarrosa, as well as the Islas Baleares terminal. No 81 goes to the university and No 11 will drop you off at the Museo de Bellas Artes. No 8 runs to the estación central de autobuses (singles 110 ptas; 10-trip *bonos* 690 ptas).

Train & Metro Valencia's metro and suburban trains are operated by Ferrocarrils de la Generalitat Valenciana (FGV; ☎ 96 362 86 48). There are five lines, although most service the outer suburbs. The closest stations to the centre are Ángel Guimerá (lines two and five), Xàtiva and Colón (both line two) and Pont de Fusta (line four).

Car International and local firms compete for car rental business. The local ones often undercut the big boys. The international ones all have offices at the airport. Other addresses include:

Atesa
    (☎ 96 395 36 05) Calle de Joaquín Costa 57
Avis
    (☎ 96 351 07 34) Calle de Isabel la Católica 17
Cuñauto
    (☎ 96 374 85 61) Calle de Burriana 51
Europcar
    (☎ 96 374 15 12) Avenida del Reino Antiguo de Valencia 7
Furgo
    (☎ 96 380 48 90) Avenida de Pérez Galdós 3

Taxi Taxis roam the streets, but should you need to book one call Radio-Taxi (☎ 96 370 33 33) or Valencia Taxi (☎ 96 357 13 13).

AROUND VALENCIA

Some of the most popular excursions from Valencia include visits to the Roman ruins at Sagunto, the beach resort of Gandia and the inland town of Játiva (see later for details).

La Albufera

About 16km south of Valencia, La Albufera is a huge freshwater lagoon separated from the sea by a strip of sand dunes and pine forests known as La Devesa. The lake and surrounding areas are a breeding ground and sanctuary for several hundred species of migrating birds, and have been protected as a natural park. Keen birdwatchers flock to the Parque Natural de la Albufera to count kingfishers, mallards, white herons, coots and red-crested pochards, among others.

The unspoiled sections of La Albufera have a serene beauty, and the area is noted for its spectacular sunsets. You can take a boat trip across the lagoon, and temporarily join the local fishers who use distinctive flat-bottomed boats and nets to harvest fish and eels from the shallow waters.

Surrounded by rice fields, La Albufera was the birthplace of paella. The villages of **El Palmar** and **El Perellonet** boast some excellent restaurants that specialise in paella and other rice and seafood dishes.

You can get to La Albufera, El Palmar and El Perellonet on the same bus as for Playa El Salér (see Beaches earlier in this section for details).

Costa del Azahar

Stretching north from Valencia is the Costa del Azahar – the orange blossom coast. Backed by a green and mountainous hinterland dominated by plantations of orange trees, the region takes its name from the spectacular displays of orange blossom that decorate the countryside each spring.

Benicasim (Benicàssim) is the best of the popular but low-key resorts along this coast; other attractions include the Roman ruins at the historic town of Sagunto and some interesting museums in the provincial and industrial capital of Castellón de la Plana.

Getting There & Away

Bus Autobuses Vallduxense has frequent services between Valencia and Sagunto (30 minutes; 280 ptas). Enatcar runs about 10 buses daily between Valencia and Barcelona.

Train RENFE's Valencia-Barcelona train line follows this coast, and regional trains pass through and stop at all the main towns (with the exception of Peñíscola). There are 12 to 15 trains daily between 6 am and 10.20 pm. Cercanías trains (line C-6) go as far as Castellón de la Plana (545 ptas). The fare to Sagunto is 355 ptas. Cercanías fares rise a little on weekends.

SAGUNTO (SAGUNT)

Sagunto, 25km north of Valencia, was a thriving Iberian community as early as the 5th century BC, when the settlers fortified their hill town with stone walls and traded with the Greeks and Phoenicians.

In 219 BC Hannibal besieged the town for eight months. The inhabitants resisted heroically against overwhelming odds but were eventually wiped out and their town destroyed, an event which led to the Second Punic War between Carthage and Rome. Rome won, named the town Saguntum and set about rebuilding.

Orientation & Information

Sagunto is a town in three parts. The Roman ruins and old town are atop an inland hill; the new town and its ugly industrial sprawl flank the highway; while on the coast is the resort of Puerto Sagunto with its sandy beaches and ritzy boat harbour.

From the train station beside the highway it's a 10 minute walk up to the old town and the tourist office (☎ 96 266 22 13) on Plaza del Cronista Chabret. The office is open Monday from 8 am to 3 pm and Tuesday to Saturday from 8 am to 3 pm and 5 to 8 pm (7 pm out of season). Another office at Puerto Sagunto is open in summer.

From the tourist office another 10 minute walk through the narrow streets of the **judería**, the former Jewish quarter, takes you up to the Roman theatre and castle.

Things to See & Do

You could easily spend a day exploring old Sagunto. The **Roman theatre** was built into a curve in the hillside during the 1st century AD. Centuries of use and disuse had left it in poor shape, but the controversial modern 'restoration' is in questionable taste. Much of the seating was covered with marble and a high cream brick and bluestone façade was tacked onto the front. Still, the acoustics remain outstanding, and it is used regularly as a theatre and music venue.

Higher up, the old stone walls of the **castle** wind around the hillside for almost a kilometre. Mostly in ruins, the castle is divided into seven different sections or plazas, each representing a different period in Sagunto's history.

The castle and Roman theatre are open Tuesday to Saturday from 10 am to 2 pm and from 4 to 6 pm (7 pm in summer), and Sunday and public holidays from 10 am to 2 pm (free).

Other monuments include the ruins of the 4th century **Templo de Diana**, the adjacent **Iglesia de Santa María**, which features Gothic and baroque doorways, and the 17th century **Ermita de la Sangre**.

Special Events
Sagunto hosts a smaller version of Valencia's Las Fallas festival each year from 15 to 19 March. The Semana Santa celebrations here are famous, and include sacred music concerts, parades and the traditional Calvary processions on Easter Friday.

The Roman theatre is the main venue for Sagunto's Escena each August, a three week open-air festival featuring opera, dance, theatre and orchestral pieces.

Places to Stay & Eat
Sagunto is mainly a day trip destination and there is no accommodation in the old town. There are three places down on the highway near the train station if you decide to stay. *Hostal Carlos* (☎ 96 266 09 02, *Avenida del País Valenciano 43*) has clean and straightforward singles/doubles at 2000/3200 ptas or 3200/4700 ptas with bathroom.

Down at Puerto Sagunto are two camping grounds and a string of beachfront hotels and apartments.

For tapas and beer, the *Tasca El Braser*, opposite the Roman theatre, is a good stop.

CASTELLÓN (CASTELLÓ) DE LA PLANA
Castellón is the provincial capital of northern Valencia. Like many Spanish cities its outskirts are drab and industrial, so the centre comes as a pleasant surprise to the few tourists who visit.

It's a prosperous commercial centre and university town with an excellent fine arts museum, interesting monuments and some fine examples of modernista architecture.

Orientation & Information
Plaza Mayor marks the centre of Castellón. The train station is almost 1km north-west of here, on the far side of the leafy Parque Ribalta. The accommodation hub, Puerta del Sol, is 200m south-west. The tourist office (☎ 964 35 86 88), Plaza de María Agustina 5, is open weekdays from 9 am to 2 pm and 4 to 7 pm and Saturday from 10 am to 2 pm.

There are several bus stations. Buses to/from Valencia operate from Plaza del País Valenciano (700m south-west of Plaza Mayor), while buses to the beaches of El Grau leave from Plaza del Juez Bornill (300m south of Plaza Mayor).

Things to See & Do
Castellón's under-visited **Museo de Bellas Artes** displays an eclectic collection, with a ceramics section that focuses on this region's major industry. It's on the corner of Calle de los Caballeros and Calle de la Gracia, and is open weekdays from 10 am to 2 pm and 4 to 6 pm (during summer from 9 am to 2 pm only) and Saturday from 10 am to 12.30 pm (free).

Also worth visiting are the **Museo Etnológico de la Diputación** at Calle de Sanchis Abella s/n (open the same hours as Bellas Artes) and the **Convento de Capuchinas** in Calle de Núñez de Arce, which houses 10 fine paintings by Zurbarán and is open Monday to Friday from 10 am to 2 pm and 4 to 6 pm (summer from 9 am to 2 pm) and Saturday from 10 am to 12.30 pm.

On Plaza Mayor is **El Fadri** (1604), an octagonal bell tower that is now the city's symbol. Beside the tower is the reconstructed **Catedral de Santa María**, which was virtually demolished in the civil war.

In the centre of the adjacent **Plaza de Santa Clara** is a modernist sculpture by Llorens Poy that depicts Castellón's history.

Four kilometres east of the centre is **El Grau de Castellón**, a huge harbour that handles this industrial region's exports as well as the local fishing fleet. Castellón's beaches start north of here.

Places to Stay & Eat

At *Hostal La Esperanza* (☎ *964 22 20 31, Calle de la Trinidad 37)* spotless rooms above a bar-restaurant cost 1700/3100 ptas. *Hotel-Residencia del Real* (☎ *964 21 19 44, Plaza Real 2)* has refurbished rooms with 70s décor, TV, phone and air-con from 4300/6500 ptas.

Comidas La Brasa (Calle de la Gracia 7), hidden away in the centre, has a good set *menú* for 950 ptas.

BENICASIM (BENICÀSSIM)

Benicasim has been a popular resort since the 19th century, when wealthy Valencian families built summer residences here. It's still the best of the Costa del Azahar resorts, despite the addition of 20th century trimmings like concrete high-rises, discos, restaurants and minigolf courses.

Unlike the Costa Blanca, it isn't completely overrun by foreigners, and many people from Madrid, Valencia and Castellón keep summer apartments here.

Orientation & Information

Benicasim's beaches and the accompanying development sprawl for 6km along the coast. The old town is about one kilometre inland, and is home to the train station and the main tourist office (☎ 964 30 38 51), inside the Ayuntamiento at Calle del Médico Segarra 4. This office is open Monday to Saturday from 9 am to 3 pm; during summer five other offices open along the beachfront.

Things to See & Do

Benicasim's 6km of beaches are the main attraction. You can hire windsurfing and other water sports gear; nearby are the Aquarama aquatic park and several golf courses.

Backing Benicasim is the mountain range known as the **Desierto de las Palmas**. In 1694 the Order of Barefooted Carmelites bought the range and built a monastery and several chapels. The area, now a natural park, isn't really a desert – the Carmelites used the term to refer to areas suitable for 'mystic withdrawal'.

Special Events

Since 1995, the first days of August have seen thousands of young people gather here for the annual Festival Internacional de Benicasim, now one of Spain's top outdoor music fests.

Places to Stay & Eat

The half-dozen camping grounds here are all within walking distance of the beaches.

Benicasim's great youth hostel, the *Albergue Argentina* (☎ *964 30 27 09, Calle de Ferrandis Salvador 40)* is a whopping whitewashed complex with games rooms, lounges, two pools and 140 bunks. Costs are 900/1100 ptas for juniors/seniors. Forget it in July and August – it's always booked solid.

Hostal Almadraba (☎ *964 30 10 00, Calle de Santo Tomás 135)*, in the old town, has comfy upstairs rooms from 2000 ptas per person.

Hotel Avenida (☎ *964 30 00 47)*, on the corner of Calle de Santo Tomás and Calle de los Cuatro Caminos, is an appealing mid-range hotel with a shady courtyard and pool. It has doubles for 4900 ptas (plus IVA).

Just north of the old town and 300m from the beach, *Hotel Vista Alegre* (☎ *964 30 04 00)* on Avenida de Barcelona is a pleasant hotel with a pool, bar and restaurant. Rooms cost 4500/7000 ptas (plus IVA).

A plethora of eateries line Calle de Santo Tomás (the main street in the old town), with *menús* ranging from 800 to 1300 ptas.

Entertainment

Particularly on weekends and during summer, Benicasim has a vibrant nightlife. Head for Plaza de los Dolores in the old town, where you'll find a good collection of bars including *Pay Pay*, *Cactus* and *Mambo*.

OROPESA (ORPESA)

It's a fine scenic drive from Benicasim to this small resort along a narrow road winding around a rocky coastline. Oropesa's development backs the two main beaches of **Morro de Gos** and **La Concha**, named after the similarly shaped bay at San Sebastián. The tourist office (π 964 31 00 20) at Avenida de la Plana 1 can help with accommodation queries.

PEÑÍSCOLA

Perched on a rocky promontory jutting into the sea, Peñíscola's old town is ringed by fortified walls and topped by a castle, with a tight cluster of narrow cobbled streets and whitewashed houses scattered below. The castle was built by the Knights Templar in the 13th century and was the home of Pedro de Luna (the deposed Pope Benedict XIII) from 1411 to 1423.

The old town is as pretty as a postcard and just as commercial, with dozens of souvenir and ceramics shops and clothes boutiques catering to the ascending hordes of tourists. In spite of the growing collection of modern high-rises in the new town, it is a pretty and manageable resort. The tourist office (π 964 48 93 92) is on the beach side of Paseo Marítimo.

The old town walls and castillo are worth exploring. From the latter in particular you have great views over the beach to the north. The beach itself is fine, but those farther north leading to the town of Benicarló are too pebbly to be much fun.

Places to Stay & Eat

The *Chiki Bar (*π *964 48 02 84, Calle Mayor 5)* is the best deal in the old town. Its modern rooms cost 1750/3500 ptas – the doubles have bathrooms. Its restaurant does reasonable set price meals.

Hotel-Restaurante Simo (π *964 48 06 20, Calle de la Porteta 5)*, at the base of the old town, offers rooms with sea views and bathroom ranging up to 5600/7000 ptas in high season.

Paseo Marítimo, the main waterfront promenade, is lined with restaurants that specialise in local seafood (and high prices).

VINARÒS

Vinaròs is a grim working city with a dreary appearance whose only redeeming feature is the sandy beaches.

Near Plaza del Ayuntamiento is the **Iglesia Arciprestal**, an interesting baroque church with a tall bell tower and elaborate main doorway decorated with candy-twist columns. From here, Calle Mayor takes you to the beaches, via an upmarket shopping zone and the Mercado Central.

Places to Stay & Eat

Pensión Casablanca (π *964 45 04 25, Calle de San Pascual 8)*, two blocks north of the tourist office, has presentable budget rooms from 1500/2500 ptas. *Hostal-Residencia El Pino (*π *964 45 05 53)* at No 47 is filled with knick-knacks and memorabilia. There's a cosy guest lounge, and pink and baby-blue rooms will cost you from 2140/3500 ptas.

You have plenty of eating choices on the waterfront, most specialising in seafood.

Inland Valencia

In Valencia the difference between Spanish holiday costa and the interior is crassly marked by a highway. Just head west of the A-7 and you find yourself alone among locals – amazing. The few tourists who venture away from the coast are richly rewarded. The best way to explore the region is with your own transport, although you can reach most of the main centres by bus or train.

Pick up the parchment-coloured series of fold-out map-brochures produced by the Comunitat Valenciana. Available in several languages from provincial tourist offices, they are full of interesting information and anecdotes.

Cycling & Hiking

The area is particularly popular with cyclists (on and off-road) and hikers. Several

VALENCIA

of Spain's long-distance *senderos de Gran Recorrido* (GR) trails pass through, linked to each other by the shorter *senderos de Pequeño Recorrido* (PR). The GR-7 crosses the Els Ports and La Tinença de Benifassá districts, while the GR-10 and GR-36 pass through El Alto Palancia region.

EL MAESTRAZGO

Straddling north-western Valencia and south-eastern Aragón (see the Aragón chapter), El Maestrazgo (El Maestrat in Catalan) is a mountainous territory dotted by ancient pueblos huddling on rocky outcrops, cones and ridges, as if seeking protection from warrior enemies and insulation from the rigours of the area's harsh winters.

One of these pueblos, Sant Mateu, was chosen in the 14th century by the *maestro* (hence the name El Maestrazgo) of the Montesa order of knights as his seat of power.

The area is a world away from the coastal resorts, little visited by foreigners and seemingly full of deep secrets. Some jewels are hidden in here. Get the *Guía de Alojamientos del Maestrazgo* from local tourist offices – it is a complete guide to all the *casas rurales* and other accommodation across the area – in Valencia and Aragón.

Morella

The fairy-tale town of Morella, commanding the southern corner of El Maestrazgo, is an outstanding example of a medieval fortress. Perched on a hill top, crowned by a castle and enclosed by a wall over 2km long, it is one of Spain's oldest continually inhabited towns.

Orientation & Information The town's walls are broken only by the seven entrance gates. Calle de la Muralla runs around the inner perimeter, but the rest of the town is a confusing (if compact) jumble of narrow streets, alleys and stairs leading up to the castle.

The tourist office (☎ 964 17 30 32) is on Plaza de la Puerta de San Miguel, just inside the main entrance gate to the old town.

Things to See Morella's **castillo**, although in ruins, is most imposing. You can almost hear the clashing of swords and clip clop of horses that were a part of life in the fortress. A strenuous climb is rewarded by breathtaking views of the town and surrounding countryside. The castle grounds are open daily from 10.30 am until 6.30 pm (7.30 pm between May and August; 200 ptas).

The old town is easily explored on foot. Three small museums have been set up in the towers of the ancient walls: the **Museo Tiempo de Imagen** has a collection of old black and white photos of Morella (100 ptas); the **Museo Tiempo de Dinosaurios** houses a handful of old bones and a video (in Spanish), but the views from the top are great (300 ptas); and the **Museo Tiempo de Historia** is in three sections devoted to prehistoric relics, the Gothic era and the Carlist Wars (100 ptas).

Morella's major church is the Gothic **Basílica de Santa María la Mayor**, which has two elaborately decorated doorways on the same façade. Inside, the **Museo Arciprestal** (100 ptas) houses a collection of religious artefacts and gold and silver pieces.

Also worth looking out for are the 14th century **Ayuntamiento**, the **Real Convento de San Francisco** and the numerous, impressive manorial houses such as the **Casa de la Cofradía de Labradores** (Farmer's Guild).

On the outskirts of town stand the arches of a 13th century **aqueduct**.

Special Events Morella's major festival is the Sexeni, held every six years (the next is in 2000) in honour of the Virgen de Vallivana. A baroque music festival takes place in August, starring the huge organ in the Basílica de Santa María la Mayor.

Places to Stay *Hostal El Cid* (☎ 964 16 01 25, Puerta de San Mateo 2) has reasonable if drab singles/doubles from 1300/2200 ptas and doubles with bath for 3500 ptas –

VALENCIA

the rooms are heated and the front ones at least have views.

A better bet is the friendly *Fonda Moreno (☎ 964 16 01 05, Calle de San Nicolás 12)* with rustic, quaint doubles only for 2150 ptas.

If you want something more modern, *Hotel La Muralla (☎ 964 16 02 43, Calle de la Muralla 12)* has good rooms with bath from 2800/3500 ptas.

Hotel Cardenal Ram (☎ 964 17 30 85, Cuesta de Suñer 1) is set in a wonderfully transformed 16th century cardinal's palace. The hotel combines the best of the old and new; ancient stone floors, high ceilings and antique furniture with modern bathrooms, TV, phone and heating. Rooms start from 5000/7000 ptas (plus IVA).

Places to Eat The upstairs restaurant at *Fonda Moreno* does a hearty *menú* for 900 ptas (drinks and IVA not included).

Restaurante Casa Roque (Calle de Segura Barreda 8) is one of the best restaurants in town. Regional dishes range from 950 ptas up to 2500 ptas for the house speciality, *cordero relleno trufado* (lamb rolled with truffles). It also offers a four course *menú* for 1500 ptas. You'll need to book on weekends.

Getting There & Away Buses run to Castellón de la Plana, Vinaròs and occasionally to Alcañiz (Aragón).

Morella is beside the N-232 highway: drivers beware in winter as the town is sometimes snowed in for days.

Els Ports

Morella is the ancient capital of Els Ports, the 'mountain passes'. This north-eastern corner of Valencia offers some outstanding scenic drives and strenuous cycling excursions, as well as excellent possibilities for hikers and mountain climbers.

Four kilometres west of Morella at **La Fábrica de Giner**, the *Hotel-Restaurante Fábrica de Giner (☎ 964 17 31 42)* is an old textile factory and village converted into an impressive accommodation complex that includes a swimming pool, walking tracks and a small textile museum. The hotel has modern, stylish rooms from 6000/7500 ptas (plus IVA). On weekends you must take half-board for 8000/11,500 ptas.

Nine kilometres farther west, **Forcall** is a quiet village set at the meeting place of the stony banks of the Río Caldés and the Río Cantavieja. Forcall is the home of the Fiesta de San Antón (aka 'La Santantonada'), held over the weekend closest to 17 January. On opposite sides of Plaza Mayor in the village centre stand two 16th century Aragonese palaces. One has been converted into an elegant hotel, the *Hotel-Restaurante Palau dels Osset Miró (☎ 964 17 75 24, Plaza Mayor 16)*. The rooms retain original features and are good value from 5200/6200 ptas (plus IVA). Half-board (8000/11,500 ptas) is compulsory on weekends.

Nearby, *Mesón de la Vila (Plaza Mayor 8)* has a mock medieval décor with terracotta floors, stone arches and whitewashed walls. The food is good and it offers a filling *menú* for 1300 ptas.

To the north is the tiny whitewashed village of **Villores**, while to the west stands the medieval castle of **Todolella**.

Mirambel

Those who make it to Todolella should go the extra mile (actually 14km) to reach this enchanting hamlet. If you want to see what a small walled medieval town looks like without the usual 20th century add-ons, this is the place. You penetrate 2.5km into Aragón to reach Mirambel, and you are bound to notice the switch in local chat from Catalan to Castellano.

Created by order of the Knights Templar in 1243, Mirambel attained a certain degree of importance, as testified by its several magnificent Aragonese mansions. HQ of the Carlist forces in Valencia, Aragón and Murcia in the 19th century, its population reached the dizzy heights of 950. Today only 150 remain.

You can stay in the modest *Fonda Guimera (☎ 964 17 82 69, Calle de Agustín*

Pastor 28). Singles/doubles with bath cost 2000/3000 ptas. It has a restaurant too.

Santuario de la Balma

For the unbelievers among you, an excursion 12km north of Villores to this sanctuary dedicated to Nuestra Señora de la Balma should be instructive. The extraordinary chapel is set inside the rock face – from which juts out a belfry. Behind the main altar is a forest of offerings to Our Lady, particularly plastic limbs, accompanied by notes of thanks to the Virgin for her intercession in the healing of diseases, operations and so on. Attached to the sanctuary is a bar/restaurant (a scrummy plate of frogs' legs costs 600 ptas).

La Tinença de Benifassà

The seven hamlets clustered in the northern-most reaches of Valencia, often snowbound in winter, have as their focal point the **Monasterio de Santa María de Benifassà**. The convent is still in use, and the nuns open their church to visitors every Thursday between 1 and 3 pm.

A couple of kilometres south-west is **La Pobla de Benifassà**, featuring distinctive local stone houses fronted by timber balconies. On the main street, *Hotel Tinença de Benifassà (☎ 977 72 90 44, Calle Mayor 50)* is set in a restored villa and has 10 rooms with heating, TV and phone. Rooms cost 6500/7800 ptas.

Most of the other villages in the area, including **Bellestar**, **Fredes** and **Coratxá** are uninhabited in winter.

Catí

About 35km south-east of Morella is the well preserved medieval village of Catí, famous for its cheeses.

Up in the mountains 5km away, the tiny spa village of **L'Avellá** consists of a dozen buildings, a 16th century chapel and a plant for bottling the local spring waters. *Fonda Miralles (☎ 964 76 50 51)* is a simple hostal that is open between July and September.

Sant Mateu

Farther east and several kilometres south of the N-232 is Sant Mateu. Its impressive mansions and elaborate façades are reminders of the town's more illustrious past. Bars and cafés surround Plaza Mayor in the centre, while signposts point you to several municipal museums, including the **Museo Paleontológico** and **Museo Arciprestal**.

Sant Mateu's tourist office (☎ 964 41 66 58) is off Plaza Mayor at Calle del Historiador Beti 4.

Places to Stay & Eat The owners of *Bar-Restaurante Moderno (☎ 964 41 62 88)* on Plaza Mayor rent out good budget rooms from 1500/3000 ptas.

There are a couple of other places near Plaza Mayor on Calle del Historiador Beti: *Hotel-Restaurante La Perdi (☎ 964 41 60 82)* at No 9 has modern and comfy rooms with bathroom, TV and heating at 2800/5600 ptas and a restaurant with a good *menú* for 900 ptas.

Set on a rocky hillside overlooking Sant Mateu is the wonderful *Restaurante Mare de Déu*. A monastery until the civil war, it remains an austere complex with a baroque chapel and several rustic dining areas with whitewashed walls, dark timber furniture and tiled floors. Meals are cooked in a huge old wood-fired oven, and you can choose between rice dishes (around 800 ptas) or *carne a la brasa* (chargrilled meats; around 1200 ptas). The restaurant is open for lunch and dinner on Saturday and lunch on Sunday (daily for lunch in summer). From Plaza Mayor in Sant Mateu, face the *pasteleria* sign, turn left and follow the unnamed, tree lined road out of town.

VILAFAMÉS

Vilafamés, a hillside town 26km north of Castellón, is topped by the ruins of a Muslim castle.

Things to See & Do

The **Museo Popular de Arte Contemporáneo**, in the Palacio del Batlle on Calle

VALENCIA

de Arriba, houses an excellent collection of paintings and sculpture. The museum is open weekdays from 11 am to 1 pm and 5 to 7 pm and weekends from 11 am to 2 pm and 4 to 7 pm.

Explore the old town, a cluttered blend of whitewashed houses and civic buildings built from rust red stone. The 18th century **Iglesia de la Asunción** features some unique ceramic artworks. From Plaza de la Sangre, stone steps take you up to the castle, with its rebuilt circular turret and sensational panoramas.

Places to Stay & Eat
Hotel El Rullo (☎ 964 32 93 84, *Calle de la Fuente 2)*, 200m below the museum, has eight rooms with bathroom, lurid bedspreads and great views at 2000/4000 ptas including breakfast. Down the road, you can get a *menú* for 1000 ptas at *Meson El Rullo*.

MONTANEJOS
It's a spectacular drive up to this popular resort town. The road follows the Río Mijares gorges to the town, surrounded by craggy, pine clad mountains. The warm springs of the nearby **Fuente de Dos Baños** and the cool fresh mountain air attract hordes of (mainly Spanish) visitors in summer. The town is plain, but a popular base for hiking, climbing, abseiling and mountain biking.

Places to Stay
Most of the six hotels in town open only in summer and on weekends. The best budget bet is the central *Hostal-Restaurante La Valenciana* (☎ 964 13 10 62) on Avenida de Elvira Peiro, with singles/doubles at 2600/3900 ptas with bath.

Another good option is *Hotel Rosaleda del Mijares* (☎ 964 13 10 79, *Carretera de Tales 28)* on the main road. Open year round, it has comfy rooms with bathroom, TV and heating for 2650 ptas per person.

EL ALTO PALANCIA
Together with nearby Montanejos, the towns along the upper reaches of the Río Palancia make up the 'route of the mountain springs'. Don't go out of your way, but if you happen to be heading along the N-234 (which links Sagunto with Teruel) there are some worthwhile stopovers.

Thirty-three kilometres north-west of Sagunto, **Segorbe** is home to an impressive Gothic cathedral with a tranquil patio. Inside one of the alcoves is the small **Museo Catedralicio**, which is open Tuesday to Sunday from 11 am to 2 pm (200 ptas). And you thought the running of the bulls in Pamplona was interesting. In the first week of September it is run here too – on horseback!

Farther north it's worth detouring just off the highway to **Navajas**, a village shaded by cypress and palm trees and surrounded by almond and olive groves and loads of springs. Navajas has a collection of charming tiled and pastel-painted villas, which were built during the 19th century by Valencian aristocrats.

On the outskirts, the excellent hillside *Navajas Camping Municipal* has modern facilities. *Hotel Navas Altas* (☎ 964 71 09 66, *Calle de Rodríguez Fornos 3)* is a modular hotel with a small pool and rooms with TV and heating from 4300/5500 ptas (plus IVA).

Jerica is dominated by an unusual *mudéjar* tower, but has little else going for it. A couple of kilometres away, **Viver** is more attractive and has a youth hostel and two camping grounds nearby.

REQUENA
On the N-111 highway 71km west of Valencia, Requena is a bustling commercial centre at whose heart lies a tangled little medina established by the Muslims in the 8th century. This is wine country, and local specialties include fruity rosé wines and sparkling *cavas*.

Orientation & Information
The centre is a five minute walk from the train station. The tourist office (☎ 96 230 38 51) is near the entrance to the old town at Calle de García Montés s/n.

Things to See

You enter the medina by the 10th century Muslim fort, or **fortaleza**. The other main monuments may be Christian, but the street plan never completely lost its Oriental touch. Look out for the Gothic **Iglesia de Santa María**, the **Iglesia de San Salvador**, and manorial houses such as the **Casa del Arte Mayor de la Seda** (silk guild house) and **Casa del Corregidor** (mayor's house).

There are also two museums, the **Museo Municipal** and the adjacent **Convento Carmelito**, both near Plaza Consistorial in the new town. Possibly more interesting is what lies below ground level. Plaza de la Villa (Plaza de Albornoz), hides in its intestines a series of *cuevas* (cellars) once used as storerooms and, during war, hideouts. Organise visits at the tourist office.

Special Events

In September, the Fiesta de la Vendimia is one of the more colourful harvest festivals in the area. Nearby Buñol has a rather unusual festival – see the boxed text 'La Tomatina' on this page.

Places to Stay & Eat

Pensión Bar Cantarranas (☎ 96 230 50 80, Calle de García Montés 43) has good rooms at 1500/3000 ptas (2000/4000 ptas with bath). Downstairs is a small bar-restaurant where you can eat well for about 1000 ptas.

Hotel Avenida (☎ 96 230 04 80, Calle de San Agustín 10), just off Avenida del Arrabal, has unexciting rooms with bath and TV from 2000/4000 (plus IVA).

If you have no luck organising a visit to the cuevas, have dinner at the *Mesón La Villa (Plaza de Albornoz 13)* and ask your hosts to let you see their cueva – once used by the local branch of the Inquisition for the cheerful business of torturing heretics.

Getting There & Away

Requena is on the Valencia-Madrid train line. Six to eight trains run daily to Valencia and three to Madrid. For Valencia *cercanías* trains (line C-3; 545 ptas) are cheaper and more frequent.

JÁTIVA (XÀTIVA)

Set at the base of the Serra Vernissa mountain range 50km south of Valencia, Játiva has a fascinating history.

In the nearby Cova Negra (black cave), archaeologists have found relics dating to

La Tomatina

If you happen to be in Valencia during the last week in August, you can participate in one of Spain's messiest and most bizarre festivals. Held in the town of Buñol (about 40km west of Valencia on the N-111 highway and the Madrid train line), La Tomatina is, believe it or not, a tomato throwing festival.

Buñol is an otherwise drab industrial town; its outskirts are overshadowed by a massive smoke-belching cement factory, while the old town is dominated by a crumbling 12th century stone castle.

The festival's origins are obscure, but who cares. And while it mightn't last long, it attracts up to 30,000 visitors to a town that normally has just 9000 inhabitants.

Here's how it goes: just before noon on the day of the festival truckloads of ripe, squishy tomatoes (125,000kg is one estimate) are delivered to (thrown at) the waiting crowd, and for the next hour or so everyone joins in a frenzied, cheerful and anarchic tomato war. The most enthusiastic participants chant *tomate, tomate, queremos tomate!* ('tomato, tomato, we want tomato!')

Apart from being pounded with pulp, you can also expect to have your clothing ripped and torn, be pelted with water bombs and drenched with hoses. Fun, fun, fun! The lunacy takes place in the town's main square and Calle del Cid.

At 1 pm an explosion signals the end, and the well-prepared change into their stash of fresh clothes. Most people come for the day, arriving on the morning train from Valencia and heading back in the afternoon.

VALENCIA

the Mousterian period (30,000 BC), along with a Neanderthal skull. Successive Iberian, Roman and Visigoth settlements were followed by the Muslims, who built Europe's first paper manufacturing plant here in the 11th century.

Játiva's importance grew after the Reconquista and it became Valencia's second largest city. Popes Calixtus III and Alexander VI were born here, but Játiva's glory days ended in 1707 when Felipe V's troops besieged and then set fire to most of the town.

Information

The tourist office (☎ 96 227 33 46) is on the main road at Alameda de Jaime I 50. It is open Monday to Saturday from 10 am to 6 pm and Sunday from 10 am to 2 pm.

Things to See & Do

Consider buying the excellent *Walking Tours Round Xàtiva* book from the tourist office.

Most of Játiva's monuments are uphill from Alameda de Jaime I. The **Museo de l'Almodí** houses a fine collection of archaeological relics and artworks, including the famed portrait of Felipe V that hangs upside down in retribution for his pyrotechnic assault. Between June and September the museum is open daily (except Monday) from 9 am to 2.30 pm. At other times it's open Tuesday to Friday from 11 am to 2 pm and 4 to 6 pm and weekends from 11 am to 2 pm (free).

It's a long climb to the **castillo** on the summit but the views are marvellous. On the way you can visit the 18th century **Ermita de San José** and the **Iglesia de Sant Feliu** (1269), Játiva's oldest church. The castle grounds are open daily (except Monday) from 10.30 am to 7 pm (6 pm in winter; free).

Places to Stay & Eat

Accommodation is limited. *Fonda El Margallonero* (☎ 96 227 66 77, *Plaza del Mercado 2*) is a family-run place with simple rooms from 1400/2800 ptas.

A charming alternative for those with fatter wallets is *Hostería de Mont Sant* (☎ 96 227 50 81, *fax 96 228 19 05*) on the road to the castle. It has seven beautifully appointed rooms with phone, TV and aircon. The views over the town and valley are superb and it has a fine restaurant. Singles/doubles cost 12,500/15,000 ptas (plus IVA) – a little less on weekends.

For snacks and a drink, sit in the courtyard of *Pub Angelus (Plaza del Padre Urios 11)*.

Getting There & Away

The train station and bus station are on Avenida del Cavaller Ximén de Tovia.

Frequent cercanías trains (line C-2) connect Játiva with Valencia (430 ptas) and Alicante (410 ptas); you can also connect with trains to Madrid from here.

Regular buses run to Valencia and Alicante, as well as a couple to Gandia on the coast.

VILLENA

Villena, on the N-330 between Alicante and Albacete, is an upbeat town with a couple of worthwhile attractions, some fine restaurants and swanky bars.

The **Museo Arqueológico**, housed in the former Palacio Municipal (now the ayuntamiento) on Plaza de Santiago, has a small but interesting collection of gold jewellery, Roman ceramics and Iberian artefacts. It's open weekdays from 9 am to 2 pm. On the other side of Plaza de Santiago, the **Iglesia de Santiago** sports a crumbling exterior and impressively restored interior. Perched high above the town, the **Castillo de la Atalya** is splendidly lit at night.

Villena's Fiesta de Moros y Cristianos is held each year from 5 to 9 September.

Places to Stay

Hotel-Restaurante Salvadora (☎ 96 580 09 50, *Avenida de la Constitución 96*) on the main road is a large hotel with pleasant rooms with TV, phone and heating from 3400/5125 ptas.

Fiestas de Moros y Cristianos

In a tradition dating back to the 13th century, more than 80 towns and villages throughout Valencia hold their own Fiesta de Moros y Cristianos (Moors and Christians festival) to celebrate their Arab heritage and to commemorate the Reconquista.

The biggest and best-known festivities are held in Alcoy (Alcoi) on 22, 23 and 24 April. Hundreds of locals dress up in elaborate traditional costumes representing different 'factions' – Muslim and Christian soldiers, slaves, guild groups, town criers, heralds, bands – and march through the streets in spectacular and colourful processions and mock battles.

A wooden fortress is erected in the main plaza, and the various processions converge on the centre from different directions. Tradition dictates who goes where when, but standing in the crowd it all feels incredibly chaotic with processions coming at you from every direction.

It's an exhilarating spectacle of sights and sounds: soldiers clad in shining armour, white-cloaked Muslim warriors carrying scimitars and shields, turban-topped Arabs, scantily clad wenches, brass bands, exploding blunderbusses, fireworks displays and confetti showering down on the crowds from above.

Each town has its own variation on the format of the festival, steeped in traditions that allude to the events of the Reconquista. For example Villena's festival (5 to 9 September) features midnight parades, while in La Vila Joiosa (24 to 31 July) you can see the re-enactment of the landing of Muslim ships on the beaches. Some of the other major festivals are those held in Bocairent (1 to 5 February), Biar (10 to 13 May) and Ontinyent (over four days from the last Friday in August – on the Valencia-Alcoy train line).

ALCOY (ALCOI)

About 50km south of Játiva, this lugubrious town is not the most exciting stop you can make, but you may pass through if you explore the region's central valleys (see later).

In the third week of April, Alcoy's Moros y Cristianos festival (see the boxed text 'Fiestas de Moros y Cristianos' on this page) is one of the region's most colourful events. Otherwise, of vague interest around here are the **Iglesia de Santa María** and **Convento de San Agustín**.

Hostal Savoy (☎ 96 554 72 72, Calle de Casablanca 5) is the cheaper of the two options here. Clean but simple singles/doubles cost 2000/3000 ptas.

Buses run regularly to Valencia and Alicante, and less regularly throughout the surrounding towns from the station on Avenida de Gil Albert, near the northern Játiva town exit. The train station is nearby – five trains run to Valencia.

CENTRAL VALLEYS
Vall de Gallirena & Vall d'Alcalá

A few kilometres north of Alcoy, a judicious right (east) turn at Muro d'Alcoy sends you down winding valley roads past a series of pueblos, mostly of Muslim origin, in the heart of Valencia's cherry growing country – *el corazón de la cereza* as local farmers say. The Vall de Gallinera is especially rich in the red fruit. Villages worth a stop include **Planes**, **Alpatró** and **Benialí**.

The occasional bus passes through between Denia and Alcoy.

A tempting detour about halfway between Muro d'Alcoy and Pego leads down a second valley, the Vall d'Alcalá. The village of the same name is 5.5km down the road, and on the way you'll pass the hilltop **Margarida**, watched over by the ruins of an old castle.

There is a modest camping ground at Vall d'Alcalá, and in Margarida you can try the *casa rural* (☎ 96 551 42 32).

VALENCIA

Guadalest

A still more spectacular route runs east from Alcoy to the coast just south of Calpe. If you can only make one excursion deep into Valencia, this should be it. About halfway along, stop at the old Muslim settlement of Guadalest, dominated by the Castillo de San José. You walk to the castillo through a natural tunnel. This is about the only place in inland Valencia that the tour buses have unfortunately discovered.

ELCHE (ELX)

Just 20km south-west of Alicante, Elche combines the historic with the industrial and is famed for its extensive palm groves, planted by the Muslims. Their irrigation systems converted the region into a rich agricultural district that now produces citrus fruit, figs, almonds, dates and cotton.

Orientation & Information

The town is divided by the Río Vinalopó, with the older town on the east side. Most of the parks and monuments are in the old town. The tourist office (☎ 96 545 27 47) is on the south-eastern corner of the Parque Municipal. It is open weekdays from 9 am to 2.30 pm and Saturday from 10 am to 1.30 pm.

The train and bus stations are both north of the centre on Avenida de la Libertad, 200m apart. From either, exit and take a left, then take the first left down Paseo de la Estación (which leads to the Parque Municipal, tourist office and town centre).

Things to See & Do

Palm groves dominate the city and environs. Some are pretty dishevelled, but the **Parque Municipal** is pleasant to stroll through. Visit the **Huerto del Cura**, a lovely private garden with tended lawns, colourful flowerbeds and a freakish eight pronged palm tree in the centre. The gardens, east of the centre on Calle de la Puerta de la Morera, open daily from 9 am to 6 pm (300/150 ptas for adults/children).

The narrow streets of the old Vila Murada (walled city) are also worth a wander. The baroque **Basílica de Santa María** is used for performances of the Misteri d'Elx (see Special Events), while the east wing of the 15th century **Palacio de Altamira** is home to the small **Museo Arqueológico Municipal**. Farther south on Carrer Major de Raval is the **Museo de Arte Contemporáneo**.

At the L'Alcúdia diggings on the southern outskirts the excellent **Museo Arqueológico** is open Tuesday to Saturday from 10 am to 2 pm and 4 to 7 pm and Sunday from 10 am to 2 pm (October to March from Tuesday to Saturday from 10 am to 5 pm; 400 ptas).

Special Events

The major festival is the Misteri d'Elx, a two act lyric drama that dates from the Middle Ages. It is performed in the Basílica de Santa María on 14 and 15 August (with rehearsals the three previous days). If you miss the real thing, you can see a video in the Museo Municipal de la Fiesta on Carrer Major 27 (about a block west of the basilica). It is shown several times daily (500 ptas). The museum also contains relevant paraphernalia and is open daily from 10 am to 1 pm and 4.30 to 8.30 pm.

Places to Stay & Eat

Budget choices are limited. *Pensión Juan* (☎ 96 545 86 09, Calle del Puente de los Ortissos 15, 3rd floor) is grim but cheap at 1000 ptas per person.

Do yourself a favour – save up, come on a weekend and book into the magnificent *Hotel Huerto del Cura* (☎ 96 545 80 40, Calle de la Puerta de la Morera 14). Set in lush gardens and shaded by huge palms, it has tennis courts, gym, sauna, solarium, a wonderful kidney-shaped pool and spa, bungalow style rooms – you're right in the city centre but it feels like a tropical island. During the week it's popular with business people and pricey at 14,500/17,000 ptas (plus IVA). But on Friday, Saturday and Sunday (and for most of August) the price of a double is often halved. The hotel restaurant, *Els Capellans*, concentrates on local cuisine.

Getting There & Away

Elche is on the Alicante-Murcia train line, with 17 to 24 trains daily to both Alicante (230 ptas) and Murcia (315 ptas). They cost a little more on weekends.

AM Molla has up to 30 buses daily to Alicante (205 ptas) and plenty to Santa Pola (125 ptas).

ORIHUELA

On the banks of the Río Segura, Orihuela is the district capital of the Vega Baja. The old quarter, set at the base of a barren mountain of rock, houses an extensive collection of Gothic, Renaissance and baroque architectural monuments. Their deteriorated appearance, together with dozens of old palm trees, give the town a decadent feel of bygone splendours.

Things to See & Do

Orihuela's old quarter includes half a dozen buildings registered as national monuments. The 16th century **Convento de Santo Domingo**, used as a university until the early 19th century, has lovely Renaissance cloisters inside. Built on the site of a Muslim mosque, the 14th century Catalan-Gothic **Catedral de San Salvador** houses the **Museo Diocesano de Arte Sacra**, with a religious art collection including Velázquez's *Tentación de Santo Tomé* (Temptation of St Thomas).

The **Iglesia de las Santas Justa y Rufina** has a Renaissance façade and a Gothic tower graced with gargoyles. Also noteworthy are the baroque **Palacio Episcopal**, the 14th century **Iglesia de Santiago Apóstol**, and the ruins of a castle dating to Muslim times farther up the mountain.

Places to Stay & Eat

One of the cheapest places is the slightly dodgy *Pensión Versalles* (☎ 96 530 29 61, Calle de San Cristóbal 10), with a couple of rooms in a family apartment at 1500 ptas

per person. It isn't in the most salubrious of areas.

Better is *Hostal-Residencia Rey Teodomiro* (☎ 96 530 03 49, Avenida de Teodomiro 10). Its rooms, with all mod cons, cost from 3500/6000 ptas (plus IVA).

Try some of the distinctive local dishes such as *cocido con pelotas* (meat stew with dumplings) and *arroz con costra* (a baked rice dish topped with an omelette).

Getting There & Away

The train station is a five minute walk from the centre at the end of Avenida de Teodomiro. Orihuela is on the Alicante-Murcia train line, and buses run all over the province.

The Costa Blanca

Alicante and the 'White Coast' are among Europe's most heavily visited regions. If you want a secluded beach in midsummer, stay away. If you are looking for a lively social life, good beaches and a suntan ...

It isn't all concrete and package deals. Although any sense of the fishing villages has long been swamped by the sprawl of resorts, holiday villas and skyscrapers, a few kernels of old towns have survived. Particularly attractive (everything is relative) are Jávea and Altea – and they're better still out of season. During July and August your chances of finding accommodation anywhere are limited if you haven't booked ahead. Out of season many places don't open, but those that do usually have rooms and charge less than in high summer (and Easter).

If you need a break from the coastal pursuits there are some fascinating inland towns worth visiting including Elche, Orihuela, Guadalest, Játiva and Villena (see Inland Valencia earlier).

Regular Ubesa buses between Alicante and Valencia connect all the towns in between. Trains connect Valencia with Gandia and FGV narrow-gauge trains run regularly between Denia and Alicante, stopping at all towns en route.

VALENCIA

GANDIA

Gandia, 65km south of Valencia, is a tale of two cities. The main town is a large and prosperous commercial centre with a rich history, and was once home to a branch of the Borja dynasty (also known as the Borgias).

Four kilometres away on the coast, Playa de Gandia's amazingly long and broad beaches are groomed daily by a fleet of tractors and backed by medium-rise hotels and apartments. It's a popular and predominantly Spanish resort with a reputation for great nightlife.

Information

The Playa de Gandia tourist office (☎ 96 284 24 07), on the waterfront at Paseo Marítimo s/n, is open weekdays from 10 am to 1 pm and 4 to 7 pm and weekends from 10 am to 2 pm. There's another tourist office (☎ 96 287 77 88) opposite the train station in the main town.

Things to See & Do

Gandia's old town has numerous historic monuments and rewards exploration. The main attraction is the magnificent **Palau Sant Duc**, which in the 15th century became the home of Duque Francisco de Borja. Derelict 100 years ago, the palace was purchased by the Jesuits and progressively restored and decorated with a collection of the duke's personal belongings. It is open for one hour tours (250 ptas) on weekdays from 11 am to 5 pm (to 6 pm in summer) and Saturday at 11 am only.

Local authorities have set up an excellent **Ruta Ecoturística Racó del Duc** 'ecotourism route' for walkers and cyclists. The 12km trail follows an old railway line through unspoiled countryside between the villages of Vilallonga (8km south of Gandia) and L'Orxa. A brochure covering the route is available from the tourist offices. Allow three to four hours on foot.

North-west of Gandia is a popular rock-climbing location, the **Penya Roja de Maxuquera**.

Places to Stay

Camping Ros (☎ 96 284 07 70) on Calle de la Armada Española is closest to the beach. **Camping L'Alqueria** (☎ 96 284 04 70) is 1km inland but has a pool in compensation.

The excellent beachfront youth hostel, the **Albergue Mar i Vent** (☎ 96 283 17 48) is 5km south in Playa de Piles. A bus from opposite the train station will get you there. Charges are 900/1100 ptas for juniors/seniors (closed in winter).

El Nido (☎ 96 284 46 40, Calle de Alcoy 22), close to the beach, is a friendly two-storey hostal with bright rooms from 3500/4500 to 5000/7000 ptas and a restaurant specialising in French cuisine (menús range from 1200 to 1500 ptas). We highly recommend this place.

On the beachfront, **Hostal Fin de Semana** (☎ 96 284 00 97, Paseo Marítimo 20) is an attractive little guesthouse with doubles from around 8000 ptas.

The modern **Hotel La Alberca** (☎ 96 284 51 63, Calle de Cullera 8), 500m back, has comfortable rooms from 2800/4500 to 3500/5800 ptas.

If you'd rather stay in the main town, **Hotel Ernesto** (☎ 96 286 40 11, Carretera de Valencia 40) has good rooms with bath from 2500/4000 ptas to 3000/5000 ptas (plus IVA).

Entertainment

There's great summer nightlife at Playa de Gandia, with around a dozen bars including **Paco Paco Paco**, **Mama Ya Lo Sabe** and **Yeyé** clustered around Plaza del Castell, 300m back from the beach. After they close (around 3 am) you can head for one of the discos that go through until dawn: **Coco Loco** is on the corner of Paseo Marítimo and Calle de Galicia.

Getting Around

Buses to Playa de Gandia depart from opposite the train station about every 15 minutes between 6.30 am and 11.30 pm (110 ptas).

DENIA

Denia is a big, popular and pricey resort town dominated by a large boat harbour and topped by a ruined castle. Flebasa Lines office (☎ 96 578 40 11) operates ferry services from here to Palma de Mallorca, Sant Antoni de Portmany and Ibiza City (see the Islas Baleares chapter for more details).

Orientation & Information

The tourist office (☎ 96 642 23 67) is in the town centre and near the waterfront at Glorieta del Oculista Buigues 9. The train station and Flebasa terminal are within 100m of the office.

Places to Stay

Conveniently placed in front of the train station, *Hotel Costa Blanca (☎ 96 578 03 36, Calle del Pintor Llorens 3)* has rooms in high season for 4800/8500 ptas or 7400/10,900 ptas with air-con. Three blocks inland, *Hostal El Comercio (☎ 96 578 00 71, Calle de la Via 43)* is harder to find but better value, offering rooms with bath, balcony and TV for 3000/5500 ptas.

JÁVEA (XÀBIA)

Jávea is worth a visit early in the season, when the sun shines but the masses haven't arrived. This laid back place is in three parts: the old town (3km inland), El Puerto (the port) and the beach zone of El Arenal, lined with pleasant bar-restaurants. If you have wheels, you might go to Cabo La Nao, where the views are spectacular, or Granadella, with its small, uncrowded beach – both are a few kilometres south of Jávea.

There is a tourist office in the centre of El Puerto (☎ 96 579 07 36) at Plaza del Almirante Bastarreche; another (☎ 96 579 43 56) in the ayuntamiento in the centre of town, at Plaza de la Iglesia 4; and one on the beach.

Places to Stay

Camping *Camping El Naranjal (☎ 96 579 10 70)* is well set up and about 10 minutes walk from the beach at El Arenal. Other-

wise try *Camping Jávea (☎ 96 579 10 70)*, run by the same people.

Other Accommodation The pleasant port area has some reasonably priced accommodation. *Fonda del Mar (☎ 96 579 01 17, Calle del Cristo del Mar 12)*, 100m back from the port, has clean singles/doubles for 2000/4000 ptas. The front rooms have sea views.

On the foreshore 200m south, *Hostal La Marina (☎ 96 579 31 39, Avenida de la Marina Española 8)* has bright rooms for 3500/5000 ptas. Doubles with bath and views of the sea cost more.

The large *Hotel Miramar (☎ 96 579 01 02, Plaza del Almirante Bastarreche 12)* has cosy, old-fashioned rooms with bath, TV and phone from 3800/6800 ptas.

Places to Eat

Finding eats on the beach is easy. In the old town, *Tasca Rebotica (Carrer de Sant Bertomeu 8)*, a block from the main church, has good paella and fish from 1100 to 1500 ptas.

CALPE (CALP)

One of the Costa's more bearable seaside resorts, Calpe is dominated by the Gibraltaresque **Peñon de Ifach**, a towering monolith that juts out into the sea. The rock is a natural park and you can follow a popular and strenuous trail to the 332m summit; it takes about half an hour to climb to the top, where you can soak up the great views.

At the base of the rock you can watch the local fish auctions or take a cruise around the bays.

Two large bays spread away from either side of the rock: Playa Arenal on the south side is backed by the old town, while Playa Levante to the north has most of the more recent development.

Information

The tourist office (☎ 96 583 85 32) on Plaza del Mosquit (100m from Plaza de la Constitución) is open weekdays from 10

VALENCIA

am to 1.30 pm and 5 to 8 pm and Saturday from 10 am to 1 pm. There's another tourist office (☎ 96 583 69 20) on Avenida de los Ejércitos Españoles near the base of the rock. American Express is represented by Gandia Travel (☎ 96 583 04 12) on Avenida de Gabriel Miró 25.

Places to Stay

There are a couple of good places to bed down. *Pensión Centrica* (☎ 96 583 55 28) on Plaza de Ifach has cosy, pretty rooms for 1600 ptas per person. A stone's throw from the beachfront, the neat *Hostal Crespo* (☎ 96 583 39 31, Calle de la Pinta 1) has eight straightforward doubles (four with sea views) ranging from 2500 to 4000 ptas.

There's also an excellent youth hostel, the modern *Albergue Abargues* (☎ 96 583 43 96) on Avenida de la Marina on the northern outskirts. It has a pool and is 200m from the beach. During summer it's usually booked out by school groups.

Places to Eat

There are plenty of restaurants, bars and *bodegas* clustered around Plaza de la Constitución and along Avenida de Gabriel Miró. The attractive *Restaurante El Pati* (Avenida de Gabriel Miró 34) has a *menú* for 1700 ptas.

ALTEA

Altea's beaches may be a blend of pebbles, rocks and sand, but the town beats Benidorm hands down when it comes to character (which, admittedly, isn't saying much). With what's left of the old town perched on a hilltop overlooking the sea, Altea is a good place to spend a few days.

The beaches and boat harbour are backed by a pleasant foreshore promenade and a strip of low-key development. Farther back you can explore the upmarket boutiques, antique shops and good restaurants of the whitewashed old town.

Altea's tourist office (☎ 96 584 41 14) is on the beachfront at Calle de San Pedro 9; it is open most days from 10 am to 2 pm and 5 to 7 pm.

Places to Stay & Eat

Pensión Fornet (☎ 96 584 01 14, Calle de Beniarda 1), in the old town, has the distinct advantage of being open all year. The rooms are clean and comfy and start at 4500 ptas for a double (6300 ptas in the high season).

On Plaza de la Iglesia, *Trattoria dels Artistes* is a surprisingly good Italian place. The number of other cute little restaurants hidden away down side streets off the square has mushroomed in the past few years.

BENIDORM

There is a morbid fascination about Tacky Town. If you're thinking about coming out of sheer curiosity – can it really be that bad? – allow us to save you the trip. It's much worse than you could have imagined. The 5km of white sandy beaches (the place's only saving grace) are backed by a jungle of concrete high-rise, and its streets are thronged with pasty tourists toting plastic beach toys.

Despite having been subjected to every derogatory cliché in the (guide) book, Benidorm continues to prosper. Most of the year it's predominantly a haven for middle-aged and elderly English, German, Dutch and Scandinavian tourists, but during summer it becomes one of Spain's premier disco hot spots with a club scene to rival Ibiza's.

The tourist office (☎ 96 585 32 24) is near the waterfront in the old town at Calle de Martínez Alejos 16. American Express is represented by Viajes Alameda (☎ 96 585 15 46), Via de Emilio Ortuno 15.

Places to Stay

Almost everyone here is on a package deal, but if you visit and decide to stay, the following hostales and hotels are all on or near the waterfront in the old town.

Hostal La Santa Faz (☎ 96 585 40 63, Calle de Santa Faz 18) has oldish rooms with bathrooms from 3000/5000 to 5000/7000 ptas – the latter also have air-con, TV and phone. *Hostal Calpi* (☎ 96 585 78 48, Costera del Barco 6) has better rooms, also with bathrooms, and charges around 3000 ptas per person, but in spring and summer you must take half-board (media pensión) – this is 12,000 ptas for a double.

Some of the big hotels are good value out of season. The two-star *Hotel Colón (☎ 96 585 04 12, Paseo de Colón 3)* has rooms with balcony and sea views starting at 4500/7000 ptas with breakfast. *Hotel Bilbaíno (☎ 96 585 08 04, Avenida de la Virgen del Sufragio 1)*, on the beachfront, charges around 7000/12,600 ptas including breakfast.

ALICANTE (ALACANT)

Alicante is a refreshing town with wide boulevards, long white sandy beaches and a number of cultural and historic attractions.

After taking a waterfront stroll beneath the palm trees that shade Explanada de España and enjoying a leisurely drink at one of the open-air cafés, you may well decide to stay the night and experience Alicante's frenetic nightlife.

Orientation

Alicante's waterfront is lined with broad, shady boulevards. Set back from the Mediterranean and clustered around the Catedral de San Nicolás are the narrow streets of El Barrio (the old quarter), where you'll find most of the cheapest accommodation places and the best nightlife. El Barrio is bordered by the Rambla de Méndez Núñez; south-west of here in the newer parts of town are the post office and bus and train stations.

Information

Tourist Offices The provincial tourist office (☎ 96 520 00 00), Explanada de España 2, is open Monday to Saturday from 10 am to 7 pm (8 pm during summer), closing between 2 and 3 pm on Saturday. Another office operates at the airport.

The municipal tourist office next to the estación de autobuses, Calle de Portugal 17 (☎ 96 514 98 20), is open weekdays from 9 am to 9 pm and Saturday from 9 am to 7.30

pm (but only Monday to Friday from 9 am to 2 pm in winter); two others are in the ayuntamiento (☎ 96 514 92 80) and on Plaza del Portal de Elche (☎ 96 514 50 03).

Post & Communications Alicante's main correos, on Plaza de Gabriel Miró, is open weekdays from 8 am to 9 pm and Saturday from 9 am to 2 pm. The post code is 03080. There's a public telephone office in the main estación de autobuses.

Medical Services & Emergency For an ambulance call the Cruz Roja on ☎ 96 525 41 41. The main hospital (☎ 96 590 83 00) is at Calle del Maestro Alonso s/n, well outside the centre. The Policía Nacional can be reached on ☎ 96 514 22 22.

Things to See & Do

The most obvious of Alicante's attractions is the **Castillo de Santa Bárbara**, a 16th century fortress overlooking the city. There is a lift shaft deep inside the mountain that will take you right to the castle (400 ptas return) – the lift entrance is opposite Playa del Postiguet. The castle is open daily from 10 am to 8 pm (October to March from 9 am to 7 pm; free).

Inside the castle the **Museo de las Hogueras** preserves some of the effigies that have been saved from the flames of the Fiesta de Sant Joan (see Special Events later in this section).

The **Colección de Arte del Siglo XX**, on Plaza de Santa María, houses an excellent collection of modern art including a handful of works by Dalí, Miró and Picasso. It is open daily from 10.30 am to 1.30 pm and 6 to 9 pm (October to April from 10 am to 1 pm and 5 to 8 pm), but is closed Monday, Sunday afternoon and public holidays (free).

On the same plaza, the **Iglesia de Santa María** has an elaborate Gothic façade, presently undergoing repairs.

The small **Museo Arqueológico**, in the impressive Diputación Provincial building near the train station on Avenida de la Estación, has well presented collections of ceramics and paintings.

VALENCIA

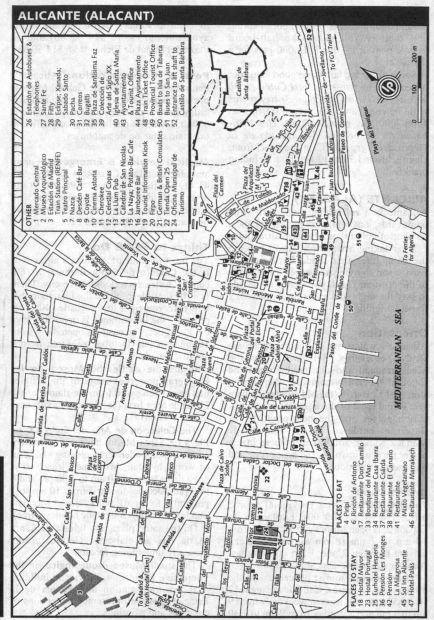

ALICANTE (ALACANT)

OTHER
1 Mercado Central
2 Museo Arqueológico
3 Estación de Madrid
  Train Station (RENFE)
5 Teatro Principal
7 Nazca
8 Desdén Café Bar
9 Coyote
10 Cinema Astoria
11 Cherokee
12 Celestial Copas
13 La Llum Pub
14 Catedral de San Nicolás
15 La Naya; Potato-Bar Cafe
16 Jamboree Bar
19 Tourist Information Kiosk
20 Firpo
21 German & British Consulates
22 Tienda Open 25
24 Oficina Municipal de
  Turismo
26 Estación de Autobuses &
  Telephones
27 Sante Fe
28 Fitty
29 Eclipse; Xanadú;
  Sabado Santo
30 Pacha
31 Correos
32 Bugatti
35 Plaza de Santísima Faz
39 Colección de
  Arte del Siglo XX
40 Iglesia de Santa María
43 Plaza Ayuntamiento
  & Tourist Office
44 Plaza Ayuntamiento
48 Train Ticket Office
49 Provincial Tourist Office
50 Boats to Isla de Tabarca
51 Buses to San Juan
52 Entrance to lift shaft to
  Castillo de Santa Barbara

PLACES TO EAT
4 Pirpi
6 Rincón de Antonio
17 Restaurante Don Camillo
33 Boutique del Mar
34 Restaurante Casa Ibarra
37 Restaurante Csárda
38 Restaurante El Canario
41 Restaurante
  Mixto Vegetariano
46 Restaurante Marrakech

PLACES TO STAY
18 Hostal Mayor
23 Hostal Portugal
25 Eurhotel Hesperia
36 Pensión Les Monges
42 Pensión
  La Milagrosa
45 Sol Inn Alicante
47 Hotel Palas

VALENCIA

Kontiki (☎ 96 521 63 96) runs boat trips most days to the popular Isla de Tabarca. The island has quiet beaches and good snorkelling and scuba diving, plus a small hotel (1700 ptas return).

A huge industrial port and ritzy boat harbour take up most of central Alicante's foreshore. Immediately north is the main city beach of Playa del Postiguet. It's sandy and has been cleaned up in recent years, but gets pretty crowded. You're better off heading farther north to the cleaner and less crowded beaches at Playa de San Juan.

Special Events

Alicante's major festival is the Fiesta de Sant Joan, held over the last week of June. On 24 June Alicante stages its own version of Las Fallas, with extensive fireworks displays and satirical effigies going up in smoke.

Places to Stay – Budget

Camping About 10km north of Alicante on Campello's outskirts, *Camping Costa Blanca* (☎ 96 563 06 70) is 200m from the beach and has a good pool and café, charging 525 ptas per car, person and tent in high season.

Youth Hostel *Residencia Universitaria Albergue Juvenil 'La Florida'* (☎ 96 511 30 44, Avenida de Orihuela 59) is an inconvenient 2km west of the centre and on a busy main road. Apart from having the longest name in Spain, it has good facilities and 204 beds in single and double rooms. Juniors/seniors pay 900/1100 ptas for bed and breakfast.

Hostales & Pensiones There are plenty of cheap hostales in El Barrio – some excellent, some appalling. The old quarter is quaint and charming by day but a little seedy by night. Standards and prices generally rise in the newer parts of town.

The outstanding *Pensión Les Monges* (☎ 96 521 50 46, Calle de Monges 2) is like a boutique hotel; walls hung with tapestries and artworks, a cosy TV lounge and sitting room for guests, and a charming owner. Each of the eight rooms is different, but they all have heating, TV, hair dryers, wash basins, piped music and air-con (the last two are optional). Singles/doubles are from 1900/3500 ptas (2200/3800 ptas with shower or 2800/4500 ptas with bathroom).

Pensión La Milagrosa (☎ 96 521 69 18, Calle de Villavieja 8) has basic but clean rooms and a small guest kitchen, and charges 1500 ptas per person. Some rooms overlook the Plaza de Santa María. It's OK but shouldn't be your first choice.

Hostal Mayor (☎ 96 520 13 83, Calle Mayor 5) has renovated rooms with modern bathrooms at 2800/4500/6000 ptas for singles/doubles/triples (cheaper out of season).

Opposite the bus station, *Hostal Portugal* (☎ 96 592 92 44, Calle de Portugal 26) is a slightly old-fashioned place with clean, spacious rooms from 2200/3400 ptas, or 3500/4200 ptas with bathroom.

Places to Stay – Mid-Range

The three-star *Hotel Palas* (☎ 96 520 93 09) on Plaza de la Puerta del Mar is a rambling place that has seen better days. The quirky, old-fashioned rooms cost 5400/8500 ptas (plus IVA).

A couple of blocks away, *Sol Inn Alicante* (☎ 96 521 07 00, Calle de Gravina 9) is a modern and stylish three-star place with rooms from 8400/9800 ptas. It has cheaper weekend rates.

Also worth considering is *Eurhotel Hesperia* (☎ 96 513 04 40, Calle del Pintor Lorenzo Casanova 33). It's a nice hotel although it isn't close to anything much except the bus station. Rooms are 10,000/11,500 ptas midweek or 6250/7500 ptas on weekends.

Places to Eat

If you're self catering, the huge *Mercado Central* up on Avenida de Alfonso X El Sabio is something of a temple to red meat but also has plenty of fresh fruit and vegies. *Tienda Open 25* is a handy 24 hour store on Calle del Pintor Lorenzo Casanova.

At *Restaurante El Canario (Calle de Maldonado 25)* is a no frills local eatery with a hearty *menú* for 900 ptas. How long since you had goulash? You can get some across the road at *Restaurante Csárda*.

Restaurante Mixto Vegetariano (Plaza de Santa María 2) is a simple low-ceilinged place with vegetarian and meat *menús* at 1000 ptas – you can choose or combine dishes from both.

Real carnivores could try *Restaurante Casa Ibarra (Calle de Rafael Altamira 19)*, which has a set *menú* for 1100. It is one of several budget places around Plaza del Ayuntamiento.

It is unusual to strike good Italian food in Spain, but a rare exception is *Restaurante Don Camillo (Plaza del Abad Penalva 2)*. Pasta dishes range up to 845 ptas.

You can try local seafood specialities at the stylish *Boutique del Mar (Calle de San Fernando 16)*. It offers arroz negro, arroz a la banda or *arroz marinera* (850 to 950 ptas), seafood dishes (750 to 1500 ptas) and the *menú* costs 1500 ptas.

For great atmosphere head up to the *Rincón de Antonio*, on Calle de Rafael in the Barrio de Santa Cruz. Here on the steep stepped lane above Plaza del Carmen is local life – *alicantinos* enjoying themselves on the street.

If you feel like Moroccan food, *Restaurante Marrakech (Calle de Gravina 15)* is not a bad bet, although a tad expensive. Hearty *tajines* (a North African stew) go for 1250 ptas.

Piripi (Calle de Oscar Esplá 30) is the place to go for stylish tapas or fine rice and seafood dishes. Expect to pay about 3500 ptas a head for some of Alicante's best food.

Entertainment

Bars & Discos It has been said elsewhere in this book (and no doubt in others), but does the expression 'wall to wall bars' mean anything to you? The old quarter around the Catedral de San Nicolás is just that, and what follows is but a taster of places where you can eliminate grey matter and/or dance yourself into oblivion. Most of the bars

open until 2 am early in the week and until 4 or 5 am on the weekends.

The *Jamboree Bar (Calle de San José 10)* is a funky stone-walled place with live jazz and blues bands. In Calle de los Labradores are the *Potato-Bar Cafe* and *La Naya*, the latter a cocktail bar with paintings by local artists.

The heavenly (and weird) *Celestial Copas* on Calle de San Pascual has a kitsch collection of religious art/junk and great music. Farther up on Calle de Santo Tomás, look out for *Cherokee* at No 8 and the nearby *Desdén Café Bar*. On the corner of Calle de Montengon and Calle del Padre Maltés, the tiny *La Llum Pub* is a sweatbox dance-bar that goes wild late in the night.

Nazca, on the corner of Calle de Argensola and Calle de Cienfuegos, plays mainly Spanish dance music and has a roof terrace if it's all getting too claustrophobic. If you want to wallow in rock 'n' roll sounds of the 60s and 70s, try *Coyote (Calle de los Santos Médicos 1)*.

The area farther west between Rambla de Méndez Núñez and Avenida del Doctor Gadea is a more concentrated but equally hectic option.

People and pounding music spill out of *Pacha* onto its open-air terrace on Explanada de España. There's more action a block back along Calle de San Fernando. *Santa Fe* on the corner of Avenida del Doctor Gadea is a sophisticated place to kick off the evening. A few steps east down Calle de San Fernando, any pretensions are left behind in a blur of mixed drinks and dancing. *Fitty* at No 57 is happening, and if for any reason it ain't you can try *Eclipse*, *Xanadu* at No 55 or *Sabado Santo* at No 53.

At No 37, the popular *Bugatti* is a slick disco with a dress code and 1000 ptas cover charge. It's open nightly but Monday until dawn (don't turn up before 3 am).

If the average partying age of about 18 is making your grey hair feel luminous – and you happen to like salsa – *Firpo (Calle de San Francisco 28)* might be the place for you.

During summer the disco scene at Playa de San Juan gets thumping. In fact there are dozens of discos along the coast from Alicante to Denia, and FGV's 'night trains' ferry party goers along this notorious section of *la ruta bakalao*. The trains operate nightly during July and August, with services hourly between 11 pm and 7 am. There is a similar bus service (Búhobus) as far as San Juan.

Theatre & Cinema The *Cinema Astoria (☎ 96 521 56 66)* 'mini twin', in El Barrio on Plaza del Carmen, screens v.o. subtitulada films.

Alicante's main venue for the performing arts is the *Teatro Principal (☎ 96 520 23 80, Calle del Teatro 16)*.

Getting There & Away

Air Alicante is the gateway to the Costa Blanca and there are frequent flights (information ☎ 96 528 50 11) to all major centres including Palma de Mallorca, Ibiza City, Valencia, Barcelona and Madrid, as well as to many destinations in Europe.

Bus The estación de autobuses (☎ 96 513 07 00) is on Calle de Portugal. Ubesa has frequent buses north to Valencia (1890 ptas) via the coastal towns along the Costa Blanca including Benidorm (420 ptas) and Calpe (605 ptas). Enatcar handles long-distance hauls to Madrid (five hours; 2895 ptas), Almería (4½ hours; 2550 ptas), Granada (six hours; 3335 ptas) and Barcelona (eight hours; 4590 ptas).

Train Alicante has two train stations. RENFE's Estación de Madrid (☎ 96 521 02 02) is on Avenida de Salamanca. Services include Madrid (four hours; 4400 ptas; seven daily); Valencia (two hours; 1½ to 2500 ptas; five daily) via Villena and Játiva; Barcelona (5½ to six hours; 4600 ptas; five daily); Murcia (1½ hours; 525 ptas); and Orihuela (one hour; 340 ptas). The high-speed Euromed train to Valencia and Barcelona leaves twice daily (see the Barcelona chapter).

RENFE has a booking office in the centre on the corner of Explanada de España and Calle de Cervantes.

The Ferrocarriles de la Generalitat Valenciana (FGV) station (☎ 96 526 27 31) is at Avenida de Villajoyosa 2, on the foreshore at the far end of Playa del Postiguet. Trains operate north along the coast as far as Denia (950 ptas) via Playa de San Juan (110 ptas), Benidorm (405 ptas) and Calpe (600 ptas), with services hourly between 6.15 am and 8.30 pm (see Entertainment earlier in this section for details of summer night trains).

Boat There is a ferry connection (☎ 96 513 00 95) to Oran (Algeria), but until things calm down there you'd be mad to get aboard.

Getting Around

El Altet airport is 12km south-west of the centre. Alcoyana has hourly buses between the airport and the bus station.

SANTA POLA

This modern seaside township sprawls around its harbour, which is home to the local fishing fleet and lined with hundreds of pleasure vessels. You can take boat trips from here across to the popular **Isla de Tabarca**, just 3.5 nautical miles offshore.

Most of Santa Pola's beaches are backed by jungles of concrete, but the sandy **Gran Playa**, **Playa Lisa** and **Santa Pola del Este** beaches are still worth a visit.

In the centre of town on Plaza de la Glorieta, the well preserved 16th century **Castillo-Fortaleza de Santa Pola** fortress stands besieged by 20th century high-rise architecture. Inside there's a sunny courtyard, a bar, a small chapel and the **archaeological museum**, open Tuesday to Saturday from 11 am to 1 pm and 4 to 7 pm and Sunday from 11 am to 1.30 pm (100 ptas).

Information

The tourist office (☎ 96 669 22 76) is at the entrance to town on Plaza de la Diputación (on the northern corner of El Palmeral park). It is open Monday to Saturday from 10 am to 2 pm and 4.30 to 7.30 pm.

VALENCIA

Places to Stay

One kilometre west of town on the C-3317 highway to Elche, **Camping Bahía de Santa Pola** (☎ 96 541 10 12) has a bar-restaurant, pool and shop.

Most of the budget options are clustered in the streets east of the tourist office, about 500m back from the waterfront. The friendly **Hostal Chez Michel** (☎ 96 541 18 42, Calle de Felipe 11) has pleasant doubles for 5300 ptas including breakfast, but in summer it doesn't have singles.

Nearby, **Hostal-Restaurante Picola** (☎ 96 541 18 68, Calle de Alicante 66) is also good, with singles/doubles for 4150/4675 ptas.

Hotel PolaMar (☎ 96 541 32 00), right on the Playa de Levante beachfront, is a big, bland three-star place with rooms for 6900/11,200 ptas (plus IVA) – ask for a room with sea views.

TORREVIEJA

A heavily developed but not completely repugnant resort, Torrevieja has good beaches and a lively nightlife, but you are unlikely to meet many Spaniards here. The tourist office (☎ 96 570 34 33) is centrally located on the waterfront at Plaza de Capdepont. It is open Monday to Friday from 9.30 am to 1 pm and 4 to 8 pm and Saturday from 9.30 am to 12 noon.

Places to Stay

On the main road into town, **Hostal Reina** (☎ 96 670 19 04, Avenida del Doctor Gre-gorio Marañón 22) is friendly, cheap and shabby. Rooms with traffic noise, tiny bathrooms and marshmallow beds (and a few with ocean glimpses) cost 1600/2800 ptas. Forget it in August though.

A better budget bet is **Hostal Fernández** (☎ 96 571 00 09, Calle de Ramón Gallud 16), central and 300m back from the beach. Freshly painted rooms with bath are 3000/6000/7500 ptas.

Near the bus station, **Hotel Cano** (☎ 96 670 09 58, Calle de Zoa 53) has modern rooms with bath and TV for 4200/6000 ptas (plus IVA).

Two blocks back from the tourist office, **Hotel Fontana** (☎ 96 670 11 25, Rambla de Juan Mateo García 19) is a big place charging 5800/11,000 ptas (plus IVA).

Places to Eat

Plenty of restaurants clustered around the waterfront offer cheap meals and international menus. One block back from the beachfront, **Restaurante Vegetariano** (Calle de Pedro Lorca 13) is a little vegetarian haven run by a Spanish-Australian couple. It offers salads and sandwiches (400 to 900 ptas) and good pizzas (around 900 ptas).

Getting There & Away

The estación de autobuses is 500m inland on Calle de Antonio Machado. Enatcar runs buses to Madrid (3580 ptas), Albacete (1610 ptas) and Villena (805 ptas). Autocares Costa Blanca has frequent buses to both Cartagena (475 ptas) and Alicante (410 ptas).

Islas Baleares (Balearic Islands)

Floating out in the Mediterranean, the Baleares (Illes Balears in Catalan) are invaded every summer by a massive multinational force of hedonistic party animals and sunseekers, as well as a minority of quieter species. This is hardly surprising when you consider what's on offer – fine beaches, relentless sunshine, good food and wild nightlife.

What *is* surprising is that, despite all this, the four main islands – Mallorca, Menorca, Ibiza and Formentera – have, to a degree, maintained their individuality and strong links with the past. Beyond the bars and beaches are Gothic cathedrals, Stone Age ruins, fishing villages, spectacular bushwalks, endless olive groves and orange orchards. Tourism hasn't *completely* consumed these islands – yet.

Including all the islets, the islands have a combined area of 5040 sq km and a population of 785,652. Mallorca is by far the largest in area (3640 sq km) and inhabitants (628,116), more than half of whom half live in Palma.

Place names and addresses in this chapter are in Catalan, the main language spoken (with slight regional variations). The major exceptions are Ibiza and Ibiza city: although both are called Eivissa in Catalan, we have used the more commonly recognised Castilian name of Ibiza.

History

Archaeologists believe the first human settlements in the Balearic Islands date from around 5000 BC. An abundance of prehistoric relics and monuments uncovered on the islands show that these communities constructed houses of stone, practised basic agriculture, domesticated animals, performed ritual burials and manufactured pottery, tools and jewellery.

The Balearics were regular ports of call for ancient Phoenician traders. They were followed by the Carthaginians, who founded

HIGHLIGHTS

- Trekking in Mallorca's Serra de Tramuntana mountains
- Palma's enormous cathedral, and the old quarter (Mallorca)
- Scenic drives and small villages along Mallorca's north-west coast
- Sunrise at the Sanctuari Puig de Maria (Mallorca)
- Ibiza's amazing discos and bars
- A *bocadillo completo* at Bar Costa in Santa Gertrudis (Ibiza)
- Formentera's beaches and walking and cycling trails
- Menorca's ancient monuments

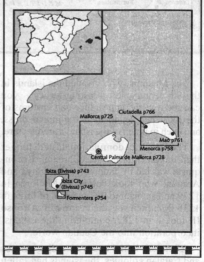

Ibiza city in 654 BC and made it one of the Mediterranean's major trading ports. Next came those compulsive road-builders the Romans, who, in turn, were conquered by the Visigoths.

ISLAS BALEARES (BALEARIC ISLANDS)

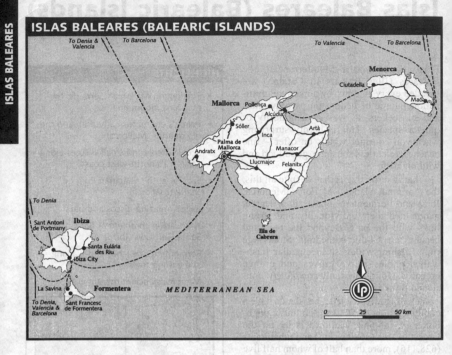

The Muslims, who invaded the islands in the 8th century, left a lasting legacy – you can see it in the appearance and customs of the local people, in their traditional dress, and even in much of the island's architecture.

The Muslim domination lasted longer than three centuries. The Christian Reconquista was led by Jaume I of Catalunya and Aragón, who took Palma de Mallorca in 1229 and sponsored the invasion of Ibiza in 1235. Menorca was the last to fall: Alfonso III took it in 1287, completing the islands' incorporation into the Catalan world.

After their initial boom as trading centres and Catalan colonies, the islands had fallen on hard times by the 15th century. Isolation from the mainland, famines and frequent raids by pirates contributed to the decline. During the 16th century, Menorca's two major towns were virtually destroyed by Turkish forces and Ibiza city's fortified

walls were built. After a succession of bloody raids, Formentera was abandoned.

The Balearics fared poorly in warfare. After backing the Habsburgs in the Spanish War of Succession, Mallorca and Ibiza were occupied by the victorious Bourbon monarchy in 1715. Menorca, on the other hand, was granted to the British along with Gibraltar in 1713 under the Treaty of Utrecht. British rule lasted until 1802, with the exception of the Seven Years War (1756-63), during which Menorca was occupied by the French.

Brief moments of recovery subsequently proved illusory and the rot was only truly stopped from the 1950s with the advent of mass tourism.

Planning

Summer (June, July and August) is the silly season in the Balearics. In July and August you'll have to put up with crowded beaches, higher prices and a shortage of accommodation. On the other hand, you can also expect plenty of sunshine, warm water, great nightlife and opportunities to meet people of all nationalities (especially Brits and Germans).

To avoid the crowds and save money, come in May-June or September-October. Winter (December, January and February) can be a peaceful time but the lack of beach weather keeps most people away and many hotels and other businesses shut between November and April.

Accommodation

Most beds are in resorts tailored to the package tourism industry, but plenty of *hostales* (budget hostels) and hotels cater for independent travellers.

Accommodation on the islands is more expensive than on the mainland, especially in summer, but occasional bargains can be found. Prices in this chapter are for the high season unless otherwise indicated – remember that in the shoulder months of June and September they can drop considerably and are often halved in winter. Lone travellers frequently find they have no choice but to pay for a double in the high season.

Getting There & Around

Air Scheduled flights from major cities on the Spanish mainland are operated by several airlines, including Iberia, Air Europa and Spanair. The cheapest and most frequent flights leave from Barcelona and Valencia.

Standard one-way fares from Barcelona are not great value – hovering around 10,000 ptas to Palma de Mallorca and costing more to the other islands. At the time of writing, however, you could get a fixed-dates return, valid for up to a month, for 13,000 ptas with Spanair. Booking at least four days ahead brought the price down to about 10,000 ptas. In the low season the occasionally truly silly offer, such as 4000 ptas one way, comes up.

From Valencia, Ibiza is marginally cheaper by air (12,450 ptas one way with Iberia) than Palma de Mallorca (13,000 ptas with Air Europa).

When on the islands, keep your eyes peeled for cheap charter flights to the mainland. At the time of writing one-way charters to Sevilla, Granada and Vigo were going for 14,900 ptas, to Málaga for 9900 ptas and to Alicante for 7900 ptas.

Inter-island flights are expensive (given a flying time of less than 30 minutes), with a trip from Palma de Mallorca to Maó or Ibiza costing 7800 ptas (return flights cost double). There are no direct flights from Ibiza to Maó.

Charter flights from Europe are usually sold as a package including accommodation. If you're looking for a cheap deal check with travel agencies, as spare seats on charter flights are often sold at substantially discounted prices. In summer masses of charter and regular flights converge on Palma de Mallorca and Ibiza. From the UK, EasyJet can get you there for a little over UK£100, while German charter airlines like Air-Berlin and LTU shuttle in thousands of passengers from cities all over Germany daily.

If your main goal in Spain is the Islas Baleares, it makes *no* financial sense to fly via the mainland.

Boat In summer 1998 a new service began operations that could revolutionise seaborne transport between the mainland and the islands. Buquebús (☎ 902-41 42 42) is a sleek high-speed ferry that rockets from Barcelona to Palma de Mallorca and back twice daily in just 3¼ hours (compare with other sailing times later). One-way tickets start at 8150 ptas. The only drawback is that you can frequently get cheaper flights (return anyway).

Otherwise, Trasmediterránea (☎ 902-45 46 45 for general information) is the major ferry company for the islands, with offices in (and services between) Barcelona (☎ 93 295 90 00), Ibiza city (☎ 971 31 51 00), Maó (☎ 971 36 60 50), Palma de Mallorca,

(☎ 971 40 50 14) and Valencia (☎ 96 367 65 12). Tickets can be purchased through any travel agency.

Scheduled services are: Barcelona-Palma (eight hours; seven to nine services weekly); Barcelona-Maó (nine hours; two to six services weekly); Barcelona-Ibiza city (9½ hours, or 14½ hours via Palma); three to six services weekly); Valencia-Palma (8½ hours; six to seven services weekly); Valencia-Ibiza city (seven hours; six to seven services weekly); Palma-Ibiza city (4½ hours; one or two services weekly); and Palma-Maó (6½ hours; one service weekly).

Prices quoted later are for one-way fares during summer; low and mid-season fares are cheaper.

Fares. from the mainland to any of the islands are 6660 ptas for a 'Butaca Turista' (seat); a berth in a cabin ranges from 10,960 ptas (four share) to 16,950 ptas (twin share) per person. Taking a small car costs 18,560 ptas or you can buy a 'Paquete Ahorro' (economy package, which includes a car and four passengers sharing a cabin) for 51,440 ptas.

The exception is the Valencia-Ibiza city trip, for which you pay 5725 ptas for a Butaca Turista, from 10,960 ptas (four-share) to 16,950 ptas (twin-share) for a cabin, 15,490 ptas for a small car and 48,370 ptas for a Paquete Ahorro.

Inter-island services (Palma-Ibiza city and Palma-Maó) both cost 2895 ptas for a Butaca Turista, 7645 ptas for a small car and 21,580 ptas for a Paquete Ahorro.

During summer, Trasmediterránea also operates the following 'Fast Ferry' services (prices quoted are for a Butaca Turista): Barcelona-Palma (4¼ hours; 8150 ptas; up to three services weekly); Valencia-Palma (6¼ hours; 8150 ptas; four services weekly); Valencia-Ibiza city (3¼ hours; 6950 ptas; four services weekly); and Palma-Ibiza city (2¼ hours; 5210 ptas; four services weekly).

Another company, Flebasa (☎ 96 578 40 11 in Denia or ☎ 971 48 00 12 in Ciutadella), operates a couple of daily ferries

from Denia on the mainland (between Valencia and Alicante) to Sant Antoni de Portmany on Ibiza and another to Palma de Mallorca via Ibiza city. They also run one between Palma de Mallorca and Vilanova i la Geltrú (just south-west of Sitges on the Catalunya coast). Flebasa has four daily car ferries between Ciutadella on Menorca and Port d'Alcúdia on Mallorca (3750 ptas one way). For details on this company's ferries between Ibiza and Formentera, see the Formentera section.

Cape Balear (☎ 971 81 86 68) operates up to three daily fast ferries to Ciutadella (Menorca) from Cala Ratjada (Mallorca) in summer for 7500 ptas return. The crossing takes 75 minutes.

Mallorca

In 1950 the first charter flight landed on a small airstrip on Mallorca, the largest of the Balearic Islands. By 1995 the number of annual visitors had topped six million – most in search of the three 's's: sun, sand and sea.

There is more to the place. Palma de Mallorca, known as Palma, is the main centre and worth visiting. The north-west coast is a world away from the concrete jungles on the other side of the island. Dominated by the Serra de Tramuntana mountains, it's a beautiful region of olive groves, pine forests and small villages, with a rugged and rocky coastline.

Most of Mallorca's best beaches are on the north and east coasts and, although many have been swallowed up by tourist developments, you can still find the occasional exception.

Orientation

The capital, Palma de Mallorca, is on the southern side of the island on a bay famous for its brilliant sunsets. A series of rocky coves and harbours punctuates the short south-western coastline. Offshore from the island's westernmost point is the large, uninhabited island of Sa Dragonera.

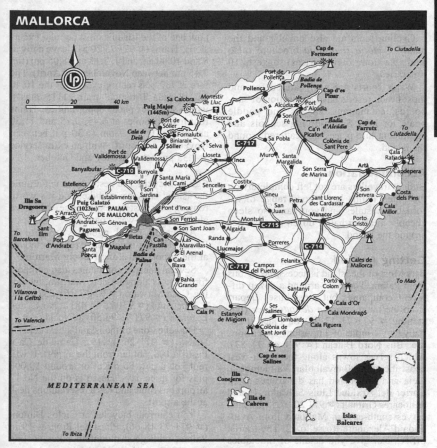

MALLORCA

The spectacular Serra de Tramuntana mountain range runs parallel with the north-western coast and includes the mountain of Puig Major (1445m), Mallorca's highest point. The north-eastern coast is largely made up of two bays, the Badia de Pollença and the larger Badia d'Alcúdia.

The eastern coast is an almost continuous string of sandy bays and open beaches, which explains the densely packed tourist developments. In contrast, most of the southern coast is lined by rocky cliffs and

the Mallorcan interior is largely made up of the flat plain known as Es Pla.

Activities

Mallorca offers some outstanding trekking in the mountainous north-west. Spring is the best time for walking, as summer is often unbearably hot and dry. The tourist office's *20 Hiking Excursions on the Island of Mallorca* brochure outlines some of the better walks and includes a locater map. For more detailed information, see one of the numerous specialist publications, including Lonely Planet's *Trekking in Spain*.

Cycling tours are also popular and the handy *Cicloturismo Guía* brochure (also available from tourist offices) suggests 10 itineraries.

Water sports are well catered for and most beach resorts have a selection of sailboards, catamarans, kayaks and paddle boats for hire. Scuba-diving schools and equipment-hire places are scattered around the island.

Accommodation

Budget travellers are not left completely on the outer. Palma has a good range of affordable hostales and you can also sleep cheaply in about half a dozen monasteries around the island.

Getting Around

Bus Most of the island is accessible by bus from Palma. There are around a dozen different companies but most buses depart from the main *estación de autobuses* (bus station; ☎ 971 71 13 93) on Plaça d'Espanya. A couple of important exceptions are: Bus Nord Balean (☎ 971 42 71 87), which serves towns along the north-west coast including Banyalbufar, Valldemossa, Deià and Sóller and has departures from Carrer del Arxiduc Lluis Salvador 1; and Autocares Grimalt (☎ 971 20 07 58), which serves south-eastern Mallorca from Avinguda d'Alexandre Rosselló 32. The tourist offices can give you details of timetables and fares.

To give you an idea of what to expect to pay, one-way fares from Palma include: Cala Ratjada (890 ptas); Ca'n Picafort (575 ptas); Port d'Alcúdia (580 ptas) and Port d'Andratx (430 ptas). About the dearest single bus ride you can make is from Ca'n Picafort along the coast to Port de Sóller (1190 ptas).

Train Two train lines run from Plaça d'Espanya in Palma – one to Sóller on the north-west coast and the other (☎ 971 75 22 45) inland to Inca.

The Palma-Sóller train line was built in 1912 to replace the local stagecoach, and is now one of the island's most popular excursions. Trains (☎ 971 75 20 51) leave daily at 8 and 10.40 am and 1, 3.15 and 8.05 pm (but 7.45 pm between November and April). The fare is 760 ptas return, except for the 10.40 am 'Parada Turística' train (1115 ptas!), which stops for photo opportunities. Trains return from Sóller at 6.45, 9.15 and 11.50 am and 2.10 and 7 pm (6.30 pm between November and April), with an extra service at 7.35 pm between May and October.

Car & Bicycle The best way to get around the island is by car or bike, and it's worth renting one just to experience the drive along the north-west coast.

About 30 rental agencies operate in Palma. The big league have representatives at the airport and along Passeig Marítim.

Several cheaper companies also compete for business along Passeig Marítim, including Casa Mascaro (☎ 971 73 61 03) at No 9, Iber-Auto (☎ 971 28 54 48) at No 13 and Entercar (☎ 971 73 94 50) at No 11.

However, one of the island's best deals is Hasso (☎ 971 26 02 19), Camí de Ca'n Pastilla 100, not far from the airport. It will rent you a new Ford Ka for around 10,000 ptas for three days. Hasso is on the No 17 airport bus route and has a reservations desk at the airport.

You can rent bicycles at Ciclos Bimont (☎ 971 73 18 66), Plaça del Progrés 19 in Palma, with good mountain bikes costing from 1200 ptas daily. Hostal Apuntadores in Palma also rents out bikes (see Places to Stay under Palma de Mallorca).

Taxi You can get around the island by taxi, but it's costly. Prices are posted at central points of many towns. You're looking at, say, 9000 ptas from the airport to Cala Ratjada.

Boat Palma and the major resorts and beaches around the island are also connected by numerous boat tours and water-taxi services. The tourist office's *Excursiones En Barca* brochure details some of these.

PALMA DE MALLORCA

Palma de Mallorca is the islands' only true city, with some 323,000 inhabitants. But people who arrive here expecting a colourless concrete jungle are often pleasantly surprised. The capital is an agreeable spot to explore for a day or two before you head off around the island.

Central Palma's old quarter is an attractive blend of tree-lined boulevards and cobbled laneways, Gothic churches and baroque palaces, designer bars and slick boutiques. It's a stylish city that buzzes by day and sizzles by night.

That's the good news. The bad news is that it's also crammed to the hilt with tourists and tacky souvenir shops. And you'll have to take a bus to get to the beaches, where you'll discover the endless sprawl of high-rise development that has engulfed the bay.

Orientation

Central Palma stretches from the harbour to Plaça d'Espanya, home to the train and bus terminals and the airport bus stops here too. It also has a tourist office and frequent buses run to the central Plaça de la Reina (otherwise it's about a 20 minute walk).

From the harbour and ferry terminals, Avinguda d'Antoni Maura runs north up to Plaça de la Reina and through the old quarter. On the western side is Palma's main restaurant and nightlife zone, while on the eastern side are the Palau de l'Almudaina and the *catedral* (cathedral). The broad boulevard of Passeig d'es Born continues north up to Plaça del Rei Joan Carles I; Avinguda de Jaume III, which runs westwards from here, is the heart of the commercial district. Farther east is the large open space of Plaça Major, from where another wide boulevard, Passeig de la Rambla, continues north-westwards.

Information

Tourist Offices The main tourist office (Turisme; ☎ 971 72 40 90) can be hard to find: it's in a pedestrian walkway just off the north-eastern end of Carrer del Conquistador at Carrer de Sant Domingo 11. It is open weekdays from 9 am to 8.30 pm and Saturday from 9 am to 1 pm.

The convenient office on Plaça d'Espanya (☎ 971 71 15 27) is open weekdays from 9 am to 8 pm and Saturday from 9 am to 1 pm. There are other offices at Plaça de la Reina 2 (☎ 971 71 22 16) and the airport.

Of the many tourist mags on sale, perhaps *Mallorca Tourist Info* (650 ptas at newsstands) is the most useful, with town maps for places all over the island and a few helpful insights.

Foreign Consulates Numerous countries maintain consular agencies here. See the Embassies & Consulates section in the Facts for the Visitor chapter.

Money You'll find plenty of banks on Avinguda de Jaume III and Passeig d'es Born. American Express has an office (☎ 971 72 23 44) at Avinguda d'Antoni Maura 10.

Post & Communications Palma's *correos* (post office; postcode 07080) is at Carrer de la Constitució 6. There is a phone office marked Teléfonos on Carrer de Paraires. It is open daily from 9 am to 8 pm.

Bookshop Book Inn is a good English-language bookshop just off Passeig de la Rambla at Carrer dels Horts 22.

Laundry There are no decent laundrettes in central Palma, so unless your hostal has washing facilities you might have to hike across to Fast Laundry (☎ 971 45 46 14) at Avinguda de Joan Miró 5.

Medical Services & Emergency The main Hospital General (☎ 971 72 84 84) is up by the Jardi Botanic. The general emergency number is ☎ 112. Otherwise you can call an ambulance on ☎ 061 or ☎ 971 73 66 94, and the police on ☎ 091.

CENTRAL PALMA DE MALLORCA

Catedral

Palma's enormous cathedral (or La Seo) is often likened to a huge ship moored at the city's edge. Construction work on what had been the site of the main mosque started in 1230 but wasn't completed until 1600. This awesome structure is predominantly Gothic, apart from the main façade (replaced after an earthquake in 1851) and parts of the interior (renovated in *modernista* style by Antoni Gaudí at the beginning of the 20th century).

Entry is via a small, three-room museum, which holds a rich collection of religious artwork and precious gold and silver effects, including two amazing candelabras.

The cathedral's interior is stunning in its sense of spaciousness, with a series of narrow columns supporting the soaring ceiling and framing three levels of elaborate stained-glass windows. The front altar's centrepiece, a twisting wrought-iron sculpture suspended from the ceiling and

CENTRAL PALMA DE MALLORCA

PLACES TO STAY

8	Hotel Barceló Cannes
9	Hotel Palladium
15	Pensión Costa Brava
16	Hostal Monleon
17	Sol Inn Jaime III
19	Hotel Saratoga
21	Hotel Residencia Almudaina
22	Hotel Born
25	Hostal Brondo
29	Hostal Pons
31	Hotel San Lorenzo
40	Hostal Apuntadores
41	Hostal Ritzi
55	Hotel Palacio Ca Sa Galesa

PLACES TO EAT

7	Restaurant Celler Sa Premsa
23	La Bodeguilla
28	Bon Lloc
30	Bar Martín
33	Vecchio Giovanni; Abaco

36	Taberna de la Boveda
38	Mario's Cafe
46	Restaurant Parlament
49	Casa Julio
50	Restaurante S'Impremta

OTHER

1	Irish Consulate
2	Bus to Airport
3	Train Stations (to Sóller & Inca)
4	Estación de Autobuses & Airport Bus
5	EMT Information
6	Tourist Office
10	Hospital General
11	Església de Santa Magdalena
12	Book Inn
13	Dutch Consulate
14	Mercat de l'Olivar
18	US Consulate
20	El Corte Inglés

24	Teatro Principal
26	Casal Solleric
27	Taxi Stand
32	Cafè-Bar Barcèlona
34	Sa Llotja Cafè
35	La Llotja
37	Gotic; Xim's Bar
39	American Express
42	German Consulate
43	Tourist Office (Turisme)
44	Main Correos
45	Telephones (Teléfonos)
47	Main Tourist Office (Turisme)
48	Ajuntament
51	Iglésia de Santa Eulalia
52	Basílica de Sant Francesc
53	Banys Àrabs
54	Museu de Mallorca
56	Museu Diocesà
57	Catedral
58	Palau de l'Almudaina
59	Taxi Stand

periodically lit with fairy lights, has been widely acclaimed, mainly because it was designed by Gaudí. Some think it looks awkward and out of place. The cathedral and museum are open weekdays from 10 am to 6 pm (10 am to 3 pm between November and March) and Saturday from 10 am to 2 pm. Entry to the museum is 400 ptas.

Palau de l'Almudaina

In front of the cathedral stands the Palau de l'Almudaina, a Muslim castle converted into a residence for the Mallorcan monarchs at the end of the 13th century. It is still occasionally used for official functions when King Juan Carlos is in town, but at other times you can join the hordes and wander through an endless series of cavernous and austere stone-walled rooms and inspect a collection of portraits of Spanish monarchs, Flemish tapestries and antique furniture. The palace is open weekdays from 10 am to 7 pm (10 am to 2 pm and 4 to 6 pm between October and March) and Saturday from 10 am to 2 pm (400 ptas, students 200 ptas).

Museu de Mallorca

A far more interesting way to spend your time and money is to visit the Museu de Mallorca at Carrer de la Portella 5. This converted 15th century palace holds an impressive collection of archaeological artefacts, religious art, antiques and ceramics. Upstairs there is a great portrait gallery of local identities and painters. Opening hours are Tuesday to Saturday from 10 am to 2 pm and 4 to 7 pm and Sunday from 10 am to 2 pm (300 ptas, students 150 ptas).

Banys Àrabs

The Arab baths, near the Museu de Mallorca, are the only extant monument to the Muslim domination of the island. All that remains are two small underground chambers, one of which has a domed ceiling supported by columns. Interestingly, each of the columns is topped by a different capital: the Muslims were great recyclers and the capitals came from demolished Roman buildings. The adjacent courtyard is pleasant. The baths are open daily from 9 am to 8 pm (150 ptas).

Museu Diocesà

Palma's Museu Diocesà, close to the cathedral (and signposted from the exit), houses a collection of religious art including paintings, ceramics and artefacts.

La Llotja

This gorgeous Gothic building, opposite the waterfront on Passeig de Sagrera, was built as a merchants' stock exchange and is now used for exhibitions. It's open Tuesday to Saturday from 11 am to 2 pm and 5 to 9 pm and Sunday from 11 am to 2 pm.

Casal Solleric

This excellent art gallery at Passeig d'es Born 27 has a good café attached. It's open from 10.30 am to 1.45 pm and 5 to 8.30 pm (closed Monday and Sunday afternoon; free).

Churches

Two of Palma's oldest churches are Església de Santa Eulalia and the nearby Basílica de Sant Francesc. The latter was begun in 1281 in Gothic style and its baroque façade was completed in 1700. Inside are the tomb of and monument to the 13th century scholar Ramon Llull, while at the front of the church is a statue of Junípero Serra, the Franciscan missionary who founded many missions in California.

Other Attractions

On the western side of the city, Poble Espanyol is a copy of the village of the same name in Barcelona. It displays replicas of famous monuments and other buildings representative of a variety of Spanish architectural styles, not to mention souvenir shops galore. Farther south, the circular Castell de Bellver is an unusual 14th century castle set in pleasant parklands.

Also worth visiting is the Fundació Pilar i Joan Miró, at Carrer de Joan de Saridakis 29 in Cala Major (about 4km south-west of the city centre). Housed in the artist's Palma studios, it exhibits a permanent collection of his works stored here at the time of his death. There are also temporary exhibitions and a shop selling Miró souvenirs, prints etc. It's open Tuesday to Saturday from 10 am to 7 pm (11 am to 6 pm during winter) and Sunday from 11 am to 3 pm (675 ptas).

Places to Stay

Central Palma is by far the best area to stay in. As well as being the oldest and most interesting part of the city, most of the major points of interest are within walking distance and the old quarter hosts Palma's best nightlife and eateries.

Avoid the string of glossy tourist hotels around the waterfront west of the centre: they're a long way from anything (except each other) and filled with package tourists.

Places to Stay – Budget

Nothing seems to have changed at *Hostal Pons* (☎ *971 72 26 58, Carrer del Vi 8*) since the 1880s. The downstairs chambers are cluttered with antiques and artworks, and the quaint bedrooms all have timber bedsteads and rickety tiled floors. Amid such charm you can almost overlook the spongy beds and queues outside the (solitary) bathroom. Singles/doubles/triples cost 2000/4000/6000 ptas.

If you want somewhere more contemporary, *Hostal Apuntadores* (☎ *971 71 34 91, Carrer dels Apuntadors 8*) is excellent. Singles/doubles start at 2200/3700 ptas; doubles with private shower are 4200 ptas. Next door, the English-run *Hostal Ritzi* (☎ *971 71 46 10*) has good security and comfortable singles/doubles at 2300/4200 ptas with shower or doubles with shower/bath for 5000 ptas. There are laundry and kitchen facilities and satellite TV in the lounge.

Hostal Monleon (☎ *971 71 53 17, Passeig de la Rambla 3*) is a big old place with dim rooms from 2200/4000 ptas (2500/4300 ptas with private shower and 2800/4700 ptas with full private bathroom).

Pensión Costa Brava (☎ *971 71 17 29, Carrer de Ca'n Martí Feliu 16*) is a backstreet cheapie with reasonable rooms from 1300/2300 ptas. On the downside, this area is somewhat seedy at night. *Hostal Brondo*

(☎ *971 71 90 43, Carrer de Ca'n Brondo 1)* is in a much better location, just off Plaça del Rei Joan Carles I . It has 10 clean rooms with bathrooms, although they're somewhat overpriced at 5000/6000 ptas (try haggling!).

Palma's youth hostel, the *Albergue Residencia d'Estudiantes* (☎ *971 26 08 92),* is at Carrer de la Costa Brava in El Arenal, a crowded and heavily developed beach suburb 11km east of the centre. It is open from June to September only.

Places to Stay – Mid-Range
Hotel Barceló Cannes (☎ *971 72 69 43, Carrer del Cardenal Pou 8),* close to Plaça d'Espanya, is an unexciting modern two-star place with rooms from 5000/7000 ptas (plus IVA) in the high season.

The superb *Hotel Born* (☎ *971 71 29 42, Carrer de Sant Jaume 3),* in the heart of the city, is set in an 18th century palace. The rooms combine elegance and history with all the mod cons. B&B rates for single rooms in the high season range from 6000 to 8500 ptas (from 9000 to 13,000 ptas for doubles).

Another good bet is the *Hotel-Residencia Almudaina* (☎ *971 72 73 40, fax 971 72 25 59, Avinguda de Jaume III 9).* It's an oldish hotel that was renovated in 1992. All rooms have air-con, heating, TV and phone; some have sea views. Rates start from 5500/10,750 ptas (plus IVA), including breakfast.

Three modern mid-range hotels line Passeig de Mallorca. They mainly cater to business clients. The best is *Hotel Saratoga* (☎ *971 72 72 40)* at No 6, with 187 stylish rooms, two pools, a restaurant, guest parking etc. Rooms start from 8500/12,900 ptas (plus IVA) in the high season. At No 14, the refurbished *Sol Inn Jaime III* (☎ *971 72 59 43)* charges from 10,900/ 13,100 ptas (plus IVA), while the impersonal *Hotel Palladium* (☎ *971 71 28 41)* at No 40 has similar prices.

Places to Stay – Top End
If you're lucky enough to get a booking and be able to afford it, stay at *Hotel San*

Lorenzo (☎ *971 72 82 00, fax 971 71 19 01, Carrer de Sant Llorenç 14)* in the old quarter. The hotel is in a beautifully restored 17th century building and has its own bar, dining room and rooftop terrace with swimming room. There are just six rooms and prices range from 14,000/17,000 to 29,000/31,000 ptas plus IVA.

The other class act in town is *Hotel Palacio Ca Sa Galesa* (☎ *971 71 54 00, fax 971 72 15 79, Carrer de Miramar 8).* It is an enchanting 16th century mansion that has been tastefully turned into a luxury hotel. It has five doubles and two singles arranged around a cool patio garden, which cost up to 28,000/32,500 ptas.

Places to Eat
For Palma's best eateries, wander through the maze of streets between Plaça de la Reina and the port. Carrer dels Apuntadors is lined with restaurants and should have something to suit everyone, including seafood, Chinese, Italian – heck, there's even a few Spanish restaurants along here! Around the corner at Carrer de Sant Joan 3 is the deservedly popular *Vecchio Giovanni.* At *Mario's Café* on Carrer de la Mar, you can have pizza or pasta from 700 ptas.

The tourist restaurants along Avinguda d'Antoni Maura (opposite the Palau de l'Almudaina) are all pretty tacky. You'll know you're in the 'Danger – Insipid and Overpriced Food' zone when you start seeing those prepared platters that show you what your meal will look like.

Just off Plaça de la Llotja, *Taberna de la Boveda* is a spacious tavern-restaurant with excellent food, reasonable prices and a lively atmosphere. For starters try the delicious *pa amb oli* – bread smeared with tomato and olive oil and topped with your choice of anchovies (1100 ptas), chorizo or cheese (800 ptas).

For a simple cheap meal with the locals, head for *Bar Martín (Carrer de la Santa Creu 2).* There's a no-nonsense set *menú* for 850 ptas.

Restaurant Parlament (Carrer del Conquistador 11), beside Palma's parliament building, has a gracious Victorian-era dining room with soaring ceilings and gilt-framed artworks. Main courses range from 950 ptas (roast chicken) to 2525 ptas (Chateaubriand).

There are a couple of good places over near Plaça de Santa Eulalia, both with cheap *menús*: the excellent **Casa Julio** *(Carrer de la Previsió 4)* specialises in local rice dishes and has great home-style cooking. It's the sort of place people keep coming back to once they've found it (it's open for lunch only, from Monday to Saturday). Nearby, **Restaurante S'Impremta** *(Carrer d'en Morey 4)* is a friendly little bar-eatery that also offers a choice between a *menú* and ordering à la carte – try the grilled sardines. **Es Cantó de S'Arc** at No 6 does a mix of local and Cuban dishes in a subdued and intimate atmosphere for moderate prices.

The rustic **Restaurant Celler Sa Premsa** *(Plaça del Bisbe Berenguer de Palou 8)* is something of a local institution, and a visit here is almost obligatory. It's a cavernous tavern filled with huge old wine barrels and has walls plastered with faded bullfighting posters. The food is hearty but basic and the set *menú* costs 1075 ptas (plus IVA). It closes on Sunday.

La Bodeguilla *(Carrer de Sant Jaume 1)* is a stylish cellar-bar cluttered with wine bottles and strings of garlic. The specialities are 'La Picada', tapas-style dishes such as *morcillo de cebolla* (black pudding with onion) and *gambas al ajillo* (garlic prawns).

For vegetarian food, try **Bon Lloc** *(Carrer de Sant Feliu 7)*.

Entertainment

The old quarter is the city's most vibrant nightlife zone. Particularly along the narrow streets between Plaça de la Reina and Plaça de la Drassana, you'll find a huge selection of bars and pubs ranging from flashy tourist haunts to stylish bodegas. For complete info on what's happening in Palma and around the island, pick up a copy of the weekly *Guía del Ocio* (200 ptas).

Abaco (Carrer de Sant Joan 1), behind a set of ancient timber doors, is the bar of your wildest dreams (with the drinks bill of your darkest nightmares). Inside, a Mallorcan patio and candle-lit courtyard are crammed with elaborate floral arrangements, cascading towers of fresh fruit and bizarre artwork, and bow-tied waiters fulfil your wishes while classical music soothes your ears. It ain't cheap – fruit cocktails are 900 ptas and alcoholic cocktails and glasses of champers cost up to 2000 ptas – but if your pocket can bear a splurge it's a great experience.

Plenty of watering holes line Carrer dels Apuntadors. The atmospheric **Café-Bar Barcelona** at No 5 has live jazz and soul most nights in its somewhat cramped upstairs bar.

If you just want a quiet drink there are several stylish bars on Plaça de la Llotja. **Gotic** and **Xim's Bar** are both fronted by rows of outdoor tables, while on the opposite corner is the smooth and popular **Sa Llotja Café**.

Palma's other supposed nightlife centre is way over on the western side of the harbour, around Avinguda de Joan Miró and Plaça de Gomila. It's actually a tremendously unexciting area that consists of a string of karaoke bars, music pubs, flamenco shows and, along S'Aigo Doka, a couple of topless bars.

You may find more life down on the waterfront on Passeig Marítim – many of the big tourist hotels along here have their own bars and discos.

Getting There & Away

The San Joan airport (☎ 971 78 90 00) is about 10km east of Palma. Iberia has an office (☎ 971 72 43 49) in Palma at Passeig d'es Born 10. Air Europa also has an office on Passeig d'es Born at No 24 (☎ 971 17 81 00). Spanair, out at the airport, is on ☎ 971 74 50 20.

Trains and buses to other parts of the island depart from terminals at or near Plaça d'Espanya (see the earlier Mallorca Getting Around section for details).

Getting Around

Bus If you're travelling by air, bus No 17 runs every half-hour between the airport and Plaça d'Espanya in central Palma (30 minutes; 290 ptas one way). Alternatively, a taxi will cost around 2000 ptas.

From the ferry terminal, bus No 1 runs around Passeig Marítim and then left up Avinguda d'Antoni Maura into central Palma.

EMT (☎ 971 29 57 00) runs some 22 local bus services around Palma and its bay suburbs. Single trip tickets cost 175 ptas, or you can buy a 10-trip card for 1500 ptas at the EMT information booth on Plaça d'Espanya.

Taxi A couple of handy ranks for the city's characteristic black and cream coloured cabs have been marked on the map. Otherwise you can call ☎ 971 75 54 40.

SOUTH-WEST COAST

A freeway skirts around the Badia de Palma towards Mallorca's south-west coast. Along the way you pass the resorts of Cala Major, Illetes and Palma Nova, which are basically a continuation of Palma's urban sprawl. From the inland town of Andratx, two turn-offs lead down to the coast: one to Port d'Andratx, the other to Sant Elm.

Port d'Andratx

Port d'Andratx is a glamorous little town set on low hills surrounding a narrow bay. The main road around the waterfront is lined with upmarket seafood restaurants, many overlooking the harbour.

Several dive schools are based here and you can rent boats and scuba-diving equipment at numerous outlets. You can also take boat trips around to Sant Elm and the island of Sa Dragonera.

One kilometre south, the **Art Forum** (signposted from Port d'Andratx as 'Cultural Centre') is an interesting series of stone buildings on a hillside above the bay of Cala Llamp. The complex includes apartments, a pool, café and restaurant, and an open-air art gallery and cinema. The owners

hail it as a 'mystic synthesis among nature, humanity and Art ...'. It's worth a look despite the pretentiousness.

Places to Stay On the waterfront, *Restaurante Las Palmeras* (☎ 971 67 20 78, Avinguda de Mateo Bosch 12) rents out good upstairs rooms with singles/doubles from 2500/4600 ptas. Some of the doubles have harbour views and shower.

A couple of hundred metres back from the harbour, *Hostal-Residencia Catalina Vera* (☎ 971 67 19 18, Carrer de Isaac Peral 63) is a lovely guesthouse retreat with rooms set around a tranquil garden courtyard. B&B starts from 4200/6000 ptas.

Places to Eat There's no shortage of good seafood eateries along the waterfront. These places have terrific outlooks but charge accordingly. If you're after somewhere more affordable you could try *Restaurante Es Porteño (Carrer de Isaac Peral 58)*, a couple of blocks inland, which has a lunch *menú* at 900 ptas.

Sant Elm

The small seaside township of Sant Elm is a popular destination for day trips from Palma. The last part of the drive across from Andratx is a spectacular climb through attractive hills. If you'd rather walk this section, take a bus to Andratx. Walk number two on the *20 Hiking Excursions on the Island of Mallorca* brochure, available from most tourist offices on the island, starts from here and takes you to the coast via the village of S'Arracó and a ruined 16th century castle.

Sant Elm's sandy beach is pleasant but can get crowded. Just offshore is a small rocky islet – within swimming distance if you've been in training. Farther north there's a small dock from where you can join a glass-bottomed boat trip or take a cruise across to the imposing and uninhabited island of **Sa Dragonera**, which is criss-crossed by good hiking trails. The *Crucero Margarita* (☎ 971 47 04 49) does daily cruises to the island (1100 ptas) and runs a service between Sant Elm and Port d'Andratx (700 ptas).

Places to Stay Several possibilities line the waterfront. *Hotel Aquamarin (☎ 971 23 91 05, Carrer de Cal Conis 4)*, a modern, circular six-storey hotel, charges 3728/7100 ptas for B&B.

Places to Eat Most of the restaurants along the main foreshore road specialise in local seafood and are pricey. At the nondescript *Bar Restaurante (Avinguda del Rei Jaume I 14)*, opposite the beach, you can get a limited but decent *menú del día* for 1000 ptas.

NORTH-WEST COAST & SERRA DE TRAMUNTANA

Dominated by the rugged Serra de Tramuntana mountain range, Mallorca's north-west coast and its hinterland make up 'the other Mallorca'. No sandy beach resorts here. The coastline is rocky and largely inaccessible, the towns and villages are mostly built of local stone (as opposed to concrete) and the mountainous interior is much loved by trekkers for its beautiful landscapes of pine forests, olive groves and spring wildflowers.

The main road through the mountains (the C-710) starts at Andratx and runs roughly parallel to the coast to Pollença. It's a stunning scenic drive and a popular cycling route, especially during spring, when the muted mountain backdrop of browns, greys and greens is splashed with the bright colours of yellow wattles and blood-red poppies. Plenty of *miradores* (lookout points) recommend themselves as stops to punctuate the trip. Unfortunately the trip can be a slow-going traffic nightmare during late spring and summer.

From Andratx the C-710 twists and turns as it climbs into the mountains. It then skirts along the top of the mountain ridges, offering tantalising glimpses of the distant deep blue sea, before finally meeting the coast.

Estellencs

Estellencs is a picturesque village of stone buildings scattered around the rolling hills below the Puig Galatzó (1025m) peak. It's a popular base for hikers and cyclists or for simply escaping Palma and relaxing. A rugged walk of about a kilometre leads down to the local 'beach', a rocky cove with crystal-clear water.

Places to Stay & Eat The popular and stylish *Hotel Maristel (☎ 971 61 85 29)* has comfortable rooms with all the mod cons, as well as a pool and a restaurant with fine views from its outdoor terrace. Singles/doubles cost 6435/9000 ptas with breakfast.

Otherwise, the owner of *Pizzeria Giardini (☎ 971 61 85 96)* has four rooms to rent out. He charges 2500 to 3000 ptas per person: the price varies, depending on the time of year and for how long you're staying.

Estellencs is also home to the excellent *Restaurant Son Llarg (☎ 971 61 85 64)*, which specialises in *cuina mallorquina* (Mallorcan cuisine). Main courses such as *faroana amb salsa de prunes* (guinea fowl in plum sauce) or *calamars amb salsa de ceba* (squid casserole Mallorcan-style) cost up to 2000 ptas.

Banyalbufar

Farther north, Banyalbufar is slightly larger than Estellencs but similarly positioned high above the coast. Surrounded by steep, stone-walled terraces carved into the hillside, the town is home to a cluster of bars and cafés and three upmarket hotels.

Places to Stay & Eat Fronted by a traditional Mallorcan patio, the family-run *Hotel Baronia (☎ 971 61 81 46)* has 36 modern rooms with fine views and a great cliff-side swimming pool. It has doubles with breakfast for 7240 ptas or with media pensión for 10,900 ptas.

Hotel Mar i Vent (☎ 971 61 80 00) has a similar setup but is more formal and a bit more expensive, with B&B at 8700/11,500 ptas for singles/doubles.

Valldemossa

Valldemossa is an attractive blend of tree-lined streets, old stone houses and impressive new villas. It owes most of its fame to the fact that the ailing composer Frédéric Chopin and his lover George Sand spent their 'winter of discontent' here in 1838-39.

They stayed in the **Cartuja de Valldemossa**, a monastery that was turned into rental accommodation after its monks were expelled in 1835. Their stay wasn't an entirely happy experience. Sand later wrote *Un Hiver à Menorque* (Winter in Mallorca), which, if nothing else, made her perennially unpopular with Mallorcans (although you'll find copies of it at some souvenir stands).

Tour buses and day-trippers now arrive in droves to visit the monastery. It's a beautiful building with lovely gardens and fine views. In the couple's former quarters are Chopin's piano (which, due to shipping delays, arrived only three weeks before their departure), his death mask and several original manuscripts. The monastery is open Monday to Saturday from 9.30 am to 1 pm and 3 to 6.30 pm (5.30 pm during winter) and mornings only on Sunday. Entry includes piano recitals (given eight times daily during summer) and admission to the local museum (1100 ptas).

The rest of the town is charming in a commercialised way, its cobblestone streets fronted by stylish bars and souvenir shops doing a brisk business. From here a torturous 7km drive leads down to **Port de Valldemossa**, where a dozen or so buildings (including two bar-restaurants) huddle around a rocky cove.

Places to Stay Most visitors make Valldemossa a day trip, but you can stay at the perfectly adequate and central *Hostal Ca'n Mário* (☎ 971 61 21 22, *Carrer de Vetam 8)*, where rooms cost 3600/6100 ptas.

Deià

Deià is perhaps the most famous village on Mallorca. Its setting is idyllic, with a cluster of stone buildings cowering beneath soaring mountains and surrounded by steep hillsides terraced with vegetable gardens, vines and fruit orchards.

Such beauty has always been a drawcard. Many visitors came, saw and *were* conquered: Deià became a second home to an international artists' colony of writers, actors, musicians etc. The most famous member was the English poet Robert Graves, who died here in 1985 and is buried in the town's hillside cemetery.

Now somewhat overrun by pretentious expats, travel writers and tourists, Deià still has something special and is worth experiencing, particularly if you can avoid the summer crowds.

Things to See & Do The C-710 passes though the town centre, where it becomes the main street and is lined with bars and shops, expensive restaurants and ritzy boutiques. Several pricey **artists' workshops and galleries** flog locally produced work.

Up beside the church, the small **Museu Parroquial** has an interesting collection of religious effects, icons and old coins (100 ptas). There's also a privately run **Archaeological Museum & Research Centre** (open by appointment) with a collection of artefacts found in the Valldemossa area.

On the coast, **Cala de Deià** has some popular swimming spots and a couple of bar-restaurants. The steep walking track from town takes about half an hour; you can also drive down, but in the high season this might take almost as long.

Some fine walks criss-cross the area: the gentle **Deià Coastal Path** to Lluc Alcari (three hours return) continues around the coast and on to Sóller, while the **Route of the Olive Trees** (number four on the hiking excursions brochure) takes you south to Valldemossa.

Places to Stay Surprisingly, Deià still has a couple of affordable places to stay. *Fonda Villa Verde* (☎ 971 63 90 37, *Carrer de Ramon Llull 19)* has charming singles/doubles with shared bathrooms for 3800/

5500 ptas, and a few doubles with private bathroom for 7500 ptas. Views from the large sunny terrace are gorgeous and prices include breakfast.

Set on a hillside overlooking the town, *Hostal Miramar* (☎ 971 63 90 84) is an appealing stone pensión with simple rooms. B&B costs 3772/7222 ptas (rooms without bathroom). Doubles with bathroom cost 8924 ptas.

Somewhat more expensive and in the old town is the superbly renovated *S'Hotel d'Es Puig* (☎ 971 63 94 09, Carrer d'Es Puig 4). Its gorgeous rooms cost 9200/13,200 ptas, including breakfast.

If you want to rub shoulders with the rich and famous, the place to stay is *La Residencia* (☎ 971 63 90 11). A short stroll from the town centre, this former 16th century manor house is now a luxurious resort hotel set in 12 hectares of manicured lawns and beautifully tended gardens. Of course, there's also the pool, tennis court, restaurant and grill-bar. B&B starts from a mere 24,500/35,000 ptas (ouch!).

Places to Eat The diverse collection of eateries along the main street includes a couple of affordable pizzerias and several expensive restaurants that claim to specialise in local cuisine.

One place everyone can afford is *Café Sa Fabrica*, where half a chicken with chips will set you back all of 600 ptas – elsewhere on this strip your wallet will be cleaned out, however pleasantly.

Lluc Alcari

On the coast 3km north of Deià is the secluded *Hotel Costa d'Or* (☎ 971 63 90 25), a popular mid-range hotel with 32 rooms, a swimming pool and a sun terrace with fine views of the coast. It's a 15-minute walk through a pine forest down to the hotel's beach. Singles/doubles cost 5100/8100 ptas with breakfast.

Sóller

Sóller's station is the terminus for the Palma-Sóller train line, one of Mallorca's most popular and spectacular excursions (see Mallorca's Getting Around section).

The town sprawls across a flat valley beneath soaring and jagged outcrops of the Serra de Tramuntana. It's a pleasant place with attractive old buildings, lush gardens and open plazas, but be prepared to cope with thick crowds of visitors during the day. Sóller is a preferred base for trekkers.

The main square, Plaça de la Constitució, is 100m downhill from the train station. It's surrounded by bars and restaurants and is home to the **ajuntament** (town hall) and the tourist office (☎ 971 63 02 00), which is open Monday to Saturday from 9.30 am to 1.30 pm. Also here is the large 16th century **Església Parroquial de San Bartolomé**, with a beautiful Gothic interior and a modernist façade.

Most visitors take a ride on one of Sóller's open-sided ex-San Francisco trams, which shuttle 2km down to Port de Sóller on the coast (115 ptas). They depart from the train station every half-hour between 6 am and 9 pm.

Places to Stay & Eat Beside the train station, the family-run *Hotel El Guía* (☎ 971 63 02 27, Carrer del Castañer 2) is a good place to meet other trekkers. Its bright rooms feature timber trim and modern bathrooms. Room prices are 5650/8600 ptas including breakfast. The set dinner *menú* costs 2300 ptas.

Nearby (go past El Guía and turn right), the cosy *Casa de Huéspedes Margarita* (☎ 971 63 42 14, Carrer Reial 3) has just seven rooms with big old beds and shared bathrooms. Singles/doubles/triples cost 2000/3000/4000 ptas.

Hostal Nadal (☎ 971 63 11 80, Carrer de Romaguera 29), a five-minute downhill walk from the town centre, is a clean and spacious hostal with singles/doubles from 1750/3000 ptas, or 2400/4000 ptas with bathroom.

Celler Cas Carrete, in an old cart workshop, is a bargain with set *menú* for 850 ptas and 1250 ptas.

Port de Sóller

Every day, Port de Sóller is invaded on all fronts by hordes of tourists: they descend from the mountains by the bus load, sail around from Palma in dozens of cruise boats and the trams trundle them in from nearby Sóller.

Why? Beats us. The harbour itself is quite scenic – the waterfront is lined with cafés and restaurants (and souvenir shops) and a fleet of boats runs excursions to Sa Calobra, Deià, Sant Elm and Illa sa Dragonera. But the 'beach' is grubby and any lingering charm has long since been swept away by that very flood of tourists. Then again, the tram ride down here can be kind of fun ...

Places to Stay If you decide to stay, the large *Hotel Generoso* (☎ 971 63 14 50), on the waterfront on Carrer del Almirante Alberzuza, has rooms with bathrooms from 4280/7290 ptas in the high season – you have a choice of sea views or mountain views.

Biniaraix & Fornalutx

From Sóller it's a pleasant 2km drive, pedal or stroll through narrow laneways up to the tiny village of Biniaraix.

From there, another narrow and scenic route continues north up to Fornalutx, taking you through terraced fields crowded with orange and lemon trees. Fornalutx is a pretty village of distinctive stone houses with green shutters, colourful flower boxes and well-kept gardens. Many of the homes are owned by expatriates, and although the village is a popular destination it's still a far cry from the hustle and bustle of Sóller.

The only place to stay is the small (and pricey) *Hostal Fornalutx* (☎ 971 63 19 97, Carrer de l'Alba 22), a delightfully converted former convent just off the main street. Singles/doubles with breakfast cost 7500/12,000 ptas.

Sa Calobra

The 12km road from route C-710 across and down to the small port of Sa Calobra is one of the most spectacular and hair-raising scenic drives you'll ever take. This serpentine road has been literally carved through the mountains, skirting over narrow ridges before it twists its way down towards the coast in an eternal series of hairpin bends.

Arriving at the coast is an anticlimax. Three or four big bar-restaurants cluster around a stony black-sand bay, catering to the steady stream of day-trippers who flock here by car, bus and boat. Some lunatics even cycle down here – definitely not recommended!

From the northern end of the road a short walking trail leads around the coast and through a series of long tunnels to a river gorge and small cove with some fabulous (but crowded) **swimming** spots.

Monestir de Lluc

Back in the 7th century, a local shepherd claimed to have seen an image of the Virgin in the sky. Later, a similar image appeared on a rock. 'It's a miracle,' everyone cried and a chapel was built near the site to commemorate it.

A monastery was established here after Jaume I reconquered Mallorca. Since then thousands of pilgrims have come every year to pay homage to the 14th century **statue of the Virgin of Lluc**, known as La Moreneta because of her dark-coloured skin.

The present monastery, a huge and somewhat austere complex, dates from the 18th century. Off the central courtyard is the entrance to the **Basílica de la Mare de Déu**, which holds the statue. It is open daily from 10 am to 5 pm (250 ptas).

Places to Stay & Eat The monastery's accommodation section, the *Santuari de Lluc* (☎ 971 51 70 25), has 97 rooms and is popular with school groups, trekkers and pilgrims. Doubles/triples with own bath start at 3000/3700 ptas. The downstairs rooms are dark and best avoided. Several restaurants and cafeterias cater to your tummy's demands.

Getting There & Away Buses connect twice daily with the Palma-Inca train.

Pollença

Next stop on the Mallorcan pilgrimage is this laid-back inland town. The devout and hardy come here to climb the **steps of Calvary**, 365 stone steps leading from the town up to a hill-top chapel and small shrine; the rest of us drive up the back road. Either way, the views from the top are great.

There isn't much to do when you get back down. You can visit a small museum in the town's convent on Tuesday, Thursday and Sunday between 10 am and 2 pm. Otherwise, the central Plaça Major is a good place to relax. *Café Espanyol* has open-air tables shaded by big old plane trees, and an interesting collection of old B&W photos of Mallorcan life inside.

Places to Stay A couple of kilometres south on the road to Palma, *Santuari Puig de Maria* has rooms. Built during the 14th and 15th centuries, this former monastery is now a somewhat chaotic retreat. Neither the food nor accommodation are anything to write home about, but the setting and views are spectacular, particularly if you manage to rise at dawn.

From the turn-off (signposted 2km south of Pollença on the Palma road), a narrow road leads two-thirds of the way up the hill; from there you'll have a steep 10 minute climb up a rocky path to the monastery. Bring a torch if you're arriving at night. We couldn't get back there this time, and their old phone number was out of order, so check with tourist offices before committing yourself!

Port de Pollença

On the northern shores of the Badia de Pollença, this resort is popular with British families (it is not strong on nightlife), soothed by all the 'English' pubs and fish and chips shops.

Sailboards and yachts can be hired on the beaches and boats run to the fine beaches of Platja de Formentor. South of town, the bay's shoreline becomes rocky and the beaches less attractive. American Express is represented by Viajes Iberia (☎ 971 86 62 62), Carrer de Joan XXIII 9.

Places to Stay Three long blocks back from the beach and on the main road, *Hostal Corro (☎ 971 86 50 05, Carrer de Joan XXIII 66)* has decent rooms above a bar. High-season doubles without bath cost 4000 ptas and 5500 ptas with. Nearby, *Hostal-Residencia Paris (☎ 971 86 40 17, Carrer de Magallanes 18)* is harder to find but better value with singles/doubles (all with private bathroom) at 4000/4500 ptas including a buffet breakfast.

Hostal-Restaurant La Goleta (☎ 971 86 59 02, Passeig de Saralegui 120) on the beachfront is an impressive small hotel with its own bar and restaurant. Rooms with bathroom cost 5500/7350 ptas (plus IVA) for B&B.

Cap de Formentor

It's a splendid drive (cyclists be warned: it is steep, narrow and often busy with four-wheeled traffic) from Port de Pollença out along this narrow, rocky promontory. Midway (on the southern side) is the *Hotel Formentor (☎ 971 89 91 00)*, a ritzy five-star place that has played host to the likes of Grace Kelly and Winston Churchill since opening in 1926. You can add yourself to the guest-list for a mere 27,300/44,000 plus IVA.

Near the hotel and backed by shady pine forests, the sandy beaches of **Platja de Formentor** are among the island's best. At your disposal are a couple of exclusive beach bars, a golf course and nearby horse-riding ranch.

From here it's another spectacular 11km out to the lighthouse on the cape that marks Mallorca's northernmost tip.

BADIA D'ALCÚDIA

This huge bay dominates Mallorca's northeast coast. It has longer and better beaches than Badia de Pollença, with broad sweeps of sand that stretch around the coast between the resorts of Port d'Alcúdia and Ca'n Picafort.

Alcúdia

Wedged between the two bays, the busy town of Alcúdia was once a Roman settlement. Remnants of the Roman theatre can be seen and the old town is still partly protected by its medieval walls. The tourist office organises walking tours of the town and publishes the handy *10 Excursions* booklet, which outlines some good walking and cycling tours to local destinations, including the **Parc Natural de l'Albufera** nature reserve and the ruins of the **Roman city of Pollèntia**.

Port d'Alcúdia

A large harbour dominates the town centre and imparts a chic maritime flavour, with boat trips leaving daily to Ca'n Picafort, Platja de Formentor and Port de Pollença. Flebasa has four daily car-ferry services to Ciutadella (Menorca). The local tourist office (☎ 971 89 26 15) is at Avinguda de Joan Carles I 68.

South of the harbour, long white-sand beaches are backed by a strip of apartments and hotels that continues for several kilometres around the bay. A good cycling path follows the coast road, so you could always hire a bike and pedal south in search of less-crowded beaches.

Places to Stay Budget options are limited. *Hostal Vista Alegre* (☎ 971 54 69 77, *Passeig Marítim 10)*, opposite the harbour and upstairs from the Pizzeria de Raffaele, is a friendly place with tidy singles/doubles with showers from 2000/3500 (no singles in summer). A couple of blocks back, the large *Hostal Puerto* (☎ 971 54 54 47, *Carrer de Teodoro Canet 29)* is an OK second choice and charges similar prices.

Campers could make for *Sun Club Picafort* (☎ 971 86 00 02), 9km south of Port d'Alcúdia. Across the road from a good beach, it's a large, first-class camping ground with excellent facilities, including tennis courts, two pools, a supermarket and

a bar. But at 2500 ptas for a site, plus an extra cost per person and car, it ain't cheap.

Ca'n Picafort

A smaller version of Port d'Alcúdia, Ca'n Picafort is a package-tour frontier town and still somewhat raw and soulless, but the beaches are pretty good and there are worse places to end up.

Colònia de Sant Pere

Beyond Ca'n Picafort the road heads inland, but midway to Artà there's a turn-off leading 5km north towards the coast. Colònia de Sant Pere is an almost deadly quiet town with a tiny beach wedged between rocky coves and a few fishing boats bobbing in the sea. Nothing much happens here, which can make for a nice change of pace.

Hostal Rocamar (☎ 971 58 93 12, *Carrer de San Mateo 9)*, two blocks back from the beach, has comfortable singles/ doubles with bathrooms and terraces for 5200/7500 ptas in the high season. It is the only accommodation in town.

EAST COAST

Most of the fine beaches along Mallorca's east coast have succumbed to the ravages of mass tourism. The northern half of this stretch of coastline is home to a series of concrete jungles that rival the worst excesses of the Costa del Sol.

Farther south the coastline is corrugated with a series of smaller coves and ports, saving it from the same fate.

Artà

The inland town of Artà is dominated by the 14th century hill-top fortress and **Església de San Salvador**. Also of interest is the **Museu d'Artà** on Plaça d'Espanya, which contains a small archaeological exhibition. It is open weekdays from 10 am to noon (100 ptas).

On the coast 10km south-east are the **Coves d'Artà**, said to be as impressive as Porto Cristo's Coves del Drac (see later) – they are certainly much less crowded. Tours

JON DAVISON

The striking hill-top fortifications at Artà

of the caves are held every half-hour between 10 am and 7 pm (to 5 pm from October to June; 1000 ptas).

Cala Ratjada

Cala Ratjada is a heavily developed and busy resort particularly popular with Germans. The main streets are wall-to-wall with souvenir shops and the beaches are nice but incredibly crowded. The tourist office (☎ 971 56 30 33) is in a glass-sided building on Plaça dels Pins. A few kilometres inland, **Capdepera** is marked by the walls of the fortress enclave above the town. See the Getting There & Around section at the beginning of this chapter for details of daily fast ferries to Ciutadella (Menorca).

Places to Stay Your chances of finding accommodation here in July and August are next to nil. At other times, one place worth a try is *Hostal Gili* (☎ 971 56 41 12, Carrer de Tamarells s/n), overlooking the small bay of Son Moll a couple of kilometres to the south. Set right on the beachfront, it has a pool, sauna, bar and disco, with B&B costing 3600 ptas per person.

Cala Millor

Stretching along the east coast's largest bay, Cala Millor is a predominantly English resort with white-sand beaches backed by some of Mallorca's blandest and most intensive developments.

Porto Cristo

During the day, Porto Cristo teems with day-trippers in town to visit the nearby underground caves. It's not good for your agoraphobia, but by late afternoon when the hordes have disappeared it can be quite nice. The town cradles a small sandy beach and boat harbour.

The **Coves del Drac** (Caves of the Dragon), on the southern outskirts, are open daily from 10 am to 5 pm. One-hour tours (900 ptas) are held hourly on the hour, the highlight being the classical music played by boat-bound musicians floating across a large subterranean lake. Nearby you can also visit Porto Cristo's large **aquarium**, which is open daily from 10.30 am to 5 pm (11 am to 3 pm in the low season; 700 ptas).

Places to Stay Opposite the entrance to the caves, *Hotel Sol i Vida* (☎ 971 82 10 74, Avinguda de Joan Servera 11) is a bright and cheerful hostal with a pool, bar-restaurant and tennis court. Rooms with bathroom cost from 2750/4500 ptas for singles/doubles. The main drawback is that it's a long walk from here to the town centre and the beach.

An alternative is to stay at the large and stylish *Hotel Felip* (☎ 971 82 07 50, Carrer de Burdils 41), on the waterfront. B&B costs 5630/10,060 ptas in the high season.

Cala d'Or

Once a quaint fishing village, Cala d'Or is now an overblown big-dollar resort. Its sleek new marina is lined with glisteningly expensive boats and the surrounding hills are crowded with blindingly whitewashed villas. Plenty of style but not much substance.

Portopetro

Immediately south of Cala d'Or (and virtually joined to it by urban sprawl) is the smaller and more tranquil port town of Portopetro. Centred around its boat-lined inlet and surrounded by residential estates, it has a cluster of harbour-side bars and restaurants and a couple of small and quiet beaches nearby.

Places to Stay A mere stone's throw from the inlet, *Hostal Nereida* (☎ 971 65 72 23) has a pool, a good restaurant and renovated rooms with bathrooms. High season singles/doubles/triples cost 6000/7000/9600 ptas, with breakfast.

Cala Mondragó

Two kilometres south of Portopetro, Cala Mondragó is one of the most attractive beaches on the east coast. Sheltered by large rocky outcrops and fringed by pine trees, this protected sandy beach has a solitary bar surrounded by deck chairs and thatched umbrellas. Development is limited to a couple of houses and one large hostal, the five-storey *Hostal Playa Mondragó* (☎ 971 65 77 52), which has good facilities including a pool, bar and restaurant. It charges 3100 ptas per person a day (including breakfast) or 4250 ptas per person for media pensión.

Cala Figuera

Compared with much of the rest of the coast, this is a little gem. The fishermen here really still fish, threading their way down the winding inlet before dawn while the predominantly German tourists sleep off the previous night's food and drink. What has probably kept the place in one piece is the fact that the nearest beach, the equally pretty little Cala Santanyí, is a few kilometres drive farther south-west. Be warned though, the place *has* been 'discovered' – even the locals seem German.

Places to Stay & Eat There's a cluster of hostales and restaurants along the southern side of the inlet. *Hostal-Restaurant Ca'n Jordi* (☎ 971 64 50 35, *Carrer de la Virgen del Carmen 58*) has good rooms with bathrooms, views and balconies from 2900/4300 ptas. It also rents out a few apartments and villas.

Another cheap option is *Hostal Oliver* (☎ 971 64 51 27, *Carrer de Bernareggi 37*) – it's on the right as you enter town. Decent rooms with own bathroom cost 2700/5000 ptas in the high season, but you can often get them cheaper. Several restaurants and bars dotted about town will keep your hunger and thirst at bay. A daily bus connects with Palma.

Colònia de Sant Jordi

On the south-east coast, the large resort town of Colònia de Sant Jordi is rather unexciting and the local beach is no great shakes either. Some good beaches lurk nearby, however, particularly Ses Arenes and Es Trenc (with a nudist strip), both a few kilometres up the coast towards Palma. The water at the latter is an impossible shade of blue and it's so popular that you pay 600 ptas to park your car here (free after 4 pm).

From Colònia de Sant Jordi itself you can take boat trips to the former prison island of Cabrera, where more than 5000 French soldiers died after being abandoned in 1809 towards the end of the Peninsular War. Cabrera and its surrounding islets now form the Parc Nacional Archipiélago de Cabrera.

Places to Stay You could try the cosy *Hostal Colonial* (☎ 971 65 52 78, *Carrer de Gabriel Roca 9*). There's a café downstairs, and rates are from 3050 ptas per person for B&B or 5900 ptas for media pensión.

THE INTERIOR

East of the Serra de Tramuntana, Mallorca's interior is a flat and fertile plain. Dominated by farmland and unremarkable agricultural townships, it holds little of interest to the average beach-bound tourist. But, for those with time, transport and an interest in discovering the traditional Mallorcan way of life, an exploration of the island's interior can be rewarding.

Several of the major inland towns are well known for their specialised products. **Inca** holds a popular market each Thursday and has numerous factory outlets selling locally produced leather goods (check out the places along Gran Via de Colón and Avinguda del General Luque). Industrial **Manacor** has a thriving manufactured pearl industry (including the famous Majorica factory, since 1890) and many of the island's furniture manufacturers. **Felanitx** is known for its ceramics showrooms and factories.

Places to Stay

If you're interested in experiencing 'the other Mallorca', numerous rural properties, mountain houses and traditional villas around the island operate as upmarket B&Bs. Pick up the *Fincas* brochure at tourist offices or at the Associació Agroturisme Balear (☎ 971 72 15 08, fax 971 71 73 17), Avinguda de Gabriel Alomar I Villalonga 8a in Palma.

Many of the properties are historic and often stylish country estates, offering outstanding facilities, including swimming pools, tennis courts and organised activities and excursions. Prices for double rooms (often with room for three) range from about 10,000 to 25,000 ptas a day.

Ibiza (Eivissa)

Ibiza is the most extreme of the islands, both in landscape and the people it attracts.

The Greeks called Ibiza and Formentera the Islas Pitiusas, or 'islands of pine trees'. The Ibizan landscape is harsh and rocky and the island receives little rainfall. Alongside the hardy pines, the most common crops are the traditionally Mediterranean olive, fig and almond trees.

A rugged coastline is interspersed with dozens of fine sandy beaches, most of them consumed by intensive tourist developments. A few out-of-the-way beaches remain but in summer you won't be doing much solitary swimming.

The island's beaches and laid-back attitude first became a major drawcard in the flower-power heyday of the 1960s: while North America's hippies were 'California dreaming', their European counterparts were heading for Ibiza to tune in, turn on and drop out. It is hard to believe that in 1956 the island boasted a total of 12 cars!

Initially a resort for the hip and fashionable, Ibiza soon discovered the financial rewards of bulk tourism and started shipping in summer sun-seekers by the thousand. Nowadays the island populace of 83,400 (34,600 of them in the capital, Ibiza city) watches more than a million visitors a year – a strange blend of hippies, gays, fashion victims, nudists, nightclubbers and package tourists – pour through. Official hopes rest with steering slowly away from the charter-flight lager louts and attracting a more culture-hungry set (with greater disposable income).

Ibiza's nightlife is renowned. The island, birthplace of the rave, is home to some of Spain's biggest and most famous discos, and its great summer club scene is complemented by a huge and diverse collection of bars.

Activities

Diving and sailing are both possible on Ibiza. You'll find plenty of schools for both activities in the main resorts – the tourist office has lists.

Accommodation

Of the five camping grounds around the island, only Camping Florida near Cala Nova is open year round. There are no grounds around the city.

Ibiza city has the most diverse range of accommodation, including good budget options, although in summer cheap beds are hard to come by. Santa Eulària also has several affordable places, but elsewhere bargains are few and far between.

As on the mainland, country homes (*casas rurales*) are beginning to win fans. For more info on the half a dozen of these

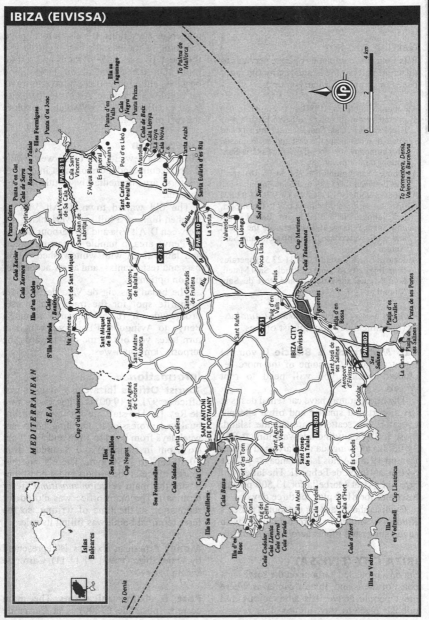

IBIZA (EIVISSA)

To Palma de Mallorca

To Formentera, Denia, Valencia & Barcelona

MEDITERRANEAN SEA

Illa sa Tagomago

Punta d'en Valls
Cala Negra
Punta Prima
La Joya
Cala Nova
Punta Arabi
Santa Eulària d'es Riu
Es Canar
Cala Llenya
Cala de Boix
Cala Mastella
Pou d'es Lleó
Xumena
Es Figueral
Cala Sant Vicent
Cala Blanca
Illes Formigues
Punta d'es Jonc
Racó de sa Talaia
Cala de Serra
Punta d'en Gat
Punta Galera
Portinatx
Cala Xarraca
Cala Xuclar
Illa d'en Calders

Sant Vicent de Sa Cala
S'Aigua Blanca
Sant Joan de Labritja
Sant Carles de Peralta
Port de Sant Miquel
S'Illa Murada
Na Xamena
Cala Benirràs
PM-811
C-733
PM-810
Sa Cala
Santa
Riu
Sant Llorenç de Balàfia
Sant Miquel de Balansat
Sant Mateu d'Aubarca
Santa Gertrudis de Fruitera

La Siesta
Valverde
Cala Llonga
Sol d'en Serra
Roca Llisa
Jesús
Cap Martinet
Cap Talamanca

Cap d'els Mussons
Illes Ses Margalides
Cap Negret
Ses Fontanelles
Santa Agnès de Corona
Punta Galera
Cala Salada
Cala Gració
SANT ANTONI DE PORTMANY
Puig d'en Valls
Figueretes
IBIZA CITY (Eivissa)
Sant Rafel
Sant Jordi de ses Salines
Aeroport d'Eivissa
C-731
PM-803
PM-802
Platja d'en Bossa
Platja d'es Cavallet
Punta de ses Portes
Platja de ses Salines
Ses Salines
La Canal

Illa Sa Conillera
Cala Bassa
Cala Conta
Port d'es Torrent
Puig del Dofí
Cala Llentia
Cala Corral
Cala Tarida
Sant Agustí
Sant Josep de sa Talaia
Cala Molí
Cala Vedella
Es Cubells
Es Codolar

Illa d'es Bosc
Cala Codolar
Cala Carbó
Cala d'Hort
Cala Vedella
Puig des Vedrà
Illa es Vedranell
Illa es Vedrà
Cap Llentisca

To Denia

Islas Baleares

0   2   4 km

attractive, quiet hideaways, approach the tourist office.

Getting Around

Bus Four bus companies operate services to different parts of the island (many run night buses in summer for party-goers):

Autobuses Empresas HF Vilas (☎ 971 31 16 01) operates from Ibiza city to Santa Eulària d'es Riu, Es Canar, Cala Sant Vicent, Portinatx and other beaches along the east and north coasts. This company also does the Santa Eulària-Sant Antoni de Portmany run.

Autobuses San Antonio (☎ 971 34 05 10) operates between Ibiza city and Sant Antoni.

Autobuses Voramar El Gaucho (☎ 971 34 03 82) operates services from Ibiza city to the airport, Ses Salines, Platja d'en Bossa, Cala Llonga and Santa Eulària. It also services the south and south-west coasts from Ibiza city and Sant Antoni.

Autocares Lucas Costa (☎ 971 31 27 55) operates from Ibiza city to Santa Gertrudis, Sant Mateu, Sant Miquel de Balansat and Port de Sant Miquel.

Pick up a copy of the *Horario de Autobuses* (bus timetable) from tourist offices.

Car, Motorcycle & Bicycle If you are intent on getting to some of the more secluded beaches you will need to rent wheels.

The big operators have car rental desks at the airport, but smaller and often cheaper operators are scattered around the island: those in Ibiza city include Valentin (☎ 971 31 08 22) at Avinguda de Bartomeu Vicent Ramón 19 and Autos Isla Blanca (☎ 971 31 54 07), at Carrer de Felipe II. The latter will hire out a Seat Marbella for 13,500 ptas or a scooter for 8100 ptas for three days.

Cyclists should ask for the tourist office's *Rutas en Mountain Bike* brochure, with seven suggested routes across the island.

IBIZA CITY (EIVISSA)

Set on a protected harbour on the south-east coast of the island, Ibiza's capital is where most people arrive. It's a vivacious and popular place to stay: unlike other resorts around the island it's a living, breathing town with an interesting old quarter and numerous attractions. It's also a focal point for some of the island's best nightlife and the most diverse range of cafés and restaurants. On the downside, it lacks good beaches, although you don't have to travel far if you want a swim. All in all, Ibiza city is an excellent base from which to explore the rest of the island.

Orientation

Most of the new city lies to the west, while the old centre and areas of most interest to visitors are immediately south of the harbour.

The old walled town, D'Alt Vila, is perched high on a hill top overlooking all. Between D'Alt Vila and the harbour lies the Sa Penya area, a jumble of narrow streets and lanes lined with whitewashed shops, bars and restaurants – and a few accommodation options.

The broad Passeig de Vara de Rey is a favourite spot for the traditional sunset promenade. It runs westwards from Sa Penya to Avinguda d'Espanya, which in turn takes you out of the city towards the airport, 7km south-west.

Information

Tourist Offices Ibiza city's main tourist office (☎ 971 30 19 00) is at Passeig de Vara de Rey 13. The staff are friendly, multilingual and professional. Opening hours are weekdays from 9 am to 1 pm and 5 to 7 pm (to 8 pm in summer) and Saturday from 10.30 am to 1.30 pm. There's another tourist office at the airport and a booth opposite the main *estación marítima* (ferry terminal). The main office was closed for renovation at the time of writing, so the ferry terminal booth was filling its role.

Money American Express is represented by Viajes Ibiza (☎ 971 31 11 11), Carrer de Vicent Cuervo 9.

Post & Communications The main *correos* (postcode 07800) is at Carrer de

IBIZA CITY (EIVISSA)

PLACES TO STAY
3 Hostal-Residencia Ripoll
8 Hostal Sol y Brisa
9 Hotel Montesol
12 Casa de Huéspedes Navarro
20 Hostal-Restaurante La Marina
22 Casa de Huéspedes La Peña
27 Casa de Huéspedes
   Vara de Rey
31 Hostal-Residencia Parque
37 Hotel El Corsario
38 Hotel El Palacio

PLACES TO EAT
4 Restaurante Hong Kong
7 Pizzería da Franco
  er Romano
10 Restaurant Victoria
11 Ca'n Costa
14 Mr Hot Dog
25 Comidas Bar San Juan
33 Restaurante El Olivo
35 El Portalon
36 La Scala

OTHER
1 Lavandería Master Clean
2 Autos Isla Blanca
5 Viajes Ibiza (American Express)
6 Valentin
13 Change Booth & Disco Tickets
15 Tourist Information Booth
16 Estación Marítima
   (Ferry Terminal) for
   Palma de Mallorca,
   Barcelona & Valencia
17 Tango
18 Bar La Biela
19 Pub Tenesse
21 Bar Mambo; Flash
23 Samsara; Capricho Bar
24 Mercat de Verdures
26 Euro Centro
28 Sunset Café
29 Main Tourist Office
30 Iberia
32 Dizzy Café
34 Museu d'Art Contemporani
39 Museu Arqueológic
40 Catedral

To Formentera Ferry Terminal, Telephones (Telefónica) & Platja de Talamanca

Carrer de Felipe II

Carrer de Carles V

To Main Correos & Bus Terminals

Avinguda de Bartomeu Rosselló

Avinguda de Bartomeu Vicent Ramón

Avinguda de Bartomeu

To Platja de Figueretes

Passeig de Vara de Rey

Carrer del Conde

Carrer de Riambau

Carrer de sa Creu

Carrera de Bisbe Torres

Carrer de Azara

Carrer de Aníbal

Carrer del Rosellón

Carrer d'Arcena

Plaça de la Font

Plaça Constitución

Plaça de sa Tertulia

Plaça d'Antoni Riquer

Avinguda dels Adenos del Porto

Carrer de Barcelona

C dels José Verdera

SA MARINA

Ganjo Ciprano

Plaça de sa Riba

Carrer d'Eming

Carrer de la Virgen

Carrera Alta

SA PENYA

Baluard de Sant Joan

Baluard de Santa Llucia

Baluard del Parque

Carrer de Cayetano Soler

Plaça del Parque

Carrer de sa Murada

Baluard d'es Portal Nou

Carrer de Rosari

Carrer de Sant Josep

Plaça de la Vila

Plaça des Desamparats

Carrer de Sant Campa

Carrer de Joan–Román

Carrer de Peña Tur

Carrer de Ponent

El Convent

Carrer d'Espanya

Carrer Major

D'ALT VILA

Baluard de Sant Jaume

Joan Baptista Calvi

Palacio Episcopal

Almudaina

Plaça de la Catedral

Es Revelli

El Castell

Baluard de Sant Jordi

Baluard de Sant Bernat

Ronda

100   200 m

Madrid s/n. There is a Telefónica phone centre opposite the Formentera ferry terminals at Avinguda de Santa Eulària 17. For your email and Internet fix, try the Euro Centro (☎ 971 30 03 54) on Carrer de Abel Matutes 4.

Laundry Lavandería Master Clean, Carrer de Felipe II 12, charges 1200 ptas to wash and dry a 5kg load. It is open weekdays from 9 am to 1 pm and 5 to 8.30 pm and Saturday from 10 am to 1 pm.

Medical Services & Emergency The Hospital Can Mises (☎ 971 39 70 00) is in the Barrio Can Mises west of Ibiza city. The Policía Nacional (☎ 971 30 53 13) are at Avinguda de la Pau s/n.

Sa Penya

When you arrive, take a stroll around Sa Penya. There's always something going on here. If you're into people-watching you'll be right at home: this small pocket must have one of the highest concentrations of exhibitionists and weirdos than anywhere else in Spain.

Shopping is a major pastime and Sa Penya is crammed with dozens of funky and trashy **clothing boutiques**. It's actually a surprisingly good place to shop for clothes: the intense competition between the locally made gear and the imports keeps prices at an almost reasonable level. The so-called **'hippy markets'**, street stalls along Carrer d'Enmig and the adjoining streets, sell just about everything under the sun. The hippies aren't too numerous but the stalls that specialise in locally made arts and crafts are worth checking out.

D'Alt Vila

From Sa Penya you can wander up into D'Alt Vila, the old walled town. The Romans were the first to fortify this hill top, but the walls you see were raised by Felipe II in the 16th century to protect against invasion by combined French and Turkish forces. A steep ramp leads from Plaça de sa Font in Sa Penya up to the **Portal de ses Taules** gateway, the main entrance to the old town. Above it hangs a commemorative plaque bearing Felipe II's coat of arms and an inscription recording the 1585 completion date of the fortification, which consists of seven artillery bastions joined by thick protective walls up to 22m in height.

Immediately inside the gateway is the expansive **Plaça de la Vila**, with its upmarket restaurants, galleries and shops. Up behind the plaza you can walk along the top of the walls and enjoy great views of the city, its harbour and the coast. Nearby, the **Museu d'Art Contemporani** is in an 18th century powder store and armoury. It features constantly changing exhibitions of contemporary art. It is open Monday to Saturday from 10 am to 1.30 pm (and 5 to 8 pm Monday to Friday in summer; 200 ptas).

A steep and well-worn route leads from Plaça de la Vila along narrow streets up to the **catedral**, which overlooks all from the top of the hill. It elegantly combines several styles: the original structure was built in the 14th century in the Catalan Gothic style,

the sacristy was added in 1592 and major renovation work in baroque style took place during the 18th century.

Adjoining the cathedral, the **Museu Arqueológic** houses a fine collection of ancient relics, mainly from the Phoenician, Carthaginian and Roman periods. It is open Tuesday to Saturday from 10 am to 1 pm and 4 to 6 pm (10 am to 2 pm and 5 to 8 pm in summer), and on Sunday from 10 am to 2 pm (300 ptas, students half-price); it is closed on Monday and public holidays.

Beaches

The closest beach to Ibiza city is **Platja de Figueretes**, about a 20 minute walk southwest of Sa Penya. The beach isn't great – a string of modernish high-rise hotels overlooks crowded strips of sand and rocks, and the water tends to be murky – but it's a pleasant walk along the waterfront. If you work up an appetite you can choose from plenty of restaurants and cafés.

In the next bay around to the north-east of Sa Penya is **Platja de Talamanca**. These beaches are OK for a quick dip, although if you have time you'd be better off heading south to the beaches at **Ses Salines** (see that section later).

Places to Stay – Budget

Quite a few reasonably priced hostales huddle around the port, although in midsummer cheap beds are as scarce as hen's teeth.

Sa Penya gets pretty rowdy at night; if you don't like the idea of staying in the heart of the nightlife zone there are a couple of quieter options a little way to the west. The friendly *Hostal Sol y Brisa (☎ 971 31 08 18, Avinguda de Bartomeu Vicent Ramón 15)* has clean singles/doubles with shared bathrooms from 2200/4000 ptas. Nearby, *Hostal-Residencia Ripoll (☎ 971 31 42 75, Carrer de Vicent Cuervo 14)* has similar rooms; its high season rates are 3000/5000 ptas.

On the waterfront (officially at Carrer de Barcelona 7), *Hostal-Restaurante La Marina (☎ 971 31 01 72)* has good doubles with harbour views for 3500 ptas. Outside peak season some rooms are let as singles for about half this price – back rooms are very noisy.

One of the most popular low-budget options is the friendly *Casa de Huéspedes La Peña* (☎ *971 19 02 40, Carrer de la Virgen 76)*. The 13 simple, tidy doubles with shared bathrooms cost from 2500 to 3500 ptas. The top rooms have great harbour views.

Casa de Huéspedes Navarro (☎ *971 31 05 31, Carrer de sa Creu 20, 3rd floor)*, in the thick of things, has 10 rooms at the top of a long flight of stairs. The front rooms have harbour views, the interior rooms are quite dark (but cool in summer) and there's a sunny rooftop terrace. This place charges between 1200 and 1800 ptas per person.

Another reasonable budget option is the well-located *Casa de Huéspedes Vara de Rey* (☎ *971 30 13 76, Passeig de Vara de Rey 7)*, one block from the tourist office; it's on the 3rd floor (no lift!). Rooms with shared bathroom cost 3000/5200 ptas.

Places to Stay – Mid-Range

Hostal-Residencia Parque (☎ *971 30 13 58, Carrer de Vicent Cuervo 3)* is quieter and a bit more upmarket than most of the other hostales. The rooms overlook the pleasant Plaça del Parque from above the café of the same name. Singles without private bath cost 3800 ptas, while singles/doubles with cost 6000/7900 ptas.

Hotel Montesol (☎ *971 31 01 61, Passeig de Vara de Rey 2)* is a comfortable one-star place. Rooms have their own bathroom, TV and phone – and most have views of the harbour or the old town. Singles/doubles cost up to 7500/11,900 ptas. The doubles are OK, but many of the singles are too pokey for the price.

Up in D'Alt Vila, *Hotel El Corsario* (☎ *971 39 32 12, Carrer de Ponent 5)* is magically located with spectacular views of the town and harbour below. The rooms are straightforward but the sprawling mansion is loaded with character and the restaurant serves fine food (admittedly for fine prices).

Doubles range from 14,000 to 18,000 ptas with breakfast (a treat on the terrace) – outside the high season you can bargain for single occupancy rates.

You could opt to stay in Platja de Figueretes. Most of the hotels in this area cater for package tourists and, although the beach is nothing special, it's a reasonable compromise if you need to be close to both beaches and nightlife. *Hotel Marítimo* (☎ *971 30 27 08, Carrer de Ramon Muntaner 48)*, right on the waterfront, is a decent two-star place with singles/doubles at 7000/11,500 ptas.

Places to Stay – Top End

Hotel El Palacio (☎ *971 30 14 78, Carrer de la Conquista 2)* in D'Alt Vila is designed for a generous wallet. Subtitled the 'Hotel of the Movie Stars', it is something of a private movie museum with a collection of signed photos, original movie posters and film awards, with seven rooms each paying homage to a different Hollywood star. It's a little glitzy but comfy all the same. The views are great, and there's a private court-yard with a bar and swimming pool. The Humphrey Bogart double is the cheapest at 27,000 ptas, and the Walt Disney room is the next up at 36,000 ptas (it has a nice terrace). The hotel is open from Easter to October.

Places to Eat

Plenty of bland and overpriced restaurants grace the streets of Sa Penya. Most serve up uniformly tasteless food and offer a similar selection – pizza, pasta, paella and seafood dishes – and many have touts who stand out the front thrusting menus at passers-by in an irritating attempt to lure them in.

Fortunately, a few exceptions are worth searching out. *Comidas Bar San Juan* (*Carrer de Guillem de Montgri 8)* is a simple, family-run operation with two small dining rooms. The décor ain't flash but the food is outstanding value, with main courses between 400 and 800 ptas – for dessert try the *manzana al horno*, a delicious baked caramelised apple. Note that the kitchen only operates between 1 and 3.15 pm and 8 and 10.15 pm.

If you just want something on the run, the hamburgers at *Mr Hot Dog* on Carrer Castelar aren't bad and cost from 300 to 500 ptas.

The friendly *Ca'n Costa (Carrer de sa Creu 19)*, a basement eatery, is another no-frills concern with good food at reasonable prices. It has a two-course *menú* for 900 ptas.

Another good budget bet is *Restaurant Victoria* on the corner of Carrer de Riambau and Carrer de Guillem de Montgri. The dining room is stark, with linoleum floors and brown checked tablecloths, but the food is hearty and cheap, with all main courses in the 400 to 850 ptas range. It's open Monday to Saturday for lunch and dinner.

The restaurant downstairs at the *Hostal-Restaurante La Marina (Avinguda de Adenos del Porto 4)*, opposite the harbour, has a good-value *menú* for 1250 ptas; the dining room has a nautical flavour, or you can eat out the front and watch the boats come in and people go by.

A good spot for brekky is the café downstairs from *Hostal-Residencia Parque (Carrer de Vicent Cuervo 3)*.

If you want better Italian food than what's on offer in the port area, head for *Pizzería da Franco er Romano* on Avinguda de Bartomeu Vicent Ramon (below Hostal Sol y Brisa). Pizzas start at 700 ptas and the pasta dishes aren't bad.

Nearby, *Restaurante Hong Kong (Carrer de Vicent Cuervo 15)* has a good if slightly expensive Chinese food *menú* for 1250 ptas. For a tastier change from local fare, try *Thai'd Up (Carrer de sa Drassana 3)*, where mains are about 1500 ptas.

Most of Ibiza's more upmarket restaurants are in D'Alt Vila. There's a cluster of places just inside the entrance to the old town, spread along Plaça de Vila. *Restaurante El Olivo* is one of the best of these: main courses like pork fillet stuffed with goat's cheese are around 1900 ptas.

There are several more restaurants along the adjacent Plaça dels Desamparats. The popular *El Portalon* is fronted by an open-sided courtyard dining area and has main courses in the 1800 to 3200 ptas range. If you're looking for somewhere intimate and romantic, head for the candle-lit *La Scala (Carrer de sa Carrossa 6)*.

You can buy fresh fruit and vegies from the small open-air *Mercat de Verdures* on Carrer de ses Verdures, opposite the entrance to D'Alt Vila.

Entertainment

Sa Penya is the nightlife centre. Dozens of bars keep the port area jumping from around sunset until the early hours. After they wind down you can continue at one of the island's world-famous discos – if you can afford the outrageous cover charges or score a free pass, that is.

Bars Carrer de Barcelona, a pedestrian-only street that runs parallel with the harbour, is lined with an impressive collection of funky bars. Most have tall tables and stools out on the street and all pump out loud music and cold drinks: *Tango*, *Bar La Biela* and *Pub Tenesse* are just a few of the places worth checking out. There are plenty more farther east along Carrer de Garijo Cipriano, including *Bar Mambo* at No 10 and *Flash* at No 9.

Don't be surprised if you receive unsolicited invitations from some attractive strangers. The local bar scene is highly competitive and lots of places employ slick and persuasive touts to 'invite' passers-by to join them for a drink, sometimes with the lure of free passes to the big discos.

If you're just after a quiet drink, *Dizzy Café* on Plaça del Parque is a laid-back place with comfy cane chairs and tables out the front. It also plays good funk and soul music, which can make for a nice change from the pounding techno-disco stuff. A slightly hipper but equally pleasant spot is *Sunset Café* across the square.

The gay scene is based towards the eastern end of Sa Penya, particularly along the far end of Carrer de la Virgen. At No 44, *Samsara* has live floor shows most nights at

12.30 pm and the *Capricho Bar* next door is a popular watering hole.

Discos Ibiza enjoys a reputation for having one of the best club scenes in Europe, and during the summer months the island is virtually a continuous party from sunset to sunrise (and beyond). Fuelled by an overdeveloped sense of competitiveness, the island's entrepreneurs have built a truly amazing collection of discos – huge, throbbing temples to which thousands of disciples flock nightly to pay homage to the gods of hedonism.

A 'disco sunrise' is definitely part of the Ibiza experience and even if you're not a disco buff you should try to check out at least one of these unique entertainment megaplexes.

With the exception of Pacha (the only club to open year round), the major discos operate nightly between June and September and most open from around midnight till dawn, although things don't usually hot up until 3 am or later. Each has something different to offer and special theme nights, fancy-dress parties, foam parties (where you are half-drowned in the stuff while you dance) and the like are regular features. Some places go a step or two further, putting on go-go girls, striptease acts and even live sex as a climax to the evening (or morning).

Entertainment Ibiza-style doesn't come cheap: most places charge between 2000 and 5000 ptas entry (and then sting you bigtime for drinks). If you hang around the right bars in Sa Penya you might score a flier that entitles you to free or discounted entry. These are handed out by club promoters, whose job it is to entice people with 'the look' (ie very hip and/or very attractive) to their discos.

The big names are *Pacha*, on the northern side of Ibiza city's port; *Privilege* (formerly known as Ku) and *Amnesia*, both 6km out of Ibiza city on the road to Sant Antoni; and *Kiss* and *Space*, both south of Ibiza city in Platja d'en Bossa. Head to

Space when everywhere else is closed – it opens at 8 am and finishes up at 6 pm!

During summer, Ibiza's 'Discobus' service operates nightly from 10 pm until sunrise, doing a continuous circuit between the major discos, bars and hotels in Ibiza city, Platja d'en Bossa, Sant Rafel and Sant Antoni.

Getting There & Away

Ibiza's airport (Aeroport d'Eivissa; ☎ 971 80 90 00) is 7km south-west of the capital. Iberia (☎ 971 30 25 80) has an office in Ibiza city at Passeig de Vara de Rey 15.

Buses to other parts of the island generally depart from a series of stops along Avinguda d'Isidoro Macabich (the western continuation of Avinguda de Bartomeu Rosselló). Tickets can be bought from the bus companies' ticket booths or on board the buses. See Ibiza's Getting Around section for more details.

Trasmediterránea (☎ 971 31 51 11) has an office in Ibiza city on the corner of Avinguda de Bartomeu Vicent Ramon and Carrer de Ramon i Cajal. See the Getting There & Away section at the beginning of this chapter for information on inter-island ferries.

Getting Around

Buses between the airport and Avinguda d'Isidoro Macabich operate hourly between 7.30 am and 10.30 pm (15 minutes; 115 ptas); otherwise, a taxi should cost around 1700 ptas.

Ibiza's commercial centre is quite compact, with most places of interest lying within five to 10 minutes walk of the harbour.

You may well want a taxi to get around the major nightclubs. You can call one on ☎ 971 330 70 00.

EAST COAST
Cala Llonga

A busy highway (C-733) speeds you north out of Ibiza city towards Santa Eulària on the east coast. Alternatively, you could take the slower but more scenic coastal road via

Cala Llonga – take the turn-off to Jesús a couple of kilometres north-west of Ibiza city. This route winds through low hills and olive groves, with detours along the way to several beaches including the pleasant **Sol d'en Serra**.

Cala Llonga is set on an attractive bay with high rocky cliffs sheltering a lovely sandy beach, but the town itself has many high-rise hotels.

Santa Eulària d'es Riu

Ibiza's third-largest town, Santa Eulària is a bustling and agreeable place with reasonable **beaches**, a large harbour and plenty of 20th century tourist-resort architecture.

Orientation & Information The main highway, known as Carrer de Sant Jaume as it passes through the town centre, is a hectic traffic artery lined with souvenir shops and restaurants.

The tourist office (☎ 971 33 07 28) is just off the highway at Carrer de Marià Riquer 4. It is open weekdays from 9.30 am to 1.30 pm and 4.30 to 7 pm and Saturday from 9.30 am to 1.30 pm. There's a telephone office next door.

Places to Stay Modern hotels and apartments crowd Santa Eulària's beachfront, but a couple of blocks inland you'll find a cluster of affordable hostales. The excellent *Hostal-Residencia Sa Rota (☎ 971 33 00 22, Carrer de Sant Vincent 59)* has bright rooms with modern bath or shower. Singles/doubles cost 3500/6000 ptas. The three-storey *Hostal Rey (☎ 971 33 0210, Carrer de Sant Josep 17)* offers decent rooms with showers and balconies for 3500/6000 ptas.

The British-run *Ca's Català (☎ 971 33 10 06, Carrer del Sol s/n)* is a find. This 12-room hotel has the feel of a private villa, with its colourful flowerpots and sunny rooms overlooking a garden courtyard and swimming pool. Singles start at 4000 ptas and doubles range from 7000 (without private bath) to 9500 ptas (plus IVA).

Places to Eat Most of the restaurants and cafés along the beachfront are either overly expensive or pretty tacky: at *Mel's English Snack Bar* you can enjoy 'home cooking at its best', with choices including beans on toast, shepherd's pie and roast dinners. Nice one, Mel.

As with accommodation, if you're after a feed you'd be better off heading inland. Four blocks back there are plenty of decent eateries along Carrer de Sant Vicent: the friendly folk at *Restaurante La Bota* at No 43 offer you a good *menú* for 950 ptas. *Taberna Andaluza*, a couple of doors up, is also recommended.

Getting There & Away The main bus stop is on Carrer del Doctor Curtoys; regular buses connect Santa Eulària with Ibiza city, Sant Antoni and the northern beaches. During summer there are also daily boat services from the harbour to Es Canar, Cala Llonga and other local beaches.

Santa Eulària to S'Aigua Blanca

North-west of Santa Eulària is the resort town of **Cala Nova**, which is heavily developed and probably best avoided, although there are several camping grounds nearby worth considering. The best is *Camping Cala Nova (☎ 971 33 17 74)*, 500m north of the main town. One kilometre south of Cala Nova and a short stroll from the popular Punta Arabi beach is *Camping Florida (☎ 971 33 16 98)*, open all year.

Farther north on the main road is the sleepy village of **Sant Carles de Peralta**. A good place to stop for a bite or a drink is the popular *Bar Anita*, opposite the church in the centre of town. Side roads lead off to the pleasant **Cala Llenya** and **Cala Mastella** beaches.

A kilometre farther along the main road a turn-off right leads to **Cala de Boix**, the only true black-sand beach in the Islas Baleares. This area is largely undeveloped and *Hostal Cala Boix (☎ 971 33 91 24)* is a good place to stay. All 14 rooms have private bathrooms and some have sea views. B&B costs 2200 ptas per person.

Back on the main road the next turning leads to the resort area of **Es Figueral**. A little farther a handwritten sign marks the turn-off to the lovely beaches of S'Aigua Blanca. There isn't too much in the way of development down this way apart from a handful of private villas and apartments. Being a bit out of the way, these beaches are particularly popular with Ibiza's 'young and restless' crowd, most of whom don't seem to bother wearing swimsuits.

A couple of hundred metres back from the beachfront is the three-storey *Pensión Sa Plana* (☎ 971 33 50 73), which is a laid-back 30-room place with a great pool, outdoor courtyard and pool-side bar and barbecue. Each room has a bathroom and a terrace with fine views. Singles/doubles cost around 4000/4700 ptas, including breakfast.

Cala Sant Vicent

The package-tour resort of Cala Sant Vicent is built around the shores of a protected bay on the north-east coast, a long stretch of sandy beach backed by a string of modern mid-rise hotels. It's not a bad place to stop for a swim if you happen to be passing by; you could join a boat trip to the islet of **Tagomago**.

NORTH COAST & INTERIOR
Cala Sant Vicent to Portinatx

The main road (PM-811) heads west from Cala Sant Vicent, passing by the unremarkable village of **Sant Vicent de sa Cala** before hitting the main north-south highway. From here you can head south to Ibiza city or north to Portinatx.

Portinatx

Portinatx is the north coast's major tourist resort, with phalanxes of hotels around its three adjoining beaches – S'Arenal Petit, S'Arenal Gran and Platja Es Port. The beaches themselves are beautiful, but unless you're looking for large crowds, beach toys or souvenirs there are better places to spend time.

Cala Xarraca

This beach, just west of Portinatx, is worth a visit. Set in a picturesque, partly protected bay with a rocky shoreline and a dark-sand beach, development is limited to a solitary bar-restaurant overlooked by a couple of private houses.

This northern part of Ibiza contains some of the island's most attractive landscapes. If you need a break from the beaches the area's coastal hills and inland mountains are popular with bushwalkers and cyclists.

Sant Llorenç de Balafia

Between Portinatx and Ibiza city and just off the main highway, Sant Llorenç is a tiny village consisting of a cluster of houses and farms surrounding a typical whitewashed Ibizan church.

Sant Miquel de Balansat & Port de Sant Miquel

One of the largest inland towns, Sant Miquel is overlooked by a box-like 14th century church but there isn't much else to the place.

Several kilometres north, Port de Sant Miquel is yet another overdeveloped resort town, dominated by the huge *Hotel Club San Miguel*, which has consumed an entire hillside above the admittedly fine beaches.

A turn-off to the right just before you enter town, coming from the south, takes you around a headland to the entrance to the **Cova de Can Marca**, a collection of underground caverns spectacularly lit by coloured lights. The caves are open daily for tours.

Beyond the caves, a *very* rough unsealed road continues 4km around the coast to the unspoiled bay of **Cala Benirrás**. A sealed road to Cala Benirrás leads off the Sant Joan-Sant Miquel road, midway between the towns.

Around the coast about 3km west of Port de Sant Miquel is Ibiza's famous cliff-top *Hotel Hacienda* (☎ 971 33 45 00). If you can afford the hefty prices and want to rub shoulders with the rich and famous, this is *the* place to stay. Rates change seasonally.

Singles cost 24,500 ptas in July and 5000 ptas more in August. Standard doubles cost 36,700/39,600 ptas in July/August, while still more luxurious ones are 43,000/45,600 ptas. Add IVA to all prices.

Santa Gertrudis de Fruitera

If you blinked at the wrong time you could easily miss tiny Santa Gertrudis, south of Sant Miquel, which would be a shame. Clustered around the central Plaça de l'Església you'll find an unusual collection of art and craft galleries and antique and bric-a-brac shops, plus several good bars. The most famous of the latter is *Bar Costa*, and while you're here it's almost obligatory to try a *bocadillo completo* – a delicious warmed roll smeared with tomato and filled with *jamón serrano* and cheese.

Sant Rafel

Midway between Ibiza city and Sant Antoni de Portmany, Sant Rafel is home to a couple of Ibiza's biggest and best discos. By day, the town is known as a craft centre and has a pretty good collection of ceramics workshops, sculpture galleries, shops and markets.

WEST COAST
Sant Antoni de Portmany

Sant Antoni, widely known as 'San An', is big, tacky and about as Spanish as bangers and mash. The locals joke (somewhat sadly) that even soccer hooligans need holidays, and somehow they all seem to end up in San An. It's the perfect destination if you've come in search of booze-ups, brawls and hangovers.

You might turn up here to use the ferry service to/from Denia in Valencia, or to sample the notorious nightlife, which is wild, to say the least.

The tourist office (☎ 971 34 33 63) is at Passeig de ses Fonts 1. Sant Antoni is connected with Ibiza city and the rest of the island by regular bus services. Boats run to local beaches like Cala Bassa and Cala Conta, as well as to Portinatx, Formentera and Denia.

Not far north of Sant Antoni are several pleasant and undeveloped beaches, such as Cala Salada, a wide bay with sandy shores backed by a pine forest. From here, a rough track continues north around the coast to the beach at Ses Fontanelles, but without a 4WD this route isn't really passable. If you're keen, access from the main road is easier.

Cala Bassa to Cala d'Hort

Heading west and south from Sant Antoni you'll come to the rocky and popular bay of Cala Bassa. Not far back from the beach, *Camping Cala Bassa* (☎ 971 34 45 99) is an OK second-class camping ground open in summer. The next few coves around the coast also hide away some very pretty beaches – Cala Conta (aka Cala Comte) is one of the best. All are accessible by bus from Sant Antoni.

Farther south, Cala Vedella is a modest resort with a fine beach in the centre of town, backed by a couple of restaurants. You could do worse than stay in *Apartmentos Puerto Cala Vedella* – an apartment sleeping up to four costs 7800 ptas. A little farther south, Cala d'Hort has a spectacular setting overlooking two rugged rocky islets, Es Vedrá and Es Vedranell. The water here is an inviting shade of blue and the beach a long arc of sand sprinkled with pebbles and rocks. The developers still haven't ruined this place, and there's nothing here apart from two good bar-restaurants, one with a few rooms.

SOUTH COAST
Ses Salines

Platja de ses Salines and the adjacent Platja d'es Cavallet, at the southernmost tip of the island, are the best and most popular beaches within striking distance of Ibiza city. You can be here in half an hour on the local bus or quicker with your own transport. The area takes its name from the salt pans that have been exploited here since Carthaginian times.

If you're taking the bus from Ibiza city you'll be dropped at the western end of Ses

Salines beside a small bar. Across the road on the other side of the sand dunes a long crescent-shaped bay stretches away into the distance, with a broad sandy beach broken by patches of rocks. These beaches are popular with Ibiza's party-hard crowd and there are four or five open-air beach bars spread around the bay. Each has a slightly different vibe and plays a different type of music. The western end is more 'family-oriented' and it seems that swimsuits become less common the farther east you go. Stroll on if the *au naturel* look appeals to you: Es Cavallet, the next bay around to the east, is Ibiza's official nudist beach.

Places to Stay There are two accommodation options immediately behind the beach (and opposite the bus stop): *Casa de Huéspedes Escandell* (☎ 971 39 65 83) is a simple little guesthouse that has six double rooms with shared bathrooms for 3800 ptas and one downstairs room with its own bathroom for 4500 ptas. It charges 3000 ptas for single occupation if a room is free. Nearby, *Hostal Mar y Sal* (☎ 971 39 65 84) has its own bar and restaurant; double rooms with bath are 4700 ptas (plus IVA) in summer.

Places to Eat All of Ses Salines' beach bars offer some type of food. About halfway along the beach, *Guaraná* is a funky tropical-style bar fronted by rows of banana lounges. It's a good spot for a drink or a bite, with timber decking shaded by palm-tree branches, good music and expensive food – a salad will set you back 1000 ptas or more.

At the eastern end of the beach, *Sa Trincha* is more casual and a bit more affordable, serving up burgers, bocadillos, salads and fruit smoothies. This place has its own DJ booth, and things can get kind of wild and crazy.

Getting There & Away Autobuses Voramar El Gaucho (☎ 971 34 03 82) runs eight to 10 buses daily to Ses Salines from Ibiza city (125 ptas).

Formentera

A short boat ride south of Ibiza, Formentera is the smallest and least developed of the four main Islas Baleares. This idyllic island boasts fine beaches and some excellent short walking and cycling trails. It's a popular day trip from Ibiza and can get pretty crowded in midsummer, but most of the time it is still possible to find yourself a strip of sand out of sight of tourist colonies and out of earshot of other tourists.

Formentera's predominantly flat landscape is rugged and at times bleak. The coast is alternately fringed with jagged rocky cliffs and beaches backed by low sand dunes. A handful of farmers scrape a living from the land in the centre and east but elsewhere the island is a patchwork of pine plantations, sun-bleached salt beds, low stone walls and vacant fields. A grand total of 5438 people reside on the island.

Orientation

Formentera is less than 20km across from east to west. Ferries arrive at La Savina, a functional harbour town wedged between two large salt lakes, the Estany d'es Peix and Estany Pudent (the aptly named 'Smelly Lake'). Three kilometres south of La Savina is the island's administrative capital, Sant Francesc Xavier, and another 5km south-west is Cap de Barbaria, the southernmost point. Es Pujols, the main tourist resort, is 3km east of La Savina.

The main road (PM-820) runs down the middle of the island, passing by the fine beaches of Platja de Migjorn along the south coast and through the fishing village of Es Caló (13km south-east of La Savina) before climbing to Sa Talaia, the island's highest point (192m). The eastern end of the island is marked by the Far de sa Mola lighthouse.

Maps The tourist office's *Green Tours* brochure includes a rundown and map of 19 excellent walking and cycling trails that take you through some of the island's most scenic areas.

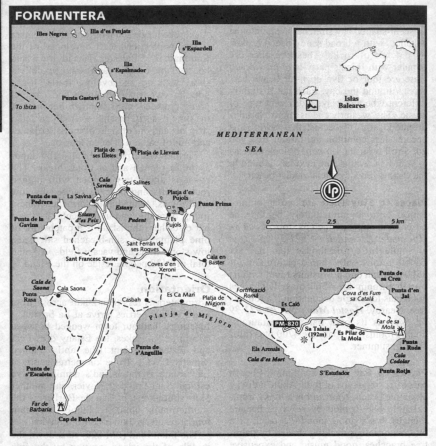

FORMENTERA

Illes Negres · Illa d'es Penjats

Illa s'Espardell

Illa s'Espalmador

Punta Gastavi · Punta del Pas

To Ibiza

MEDITERRANEAN SEA

Platja de ses Illetes · Platja de Llevant

Cala Savina · Ses Salines

Punta de sa Pedrera · La Savina

Platja d'es Pujols · Punta Prima

Punta de la Gavina · *Estany d'es Peix* · *Estany Pudent* · Es Pujols

Sant Ferrán de ses Roques

Sant Francesc Xavier · Coves d'en Xeroni · Cala en Baster

Punta Palmera · Punta de sa Creu

Cala de Saona · Cala Saona · Casbah · Es Ca Marí · Platja de Migjorn · Fortificació Romà · Es Caló

Cova d'es Fum sa Catalá · Punta d'en Jal

Punta Rasa

Cap Alt

Punta de s'Escaleta

Platja de Migjorn

PM-820

Sa Talaia (192m) · Es Pilar de la Mola · Far de sa Mola · Punta sa Ruda

Punta de s'Anguilla

Els Arenals · *Cala d'es Mort* · *Cala Codolar* · Punta Rotja

S'Estufador

Far de Barbaria · Cap de Barbaria

Islas Baleares

0   2.5   5 km

Information

Formentera's tourist office (☎ 971 32 20 57) is in La Savina, hidden behind the row of rental agencies that line the port. Opening hours vary seasonally: during summer it is open from 10 am to 2 pm and 5 to 7 pm (closed Saturday afternoon and Sunday). Most of the banks are in Sant Francesc Xavier. You'll find a Telefónica phone centre and laundrette in Es Pujols. There is a Centro Médico (☎ 971 32 23 69) 3km south of La Savina.

Things to See & Do

Apart from walking, cycling and lying on beaches, activities are fairly limited. Points of interest include a series of crumbling **stone watchtowers** along the coastline, a ruined **Roman fortress** on the south coast and another 40 minor **archaeological sites** (most are signposted off the main roads).

Beaches Among the island's best beaches are **Platja de Llevant** and **Platja de ses Illetes** – beautiful strips of white sand that line the eastern and western sides, respectively, of the narrow promontory stretching north towards Ibiza. A 2km walking trail leads from the La Savina-Es Pujols road to the far end of the promontory, from where you can wade across a narrow strait to S'Espalmador, a tiny islet with beautiful, quiet beaches. The promontory itself is largely undeveloped.

East of Sant Ferrán, towards Es Caló, a series of bumpy roads and unsealed tracks lead to the south coast beaches, known collectively as **Platja de Migjorn**. They are secluded and popular with nudists, despite their sometimes rocky and seaweed-strewn shorelines. Most of these beach settlements consist of a handful of houses and apartments, a couple of bar-restaurants and the odd hostal.

San Francesc Xavier Formentera's capital, San Francesc Xavier, is an attractive whitewashed village with some good cafés overlooking small, sunny plazas. The town's older buildings include a 14th century chapel, an 18th century fortress, and an interesting Ethnological Museum.

Cap de Barbaria A narrow sealed road heads south out of the capital and winds through stone-walled farmlands to Cap de Barbaria, the island's southernmost point. It's a pleasant ride or drive down to the lonely white lighthouse at the road's end, although there isn't much to do once you get there. From the lighthouse a 10-minute walking track leads east to the **Torre d'es Cap de Barbaria**, an 18th century watchtower.

Cala Saona One-third of the way to Cap de Barbaria, you can turn west to the small and lovely settlement of Cala Saona. The beach is one of the island's best, with just one big hotel (see Places to Stay & Eat) and a couple of bar-restaurants overlooking the clear, pale aqua and blue-black waters.

Coves d'en Xeroni Beside the main road just east of Sant Ferrán are the Coves d'en

Xeroni, an unexceptional series of underground caves. The caves are open daily from 10 am to 8 pm between May and October (500 ptas, children 250 ptas).

Es Caló This small (but expanding) fishing settlement is set on a tiny rocky cove ringed by faded timber boat shelters. The coastline here is jagged but immediately west of Es Caló you'll find some good swimming holes and rock pools with small patches of sand.

From Es Caló, the road twists its way up to the island's highest point. Close to the top, *Bar-Restaurant El Mirador* offers spectacular views along the length of the island. Eating here isn't cheap, but for the price of a beer you can enjoy the same views.

Eastern End The eastern end of the island is an elevated limestone plateau. It doesn't hold much interest: most of the coastline is only accessible by boat, and the interior is mainly taken up by pine forests and farms. A road runs arrow-straight to the island's eastern tip, passing through the nondescript town of Es Pilar de la Mola. At the end of the road stand the Far de sa Mola lighthouse and a monument to Jules Verne, who used this setting in one of his novels.

Places to Stay & Eat

Camping is prohibited on Formentera. And sad to say, most of the accommodation on the coast caters mainly to German and English package-tour agencies – so is overpriced and/or booked out in summer. Base yourself in an inland town and cycle to the beaches.

If you decide to stay longer, agencies in the main towns can help you rent an apartment, as can the tourist office.

Es Pujols Once a sleepy fishing village, Es Pujols has been radically transformed by Spain's tourism boom. Rows of sun-bleached timber boat shelters still line the beachfront, but nowadays they are overshadowed by modern hotels, apartments and restaurants, and tourism has all but replaced fishing as the town's main source of income. Nevertheless, the scale of development remains low-key compared with that on Ibiza or Mallorca. And if the town's sandy beaches are too crowded for your liking, more secluded options lie within easy striking distance.

Es Pujols' popularity makes it a relatively pricey place to stay and unless you have an agency booking you may have trouble getting a room during summer.

Right on the beachfront, *Hostal Tahiti* (☎ 971 32 81 22, Carrer de Fonoll Marí 16) is a large, modern three-star place charging 5500/9200 ptas for singles/doubles with B&B. Three other similar hostales line Carrer de Miramar (the main street): *Hostal Voramar* (☎ 971 32 81 19), 100m inland, has double rooms in July for 7600 ptas and 8800 ptas in August; *Hostal Rosales* (☎ 971 32 81 23), 50m farther back, has rooms for 11,000/15,000 ptas in August, but half that outside the high season; and *Hostal-Residencia Sa Volta* (☎ 971 32 81 25), on the corner of Carrer d'Espalmador, charges 4500/8000 ptas.

Another cluster of hostales lurks a kilometre around the coast west of Es Pujols, including *Hostal Sa Roqueta* (☎ 971 32 85 06), with singles/doubles from 3600/6600 ptas.

On the beachfront the popular *Caminito* serves up excellent Argentine food – the *churrasco* is great for meat-eaters at 2100 ptas. *The Grapevine*, a tiny and affordable bar-eatery just back from the beach on Carrer de Punta Prima, is a good spot for a burger or a snack.

Sant Francesc Xavier There's only one hostal here: the friendly *Restaurant-Casa Rafal* (☎ 971 32 22 05) on Carrer d'Isidoro Macabich has doubles without/with bathroom for 4500/6500 ptas, including breakfast. Out of the high season they let some rooms out as singles.

Sant Ferrán de ses Roques Just 1.6km south of Es Pujols, this unassuming little

town has a couple of decent budget hostales. The popular *Hostal Pepe* (☎ 971 32 80 33, Carrer Major 68) has 45 simple and breezy rooms with bath – B&B costs 3470/5540 ptas. The hostal's legendary bar has been a popular hippy hangout since the 1960s. On the main road, *Hostal Illes Pitiuses* (☎ 971 32 81 89) has modern rooms with bath costing up to 5000/7300 ptas in August.

La Savina Formentera's port town isn't the most thrilling place, but if you decide to opt for convenience there are a couple of choices. Closest to the ferry docks, *Hostal Bahia* (☎ 971 32 21 42) has singles/doubles for 4000/5250 ptas (doubles only in August for 6000 ptas). A better bet is the impressive *Hostal La Savina* (☎ 971 32 22 79), overlooking the Estany d'es Peix from Avinguda Mediterránea 22 (on the main road out of town). Singles/doubles with breakfast cost up to 5000/7800 ptas.

Cala Saona The only accommodation is *Hotel Cala Saona* (☎ 971 32 20 30), a modernish if somewhat bland place with 116 air-con rooms, a pool, tennis courts, restaurant etc. Rooms (including breakfast) go for 11,750/16,000 ptas, plus IVA, in the high season.

South Coast There are numerous hostales spread along Formentera's south coast (otherwise known as Platja de Migjorn).

Es Ca Marí is a small resort with a cluster of places and reasonable beaches. *Hostal Ca Marí* (☎ 971 32 81 80) is actually three hostales in one: their rooms and apartments all share a central bar, restaurant, pool and grocery shop. B&B rates are 6100 ptas per person per day. Nearby, the mid-range *Hostal Costa Azul* (☎ 971 32 82 24) also has rooms or apartments at similar prices.

There is a couple of other secluded hostales farther along this stretch of coast. The exclusive *Hostal Santi* (☎ 971 32 83 75) has its own bar-restaurant and charges 7500/11,500 ptas a double (plus IVA; doubles only in August), while several hundred metres farther east, *Hostal Maysi* (☎ 971 32 85 47) is better value, charging 6000/8400 ptas at the height of summer.

Es Caló Overlooking a small rocky harbour, *Fonda Rafalet* (☎ 971 32 70 16) has good rooms (some with sea views) costing up to 4500/8000 ptas in August. It also incorporates a bar and a pricey seafood restaurant.

Across the (main) road, *Casa de Huéspedes Miramar* (☎ 971 32 70 60) has eight simple upstairs rooms sharing a communal bathroom. Nightly costs are 2000/3200 ptas for singles/doubles; the front rooms have sea views (and traffic noise), while the back rooms have bush views. It is often booked up for August.

Es Pilar de la Mola Formentera's easternmost town has a handful of bars and restaurants. You can sit out the front of *Bar Can Toni* and watch the lighthouse-bound traffic go back and forth while you tuck into a good value meal (about 1200 ptas a head). Two kilometres farther east, near the lighthouse itself, *Bar Es Puig* specialises in mixed platters of hams, sausages and cheeses, herbal liquors and local wines. But ask '*¿Cuánto cuesta?*' before you order – the menu is 'priceless'.

Entertainment
Es Pujols has the only nightlife to speak of. In summer the town is pretty lively, with a cluster of bars along Carrer de Miramar that stay open until 3 or 4 am. Close to the beachfront, Carrer d'Espardell has a couple of popular watering holes, including the *Tennis Bar* and the small *Indiana Café*. Two good discos, *Magoos* and *Tipik*, take you through until sunrise.

Getting There & Away
Flebasa Lines (☎ 971 31 07 11) operates at least nine ferry services, six of them in fast passenger-only vessels (25 minutes) daily between Ibiza city and Formentera. The first ferry leaves Ibiza city at 8 am and the last returns from Formentera at around 8 pm. Services are more frequent during summer.

The fast ferries charge 1900 ptas each way, while the car ferries take about an hour and charge 1100 ptas each way (or 2000 ptas return). Return fares for vehicles are 9000 ptas for a small car, 1200 ptas for a scooter and 700 ptas for a bike.

At least two other companies, Umafisa Lines (☎ 971 31 45 13) and Inserco (☎ 971 32 22 10), compete with Flebasa. The former has up to three car-ferry departures on weekdays (one on weekends), while the latter runs two car-ferries daily. Prices are the same.

Pitra (☎ 96 642 31 20, 971 32 30 07) operates ferries once or twice a week from Denia on the mainland to Formentera (via Sant Antoni de Portmany on Ibiza).

If money is no object and you need to cross between Ibiza and Formentera *now*, try the Taxi Nautico (☎ 908-73 27 20 or ☎ 908-53 38 64).

Getting Around
Pedal power is the best way to get around this little island but Autocares Paya (☎ 971 32 31 81) runs a regular bus service connecting all the main towns.

If you need to hire transport you'll find rental agencies all over the island, including a string of places opposite the harbour in La Savina. Avis and Hertz have representatives here: local agencies include Moto Rent Mitjorn (☎ 971 32 22 55), Autos Isla Blanca (☎ 971 32 25 59) and Moto Rent La Savina (☎ 971 32 22 75). Daily rates are around 500 ptas for a bike, 800 ptas for a mountain bike, 1400 ptas for a motor scooter and up to 4000 ptas for motorbikes, 5000 to 7000 ptas for small cars and 7000 to 10,000 ptas for a Suzuki 4WD.

Menorca

Menorca, with a population of 68,700, is perhaps the least overrun of the Islas Baleares. In 1993 the island was declared a Biosphere Reserve by UNESCO, with the aim of preserving important environmental

MENORCA

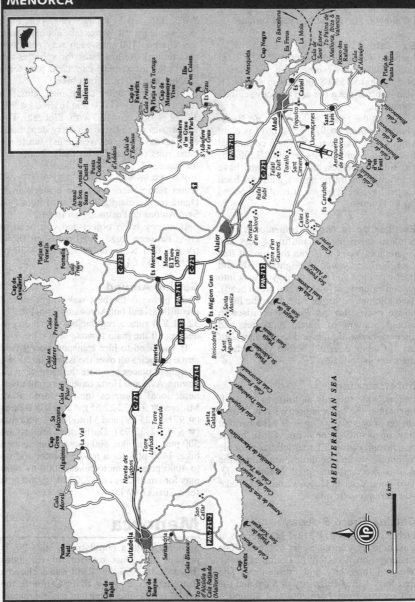

areas such as the S'Albufera d'es Grau wetlands and its unique archaeological sites.

Not the island of choice for all-night party-goers, Menorca is probably the least affected of the islands. The untouched beaches, coves and ravines around its 216km coastline even allow the more adventurous the occasional sense of discovery! This must be one of the few places in the Mediterranean where it is possible to have a beautiful beach largely to yourself in summer.

The second-largest and northernmost of the Baleares, Menorca also has a wetter climate and is usually a few degrees cooler than the other islands – which can be a blessing in summer. Particularly in cooler months, the 'windy island' is relentlessly buffeted by chilling *tramuntana* winds.

Orientation

The capital, Maó (Mahón in Castilian), is at the eastern end of the island. Ferries from the mainland and Palma de Mallorca arrive at Maó's busy port, and Menorca's airport is 7km south-west of the city. The main road (C-721) runs along the middle of the island to Ciutadella, Menorca's second town, with secondary roads leading north and south to the resorts and beaches.

The northern half of the island is an undulating area of green, rolling hills with a rugged, rocky coastline. The southern half is flatter and drier, with a smoother coastline and sandy beaches between high cliffs.

Activities

Maó, Ciutadella, Fornells and Es Castell all have yacht clubs. Many resorts have boats and sailboards for hire. There are several scuba-diving centres around the island, as well as a couple of horse-riding ranches.

Special Events

Each town has a festival to celebrate the feast day of its patron saint. The biggest is the Festa de Sant Joan, held in Ciutadella in the last week in June. The season finishes with the Festa de Mare de Déu de Gràcia in Maó on 8 September.

Menorca's festivals are steeped in traditions dating to the Middle Ages: jousting tournaments and other medieval games are common fare. The locals pride themselves particularly on their riding skills, and during the fiestas prancing horses are ridden into the crowds, rearing on their hind legs and spinning in circles.

Accommodation

Maó and Ciutadella have a handful of good, affordable hostales, but elsewhere bargains are few and far between.

Menorca's two camping grounds are near the resorts of Santa Galdana, about 8km south-west of Ferreries, and Son Bou. They open in summer only.

Getting Around

To/From the Airport Menorca's airport (☎ 971 36 01 50) is *not* served by buses, so you'll have to settle for a taxi, which into central Maó will cost around 1200 ptas.

Bus Three bus companies operate on Menorca. For more details, see the destination entries later.

Car, Motorcycle & Bicycle Rental If you're planning to hire a car, rates vary from around 3500 to 8000 ptas a day, depending on the season and the type of car. During summer, minimum hire periods sometimes apply.

In Maó, places worth trying include Autos Valls (☎ 971 36 84 65), Plaça d'Espanya 13, and Autos Isla (☎ 971 36 65 69), Avinguda de Josep Maria Quadrado 28.

See Getting Around under Maó and Ciutadella for details of motorcycle and bicycle rentals.

MAÓ

The British have invaded Menorca four times (if you count the modest campaign that began with the first charter flight from London in 1953). As a result Maó, the capital (population 23,200), is an unusual blend of Anglo-Spanish characteristics.

The British made it the capital in 1713, and the influence of their almost hundred-year rule is still evident in the town's architecture, traditions and culture. Even today, the majority of its visitors come from Britain.

It's a pleasant and relaxed town and a good place to base yourself when you first arrive. Good beaches are a short bus ride away.

Maó's harbour is its most impressive feature. The deep, well-protected waters handle everything from small fishing boats to car ferries, cruise ships and tankers.

The town was built atop the cliffs that line the harbour's southern shore. Although some older buildings remain, the majority of the architecture is in the restrained 18th century Georgian style.

Information
Tourist Office Menorca's main tourist office (☎ 971 36 37 90) is at Plaça de s'Esplanada 40. It is open Monday to Friday from 8.30 am to 7.30 pm and Saturday from 9 am to 2 pm.

Post & Communications Maó's correos (postcode 07700) is on the corner of Carrer del Bon Aire and Carrer de l'Església.

Medical Services & Emergency Hospital Verge del Toro (☎ 971 36 35 00) is at Carrer de Barcelona s/n. The Policía Nacional (☎ 971 36 37 12) are at Carrer de la Concepciò 1.

Old Quarter
Maó's main plaza is the large Plaça de s'Esplanada. A **craft and clothing market** is held here every Saturday.

The narrow streets to the east of here comprise the oldest part of Maó. The **Arc de Sant Roc**, a 16th century archway at the top end of Carrer de Sant Roc, is the only remaining relic of the medieval walls that once surrounded the old city.

Església de Santa Maria la Major, farther east on Plaça de la Constitució, was originally completed in 1287 but largely rebuilt during the 18th century. It houses a massive organ built in Barcelona and shipped across

in 1810. On the northern end of this plaza is the **ajuntament**.

Plaça d'Espanya
Just off Plaça d'Espanya is the **Mercat Claustre del Carme**, where former church cloisters have been imaginatively converted into a produce market. It is open Monday to Saturday from dawn until 2 pm. From Plaça d'Espanya, the winding Costa de ses Voltes leads down to the harbour.

Museu de Mallorca
After being closed for 23 years, this collection housed in a former 15th century Franciscan monastery off Plaça d'es Monestir was finally reopened in 1998. From the time the Franciscans were obliged to abandon the premises in 1835 after Mendizábal's expropriations, the buildings have had a chequered history – ranging from nautical school and public library to high school and children's home. The permanent collection covers the earliest history of the island, the Roman and Byzantine eras and Muslim Menorca, and includes paintings and other material from more recent times too. It is well set up with explanations in English. The museum is open Tuesday to Friday from 10 am to 1 pm and 5.30 to 8 pm and weekends from 10.30 am to 1 pm (free).

Xoriguer Gin Distillery
From the old quarter, head north up to the Xoriguer distillery at Moll de Ponent 93, where you can try the local gin, another legacy of the Brits. At the front is a liquor outlet and souvenir shop where visitors can help themselves to free samples. Menorcan gin is distinctively aromatic and very tasty; you can also try various strange liqueurs and tonics. The distillery is open weekdays from 8 am to 7 pm and Saturday from 9 am to 1 pm.

Acuarium Menorca
Not far from the distillery at Moll de Ponent 73, the aquarium houses a rather unexciting

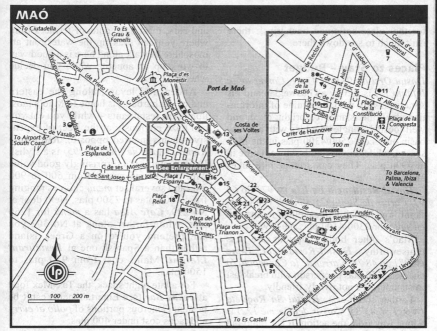

MAÓ

PLACES TO STAY
19 Hostal Orsi
20 Hostal-Residencia Jume
25 Hostal-Residencia La Isla
30 Hotel Port Mahón
31 Hostal Sa Roqueta

PLACES TO EAT
9   La Dolce Vita
18 American Bar
27 Ristorante Roma
28 Café Alba
29 Restaurant Llevant

OTHER
1   Museu de Mallorca
2   Autos Isla
3   Estación de Autobuses (TMSA)
4   Main Tourist Office
5   Xoriguer Gin Distillery
6   Acuarium Menorca
7   Berri; Tse-Tse Bar
8   Arc de Sant Roc
10 Correos
11 Ajuntament

12 Església de Santa Maria la Major
13 Estació Marítim (Main Ferry Terminal)
14 Akelarre
15 Mercat Claustre del Carme
16 Nou de Copes
17 Autos Valls
21 Policía Nacional
22 Motos Rayda
23 Texas Bar; Martin's Mô
24 Nashville Beer & Soundhouse
26 Hospital Verge del Toro

collection of disinterested fish. It was shut at the time of writing.

Beaches

The closest decent beaches to the capital are **Es Grau** to the north and **Punta Prima** to the south. Both are connected to Maó by regular bus services.

Organised Tours

Numerous operators offer boat cruises around the harbour. These can be a pleasant way to kill a few hours, but don't pay extra for the 'glass-bottomed boat trips': there isn't much to see down there.

Places to Stay – Budget

Hostal Orsi (☎ 971 36 47 51, *Carrer de la Infanta 19*) is run by a Glaswegian and his American wife who are a mine of information about the island. It's bright, clean and well located. Singles/doubles with a washbasin only cost 2500/4300 ptas in the high season, while doubles with shower come in at 4900 ptas. They can arrange hire bikes and cars.

Hostal-Residencia La Isla (☎ 971 36 64 92, *Carrer de Santa Catalina 4*) is a large, family-run hostal with excellent rooms and *en suite* for 2300/4100 ptas plus IVA.

Maó's other budget options are less praiseworthy. *Hostal-Residencia Jume* (☎ 971 36 48 78, *Carrer de la Concepció 6*) charges 2650 ptas per person with breakfast in summer. It's not overly friendly.

Farther south-east, *Hostal Sa Roqueta* (☎ 971 36 43 35, *Carrer del Carme 122*) is a long way from the action. It has plain but clean rooms at 2200/3200 ptas.

Places to Stay – Top End

The *Hotel Port Mahón* (☎ 971 36 26 00, *Avinguda del Port de Maó*) is a sleek four-star hotel with 74 marble-clad rooms, a pool and pleasant gardens. Rooms start at 9000/14,000 ptas with breakfast. Doubles with sea views are 20,000 ptas.

Places to Eat

Maó's architecture may have an English flavour, but it seems every second restaurant is an Italian bistro. One of the best is *La Dolce Vita* (*Carrer de Sant Roc 25*), which has great home-made bread, fresh salads, pastas and pizzas (500 to 900 ptas) and an excellent *menú* at 1150 ptas. It is open for dinner only.

The *American Bar* on Plaça Reial is a spacious café fronted by open-air tables. It's a good place to linger over the newspaper or write postcards and has reasonable food with mains costing under 1000 ptas.

Maó's harbour is lined with restaurants and bars; most have outdoor terraces from where you can soak up the waterfront atmosphere. A walk along here is a good way to work up an appetite while you decide where to eat.

Andén de Llevant, along the eastern end of the harbour, is home to Maó's most upmarket restaurants – while you eat you can gaze enviously at the fleet of expensive yachts moored opposite. *Ristorante Roma* (*Andén de Llevant 295*) is a stylish Italian eatery; it's surprisingly good value with pizzas and pastas from 600 to 900 ptas and several set *menú* choices ranging from 1500 ptas to 2300 ptas. Next door at No 299, *Café Alba* has a *menú* for 1250 ptas, while farther along at No 302 you can pretend you're on a Greek island rather than a Spanish one at *Restaurant Llevant*. Mains cost from 950 ptas to 1500 ptas.

For a late night snack, the Tex-Mex food at *Texas Bar* (see Entertainment) can't be beaten. Generous portions of *pollo al curry* and tacos cost under 400 ptas.

Entertainment

Nightlife in Maó is low-key in comparison to Mallorca or Ibiza. Most of the bars and discos are down along the waterfront, but you'll need to wear your walking boots as they are well spread out.

Heading east along the Andén de Llevant, one of the first places you'll come to is the *Texas Bar*, a lively wood-panelled country and/or western joint at No 65 (Yeeha!). Tacky but fun. It closes at 4 am but you can get in another tipple next door at *Martin's Mô*. Farther along, the *Nashville Beer & Soundhouse* is a large tavern featuring mainstream rock.

You'll find a string of places opposite the estación marítima. *Akelarre* (*Moll de Ponent 42*) is a hip place with a mixed crowd. *Berri* (*Costa d'es General 14*) is a dance bar playing standard rock faves, while *Tse-Tse Bar* next door is a funkier, upstairs place that doesn't get going until around 3 am.

Nou de Copes, in a laneway between the top of Costa de ses Voltes and the Claustre del Carme, is a popular little music bar with a cave-like interior carved out of the old walls above the harbour.

Getting There & Away

TMSA (☎ 971 36 03 61) buses depart from either its estación de autobuses at Avinguda de Josep Maria Quadrado 7 or from nearby Plaça de s'Esplanada. Six go to Ciutadella (550 ptas) via Alaior (170 ptas), Es Mercadal (285 ptas) and Ferreries (375 ptas). It also has regular services to the south-coast beaches including Punta Prima (200 ptas) and Cala Tomas (345 ptas).

Getting Around

Motos Rayda (☎ 971 35 47 86) at Andén de Llevant 35-36 hires out mountain bikes (1000 ptas per day), scooters and Vespas (2400 to 2900 ptas daily). Just Bicicletas also rents out bikes (for details inquire at Hostal Orsi).

THE INTERIOR – MAÓ TO CIUTADELLA

Menorca's main road, from Maó to Ciutadella, divides the island into north and south. It passes through the towns of Alaior, Es Mercadal and Ferreries, and along the way smaller roads branch off towards the beaches and resorts of the north and south coasts.

Many of the island's most significant archaeological relics are signposted off the main road (see the boxed text 'Menorca's Prehistoric Heritage' for details).

The small town of **Alaior** is home to the (rundown) local cheese and shoe industries. Cheeses from the Quesos Coinga factory are sold all over Menorca, but if you're passing through you can visit the tasting and sales room at the front of the factory; it's open weekdays from 9 am to 1 pm and 5 to 8 pm and Saturday from 9 am to 1 pm.

In the centre of the island **Es Mercadal** is perhaps most notable as the turn-off for Fornells. You also turn here to get to **Monte El Toro**, Menorca's highest point at 357m. A steep and twisting road leads to the summit, shared by a 16th century church and Augustine monastery, a cluster of satellite dishes and radio towers, and a statue of Christ (built to honour the islanders who died defending the Republican cause during the civil war). You can see right across the islands in all directions and on a clear day as far as Mallorca.

Ferreries is Menorca's highest town. On Saturday morning the excellent Mercat de Ferreries is held, with stall holders selling fresh produce as well as traditional Menorcan crafts and artworks. On other days there are few reasons to linger. The turn-off to the resort of Santa Galdana is just west of here.

CIUTADELLA

Founded by the Carthaginians and known to the Muslims as Medina Minurqa, Ciutadella was virtually destroyed following the Turkish invasion of 1558 and much of the city was subsequently rebuilt during the 17th century. It was the capital of Menorca until the arrival of the British.

Known as 'Vella i Bella' (the Old and the Beautiful), it's an attractive and distinctly Spanish city with a picturesque port and an historic old quarter.

Information

Tourist Office Ciutadella's tourist office (☎ 971 38 26 93) is opposite the cathedral on Plaça d'es Born. During summer it is open on weekdays from 9 am to 1.30 pm and 6 to 8 pm, and on Saturday from 9 am to 1 pm.

Post & Communications The correos (postcode 07760) is at the southern end of Plaça d'es Born.

Things to See & Do

Ciutadella has few outstanding 'sights', which in a way is part of its appeal. It's an attractive town that simply goes about its business without too many concessions to tourism. It's a pleasure to explore the old quarter and port.

Menorca's Prehistoric Heritage

Menorca's beaches aren't its only attractions. The interior is liberally sprinkled with reminders of its rich and ancient heritage.

Many of the most significant sites and monuments are open to the public (and free!), although some are on private property and you'll need to ask permission before visiting.

Menorca's tourism promoters often liken the island to an open-air museum and the main sites have been made readily accessible to visitors – sometimes to their detriment. These places provide fascinating insights into the past, but most aren't as well presented as they could be. The major monuments are definitely worth a look, but many of the minor sites present little to see but crumbling ruins.

The monuments are linked to three main periods: the Pre-Talayotic Period (or cave era) from 2000 to 1300 BC; the Talayotic Period (or Bronze Age) from 1300 to 800 BC; and the Post-Talayotic Period (or Iron Age) from 800 to around 100 BC. Similarly, there are three types of structures: navetas, talayots and taulas.

Navetas, built from large rocks in the shape of upturned boat hulls, are thought to have been used as either tombs or meeting places – perhaps both.

Talayots, large stone mounds found all over the island, were perhaps used as watchtowers for each settlement.

Unique to Menorca, **taulas** are huge stone tablets precisely balanced in the shape of a 'T'. It has been suggested they could have been used as sacrificial altars but, as with Stonehenge, nobody is sure how these enormous slabs of stone were moved into position or what they signify.

Just off the main road 3km west of Maó, the talayotic settlement known as **Talatí de Dalt** is one of the most interesting sites. It's about five minutes walk from the car park to the main feature, a well-preserved taula. Unusually, it has an attached column, probably a second taula that fell here by accident.

The main square, Plaça d'es Born, is surrounded by palm trees and gracious 19th century buildings including the **ajuntament**, the correos and the **Palau Torresaura**. In the centre of the square is a tall, thin obelisk, built to commemorate those townsfolk who died trying to ward off the Turks on 9 July 1558.

Costa d'es Moll takes you down to the port from Plaça d'es Born. Heading in the other direction, the cobbled laneways and streets between Plaça d'es Born and Plaça d'Alfons III hold plenty of interest, with simple whitewashed buildings alongside ornate churches and elegant palaces. The pedestrian walkway of **Ses Voltes**, the heart of the commercial district, is lined with glamorous shops and boutiques, restaurants and smoky bars.

Architectural landmarks worth looking out for include the 14th century **catedral**, built in Catalan Gothic style on the original site of Medina Minurqa's central mosque; the baroque 17th century churches **Església dels Socors** and **Església del Roser** (now used as an exhibition gallery); and impressive noble families' mansions such as **Palau Martorell** and **Palau Saura**.

Special Events
The Festa de Sant Joan de Ciutadella, held in the last week of June, is one of Spain's best-known and most traditional festivals.

Places to Stay – Budget
Hostal-Residencia Oasis (☎ 971 38 21 97, Carrer de Sant Isidre 33) is set around a spacious garden courtyard and has pleasant

Menorca's Prehistoric Heritage

About 4km farther along on the north side of the road is the **Rafal Rubí**, a pair of well-preserved burial navetas.

The nearby **Torralba d'en Salord** is another talayotic settlement. It also features an impressive taula, but the rest of the settlement is in poor repair.

South of Alaior is the large **Torre d'en Gaumes** settlement, which now has its own car park, kiosk and a signposted walking trail that leads you around the site. It includes three talayots on a hilltop and a collection of circular dwellings.

Farther south on the coast at **Cales Coves** some 90 caves dug into the coastal cliffs were apparently used for ritual burials. More recently some of the caves have been homes to hippy colonies, and nearby the large **Cova des Xoroi** has been enterprisingly converted into a disco.

South of Ciutadella, **Son Catlar** is the largest talayotic settlement in the Balearic Islands. Its five talayots and the remains of its dwellings cover around six hectares. East of Ciutadella (near the 40km road marker), the **Naveta des Tudons** is a stone burial chamber that was restored in 1961.

The tourist office's excellent *Archaeological Guide to Menorca* is a handy guide.

JON DAVISON

Prehistoric Menorcans are thought to have used these talayots near Binebeca as tombs and meeting places

---

rooms, most with bathrooms. It charges up to 5500 ptas (no singles).

Café Ses Persianes (☎ 971 38 14 45), a hip little bar on Plaça d'Artrutx, has rooms upstairs at 4000 ptas a double.

Places to Stay – Mid-Range
Hotel Gèminis (☎ 971 38 58 96, Carrer de Josepa Rossinyol 4) is a friendly and stylish two-star place. Excellent rooms with bathroom, TV, phone and heating cost from 4000/7000 ptas (plus IVA).

The well-located *Hostal-Residencia Ciutadella* (☎ 971 38 34 62, Carrer de Sant Eloi 10) is another good mid-range option. Cosy rooms with timber furniture, a phone and bathroom cost up to 8500 ptas including breakfast. Prices drop dramatically out of season, when single rates also become available.

If the other two are full, there's always the big and bland *Hotel Alfonso III* (☎ 971 38 01 50, Camí de Maó 53) on the main road into town. Rooms with bath cost 3600/6400 ptas (plus IVA).

Places to Eat
Ciutadella's small port is teeming with little restaurants and cafés, many of them set in the old city walls or carved out of the cliffs that line the waterfront. If you join the evening *paseo* you won't have any trouble finding somewhere to eat.

For a good Italian feed, try *Il Palato Fino* – it's out the back of Hostal Oasis' courtyard at Carrer de Sant Isidre 33.

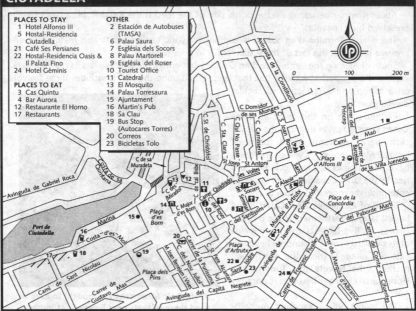

CIUTADELLA

PLACES TO STAY
1 Hotel Alfonso III
5 Hostal-Residencia
   Ciutadella
21 Café Ses Persianes
22 Hostal-Residencia Oasis &
   Il Palata Fino
24 Hotel Gèminis

PLACES TO EAT
3 Cas Quintu
4 Bar Aurora
12 Restaurante El Horno
17 Restaurants

OTHER
2 Estación de Autobuses
  (TMSA)
6 Palau Saura
7 Església dels Socors
8 Palau Martorell
9 Església del Roser
10 Tourist Office
11 Catedral
13 El Mosquito
14 Palau Torresaura
15 Ajuntament
16 Martin's Pub
18 Sa Clau
19 Bus Stop
  (Autocares Torres)
20 Correos
23 Bicicletas Tolo

Cas Quintu's corner bar on the central Plaça d'Alfons III has a great tapas selection – try the *calamar a la plancha* (grilled calamari; 500 ptas) or the tasty *albóndigas* (meatballs; 250 ptas). The adjoining restaurant offers a *menú* for 1300 ptas. *Bar Aurora* next door is also worth a visit.

The tucked away *Restaurante El Horno (Carrer d'es Forn 12)* is a cosy little place where you can dine equally well on seafood and meat dishes – most mains go from 1500 to 2200 ptas.

Entertainment

After dinner, check out *Sa Clau*, on the waterfront at the bottom of Costa d'es Moll. Set in the old city walls, it's a hip piano bar that features live jazz and blues.

Halfway up Costa d'es Moll, *Martin's Pub* pumps out throbbing *bakalao* music most nights until around 4 am.

A little farther north at the top of Carrer de sa Muradeta, *El Mosquito* is a funky salsa club with a great vibe.

Getting There & Away

TMSA (☎ 971 38 03 03) runs buses between Ciutadella and Maó; its depot is close to the centre at Carrer de Barcelona 8. Autocares Torres (☎ 971 38 47 20) serves the coast south of Ciutadella; its buses leave from the estación de autobuses on Plaça dels Pins.

Getting Around

Bicicletas Tolo (☎ 971 38 15 76), opposite Hostal Oasis at Carrer de Sant Isidre 28, rents out mountain bikes (800 ptas per day) as well as Vespas and scooters (1700 to 4600 ptas per day, with a two-day minimum).

NORTH COAST

Menorca's north coast is rugged and rocky, dotted with small and scenic coves. It's much less developed than the south coast and, with your own transport and a bit of footwork, you'll discover some of the Baleares' best off-the-beaten-track beaches.

Maó to Fornells

The closest beach to the north of Maó, **Sa Mesquida**, isn't appealing. Farther north is **Es Grau**, a plain little village on an open bay. The beach is OK, and there is a couple of bar-restaurants.

Inland from Es Grau and separated from the coast by a barrier of high sand dunes is **S'Albufera d'es Grau**, the largest freshwater lagoon in the Islas Baleares. Home to many species of wetland birds and an important stopover for migrating species, S'Albufera and the surrounding countryside have been designated the 'nucleus zone' of Menorca's Biosphere Reserve, a natural park protected from the threat of development. **Illa d'en Colom**, a couple of hundred metres offshore, is considered part of the park. Boats splutter across to the island from Es Grau.

Continuing north, it's a great drive from Maó up to **Cap de Favàritx**, a narrow rocky cape at the top of the S'Albufera d'es Grau zone. The last leg of the drive is across a lunar-like landscape of black rock. At the end of the road a lighthouse stands watch while a relentless sea pounds the impassive cliffs.

South of the cape you can reach some fine sandy bays and beaches, including **Cala Presili** and **Platja d'en Tortuga**, on foot. If you park just before the gate to the lighthouse and climb up the rocks behind you, you'll see a couple of them.

Fornells

The picturesque whitewashed town of Fornells is on a large, shallow bay popular with windsurfers. A former fishing village, Fornells has been made famous by its waterfront seafood restaurants, most of which serve up the local speciality *caldereta de llagosta*, a lobster stew.

It's a nice place – perhaps too nice, to judge by the steady stream of white-shoed tourists. Another downside of its 'discovery' is that it's an expensive spot to eat or sleep in.

Things to See & Do If the sight of those fishing boats bobbing in the bay conjures up romantic fantasies, you could always hire one of Servinautic's (☎ 971 37 66 36) small motor boats and go exploring. There's also a windsurfing school just south of town.

A couple of kilometres west at **Platjas de Fornells**, the development frenzy has been unleashed on the coastal hills surrounding a small beach. The exclusive villas of the Menorca Country Club resort dominate this ritzy *urbanització* (suburban development).

If you want to escape the crowds, continue west to the beach of **Binimella**, from where you can walk around to the unspoilt beaches at **Cala Pregonda**.

Places to Stay *Hostal La Palma* (☎ 971 37 66 34, Plaça S'Algaret 3) offers the best value. Out the back of this bar-restaurant are cheerful rooms with private bathrooms, balconies and views of the surrounding countryside. Singles (not available during summer) cost 3000 ptas and doubles are up to 6250 ptas.

Next door, *Hostal-Residencia S'Algaret* (☎ 971 37 65 52) is relatively overpriced at 6250/10,300 ptas. Fifty metres on is *Hostal Fornells* (☎ 971 37 66 76, Carrer Major 17), a slick place with a good pool, bar and restaurant. High season (in this case the first three weeks of August form a kind of super high season with even higher prices) rooms start at 7820/12,580 ptas and reach 10,500/17,500 ptas if you want sea views. Add IVA to these prices. Prices drop heavily in the off season.

Places to Eat The restaurants along the foreshore are all pretty expensive and if you're here to try *caldereta de llagosta* you're up for around 5500 ptas.

If you're planning to spend that sort of money head for *Es Cranc (Carrer de Tra-*

muntana 31), a couple of hundred metres north of the centre. It has a simple dining room, but the food is good, and it's less touristy than the waterfront places. Steak and seafood dishes mostly cost from 1400 to 2500 ptas, or you could splash out on caldereta de llagosta (6200 ptas) or perhaps *paella de llagosta* (12,400 ptas for two people).

Near Ciutadella

Newly paved and well-signposted roads invariably lead to heavily developed *urbanizaciones*. If you find yourself bouncing along a narrow, pot-holed shocker lined with crumbling stone walls, it probably leads somewhere interesting.

A good example is the road from Ciutadella to **Cala Morell**. It's hard to find and bumpy as hell, but it leads to a low-key, tasteful development of whitewashed villas. Steep steps lead to the small port-beach, backed by a couple of bar-restaurants. A track leads around the cliffs to the **Cala Morell Necropolis**, burial caves hacked into the coastal cliffs in prehistoric times.

Instead of turning left to Cala Morell, you could also continue straight on to **La Vall**. At the end of the road you come to a set of gates, beyond which is a privately owned nature and wildlife park with a parking area, a small lake and good, untouched beaches. The owners charge 600 ptas entry per car. La Vall is open daily from 10 am to 7 pm.

SOUTH COAST

Menorca's southern coastline tends to have the better beaches – and thus the greater concentration of development. The recurring image is of a jagged coastline, occasionally interrupted by a small inlet with a sandy beach and backed by a growing cluster of modern whitewashed villas. Menorca has opted for small-scale developments in the 'Moorish-Mediterranean' style, largely modelled on the resort of Binibèquer (or Binibeca) Vell (south of Maó), designed by the architect Antonio Sintes in 1972.

Although comparatively easy on the eye, these resorts remain the domain of package tourists and time-share touts.

The rugged coastline south of Ciutadella gives way to a couple of smallish beaches at the resorts of **Santandria** and **Cala Blanca**. On the island's south-western corner looms the large resort of **Cala en Bosc**, a busy boating and diving centre. Not far east are the popular sandy beaches of **Son Xoriguer**, which are connected to Ciutadella by frequent buses.

Between Son Xoriguer and Santa Galdana lies some of the least accessible coast, and hence least spoiled beaches, in the south. A series of rough tracks and walking trails lead to the lovely beaches of **Son Saura**, **Cala en Turqueta** and **Es Castellet de Macarelleta**. Some of these pass through private property; you'll need to ask permission to use them.

South-west of Ferreries is the big resort of Santa Galdana. Two-thirds of the way down this road, *Camping S'Atalai (☎ 971 37 30 95)* is a simple, pleasant camping ground shaded by pine trees.

Santa Galdana is just the place to go if karaoke bars, English pubs and mini-golf courses are your idea of a good holiday. A walking track leads west around the coast to the popular **Macarella**, which has a couple of beach bars, and a little farther on is the previously mentioned Es Castellet de Macarelleta. To the east of Santa Galdana is the fine beach of **Cala Mitjana**.

The resort of **Son Bou**, south of Alaior, boasts the island's longest beach and most depressing development. A few kilometres up the road towards Alaior is *Camping Son Bou (☎ 971 37 26 05)*, a first-class place with everything from pool to horse riding and outdoor cinema.

Most of the coast south of Maó is more intensively developed. There are regular buses down to the resort of **Punta Prima**, which has a nice beach. West around the coast is **Binibèquer Vell**, already mentioned above. It is touted as a charming old fishing town. It has been given several coats of whitewash and turned into a tourist beehive

Detail from the *modernisme* Mercado Central, Valencia City (Valencia)

BETHUNE CARMICHAEL

The fishing port of Castro Urdiales (Cantabria)

DAMIEN SIMONIS

La Coruña's impressive ayuntamiento (Galicia)

DAMIEN SIMONIS

Ibiza City's harbour area has lanes lined with bars, shops and restaurants (Islas Baleares)

Fornells, Menorca (Islas Baleares)

Sun-seekers at Es Canar, Ibiza (Islas Baleares)

Menorca has many lovely secluded beaches and coves (Islas Baleares)

but the curious houses and narrow lanes, not to mention the little boat harbour with its transparent water (fine for swimming), *are* attractive. A few kilometres farther west

lies **Binidalí**. The village is no big deal and the beach small, but the water so azure it makes you want to swim out of the inlet and into the open sea.

Murcia

This must be one of the least visited corners of Spain. Walled off to the east and south by the arid steppes and mountains of inland Andalucía and Castilla-La Mancha and to the north by the equally dry southern end of Valencia, Murcia finds its only relief in the 250km of Mediterranean coastline called the Costa Cálida.

Long occupied by the Muslims, whose ancestors in North Africa and the Middle East knew a thing or two about heat, Murcia inherited systems of irrigation comprising waterwheels, aqueducts and even restored Islamic-era canals *(acequias)*. These help to distribute the parsimonious 300mm annual rainfall, allowing at least some of the otherwise untilled land to be cultivated intensively – notably for citrus crops in the El Guadalentín valley, fed by the Río Segura and Río Mula. Wine grapes are also grown.

Of the more than 300 peaks, the highest lie in the north-western Moratalla uplands. Farther north still, the La Puerta district is notable for its pine forest. In the middle of the province is the Segura valley, its ancient Muslim villages dotted around the rugged countryside and sheltered by the ochre rock of the Sierra de Ricote.

More than 310,000 people crowd the busy capital, also called Murcia, and the local orchards and canning industry are their main employers. Cartagena is the second city, with 175,000 people and one of the country's major ports. Inland, the former frontier town of Lorca is famous for its spectacular Semana Santa processions.

The Parque Natural de Sierra Espuña is popular with climbers and hikers, while beach and sun-seekers prefer the tepid waters of the Mar Menor.

MURCIA CITY

Founded in 825 AD by Abd ar-Rahman II, caliph of Córdoba, the Islamic town of Mursiya and its territories became an independent kingdom in 1224, only to be

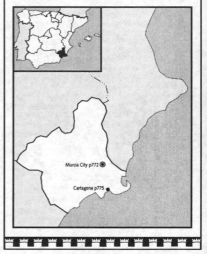

HIGHLIGHTS

- Semana Santa celebrations in the town of Lorca
- Murcia's Catedral de Santa María
- Hiking in the Parque Natural de Sierra Espuña
- A swim in the Mar Menor

Murcia City p772

Cartagena p775

conquered by Castilla in 1243. Over the years much of its land was lost to Jaén, Valencia, Albacete, Cuenca, Granada and Almería, until the province was reduced to its present size of 11,300 sq km in 1833.

During the War of the Spanish Succession, the countryside surrounding the city was flooded to defend it against attack by the Austrians. In 1936, during the Spanish Civil War, it was the scene of bitter fighting and many of its churches were burnt down.

Despite industrial growth on the outskirts, Murcia remains an attractive university city, with several important Renaissance monuments intact.

Orientation

The city centre is immediately north of the Río Segura, across the Puente Viejo (old bridge). The *estación de autobuses* (bus station) on Calle de la Sierra de la Pila is a 20 minute walk west from the centre. The RENFE train station is still farther out, south of the Puente Viejo. Gran Vía del Escultor Francisco Salzillo, the main commercial thoroughfare and known to locals simply as the Gran Vía, runs north from the Puente Viejo.

All of Murcia's sights are within walking distance of each other, mostly between the river and the university. From the cathedral on Calle de la Trapería, the pedestrianised *calle mayor* (main street) of medieval and Renaissance Murcia runs north through the old town.

Information

Tourist Offices The municipal tourist office (☎ 968 21 98 01), Calle del Plano de San Francisco 8, is open Monday to Friday

MURCIA

To Albacete &
Madrid

CASTILLA -
LA MANCHA

VALENCIA

Yecla

Jumilla

Casas
del Puerto

0   20   40 km

N-301

To Alicante &
Valencia

Río   Benamor   Río   Segura   Cieza

Moratalla   Calasparra

Blanca

Fortuna

Elche (Elx)

Caravaca
de la Cruz   Cehegín

Sierra de Ricote

Archena

Molina

Orihuela   Río   Segura

A-7

▲ Revolcadores
(2001m)

Barranda   Bullas   Río   Mula   Pliego   Mula

Alcantarilla

Murcia

El Moral

Parque Natural de
Sierra España   España
(1585m)   Librilla

Torrevieja

Zarcilla de
Ramos   La Paca   ▲ Alhama
de Murcia

Casas
Nuevas   Aledo   N-340   Gañuelas   Corvera   Balsicas

Sucina

San Pedro
del Pinatar

Vélez Blanco   Baños
de la Fuensanta   Lorca   Totana   N-301   Lo Pagán
Santiago de la Ribera

Vélez Rubio   Fuente
Álamo   Los Alcázares

Mar   La Manga
Menor   La Manga
del Mar Menor

To Granada   N-342   Puerto
Lumbreras   Mazarrón   Cartagena   N-332   La
Unión

ANDALUCÍA   N-332   Puerto de
Mazarrón

Golfo de Mazarrón   C á l i d a

Cope   C o s t a

N-340   Águilas

MEDITERRANEAN
SEA

To Almería

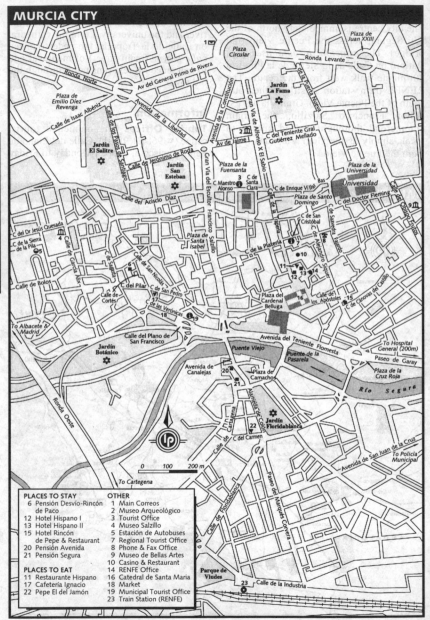

MURCIA CITY

Plaza de Juan XXIII

Plaza Circular

Ronda Levante

Ronda Norte

Av del General Primo de Rivera

Plaza de Emilio Díez Revenga

Jardín La Fama

Avenida de la Libertad

Calle de Isaac Albéniz

Calle de los Pasos de Santiago

Jardín El Salitre

Calle de Jerónimo de Roda

Jardín San Esteban

Gran Vía del Escultor Francisco Salzillo

Gran Vía de Alfonso X El Sabio

C del Teniente Gral Gutiérrez Mellado

Av de Jaime I

Plaza de la Fuensanta

Plaza de la Universidad

Universidad

C de Enrique Villar

Calle del Acisclo Díaz

Maestro Alonso

C de Santa Clara

Plaza de Santo Domingo

C del Doctor Fleming

C del Dr Jesús Quesada

C de la Sierra de la Pila

Calle de García Alix

Calle de Sagasta

Plaza de Santa Isabel

C de San Cristóbal

C de la Platería

C de Alejandro Séiquer

Calle de Bolos

C de San Nicolás

C del Pilar

C de San Pedro

Plaza del Cardenal Belluga

Calle del los Apóstoles

C de Cánovas del Castillo

Calle de Cortés

de las Verónicas

Calle del Plano de San Francisco

Market

Avenida del Teniente Flomesta

To Albacete & Madrid

Jardín Botánico

Ronda Oeste

Avenida de Canalejas

Puente Viejo

Puente de la Pasarela

To Hospital General (200m)

Paseo de Garay

Plaza de la Cruz Roja

Río Segura

Plaza de Camachos

Alameda de Colón

Calle de Cartagena

Jardín Floridablanca

C del Carmen

Avenida de San Juan de la Cruz

To Policía Municipal

0   100   200 m

To Cartegena

Calle de Rondablanca

Paseo del Marqués Corvera

Parque de Viudes

Calle de la Industria

PLACES TO STAY	OTHER
6 Pensión Desvío-Rincón de Paco	1 Main Correos
12 Hotel Hispano I	2 Museo Arqueológico
13 Hotel Hispano II	3 Tourist Office
15 Hotel Rincón de Pepe & Restaurant	4 Museo Salzillo
20 Pensión Avenida	5 Estación de Autobuses
21 Pensión Segura	7 Regional Tourist Office
	8 Phone & Fax Office
	9 Museo de Bellas Artes
PLACES TO EAT	10 Casino & Restaurant
11 Restaurante Hispano	14 RENFE Office
17 Cafetería Ignacio	16 Catedral de Santa María
22 Pepe El del Jamón	18 Market
	19 Municipal Tourist Office
	23 Train Station (RENFE)

from 9 am to 3.30 pm and 5 to 7.30 pm. An alternative office is on Calle del Maestro Alonso. It is open daily from 10 am to 1.30 pm and from 5 to 7.30 pm from Monday to Saturday.

The regional tourist office (☎ 968 36 61 00), Calle de San Cristóbal 5, is open Monday to Friday from 10 am to 2 pm and 5 to 7 pm and Saturday from 11 am to 1 pm.

Money Banks with ATMs throng Gran Vía del Escultor Francisco Salzillo and Calle de la Trapería.

Post & Communications The main *correos* (post office; postcode 30080) is on Plaza Circular. The phone and fax office on Calle de San Lorenzo is open Monday to Friday from 10 am to 2 pm and 6 to 9 pm.

Medical Services & Emergency In a medical emergency call the Cruz Roja on ☎ 968 22 22 22. The Hospital General (☎ 968 25 69 00) is north of the river at Avenida del Intendente Jorge Palacios 1.

The Policía Municipal (☎ 968 26 66 00) are at Avenida de San Juan de la Cruz 12. In an emergency ring ☎ 092.

Catedral de Santa María

Murcia's sumptuous cathedral was raised on the site of a mosque in 1358. Building began in Gothic style, but alterations were made in the 16th century and from 1748 came dramatic changes, including addition of the baroque façade.

Inside, don't miss the 16th century **Capilla de Junterón**, built in Renaissance style by Jerónimo Quijano, also responsible for the panelling in the sacristy. For spectacular views of the city, climb the 92m tower (closed at the time of writing).

In the 19th century cloister and chapterhouse, the **museo** contains many treasures, including a Roman sarcophagus, an 18th century silver monstrance by Antonio Pérez and a 14th century altarpiece by Bernabé de Módena. The cathedral and museum are open daily from 10 am to 1 pm and 5 to 7 pm (200 ptas).

Casino

The casino, Calle de la Trapería 22, opened as a gentlemen's club in 1847. Its decorative façade, completed in 1901, is the work of architect Don Pedro Cerdán Martínez, while the vestibule and Arabic patio were designed by *madrileño* artist Manuel Castraños. It is open daily to nonmembers from 9.30 am to 9 pm (100 ptas).

Museums

The **Museo Arqueológico**, in the Casa de la Cultura at Gran Vía de Alfonso X El Sabio 9, has a fine collection of prehistoric, Roman and Islamic artefacts. It is open Monday to Friday from 9 am to 2 pm and 4 to 8 pm and Saturday from 10 am to 1.30 pm (free). From July to September it is only open from 9 am to 2 pm on weekdays.

The **Museo de Bellas Artes**, Calle del Obispo Frutos 12, contains works by José de Ribero, Hernández Amores and Martínez Pozo and has a good selection of contemporary art. It is open Monday to Friday from 9 am to 2 pm and 5 to 8.30 pm, and Saturday from 10 am to 2 pm (mornings only in July and August). Entry is free.

The Ermita de Jesús is a baroque chapel in the west of town. It houses the **Museo Salzillo**, devoted to the Murcian sculptor Francisco Salzillo (1707-83). Here you can see his impressive *pasos*, the figures carried in the Semana Santa processions. The exhibition also features his superb Nativity scene, with more than 500 figures in 18th century Murcian dress. It is open Tuesday to Saturday from 9.30 am to 1 pm and 4 to 7 pm (3 to 6 pm in winter) and Sunday (except in July and August) from 11 am to 1 pm (200 ptas).

Places to Stay

There is no shortage of budget pensiones. *Pensión Desvío-Rincón de Paco (☎ 968 21 84 36, Calle de Cortés 27)*, near the food market, is as basic as you can get in terms of décor, with singles for 1500 ptas or doubles with bath for 2900 ptas.

A better option is *Pensión Avenida (☎ 968 21 52 94, Avenida de Canalejas 10)*, just south of the Puente Viejo. Singles/doubles cost 1500/3000 ptas.

By comparison, *Pensión Segura (☎ 968 21 12 81, Plaza de Camachos 19)*, a few doors down, is luxurious, with singles/doubles for just 2300/3600 ptas, all with private bath and TV.

The two-star *Hotel Hispano I (☎ 968 21 61 52, Calle de la Trapería 8)*, closed July and August, has a bar and car park. Rooms cost 3500/5000 ptas plus IVA.

Hotel Hispano II (☎ 968 21 61 52, Calle de Radio Murcia 3) is more upmarket. Rooms with TV and phone cost 7500/9500 ptas plus IVA.

At the top of the range is *Hotel Rincón de Pepe (☎ 968 21 22 39, fax 968 22 17 44, Calle de los Apóstoles 34)*. Doubles cost from 10,000 to 17,600 ptas plus IVA.

Places to Eat

A lively *market* is sandwiched between Calle de las Verónicas and Calle del Plano de San Francisco.

Cafetería Ignacio on the corner of Calle de los Desamparados and Calle de San Pedro has great tapas from 175 ptas and spectacular cakes.

Pepe El del Jamón (Calle del Carmen 4), or Pepe the Ham Man, is a rough and ready locals' hangout where a set lunch costs 900 ptas.

Clamped between hotels Hispano I and Hispano II, on Calle del Arquitecto Cerdán, is the smart *Restaurant Hispano*. It has a fabulous display of fresh fish and looks expensive – but isn't. The food is superb, but a three-course set *menú* costs as little as 1000 ptas.

The *casino's restaurant* on Calle de la Trapería has a three-course set *menú* for 1100 ptas.

The *Hotel Rincón de Pepe's restaurant* is renowned throughout Spain. It's good for a splurge, but it's not necessary to spend a fortune: main courses start at 1450 ptas.

Entertainment

Most of the nightlife is concentrated around the *universidad* (university), particularly in the area between Calle de Saavedra Fajardo and the Museo de Bellas Artes. Later on, move to the side streets off Gran Vía de Alfonso X El Sabio, between Plaza Circular and the Museo Arqueológico.

Getting There & Away

Bus There are 20 buses a day to Cartagena (415 ptas), seven to Alicante (600 ptas), two to Águilas (735 ptas), four to Almería (2110 ptas) and Málaga (3815 ptas) and five to Barcelona (5255 ptas). For info call ☎ 968 29 22 11.

Train RENFE has an office (☎ 968 25 21 54) at Calle de Barrionuevo 4. The five trains to Cartagena (1200 ptas) are Talgos. Four run to Madrid (4900 ptas) via Albacete (2400 ptas). Four *cercanías* trains head for Águilas (720 ptas) and up to 17 a day travel to Alicante (525 ptas; more frequently on weekends). The cheapest seat to Valencia is 3200 ptas, where you can connect for Barcelona (4700 ptas).

Car & Motorcycle For Cartagena, take the N-301 southbound. If you're heading north-west, the N-301 also takes you to Albacete and on to Madrid. For the Parque Natural de Sierra Espuña you need the N-340 to Alhama de Murcia and Almería.

Getting Around

To get into town from the estación de autobuses take the No 3 bus. From the train station take No 9 or No 11.

CARTAGENA

In 223 BC, Hasdrubal marched into the Iberian settlement of Mastia at the head of his Carthaginian army and renamed it Carthago Nova. It continued to flourish under the Romans, and under Muslim rule became the independent emirate of Cartajana. The Arabs improved its agriculture and established its reputation for building warships. In 1242 Fernando III of Castilla evicted Murcia's Muslim rulers for good.

Cartagena remains one of Spain's most important ports, although in 1998 the US

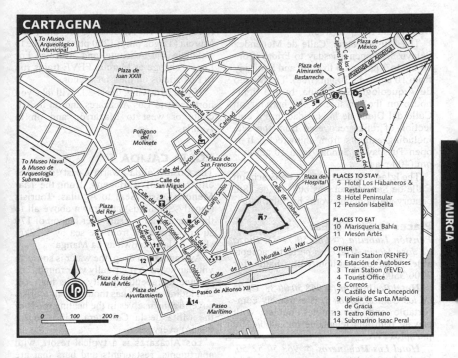

CARTAGENA

PLACES TO STAY
5 Hotel Los Habaneros &
   Restaurant
8 Hotel Peninsular
12 Pensión Isabelita

PLACES TO EAT
10 Marisquería Bahía
11 Mesón Artés

OTHER
1 Train Station (RENFE)
2 Estación de Autobuses
3 Train Station (FEVE)
4 Tourist Office
6 Correos
7 Castillo de la Concepción
9 Iglesia de Santa María
   de Gracia
13 Teatro Romano
14 Submarino Isaac Peral

MURCIA

navy decided not to dock its big nuclear-powered warships here any more. The previous year the aircraft carrier USS Theodore Roosevelt had been unable to squeeze into port, so its 5000 crew were obliged to stay on board out at sea – frustratingly close to land after months at sea. What this will mean for business in the local bars remains to be seen, although Washington promised 'smaller vessels' would continue to visit.

Apart from the occasional appearance of dollar-laden sailors, mining still plays a part in the local economy – as it has done since ancient times.

Information

The tourist office (☎ 968 50 64 83), Plaza del Almirante Bastarreche s/n, is open Monday to Friday from 10 am to 1 pm and 5 to 8 pm and Saturday from 10 am to 2 pm.

The correos (postcode 30200) is on Calle del Arco de la Caridad. In a medical emergency call the Cruz Roja on ☎ 968 50 27 50.

Things to See

Right by the quay, at the western end of Paseo de Alfonso XII, is the **Submarino Isaac Peral**, one of the oldest submarines in the world, built in 1888 by an eccentric Catalan who failed to interest the navy sufficiently to get funding for his schemes. Nearby, to the north-west, are the remains of the **Teatro Romano**, discovered in 1987. Inscriptions indicate it was built in 1 BC.

The **Museo Arqueológico Municipal**, Calle de Ramón y Cajal 45, stands on the site of the 4th century Roman necropolis of San Antón and contains Carthaginian, Roman, Visigothic and Muslim antiquities. It is open Tuesday to Friday from 10 am to

1 pm and 4 to 6 pm, Saturday and Sunday from 10 am to 1 pm (free).

The **Museo Naval**, Calle de Menéndez Pelayo 8, is open Tuesday to Friday from 10 am to 3 pm and 4 to 6 pm and Saturday from 10 am to 12.30 pm (free). The **Museo de Arqueología Submarina**, by the lighthouse on the far side of the harbour on Calle del Dique de la Navidad, has a collection of relics recovered from the sea, including exhibits from shipwrecks. It is open Tuesday to Sunday from 10 am to 3 pm (400 ptas).

The **Iglesia de Santa María de Gracia** on Calle de San Miguel was built in the 18th century and contains works by Salzillo.

Places to Stay & Eat

Pensión Isabelita (☎ 968 50 77 35, Plaza de José María Artés) has perfectly acceptable doubles without/with bath for 3000/3500 ptas.

Hotel Peninsular (☎ 968 50 00 33, Calle de los Cuatro Santos 3) is extremely comfortable and has singles/doubles with private bath and telephone for 3000/4500 ptas plus IVA.

Hotel Los Habaneros (☎ 968 50 52 50, Calle de San Diego 60) is a step up in luxury, with doubles for 6000 ptas plus IVA.

Most of the bars and restaurants are concentrated around Plaza del Ayuntamiento, Plaza de José María Artés and the side streets off Calle Mayor.

Virtually opposite Pensión Isabelita is *Mesón Artés*, where you can get a *menú del día* for 1000 ptas. Highly rated is the traditional *Marisquería Bahía (Calle del Escorial 6)*, which specialises in paella and fresh fish. A *menú* costs 1275 ptas. For more upmarket surroundings, try the restaurant at *Los Habaneros*, where a *menú* costs 1300 ptas.

Getting There & Away

At least 18 buses run daily to Los Alcázares (220 ptas) on the Mar Menor, two to Águilas and up to eight to Lorca (690 ptas).

There are four trains a day to Madrid (5400 ptas) via Albacete (3100 ptas) and Murcia (Talgos only; 1200 ptas), and one to Valencia via Alicante and Murcia. For Lorca, change at Murcia. FEVE trains run to Los Nietos on the Mar Menor.

If you're driving, the N-332 will take you north-east to Los Alcázares and on to Alicante or west to Mazarrón and on to Águilas.

COSTA CÁLIDA

The Costa Cálida (Warm Coast) stretches either side of Cartagena, from the **Mar Menor** (Lesser Sea) to **Águilas**. Tourists (mostly Spaniards) are drawn above all to the Mar Menor – a saltwater lagoon of 170 sq km, separated from the sea by a 22km sliver of land known as **La Manga**.

Averaging 7m deep, the water is so warm you can swim in it virtually year round. The reputed therapeutic quality of its high salt and iodine content has thousands of tourists covering themselves in the healing muds of the Mota de la Calcetera (close to Lo Pagán) every year.

Los Alcázares is a typical resort, with apartments, restaurants and bars that are hard to squeeze into in the tourist season and empty the rest of the year.

West of Cartagena, on the Golfo de Mazarrón, the coast is quieter. The main resorts are Puerto de Mazarrón and Águilas, with little development in between and some beautiful, unspoilt beaches.

LORCA

Illurco was to the Romans a modest stopover on the road between the Pyrenees and Cádiz, but for the Visigoths it became a key bastion in the vain attempts to hold off the invading Muslim armies. It fell to them in around 780 AD, from when it was known as Lurka.

On 23 November 1243, the same day his father, Fernando III, took Sevilla, the future Alfonso X El Sabio reconquered Lorca, although Muslims continued to raid it until the fall of Granada in 1492.

Orientation & Information

Lorca sits on the banks of the Río Guadalentín and is overlooked by a 13th century castle (whose Torre Alfonsina is the outstanding remnant). The tourist office (☎ 968 46 61 57) at Calle de Lope Gisbert 12 is open Monday to Friday from 9.30 am to 2 pm and 5 to 7.30 pm and Saturday from 11 am to 2 pm. The correos (postcode 30800) is at Calle de Musso Valiente 1.

Things to See

The **Centro de Artesanía**, beside the tourist office, sells traditional arts and crafts and some fairly funky stuff too. It is open Monday to Friday from 10 am to 2 pm and 4 to 7.30 pm.

The 17th century **Casa de los Guevara** is a splendid example of baroque architecture; unfortunately, all you can see of it is the inside of the tourist office as the rest of the building is undergoing restoration.

There are more baroque buildings around the **Plaza de España**, otherwise known as Plaza Mayor, in the centre of town. These include the **Pósito y Juzgados**, a 16th century public granary, now the courthouse, and the **Casa Consistorial**, which is now the *ayuntamiento* (town hall). Most impressive of all is the **Colegiata de San Patricio**: its façade is baroque but the interior is mostly Renaissance. It is open daily from 11 am to 1 pm and 4.30 to 6.30 pm.

Peculiar to Lorca are two extraordinary museums – one for the Blancos and another for the Azules (see Special Events) – featuring the magnificent embroidery used in the Semana Santa processions. The **Museo de Bordados del Paso Blanco** on Plaza de Santa Domingo is open Monday to Friday from 11 am to 1 pm and 5.30 to 7.30 pm (free). The **Museo de Bordados del Paso Azul** at Calle de Nogalte 7 is open Tuesday to Friday from 11 am to 1 pm and 5.30 to 8.30 pm and Saturday from 11 am to 1 pm (free).

The **Museo Arqueológico**, in the grand 16th century Casa de los Salazar on Plaza de Juan Moreno, is open Monday to Friday from 11 am to 2 pm and 5 to 8 pm and Saturday and Sunday from 11 am to 2 pm (free).

Special Events

Lorca is renowned throughout Spain for its Semana Santa celebrations, in which two brotherhoods – the Azules (Blues) and the Blancos (Whites) – have competed every year since 1855 to see who can put on the most lavish display.

Places to Stay & Eat

For some bizarre reason there is only one pensión in the centre of town: the spotless *Hostal del Carmen* (☎ 968 46 80 06, *Rincón de los Valientes 3*). Rooms with bath cost about 2000 ptas per person. To find it, turn onto Cuesta de San Francisco from the underground car park, then take a left. The *hostal* is in a tiny square on the right after Calle de Andrés Pascual – the fifth turning on the right from the Cruz Roja building.

The other options are quite a hike over the other side of the river. The three-star *Hotel Alameda* (☎ 968 40 66 00, *Calle de Musso Valiente 8*) has rooms for 5000/7000 ptas plus IVA, and the modern, four-star *Jardines de Lorca* (☎ 968 47 05 99) on Alameda de Rafael Méndez has doubles for 7000/8800 ptas plus IVA.

One of the better restaurants in town is *Casa Roberto (Calle de Musso Valiente 7)*. Its set *menú* costs 1200 ptas. *Rincón de los Valientes*, right next to Hostal del Carmen, serves fine fare, with a *menú* for 1100 ptas. *Jardines de Lorca* has its own excellent restaurant with a *menú* for 1500 ptas plus IVA.

Getting There & Away

There are eight buses a day to Murcia (600 ptas on the nonstop service), two to Almería (1125 ptas) and three to Granada (1875 ptas). At least 10 cercanías trains a day run to Murcia (525 ptas). The train and bus stations are next door to one another about 200m south-west of the tourist office. By road, the N-340 runs south-west to Almería or north-east to Murcia via Totana.

PARQUE NATURAL DE SIERRA ESPUÑA

A 40 minute drive south-west of Murcia towards Lorca, just north of the N-340, the Parque Natural de Sierra Espuña is a paradise for hikers and climbers, with 240 sq km of unspoilt highlands.

Above the sprawling pine forests tower limestone formations, of which the most impressive is **La Pared Sur del Valle de Leiva** (the southern wall of the Leiva valley).

In the north-west of the park you can see the Pozos de la Nieve (snow wells), which were built in the 16th century. The snow was compressed into ice and transported to nearby towns and cities in the summer – a practice that lasted until earlier this century.

Access to the park is best via Alhama de Murcia or Totana. Ask for more details at the tourist offices in Murcia or Lorca.

Andalucía

This large region stretching across southern Spain is one of the country's most diverse and exciting. Andalucía's famously vibrant people are perhaps even more in love with fiestas, music, spectacle and fun than other Spaniards. This is the home of flamenco, sherry and some of the country's biggest and most spectacular festivities, a heartland of bullfighting and the birthplace of the guitar. Cities such as Sevilla, Granada, Málaga, Córdoba and Cádiz present not only a fascinating historic and artistic heritage but also a vibrant entertainment scene and a nightlife which often kicks on till dawn.

In basic geographic terms, Andalucía consists of two east-west mountain chains separated by the fertile valley of the Río Guadalquivir, plus a narrow coastal plain along the Mediterranean and a broader one facing the Atlantic. Of the two mountain chains, the Sierra Morena rolls along Andalucía's northern borders, while the Cordillera Bética is a complicated mass of rugged, dramatic *sierras* broadening out from the south-west to the east; it includes mainland Spain's highest peak, Mulhacén (3478m), in the Sierra Nevada south-east of Granada. This framework encompasses a huge variety: the Sierra de Grazalema in the south-west, exposed to Atlantic winds, is the wettest part of Spain; the deserts of Almería in the east are the driest. And while inland cities like Sevilla and Córdoba are notorious for their extreme heat in summer, snow lies most of the year on the heights of the Sierra Nevada.

The coasts include not only the intensively developed Costa del Sol west of Málaga, but also – you'll be delighted to discover – some very beautiful and relatively little developed beaches on rugged Cabo de Gata east of Almería and along the Atlantic Costa de la Luz. Andalucía's hill country and its picturesque white villages present scenes of endless and varied beauty,

HIGHLIGHTS

- Sevilla, the magical capital of the south
- Granada, with the Alhambra, Albayzín and a buzzing modern life
- Beautiful Parque Natural de Cazorla – Spain's biggest protected area
- The pretty patios and mesmerising Mezquita of Córdoba
- The mysterious Las Alpujarras valleys, huddled beneath the snow-capped Sierra Nevada
- Cabo de Gata, where semidesert meets the Mediterranean, boasting isolated beaches and dramatic cliffs
- The Costa de la Luz – long, sandy, little-developed Atlantic beaches
- Fiestas: Semana Santa or the Feria de Abril in Sevilla, *carnaval* in Cádiz, the Horse Fair at Jerez de la Frontera, Málaga's August *feria* and many, many more

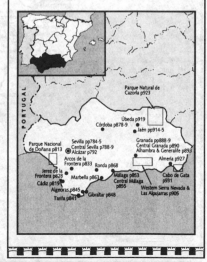

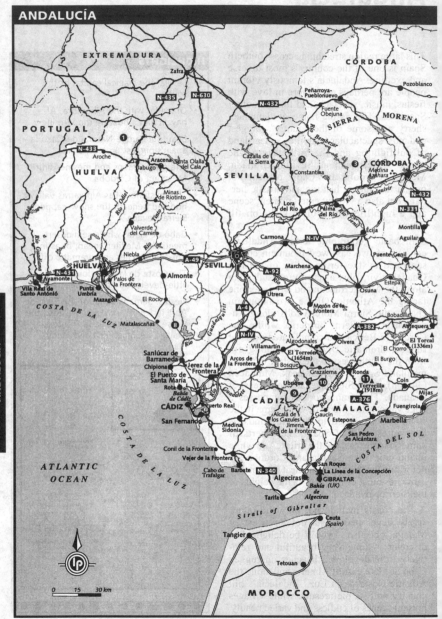

ANDALUCÍA

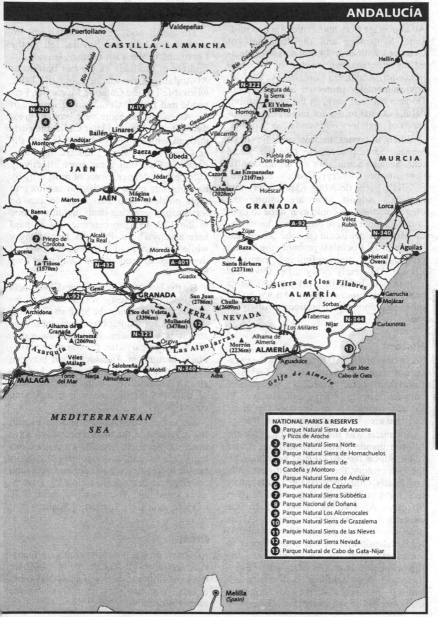

ANDALUCÍA

NATIONAL PARKS & RESERVES

1. Parque Natural Sierra de Aracena y Picos de Aroche
2. Parque Natural Sierra Norte
3. Parque Natural Sierra de Hornachuelos
4. Parque Natural Sierra de Cardeña y Montoro
5. Parque Natural Sierra de Andújar
6. Parque Natural de Cazorla
7. Parque Natural Sierra Subbética
8. Parque Nacional de Doñana
9. Parque Natural Los Alcornocales
10. Parque Natural Sierra de Grazalema
11. Parque Natural Sierra de las Nieves
12. Parque Natural Sierra Nevada
13. Parque Natural de Cabo de Gata-Níjar

ANDALUCÍA

and a wealth of excellent walking routes. (The best seasons for walking in most of Andalucía are from about mid-April to mid-June, September and the first half of October.) With over 14,000 sq km protected as *parques nacionales* or *parques naturales*, Andalucía contains 60% of all environmentally protected land in Spain. Doñana national park, in the Guadalquivir delta, is a vital refuge for hundreds of thousands of migratory birds and other wildlife.

When it comes to festivals, Sevilla's Semana Santa processions (see the boxed text 'Semana Santa') are the most magnificent in the country; Cádiz's *carnaval*, Sevilla's Feria de Abril (April Fair) and Málaga's August *feria* are among the biggest parties you could ever hope to find; and the annual festive pilgrimage known as the Romería del Rocío (see the boxed text 'Romería del Rocío') is probably the largest religious (or quasi-religious) event in Europe. Yet nearly every other town and village, too, holds its own Semana Santa processions, summer feria and a variety of other full-blooded celebrations through the year.

History

Some time around 1000 to 600 BC the mysterious vanished civilisation of Tartessos flourished here, probably somewhere between Sevilla, Cádiz and Huelva. In Roman times Andalucía was the most civilised area in the empire west of Italy.

Andalucía was the obvious base for the Muslim invaders who arrived from Africa in the 8th century AD. First Córdoba, until the 11th century, then Sevilla until the 13th, and finally Granada until the 15th century took turns to be the leading city of Muslim Spain – Al-Andalus (from which the modern name Andalucía comes). At its peak, Córdoba ruled most of Spain and Portugal. Islamic civilisation lasted longer in Andalucía than anywhere else on the Iberian peninsula and its Islamic heritage – including great buildings such as the Alhambra in Granada, the Mezquita in Córdoba and the Alcázar and Giralda in

Sevilla – is one of Andalucía's most fascinating aspects today.

The north and west of Andalucía, including Córdoba and Sevilla, fell to the Christians in the 13th century, leaving the Emirate of Granada as the last bastion of Al-Andalus. Granada held out till 1492, when it fell to the Catholic Monarchs, Fernando and Isabel. Columbus' discovery of the Americas the same year brought great wealth to Sevilla, and later Cádiz, the ports through which most of the trade with the new continent was conducted. But Andalucía's Castilian conquerors effectively killed off its deeper source of prosperity by handing out great swathes of territory to their nobles, who set sheep to run on former food-growing lands. Spain's decline in the 17th to 19th centuries bit as hard here as anywhere. Peasants went hungry while the owners of huge estates either let the land go to seed or sold away what they produced.

By the late 19th century, rural Andalucía – especially the west – was a hotbed of anarchist unrest. During the Spanish Civil War Andalucía split along class lines and savage atrocities were committed by both sides. The hungry years after the war were particularly hungry in Andalucía, and between 1950 and 1970 some 1.5 million Andalucians left to find work in the industrial cities of northern Spain, and other European countries.

Since the 1960s tourism and the overall improvement in the Spanish economy have made a difference. Andalucía's major cities today are bright, cosmopolitan places, its people increasingly well educated, and rural poverty has been dealt a blow by government subsidies. Yet, unemployment, 31% in 1997, is still the highest in Spain.

Press

El Giraldillo, a monthly what's-on magazine covering all Andalucía, is useful for tracking down concerts, fiestas and other events. You can pick it up free at some tourist offices.

Medical Services & Emergency

Throughout Andalucía, you can call ☎ 061 for an ambulance.

Accommodation

Hotel and *hostal* (budget hotel) prices given in this chapter are generally for the high season (July and August in most places). Room prices can be 30% less in winter.

Youth Hostels The 20 or so hostels of the official Andalucian youth hostel organisation, Inturjoven, are mostly good, modern places with a high proportion of twin rooms. Sheets are provided and many rooms have private bathrooms. The hostels don't have cooking facilities but they do have *comedores* (dining rooms), usually serving all meals at good prices.

Inturjoven has a central booking office (☎ 95 455 82 93) at Calle del Miño 24, Los Remedios, 41011 Sevilla. You can also book with the hostels themselves. Prices in all Inturjoven hostels are 900/1300 ptas in the low/high season for under-26s (1075/1475 ptas with breakfast), and 1200/1600 ptas for 26 and overs (1375/1775 ptas with breakfast) – plus IVA in all cases.

At the Córdoba, Granada, Huelva, Málaga, Almería and Sevilla hostels the high season is all year; at Jerez de la Frontera it's April to September; at Sierra Nevada it's when the ski station is open (normally from early December to early May); at the other hostels it's from mid-June to mid-September, long weekends year round, and Semana Santa.

Sevilla Province

The wonderful city of Sevilla overshadows the rest of the province, but country-lovers could head out to the Parque Natural Sierra Norte, while east of the city you can stop off at interesting old towns such as Carmona and Osuna.

SEVILLA

Sevilla, capital of the south with 697,000 people, is one of the most exciting cities in Spain. It takes a stony heart not to be captivated by its unique atmosphere – stylish and proud yet also relaxed and fun-loving. One of the first people recorded as falling in love with Sevilla was the Muslim poet-king Al-Mutamid in the 11th century. The place works its old enchantment every bit as well today.

Except along the banks of the Río Guadalquivir – navigable to the Atlantic Ocean 100km away and source of Sevilla's greatness in times past – this is not a city of great long vistas. Its dense centre unfolds more subtly as you wend your way around its narrow streets and small plazas.

A great city in Muslim times and again in the 16th century, Sevilla has known bad times, too, so it knows how to enjoy the good ones when they come. The year 1992, when the eyes of the world turned on Sevilla's World Expo, was one of the best. But Sevilla has been throwing one of Spain's biggest parties, the Feria de Abril, every year for more than a century, and shortly before the feria it stages Semana Santa processions which are probably the most magnificent in the country.

Aside from its fascinating inner city, Sevilla has some good green parks on the fringes of the centre. It's also one of the homes of flamenco and bullfighting, and has wonderful nightlife. But above all, Sevilla is an atmosphere. Being out among its happy, celebratory crowds on a warm night is a not-to-be-forgotten experience.

There are a couple of catches, of course. One is that Sevilla is expensive. You might pay 5000 or 6000 ptas for a room that would cost 3000 ptas elsewhere. And prices go even higher around the two big festivals (if you can get a room). Another thing to bear in mind is that Sevilla gets *very* hot in July and August.

History

The Taifa Kings Roman Hispalis was a significant town, but overshadowed by Córdoba. Come the Muslims, who called it Ishbiliya, Sevilla continued to play second fiddle to Córdoba. After the collapse of the

ANDALUCÍA

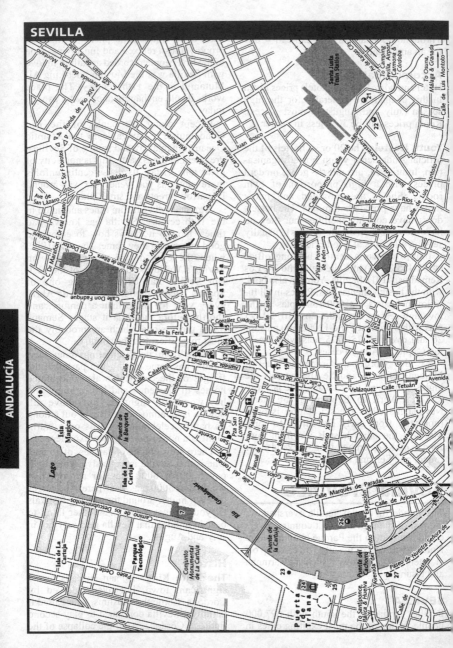

SEVILLA

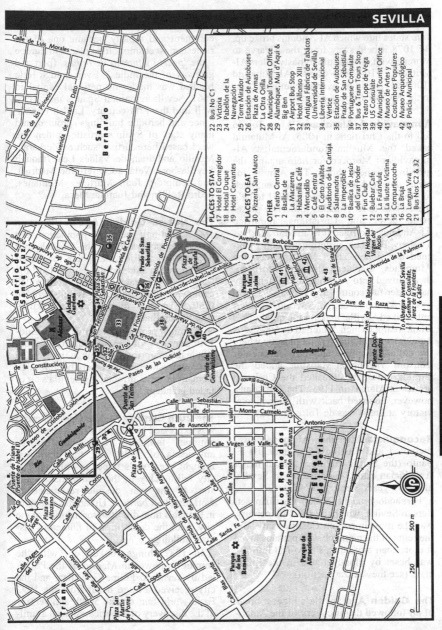

PLACES TO STAY
17 Hotel El Corregidor
18 Hostal Duque
19 Hotel Cervantes

PLACES TO EAT
30 Pizzeria San Marco

OTHER
1 Teatro Central
2 Basílica de La Macarena
4 Mercadillo
5 Habanilla Café
6 Café Central
7 El Corto Maltés
8 Auditorio de la Cartuja
9 Salamandra
10 La Imperdible
10 Basílica de Jesús del Gran Poder
11 Fun Club
12 Bulebar Café
13 La Farándula
14 La Ilustre Víctima
15 Compartecoche
16 La Bruja
20 Lengua Viva
21 Bus Nos C2 & 32
22 Bus No C1
23 Victoria
24 Pabellón de la Navegación
25 Torre Mirador
26 Estación de Autobuses Plaza de Armas
27 La Otra Orilla
28 Municipal Tourist Office
29 Alambique, Mui d'Aquí & Big Ben
31 Airport Bus Stop
32 Hotel Alfonso XIII
33 Antigua Fábrica de Tabacos (Universidad de Sevilla)
34 Librería Internacional Vertice
35 Estación de Autobuses Prado de San Sebastián
36 Portuguese Consulate
37 Bus & Tram Tours Stop
38 Teatro Lope de Vega
39 US Consulate
40 Municipal Tourist Office
41 Museo de Artes y Costumbres Populares
42 Museo Arqueológico
43 Policía Municipal

ANDALUCÍA

Córdoba Caliphate in 1031, however, Sevilla became the most powerful of the *taifa* states into which Al-Andalus broke up. By 1078 it held sway from the Algarve to Murcia, with its Abbadid dynasty rulers Al-Mutadid (1042-69) and Al-Mutamid (1069-91) presiding over a hedonistic court in the Alcázar fortress-palace.

Almoravids & Almohads When Toledo fell to the Christians in 1085, Al-Mutamid asked the Muslim fundamentalist Almoravids of Morocco for help against the growing northern threat. The Almoravids came, defeated Alfonso VI, and went back to Morocco – then returned in 1091 to help themselves to Al-Andalus too. They persecuted Jews and Christians, reunified Al-Andalus and ruled it from Marrakesh as a colony. But their austere grip soon weakened and a new strict Muslim sect, the Almohads, displaced them in Morocco, then moved into Al-Andalus, which they had under full control by 1173.

The Almohad caliph Yacoub Yousouf rather liked Sevilla, making it capital of his whole realm (which stretched as far east as Tunisia) and building a great mosque where the cathedral now stands. His successor Yousouf Yacoub al-Mansour added the Giralda tower and thrashed the Christian armies at Alarcos in 1195. The Christians, however, bounced back with their pivotal victory at Las Navas de Tolosa (1212).

Reconquista After this, Almohad power dwindled and Castilla's Fernando III El Santo (the Saint) captured several major Andalucian cities, culminating in Sevilla, after two years' siege, in 1248.

Fernando brought 24,000 Castilian settlers to Sevilla, which, by the 14th century, was the most important Castilian city. But the reign of the monarch who perhaps loved it more than any other, Pedro I (1350-69), was beset by bloody feuds in the ruling class (see the Alcázar section).

The Golden Age Sevilla's biggest break of all followed the discovery of the Ameri-

cas in 1492. In 1503 the city was given a monopoly on Spanish trade with the new continent and rapidly became one of the richest, most cosmopolitan places in Europe – the *'puerto y puerta de Indias'* (port and gateway of the Indies). Even though little Madrid was made the national capital in 1561, Sevilla remained Spain's major city well into the 17th century. Lavish Renaissance and baroque buildings sprouted, and many stars of Spain's artistic golden age were based here: artists such as Zurbarán, Murillo and Juan de Valdés Leal (though Sevilla-born Velázquez left for Madrid), and sculptors Juan Martínez Montañés, Pedro Roldán and Juan de Mesa.

The Not-so-Golden Age A plague in 1649 killed half the city's population, and as the century wore on, the Guadalquivir became less and less navigable for the increasingly big ships of the day. In 1717 the Casa de la Contratación, which controlled commerce with America, was transferred to Cádiz. Another plague in 1800 killed 13,000 Sevillians.

A limited prosperity returned in the mid-19th century with early industrialisation. While the majority of people in the city and the countryside remained very poor, foreign Romantics were attracted by Sevilla's air of faded grandeur.

The 20th Century Middle-class optimism was expressed by Sevilla's first great international fair, the Exposición Iberoamericana of 1929, but the civil war brought everyone's hopes to nothing. The city fell quickly to the Nationalists at the start of the war despite resistance in working class *barrios*. Urban development in Franco's time did little for the look of the city, with the demolition of numerous historic buildings.

In 1982 things looked up, with the coming to power in Madrid of the PSOE, led by *sevillano* Felipe González, and the city received a huge boost from the 1992 Expo world fair, on the 500th anniversary of the discovery of America. As well as millions of visitors that year, Sevilla got eight new bridges across the Guadalquivir, the new, super-fast AVE rail link to Madrid, and many thousand new hotel rooms.

Orientation

Sevilla straddles the Río Guadalquivir, with most of the interest on the east side. The centre is a tangle of narrow, twisting old streets and small plazas, with the exception of Plaza Nueva and Avenida de la Constitución which runs south from Plaza Nueva. Just east of Avenida de la Constitución are the cathedral, the Giralda tower and the Alcázar fortress-palace, the city's major monuments. The quaint Barrio de Santa Cruz, east of the cathedral and Alcázar, has a good many budget lodgings. The true centre of Sevilla (El Centro) is a bit farther north, around plazas such as Plaza de San Francisco and Plaza Salvador and streets such as Calle Sierpes.

The main transport terminals are on the periphery of the central area: Santa Justa train station 1.5km north-east of the cathedral, Estación de Autobuses Plaza de Armas, 1km north-west of the cathedral, and Estación de Autobuses Prado de San Sebastián, 750m south-east of the cathedral.

Information

Tourist Offices The main tourist office is at Avenida de la Constitución 21 (☎ 95 422 14 04). Open Monday to Saturday from 9 am to 7 pm and Sunday from 10 am to 2 pm (closed on holidays), it's often very busy. It has a list of over 30 foreign consulates in the city. There are also two municipal tourist offices: one south of the centre at Paseo de las Delicias 9 (☎ 95 423 44 65) is open Monday to Friday from 8.30 am to 6.30 pm, the other at Calle de Arjona 28 by the Puente de Triana (☎ 95 450 56 00) is open Monday to Friday from 9 am to 8.45 pm and weekends from 9 am to 2 pm. There are also tourist offices at the train station and airport.

Money There's no shortage of banks and ATMs in the central area. American Express on Plaza Nueva cashes banknotes and travellers' cheques commission-free. Santa Justa station has ATMs.

Post & Communications The main *correos* (post office; postcode 41080), at Avenida de la Constitución 32, is open Monday to Friday from 8.30 am to 8.30 pm and Saturday from 9.30 am to 2 pm.

Finding an unvandalised coin pay phone in the city centre can take a long time, so a phonecard is handy.

Public Internet and email services include Alfalfa 10 (☎ 95 421 38 41), an Internet café at Plaza de la Alfalfa 10, and the Cibercenter (☎ 95 422 88 99), Calle Julio Cesar 8.

Bookshops Librería Beta at Avenida de la Constitución 9 and 27 and Calle Sierpes 81 has guidebooks and novels in English, and maps. Librería Internacional Vértice, Calle San Fernando 33, has a large range of books in English, French and German.

Laundry Tintorería Roma, Calle Castelar 4, will wash, dry and fold a load of washing in one hour for 1000 ptas. It's open weekdays from 9.30 am to 1.30 pm and 5 to 8.30 pm and Saturday from 10 am to 2 pm.

Medical Services & Emergency There's a first aid post (☎ 95 441 17 12) on Calle de Menéndez Pelayo at the corner of Avenida Málaga. The main general hospital is the Hospital Virgen del Rocío (☎ 95 424 81 81) at Avenida Manuel Siurot s/n, 1km south of the Parque de María Luisa. For an ambulance call ☎ 95 442 55 65. The Policía Municipal (☎ 95 461 54 50) are in the Pabellón de Brasil, Paseo de las Delicias 15, and the Policía Nacional (☎ 95 422 88 40) are on Plaza Concordia.

Dangers & Annoyances Sevilla has a reputation for petty crime against tourists – pickpockets, bag-snatchers and the like – so take care.

ANDALUCÍA

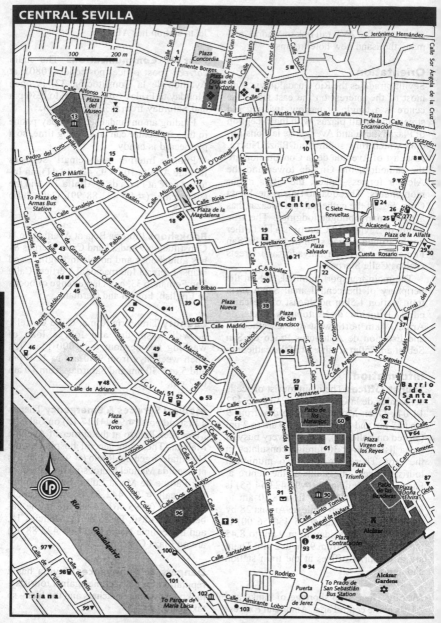

CENTRAL SEVILLA

0   100   200 m

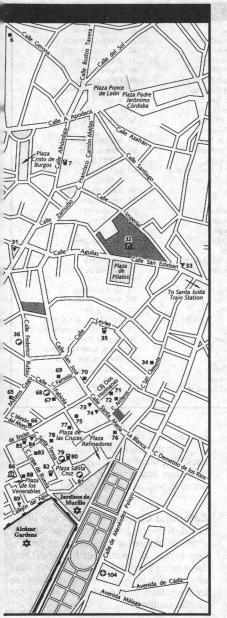

Catedral & La Giralda

After Sevilla fell to the Christians in 1248 the city's main mosque was used as a church until 1401, when in view of its decaying state the church authorities decided to knock it down and start again. 'Let us create such a building that future generations will take us for lunatics,' they agreed – or so legend has it. They certainly got themselves a big church. In fact, some 160m wide and 140m long, it's one of the three largest cathedrals in the world, along with St Peter's (Rome) and St Paul's (London). The building was completed by 1507 and was originally all Gothic, though later work after its central dome collapsed in 1511 was mostly in Renaissance style.

Exterior The cathedral's bulky exterior, seen from ground level, gives few hints of the treasures within, apart from the La Giralda tower on the cathedral's east side and the Puerta del Perdón on Calle Alemanes (two survivals from the Islamic building) and the one neo-Gothic and two Gothic doorways on Avenida de la Constitución.

Entry The entrance to the cathedral and Giralda is beside the Giralda, on Plaza Virgen de los Reyes; it's open Monday to Saturday from 10.30 am to 6 pm and Sunday from 2 to 5 pm, with last entry one hour before closing time (600 ptas, students 200 ptas).

Patio de los Naranjos Immediately inside the entrance and planted with over 60 orange trees, this was originally the courtyard where Muslims performed ablutions before entering the mosque. You enter the cathedral proper by the Puerta de la Granada in the patio's south-east corner. Hanging from the roof just outside this entry are a stuffed crocodile – a gift in 1260 to Alfonso X from the Sultan of Egypt – and an elephant's tusk, supposedly found in the Roman amphitheatre at nearby Itálica.

La Giralda Over 90m high, La Giralda was the minaret of the mosque, constructed in brick over 14 years from 1184 to 1198. Its

ANDALUCÍA

CENTRAL SEVILLA

PLACES TO STAY
4 Hostal Pino
5 Hotel Sevilla
8 Hostal Lis
14 Hostal Londres
15 Hotel Zaida
16 Hostal Lis II
34 Huéspedes La Montoreña
37 Hostal Sánchez Sabariego
42 Hostal Central
44 Hotel Becquer
45 Hotel Puerta de Triana
49 Hotel La Rábida
56 Hotel Simón
63 Hotel Doña María
65 Hostal Goya
66 Pensión Vergara
67 Pensión Fabiola
69 Hostal Córdoba
70 Hotel Fernando III
71 Las Casas de la Judería
72 Hostal Bienvenido
75 Pensión San Pancracio
76 Hostal Santa María La Blanca
77 Pensión Cruces El Patio
78 Hostal Toledo
83 Hotel Murillo
88 Hostería del Laurel

PLACES TO EAT
9 Sopa de Ganso
10 Restaurante San Marco
11 Patio San Eloy
12 Bodegón Alfonso XII
22 Café Universal
26 Restaurante Bar Zucchero
28 Alfalfa 10

29 La Bodega
30 La Bodega Extremeña
31 La Trastienda
33 Bodega Extremeña
48 Casa Pepe-Hillo
50 Bodega Paco Góngora
55 Mesón del Serranito
62 Cervecería Giralda
64 Bodega Santa Cruz
73 Alta-Mira Café Bar
74 Bar Casa Fernando
84 Café Bar Las Teresas
87 El Rincón de Pepe
89 Corral del Agua
97 Pizzería O Mamma Mia
99 Ristorante Cosa Nostra

OTHER
1 Policía Nacional
2 El Corte Inglés
3 El Corte Inglés
6 CLIC
7 Café Lisboa
13 Museo de Bellas Artes
17 El Corte Inglés
18 El Corte Inglés
19 Capilla de San José
20 Halcón Viajes
21 Librería Beta
23 Parroquia del Salvador
24 El Mundo
25 Bare Nostrum & Cabo Loco
27 La Rebótica
32 Casa de Pilatos
35 La Carbonería
36 Australian Consulate

38 Ayuntamiento
39 British Consulate
40 American Express
41 RENFE Office
43 Cibercenter
46 Café Isbiliyya
47 Mercado del Arenal
51 Arena
52 Bar Populus
53 Tintorería Roma
54 A3
57 Hijos de E Morales
58 Librería Beta
59 P Flaherty Irish Pub
60 La Giralda
61 Catedral
68 Italian Consulate
79 French Consulate
80 El Tamboril
81 Irish Consulate
82 Los Gallos
85 Bar Entrecalles
86 Hospital de los Venerables Sacerdotes
90 Archivo de Indias
91 Correos
92 Sevilla Mágica
93 Main Tourist Office
94 Librería Beta
95 Hospital de la Caridad
96 Teatro de la Maestranza
98 Café La Pavana
100 Bus & Tram Tours Stop
101 Embarcadero (Boats)
102 Torre del Oro
103 Iberia
104 First Aid Post

proportions, decoration and colour – which changes with the light – make it perhaps Spain's most perfect Islamic building. The topmost parts (from the bell level up) were added in the 16th century, when Spanish Christians were busy 'improving on' surviving Islamic buildings. El Giraldillo, a bronze weathervane representing Faith which had topped the Giralda for four centuries, was removed in 1997 to prevent further damage by the elements. A copy is to be put in its place.

Turn left inside the cathedral to climb up to the Giralda's belfry. The ascent is quite easy as there's a series of ramps all the way up, so that guards could ride up on horseback. The climb affords great views of the buttresses and pinnacles around the cathedral, as well as the city beyond.

Cathedral Chapels The sheer size of the broad, five-naved cathedral is obscured by a welter of interior structures and decoration typical of Spanish cathedrals. These constitute a storehouse of art work as rich as any church's in Spain – but don't forget to look up from time to time to admire the Gothic vaulting.

The sculpture, stained glass and painting in the chapels along the north and south sides have filled books of their own. Near the west end of the north side is the Capilla de San Antonio with Murillo's large 1666 canvas depicting the vision of St Anthony of Padua; thieves cut out the kneeling saint in 1874 but he was later found in New York and put back.

Columbus' Tomb Inside the cathedral's south door, the Puerta de los Príncipes, stands the tomb of Christopher Columbus. The great sailor's remains – or rather, his probable remains, for no one's 100% sure that the real ones didn't get mislaid somewhere in the Caribbean – were brought here from Cuba in 1899. The monument shows four pallbearers representing the four kingdoms of Spain at the time of Columbus' 1492 voyage: Castilla (carrying Granada on the point of its spear), León, Aragón and Navarra.

Coro Right in the middle of the cathedral is the large *coro* (choir) with 117 carved Gothic-*mudéjar* stalls. The lower ones have marquetry representations of La Giralda on their seats and show vices and sins on the misericords (the front bits of the movable parts).

Capilla Mayor East of the coro is the Capilla Mayor whose Gothic retablo is the jewel of the cathedral and reckoned to be the biggest altarpiece in the world. Begun by the Flemish sculptor Pieter Dancart in 1482 and completed by others in 1564, this sea of gilded and polychromed wood holds more than 1000 carved biblical figures. At the centre of the lowest level is the 13th century image of the Virgen de la Sede, patron of the cathedral.

Eastern Chapels In the east wall of the cathedral are more chapels. The central one of these is the Capilla Real (Royal Chapel) containing the silver and bronze tomb of Fernando III in front of the altar (he's mummified inside), and the tombs of Fernando's wife, Beatrice of Swabia, and son, Alfonso X, at the sides. The Capilla de San Pedro, immediately north, has a retablo with nine Zurbarán paintings of St Peter's life.

Sacristía de los Cálices South of the Capilla Mayor is the entrance to a group of rooms with some of the cathedral's main art treasures. Westernmost of these is the Sacristía de los Cálices, where Goya's painting of the Sevilla martyrs *Santas Justa y Rufina* (1817) hangs above the altar; this pair of potters died at the hands of the Romans in 287 AD but that didn't stop Goya anachronistically putting the Giralda and cathedral in the background.

Sacristía Mayor This large domed room east of the Sacristía de los Cálices is a plateresque creation of 1528-47: the arch over its portal has carvings of 16th century foods. Pedro de Campaña's 1547 *Descendimiento* (Descent from the Cross), above the central altar at the south end, and Zurbarán's *Santa Teresa* to its right, are two of the cathedral's masterpieces. Murillo's *San Isidoro* (reading) and *San Leandro* face each other across the room (the pair were leading figures of the Visigothic church in Sevilla). This room also holds a huge 475kg silver monstrance made in the 1580s by Juan de Arfe; 17th century images of San Fernando (Fernando III) and La Inmaculada which, like the monstrance, are carried in Sevilla's Corpus Christi processions; and, in one of the glass cases, the city keys handed over to Fernando III when he captured Sevilla in 1248.

Cabildo This beautifully domed chapter house, in the south-east corner of the cathedral, was built between 1558 and 1592 to the designs of Hernán Ruiz, architect of the Giralda belfry. High above the archbishop's throne at the south end is a Murillo masterpiece, *La Inmaculada*. There are eight Murillo saints around the dome at the same level.

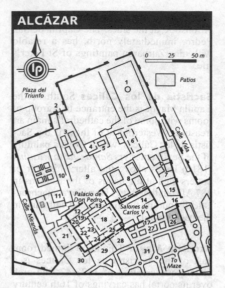

ALCÁZAR

1	Patio de las Banderas
2	Puerta del León (Entrance)
3	Patio del León
4	Sala de la Justicia
5	Patio del Yeso
6	Apeadero
7	Jardín de la Alcabilla
8	Patio del Crucero
9	Patio de la Montería
10	Salón del Almirante
11	Sala de Audiencias
12	Cuarto del Príncipe
13	Cámara Regia
14	Salón de Tapices
15	Jardín del Chorrón
16	Puerta del Palacio de los Duques de Arcos
17	Baños de Doña María de Padilla (Entrance)
18	Patio de las Doncellas
19	Patio de las Muñecas
20	Cuarto del Techo de los Reyes Católicos
21	Jardín del Príncipe
22	Salón del Techo de Felipe II
23	Salón de Embajadores
24	Sala de Infantes
25	Salón del Techo de Carlos V
26	Estanque de Mercurio
27	Jardín de las Danzas
28	Jardín de Troya
29	Jardín de las Galeras
30	Jardín de las Flores
31	Jardín de las Damas

Alcázar

Built originally as a fort for the Córdoban governors of Sevilla in 913, the Alcázar has been adapted and/or enlarged in almost every century since, and today is more palace than fort. It's an intriguing and beautiful place that shouldn't be missed, not least for its associations with the lives and loves of several Muslim and Christian rulers, above all the extraordinary Pedro I (1350-69), known either as El Cruel or El Justiciero – the Justice-Dispenser – depending which side you were on.

History As Sevilla prospered in the 11th century, its Muslim taifa rulers built themselves a palace called Al-Muwarak (The Blessed) in what's now the western part of the Alcázar. East of this, the 12th century Almohad rulers added another palace around the Patio del Crucero. When Sevilla fell to the Christians in 1248, Fernando III moved into the Alcázar, dying here in 1252. His son, Alfonso X, replaced much of the Almohad palace with a Gothic one, now called the Salones de Carlos V.

In 1364-66 Pedro I created the sumptuous mudéjar Palacio de Don Pedro, partly on the site of the old Al-Muwarak palace. The Catholic Monarchs, Fernando and Isabel, set up court in the Alcázar for several years as they prepared the conquest of Granada. The whole complex was further adapted and expanded by later rulers, who also created the Alcázar's beautiful gardens.

Entry The entrance is the Puerta del León at the southern corner of Plaza del Triunfo. The Alcázar is open Tuesday to Saturday from 9.30 am to 7 pm (to 5 pm from October to March) and Sunday and holidays from 9.30 am to 5 pm (to 1.30 pm from October to March). Entry is 600 ptas (students free).

Patio del León This was the garrison yard of the Al-Muwarak palace. Off its southeast corner is the **Sala de la Justicia**, with beautiful mudéjar plasterwork and an *artesonado* ceiling. It was built in the 1340s by Alfonso XI, who disported here with his mistress Leonor de Guzmán. Alfonso's sexual exploits left his heir Pedro I with five half-brothers and a severe case of sibling rivalry. Pedro had a dozen friends, cousins and half-brothers murdered in his efforts to hang on to the throne. One of the half-brothers, Don Fadrique, met his maker right here in the Sala de la Justicia. The room leads on to the pretty **Patio del Yeso**, one of the few surviving parts of the Almohad palace.

Patio de la Montería The rooms on the west side of this courtyard were part of the Casa de la Contratación founded by the Catholic Monarchs in 1503. The **Salón del Almirante** has 19th and 20th century paintings which show historical events associated with Sevilla. The **Sala de Audiencias** contains the earliest known painting on the discovery of the Americas (by Alejo Fernández, 16th century), in which Columbus, Fernando El Católico, Carlos I, Amerigo Vespucci and American Indians can be seen sheltered beneath the cloak of the Virgen del Buen Aire. Also here is a model of Columbus' ship, the *Santa María*.

Patio del Crucero The passage off the Patio de la Montería's east side leads onto this garden, which was originally the upper level of the patio of the 12th century Almohad palace. At first this upper level consisted only of raised walkways which met in the middle. On the lower level grew orange trees, whose fruit could be plucked at hand height by the privileged folk strolling above. The lower level was built over in the 18th century after earthquake damage. Pedro I gave his beloved mistress María de Padilla the Salones de Carlos V, on the south side of the patio, to live in. María must have liked strolling around picking oranges for the patio is also known as the Patio de María de Padilla.

The Red King, The Black Prince & A Big Red Stone

Three centuries before Pedro I set to work on the Salón de Embajadores, the *taifa* poet-king Al-Mutamid had held literary soirées here and sung of his beloved, Rumaykka. Pedro put the room to other uses.

When his buddy Mohammed V was deposed in Granada by a rival known as the Red King, Pedro invited the Red King to a banquet in the Salón de Embajadores. Armed men suddenly leapt from hiding and seized the Red King and his retinue of 37. All were killed outside the city a few days later.

Legend has it that Pedro's real aim was to get his hands on a particularly fabulous ruby in the Red King's possession. Later Pedro gave the jewel to England's Edward, the Black Prince, an ally in his struggles with his most troublesome half-brother, Enrique de Trastámara (known through history as Henry the Bastard).

Mohammed V got his kingdom back and the Black Prince helped Pedro keep a lid on Enrique. But when the Black Prince eventually went home (with the ruby), Enrique turned nasty again, and Pedro wound up being stabbed to death by his sibling in a tent.

Enrique founded the Trastámara dynasty that ruled Castilla until 1516, and the ruby – worn by England's Henry V at Agincourt and described by Elizabeth I as 'great as a racket ball' – today sits in the Tower of London as part of the English royal crown.

ANDALUCÍA

Palacio de Don Pedro Whatever else Pedro I may have done, posterity owes him a big thank you for creating this palace.

Unable to trust 'friends' from closer to home, Pedro maintained an alliance with Mohammed V of Granada, the man chiefly responsible for the decoration of the Alhambra's Palacio Nazaries. So when in 1364 Pedro decided to build himself a new palace in the Alcázar, Mohammed sent along many of his best artisans to help. These were joined by Jews and Muslims from Toledo, and others, mainly Muslim, from Sevilla. Their work represented the best of contemporary architecture and design and also drew on the earlier traditions of the Almohads and caliphal Córdoba. What resulted is a unique synthesis of Iberian Muslim art.

Inscriptions on the palace's façade on the Patio de la Montería encapsulate the unusual nature of the whole enterprise. While one records that the building's creator was 'the very high, noble and conquering Don Pedro, by the grace of God king of Castilla and León', another states repeatedly 'There is no conqueror but Allah'.

At the heart of the palace is the wonderful **Patio de las Doncellas**, surrounded by beautiful arches and with exquisite plasterwork and tiling. The doors at the two ends are among the finest ever produced by Toledo's carpenters.

The **Cámara Regia** on the north side of the patio has two rooms with incredibly beautiful ceilings and more wonderful plaster and tilework. The rear room was probably the monarch's bedroom. From here you can move west into the small **Patio de las Muñecas**, the heart of the palace's private quarters, with delicate Granada-style decoration on its lowest level. The mezzanine and top gallery were built in the 19th century for Isabel II, using plasterwork brought from the Alhambra. The **Cuarto del Príncipe** to the north has superb ceilings and was probably the queen's bedroom.

The spectacular **Salón de Embajadores** (Hall of Ambassadors), on the west side of the Patio de las Doncellas, was Pedro I's throne room – as it had been, in earlier form, of the Al-Muwarak palace. Its fabulous wooden dome of multiple star patterns, symbolising the universe, was added in 1427. The dome's shape gives the room the alternative name Sala de la Media Naranja (Hall of the Half Orange). The coloured plasterwork is equally magnificent. The door arches, strongly reminiscent of the Medina Azahara palace near Córdoba, were retained by Pedro I from the Al-Muwarak building. On the west side the beautiful **Arco de Pavones** archway, with peacock motifs, leads into the **Salón del Techo de Felipe II**, with a Renaissance ceiling from 1589-91.

Salones de Carlos V Reached by a staircase from the south-east corner of the Patio de las Doncellas, these are the much remodelled rooms of the 13th century palace built by Alfonso X. It was here that Alfonso's intellectual court gathered and, a century later, Pedro I installed María de Padilla. The Salón de Tapices or Sala Grande has a collection of huge tapestries showing Carlos I's 1535 conquest of Tunis from the Turkish-backed pirate Barbarossa.

Gardens From the Salones de Carlos V you can make your way out into the Alcázar's large gardens, a perfect place to relax. The gardens in front of the Salones de Carlos V and Palacio de Don Pedro go back to Muslim times but were mostly brought to their present form in the 16th and 17th centuries, while those to the east, beyond a long Almohad wall, are 20th century creations. Immediately in front of the Salones de Carlos V and Palacio de Don Pedro is a series of small linked gardens, some with pools and fountains. From one, a passage runs beneath the Salones de Carlos V to the so-called **Baños de Doña María de Padilla**. Here, beneath the Patio del Crucero, is a grotto which replaced that patio's original pool in which, we imagine, María de Padilla liked to bathe.

From the new gardens you can return to the corner of the Salones de Carlos V, whence a passage leads north to the **Apeadero**, built between 1607 and 1609 as an entrance hall for the Alcázar and now housing a collection of carriages. From here you leave the Alcázar by the **Patio de las Banderas**.

Archivo de Indias

Since 1785 this building on the west side of Plaza del Triunfo has been the main archive on the conquest and colonisation of Spain's American empire. It houses over 80 million pages of documents dating from 1492 through to the end of the empire in the 19th century. There are rotating displays of fascinating maps and historic documents, and is open Monday to Friday from 10 am to 1 pm (free). The 16th century building, by Juan de Herrera, was originally Sevilla's Lonja (Exchange) for commerce with the Americas.

Barrio de Santa Cruz

Sevilla's medieval *judería* (Jewish quarter), immediately east of the cathedral and Alcázar, is today a tangle of quaint, winding streets and lovely plant-decked plazas. The judería, which extended to just east of Calle Santa María La Blanca, came into existence after the Reconquista and was emptied by a pogrom in 1391. Its most characteristic plaza today is Plaza de Santa Cruz, with a central cross made in 1692 which is one of the finest examples of Sevilla wrought-iron work. Plaza Doña Elvira is another quaint spot.

The 17th century **Hospital de los Venerables Sacerdotes** on Plaza de los Venerables, a former residence for aged priests, is open most of the year for guided visits daily from 10 am to 2 pm and 4 to 8 pm (600 ptas). You visit the lovely central courtyard, old living quarters, several art exhibition rooms, and the church with murals by Juan de Valdés Leal and fine sculptures by Pedro Roldán.

El Centro

The real centre of Sevilla, north of the cathedral, is a densely packed zone of narrow, crooked streets, broken up here and there by plazas around which the city's life has revolved for aeons.

Plaza de San Francisco & Calle Sierpes Site of a market in Muslim times, Plaza de San Francisco has been Sevilla's main public square since the 16th century and was once the scene of Inquisition burnings. The southern end of the **Ayuntamiento** (City Hall) here is encrusted with lovely Renaissance carving from the 1520s and 30s.

Pedestrianised Calle Sierpes, heading north from the plaza, is Sevilla's fanciest shopping street. Take a few steps off Sierpes along Calle Jovellanos to the **Capilla de San José**, an 18th century chapel with amazingly intense baroque ornamentation (open for mass daily at 8 pm and Monday to Saturday hourly from 9 am to noon).

Plaza Salvador This was the forum of Roman Hispalis. The plaza is dominated by the **Parroquia del Salvador** (open daily from 6.30 to 9 pm), a big red baroque church built between 1674 and 1712 on the site of a mosque. Inside are three huge, profuse baroque retablos, and on the north side are the remains of the mosque's small patio, with a few half-buried Roman columns.

Casa de Pilatos This finest of Sevilla's noble mansions, on Plaza Pilatos, is still occupied by the ducal Medinaceli family. This 16th century building is a handsome mixture of diverse architectural styles, with some beautiful tilework, artesonado ceilings and gardens, though the overall effect is not unlike that of the Alcázar. The Patio Principal, for instance, has intricate mudéjar plasterwork, 16th century tiling, a Renaissance fountain and Roman sculpture. The staircase from here to the upper floor has the most magnificent tiles in the building, with a great golden artesonado dome above.

The Casa de Pilatos is open daily from 9 am to 7 pm, at 500 ptas for each of the two floors – if time or money are short, skip the top floor.

ANDALUCÍA

Río Guadalquivir

A short walk west from the south end of Avenida de la Constitución brings you to the east bank of the Guadalquivir, a pleasant place for a stroll.

Torre del Oro

This 13th century riverbank Muslim watchtower once crowned a corner of the Almohad city walls. It was supposedly originally covered in golden tiles, hence its name. Inside is the small, crowded Museo Marítimo (Maritime Museum), which is open Tuesday to Friday from 10 am to 2 pm and Saturday and Sunday from 11 am to 2 pm (100 ptas).

Hospital de la Caridad

A block back from the river at Calle Temprado 3, this hospice for the elderly was founded in the 17th century by Miguel de Mañara. According to legend, he was a notorious libertine who changed his ways after experiencing a vision of his own funeral procession.

Its church is adorned with a collection of top-class 17th century Sevillian art on the theme of death and redemption through mercy, commissioned by Mañara. Valdés Leal's frightening masterpieces *In Ictu Oculi* (In the Blink of an Eye) and *Finis Gloriae Mundi* (The End of Earthly Glory) face each other across the west end of the church, chillingly illustrating the futility of worldly success in the face of death.

Four Murillo paintings along the side walls illustrate the mercy theme. They show Moses drawing water from the rock, the miracle of the loaves and fishes, St John of God (San Juan de Dios) caring for an invalid, and Isabel de Hungría curing the sick.

Mañara is buried in the crypt beneath the main altar, on which Pedro Roldán's masterly sculpture illustrates the ultimate act of mercy: the burial of the dead – in this case, of Christ himself.

The Hospital de la Caridad is open Monday to Saturday from 9 am to 1.30 pm and 3.30 to 6.30 pm and Sunday and holidays from 10 am to 1 pm (400 ptas).

Plaza de Toros de la Real Maestranza

Sevilla's bullring on Paseo de Cristóbal Colón is one of the handsomest in Spain, and probably the oldest (building began in 1758). Sevilla is one of Spain's bullfighting capitals, and it was in rings such as this that bullfighting on foot (instead of horseback) took off in the 18th century. Interesting guided tours of the ring and its museum are given in English and Spanish every 20 minutes daily from 10 am to 1.30 pm, and Monday to Friday (except holidays) from 4 to 5.30 pm (300 ptas).

Museo de Bellas Artes

The Fine Arts Museum, in a beautiful former convent at Plaza del Museo 9, does full justice to Sevilla's leading role in Spain's artistic golden age. The 17th century Sevillian masters Murillo, Zurbarán and Valdés Leal are particularly well represented, but the museum also holds interesting antecedents to the Sevillian golden age and some works by great artists who worked elsewhere such as El Greco and Ribera. It's open Tuesday from 3 to 8 pm, Wednesday to Saturday from 9 am to 8 pm and Sunday from 9 am to 3 pm, and is free with an EU passport (250 ptas otherwise).

Highlights include Pedro Millán's 15th century terracotta sculptures (Room I); El Greco's portrait of his son Jorge Manuel, and the influential Renaissance sculpture *San Jerónimo Penitente* by Pedro Torrigiano (Room II); paintings by Velázquez and Alonso Cano (Room III); Zurbarán's masterpiece *Apoteosis de Santo Tomás de Aquinas* and numerous paintings by Murillo (Room V); Ribera's very Spanish-looking *Santiago Apóstol* and Zurbarán's disturbing little *Cristo Crucificado Expirante* (Room VI); and several major works by Zurbarán (Room X).

South of the Centre

Antigua Fábrica de Tabacos

Sevilla's massive former tobacco factory on Calle San Fernando – workplace of Bizet's operatic heroine, Carmen – was built in the 18th century and served its original purpose until the mid-20th century. The factory had its own jail, stables for 400 mules, 24 patios and even a nursery since most of its workers were women. Now part of the Universidad de Sevilla, it's an impressive if rather gloomy building. You can wander in daily any time between 9 am and 9 pm.

Parque de María Luisa & Plaza de España A large area south of the Fábrica de Tabacos was transformed for the 1929 Exposición Iberoamericana. It's spattered with all sorts of fancy and funny buildings, many of them harking back to eras of past glory. In its midst, the large, leafy Parque de María Luisa is a fine respite from the hustle of the city, and is open daily from 8 am to 10 pm.

Facing the park across Avenida de Isabel la Católica, Plaza de España is one of the city's favourite relaxation spots, with fountains and mini-canals where people splash around in rowing boats. Around it is the most grandiose of the 1929 buildings, a semicircular brick and tile confection featuring Sevilla tilework at its gaudiest.

On Plaza de América in the south end of the park is Sevilla's **Museo Arqueológico** with a big collection that includes a room of gold jewellery from the mysterious Tartessos culture and fine collections of Iberian animal sculptures and beautiful Roman mosaics. Facing it is the **Museo de Artes y Costumbres Populares**, with mock-up workshops of local crafts such as guitar-making, ceramics and wrought iron, and some beautiful old bullfighting and feria costumes. Both museums are open on Tuesday from 3 to 8 pm, Wednesday to Saturday from 9 am to 8 pm, and Sunday and holidays from 9 am to 2.30 pm (250 ptas each museum, free with an EU passport and for students).

Isla de La Cartuja

Not quite an island, this tongue of land between two branches of the Guadalquivir, north-west of the centre, was the site of Expo 92. Since the big year the site has had a chequered history, and expanses of it now lie decaying – but there's still plenty to see and do.

The southern **Puerta de Triana** area, across the Puente del Cachorro from the city centre, features a Pabellón de la Navegación (Shipping Pavilion) with exhibits on sea exploration focusing on Sevilla's role (500 ptas), a replica of Magellan's ship the *Victoria* (250 ptas), and a Torre Mirador (Lookout Tower; 250 ptas). They are all open Tuesday to Friday from 10.30 am to 1 pm and 4.30 to 7 pm and weekends and holidays from 11 am to 2.30 pm and 4.30 to 8 pm.

Just north is the **Conjunto Monumental de La Cartuja**, a 15th century monastery where Columbus used to stay. His body lay here from 1509 to 1536. In 1839 the monastery was bought by a Liverpudlian, Charles Pickman, who turned it into a ceramics factory and built the five tall kilns which stand incongruously beside the monastery buildings. The whole complex was restored for Expo. It's open daily except Monday from 11 am to 9 pm (October to March, to 7 pm). Entry is 300 ptas (free on Tuesday for EU citizens).

From here you can wander farther north among the exotic exhibition buildings. Some are being turned into a technology industries park; others are starting to rot away.

On the eastern side of the island near the Puente de la Barqueta is the big **Isla Mágica** amusement park. The theme is the 16th century Spanish colonial adventure, and highlight rides include the El Jaguar roller-coaster, with high-speed 360° turns, and the Iguazú in which you descend an Amazon jungle waterfall. Isla Mágica is open March to October, daily from 11 am to midnight or 1 am. The charge of 3100 ptas for adults, and 2100 ptas for children from five to 12 and over-65s, includes all main attractions. *Tarde* tickets, valid from 5, 6 or 7 pm depending on the season, are 2100/1500 ptas.

Getting There & Away Bus Nos C1 and C2 (see Getting Around) stop at Puerta de

Triana and Isla Mágica. No C3, and No 5 from Puerta de Jerez, also go to Puerta de Triana.

Courses

For information on Spanish-language courses at the university, contact the Instituto de Idiomas, Universidad de Sevilla (☎ 95 455 14 93, fax 95 456 04 39), Calle Palos de la Frontera s/n, 41004 Sevilla. The main tourist office can give you a list of private colleges. Two that we have heard good things about are CLIC, Calle Sor Ángela de la Cruz 18 (☎ 95 456 15 14, 95 456 19 96); and Lengua Viva (☎ 95 490 51 31), Calle Viriato 22.

The main tourist office has a list of several *academias de baile* giving courses in Spanish dance or guitar. You'll also find ads in *El Giraldillo*.

Organised Tours

Open-topped double deck buses run by Sevirama/Guide Friday and the converted trams of Compañía Hispalense de Tranvías both do several daily city tours of about one hour from Paseo de Cristóbal Colón, 100m north of the Torre del Oro. The price for either is 1300 ptas, but you can usually pick up 200 or 300 ptas discount coupons at the main tourist office and elsewhere. Sevirama has earphone commentary in eight languages and children under 12 ride free; Hispalense has commentary in English and Spanish and charges children and students 500 ptas. Their routes are broadly similar: Antigua Fábrica de Tabacos, Parque de María Luisa, Plaza de Toros, Expo 92 site etc.

There are one hour river at least hourly from 11 am to 7 pm, by Cruceros Turísticos Torre del Oro from the Torre del Oro cruises (1200 ptas).

Special Events

Sevilla's Semana Santa processions (see the boxed text 'Semana Santa in Sevilla') and its Feria de Abril, which follows a week or two later, are two of Spain's most famous and exciting festivals.

Feria de Abril Sevilla's April Fair, in the second half of the month, is a kind of release after the solemnity of Semana Santa. It takes place on a special *recinto* (site), El Real de la Feria, in the Los Remedios area west of the Guadalquivir. The ceremonial lighting of the feria grounds on the Monday night is the starting gun for six nights of eating, drinking, fabulous flouncy dresses, and music and dancing till dawn. Much of the recinto is occupied by private *casetas* (enclosures for associations and groups), but there are public casetas, too, where much the same fun goes on. There's also a huge fairground.

In the afternoons, from about 1 pm, those who have horses and carriages parade about the feria grounds in their finery (many of the horses are dressed up too). And it's during the feria that Sevilla's major bullfight season takes place.

Places to Stay

During and around Semana Santa and the Feria de Abril, room prices in many places go up by anything from 20% to 200%, and you should book far ahead. Even at normal times, Sevilla accommodation is fairly expensive – and often in heavy demand, so it's advisable to ring ahead. But the summer prices given here can come down significantly from October to March.

Places to Stay – Budget

Camping *Camping Sevilla* (☎ 95 451 43 79) is about 6km out on the N-IV to Córdoba, just before Sevilla airport. It's open all year at 460 ptas per person and per car, and 400 ptas per tent, plus IVA.

Youth Hostel The Inturjoven *Albergue Juvenil Sevilla* (☎ 95 461 31 50, Calle Isaac Peral 2), south of the centre just off Avenida de la Palmera, has room for 188, mostly in twin rooms. It's about 10 minutes by bus No 34 from opposite the main tourist office. For prices, see this chapter's introductory Youth Hostels section.

Hostales & Pensiones The attractive Barrio de Santa Cruz, close to the cathedral, has lots of places. There are many others north of Plaza Nueva, which is still pretty central.

Barrio de Santa Cruz & Around The 14-room *Hostal Santa María La Blanca* (☎ 95 442 11 74, Calle Santa María La Blanca 28), has clean, modern singles/doubles for 1500/3000 ptas, or doubles with bath for 4000 ptas. Among several places on Calle Archeros, friendly *Hostal Bienvenido* (☎ 95 441 36 55), at No 14, charges 1700/3200 ptas. Just east, little *Huéspedes La Montoreña* (☎ 95 441 24 07, Calle San Clemente 12) has clean, simple rooms at 1500/3000 ptas.

Pensión San Pancracio (☎ 95 441 31 04, Plaza de las Cruces 9) has poky singles for 1800 ptas and bigger doubles for 3200 or 4000 ptas. *Pensión Cruces El Patio* (☎ 95 422 96 33, Plaza de las Cruces 10) has a dorm room with beds at 1300 ptas, singles at 2500 ptas, and doubles at 4000 and 5000 ptas.

Pensión Fabiola (☎ 95 421 83 46, Calle Fabiola 16) with a plant-filled courtyard, has simple, well-kept singles/doubles for 2000/4000 ptas, and doubles with bath for 6000 ptas. *Hostal Córdoba* (☎ 95 422 74 98, Calle Farnesio 12) nearby, has nice air-con rooms for 2500/4000 ptas.

Some of the cheapest rooms are at little *Pensión Vergara* (☎ 95 422 47 38, Calle Ximenez de Enciso 11), with only a 'Camas Rooms Chambres' sign. Adequate singles/doubles will cost you as little as 1300/2500 ptas.

The well kept *Hostal Toledo* (☎ 95 421 53 35, Calle Santa Teresa 15) has 10 rooms with bath for 2500/5000 ptas. *Hostal Goya* (☎ 95 421 11 70, Calle Mateos Gago 31) has nice clean rooms with bathroom at 4175/6500 ptas, doubles with shower for 5775 ptas, and a pleasant sitting area. To the north, the friendly little *Hostal Sánchez Sabariego* (☎ 95 421 44 70, Corral del Rey 23) has decent rooms, most with bath, for around 2000/4500 ptas.

North of Plaza Nueva *Hostal Central* (☎ 95 421 76 60, Calle Zaragoza 18), a three minute walk from Plaza Nueva, has well-kept, decent-sized singles/doubles with bath for around 3500/5000 ptas.

Hostal Lis II (☎ 95 456 02 28, Calle Olavide 5), in a beautiful house, charges 1700 ptas for small singles, and 3500 ptas for doubles with toilet.

Hotel Zaida (☎ 95 421 11 38, Calle San Roque 26) occupies an 18th century house with a lovely patio. The 27 rooms are plain but decent, with bath, for 3000/5000 ptas plus IVA.

Hostal Londres (☎ 95 421 28 96, Calle San Pedro Mártir 1) has plain, clean rooms with private bath at around 3500/5000 ptas.

Farther east, the 10-room *Hostal Lis* (☎ 95 421 30 88, Calle Escarpín 10) has a nice tiled lobby, and singles/doubles with shower for 2000/3500 ptas.

Near Plaza del Duque de la Victoria, *Hostal Pino* (☎ 95 421 28 10, Calle Tarifa 6) has decent, sizable rooms for 1700/2700 ptas or 2200/3500 ptas with shower. The 36 varied rooms at friendly *Hostal Duque* (☎ 95 438 70 11, Calle Trajano 15) are 1800/3500 ptas, or 3000/5000 ptas with private bath. *Hotel Sevilla* (☎ 95 438 41 61, Calle Daóiz 5), has 30 clean, plain, medium-sized rooms with bath for 3745/5885 ptas.

Places to Stay – Mid-Range

Hotels There is plenty of middle range accommodation on offer in Sevilla's more central areas.

Barrio de Santa Cruz The first two places here both cut prices in July and August. *Hostería del Laurel* (☎ 95 422 02 95, Plaza de los Venerables 5) has 21 simple, attractive rooms at 7000/9500 ptas plus IVA. *Hotel Murillo* (☎ 95 421 60 95, Calle Lope de Rueda 7) has a lobby like an antiques showroom and 57 rooms for 4500/7800 ptas plus IVA. The bigger *Hotel Fernando III* (☎ 95 421 73 07, Calle San José 21) charges 9200/11,500 ptas plus IVA.

West of Avenida de la Constitución This is a good central location. *Hotel Simón*

Semana Santa In Sevilla

Every day from Palm Sunday to Easter Sunday, large, richly bedecked images and whole life-size tableaux from the Easter story are carried from Sevilla's churches through the streets to the Catedral, accompanied by long processions which may take more than an hour to pass, and watched by vast crowds. These rites go back to the 14th century but they took on their present form in the 17th, when many of the images – some of which are supreme works of art – were created.

The processions are organised by over 50 different *hermandades* or *cofradías* (brother-hoods, some of which include women), each normally with two *pasos*, as the lavishly decorated platforms bearing the images are called. The first paso carries an image of Christ, crucified or bearing the cross, or in a scene from the Passion; the second holds an image of the Virgin. The pasos are carried by teams of about 40 bearers called *costaleros*, who work in relays. The pasos are heavy – each costalero normally carries about 50kg – and they move with a hypnotic swaying motion to the rhythm of their accompanying bands and the commands of their *capataz* (leader), who strikes a bell to start and stop the paso.

Each pair of pasos has between 400 and 2500 costumed followers, known as *nazarenos*. Many of these wear tall Ku Klux Klan-like capes which cover their heads except for narrow eye slits, symbolising that the identity of the penitent is known only to God. The most contrite go barefoot and carry crosses.

Each day from Palm Sunday to Good Friday, seven or eight hermandades leave their churches in the afternoon or early evening and arrive between 5 and 11 pm at Calle Campana at the north end of Calle Sierpes. This is the start of the *carrera oficial* which all then follow: along Calle Sierpes, through Plaza San Francisco and along Avenida de la Constitución to the Catedral, which they enter at the west end and leave at the east, emerging on Plaza Virgen de los Reyes. They get back to their churches some time between 10 pm and 3 am.

The climax of the week is the *madrugada* (early hours) of Good Friday, when some of the most respected and/or popular hermandades file through the city. The first of these to reach the carrera oficial, at about 1.30 am, is the oldest hermandad, El Silencio, which goes in complete silence. Next, at about 2 am, comes Jesús del Gran Poder, whose 17th century Christ, sculpted by Juan de Mesa, is one of the masterpieces of Sevillan sculpture. This is followed at about 3 am by La Macarena, whose Virgin is the most passionately adored of all. Created by an unknown sculptor in, it's believed, the mid-17th century, she's the patron of bullfighters and the city's supreme representation of the grieving yet hoping mother of Christ. Then come El Calvario from the Iglesia de la Magdalena, Esperanza de Triana, and finally at about 6 am Los Gitanos, the *gitano* hermandad.

On the Saturday evening, just four hermandades make their way to the Catedral, and finally, on Easter Sunday morning, only one, the Hermandad de la Resurrección.

(☎ 95 422 66 60, *Calle García de Vinuesa 19*), in a fine 18th century house, has 29 pleasant singles/doubles at 5500/7500 ptas. It's extremely popular, so book ahead. The bigger **Hotel La Rábida** (☎ 95 422 09 60, *Calle Castelar 24*) has good rooms at 5700/8750 ptas plus IVA.

North & West of Plaza Nueva Hotel Puerta de Triana (☎ 95 421 54 04, *Calle Reyes Católicos 5*) is a good 65-room hotel in a modernised old house. You can get singles/doubles for 6500/10,000 ptas plus IVA. Farther north, **Hotel El Corregidor** (☎ 95 438 51 11, *Calle Morgado 17*) has 77

The Alhambra, a delightful palace-fortress complex built by the Nasrid dynasty in the 13th and 14th centuries. It dominates Granada, Andalucía, from a hill top in the north-east of the city.

DAMIEN SIMONIS

BETHUNE CARMICHAEL

DAMIEN SIMONIS

DAMIEN SIMONIS

Intricate detailing, colourful tiles and serene water: the Alhambra is a world away from bustling Granada

Semana Santa In Sevilla

There are marked differences between the styles of the hermandades. City centre hermandades, such as El Silencio, are traditionally linked with the bourgeoisie. They're serious and austere, with little or no music, and wear black tunics, usually without capes and tied with esparto grass. Hermandades from the working class *barrios* outside the centre, such as La Macarena, have brass and drum bands accompanying more brightly bedecked pasos. Their nazarenos wear coloured, caped tunics, often of satin, velvet or wool. They also have to come from farther away, and some are on the streets for more than 12 hours.

Programs giving each hermandad's schedule and route are widely available during Semana Santa. The best source of information is the *ABC* newspaper. It's not too hard to work out which procession will be where and when, and pick one up on the way through its own barrio or even as it leaves or re-enters its church, which are always emotional moments.

Crowds along most of the carrera oficial make it hard to get much of a view there, unless you manage to get one of the seats, which go for anything from about 900 ptas on Plaza de la Virgen de los Reyes behind the Catedral to 3000 ptas on Good Friday morning at the top of Calle de Sierpes. But if you arrive early enough in the evening, you can usually get close enough to the cathedral to see plenty without paying.

If you're not in Sevilla for Semana Santa, you can get an inkling of what it's about by visiting some of the churches where the famous images are housed. The Basílica de La Macarena, Calle Bécquer 1, and the Basílica de Jesús del Gran Poder, on Plaza de San Lorenzo, are both in the north of the city, within about 600m of the Alameda de Hércules. The Iglesia de la Magdalena is farther south on Calle de San Pablo. All three churches are normally open daily from at least 9 to 11 am and 6.30 to 9 pm, and La Macarena has a museum too.

La Macarena, Sevilla's most adored image of the Virgin and the city's patron saint

ANDALUCÍA

comfortable, clean rooms for 6420/9630 ptas.

Places to Stay – Top End

In the Barrio de Santa Cruz, *Las Casas de la Judería* (☎ 95 441 51 50, Callejón de Dos Hermanas 7), is a group of charming-ly restored old houses around several patios and fountains. The 56 cosy singles/doubles cost from 8500/14,500 to 11,000/17,000 ptas plus IVA (less in July and August).

A few steps from the cathedral, *Hotel Doña María* (☎ 95 422 49 90, Calle Don Remondo 19) has 60 varied rooms and suites in comfy, old-fashioned style from 11,000/18,000 to 13,000/23,000 ptas plus IVA (less in July and August).

Farther north, **Hotel Becquer** (☎ 95 422 89 00, Calle Reyes Católicos 4) has 120 comfy, modern rooms for 8000/13,000 ptas plus IVA, while **Hotel Cervantes** (☎ 95 490 02 80, Calle Cervantes 10) is a charming medium-sized hotel charging 9500/13,000 ptas plus IVA (less at weekends and in July and August).

Places to Eat

Sevilla is one of Spain's tapas capitals, with scores and scores of bars serving all sorts of tasty light bites. To catch the atmosphere of the city, you should certainly do some of your eating in bars.

Restaurants and Cafés Don't bother looking for dinner till at least 8 pm – very few kitchens get going for the evening before then.

Barrio de Santa Cruz Near the Alcázar, *El Rincón de Pepe (Calle Gloria 6)* has pretty, folksy décor and does a lunch *menú del día* of gazpacho or salad, paella and dessert for 1050 ptas. **Hostería del Laurel** (Plaza de los Venerables 5) has an atmospheric old bar with a wide range of good *media-raciones* (550 to 1450 ptas) and *raciones*.

Cervecería Giralda (Calle Mateos Gago 1) is a great spot for breakfast. *Tostadas* are from 95 to 275 ptas, or there's bacon and eggs for 450 ptas.

Calle Santa María La Blanca has several good-value places: at the **Alta-Mira Café Bar**, No 6, a media-ración of *tortilla Alta-Mira* (with potatoes and vegetables) is almost a meal for 600 ptas, while the busy little **Bar Casa Fernando** round the corner has a decent 800 ptas lunch *menú*.

For something fancier, **Corral del Agua** (Callejón del Agua 6) has fine, inventive food. Its cool, green courtyard is great on a hot day, if you can get a table. Main courses (1800 to 2500 ptas) include some good fish choices and varied dishes of the day.

West of Avenida de la Constitución
Mesón del Serranito (Calle Antonio Díaz 9) has a good selection of *platos combinados* from 750 ptas. Busy **Bodega Paco Góngora** (Calle Padre Marchena 1) does a huge range of good seafood at decent prices – media-raciones of fish *a la plancha* (grilled) are mostly 600 ptas. It's open daily from 11 am to 4 pm and 7 pm to midnight.

El Centro *Restaurante San Marco (Calle de la Cuna 6)*, in an 18th century mansion, does good pizza and pasta around 1000 ptas, plus a big choice of fish and meat from 1000 to 2000 ptas. It's open daily for lunch and dinner.

Restaurante Bar Zucchero (Calle Golfo) near Plaza de la Alfalfa, is a little haven for vegetarians, doing a lunch *menú* Monday to Friday for 950 ptas. It's open daily except Tuesday from 1.30 to 4.30 pm and 9 pm to midnight.

Elsewhere *Bodegón Alfonso XII (Calle Alfonso XII 33)* near the Museo de Bellas Artes, is good value with deals like scrambled eggs with mushrooms, ham and prawns for 475 ptas and a *menú* for 800 ptas.

Calle del Betis on the west bank of the Río Guadalquivir, with views across the river to the city centre, has several popular Italian spots: at No 68 *Pizzeria San Marco* does most pizzas and pasta around 800 ptas plus IVA. Up the street, the good **Ristorante Cosa Nostra** has pizza for 550 to 900 ptas, pasta 600 to 1000 ptas, while *Pizzeria O Mamma Mia* at No 33 is slightly more economical.

The **Mercado del Arenal** (Calle Pastor y Landero) is the only food market in the central area.

Tapas Bars An evening of tapas-hopping round Sevilla's bars is one of the city's most enjoyable experiences. Most of these places are good for popping into at other times of day too, though from about 4 to 8 pm only cold tapas are available at many.

Barrio de Santa Cruz Bodega Santa Cruz *(Calle Mateos Gago)*, a bar popular with visitors and locals, has a big choice of decent-sized tapas, most at 185 to 210 ptas. **Cervecería Giralda** *(Calle Mateos Gago 1)* has a wonderful variety of good tapas, some pretty exotic, for 250 to 300 ptas. Some are tiny, though. **Café Bar Las Teresas** *(Calle Santa Teresa 2)* is an atmospheric old-style bar with good tapas from 160 to 200 ptas and media-raciones around 600 ptas.

West of Avenida de la Constitución The relaxed **Casa Pepe-Hillo** *(Calle de Adriano 24)* does some mouth-watering tapas from 250 to 325 ptas – try mushroom-filled artichoke hearts.

El Centro Just off Plaza Salvador, **Café Universal** is thronged at tapas times with people tucking into delicious, generous offerings such as *pinchos de solomillo a la pimienta* (pepper steak kebabs) or *patatones* (fried potato chunks with a variety of succulent dips) for 250 to 375 ptas.

Alfalfa 10 *(Plaza de la Alfalfa 10)* has some good tapas for 250 to 350 ptas. Just north, **Sopa de Ganso** *(Calle Pérez Galdós 8)*, and **Restaurante Bar Zucchero**, Calle Golfo, do vegetarian tapas. Just east on Calle Alfalfa, **La Bodega** deals in *jamón* and sherry, **La Bodega Extremeña** sticks to cheese, and **La Trastienda** offers crab. For succulent grilled meat tapas for 250 ptas, head a little farther east to another **Bodega Extremeña** *(Calle San Esteban 17)*.

Elsewhere Patio San Eloy *(Calle San Eloy 9)* is a bright, busy place, popular with a young crowd. Tapas of ham, cheese, smoked salmon, pork and more go for 110 to 185 ptas. It's open daily from 11.30 am to 4 pm and 6.30 pm to 11.30 pm.

Entertainment

Several free publications have what's-on listings: look for *Casco Antiguo*, *El Giraldillo*, *Sevilla Welcome & Olé* and *The Tourist Sevilla*. Live music schedules are changeable, of course.

Tapas in Sevilla

A few Sevilla tapas favourites to look for are:

caña de lomo
   pork loin (can be expensive)
cazón en adobo
   a white fish marinated in vinegar, salt, lemon and spices, then deep fried (delicious)
espinacas con garbanzos
   spinach and chick peas
papas aliñás
   sliced potatoes and boiled eggs, with vegetable garnish and a vinaigrette dressing
pavía
   battered fish or seafood
puntillitas
   baby squid, usually deep fried

Bars Sevilla's bar and music scene is among the liveliest in Spain. It really gets going at about midnight or 1 am, and the best action is on Friday and Saturday nights. But bars begin to fill from 10 pm most nights. In summer dozens of open-air late-night bars *(terrazas de verano)*, many with live music, spring up beside the Guadalquivir.

Barrio de Santa Cruz There are several hugely popular bars just north of the cathedral: **P Flaherty Irish Pub** *(Calle Alemanes)* gets packed with locals and visitors alike – 500 ptas for your pint of Guinness.

In the heart of Barrio de Santa Cruz, small bars such as **Bodega Santa Cruz**, on Calle Mateos Gago, and **Bar Entrecalles**, Calle Ximenez de Enciso, can get pretty lively with a mixed crowd of visitors and locals.

La Carbonería *(Calle Levíes 18)* is thronged nearly every night with visitors and locals come to enjoy the scene and hear varied live music – including, at our last check, blues on Wednesday, flamenco on

ANDALUCÍA

Thursday and rock on Saturday – from around 10 pm to 4 am.

West of Avenida de la Constitución
Hijos de E Morales (Calle García de Vinuesa 3), is an old-fashioned *bodega* with wine and sherry from the barrel in a large back room where old wine casks serve as tables. A little farther west, on Calle de Adriano, the crowds (mostly young) some nights have to be seen to be believed. Busy music bars include *A3*, *Bar Populus* and *Arena*.

Café Isbiliyya (Paseo de Colón 2), near the Puente de Triana, is a bustling gay music bar – mostly men – overflowing on to the street on busy nights.

El Centro From mid-evening to around 1 am, Plaza Salvador is a very popular spot for an open-air drink, with a studenty crowd and a couple of little bars selling 'takeaway' drinks. Calle Pérez Galdós, off Plaza de la Alfalfa, has at least four throbbing music bars.

Alameda de Hércules & Around Several excellent bars and some live music attract an offbeat crowd to this former red-light district north of the centre.

The *Fun Club (Alameda de Hércules 86)* is a small, busy dance warehouse, open Thursday to Sunday from 11.30 pm (9.30 pm on live-band nights) till late. There's live rock Friday and/or Saturday (500 to 1000 ptas entry). Drinks are 250 ptas-plus. Also on this east side of the Alameda, *Bulebar Café* is a more relaxed place for a drink, with a good courtyard out the front, while *El Corto Maltés*, *Café Central* and *Habanilla Café* are busy, pub-like, somewhat aromatic places that spill out on to the street.

East of the Alameda, *La Ilustre Víctima (Calle Dr Letamendi 35)* plays a lot of jazz and does some great tapas. It's open daily from 4 pm to 2 or 3 am (beer is 125 ptas). Nearby, *La Farándula (Calle Cruz de la Tinaja 5)* has live music Tuesday to Thursday. It's open daily from 10 pm till very late

(beer 125 is ptas). At *La Bruja* on little Plaza Europa, the long-haired heavy-rock crowd sit around on the floor rolling joints (beer is 150 ptas).

West of the Alameda, the arts centre *La Imperdible (Plaza San Antonio de Padua 9)* has a mellow bar, the Almacén, where you'll often find free live jazz on Tuesday, Friday or Saturday from 10.30 pm. The *Salamandra (Calle del Torneo 43)* has varied bands – soul, blues, Latin, ethnic – Thursday and/or Friday from around 10.30 pm (entry is usually 600 to 1000 ptas).

Triana On the west bank of the Guadalquivir, Calle del Betis has a string of lively bars – including *Alambique*, *Mui d'Aqui*, *Big Ben* and *Café La Pavana* – all playing good music and attracting an interestingly mixed crowd. They open at about 9 pm. Northward, Calle Castilla has yet more good bars. *La Otra Orilla (Paseo de Nuestra Señora de la O)* is a buzzing music bar with a great terrace overlooking the river.

Flamenco Venues Sevilla's Triana barrio was one of flamenco's birthplaces, but most flamenco goes on elsewhere in the city these days. Hotels and tourist offices will steer you towards the tourist-oriented *tablaos*. These can be unauthentic and lacking in atmosphere, but *Los Gallos* (☎ 95 421 69 81, Plaza de Santa Cruz 11) is an honourable exception. It puts on two-hour shows nightly at 9 and 11.30 pm for 3000 ptas including one drink.

In general you'll catch a more genuine atmosphere – though unpredictable quality – in one of the bars that stage regular nights of flamenco or *sevillana* music. *El Mundo (Calle Siete Revueltas 5)* near Plaza Salvador, has flamenco on Tuesday at around 11 pm (entry is 300 ptas including one drink). Entry is free at *El Tamboril* bar on Plaza de Santa Cruz, with jolly crowds enjoying its live sevillana and rumba music nightly from midnight; at *Café Lisboa (Calle Alhóndiga 43)* with live flamenco most Thursdays from 11 pm; and at three places mentioned earlier: *La Farándula* (flamenco on Wednesday); *La Carbonería* (Monday and Thursday); and *Salamandra* (Wednesday, 10.30 pm).

There are fairly frequent appearances by big-name flamenco artists at some of Sevilla's theatres, especially the *Teatro Central* on Isla de La Cartuja. Sevilla also stages a major flamenco festival, the Bienal de Flamenco, in September of even-numbered years.

Spectator Sports

Sevilla's Plaza de Toros on Paseo de Cristóbal Colón, which holds 14,000 spectators, is one of the country's oldest and most elegant bullrings, and its crowds among the most knowledgeable. The season runs from Easter to October, with fights every Sunday, usually at 6.30 pm, and almost every day during the Feria de Abril and the week before it. Up to late June/early July, nearly all fights are by fully-fledged matadors and often only *sol* (sun) seats – from 3000 ptas – are available to non-season-ticket-holders. Most of the rest of the season, junior matadors fight young bulls: tickets cost from 1500 ptas.

Shopping

Some of the tourist-oriented craft shops in the Barrio de Santa Cruz sell some excellent local pottery.

Pedestrianised Calle Sierpes in the city centre is the fanciest, most varied shopping street, lined with shops devoted to a wide range of everyday and luxury goods. The large El Corte Inglés department store occupies four separate buildings a little west, on Plaza de la Magdalena and Plaza del Duque de la Victoria.

The large Thursday *mercadillo* on Calle de la Feria, east of the Alameda de Hércules, is a colourful flea market well worth a visit.

Getting There & Away

Air Sevilla airport (☎ 95 451 25 78) has quite a range of domestic and international flights. Air Europa flies most days to/from Barcelona (19,200 ptas one way) and Palma de Mallorca. You can get tickets at Halcón Viajes (☎ 95 421 44 56), Calle Almirante Bonifaz 3. Iberia (☎ 95 422 89 01), Calle Almirante Lobo 2, flies to/from Madrid, Barcelona, Valencia, London, Paris, Amsterdam, Brussels, Dusseldorf, Frankfurt, Munich and Rome.

Bus From Estación de Autobuses Prado de San Sebastián (☎ 95 441 71 11) on Plaza San Sebastián, there are nine or more daily buses to Córdoba (two hours; 1200 ptas), Granada (four hours; 2710 ptas), Málaga (3½ hours; 2245 ptas), Jerez de la Frontera, Sanlúcar de Barrameda and Cádiz (one hour; 1200 to 1300 ptas); and a few to Arcos de la Frontera and Ronda (2½ hours; 1235 ptas). This is also the station for buses to Tarifa, Algeciras, La Línea, the Costa del Sol, Antequera, Jaén, Almería, Alicante, Valencia and Barcelona.

From Estación de Autobuses Plaza de Armas (☎ 95 490 80 40), just east of Puente del Cachorro, there are frequent buses to Huelva, a few daily to El Rocío and Matalascañas, and 11 to Madrid (six hours; 2715 ptas). Northward, there are frequent buses to Zafra, about 12 daily to Mérida (3¼ hours; 1600 ptas), five or more to Cáceres (four hours; 2170 ptas) and Salamanca, and a few as far as Galicia. To Lisboa there are direct buses five days a week (nine hours; 4350 to 4510 ptas) and daily buses with a transfer at the border (10 hours; 2875 ptas). One or two buses run daily to/from Faro on the Algarve (four hours; 1570 ptas).

Train The central RENFE office, Calle Zaragoza 31, is open Monday to Friday, from 9 am to 1.15 pm and 4 to 7 pm. Santa Justa train station (☎ 95 454 02 02) is about 1.5km north-east of the centre on Avenida Kansas City.

Fourteen super-fast AVE trains daily cover the 471km to Madrid in just 2½ hours, costing 8100 or 9500 ptas in the cheapest class *(turista)*; a couple of Talgos take about 3¾ hours for 7000 to 7900 ptas in 2nd class; and the evening Tren Hotel takes 3¾ hours for 5400 ptas in a seat. The

AVE service is the pride of Spain's rail network: the trains reach speeds of 280km/h and if they arrive more than five minutes late, you get your money back. (Don't get excited: this only happens to 1 train in 250.) Inter-Rail cards are not valid on trains from Sevilla to Madrid or vice-versa; Eurail pass-holders pay 1200 ptas on AVEs.

Other daily trains from Sevilla include about 20 to Córdoba (45 minutes to 1¼ hours; 1050 to 2700 ptas); up to 15 to Jerez de la Frontera and Cádiz (1½ to two hours; 1085 to 1600 ptas); three each to Granada (four hours; 2280 ptas), Málaga (three hours; 1825 ptas), Huelva (1½ hours; 820 to 945 ptas), Ronda (three hours; 1860 ptas) and Algeciras (five hours; 2635 ptas), with a change at Bobadilla for the last two places; two to Valencia (nine hours; 5200 ptas); four to Barcelona (11 to 14 hours; from 6400 ptas); one to Jaén; and one north to Zafra, Mérida and Cáceres. For Lisbon you must change at Cáceres (16 hours; 6800 ptas in 2nd class).

Car & Motorcycle If you're staying in the Barrio de Santa Cruz, you can usually park on the street five minutes walk away, east of Calle de Menéndez Pelayo in streets such as Avenida de Cádiz.

Car rental is expensive. Several local rental firms are in Calle Almirante Lobo.

Car Pooling Compartecoche (☎ 95 490 75 82), Calle González Cuadrado 49, is an intercity car-pooling service. Its service is free to drivers, while passengers pay an agreed transfer rate. Ring or visit between 10 am and 1.30 pm or 5 and 8 pm for details.

Boat From around April to October, several companies run day cruises from the *embarcadero* by the Torre del Oro to Sanlúcar de Barrameda, for around 3500 ptas. Early and late in the season cruises may only go at weekends. It's 4½ hours each way, usually with 4½ hours in Sanlúcar in between.

Getting Around

To/From the Airport Sevilla airport is about 7km from the centre off the N-IV Córdoba road. Amarillos buses (☎ 902-21 03 17) make the 30 minute trip (750 ptas) between the airport and the Puerta de Jerez, in front of the Hotel Alfonso XIII, at least nine times daily. A taxi is about 1200 ptas.

Bus Bus Nos C1, C2, C3 and C4 do circular routes linking the main transport terminals and the city centre. There's been talk of changing their routes, so check that they're going where you want to go. From Santa Justa train station the eastbound C1 follows a clockwise route via Avenida de Carlos V (close to Estación de Autobuses Prado de San Sebastián), Avenida de María Luisa, Triana, Puerta de Triana and Isla Mágica. No C2 follows the same route in reverse. Bus No 32, from the same stop as No C2, runs to/from Plaza de la Encarnación in the city centre.

The clockwise No C3 goes from Calle de Menéndez Pelayo (near Estación de Autobuses Prado de San Sebastián) to Puerta de Jerez, Triana, Puerta de Triana, Estación de Autobuses Plaza de Armas, Calle del Torneo, Calle de Resolana and Calle de Recaredo. The C4 does the same circuit anti-clockwise except that from Estación de Autobuses Plaza de Armas it heads south along Paseo de Cristóbal Colón to Puerta de Jerez, instead of crossing the river to Puerta de Triana and Triana.

A single bus fare is 125 ptas.

Bicycle Sevilla Mágica (☎ 95 456 38 38), Calle Miguel de Mañara 11B near the main tourist office, rents out decent bikes for 1200 ptas a half-day or 1800 ptas a day (open daily).

AROUND SEVILLA
Itálica

Itálica, 8km north-west of Sevilla on the north-west edge of the small town of Santiponce, was the first Roman town in Spain – founded in 206 BC for veterans of the Roman victory over Carthage at nearby

Ilipa. Itálica was also the home town of the 2nd century Roman emperors Trajan and Hadrian. The partly-reconstructed ruins include one of the biggest of all Roman amphitheatres, a large public bathhouse, some excellent mosaics and a theatre. The site is open Tuesday to Saturday from 9 am to 5.30 pm, and Sunday and holidays from 9 am to 2 pm (250 ptas, free with an EU passport).

Frequent buses run to Santiponce from Estación de Autobuses Plaza de Armas.

LA CAMPIÑA

This rolling, fertile area east of Sevilla and south of the Río Guadalquivir, crossed by the main roads to Córdoba, Granada and Málaga, can be oddly bleak country: a land of huge agricultural estates with hardly a soul in sight between the few towns. But the surprisingly grand architecture of some towns makes them well worth a detour.

Carmona

Carmona is just off the N-IV, 38km east of Sevilla. Frequent buses from Sevilla (Prado de San Sebastián) normally stop 300m west of the old town on Paseo del Estatuto, but at the time of writing were forced by roadworks to terminate 500m farther west on Avenida de Jorge Bonsor (close to the Necrópolis Romana). The helpful tourist office (☎ 95 419 09 55), in the Puerta de Sevilla at the west end of the old town, is open Monday to Saturday from 10 am to 6 pm, and Sunday and holidays from 10 am to 3 pm.

Things to See In the new part of town at Avenida de Jorge Bonsor 9, just over 1km west of the Puerta de Sevilla, is the **Necrópolis Romana**. Here you can climb down into a dozen or more elaborate Roman tombs hewn from the rock. From 15 June to 15 September, the necropolis is open Tuesday to Friday from 9 am to 2 pm, and Saturday from 10 am to 2 pm; the rest of the year, daily except Monday from 10 am to 2 pm, plus Tuesday to Friday from 4 to 6 pm (closed holidays). It's free for EU passport-holders, 250 ptas for others.

The tourist office in the **Puerta de Sevilla**, the impressive main gate of the old town, sells tickets (200 ptas) for the interesting upper levels of the structure, the Alcázar de la Puerta de Sevilla, which includes an Almohad patio with traces of a Roman temple. Up into the old town from here, the patio of the 18th century **Ayuntamiento** on Calle El Salvador (open Monday to Friday from 8 am to 3 pm) contains a large, very fine Roman mosaic. Nearby Calle Martín López de Córdoba leads to the **Iglesia Prioral de Santa María**, the town's most splendid church, open daily from 9 am to noon and 6 to 9 pm, which was built mainly in the 15th and 16th centuries in a typical Carmona combination of brick and stone. Its Patio de los Naranjos, originally a mosque's courtyard, has a Visigothic calendar carved into one of its pillars. Continuing along the same street you reach the **Puerta de Córdoba**, an originally Roman gate through which there are fine panoramas. South of here is the **Alcázar**, an Almohad fort which Pedro the Cruel turned into a country palace in a style similar to his parts of the Sevilla Alcázar. Ruined by an earthquake in 1504, it was restored as a *parador* in the 1970s.

Places to Stay *Pensión Comercio* (☎ 95 414 00 18, Calle Torre del Oro 56), just north of the Puerta de Sevilla, is a lovely old building with a brick-pillared patio and 14 well-kept rooms for 2000/3500 ptas plus IVA a single/double, or 4500 ptas plus IVA for doubles with bath. It also has a well-priced restaurant. *Hostal San Pedro* (☎ 95 414 16 06, Calle San Pedro 3), outside the Puerta de Sevilla, has comfy doubles with bath for 6000 ptas. The *Parador Alcázar del Rey Don Pedro* (☎ 95 414 10 10) has doubles at 18,000 ptas plus IVA. Even more charming and luxurious is the *Casa de Carmona* (☎ 95 414 33 00, Plaza de Lasso 1) with doubles from 22,000 ptas plus IVA.

Osuna

Osuna, 91km from Sevilla just off the A-92, is a pleasant place with some impressive buildings, several of them created by the ducal family of Osuna, one of Spain's richest since the 17th century. The tourist office (☎ 95 481 16 17) on the handsome plaza mayor is open Monday to Friday from 9 am to 2 pm and 5 to 7 pm.

Things to See Most impressive are the big buildings on the hill overlooking the centre. On the way up from the plaza mayor, there's a **Museo Arqueológico**, open daily (300 ptas). Above here is the 16th century **Colegiata de Santa María** church, containing a wealth of sacred art including several paintings by José de Ribera. It's open for guided tours daily except Monday from 10 am to 1.30 pm and 4 to 7 pm (October to April from 11.30 am to 1.30 pm and 3.30 to 5.30 pm). The tour includes the lugubrious Sepulcro Ducal, the family vault of the Osuna family (300 ptas). Opposite is the **Convento de la Encarnación**, now a museum with mainly religious art and artefacts; open similar hours to the Colegiata (250 ptas). Behind the Colegiata, the **Antigua Universidad** (Old University) was founded in 1549.

Places to Stay *Hostal 5 Puertas* (☎ 95 481 12 43, Calle Carrera 79), five minutes walk north of the plaza mayor, has decent rooms for 2000/4000 ptas (more in April and May). *Hostal Caballo Blanco* (☎ 95 481 01 84, Calle Granada 1), an old coaching inn across the street, charges 3000/5000 ptas. Both have food.

Getting There & Away Half a dozen daily buses run to/from Sevilla (Prado de San Sebastián), four to/from Antequera, and a few to/from Málaga. Three trains daily run to/from Sevilla, Antequera, Granada and Málaga.

PARQUE NATURAL SIERRA NORTE

If you're looking to get off the regular foreign tourist's trail, this 1648 sq km area of the Sierra Morena, stretching across the north of Sevilla province, fits the bill nicely.

It's a sparsely populated, in places wild, region, much of it covered in *dehesas*, woodlands of scattered evergreen oaks rising from scrub or pasture. Many of the villages and small towns bear a clear Islamic imprint, with old forts, part-mudéjar churches and narrow, zigzagging white streets. There are good walks in several areas.

A convenient base is the small town of **Cazalla de la Sierra**, though the park information centre, Centro de Interpretación El Robledo (☎ 95 588 15 97), is just outside Constantina (which is 1km along the A-452 El Pedroso road). In Cazalla, tourist information is available Monday to Friday from 9 am to 2 pm at the ayuntamiento (☎ 95 488 40 00) at Plaza de Manuel Nosea 1.

Two or more daily buses to Cazalla de la Sierra and Constantina leave from Sevilla's Estación de Autobuses Plaza de Armas, and two trains daily from Sevilla go to Cazalla-Constantina station, on the A-455 between the two towns (local buses link the station with Cazalla).

Things to See & Do

The most impressive building in Cazalla's tangled streets is the fortress-like 14th century **Iglesia de Nuestra Señora de la Consolación** on the plaza mayor. **La Cartuja de Cazalla** is a large, ruined 15th century monastery in a beautiful nook of the Sierra Morena, 4km east. Now under restoration, it's open for visits daily from 10 am to 2 pm and 5 to 9 pm (500 ptas).

Huéznar Valley Walk Two tracks lead east from Cazalla down to the pretty Huéznar valley and by combining them you can enjoy a round-trip walk of about 8km. One, the Sendero de las Laderas (or Vereda del Valle), starts at a fountain, El Chorrillo, at the foot of Calle Parras. The other is the Camino Viejo. You can join this walk from Cazalla-Constantina station by following the 'Molino del Corcho' path down the Huéznar for about 1km.

Places to Stay

Camping La Fundición (☎ 95 595 41 17) is beside the Río Huéznar, 2km up the San Nicolás del Puerto road from Cazalla-Constantina station. The price is 250 ptas per person and per car and 300 ptas per tent, plus IVA.

The Inturjoven *Albergue Juvenil Constantina* youth hostel (☎ 95 588 15 89, *Cuesta Blanca s/n*), Constantina, has room for 93 people. For prices, see this chapter's introductory Youth Hostels section.

In Cazalla, *Hospedaje La Milagrosa* (☎ 95 488 42 60, *Calle Llana 29*) has small singles/doubles for 2000/3500 ptas; *Posada El Moro* (☎ 95 488 43 26, *Paseo El Moro s/n*) has a pool and comfortable rooms with bath for 5000/8000 ptas. *Hospedería La Cartuja* (☎ 95 488 45 16, *La Cartuja de Cazalla*) has a pool and eight good rooms at 8500/12,000 ptas including breakfast (less for more than one night).

Huelva Province

Andalucía's westernmost province includes most of the Parque Nacional de Doñana, whose famous wetlands are a bird habitat of huge international importance. The *lugares colombinos* (Columbus sites) east of Huelva city, where Columbus planned his 1492 voyage and set sail, will fascinate anyone with a historical leaning. Also along Huelva's coasts are around half the excellent beaches of the Costa de la Luz. West of Aracena in the north is a large area of beautiful, verdant hill country.

HUELVA

The province's capital is a port and industrial city of 141,000 people. It was probably founded by the Phoenicians as a trading settlement about 3000 years ago, but much of it was destroyed by the Lisbon earthquake of 1755.

Orientation

The central area is about 1km square, with the estación de autobuses on its western edge on Calle Doctor Rubio, and the train station on its southern edge on Avenida de Italia. South-east from Plaza de las Monjas, the central square, leads the main street Avenida Martín Alonso Pinzón – also called Gran Vía – which becomes Alameda Sundheim.

Information

The tourist office (☎ 959 25 74 03) is just across the way from the bus station at Avenida de Alemania 12. It's open Monday to Friday from 9 am to 7 pm and Saturday and Sunday from 10 am to 2 pm.

The main correos (post office; postcode 21080) is on the corner of Avenida de Italia and Avenida Tomás Domínguez.

The Cruz Roja (Red Cross, ☎ 959 22 22 22) is on Avenida de Buenos Aires near the cathedral. The Policía Local (☎ 959 21 02 21) are on Avenida Tomás Domínguez, across the street from the post office.

Things to See

The **Museo Provincial**, Alameda Sundheim 13, has an impressive archaeological collection ranging from the early Stone Age to Muslim times. There's abundant Tartessos culture material and plenty on the province's mining history including a huge Roman water wheel found at Minas de Riotinto. It's open Monday to Friday from 9 am to 2 pm (free).

The **Santuario de Nuestra Señora de la Cinta**, a chapel 2km north of the centre off Avenida de Manuel Siurot, with good views over the Odiel estuary, was visited by Columbus before he embarked on his momentous voyage, an event portrayed in tiles by artist Daniel Zuloaga. Bus No 6 from outside the main bus station will take you there.

Places to Stay

The modern Inturjoven *Albergue Juvenil Huelva* youth hostel (☎ 959 25 37 93, *Avenida Marchena Colombo 14*) is 2km north of the bus station. Bus No 6, every 25 minutes from outside the main bus station, stops round the corner, on Calle JS Elcano.

See this chapter's introductory Youth Hostels section for prices.

Pensión La Vega (☎ *959 24 15 63, Paseo de la Independencia 15)* near the cathedral, is the best budget option, albeit noisy on weekend nights. Singles/doubles are 1750/3500 ptas; doubles with private bath are 4000 ptas. *Hostal Andalucía* (☎ *959 24 56 67, Calle Vázquez López 22)*, also central, has doubles from 3100 to 4100 ptas plus IVA. *Hostal Virgen del Rocío* (☎ *959 28 17 16, Calle Tendaleras 14)*, in a dingier area off Avenida de Italia near the fish market, has singles for 1800 ptas and doubles with bath for 4500 ptas. Nearby, *Hostal La Cinta* (☎ *959 24 85 82, Calle Rascón 29)* and *Hostal Calvo* (☎ *959 24 90 16, Calle Rascón 33)* are about half that price but very basic.

Hotel Los Condes (☎ *959 28 24 00, Alameda Sundheim 14)* has 53 air-con rooms with bath for 4200/7500 ptas plus IVA. The modern *Hotel Tartessos* (☎ *959 28 27 11, Avenida Martín Alonso Pinzón 13)* has 112 comfy, air-con rooms, with doubles at 12,000 ptas plus IVA.

Places to Eat

Los Encinares on the corner of Avenida Martín Alonso Pinzón and Calle Sor Ángela de la Cruz does excellent grills for around 1600 ptas. Just south on Calle Sor Ángela de la Cruz, the straightforward *Cafetería Parra I* has platos combinados for 600 to 750 ptas. A few steps away, *Oh La La (Calle Berdigón 26)* packs 'em in for its baguettes (350 to 400 ptas) and pizza and pasta (500 to 850 ptas). Nearby, *La Cazuela (Calle Garci-Fernández 5)* is a classier place specialising in fish, with a *menú* for 1600 ptas plus IVA.

To the north, Avenida Pablo Rado is lined with popular eateries, many of them with *terrazas*. Westward, *Camillo e Peppone (Calle Isaac Peral)* serves up excellent pasta and pizza for 550 to 1000 ptas.

Entertainment

From around 9 to 11 pm some of the bars off Avenida Martín Alonso Pinzón such as *Los Encinares* and *Cafetería Parra I* (see Places to Eat) and *Taberna El Condado*, opposite the Parra I, get quite lively. Later, crowds flock to the bars and terrazas lining Avenida Pablo Rada and the bars in the streets south of the cathedral.

Getting There & Away

Bus From the estación de autobuses (☎ 959 25 69 00), frequent buses head to/from Sevilla (1¼ hours; 875 ptas), and three or four daily to Madrid. For Portugal, Transportes Agobe runs buses on Monday, Wednesday and Friday to Albufeira and Lisbon, and Damas has one or two buses daily to Faro.

Train From the train station (☎ 959 24 56 14), there are three daily trains to Sevilla (1½ hours; 820 to 945 ptas), and one to Córdoba (two hours; 2700 ptas) and Madrid.

AROUND HUELVA
Paraje Natural Marismas del Odiel

The Odiel *marismas* (marshes), across the Odiel estuary from Huelva, are remarkably wild and peaceful, with a large, varied bird population, some of which is easily viewed from a 20km road that runs right down their length. In winter there are up to 1000 greater flamingos here. Several paths strike off from the road.

Huelva Turistica at the Centro de Visitantes Calatilla (☎ 959 50 03 25), towards the north end of the marismas, runs guided trips by boat (1500 to 3000 ptas per person), 4WD or horse. If there are enough people, they will usually pick you up by boat at Huelva port. In your own vehicle, take the A-497 Punta Umbría road west from Huelva: at the far end of the Odiel bridge, fork right for 'Ayamonte, Corrales, Dique Juan Carlos I' then immediately left for 'Aljaraque, Espigón', then right for 'Dique Juan Carlos I'.

Lugares Colombinos

La Rábida, Palos de la Frontera and Moguer, three of the key sites in the Columbus story, lie along the east bank of the Río Tinto estuary and can all be visited in a 40km return trip from Huelva. At least 10 buses daily run from the estación de autobuses in Huelva to La Rábida and Palos, many of them continuing to Moguer.

La Rábida Columbus visited the **Monasterio de La Rábida** several times while planning his voyage, and won influential support from a monk here, Antonio de Marchena, and the abbot Juan Perez, who happened to be a former confessor of Queen Isabel La Catolica. Absorbing monk-guided tours of the monastery are given in simple Spanish daily except Monday, every 45 minutes from 10 am to 1 pm and 4 to 6.15 pm. You pay by donation at the end of the tour.

On the waterfront below the monastery is the **Muelle de las Carabelas** (Wharf of the Caravels), with replicas of Columbus' three ships, the *Santa María*, *Niña* and *Pinta*. It's open daily except Monday from 10 am to 2 pm and 5 to 9 pm (late September to late April from 10 am to 7 pm), for 420 ptas.

Hostería de La Rábida (☎ 959 35 03 12) next to the monastery has five rooms with bath at 7500 ptas a double – a nice place but often booked up.

Palos de la Frontera This small town was the port where Columbus set sail and which provided two of his ships and more than half his crew. Palos' access to the Tinto is now silted up, but it remains proud of its role in the discovery of the Americas, especially the cousins Vicente Yañez Pinzón and Martín Alonso Pinzón, respectively the captains of the *Niña* and the *Pinta*.

Buses stop on the central plaza. The **Casa Museo Martín Alonso Pinzón**, a short walk uphill at Calle Colón 24, open Monday to Friday from 10 am to 2 pm (free), was the home of Martín Alonso Pinzón. Farther along Calle Colón is the 14th century **Iglesia de San Jorge**, open Monday to Friday from 10.30 am to 1 pm and 7 to 8 pm. Columbus and his men took communion here before embarking on 3 August

1492. In a park down the street is **La Fontanilla**, a well where Columbus' crew drew water for their voyage. A plaque marks the site of the *embarcadero* from which they sailed.

Places to Stay Just off the central plaza, *Pensión Rábida* (☎ 959 35 01 63, Calle Rábida 9) has doubles with shared bathroom at 3000 ptas. Farther along the same street at No 79, the good *Hotel La Pinta* (☎ 959 35 05 11) has doubles for 10,000 ptas plus IVA.

Moguer

The pleasant town of Moguer provided many of Columbus' crew. There's a tourist office at Calle Andalucía 5, a few steps off the central Plaza del Cabildo.

The **Convento de Santa Clara** on Plaza de las Monjas, up the street almost opposite the tourist office, is where Columbus kept vigil the night after returning from his voyage. It's open for guided visits Tuesday to Saturday at 11 am, noon and 1, 4.30 and 7.30 pm, and on Sunday and holidays at 11 am, noon and 1 pm (250 ptas).

Moguer was the birthplace of the 1956 Nobel literature laureate Juan Ramón Jiménez, author of *Platero y Yo* (Platero and I), which tells touchingly of his childhood wanderings around Moguer with his donkey Platero. The **Casa Museo Juan Ramón Jiménez** on Calle Juan Ramón Jiménez, a five minute walk from Plaza del Cabildo, is open for 45 minute guided visits daily, every hour from 10.15 am to 1.15 pm and 5.15 to 7.15 pm (except Sunday afternoons and holidays; 250 ptas).

Places to Stay Three central hostales, *Hostal Lis* (☎ 959 37 03 78, Calle Andalucía 6), *Hostal Pedro Alonso Niño* (☎ 959 37 23 92, Calle Pedro Alonso Niño 13) and *Hostal Platero* (☎ 959 37 21 59, Calle Sor Ángela de la Cruz 4) all have rooms for between 2200 to 3000 ptas a double.

ANDALUCÍA

EASTERN COAST

A wide, sandy, dune and pine-backed beach runs 60km south-east from Huelva to the mouth of the Río Guadalquivir. Apart from two seaside resorts, the coast is almost un-inhabited. Of the two resorts, the fairly low-key **Mazagón** is the more pleasant. It has a tourist office on Carretera de la Playa, three year-round camp sites between the road and beach within 7km east, and a couple of hostales and hotels. The luxurious *Parador de Mazagón (☎ 959 53 63 00)* is set in cliff-top gardens above the beach 3km east of Mazagón, with doubles from 16,500 ptas plus IVA. At least three buses run daily from Huelva to Mazagón, and a few from Palos de la Frontera.

Matalascañas This is a modern resort stretching 4km along the coast with a number of tall hotels, but could hardly be in greater contrast to the wildernesses of the adjoining Doñana national park. The tourist office (☎ 959 43 00 86) is on Avenida de las Adelfas at the west end of town, with the huge *Camping Rocío Playa (☎ 959 43 02 38)* just above the beach 1km west. There are a few hostales near the tourist office; *Pensión Rocío (☎ 959 43 01 41)* has doubles with bath for 4000 ptas a double in the high season. One bus runs to/from Huelva via Mazagón daily except Saturday. Buses also link Matalascañas with El Rocío and Sevilla – see the next section.

PARQUE NACIONAL DE DOÑANA

The Doñana national park, one of Europe's most important wetlands, covers 507 sq km in the south-east of Huelva province and neighbouring Sevilla province. It's not only a vital refuge for such endangered species as the pardel lynx and Spanish imperial eagle (both with populations of about 40 here), but also a crucial habitat for hundreds of thousands of other birds, many of them migratory. Bordering the national park are four discrete zones making up the separate, 540 sq km Parque Natural Entorno de Doñana.

Since its creation in 1969 the national park has had to continue battling against agricultural and tourism schemes around its fringes which threaten to reduce the wetlands' water supplies. But the biggest threat to its delicate balance came in 1998 when a dam broke at a mine at Aznalcóllar, 50km north. Five million cubic metres of water and mud loaded with acids and heavy metals flooded into the Río Guadiamar, one of the chief waterways feeding Doñana's wetlands. Hastily erected dykes prevented the flood entering the national park itself, but up to 100 sq km of wetlands to its north-east were contaminated, and agricultural land bordering about 45km of the river was devastated. Biologists and environmentalists fear that the effects may be felt for decades to come through poisons entering Doñana's water table and the food chain of its birds and animals.

Visiting the national park itself requires booking ahead for a guided tour. These can be made either from the Centro de Recepción El Acebuche on the west side of the park (see later), or from Sanlúcar de Barrameda (see the Cádiz Province section). But there are also some interesting surrounding areas for which you don't need to book (or pay).

Flora, Fauna & Ecosystems

Doñana counts 125 resident and 125 migratory bird species and is a major habitat for greater flamingos, ducks, herons, stilts, vultures, birds of prey and many more.

Half the national park consists of the marismas (marshes) of the Guadalquivir delta. The park contains only about one-tenth of the Guadalquivir marismas but most of those outside it have been drained or channelled for agriculture. The park's marismas are almost dry from July to October. In autumn they start to fill with water, eventually leaving only a few islets of dry land. Hundreds of thousands of water birds arrive from the north to winter here, including an estimated 80% of western Europe's wild ducks. As the waters sink in spring, other birds – greater flamingos,

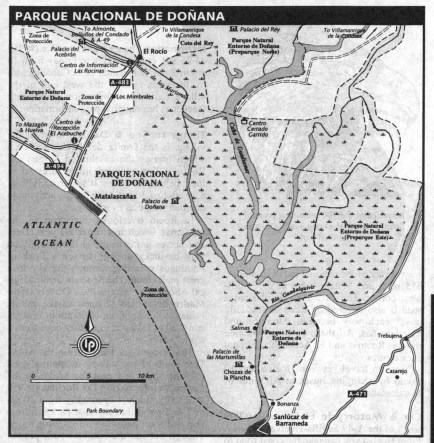

PARQUE NACIONAL DE DOÑANA

To Almonte,
Bollullos del Condado
& A-49

Zona de
Protección

Palacio del
Acebrón

Centro de Información
Las Rocinas

Parque Natural
Entorno de Doñana

Zona de
Protección

Los Mimbrales

To Mazagón
& Huelva

Centro de
Recepción
El Acebuche

A-494

PARQUE NACIONAL
DE DOÑANA

Matalascañas

Palacio de
Doñana

**ATLANTIC
OCEAN**

Zona de
Protección

To Villamanrique
de la Condesa

El Rocío

Coto del Rey

Palacio del Rey

Parque Natural
Entorno de Doñana
(Preparque Norte)

To Villamanrique
de la Condesa

A-483

Caño de Guadiamar

Madre de las Marismas

Centro
Cerrado
Garrido

Parque Natural
Entorno de Doñana
(Preparque Este)

Río Guadalquivir

Salinas

Palacio de
las Marismillas

Chozas de
la Plancha

Bonanza

Sanlúcar de
Barrameda

Parque Natural
Entorno de Doñana

Trebujena

Casarejo

A-471

0   5   10 km

Park Boundary

ANDALUCÍA

spoonbills, storks, herons, hoopoes, bee-eaters – arrive, many of them to nest. In summer great flocks crowd around the shrinking *lucios* (ponds), and in July, herons, storks and kites move in to take bountiful catches of trapped perch.

Between the park's 25km Atlantic beach and the marismas is a band of moving sand dunes, up to 5km wide, which are blown inland at a rate of up to 6m a year. When dune sand reaches the marismas, it is carried back down to the sea, which washes it up on the beach where wind begins the cycle all over again. The beach and moving dunes together make up 102 sq km of the park.

In other parts of the park, stable sand supports 144 sq km of *coto,* woodland and scrub, which is the favoured habitat of an abundant mammal population, including deer, wild boar and feral camels.

Getting There & Away

Bus Damas runs three or four daily buses from Sevilla to/from El Rocío at the north-

About 20 of the 100 remaining pairs of Spanish imperial eagles live in Doñana national park

west corner of the national park (1½ hours; 615 ptas) and Matalascañas at the south-west corner. The El Rocío-Matalascañas road is also covered by three to six daily buses each way between Almonte and Matalascañas. All these will stop outside the Las Rocinas and El Acebuche national park centres.

You can travel between Huelva and El Rocío by changing buses at Almonte or Matalascañas.

Car & Motorcycle El Rocío is 27km south of the A-49 Sevilla-Huelva highway. From Huelva you can take the coast road to Matalascañas, then head north.

El Rocío

Overlooking the marismas at the north-west corner of the national park, El Rocío's sandy streets bear almost as many hoof-prints as tyre marks, and are lined by rows of verandahed buildings which usually stand empty. But this is no ghost town: most of the houses belong to the 90-odd *hermandades* of pilgrim-revellers who converge on El Rocío every year for the Romería del Rocío (see the boxed text 'Romería del Rocío'). Indeed, a fiesta atmosphere per-vades the village most weekends as her-mandades arrive to carry out lesser rituals.

Information There's a tourist office (☎ 959 44 26 84), open Monday to Friday from 10 am to 2 pm, at Avenida de la Canaliega s/n by the main road at the west end of the village. Centro de Información Las Rocinas (see later) has national park information.

Things to See & Do The heart of the village is the **Ermita del Rocío**, a church which houses the celebrated Virgen del Rocío, a tiny wooden image dressed in long, bejewelled robes. It's open daily from 8.30 am to 7.30 pm, with people arriving to pay their respects every day.

El Rocío overlooks a section of the **marismas** which has water all year. Deer and horses graze in the shallows and you may be lucky enough to see a flock of flamingos wheeling through the sky in a great pink cloud. The Spanish Ornithological Society's waterside **Observatorio Madre del Rocío** is open to the public Friday to Sunday from 10.30 am to 1.30 pm and 2.30 to 5.30 pm, and other days from 9 am to 3 pm.

The bridge over the river on the A-483 1km south of the village is another good viewing spot. Just past the bridge is the **Centro de Información Las Rocinas** (☎ 959 44 23 40) which is open daily from 10 am to 7 or 8 pm. It has national park information and short paths to birdwatching hides. Though outside the national park proper, there's abundant birdlife here.

For a longer walk from El Rocío, head across the Puente del Ajolí at the north-east edge of the village and into the woodland ahead. This is the beginning of the **Coto del Rey**, a large woodland zone where in early morning or late evening you may spot deer or boar.

You can hire **horses** at various places in El Rocío.

Places to Stay & Eat Don't bother even trying for a room at Romería time. *Hostal Vélez (☎ 959 44 21 17, Calle Algaida 2),*

The Romería del Rocío

Like most of Spain's holiest images, Nuestra Señora del Rocío, or La Blanca Paloma (White Dove), has legendary origins from soon after the Reconquista. Back in the 13th century, the story goes, a hunter from the village of Almonte found her in a tree in the marismas. Carrying her home he stopped for a rest, but while he dozed the Virgin made her own way back to the tree.

Before long a chapel was built on the spot (El Rocío) and pilgrims were making for it. By the 17th century *hermandades* were forming in nearby towns to make an annual pilgrimage to El Rocío at Pentecost, the seventh weekend after Easter (22 to 24 May in 1999, 10 to 12 June in 2000). Today the Romería del Rocío has mushroomed into a vast festive cult that pulls people from all over Spain. There are over 90 hermandades, some of several thousand men and women, and they still reach El Rocío on foot, on horseback, and in gaily decorated covered wagons pulled by cattle or horses, using cross-country tracks and camping along the way.

Solemn is the last word you'd apply to this quintessentially Andalucian event. In an atmosphere similar to Sevilla's Feria de Abril, participants dress in bright Andalucian costume and sing, dance, drink and romance their way to El Rocío. Hundreds of thousands of *'rocieros de fin de semana'* (weekend rocieros) converge on the village by other means, pushing the total number up to about a million.

The weekend comes to an ecstatic climax in the early hours of the Monday, by which time a million people's senses have been stretched by at least 40-odd hours of little sleep and a lot of alcohol. Members of the hermandad of the nearby town of Almonte, which claims the Virgin for its own, barge into the church and bear her out on a float. Violent struggles ensue as others literally battle with the Almonte lads for the honour of carrying La Blanca Paloma. With everyone else trying to get within touching distance, the crush and chaos is immense but somehow good humour survives and the Virgin is carried round to each of the hermandad buildings, finally being returned to the Ermita in the afternoon.

with no sign, next to Cerámicas La Carreta one block north of Ermita, has clean, basic singles/doubles for 1500/2500 ptas.

Pensión Cristina (☎ 959 40 65 13, Calle Real 32), a short distance east of the Ermita, has reasonable rooms with bath for 3000/4000 ptas, and a decent restaurant where paella, or veal/lamb/venison and chips, are 700 ptas.

Hotel Toruño (☎ 959 44 23 23, Plaza Acebuchal 22), a little farther east, has 30 attractive air-con rooms with bath at 5500/7500 ptas. Some have marismas views.

Hotel Puente del Rey (☎ 959 44 25 75, Avenida de la Canaliega s/n), by the main road, is a larger place charging 6800/8600 ptas plus IVA.

There are several cafés, bars and restaurants around the village.

Centro de Recepción El Acebuche

Twelve kilometres south on the A-483 from El Rocío, then 1.6km west, El Acebuche (☎ 959 44 87 11) is the national park's main visitor centre and the starting point for tours into the park. Open daily from 8 am to 7 or 8 pm, it also has footpaths to birdwatching hides overlooking a lagoon.

National Park Tours Trips by 4WD from El Acebuche are the only way for ordinary folk to get inside the park from the west side. You need to book ahead on ☎ 959 43 04 32; spring, summer and holiday times

ANDALUCÍA

the trips can get booked up a month ahead, but otherwise a week or less is usually adequate. The trips go at about 8.30 am and 4 pm except Monday, last about four hours and cost 2500 ptas per person. They normally begin with a long beach drive to the mouth of the Guadalquivir, before taking in moving dunes, marismas, and woods where you can be pretty certain of seeing deer and boar.

WEST OF HUELVA

The coast between Huelva and the Portuguese border, 53km west, alternates between estuaries, wetlands, good sandy beaches, small and medium-sized resorts (packed in the second half of July and August) and fishing ports. A few daily buses run from Huelva to all the places mentioned below. From Ayamonte there are also buses to the Algarve and Lisbon.

Punta Umbría, Huelva's summer playground, stands on a point of land between the Marismas del Odiel and a good Atlantic beach. Farther west, **La Antilla** fronts a wide, sandy beach that runs all the way from the Río Piedras to Isla Cristina. **Isla Cristina**, enlivened by a sizable fishing fleet, has a tourist office near the centre at Avenida de España 4. Its best beach is Playa Central, about 2km east of the centre.

Ayamonte   Ayamonte stands beside the broad Río Guadiana which divides Spain from Portugal. A free road bridge crosses the river 2km north, but there's also a ferry from the town (525 ptas for a car and driver, 125 ptas for everyone else). Ayamonte's tourist office is on Avenida Alcalde Navarro just south of the centre.

Places to Stay

In La Antilla, at least six hostales are bunched near the beach on Plaza La Parada, most with doubles for around 6000 ptas plus IVA in summer (but you'd be lucky to get a room in August).

In central Isla Cristina, *Pensión Maty* (☎ 959 33 11 30, Calle Catalanes 7) charges 3500 ptas plus IVA a double in high

season, and *Hostal Gran Vía* (☎ 959 33 07 94, Gran Vía Román Pérez 10) charges 5500 ptas plus IVA. The best hotels are along Camino de la Playa near Playa Central: *Hotel Paraíso Playa* (☎ 959 33 18 73), *Hotel Los Geranios* (☎ 959 33 18 00) and *Hotel Sol y Mar* (☎ 959 33 20 50), all with doubles around 8000 ptas plus IVA.

In Ayamonte, the central *Hotel Marqués de Ayamonte* (☎ 959 32 01 25, Calle Trajano 14) has adequate singles/doubles with bath for 2500/5000 ptas plus IVA.

MINAS DE RIOTINTO

Minas de Riotinto (population 5000), 68km north-east of Huelva, makes a fascinatingly unusual stop. Silver was being extracted locally well before the Phoenicians came here, and iron has been mined since at least Roman times. In the late 19th century the British-dominated Río Tinto Company turned the area into one of the world's great copper mining centres. The mines returned to Spanish control in 1954.

Things to See & Do

The good **Museo Minero**, Plaza del Museo s/n, covers the geology and history of the mines. Pride of place goes to the Vagón del Maharajah, a luxurious carriage built for British Queen Victoria's tour of India and used by Spain's Alfonso XIII to visit the mines. The museum (200 ptas) is normally open Tuesday to Friday from 10 am to 2 pm, and Saturday, Sunday and holidays from 10 am to 6 pm, but from 16 June to 30 September it always closes at 2 pm.

The museum is also the ticket office for guided visits to the **Corta Atalaya** 1km west of the town, claimed to be the world's biggest opencast mine, and for rides on the **Ferrocarril Turístico-Minero** railway, with refurbished early 20th century carriages and steam engine. Corta Atalaya hourly trips go Tuesday to Sunday, hourly from 11 am to 2 pm; and at 4 and 5 pm on Saturday, Sunday and holidays from 1 October to 15 June (600 ptas). The train trips go daily except Monday at 2 pm from 16 June to 30 September, and for the rest of the year, on

Saturday, Sunday and holidays only, at 4 or 5 pm (1100 ptas).

About 1km north of Minas de Riotinto, the Aracena road passes the **Corta Cerro Colorado**, a vast opencast mine which a century ago was a hill.

Places to Stay & Eat
Hostal Galán (☎ 959 59 18 52, Calle Romero Villa s/n), outside the Museo Minero, has doubles with bath at 4250 ptas plus IVA, and a decent restaurant and bar.

Getting There & Away
Three or more Damas buses daily run to/from Huelva (670 ptas). Casal has two buses to/from Aracena Monday to Friday and one on Saturday. From Sevilla (Plaza de Armas) there are two or more daily Casal buses.

ARACENA
This attractive, whitewashed town of 6700 people in the north of the province spreads beneath the Cerro del Castillo, a hill topped by a medieval church and ruined castle. The main tourist office is the Centro de Turismo Rural y Reservas (☎ 959 12 83 55) on Calle Pozo de la Nieve. The Centro de Visitantes Cabildo Viejo (☎ 959 12 82 25) on Plaza Alta is the main information centre of the Parque Natural Sierra de Aracena y Picos de Aroche.

Things to See & Do
The **Gruta de las Maravillas** (Cave of Marvels) ranks among the most spectacular caves in Spain. The entrance is on Calle Pozo de la Nieve. It's open daily from 10.30 am to 1.30 pm and 3 to 6 pm, with visits (875 ptas) by guided tour in Spanish, when there are at least 25 people.

The **Cerro del Castillo** is surmounted by a beautiful church and a ruined castle, both built around 1300.

Places to Stay
Camping Aracena (☎ 959 50 10 05), open all year, is 4km south-east of town off the N-433.

The only budget beds are at the friendly *Casa Manolo (☎ 959 12 80 14, Calle Barbero 6)*, just south of the central Plaza del Marqués de Aracena. Seven basic but adequate rooms cost 3200 ptas a double.

The centrally located *Hotel Sierra de Aracena (☎ 959 12 61 75, Gran Vía 21)* has 43 comfy singles/doubles at 4200/6300 ptas plus IVA. *Hotel Los Castaños (☎ 959 12 63 00)*, nearby on Calle Rosal, is the best in town, with doubles at 7000 ptas plus IVA, and a good restaurant.

Getting There & Away
Casal (☎ 959 12 81 96) on Avenida de Andalucía, a few minutes walk south-east of Plaza del Marqués de Aracena, runs two or three daily buses to/from Sevilla (Plaza de Armas), and a daily bus to Rosal de la Frontera near the Portuguese border, where you can change to a bus for Lisbon. From the Casal station, Damas runs daily buses to/from Huelva (1050 ptas).

WEST OF ARACENA
The verdant valleys, at times dramatic hills and stone-built villages of Huelva's portion of the Sierra Morena form one of Andalucía's most surprisingly beautiful landscapes. **Linares de la Sierra**, **Alájar**, **Fuenteheridos** and **Almonaster la Real** are all intriguingly old-fashioned little places, and Almonaster's 10th century Mezquita (mosque) is one of Spain's most perfect little gems of Islamic architecture (collect the key from the ayuntamiento). The ham from **Jabugo** is acclaimed as the best in Spain (see the boxed text 'Jamón Jamón' in the Food & Wine special section), and a line of bars and restaurants along Carretera San Juan del Puerto waits for you to sample it. Castle-topped **Cortegana** and **Aroche** are two of the bigger places in the district.

There's an extensive web of marked **walking trails** throughout the Parque Natural Sierra de Aracena y Picos de Aroche, particularly between Aracena and Aroche. You should be able to pick up enough maps and leaflets from tourist offices in Aracena and village ayuntamientos to find your way around.

Hostales at Alájar, Santa Ana La Real, Fuenteheridos, Galaroza, Jabugo, Almonaster la Real, Cortegana and Aroche, all with doubles for between 2600 and 5000 ptas, provide accommodation.

Casal (see Getting There & Away under Aracena) runs two or more buses daily from Aracena, and one or more from Sevilla (Plaza de Armas), to nearly all these *pueblos*. Two daily trains run from Huelva to Almonaster-Cortegana and Jabugo-Galaroza stations.

Cádiz Province

The province of Cádiz reaches from the mouth of the Río Guadalquivir to the Strait of Gibraltar and inland to the rainy Sierra de Grazalema. It's a region of great and varied attractions, from the historic port of Cádiz itself and the nearby triangle of sherry towns (Jerez de la Frontera, Sanlúcar de Barrameda and El Puerto de Santa María), to the little-developed Atlantic beaches along the Costa de la Luz and the green Sierra de Grazalema with its remote white towns and villages.

The proliferation of 'de la Frontera' place names here stems from the days of the Reconquista. Castilla took most of Cádiz province from the Muslims in the 13th century, but the south was raided repeatedly by the Merenids of Morocco, while to the east lay the Emirate of Granada. Hence for over two centuries this region was one of the *fronteras* (frontiers) of Christian-held territory. It retains an untamed feel, with large tracts of sparsely inhabited sierra, windy coasts and big lowland ranches which breed famous fighting bulls.

CÁDIZ

Few people remember Cádiz when they list the great cities of Andalucía, and yet this port is as famous and historic as almost any of them.

Past the desolate coastal marshes and industrial sprawl of the approach to Cádiz, you emerge into a largely 18th century city of decayed grandeur, crammed on to the head of a peninsula like some huge, overcrowded Atlantic-going ship. Its 146,000 people, called *gaditanos*, are a mostly unassuming and tolerant lot whose main concern is to make the best of life – whether staying out late in the sweltering summer months, or indulging in Spain's most riotous carnaval in spring.

History

Cádiz may be the oldest city in Europe. It was founded, tradition says, in 1100 BC by the Phoenicians, who called it Gadir and traded Baltic amber as well as Spanish silver and tin here. Later a naval base for the Romans, who heaped praise on its culinary, sexual and musical delights, Cádiz then faded into obscurity until 1262, when it was taken from the Muslims by Alfonso X.

Cádiz began to boom with the discovery of America. Columbus sailed from here on his second and fourth voyages. It attracted Spain's enemies too: in 1587 England's Sir Francis Drake 'singed the King of Spain's beard' with a raid on the harbour which delayed the Armada, then in 1596 Anglo-Dutch attackers burnt almost the entire city.

Cádiz's golden age was the 18th century, when it enjoyed 75% of Spanish trade with the Americas. It grew into Spain's richest, most cosmopolitan city, and gave birth to Spain's first liberal middle class. Most of its fine buildings date from this era.

The Napoleonic Wars brought British warships back, to blockade and bombard the city. After Spain turned against Napoleon in 1808, Cádiz was one of the few cities that never fell to the French, withstanding a two-year siege from 1810. During this time a national *cortes* (parliament) convened here and adopted Spain's liberal 1812 constitution, setting the scene for a century of struggle between Spanish liberals and conservatives.

The loss of the American colonies in the 19th century plunged Cádiz into a decline from which it has recovered only in the past few decades.

CÁDIZ

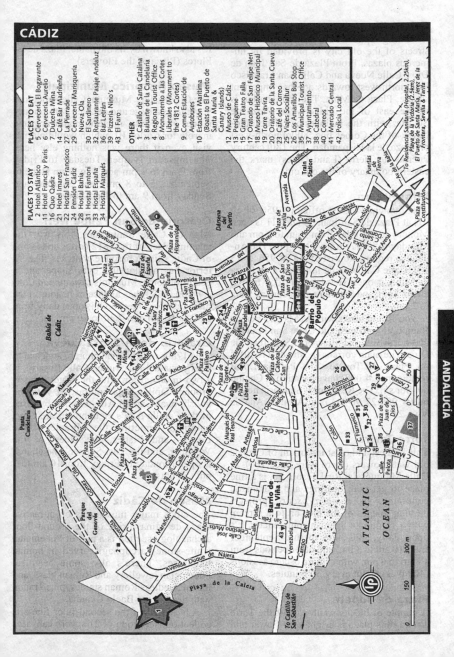

ANDALUCÍA

Orientation

Breathing space between the huddled streets of the old city is provided by numerous plazas. From Plaza de San Juan de Dios, Calle Nueva and Calle San Francisco lead north-west towards another important square, Plaza de Mina. The train station is in the east of the old city on Plaza de Sevilla, with the main estación de autobuses, of the Comes line, 800m north-west on Plaza de la Hispanidad. The 18th century Puertas de Tierra (Land Gates) mark the eastern boundary of the old city.

Information

The municipal tourist office (☎ 956 24 10 01) at Plaza de San Juan de Dios 11 is open Monday to Saturday from 9 am to 2 pm and Monday to Friday from 5 to 8 pm. The Andalucía regional tourist office (☎ 956 21 13 13), Calle Calderón de la Barca 1 on Plaza de Mina, is open Tuesday to Friday from 9 am to 7 pm, and Saturday and Monday 9 am to 2 pm.

You'll find banks with ATMs on Avenida Ramón de Carranza and Calle San Francisco, north-west of Plaza de San Juan de Dios. The main correos (postcode 11080) is on Plaza de Topete. The Policía Local (emergency ☎ 092) have a station at Campo del Sur s/n. The Residencia Sanitaria hospital (☎ 956 27 90 11) is at Avenida Ana de Viya 21.

Torre Tavira

This highest and most important of Cádiz's old watchtowers (there were once 160), at Calle Marqués del Real Tesoro 10, is a fine place to get your bearings and a dramatic panorama. Its *cámara oscura* projects moving images of the city on to a screen, with a 15 minute Spanish commentary. It's open daily, mid-June to mid-September from 10 am to 8 pm, and other periods from 10 am to 6 pm, with cámara oscura sessions (400 ptas) about every 30 minutes.

Plaza de Topete

A couple of blocks south-east of the Torre Tavira, this plaza is bright with flower and cage-bird stalls and adjoins the large, covered Mercado Central (Central Market). It's also known by its old name, Plaza de las Flores (Plaza of the Flowers).

Museo Histórico Municipal

The City History Museum, Calle Santa Inés 9, contains a large and detailed 18th century model of the city, made in mahogany and marble for Carlos III, which would merit a visit even if there was nothing else here. The museum is open Tuesday to Friday from 9 am to 1 pm and 4 to 7 pm (June to September, 5 to 8 pm), and Saturday and Sunday from 9 am to 1 pm (free).

Oratorio de San Felipe Neri

Also on Calle Santa Inés, this was the meeting place of the 1812 cortes and is one of Cádiz's finest baroque churches. The interior has an unusual oval shape and a beautiful dome. Murillo's *Inmaculada Concepción* (1680) has a place of honour in the main retablo. The church is open daily from 8.30 to 10 am and 7.30 to 10 pm.

Oratorio de la Santa Cueva

This 1780s neoclassical church, attached to the Iglesia del Rosario on Calle Rosario, is a two-in-one affair, with the austere underground Capilla Baja contrasting with the lavish, oval Capilla Alta. Framed by three of the Capilla Alta's eight arches are Goya paintings depicting the Miracle of the Loaves and Fishes, the Guest at the Wedding, and the Last Supper. The church is open Monday to Friday from 10 am to 1 pm (50 ptas).

Museo de Cádiz

The city's major museum is on attractive Plaza de Mina. Pride of the ground-floor archaeology section is a pair of Phoenician white-stone sarcophagi carved in human likenesses. There's also some beautiful Phoenician jewellery and Roman glass, and lots of headless Roman statues, plus Trajan, with head, from Baelo Claudia.

A highlight of the second-floor fine arts collection is a group of 21 superb canvases of saints, angels and monks by Zurbarán. The museum also has a room of beautiful old puppets used in satirical theatre in Cádiz. It's open daily from 9.30 am to 2.30 pm, and Monday to Friday from 5.30 to 8.30 pm (free with an EU passport, 250 ptas otherwise).

Coastal Walk

One block north of Plaza de Mina is the city's northern seafront, with views over the Bahía de Cádiz. From here you could head west along the **Alameda** garden, with the **Baluarte de la Candelaria** bastion at its end, then south-west beside the sea wall to the **Parque del Genovés**. From here Avenida Duque de Nájera leads south to **Playa de la Caleta** beach (very crowded in summer). The star-shaped **Castillo de Santa Catalina** at the north end of this bay, built in 1598 and for a long time Cádiz's main citadel, is open for guided visits every 30 minutes, Monday to Friday from 10 am to 6 pm, and Saturday and Sunday from 10 am to 2 pm. The **Castillo de San Sebastián**, out on the south side of the bay, is in military use and not visitable. From Playa de la Caleta you can follow the coast eastward to the cathedral.

Catedral & Around

The decision to build Cádiz's yellow-domed cathedral was taken in 1716 on the strength of the imminent transfer from Sevilla to Cádiz of the Casa de la Contratación, which controlled Spanish trade with the Americas. But the cathedral wasn't finished till 1838, by which time neoclassical elements had diluted Vicente Acero's original baroque design, and a drying-up of funds had forced cutbacks in size and quality.

It's still a big and impressive construction, with a grand marble and stone interior, lit from the 50m high dome. The Cádiz-born composer Manuel de Falla is buried in the crypt. The cathedral is open Monday to Saturday from 10 am to 1.30 pm.

Plaza de San Juan de Dios & Around

This large plaza is dominated by the neo-classical **Ayuntamiento**, built at its south end around 1800. If by now you need a cool, quiet resting spot, the bougainvillea-shaded benches in **Plaza Candelaria** fit the bill nicely.

Playa de la Victoria

This wide beach stretches many kilometres down the ocean side of the peninsula, beginning about 1km beyond the Puertas de Tierra. On summer weekends the whole city seems to be out here. Bus No 1 'Plaza España-Cortadura' from Plaza de España runs along the peninsula one or two blocks inland.

Special Events

No other Spanish city celebrates carnaval with the verve of Cádiz, where it turns into a 10 day singing, dancing and drinking fancy-dress party that continues until the weekend after the normal Shrove Tuesday close of carnaval. Everyone dresses up, and the fun, abetted by huge quantities of alcohol, is wholly infectious. Costumed groups called *murgas* tour the city on foot or on floats, singing witty satirical ditties, dancing or performing sketches. In addition to the 300 or so officially recognised murgas, whose efforts go before judges in the Gran Teatro Falla, there are also the *ilegales* – any group that fancies taking to the streets and trying to play or sing.

Some of the liveliest scenes are in the working-class Barrio de la Viña, between the Mercado Central and Playa de la Caleta, and on Calle Ancha and Calle Columela, where ilegales tend to congregate.

Rooms in Cádiz for carnaval get booked months in advance. Assuming you haven't managed this, you could just go for the night from somewhere else within striking distance. You'll find plenty of other people do this – in fancy dress.

Places to Stay – Budget

Youth Hostel Cádiz's excellent independent youth hostel *Quo Qádiz* (☎ *956 22 19*

39, Calle Diego Arias 1) is in a revamped old house a block south of Gran Teatro Falla. A dorm bed costs 1000 ptas, singles/doubles 2100/3200 ptas, including a decent breakfast.

Hostales & Pensiones Cheaper places mostly cluster just west of Plaza de San Juan de Dios. A good choice is the friendly *Hostal Fantoni (☎ 956 28 27 04, Calle Flamenco 5)*, in an old house. Very clean and with a roof terrace catching a bit of summer breeze, it has singles/doubles for 1600/3200 ptas, and doubles with bath for 5000 ptas. *Hostal Marqués (☎ 956 28 58 54, Calle Marqués de Cádiz 1)* has slightly ageing but clean singles/doubles, with balcony, for 2000/3500 ptas. *Hostal España (☎ 956 28 55 00)* at No 9 on the same street has nice rooms from 2800/3800 ptas.

A bit farther north-west, *Pensión Cádiz (☎ 956 28 58 01, Calle Feduchy 20)*, is a popular little place with doubles/triples only, at 3000/4500 ptas with shared bathroom.

A good choice farther into the old city is *Hostal San Francisco (☎ 956 22 18 42, Calle San Francisco 12)*, with singles/doubles from 2300/3900 ptas. Rooms at *Hotel Imares (☎ 956 21 22 57)*, across the street at No 9, range from airless interior ones to bright, breezy ones overlooking the street. They cost from 2800/4700 to 3500/5700 ptas.

Places to Stay – Mid-Range & Top End

Hostal Bahía (☎ 956 25 90 61, Calle Plocia 5), just off Plaza de San Juan de Dios, has comfortable air-con rooms with TV at 5200/6500 ptas. *Hotel Francia y París (☎ 956 21 23 18, Plaza San Francisco 2)*, is bigger (57 rooms) and more luxurious, with rooms for 7100/9500 ptas plus IVA. The modern *Hotel Atlántico* parador *(☎ 956 22 69 05, Avenida Duque de Nájera 9)* is on the seafront. Rooms start at 10,000 ptas plus IVA.

Places to Eat

Naturally, Cádiz is strong on seafood, particularly *pescado frito* (fried fish) and shellfish. *Erizos* (sea urchins) are a local favourite. Head for the bar at *El Faro (Calle San Felix 15)* in the Barrio de la Viña, to sample exquisite but moderately-priced seafood tapas.

Plaza de San Juan de Dios If price is crucial, *Restaurante Pasaje Andaluz* has *menus* from 850 ptas and mains from 500 ptas. *El Sardinero* does similar fare better but for almost twice the price. *Bar Letrán* does platos combinados from 550 to 1000 ptas. *Cervecería Marisquería Nueva Ola* has good seafood and fish raciones or platters from 750 ptas, and platos combinados from 550 to 1000 ptas. *La Pierrade (Calle Plocia 2)*, off the plaza, is a bit more adventurous. The three-course *menú* might offer *mejillones* (mussels) al Roquefort, or *brocheta de cordero* (lamb kebab) and includes wine and bread.

Plaza de Mina & Around *Café Bar Madrileño* has a wide choice at reasonable prices: tapas at 150 to 200 ptas, salads around 350 ptas, stuffed peppers or pork brochettes for 700 ptas. *Dulcería Mina (Calle Antonio López 2)* has good pastries, baguettes, or breakfast (tea/coffee, juice and tostada for 300 ptas; bacon and eggs 450 ptas). Off another side of the plaza, it's hard to pass by the fresh seafood tapas at *Cervecería Aurelio (Calle Zorrilla 1)*. Down at the end of this street, you can enjoy the bay views at *Cervecería El Bogavante* while attentive waiters serve up big salads for 600 ptas, or good mains from 800 to 1200 ptas.

Plaza de Topete *Pizzeria Nino's (Calle Columela)*, just off the plaza, does tasty pizzas from 740 ptas, and pasta, Tex-Mex and burgers from 625 ptas. The nearby *Mercado Central* sells *churros* which you can take to cafés to accompany hot chocolate for breakfast.

Entertainment

There's a great atmosphere in some of the old city's plazas on hot summer nights, with all ages out enjoying the relative cool. From midnight or so in summer the real scene migrates to the Paseo Marítimo along Playa de la Victoria, about 3km from the Puertas de Tierra, past the big Hotel Playa Victoria. Here you'll find lively music bars like *La Jarra* and *El Cobertizo Pub*, while on Calle Villa de Paradas throngs of people stand in the street with 250 ptas *macetas* of beer. A taxi from the old city to this area costs around 600 ptas. Until about 1.30 am you could get here on bus No 1 from Plaza de España.

A few places in the centre have live music. *Café del Correo (Calle Cardenal Zapata 6)* is a popular spot with good music (closed Monday and Tuesday). *Persígueme* on the corner of Calle Tinte and Calle Sagasta is another good music bar, with live sounds on Thursday. Plaza de España, and around, is where it all happens (late) on winter weekends.

Getting There & Away

Bus Most buses are run by Comes (☎ 956 21 17 63) from Plaza de la Hispanidad. There are at least seven daily to Sevilla (one hour; 1330 ptas), El Puerto de Santa María, Jerez de la Frontera and Tarifa, three or more to Arcos de la Frontera, Ronda and Málaga, and one or more to Córdoba and Granada.

Los Amarillos runs up to 10 daily buses to El Puerto de Santa María and Sanlúcar de Barrameda, and two or three to Arcos de la Frontera and El Bosque, from its stop by the south end of Avenida Ramón de Carranza. Tickets can be bought at Viajes Socialtur (☎ 956 28 58 52), Avenida Ramón de Carranza 31.

Train From the station (☎ 956 25 43 01) up to 20 trains run daily to/from El Puerto de Santa María and Jerez de la Frontera (40 minutes), and up to 12 to/from Sevilla (two hours; 1080 to 1240 ptas). There are four trains daily to/from Córdoba, and two each for Madrid (five hours) and Barcelona.

Car & Motorcycle The A-4 *autopista* from Sevilla to Puerto Real on the east side

of the Bahía de Cádiz carries a toll of 783 ptas. The toll-free N-IV is much slower.

Boat Trasmediterránea (☎ 956 22 74 21) at the Estación Marítima operates a vehicle ferry to the Canary Islands, leaving Cádiz on Saturday and arriving in Santa Cruz de Tenerife and Las Palmas 1½ and two days later, respectively. The one-way passenger fare is from 29,000 to 35,250 ptas.

EL PUERTO DE SANTA MARÍA

The town of El Puerto de Santa María, 10km north-east of Cádiz across the Bahía de Cádiz (22km by road), makes an interesting side trip, best enjoyed by taking the ferry *El Vapor*. It was here that Columbus met the owner of his flagship the *Santa María*, Juan de la Cosa, who was his pilot in 1492. Later many palaces were built in El Puerto on the proceeds of American trade. Recent prosperity has come from sherry.

Orientation & Information

Most of the town is on the north bank of the Río Guadalete. *El Vapor* puts in dead in the centre at the Muelle del Vapor jetty, beside Plaza de las Galeras Reales. The tourist office (☎ 956 54 24 13), open daily from 10 am to 2 pm and 6 to 8 pm, is close by at Calle Guadalete 1. Calle Luna, the main drag with shops and banks, is straight ahead of the jetty. Calle Palacios runs parallel, one block to the left.

Buses come and go from stops outside the Plaza de Toros, off Calle Los Moros about 800m north-west of the Muelle del Vapor. Calle Los Moros runs all the way to the riverfront. The train station is to the east on Plaza de la Estación, a 10 minute walk from the centre.

Things to See & Do

Most of the sights are between the river and Plaza España, seven blocks north of the Muelle del Vapor at the top of Calle Palacios. The **Iglesia Mayor Prioral**, with a baroque façade, dominates Plaza España. The little **Museo Municipal** at Calle Pagador 1, just off Plaza España, has interesting

Sherry

Sherry is fortified wine produced in the towns of Jerez de la Frontera, El Puerto de Santa María and Sanlúcar de Barrameda, plus five other areas in Cádiz province and Lebrija in Sevilla province. A combination of climate, chalky soils that soak up the sun but retain moisture, and a special ageing process called the *solera* system produce this unique wine. Some 95% of sherry is made from the Palomino grape variety.

There are endless varieties of sherry but the main distinction is between *fino* (dry and the colour of straw) and *oloroso* (sweet, dark and with a strong bouquet). Both varieties have several subdivisions. An *amontillado* is an amber, moderately dry fino with a nutty flavour and a higher alcohol content than the paler finos. An *oloroso* combined with a sweet wine results in a potent 'cream sherry'. A *manzanilla* – not strictly sherry but very similar – is an unfortified camomile-coloured fino from Sanlúcar de Barrameda; its delicate flavour is reckoned to come from sea breezes wafting into the bodegas.

Sherry, especially fino, goes brilliantly with many tapas, but it can also accompany a meal: manzanilla is great with seafood and olorosos are excellent with red meat.

Once sherry grapes have been harvested, they are pressed and the resulting must is left to ferment. Within a few months a frothy veil of yeast called *flor* appears on the surface. The wine is transferred to the *bodegas* (wineries) in big barrels of American oak, which add to its flavour.

Wine enters the solera process when it is a year old. The barrels, about five-sixths full, are lined up in rows, called *escalas*, at least three barrels high: the barrels on the bottom layer, called the solera (from *suelo*, floor), contain the oldest wine. From these, around three times a year 10% of the wine is drawn off. This is replaced with the same amount of wine from the barrels in the layer above, which is in turn replaced from the next layer. The wines are left to age for between three and seven years. A small amount of brandy is added to stabilise the wine before bottling, bringing the alcohol content to 16-18%, which stops fermentation. (This constitutes the 'fortification' of the wine.)

Sherry houses are often beautiful buildings in attractive gardens. A tour will take you through the bodegas where the wine is stored and aged, inform you about the process and the history of the sherry producers, and give you a bit of a tasting. You'll be given a demonstration of the use of a *venencia*, a long-handled cup for sampling sherry from the barrel. The venencia is expertly manipulated, with the sherry cascading from head level into a glass held at waist level.

archaeological and fine arts sections. It's open Monday to Saturday from 10 am to 2 pm (free). Back towards the river the **Castillo San Marcos** was built by Alfonso X after he took the town in 1260. Right by the river, **Plaza de las Galeras Reales** takes its name from the America-bound ships *(galeras)* which drew their water from its fountain. A couple of blocks west on Calle Aramburu de Mora is the lovely old fish exchange, the **Antigua Lonja de Pescado**, which is now a restaurant.

The tourist office can help with information about visiting several **18th century palaces** around town.

Phone ahead if you want to visit one of El Puerto's **sherry bodegas**. Bodegas Osborne (☎ 956 85 52 11) is open for visits (300 ptas) Monday to Friday from 9 am to 1 pm. Bodegas Terry (☎ 956 48 30 00) welcomes visitors Monday to Friday at 9.30 am, 11 am and 12.30 pm.

The pine-backed **Playa de la Puntilla**, a 30 minute walk south-west of the centre, is the most appealing beach. Bus No 26 from Plaza de las Galeras Reales stops here.

Special Events

El Puerto's early-May Feria de la Primavera is in large measure dedicated to sherry, with around 180,000 half-bottles being drunk in a week.

Places to Stay

Camping Playa Las Dunas (☎ 956 87 22 10, *Paseo Marítimo La Puntilla*), Playa de la Puntilla, has shade and is open year round. The cost is 535 ptas per tent and per adult, and 480 ptas per car.

Las Columnas (☎ 956 85 20 19, *Calle Vicario 8*), a rambling old house a few steps east of Plaza España, has clean rooms with shared bathroom at 1200 ptas per person. *Hostal Santamaría* (☎ 956 85 36 31, *Calle Pedro Muñoz Seca 38*), two blocks towards the river from Plaza España, has reasonable singles/doubles at 1500/3000 ptas. The better *Hostal Manolo* (☎ 956 85 75 25, *Calle Jesús de los Milagros 18*), a block inland from Plaza de las Galeras Reales, has singles/doubles at 2900/4300 ptas, while the nearby *Hostal Loreto* (☎ 956 54 24 10, *Calle Ganado 10*) charges 3000/5000 ptas for rooms with bathroom around a leafy courtyard.

The top place is the *Monasterio San Miguel* (☎ 956 54 04 40, *Calle Virgen de los Milagros 27*) with rooms from 12,400/17,300 ptas plus IVA.

Places to Eat

Crowds flock for the take-away seafood at the *Romerijo* and *Romerijo 2* on Calle Ribera del Marisco, near the Muelle del Vapor. The Romerijo specialises in boiled seafood while Romerijo 2 fries it; a quarter-kilo of prawns is 700 ptas, *choco* (cuttlefish) is 600 ptas. Just back from here, *Café Bar Herrera* has good food and prices, with a nice little salad at 275 ptas and *pinchitos morunos* at 800 ptas. *Restaurante El Resbaladero* in the Antigua Lonja de Pescado offers air-con comfort and a medium-to-expensive *menú* with lots of

seafood. *Cafetería las Capuchinas* in the Monasterio San Miguel hotel provides welcome air-con and has a three-course *menú* for 1250 ptas plus IVA.

Entertainment

El Puerto is a lively place with plenty of bars, and quite a lot more going on in summer. Ask at the tourist office what's coming up at the flamenco clubs *Tertulia Flamenca Tomás El Nitri* and *Peña Flamenca El Chumni*. There are also *night boat trips* (two hours; 600 ptas) on the Bahía de Cádiz from July to September.

Getting There & Away

Bus A timetable is posted on the window of Bar Sol y Sombra, close to the Plaza de Toros bus stops. There are buses for Cádiz almost half-hourly Monday to Friday from 6.30 am to 9.30 pm (fewer at weekends) and up to 10 daily to Jerez de la Frontera and Sanlúcar de Barrameda.

Train El Puerto station (☎ 956 54 25 85) is on the Cádiz-Sevilla line, half an hour from Cádiz, with up to 33 trains daily in each direction.

Boat *El Vapor* (☎ 956 87 02 70) sails from the Estación Marítima in Cádiz daily except Monday at 10 am, noon, and 2, 6.30 and 8.30 pm, with an extra trip on Sunday at 4.30 pm. Trips back from El Puerto are at 9 and 11 am and 1, 3.30 and 7.30 pm, plus 5.30 pm on Sunday. The 45 minute crossing costs 250 ptas one way.

SANLÚCAR DE BARRAMEDA

The northern tip of the sherry triangle and a flourishing summer resort, Sanlúcar is 23km north-west of El Puerto de Santa María. It has a likeable atmosphere and a fine location on the Guadalquivir estuary looking across to the Parque Nacional de Doñana.

Columbus sailed from Sanlúcar in 1498 on his third voyage to the Caribbean. So, in 1519, did the Portuguese Ferdinand Magellan, seeking – as Columbus had – a westerly

ANDALUCÍA

route to the Asian spice islands. Magellan achieved the first-known voyage round the bottom of South America but was killed in the Philippines. By the time his pilot Juan Sebastián Elcano completed the first circumnavigation of the globe by returning to Sanlúcar in 1522, just one of their five ships, the *Victoria*, and 17 sailors were left.

Orientation

Sanlúcar stretches about 2.5km along the south-east side of the estuary. Calzada del Ejército, running inland from the seafront Paseo Marítimo, is the main avenue. A block beyond its inland end is Plaza del Cabildo, the central square. The Los Amarillos bus station is on Plaza La Salle, 500m south-west of Plaza del Cabildo along Calle San Juan.

The old fishing quarter, Bajo de Guía, site of Sanlúcar's best restaurants and Doñana boat departures, is 750m north-east along the riverfront from Calzada del Ejército.

Information

The tourist office (☎ 956 36 61 10) is towards the inland end of Calzada del Ejército. It's open Monday to Friday from 10 am to 2 pm and 6 to 8 pm (from 5 to 7 pm in winter) and Saturday and Sunday from 10 am to 1 pm.

The **Centro de Visitantes Fábrica de Hielo** (☎ 956 36 38 13) at Bajo de Guía has displays and information on the Parque Nacional de Doñana and related topics. It's open daily from 9 am to 2.30 pm and 4 to 7 pm (to 8 pm from May to September).

Things to See & Do

Walking Tour A tour of the sights doesn't take long as few are open to visitors. From Plaza del Cabildo, cross Calle Ancha to Plaza San Roque and head uphill on Calle Bretones, where you can look into the **mercado** just before reaching **Las Covachas**, a set of 15th century wine cellars (closed for restoration). Here the street becomes Calle Cuesta de Belén where, Monday to Friday from 10 am to 2 pm, you can look into the

Palacio de Orleans y Borbón, a neo-mudéjar fantasy created for the Montpensier family in the 19th century, and now the ayuntamiento.

From the top of Calle Cuesta de Belén, a block to the left along Calle Caballeros is the 15th century **Iglesia de Nuestra Señora de la O**, with a mudéjar façade and ceiling. Adjoining is the **Palacio de los Duques de Medina Sidonia** (not open to visitors), home of the aristocratic family who were Spain's largest landowners until well into the 20th century. Some 200m farther along the street is the 15th century **Castillo de Santiago** (closed for restoration), amid buildings of the Barbadillo sherry company. From the castle you can return directly downhill to the town centre.

Beach Sanlúcar's sandy beach runs along the riverfront and several kilometres beyond to the south-west.

Sherry Bodegas Sanlúcar produces a distinctive sherry, *manzanilla* (see the boxed text 'Sherry'). Tours of Bodegas Barbadillo, the town's biggest firm, at Calle Luis de Eguilaz 11, are given every Thursday at noon for 200 ptas (book in advance on ☎ 956 36 08 94, or through the tourist office). Other manzanilla houses do some tours on other weekday mornings – inquire and book at the tourist office.

Parque Nacional de Doñana Trips to the national park are made by the boat *Real Fernando* from Bajo de Guía. The four hour trip ventures 10km up the Guadalquivir with stops for guided walks at some salt lagoons with plentiful bird life and a restored farmhouse in pine woods. Guides speak Spanish and English. The trips leave Tuesday to Sunday, May to October at 9.30 am and 5 pm, other months at 10 am. Tickets (2100 ptas) are sold at the Centro de Visitantes Fábrica de Hielo (see Information). From May to October and at holiday times, you should book one week ahead; at other times book two to three days ahead.

Tourafrica (☎ 956 36 25 40), Calle San Juan 20, operates 3½ hour guided tours (3700 ptas per person) into the national park on Tuesday and Friday, May to September, leaving Bajo de Guía at 8.30 am and 4.30 pm. After the river crossing, the trip is by 4WD taking in around 70km.

Doñana mosquitoes can be savage: take a repellent.

Special Events

The Sanlúcar summer gets going with a sherry festival, the Feria de la Manzanilla, in late May or early June, and blossoms in July and August with happenings like the Noches de Bajo de Guía flamenco season (late July), jazz and classical music festivals, and Sanlúcar's unique horse races, in which real thoroughbred racehorses thunder along the beach during a couple of three or four-day evening meets in August.

Places to Stay

Book well ahead for a room at holiday times. At other times, expect about 20% off prices given here. *Hostal La Blanca Paloma (☎ 956 36 36 44, Plaza San Roque 15)* has adequate singles/doubles for 2500/4000 ptas. *Hostal Bohemia (☎ 956 36 95 99, Calle Don Claudio 5)*, off Calle Ancha 300m north-east of Plaza del Cabildo, has better rooms with bath at 2500/5500 ptas.

Hotel Los Helechos (☎ 956 36 76 55, Calle Madre de Dios 9), off Calle San Juan, is an excellent middle-range choice with rooms with bathroom round two pretty courtyards for 5000/7000 ptas plus IVA. *Hotel Tartaneros (☎ 956 36 20 44, Calle Tartaneros 8)* at the inland end of Calzada del Ejército, is a turn-of-the-century mansion with solidly comfy rooms at 6500/10,000 ptas plus IVA.

Places to Eat

Spain holds few more idyllic dining experiences than watching the sun go down over the Guadalquivir while tucking into the succulent fresh fare at one of the seafood restaurants facing the river at Bajo de Guía

and washing it down with a glass or two of manzanilla. Just wander along and pick a restaurant that suits your pocket. At the *Restaurante Virgen del Carmen*, for instance, most fish mains, plancha (grilled) or frito (fried), are 1000 to 1400 ptas. Don't miss out on the starters: *langostinos* (king prawns) and the juicy *coquines al ajillo* (cockles in garlic), both 1000 ptas, are specialities. A half-bottle of manzanilla is 600 ptas.

There are lots of cafés and bars, many serving manzanilla from the barrel, around Plaza del Cabildo – *Casa Balbino* is a must for tapas. *Bar El Cura (Calle Amargura 2)*, between Calle San Juan and Plaza San Roque, does platos combinados for 500 ptas.

Entertainment

There are some lively music bars and discos on and around Calzada del Ejército and Plaza del Cabildo.

Getting There & Away

Bus Los Amarillos (☎ 956 36 04 66) runs up to nine buses daily to/from El Puerto de Santa María, Cádiz and Sevilla. Linesur-Valenciana, at Bar La Jaula behind the tourist office, runs at least seven buses daily to/from Jerez de la Frontera.

Boat Though you can visit Sanlúcar on excursion boats from Sevilla, you can't take a one-way ride upriver from Sanlúcar.

JEREZ DE LA FRONTERA

The large town of Jerez (population 180,000), 36km north-east of Cádiz, is world-famous for its wine, sherry, made from grapes grown on the area's chalky soil. Many people come here to visit its bodegas, but Jerez is also Andalucía's horse capital and supports a *gitano* community which is one of the hotbeds of flamenco.

British money was largely responsible for the development of the wineries from around the 1830s, and Jerez high society today is a mixture of *andaluz* and British due to intermarriage among sherry families

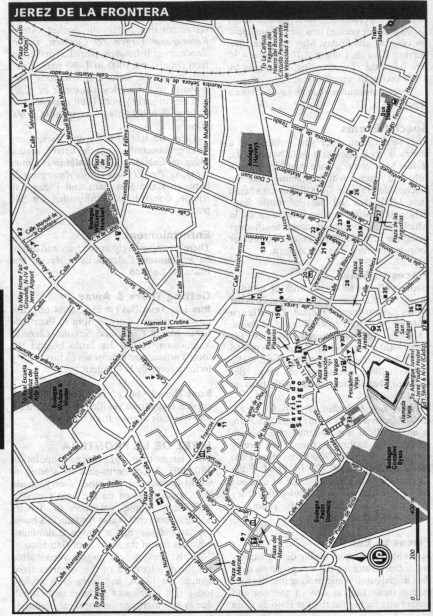

JEREF DE LA FRONTERA

JEREZ DE LA FRONTERA

PLACES TO STAY
2   Hotel Avenida Jerez
13 Hostal/Hotel
     San Andrés
24 Hostal Las Palomas
25 Hotel Serit
26 Hotel Trujillo
35 Nuevo Hotel
37 Hostal San Miguel

PLACES TO EAT
1   Restaurante La Mesa
     Redonda
3   Telepizza
5   Gaitán

12 La Rotonda
17 Bar
19 La Canilla
22 Mesón la Alcazaba
23 Patissería
29 El Almacén
30 Bar Juanita
31 Las Almenas

OTHER
4   La Plaza de Canterbury
6   Iglesia de Santiago
7   El Lago Tío Parrilla
8   Iglesia de San Mateo
9   Museo Arqueológico

10 Centro Andaluz de
     Flamenco
11 Cine Astoria
14 RENFE Office
15 Tourist Office
16 Iglesia de San Dionisio
18 Antiguo Cabildo
20 Correos
21 Teatro Villamarta
27 Bus No 9 to Youth Hostel
28 Mercado
32 Bar Dos Deditos
33 Catedral
34 Bus No 13 to Youth Hostel
36 Iglesia San Miguel

over the past 150 years. Since the 1980s most of the wineries have been bought out by multinational companies. Jerez reeks of money with lots of fancy shops, well-heeled residents, wide, spacious streets, old mansions and beautiful churches in its interesting old quarter. It puts on fantastic fiestas with sleek horses, beautiful people and flamenco.

History
The Muslims called the town Scheris, from which 'Jerez' and 'sherry' are derived. The drink was already famed in England in Shakespeare's time.

Jerez had its share of strife in the late 19th century when anarchy gained ground in Andalucía; thousands of peasants armed with scythes and sticks occupied the town for a few hours during one day in 1891 succeeding only in bringing down further repression on their heads.

The sherry industry has brought greater prosperity in more recent times. Jerez brandy, popular in Spain, is also a profitable product.

Orientation
Jerez centres on the Alameda Cristina and Plaza del Arenal, connected by Calle Larga and Calle Lancería (both pedestrianised). Budget accommodation clusters east of Calle Larga, around Avenida de Arcos and

Calle Medina. West of Calle Larga is the old quarter.

Information
The tourist office (☎ 956 33 11 50), Calle Larga 39, has an energetic, multilingual staff with mountains of information. It's open Monday to Friday from 8 am to 2 or 3 pm and 5 to 8 pm (from 4 to 7 pm in winter) and Saturday from 10 am to 2 pm and 5 to 8 pm (to 7 pm in winter).

There are plenty of banks and ATMs on and around Calle Larga. The correos (postcode 11400) is on Calle Cerrón.

The Old Quarter
The obvious place to start a tour of the old town is the **Alcázar**, the 12th century Almohad fortress south-west of Plaza del Arenal. Inside are the **Capilla Santa María la Real**, a chapel converted from a mosque by Alfonso X in 1264, a Muslim bathhouse (closed) and an 18th century palace (under restoration). The orange-tree-lined plaza outside has good vistas with the mainly 18th century **Catedral** in the foreground, which was built on the site of the main mosque. Note the 15th century mudéjar belfry, set slightly apart.

A couple of blocks north-east of the cathedral is Plaza de la Asunción, with the splendid 16th century **Antiguo Cabildo** (old

ANDALUCÍA

Town Hall) and lovely 15th century mudéjar **Iglesia de San Dionisio**.

North-west is the **Barrio de Santiago**, one of the epicentres of flamenco. The barrio has churches dedicated to all four evangelists: the Gothic **Iglesia de San Mateo**, with mudéjar chapels, is on Plaza del Mercado, where you'll also find the **Museo Arqueológico**, with a 7th century BC Greek helmet found in the Río Guadalete. In summer, the museum is open daily except Sunday from 10 am to 2.30 pm; in other seasons, Tuesday to Friday from 10 am to 2 pm and 4 to 7 pm, and Saturday and Sunday from 10 am to 2.30 pm (250 ptas).

Also in this area is the **Centro Andaluz de Flamenco** (Andalucian Flamenco Centre), in the Palacio de Pemartín on Plaza de San Juan. Jerez is at the heart of the Sevilla-Cádiz axis where flamenco began and which remains its heartland today. The centre is a kind of flamenco library-museum and school, open Monday to Friday from 10 am to 2 pm, with an audio-visual presentation hourly from 10 am to 1 pm in the main tourist seasons (free).

Just east of Plaza del Arenal is one of Jerez's loveliest churches, the 16th century **Iglesia de San Miguel**, in Isabelline Gothic style and with superb stained-glass windows.

Sherry Bodegas

For most of the bodegas you need to phone ahead to book your visit. The two biggest companies, both handily located west of the Alcázar, are **González Byass** (☎ 956 35 70 00), Calle Manuel González s/n, and **Domecq** (☎ 956 15 15 00), Calle San Ildefonso 3. González Byass is open for visits Monday to Friday at 10 and 11 am, noon, 1, 4.30 and 5.30 pm (400 ptas), Saturday 10 and 11 am, noon and 1 pm (500 ptas). Domecq has several tours Monday to Friday from 9 am to 1 pm, and Saturday and Sunday from 10 am to 1 pm (375 ptas). The tourist office has a complete list of bodegas that welcome visitors.

Other Attractions

One of Jerez's main attractions is the **Real Escuela Andaluz del Arte Ecuestre** (Royal Andalucian School of Equestrian Art) on Avenida Duque de Abrantes in the north of town. The school trains horses and riders in dressage, and you can watch them going through their paces in training on Monday, Tuesday, Wednesday and Friday from 11 am to 1 pm (450 ptas). On Thursday at noon there's an official show where the handsome horses perform to classical music (1500 to 2400 ptas). A couple of kilometres west of the centre is the **Parque Zoológico**, or Zoo Jerez, with lovely gardens and a wild animal recuperation centre. It's open Tuesday to Sunday from 10 am to 6 pm, to 8 pm in summer (600 ptas, children 400 ptas).

Special Events

Jerez's *Feria del Caballo* (Horse Fair) in early May is one of Andalucía's biggest festivals, with music and dance as well as all kinds of equestrian competitions. Colourful parades of horses and finely-dressed riders pass through the Parque González Hontoria fairgrounds in the north of town. Preceding the horse fair is the two-week *Festival de Jerez* dedicated to music and dance, particularly flamenco.

The *Fiestas de Otoño* from mid-September to mid-October, celebrating the grape harvest, range from cultural events to horse races and dressage competitions, concluding with a massive parade of horses and riders.

Places to Stay

Rates go sky-high during the Feria del Caballo, and you need to book ahead.

Places to Stay – Budget

The modern Inturjoven *Albergue Juvenil Jerez* youth hostel (☎ 956 34 28 90, Avenida Carrero Blanco 30) is 1.5km south of the centre. For prices, see this chapter's introductory Youth Hostels section. Bus No 13 from Plaza del Arenal, or bus No 9 with stops near the train and bus stations and on

Plaza de las Angustias, will take you there. Get off at the Continente stop.

The friendly *Hostal/Hotel San Andrés* (☎ 956 34 09 83, Calle Morenos 12) is a good choice. Singles/doubles with bathroom and TV cost 2500/4500 ptas; rooms with shared bath are 1600/2500 ptas. *Hostal Las Palomas* (☎ 956 34 37 73, Calle Higueras 17) has spacious rooms for 1500 ptas per person; some doubles have private bath. *Nuevo Hotel* (☎ 956 33 16 00, Calle Caballeros 23), in an old mansion, has roomy singles/doubles with bath from 2500/3500 ptas. *Hostal San Miguel* (☎ 956 34 85 62, Plaza San Miguel 4) costs 1500/3000 ptas, or 2500/4500 ptas with attached bath.

Places to Stay – Mid-Range & Top End

Add IVA to the following prices. *Hotel Trujillo* (☎ 956 34 24 38, Calle Medina 3) has rooms with all mod cons at 5900/9800 ptas (3500/5500 ptas from November to April). Nearby, *Hotel Serit* (☎ 956 34 07 00, Calle Higueras 7) has similar rooms for 5000/7000 ptas, doubles from 8000 to 15,000 ptas at peak periods. *Hotel Avenida Jerez* (☎ 956 34 74 11, Avenida Álvaro Domecq 10) has doubles for 15,000 ptas. There are more top end places on this road.

Places to Eat

Sherry is used to flavour local dishes and the sherry trade has introduced English and French elements into the local cuisine. A good, but pricey, place to try Jerez specialities is little *La Mesa Redonda* (Calle Manuel de la Quintana 3), just north-east of the centre.

The restaurants on Pescadería Vieja, a small alley off Plaza del Arenal which catches a refreshing breeze, are moderate to expensive. *Las Almenas* has three-course *menús* from 850 ptas. *Bar Juanita*, and *El Almacén* round the corner on Calle Ferros, are local tapas haunts, and good places to sample a fino.

La Canilla (Calle Larga 8) is fine for a simple breakfast. The stylish *La Rotonda* at the north end of Calle Larga does excellent breakfasts from 475 to 750 ptas, and other meals. Cheaper breakfasts can be had in the *Bar (Plaza de Plateros)*, behind Iglesia de San Dionisio.

Mesón la Alcazaba (Calle Medina 19), with a covered patio, has cheap and filling food; *menús* from 800 ptas offer plenty of choice. Platos combinados are 500 ptas. The *Patissería* on the corner of Calles Medina and Higueras has good cakes, pastries and baguettes. *Telepizza* on Calle Salvatierra, north of the bullring in the heart of the small nightlife area, has cheap deals and does a roaring trade.

For a splash-out meal at *Gaitán (Calle Gaitán 3)*, two blocks west of the Alameda Cristina, expect to pay around 1250 ptas for starters such as seafood cocktails, a little less for soups, and 1675 to 2100 ptas for main courses.

Entertainment

Check at the tourist office and watch out for posters advertising upcoming events. *Diario de Jerez* newspaper has some what's-on information and the Teatro Villamarta on Calle Medina puts out a monthly program. *Cine Astoria* on Calle Francos is an outdoor cinema and concert area where there's often live music from blues to flamenco. *Bar Dos Deditos*, Plaza Vargas 1, behind Pescadería Vieja, has live music some nights, including blues; if there's something on, you can't miss the crowd spilling on to the pavement.

North-east of the centre just before the bullring, La Plaza de Canterbury, with loads of bars around a courtyard, attracts a young crowd. Between the bullring and Plaza Caballo is a small nightlife area centred on Calle Salvatierra, with bars and a couple of clubs for dancing until late at weekends and fiestas.

For flamenco, there are several *peñas* in the Barrio de Santiago; sometimes they're listed on the tourist office map – if not, ask at the tourist office. *El Laga Tío Parrilla* on Plaza del Mercado has more tourist-oriented flamenco performances Monday to Saturday

ANDALUCÍA

from 11 pm but you may experience something more authentic there out of the main tourist seasons.

Spectator Sports
Jerez's Circuito Permanente de Velocidad, on the A-382 10km east of town, stages motorcycle races throughout the year including, on a Sunday in May, one of the *grands prix* of the World Motorcycle Championship. There are around three car races annually.

Getting There & Away
Air Jerez airport (☎ 956 15 00 00) is 7km north-east of town on the N-IV. Iberia (☎ 956 15 00 10) has daily flights to/from Madrid. British Airways (☎ 956 15 00 93) flies to/from London twice a week.

Bus The estación de autobuses (☎ 956 34 52 07) is on Calle Cartuja, about 1km south-east of the centre. Comes has buses for Cádiz (up to 18 daily; 350 ptas), El Puerto de Santa María (up to six daily; 150 ptas), Ronda (four daily; 1255 ptas, with one continuing to Málaga; 1850 ptas) and Córdoba (one daily; 1850 ptas). There are plenty of buses to Sevilla (875 ptas) by Linesur-Valenciana and Comes. Linesur-Valenciana also runs to Sanlúcar de Barrameda hourly from 7 am to 8 pm (205 ptas). Los Amarillos handles buses to inland towns with plenty to Arcos de la Frontera (280 ptas), and up to six daily to El Bosque.

Train Jerez station, at the end of Calle Cartuja, is on the Cádiz-Sevilla line with plenty of trains in both directions. The central RENFE office is at Calle Larga 34.

ARCOS DE LA FRONTERA
Arcos (population 28,000) is 30km east of Jerez along the A-382 across rolling country of wheat and sunflower fields, vineyards and fruit orchards. Arcos' ridge-top old town, with the Río Guadalete meandering below, makes a striking sight, though the modern suburbs spilling out below are less enchanting. Arcos is said to have a dark,

sinister side: there are tales of strange vibes, madness and witchcraft. Whether or not you detect anything mysterious in the atmosphere, the old town is well worth visiting, with a street plan little changed since medieval times and some lovely post-Reconquista buildings.

History
In the 11th century Arcos was for a time an independent Muslim taifa until absorbed by Sevilla. In 1255 Alfonso X took the town and repopulated it with Castilians and Leonese. Some Muslims stayed but rebelled in 1261 and were evicted. In 1440 the town passed to the Ponce de León family, the Duques de Arcos. When the last duke died heirless in 1780, his cousin, the Duquesa de Benavente, took over his lands. She was partly responsible for replacing sheep farming with cereals, olives, vines and horse breeding as the area's dominant economic activities.

Orientation & Information
From the estación de autobuses on Calle Corregidores it's a 1km uphill walk to the old town. About halfway up is the leafy Paseo de Andalucía. From the Plaza España roundabout at the top of Paseo de Andalucía, Paseo de los Boliches and Calle Debajo del Corral (becoming Calle Corredera) both head east up to the old town's main square, Plaza del Cabildo.

The tourist office (☎ 956 70 22 64) on Plaza del Cabildo, open Monday to Saturday from 9 am to 2 pm and 5 to 7 pm, and Sunday from 11 am to 1.30 pm, has lively staff who can provide a useful map.

Banks and ATMs, on Calle Debajo del Corral and Calle Corredera, and the correos (postcode 11630) on Paseo de los Boliches, are down to the west of the old town.

Things to See & Do
The best thing to do in Arcos is simply wander the old town with its narrow cobblestone streets, Renaissance buildings and whitewashed houses. **Plaza del Cabildo** is surrounded by fine old buildings and has a

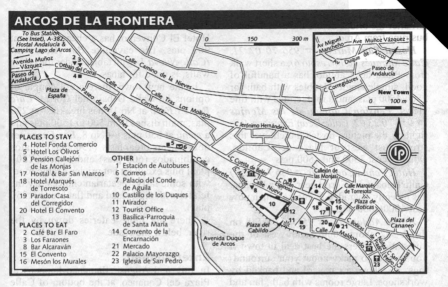

ARCOS DE LA FRONTERA

PLACES TO STAY
4 Hotel Fonda Comercio
5 Hotel Los Olivos
9 Pensión Callejón
   de las Monjas
17 Hostal & Bar San Marcos
18 Hotel Marqués
   de Torresoto
19 Parador Casa
   del Corregidor
20 Hotel El Convento

PLACES TO EAT
2 Café Bar El Faro
3 Los Faraones
8 Bar Alcaraván
15 El Convento
16 Mesón los Murales

OTHER
1 Estación de Autobuses
6 Correos
7 Palacio del Conde
   de Aguila
10 Castillo de los Duques
11 Mirador
12 Tourist Office
13 Basílica-Parroquia
   de Santa María
14 Convento de la
   Encarnación
21 Mercado
22 Palacio Mayorazgo
23 Iglesia de San Pedro

mirador with panoramic views over the river and countryside. On the west side of the plaza, Arcos' crowning glory, the **Castillo de los Duques**, dating from the 11th century, is not open to the public. On the north side, take a look at the **Basílica-Parroquia de Santa María**, begun in the 13th century, which is open daily from 10 am to 1 pm and 4 to 7 pm (150 ptas). On the east side, the **parador**, with striking views from its restaurant and terrace, is a 1960s reconstruction of a 16th century magistrate's house, the **Casa del Corregidor**.

On the streets east of here stand some lovely buildings such as the 16th century **Convento de la Encarnación** on Calle Marqués de Torresoto, with a Gothic façade. On Calle Núñez de Prado is the **Iglesia de San Pedro**, in 15th century Gothic style but with an impressive baroque façade and bell tower (the latter currently closed); the Iglesia is open Monday to Saturday, from 10 am to 1 pm and 4 to 7 pm (150 ptas). Nearby, the 17th century **Palacio Mayorazgo** with a Renaissance façade is now a senior citizens' centre.

The 15th century Gothic/mudéjar **Palacio del Conde del Águila**, on Calle Cuesta de Belén, has the town's oldest façade.

Organised Tours
The tourist office organises hour-long guided tours of the old town and its patios, Tuesday to Saturday at 10.30 am, noon, 5 and 6.30 pm (300 ptas).

Special Events
Semana Santa processions through the town's old streets are dramatic. At the beginning of August, the three-day Fiesta de la Virgen de las Nieves includes late-night live music in Plaza del Cabildo. On 29 September, during the feria dedicated to Arcos' patron saint San Miguel, there's a hair-raising running of the bulls.

Places to Stay – Budget
Camping Lago de Arcos (☎ 956 70 05 14), open year-round, is in El Santiscal near the Lago de Arcos reservoir north-east of the old town. The most straightforward route to drive from the old town is by the A-382 and

Bosque y Ubrique. Turn ge across the dam. A local cos.

Marcos (☎ *956 70 07 21, Calle Marques ae Torresoto 6)*, a short walk from Plaza del Cabildo, has a handful of good, simple singles/doubles with bath for 2500/4500 ptas, and a roof terrace with fine views. *Pensión Callejón de las Monjas* (☎ *956 70 23 02, Calle Deán Espinosa 4)* is right by the picture-postcard arch over this street, just west of Plaza del Cabildo. Doubles cost 3500 and 4500 ptas.

Hotel Fonda Comercio (☎ *956 70 00 57)* Calle Debajo del Corral near Plaza España, has recently upgraded its rooms which now cost 4000/6000 ptas.

Hostal Andalucía (☎ *956 70 07 14)*, on the A-382 about 300m south-west of the bus station, offers the best deal in town if you're not too picky about your surroundings: it's above a car yard and backed by workshops. Large rooms with bath, fan and TV cost 1500 ptas per person.

Places to Stay – Mid-Range & Top End

Arcos has some charming places in this category. Add IVA to prices. *Hotel El Convento* (☎ *956 70 23 33, Calle Maldonado 2)*, in a 17th century convent just east of Plaza del Cabildo, has great views. Fine singles/doubles are 5000/10,000 ptas. Nearby in a converted mansion, *Hotel Marqués de Torresoto* (☎ *956 70 07 17, Calle Marqués de Torresoto 4)* charges 6600/8600 ptas. The friendly, attractive *Hotel Los Olivos* (☎ *956 70 08 11, Paseo de los Boliches 30)* has rooms at 5000/9000 ptas. *Parador Casa del Corregidor* (☎ *956 70 05 00)* Plaza del Cabildo, offers typical parador luxury at 13,000/17,500 ptas.

Places to Eat

In the old town the homy *Bar San Marcos* (*Calle Marqués de Torrosoto 6)* does platos combinados from 500 to 900 ptas, tapas around 200 ptas and a *menú* at 800 ptas. Opposite, the classy *El Convento* turns out interesting fare – the three-course *menú* is

2500 ptas including a drink. *Mesón Los Murales (Plaza de Boticas 1)*, near the Hotel El Convento, has a cheaper *menú* at 900 ptas. The cave-like *Bar Alcaraván (Calle Nueva 1)* with tables under the castle walls, is good for tapas.

In the new town, there are a couple of options on Calle Debajo del Corral. *Café Bar El Faro* at No 14 has breakfast at 225 ptas, main dishes from 500 to 1500 ptas and a *menú* at 850 ptas. At No 8, *Los Faraones* does cheap breakfasts (150 ptas), platos combinados (600 ptas) and a *menú* (800 ptas) plus excellent but pricier Arabic food, with some tasty vegetarian choices: try the felafel with dips, salad and flat bread (1350 ptas).

There are more eateries down by the river, below the castle.

Entertainment

In July and August, flamenco happens at Plaza del Cananeo, at the bottom of Calle Cadenas in the old town, on Thursday from 10.30 pm.

Getting There & Away

Buses departing from Calle Corregidores Monday to Friday include 19 daily to Jerez, six to El Bosque, and a few each to Cádiz, Sevilla and Ronda. On most routes there are fewer buses on weekends. For information you can call ☎ 956 70 20 15.

PARQUE NATURAL SIERRA DE GRAZALEMA

The mountainous Parque Natural Sierra de Grazalema in north-east Cádiz province, dotted with attractive white towns and villages, is the wettest part of Spain and one of Andalucía's most beautiful and green areas. This is fine walking country, and there are opportunities for a range of other activities from rock climbing and caving to paragliding and trout fishing. The best times to visit are spring, early summer and autumn. The park extends into north-western Málaga province, where it includes the Cueva de la Pileta with ancient rock paintings (see Around Ronda in this chapter).

The *pinsapo* (Spanish fir), a relic of forests more than 2 million years old, dominates the land above 1000m. Other vegetation is typically Mediterranean and includes evergreen oaks, wild olive and riverside forest. Among the park's fauna are the ibex, chamois and roe deer. Birds of prey include Bonelli's eagle, golden eagle, Egyptian vulture and one of Europe's largest colonies of common vultures, which feed on the carcasses of the area's livestock.

Plenty of maps and printed information on the park are available, including suggested walks and drives. Many of the best walking routes are in the north of the park, around and between the villages of El Bosque, Benamahoma, Grazalema and Zahara de la Sierra, which can be linked in circuits of three or four days. Highlight walks include the route through the *pinsapar* (pinsapo forest) between Grazalema and Benamahoma, the ascent of the highest peak in Cádiz province, El Torreón, also called El Pinar (1654m), between the same two villages, and the trip into the Garganta Verde gorge south of Zahara.

For some walking routes, including several peaks and entry to the pinsapares, permission is needed. At our last check, entry to the pinsapares was in guided groups of 15 (900 ptas per person). Places needed to be reserved at the park information office in El Bosque (☎ 956 71 60 63, 956 72 70 29) at least 48 hours ahead. Contact this office for up-to-date information, or check at the information offices in Benamahoma, Grazalema or Zahara.

El Bosque

From Arcos de la Frontera, the A-372 heads 33km east to El Bosque across rolling country which gradually becomes more treed. El Bosque, prettily situated below the Sierra de Albarracín, grew up around the Palacio de Marcenilla, which was owned by the Duques de Arcos. There's a take-off point for hang-gliders and paragliders in the Sierra de Albarracín, plenty of trout to be fished in the streams near the village, and some good walking.

Orientation & Information Most places you'll need are close to the A-372 (Avenida Diputación) on the west side of the village, including the park information office, the Centro de Información El Bosque (☎ 956 71 60 63, 956 72 70 29), opposite the Hotel Las Truchas. It's open daily from 9am to 2 pm, plus Friday to Sunday from 4 to 6 pm. El Bosque's large public swimming pool (350 ptas), with shade, is between the park office and the little stone bridge over the river.

Places to Stay & Eat The Inturjoven *Albergue Campamento El Bosque* youth hostel (☎ 956 71 62 12, Molino de Enmedio s/n) is pleasantly situated by a trout stream 800m from the A-372 on the west side of the village. Turn off by the Hotel Las Truchas. There are bungalows and a shady camping area as well as doubles and triples in the main block. There's a swimming pool too. For prices, see this chapter's introductory Youth Hostels section. Various walks start on a track beside the hostel; there's an information board showing the routes.

Camping La Torrecilla (☎ 956 71 60 95) Carretera Antigua El Bosque-Ubrique, is on the far side of the village, 1km off the A-372. The cost for two adults with tent and car is 1500 ptas.

Hostal Enrique Calvillo (☎ 956 71 61 05, Avenida Diputación 5) has singles/doubles with bath for 2000/4500 ptas. Reception is in the *Casa Calvillo* restaurant a few doors away.

Hotel Las Truchas (☎ 956 71 60 61, Avenida Diputación s/n) nearby has comfy rooms with bath for 4100/7150 ptas plus IVA and a restaurant terrace overlooking the village and countryside. Try the trout, the local speciality.

Getting There & Away Up to six buses daily run from Arcos de la Frontera and Jerez de la Frontera, and a few from Cádiz and Grazalema.

Benamahoma

The village of Benamahoma, 4km from El Bosque on the A-372 to Grazalema, is known for its market gardens, trout farm and a cottage industry of rush-backed chairs. There's a park information office (☎ 956 71 60 63) and museum in an old mill. Nearby on Camino del Nacimiento, *Camping Los Linares* (☎ 956 71 62 75) has good facilities including a pool.

Grazalema

From Benamahoma the A-372 winds east up to Puerto del Boyar at 1103m, where there's a lookout point, before the descent to Grazalema (823m); when the mist comes down, this road is dangerous. Grazalema nestles into a hillside, surrounded by beautiful mountain country, with the Sierra del Pinar to the north-west and the Sierra del Endrinal to the south. Towering Pico San Cristóbal (1525m), to the north-west, provided the first glimpse of home for Spanish sailors returning with their treasure troves from the Americas.

A haunt of nature-lovers and artists, Grazalema is a neat, pretty, picture-postcard village. Its steep, cobblestone streets, whitewashed houses and flowery window boxes reflect its Muslim heritage. Local products include pure wool blankets and rugs.

Information On the central Plaza de España you'll find the tourist office (☎ 956 13 22 25) with information about the natural park, details of houses to rent, and local crafts and produce for sale. It's open Tuesday to Sunday from 10 am to 2 pm and 4 to 6 pm (summer 6 to 8 pm). Unicaja bank, right by Plaza de España, has an ATM.

Things to See & Do There are a couple of lovely 17th century churches, the **Iglesia de la Aurora** on Plaza de España and the nearby **Iglesia de la Encarnación**.

Horizon (☎ 956 13 23 63), Calle Doctor Mateos Gago 12, offers activities from horse riding (1500 ptas an hour) and rock climbing to hot-air balloon trips and paragliding. It's open Tuesday to Friday from 10 am to 2 pm, and at weekends from 3.30 to 5.30 pm.

Grazalema's public swimming pool, with good views, is below Restaurante El Tajo at the east end of the village.

Special Events *Las Fiestas del Carmen*, from around 12 to 20 July, include plenty of late-night music and dance performances. The festivities end on a Monday with a bull-running through the streets.

Places to Stay & Eat *Camping Tajo Rodillo* (☎ 956 13 20 63) is 1km above the village on the A-372 to El Bosque. It's closed in winter. Cost for two adults, a tent and a car is 1515 ptas.

In the centre, *Casa de las Piedras* (☎ 956 13 20 14, Calle las Piedras 32) has plenty of singles/doubles for 1500/3000 ptas, or 3600/4800 ptas with bath. Its restaurant serves a range of hearty, medium-priced breakfasts, and platos del día such as *pisto* (mixed vegetables, 450 ptas) and stuffed pork (900 ptas).

The *Villa Turística* (☎ 956 13 21 62, El Olivar s/n) above the village to the north, has manicured lawns with a pool and great views. Rooms with all mod cons cost from 4400/7150 ptas plus IVA.

There are plenty more places to eat and drink on Calle Agua, off Plaza de España. *Restaurante El Tajo*, with panoramic views at the east end of the village, has classy airs. The buffet lunch (not served in winter) is around 1100 ptas; trout stuffed with ham is 1250 ptas.

Getting There & Away There are two buses daily from El Bosque, several from Ubrique, and two from Ronda.

Zahara de la Sierra

Topped by a crag with a ruined castle, Zahara de la Sierra (551m) is one of the most dramatic and pretty of all the white villages. It feels quite otherworldly, especially if you've driven through heavy mist over the high and potentially dangerous road from Grazalema by the 1331m Puerto de los Palomas ('Doves' Pass', but there are more vultures than doves). Zahara is well set up for those wanting to explore the surrounding country.

Zahara's recapture from the Christians by Abu al-Hasan of Granada in a daring night raid in 1481 sparked the last phase of the Reconquista, which ended with the fall of Granada. In the late 19th century Zahara was a noted hotbed of anarchism.

Information The village centres on Calle San Juan, a cobblestone street with a church at each end. Here you'll find Turismo Rural Bocaleones (☎ 956 12 31 14), a tourist office-cum-activities cooperative, open daily from 9.30 am to 2 pm, plus Saturday and Sunday from 4 to 7 pm. For most walks in the park from Zahara, you need to get permission here. The office can organise horse rides, canoe trips, bicycle and 4WD rental and more.

Things to See & Do You can climb up to the 12th century **Castillo**, of which one tower survives, by a dirt track beside the 18th century baroque **Iglesia de Santa María de la Mesa** on Calle San Juan or, more easily, by a new path with steps from the main road below the village. There's also a **mirador** on Calle San Juan. Zahara's steep streets invite investigation, with pretty views framed by tall palm trees or hot-pink bougainvillea.

There are five major walking routes in the natural park, some also open to 4WD, bicycles and horses. There are also caving possibilities.

Places to Stay & Eat *Camping Cortijo*, 3km from the village at Arroyomolinos, charges around 1000 ptas for two adults with tent and car. The unsigned, friendly little *Pensión González* (☎ 956 17 32 17, Calle San Juan 9) has a few singles/doubles with shared bathroom at 2000/3000 ptas. *Hostal Marqués de Zahara* (☎ 956 12 30 61, Calle San Juan 3), a converted mansion, has 10 comfy rooms for 3750/5650 ptas. Its restaurant, with a 1500 ptas *menú*, is for guests only, but there are other places to eat on this street and a *supermarket* nearby.

Other hostales include *Los Estribos* (☎ 956 13 74 45, Calle Fuerte 3) and *Los Tadeos* (☎ 956 13 78 86, Paseo de la Fuente s/n).

Getting There & Away The Comes line operates two buses Monday to Friday to/from Ronda via Algodonales.

COSTA DE LA LUZ

The 90km coast between Cádiz and Tarifa can be windy and its Atlantic waters are a shade cooler than the Mediterranean, but these are small prices to pay for an unspoiled, often wild shore, strung with long, clean white-sand beaches. Andalucians flock down here in July and August, bringing a vibrant fiesta atmosphere to the scattered, normally quiet coastal towns and villages.

The three finest places to head for are the villages of Los Caños de Meca, Zahara de los Atunes and Bolonia. It's advisable to ring ahead for rooms anywhere in July and August.

Vejer de la Frontera

This isolated, old-fashioned white town looms atop a rocky hill 200m above the busy N-340, 50km from Cádiz and 10km inland.

The narrow, winding streets of the oldest part of town, still partly walled, spread over the highest part of the hill. Just below this are the Plazuela (more or less the heart of town) with the Hotel Convento de San Francisco, and the tourist office (☎ 956 45 01 91) at Calle Marqués de Tamarón 10, which is open Monday to Friday from 8 am to 3 pm (to 2 pm in summer). Buses stop on Avenida de Remedios, the road up from the N-340, about 500m below the Plazuela.

Within the walled area, seek out the **Iglesia del Divino Salvador**, whose interior is mudéjar at the altar end and Gothic at the other; and the much-reworked **Castillo**, open from 11 am to 2 pm and 5 to 10 pm, which has great views and a small museum that preserves one of the black cloaks, covering everything but the eyes, that Vejer women wore until just a couple of decades ago.

Places to Stay *Hostal La Janda* (☎ 956 45 01 42), across town at the meeting of Calle San Ambrosio and Calle Cerro Clarinas, has singles/doubles with bath for 2000/4000 ptas. Down a side street nearby, *Hostal Buena Vista* (☎ 956 45 09 69, Calle Manuel Machado 20) has good-value doubles with bath for 5000 ptas. *Hotel Convento de San Francisco* (☎ 956 45 10 01, Plazuela s/n), in a restored 17th century convent, has singles/doubles at 6600/8800 ptas plus IVA.

Getting There & Away Comes buses run to/from Cádiz and Barbate up to nine times daily. More buses for the same places, plus Tarifa and Algeciras (about 10 daily), La Línea, Málaga and Sevilla (all three or more) stop at La Barca de Vejer, on the N-340 at the bottom of the hill.

Barbate

A fishing and canning town with a long sandy beach and a big harbour, Barbate becomes a fairly lively resort in summer, but it's mostly a drab place. You might need to change buses here. The only tourist office (☎ 956 43 10 06) for the Los Caños de Meca-Zahara area is on Calle Ramón y Cajal, just back from the beachfront Paseo Marítimo towards its east end.

The Comes bus station (☎ 956 43 05 94) is over 1km back from the beach at the north end of the long main street, Avenida del Generalísimo. Buses run to/from La Barca de Vejer (see Vejer de la Frontera) and Cádiz up to 12 times daily, Vejer de la Frontera four to nine times, Sevilla once (not Sunday), and Tarifa once.

Los Caños de Meca

Los Caños, once a hippy hideaway, straggles untidily along a series of sandy coves beneath a pine-clad hill 12km west of Barbate. It maintains its laid-back air even at the height of summer.

The road from Barbate emerges towards the east end of Los Caños' single street, which mostly seems to be called Avenida Trafalgar. The main beach is straight in

front of you. At the west end of the village a side road leads out to a lighthouse on a low spit of land with a famous name: Cabo de Trafalgar. Off here, Spanish naval power was terminated in a few hours one day in 1805 by a British fleet under Nelson. There are further decent beaches either side of Cabo de Trafalgar.

Places to Stay *Camping Camaleón* (☎ 956 43 71 54, Avenida Trafalgar s/n), about 1km west from the Barbate road corner, has a shady site at about 2200 ptas for two people with a car and tent. This and two slightly cheaper camp sites within the next 2km along the road open from about April to September and get pretty crowded in high summer.

About 10 hostales are strung along Avenida Trafalgar, and there are more at Zahora, 2km west. Most are pretty similar and have decent rooms with private bath.

The quieter end of the village is east from the Barbate road corner. *Hostal Fortuna* (☎ 956 43 70 75), about 200m along, has doubles for 5000 ptas (8000 ptas in August). Farther on, the quaint, turreted *Hostal Los Castillejos* has lingering hippy vibes and doubles for around 4000 ptas.

West from the Barbate road corner, *Hostal Miramar* (☎ 956 43 70 24, Avenida Trafalgar 100) boasts a pool and restaurant and has singles/doubles with bath for 4000/5300 ptas. Past the Camping Camaleón turning, *Hostal El Ancla* (☎ 956 43 71 00) has doubles or triples with bath for around 5000 ptas. Both these places close in winter.

Places to Eat *Restaurante El Caña*, just east of the Barbate road corner, has a fine position above the beach. Most seafood is around 1000 ptas. The *supermarket* across the road has an attached café (open all year).

In season, *El Pirata*, above the beach a couple of hundred metres west, is a good bet with salads from 300 ptas and seafood media-raciones at 500 or 600 ptas.

Entertainment In high summer, good bars include the cool *Bar Araña* next to Hostal Los Castillejos, *Café-Bar Ketama* across the street from El Pirata, and a couple of places with music on the road out to Cabo de Trafalgar. *Sajorami* restaurant-bar at Playa Zahora often has live rock, blues or flamenco on summer nights.

Getting There & Away Buses to Los Caños run in summer only. In 1997 the Comes line ran buses from Sevilla from mid-June to early September, daily at 9 am. From Barbate there was a daily bus to Los Caños from mid-June to early September at 7 pm.

Zahara de los Atunes

Plonked in the middle of nothing except a broad, 12km sandy beach, Zahara is an elemental sort of place. At the heart of the village stand the crumbling walls of the old Almadraba, once a depot and refuge for the local *atún* (tuna) fishers, who were an infamously rugged lot. Cervantes wrote that no-one deserved the name *pícaro* (low-life scoundrel) unless they had spent two seasons fishing for tuna at Zahara. Records state that in 1541 no fewer than 140,000 tuna were brought into Zahara's Almadraba. Today the nearest tuna fleet is at Barbate, but Zahara has revived as an almost fashionable Spanish summer resort. With an old-fashioned core of narrow streets, it's altogether a fine spot to let the sun, sea and wind – and, in summer, a spot of lively nightlife – batter your senses.

Unicaja bank on Calle María Luisa has an ATM.

Places to Stay *Camping Bahía de la Plata* (☎ 956 43 90 40), near the beach at the south end of Zahara, is open all year, charging 2000 ptas for two people with car and tent.

The cheapest rooms, and the most likely vacancies when everywhere seems full, are at *Hostal Monte Mar* (☎ 956 43 90 47, Calle Peñón 12) at the northern tip of the village. The rooms are fine, at 4500 ptas a

double with bath. The small *Hotel Nicolás* (☎ 956 43 92 74, Calle María Luisa 13) has simple but attractive singles/doubles with TV and bath for 4000/5700 ptas plus IVA, and a restaurant.

Hotel Gran Sol (☎ 956 43 93 01, Calle Sánchez Rodríguez s/n), with the prime beach position, has large, comfortable doubles at 9500 ptas plus IVA. *Hotel Doña Lola* (☎ 956 43 90 09, Plaza Thompson 1) is a modern place in old-fashioned style, with good doubles at 10,000 ptas.

Places to Eat Most restaurants are on or near Plaza de Tamarón near the Hotel Doña Lola, and most offer similar lists of fish, seafood, salads, meat and sometimes pizzas. *Patio la Plazoleta (Plaza de Tamarón)* is a good one, open to the air; a media ración of *pez limón a la plancha* (grilled tuna with vegetables and lemon) is 600 ptas.

Entertainment In July and August a line of marquees and shacks along the beach south of the Almadraba serve as bars, discos and *teterías*. They get busy from about midnight. Some have live flamenco or other music.

Getting There & Away Comes runs two buses daily to/from Cádiz (one on Sunday), three daily to/from Barbate (one on Sunday), one daily except Sunday to/from Tarifa and, from mid-June to early September, one daily to/from Sevilla via Los Caños de Meca.

Bolonia

This tiny village, 10km down the coast from Zahara and about 20km from Tarifa, has a fine white-sand beach, a handful of restaurants and small hostales, and the ruins of the Roman town of Baelo Claudia. The ruins include a theatre, a forum surrounded by temples and other buildings, and workshops which turned out the products that made Baelo Claudia famous in the Roman world: salted fish and *garum*, a prized condiment made from fish entrails – an

ANDALUCÍA

ancestor of the fish sauce of South-East Asian cuisine. The site is open for guided visits, which cost 250 ptas for foreigners, Tuesday to Sunday at 10 and 11 am, noon, 1 pm and (except Sunday) 4 and 5 pm (5 and 6 pm from July to mid-September).

The hostales are all around 5000 ptas for a double with bath in summer.

The road to Bolonia heads west off the N-340, 15km from Tarifa. If you don't have wheels, it's a 7km hilly walk from the main road. There's no regular bus service. You can also walk the 8km along the coast from Ensenada de Valdevaqueros via Punta Paloma (see Tarifa).

TARIFA

Even at peak times, Tarifa is an attractive, laid-back town. Until 10 years or so ago it was relatively unknown but it has since become a mecca for windsurfers. The beaches have clean, white sand and good waves, and inland the country is green and rolling. Then there's the old town to explore, with its narrow streets, white-washed houses and cascading flowers. The only negative, though not for windsurfers or the hundreds of windmills inland, is the wind; for much of the year, either the *levante* (easterly) or *poniente* (westerly) is blowing, ruinous for a relaxed sit on the beach and tiring if you're simply wandering around. When the levante is blowing or there's little wind, the Tarifa area, including the spectacular Mirador del Estrecho lookout point 7km east on the N-340, is good for watching bird migrations across the Strait of Gibraltar (see the Gibraltar section for more on these).

History

Tarifa takes its name from Tarif ibn Malik who led a Muslim raid in 710, the year before the main Islamic invasion of the peninsula. The Christians took the town in 1292. Tarifa was active in the colonisation of the Americas: many of its population left for Peru in the 16th and 17th centuries.

Orientation

Two roads lead into Tarifa from the N-340. The one from the north-west becomes Calle Batalla del Salado, which ends at Avenida de Andalucía where the Puerta de Jerez leads through the walls into the old town. The one from the north-east meets Avenida de Andalucía at the Puerta de Jerez. The main street of the old town is Calle Sancho IV El Bravo. To the south-west protrudes the Punta de Tarifa, a military-occupied promontory that is the southernmost point of continental Europe.

Information

The tourist office (☎ 956 68 09 93) is near the top end of the palm-lined Paseo de la Alameda on the west side of the old town. It's open Monday to Friday from 10.30 am to 1.30 pm and 5 to 7 pm (from 6 to 8 pm in summer).

There are banks and ATMs on Calle Sancho IV El Bravo and Calle Batalla del Salado. The correos (postcode 11380) is at Calle Coronel Moscardó 9. The Policía Local (☎ 956 61 41 86) are in the ayuntamiento on Plaza de Santa María. The Cruz Roja (Red Cross; ☎ 956 64 48 96) is at Calle Alcalde Juan Núñez 5.

International newspapers and books in English and German are available at the News Stand on Calle Batalla del Salado. SYP supermarket on Calle San José, will wash and dry a load of laundry for roughly 1000 ptas.

Things to See & Do

Tarifa is best enjoyed by exploring the tangled streets of the old town, stopping in at the busy fishing port and sampling the beaches.

Old Town The mudéjar **Puerta de Jerez** was built after the Reconquista. Look in at the bustling **mercado** on Calle Colón before wending your way to the mainly 15th century **Iglesia de San Mateo** at the end of Calle Sancho IV El Bravo. The streets south of the church are little changed since

TARIFA

Calle General Primo de Rivera

Parque Feria

Plaza de Toros

Calle Callao

Calle Navas de Tolosa

Calle San José

Calle San José

Calle San Sebastián

Calle San José

Calle Batalla del Salado

Calle Otumba

Calle Antonio Maura

To Marruecotur, N-340, Camping Grounds & Cádiz

To N-340 (Algeciras & Málaga)

Calle Amador de los Ríos

Calzadilla de Teller

Avenida de Andalucía

Avenida de la Constitución

Paseo de la Alameda

Calle Colón

Calle Peso

C Nuestra Señora de la Luz

Calle Silos

Calle

Calle Castelar

Plaza San Hiscio

Bravo

C San Francisco

Calle Santísima Trinidad

Calle Cervilles

Calle San

Calle Guzmán

Calle Coronel Moscardó

Calle María Coronel

Plaza de Santa María

Calle Aljaranda

C General Copons

C María de Molina

C Alcalde Juan Núñez

Port

To Punta de Tarifa & Playa Chica

Playa de los Lances

PLACES TO STAY
1 La Mirada
3 Casa Facundo
8 Hostal Villanueva
15 La Casa Amarilla &
   Bodega de Casa Amarilla
18 Pensión Correo
22 Hostal Alameda

PLACES TO EAT
12 La Capricciosa
13 Café Central
14 Ali Baba
17 Mandrágora
20 Bar El Sevilla

OTHER
2 SYP Supermarket &
   Laundrette
4 Comes Bus Stop
   and Office
5 Hospital
6 Newsstand
7 Puerta de Jerez
9 Tourist Office
10 Mercado
11 Tanakas
16 Iglesia de San Mateo
19 Correos
21 Café Continental
23 Bus Stop for West
   Coast Beaches
24 Entrance to Castillo
   de Guzmán
25 Castillo de Guzmán
26 Museo Municipal
27 Ayuntamiento &
   Policía Local
28 Mirador El Estrecho
29 Ferry Ticket Offices
30 Cruz Roja

0   50   100 m

ANDALUCÍA

Islamic times. The **Mirador El Estrecho** atop part of the castle walls has spectacular views across to Africa.

The **Castillo de Guzmán**, extending west from here, is named after the Reconquista hero Guzmán El Bueno. In 1294, when threatened with the death of his kidnapped son unless he relinquished the castle to Islamic forces trying to recapture Tarifa, he threw down his own dagger to be used at the execution. Guzmán's descendants became the Duques de Medina Sidonia (see

Sanlúcar de Barrameda). The imposing fortress, originally built in 960 on orders of the Córdoban caliph, Abd ar-Rahman III, is open Tuesday to Sunday from 10 am to 1.30 pm and 5 to 8 pm (Sunday afternoon from 4 to 5 pm), for 200 ptas. The entrance is on Calle Guzmán. Inside, you can walk along the parapets and stand atop a couple of the towers.

The small **Museo Municipal** on Plaza de Santa María is open Monday to Friday from 10 am to 1.30 pm.

Beaches The popular town beach is the sheltered Playa Chica, on the isthmus leading out to Punta de Tarifa. From here Playa de los Lances stretches 10km north-west to the huge sand dune at Punta Paloma.

Windsurfing Conditions are often right for the sport on Tarifa's town beaches, but most of the action occurs along the coast between Tarifa and Punta Paloma. El Porro on Ensenada de Valdevaqueros, the bay formed by Punta Paloma, is one of the most popular spots, with easy parking and plenty of space to set up.

You can buy new and second-hand windsurfing gear in Tarifa at the shops along Calle Batalla del Salado. For board rental and classes you need to try places up the coast such as Club Mistral at the Hurricane Hotel (see Places to Stay), or Spin Out in front of Camping Torre de la Peña II, near El Porro. At Club Mistral board rental costs 2500 ptas an hour or 7000 ptas a day; a six-hour beginner's course is 19,500 ptas.

Competitions are held year round with two big events in summer: the World Speed Cup (July) and the World Cup (Formula 42) (July or August).

Places to Stay

Camping There are six year-round camp sites on or near the beach between Tarifa and Punta Paloma, 10km north-west along the N-340. All charge around 2200 ptas for two people with a tent and a car.

Hostales & Hotels It's best to phone ahead in summer, when rooms can be tight.

In Town Pensión Correo (☎ *956 68 02 03, Calle Coronel Moscardó 9*) has attractive rooms from 1500 to 3000 ptas per person. *La Casa Amarilla* (☎ *956 65 19 93, Calle Sancho IV El Bravo s/n*) has better rooms, most with kitchenette and all with bath, with singles/doubles from 2500/5000 to 3500/7000 ptas. The friendly *Hostal Villanueva* (☎ *956 68 41 49, Avenida de Andalucía 11*) is built into the city walls west of the Puerta de Jerez. Good, clean rooms are 3500/4500 ptas in summer. *Hostal Alameda* (☎ *956 68 11 81, Paseo de la Alameda 4*) has doubles with bath and air-con for 4000 to 6000 ptas depending on season.

Popular *Casa Facundo* (☎ *956 68 42 98, Calle Batalla del Salado 47*), is geared up for windsurfers and even has board storage space. Doubles with bath are 5000 ptas from July to October; other rooms are 2500/4000 ptas. If you're after sea views, *La Mirada* (☎ *956 68 06 26, Calle San Sebastián 41*) has doubles for 7500 ptas in the high season.

Along the Coast At least nine places are dotted along the beach and the inland side of the N-340 within 10km north-west of Tarifa, but none is cheap. All have rooms with private bath.

Hostal Millón (☎ *956 68 52 46*), 5km from the town centre, has a nice little beachside garden, its own small restaurant, and reasonable doubles at 9000 ptas (7000 ptas from October to June).

The *Hurricane Hotel* (☎ *956 68 49 19*), in beachside semitropical gardens 6km out, has 33 large, comfy rooms, two pools, a health club, and a windsurfing school and board rental. Singles/doubles range seasonally from 9000/12,000 to 13,125/17,500 ptas on the ocean side, and 6750/9000 to 10,675/14,500 ptas on the land side (all plus IVA and including an excellent buffet breakfast).

Hostal Oasis (☎ *956 68 50 65*) and *Hotel La Ensenada* (☎ *956 68 06 37*), both about 8km out, are two of the less pricey places, with doubles from 5000 to 8500 ptas depending on the season.

Places to Eat

In Town Calle Sancho IV El Bravo has plenty of takeaway options including popular *Ali Baba* with filling, tasty Arabic food. Excellent felafels are 375 ptas; kebabs and *kebes* (spicy meatballs) are a bit more. A few doors away, *Café Central* has good *churros y chocolate* and a good range of breakfasts from 375 ptas. Main meals are around 950 ptas.

There's excellent food at *Mandrágora (Calle Independencia 3)* behind the Iglesia de San Mateo. Delicious options include *bacalao*-stuffed peppers (1000 ptas) and cheese-stuffed chicken breasts (900 ptas). For pizzas, head to *La Capricciosa (Calle San Francisco)*.

The best-value seafood in town is at *Bar El Sevilla (Calle Inválidos)* west of the centre. There's no name outside, some locals call it El Gallego. Mixed fish and seafood fry-ups cost 150 ptas for a generous tapa, 850 ptas for a ración (enough for two people) – excellent with a beer!

Along the Coast Most hotels and hostales have restaurants. The Hurricane Hotel's *Terrace Restaurant* is good for lunch (home-made pasta, local fish and seafood). *Mesón El Toro*, on the inland side of the N-340 4km from Tarifa, is a good steak and fish house with mains around 1200 to 1500 ptas. It is open from 7 pm to 1 am (closed Monday).

Entertainment
Except in summer, nightlife is mostly limited to the bars in town and up the beach, though the town's big disco *Tanakas*, on Plaza San Hiscio, is lively until 5 am on Friday and Saturday year-round. *Bodega de Casa Amarilla* in the centre is good for a drink from Thursday to Sunday and sometimes has live music, including flamenco. On summer weekends, several places have live music – try *Café Continental* on Paseo de la Alameda.

Getting There & Away
Bus The Comes line (☎ 956 68 40 38), on Calle Batalla del Salado 1½ blocks north of Avenida de Andalucía, runs six or more daily buses to Cádiz, Algeciras and La Línea; a few to Jerez de la Frontera, Sevilla and Málaga; and one each to Facinas (see Parque Natural Los Alcornocales) and (except Sunday) Barbate and Zahara de los Atunes.

Boat Isleña de Navegación (☎ 956 65 28 00) and Transtour each operate one ferry daily between Tarifa and Tangier, leaving Tarifa at 9.30 am and 10 am respectively. Return sailings are at 3.30 and 4 pm (Moroccan time). The one-way passenger fare for the one-hour crossing is 2960 ptas; a car and driver is 9300 ptas and a motorcycle 2650 ptas. Buy your ticket at the port or from Marruecotur, Calle Batalla del Salado 57.

PARQUE NATURAL LOS ALCORNOCALES
This 1700 sq km natural park stretches 75km north from the Strait of Gibraltar across a sparsely populated jumble of sierras of medium height. Much of it is covered in Spain's most extensive *alcornocales* (cork oak woodlands).

There are plenty of walks and possibilities for other activities in the park, but you need your own wheels to make the most of it. The Centro de Visitantes Huerta Grande information office (☎ 956 67 91 61) is beside the N-340 at Pelayo, some 12km east of Tarifa and about 750m east of the Inturjoven *Albergue Juvenil Algeciras* (☎ 956 67 90 60) youth hostel, which has singles, doubles, four-person rooms and a swimming pool. For prices, see this chapter's introductory Youth Hostels section. There's a bus stop in front of the hostel.

One road into the south of the park goes through the village of Facinas, off the N-340 20km north of Tarifa. Here Turismo Rural, (☎ 956 68 74 29), Calle Divina Pastora 6, runs varied trips into the park.

The small town of **Jimena de la Frontera**, on the A-369 on the park's eastern boundary, is a good base for the generally higher and more rugged northern part of the park. Jimena is crowned by a fine Muslim castle, has a couple of hostales, and is served by train and bus from Algeciras and Ronda, and bus from La Línea.

ALGECIRAS
Algeciras, the major port linking Spain with Africa, is an unattractive, industrial and

fishing town and a drug-smuggling centre. During the summer, the port is hectic with large numbers of Moroccan workers heading home from Europe for their holidays.

History
Taken by Alfonso XI from the Merenids of Morocco in 1344, Algeciras was later razed by Mohammed V of Granada. In 1704 it was repopulated by many of those who left Gibraltar after it was taken by the British.

Orientation
Algeciras faces Gibraltar across the Bahía de Algeciras. Avenida Virgen del Carmen runs north-south along the seafront, becoming Avenida de la Marina around the entrance to the port. From here Calle Juan de la Cierva (becoming Calle San Bernardo) runs inland to the Comes bus station (about 350m) and the train station (400m). The central square is Plaza Alta. Plaza Palma stages a bustling market daily except Sunday.

Information
Tourist Offices The English-speaking main tourist office (☎ 956 57 26 36), Calle Juan de la Cierva s/n, is open Monday to Friday from 9 am to 2 pm. The Spanish-speaking municipal tourist office, outside the port entrance, is open Monday to Friday from 10 am to 2 pm, and extra hours in July and August.

Money Ignore money-changing touts around the port; they're a rip-off for pesetas and you'll get a better deal buying dirham in Morocco. There are banks and ATMs on Avenida Virgen del Carmen and around Plaza Alta, plus an ATM inside the port.

Medical Services & Emergency The Policía Nacional (☎ 956 66 04 00) are at Avenida de las Fuerzas Armadas 6. For an ambulance dial ☎ 956 65 15 55. The Hospital Cruz Roja (☎ 956 60 31 44) is central at Paseo de la Conferencia s/n, on the southern extension of Avenida de la Marina.

Left Luggage The train station has plenty of *consigna* lockers (400 ptas daily). In the port, storage is available from 7.30 am to 10 pm at 100 ptas a bag, but there are no lockers.

Things to See & Do
If you have to spend time in Algeciras, wander up to palm-fringed **Plaza Alta**, which has a lovely tiled fountain. On its west side is the 18th century **Iglesia Nuestra Señora de la Palma** and on its east the 17th century **Santuario Nuestra Señora de Europa**, both worth a look. The leafy **Parque de María Cristina** is a few blocks north.

Places to Stay
Camping There are two sites, both north of the town: *Camping Costa del Sol* (☎ 956 66 02 19), N-340 Km 108, and *Camping Bahía* (☎ 956 69 19 58), on the N-340 at Km 109, by Playa del Rincóncillo.

Hostales & Hotels There's loads of budget accommodation in the streets behind Avenida de la Marina, but market traffic in the small hours renders a good night's sleep near-impossible. If it's not too hot, try for an interior room. *Hostal González* (☎ 956 65 28 43, Calle José Santacana 7) is perhaps the pick of this bunch. Good, clean singles/doubles with shared bath are 1700/3500 ptas plus IVA in summer. *Hostal España* (☎ 956 66 82 62, Calle José Santacana 4) has large, clean rooms at 1000 ptas per person but it's right by the market. *Hostal Nuestra Señora de la Palma* (☎ 956 63 24 81, Plaza Palma 12) has comfortable rooms with bath for 2000/4000 ptas. *Hostal Levante* (☎ 956 65 15 05, Calle Duque de Almodóvar 21) is a little removed from the thick of things; reasonable rooms with a shower are 1500/2500 ptas though the corridors are a bit musty.

Hotel Reina Cristina (☎ 956 60 26 22, Paseo de la Conferencia s/n), a brisk five minute walk south of the port, is an old colonial-style hotel with tropical gardens. Doubles cost 20,000 ptas, or 14,500 ptas in winter, plus IVA.

ALGECIRAS

PLACES TO STAY
9 Hostal Nuestra Señora
de la Palma
10 Hostal España
14 Hostal González
15 Hostal Levante

PLACES TO EAT
6 Bar Montes &
Restaurante Montes
7 Casa María
11 Panadería/Café
16 Bar Restaurante Casa
Arturo
17 Restaurante Casa Blanca

OTHER
1 Policía Nacional
2 Iglesia Nuestra Señora
de la Palma
3 Correos
4 Santuario Nuestra
Señora de Europa
5 Portillo Estación de
Autobuses
8 Mercado
12 Municipal Tourist Office
13 Estación Marítima (Port)
18 Viajes Kontubia
19 Main Tourist Office
20 Train Station
21 Comes Estación de
Autobuses

Places to Eat

The *mercado* has wonderful fresh produce. The excellent *Panadería-Café*, open from early, at the market end of Calle José Santacana is good for breakfast. *Restaurante Casa Blanca (Calle Juan de la Cierva 1)* is popular for its 800 ptas *menú* of two courses, bread, drink and dessert; other options are moderately priced. *Bar Restaurante Casa Arturo*, Calle Segismundo Moret, has a reasonable *menú* at 900 ptas and a long list of platos combinados from 575 ptas.

In the evening you can sample tapas at *Bar Montes (Calle Emilio Castelar 36)*, several blocks north-west. Tapas keep appearing from the kitchen after 7 pm; the bar is the best place to keep an eye on what tantalising morsel will emerge next. The adjacent *Restaurante Montes* has a 1100 ptas *menú* with quite a wide choice, and à

la carte seafood. Across the road, popular *Casa María (Calle Emilio Castelar 53)* has a *menú* for 975 ptas.

Entertainment

In summer there are flamenco, rock and other concerts at some of the more pleasant spots in town: the Plaza de Toros, Parque de María Cristina, Plaza de Andalucía and Playa del Rincóncillo.

Getting There & Away

The daily paper *Europa Sur* has up-to-date transport details.

Bus The Comes bus station (☎ 956 65 34 56) is under the Hotel Octavio on Calle San Bernardo. To Tarifa there are 10 buses daily Monday to Saturday but only four on Sunday and holidays (215 ptas). Buses run to La Línea every half-hour from 7 am to

9.30 pm (40 minutes; 220 ptas). Other daily buses include 10 to Cádiz, four to Sevilla, three to Jimena de la Frontera (two on Saturday, one on Sunday), and two to Madrid (3283 ptas). There's one bus (except Sunday) to Zahara de los Atunes and Barbate.

Portillo (☎ 956 65 10 55), Avenida Virgen del Carmen 15, operates nine buses daily to Málaga via Estepona, Marbella, Fuengirola and Torremolinos (2½ hours; 1290 ptas), and two to Granada (2455 ptas).

Bacoma (☎ 956 66 65 89), inside the port, runs up to four services daily to Alicante, Valencia and Barcelona (9785 ptas).

There are buses to France, Germany and Holland from Viajes Kontubia, next to the main tourist office.

Train Three or four trains daily run between Algeciras and Bobadilla via Ronda from the station (☎ 956 63 02 02) adjacent to Calle San Bernardo. At Bobadilla, you can change for Granada, Málaga, Sevilla and Madrid. A train to Madrid leaves Algeciras at 9.30 pm.

Boat Trasmediterránea (☎ 956 66 52 00), Isleña de Navegación (☎ 956 65 20 00) and Moroccan companies operate frequent daily car ferries and hydrofoils (also called fast ferries or *rápidos*) to/from Tangier and Ceuta, the Spanish enclave on the Moroccan coast. Usually at least 14 sailings daily go to Tangier and 20 or more to Ceuta. From late June to September there are ferries almost round the clock to cater for the Moroccan migration, and you may have to queue three hours to get on board. Buy your ticket in the port or at the agencies on Avenida de la Marina – prices are the same everywhere.

To Tangier, one adult pays 2960 ptas one-way by ferry (two hours), or 3440 ptas by hydrofoil (one hour). A car costs 9300 ptas, a motorcycle 2650 ptas.

To Ceuta, it's 1801 ptas by ferry (90 minutes), 2945 ptas by hydrofoil (40 minutes). Cars cost 8223 ptas, motorcycles 1370 to 2263 ptas.

LA LÍNEA

La Línea de la Concepción (to give it its full name), 20km east of Algeciras, is the unavoidable stepping stone to Gibraltar. A left turn as you exit the estación de autobuses will bring you out on Avenida 20 de Abril, which runs the 300m or so from the main square, Plaza de la Constitución, to the Gibraltar border. There's a tourist office (☎ 956 76 99 50) on the plaza.

Places to Stay

Pensión La Perla (☎ 956 76 95 13, Calle Clavel 10), two blocks north of Plaza de la Constitución, has clean, spacious singles/doubles for 2000/3000 ptas. *Hostal La Esteponera* (☎ 956 17 66 68, Calle Carteya 10), several blocks west, has doubles from 1875 ptas plus IVA. *Hostal La Campana* (☎ 956 17 30 59, Calle Carboneros 3), off the west side of Plaza de la Constitución, has decent rooms with bath for 3800 ptas a double (4800 ptas in summer).

Getting There & Away

Bus There are four buses daily to/from Málaga (three hours; 1225 ptas), stopping in the Costa del Sol towns; five to/from Cádiz (2½ hours; 1440 ptas), three to/from Sevilla (four hours; 2500 ptas), two to/from Granada (2360 ptas), one (except Sunday) to/from Ronda (990 ptas), and buses every 30 minutes to/from Algeciras.

Car & Motorcycle To avoid vehicle queues at the Gibraltar border, many visitors park in La Línea, then walk across. The underground Parking Fo Cona just off Avenida 20 de Abril charges 150 ptas an hour or 1000 ptas for 24 hours; parking meters cost 115 ptas an hour or 680 ptas for 10 hours (free from 10.30 pm to 9.30 am).

Gibraltar

Looming like some great ship off almost the southernmost tip of Spain, the British colony of Gibraltar is such a compound of curiosities that a visit can hardly fail to stir one's interest.

Gibraltar's territory is 5km long and 1km wide and most of it is one huge lump of limestone, 426m high. To the ancient Greeks and Romans, Gibraltar was one of the two Pillars of Hércules, set up by the mythical hero to mark the edge of the known world. (The other pillar was the coastal mountain Jebel Musa in Morocco, 25km south.)

History

In 711 AD Tariq ibn Ziyad, the Muslim governor of Tangier, landed at Gibraltar to launch the Islamic invasion of the Iberian Peninsula. The Rock has carried his name ever since: Jebel Tariq (Tariq's Mountain).

Castilla wrested the Rock from the Muslims in 1462. Then in 1704 an Anglo-Dutch fleet captured Gibraltar during the War of the Spanish Succession. Spain ceded the Rock to Britain in 1713, but didn't end military attempts to regain it until the failure of the Great Siege of 1779-83. Britain developed it into an important naval base. During the Franco period Gibraltar was an extremely sore point between Britain and Spain: the border was closed from 1967 to 1985. In 1969, Gibraltarians voted by 12,138 to 44 in favour of British rather than Spanish sovereignty, and a new constitution gave Gibraltar domestic self-government. Today Spain offers Gibraltar autonomous-region status within Spain, but Britain and the Gibraltarians continue to reject any compromise over sovereignty. The British garrison was withdrawn in the early 1990s but the British navy continues to use Gibraltar.

Population & People

Gibraltar has some 30,000 people, of whom 75% are classed as Gibraltarians, 14% British, and 7% Moroccan. The Gibraltarians are of mixed Genoese, Jewish, Spanish and British ancestry (the Genoese element comes from the 18th century ship repairers). The Moroccans are mostly temporary workers.

Gibraltarians speak both English and Spanish and, at times, a curious mix of the two. Signs are in English.

Orientation

To reach Gibraltar by land you must pass through the Spanish border town of La Línea (see that section earlier in this chapter). Immediately south of the border, the road crosses Gibraltar airport runway. The town and harbours of Gibraltar lie along the Rock's less steep west side, facing the Bahía de Algeciras (or Bay of Gibraltar).

Information

Tourist Offices Gibraltar has several helpful tourist offices. One (☎ 50762) is in the customs and immigration building at the border, open Monday to Friday from 9 am to 4.30 pm, and Sunday from 10 am to 1 pm; the main office (☎ 45000) is in Duke of Kent House, Cathedral Square, open Monday to Friday from 9 am to 5.30 pm; another is at The Piazza, Main St (☎ 74982), open Monday to Friday from 9 am to 5.30 pm, and Saturday from 10 am to 2 pm.

Visas & Documents To enter Gibraltar you need a passport or EU national identity card. EU, USA, Canada, Australia, New Zealand, Israel and South Africa passport-holders are among those who do not need visas for Gibraltar. For further information contact Gibraltar's police headquarters (☎ 72500).

Those who need visas for Spain should have at least a double-entry Spanish visa so that they can return to Spain from Gibraltar.

Money The currencies are the Gibraltar pound (£) and pound sterling, which are interchangeable. You can use pesetas (except in pay phones and post offices) but conversion rates aren't in your favour. Change any unspent pounds before leaving.

Banks are generally open Monday to Friday from 9 am to 3.30 pm. There are several on Main St. *Bureaux de change* are open longer hours.

Post & Communications The main post office, open Monday to Friday from 9 am to 4.30 pm (in summer to 2.15 pm), and Saturday from 10 am to 1 pm, is at 104 Main St.

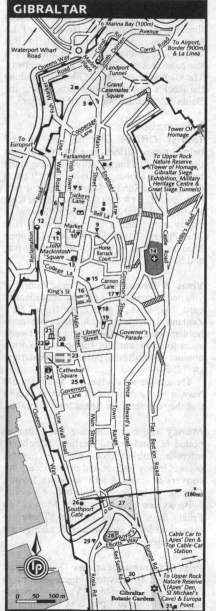

GIBRALTAR

PLACES TO STAY
2	Emile Youth Hostel
4	Continental Hotel
15	Cannon Hotel
19	Eliott Hotel
20	Bristol Hotel
26	Toc H Hostel
28	Queen's Hotel
31	Rock Hotel

PLACES TO EAT
5	House of Sacarello
6	The Clipper
9	Viceroy of India
10	The English Tea Room
17	Three Roses Bar
18	Cannon Bar
29	Piccadilly Gardens

OTHER
1	Bus No 9
3	Tourafrica
7	Post Office
8	Bell Books
11	Policía Nacional
12	Bus No 10
13	Tourist Office
14	St Bernard's Hospital
16	Roman Catholic Cathedral
21	Gibraltar Museum
22	Bus No 3
23	Anglican Cathedral
24	Tourist Office
25	Gibraltar Bookshop
27	Trafalgar Cemetery
30	Lower Cable-Car Station

To phone Gibraltar from Spain, precede the five-digit local number with the code ☎ 9567; from other countries dial the international access code, then the ☎ 350 Gibraltar country code and the local number.

To phone Spain from Gibraltar, just dial the nine-digit Spanish number.

Bookshops You can stock up on English-language reading material at Bell Books, 11 Bell Lane, and Gibraltar Bookshop, 300 Main St.

Medical Services & Emergency St Bernard's Hospital (☎ 79700) on Hospital

Hill has 24-hour emergency facilities. The police (☎ 72500) have a station at 120 Irish Town. In an emergency call ☎ 199 for police or ambulance.

Electricity Electric current is the same as in Britain, 220V or 240V, with plugs of three flat pins.

Town Centre

Most Spanish and Islamic buildings were destroyed in 18th century sieges, though British fortifications, gates and gun emplacements are all over the place.

The **Gibraltar Museum** on Bomb House Lane has good historical, architectural and military displays, including a well-preserved Muslim bathhouse and a detailed model of the Rock made in the 1860s. The museum is open Monday to Friday from 10 am to 6 pm, and Saturday from 10 am to 2 pm (£2).

Many of the graves in the **Trafalgar Cemetery** are of British sailors who died at Gibraltar after the Battle of Trafalgar (1805). A short distance south are the **Gibraltar Botanic Gardens**, open daily from 8 am to sunset (free).

At **Europa Point**, the southern tip of Gibraltar, are a lighthouse, the Christian Shrine of Our Lady of Europe, and a handsome new mosque. Free guided tours of the mosque are given; tourist offices can tell you the current hours.

Upper Rock Nature Reserve

Most of the upper Rock, starting just above the town, is a nature reserve, with spectacular views and several interesting spots to visit. The Rock is home to 600 plant species and, when the wind is westerly, is often a fine spot for observing migrations of birds, especially raptors and storks, between Africa and Europe. January to early June is the time for northbound migrations, and late July to early November for southbound. When the wind is calm or easterly, the Tarifa area is usually better. White storks sometimes congregate in flocks of up to 3000 to cross the strait.

The reserve is officially open from 9.30 am to 7 pm. Entry by road at £5 an adult, £2.50 a child and £1.50 a vehicle includes all the sights mentioned in what follows. These are open to 6.15 or 6.30 pm. Cable-car tickets (see Getting Around) include entry to the reserve, the Apes' Den and St Michael's Cave.

The Rock's most famous inhabitants are its colony of **Barbary macaques**, the only wild primates (apart from *Homo sapiens*) in Europe. Some of these hang around the **Apes' Den** near the middle cable-car station; others can often be seen at the top cable-car station or Great Siege Tunnels. Legend has it that when the apes (probably introduced from North Africa in the 18th century) disappear from Gibraltar, so will the British.

From the **top cable-car station**, you can see Morocco in clear weather. Down the

No vertigo! Barbary macaques at the Upper Rock Nature Reserve

precipitous east side of the Rock is the biggest of the old **water catchments** which channelled rain into underground reservoirs. Today these have been replaced by desalination plants. About 20 minutes walk south down St Michael's Rd (or 20 minutes up from the Apes' Den), **St Michael's Cave** is a big, impressive natural grotto that was once home to Neolithic inhabitants of the Rock. Today, apart from attracting tourists in droves, it's used for concerts, plays, even fashion shows. There's a café outside.

Princess Caroline's Battery, about 30 minutes walk north (downhill) from the top cable-car station, houses a **Military Heritage Centre**. From here a road leads up to the impressive **Great Siege Tunnels**, hewn out by hand by the British during the 1779-83 siege for gun emplacements. They constitute a tiny proportion of the more than 70km of tunnels in the Rock, most of which are off limits to the public.

On Willis' Rd, which leads down to the town from Princess Caroline's Battery, are the **Gibraltar, A City Under Siege** exhibition and the **Tower of Homage**, the last vestige of Gibraltar's Muslim castle built in 1333.

Dolphin-Watching

The Bahía de Algeciras has a sizable population of dolphins, and from about April to September, several boats make two or more daily trips out to see them; at other times of year there's usually at least one in daily operation. Most go from Watergardens Quay or adjacent Marina Bay. The trips last about 2½ hours and adult prices range from £11.50 to £20. Tourist offices have full details. You'll be unlucky if you don't get plenty of close-up dolphin contact.

Work

Gibraltar is better than anywhere in Spain except Palma de Mallorca for finding an unpaid yacht crew place. Yachting (Gibraltar) Ltd (☎ 73736) at Marina Bay runs a crew register.

Places to Stay

The independent *Emile Youth Hostel* (☎ 51106, Montagu Bastion, Line Wall Rd) has 43 places in two to eight-person rooms, for £10 including continental breakfast. The ramshackle old *Toc H Hostel* (☎ 73431), tucked into the city walls at the south end of Line Wall Rd, has beds at £5 a night and cold showers.

The *Queen's Hotel* (☎ 74000, 1 Boyd St) has a restaurant, bar and singles/doubles at £16/24 (£20/36 with private bath or shower). Reduced rates of £14/20 and £16/24 are offered for students and young travellers. All rates include English breakfast. The *Cannon Hotel* (☎ 51711, 9 Cannon Lane) also has decent rooms, each sharing a bathroom with one other, for £20/30 including English breakfast.

The rooms at the *Bristol Hotel* (☎ 76800, 10 Cathedral Square) are pleasant enough but expensive at £47/61 interior or £51/66 exterior. The *Continental Hotel* (☎ 76900, 1 Engineer Lane) has cosy rooms at £42/55 including continental breakfast.

In the luxury bracket, the central *Eliott Hotel* (☎ 70500, 2 Governor's Parade) charges £120 to £200 per room. The more venerable *Rock Hotel* (☎ 73000, 3 Europa Rd) has singles/doubles from £65/85 to £105/110, including English breakfast. Both hotels have good restaurants and pools.

If Gibraltar prices don't grab you, there are some economical options in La Línea.

Places to Eat

Most of the many pubs do British pub meals. One of the best is *The Clipper (78B Irish Town)*, where a generous serve of fish and chips and a pint of beer will set you back £6. *Three Roses Bar (60 Governor's St)* does a big all-day breakfast for £2.80. The *Cannon Bar (27 Cannon Lane)* has some of the best fish and chips in town, with big portions for £4.50. At the popular *Piccadilly Gardens* pub on Rosia Rd you can sit outside and have a three course lunch for £6.

For a restaurant meal, the chic *House of Sacarello (57 Irish Town)* is a good bet, with good soups for around £2 and some excellent daily specials from £4.95 to £5.75. The Indian food at the *Viceroy of India (9/11 Horse Barrack Court)* is usually pretty good; it has a three-course lunch special for £6.75; à la carte there are vegetarian dishes for £2 to £3 and main courses from £6 to £10.

The English Tea Room (9 Market Lane), open from 9 am to 7 pm, isn't much to look at but the scones, jam and cream are great at £1.80 a serve (tea included!).

There's a line of pleasant waterside eateries at Marina Bay, among them *Bianca's*, open noon to 2.45 pm and 7.30 to 10.45 pm, with fish and meat main dishes from £6 to £10, and pasta or burgers around £5.

Shopping

Gibraltar has lots of British high street chain stores, such as Marks & Spencer, Mothercare and The Body Shop (all on Main St) and Safeway (in the Europort development at the north end of the main harbour). Shops are normally open Monday to Friday from 9 am to 7.30 pm, and Saturday morning.

Getting There & Away

The border is open 24 hours.

Air There is a departure tax of £7 on flights from Gibraltar to the UK and £3 on flights to Morocco. The tax appears as a separate item on tickets.

GB Airways (☎ 79300, in Britain ☎ 0345-222111) flies daily to/from London. Return fares from London range from around £160 to more than double that, depending on the season. From Gibraltar, one-way/return fares are about £100/180. GB Airways also flies to Casablanca most days for £99/146 one-way/return.

Monarch Airlines (☎ 47477, in Britain ☎ 01582-398333) flies up to four times a week to/from Luton, for between about £65/130 and £115/230 one-way/return.

Bus Apart from excursion buses from Costa del Sol resorts, there are no regular buses to Gibraltar, but the bus station in La Línea is only a five minute walk from the border.

Car & Motorcycle Vehicle queues at the border often make it less time-consuming to park in La Línea, then walk across the border. To take a car into Gibraltar you need an insurance certificate, registration document, nationality plate and driving licence.

Boat There are normally three ferries a week each way between Gibraltar and Tangier, taking two hours for £18/30 one way/return per person and £40/80 per car. In Gibraltar, buy tickets at Tourafrica (☎ 77666), ICC Building, Main St.

Getting Around

The 1.5km walk from border to town centre is quite fun as it crosses the airport runway. A left turn off Corral Rd takes you through the pedestrian Landport Tunnel into Grand Casemates Square. Alternatively, several bus lines run from the border into town about every 15 minutes from about 8 am to 9 pm. No 9 goes to Market Place; No 3 stops at Cathedral Square and the bottom cable-car station, then goes on to Europa Point; No 10 runs to Europort (stopping at Safeway), then Reclamation Rd near the centre. Buses are 40p a ride. On Sunday services are limited.

All of Gibraltar can be covered on foot, and much of it (including the upper Rock) by car or motorcycle. You can also ascend the rock by the cable car which, weather permitting, leaves Red Sands Rd Monday to Saturday every few minutes between 9.30 am and 5.15 pm. Adult fares are £3.45/4.90 one way/return. For the Apes' Den, disembark at the middle station.

Taxi drivers will take you on a 90 minute 'Official Rock Tour' of a set list of sights for £20 plus the cost of entry into the Upper Rock Nature Reserve.

Málaga Province

Málaga province in south central Andalucía is best known for the Costa del Sol, Spain's most densely packed holiday coast. But it's much more than that. The province includes some wild, dramatic hill country, a vibrant capital city and fascinating towns such as Ronda and Antequera. Málaga's international airport is many people's point of entry into Spain.

MÁLAGA

Málaga is ignored by many visitors who slip straight off from its airport to the Costa del Sol resorts. But this thriving, cosmopolitan port city of 556,000 people is well worth investigating. Its centre, with the backdrop of a sparkling blue Mediterranean, has wide, leafy boulevards, good museums, a handful of impressive monuments and some charmingly dilapidated streets. A lively city with a liberal tradition, Málaga stays open late and inspires a fierce devotion among its citizens.

History

Phoenician traders are credited with planting the area's first vineyards. The city flourished in the Muslim era, especially under the Granada taifa in the 11th century and later the Emirate of Granada. Its fall to the Christians in 1487 was a big nail in the emirate's coffin.

The expulsion of the *moriscos* (christianised Muslims), who had been active in agriculture, contributed to famine in the 17th century, but prosperity arrived in the 19th century with a dynamic middle class, led by the Larios and Heredia families, who founded varied industries. The popularity of Málaga dessert wine ('mountain sack') in Victorian England was also profitable until the phylloxera bug devastated the vineyards in the late 19th century. Málaga's first tourism drive helped to compensate: the city had been popularised by the Romantic movement and in the 1920s it became the favourite winter resort of rich *madrileños*.

In the civil war Málaga, which had a strong anarchist movement, was initially a Republican stronghold. Hundreds of Nationalist sympathisers were killed before the city fell to the Nationalists in February 1937 after being bombed by Italian planes. Particularly vicious reprisals followed.

In the 1960s Franco flogged tourism on the Costa del Sol and Málaga has since flourished, but youth unemployment is high.

Orientation

The central thoroughfare is the Alameda Principal, which continues eastward as the leafy Paseo del Parque and westward as Avenida de Andalucía. The main streets north off the Alameda are Calle Molina Lario, with the cathedral; Calle Marqués de Larios, ending at the central Plaza de la Constitución, around which is what remains of the old quarter; and Calle Puerta del Mar, the centre of the shopping district.

Information

Tourist Offices The Junta de Andalucía's helpful, multilingual tourist office (☎ 95 221 34 45) is at Pasaje Chinitas 4, off Plaza de la Constitución. It's open Monday to Friday from 9 am to 7 pm, Saturday from 10 am to 7 pm, and Sunday from 10 am to 2 pm, and has details of the many foreign consulates in Málaga. The main municipal tourist office (☎ 95 260 44 10), Avenida de Cervantes 1, is also helpful, and open Monday to Friday 8.15 am to 2 pm and 4.30 to 7 pm, Saturday 9.30 am to 1.30 pm. There are smaller tourist offices at the airport, bus station, Plaza de la Merced and outside the post office.

Money There are plenty of banks with ATMs on Calle Puerta del Mar and Calle Marqués de Larios.

Post The main correos (postcode 29080) is at Avenida de Andalucía 1.

Bookshops Librería Jabega, Calle Santa María 17, and Librería de Ocasión, Calle Sancha de Lara 9, have English-language

Alcazaba

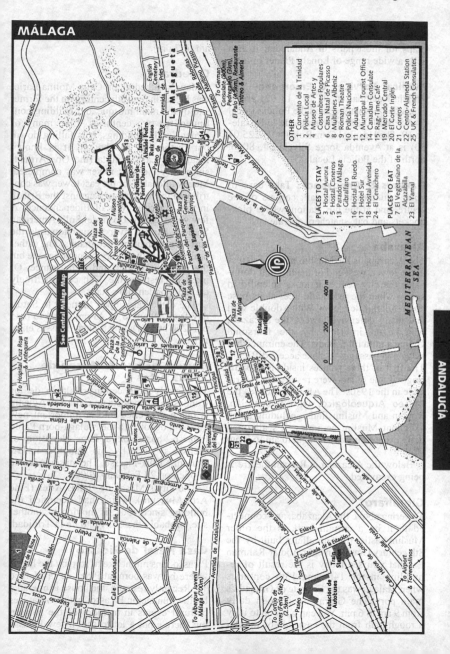

MÁLAGA

OTHER
1 Convento de la Trinidad
2 Policía Local
4 Museo de Artes y Costumbres Populares
6 Multicines Albéniz
8 Casa Natal de Picasso
9 Roman Theatre
10 Policía Nacional
11 Aduana
12 Municipal Tourist Office
14 Canadian Consulate
15 Rag-Time Café
19 Mercado Central
20 El Corte Inglés
21 Correos
22 Centro-Alameda Station
25 UK & French Consulates

PLACES TO STAY
3 Hostal Aurora
5 Hostal Cisneros
13 Parador Málaga Gibralfaro
16 Hostal El Ruedo
17 Hotel Sur
18 Hostal Avenida
24 El Cenachero

PLACES TO EAT
7 El Vegetariano de la Alcazábila
23 El Yamal

MEDITERRANEAN SEA

ANDALUCÍA

novels. Atlante Mapas, Calle Echegaray 7, is an excellent source of city and hiking maps for most parts of Andalucía; it also sells a wide range of Lonely Planet guides.

Medical Services & Emergency The Policía Nacional (☎ 95 221 13 02) are at Plaza de la Aduana 1, and the Policía Local (☎ 95 260 00 92) at Avenida de la Rosaleda 19. The Hospital Cruz Roja (☎ 95 225 04 50) is at Avenida Jorge Silvela 64, 800m north of the Policía Local.

Dangers & Annoyances Take care of your valuables in the dark corners of the centre, and at the bus station, where pickpockets and bag-snatchers operate.

Alcazaba

The Alcazaba is the Muslim palace-fortress at the lower, west end of the hill that dominates the city centre. It looks splendid in spring when the jacaranda trees at its base are in full purple bloom. With a double wall and many defensive towers, the Alcazaba was begun in 1057 by the fearsome Granada taifa ruler Badis. The entrance has staggered passages to make access difficult. The first of three palaces inside is a Badis original; the others were restored in Nasrid style in the 1930s. The Alcazaba houses the **Museo Arqueológico**, with Phoenician, Roman and Muslim finds, including some excellent Muslim ceramics. It's all open daily except Tuesday from 8.30 am to 7 pm (free).

Below the Alcazaba, a Roman theatre is being excavated.

Gibralfaro

Towering above the Alcazaba, and connected to it by a curtain wall, is the older Muslim castle, the Gibralfaro, built by the 8th century Córdoban emir Abd ar-Rahman I. What you see today is the result of rebuilding in the 14th and 15th centuries when Málaga was the Emirate of Granada's main port. The Gibralfaro is open daily from 9 am to 6 pm. You can walk up to it by a rough path from the east side of the Al-

cazaba or take bus No 35 from Paseo del Parque (roughly every 45 minutes from 11 am to 7 pm).

Catedral

Málaga's cathedral, on Calle Molina Lario, was begun in the 16th century on the former site of the main mosque and building continued for two centuries. Like many of Málaga's old buildings, it is falling down, but restoration has begun. It is known locally as La Manquita (the One-Armed) since only the west tower was completed. Money allocated for the east tower was contributed to the campaign against the British in the American War of Independence. A few years ago the Costa del Sol's American Society handed over money towards the current repairs in belated thanks. The cathedral has an 18th century baroque façade but the inside is Gothic and Renaissance. Of most interest are the 17th century finely carved wooden choir stalls.

The cathedral is open Monday to Saturday from 10 am to 12.45 pm and 4 to 6.45 pm (200 ptas). During Sunday Masses entry is free.

Museo Picasso & Museo de Bellas Artes

The lovely 16th century Palacio de los Condes de Buenavista on Calle San Agustín is being converted into an important new museum devoted to the Málaga-born Pablo Picasso, based on a large donation of Picasso's work by his daughter-in-law Christine Ruiz-Picasso. The museum is due to open on 28 February 2000.

The city's Museo de Bellas Artes (Fine Arts Museum), which had occupied the building since 1961, is moving to another site, probably the Convento de la Trinidad.

Casa Natal de Picasso

Picasso fans might like to stop by the house where he was born, at Plaza de la Merced 15. Recently restored, the house is operated by the Fundación Picasso, which organises cultural events in memory of the painter, but there's not a lot to see: a few Picasso

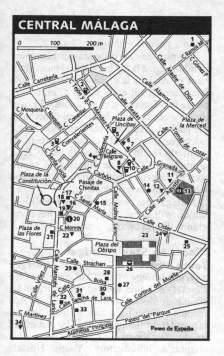

CENTRAL MÁLAGA

0   100   200 m

PLACES TO STAY
17 Hostal Lampérez
19 Hostal Chinitas
21 Hotel Larios
25 Hotel Carlos V
28 Hostal Córdoba
31 Hotel Don Curro
32 Hostal Victoria
33 Hostal Derby

PLACES TO EAT
4 Café Bar La Nueva Cabaña
6 Asador Cervecería Plaza Mayor
7 Cervecería Uncibay
8 La Cancela
11 Tetería
12 Bar Restaurant Tormes
16 Málaga Siempre Bar
18 Café Central
22 Bar Restaurant Mesón El Chinitas
24 El Jardín
34 Marisquerías

OTHER
1 Teatro Cervantes
2 ZZ Pub
3 Siempre Así
5 Discoteca Anden
9 Salsa
10 Barsovia
13 Museo Picasso (opening in 2000)
14 Atlante Mapas
15 Librería Jabega
20 Junta de Andalucía Tourist Office
23 Catedral
26 Bus Stop to Airport
27 Iberia; Binter Mediterráneo
29 RENFE Office
30 Librería de Ocasión

ANDALUCÍA

sketches and paintings, articles about him and a video about his life. Current opening times are Monday to Friday from 11 am to 2 pm and 5 to 8 pm.

Alameda Principal & Paseo del Parque

The Alameda Principal, now a busy thoroughfare, was constructed in the late 18th century as a boulevard over what were then the sands of the Guadalmedina estuary. Until Paseo del Parque was built, it was the city's main gathering and strolling place. It's lined with old trees from the Americas.

The palm-lined Paseo del Parque was laid out in the 1890s on land reclaimed from the sea. Over time the garden along its south side has been filled with tropical plants, making a pleasant refuge from the bustle of

the city. The 18th century **aduana** (customs house) on the paseo's north side originally had the sea lapping at its doors.

Museo de Artes y Costumbres Populares

The Museum of Popular Arts, in an old inn on Pasillo Santa Isabel, is a fun place to visit, especially for children. The collection focuses on everyday life and includes items connected with farming and fishing. Note the cabinets containing *barros* (painted clay figures) of the highwayman, the couple dancing, the rider from Ronda and other characters from malagueño folklore. Barros of this type fascinated 19th and early 20th century travellers influenced by the Romantic movement. The museum is open Monday to Friday from 10 am to 1.30 pm and 4 to 7 pm (200 ptas, students and children under 14 free).

English Cemetery

The leafy English Cemetery on Paseo de Reding was founded in 1829 on land ceded to the British consul for this purpose. (Prior to this, non-Catholic bodies were buried at night upright in the sand at the foot of the beach, where the corpses were liable to be ravaged by dogs, washed out to sea or back to shore.) Some of the graves and monuments have fascinating inscriptions. A variety of people of many nationalities, from poets to consuls to children, are buried here.

The cemetery is open daily from 8 am to 1 pm, and Monday to Friday from 2.30 to 6 pm.

Language Courses

We've had good reports about Spanish courses run by the Universidad de Málaga (☎ 95 227 82 11, fax 95 227 97 12). Two-week intensive courses cost around 45,000 ptas and accommodation with a Spanish family (3000 ptas daily) can be arranged. For more information, write to Universidad de Málaga, Cursos de Español para Extranjeros, Apartado 310, 29080 Málaga.

There are also some good private language schools in Málaga; the main tourist offices can help with information.

Special Events

Semana Santa processions in Málaga are among the most solemn and spectacular in Spain. The platforms bearing the holy images, known as *tronos*, are large and heavy, some needing up to 150 people to carry them. Each night from Palm Sunday to Good Friday, six or seven *cofradías* bear their holy images through the city, watched, and in some cases followed, by big crowds.

A good place to watch is the Alameda Principal, where they pass through between about 7 pm and midnight.

The nine-day Feria de Málaga beginning in mid-August is the biggest and most ebullient of Andalucía's summer ferias. From late morning till early evening, especially on the two Saturdays, celebrations take over the city centre, with music and dancing in the packed streets and bars, and horses and riders parading round a circuit of streets. At night the action switches to large feria grounds at Cortijo de Torres 4km southwest of the centre, with fairground rides and lots more music and dancing.

Málaga also stages its main bullfight season at this time. Tourist offices have programs of feria events.

Places to Stay – Budget

Youth Hostel The Inturjoven *Albergue Juvenil Málaga (☎ 95 230 85 00, Plaza Pío XII)* is 1.5km west of the centre and a couple of blocks north of Avenida de Andalucía, on the right side of town for the bus and train stations. It has 100 places, all in double rooms. For prices, see this chapter's introductory Youth Hostels section. Bus No 18 from the Alameda Principal along Avenida de Andalucía goes most of the way.

Hostales Most hostales are in the blocks north and south of the Alameda Principal. Budget rooms are on the whole tatty. Expect to pay more than the prices quoted during July, August and Semana Santa.

North of the Alameda *Hostal Chinitas (☎ 95 221 46 83, Pasaje Chinitas 2)*, off Plaza de la Constitución, is run by a friendly family and has clean, basic singles/ doubles for 1700/3400 ptas plus IVA. Nearby, *Hostal Lampérez (☎ 95 221 94 84, Calle Santa María 6)* costs 1500/2500 ptas. Rooms vary; the bathroom is a bit grim.

West of Plaza de la Constitución, the welcoming *Hostal Aurora (☎ 95 222 40 04, Calle Muro de Puerta Nueva 1)* has six clean, attractive rooms for 2300/4500 ptas plus IVA. *Hostal Cisneros* (☎ 95 221 26 33, *Calle Cisneros 7*) is spotless and friendly, with rooms from 2500/4500 ptas plus IVA.

Close to the Alameda Principal, the friendly *Hostal Derby* (☎ 95 222 13 01, *Calle San Juan de Dios 1*) has spacious rooms with bath from 3200/4500 ptas. One block north, Calle Bolsa has more possibilities. The homy *Hostal Córdoba* (☎ 95 221 44 69) at No 9 has rooms with shared bath from 1300/2500 ptas.

South of the Alameda Hostal Avenida (☎ 95 221 77 28, *Alameda Principal 5*) has clean, basic rooms at 1500/2900 ptas plus IVA. The friendly old *Hostal El Ruedo* (☎ 95 221 58 20, *Calle Trinidad Grund 3*) charges 1700/3200 ptas. *El Cenachero* (☎ 95 222 40 88, *Calle Barroso 5*) is a good bet at 3200/4800 ptas for rooms with bath, or doubles with shared bathroom for 3700 ptas.

Places to Stay – Mid-Range

All these have private bathroom and TV. Expect to pay more in July and August. A few steps west of the cathedral, *Hotel Carlos V* (☎ 95 221 51 27, *Calle Cister 10*) has comfortable singles/doubles for 3600/7000 ptas. The popular *Hostal Victoria* (☎ 95 222 42 24, *Calle Sancha de Lara 3*) has 16 rooms at 4000/5900 ptas plus IVA. *Hotel Sur* (☎ 95 222 48 03, *Calle Trinidad Grund 13*) has similar rates.

Places to Stay – Top End

Add IVA to all prices. In the centre, *Hotel Larios*, (☎ 95 222 22 00, *Calle Marqués de Larios 2*) has doubles for 17,000 ptas (35,000 ptas in Semana Santa). The large *Hotel Don Curro* (☎ 95 222 72 00, *Calle Sancha de Lara 9*) has singles/doubles from 8500/12,000 ptas.

The recently refurbished *Parador Málaga Gibralfaro* (☎ 95 222 19 02) has an unbeatable location on the Gibralfaro hill, and a pool. Doubles are 16,500 ptas but there are winter discounts.

Places to Eat

The colourful *Mercado Central*, built in the 19th century in a mudéjar-influenced style, has terrific fresh produce. Malagueño cuisine concentrates on fish fried quickly in olive oil. *Fritura malagueño* consists of fried fish, anchovies and squid. Cold soups are popular. As well as gazpacho (in the tomato season) and *sopa de ajo* (garlic soup), try *sopa de almendra con uvas* (almond soup with grapes).

Restaurants & Bars Near Plaza de la Constitución there are lots of places to try. *Café Central* on the busy east side of the plaza is a noisy local favourite: its coffee will satisfy any caffeine addict. Prices for food are reasonable, and there's plenty of choice. Round the corner on Pasaje Chinitas, *Málaga Siempre Bar* serves up a good range of tapas (150 ptas including a beer), and coffee. Nearby, *Bar Restaurante Mesón El Chinitas* on Calle Monroy is a fancy place with many typical andaluz dishes from 1250 to 2100 ptas plus IVA.

Café Bar La Nueva Cabaña on Calle Calderería, open till late on weekdays and to 4 pm on weekends, is good for tea, coffee and pastries. *La Cancela* (*Calle Belgrano 5*) nearby has an appetising *menú* at moderate prices.

There are several popular tapas bars on nearby Plaza de Uncibay: *Cervecería Uncibay* has *embutidos*, cheeses, pâtés and *pulpo a la gallega* (Galician-style octopus), while *Asador Cervecería Plaza Mayor* specialises in *asados* (roasted meats).

Near the cathedral *El Jardín* on Calle Cister, with a pleasant terrace facing the cathedral, has a fancy interior and lots of seafood; the *menú* is 1100 ptas and platos combinados are 600 to 1000 ptas. It's open daily from 8 am to late. The *Tetería* on Calle San Agustín does all manner of teas, including an 'antidepresivo', plus crêpes, pastries and sorbets. Open daily from 4 pm until late, it's popular with students. *Bar Restaurante Tormes* (*Calle San Agustín 13*) is open for late breakfast, lunch and dinner; the three course *menú* is 1100 ptas.

ANDALUCIA

The *cafés* on Calle Herrederia del Rey, near the Market, open early and pack up promptly at 1 pm. There are also some atmospheric *bars* serving local wine from barrels, among them one on the corner of Calles Puerta del Mar and Herrederia del Rey.

South of the Alameda, the relaxed *El Yamal (Calle Blasco de Garay 3)* cooks up excellent Moroccan food: couscous with vegetables costs 1100 ptas; a tasty salad with hummus and flat bread is 600 ptas. It's closed on Sunday evening.

Seafood Sample fish dishes at the *marisquerías* (seafood eateries) with outside tables on slightly seedy Calle Comisario, off the north side of the Alameda Principal. The seafront eateries at Pedregalejo, 4.5km east of the centre, do good fish, or you could continue 1km east to *Restaurante Tintero* on the seafront at El Palo, where plates of seafood (most 600 ptas) are brought out by the waiters and you call for ones you fancy.

Vegetarian *El Vegetariano de la Alcazabilla (Calle Pozo del Rey 5)*, opposite Multicines Albéniz, has a good range of dishes between 800 and 1100 ptas including a very nice Greek salad, wholemeal pasta and *empanadillas de espinacas* (spinach pies).

Entertainment

Three monthly publications, *Guía del Ocio* (200 ptas) from kiosks, and *¿Qué Hacer? ¿Dónde Ir?* and *Málaga, Tan Cerca*, free from tourist offices, have entertainment listings.

Nightlife in the centre clusters around Plaza Uncibay, where *Discoteca Anden* rages Thursday to Saturday from midnight to dawn. On little Calle Belgrano, *Barsovia*, has recorded dance music (80s and 90s) and gets pretty crowded on weekends, and *Salsa* has live salsa on Wednesday from midnight and occasional party nights. A few blocks farther north, *ZZ Pub* on Calle Tejón y Rodríguez has live music, mainly rock,

several nights a week. *Siempre Asi (Calle Convalecientes 5)*, with mostly Spanish music, has a good atmosphere and a varied clientele (25 to 40 years). It's open Thursday to Sunday from 9.30 pm.

Rag-Time Café (Calle Reding 12) in La Malagueta, near the seafront immediately east of the centre, has blues, jazz or flamenco depending on the night. Pedregalejo suburb, 4.5km east of the centre, with numerous bars and discos, buzzes until late on weekends, and most nights in summer.

Multicines Albéniz (Calle Alcazabilla 4) screens international films with subtitles most nights at 10 pm (400 ptas).

The *Teatro Cervantes* on Calle Ramos Marín has a regular program of classical music, opera, dance and theatre.

Getting There & Away

Air Málaga's busy airport (☎ 95 224 88 04), receiving scheduled and charter flights from many European cities, is 10km west of the centre. The city office of Iberia and Binter Mediterráneo (☎ 95 213 61 46) is at Calle Molina Lario 13.

Discounted return flights from London range between about £80 and £150 depending on the season. Iberia and Royal Air Maroc (☎ 91 541 51 58) fly to Casablanca for around 20,000 ptas one-way. Binter Mediterráneo and Pauknair (☎ 95 204 82 65) fly to Melilla.

Iberia flies daily to/from Madrid, Barcelona and Valencia. To Barcelona, a one-way ticket and the cheapest return both cost around 24,000 ptas. Air Europa (☎ 95 237 30 00), which flies to/from Madrid and Barcelona most days, is a few thousand pesetas cheaper. Spanair (☎ 902-13 14 15) also flies to/from Madrid and Barcelona. Its last-minute offers can give you a Madrid-Málaga return for 10,000 ptas. Pauknair has a few flights a week to/from Barcelona, Bilbao, Madrid, Santiago de Compostela and Palma de Mallorca.

For a flight out of Spain, check the ads in the free newspaper *Sur in English*. Agencies such as Servitour (☎ 95 256 60 00) and Flight-Line International (☎ 95 204 83 40) offer occasional one-way flights to London for 6500 ptas (but more often between 10,000 and 12,000 ptas).

Bus The estación de autobuses (☎ 95 235 00 61) is on Paseo de los Tilos, 1km west of the centre. Frequent buses run along the coast in both directions and to Sevilla (3½ hours; 2245 ptas) and Granada (2½ hours; 1175 ptas), and several daily go to inland towns including Córdoba (2½ hours; 1515 ptas), Antequera and Ronda. At least three buses daily run to Madrid (8½ hours; 2629 to 4480 ptas), Valencia (11 hours; 5960 ptas) and Barcelona (18 hours; 8495 ptas). There are also buses to Germany, Switzerland, Britain, Portugal, France and the Netherlands.

Train The train station (☎ 95 236 02 02) is on Explanada de la Estación round the corner from the bus station. The city centre RENFE office (☎ 95 221 41 27), Calle Strachan 2, is open Monday to Friday from 9 am to 1.30 pm and 4.30 to 7.30 pm.

Most days there are five trains to Madrid: three Talgo 200s (four hours; 6800 to 8000 ptas), one InterCity (6½ hours; 4800 ptas) and one 1st class night train.

Several daily trains to Córdoba take two to three hours for 1550 to 2200 ptas. To Sevilla (three hours; 1825 ptas) there are four regionales daily, one requiring a change at Bobadilla. For Granada there are three trains daily (three to four hours; 1520 to 2600 ptas). For Ronda you must change at Bobadilla.

For Valencia and Barcelona (14 hours; 6500 ptas) there are two or three 2nd class trains daily, one of them overnight.

Car Rental There are several agencies at the airport, many with cars for under 20,000 ptas a week.

Boat Trasmediterránea (☎ 95 222 48 83), Estación Marítima, Local E1, operates ferries daily (except Sunday from mid-September to mid-June) to/from Melilla. The trip takes 6½ hours and costs 3760 ptas in

the cheapest seat and 15,355 ptas for a car. Buy your tickets at the Estación Marítima, more or less directly south of the town centre.

Getting Around

To/From the Airport Buses to the city centre (135 ptas), from outside the airport arrivals hall, go about every half-hour between 6.30 am and 11.30 pm, stopping at the city bus and train stations en route. Going out to the airport you can pick them up on the south side of the cathedral.

The Aeropuerto train station is a five minute walk from the airport's departures (salidas) hall. Trains run every half-hour from 7.15 am to 11.45 pm to Málaga's main station (11 minutes; 135 ptas) and the Centro-Alameda station on the west side of the Río Guadalmedina. Departures from the city to the airport are from 6 am to 10.30 pm. Fares are slightly higher on weekends and holidays.

A taxi between the airport and city costs around 1300 ptas.

Bus Useful buses around town (115 ptas) include No 4 from the train station to the centre and No 11 from Paseo del Parque to Pedregalejo and El Palo.

COSTA DEL SOL

The much-maligned Costa del Sol might best be described as an international strip stuck on the bottom of Spain, home to perhaps 300,000 expatriates, particularly from Britain, Germany and Scandinavia.

Comprising a string of resorts running from Málaga towards Gibraltar, the Costa del Sol pulls in package tourists and the time-share crowd because of its weather, beaches, warm Mediterranean water, cheap package deals, entertainment and leisure attractions. It also attracts the jet set with some exclusive facilities.

The resorts were once fishing villages, but there's little sign of that now. Instead, the Costa del Sol is arguably the finest example in Europe of how overdevelopment can ruin a spectacular landscape. It

ANDALUCÍA

has become a series of townscapes from one end to the other, all heaving with humanity in summer.

Activities

The Costa del Sol is good for sport lovers, with nearly 40 golf clubs, several busy marinas, tennis and squash courts, riding schools, swimming pools and gymnasiums. Many beaches have facilities for water sports such as windsurfing, sailing, water-skiing and paragliding.

Accommodation

In August and the second half of July, it's a very good idea to ring ahead for a room. The costa has about 15 camp sites, nearly all on or just off the N-340.

Getting There & Away

Trains run every half-hour, from 6 am to 10.30 pm, from Málaga city and airport stations to Torremolinos and Fuengirola. There are also frequent buses from Málaga along the coast, linking the resorts, and services to places such as Ronda, La Línea, Cádiz, Sevilla and Granada from the main resorts.

Rental cars for 16,000 to 20,000 ptas a week can be found from local firms in the main resorts.

Torremolinos & Around

'Torrie', which led the Costa del Sol's mass tourist boom of the 1950s and 60s, is a concrete high-rise jungle basically designed to squeeze as many paying customers as possible into the smallest possible space. It has made an effort to spruce itself up in the 90s.

Orientation Calle San Miguel, running most of the 500m from Plaza Costa del Sol down to Playa del Bajondillo, is Torremolinos' main pedestrian artery. South-west of Playa del Bajondillo is Playa de la Carihuela, once the fishing quarter. The estación de autobuses (☎ 95 238 24 19) is on Calle Hoyo north-east of Plaza Costa del Sol. Buses to Málaga stop on Avenida Palma de Mallorca, 200m south-west of Plaza Costa

del Sol. The train station is on Avenida Jesús Santos Rein, off Calle San Miguel.

Information There are tourist offices in the ayuntamiento on Plaza de la Independencia, a block inland of Plaza Costa del Sol (☎ 95 237 95 51); on Plaza de las Comunidades Autónomas facing Playa del Bajondillo (☎ 95 237 19 09); and on Calle Borbóllon Bajo in La Carihuela. They are all open daily from 10 am to 2 pm, except that the ayuntamiento one closes on Sunday.

Things to See & Do Torremolinos' beaches are wider, longer and a paler shade of grey-brown than most on the costa – which is why they pull in so many people.

In the swish marina at Benalmádena Costa, just south-west of Torremolinos, Sea Life is a good modernist aquarium of mainly Mediterranean marine creatures. It's open daily from 10 am to 6 pm (975 ptas, 675 ptas for children). Tivoli World, five minutes walk from Benalmádena-Arroyo de la Miel train station, is the costa's biggest amusement park. From early to late summer, it's open daily, late afternoon to after midnight; at other times on Saturday, Sunday and holidays only.

Places to Stay & Eat There are a couple of dozen hostales and hotels within a few minutes walk of Torremolinos' train and bus stations. The tourist offices can supply lists of options. Pleasant *Hostal Micaela* (☎ 95 238 33 10, Calle Bajondillo 4), near Playa del Bajondillo, has doubles with bath for 4000 ptas plus IVA.

In La Carihuela, 1.5km south-west of the centre, *Hostal Prudencio* (☎ 95 238 14 52, Calle Carmen 43) has some rooms facing the beach at 3000/6000 ptas for singles/doubles. Nearby *Hostal Pedro* (☎ 95 238 54 79, Calle Bulto 1), also facing the beach, is smaller and cheaper. *Hotel Miami* (☎ 95 238 52 55, Calle Aladino 14), a few blocks back, is a quaint old villa turned into a small hotel with nice gardens and doubles for 6800 ptas.

Carretera de Confusión

Although a new autopista is being built from Málaga to Estepona, for now life on the Costa del Sol continues to revolve around the existing main road: the N-340, without which it is impossible to get from A to B. So pivotal is the N-340 to everyday life that even luxury hotels use a Km mark on it as their address. They may call it the CN-340, or the Carretera de Cádiz, or the Carretera Málaga-Cádiz, but they're all talking about the same road – which also used to glory in the nickname 'Death Highway' due to the number of fatalities on it.

Much has been done in recent years to make the N-340 safer. Town bypasses have been opened, barriers have been put up to prevent dangerous turn-offs, bridges and underpasses have been built to enable motorists supposedly safe access to the *urbanizaciones*. Yet it's still a hair-raisingly busy road on which many vehicles travel far too fast.

Many visitors don't spot their turn-off until the last minute – or miss it altogether – which leads to panic-stricken driving manoeuvres. The confusion is compounded by the fact that with the bypasses there are now often two, and in some places three, parallel roads all named N-340 or Carretera de Cádiz.

The N-340 that's usually referred to in addresses is the one that forms Torremolinos' *inner* bypass, then runs through Fuengirola and Marbella. It is *not* the autovía which bypasses Torremolinos, Fuengirola and Marbella, as much as 4km inland in places, even though that road is also numbered N-340.

Km markers aside, undoubtedly the most useful sign for the motorist is 'Cambio de Sentido', which appears every couple of kilometres and tells you where you can change direction to get back to a turning you have missed. Meanwhile, beware of other motorists and watch out for cats, dogs and/or inebriated pedestrians trying to cross.

Take special care in the rain: the roads are lethal when wet after months of hot weather. You'd expect people to slow down in these conditions, but they don't.

The new autopista, due to open in 1999, will incorporate the existing Torremolinos, Fuengirola and Marbella bypasses, and there will be tolls on some stretches.

Besides British bars with British breakfasts and British beer, Torremolinos has no shortage of good seafood places, many of them lining the Paseo Marítimo in La Carihuela.

Entertainment Torremolinos' nightlife can be wild and has a big gay and transvestite scene; most gay bars are on Calle Nogalera off Avenida Jesús Santos Rein. Discos are mainly on Avenida Palma de Mallorca.

Fuengirola

Fuengirola, 18km down the coast from Torremolinos, has more of a family scene but is just as densely packed. The narrow streets in the few blocks between the beach and Avenida Matías Sáenz de Tejada (where the estación de autobuses is) constitute what's left of the old town. The train station is a block farther inland on Avenida Jesús Santos Rein. At the old town's centre is Plaza de la Constitución. The tourist office (☎ 95 246 74 57), Avenida Jesús Santos Rein 6, can supply a full list of accommodation options.

Places to Stay & Eat The English-run *Pensión Coca* (☎ 95 247 41 89, Calle de la Cruz 3), close to both Plaza de la Constitución and the beach, has decent singles/doubles at 3600/5800 ptas (cheaper outside August). The friendly *Hostal Italia* (☎ 95 247 41 93, Calle de la Cruz 1) has doubles for 4580 ptas plus IVA. *Hostal*

Marbella (☎ 95 266 45 03, Calle Marbella 34), just south-west of Plaza de la Constitución, is friendly and clean with singles/doubles for 3950/5950 ptas.

Along Calle Moncayo, a block back from the beachfront in the centre, you can choose from a host of British bars and Italian, Chinese, Indonesian and even Spanish *restaurants*, many with *menú*s for 800 or 900 ptas. *El Tomate (Calle Troncón 19)*, near Plaza de la Constitución, is a fine international restaurant, with a good 1600 ptas *menú*.

Mijas

A village of Muslim origin in the hills 8km north of Fuengirola, Mijas is surrounded by villas and urbanisations but remains a pretty place, with narrow streets, panoramic views, and whitewashed houses covered with bougainvillea and jasmine. It's also full of souvenir and craft shops and has a gamut of restaurants and cafés. Busloads of tourists come up here in search of 'the typical Andalucian village'. Frequent buses run from Fuengirola.

Marbella

Marbella, sheltered by the beautiful Sierra Blanca 25km west of Fuengirola, has always been the Costa del Sol's glossiest resort. It was the building of the exclusive Marbella Club Hotel in the 1950s by the part-Spanish, part-Austrian Alfonso von Hohenlohe that turned Marbella into a playground of the international jet set. In the 1980s Marbella went into decline, but in 1991 Jesús Gil y Gil, a controversial businessman, won a landslide victory to become mayor. Gil's police, at times notoriously heavy-handed, cleansed Marbella's streets of petty criminals, prostitutes and drug addicts. Avenues were lined with palms, marble pavements laid and plazas spruced up. Today Marbella has regained its reputation as the Costa del Sol's quality resort.

Orientation The N-340 through town goes by the names Avenida Ramón y Cajal and Avenida Ricardo Soriano. The old town is centred on Plaza de los Naranjos. The estación de autobuses is on the north side of the N-340's Marbella bypass, 1.2km from Plaza de los Naranjos.

Information The main tourist office (☎ 95 277 14 42), on Glorieta Fontanilla, is open Monday to Friday from 9.30 am to 8 pm, and Saturday from 10 am to 2 pm. A smaller office (☎ 95 282 35 50) at Plaza de los Naranjos 1 is open similar hours.

The Policía Nacional (☎ 091) are on Avenida Doctor Viñals in the north of town. The Ambulatorio Leganitos public clinic (☎ 95 277 81 24) is on Plaza Leganitos.

Things to See & Do Pretty **Plaza de los Naranjos**, with its 16th century ayuntamiento, is the heart of the largely pedestrianised old town. Nearby on Plaza de la Iglesia is the **Iglesia de Nuestra Señora de la Encarnación**, begun in the 16th century. A little farther east, the **Museo del Grabado Español Contemporáneo**, on Calle Hospital Bazán, houses work by Picasso, Miró and Dalí. It is open daily except Saturday. Just to the north, along streets such as Calle Arte and Calle Portada, are remains of Marbella's old **Muslim walls**.

Down to the east of the old town, in attractive Parque de la Represa, is the charming **Museo Bonsai**, devoted to the Japanese miniature-tree art, open daily from 10 am to 1.30 pm and 4 to 7 pm (400 ptas).

The best stretch of town beach is **Playa de Venus**, east of the Puerto Deportivo.

Places to Stay *Camping Marbella 191 (☎ 95 277 83 91)* on the N-340 at Km 184.5, on the beach 3km east of the centre, charges 3000 ptas a site in the high season. There are three bigger sites in the next 10km of the N-340 east.

The modern Inturjoven *Albergue Juvenil Marbella* youth hostel *(☎ 95 277 14 91, Calle Trapiche 2)*, above the old town, has room for 100 people in rooms with two or three beds. Half have private bath. There's

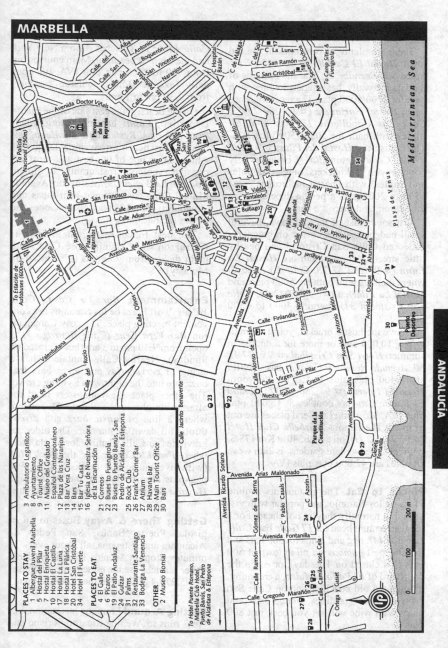

MARBELLA

PLACES TO STAY
1. Albergue Juvenil Marbella
5. Hostal del Pilar
7. Hostal Enriqueta
10. Hostal El Castillo
17. Hostal La Luna
18. Hostal La Pilárica
20. Hotel San Cristóbal
34. Hotel El Fuerte

PLACES TO EAT
4. El Gallo
6. Picaros
19. El Patio Andaluz
24. Gulzar
31. Palms
32. Restaurante Santiago
33. Bodega La Venencia

OTHER
2. Museo Bonsai
3. Ambulatorio Leganitos
8. Ayuntamiento
9. Tourist Office
11. Museo del Grabado
    Español Contemporáneo
12. Plaza de los Naranjos
13. Bar Vera Cruz
14. Bars
15. Bar Tu Casa
16. Iglesia de Nuestra Señora
    de la Encarnación
21. Correos
22. Buses to Fuengirola
23. Buses to Puerto Banús, San
    Pedro de Alcántara, Estepona
25. Rock Club
26. Frank's Corner Bar
27. Atrium
28. Havana Bar
29. Main Tourist Office
30. Bars

To Hotel Puente Romano,
Marbella Club Hotel,
Puerto Banús, San Pedro
de Alcántara & Estepona

a pool. For prices, see this chapter's introductory Youth Hostels section.

There are plenty of pensiones in the old town. **Hostal El Castillo** (☎ *95 277 17 39, Plaza San Bernabé 2)*, near the remains of the Islamic walls, has singles/doubles with bath for 2700/5000 ptas. The recently renovated **Hostal Enriqueta** (☎ *95 282 75 52, Calle Los Caballeros 18)* has doubles/triples with bath for 5000/7500 plus IVA. The British-run **Hostal del Pilar** (☎ *95 282 99 36, Calle Mesóncillo 4)* is deservedly popular with backpackers. Singles, doubles and triples, with shared bathrooms, cost 1500 to 2000 ptas a person depending on the season, and there's a bar.

Just south-east of the old town, several small budget hostales cluster on greenery-bedecked Calle San Cristóbal and nearby little streets. Among them are **Hostal La Luna** (☎ *95 282 57 78, Calle La Luna 7)* where doubles with bath are 5000 ptas; and **Hostal La Pilárica** (☎ *95 277 42 52, Calle San Cristóbal 31)* charging 4000 to 4500 ptas.

Above the hostal bracket, you'll normally pay 10,000 ptas or more for a double in summer. **Hotel San Cristóbal** (☎ *95 277 12 50, Avenida Ramón y Cajal 3)* has doubles at 10,400 ptas plus IVA. The 263-room **Hotel El Fuerte** (☎ *95 286 15 00, Avenida El Fuerte s/n)* has doubles at 15,000 ptas plus IVA. Most other top-end places are out of town. The famous **Marbella Club Hotel** (☎ *95 282 22 11),* on the N-340 at Km 178.5, with its large, verdant gardens, is 2km west. Doubles are 42,000 ptas plus IVA.

Places to Eat The restaurants around Plaza de los Naranjos are popular with visitors, but naturally they're not cheap. For a local adventure head for **El Gallo** bar *(Calle Lobatos 44)*: egg and chips for 300 ptas and the cheapest *gambas pil pil* in town at 500 ptas (it's closed on Tuesday); or eat in the courtyard of **El Patio Andaluz**, a charming, dilapidated old coaching inn on Calle San Juan de Dios: sardines, *boquerones* and chips with wine will set you back just 800 ptas.

For something more up-market book a patio table at **Pícaros** (☎ *95 282 86 50, Calle Aduar 1)*. The chef is from New York and the décor is beautiful. Main courses run from 900 to 2300 ptas plus IVA. It's open daily (except Monday outside summer) from 7.30 pm to 1 am.

On the beach at the east side of the Puerto Deportivo, **Palms** has interesting salads from 850 ptas. **Restaurante Santiago**, just behind this beach on Avenida Duque de Ahumada, is one of the best and most expensive seafood restaurants in town. **Bodega La Venencia**, nearby on Avenida Miguel Cano, serves great ham tapas and *montaditos* from 125 ptas, plus raciones and media-raciones.

The best Indian restaurant in town is **Gulzar** on Calle Camilo José Cela, with main dishes from 750 ptas (it's closed on Monday).

Entertainment **Bar Tu Casa** *(Calle Valdés 2)* off Plaza de los Naranjos is a convenient meeting place. The cosy Canadian-run **Bar Vera Cruz** *(Calle Buitrago 7)* is open from 7.30 pm to 3 am (but is closed on Sunday). Nearby Calle Pantaleón has a string of *cervecerías* and other bars that buzz late into the night with a young crowd. The other place the youngsters head for after midnight is the Puerto Deportivo, where a line of *music bars* and *discos* throbs till dawn in summer. The older set gravitates to Calle Camilo José Cela area, where **Frank's Corner Bar**, the **Rock Club** (with live music and drinks costing 500 ptas-plus after midnight), the **Atrium** and **Havana Bar** are among the main hang-outs.

Getting There & Away Buses to Fuengirola, Puerto Banús, San Pedro de Alcántara and Estepona, all about every 30 minutes, stop on Avenida Ricardo Soriano. Other services use the estación de autobuses (☎ 95 276 44 00) up in the north of town.

Getting Around From the bus station, bus No 7 runs to Avenida Ricardo Soriano and

A 'verdiales' group beats up a storm with its exhilarating folk music, unique to the Málaga area (Andalucía)

Feria de Málaga: even horses dress up (Andalucía)

Festa de la Mercè, Barcelona

Andalucian dancers perform in public from early childhood

Horse and buggy, Sevilla (Andalucía)

Tiled balustrade, Plaza de España, Sevilla (Andalucía)

The peaceful gardens of the Alcazar, Sevilla (Andalucía)

MARK DAFFEY

JOHN NOBLE

BETHUNE CARMICHAEL

No 2 stops on Calle Jacinto Benavente on the north-west edge of the old town.

Ojén & Around

The picturesque mountain village of Ojén is 10km inland from Marbella, with panoramic views along the way. About 4km north of Ojén, a left turn off the Coín road heads 6km west up an isolated valley to the *Refugio de Juanar* (☎ 95 288 10 00). This comfortable hotel (doubles 9800 ptas plus IVA) is a starting point for some good walks in the forested Sierra Blanca, including to a marvellous 1,000m *mirador* 2km away.

Several buses daily run from Marbella to Ojén.

Puerto Banús

The coastal strip between Marbella and Puerto Banús, 5km west, is called the 'Golden Mile' for its number of super-luxury properties. Puerto Banús itself is the flashiest marina on the Costa del Sol, often a port of call for gin palaces that moor in Monte Carlo at other times of year. By the control tower at the west end of the harbour – where the swankiest boats tie up – is the **Aquarium de Puerto Banús**, similar to Sea Life at Benalmádena Costa (opens daily from 11 am to 6 pm).

Towards the west end of the marina you'll find *Salduba Pub* and *Sinatra Bar*, two of the most popular bars. Just east is the Greek *Red Pepper* with a spectacular display of live seafood and most main courses over 2000 ptas. Farther east, *Don Leone* is the best Italian restaurant, with a *menú* for 1950 ptas. A little farther on, *Pizzeria Picasso* is popular for its pizzas and pasta (from 675 to 950 ptas).

Puerto Banús is a nightlife centre, though prices are on the expensive side. *Old Joy's Pub*, just east of Pizzeria Picasso, and, behind it, the *Navy*, are two popular haunts. *Bang & Olufsen*, by the marina's main entrance, has a classy late-night bar upstairs. *La Comedia* on Calle de Ribera behind the Red Pepper is a lively disco.

San Pedro de Alcántara

It's difficult for San Pedro, a couple of kilometres west of Puerto Banús, to compete as a resort when the beach – albeit one of the nicer on the costa – is a 1km hike from the town. The central tourist office (☎ 95 278 52 52) at Calle Marqués del Duero 69 can tell you about places to stay.

Estepona

Estepona has controlled its development carefully and remains an agreeable seaside town. It has a sizable fishing fleet, sharing the port beyond the lighthouse at the west end of town with a marina.

The tourist office (☎ 95 280 09 13) is at Avenida San Lorenzo 1 in the west of the centre. The estación de autobuses (☎ 95 280 02 49) is 400m west, on the seafront Avenida de España.

There are plenty of places to stay. *Hostal El Pilar* (☎ 95 280 00 18, Plaza Las Flores 10) overlooks the central square and has singles/doubles for 2100/3500 ptas, and doubles with bath for 4500 ptas. Friendly *Pensión San Antonio* (☎ 95 280 14 76, Calle Adolfo Suárez 9), a block east of the plaza, has basic rooms for 1900/3500 ptas. On the seafront, *Hotel Buenavista* (☎ 95 280 01 37, Paseo Marítimo 180) has doubles with bath for 6500 ptas.

Plaza Las Flores is surrounded by tapas bars and restaurants. Nightlife focuses on the marina.

Casares

Eight kilometres south-west of Estepona on the N-340 is the turning for Casares, 10km inland. Dubbed 'the hanging village' for the way it clings to the edge of a cliff below the well-preserved remains of a Muslim castle, it's well worth an excursion, with wonderful views and good hiking opportunities in the surrounding hills.

Hostal Plaza (☎ 95 289 40 88) on the central Plaza de España has decent rooms with bath for 2700 ptas a double.

There are buses (except on Sunday) from Estepona at 11 am, 1.30 pm and 7pm. The last one back leaves Casares at 4.30 pm.

EL CHORRO & AROUND

Fifty kilometres north-west of Málaga the Río Guadalhorce carves its way through the awesome **Garganta del Chorro** (El Chorro Gorge), 4km long, up to 400m deep and as little as 10m wide. The gorge is traversed not only by the main railway in and out of Málaga but also by a footpath, the **Camino del Rey** (King's Path), which for long stretches becomes a concrete catwalk clinging to the gorge wall 100m above the river. The gorge provides marvellous rock climbing, and there are other good walks in the area.

The Camino del Rey is in a state of serious disrepair and has been officially closed since 1992, but nothing stops adventurous folk from walking parts of it. We can't actually recommend it, but we have done it. Starting from tiny El Chorro village, above a dam just south of the gorge, you can follow the road up the east side of the reservoir for 600m, then go 2.25km north along the railway (passing through several tunnels, with plenty of space at the side should a train come). Between tunnels Nos 7 and 6 a narrow, parapetless footbridge crosses the gorge, then a 1.5km walk along the catwalk brings you to another dam. From here, a broad 1.5km track up to the left meets a road which leads 1.6km down to the Parque Ardales camp site (see Places to Stay & Eat).

Not far from El Chorro is **Bobastro**, the hill-top redoubt of the 9th century rebel Omar ibn Hafsun (see the boxed text 'Bandoleros & Guerrilleros'). From El Chorro station, take the road up the far (west) side of the valley and after 3km take the signposted Bobastro turning. Three kilometres up here, an 'Iglesia Mozárabe' sign indicates a path to the remains of a remarkable little Mozarabic church cut from the rock. It's thought that Ibn Hafsun, originally a Muslim, converted to Christianity (thus becoming a Mozarab) before his death in 917, and was buried here. When Bobastro was finally conquered in 927, his remains were taken for posthumous crucifixion outside Córdoba's Mezquita. A

farther 2.5km up the road is the top of the hill, with faint traces of Ibn Hafsun's *alcázar* (fortress) and magnificent views.

Places to Stay & Eat

At El Chorro village, **Refugio de Escalada La Garganta** (☎ 95 249 51 19) has beds for 600 ptas; **Pensión Estación** (☎ 95 249 50 04) has four clean little singles/doubles for 2000/3500 ptas; and **Apartamentos La Garganta** (☎ 95 249 51 19) has rooms with small kitchens and bathrooms at 4000 ptas single or double, plus a pool and restaurant. **Restaurante Estación** (or **Bar Isabel**), a popular climbers' gathering spot, does platos combinados from 375 to 550 ptas. Accommodation at **Finca La Campana** (☎ 95 211 20 19), up a dirt road 2km from the station, ranges from bunks for 1500 ptas to an apartment costing 4000/6000 ptas for two/four people. It also offers climbing courses, and guided climbs, walks and other activities.

Overlooking the picturesque Embalse del Conde del Guadalhorce reservoir west of Bobastro, **Parque Ardales** (☎ 95 211 24 01) has a large, shady camp site, apartments, and mountain bikes to rent (300 ptas an hour). The friendly **Pensión Bobastro** (☎ 95 245 91 50, Plaza de San Isidro 13) in Ardales village 9km south, has singles/doubles for 1500/3000 ptas. Several restaurants overlooking the reservoir north of Parque Ardales get busy at weekends and holiday times.

Getting There & Away

Los Amarillos runs several daily buses from Málaga and Ronda to Ardales. To El Chorro village there's just one train daily from Málaga (455 ptas).

RONDA

Though only an hour or so from the Costa del Sol, Ronda (population 34,000) is a world away from the coastal hustle. Set astride the awesome, 100m-deep El Tajo gorge amid the beautiful Serranía de Ronda mountains, it attracts its quota of visitors,

Bandoleros & Guerrilleros

Andalucía's complicated sierras, full of ravines, caves, and hidden valleys, are an age-old refuge for those who didn't get on with the authorities of the day. As long ago as the 9th century the hill fortress of Bobastro, near El Chorro gorge, was the epicentre of prolonged, widespread opposition to Cordoban rule led by a sort of Islamic Robin Hood, Omar ibn Hafsun. Ibn Hafsun came from a landed family of *muwallads* (Christian converts to Islam) but turned to banditry after being disowned by his father for killing a neighbour. Quickly gaining followers and popular support – partly, it's said, because he defended the peasants against taxes and forced labour – he at one stage controlled territory from Cartagena to the Strait of Gibraltar.

In the 19th century the bandits *(bandoleros)* who preyed on the rich also became folk heroes of a kind. The most famous was El Tempranillo (the Early One), born in 1800 at Jauja, near Lucena in Córdoba province. By the age of 22 he claimed: 'The king may reign in Spain, but in the sierra I do'. Blond and courteous to women, El Tempranillo reputedly demanded an ounce of gold for each vehicle crossing his domain.

It was the activities of these bandits that led the government to set up the Guardia Civil, Spain's rural police force, in 1844. Many bandoleros were then forced into the service of the *caciques* (local landowners and political bosses), or even of the guardia civil itself. El Tempranillo met his end this way, murdered by an old comrade.

The last of the bandolero breed was Pasos Largos (Big Steps), a murderous, agile and clever poacher who haunted the area between El Burgo and Yunquera, east of Ronda. He was killed in 1934, officially in a cave shoot-out with the guardia civil, though some say his killer was a traitorous companion.

After the civil war the Andalucian sierras became the refuge of a new kind of outlaw: communist *guerrilleros* waging the last resistance to Franco. The Sierra Bermeja, north of Estepona, and the mountains of La Axarquía, east of Málaga, were among their hide-outs. This little-known chapter of Spanish history closed in the 1950s. But on the panoramic peak of one of La Axarquía's mountains, El Lucero, remain the ruins of a guardia civil post built to watch for just such guerrilleros.

but many of them return to the coast in the afternoon.

For most of the Muslim period, Ronda was capital of its independent, or almost independent, statelet. Its near-impregnable position kept it out of Christian hands until 1485.

Orientation

The old Muslim town, known as La Ciudad, stands on the south side of El Tajo, with the newer town to the north. Three bridges cross the gorge, the main one being the Puente Nuevo. Both parts of town come to an abrupt end on their west side with cliffs plunging away to the valley of the Río Guadalevín. Most places to stay and eat, and the bus and train stations, are in the newer part of town.

Information

The tourist office (☎ 95 287 12 72), Plaza de España 1, is open Monday to Friday from 10 am to 2 pm and 4 to 6.30 pm, Saturday from 10.30 am to 2.30 pm, and sometimes longer in summer.

Banks and ATMs are mainly on Calle Virgen de la Paz and Plaza Carmen Abela. The main correos (postcode 29400) is at Calle Virgen de la Paz 18-20. The Policía

RONDA

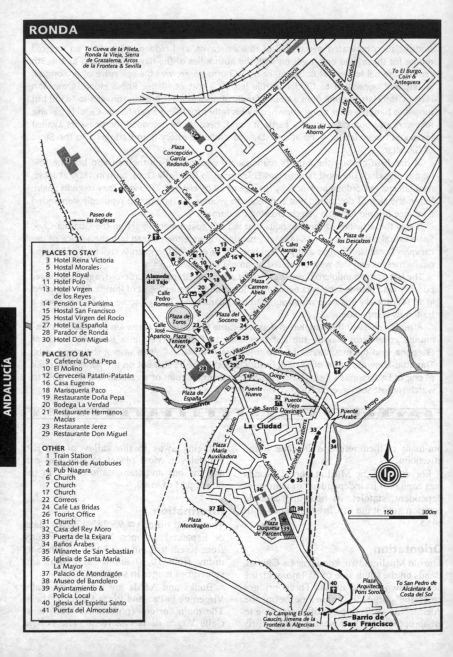

To Cueva de la Pileta,
Ronda la Vieja, Sierra
de Grazalema, Arcos
de la Frontera & Sevilla

To El Burgo,
Coín &
Antequera

Plaza del
Ahorro

Plaza
Concepción
García
Redondo

Paseo de
las Inglesas

Plaza de
los Descalzos

Alameda
del Tajo

Plaza
Carmen
Abela

Plaza del
Socorro

Plaza de
Toros

Plaza
Teniente
Arce

Tajo Gorge

Plaza de
España

Puente
Nuevo

Puente
Viejo

Puente
Árabe

La Ciudad

Plaza
María
Auxiliadora

Plaza
Mondragón

Plaza
Duquesa
de Parcent

Plaza
Arquitecto
Pons Sorolla

To San Pedro de
Alcántara &
Costa del Sol

To Camping El Sur,
Gaucín, Jimena de la
Frontera & Algeciras

Barrio de
San Francisco

0   150   300m

PLACES TO STAY
3 Hotel Reina Victoria
5 Hostal Morales
8 Hotel Royal
11 Hotel Polo
13 Hotel Virgen
   de los Reyes
14 Pensión La Purísima
15 Hostal San Francisco
25 Hostal Virgen del Rocío
27 Hotel La Española
28 Parador de Ronda
30 Hotel Don Miguel

PLACES TO EAT
9 Cafetería Doña Pepa
10 El Molino
12 Cervecería Patatín-Patatán
16 Casa Eugenio
18 Marisquería Paco
19 Restaurante Doña Pepa
20 Bodega La Verdad
21 Restaurante Hermanos
   Macías
23 Restaurante Jerez
29 Restaurante Don Miguel

OTHER
1 Train Station
2 Estación de Autobuses
4 Pub Niagara
6 Church
7 Church
17 Church
22 Correos
24 Café Las Bridas
26 Tourist Office
31 Church
32 Casa del Rey Moro
33 Puerta de la Exijara
34 Baños Árabes
35 Minarete de San Sebastián
36 Iglesia de Santa María
   La Mayor
37 Palacio de Mondragón
38 Museo del Bandolero
39 Ayuntamiento &
   Policía Local
40 Iglesia del Espíritu Santo
41 Puerta del Almocabar

Local (☎ 092) are at Plaza Duquesa de Parcent s/n.

Plaza de España & Puente Nuevo

Chapter 10 of Hemingway's *For Whom the Bell Tolls* tells how at the start of the Spanish Civil War the 'fascists' of a small town were rounded up in the town hall, then clubbed and flailed as they ran the gauntlet between two lines of townspeople 'in the plaza on the top of the cliff above the river'. At the end of the line the victims, dead or still alive, were thrown over the cliff. The episode was based on events in Ronda, though the actual perpetrators were apparently a gang from Málaga. The Parador de Ronda on Plaza de España was once the town hall.

The majestic Puente Nuevo spanning El Tajo from Plaza de España is two centuries old. A Ronda tradition relates that its architect, Martín de Aldehuela, fell to his death in 1793 while trying to engrave the completion date on the bridge. The word *año* (year) and some other, incomplete hieroglyphics by the shield on the bridge's side, may encourage you to disbelieve historians who say that Aldehuela died in 1802.

La Ciudad

The old Muslim town retains a typical *medina* character of narrow streets twisting between white buildings.

The first street to the left after you cross the Puente Nuevo, Calle Santo Domingo, leads to the **Casa del Rey Moro**. This 18th century house, supposedly built over remains of a Muslim palace, is itself closed, but for 500 ptas you can visit its terraced gardens in the gorge, and La Mina, an old underground stairway cut by slaves out of the rock right down to the river. They are open daily from 10 am to 7 pm.

From the Casa del Rey Moro head back up towards **Plaza María Auxiliadora**, which has fine views, then continue to the **Palacio de Mondragón**, thought to have been originally built for Abomelic, ruler of Ronda in 1314. The ground floor has three court-

yards, of which only the Patio Mudéjar preserves an Islamic character with its rich tiling and arches, one of which leads into a small cliff-top garden. Some rooms house a museum of prehistoric life in the Ronda area. The palace is open daily from 10 am to 7 pm (Saturday and Sunday to 3 pm). Entry is 200 ptas.

A minute's walk beyond is Plaza Duquesa de Parcent, where the **Iglesia de Santa María La Mayor** stands on the site of Muslim Ronda's main mosque. The tower betrays clear Islamic origins, and the handsome galleries beside it, built for viewing festivities, also date from Muslim times. Just inside the entrance is an arch covered with Arabic inscriptions which was the mosque's mihrab. The church was begun in Gothic style, but as building went on over the centuries, tastes changed so that it would wound up with an 18th century baroque north end. It's open daily from 10 am to 8 pm (6 pm in winter) for 200 ptas.

Nearby at Calle Armiñán 65, the Museo Histórico-Popular de la Serranía, more often called the **Museo del Bandolero**, is dedicated to the banditry for which the Ronda area was once renowned (see the boxed text 'Bandoleros & Guerrilleros'); it's open daily from 10 am to 8 pm (6 pm in winter) for 200 ptas. Just off the same street, the little **Minarete de San Sebastián** was built in Granada style, as part of a mosque, in the 14th century. Beside the museum, steps lead down to an impressive stretch of the old **walls** of La Ciudad. Follow them down to the **Puerta de la Exijara**, originally the gate of Islamic Ronda's Jewish quarter. From here a path leads down the hillside to the beautiful, almost intact **Baños Árabes** (Arab Baths), built in the 13th and 14th centuries. Open daily except Monday from 9 am to 2 pm and 4 to 6 pm, entry is free. Just north is the old **Puente Árabe** over the Río Guadalevín, immediately downstream of which, at the start of the gorge, is the **Puente Viejo**, dating in its current version from 1616. From the north side of the Puente Viejo you can make your way back up to Plaza de

ANDALUCÍA

España via a small park along the gorge's edge.

Plaza de Toros & Around

Ronda's elegant bullring on Calle Virgen de la Paz is a mecca for aficionados. Opened in 1785, it's one of the oldest in Spain, and has seen some of the most important events in bullfighting history (see the boxed text 'Ronda's Fighting Romeros'). Open daily from 10 am to 6 pm (275 ptas), it contains a small **Museo Taurino** which includes photos of famous visitors including Ernest Hemingway and Orson Welles.

Behind the Plaza de Toros, you can walk along from the cliff-top **Plaza Teniente Arce** to the shady **Alameda del Tajo** park.

Walks

A path leads down into the valley at the foot of the gorge from Plaza María Auxiliadora.

Ronda's Fighting Romeros

Ronda can justly claim to be the home of bullfighting. A company of knights, the Real Maestranza de Caballería, was formed here in 1572 to supervise the activity, and in the 18th and 19th centuries three generations of the Romero family established most of the basics of modern bullfighting on foot. Previously it had been done on horseback as a kind of cavalry training-cum-sport for the nobility.

Francisco Romero, born in 1698, invented the use of the cape to attract the bull, and its cloth replacement in the kill, the *muleta*; his son Juan introduced the matador's supporting team, the *cuadrilla*; and his grandson Pedro (1754-1839) perfected a strict classical style still known as the Ronda School before becoming director of the country's first bullfighting college (in Sevilla) at the age of 77.

Pedro's skill was such, it's said, that outlaws from the bandit-ridden mountains around Ronda would risk capture to see him in action.

From the bottom a road leads up to the Barrio de San Francisco, at the south end of town, or you could work your way north, crossing the river, up to the Hotel Reina Victoria.

Special Events

Ronda's bullring stages relatively few fights, but in early September it holds some of the most unusual anywhere, the Corridas Goyescas, in which top matadors fight in 19th century costumes as portrayed in Goya's Ronda bullfight scenes. These are the excuse for a general fiesta, the Feria de Pedro Romero.

Places to Stay – Budget

Camping El Sur (☎ 95 287 59 39), in a pleasant setting 2km south-west of town on the Algeciras road, has a pool and restaurant and is open all year, charging 1650 ptas plus IVA for two adults with a car and tent.

The bright *Pensión La Purísima* (☎ 95 287 10 50, Calle Sevilla 10) has nine rooms at 2000/3000 ptas. *Hostal Morales* (☎ 95 287 15 38, Calle Sevilla 51) is reasonable value at 1200/2400 ptas. *Hostal Virgen del Rocío* (☎ 95 287 74 25, Calle Nueva 18) and *Hostal San Francisco* (☎ 95 287 32 99, Calle María Cabrera 18) both have singles/doubles with bath for 1800/3600 ptas plus IVA.

Places to Stay – Mid-Range

The 30 room *Hotel Virgen de los Reyes* (☎ 95 287 11 40, Calle Lorenzo Borrego Gómez 13) has solid singles/doubles with small bathrooms for 3000/5000 ptas. *Hotel Royal* (☎ 95 287 11 41, Calle Virgen de la Paz 42) has similar standards and prices.

Hotel Polo (☎ 95 287 24 47, Calle Mariano Soubirón 8) is a bit better. Its 33 rooms, at 6300/9000 ptas plus IVA, have air-con, and there's a restaurant. The least expensive gorge views are at the *Hotel Don Miguel* (☎ 95 287 77 22, Calle Villanueva 8), where doubles are 9000 ptas plus IVA. The well located *Hotel La Española* (☎ 95 287 10 52, Calle José Aparicio 3) has similar prices.

Places to Stay – Top End

Hotel Reina Victoria (☎ 95 287 12 40, *Avenida Doctor Fleming 25)*, was built by a British company in the 1900s and has fine cliff-top gardens. The air of faded comfort recalls hill-station hotels in far-flung parts of the British Empire. Singles/doubles with shower are 9000/16,800 ptas plus IVA; bigger ones with bath, balcony and view are 11,000/16,800 ptas plus IVA.

The stylish, modern *Parador de Ronda* (☎ 95 287 75 00, *Plaza de España s/n)* is right on the edge of the gorge with a pool almost on the cliff top. Standard singles/doubles are 14,800/18,500 ptas plus IVA.

Places to Eat

Typical Ronda food is hearty mountain fare, strong on stews, trout, game such as rabbit, partridge and quail, and, of course, oxtail.

Restaurante Jerez is the best (and most expensive) of a line of touristic restaurants on Calle José Aparicio, with offerings from soups and salads (450 to 650 ptas) to oxtail (1600 ptas) or partridge (2200 ptas). *Restaurante Don Miguel* on Plaza de España has tables overlooking El Tajo and huntin' and shootin' fare such as partridge stew or roast stag leg for 1500 to 2000 ptas.

You'll find generally better value on and around Plaza del Socorro. *Marisquería Paco* here does good seafood and jamón tapas. *El Molino* is popular for its pizzas and pasta at 500 to 700 ptas and platos combinados from 600 ptas. The reliable, old-fashioned *Restaurante Doña Pepa* has *menús* for 1300 and 1750 ptas. Its nearby sibling *Cafetería Doña Pepa* *(Calle Marina 1)* is slightly cheaper, and open for breakfast. Vegetarians have options at both these places.

Bodega La Verdad *(Calle Pedro Romero 5)*, just off Plaza del Socorro, is a good, inexpensive tapas joint, popular with young locals. *Restaurante Hermanos Macías* on the same street does a reasonably-priced, typically *rondeño menú*. The bright *Cervecería Patatín-Patatán* *(Calle Lorenzo Borrego Gómez 7)* has sherry and very tasty

tapas, mostly between 75 and 150 ptas and featuring *filetito* (a small slice of steak).

Casa Eugenio *(Calle de Sevilla 7)* must have the cheapest platos combinados in town – eg bacon, egg and chips for 350 ptas.

Entertainment

Café Las Bridas *(Calle Los Remedios 18)* usually has live flamenco or rock on Friday and Saturday around midnight. *Pub Niagara* on Avenida Doctor Fleming plays some good music.

Getting There & Away

Bus The estación de autobuses is at Plaza Concepción García Redondo 2. Los Amarillos (☎ 95 287 22 64) goes to Málaga (two hours; 1075 ptas) six times daily and Sevilla (2½ hours; 1235 ptas) three to five times. Comes (☎ 95 287 19 92) has buses to Arcos de la Frontera, Jerez de la Frontera and Cádiz three to five times daily; and Jimena de la Frontera and La Línea de la Concepcion (990 ptas) Monday to Friday at 4 pm. Portillo (☎ 95 287 22 62) runs to San Pedro de Alcántara, Marbella (585 ptas), Fuengirola and Torremolinos three to five times daily. There are further services to other sierra towns and villages.

Train Ronda is on the scenic Bobadilla-Algeciras line, served by three or four trains each way daily. Change at Bobadilla for Sevilla (around three hours from Ronda; 1860 ptas), Málaga (2½ hours; 1130 ptas), Granada (3½ hours; 1550 ptas) and Córdoba (three hours; 1550 ptas). The station (☎ 95 287 16 73) is on Avenida de Andalucía.

Getting Around

Occasional buses run to Plaza de España from Avenida Martínez Astein, across the road from the train station.

AROUND RONDA

Beautiful green hill country, dotted with isolated towns and villages, stretches in all directions from Ronda, continuing west-

ANDALUCÍA

ward into the remote north-east of Cádiz province (see the Parque Natural Sierra de Grazalema section earlier in this chapter).

Parque Natural Sierra de las Nieves

This craggy 180 sq km natural park southeast of Ronda encompasses some good walking country. These mountains are noted for their stands of rare Spanish fir (pinsapo) and fauna that includes ibex and mouflon (wild sheep).

You can walk to the top of the highest peak, Torrecilla (1918m), in five or six hours return from the Área Recreativa Los Quejigales, which is 10km east by dirt road from the A-376 12km south of Ronda. For information on the park and walking routes, contact the Ronda tourist office or the tourist offices or ayuntamientos in small towns just north and east of the park: Calle Real 22, El Burgo (☎ 95 216 02 77); Calle del Pozo 17, Yunquera (☎ 95 248 25 01); Calle Coín 10, Alozaina (☎ 95 248 10 17); Plaza Alta 5, Tolox (☎ 95 248 73 33).

Places to Stay Camping is not allowed in the park but *Camping Pinsapo Azul* (☎ 95 248 27 54) is just outside Yunquera.

At Km 135 on the A-376, 1km north of the Los Quejigales turn-off, *Pensión Restaurante Navasillo* (☎ 95 211 42 35) has a few singles/doubles with bathroom for 2000/4500 ptas.

La Posada del Canónigo (☎ 95 216 01 85, Calle Mesónes 24, El Burgo) is a cosy small hotel charging 4000/6000 ptas. There are hostales with doubles between 3000 and 4000 ptas at El Burgo, Yunquera and Tolox. Those at Tolox open only from mid-June to mid-October.

Getting There & Away Portillo runs up to six buses each way between Málaga and Ronda via Marbella and San Pedro de Alcántara, stopping at Cruce La Ventilla on the A-376, 2km north of the Los Quejigales turning. Ferron Coín (☎ 95 235 54 90) runs daily buses between Ronda and Málaga via El Burgo and Yunquera, and a Ronda-Tolox

bus daily except Sunday and holidays. Portillo (☎ 95 236 01 91) runs daily buses from Málaga to Tolox.

Cueva de la Pileta

Some of Spain's most fascinating prehistoric rock art lies within this impressive cave some 15km south-west of Ronda. The entrance is on a rocky hillside and you'll be guided by lamplight by one of the Bullón family, from the only farmhouse in the valley. One of the family discovered the paintings in 1905 when searching for batdung fertiliser. The paintings include an archer, a pregnant horse and other animals, fish and abstract symbols.

Cueva de la Pileta is signposted from the Benaoján-Cortes de la Frontera road about 4km from Benaoján. One-hour tours are given daily at 10 and 11 am, noon, and 1, 4 and 5 pm, for 600 to 800 ptas per person, depending on the size of the group.

The nearest you can get by public transport is Benaoján. From Ronda there are four daily trains, and Los Amarillos buses Monday to Friday at 8.30 am and 1 pm.

ANTEQUERA

Antequera (population 40,000), 50km inland from Málaga, is one of Andalucía's most attractive towns. It's set on the edge of a plain 540m above sea level, with rugged mountainous country to the south and east.

Orientation & Information

The old heart of the town is below the north-west side of the hill-top Muslim Alcazaba. The main street, Calle Infante Don Fernando, begins here on Plaza San Sebastián and runs west. The tourist office (☎ 95 270 25 05), at Plaza San Sebastián 7, is open Monday to Saturday from 9.30 am to 1.30 pm and 4 to 7 pm, and Sunday and holidays from 10 am to 2 pm.

Things to See

The Muslim castle, the **Alcazaba**, affords great views, and its gardens sport a nice line in topiary. It's open daily except Monday from 10 am to 2 pm (free). Antequera was a favourite spot of the emirs of Granada before it became the first of their towns to fall to Castilla, in 1410. Two impressive 16th century structures up here are the **Arco de los Gigantes** gate, incorporating inscribed stones from Roman Antequera, and the Renaissance **Colegiata de Santa María la Mayor** church, open the same hours as the Alcazaba.

The pride of the **Museo Municipal**, in the Palacio de Nájera on Plaza Coso Viejo, is the 1.5m bronze Roman statue of a boy, 'Efebo', found near Antequera in the 1970s. The museum is open daily from 10 or 11 am to 1 or 1.30 pm (200 ptas).

The finest of Antequera's many churches is the 16th century mudéjar **Iglesia del Carmen**, with a lavish 18th century baroque interior, a couple of blocks east of the museum. It's open on Monday from 11.30 am to 2 pm and other days from 10 am to 2 pm, plus Saturday from 4 to 7 pm (200 ptas).

Some of Europe's largest megalithic dolmens stand on the fringes of Antequera. The **Cueva de Menga** and **Cueva de Viera** are about 1.5km from the centre on the road leading north-east out to the N-331. In around 2500 or 2000 BC the local folk managed to quarry huge blocks of stone from nearby hills and transport them here to construct these tombs, originally covered in earth, for their chieftains. Menga is 25m long, 4m high and composed of 31 slabs, the largest weighing 180 tonnes. At midsummer, the sun rising behind the 'head' on the landmark Peña de los Enamorados mountain to the north-east shines directly into its mouth. Menga and Viera are open daily except Monday from 10 am to 2 pm, and also Tuesday to Friday from 3 to 5.30 pm (free). Ask here or at the tourist office whether a third big dolmen a farther 3.5km out of town, the **Cueva del Romeral**, is open.

Places to Stay

The no-frills **Camas El Gallo** (☎ 95 284 21 04, Calle Nueva 2), just south of Plaza San Sebastián, has small singles/doubles for 1300/2200 ptas. Half a kilometre west, **Hostal Reyes** (☎ 95 284 10 28, Calle Tercia 4), off Calle Infante Don Fernando, has rooms from 1450/2900 ptas.

Pensión Madrona (☎ 95 284 00 14, Calle Calzada 31), also fairly central, has doubles with bath for 3800 ptas plus IVA.

Hostal Manzanito (☎ 95 284 10 23, Plaza San Sebastián 4) charges 2600/4500 ptas plus IVA for singles/doubles. The larger **Hostal Colón** (☎ 95 284 00 10, Calle Infante Don Fernando 29) has doubles from 3200 to 5000 ptas plus IVA. The **Parador de Antequera** (☎ 95 284 02 61, Paseo Calle García del Olmo s/n), in a quiet area north of the bullring, has doubles for 12,500 ptas plus IVA.

Places to Eat

Bar Manzanito on Plaza San Sebastián has reasonably priced meals. **Mesón Papabellotas** on Calle Encarnación facing the lovely Plaza Coso Viejo is more expensive: you could just have a drink and tapas and admire the interesting old photos. **Copa-Así** (Calle Lucena 10) off the west end of Plaza San Sebastián, does good-value tapas for 50 to 100 ptas. **La Espuela** in the 19th century bullring at the west end of Calle Infante Don Fernando has good local cooking and a fairly economical menú.

Getting There & Away

The estación de autobuses is located about 1km north-west of the centre at Campillo Alto s/n.

Several daily buses run to/from Málaga, and three or more to Osuna, Sevilla (Prado de San Sebastián), Granada and Córdoba.

The train station is about 2km north-west of the centre at Calle Divina Pastora 8. Two or three trains daily run to/from Granada, Sevilla, Málaga and Córdoba (with a change at Bobadilla for the latter pair).

AROUND ANTEQUERA
El Torcal

Millions of years of wind and water action have sculpted this 1336m mountain south of Antequera into some of the most weird and wonderful rock formations you'll see anywhere. The 12 sq km of gnarled, serrated, pillared and deeply fissured limestone were originally formed as sea bed 150 million years ago. A visitors centre (☎ 95 203 13 89) here is open daily from 10 am to 2 pm and 4 to 6 pm.

A few marked – and sometimes busy – walking trails set off from the visitors centre. There's an intermittently functioning camp site on the road from Antequera.

Getting There & Away Unless you walk to or from Antequera (16km), you need a vehicle if you're to get more than an hour at El Torcal. Monday to Friday only, a bus at 1 pm from Antequera to Villanueva de la Concepción will drop you at the Cruce del Torcal junction, from which it's a 4km uphill walk to the visitors centre. The return bus passes the Cruce at about 4.20 pm.

Laguna de Fuente de Piedra

When it's not dried up by drought, this shallow lake, close to the A-92 about 20km north-west of Antequera, is one of Europe's two main breeding grounds for the spectacular greater flamingo (the other is the Camargue in France). In 1996 and 1997 record numbers of flamingo chicks – more than 13,000 each year – hatched here. The birds arrive in January or February, with the chicks hatching in April and May, and stay till about August. The Centro de Información Fuente de Piedra (☎ 95 211 10 50) at the lake is open daily except Monday from 9 am to 2 pm and 4 to 7 pm. You may find however that nearly all the birds are congregating on the far side of the lake, several kilometres from the Centro de Información and Fuente de Piedra village. The inexpensive *Camping La Laguna* (☎ 95 273 52 94), on the edge of nearby Fuente de Piedra village, is open all year. *Hostal La Laguna* (☎ 95 273 52 92), just off the A-92 in Fuente de Piedra, has doubles for 5000 ptas.

Getting There & Away Buses run between Antequera estación de autobuses and Fuente de Piedra village, a few minutes

walk from the visitors centre, at least three times daily.

EAST OF MÁLAGA

The coast east of Málaga, sometimes described as the Costa del Sol Oriental, is less developed than the coast to the west.

Behind the coast, the attractive La Axarquía region, riven by deep valleys and dotted with white villages of Muslim origin linked by snaking mountain roads, climbs to the sierras along the border of Granada province. There's good walking here (best in April and May and from mid-September to late October). Information on La Axarquía is available at the tourist offices in coastal towns such as Nerja, Torre del Mar and Torrox.

Nerja

Nerja, 56km from Málaga, is older, whiter and more charming than the towns to its west, though inundated by tourism. The tourist office (☎ 95 252 15 31) is in the centre at Puerta del Mar 4, near the Balcón de Europa lookout point, which has good coastal views. The best beach is Playa Burriana, on the east side of town.

Places to Stay The pleasant *Nerja Camping* (☎ 95 252 97 14), about 4km east on the N-340, charges 2000 ptas for two people with tent and car.

In July and August, try to arrive early in the day to ensure a room in town. A good, economical choice is *Hostal Mena* (☎ 95 252 05 41, Calle El Barrio 15), a short distance west of the tourist office. Its 14 singles/doubles cost from 1000/2000 to 1250/2500 ptas (add about 60% in high season). Nearby and a bit more expensive, with doubles from about 3000 to 5000 ptas depending on the season, are *Hostal Atenbeni* (☎ 95 252 13 41, Calle Diputación Provincial 12) and *Hostal Alhambra* (☎ 95 252 21 74) on Calle Antonio Millón.

Hotel Cala Bella (☎ 95 252 07 00) and *Hotel Portofino* (☎ 95 252 01 50) on Puerta del Mar have some rooms with good beach views – respectively 6000 and 8000 ptas a double plus IVA in the high season. *Hotel Balcón de Europa* (☎ 95 252 08 00), next to the Balcón itself, has doubles for 14,900 ptas plus IVA in the high season. The *Parador de Nerja* (☎ 95 252 00 50, Calle Almuñécar 8), above Playa Burriana, charges 18,000 ptas plus IVA.

Places to Eat One of the best feeds is at the open-air *Merendero Ayo* towards the east end of Playa Burriana, where a plate of paella, cooked on the spot in great sizzling pans, is 675 ptas.

Haveli (Calle Cristo 44), north off Puerta del Mar, is a good, medium-priced Indian restaurant. *Ostería di' Mamma Rosa* in Edificio Corona, Calle Chaparil, about a 10 minute walk west of Puerta del Mar, is another good medium-priced option.

Getting There & Away Alsina Graells (☎ 95 252 15 04), on the N-340 near the top of Calle Pintada, has around 12 daily buses to/from Málaga, eight to/from Almuñécar, several to/from Almería, and two to/from Granada.

Around Nerja

The big tourist attraction is the **Cueva de Nerja**, 3km east of town just off the N-340. This enormous set of caverns remains very impressive despite the crowds traipsing continually through it; they are open daily from 10.30 am to 2 pm and 3.30 to 6 pm (500 ptas). About 11 buses daily run from Nerja; others run from Málaga.

Farther east the coast becomes more rugged and scenic and with your own wheels you can head out to some good **beaches** reached by tracks down from the N-340 around 8 to 10km from Nerja.

Seven kilometres inland from Nerja and linked to it by several buses daily (except Sunday), the pretty village of **Frigiliana** is another worthwhile outing.

Cómpeta & Around

A good base for exploring La Axarquía and walking in the mountains is the village of Cómpeta, 17km inland. Cómpeta produces some of the best of La Axarquía's sweet white wine, and has a range of places to stay and eat.

Things to See & Do Perhaps the most exhilarating walk in the area is up the dramatically peaked **El Lucero** (1779m). From its summit, on a clear day, there are views to Granada in one direction and Morocco in the other. This is a very full day's round-trip walk from Cómpeta, with an ascent of 1150m. It is, however, possible to drive as far up as the Puerto Blanquillo pass (1200m), on a mountain track from Canillas de Albaida, 3km north-west of Cómpeta. The booklet *25 Walks in and around Cómpeta & Canillas de Albaida* by Albert & Dini Kraaijenzank, available locally, covers a range of other day walks.

Árchez, a few kilometres down the valley from Cómpeta, has a beautiful Almohad minaret next to its church. From Árchez a road winds 8km south-west to **Arenas**, where a steep but driveable track climbs to the ruined Muslim **Castillo de Bentomiz**, crowning a hill top.

Places to Stay *Hostal Alberdini* (☎ 95 251 62 41) at La Lomilla, 1km south-east of Cómpeta, with spectacular views, has singles/doubles with bathroom for 3000/4500 ptas (less if you stay more than one night), and a reasonably priced restaurant. *Hostal Los Montes* (☎ 95 251 60 15) on Cómpeta's Plaza Almijara has rooms for 1500/3000 ptas.

Getting There & Away Two or three buses daily run from Málaga to Cómpeta and Canillas de Albaida, via Torre del Mar.

Córdoba Province

The big draw here is the city of Córdoba, capital of Al-Andalus when it was at its peak. Córdoba's Mezquita (Mosque) is one of the most magnificent of all Islamic buildings. North of the city rises the Sierra Morena. To the south is a fertile rolling area

ANDALUCÍA

called La Campiña, rising to the Sierras Subbéticas in the south-east.

CÓRDOBA

Standing on a sweep of the Río Guadalquivir with countryside stretching far in every direction around, Córdoba (population 306,000) is both provincial and sophisticated. Its labyrinthine old quarter, centred on the Mezquita, is fascinating to explore, while the modern city, farther north, brings you back to the 20th century with its bustle, shops and traffic.

The most popular time to visit is from about mid-April to mid-June, when the skies are big and blue but the heat tolerable and the old town's beautiful patios are at their best, dripping with foliage and blooms.

History

The thriving Roman colony of Corduba, founded in 152 BC, was the capital first of Hispania Ulterior province then, after a re-organisation in the 1st century BC, of Baetica province. In this major cultural centre were born both the famous Latin author and philosopher Seneca, and his nephew, the poet Lucan. In 711 AD Córdoba fell to the Islamic invaders and soon became the Muslim capital on the peninsula. At first it was subordinate to the Omayyad caliphate in Damascus, but after this was overthrown in 750, an Omayyad survivor made his way to Córdoba and set himself up in 756 as the independent emir of Al-Andalus, Abd ar-Rahman I.

Córdoba's heyday came under Abd ar-Rahman III (912-61). In 929 he gave himself the title Caliph, setting the seal on Al-Andalus' de facto independence of the Abbasid caliphs in Baghdad. Córdoba was then the biggest city in western Europe, with a population estimated at somewhere between 100,000 and 500,000. It had dazzling mosques, patios, gardens, public baths, libraries, observatories, aqueducts and a university. Its economy flourished on the agriculture of its irrigated hinterland and the products of its skilled artisans: leather and metal work, textiles, glazed tiles and

more. The court of Abd ar-Rahman III was frequented by Jewish, Arab and Christian scholars.

The Omayyads unified Al-Andalus for long periods and for most of their rule Muslims, Jews and Christians co-existed in reasonable harmony. At its peak, the caliphate encompassed most of the Iberian peninsula south of the Río Duero, plus the Balearic Islands and some of North Africa. Córdoba became a place of pilgrimage for Muslims who could not reach Mecca or Jerusalem.

Towards the end of the 10th century, Al-Mansour (Almanzor), a fearsome general, took over the reins of power and struck terror into Christian Spain, making over 50 forays (razzias) in 20 years. He destroyed the cathedral at Santiago de Compostela, forcing Christian slaves to bring its bells to Córdoba where they were hung upside-down as gigantic oil lamps in the Mezquita.

After the death of Al-Mansour's son in 1008 the caliphate descended into anarchy. Berber troops terrorised and looted the city and in 1031 the caliphate finally collapsed into dozens of taifas. Córdoba became a part of the Sevilla taifa in 1069.

Its intellectual traditions, however, continued. In the 12th century Córdoba produced two of the most celebrated of all Al-Andalus' scholars: the Muslim Averroës (Ibn Rushd) and the Jewish Moses Maimonides, both men of multifarious talents best remembered for their philosophical efforts to harmonise religious faith with reason.

Córdoba was taken in 1236 by Fernando III, who returned the bells to Santiago de Compostela, and became a provincial town of shrinking importance. The decline only began to be reversed with the coming of industry in the late 19th century.

Orientation

Immediately north of the Río Guadalquivir is the old city, a warren of narrow streets focused on the Mezquita. The area northwest of the Mezquita was the Judería (Jewish quarter). The main square of the modern city is Plaza Tendillas, 500m north of the Mezquita.

Information

Tourist Offices The helpful Junta de Andalucía tourist office (☎ 957 47 12 35) faces the Mezquita at Calle de Torrijos 10. In summer it's open Monday to Saturday from 9 am to 8 pm and Sunday and holidays from 10 am to 2 pm. In other seasons it closes earlier on Monday to Saturday (5 pm in winter). The municipal tourist office (☎ 957 20 05 22) is on Plaza de Judá Levi, a block west of the Mezquita and is open Monday to Friday from 9 am to 2 pm and 4.30 to 6.30 pm, Saturday from 8.30 am to 2.30 pm and Sunday from 9 am to 2 pm. Staff speak only Spanish.

Money The main concentration of banks and ATMs is in the new town, around Plaza Tendillas and Avenida del Gran Capitán.

Post & Communications The main correos (postcode 14080) is on Calle José Cruz Conde, off Plaza Tendillas.

Books & Maps Librería Luque, Calle Conde de Gondomar 13, has a good range of maps and a decent selection of novels in English.

Medical & Emergency Services The main general hospital, Hospital Reina Sofia (☎ 957 21 70 00), is 1.5km south-west of the Mezquita at Avenida de Menéndez Pidal s/n. For an ambulance call ☎ 061. The Policía Nacional (☎ 957 47 75 00, ☎ 091 in emergency) are at Avenida Doctor Fleming 2.

Opening Hours Opening times for Córdoba's sights rarely remain static – check with the tourist offices for the latest times. Most places except the Mezquita close on Mondays, and closing times are generally earlier in winter than summer.

Mezquita

This astonishing building can seem rather bewildering at first. Because of the Christ-

ian alterations to the original Islamic structure and the darkness they imposed, you need a bit of imagination to picture the Mezquita as it was in Muslim times, open to and in harmony with its surroundings. It has some truly beautiful architectural features, among them the famous rows of two-tier arches in mesmerising stripes of red brick and white stone, and the more elaborate arches, domes and decoration around the splendid *mihrab* (prayer niche). The outside of the building has thick stone walls punctuated by ornate gates.

History Abd ar-Rahman I founded the Mezquita in 785 on the site of a church which for 50 years had been partitioned between Muslims and Christians. Abd ar-Rahman I purchased the Christian half from the Christian community. Abd ar-Rahman II in the 9th century and Al-Hakim II in the 960s extended the Mezquita southwards to cater for Córdoba's expanding population. Al-Hakim II also created the existing mihrab and its surrounds. Under Al-Mansour, extensions were made to the east.

What you see today is the Mezquita's final Islamic form with one marked alteration: a 16th century cathedral right in the middle (hence the often-used description 'Mezquita-Catedral').

Entry The main entrance is the Puerta del Perdón, a 14th century mudéjar gateway on Calle Cardenal Herrero. The Mezquita is open Monday to Saturday from 10 am to 7.30 pm (October to March, to 5 pm) and Sunday from 2 to 7 pm (October to March from 3.30 to 5.30 pm). Entry is 750 ptas. You can enter free during Mass from 9 to 10 am but most of the building will not be lit.

Beside the Puerta del Perdón is a 16th century tower which replaced the original minaret. Inside is the pretty **Patio de los Naranjos** (Courtyard of the Orange Trees), from which a door leads into the Mezquita itself.

Inside the Mezquita Straight ahead from the entrance door, in the far (south) wall,

ANDALUCÍA

CÓRDOBA

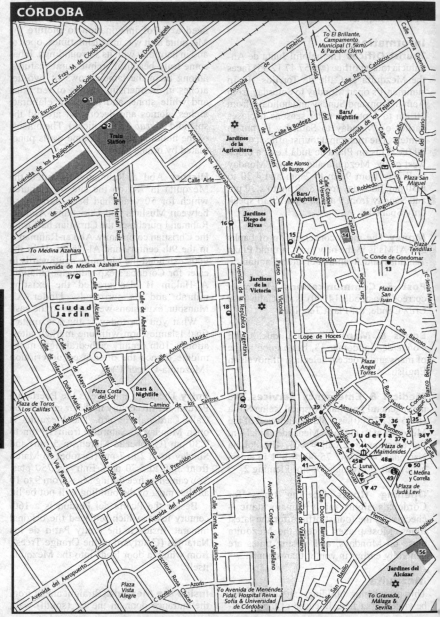

CÓRDOBA

1
2 Train Station

Jardines de la Agricultura

To El Brillante, Campamento Municipal (1.5km) & Parador (3km)

Bars/Nightlife

3
4 Plaza San Miguel

Calle Arfe

16

Jardines Diego de Rivas

Bars/Nightlife

15
14

13

Plaza Tendillas

Plaza San Juan

To Medina Azahara

Avenida de Medina Azahara

17

Ciudad Jardín

Jardines de la Victoria

18

Plaza Costa del Sol

Bars & Nightlife

Plaza de Toros Los Califas

Plaza Angel Torres

Plaza Buen Pastor

40

39

38 36
35
34
33

Juderia

37

42
44
43
41
45 48
46 Luna
47 49
50

Plaza de Maimónides

C Medina y Corella

Plaza de Judá Leví

56

Jardines del Alcázar

To Avenida de Menéndez Pidal, Hospital Reina Sofía & Universidad de Córdoba

Plaza Vista Alegre

To Granada, Málaga & Sevilla

ANDALUCÍA

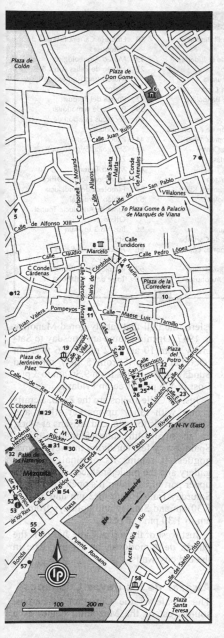

you can see the mihrab. The first 12 aisles inside the entrance, a forest of pillars and arches, comprise the original **8th century mosque**. This incorporated columns and capitals – of various coloured marbles, granite and alabaster – from the site's previous Visigothic church, from Roman buildings in Córdoba and farther afield, and even from ancient Carthage. The columns support two tiers of arches, giving an effect reminiscent of aqueducts and/or date palms. The use of bicoloured materials for the arches was inspired. Subsequent extensions required more columns, most made locally. The final Islamic building had 1300 columns, of which 850 remain.

In the centre of the building is the Christian cathedral, surrounded by Islamic aisles, pillars and arches. Just past the right-hand (west) end of the cathedral begins the approach to the mihrab, marked by heavier, more elaborate arches.

The bay immediately in front of the mihrab and the bay to each side form the **maksura**, where the caliphs and their retinues would have prayed (today enclosed by railings). Each of the maksura's three bays has a skylit dome with star-pattern vaulting: the mosaic decoration on the central dome is particularly beautiful. The horseshoe-arched entrance to the **mihrab** itself (which you cannot enter) is superbly decorated with floral-motif mosaics by Byzantine craftsmen, rich stucco work and mosaic inscriptions from the Qur'an, all in gold, purple, green, blue and red.

Wandering around the rest of the Mezquita, it's possible to lose yourself in the aisles with views of only the incredible columns and arches. In Muslim times the Mezquita would have been better lit, with doors open along its sides.

Early modifications after the Mezquita was turned into a cathedral in 1236 were carried out with restraint, but in the 16th century its centre was ripped out to allow construction of the **Capilla Mayor** and **coro** (choir). The Capilla Mayor has a rich 17th century jasper and marble retablo; the coro's fine mahogany stalls were carved in

ANDALUCÍA

CÓRDOBA

the 18th century by Pedro, Duque Cornejo y Roldán. The forests of Islamic arches and pillars provide a magnificent setting for the Christian structures, but if you think of the building in its original terms, the Christian additions undeniably destroy the whole conception of the place.

There are further chapels, one next to the mihrab and others lining the east and west walls of the building.

Judería

The Judería, extending from the Mezquita almost to Avenida del Gran Capitán, is a maze of narrow streets and small plazas, of whitewashed buildings with flowers dripping from window boxes, and wrought-iron doorways giving glimpses of plant-filled patios.

The **Museo Taurino** (Bullfighting Museum) on Plaza de Maimónides celebrates Córdoba's legendary *toreros*: there are rooms dedicated to El Cordobés and Manolete, even with the skin, tail and ear of Islero, the bull that fatally gored Manolete in 1947. Opening hours are Tuesday to Saturday from 10 am to 2 pm and 6 to 8 pm (October to April from 5 to 7 pm) and Sunday and holidays from 9.30 am to 3 pm. Cost is 425 ptas (free on Friday).

Just up Calle Judíos are the **Zoco**, a crafts centre with fairly up-market silver and leather goods for sale, and artisans at work, and the small 14th century **Sinagoga**, one of Spain's very few surviving medieval synagogues. It retains its original women's gallery and the mudéjar stucco work on the upper part of its walls; it's open Tuesday to Saturday from 10 am to 2 pm and 3.30 to 5.30 pm and Sunday and holidays from 10 am to 1.30 pm (50 ptas).

Just west of the top of Calle Judíos is the **Puerta de Almodóvar**, an Islamic gate in the old city walls.

Alcázar de los Reyes Cristianos

The Castle of the Christian Monarchs, south-west of the Mezquita, began as a palace and fort for Alfonso X in the 13th century. Isabel and Fernando once received Columbus here, and from 1490 to 1821 the Inquisition operated from here. The Alcázar is undergoing renovations which means you can't explore its four watchtowers or its ramparts; but its extensive, beautiful gardens, full of fishponds, fountains, orange trees, flowers and topiary are among the most beautiful in Andalucía. The Alcázar also houses a royal bathhouse and a museum, with some Roman mosaics of most interest. It's open Tuesday to Saturday from 10 am to 2 pm and 6 to 8 pm (October to April from 4.30 to 6.30 pm) and Sunday and holidays from 9.30 am to 3 pm. Entry is 300 ptas (free on Friday).

Río Guadalquivir & Torre de la Calahorra

Just south of the Mezquita, the Guadalquivir is crossed by the much-restored **Puente Romano** (Roman Bridge). Just downstream, near the north bank, is a restored **Islamic water wheel**.

At the south end of the bridge is the **Torre de la Calahorra**, a 14th century tower housing a museum highlighting the intellectual achievements of Islamic Córdoba and focusing rather rose-tintedly on its reputation for religious tolerance. A 55 minute taped commentary, available in several languages, guides you through the displays. The museum contains good models of the Mezquita and Granada's Alhambra. It's open daily from 10 am to 2.30 pm and 5.30 to 8.30 pm (October to April from 10 am to 6 pm) and costs 500 ptas.

Museo Arqueológico

Córdoba's Archaeological Museum, in a Renaissance mansion on Plaza de Jerónimo Páez, has an extensive collection ranging from Palaeolithic to Islamic times. A reclining stone lion takes pride of place in the Iberian section, and the Roman period is well represented with large mosaics, elegant ceramics and tinted glass bowls. The upstairs is devoted to medieval Córdoba, including bronze animals from

the caliphs' palace at Medina Azahara. The museum is open Tuesday from 3 to 8 pm, Wednesday to Saturday from 9 am to 8 pm and Sunday and holidays from 9 am to 3 pm (free with an EU passport, 250 ptas otherwise).

Plaza del Potro

This attractive plaza 400m east of the Mezquita was a hangout for traders and adventurers in the 16th and 17th centuries. The former Hospital de la Caridad here houses the **Museo de Bellas Artes**, with the same hours and prices as the Museo Arqueológico and a collection of paintings by mainly Córdoban artists; and the **Museo Julio Romero de Torres**, which includes a wonderful collection of dark, sensual portraits of Córdoban women by Romero de Torres (1880-1930). It is open Tuesday to Saturday from 10 am to 2 pm and 6 to 8 pm (October to April from 5 to 7 pm) and Sunday and holidays from 9.30 am to 3 pm (425 ptas, free on Friday).

Plaza de la Corredera

This handsome square 200m north of Plaza del Potro was the site of Córdoba's Roman amphitheatre and later of Inquisition burnings and bullfights. Nearby on Calle Claudio Marcelo, a ruined **Roman temple** has been partly restored.

Palacio de Viana

This Renaissance palace at Plaza de Don Gome 2, 500m north of Plaza de la Corredera, has 12 patios and a garden, some of which are outstandingly beautiful. It's also packed with a rich collection of antique furniture, art and crafts; it is open Monday to Saturday (except Wednesday) from 10 am to 1 pm and 4 to 6 pm and Sunday from 10 am to 2 pm (500 ptas).

Language Courses

Centro de Idiomas Klack (☎/fax 957 49 13 03, klack@arrakis.es), Calle Manchado 9, runs courses from two to 16 weeks for 32,000 to 197,000 ptas. For information on

ANDALUCÍA

courses at the university contact the Servicio de Lenguas y Traducción Técnica (☎ 957 21 89 97, fax 957 21 89 96), Universidad de Córdoba, Avenida Menéndez Pidal, 14071 Córdoba.

Organised Tours

Córdoba Vision (☎ 957 23 17 34) operates 2½ hour city tours for 2650 ptas. Book at major hotels and agents around town.

Special Events

Semana Santa is one of Córdoba's major festivals, with big processions every evening from Palm Sunday to Good Friday. But early summer is the chief festival time. Events include:

First half of May
  Concurso & Festival de Patios Cordobeses (see the boxed text 'Córdoba's Patios'); at the same time there's a busy cultural program

---

Córdoba's Patios

SUSAN FORSYTH

A fleeting glimpse of one of Córdoba's garden havens

Córdoba's patios have two roots: Roman and Muslim. For the Romans, the patios provided a meeting place; during Islamic times, patios were used for rest and recreation. Today, both these trends continue – patios provide a haven of peace and quiet, shade during the searing heat of the summer, and a place to entertain.

As you wander the streets and alleys of Córdoba in the first half of May, you'll notice 'Patio' signs; this means that you're invited to view what is for the rest of the year closed to the world by heavy wooden doors or partly hidden by wrought-iron gates. At this time of year the patios are at their prettiest as new blooms proliferate, though not all displays are on a grand scale.

Around 50 patios are entered in the annual Concurso de Patios Cordobéses, a competition with prizes for the best patios. The tourist office can provide a map of patios open for viewing. If you don't have a lot of time, those in the vicinity of Calle de San Basilio, about 400m west of the Mezquita, are some of the best.

During the concurso, the patios are generally open Monday to Friday from 5 pm to midnight and Saturday and Sunday from noon to midnight. Entry is usually free but sometimes a container is placed at the exit for donations.

If you're not here for the concurso, the Palacio de Viana, with its 12 lovely patios, is open year round.

Late May/early June

Feria de Nuestra Señora de la Salud: 10 days of party time for Córdoba

Late June/first half of July

Festival Internacional de Guitarra: a two-week celebration of the guitar with live performances of classical, flamenco, rock, blues and more in the Alcázar gardens.

Places to Stay

Many of Córdoba's lodgings are built around charming patios. Single rooms for a decent price are in short supply. It's best to ring ahead at peak times including Semana Santa and during the festivals from late April to early June.

Places to Stay – Budget

Camping The *Campamento Municipal* (☎ 957 28 21 65, *Avenida del Brillante 50)*, on the road to Villaviciosa, is about 1.5km north of the train station. It costs 532 ptas plus IVA per adult, per car and per tent.

Youth Hostel The ultramodern Inturjoven *Albergue Juvenil Córdoba* (☎ 957 29 01 66), perfectly positioned on Plaza de Judá Levi, has room for 94 people in double, triple and four-person rooms. For prices, see this chapter's introductory Youth Hostels section.

Hostales *Huéspedes Martínez Rücker* (☎ 957 47 25 62, *Calle Martínez Rücker 14)*, with singles/doubles for 1750/3500 ptas, is particularly friendly and only a stone's throw east of the Mezquita. A short walk east, *Hostal Santa Ana* (☎ 957 48 58 37, *Calle Cardenal González 25)* has one single at 1750 ptas and doubles at 3500 or 4500 ptas. A little to the north-west, the friendly *Hostal Rey Heredia* (☎ 957 47 41 82, *Calle Rey Heredia 26)* has singles/doubles around a plant-filled patio for 1500/3000 ptas.

There are some good hostales to the east, farther from the tourist masses. *Pensión San Francisco* (☎ 957 47 27 16, *Calle de San Fernando 24)* has one small single at 2000 ptas and doubles from 4500 ptas. *Hostal La Fuente* (☎ 957 48 78 27, *Calle de San Fernando 51)* has compact singles at 2000 ptas and doubles with bath at 5500 ptas; its café serves a decent breakfast. *Hostal Los Arcos* (☎ 957 48 56 43, *Calle Romero Barros 14)* has singles/doubles round a pretty courtyard for 2000/3500 ptas, and doubles for 4500 ptas with bath. Next door at No 16, *Hostal Maestre* (☎ 957 47 53 95)* has plenty of clean, spacious rooms with bath at 2500/4500 ptas.

A short distance north of the Mezquita, *Hostal Séneca* (☎ 957 47 32 34, *Calle Conde y Luque 7)* is charming with friendly management, a *típico* patio and a breakfast room; rooms with shared bathroom cost 2450/4600 ptas, with attached bath 5600 ptas, including breakfast. Phone ahead.

Places to Stay – Mid-Range

Hostal El Triunfo (☎ 957 47 55 00, *Calle Corregidor Luis de la Cerda 79)*, just south of the Mezquita, has singles/doubles with air-con and TV for 3700/6200 ptas plus IVA. Half a block from the Mezquita, *Hotel Los Omeyas* (☎ 957 49 22 67, *Calle Encarnación 17)* is attractive with doubles at 7000 ptas plus IVA. *Hotel Maestre* (☎ 957 47 24 10, *Calle Romero Barros 4)* has bright singles/doubles with attached bath for 3500/6000 ptas.

Places to Stay – Top End

Add IVA to prices quoted. *Hotel El Conquistador* (☎ 957 48 11 02, *Calle Magistral González Francés 15-17)*, facing the Mezquita, has very comfortable doubles for 15,500 ptas. *Hotel Amistad Córdoba* (☎ 957 42 03 35, *Plaza de Maimónides 3)*, occupying two converted mansions, has singles/doubles for 12,300/15,000 ptas but from Friday to Sunday doubles are just 9800 ptas. Córdoba's modern *Parador* (☎ 957 27 59 00, *Avenida de la Arruzafa s/n)* is 3km north of the centre on the site of Abd ar-Rahman I's country palace. Doubles are 16,500 ptas (14,500 ptas in July and August).

Places to Eat

A couple of dishes are common to most Córdoban restaurants. *Salmorejo* is a type of gazpacho with chopped hard-boiled eggs floating on top. *Rabo de toro* is oxtail stew. Some top restaurants feature recipes from Al-Andalus such as garlic soup with raisins, honeyed lamb, or meats stuffed with dates and pine nuts. The local tipple is wine from nearby Montilla and Moriles, similar to sherry.

There are lots of places to eat right by the Mezquita, some expensive, some mediocre, some awful. Some better-value places are a short walk west into the Judería. A longer walk east or north will produce even better options for the budget-conscious and/or inquisitive.

Around the Mezquita *Self-Service Los Patios (Calle Cardenal Herrero 14)* has functional main courses and desserts with nothing over 700 ptas plus IVA. A typical main dish is fried *merluza* (hake) and salad. The lovely covered patio offers respite from the heat.

El Caballo Rojo (Calle Cardenal Herrero 28) specialises in food from the time of the caliphs. The *menú* is a hefty 2950 ptas plus IVA and mains start at about 1600 ptas, but here you're guaranteed something different from the usual fare. There's also good food at *Restaurante Bandolero (Calle de Torrijos 6)*, which has media-raciones from 250 ptas and platos combinados from 975 to 1100 ptas; á la carte, you could expect to pay 3000 to 4000 ptas for three courses with drinks.

Judería *Casa Pepe de la Judería (Calle Romero 1)* does excellent tapas and raciones in its bar and has a good restaurant with typical main dishes in the 1500 ptas zone. On the same street, *Restaurante El Rincón de Carmen* has an open-air patio with a *menú* for 1500 ptas and an attached café that does good snacks and breakfasts. *El Churrasco (Calle Romero 16)* is one of Córdoba's best restaurants, with rich food, generous portions and attentive service. The *menú* is 3000 ptas; most mains are around 2000 ptas, though some are only 1200 ptas.

Mesón de la Luna and *Mesón la Muralla*, in the city walls on Calle de la Luna, share a courtyard and have *menús* from 1200 to 1900 ptas which feature local specialities.

East of the Mezquita *Taberna Sociedad de Plateros (Calle San Francisco 6)* is a popular tavern with a good range of tapas and raciones (nothing over 700 ptas). Just east, on pedestrian Calle Enrique Romero de Torres, are two bar/restaurants with outside tables looking on to Plaza del Potro. This is a fine place to sit on a balmy evening at sunset. *Bar Callejón* has egg dishes around 400 ptas, or a three-course *menú* for 1000 ptas.

The homy *Taberna Salinas (Calle Tundidores 3)*, a little farther north, offers good, inexpensive Córdoban fare. *Revuelto de ajetes, gambas y jamón* (scrambled eggs with garlic shoots, prawns and ham), *chuletas de cordero* (lamb chops) and pisto (fried vegetables) cost 625 to 725 ptas (closed Sunday).

City Centre There are several reasonably priced eateries on Plaza Tendillas and Calle Claudio Marcelo. *Casa El Pisto*, officially *Taberna San Miguel, (Plaza San Miguel 1)* is an atmospheric old watering hole with a great range of tapas, media-raciones (500 to 900 ptas) and raciones, and good Moriles wine; it's open Monday to Saturday from noon to 4 pm and 8 pm to midnight.

Self-Catering There's a *food market* on Plaza de la Corredera, which is open Monday to Saturday. *Simago* is a handy supermarket on Calle Jesús María, just south of Plaza Tendillas.

Entertainment

Córdoba's lively music bars and late-night bars are scattered around the north and west of town. One lively street is Calle Reyes Católicos, off Plaza de Colón; there are more bars in Calle Cordova de Veracruz and Calle Alonso de Burgos, south of Avenida Ronda de los Tejares. A third nightlife area is the Ciudad Jardín suburb around Plaza

ANDALUCÍA

Costa del Sol, 350m west of Avenida de la República Argentina; and finally there's the northern El Brillante suburb, especially along Avenida del Brillante (the continuation of Avenida del Gran Capitán) and in the El Tablero urbanisation. There's generally little action early in the week.

Most bars in the old town close by about midnight, but there's a fairly good flamenco show at *Tablao Cardenal (Calle de Torrijos 10)* on Tuesday to Saturday at 10.30 pm for 2400 ptas including one drink.

The *Gran Teatro de Córdoba* has a busy program ranging from varied concerts and theatre to dance and film festivals. The *Filmoteca de Andalucía* regularly shows subtitled foreign films.

Shopping
Córdoba is known for its leather goods, silver jewellery (particularly filigree) and attractive pottery. Plenty of these can be found in the tourist shops around the Mezquita, but prices are lower in the central shopping district around Plaza Tendillas. The Zoco on Calle Judíos has good but pricey products.

Plaza de la Corredera has a few shops selling boots, music and bric-a-brac but becomes a lively mercadillo on Saturday morning.

Getting There & Away
Bus A new estación de autobuses, behind the train station, is due to open maybe in 1999, but until then the different bus companies use different stations around town.

The major one is at Avenida de Medina Azahara 29, 500m west of Avenida de la República Argentina. Alsina Graells (☎ 957 23 64 74) has several daily buses to Sevilla (1200 ptas), Granada (1765 ptas), Málaga (1515 ptas) and Jaén, and has daily service to Cádiz and Almería. From this same station Bacoma (☎ 957 45 65 14) runs to Baeza, Úbeda, Alicante, Valencia and Barcelona.

Empresa Carrera (☎ 957 23 14 01), Avenida de la República Argentina 30, serves the south of Córdoba province, including Priego de Córdoba, Montilla, Cabra, Luque and Zuheros.

Auto-Transportes López (☎ 957 47 45 92), Paseo de la Victoria 15, serves Extremadura. Buses to Madrid (at least six daily; 1580 ptas) are run by Secorbus (☎ 957 46 80 40), Camino de los Sastres 1.

Train The station (☎ 957 40 02 02) is on Avenida de América, 1km north-west of Plaza Tendillas.

About 20 trains daily run to/from Sevilla, taking from 45 minutes to 1¼ hours for 1050 to 2700 ptas. The numerous services to/from Madrid range from a single Inter-City (4¼ hours; 3700 ptas) to several AVEs (1¾ hours; 5900 to 7000 ptas).

There are several daily trains to Málaga (2¼ hours; 1900 to 2200 ptas) and Cádiz, and one each to Jaén and Huelva. For Granada (four hours; 1800 ptas), you must change at Bobadilla.

Getting Around
Bus No 3 (110 ptas) from behind the train station (and in front of the new bus station when it opens) runs to Plaza Tendillas and down Calle de San Fernando, east of the Mezquita. For the return trip, you can pick it up on Ronda de Isasa, just south of the Mezquita.

Taxis cost around 450 ptas from the train station or Alsina Graells bus station to the centre or Mezquita.

AROUND CÓRDOBA
Medina Azahara
In 936 Abd ar-Rahman III began the building of a magnificent new capital for his new caliphate, 8km west of Córdoba, and by 945 was able to install himself and his retinue there. The glory of the new city, called Medina Azahara, or Madinat al-Zahra, was short-lived, however. Between 1010 and 1013 Medina Azahara was wrecked by Berber soldiers who occupied it during the caliphate's collapse.

Though less than one-tenth of the city has been excavated, and what's open to visitors is only about a quarter of that, Medina

Azahara is still an intriguing place to visit, and its hillside location in pleasant countryside adds to the appeal. It's open Tuesday to Saturday from 10 am to 2 pm and 6 to 8.30 pm (October to April from 4 to 6.30 pm) and Sunday from 10 am to 2 pm. Entry is free with an EU passport, 250 ptas otherwise.

The visitor route takes you through the north gate of the city to the **Dar al-Wuzara** (House of the Viziers), a substantial building with several horseshoe arches, fronted by a square garden. Down to the east from here is a **Portico**, a row of arches similar to those of the Córdoba Mezquita, which fronted a military parade ground. From here you follow the path downhill, with views over the ruins of a mosque, to the most impressive building, the **Salón de Abd ar-Rahman III**. This was the caliph's throne hall, with beautiful horseshoe arching and carved stone decoration of a lavishness unprecedented in the Islamic world.

Getting There & Away Córdoba Vision (see Organised Tours under Córdoba) runs tours to Medina Azahara twice daily, except Sunday afternoon and Monday, for 2150 ptas. The nearest you can get by bus is the Cruce de Medina Azahara turn-off on the A-341, a 3km walk from the site. City bus No 0-1 from Avenida de la República Argentina will drop you at the Cruce (☎ 957 25 57 04 for schedule information in Spanish).

Driving, take Avenida de Medina Azahara west from the city centre. The Medina Azahara turn-off is signposted some 5km out.

SOUTH OF CÓRDOBA
Towards Málaga
Just east of the N-331 and on the Córdoba-Málaga railway, **Montilla** is the main production centre for Córdoba's sherry-like wines. You can visit Bodegas Alvear (☎ 957 65 01 00), Avenida María Auxiliadora 1 – call for times.

Farther south, **Cabra**, 10km east of the N-331, has a pretty old quarter, the Barrio del Cerro, some handsome old mansions and churches, and an archaeological museum on Calle Martín Belda. Winding roads lead 15km east up to 1217m **El Picacho**, with great panoramas. *Fonda Guerrero (☎ 957 52 05 07, Calle Pepita Jiménez 5)* has doubles with bath for 3800 ptas.

Towards Granada
Beyond the olive-oil-producing town of Baena on the N-432, the mountains of the Sistema Subbética rise up from the campiña. The picturesque mountain villages of **Luque** and **Zuheros** and the town of **Priego de Córdoba**, all south of the N-432, have accommodation and can act as bases for walks in the rugged hills and wooded river valleys of the **Parque Natural Sierra Subbética**. Priego also has a very helpful tourist office (☎ 957 54 09 47) at Carrera de las Monjas 16, a series of gloriously lavish 18th century baroque churches, a very pretty old Muslim quarter, the Barrio de La Villa, and a wonderfully elegant 1780s fountain, the Fuente del Rey.

Granada Province

As well as the world-famous city of Granada, the province includes the highest parts of mainland Spain's highest mountain range, the Sierra Nevada, and, south of the Sierra Nevada, the beautiful, mysterious valleys known as Las Alpujarras.

GRANADA
At first, modern Granada with its traffic-choked main streets and high-rise apartment blocks seems a disappointing world away from its Muslim past. However, the famous Alhambra, dominating the skyline from its hill-top perch, and the fascinating Albayzín, the old Islamic quarter also rising above the modern city, are highlights of a visit to Spain.

The city has more to offer. Its setting, with the backdrop of the often snow-clad Sierra Nevada, is magnificent; its greenness is a delight and the climate pleasant especially in spring and autumn. Granada also has some impressive and historic post-

Reconquista buildings, and, thanks to its university, a vibrant, youthful population, a buzzing cultural life and a hopping nightlife.

A wealthy city of 246,000 people, Granada has an international feel and seems to absorb tourism well except for peak periods inside the Alhambra and the Capilla Real. In tandem with its wealth subsists a whole underclass: you'll see quite a few beggars.

History

The Romans settled in the vicinity of the Alcazaba (part of the Alhambra) and Albayzín. The Visigoths built city walls and laid the foundations of the Alcazaba. Muslim forces, with the help of the city's Jews, took Granada in 711. It was ruled from Córdoba until 1031, and later from Sevilla by the Almoravids and then the Almohads. The Islamic city was called Karnattah, from which 'Granada' is derived; (*granada* also happens to be the Spanish for pomegranate, a fruit which appears on the city's coat of arms).

After the fall of Córdoba (1236) and Sevilla (1248), Muslims sought refuge in Granada, where the founder of the famous Nasrid dynasty, Mohammed ibn Yousouf ibn Nasr (Mohammed al-Ahmar), had recently established an independent emirate. Stretching from the Strait of Gibraltar to east of Almería, this became the final remnant of Al-Andalus, ruled by the Nasrids from the lavish Alhambra palace for 250 years. The Nasrids paid tribute to Castilla until 1476 but also played off Aragón against Castilla and at times sought assistance from the Merenid rulers of Morocco.

Nasrid Granada became one of the richest and most populous cities in medieval Europe, flourishing on the talents of its swelled population of traders and artisans. Two centuries of artistic and scientific splendour peaked under Yousouf I and Mohammed V in the 14th century.

But by the late 15th century the economy had stagnated, the rulers had retreated into a hedonistic existence inside the Alhambra, and violent rivalry had developed over the succession. One faction supported the emir, Abu al-Hasan, and his harem favourite Zoraya. The other faction backed Boabdil, Abu al-Hasan's son by his wife Aixa. In 1482 Boabdil rebelled, setting off a confused civil war. The Christian armies which invaded the emirate the same year took full advantage. The scene had been set for war by the unification of Castilla and Aragón and by Abu al-Hasan's refusal to pay tribute to Castilla from 1476.

The Christians pushed across the emirate, besieging towns and devastating the countryside, and in 1491 they finally laid siege to Granada. After eight months, Boabdil agreed to surrender the city in return for the Alpujarras valleys and 30,000 gold coins, plus political and religious freedom for his subjects. He allowed Castilian troops into the Alhambra on the night of 1-2 January 1492. Next day Isabel and Fernando entered the city ceremonially in Muslim dress. They set up court in the Alhambra for several years.

Religious persecution soon soured the scene. Jews were expelled from Spain soon after the city's conquest, and before long persecution of Muslims led to revolts across the former emirate and finally their expulsion from Spain in the early 17th century. (See History in Facts about Spain and under Las Alpujarras in this chapter).

Having lost much of its talented populace, Granada fell into a decline which was only arrested by the interest drummed up by the romantic movement in the 1830s. This set the stage for the restoration of Granada's Islamic heritage and the arrival of tourism. Many historic buildings were, however, torn down to make way for wide thoroughfares.

Early 20th century Granada frowned on liberalism, leading to the horrors unleashed after the Nationalists took over the city at the start of the civil war in 1936. An estimated 4000 *granadinos* with left or liberal connections were killed, among them Federico García Lorca, Granada's most famous

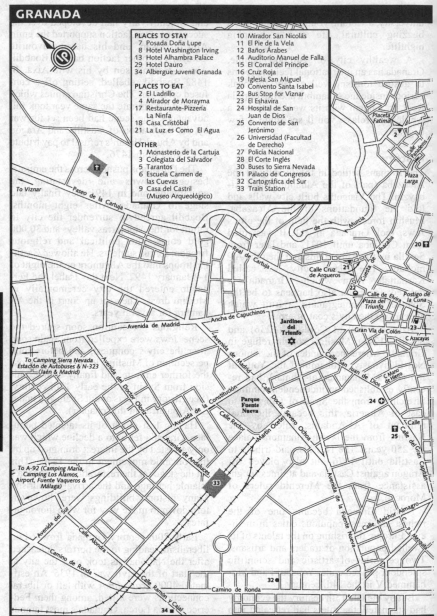

ANDALUCÍA

GRANADA

PLACES TO STAY
7 Posada Doña Lupe
8 Hotel Washington Irving
13 Hotel Alhambra Palace
29 Hotel Dauro
34 Albergue Juvenil Granada

PLACES TO EAT
2 El Ladrillo
4 Mirador de Morayma
17 Restaurante-Pizzería
    La Ninfa
18 Casa Cristóbal
21 La Luz es Como El Agua

OTHER
1 Monasterio de la Cartuja
3 Colegiata del Salvador
5 Tarantos
6 Escuela Carmen de
    las Cuevas
9 Casa del Castril
    (Museo Arqueológico)

10 Mirador San Nicolás
11 El Pie de la Vela
12 Baños Árabes
14 Auditorio Manuel de Falla
15 El Corral del Príncipe
16 Cruz Roja
19 Iglesia San Miguel
20 Convento Santa Isabel
22 Bus Stop for Viznar
23 El Eshavira
24 Hospital de San
    Juan de Dios
25 Convento de San
    Jerónimo
26 Universidad (Facultad
    de Derecho)
27 Policía Nacional
28 El Corte Inglés
30 Buses to Sierra Nevada
31 Palacio de Congresos
32 Cartográfica del Sur
33 Train Station

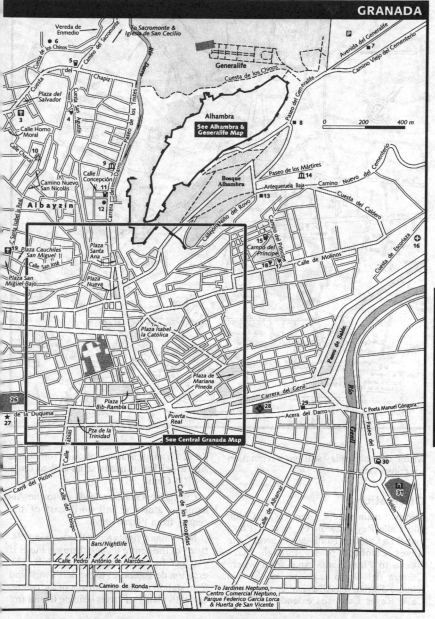

GRANADA

ANDALUCÍA

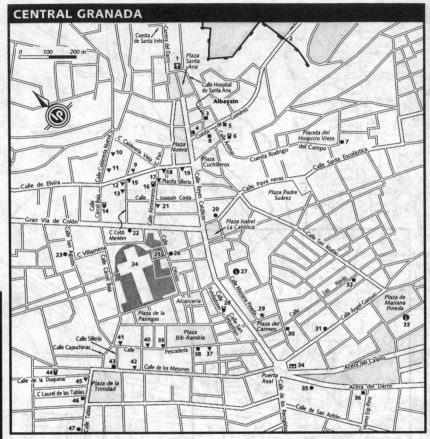

CENTRAL GRANADA

writer. Granada today still has a reputation for conservatism.

Orientation

The two main streets, Gran Vía de Colón and Calle Reyes Católicos, meet at Plaza Isabel La Católica. North-east of here, Calle Reyes Católicos passes through Plaza Nueva to Plaza Santa Ana, from where Carrera del Darro leads up to the old Islamic district, the Albayzín. To the south, Calle Reyes Católicos extends to Puerta

Real, Granada's main plaza. From here, Acera del Darro heads south-east to cross the Río Genil.

Cuesta de Gomérez leads up to the Alhambra, atop the hill north-east of the centre, from Plaza Nueva.

Most major sights are within walking distance of the centre though there are buses if you get fed up with walking uphill. The estación de autobuses to the north-west and train station to the west are out of the centre, but with plenty of buses heading to and fro.

CENTRAL GRANADA

PLACES TO STAY
3 Hostal Vienna
4 Hostal Britz
5 Hostal Gomérez
8 Hostal Austria
30 Hostal-Residencia Lisboa
31 Hostal Fabiola
32 Hotel Dauro II
36 Hotel Montecarlo
38 Hotel Los Tilos
43 Pensión Romero
46 Hostal Zurita

PLACES TO EAT
9 Boabdil
10 El Panadero Loco
11 Naturii Albayzín
12 La Nueva Bodega
13 Café-Bar Nueva Riviera

15 Mesón Andaluz
17 Bodegas Castañeda
18 Antigua Castañeda
19 Café-Bar Al Andalus
21 Jamones Castellano
37 Café Bib-Rambla
39 Pizzeria Gallio
40 Cunini
41 El Cepillo
42 Mesón El Patio
45 Bar-Cervecería Reca

OTHER
1 Iglesia de Santa Ana
2 Puerta de las Granadas
6 Café Aljibe
7 Universidad – Centro de
  Lenguas Modernas
14 Granada 10

16 La Taberna del Irlandés
20 Iberia Office
22 Librería Atlántida
23 Mercado
24 Catedral
25 Capilla Real
26 La Madraza
   (Casa del Cabildo Antiguo)
27 Corral del Carbón;
   Junta de Andalucía Tourist
   Office
28 La Sabanilla
29 Policía Local
33 Provincial Tourist
   Office
34 Main Post Office
35 Librería Continental
44 Pub Librería
47 Librería Urbano

Information

Tourist Offices The helpful, English-speaking provincial tourist office (☎ 958 22 66 88), on Plaza de Maríana Pineda, east of Puerta Real, has plenty of give-away information about Granada and Granada province. It is open Monday to Friday from 9.30 am to 7 pm and Saturday from 10 am to 2 pm. Open the same hours, the Junta de Andalucía's more central tourist office (☎ 958 22 59 90) is in the Corral del Carbón on Calle Maríana Pineda. Staff here are more pressed, and charge for maps and other printed material. Bus and train information is posted outside.

Money There are several banks with ATMs on Gran Vía de Colón, Plaza Isabel La Católica and Calle Reyes Católicos.

Post The main correos (postcode 18080) is at Puerta Real s/n.

Books & Bookshops *Tales of the Alhambra* by Washington Irving makes a great read while on site in Granada. Librería Urbano, Calle Tablas 6, south-west off Plaza de la Trinidad, Librería Continental, Puerta Real, and Librería Atlántida, Gran

Vía de Colón 9, stock books in English. Cartográfica del Sur, Calle Valle Inclán 2, off Camino de Ronda about 1.5km west of the cathedral, is the best map shop in Granada.

Medical & Emergency Services The Policía Local (☎ 092) are at Plaza del Carmen 5. The Policía Nacional (☎ 091) are at Calle de la Duquesa 15. For urgent medical help, the Cruz Roja (☎ 958 22 22 22) is at Cuesta de Escoriaza 8, near Paseo de la Bomba and the Río Genil. The Hospital Universitario de San Juan de Dios (☎ 958 24 11 00) is fairly central at Calle San Juan de Dios 15.

Alhambra & Generalife

Perched on top of La Sabika, the hill which overlooks Granada, this monument is the stuff of fairy tales. It may initially disappoint with its simple, unadorned red fortress towers and walls, though its Sierra Nevada backdrop and the cypresses and elms in which it nestles are undeniably magnificent. Inside the marvellously decorated Palacio Nazaries (Nasrid Palace) and the Generalife (the Alhambra's gardens), you're in for a treat. Water has been used as an art form in both places, and even around the exterior of the Alhambra the sound of running water and the greenness contribute to a sense of calm, a world away from the bustle of the city and the general dryness of much of Spain.

This tranquillity can be completely shattered by the hordes of visitors who traipse through the complex, so try to visit first thing in the morning, late in the afternoon or – a magical experience – at night. (Note that for night visits, only the major rooms of the Palacio Nazaries are open.)

The Alhambra has two main parts, the Alcazaba (Fortress) and the Palacio Nazaries. Also within it are the Palacio de Carlos V, the Iglesia de Santa María de la Alhambra, two hotels, a few restaurants, souvenir shops and refreshment stalls. The Generalife is a short walk east.

History The Alhambra, from the Arabic *al-qala'at al-hamra* (red castle), was a fortress from the 9th century. The Nasrids of the 13th and 14th centuries turned it into a fortress-palace complex adjoined by a small city (medina), of which nothing remains. The founder of the Nasrid dynasty, Mohammed ibn Yousouf ibn Nasr, set up home on the hill top, restoring and expanding the Alcazaba. His 14th century successors, Yousouf I and Mohammed V, built the Palacio Nazaries: Mohammed V was responsible for much of palace's decoration.

In 1492 the Catholic Monarchs moved in after their conquest of Granada, appointing a morisco to restore the decoration of the Palacio Nazaries. In time the palace mosque was replaced with a church, and a convent, the Convento de San Francisco, was built. In the 16th century Carlos I had a wing of the Palacio Nazaries destroyed to make space for a huge Renaissance palace, which is called the Palacio de Carlos V using his title as Holy Roman Emperor.

In the 18th century the Alhambra was abandoned to thieves and beggars, and during the Napoleonic occupation it was used as a barracks and narrowly escaped being blown up. In 1870 it was declared a national monument after the huge interest taken in it by romantic writers such as Washington Irving, who had written his wonderful *Tales of the Alhambra* in his study in some of the palace rooms during his stay in the 1820s. Since then it has been salvaged and heavily restored.

Getting There & Away The Alhambra bus (No 2) from Plaza Nueva (every 35 minutes, every 12 minutes from July to September) heads up to the Alhambra ticket office. The Tren Alhambra (100 ptas), a little road train, runs every 15 minutes between the Alhambra ticket office/car parks and the Palacio de Carlos V.

Walking up Cuesta de Gomérez from Plaza Nueva you soon reach the **Puerta de las Granadas** (Gate of the Pomegranates), a solid gateway with three pomegranates, built by Carlos I. Above the gate are the Bosque Alhambra woods. Here a path to the left rises steeply to the austere **Puerta de la Justicia** (Gate of Justice), constructed by Yousouf I in 1348, originally the main entrance to the Alhambra. From the gate, a passage leads to Plaza de los Aljibes, with a tourist office and the ticket office for night visits to the Palacio Nazaries.

The main ticket office and entrance, and another tourist office, are 800m south-east of the Puerta de la Justicia, outside the Generalife and adjacent to the car parks. On foot, don't head up to the Puerta de la Justicia but continue ahead outside the Alhambra walls.

From April to September, the Alhambra and Generalife are open Monday to Saturday from 9 am to 8 pm and Sunday from 9 am to 6 pm; the Palacio Nazaries is also open Tuesday, Thursday and Saturday from 10 pm to midnight. Hours from October to March are from 9 am to 6 pm daily, with the Palacio Nazaries also open on Saturday from 8 to 10 pm. You can buy your ticket (725 ptas; free for the disabled and children under eight) from 8.30 am until one hour before closing time; 8000 tickets are allotted for each day. It's advisable to go early: at busy times of year (roughly April to early

ALHAMBRA & GENERALIFE

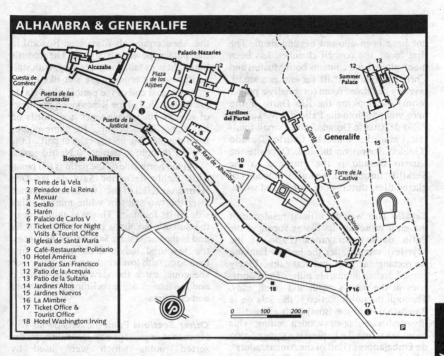

1 Torre de la Vela
2 Peinador de la Reina
3 Mexuar
4 Serallo
5 Harén
6 Palacio de Carlos V
7 Ticket Office for Night
    Visits & Tourist Office
8 Iglesia de Santa María
9 Café-Restaurante Polinario
10 Hotel América
11 Parador San Francisco
12 Patio de la Acequia
13 Patio de la Sultana
14 Jardines Altos
15 Jardines Nuevos
16 La Mimbre
17 Ticket Office &
    Tourist Office
18 Hotel Washington Irving

0   100   200 m

ANDALUCÍA

September) two-hour queues can form and the daily ticket allocation is sometimes sold out a few hours before closing time.

Tickets are stamped with a half-hour time slot in which you must enter the Palacio Nazaries, though you can spend as long as you like in there. From April to September, even if you buy your ticket at 8.30 am, you may have several hours to wait until you can enter the Palacio Nazaries. You can book a time for your visit on ☎ 958 22 09 12 or fax 958 21 05 84 anything from one week to a year ahead.

Ticketing arrangements change occasionally as the authorities strive to cope with the huge numbers of visitors. Ticket sales points in the city centre are planned.

Alcazaba What remains are the ramparts and several towers. The most important and tallest is the **Torre de la Vela** (Watchtower),

with a narrow, winding staircase up to the top terrace, which has splendid views. It was here that the cross and banners of the Reconquista were raised in January 1492. The tower's bell is rung on festive occasions only, but in the past it tolled to control the irrigation system of the Vega, the fertile cultivated plain surrounding Granada.

Palacio Nazaries The Nasrid Palace (also called the Casa Real, Royal House), with its intricately-carved stucco walls, fine knotted wooden ceilings, elaborate honeycomb vaulting and beautifully proportioned rooms and courtyards, stands in marked contrast to the austere walls and towers of the fortress. Arabic inscriptions recur in the stucco work.

Mexuar These rooms through which you normally enter the palace date from the 14th century and were used for bureaucratic and judicial purposes. The general public would not have been allowed beyond them. The first room, the council chamber, has been much altered and contains both Muslim and Christian motifs. At its far end is a small, lavishly decorated room (originally a prayer room) overlooking the Río Darro. From here you pass into the **Patio del Mexuar** or Patio del Cuarto Dorado, with a small fountain, and the mudéjar **Cuarto Dorado** (Golden Room) on the left. Opposite the Cuarto Dorado is the entrance to the Serallo, through a beautiful façade of glazed tiles, stucco work and carved wood.

Serallo This was the official residence of the emir or sultan. Its rooms surround the **Patio de los Arrayanes** (Patio of the Myrtles), named after the hedges flanking its rectangular pool and fountains. Finely carved arches on marble pillars form porticoes at the patio's north and south ends. Through the north portico is the **Sala de la Barca** (Salón of the Boat) with a beautiful inverted-boat-shaped wooden ceiling. This room leads into the impressive square **Salón de Embajadores** (Hall of the Ambassadors), where the emirs conducted their negotiations with Christian emissaries. Its domed cedar ceiling is remarkable, the repeating patterns of the stuccoed and tiled walls mesmerising. The south end of the patio is marred by the gloomy grey walls of the Palacio de Carlos V.

Harén The harem, surrounding the celebrated **Patio de los Leones** with its fountain feeding water through the mouths of 12 stone lions, was built during Mohammed V's reign. The patio's gallery, including the beautiful structures protruding at its east and west ends, is supported by 124 slender marble columns which produce a delicate oriental effect with a hint of a medieval monastery cloister.

Of the four halls bordering the patio, the **Sala de los Abencerrajes** on the south side is legendary for the murders of the noble Abencerraj family, whose head, the story

goes, dared to dally with Zoraya, the harem favourite of Abu al-Hasan. (Historians say the Abencerrajes also favoured Boabdil in the palace power struggle.) The room's highlight is its tall, domed ceiling, with stalactite vaulting producing a star-like effect.

At the east end of the patio is the **Sala de los Reyes** (Hall of the Kings) with paintings of royalty, medieval scenes and motifs on its leather-lined ceiling. Its name comes from the painting on the central part of the ceiling, thought to depict 10 Nasrid emirs.

On the north side of the patio is the beautiful, richly decorated **Sala de las Dos Hermanas** (Hall of the Two Sisters), named after the two slabs of white marble either side of its fountain. This was the room of the sultan's favourite paramour. At its far end is the enchanting **Sala de los Ajimeces**, the favoured lady's dressing room and bedroom, with low windows through which she could catch the view of the Albayzín and mountains while reclining on ottomans and cushions.

Other Sections From the Sala de las Dos Hermanas, a passageway leads through deserted rooms which were used by Washington Irving. The **Peinador de la Reina** (Queen's Dressing Room), the last of these, was a dressing room for Isabel, wife of Carlos I. From here you descend to the **Patio de los Cipreses** (Patio of the Cypresses), off which are the richly decorated **Baños Reales** (Royal Baths), currently closed.

Outside the palace is a group of recent terraced gardens, the **Partal**, bordered by the palace towers and ramparts. From the Partal there is an exit to the Palacio de Carlos V, or you can continue along a path to the Generalife.

Palacio de Carlos V This huge Renaissance palace is the dominant Christian building in the Alhambra. Begun in 1527 by Pedro Machuca, a Toledo architect and painter who studied under Michelangelo, it was never completed. The building is square, but contains a surprising two-tiered circular courtyard with 32 columns. Were the palace in a different setting its merits would be more readily appreciated, but here it seems intrusive.

On the ground floor, the **Museo de la Alhambra** concentrates on the Muslim period with a wonderful collection of artefacts from the Alhambra, Granada province and Córdoba. Its highlight is the tall, elegant, blue, white and gold Alhambra Vase, decorated with gazelles. The museum is open Tuesday to Saturday from 9 am to 2.30 pm (free).

Upstairs, the **Museo de Bellas Artes** has an impressive collection of paintings and sculptures. Most notable are a carved wooden relief of the Virgin and Child by Diego de Siloé, a small enamelled screen of around 1500 that belonged to El Gran Capitán (Gonzalo Fernández de Córdoba), the military right-hand man of Isabel and Fernando, and various pieces by Alonso Cano. Opening hours are Tuesday to Saturday from 10 am to 2 pm (free).

Other Christian Buildings The **Iglesia de Santa María** was built between 1581 and 1617 on the site of the former palace mosque. The **Convento de San Francisco**, now a parador, was erected upon an Islamic palace. Isabel and Fernando were buried in a sepulchre in the parador's patio before being transferred to the Capilla Real. Today, the outdoor terrace bar makes a fine setting for refreshments.

Generalife The name means 'Garden of the Architect'. These palace gardens on the hillside facing the Palacio Nazaries are a beautiful, soothing composition of terraces, patios, fountains, trimmed hedges, tall, long-established trees, especially cypresses, and flowers, in season, of every imaginable hue. The Muslim rulers' summer palace is in the farthest corner. Within it, the **Patio de la Acequia** (Court of the Long Pond) has a long pool framed by flowerbeds and fountains whose shapes sensuously echo the arched porticoes at each end. Off the Patio de la Acequia is the **Patio de la Sultana**, almost as lovely and with the trunk of a 700-year-old cypress tree where Abu al-Hasan supposedly caught his lover, Zoraya, with the chief of the Abencerraj clan, leading to the murders in the Sala de los Abencerrajes of the Palacio Nazaries. Above here are the modern **Jardines Altos** (Upper Gardens), and a stairway with cascading waterfalls. Back towards the entry are the **Jardines Nuevos** (New Gardens). A pleasant alternative route back to town is along Cuesta de los Chinos, which runs down a gully between the Generalife and the Alhambra proper, to the Río Darro.

Capilla Real

The Royal Chapel, on Calle Oficios adjoining the cathedral, is Granada's outstanding Christian building. Built in elaborate Isabelline Gothic style, it was commissioned by the Catholic Monarchs as their mausoleum, but not completed until 1521 – hence their temporary interment in the Convento de San Francisco.

The illustrious monarchs lie in simple lead coffins in the crypt beneath their marble monuments in the chancel, which is enclosed by a stunning gilded wrought-iron screen created in 1520 by Bartolomé de Jaén. The coffins, from left to right, are those of Felipe El Hermoso (husband of the monarchs' daughter Juana la Loca), Fernando, Isabel, Juana la Loca (the Mad) and Miguel, the eldest grandchild of Isabel and Fernando. The carved effigies reclining above the crypt were the idea of Carlos I as a tribute to his parents and grandparents. The representations of Isabel and Fernando are slightly lower than those of Felipe and Juana, apparently because Felipe was the son of the Holy Roman Emperor, Maximilian. The chancel's densely decorated plateresque retablo (1522) is the work of Felipe de Vigarni. Note its kneeling figures of Isabel and Fernando, attributed to Diego de Siloé, and the paintings below depicting the defeat of the Muslims and subsequent conversion to Christianity.

ANDALUCÍA

In the sacristy is a museum with an impressive collection including Isabel's sceptre and silver crown and Fernando's sword. Isabel's personal art collection, mainly Flemish, occupies one room; there's also Botticelli's *Prayer in the Garden of Olives*, and two fine statues of the kneeling monarchs by Vigarni.

The Capilla Real is open Monday to Saturday from 10.30 am to 1 pm and 4 to 7 pm (winter 3.30 to 6.30 pm) and Sunday from 11 am to 1 pm (300 ptas).

Catedral

Adjoining the Capilla Real, the chunky Gothic/Renaissance cathedral, with its cavernous interior, was begun in 1521, and directed by Diego de Siloé from 1528 to 1563. Work was not completed until the 18th century. The main façade on Plaza de las Pasiegas, with its four heavy buttresses and arched doorway, was designed by Alonso Cano. The lavish Puerta del Perdón on the north-west façade has statues carved by Diego de Siloé. Much of the interior is also the work of de Siloé, including the gilded and painted Capilla Mayor where you'll find the Catholic Monarchs at prayer carved by Pedro de Mena – look to each side of the tabernacle above the lovely carved and painted pulpits – and Cano's busts of Adam and Eve.

The Catedral is open for tourist visits Monday to Saturday from 10.30 am to 1 pm and daily from 4 to 7 pm (winter 3.30 to 6.30 pm; 300 ptas). Entry is from Gran Vía de Colón.

Islamic Buildings near the Capilla Real

La Madraza Opposite the Capilla Real remains part of the old Muslim university, La Madraza. The much-altered building, now with a painted baroque façade, retains an octagonal domed prayer room with stucco lacework and pretty tiles. The building is now part of the modern university, but you can take a look at most times during the day.

Corral del Carbón Originally a 14th century *caravanserai* or inn for merchants, this building has also been an inn for coal dealers (hence its modern name, which means Coal Yard) and a theatre. It retains a lovely Islamic façade with an elaborate horseshoe arch, and houses a tourist office and government-run crafts shop. To find it, cross Calle Reyes Católicos from Capilla Real and look for the sign that points down an alley.

Alcaicería Just south-west of the Capilla Real, the Alcaicería was the Muslim silk exchange, but what you see now is a restoration after a 19th century fire, filled with tourist shops. The buildings, separated by narrow alleys, are charming in the light and quiet of early morning.

Albayzín

A wander around the hilly streets and narrow, aged alleys of the Albayzín, Granada's old Muslim quarter, is a must. The Albayzín covers much of the hill that faces the Alhambra across the Darro valley. Its name derives from 1227 when Muslims from Baeza populated the district after their city was conquered by the Christians. For a few decades after the Reconquista it survived as the city's Muslim quarter. Muslim ramparts, cisterns, gates, fountains and houses remain, and many of the Albayzín's churches and *cármenes* (large walled villas with gardens) stand on the sites of, or incorporate parts of, Islamic buildings.

Carrera del Darro One way to approach the Albayzín is up Carrera del Darro from Plaza Nueva. On Plaza Santa Ana is the **Iglesia de Santa Ana**, which incorporates a former mosque's minaret in its bell tower, as do several churches in the Albayzín. Stop by at Carrera del Darro 31 to see the remains of the 11th century **Baños Árabes** (Muslim baths), which are open Tuesday to Saturday from 10 am to 2 pm (free). Entry is through a pretty patio complete with plants, birds in cages and a pond.

within 14 days.

For any return you may be asked for acceptable identification.

Items purchased at Walgreens may be returned to any of our stores within 30 days of purchase.

Items with a receipt will be exchanged, refunded in cash or credited to your account.

Items without a receipt, will be exchanged or refunded by mail within 14 days.

For any return you may be asked for acceptable identification.

Items purchased at Walgreens may be returned to any of our stores within 30 days of purchase.

Items with a receipt will be exchanged, refunded in cash or credited to your account.

Items without a receipt, will be exchanged or refunded by mail within 14 days.

For any return you may be

Camino del Rey, El Chorro Gorge (Andalucía)

Cascada de Linarejos, Parque Natural de Cazorla

The Embalse del Tranco de Beas, Parque Natural de Cazorla, in autumn (Andalucía)

Spring colours near Ronda (Andalucía)

At Carrera del Darro 43 is the Renaissance Casa del Castril, home to the **Museo Arqueológico**, with some interesting finds from Granada province. Upstairs, the Islamic room has some lovely *azulejos*, carved wood and fine ceramics. It's open Tuesday to Sunday from 10 am to 2 pm (250 ptas, free with an EU passport).

Paseo de los Tristes Shortly after the museum, Carrera del Darro becomes Paseo de los Tristes (also called Paseo del Padre Manjón), with a number of cafés and restaurants with outdoor tables, and a dramatic view of the Alhambra's fortifications directly above.

Upper Albayzín From the top end of Paseo de los Tristes, Cuesta del Chapiz heads north, uphill, then curves west into Plaza del Salvador, where the **Colegiata del Salvador**, a 16th century church, still contains the Islamic courtyard of the mosque it replaced; it's open daily from 10 am to 1 pm and 4 to 7 pm (100 ptas). From here Calle Panaderos leads to **Plaza Larga**, with an Islamic gateway at the top end of the Albayzín's surviving Muslim ramparts, and lively bars offering cheap *menús*. From Calle Panaderos, Calle Horno Moral and Calle Charca lead to the **Mirador San Nicolás**, which has fantastic views of the Alhambra and Sierra Nevada.

Descent from Mirador San Nicolás Descending from the mirador along Camino Nuevo San Nicolás, which becomes Calle Santa Isabel la Real, you pass the **Convento Santa Isabel**, a former Islamic palace. Its church, ostensibly open daily from 10 am to 6 pm, has a mudéjar ceiling. Nearby is **Plaza de San Miguel Bajo**, where the **Iglesia San Miguel** occupies the site of a former mosque. To wend your way back to the centre, follow Plaza Cauchiles San Miguel and then Calle San José. Calle San José ends near the top end of picturesque **Calle Calderería Nueva**, a stone's throw from Plaza Nueva. Alternatively, enjoy getting lost – but not too late at night.

Sacromonte

Camino del Sacromonte leads from Cuesta del Chapiz up Sacromonte hill to the **Iglesia de San Cecilio**, passing caves dug into the hillside which have been occupied by gitanos since the 18th century.

Plaza Bib-Rambla, Plaza de la Trinidad & Around

Just south-west of the Alcaicería is the large, pleasant **Plaza Bib-Rambla**, with restaurants, flower stalls and a central fountain with statues of giants at its base. This was the scene of Inquisition lashings and burnings, jousting and bullfights. Today buskers, mime artists and street sellers provide more gentle entertainment.

A block south-west is pedestrianised Calle de los Mesones with modern shops. At its north-west end is leafy **Plaza de la Trinidad**, from which Calle de la Duquesa leads past the university founded by Carlos I (now the Law Faculty, with the main campus out of the centre to the north) to the 16th century **Convento de San Jerónimo** on Calle del Gran Capitán. This features more work by the talented Diego de Siloé, including the larger of the convent's two cloisters and much of the attached church. Either side of the church's altar are statues of El Gran Capitán and his wife María; El Gran Capitán is reputedly buried beneath the altar. The convent is open daily from 10 am to 1.30 pm and 4 to 7 pm (in winter from 3.30 to 6 pm) (300 ptas).

Monasterio de La Cartuja

The impressive, ornate La Cartuja Monastery is a 20 minute walk north of the Convento de San Jerónimo (or take bus No 8 from Gran Vía de Colón). The monastery, with an imposing sand-coloured stone exterior, was built between the 16th and 18th centuries. Its baroque interior oozes wealth, especially the astonishingly lavish sacristy, decorated in brown and white marble and stucco, and the adjacent sanctuary (*sanctum*

ANDALUCÍA

sanctorum), a riot of colour and patterns with its twisted marble columns, loads of statues, paintings, gilt and beautiful frescoed cupola. The monastery is open daily from 10 am to 1 pm (Sunday to noon) and 4 to 8 pm (in winter from 3.30 to 6 pm) (300 ptas).

Huerta de San Vicente

This house where Federico García Lorca spent summers and wrote some of his well-known works is a 15 minute walk from the centre and was once surrounded by orchards. Today the new Parque Federico García Lorca separates it from whizzing traffic in an attempt to recreate the tranquil rural environment that inspired Lorca. The house contains some original furnishings including Lorca's desk and piano, some of his drawings and other memorabilia, and exhibitions connected with his life and work. To find it, head down Calle de las Recogidas from Puerta Real and cross Camino de Ronda. A block farther on is Calle del Arabial, and the park is just along it to the right.

It's open Tuesday to Sunday from 10 am to 1 pm and 5 to 8 pm (in winter from 4 to 7 pm), with guided tours (300 ptas) in Spanish on the hour. See Around Granada for more Lorca sites.

Courses

With the city's attractions and youthful population, Granada makes a good place to study Spanish. The university offers a variety of intensive programs with a four week course priced at 58,000 ptas; contact Universidad de Granada, Centro de Lenguas Modernas, Cursos Para Extranjeros, Placeta del Hospicio Viejo s/n (Realejo), 18071 Granada (☎ 958 22 07 90, fax 958 22 08 44). There are many other language schools. Escuela Carmen de las Cuevas (☎ 958 22 10 62, fax 958 22 04 76, info@carmencuevas.com), Cuesta de los Chinos 15 in the Albayzín, caters for all levels of Spanish language, and offers courses in history, culture, flamenco dance,

guitar and song, but it's pricier than the university.

Organised Tours

Grana Vision (☎ 958 13 58 04) does guided tours of the Alhambra and Generalife (3700 ptas), Granada Histórica tours (3900 ptas), flamenco shows (3800 ptas) and excursions farther afield. Phone direct or book through any travel agent.

Special Events

Semana Santa and the Corpus Christi feria nine weeks later are the big two. Benches are set up in Plaza del Carmen for viewing the Semana Santa processions. At Corpus Christi, fairgrounds, drinking and dancing sevillanas are the go.

Around 3 May, the Día de la Cruz (Day of the Cross), squares, patios and balconies are adorned with crosses (the 'Cruces de Mayo') made of flowers. Horse riders, polka-dot dresses and sevillana dancing add to the colour. The Festival Internacional de Música y Danza in late June/early July features open-air performances (some free) in historic sites.

Places to Stay

There should be no problem finding a room in Granada except during Semana Santa. Unless stated otherwise, expect to pay more than the prices given during Semana Santa, July and August.

Places to Stay – Budget

Camping There are several camp sites within about 5km of Granada, all accessible by bus. All charge around 500 ptas per adult, per tent and per vehicle. Closest and biggest, though closed from November to February, is *Camping Sierra Nevada* (☎ 958 15 00 62, Avenida de Madrid 107) 3km north-west of the centre and 200m along the road from the estación de autobuses. There are big, clean bathrooms, a pool and a laundry. From the city centre take bus No 3 from Gran Vía de Colón.

Two camp sites in the Vega en route to Santa Fe are *Camping María Eugenia*

(☎ 958 20 06 06) on the A-92, at Km 286 and *Los Álamos* (☎ 958 20 84 79) on the A-92, at Km 290.

Youth Hostel The Inturjoven *Albergue Juvenil Granada* (☎ 958 27 26 38, *Calle Ramón y Cajal 2*) is just off Camino de Ronda, 1.7km west of the centre and a 600m walk south-west of the train station. It's a large, modern building with 60 double rooms, and a pool. For prices, see the introductory Youth Hostels section in this chapter. From the bus station, you can take bus No 3 to the centre then pick up bus No 11 outside the cathedral: it runs a circular route and will drop you at the hostel.

Hostales & Pensiones Cheap hostales are mainly located near Plaza Nueva, around Plaza de la Trinidad and near Plaza del Carmen. One exception, handy for the Alhambra, is *Posada Doña Lupe* (☎ 958 22 14 73, *Avenida del Generalife s/n*), with more than 40 rooms. English is spoken and there's a small pool on a large roof-terrace. Clean, interior singles/doubles/triples with bathroom cost 1000/1950/2952 ptas, or 700 ptas per bed with your own bedding. Better doubles are 3900 and 4950 ptas. All prices include a light breakfast. The Alhambra Bus from Plaza Nueva stops outside.

Near Plaza Nueva There's plenty of choice on Cuesta de Gomérez, running from Plaza Nueva up to the Alhambra. The friendly *Hostal Britz* (☎ 958 22 36 52) at No 1 has clean, adequate singles/doubles for 2300/3500 ptas, or 3600/5000 ptas with bath. *Hostal Gomérez* (☎ 958 22 44 37) at No 10, with a lively, multi-lingual owner, has nine well-kept rooms at 1500/2500 ptas. *Hostal Vienna* (☎ 958 22 18 59, *Calle Hospital de Santa Ana 2*), just off Cuesta de Gomérez, is a popular choice. Singles/doubles/triples, some with bath, cost 1500/3000/4000 ptas. English and German are spoken. The same people run *Hostal Austria* (☎ 958 22 70 75, *Cuesta de Gomérez 4*), where all rooms have attached bath and cost a little more.

Near Puerta Real & Plaza del Carmen
Hostal Fabiola (☎ 958 22 35 72, *Calle Ángel Ganivet 5, 3rd floor*) is a friendly, family-run place. The 19 good rooms, some with balcony and all with private bathroom, cost 1800/3500/5000 ptas for singles/doubles/triples. Two blocks north, the friendly *Hostal-Residencia Lisboa* (☎ 958 22 14 13, *Plaza del Carmen 27*) has singles/doubles for 3300/4700 ptas with bath, less without.

Near Plaza de la Trinidad Some of the many hostales in this area are full up with university students in term-time. The following should have rooms year-round. The good, family-run *Pensión Romero* (☎ 958 26 60 79, *Calle Sillería 1*), on the corner of Calle Los Mesónes, opposite Plaza de la Trinidad, has singles/doubles for 1500/2700 ptas, some with balconies. *Hostal Zurita* (☎ 958 27 50 20, *Plaza de la Trinidad 7*), has good-value rooms for 1875/3750 ptas, and doubles for 4500 ptas with bathroom.

Places to Stay – Mid-Range
Many of the middle-range hotels are on or near busy Acera del Darro. Others are in the Alhambra vicinity. Add IVA to all prices given here.

Hotel Montecarlo (☎ 958 25 79 00, *Acera del Darro 44*) has good singles/doubles with all mod cons for 4700/6800 ptas. *Hotel Los Tilos* (☎ 958 26 67 12, *Plaza Bib-Rambla 4*) costs 4700/7000 ptas. Up the scale a bit, *Hotel Dauro* (☎ 958 22 21 55, *Acera del Darro 19*) and *Hotel Dauro II* (☎ 958 22 15 81, *Calle de Las Navás 5*) both charge 8000/11,500 ptas.

Rooms at *Hotel América* (☎ 958 22 74 71, *Real da Alhambra 53*), within the Alhambra grounds but only open from March to October, cost 6,500/11,000 ptas. Reserve well in advance as there are only 13 rooms. *Hotel Washington Irving* (☎ 958 22 75 50, *Paseo del Generalife 2*), near the Bosque Alhambra, has been around since last century. Rooms are 8000/10,500 ptas.

ANDALUCÍA

Places to Stay – Top End

Again, add IVA. *Parador San Francisco* (☎ 958 22 14 40, Real de Alhambra s/n) is the top hotel in Granada. The converted monastery can't be beaten for its location within the Alhambra and its historical connections. Singles/doubles cost 26,400/ 33,000 ptas. Book well ahead. The distinctive neo-Islamic *Hotel Alhambra Palace* (☎ 958 22 14 68, Peña Partida 2), close to the Alhambra, has wonderful views over the city. Rooms are 16,000/20,500 ptas.

Places to Eat

For fresh fruit and vegetables, the produce *mercado* spills down Calle San Agustín a block west of the cathedral. A new covered market is being built here. Basic groceries can be bought at *Jamónes Castellano* on the corner of Calle Almireceros and Calle Joaquín Costa. *El Panadero Loco (Calle Calderería Nueva 14)* stocks good wholemeal bread and cakes (closed on Sunday).

Granadino cuisine uses seafood and tropical fruits from the nearby coast and the meats and sausages of the interior. A hint of the Muslim past is evident in seasonings and desserts. Rabo de toro (oxtail stew) and *habas con jamón* (broad beans with ham) are platos típicos. A tortilla Sacromonte is an omelette combining jamón, prawns or oysters, greens and offal. Bar flies will be pleased to find that tapas are often free at night.

Plaza Nueva & Around *La Nueva Bodega (Calle Cetti Meriém 3)* and *Café/Bar Nueva Riviera* next door have similar fare and prices, with *menús* starting at 850 ptas, and options for vegetarians. Roquefort salad (550 ptas), excellent spinach soup (425 ptas), bacalao, and trout with mushrooms enliven the *menús*. Across the road on the corner of Calle de Elvira, *Mesón Andaluz* is more expensive with mains around 1300 ptas and *menús* from 1250 ptas, all plus IVA. Round the corner on Calle de Elvira, *Boabdil* has reasonable food with *menús* from 725 ptas. A line of

blackboards out the front display the options.

On Plaza Nueva, *Café/Bar Al-Andalus* has good, cheap Arabic food to take away, or consume at the few tables inside or on the plaza. Tasty felafel in pitta bread costs 275 ptas, kebabs or hummus 350 ptas, and spicy meat mains are 800 ptas.

Classy food in a típico setting can be had at *Bodegas Castañeda* (an institution among locals and tourists alike) and *Antigua Castañeda*, back to back on Calle Almireceros and Calle de Elvira. Both have barrels of Alpujarras wine and offer delicious, beautifully presented food. Try the *montaditos* (250 ptas), slices of bread with toppings such as smoked salmon with a touch of caviar. More elaborate meals cost around 1700 ptas.

Alhambra Even the kiosks inside the Alhambra complex charge marked-up prices. *Café-Restaurante Polinario*, opposite the Iglesia de Santa María, has a buffet lunch at 1500 ptas plus IVA, and *bocadillos*. *Parador San Francisco* has a pricey restaurant and a slightly more affordable terrace bar out the back with a lovely view, open daily from 11 am to 11 pm.

La Mimbre on the corner of Avenida del Generalife and Cuesta de los Chinos has outdoor tables in a leafy garden under the Alhambra walls. It specialises in granadino fare, with main dishes from 950 ptas and a 1500 ptas *menú*.

Albayzín A couple of blocks from Plaza Nueva, atmospheric Calle Calderería Nueva has several restaurants, *teterías* (Arabic-style tea shops), health-food shops and takeaway food places. The cosy, intimate *Naturii Albayzín (Calle Calderería Nueva 10)* has an interesting veggie *menú* with an Arabic twist. No alcohol is served. Hunks of delicious wholemeal bread accompany the *menú* (950 or 1150 ptas, plus IVA). Mains (try the couscous) are 750 to 900 ptas, plus IVA.

Near the top of the Albayzín, Plaza Larga and nearby Calle Panaderos have lively café-bars with cheap *menús* around 750 ptas. A couple of blocks north, *El Ladrillo* on Placeta Fátima spills out into the street in fine weather. It's a popular seafood place open for lunch and dinner. Big platters of seafood called *barcos* go for 1200 ptas. For a splash-out, try the highly regarded *Mirador de Morayma (Calle Pianista Carrillo 2)*, off Cuesta San Agustín on the west side of Cuesta del Chapiz. It occupies a lovely *carmen*.

On the south-west edge of the Albayzín, Plaza San Miguel Bajo has a couple of lively bars with meals and tapas, popular with students. Down from here, close to Plaza del Triunfo, *La Luz es Como el Agua (Cruz de Arqueros 3)* is a small restaurant serving up good, cheap pastas and salads nightly from Wednesday to Saturday, plus Sunday afternoon.

Plaza Bib-Rambla & Around *Café Bib-Rambla* is great for breakfast. Coffee and toast with butter and excellent marmalade cost 400 ptas at its outside tables. *Pizzeria Gallio (Plaza Bib-Rambla 10)* does tasty Italian food. Try pizza Florentina, with spinach and béchamel sauce (785 ptas plus IVA). Drinks are expensive. A little west on Calle Pescadería is *Cunini*, an expensive seafood restaurant with tables outside – prices are lower inside at the bar. A few doors away is *El Cepillo*, a popular cheaper seafood restaurant with *menús* at 775 ptas (closed on Sunday).

Plaza de la Trinidad & Around *Bar-Cervecería Reca* on the plaza is full to overflowing at peak times due to its tasty free tapas. Raciones are 500 to 1000 ptas. *Mesón El Patio (Calle de Los Mesónes 50)* is a medium-priced restaurant with the usual Spanish-granadino mix of food, and a pleasant patio.

Campo del Príncipe South of the Alhambra is Campo del Príncipe, another area that buzzes at night. Of its several restaurants, *Casa Cristóbal* has *menús* from 850 ptas and does wonderful sangría. *Restau-rante-Pizzería La Ninfa* at No 14 is an excellent Italian place.

Entertainment

Guía del Ocio, available at kiosks at the beginning of each month, and the daily newspaper *Ideal* have what's-on listings.

Bars, Live Music & Discos Granada is reputed to have a sedate nightlife, but you can as easily dance the night away here as in most places in Spain. Watch for posters advertising live music and non-touristy flamenco.

Around Plaza Nueva The streets just west of Plaza Nueva are lively on weekend nights. *Bodega Castañeda* and *Antigua Castañeda* (see Places to Eat), with free tapas, make a good start to the evening. Nearby, there are popular bars with good music on Placita Sillería and Calle Joaquín Costa, while *La Taberna del Irlandés* on Calle Almireceros offers Tetley's Bitter, Guinness and Fosters as well as Spanish tipples. *Granada 10* disco on Calle Cárcel Baja has varied dance music. It is open at about midnight and gets going at about 2 am. Don't look too scruffy. Cover is 1000 ptas including a *copa*; subsequent drinks are expensive.

Café Aljibe (Calle Ánimas 7), just above Plaza Cuchilleros on the south side of Plaza Nueva is great for late live music, though this is only sporadic. *La Sabinilla (Calle San Sebastián 14)*, near the Alcaicería, is Granada's oldest bar and, though showing its age, is still worth a visit.

Elsewhere Don't miss *El Eshavira (Postigo de la Cuna 2)*, a basement jazz and flamenco club down a dark alley towards the north end of Calle de Elvira. It's open nightly, with live music several nights a week.

El Pie de la Vela, on Carrera del Darro near Calle Concepción, is another popular bar. There are more places to check out farther up on Paseo de los Tristes.

Pub Librería (Calle de la Duquesa 8), near Plaza de la Trinidad, celebrates the blues. The music (free) starts at about 11 pm on Thursday and Friday.

From about 11 pm at weekends, you can't miss the crowds heading for Calle Pedro Antonio de Alarcón, a kilometre or so south-west of the centre, where a string of disco-bars offer cheap deals on drinks with tapas thrown in.

Some of the Sacromonte caves turn into discos during university terms.

Flamenco It's difficult to see flamenco that's not geared to tourists, but some shows are more authentic than others and attract Spaniards as well as foreigners. These include the almost-nightly ones (summer only) at *El Corral del Príncipe* on Campo del Príncipe (4000 ptas), and the Friday and Saturday midnight shows at *Tarantos (Camino del Sacromonte 9)* (3500 ptas). Tarantos' 10 pm shows attract more foreigners. *Jardines Neptuno* on Calle del Arabial has a tourist-oriented flamenco performance at 10.15 pm daily (3500 ptas).

For all of these places you can book at the venues or through hotels and travel agents. Some travellers go to the Sacromonte caves to see impromptu flamenco but it is extremely touristy and a bit of a rip-off.

Other Entertainment The notice board in the foyer of La Madraza, on Calle Oficios, has large posters listing forthcoming cultural events. *Auditorio Manuel de Falla (Paseo de los Mártires s/n)*, near the Alhambra, is the venue for orchestral concerts a couple of nights weekly from around 9 pm.

Shopping

A distinctive local craft is marquetry *(taracea)*, used on boxes, tables, chess sets and more – the best has shell, silver or mother-of-pearl inlays. Other granadino crafts include embossed leather, guitars, wrought iron, brass and copperware, basket-weaving, textiles and, of course, pottery. Places to look include the Al-caicería, the Albayzín and Cuesta de Gomérez. Watch marquetry experts at work in the shop opposite the Iglesia de Santa María in the Alhambra, and in a shop on Cuesta de Gomérez. There are also a couple of guitar-makers on Cuesta de Gomérez.

Getting There & Away

Air Iberia (☎ 958 22 75 92) at Plaza Isabel La Católica 2 flies daily to/from Madrid and Barcelona. Air Europa (☎ 902 24 00 42) has daily flights (except Saturday) to/from Barcelona. You can buy tickets at Halcón Viajes, Calle de los Recogidas 2.

Bus Granada's estación de autobuses is at Carretera de Jáen s/n, the continuation of Avenida de Madrid, 3km north-west of the centre. All services operate from here except a few to nearby destinations such as Fuente Vaqueros, Viznar and the Estación de Esquí Sierra Nevada (for these, see the relevant sections in this chapter). Alsina Graells (☎ 958 18 50 10) runs to Córdoba (eight daily; 3½ hours; 1735 ptas), Sevilla (nine daily; four hours; 2710 ptas), Málaga (14 daily; 2½ hours; 1165 ptas), Las Alpujarras (see the Las Alpujarras section for details), Jaén, Baeza, Úbeda, Cazorla, Almuñécar and Nerja. There are at least nine buses daily to Madrid (six hours; 1945 ptas). Bacoma (☎ 958 15 75 57) has daily services to Alicante, Valencia, Barcelona and Madrid (four daily). Buses to Guadix, Almería (3½ hours) and Mojácar are run by Autedia (☎ 958 15 36 36).

Train The station (☎ 958 27 12 72) is 1.5km west of the centre on Avenida de Andaluces, off Avenida de la Constitución.

Three trains daily run to/from Antequera (1¾ hours) and Sevilla (four hours; 2280 ptas), and to/from Almería (2¾ hours; 1550 ptas) via Guadix. For Málaga (1520 to 2600 ptas) and Córdoba (1900 to 2400 ptas), both four hours, there are two or three trains daily, all involving a change at Bobadilla. For Linares-Baeza there are at least four trains daily.

To Madrid there's a daily Talgo at 3.40 pm (six hours; 3200 ptas) and a night train (9½ hours; 3000 ptas). One train daily goes to Valencia and Barcelona.

Getting Around

The Airport The airport (☎ 958 44 64 11) is 17km west of the centre on the A-92. Five airport buses (☎ 958 13 13 09) daily except Saturday leave from Plaza Isabel La Católica. A taxi will set you back 2500 ptas.

Bus City buses cost 125 ptas. The tourist offices have a handy map showing all routes. Bus No 3 runs from the bus station to the centre. You may have to wait up to 20 minutes. Get off at the Catedral stop – you can't see the cathedral itself from the bus. To reach the centre from the train station, walk straight ahead to Avenida de la Constitución and pick up bus No 3 or 11 going to the right (south-east).

Taxi Taxis line up on Plaza Nueva. Most fares within the city are 400 to 600 ptas.

AROUND GRANADA

Granada is surrounded by a fertile plain known as La Vega, planted with poplar groves and crops ranging from potatoes and maize to melons and tobacco. The Vega has always been vital to the city and was an inspiration to Federico García Lorca, who was born and, as fate had it, killed here.

Fuente Vaqueros

The house where Lorca was born in 1898, in this village 17km west of Granada, is now the **Casa Museo Federico García Lorca**. The place really makes his spirit come alive, with numerous charming photos, posters and costumes for plays that he wrote and directed, and paintings illustrating some of his poems. A short video at the end of the visit captures him in action with the touring Teatro Barraca.

The museum is open for guided tours in Spanish Tuesday to Sunday, hourly from 10 am to 1 pm and 4 to 6 pm (6 to 8 pm from July to September) (200 ptas). To get there

take an Ureña bus from outside Granada train station. In summer from Monday to Friday, these depart almost hourly from 9 am to 9 pm; on weekends it's every two hours. There are fewer buses in winter. There's a timetable at the roundabout in the village centre.

Viznar

To follow the Lorca trail to the bitter end you have to make your way out to this village 8km north-east of the city. When the civil war broke out and the Nationalists took over Granada in 1936, Lorca was arrested and taken with hundreds of others to Viznar to be shot. Outside the village, on the road to Alfacar, is the **Parque Lorca**, with a granite block marking the spot where he is believed to have been killed. His body has never been found.

The Inturjoven *Albergue Juvenil Viznar* *(☎ 958 54 33 07, Camino de la Fuente Grande s/n)* is a good, modern youth hostel accommodating 111, with a pool. For prices see this chapter's introductory Youth Hostels section. Buses to Viznar leave Plaza del Triunfo Monday to Friday at 12.30, 2.45 and 8 pm, returning from Viznar at 7.45 am, 12.30 and 4 pm. On Saturday there's one bus at 1.30 pm from Granada and 8.30 am from Viznar. There are no buses on Sunday. Call ☎ 958 15 12 49 for information.

ALHAMA DE GRANADA

This picturesque ancient spa town, on a back-country route to the Málaga area, stands at the top of a ravine 53km from Granada. There's a tourist office (☎ 958 36 06 86) on Calle Vendederas, uphill east of the central Plaza de la Constitución.

Things to See & Do

The centre is of Muslim origin, with narrow zigzagging streets. Close to the gorge's edge is the pretty, 16th century **Iglesia del Carmen**, with some fine stone carving. The **Iglesia de la Encarnación** on Plaza de los Presos was a gift from the Catholic Monarchs, whose conquest of Alhama in 1482 was a key step in their war against Granada.

ANDALUCIA

There's a **Roman bridge** about 1km below the town, near the modern bridge on the Granada road.

Beside the latter bridge is the turning to the **balneario** (spa), 1km away. The warm springs here have been channelled into baths since Roman times, and daily at around 12.30 pm during the spa's season (10 June to 10 October) you can visit the Muslim bathhouse inside the Hotel Balneario (100 ptas). In the park in front of the hotel is an open-air pool with lovely hot waters, open daily in the season from 11 am to 2 pm and 4.30 to 7.30 pm (500 ptas; tickets from the hotel).

Places to Stay

Hostal San José (☎ 958 35 01 56, Plaza de la Constitución 27) has reasonable rooms from 2800 to 3500 ptas plus IVA a double. At the balneario, *Hotel Baño Nuevo (☎ 958 35 00 11)* has doubles for 4700 ptas plus IVA, while *Hotel Balneario (same ☎)* charges 8900 ptas plus IVA. Both open from 10 June to 10 October.

Getting There & Away

Alsina Graells runs three daily buses (two on Saturday, one on Sunday) to/from Granada and one to/from Málaga via Torre del Mar.

GUADIX

The A-92 north-east from Granada starts off through forested, mountainous country before entering an arid, almost lunar landscape. The rather shabby town of Guadix, 55km from Granada, is famous for its cave dwellings – not prehistoric remnants but modern-day homes of the ordinary townsfolk, nearly half of whom inhabit Guadix's cave quarter, the Ermita Nueva or Barrio de Santiago. There's a tourist office (☎ 958 66 26 65) at Carretera de Granada s/n.

Things to See

Your average modern cave home has a whitewashed wall across the front and a chimney – often with TV aerial attached –

sticking out the top. Some have many rooms and all mod cons. The **Cueva Museo** on Plaza de Ermita Nueva recreates typical cave life and is open Monday to Friday from 10 am to 2 pm and 4 to 6 pm, and Saturday from 10 am to 2 pm.

Guadix has an interesting 16th century sandstone **catedral** designed by Diego de Siloé. It's open Monday to Saturday from 11 am to 1 pm and 4.30 to 7 pm and Sunday from 10.30 am to 2 pm. Also have a look at the remains of the Muslim fort, the **Alcazaba**, with views over the Ermita Nueva; it's open daily except Sunday (and Saturday afternoon) from 9.30 am to 1.30 pm and 3.30 to 6.30 pm.

Places to Stay

Cuevas Pedro Antonio de Alarcón (☎ 958 66 49 86), a modern cave hotel in Barrio San Torcuato about 1km from the centre, has comfortable modern grottoes at 6000/7600 ptas plus IVA for singles/doubles – plus a pool and a good restaurant.

Doubles with bath are 5500 ptas plus IVA in the good central *Hotel Comercio (☎ 958 66 05 00, Calle Mira de Amezcua 3)*.

Getting There & Away

Guadix is about 1½ hours from both Granada and Almería by several daily buses or three daily trains.

SIERRA NEVADA

The Sierra Nevada, which includes mainland Spain's highest peak, Mulhacén (3478m), forms an almost year-round snowy backdrop to Granada. The range extends about 75km from west to east, extending into Almería province. All its highest peaks (3000m or more) are towards the Granada end. The range's upper reaches are home to about 60 endemic plant species. Nearly half the 1710 sq km Parque Natural Sierra Nevada, which covers most of the range, is being upgraded to Parque Nacional. The Centro de Visitantes El Dornajo (☎ 958 34 06 25), on the A-395 about 10km before the Estación de Esquí Sierra Nevada,

WESTERN SIERRA NEVADA & LAS ALPUJARRAS

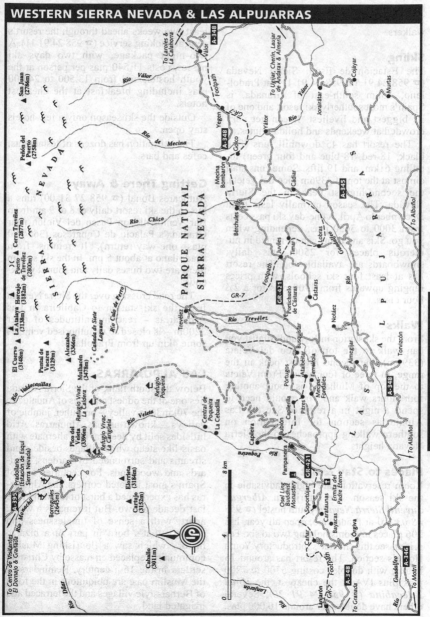

ANDALUCÍA

has plenty of information on the Sierra Nevada, including on mountain *refugios* for walkers.

Skiing

The Estación de Esquí Sierra Nevada (☎ 958 24 91 19, 958 24 91 11), at Pradollano, 33km south-east of Granada, is Spain's most southerly ski resort and one of its biggest and liveliest. It can get very crowded at weekends and holiday times.

The resort has 45 downhill runs (five black, 18 red, 18 blue and four green) totalling 61km, and 19 lifts. Some runs start almost at the top of 3396m Pico del Veleta, the second-highest peak in the Sierra Nevada. The season normally lasts from December to April. A one-day ski pass costs from 3000 to 3650 ptas, depending when you go. Skis and boots can be rented in numerous places for 2500 ptas daily; snowboards are available too. The resort has at least four ski schools, with prices ranging upwards from 1700 ptas for a 2½ hour class.

Walks

From the ski station in July and August you can walk to the top of Pico del Veleta (3396m), the second highest peak in the range, in three or four hours. From Veleta to the top of Mulhacén is about another four hours walk and you would need to spend a night in a refugio. See the Las Alpujarras section for information on southern walking approaches to the Sierra Nevada heights.

Places to Stay & Eat

Room reservations are highly advisable in the ski season. The Inturjoven *Albergue Juvenil Sierra Nevada* youth hostel *(☎ 958 48 03 05)* at Pradollano, open all year, has 206 places in rooms holding two to six. For prices, see this chapter's introductory Youth Hostels section. The resort has around 15 hotels, with doubles costing 5700 to 7200 ptas plus IVA at the cheapest, the *Hotel Telecabina (☎ 958 24 91 20)*. Several others have doubles for around 10,000 ptas.

If you're here to ski, the best deals are packages, which you should try to book at least two weeks ahead through the resort's central booking service (☎ 958 24 91 11). A two-night package, with two days ski passes, costs 11,540 ptas per person at the youth hostel, and from 13,500 to 24,000 ptas including breakfast at the cheapest hotels.

Outside the ski season only a few hotels stay open.

The ski station has dozens of restaurants, cafés and bars.

Getting There & Away

Autocares Bonal (☎ 958 27 31 00) runs a bus to the ski resort daily at 8 or 9 am from Bar Ventorrillo on Paseo del Violón near Granada's Palacio de Congresos (365/700 ptas one-way/return). It returns from Pradollano at about 5 pm. In the ski season there are two buses daily and four at weekends.

The road crossing over the Sierra Nevada from the ski station to Capileira in Las Alpujarras – reaching altitudes of over 3200m – is closed to unauthorised vehicles some 4km up from Pradollano.

LAS ALPUJARRAS

Below the south flank of the Sierra Nevada lies one of the oddest crannies of Andalucía, the 70km long valley – or, rather, jumble of valleys – known as Las Alpujarras. Arid hillsides split by deep ravines alternate with oasis-like steep white villages beside rapid streams and surrounded by gardens, orchards and woodlands. For centuries one of Spain's most isolated corners, the Alpujarras has experienced a burst of tourism in the last decade or two. But it remains a world apart, with a sense of timelessness and mystery that's born in part of a bizarre history which saw a flourishing Muslim community replaced en masse by Christian settlers in the 16th century. Reminders of the Muslim past are ubiquitous in the form of Berber-style villages and the terraced and irrigated land.

History

The Alpujarras rose to prominence in the 10th and 11th centuries as a great silkworm farm for the silk workshops of Almería. This activity went hand in hand with a wave of Berber settlers in the area. Together with irrigation and agriculture, it supported at least 400 villages and hamlets by the late 15th century.

On his surrender to Fernando and Isabel in 1492, Boabdil, the last Granada emir, was awarded the Alpujarras as a personal fiefdom. He settled at Laujar de Andarax, east of Ugíjar, but left for Africa the next year. As Christian promises of tolerance gave way to forced mass conversions and land expropriations, in 1500 Muslims rebelled right across the former Granada emirate, with the Alpujarras in the thick of things. When the revolt failed, Muslims were given the choice of exile or conversion. Most converted, but the change was barely skin-deep. The Christians contented themselves with repressing outward signs of Islamic culture, until a particularly repressive decree by Felipe II in 1567, forbidding Arabic names and dress and even the Arabic language, brought a new revolt in the Alpujarras in 1568. Two years of vicious guerrilla war ensued, until Don Juan of Austria, Felipe's half-brother, was finally brought in to quash the insurrection.

Almost the whole Alpujarras population was deported to western Andalucía and more northerly parts of Castilla, and most of the villages were repeopled with settlers from the north. The rest were abandoned. The Alpujarras returned to the footnotes of history. Over the centuries, the silk industry fell by the wayside and great swathes of the Alpujarras' woodlands were lost to mining and cereal growing.

Books

South From Granada by Gerald Brenan, an Englishman who lived in the Alpujarras village of Yegen in the 1920s and 30s, is full of fascinating, amusing detail on what was then a very isolated, superstitious corner of Spain.

Special Events

The Alpujarras calendar is replete with village fiestas. Among the most interesting are the annual Moros y Cristianos (Muslims and Christians) festivities in several villages, recreating events of the 1568 rebellion. The best known are those at Válor, birthplace of the rebellion's leader Aben Humeya, on 14 and 15 September. Costumed 'armies' battle it out intermittently all day from midday to evening.

On 5 August, or the Sunday before, villagers from Trevélez stage a *romería* to the top of Mulhacén to honour the Virgen de las Nieves (Virgin of the Snows).

Walking

Innumerable good walks link valley villages or head up into the Sierra Nevada. Lonely Planet's *Walking in Spain* details two good four-day routes in the Alpujarras and Sierra Nevada. The GR-7 long-distance footpath from Greece to Algeciras runs through the Alpujarras and its section of six days or so from the Puerto de la Ragua pass to Lanjarón – via Bayárcal, Laroles, Válor, Yegen, Bérchules, Cádiar, Trevélez, Busquístar, Pitres, Bubión, Pampaneira, Soportújar and Cañar – is marked most of the way by posts with red and white rings.

The best conditions in the high mountains – July, August and early September – unfortunately don't coincide very well with the most pleasant periods in the valleys (April to mid-June, and mid-September to early November). In the Sierra Nevada – which are serious mountains – you have to be prepared for cloud, rain or strong cold winds any day, and should come well equipped.

The best overall map of the western halves of the Sierra Nevada and Las Alpujarras is the CNIG's 1:50,000 *Sierra Nevada*, though it certainly doesn't show every path or even track. Unfortunately this is increasingly hard to find as it recently went out of print pending production of an updated version. CNIG 1:25,000 sheets have their inadequacies too but are certainly better than nothing. You can normally

ANDALUCÍA

buy them at the information office in Pampaneira.

Accommodation

It's worth booking ahead for rooms in Semana Santa and from June to September. In addition to hotels or hostales, many villages have apartments and houses for short-term rental.

Food

Alpujarras food is basically hearty country fare, with lots of good meat and also local trout. Trevélez is famous for its *jamón serrano*, but many other villages produce good hams too. The *plato alpujarreño*, which you'll find on almost every *menú*, consists of fried potatoes, fried eggs, sausage, ham and maybe a black pudding, usually for around 700 ptas.

Getting There & Away

Buses to the Alpujarras are run by Alsina Graells (☎ 958 78 50 02 in Órgiva). From Granada, they run three times daily to Órgiva (1½ hours), Pampaneira (two hours), Bubión, Capileira and Pitres (2¾ hours), with two continuing to Trevélez (3¼ hours) and Bérchules (3¾ hours). There are also a twice daily Granada-Ugíjar service via Órgiva, Cádiar and Yegen; a Málaga-Órgiva bus daily except Sunday; an Almería-Ugíjar bus daily except Sunday; and an Almería-Bérchules service via Ugíjar and Yegen daily except Sunday. Other daily services link Órgiva and other villages with Bérchules and Ugíjar.

Órgiva

The scruffy main town of the western Alpujarras (population 5,000) is at its most interesting on Thursday morning, when locals and the Alpujarras' sizable international community converge to buy and sell everything from vegetables to hippie jewellery at a colourful market by the Río Chico on the west side of town.

There are banks, some with ATMs, on and near the main street, Calle Doctor Fleming, and a correos (postcode 18400)

towards the top of town at Calle Mulhacén 5. The Policía Local (☎ 958 78 52 12) are at Calle Doctor Fleming 1.

Places to Stay & Eat *Camping Órgiva* *(☎ 958 78 43 07)* has a pool and restaurant but only a small area for camping. Two adults with a car and tent pay around 1900 ptas. It's open all year, 2km south of the centre on the A-348.

Pensión Alma Alpujarreña (☎ 958 78 40 85, Avenida González Robles 49), just below the traffic lights at the foot of Calle Doctor Fleming, has singles/doubles for 2000/4000 ptas, or doubles with bath for 5000 ptas, and a three course *menú* for 1200 ptas.

Hostal Mirasol (☎ 958 78 51 59, Avenida González Robles 3), overlooking the Thursday market site, has adequate singles/doubles with bath for 2000/4000 ptas plus IVA. The adjacent *Hotel Mirasol (☎ 958 78 51 08)* has newer, more comfortable rooms for 5000/8000 ptas plus IVA.

La Zahona bakery on Calle Doctor Fleming does good cakes and pastries, which go well with a drink at the pavement tables of *Café Heladería Galindo*, which shares the same premises. The Galindo has pizzas for 950 ptas.

Pampaneira, Bubión & Capileira

This trio of villages clinging to the side of the deep Barranco de Poqueira ravine, 14 to 20km north-east of Órgiva, are three of the prettiest, most dramatically sited – and most touristed – in Las Alpujarras. Their white-washed stone houses seem to clamber over each other in an effort not to slide down into the gorge, while streets decked with flowery balconies climb haphazardly in between.

Capileira, the highest of the three at 1440m, is the best base for walks in the surrounding valleys and mountains.

Information The Centro de Visitantes de Pampaneira (☎ 958 76 31 27), on Pampaneira's square, Plaza de la Libertad, has a wealth of information on the Alpujarras and Sierra Nevada, including maps for sale, and

Alpujarras Houses

Travellers who have been to Morocco may notice a resemblance between villages in the Alpujarras and those in the Atlas mountains, from where the Alpujarran style was introduced in Muslim times by Berber settlers.

Most houses are of two storeys, with the lower one used for storage and animals. The characteristic *terraos* or flat roofs, with their protruding chimney pots, consist of a layer of *launa* (a type of clay) packed on to flat stones which are themselves laid on beams of chestnut, ash or pine. Nowadays there's often a layer of plastic between the stones and the launa for extra waterproofing.

Whitewash is a fairly modern introduction too: nearly all houses used to be stone-coloured.

can put you in the picture about walks and mountain refuges. It's normally open Wednesday to Saturday from 10 am to 2 pm and 4 to 6 pm and other days from 10 am to 3 pm, and English is spoken. There's an information kiosk by the main road in Capileira.

There's an ATM just outside the car park in Pampaneira. La General bank on Calle Doctor Castilla in Capileira has one too. All three villages have small supermarkets.

Things to See & Do All three villages have solid 16th century **mudéjar churches** (open only at Mass times). They also have small **weaving workshops**, descendants of a textile tradition that goes back to Muslim times, and plentiful craft shops.

Given the somewhat Himalayan character of the Poqueira landscape, it's not entirely surprising that there's a small Tibetan Buddhist monastery, **Osel Ling** (Place of Clear Light), high on the far side of the valley from Pampaneira. The monastery welcomes visitors at certain times (call ☎ 958 34 31 34 for current

hours). You can walk to it from any of the three villages, or drive up from the turning marked 'Camino Forestal a la Casa 4340m' opposite the Ermita del Padre Eterno chapel on the GR-421.

Walks Eight trails ranging from 4 to 23km (1½ to eight hours) are marked out in the Barranco de Poqueira with little colour-coded posts. Their outlines are shown on rather rough maps posted in all three villages. Most start from Capileira, though No 1 (6km; 2½ hours) is a circuit from Pampaneira, and No 6 (14km; 4½ hours) is a circuit from Bubión.

Route No 4 from Capileira (8km; 2½ hours) takes you up to the hamlet of La Cebadilla, then down the west side of the valley and back up to Capileira. To find its start, walk to the end of Calle Cubo, turn right at Apartamentos Vista Veleta and keep going. Route Nos 7 and 8 both continue up the valley from La Cebadilla. Nos 2 and 5 start from the end of Calle Cerezo in Capileira.

You can walk from Capileira to Trevélez in four or five hours by taking the broad track heading to the right 4km up the Mulhacén road from the village, a couple of hundred metres after the 8km marker. It's marked by red and white paint on a rock a few metres along the track.

At the information office in Pampaneira, Nevadensis (☎ 958 76 31 27, nevadensis@ arrakis.es) and, by the main road at the bottom of Bubión, Rustic Blue (☎ 958 76 33 81) both offer a range of guided hikes and treks, with vehicle support where needed. Nevadensis day walks cost from 2300 to 4000 ptas a person, with a minimum of five people usually needed.

Other Activities Nevadensis and Rustic Blue can set you up with horse riding (around 4000 ptas for two hours or 8000 ptas a day) or, in winter, ski touring. Rustic Blue also offers courses in sevillana dancing, painting, photography and cooking. Nevadensis arranges mountain biking, climbing, paragliding, canyoning and 4WD trips.

ANDALUCÍA

Places to Stay & Eat

Pampaneira Two good hostales face each other across Calle José Antonio at the entrance to the village. **Hostal Pampaneira** (☎ 958 76 30 02) has singles/doubles with bathroom for 2000/3000 ptas, and the cheapest restaurant in the village (trout 550 ptas, pork chops 650 ptas). **Hostal Ruta del Mulhacén** (☎ 958 76 30 10) has rooms with bath for 2900/4000 ptas. Of the three restaurants along the street on Plaza de la Libertad, **Restaurante Casa Diego**, with a pleasant upstairs terrace, is a good choice. Main dishes are from 650 to 1100 ptas: trout with ham, and local ham and eggs, are among the cheaper dishes.

Bubión Hostal Las Terrazas (☎ 958 76 30 34 Plaza del Sol 7), below the main road, has pleasant singles/doubles with bath for 2350/3300 ptas plus IVA, and apartments nearby. The **Villa Turística de Bubión** (☎ 958 76 31 11), at the top of the village, has comfortable self-catering apartments for up to six people. Cost for two or three people is 12,000 ptas plus IVA. There's a restaurant too. Rustic Blue (see Other Activities in Things to See & Do earlier) offers houses to rent here and elsewhere in the Alpujarras, generally from 6000 ptas for two or three people.

Restaurante Teide by the main road is good, with a three-course *menú* for 1100 ptas. À la carte there are several mains under 800 ptas, including trout with ham. Add IVA to prices. Up the road are a few convivial bars such as the pub-like **Restaurante Fuenfria** and **Taberna Boabdil**.

Capileira Mesón Hostal Poqueira (☎ 958 76 30 48, Calle Doctor Castilla 6), just off the main road, has good singles/doubles with bath for 2400/4000 ptas, and a popular restaurant. **Hostal Atalaya** (☎ 958 76 30 25, Calle Perchel 3), 100m down the main road, has similar prices. **Hostal Paco López** (☎ 958 76 30 11, Carretera de la Sierra 5), just up the main road, has decent rooms for 2000/3000 ptas with bathroom. **Café Bar Rosendo** (☎ 958 76 30 70), a little farther up the road, has apartments for three to six people at 6000 to 10,800 ptas.

Bar El Tilo on Plaza Calvario, just down from the far end of Calle Doctor Castilla, has good-value raciones. **Casa Íbero** below the church (follow signs from the end of Calle Doctor Castilla) does good, original food ranging from vegetarian croquettes (650 ptas) or cous cous (700 to 1100 ptas) to lamb with ginger sauce (1100 ptas).

Mulhacén

Rising above the top of the Poqueira valley are the Sierra Nevada's two highest peaks: Mulhacén (3478m) and Pico del Veleta (3396m).

Very strong hikers could make it from Capileira to the summit of Mulhacén in a long day (with over 2000m of ascent), but a better plan is to overnight at the 87-place **Refugio Poqueira** (☎ 958 34 33 49) towards the top of the Poqueira valley at 2500m. The refugio is open all year at 1000 ptas per person, and has prepared meals available (breakfast 550 ptas, dinner 1600 ptas). Blankets are provided. From the refugio you can reach the top of Mulhacén in about three hours.

An alternative walker's approach to Mulhacén, and other high Sierra Nevada peaks, is from Trevélez to their south-east, by the Trevélez valley and the Cañada de Siete Lagunas, a lake-dotted basin below the east side of Mulhacén. The important thing on this route is to steer clear of the boggy bottom of the valley of the Río Culo de Perro (Dog's Arse River). Again, it's possible to reach the peak in one hard day, but better is to camp in the *cañada*, five or six hours up from Trevélez.

The road climbing over the mountains from Capileira to the Estación de Esquí Sierra Nevada is closed to unauthorised vehicles some 12km up from Capileira (in winter snow may prevent you driving even that far).

Pitres & Around

Pitres is almost as pretty as the Poqueira gorge villages but less touristed. It has a bank (no ATM) on the main square. *Camping El Balcón de Pitres* (☎ 958 76 61 11), by the GR-421 on the west side of the village, is open from March to October and charges 1700 ptas plus IVA for two adults with a car and tent. It has a decent restaurant and a pool. *Refugio Los Albergues* (☎ 958 34 31 76), two minutes walk (signposted) down a path from the GR-421 on the east side of the village, is a small, privately run hikers' hostel, with bunks at 1000 ptas, one double room for 3000 ptas, and an equipped kitchen. It's open all year except 10 January to 15 February. The friendly German owner is full of information on the locality and the many good walks in it. *Fonda Sierra Nevada* (☎ 958 76 60 17) on Pitres' plaza has singles/doubles at 1700/3400 ptas. There's a handful of cafés and restaurants around the plaza.

Trevélez

Trevélez (1476m; population 800), in a valley almost as impressive as the Poqueira gorge, claims to be the highest village in Spain (Taüll in Cataluña, at 1495m, might have something to say about that), and produces some of the country's best jamón serrano. Hams are trucked in from far and wide for curing in Trevélez's dry mountain air.

First impressions of Trevélez are disappointing as you're confronted by a welter of jamón and souvenir shops along the main road, but a wander into the upper parts reveals a lively village of typical Alpujarran quaintness. La General bank just above the main road has an ATM.

Places to Stay & Eat *Restaurante González* (☎ 958 85 85 33) on Plaza de Don Francisco Abellán, by the main road at the foot of the village, has doubles for 2500 ptas and a good restaurant with chicken, trout or a plato alpujarreño for 700 to 800 ptas. There are three or four other places with rooms just along the road.

Hostal Fernando (☎ 958 85 85 65, *Pista del Barrio Medio s/n*), by the road going up towards the top of the village, has decent

doubles with bath for 3200 ptas, or two-person apartments with terraces for 4200 ptas. Past here, the road reaches Plaza Barrio Medio, with signs to the *Hotel La Fragua* (☎ 958 85 86 26, *Calle San Antonio 4*), which has the most comfortable rooms in town at 5500 ptas with bath. Its nearby restaurant, *Mesón La Fragua*, offers relatively exotic fare such as partridge in walnut sauce (1400 ptas) as well as trout, ham, pork etc. Just below, *Café Bar Castellón* on Calle Cárcel has singles/doubles for 1250/2500 ptas.

Mesón Haraicel, just above Plaza de Don Francisco Abellán, has a few outside tables and good food, with several trout and meat main courses for 775 to 850 ptas. *Jamón de Trevélez* crops up on every *menú*. If you want some to take away, the shops up in the village tend to be cheaper than those on the main road. You should be able to get 1kg for 1000 ptas or less (double for the special *ibérico* and *pata negra* varieties).

East of Trevélez

Seven kilometres south of Trevélez, the GR 421 crosses the low Portichuelo de Cástaras pass and turns east into a barer landscape. Yet there are still oases of greenery around the villages, and these central and eastern parts of the Alpujarras are in their own way just as impressive as the west. They pull in far fewer tourists.

Bérchules Seventeen kilometres from Trevélez, Bérchules is an attractive spot in a green valley which stretches far back into the hills. *Casa Resu* (☎ 958 76 90 92, *Calle Iglesia 18*) has basic singles/doubles for 1000/2000 ptas. *Hotel Los Bérchules* (☎ 958 85 25 30) down on the main road has doubles for 5000 ptas.

Cádiar Down in the valley 8km south of Bérchules, Cádiar is more appealing than it looks from afar. *Hostal Montoro* (☎ 958 75 00 68, *Calle San Isidro 20*) has doubles with bath for just 1900 ptas plus IVA. The *Alqueria de Morayma* (☎ 958 34 33 03), 2km south, is a beautifully renovated old farmhouse with a good, inexpensive restaurant and a library of Alpujarras information. Singles/doubles in rooms and apartments, some with a small kitchen, are from 4800/6000 to 6700/8300 ptas plus IVA. The friendly owners offer a variety of interesting outings.

Yegen Twelve kilometres east of Bérchules is Yegen, where Gerald Brenan's house, just off the main plaza, has a plaque. This typically pretty Alpujarras village is another good walking or touring base. *Café-Bar La Fuente* on the plaza has singles/doubles for 1300/2600 ptas. *El Tinao* (☎ 958 85 12 12) on the road has good rooms with bath for 2000/3500 ptas, and also food, bicycles, and apartments and houses to rent; *El Rincón de Yegen* (☎ 958 85 12 70) by the road on the east edge of the village has more rooms and apartments.

Válor At Válor, a quiet place 5km east of Yegen, *Hostal Las Perdices* (☎ 958 85 18 21) on Calle Torrecilla has good rooms with bath for 3000 ptas a double.

Ugíjar Seven kilometres south-east of Válor, Ugíjar (population 2,600) is the main market town hereabouts, with two hostales. From here the Alpujarras, and the A-348, continue east into Almería province.

THE COAST
Granada's rugged, cliff-lined, 80km coast has a few reasonably attractive beach towns, all linked by several daily buses to Granada, Málaga and Almería.

Salobreña
Salobreña's huddle of white houses rises on a crag between the N-340 and the sea. The helpful tourist office (☎ 958 61 03 14) on Plaza de Goya, 200m off the N-340, is open daily except Sunday. Up at the top of the village is the impressive 13th century **Castillo Árabe**, which is open Monday to Friday from 10 am to 1.30 pm and 4 to 8 pm (200 ptas), and below is a long dark-sand **beach**.

Pensión Mari Carmen (☎ 958 61 09 06, Calle Nueva 30) and *Pensión Arnedo* (☎ 958 61 02 27, Calle Nueva 15) have reasonable doubles for under 3000 ptas. Little *Restaurante Pesetas* on Calle Bóveda serves up good tapas and meals. *Restaurante El Peñón*, by the big rock which divides Salobreña's main beach, does good fish and seafood.

Almuñécar
Almuñécar appears from the road as an uninviting agglomeration of apartment blocks, but it has a more attractive older heart around the 16th century Castillo San Miguel. Popular with Spanish tourists, it's a bright and not-too-expensive resort, though its beaches are pebbly.

Orientation & Information The estación de autobuses is at Avenida Juan Carlos I 1, just south of the N-340. The tourist office (☎ 958 63 11 25), open daily, is on Avenida de Europa, just back from Playa de San Cristóbal.

Things to See On Playa de San Cristóbal is an aviary with 120 types of tropical bird, the **Parque Ornitológico Loro Sexi**. (*Loro* means parrot and Sexi was the Phoenician name for Almuñécar). Antiquity-lovers should visit the **Museo Arqueológico**, in a set of Roman galleries called the Cueva de Siete Palacios (open daily except Monday), and seek out the **Tumbas Fenicias Puente de Noy**, a Phoenician and Roman necropolis, and the Roman **Acueducto de la Carrera**.

Places to Stay & Eat There are two year-round camp sites on the N-340 east of the centre.

Hotel Victoria II (☎ 958 63 17 34, Plaza de la Victoria 22), a few minutes walk south of the bus station, has decent singles/doubles from 1800/3200 to 3000/4800 ptas. The good *Hostal Plaza Damasco* (☎ 958 63 01 65, Calle Cerrajeros 8), almost next door, and *Hostal Tropical* (☎ 958 63 34 58) and *Hotel Goya* (☎ 958 63 05 50), both on Avenida de Europa, are all in a similar price range. By Playa de San Cristóbal, *Hotel Casablanca* (☎ *958 63 55 75, Plaza San Cristóbal 4)* has comfortable doubles at 9000 ptas plus IVA.

Plaza de la Constitución, the main plaza of the older part of town, a few minutes walk south of the bus station, has a few popular restaurants. Nearby, *Pizzería Il Grillo (Plaza de Damasco 5)* serves up good Italian food, and Plaza Kelibia, with several bars with tables out on the plaza, buzzes at night – *La Trastienda* has excellent tapas. Or you could head for the restaurants opposite the seafront on Paseo de las Flores and Paseo de San Cristóbal.

La Herradura

The little resort of La Herradura, 7km west of Almuñécar, has a windsurfing school, a few diving outfits (two of them at the beautifully sited Marina del Este, off the N-340 between the two towns), and a string of good seafront restaurants. Two summer camp sites and a couple of hostales, charging 6000 ptas plus IVA for doubles with bath in summer, are opposite the beach on Paseo Andrés Segovia.

Jaén Province

The Jaén landscape alternates between rolling country covered with olive trees (the province produces about 10% of the world's olive oil), and impressive mountain ranges. The Parque Natural de Cazorla is perhaps the most beautiful of all Andalucía's mountain regions. Another highlight of Jaén province is the marvellous Renaissance architecture of 16th century master Andrés de Vandelvira, especially in Úbeda.

The N-IV from Madrid enters Andalucía through the Desfiladero de Despeñaperros pass in the Sierra Morena. The rout of the Almohad army by Christian forces in 1212 at Las Navas de Tolosa, a few kilometres south of the pass, was a key event of the Reconquista, opening the doors of Andalucía to the Christians.

The Jaén diet is pretty traditional but richly varied, with plenty of game (par-

tridge, venison, wild boar) available, especially in the mountains. An endearingly old-fashioned habit throughout much of the province is that of serving free tapas with drinks in bars.

JAÉN

The provincial capital (population 105,000) has enough interest to hold you for a day or so.

Orientation

Old Jaén huddles around the foot of the high, castle-topped Cerro de Santa Catalina. From Plaza de la Constitución, the focal point of the newer part of town, Calle Roldán y Marín (becoming Paseo de la Estación) heads north-west to the train station, 1km away. The estación de autobuses is on Plaza de Coca de la Piñera, 250m north of Plaza de la Constitución.

Information

The helpful Junta de Andalucía tourist office (☎ 953 22 27 37), Calle del Arquitecto Berges 1, is open Monday to Friday from 9 am to 7 pm and Saturday from 9 am to 2 pm. The Oficina Municipal de Turismo (☎ 953 21 91 16), Calle de la Maestra 16, is open Monday to Friday from 9 am to 2 pm.

There's no shortage of banks or ATMs on Plaza de la Constitución and Calle Roldán y Marín. The main correos (postcode 23080) is on Plaza de los Jardinillos.

The main general hospital is the Hospital Ciudad de Jaén (☎ 953 22 24 08) on Avenida del Ejército Español. The Policía Municipal (☎ 953 21 91 05) are on Carrera de Jesús, just behind the ayuntamiento.

Things to See

Jaén's huge **Catedral** was built mainly in the 16th and 17th centuries, and mainly to the designs of Andrés de Vandelvira. Its highlight is the superb south-west façade on Plaza de Santa María, with an array of 17th century statuary, much of it by Sevilla's Pedro Roldán. The interior is open Monday to Saturday from 8.30 am to 1 pm and 4 to 7 pm (from 5 to 8 pm in summer) and

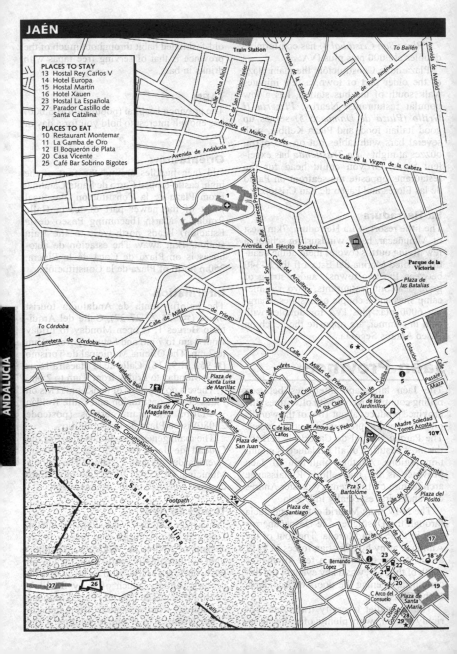

JAÉN

PLACES TO STAY
13 Hostal Rey Carlos V
14 Hotel Europa
15 Hostal Martín
16 Hotel Xauen
23 Hostal La Española
27 Parador Castillo de
   Santa Catalina

PLACES TO EAT
10 Restaurant Montemar
11 La Gamba de Oro
12 El Boquerón de Plata
20 Casa Vicente
25 Café Bar Sobrino Bigotes

Train Station

To Bailén

Avenida de Madrid

Calle Santa Alicia

C de San Francisco Javier

Paseo de la Estación

Avenida de Ruiz Jiménez

Avenida de Muñoz Grandes

Avenida de Andalucía

Calle de la Virgen de la Cabeza

Calle Alféreces Provisionales

Avenida del Ejército Español

Calle del Arquitecto Berges

Calle Puerta del Sol

Parque de la Victoria

Plaza de las Batallias

To Córdoba

Calle de Millán de Priego

Carretera de Córdoba

Calle de la Magdalena Baja

Paseo de la Estación

Calle de Millán de Priego

Calle de San Andrés

Plaza de Santa Luisa de Marillac

Calle Santo Domingo

C. Juanito el Practicante

Plaza de Magdalena

Carretera de Circunvalación

C de la Sta Cruz

C de Sta Clara

Calle Arroyo de S Pedro

Plaza de los Jardinillos

Calle de Castilla

Pasaje Maza

Plaza de San Juan

C de los Caños

Calle de San Bartolomé

Calle Doctor Eduardo Arroyo

Madre Soledad Torres Acosta

C de San Clemente

Cerro de Santa Catalina

Footpath

Calle Almendros

Calle Martínez Molina

Aguilar

Pza S Bartolomé

Plaza del Pósito

Plaza de Santiago

Calle de Buenavista

Calle de Colón

Calle de los Álamos

Calle del Cerón

Walls

C Bernardo López

C de Maestra

Plaza de Santa María

C Arco del Consuelo

Obispo González

Plaza de Santa María

Walls

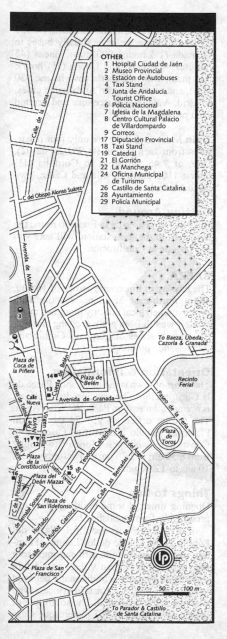

OTHER
1 Hospital Ciudad de Jaén
2 Museo Provincial
3 Estación de Autobuses
4 Taxi Stand
5 Junta de Andalucía
  Tourist Office
6 Policía Nacional
7 Iglesia de la Magdalena
8 Centro Cultural Palacio
  de Villardompardo
9 Correos
17 Diputación Provincial
18 Taxi Stand
19 Catedral
21 El Gorrión
22 La Manchega
24 Oficina Municipal
   de Turismo
26 Castillo de Santa Catalina
28 Ayuntamiento
29 Policía Municipal

Sunday and holidays from 8.30 am to 1.30 pm and 5 to 7 pm.

The **Centro Cultural Palacio de Villardompardo**, in a Renaissance palace on Plaza de Santa Luisa de Marillac, houses the **Museo Internacional de Arte Naif**, with a large international collection of colourful, easily accessible naïf art; the beautiful 11th century **Baños Árabes** (Arab Baths), one of Spain's biggest Islamic bathhouses; and the **Museo de Artes y Costumbres Populares**, devoted to pre-industrial life in Jaén province. It's all open Tuesday to Friday from 10 am to 2 pm and 5 to 8 pm and Saturday and Sunday from 10.30 am to 2 pm (free with an EU passport, 100 ptas otherwise).

Jaén's oldest church, the **Iglesia de la Magdalena** on Calle Santo Domingo, has a Gothic main façade and interior but its tower is a mosque's minaret, reworked in the 16th century. You can enter the church, and view its lovely Islamic courtyard with Roman tombstones daily from 6 to 8 pm.

The **Museo Provincial**, Paseo de la Estación 27, has a good archaeological section with a fine collection of Iberian sculpture; it's open Tuesday to Friday from 10 am to 2 pm and 4 to 7.30 pm and Saturday and Sunday from 10 am to 2 pm (free with an EU passport, 100 ptas otherwise).

Undoubtedly Jaén's most exhilarating spot is the top of the **Cerro de Santa Catalina**, a circuitous 4km drive up from the city centre (800 ptas by taxi). You can walk up in about an hour using a steep path almost opposite the top of Calle de Buenavista. The **Castillo de Santa Catalina** up here was surrendered to Fernando III in 1246 by the emir of Granada after a six-month siege. It's open daily except Wednesday from 10 am to 1.30 pm (free). If you have walked up, you deserve to treat yourself to a drink in Parador Castillo de Santa Catalina next door!

Places to Stay

Mosquitoes can be a nuisance in Jaén hotels, especially the cheaper ones.

ANDALUCÍA

Hostal Rey Carlos V (☎ *953 22 20 91, Avenida de Madrid 4)*, near the bus station, has basic singles/doubles for 2300/3200 ptas. *Hostal Martín* (☎ *953 24 36 78, Calle Cuatro Torres 5)*, just off Plaza de la Constitución, is shabby but adequate, charging 2000/3000 ptas. *Hostal La Española* (☎ *953 23 02 54, Calle Bernardo López 9)*, in a sizable old house, has much more character, and rooms for 1600/3000 ptas, or doubles with bathroom for 4000 ptas.

Hotel Europa (☎ *953 22 27 00, Plaza de Belén 1)* has decent rooms with air-con and bath for 5000/7490 ptas, and a garage. Better still is *Hotel Xauen* (☎ *953 24 07 89, Plaza del Deán Mazas 3)*, charging 5200/7000 ptas plus IVA.

The *Parador Castillo de Santa Catalina* (☎ *953 23 00 00)*, atop the Cerro de Santa Catalina, has spacious, comfortable rooms at 13,200/16,500 ptas plus IVA, and a pool.

Places to Eat

Several of the atmospheric old bars on Calle de Arco del Consuelo and Calle Bernardo López, near the cathedral, serve decent raciones and tapas. Nearby, *Casa Vicente*, in a restored mansion on Calle Francisco Martín Mora, is one of Jaén's best restaurants, specialising in pork and venison: a three-course meal will be around 2500 to 3000 ptas.

Restaurant Montemar (Calle Roldán y Marín 7) serves up lots of Jaén specialities, with a three-course *menú* with wine for 1500 ptas, or à la carte mains from 850 ptas. Opposite, short Calle Nueva is packed with bright, lively spots to eat and drink. Excellent seafood raciones are 750 to 1000 ptas at *El Boquerón de Plata*, a little more at *La Gamba de Oro*.

A three-course meal at the *Parador de Santa Catalina's* excellent restaurant will set you back around 3500 ptas, plus drinks.

Entertainment

Some of the bars on Calle de Arco del Consuelo, Calle Bernardo López and Calle Nueva (see Places to Eat) are excellent for drinks and tapas.

Getting There & Away

Bus From the estación de autobuses (☎ 953 25 01 06) there are several daily buses to Granada (1½ hours; 900 ptas), Baeza (45 minutes; 450 ptas) and Úbeda (1¼ hours; 535 ptas), two to Cazorla (two hours; 930 ptas), and others to main Andalucian cities, Madrid, Valencia, Barcelona and around Jaén province.

Train Most days there are only four departures from Jaén station (☎ 953 27 02 02). One, at 7.45 am, goes to Córdoba (1½ hours; 1105 ptas), Sevilla and Cádiz. Two go to Madrid.

Getting Around

Bus No 1, on Paseo de la Estación round the corner from the train station, will take you to Plaza de la Constitución.

BAEZA

The heyday of this country town of 16,000, 48km north-east of Jaén, was the 16th century, when local nobility ploughed much of their wealth from grain growing and textiles into a series of gorgeous Gothic and Renaissance buildings.

Orientation & Information

The heart of town is the long, wide Paseo de la Constitución. The estación de autobuses is about 700m east on Paseo Arco del Agua. The tourist office (☎ 953 74 04 44), on Plaza del Pópulo just west of Paseo de la Constitución, is open Monday to Friday from 8.30 am to 2.30 pm and Saturday from 10 am to 12.30 pm.

Things to See

Opening times of some buildings vary unpredictably from published hours.

In the centre of beautiful **Plaza del Pópulo** is the Fuente de los Leones (Fountain of the Lions), built with carvings from the Iberian and Roman village of Cástulo and topped by a statue traditionally believed to represent Imilce, a Cástulo princess who was married to Hannibal. The south side of the plaza is lined by the plateresque Casa del Populo of about 1540 (housing Baeza's tourist office), and on the east side stands the Antigua Carnicería (old slaughterhouse) of 1548.

Baeza's **Antigua Universidad** (old University) on Calle del Beato Juan de Ávila was founded in 1538 and closed in 1824. Today it's a high school, which you can enter Monday to Friday from 9 am to 2 pm. The main patio has two levels of elegant Renaissance arches. Round the corner on Cuesta de San Felipe stands the early 16th century **Palacio de Jabalquinto**, a mansion with a flamboyant Isabelline Gothic façade and lovely Renaissance patio. It's open Monday to Friday from 11 am to 1 pm and 5 to 7 pm (free). Across the square, the mid-13th century **Iglesia de la Santa Cruz** may be the only Romanesque church in Andalucía.

The main façade of Baeza's **Catedral**, on Plaza de Santa María, is in 16th century Renaissance style, as is the basic design of the interior (by Andrés de Vandelvira and Jerónimo del Prado). But the building also has earlier Gothic features such as the 13th century Puerta de la Luna (Moon Doorway) at the west end. The interior is open daily from 10.30 am to 1 pm and 5 to 7 pm.

A block north of Paseo de la Constitución at Paseo del Cardenal Benavides 9, the **Ayuntamiento** has a marvellous plateresque façade.

Places to Stay

Some prices go up a few hundred pesetas from about June to September.

The friendly *Hostal El Patio (☎ 953 74 02 00, Calle Conde Romanones 13)* occupies a 17th century mansion with a large covered patio. Varied singles/doubles cost 1500/2500 to 2000/3500 ptas. Another friendly place, *Hostal Comercio (☎ 953 74 01 00, Calle San Pablo 21)* has decent rooms from 1500/2900 to 1700/3300 ptas.

Hotel Baeza (☎ 953 74 81 30, Calle de la Concepción 3) has cosy rooms for 6300/9600 ptas plus IVA, including breakfast. The relaxed *Hospedería Fuentenueva (☎ 953 74 31 00, Paseo Arco del Agua s/n)*, about 300m beyond the bus station, has 12 rooms for 5700/8000 ptas plus IVA, including breakfast. *Hotel Juanito (☎ 953 74 00 40)* 450m farther along Paseo Arco del Agua, offers comfy rooms for 4600/5400 ptas plus IVA.

Places to Eat

Cafetería Churrería Benjamín (Calle Patrocinio Biedma 1), on the corner of Calle San Pablo, is a fine place for a breakfast of good crisp churros y chocolate.

Cafetería Mercantil (Plaza de España), at the top end of Paseo de la Constitución, is always busy with amiable *baezanos* and serves a long list of tapas and generous raciones for 900 to 1200 ptas. In the Hotel Baeza, the popular *Restaurante La Cazuela* is a step up in quality, but moderately priced.

Hospedería Fuentenueva has a good restaurant with a three-course lunch for 2100 ptas including drinks, and a bar/café with some tasty snacks.

People come from far and wide to enjoy the Jaén specialities at *Restaurante Juanito* in the Hotel Juanito. A three-course meal is likely to set you back 4000 ptas or more, plus drinks (closed Sunday and Monday evenings).

Getting There & Away

From the estación de autobuses (☎ 953 74 04 68), there are 12 or more daily buses to Jaén and Úbeda, two to Cazorla and at least five to Granada. Others go to Madrid, Córdoba, Sevilla and Málaga.

The nearest train station is Linares-Baeza (☎ 953 65 02 02), 13km north-west. There are connecting buses for most trains Monday to Saturday.

ÚBEDA

Just 9km east of Baeza, Úbeda (population 32,000) has an even finer heritage of marvellous buildings from bygone centuries. In the 16th century Francisco de los Cobos y Molina, from an Úbeda noble family, became first secretary to Carlos I; his nephew Juan Vázquez de Molina succeeded him in

ANDALUCÍA

the job and kept it under Felipe II. Much of the wealth that these men and flourishing local agriculture brought to Úbeda was spent on a profusion of Renaissance mansions and churches that remain its glory today. A great many of them were designed by Andrés de Vandelvira, born in 1509 at Alcaraz, 150km north-east.

Orientation

Most of the fine architecture is in the old part of town in the south-east, a warren of narrow streets and expansive plazas. Budget accommodation and the estación de autobuses are in the drab new town in the west and north. Plaza de Andalucía marks the boundary between old and new.

Information

The tourist office (☎ 953 75 08 97) is in the Hospital de Santiago on Calle Obispo Cobos in the new town and is open Monday to Saturday from 8 am to 3 pm.

You'll find the biggest concentration of banks and ATMs on Plaza de Andalucía and nearby Calle Rastro. The correos (postcode 23400) is at Calle Trinidad 4.

There's a Centro de Salud (☎ 953 75 11 03), with an emergency section, in the new town on Calle Explanada. The Policía Nacional (☎ 091) occupy the Antiguo Pósito on Plaza Vázquez de Molina.

Plaza Vázquez de Molina

This plaza is almost entirely surrounded by beautiful stone buildings from the 15th and 16th centuries.

Capilla de El Salvador Facing along the plaza from its east end, this 1540s church, founded by Francisco de los Cobos y Molina as his family funerary chapel, was Vandelvira's first commission in Úbeda. The basic design is by Diego de Siloé but Vandelvira added plenty of his own touches, including the portal on the elaborate main façade which is an outstanding piece of plateresque design.

To enter the church, knock on the sacristy door along the street on the north side (the door has a five-lion shield above it). You'll be shown round by the caretaker, who at the end will appreciate a donation towards upkeep. You first enter the sacristy, by Vandelvira, which contains a portrait of Francisco de los Cobos y Molina. The richly decorated chancel of the main church is modelled on Siloé's Capilla Mayor in Granada's cathedral, with a frescoed dome. The Cobos family crypt is beneath the nave.

Palacio del Deán Ortega Next to the Capilla de El Salvador stands what was the abode of its chaplains – in fact one of Vandelvira's finest palaces, and at least as big as their church. The mansion is now Úbeda's parador, and its courtyard is the finest spot for a drink in town (a beer is 250 ptas).

Palacio de Vázquez de Molina The harmonious proportions of this Italian-influenced Vandelvira mansion at the west end of the plaza, now Úbeda's ayuntamiento, make it perhaps the most magnificent building in the town. Vandelvira built it in about 1562 for Juan Vázquez de Molina, whose coat of arms surmounts the doorway. You can enter any day from 10.30 am to 2 pm and 4.30 to 9 pm to admire the patio.

Santa María de los Reales Alcázares This fine church, built mainly in the 15th century on the site of Muslim Úbeda's main mosque, has recently been closed for restoration. Inside is a lovely Gothic cloister.

Plaza 1° de Marzo & Around

A couple of blocks north-east of Plaza Vázquez de Molina, Plaza 1° de Marzo used to be Úbeda's market square and bullring, and the Inquisition burnt heretics where the kiosk now stands. Worthies could watch the merry events from the gallery of the elegant 16th century **Antiguo Ayuntamiento** (old town hall) in the south-west corner. Along the top (north) side of the square is the Iglesia de San Pablo, with a

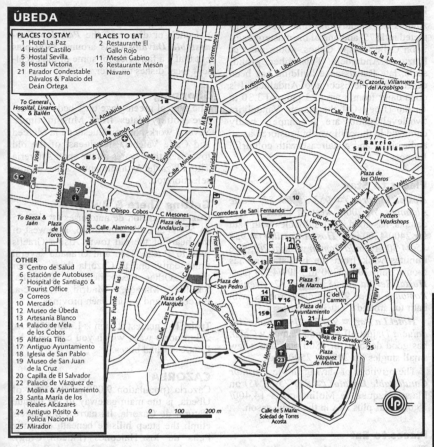

ÚBEDA

PLACES TO STAY
1 Hotel La Paz
4 Hostal Castillo
5 Hostal Sevilla
8 Hostal Victoria
21 Parador Condestable Dávalos & Palacio del Deán Ortega

PLACES TO EAT
2 Restaurante El Gallo Rojo
11 Mesón Gabino
16 Restaurante Mesón Navarro

OTHER
3 Centro de Salud
6 Estación de Autobuses
7 Hospital de Santiago & Tourist Office
9 Correos
10 Mercado
12 Museo de Úbeda
13 Artesanía Blanco
14 Palacio de Vela de los Cobos
15 Alfarería Tito
17 Antiguo Ayuntamiento
18 Iglesia de San Pablo
19 Museo de San Juan de la Cruz
20 Capilla de El Salvador
21 Palacio de Vázquez de Molina & Ayuntamiento
23 Santa María de los Reales Alcázares
24 Antiguo Pósito & Policia Nacional
25 Mirador

fine late Gothic portal of 1511 (open daily from 7 to 9 pm).

Just north at Calle Cervantes 4, the **Museo de Úbeda** has archaeological exhibits from Neolithic to Muslim times in a 14th century mudéjar house; it's open daily except Monday from 10 am to 2 pm and 5 to 9 pm (free).

The **Museo de San Juan de la Cruz** on Calle del Carmen, a block east of Plaza 1° de Marzo, is devoted to the mystic and religious reformer St John of the Cross (see

Ávila in the Castilla y León chapter), who died here in 1591. It's open daily except Monday from 11 am to 1 pm and 5 to 7 pm, with interesting free visits guided by Spanish-speaking monks. Those who can follow them will get not only an idea of St John's teachings – he wrote of the 'dark night of the soul' leading to the bright dawn of the experience of God – but also a look at a couple of his fingers and some of his bones, preserved in cabinets, and other memorabilia.

ANDALUCÍA

Hospital de Santiago

Andrés de Vandelvira's final work, completed in 1575, and one of his masterpieces, is on Calle Obispo Cobos, 400m west of Plaza de Andalucía. This sober, grand-scale, late Renaissance building has been described as the Escorial of Andalucía. It's open daily from 8 am to 3 pm and 3.30 to 10 pm (free). Off the classic Vandelvira two-level patio are a chapel, badly damaged in the civil war but restored as an auditorium, and a staircase with colourful frescoes.

Places to Stay

Hostal Victoria (☎ 953 75 29 52, *Calle Alaminos 5*), 200m west of Plaza de Andalucía, has good singles/doubles with bath for 2400/4300 ptas. *Hostal Castillo* (☎ 953 75 04 30, *Avenida Ramón y Cajal 20*), five minutes walk from the bus station, has rooms from 2000/3300 to 2400/4300 ptas. *Hostal Sevilla* (☎ 953 75 06 12, *Avenida Ramón y Cajal 9*), has clean rooms with bath for around 2000/3800 ptas.

Hotel La Paz (☎ 953 75 21 40, *Calle Andalucía 1*), just off Avenida Ramón y Cajal, has good doubles for 6800 ptas and a few small singles for 2000 to 2500 ptas.

The privilege of staying in the *Parador Condestable Dávalos* (☎ 953 75 03 45) on Plaza Vázquez de Molina costs 14,400/18,000 ptas plus IVA in the high season.

Places to Eat

The restaurant at the *Hostal Castillo* does a good three-course *menú* for 1000 ptas. The good *Restaurante El Gallo Rojo* (*Calle Manuel Barraca 3*), just off the top end of Avenida Ramón y Cajal, has meat and fish main dishes from 800 to 1800 ptas, and a three-course *menú* with lots of choice and a drink for 1100 ptas.

In the old town, *Restaurante Mesón Navarro* (*Plaza del Ayuntamiento 2*) has a bar that's good for a range of raciones (tortilla española 600 ptas) and bocadillos, and a restaurant serving typical local fare at the back. *Mesón Gabino* on Calle Fuente Seca is a cellar-type restaurant with decent food at middling prices.

Lunch or dinner in the *Parador Condestable Dávalos* costs around 3500 ptas but that's a fair price for some of the excellent local dishes on offer.

Shopping

The typical green glaze on Úbeda's attractive pottery dates from Muslim times. Several workshops on Cuesta de la Merced and Calle Valencia, north-east of the old town, sell their wares on the spot. Alfarería Tito, Plaza del Ayuntamiento 12, has a large selection too.

Getting There & Away

Bus The estación de autobuses (☎ 953 75 21 57) is at Calle San José 6, 1km west of the heart of the old town. Alsina Graells runs to Baeza, Jaén and Granada several times daily, and to Cazorla three or four times. Other buses head to Córdoba, Sevilla, Málaga, Madrid, Valencia, Barcelona and around Jaén province.

Train The nearest station is Linares-Baeza, 21km north-west, which you can reach by Linares-bound buses.

CAZORLA

Cazorla (population 9,000), 45km east of Úbeda, is the main gateway to the Parque Natural de Cazorla. Its narrow old streets climb the steep hillside beneath dramatic Peña de los Halcones (Falcon Crag). Cazorla can get very busy at Spanish holiday times and on fine weekends.

Orientation

Plaza de la Constitución is the main square of the northern, newer part of town. Plaza de la Corredera is 150m south along Calle Doctor Muñoz. Plaza de Santa María, 300m farther south-east, is the heart of the oldest part of town.

Information

The Oficina de Turismo Municipal (☎ 953 71 01 12), Paseo del Santo Cristo 17, 200m north of Plaza de la Constitución, has some information on the Parque Natural as well as Cazorla town. Quercus (☎ 953 72 01 15), Calle Juan Domingo 2 (just off Plaza de la Constitución), provides some tourist information as well as selling maps and excursions.

There are several banks in the town centre. The health centre, Centro de Salud Dr José Saldedocano (☎ 953 72 10 61), is at Calle Ximénez de Rada 1.

Things to See

Calle Gómez Calderón heads south from Plaza de la Corredera to the **Balcón de Zabaleta** lookout point. Down to the left is the lovely **Plaza de Santa María** (or Plaza Vieja), with the large shell of the **Iglesia de Santa María**, built by Andrés de Vandelvira in the 16th century but wrecked by Napoleonic troops. A short walk up from here, the impressive **Castillo de la Yedra** houses the Museo del Alto Guadalquivir, with art and relics of past local life (open daily except Monday, the hours vary).

Places to Stay

Tiny *Camping Cortijo San Isicio* (☎ 953 72 12 80), off the Úbeda road about 2km from Cazorla, charges 1400 ptas plus IVA for two adults with a tent and car. You should find it open from March to early November.

The spick-and-span Inturjoven *Albergue Juvenil Cazorla* youth hostel (☎ 953 72 03 29, Plaza Mauricio Martínez 6), 200m uphill from Plaza de la Corredera, accommodates 97. For prices, see this chapter's introductory Youth Hostels section.

The friendly, clean *Hostal Betis* (☎ 953 72 05 40, Plaza de la Corredera 19) has singles/doubles from 1200/2500 to 1500/2700 ptas. *Pensión Taxí* (☎ 953 72 05 25, Travesía de San Anton 7), just off Plaza de la Constitución, and *La Cueva de Juan Pedro* (☎ 953 72 12 25) on Plaza de Santa María charge 1500/3000 ptas.

Hostal Guadalquivir (☎ 953 72 02 68, Calle Nueva 6), just off Calle Doctor Muñoz, is a grade better, with doubles with bath from 3800 ptas plus IVA.

Hotel Andalucía (☎ 953 72 12 68, Calle Martínez Falero 48) has nice, sizable rooms with bath at decent prices of 3400/4400 ptas for singles/doubles.

Hotel Peña de los Halcones (☎ 953 72 02 11, Travesía del Camino de La Iruela 2), 400m uphill from Plaza de la Corredera, has good-sized, pleasant rooms for 5000/6400 ptas plus IVA, and a restaurant and pool.

Places to Eat

Mesón Don Chema (Calle Escaleras del Mercado 2), off Calle Doctor Muñoz, does typical local fare from 700 to 1500 ptas.

La Forchetta (Calle de las Escuelas 2), down from Plaza de la Constitución, serves up pizzas and pasta for 450 to 700 ptas. Nearby on Plaza del Mercado, the classier *Restaurante La Sarga* does a 1700 ptas, four-course *menú*, and individual mains for around 1200 to 1500 ptas.

Down on Plaza de Santa María, ancient, wood-beamed *La Cueva de Juan Pedro* serves up very traditional Cazorla fare such as rabbit, trout, *rin-rán* (a mash of bacalao, potato and dried peppers), wild boar and venison as raciones for 900 ptas.

Several of the bars on Cazorla's plazas serve fine tapas – among them *Café-Bar Las Vegas* (Plaza de la Corredera 17). There's a daily **market** on Plaza del Mercado.

Getting There & Away

Alsina Graells runs two daily buses to/from Úbeda, Baeza, Jaén and Granada. The main stop in Cazorla is Plaza de la Constitución. Quercus has timetable information. A couple of other buses run just between Úbeda and Cazorla.

AROUND CAZORLA

The footpaths and dirt roads working their way between the forests, meadowlands, crags, streams and valleys of the Sierra de Cazorla, immediately east of Cazorla, offer heaps of scope for day walks or drives.

ANDALUCÍA

La Iruela This village is less than 1km up from Cazorla, to the east. The picturesque ruins of a Knights Templar castle stand atop a sheer crag at the east end of the village. If you turn right just after entering La Iruela from Cazorla (follow the 'Ermita' sign), you reach the Merenderos de Cazorla mirador after about 700m. Here a track heads 500m left up to a white church, the **Ermita de la Virgen de la Cabeza**.

Some 7.5km farther along the road, which becomes dirt, is **El Chorro**, a gorge which is an excellent spot for watching vultures.

Walks

The Ermita de la Virgen de la Cabeza is a starting point for many walks into the Parque Natural. A path behind the *ermita* climbs along the edge of a pine forest, then ascends a stream bed to join a north-south path about 1.5km (300m ascent) from the ermita. Heading south then south-east from here, the path loops around crags and brings you, after about 3km (250m ascent), to the 1550m **Puerto del Tejo** pass, three to four hours from Cazorla.

From Puerto del Tejo one track heads eastward down to the **Parador El Adelantado**, a little over a kilometre away. Just over 3km down the road from the parador towards Vadillo Castril is the **Fuente del Oso** fountain, from which the **Sendero de la Fuente del Oso** path goes 1.4km south-east down to the Puente de las Herrerías in the upper Guadalquivir valley. Another easy path, the Sendero de El Empalme del Valle, heads 1.5km north-west from the Fuente del Oso to **Empalme del Valle** on the A-319, a stop for Cazorla-Coto Ríos buses.

Another path from Puerto del Tejo, southward, runs 4km fairly level via **Loma de los Castellones**, a grassy area frequented by deer, to the **Collado del Gilillo** pass. From here it's a short detour up 1847m **Gilillo**, the highest peak in this area. A north-westward path from the *collado* leads 3km down to Ríogazas on the La Iruela-El Chorro road. You should get back to Cazorla seven or eight hours after leaving it.

PARQUE NATURAL DE CAZORLA

The 2140 sq km Parque Natural de las Sierras de Cazorla, Segura y Las Villas (to give it its full title) is the biggest protected area in Spain. It's a crumpled, memorably beautiful region of several rugged mountain ranges, divided by high plains and deep valleys, and in many places thickly forested. You stand a chance of seeing ibex, mouflon, red or fallow deer or wild boar here. The ibex lives mainly on rocky heights; the others prefer forests, but you may come across deer or boar near some of the main roads. Some 140 bird species nest in the park, with such as the golden eagle, Bonelli's eagle, griffon vulture, Egyptian vulture and peregrine falcon haunting rocky crags. The lammergeier disappeared from the park in 1986, but is being reintroduced.

In spring, the wild flowers are magnificent, and in autumn deciduous trees provide another feast of colour. Of the park's 2300 plant species, 24 are unique to it including the beautiful Cazorla violet, a very bright violet colour.

The Guadalquivir, Andalucía's longest river, rises in the south of the park and flows north into the Embalse del Tranco de Beas reservoir, then west towards the Atlantic Ocean.

The best times to visit are late April to late June, and September and October, when the vegetation is at its most colourful and the weather at its best. The park attracts an estimated 600,000 visitors a year, with the peak periods being Semana Santa, July, August, and weekends from April to October.

Information

The main information centre is the Centro de Interpretación Torre del Vinagre, 16km north of Empalme del Valle on the A-319; it's open daily except winter Mondays from 11 am to 2 pm and for two or three hours from 4 or 5 pm. In an adjoining building is

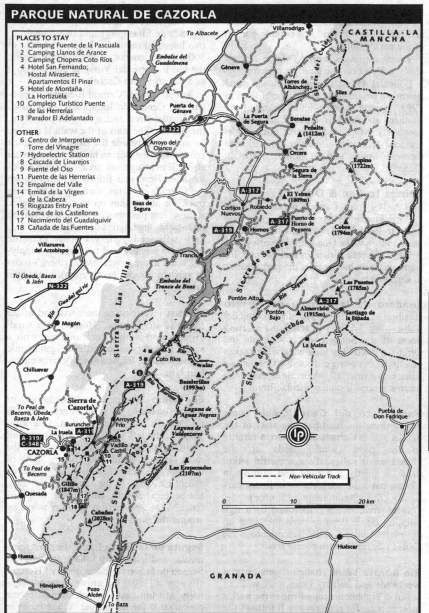

PARQUE NATURAL DE CAZORLA

PLACES TO STAY
1 Camping Fuente de la Pascuala
2 Camping Llanos de Arance
3 Camping Chopera Coto Ríos
4 Hotel San Fernando;
  Hostal Mirasierra;
  Apartamentos El Pinar
5 Hotel de Montaña
  La Hortizuela
10 Complejo Turístico Puente
  de las Herrerías
13 Parador El Adelantado

OTHER
6 Centro de Interpretación
  Torre del Vinagre
7 Hydroelectric Station
8 Cascada de Linarejos
9 Fuente del Oso
11 Puente de las Herrerías
12 Empalme del Valle
14 Ermita de la Virgen
  de la Cabeza
15 Riogazas Entry Point
16 Loma de los Castellones
17 Nacimiento del Guadalquivir
18 Cañada de las Fuentes

ANDALUCÍA

a Museo de Caza (Hunting Museum) with stuffed specimens of some park wildlife, and just along the road is a botanic garden of the park's flora.

There are banks with ATMs in Burunchel, Arroyo Frío and Cortijos Nuevos.

Editorial Alpina's Sierra de Cazorla and Sierra de Segura map/guides, published in 1998, include good 1:40,000 maps of the southern and northern parts of the park respectively. Maps and Spanish guidebooks are sold at tourist offices in the park and Cazorla town, and at some shops in Cazorla.

Things to See & Do

The A-319 from Cazorla winds over the 1200m Puerto de las Palomas pass and down to Empalme del Valle, where it turns north to follow the Guadalquivir valley. See Around Cazorla earlier in this chapter for some walks in the areas of the park nearest to Cazorla.

Sendero de la Cerrada del Utrero

Heading east off the A-319 at Empalme del Valle, after 3.5km you reach the starting point of the Sendero de la Cerrada del Utrero, a good 2km loop walk which takes you under imposing cliffs to the Cascada de Linarejos waterfall, then along above a narrow reservoir on the Guadalquivir.

Nacimiento del Guadalquivir

Some 400m along the road past the start of the Sendero de la Cerrada del Utrero, a turning to the right (south) leads up the Guadalquivir valley. It's a beautiful 14km drive – mostly dirt road and bumpy in places, but quite passable for ordinary cars – to the Nacimiento (Source) del Guadalquivir, which is indicated by a sign pointing down steps towards the river on your left. A little past the Nacimiento is the Cañada de las Fuentes picnic area.

Río Borosa Walk

Though it gets busy at weekends and holiday times, this walk of seven or eight hours round-trip is the park's most popular for good reason. It follows the tumbling, exuberantly vegetated course of the Río Borosa upstream, via the 1km Cerrada de Elías gorge and two tunnels, to two beautiful mountain lakes; an ascent of 500m in the course of about 11km. Using the bus to Torre del Vinagre, you can do it as a day trip from Cazorla.

A road signed 'Central Eléctrica', opposite the Centro de Interpretación, crosses the Guadalquivir and, after just over 1km, the Borosa. The start of the walk is marked on your right beside the Borosa. The track crisscrosses the Borosa before arriving after about 3km at a grassy area, the Vado de los Rosales. Here you follow a path through the Cerrada de Elías, then rejoin the main track for about 3km up to a hydroelectric station. Just past this, a sign points you on up towards the Laguna de Valdeazores. This path will lead you, via some dramatic mountain scenery and two tunnels supplying water to the power station (there's room to stay dry as you go through), to the two lakes.

Hornos

Overlooking the north end of the Embalse del Tranco, Hornos is a small village atop a high rock outcrop with a small, ruined Islamic castle and panoramic views. Casa El Rápido grocery rents mountain bikes.

El Yelmo

About 10km north-east of Hornos on the A-317 is the Puerto de Horno de Peguera pass and junction. One kilometre to the left here, a dirt road turns left to the top of El Yelmo (1809m), one of the most distinctive mountains in the north of the park. It's little more than 2km, and an ascent of 350m, to the top – OK for cars, but better as a walk, with superb long-distance views and griffon vultures wheeling around the skies.

Segura de la Sierra

Easily the most spectacular and interesting village in the park, Segura de la Sierra, 20km north of Hornos, sits atop a 1100m hill crowned by an originally Muslim castle which dominates the countryside for far around. When taken in

1214 by the Knights of Santiago, Segura was one of the very first Christian conquests in Andalucía.

As you approach the upper, older part of the village, there's a tourist office (☎ 953 48 02 80), which is open in Semana Santa and summer only, beside the Puerta Nueva arch. If the tourist office is open, ask about access to any buildings you want to visit. Through the Puerta Nueva is the **Iglesia de Nuestra Señora del Collado**, built about 1400. Below, on Calle Caballeros Santiaguistas, is the **Baño Moro** (Muslim Bathhouse) of about 1150. Near the Baño Moro is the **Puerta Catena**, the best preserved of Segura's four Muslim gates.

To visit the **castle**, you must borrow its outsize key from the tourist office (or the Cafe-Bar Casino just down the hill from the tourist office), in exchange for your passport. From the castle's three-storey keep there are great views across to El Yelmo and far to the west.

Activities & Organised Tours A number of operators offer trips to some of the park's less accessible areas, plus other activities. Several hotels and camp sites in the park can arrange for you to be picked up.

The most high-profile operator is Quercus (☎ 953 72 01 15), some of whose guides speak English or French. It has offices in Cazorla and at the Centro de Interpretación Torre del Vinagre. Quercus offers 4WD trips from these centres to *zonas restringidas* (where vehicles are not normally allowed) for around 3000 ptas a half-day or 5000 ptas a full day, as well as guided hikes and photographic outings.

Places to Stay

There's plenty of accommodation in the park but little in the budget bracket except about a dozen camp sites. At peak times it's worth booking ahead.

The *Complejo Turístico Puente de las Herrerías* camp site (☎ 953 72 70 90), on the road to the Nacimiento del Guadalquivir, open about mid-April to early December, has room for about 1000 people at 425 ptas per adult, per tent and per car. It also has cabañas and a restaurant, and offers activities from horse riding to canoeing or climbing.

Also in the south of the park, *Parador El Adelantado* (☎ 953 72 70 75) has all the parador comforts in a pine forest setting at 13,500 ptas a room.

Most accommodation is dotted along the A-319 north of Empalme del Valle. At Arroyo Frío, 6km from Empalme del valle, the modern *Complejo Turístico Los Enebros* (☎ 953 72 71 10), *Hotel Cazorla Valle* (☎ 953 72 71 00) and *Hotel Montaña* (☎ 953 72 70 11) all have doubles between 6300 and 7000 ptas plus IVA. Los Enebros also has apartments, wooden cabins and a small camp site.

Two kilometres north of the Centro Torre del Vinagre is the turning to the 27-room *Hotel de Montaña La Hortizuela* (☎ 953 71 31 50), in a tranquil setting 1km off the A-319, where singles/doubles with bath are 4000/5000 ptas plus IVA. It has a good restaurant and a pool.

A farther 1km north on the A-319 are *Hotel San Fernando* (☎ 953 71 30 69), with doubles at 9000 ptas plus IVA, and the older *Hostal Mirasierra* (☎ 953 71 30 44) where singles/doubles with bath are 3800/4800 ptas plus IVA. Both have pools. Adjoining the Mirasierra is *Apartamentos El Pinar* (☎ 953 71 30 68) with four-person apartments for 8000 ptas.

Within the next 4km on (or just off) the A-319 are three medium-sized *camp sites* beside the Guadalquivir, all charging around 1300 ptas for two adults with a car and tent.

In Hornos, *Bar El Cruce* (☎ 953 49 50 35, Puerta Nueva 45) has a few decent rooms with bath at 3500 ptas a double, and good food. Round the corner, *El Mirador* restaurant (☎ 953 49 50 19) has eight rooms with bath for 3700 ptas.

The only accommodation in Segura de la Sierra is the *Mesón Jorge Manrique* (☎ 953 48 03 80, Calle de las Ordenanzas del Común 2), with just a few rooms at

ANDALUCÍA

1800/3500 ptas for singles/doubles, and a small restaurant.

Getting There & Away

Bus Carcesa (☎ 953 72 11 42) runs two buses daily except Sunday – one in the early morning, one in the early afternoon – from Cazorla's Plaza de la Constitución to Empalme del Valle, Arroyo Frío, Torre del Vinagre and Coto Ríos. Quercus in Cazorla has current timetables. The run to Coto Ríos takes 1¼ hours. At our last check buses back from Coto Ríos left at 7 or 8 am and 4.30 pm.

Daily at 9.30 am, an Alsina Graells bus leaves Jaén for Baeza, Úbeda and La Puerta de Segura, where (except Sunday and holidays) you can switch to the 12.30 pm bus by Gil San (☎ 953 49 60 27) to Segura de la Sierra.

No buses link the northern part of the park with the centre and south.

Car & Motorcycle There are at least seven petrol stations in the park.

Almería Province

Andalucía's easternmost province is the most parched part of Spain, with large expanses of rocky semidesert, particularly north and east of Almería city. On the Cabo de Gata promontory, this stark landscape meets the coast in majestic fashion, with excellent beaches strung between dramatic cliffs and headlands.

Remote and for long forgotten and impoverished, the province has used its main natural resource, sunshine, to stage a bit of a comeback in recent decades through tourism and intensive horticulture in plastic greenhouses, a distinctly unattractive feature of the landscape.

ALMERÍA

As the chief port of the Córdoba caliphate and, later, capital of an independent taifa, the Islamic city of Al-Mariyat grew wealthy weaving silk from the silkworms of the Alpujarras. Devastated by an earthquake in 1522, Almería is today a mostly modern and likeable enough city of 171,000, hub of a mining and horticultural region.

Orientation

The centre lies between the Alcazaba and the Rambla de Belén, a *paseo* created from a dry river bed. Paseo de Almería, cutting north-west from Rambla de Belén to the Puerta de Purchena intersection, is the main artery.

Information

The helpful tourist office (☎ 950 27 43 55), Parque de Nicolás Salmerón s/n, is open Monday to Friday from 9 am to 7 pm and Saturday and Sunday from 9 am to 1 pm.

There are numerous banks on Paseo de Almería. The Policía Local (☎ 950 21 00 19) are at Calle Santos Zárate 11. The Hospital Torrecárdenas (☎ 950 21 21 19) is on Pasaje Torrecárdenas in the north of the city.

Alcazaba

The hefty hill-top Alcazaba on Calle Almanzor, founded in the 10th century by the Córdoba caliph Abd ar-Rahman III, still dominates Almería and commands great views, though earthquakes and time have spared little of its once Alhambra-like internal splendour. It's open daily: from mid-June to September from 10 am to 2 pm and 5 to 8.30 pm; otherwise from 9 am to 1.30 pm and 3.30 to 6.30 pm (free to EU passport holders, 250 ptas otherwise).

The lowest of the three compounds, the Primer Recinto, is mainly gardens. Originally it served as a military camp and a refuge in times of siege. The Segundo Recinto was the heart of the Alcazaba. At its eastern end is the Ermita de San Juan chapel, converted from a mosque by the Catholic Monarchs, who took Almería in 1489. On the northern side is the Muslim rulers' palace, the Palacio de Almotacin. The Ventana de la Odalisca (Concubine's Window) here gets its name from a slave girl who, according to legend, jumped to her death after her Christian prisoner lover

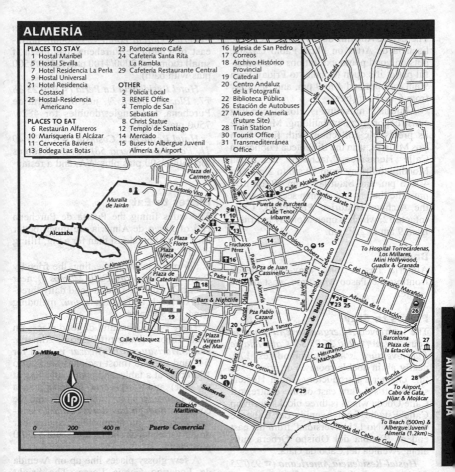

ALMERÍA

PLACES TO STAY
1. Hostal Maribel
5. Hostal Sevilla
7. Hotel Residencia La Perla
9. Hostal Universal
21. Hotel Residencia Costasol
25. Hostal-Residencia Americano

PLACES TO EAT
6. Restaurán Alfareros
10. Marisquería El Alcázar
11. Cervecería Baviera
13. Bodega Las Botas

23. Portocarrero Café
24. Cafetería Santa Rita La Rambla
29. Cafetería Restaurante Central

OTHER
2. Policía Local
3. RENFE Office
4. Templo de San Sebastián
8. Christ Statue
12. Templo de Santiago
14. Mercado
15. Buses to Albergue Juvenil Almería & Airport

16. Iglesia de San Pedro
17. Correos
18. Archivo Histórico Provincial
19. Catedral
20. Centro Andaluz de la Fotografía
22. Biblioteca Pública
26. Estación de Autobuses
27. Museo de Almería (Future Site)
28. Train Station
30. Tourist Office
31. Transmediterránea Office

had been thrown from the window when he was caught attempting to escape.

The Tercer Recinto, at the top end of the Alcazaba, is a fortress added by the Catholic Monarchs.

Catedral

Almería's weighty cathedral is at the heart of the old part of the city below the Alcazaba. Begun in 1524, its fortress-like appearance, with six towers, was necessitated by raids by pirates from North Africa.

The spacious interior has a Gothic ribbed ceiling and makes use of jasper and local marble in some of its trimmings. The chapel behind the main altar contains the tomb of Bishop Villalán, the founder of the cathedral, whose broken-nosed image is a work of Juan de Orea, who also created the Sacristía Mayor with its fine stone carving.

The cathedral is open for tourist visits Monday to Friday from 10 am to 5 pm and Saturday from 10 am to 1 pm (300 ptas).

Other Things to See

The **Centro Andaluz de la Fotografía**, in the Escuela de Artes on Plaza Pablo Cazard, puts on good photo exhibitions in a beautiful patio; it's open Monday to Friday from 9 am to 2 pm and 4 to 9 pm, and Saturday from 6 to 9 pm (free).

Almería's **museum** is closed pending construction of a new building. Meanwhile its prehistoric collection, with finds from Los Millares, is in the Biblioteca Pública on Calle Hermanos Machado. It's open Monday to Friday from 10 am to 2 pm and 4 to 6 pm, and Saturday from 10 am to 1 pm. The Iberian and Roman sections are in the **Archivo Histórico Provincial**, Calle Infanta 12, which is open Monday to Friday from 9 am to 2.30 pm.

Beach

Almería has a long grey-sand beach fronting the Paseo Marítimo, east of the centre.

Places to Stay

The Inturjoven *Albergue Juvenil Almería* youth hostel (☎ 950 26 97 88, Calle Isla de Fuerteventura s/n) accommodates 170, nearly all in double rooms. For prices, see this chapter's introductory Youth Hostels section. It's 1.5km east of the centre, off Calle Úbeda which is three blocks north up Calle Estadio from Avenida del Cabo de Gata. Bus No 1 'Universidad' from the east end of Rambla del Obispo Orbera runs along Avenida del Cabo de Gata.

Hostal-Residencia Americano (☎ 950 25 80 11, Avenida de la Estación 6) is a good choice near the bus and train stations. Well-kept singles/doubles are from 2200/4200 ptas with washbasin to 2800/5000 ptas with bath.

Hostal Universal (☎ 950 23 55 57, Puerta de Purchena 3), in the centre, has about 20 simple but sizable rooms for 1500/3000 ptas, with shared bathrooms. The building was once a minor mansion.

Nearby, the better *Hostal Sevilla* (☎ 950 23 00 09, Calle de Granada 23) has rooms with TV and bath for 3200/5000 ptas.

Hostal Maribel (☎ 950 23 51 73, Avenida Federico García Lorca 153), 600m northeast of Puerta de Purchena, has clean if small rooms for 2000/4100 ptas (2300/4500 ptas with bath).

Hotel Residencia La Perla (☎ 950 23 88 77, Plaza Carmen 7), just off Puerta de Purchena, has singles/doubles for 4825/7500 ptas plus IVA.

Hotel Residencia Costasol (☎ 950 23 40 11, Paseo de Almería 58) has good rooms for 7600/9500 ptas plus IVA, and a restaurant.

Places to Eat

The cafés lining the Puerta de Purchena end of Paseo de Almería are much better for a spot of breakfast than for a big, filling meal.

For more substantial eating, the friendly *Restaurán Alfareros (Calle Marcos 6)*, near Puerta de Purchena, has a good daily three-course lunch and dinner *menú*, including wine, for 950 ptas.

There's also a handful of good places on Calle Tenor Iribarne off Paseo de Almería. Here, *Marisquería El Alcázar* is good for fish and seafood (most raciones are 800 to 1000 ptas at a table, and about 20% less at the bar) and *Cervecería Baviera* has a three-course *menú* for 1000 ptas. Round the corner is *Bodega Las Botas (Calle Fructuoso Pérez 3)*, an atmospheric sherry bar doing varied tapas and raciones and a 2000 ptas *menú*.

A few glossy places line up on Avenida de Federico García Lorca. The bright *Cafetería Restaurante Central* does platos combinados from 975 ptas and main dishes from 600 to 1900 ptas. The *Portocarrero Café* and *Cafetería Santa Rita La Rambla* are nice for a lighter bite.

Entertainment

There are a dozen or two music bars and discos on streets like Calle Padre Luque, Calle San Pedro and Calle Real, between the post office and cathedral. Some open from late afternoon.

Getting There & Away

Air Almería airport (☎ 950 22 41 14) receives charter flights from several European countries and has daily scheduled services to/from Barcelona and Madrid by Iberia and to/from Melilla by Binter Mediterráneo (both airlines are on ☎ 950 21 37 90 at the airport). Pauknair (☎ 950 21 37 88 at the airport) flies Monday to Friday to/from Barcelona and Melilla. You can pick up one-way international fares from agencies such as Viajes Cemo (☎ 950 21 38 47) or Viajes Mundial (☎ 950 21 37 45) at the airport.

Bus The estación de autobuses (☎ 950 21 00 29) is 400m east of Rambla de Belén on Plaza Barcelona. Five or more daily buses run to Granada (2¼ hours; 1285 ptas), eight to Málaga (3¼ hours; 1915 ptas) and three to Sevilla (6¼ hours), plus at least one each to Jaén, Úbeda, Córdoba, Madrid, Murcia, Valencia, Barcelona and – except Sunday – Ugíjar (via Berja) and Bérchules.

Train The train station (☎ 950 25 11 35) is on Plaza de la Estación, 200m south of the bus station. Three daily trains run to/from Granada (2¾ hours; 1550 ptas) and two to/from Madrid. All go through Guadix.

Car & Motorcycle East of Almería, the N-344 is a faster and better road than the N-340.

Boat Trasmediterránea sails to Melilla six days a week, and three times daily from mid-June to the end of August. The trip takes up to eight hours. The cheapest passenger accommodation, a *butaca* (seat), is 3760 ptas one way; a car is 15,355 ptas. You can buy tickets at the Estación Marítima (Port) or at Trasmediterránea (☎ 950 23 61 55), Parque de Nicolás Salmerón 19.

Getting Around

The airport is 9km east of the city: the No 14 'El Alquián' bus runs between the city (east end of Rambla del Obispo Orbera) and airport every 30 to 45 minutes from 7 am to 9.30 pm.

AROUND ALMERÍA
Los Millares

Los Millares, occupied from about 2700 to 1800 BC, was probably Spain's first metalworking culture: its people's ability to smelt and shape copper made it a crucial stepping stone between the Stone and Bronze Ages. This large archaeological site, 20km northwest of Almería, contains remains of four lines of defensive walls, round dwelling huts, a foundry and over 100 tombs (some reconstructed). Opening hours are changeable – check with the Almería tourist office or by ringing the site (☎ 908-95 70 65).

In your own vehicle, head north to Benahadux, then north-west on the A-348. Signs indicate the Los Millares turning shortly before Alhama de Almería. You may get a bus bound for Alhama de Almería to drop you at the Los Millares turn-off, a few hundred metres from the site. But you may have to walk into Alhama, about 4km, to get a bus back – and these are rare.

Mini Hollywood

North of Benahadux, the landscape becomes a series of canyons and rocky wastes that look straight out of the Arizona badlands, and in the 1960s Western movie makers shot dozens of films here. Locals played Indians, outlaws and US cavalry while Clint Eastwood, Raquel Welch, Charles Bronson and co did the talking bits. The movie industry has left behind three Wild West town sets which are open as tourist attractions.

Mini Hollywood (☎ 950 36 52 36), the best known and best kept, is 24km from Almería on the N-340 to Tabernas. Parts of more than 100 films, including *A Fistful of Dollars*, *The Magnificent Seven* and *The Good, the Bad and the Ugly*, were shot here. Also here is a Reserva Zoológica with 100-odd species of African and Iberian fauna. Both are normally open daily from April to October from 10 am to 9 pm, and daily except Monday in other months from 10 am to 7 pm. At noon and 5 pm a mock bank hold-up and shoot-out is staged in Mini Hollywood. Adult/child tickets cost 995/

600 ptas for Mini Hollywood, 1195/650 ptas for the Reserva Zoológica, 1800/950 ptas for both.

You really need your own vehicle to visit. Buses to Tabernas might drop you at Mini Hollywood, but are unlikely to stop on the way back.

Níjar

Some of Andalucía's most attractive and unusual glazed pottery, and colourful striped cotton rugs known as *jarapas*, are made in this small town 31km north-east of Almería. It's well worth a little detour if you're driving this way. Shops selling the products, many of which are quite affordable, line the main street, Avenida García Lorca.

CABO DE GATA

Some of Spain's most beautiful and least crowded beaches are strung between cliffs and capes of awesome grandeur around this arid promontory east of Almería city. Though Cabo de Gata is certainly not undiscovered, it has a wild, elemental feel and is far enough from the beaten track to seem positively deserted compared with most Andalucian beach areas. With a couple of exceptions in July and August, its scattering of villages remain very low-key.

It's possible to walk along, or not far from, the coast from Retamar in the northwest to Agua Amarga in the north-east, but there's very little shade.

It's worth calling ahead for accommodation anywhere on Cabo de Gata during Semana Santa and in July and August. Camping is only officially allowed in the four organised camp sites.

Getting There & Away

From Almería estación de autobuses there are four or more buses daily to San Miguel de Cabo de Gata by Autocares Becerra (☎ 950 22 44 03); two daily Monday to Friday, one on Saturday, and one on Sunday from about June to September, to San José by Autocares Bernardo (☎ 950 25 04 22); and one daily except Sunday to Las Negras

and Rodalquilar by Tomás Marín Amat (☎ 950 22 81 78).

There's no bus service from Mojácar.

The only petrol station on Cabo de Gata is between Ruescas and San José.

Centro de Interpretación Las Almoladeras

About 2.5km north-west of Ruescas, this is the main information centre for the **Parque Natural de Cabo de Gata-Níjar**, which covers the 60km or so of coast around Cabo de Gata, plus a thick strip of hinterland. The centre (☎ 950 16 04 35) has displays on the area as well as tourist information. It is open daily, except Monday, in Semana Santa and July to September, from 10 am to 2 pm and 5 to 9 pm; and otherwise from 9.30 am to 3.30 pm.

San Miguel de Cabo de Gata

Fronted by a long straight beach, this village is composed largely of holiday houses and apartments, but has an old nucleus, with a small fishing fleet, at the south end. Caja Rural bank on Calle Iglesia has an ATM.

South of the village stretch the **Salinas de Cabo de Gata** salt-extraction lagoons. In spring many greater flamingos and other birds call in here while migrating to breeding grounds farther north. A few flamingos and many others stay on here to breed, then others arrive in summer: by late August there can be 1000 flamingos here. There's a hide just off the road 3km south of the village. Autumn brings the biggest numbers of migratory birds, but you should see a good variety any time except winter, when the salinas are drained after the autumn salt harvest.

Places to Stay & Eat *Camping Cabo de Gata* (☎ *950 16 04 43*), near the beach, 2km down a side road south of Ruescas, is open all year, charging around 1350 ptas plus IVA for two adults with a car and tent.

Restaurante Mediterráneo (☎ 950 37 11 37), towards the south end of the village seafront, has a handful of singles/doubles

CABO DE GATA

To Sorbas
To Murcia
Venta del Pobre
To Mojácar
Carboneras

Níjar
N-341
Agua
Amarga
Playa de los
Muertos
Faro de la
Mesa Roldán
Punta de la
Media Naranja

Campohermoso
Cala del Plomo

To Granada
& Málaga
San Isidro
de Níjar
Fernán Pérez
Playa de Cala
San Pedro
Punta Javana

N-344
Parque Natural
de Cabo de
Gata-Níjar
Punta del Cerro Negro
Las Negras

To Almería
Retamar
Los
Albaricoques
Hortichuelas
Playa del Playazo
Punta de la Polacra

El Barranquete
Rodalquilar
Lobos (265m)

Centro de Interpretación
Las Almoladeras
Petrol Station
Cala del Carnaje
Mirador de la Amatista
Playa del Peñón Blanco
La Isleta del Moro

Golfo de
Almería
Ruescas
Pujaire
El Pozo de
los Frailes
El Fraile
(493m)
Los Escullos
Parque Natural
de Cabo de
Gata-Níjar

Camping
Cabo de Gata
San Miguel de
Cabo de Gata
Salinas de Cabo
de Gata
Cerro de
Santa Cruz
(432m)
Punta de
Loma Pelada

Parque Natural
de Cabo de
Gata-Níjar
La Almadraba
de Monteleva
Cerro de
la Testa
(343m)
San José
Cala Higuera
Playa de los Genoveses
MEDITERRANEAN
SEA

Faro de
Cabo de Gata
Punta Negra
Playa de Mónsul

0   2.5   5 km

for 2500/4000 ptas. It serves decent seafood and meat for 700 to 1000 ptas. On the left as you enter the village from Ruescas, *Hostal Chiri-Bus (☎ 950 37 00 36, Calle La Sardina 2)* has five nice, modern rooms with bathroom for 3500/5000 ptas. This place was so new at the time of writing that it had no name sign. There are excellent pizzas nearby at *Pizzeria Pedro (Calle Islas de Tabarca 2)*, across the main road. *Hostal Las Dunas (☎ 950 37 00 72, Calle Barrionuevo 5)*, about 250m from the beach at the north end of the village, is a clean, modern place where singles/doubles with bath are 4500/6500 ptas plus IVA.

Faro de Cabo de Gata & Around

Beyond the Salinas de Cabo de Gata, the road winds 4km round the cliffs to the **Faro de Cabo de Gata**, the lighthouse at the promontory's tip. A turning by *Bar José y María* (serving seafood), just before the lighthouse, leads up to **Punta Negra**, 3.5km east, with an old Arab watchtower and awesome panoramas. Here the road ends but a walking track continues to Playa de Mónsul.

San José & Around

San José, spreading round a bay on the east side of Cabo de Gata, becomes a mildly chic little resort in summer, but it's still a small, rambling place with sandy streets and no high-rise development.

Orientation & Information The road from the north becomes San Josés main street, Calle Correo, with the beach a couple of blocks down to the left. On Calle Correo you'll find an information office (☎ 950 38 02 99), open daily except Sunday from

10.30 am to 2 pm (longer in summer), an ATM and a *Spar supermarket*. The information office can tell you about bicycle rental, horse riding, boat trips, windsurfing or diving.

Beaches San José has a sandy beach but two of the finest beaches on Cabo de Gata lie south-west along a dirt road. **Playa de los Genoveses**, a broad strip of sand about 1km long, with shallow waters, is 4.5km from San José. **Playa de Mónsul**, 2.5km farther on, is a shorter length of grey sand, backed by huge lumps of volcanic rock.

Places to Stay *Camping Tau* (☎ 950 38 01 66), open April to September, has a shady site about 300m from San José beach, with room for 185 people at around 450 ptas per person, per tent and per car. Follow the 'Albergue' sign pointing left as you enter San José from the north, and go about 800m.

The *Albergue Juvenil de San José* (☎ 950 38 03 53, Calle Montemar s/n) is a friendly independent youth hostel holding 86 people in bunk rooms of up to eight, at 1000 to 1300 ptas depending on the season. It is open from Semana Santa to 1 October, and also for Christmas-New Year and long weekends. Heading towards Camping Tau, turn right after crossing a river bed, then first left.

On Calle Correo, *Café Bar Fonda Costa Rica* (☎ 950 38 01 03) has eight decent doubles with bath for 5500 ptas plus IVA, and *Hostal Bahía* (☎ 950 38 03 07) has attractive singles/doubles for 5000/7500 ptas. There are half a dozen other hostales and hotels at similar or higher prices. If you fancy staying a while, consider renting an apartment.

For a bit of a hideaway, head for the friendly *Refugio Mediterráneo de Gata* (☎ 950 52 56 25) on Cala Higuera, a pebbly bay just east of San José. Eight rustic but cosy rooms for two or three people, some with kitchen, cost from 3000 to 6000 ptas, and there's a summer terrace bar with food. To find it, continue past Camping Tau to a

T-junction with a wooden fence in front of you, then go right for 1km, following 'Bungalow' signs.

Places to Eat *Bar-Restaurante El Emigrante* facing Hostal Bahía does good fish and meat mains around 850 to 1100 ptas, and omelettes or a big mixed salad for 350 to 500 ptas. Just back from the far end of San José beach, the popular *El Ancla* has seafood between 1100 and 2000 ptas. Just beyond, near the harbour, there's a line of eateries with outdoor tables including two Italian places (pizza or pasta 600 to 900 ptas).

San José to Las Negras

The rugged coast north-east of San José allows only two small settlements, the odd old fort and a few beaches before the village of Las Negras, 17km away as the crow flies. The road spends most of its time ducking inland, though you can walk nearer the coast most of the way.

The hamlet of **Los Escullos** has a short beach. The large *Camping Los Escullos* (☎ 950 38 98 11), 900m from the beach, is open all year and has a pool and supermarket. *Hotel Los Escullos* (☎ 950 38 97 33), by the beach, has about 20 rooms at 8000 or 9000 ptas; *Casa Emilio* (☎ 950 38 97 32) behind it has eight singles/doubles for 4000/6000 ptas. All three places have restaurants.

Two kilometres farther north-east, **La Isleta del Moro** is a tiny pueblo with a couple of fishing boats. Playa del Peñón Blanco stretches east. *Hostal Isleta del Moro* (☎ 950 38 97 13) has rooms with bath for 3000/5000 ptas, and a restaurant with fresh seafood. *Casa Café de la Loma* (☎ 950 52 52 11) just above the village, run by a friendly young German, has a few singles/doubles at 3000/4500 ptas, and a vegetarian restaurant in summer.

From here the road climbs to the **Mirador de la Amatista** lookout point before heading inland past the former gold-mining village of Rodalquilar. The turning to **Playa del Playazo** is 300m after a turn marked 'La

Polacra' just past Rodalquilar. It's 2km along a level track to this good beach between two headlands. From here walkers can stick close to the coast as far as **Las Negras**, which is on a pebbly beach, with several holiday apartments and houses to let. *Camping Náutico La Caleta (☎ 950 52 52 37)*, open all year, 1km south of Las Negras, has little shade but a nice pool. *Restaurante La Palma* on the village beach serves good medium-priced food.

Las Negras to Agua Amarga

There's no road along this secluded, cliff-lined stretch of coast, but walkers can take an up-and-down path of about 11km giving access to several beaches. **Playa de Cala San Pedro** nudist beach is about 4km from Las Negras. **Cala del Plomo** is about 3.5km farther on.

Drivers must head inland through Hortichuelas. A dirt road heads north-east across country from the bus shelter in Fernán Pérez. Keep to the main track at all turnings and after 10km you'll reach a paved road running down to Agua Amarga from the N-341.

Agua Amarga

Agua Amarga is a pleasant fishing-cum-tourist settlement stretched along a straight sandy beach. It has a supermarket and correos.

Three kilometres up the road to the east, there's a turning to the cliff-top Faro de la Mesa Roldán lighthouse (1.25km), with an old watchtower for a neighbour. The views up here are marvellous. From the turning you can walk down to the Playa de los Muertos nudist beach.

Places to Stay & Eat *Hostal Restaurante La Palmera (☎ 950 13 82 08)* on the beach has 10 pleasant rooms with bath for 10,000 ptas plus IVA (a bit less without sea view). On Calle La Lomilla just up from the west end of the beach, *Restaurante-Hostal René y Michèle 'El Family' (☎ 950 13 80 14)* has nine lovely doubles with bath for 10,000 ptas including a big breakfast

(half price from mid-September to February), plus a pool and an excellent 2000 ptas four-course *menú*, including drinks. The restaurant is open nightly at 7 pm, and Saturdays and Sundays at 1 pm. There are also houses and apartments for rent in Agua Amarga.

MOJÁCAR

Mojácar, north-east of Cabo de Gata, is two towns: Mojácar Pueblo, a jumble of white, cube-shaped houses on a hill top 2km inland, and Mojácar Playa, a modern beach resort strip, 7km long but only a couple of blocks wide. Though dominated by tourism, the Pueblo remains picturesque, and Mojácar Playa has been developed in a less intense way than other Spanish package-tourism honey-pots.

From the 13th to 15th centuries, Mojácar found itself on the Granada emirate's eastern frontier, finally falling to the Catholic Monarchs in 1488. Tucked away in an isolated corner of one of Spain's most backward regions, it was decaying and half-abandoned by the 1960s, before the mayor started luring outsiders with give-away property offers. Mojácar became chic and trendy, then a holiday resort. Today its two parts have a permanent population of around 4,000.

Orientation & Information

Pueblo and Playa are joined by a road which heads uphill from a junction known as El Cruce, by the Parque Comercial shopping centre towards the north end of Mojácar Playa.

The tourist office (☎ 950 47 51 62) is on Calle Glorieta, just off Mojácar Pueblo's main square Plaza Nueva, in the same building as the correos (postcode 04638) and Policía Local (☎ 950 47 20 00). It's open Monday to Friday from 10 am to 2 pm and 5 to 7 pm (in winter from 9 am to 3 pm) and Saturday from 10 am to 1 pm. Banesto next door has an ATM, as does Banco Andalucía in the Parque Comercial at El Cruce.

ANDALUCÍA

Things to See & Do

Exploring the Pueblo is mainly a matter of wandering the winding streets with their flower-decked balconies and nosing into the craft shops, galleries and boutiques. **El Castillo** at the topmost point is private property, but there are good views from the walkway around it. The fortress-style **Iglesia de Santa María** dates from 1560 and may have once been a mosque. The **Puerta de la Ciudad** gate on Calle La Guardia is one of the few vestiges of Muslim Mojácar.

The most touching spot is the **Fuente Público** in the lower part of the Pueblo. Though remodelled in modern times, it maintains the Muslim tradition of turning water into art. An inscription records the speech made here, according to legend, in 1488 by Alavez, the last Islamic governor of Mojácar, to the envoy of the Catholic Monarchs. It translates, in part:

Though my people have lived in Spain for more than 700 years, you say to us: 'You are foreigners, go back to the sea'. In Africa an inhospitable coast awaits us, which will surely tell us, as you do – and certainly with more reason – 'You are foreigners: cross the sea by which you came and go back to your own land'. Treat us like brothers, not enemies, and let us continue working the land of our ancestors.

Places to Stay

Mojácar Pueblo *Pensión Casa Justa* (☎ 950 47 83 72, Calle Morote 7) is good value with singles/doubles from 2000/4000 ptas. Nearby, *Hostal La Esquinica* (☎ 950 47 50 09, Calle Cano 1) charges 1750/3500 ptas. *Pensión La Luna* (☎ 950 47 80 32, Calle Estación Nueva 15) is more comfortable, with 10 doubles with bath for 6000 ptas including breakfast, and other good meals available.

Hotel Mamabel's (☎ 950 47 24 48, Calle Embajadores 3) has just four big, characterful rooms, with sea views and bath, for 6500 ptas. *Pensión El Torreón* (☎ 950 47 52 59, Calle Jazmín s/n) is another beautiful house with great views, and just five good rooms, with shared bathroom, at 6000

ptas a double. Apparently Walt Disney was born here!

Mojácar Playa The shady *Camping El Cantal* (☎ 950 47 82 04), 1km south of El Cruce at the El Cantal bus stop, has room for 800 people at around 2050 ptas plus IVA for two adults with a car and tent. *Hotel Bahía* (☎ 950 47 80 10), just south, has doubles from 4000 ptas.

Hotel El Puntazo (☎ 950 47 82 65), 2km south of El Cruce, is a decent medium-sized hotel with doubles from 6730 to 10,200 ptas, all with bath and breakfast, and a pool.

Hotel Playa Río Abajo (☎ 950 47 89 28) at the north end of town has 19 nice rooms in a pleasant garden fronting the beach for 6500 ptas (8500 ptas with TV and beach view). It has a pool, restaurant and bar. From La Rumina bus stop, head towards the beach and you'll find it.

Places to Eat

Mojácar Pueblo *Restaurante El Viento del Desierto* on Plaza Frontón is good value with main courses such as beef bourguignon or rabbit in mustard for 600 to 750 ptas. *Café Bar El Rincón de Embrujo (Calle Iglesia 4)* does platos combinados and seafood raciones from only 500 ptas.

Bar Aquelarre up in the shopping precinct above Plaza Nueva serves up reasonable meat and seafood dishes from 550 ptas.

Hotel Mamabel's serves up some of the best food in Mojácar, with main dishes from 1250 ptas.

Mojácar Playa *Restaurante Chino La Gran Muralla*, 2km south of El Cruce near Pueblo Indalo bus stop, has fair-value Chinese set meals from 625 to 1750 ptas. *Antonella*, just above the beach near Cueva del Lobo bus stop, pulls in the customers with its medium-priced pizzas and pasta. Out of season it usually is open evenings only. Farther south, *Mesón Casa Egea* at Las Ventánicas bus stop is popular for its fish and meat main courses from about 500 to 800 ptas.

Entertainment

Lively bars in Mojácar Pueblo include *La Escalera* on Calle Horno, *Budú Pub* on Calle Estación Nueva, *La Muralla* on Calle Aire Alto, and *Sahara* on Calle Cuesta de la Fuente. To burn up some energy after midnight in the high season, head down to one of Mojácar's open-air discos: *Master Disco* halfway between Mojácar Pueblo and Playa, *Pascha* by the beach just north of Camping El Cantal, or *Tuareg*, on the Carboneras road 3.5km out of Mojácar Playa. But bear in mind that these may only open on Friday and Saturday nights. *Tito's* towards the south end of Mojácar Playa, near Las Ventánicas bus stop, is a good lounge-type bar, sometimes with live music.

Getting There & Away

Buses stop at the Parque Comercial at El Cruce and at the Fuente stop by the Centro de Artesanía at the foot of Mojácar Pueblo. The tourist office has some timetables. Cafetería San Bernabé at the seaward end of the Parque Comercial sells tickets. At least three buses a day run to/from Almería (1¾ hours) and Murcia (2½ hours), two each travel to/from Granada (4½ hours) and Madrid, while another goes to Alicante.

Getting Around

The 'Mojácar Bus' runs from Mojácar Pueblo down to El Cruce, then to the south end of Mojácar Playa (Hotel Indalo stop), then to the north end of Mojácar Playa (La Rumina stop), then back to El Cruce and the Pueblo. It goes about every half-hour from 9 am to 11 pm in summer, and about every hour from 10 am to 6.30 pm in winter.

Extremadura

Extremadura, a large, sparsely populated tableland bordering Portugal, is one of Spain's least-known gems. It's not totally without tourists but is far enough from the beaten track to give you a genuine sense of exploration. The *extremeños* themselves have a flair for this: many epic 16th century conquistadors of the Americas, including Francisco Pizarro and Hernán Cortés, sprang from this land.

Though much of Extremadura is flat, wooded sierras rise up along its northern, eastern and southern fringes. The north, particularly, is a sequence of beautiful ranges and green valleys, dotted with old-fashioned villages that make for great exploring.

Extremadura's most interesting towns form a convenient triangle in the centre. Cáceres and Trujillo are full of reminders of the conquistadors and the Reconquista. Mérida was the main city of the Iberian Peninsula in Roman times and today has Spain's finest collection of Roman ruins.

Two of Spain's major rivers, the Tajo and the Guadiana, cross Extremadura from east to west. Those with an interest in wildlife should do their utmost to get to the craggy Parque Natural Monfragüe, straddling the Tajo between Plasencia and Trujillo, which has some of Spain's most spectacular bird life.

The name Extremadura probably means 'beyond the Río Duero'. In the 10th and 11th centuries the name was given to territory held by Christians in what's now southern Castilla y León.

In the 13th century, when most of Extremadura fell to Alfonso IX of León, the name was transferred to the newly acquired lands. Huge tracts of territory, granted to the knightly orders and nobility who had led the Reconquista, were turned over to livestock, especially sheep, leaving scant chance of gain for the rest of the population. Thus it was that so many extremeños were willing

HIGHLIGHTS

- Charming Trujillo, cradle of conquistadors
- Spain's finest Roman remains at Mérida
- Spectacular birds of prey at Parque Natural Monfragüe
- Exploring the lush valleys, ancient villages and high ranges of the north
- Cáceres' perfectly preserved medieval centre
- The biggest meal you may ever eat, at *Restaurante La Troya* in Trujillo

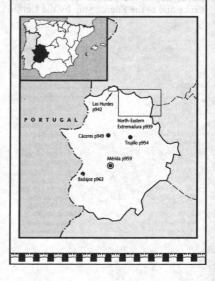

to try their luck in the Americas in the 16th century (see the boxed text 'Extremadura & America'). The riches some of these folk brought back turned Extremadura briefly into a prosperous place, but Spain's expulsion of the *moriscos* (christianised Muslims) in the 17th century contributed to a decline.

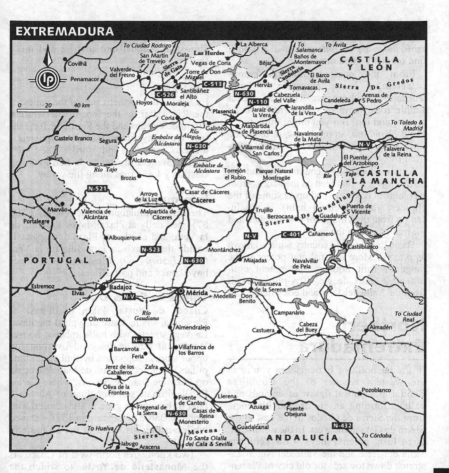

EXTREMADURA

In the 1970s a new wave of emigration took many hard-up extremeños to jobs in northern Spain and abroad. There's still minimal industry: sheep and pig farming, and olive, cork and fruit-growing are among the region's most important economic activities.

Extremadura is very hot in high summer and can be bitingly chilly in winter. Climatically, the best times to come are the second half of April, May, September and the first half of October. From May to late

June you could have a ball touring the main towns' major fiestas. Among other diversions, this is when Spain's top matadors head for extremeño bullrings.

Food & Drinks

Extremadura is often said to have two types of food: the fine fare that originated in its wealthy monasteries and convents, and a more rough and ready peasant cuisine. The Convento de San Benito at Alcántara concocted recipes so good that even the French borrowed them when their armies came this way early in the 19th century. *Perdiz al estilo/modo de Alcántara* is a dish you'll find on many good menus.

From the peasant tradition comes *caldereta*, a hearty casserole of lamb *(cordero)* or kid *(cabrito)*. You can expect simple roast lamb *(cordero asado)* to be pretty good too. But you might think twice about *chanfaina*, an offal stew, or *ancas de rana*, frogs' legs, which usually come deep-fried *(rebozadas)*.

Extremadura is pig country too and the *cerdos ibéricos* that feed on the acorns from its plentiful oak trees end up as some of the choicest *jamón* (cured ham) in Spain. Jamón from the villages of Montánchez and Piornal is among the best.

Basic Extremadura country wine is known as *pitarra*. More unusual and potent is the range of fruit liqueurs and potent *aguardientes* (eaux de vie, 40%-plus alc/vol) from the Valle del Jerte and elsewhere.

Northern Extremadura

In the far north of Extremadura you're in the western reaches of the Cordillera Central, a beautiful jigsaw of uplands and valleys forming an arc around Plasencia from the Sierra de Gredos in the east to the Sierra de Gata in the west. In the north-east, three lush, green valleys – La Vera, the Valle del Jerte and the Valle del Ambroz – stretch down towards the old city of Plasencia. Watered by rushing mountain streams called *gargantas*, and dotted with almost medieval villages, these valleys have a good network of places to stay and some excellent walking routes. A useful tool is the Editorial Alpina guide booklet *Sistema Central: Valle del Jerte, Valle del Ambroz, La Vera*, which includes a map showing many walking routes. Try to get it before you come: if not, the tourist office in Cabezuela del Valle may have copies.

The remote and mysterious Las Hurdes region in the northernmost tip of Ex-

tremadura has a harsher sort of beauty, while the Sierra de Gata in the north-west is almost as isolated but prettier and more fertile.

LA VERA
La Vera is the northern side of the valley of the Río Tiétar, at the foot of the western Sierra de Gredos and the Sierra de Tormantos. Its many crops include raspberries, tobacco, asparagus and paprika. The C-501 from Plasencia to Arenas de San Pedro in Castilla y León runs along the valley.

Information
There's a helpful tourist office (☎ 927 17 05 87) open daily at Plaza Mayor 1, Jaraíz de la Vera, and another at Plaza de España 1, beside the church in Jarandilla de la Vera (☎ 927 56 04 60). Most sizable villages have banks and post offices.

Things to See & Do
Cuacos de Yuste, 45km north-east of Plasencia, has its share of typical medieval La Vera streets, with half-timbered houses leaning at odd angles, and overhanging upper storeys supported by timber or stone pillars. Look for the Casa de Juan de Austria on Plaza de Juan de Austria, where Carlos I's illegitimate son Don Juan of Austria – later a charismatic general and admiral who won the Battle of Lepanto in 1571 – stayed while visiting his father at the Monasterio de Yuste.

Two kilometres north-west of Cuacos is the **Monasterio de Yuste**, to which the gouty Carlos I, having handed over the world's biggest empire to his legitimate sons, retired in 1557 to spend his dying years. The serenity of the setting makes it easy to understand his choice. The monastery is occupied by a closed order of Hieronymite monks, but the church and the simple royal chambers – with the ailing monarch's bed placed to give him a direct view of the altar – are open Tuesday to Saturday from 9.30 am to 12.30 pm and 3.30 to 6 pm and Sunday from 9.30 to 11.30 am and 1 to 1.30 pm and the same afternoon

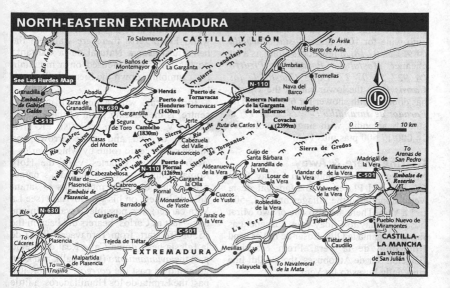

NORTH-EASTERN EXTREMADURA

hours. Entry is by guided tour in Spanish (100 ptas).

The road to the monastery continues 7km to **Garganta la Olla**, another picturesque village, from where you can head over the 1269m **Puerto de Piornal** pass to Piornal and the Valle del Jerte.

Jarandilla de la Vera, 10km north-east of Cuacos de Yuste, is a bigger village, with a 15th century fortress-church on the main square (below the main road), and a *parador* occupying the 15th century castle where Carlos I stayed for a few months while Yuste was being readied for him. A Roman bridge over the Garganta Jaranda below the village makes a focus for short rambles. Of the longer hikes, the Ruta de Carlos V (see Valle del Jerte later in this chapter) is one of the most enticing. To start this walk from the Jarandilla end, head north-west out of the village along the C-501 for a few minutes. Opposite the 'Camping Jaranda 300m' sign is a curve of disused road on the right, with a track off it that runs up between a hedge and a red-brick building. At the end of the hedge the

track bends left, then right. At this second bend look for a faint arrow on the wall pointing you up a path to the left beside a wire fence. This is the Ruta de Carlos V.

Other La Vera villages with particularly fine traditional architecture are **Jaraíz de la Vera**, **Valverde de la Vera** and **Villanueva de la Vera**.

Places to Stay & Eat

There are camping grounds – often with good riverside positions – in many villages. Most only open from March/April to September/October, but *Camping Godoy* (☎ 927 57 08 38) at Losar and *Camping La Vera* (☎ 927 56 06 11) at Jarandilla stay open all year.

On the main road in Cuacos de Yuste, *Pensión Sol* (☎ 927 17 22 41) has good singles/doubles for 1900/2700 ptas; *Hostal Moregón* (☎ 927 17 21 81), two doors along, gives you private bath for 3800/6600 ptas. Both have restaurants.

In Jarandilla de la Vera, *Hostal Jaranda* (☎ 927 56 02 06, Avenida Soledad Vega Ortiz 101), on the main road, has big, bright

EXTREMADURA

rooms with bath for 3250/6500 ptas, and an excellent value three-course *menú del día* with wine for 1000 ptas. *Hostal Marbella* (☎ 927 56 02 18), a few doors along, is a bit cheaper. *Hostal La Posada de Pizarro* (☎ 927 56 07 27, Calle Cuesta de los Carros 1)*, in the lower part of the village, has doubles with shower for 6500 ptas. The *Parador de Jarandilla* (☎ 927 56 01 17) is suitably splendid, with singles/doubles for 14,000/17,500 ptas plus IVA.

Getting There & Away

Mirat runs a bus Sunday to Friday from Cáceres and Plasencia to Madrigal de la Vera, stopping at the villages on the C-501 in La Vera. There are also one or two Mirat buses Monday to Friday from Plasencia as far as Garganta la Olla, Losar de la Vera and Robledillo de la Vera. From Madrid's Estación Sur de Autobuses, the Doaldi line runs daily buses to La Vera.

VALLE DEL JERTE

This valley, separated by the Sierra de Tormantos from La Vera, grows half Spain's cherries and turns into a sea of white blossom in April. The N-110 Plasencia-Ávila road runs up the valley, crossing into Castilla y León by the 1275m Puerto de Tornavacas pass. Tourist information is available from the Asociación de Turismo Rural del Valle del Jerte (☎ 927 47 21 22), Paraje de Peñas Albas s/n, Cabezuela del Valle.

Things to See & Do

The village of Piornal, at a height of 1200m on the south-eastern flank of the valley, is a good base for walks along the Sierra de Tormantos by the PR-19 path, or down to Navaconcejo in the valley by the PR-15. The lower part of the village, below the main road, is the more old-fashioned. Piornal temperatures can be pleasant in August but cold in September.

In the valley, **Cabezuela del Valle** has a particularly medieval main street, Calle El Hondón. A 35km road crosses from just north of Cabezuela over the 1430m Puerto de Honduras to Hervás in the Valle del

Ambroz. For hikers, the PR-10 trail to Gargantilla climbs roughly parallel – a one-day walk. From **Jerte** there are walks in the beautiful **Reserva Natural de la Garganta de los Infiernos**, focused on a mountain river tumbling down the Sierra de Tormantos.

Tornavacas, with a huddled, medieval centre, is the starting point of the **Ruta de Carlos V**. This 28km trail (No PR-1) is marked by red and white arrows and follows the scenic route by which Carlos I (who was also Charles V of the Holy Roman Empire – hence the path's name) was carried over the mountains to Jarandilla de la Vera on his way to Yuste (see La Vera earlier). It's possible to walk it in one day – just as Carlos' bearers did back in the 1550s. To start, from Tornavacas' Plaza de la Iglesia head down Calle Real de Medio past the *ayuntamiento* (town hall), and keep going down past the *correos*. Turn left just past the Ermita de los Humilladeros, a little chapel with black railings, cross a small bridge and turn right. The route crosses the Sierra de Tormantos by the 1479m Collado (or Puerto) de las Yeguas.

Places to Stay & Eat

Camping Río Jerte (☎ 927 17 30 06), 1.5km south-west of Navaconcejo, is open all year; *Camping Valle del Jerte* (☎ 927 47 01 27) by the Río Jerte 2km south-west of Jerte village, near the entrance to the Reserva Natural de la Garganta de los Infiernos, is open from mid-March to September.

In Piornal, *Casa Verde* (☎ 927 47 63 95, Calle Libertad 38) is a friendly hostel-style place charging 2500 ptas a person, including breakfast, in decent doubles with private bath. To find it, follow Calle Cuesta up from the plaza where the bus stops. It's advisable to ring ahead as it's often full, especially in spring. *Pensión Los Piornos* (☎ 927 47 60 55), on Plaza de las Eras near the bus stop, charges 2000/2500 ptas for plain singles/doubles.

In Cabezuela del Valle, *Hotel Aljama* (☎ 927 47 22 91, Calle Federico Bajo s/n), almost touching the church across the street, has nice rooms for 3000/4900 ptas plus IVA. There are numerous places to eat and drink on nearby Calle El Hondón.

Hotel Los Arenales (☎ *927 47 02 50)*, 2km south-west of Jerte on the N-110, has good rooms with bath for 4000/6000 ptas plus IVA, and a restaurant.

Hostal Puerto de Tornavacas (☎ *927 17 73 13)*, a couple of kilometres up the N-110 from Tornavacas, is an inn-style place with rooms for 2500/4600 ptas, and a restaurant specialising in extremeño food.

Good local trout is available in almost every eatery in the Valle del Jerte.

Getting There & Away

From Plasencia, there's one bus a day, Monday to Friday, to Piornal, and four a day, Monday to Friday (one on Saturday and Sunday) up the Valle del Jerte to Tornavacas.

VALLE DEL AMBROZ

This broader valley west of the Valle del Jerte is the route of the N-630 running north from Plasencia to Béjar and Salamanca in Castilla y León.

Hervás

The valley's main focus of interest is this pleasant small town with the best surviving 15th century **barrio judío** (Jewish quarter) in Extremadura, where many Jews took refuge in the hope of avoiding the Inquisition. There's a tourist office (☎ 927 48 10 45) on Plaza de González Fiori. El Lagar crafts shop on Rincón de Don Benito has displays on old Jewish life. You can climb up to the **Iglesia de Santa María**, on the site of a ruined Knights Templar castle at the top of the town, to get your bearings. The **Museo Pérez Comendador-Leroux** in an 18th century mansion on the main street, Calle de Asensio Neila, houses works of the interesting Hervás-born sculptor Enrique Pérez Comendador (1900-81) and his wife, the French painter Magdalena Leroux. It is open daily except Monday for varying hours (free).

Granadilla

About 22km west of Hervás, Granadilla is a picturesque old fortified village that was abandoned after the creation in the 1960s of the Embalse de Gabriel y Galán reservoir, which almost surrounds it. Since then it has been restored as an educational centre and you can visit from 10 am to 1 pm and 4 to 6 pm daily except Sunday afternoon and Monday (free).

Places to Stay

Camping El Pinajarro (☎ *927 48 16 73)*, 1.5km from Hervás on the more southerly of the two approach roads from the N-630, is open from mid-March to late September, charging 485 ptas plus IVA per adult, per car and per tent. *Hostal Sinagoga* (☎ *927 48 11 91, Avenida de la Provincia 2)*, outside Hervás centre, is adequate but dull, charging 3000/6000 ptas for singles/doubles with bath and TV. You may find the odd house with an 'Habitaciones' or 'Camas' sign in Hervás' *barrio judío*.

Getting There & Away

Los Tres Pilares runs two buses Monday to Friday between Plasencia and Hervás. Enatcar has a few services daily between Cáceres, Plasencia and Salamanca via the Valle del Ambroz, stopping at the Empalme de Hervás junction on the N-630, 2km from the town.

LAS HURDES

Las Hurdes was long synonymous with grinding poverty and disease and chilling tales of witchcraft, evil spirits and even cannibalism. In the 16th century a Carmelite monastery was founded in the Valle de Las Batuecas, across the border in Castilla y León, to counteract the demons. In 1922 the miserable existence of the *hurdanos* prompted Alfonso XII to declare during a horseback tour 'I can bear to see no more'. In the 1930s Luis Buñuel made Las Hurdes the subject of his film about rural poverty, *Las Hurdes – Terre Sans Pain*. Today Las Hurdes has shaken off the worst of its poverty, but the atmosphere in some of its

EXTREMADURA

more isolated and inbred villages remains a little spooky.

The rocky terrain yields only small terraces of cultivable land along the river banks, but has an austere beauty. The huddles of small stone houses look almost as much like slate-roofed sheep pens as human dwellings. Here and there are clusters of beehives that produce high-quality honey.

Things to See & Do

The heart of Las Hurdes is the valley of the Río Hurdano, north-west from Vegas de Coria on the C-512 Coria-Salamanca road.

From Nuñomoral, 7.5km up the valley, a road heads west up a side valley to such isolated and old-fashioned villages as **Fragosa** (turn south at Martinlandrán), **Cottolengo** and **El Gasco**. Various tracks head off into the hills from this valley: there's a good

walk from El Gasco to the 70m waterfall **El Chorro de la Miacera**.

Back in the main valley, **Asegur**, 5km north-west of Nuñomoral, has many stone houses that look as though they grew out of the hillside. Four kilometres up, **Casares de las Hurdes** is almost cosmopolitan. Between Asegur and Casares, another side road heads west to **Casabrubia** and **La Huetre**, from where you could head off for more walks into the hills.

Beyond Casares de las Hurdes, the road winds up through Carabusino and Robledo to the border of Salamanca province. Drivers could continue to Ciudad Rodrigo (25km), but a right turn just 20m before the border marker will take you winding 9km down through forest to the picturesque, isolated village of **Riomalo de Arriba**. From Riomalo de Arriba the road continues through Ladrillar and Cabezo to **Las**

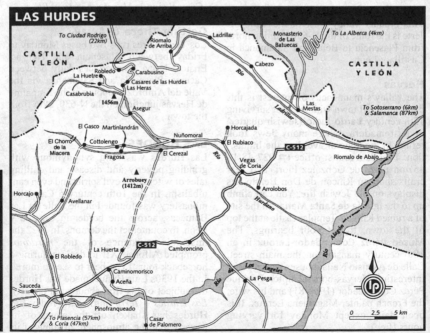

LAS HURDES

Mestas, a relatively lively place in the evenings. From Las Mestas you can turn north to the Valle de las Batuecas and La Alberca (see the Sierra de la Peña de Francia section in the Castilla y León chapter), or continue 3.5km down to rejoin the C-512.

Places to Stay & Eat

You'll find the closest camping grounds on the C-512 at Riomalo de Abajo and Pinofranqueado. *Camping Del Pino (☎ 927 67 41 41)* at Pinofranqueado is open from April to mid-October.

Pensión El Abuelo (☎ 927 43 51 14) in Caminomorisco has doubles for 2000 ptas plus IVA, and singles/doubles with shower for 1700/2800 ptas plus IVA. *Hostal Riomalo (☎ 927 43 40 20)* in Riomalo de Abajo has singles/doubles with shower or bath for 3000/3500 ptas. Also on the C-512 there are *hostales* in Pinofranqueado and Vegas de Coria.

Pensión Hurdano (☎ 927 43 30 12) in Nuñomoral has decent singles/doubles, some with bath, for 1600/2500 ptas. *Hostal Montesol (☎ 927 67 61 93, Calle Lindón 7)* in Casares de las Hurdes has doubles for 3000 or 3500 ptas plus IVA.

Nearly all the places to stay have reasonably priced restaurants or *comedores*.

Getting There & Away

Autocares Cleo runs a daily bus Monday to Friday from Plasencia to Vegas de Coria, La Huetre, Casares de las Hurdes (775 ptas) and back, and another (also Monday to Friday) to El Gasco and back.

SIERRA DE GATA

The Muslims built several castles here, and after the Reconquista, in 1212, the area was controlled by the Knights Templar and Knights of Alcántara. The traditional architecture features a lot of granite stonework with external staircases, and several villages have impressive 16th century churches. Olives and other fruit are grown in the lower parts of the area's wooded valleys. There's a tourist office (☎ 927 14 70 88) by the C-526 in Moraleja.

The two main roads through the region – the C-526 north from Coria to Ciudad Rodrigo and the C-513 west from the Valle del Ambroz to Penamacor in Portugal – cross near the biggest and one of the most attractive villages, Hoyos, which has some impressive *casas señoriales* (mansions) and a ruined 16th century convent. To the east, Santibáñez el Alto has a substantial castle dating back to the 9th century, with fine views; Torre de Don Miguel has more casas señoriales and an elm tree in its plaza said to be 500 years old; Gata has some of the best traditional architecture and another ruined convent.

In the west, locals speak a unique dialect thought to stem from Asturian and Leonese settlers in the Reconquista. San Martín de Trevejo is a pretty place with traditional buildings amid a landscape of oak and chestnut woods. Valverde del Fresno is larger but also picturesque, with a ruined castle and a handsome *plaza mayor*.

Places to Stay

At Gata, *Camping Sierra de Gata (☎ 927 67 21 68)* is open from mid-March to mid-October, and charges around 475 ptas per adult, per car and per tent.

In Hoyos, *Pensión El Redoble (☎ 927 51 40 18, Plaza de la Paz 14)* has singles/doubles for 1500/2500 ptas.

Pensión Avenida (☎ 927 67 22 71, Avenida de Almenara 12) in Gata is a little more comfortable charging 2500/3000 ptas plus IVA.

In Valverde del Fresno *Pensión Sajeras (☎ 927 51 02 49, Calle Francisco Pizarro 43)* has basic rooms for 1300/2600 ptas; *Hotel La Palmera (☎ 927 51 03 23, Avenida Santos Robledo 10)* has rooms with bath for 3000/5000 ptas.

Getting There & Away

There are one or two daily buses into the region from Plasencia and (except Saturday) from Coria and Cáceres.

EXTREMADURA

CORIA & AROUND

South of the Sierra de Gata, the old part of Coria (population 12,000) is still surrounded by what are claimed to be Europe's most perfectly preserved **Roman walls**. The most impressive stretch of walls is along Calle Horno. There's a tourist office (☎ 927 50 13 51) at Avenida de Extremadura 39A, open daily.

The impressive **catedral** on Plaza Catedral, open daily from 9 am to 12.50 pm and 4 to 7 pm, was built between the 14th and 17th centuries. Primarily a Gothic construction, it has platesresque decoration around the portals, a tall tower and a very wide nave. Below the cathedral stands a fine old stone bridge, abandoned in the 17th century by the Río Alagón, which now takes a slightly more southerly course.

Galisteo village, 26km east of Coria, is worth popping into for a look at its intact Almohad walls, the remains of a 14th century fort known as the Palacio, with a curious octagonal cone-shaped tower, and the *mudéjar* brick apse on its old church.

Coria's Fiestas de San Juan around 24 June feature bull running in the streets of the old town.

Places to Stay & Eat

In Coria, *Pensión Piro (☎ 927 50 00 27, Plaza del Rollo 6)*, just outside the old walls, has singles/doubles for 1500/2000 ptas and decent, inexpensive food. *Hotel Montesol (☎ 927 50 10 49)*, by the Río Alagón just off the Cáceres road, has rooms with bath for 2800/4000 ptas plus IVA.

Getting There & Away

The *estación de autobuses* is on Calle Chile in the new part of town, about 1km from the old part. There are buses at least once daily to/from Plasencia, Cáceres, Salamanca and Madrid.

PLASENCIA

This bustling and pleasant old town of 37,000, rising above a bend of the Río Jerte, is the natural hub of northern Extremadura. Founded in 1186 by Alfonso VIII of Castil-la, Plasencia only lost out to Cáceres as northern Extremadura's most important town in the 19th century. It retains a very attractive old quarter of narrow streets with some stately stone buildings.

Orientation & Information

The heart of town is the lively, arcaded Plaza Mayor, meeting place of 10 streets and the scene of a Tuesday market since the 12th century. The estación de autobuses is at Calle Tornavacas 2, about 1km east, and the train station is off the Cáceres road about 1km south-west.

There are tourist offices at Calle del Rey 8, a few steps east off Plaza Mayor (☎ 927 42 21 59), and on Plaza de la Catedral facing the cathedral (☎ 927 42 38 43). You'll find one or both open daily from 9 am to 2 pm and (except Sunday and holidays) 5 to 7.30 pm.

Things to See

The **catedral** on Plaza de la Catedral, a quick wiggle south-west from Plaza Mayor, is actually two cathedrals: the 13th and 14th century Romanesque Catedral Vieja round the side, and the 16th century Catedral Nueva, a mainly Gothic building with a handsome platesresque façade. Both are open Monday to Saturday from 9 am to 12.30 pm and 5 to 7 pm (4 to 6 pm in winter) and Sunday from 9 am to 1 am (free for the Catedral Nueva, 150 ptas for the Catedral Vieja). The Catedral Nueva was never finished, so seems disproportionately tall for its length. The carvings on its early 16th century choir stalls alternate between the sacred and the obscene: their carver, Rodrigo Alemán, is said to have been an unwillingly converted Jew who took the chance to mock the Christian church. They're behind a locked *reja* (grille), dividing the choir from the rest of the church, but the attendant may be willing to open it for you. In the Catedral Vieja, check out the fine Capilla de San Pablo and the lovely cloister.

Nearby on Plazuela del Marqués de la Puebla is the **Museo Etnográfico-Textil** with an interesting display of local crafts and costumes, open Wednesday to Sunday (free). The 16th century **Palacio del Marqués de Mirabel** on Plaza de San Vicente Ferrer houses the Duque de Arión's one room Museo Cinegético, a museum of hunting trophies and weapons (normally open daily till about 7 pm).

Among the numerous old churches and mansions in town, some of those most worth a look are the **Casa de las Dos Torres** on Calle Santa Isabel, the **Iglesia de San Nicolás** on Plaza de San Vicente Ferrer, and the **Iglesia de San Martín** on Plazuela de San Martín, all dating from the 13th or 14th century. San Martín, now an exhibition hall, has a retablo with paintings by the noted 16th century extremeño artist Luis Morales, known as El Divino Morales. At the east end of town is a series of pleasant **parks** crossed by a 16th century **aqueduct**.

Special Events
Plasencia stages its lively Feria y Fiestas de Junio over a few days in the first 10 days of June.

Places to Stay & Eat
Camping La Chopera (☎ 927 41 66 60), about 4km north-east on the N-110, has a shady site and a restaurant and pool, charging around 450 ptas per adult, per car and per tent.

There are four places to stay in the centre. The first three are all within two blocks north of Plaza Mayor. *Pensión Blanco (☎ 927 41 04 09, Resbaladero de las Capuchinas 5)* has simple singles/doubles for 1500/2500 ptas, or 1800/2800 ptas with shower. *Hostal La Muralla (☎ 927 41 38 74, Calle de Berrozana 6)* charges from 1700/3000 to 3350/3950 ptas plus IVA for a range of rooms. *Hotel Rincón Extremeño (☎ 927 41 11 50, Calle Vidrieras 6)* has good rooms with shower or bath for 4000/5400 ptas. *Hotel Alfonso VIII (☎ 927 41 02 50, Avenida Alfonso VIII 34)* charges from 6000/9500 ptas plus IVA.

The cafés under the arches on Plaza Mayor are a fine place to watch Plasencia

go by. *La Taberna Extremeña* on Calle Vidrieras, just off Plaza Mayor, and *Bar La Muralla*, next to Hostal La Muralla, serve reasonably priced *platos combinados* and *raciones*. Many of the dozens of bars in the centre serve free tapas with drinks.

Entertainment
There are plenty of lively bars in the streets either side of Calle Talavera, south off Plaza Mayor, and on Callejón de San Martín, north-west off Plaza Mayor.

Getting There & Away
From the estación de autobuses (☎ 927 41 45 50) there are up to 12 daily buses to Cáceres and Salamanca, up to six to Mérida and four to Sevilla (2850 ptas), and other services – but not always daily – as far afield as Madrid, Badajoz, Valladolid, Bilbao, San Sebastián and Barcelona. Direct buses to Trujillo, via the Parque Natural Monfragüe, only go on Monday and Friday.

From the train station (☎ 927 41 00 49) there are two or three trains daily to/from Madrid (3½ hours), Cáceres (1½ hours), Mérida (2½ hours) and Zafra, and trains six days a week to/from Sevilla (seven hours) and Badajoz.

PARQUE NATURAL MONFRAGÜE
This natural park straddling the Tajo valley is home to some of Spain's most spectacular colonies of birds of prey. Among its 178 feathery species are over 200 pairs of black vultures (the largest concentration of Europe's biggest bird of prey) and important populations of two other rare large birds, the Spanish imperial eagle (about 10 pairs) and the black stork (about 20 pairs). March to October are the best months to come, as the vultures, storks and others spend winter in Africa.

Orientation & Information
At the hamlet of Villarreal de San Carlos on the C-524/EX-208 Plasencia-Trujillo road is an information centre (☎ 927 19 91 34)

EXTREMADURA

Woolly Wanderers

If you travel the byways of Extremadura, Castilla y León, Castilla-La Mancha or western Andalucía you may find your road crossing or running beside a broad grassy track, which might have signs saying *cañada real* or *vía pecuaria*. What you've stumbled upon is one of Spain's age-old livestock migration routes. The Visigoths are reckoned to have been the first to take their flocks and herds south from Castilla y León to winter on the plains of Extremadura – a practice which not only avoided the cold northern winters but also allowed pastures to regenerate.

This twice-yearly *trashumancia* (migration of herds) grew to epic proportions in the late Middle Ages when sheep became Spain's economic mainstay. Huge clouds of dust raised by the migrating flocks were a characteristic sight in a countryside that was now often emptied of other agriculture and human habitation by the dominance of this single beast. (Don Quijote thought one pair of such dust clouds were armies advancing to do battle with each other and charged into the fray, only to find he was spearing sheep instead of valiant knights.) The powerful sheep owners' guild known as the Mesta established a vast network of drove roads which is said eventually to have totalled 124,000km.

The biggest drove roads – veritable sheep freeways up to 75m wide – were the *cañadas reales* (royal drove roads). The Cañada Real de la Plata – roughly following the Roman Via Lata from north-west to south-west Spain – passes just west of Salamanca, enters Extremadura by the Valle del Ambroz, crosses the Parque Natural Monfragüe and is then used by stretches of the C-524/EX-208 to Trujillo.

Come the easy truck and train transport of modern times, and a decline in the importance of sheep and in the attractions of the shepherd's life, the trashumancia has dwindled to a trickle. Many of the cañadas have been made unusable by new roads, spreading towns, reservoirs, rubbish tips and farms. The nearest most Spaniards come to a migrating sheep today is when Proyecto 2001, a campaign dedicated to keeping the drove roads open, takes a flock of 2000 or so through downtown Madrid each October. Proyecto 2001 has staged full-scale trashumancias of thousands of sheep each year since 1993, aiming to revitalise the trashumancia, arrest the loss of public land, and maintain the drove roads for their environmental value.

open daily from 9 am to 2.30 pm and 4 to 6 pm (June to September from 5 to 7 pm). From Villarreal several marked walking trails take you to some good lookout points, some of which you can drive to as well. Villarreal is near the confluence of the Tajo and Tiétar rivers, both of which are dammed not far upstream.

Things to See & Do

One of the best spots to head for is the hilltop **Castillo de Monfragüe**, a ruined 9th century Muslim fort about 1½ hours walk south from Villarreal (or a few minutes drive). This is a great spot for watching birds in flight from the Peña Falcón crag on the opposite (west) bank of the Río Tajo. Peña Falcón's residents at the last count included 80 pairs of huge griffon vultures, three pairs of black storks, and one pair each of Egyptian vultures, peregrine falcons, golden eagles and eagle owls – the latter another giant of the bird world with a 1.5m wingspan. You can get a closer look at Peña Falcón from Salto del Gitano, by the road below the Castillo de Monfragüe.

Another walk (2½ hours return) goes west from Villarreal de San Carlos to **Cerro**

Gimio, where you may see black vultures nesting. This bird is distinguishable from the griffon vulture by being all black. A further good bird-viewing spot is the **Mirador de la Tajadilla**, about a three hour round-trip walk from Villarreal (you can also drive there), which is noted for griffon vultures and Egyptian vultures in flight (the griffon is the bigger).

Places to Stay & Eat
You can get a bite to eat at a couple of bars at Villarreal de San Carlos, but the nearest place to stay is *Camping Monfragüe* (☎ *927 45 92 33)*, open all year, 14km north on the C-524/EX-208. Camping costs 450 ptas plus IVA per adult, per tent and per car, and there are six four-person bungalows for 6500 ptas plus IVA, a restaurant and pool, and bicycles for rent at 2000 ptas a day. At Monfragüe train station, 1.5km off the C-524/EX-208 from Camping Monfragüe, the recently opened *Residencial Parque Natural Monfragüe* (☎ 927 45 94 48, ☎ 989 31 45 12) has bunk rooms for two or four people at 2000 ptas a person, meals available, and says it can organise bicycles to rent or horse rides. Initially it was open some weekends only, so ring ahead.

The nearest hostales are in the village of Torrejón el Rubio, 16km south of Villarreal de San Carlos. *Pensión Avenida* (☎ *927 45 50 50, Calle San José s/n)* and *Pensión Monfragüe* (☎ *927 45 50 26, Paseo de Pizarro 25)*, on the C-524/EX-208, both have decent rooms with shared bathroom at around 3000 ptas a double, and restaurants. *Casa Rural La Cañada* (☎ *927 45 52 54, Avenida Virgen de Guadalupe 5)* has doubles with bath for 6000 ptas.

Getting There & Away
The only bus service is by the Izquierdo company, which runs buses on Monday and Friday only from Trujillo to Plasencia and back, with stops at Torrejón el Rubio and Villarreal de San Carlos, and a bus on Tuesday from Torrejón el Rubio to Plasencia and back. Schedules at the time of writing would give you a worthwhile six or

seven hours at Monfragüe before returning the same day.

Monfragüe train station (☎ 927 45 92 32, called Palazuelo-Empalme on some maps) is 16km north of Villarreal de San Carlos and 1.5km west of the C-524/EX-208 and Camping Monfragüe. It's served by two or three trains daily to/from Madrid and Plasencia, and one or two daily to/from Cáceres, Mérida and Zafra.

Central Extremadura

CÁCERES
At the heart of Cáceres, Extremadura's second biggest city with 78,000 people, stands an old town so little changed since the 15th and 16th centuries that it's often used as a film set. Cáceres is a pleasant and lively place, with a sizable student population.

A key goal for anyone hoping to control Extremadura, the city was captured from the Muslims by the Christian kingdom of León three times between 1142 and 1184 but was retaken by the Muslims each time. The fourth conquest, by Alfonso IX of León in 1227, proved permanent. Noble Leonese families started settling here in the late 13th century, and during the 15th and 16th centuries they turned its walled nucleus into one of the most impressive concentrations of medieval stonemasonry in Europe.

Orientation
The heart of Cáceres is the 150m-long Plaza Mayor, with the walled old city, the Ciudad Monumental, rising on its east side. Around Plaza Mayor and the Ciudad Monumental extends a tangle of humbler old streets that give way, about 450m to the south-west, to the straight Avenida de España lining the Parque Calvo Sotelo and Paseo de Cánovas. This is the modern half of central Cáceres. From the south end of Paseo de Cánovas, Avenida de Alemania runs 1km south-west to the train and bus stations.

EXTREMADURA

Dehesas

The Spanish word dehesa means, simply, pastureland, but in parts of Extremadura and the Sierra Morena, where the pastures are often dotted with evergreen oaks, it takes on a dimension that sends environmentalists into raptures of delight. Dehesas of encina (holm oak) or alcornoque (cork oak) are a textbook case of sustainable exploitation. The bark of the cork oak can be stripped every nine years for cork (corcho) – you'll see the scars on some trees, a bright terracotta colour if they're new. The holm oak can be pruned about every four years and the wood used for charcoal. Meanwhile livestock can graze the pastures and in autumn pigs are turned out to gobble up the fallen acorns (bellotas) – a diet considered to produce the best ham of all.

Such, at least, is the theory. In practice a growing number of Extremadura's dehesas are used to far less than their full potential. Some belong to absentee landlords who use them only for shooting; others are left untended simply because people are finding easier ways of earning a crust.

Information

The tourist office (☎ 927 24 63 47) at Plaza Mayor 3 is open Monday to Friday from 9 am to 2 pm and 5 to 7.30 pm and weekends and holidays from 9.15 am to 2 pm. Tourist information is also available in the Palacio Carvajal in the Ciudad Monumental Monday to Friday from 8 am to 9 pm and weekends and holidays from 10 am to 2 pm.

You'll find banks and ATMs along Calle Pintores, off Plaza Mayor. The main correos (postcode 10080) is at Paseo Primo de Rivera 2 facing Parque Calvo Sotelo.

The Policía Nacional (☎ 091) are at Avenida Virgen de la Montaña 3, off Parque Calvo Sotelo. The Hospital Provincial (☎ 927 25 68 00) is on the western side of Parque Calvo Sotelo.

Ciudad Monumental

The Ciudad Monumental is worth two visits – one by day to look around and visit such buildings as you can, and one by night to soak up the atmosphere of accumulated ages. Many of its mansions – all carved with the heraldic shields of their founding families – are still in private (often absentee) hands; others are used by the provincial government, the local bishop and sections of the Universidad Extremeña.

The Ciudad Monumental is still almost surrounded by **walls** and **towers** rebuilt by the Almohads about 1184.

Plaza de Santa María Entering the Ciudad Monumental from Plaza Mayor through the 18th century **Arco de la Estrella** arch, you'll see ahead the **Iglesia de Santa María**, Cáceres' 15th century Gothic cathedral. From February to September, Santa María's tower will be topped by the ungainly nests of the white storks which make their homes on every worthwhile vertical protuberance in the old city. The clacking beaks of the chicks demanding food are sometimes the loudest sound you'll hear. On the outside corner of the church is a statue of San Pedro de Alcántara, a 16th century extremeño ascetic who dedicated himself to reforming the Franciscan order. Inside the church, stick 100 ptas in the slot to the right of the sacristy/museum door to light up the fine carved cedar retablo of 1549-51.

The cathedral stands on one of the Ciudad Monumental's handsomest plazas, Plaza de Santa María, which is also fronted by such other fine buildings – all in 16th century Renaissance style – as the **Palacio Episcopal** (Bishop's Palace), the **Palacio de Mayoralgo**, and the **Palacio de Ovando**, this last built by Cáceres' leading clan of the 16th and 17th centuries. Just off the northeast corner of the plaza is the **Palacio Carvajal**, another old mansion now used to lodge visiting dignitaries and as the offices

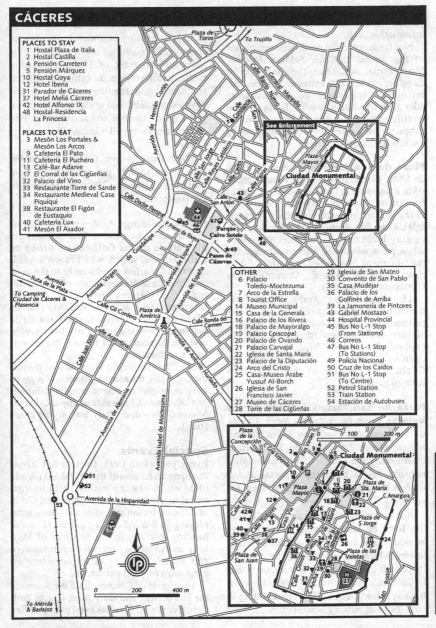

CÁCERES

PLACES TO STAY
1 Hostal Plaza de Italia
2 Hostal Castilla
4 Pensión Carretero
5 Pensión Márquez
10 Hostal Goya
12 Hotel Iberia
31 Parador de Cáceres
37 Hotel Meliá Cáceres
42 Hotel Alfonso IX
48 Hostal-Residencia
   La Princesa

PLACES TO EAT
3 Mesón Los Portales &
   Mesón Los Arcos
9 Cafetería El Pato
11 Cafetería El Puchero
13 Café-Bar Adarve
17 El Corral de las Cigüeñas
32 Palacio del Vino
33 Restaurante Torre de Sande
34 Restaurante Medieval Casa
   Piquiqui
38 Restaurante El Figón
   de Eustaquio
40 Cafetería Lux
41 Mesón El Asador

OTHER
6 Palacio
   Toledo-Moctezuma
7 Arco de la Estrella
8 Tourist Office
14 Museo Municipal
15 Casa de la Generala
16 Palacio de los Rivera
18 Palacio de Mayoralgo
19 Palacio Episcopal
20 Palacio de Ovando
21 Palacio Carvajal
22 Iglesia de Santa María
23 Palacio de la Diputación
24 Arco del Cristo
25 Casa-Museo Árabe
   Yussuf Al-Borch
26 Iglesia de San
   Francisco Javier
27 Museo de Cáceres
28 Torre de las Cigüeñas
29 Iglesia de San Mateo
30 Convento de San Pablo
35 Casa Mudéjar
36 Palacio de los
   Golfines de Arriba
39 La Jamonería de Pintores
43 Gabriel Mostazo
44 Hospital Provincial
45 Bus No L-1 Stop
   (From Stations)
46 Correos
47 Bus No L-1 Stop
   (To Stations)
49 Policía Nacional
50 Cruz de los Caídos
51 Bus No L-1 Stop
   (To Centre)
52 Petrol Station
53 Train Station
54 Estación de Autobuses

EXTREMADURA

of the local tourism department. Free guided visits are available daily: ask at the information desk.

Not far away in the north-western corner of the walled city, the **Palacio Toledo-Moctezuma** was once the home of a daughter of the Aztec emperor Moctezuma, brought to Cáceres as the bride of conquistador Juan Cano de Saavedra. Today it's the Archivo Histórico Provincial and sometimes stages exhibitions: otherwise, only the unexciting patio is open.

Plaza de San Jorge South-east of Plaza de Santa María, past the fine Renaissance-style **Palacio de la Diputación** (the Cáceres provincial government headquarters), is Plaza de San Jorge, above which rises the **Iglesia de San Francisco Javier**, an 18th century Jesuit church. The church's coat of white paint was added a few years ago for the filming of *1492, The Conquest of Paradise* starring Gerard Depardieu as Christopher Columbus.

The **Casa-Museo Árabe Yussuf Al-Borch**, nearby at Cuesta del Marqués 4, is a private house decked out by its owner with all sorts of oriental and Islamic trappings to capture the feel of Muslim times. Its opening hours are erratic. The **Arco del Cristo** at the bottom of this street is a Roman gate.

Plaza de San Mateo & Plaza de las Veletas From Plaza de San Jorge, Cuesta de la Compañía climbs to Plaza de San Mateo, where the **Iglesia de San Mateo**, traditionally the church of the landowning nobility, has a plateresque portal and a rococo retablo (it's usually only open for services).

Just to the east on Plaza de las Veletas is the **Torre de las Cigüeñas** (Tower of the Storks). This is the only one of Cáceres' many towers which did not have its battlements lopped off in the late 15th century, on Isabel la Católica's orders, to stop rivalry between the city's fractious nobility. The building is now the local military headquarters.

Also on Plaza de las Veletas is the excellent **Museo de Cáceres**. This museum is housed in a 16th century mansion built over an elegant 12th century cistern *(aljibe)* – the only surviving bit of Cáceres' Muslim castle – which is its prize exhibit. It also has an interesting archaeological section, rooms devoted to traditional crafts and costumes, and a good little fine arts section which includes works by El Greco, Picasso and Miró.

The museum is open Tuesday to Saturday from 9 am to 2.30 pm and Sunday from 10.15 am to 2.30 pm (200 ptas, free with an EU passport).

Other Buildings Also worth a look as you wander the Ciudad Monumental are the **Palacio de los Golfines de Arriba** on Calle Olmos, which was Franco's headquarters for a few weeks early in the civil war; the **Casa Mudéjar**, one of few buildings in Cáceres to show Muslim influence, on Cuesta de Aldana; and, on Plaza de los Caldereros, the **Casa de la Generala**, now the university law faculty, and the **Palacio de los Rivera**, the university's rectorate.

On Plaza de Publio Hurtado just outside the old walls, the **Museo Municipal** is given over to bright, attractive, acrylic paintings of Cáceres and Extremadura by local artist Massa Solís – open daily for varying hours (free).

Special Events

Every year since 1992, Cáceres has staged the Spanish edition of the WOMAD (World of Music & Dance) festival, with international bands ranging from reggae and Celtic to African, Indian and Australian aboriginal playing in the old city's squares. If you're heading this way in the first half of May, keep an eye on the papers for information or call ☎ 927 21 56 51 or try www.bme.es/granteatro on the Internet.

The Ferias de Cáceres, for a week around the end of May and early June, feature bullfights, concerts, fireworks and plenty of fun.

Places to Stay – Budget

Camping Ciudad de Cáceres (☎ 927 23 04 03) is 3km from the centre on the N-630 to Plasencia. It's quite a pleasant site, set back from the road, and open all year at 450 ptas plus IVA per adult, per car and per tent.

There's plenty of choice for rooms around Plaza Mayor, though the area can get noisy on weekend nights. The nine-room *Pensión Márquez* (☎ 927 24 49 60, *Calle Gabriel y Galán 2*), just off the plaza, is a friendly family-run place with clean singles/doubles at 1500/3000 ptas. *Pensión Carretero* (☎ 927 24 74 82, *Plaza Mayor 23*) has simple, decent rooms for 2000/3000 ptas. Outside summer it usually closes during the week. *Hostal Castilla* (☎ 927 24 44 04, *Calle Ríos Verdes 3*), one block from the plaza, has adequate rooms for 2000/4000 ptas.

Away from Plaza Mayor, *Hostal-Residencia La Princesa* (☎ 927 22 70 00) on Calle Camino Llano has 34 ordinary but adequate rooms. Singles, with shared bathrooms, are 2100 ptas; doubles are 3400 or 3750 ptas, with shower or bath. *Hostal Plaza de Italia* (☎ 927 24 77 60, *Calle Constancia 12*), away from the hustle and bustle, has clean, pleasant rooms with shower and TV for 3500/5000 ptas.

Places to Stay – Mid-Range & Top End

Hotel Iberia (☎ 927 24 76 34, *Calle Pintores 2*), just off Plaza Mayor in a 17th century building, is good value and full of character, with lounge and rooms with bathroom and TV, for 3000/6000 ptas plus IVA.

Hostal Goya (☎ 927 24 99 50, *Plaza Mayor 31*) has pleasant rooms with TV for 6500 ptas a double with shower, 7500 ptas with bath. *Hotel Alfonso IX* (☎ 927 24 64 00, *Calle Moret 22*) has reasonable rooms from 4400/6900 ptas. A good 450 ptas breakfast is available.

The *Parador de Cáceres* (☎ 927 21 17 59, *Calle Ancha 6*), in the Ciudad Monumental, occupies a 14th century mansion and has all mod cons, with singles/doubles from 12,000/17,000 ptas plus IVA. *Hotel*

Meliá Cáceres (☎ 927 21 58 00, *Plaza de San Juan 11*), in a 16th century mansion just outside the Ciudad Monumental, has good modern rooms at 15,000/19,300 ptas plus IVA, and all the appropriate services.

Places to Eat

Plaza Mayor & Around *Cafetería El Puchero (Plaza Mayor 33)* is a popular hang-out with a huge variety of eating options, from good *bocadillos* (around 400 ptas) and raciones to solid platos combinados (675 to 900 ptas) or à la carte fare. *Cafetería El Pato*, a block down the arcade, has excellent coffee and an upstairs restaurant with good three-course *menús*, including wine, for 1200 and 1800 ptas plus IVA.

Mesón Los Portales and *Mesón Los Arcos* at the bottom of Plaza Mayor and *Cafetería Lux (Calle Pintores 32)* all do platos combinados from 550 to 850 ptas. *Mesón El Asador (Calle Moret 34)*, just off Calle Pintores, is good for roast and grilled meat, with most main dishes from 1600 ptas though chicken and *solomillo* (pork sirloin) are considerably less. Its bar serves bocadillos from 300 ptas and dozens of raciones and tapas.

Café-Bar Adarve off Calle Pintores is not a bad spot for breakfast – 175 to 225 ptas for coffee and a *tostada* or croissant.

Restaurante El Figón de Eustaquio (Plaza de San Juan 12) is a good bet for a traditional extremeño meal. The three-course *menú de la casa*, with wine, is 1650 ptas plus IVA, or there's a *menú regional* at 2600 ptas plus IVA. À-la-carte mains are between 750 and 1700 ptas plus IVA.

Good shops to inspect local hams, sausages, cheeses and fruit liquor are *La Jamonería de Pintores* on Calle Pintores, and *Gabriel Mostazo* at the corner of Calle San Pedro and Calle San Antón.

Ciudad Monumental The Ciudad Monumental has several medium to expensive restaurants serving mainly traditional food in suitably ancient surroundings. *Menús* are 2000 to 2800 ptas plus IVA at the *Palacio* *del Vino* on Calle Ancha (also with a bar serving tapas and raciones); 2500 and 3900 ptas at *Restaurante Medieval Casa Piquiqui (Calle Orellana 1)*; and 3500 or 4000 ptas plus IVA at *Restaurante Torre de Sande*, with tables in a nice courtyard, on Calle de los Condes. If you intend to splash out, the restaurant at the *Parador de Cáceres (Calle Ancha 6)* is pretty good – especially its *caldereta de cordero*. The *menú* is 4250 ptas plus IVA.

For a more economical bite, *El Corral de las Cigüeñas* on Cuesta de Aldana has raciones from 500 ptas. Or visit the *Convento de San Pablo* on Plaza de San Mateo, where the nuns bake and sell tasty snacks such as *pastas con almendra* (almond pastries; 475 ptas) and *yemas de San Pablo* (candied egg yolks; 650 ptas). A revolving dumb waiter enables the nuns, who are members of a closed order, to sell the goodies without seeing or being seen by customers. Hours are Monday to Friday from 9 am to 1 pm and 5 to 8 pm and Saturday from 9 am to 1 pm.

Entertainment

The bottom (north) end of Plaza Mayor, and nearby streets such as Calle Gabriel y Galán and Calle General Ezponda, are full of lively *late night bars*, most with recorded music. At weekends during university terms, you can party here most of the night.

El Corral de las Cigüeñas in the Ciudad Monumental is a popular place for a drink on a summer evening, with a couple of palm trees poking out of its old courtyard and occasional live music from flamenco to blues.

Getting There & Away

Bus Minimum daily services from the estación de autobuses (☎ 927 23 25 50) include at least six to Trujillo (400 ptas) and Madrid (3½ hours; 2385 ptas); five each to Mérida (1¼ hours; 650 ptas) and Plasencia; three each to Salamanca (three to four hours; 2000 ptas), Zafra and Sevilla (four hours; 2170 ptas); two to Badajoz (825 ptas); and one each to Córdoba and Barcelona. To most places there are more services Monday to Friday.

Train There are three to five trains a day to/from Madrid (3½ to five hours; from 2300 ptas) and Mérida (one hour); two or three each to/from Plasencia (1¼ hours), Badajoz (two hours) and Barcelona; and one to/from Sevilla (5½ hours; 2165 ptas). The single daily train to Lisbon (six hours; from 4400 ptas) leaves in the middle of the night. The station is on ☎ 927 23 37 61.

Getting Around

Bus No L-1 from the stop beside the petrol station by the roundabout outside the train station – also close to the bus station – will take you into town. The nearest stop to the centre is the third, on Paseo Primo de Rivera. Returning to the stations, you can catch this bus by the Kiosco Colón on Avenida de España.

ALCÁNTARA

This historic and pleasant small town is 62km north-west of Cáceres on a route to Portugal, the C-523. There's a tourist office (☎ 927 39 08 63) on the way in from Cáceres at Avenida de Mérida 21.

Alcántara is Arabic for 'the bridge'. The finest **Roman bridge** in Spain – 204m long, 61m high and built without mortar – spans the Río Tajo west of the town, below a huge modern dam holding back the Embalse de Alcántara reservoir. There's a memorial to the bridge's architect, Caius Julius Lacer, in a small Roman temple on the river bank.

The town itself has old walls, remains of a castle, and numerous fine old buildings. From 1218 it was the headquarters of the Orden de Alcántara, an order of Reconquista knights that ruled much of western Extremadura as a kind of private kingdom. The order built the 16th century **Convento de San Benito**, famous for its recipes, with Renaissance exterior, Gothic cloister, plateresque church interior and beautiful three-tier gallery. The 13th century **Iglesia de Santa María de Almócovar**, a mix of Romanesque and Herreran styles, contains tombs of masters of the Orden de Alcántara and paintings by El Divino Morales.

Hostal Kantara Al Saif (☎ 927 39 08 33, Avenida de Mérida s/n) has doubles with bath from 4500 to 6500 ptas plus IVA, depending on the season.

Buses run daily except Sunday from Cáceres.

TRUJILLO

Trujillo is one of the most perfect little towns in Spain. With just 9000 people, it can't be much bigger now than it was in 1529 when its most famous son, Francisco Pizarro, set off with his four half-brothers and a few other local buddies for an expedition that culminated in the bloody conquest of the Inca empire (see the boxed text 'Extremadura & America').

Trujillo is blessed with a broad and fine plaza mayor, from which rises its remarkably preserved old town, packed with aged buildings exuding history. If you arrive from the Plasencia direction you might imagine that you've driven through a time warp into the 16th century.

Information

The tourist office (☎ 927 32 26 77) on Plaza Mayor is open Monday to Friday from 9 am to 2 pm and 5 to 7.30 pm and weekends and holidays from 9.15 am to 2 pm. The correos (postcode 10200) is at Calle Encarnación 28, south of the centre.

The Policía Local are in an alley off Plaza Mayor.

Things to See

Plaza Mayor A large equestrian **statue of Pizarro**, done by an American, Charles Rumsey, in the 1920s, dominates Plaza Mayor. There's a tale that Rumsey originally did the piece as a statue of Hernán Cortés, to present to Mexico, but Mexico (which takes a poor view of Cortés) didn't want it, so it was given to Trujillo as Pizarro instead!

On the plaza's south side, the corner of the **Palacio de la Conquista** sports the carved images of Pizarro and his lover Inés

Yupanqui (sister of the Inca emperor Atahualpa) and, to the right, their daughter Francisca Pizarro Yupanqui with her husband (and uncle) Hernando Pizarro. The mansion was built in the 1560s for Hernando and Francisca after Hernando – the only Pizarro brother not to die a bloody death in Peru – had done 20 years in jail in Spain for the killing of Diego de Almagro. Above the corner balcony another carving shows the Pizarro family shield – two bears and a pine tree – surrounded by the walls of Cuzco, plus Pizarro's ships at Tumbes, and Atahualpa with his hands in two chests of gold surrounded by seven Inca chiefs. The inside of the palacio is not open to visitors.

Overlooking the Plaza Mayor from the north-east corner is the mainly 16th century **Iglesia de San Martín**, with a number of noble tombs inside (normally only open for services). Its towers, like many in Trujillo, support the precarious nests of storks for much of the year. Across the street from the church is the 16th century **Palacio de los Duques de San Carlos**, now a convent but open for visits daily (100 ptas). It has a classical-style patio and a very grand staircase.

Through an alley from the south-west corner of Plaza Mayor is the **Palacio Juan Pizarro de Orellana**, which was converted from a miniature fortress into a Renaissance mansion by a cousin of the Pizarros who took part in the conquest of Peru and lived to reap the benefits back home. It's now a school and you can visit its patio, decorated with Pizarro and Orellana coats of arms, daily from 9.30 am to 2 pm and 4.30 to 7 pm (free).

Upper Town The 900m of **walls** circling the upper town date from Muslim times. It was here that after the Reconquista the newly settled noble families erected their mansions and churches.

The **Iglesia de Santiago** on Plaza Santiago was founded in the 13th century by the Knights of Santiago, and their conchshell emblem is a recurring motif. It's open from 11 am to 5 pm (50 ptas).

TRUJILLO

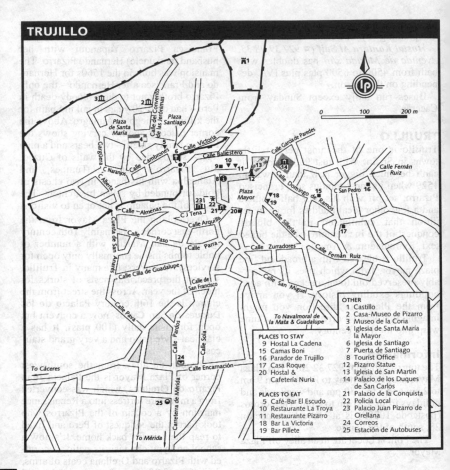

0   100   200 m

OTHER
1 Castillo
2 Casa-Museo de Pizarro
3 Museo de la Coria
4 Iglesia de Santa María
   la Mayor
6 Iglesia de Santiago
7 Puerta de Santiago
8 Tourist Office
12 Pizarro Statue
13 Iglesia de San Martín
14 Palacio de los Duques
   de San Carlos
21 Palacio de la Conquista
22 Policia Local
23 Palacio Juan Pizarro de
   Orellana
24 Correos
25 Estación de Autobuses

PLACES TO STAY
9 Hostal La Cadena
15 Camas Boni
16 Parador de Trujillo
17 Casa Roque
20 Hostal &
   Cafetería Nuria

PLACES TO EAT
5 Café-Bar El Escudo
10 Restaurante La Troya
11 Restaurante Pizarro
18 Bar La Victoria
19 Bar Pillete

The **Iglesia de Santa María la Mayor** on Plaza de Santa María is a hotchpotch of 13th to 16th century styles, with a Romanesque tower. Inside are the tombs of leading Trujillo families of the Middle Ages, plus that of Diego García de Paredes (1466-1530), a Trujillo warrior of legendary strength who, according to Cervantes, could stop a mill wheel with one finger. The church has a fine retablo with Flemish-style paintings done in about 1485 by Fernando Gallego from Salamanca. It's open from 10.30 am to 2 pm and 4.30 to 6 pm (50 ptas).

A little higher, the 15th century **Casa-Museo de Pizarro** was the ancestral home of the great conquistador family. Recently restored in the style of the 15th and 16th centuries, the house contains informative displays (in Spanish) on the Inca empire and the Pizarros. Whether Francisco Pizarro ever lived here is doubtful. Though the eldest of his father Gonzalo's nine children (by four women) Francisco was illegitimate and not accepted as an heir. However it was to this house that Francisco was brought in triumph by his siblings on his visit to Trujillo in 1529. The house is open Tuesday to Sunday from 11 am to 2.30 pm and 3.30 to 8.30 pm (250 ptas).

The **Museo de la Coria** has further displays on the conquest of the Americas, in a restored former convent. It's only open weekends and holidays from 11.30 am to 2 pm (free).

At the top of the hill and affording great views, Trujillo's **castillo**, of 10th century Muslim origin and strengthened later by the Christians, is impressive though empty. It's open daily till dusk (free).

Special Events
The Feria y Fiestas de Trujillo, with bull-fights, music and partying, last for a few days in early June.

Places to Stay
Camas Boni (☎ 927 32 16 04, Calle Domingo de Ramos 7) is good value with small but well kept singles/doubles from 2000/3000 ptas, and doubles with bathroom for 4500 ptas. *Casa Roque (☎ 927 32 23 13, Calle Domingo de Ramos 30)* has singles at 1500 ptas, and doubles with bath at 3500 ptas. *Hostal Nuria (☎ 927 32 09 07, Plaza Mayor 27)* has nice rooms with bath for 3000/5000 ptas. The friendly eight-room *Hostal La Cadena (☎ 927 32 14 63, Plaza Mayor 8)* is also good, charging at 4500/5500 ptas.

The *Parador de Trujillo (☎ 927 32 13 50)* on Plaza de Santa Clara is in a beautiful former convent dating from the 16th century. Rooms are 12,000/15,000 ptas plus IVA.

Places to Eat
If you're a meat-eater, the 1990 ptas *menú* at *Restaurante La Troya (Plaza Mayor 10)* will save you from eating much else for the next couple of days. What the bare three-course list of offerings doesn't tell you is that portions are gigantic and that they also give you a large potato omelette and salad

for starters, and an extra main course later on! Caldereta is a main course speciality. If you're not *that* hungry there are great tapas here too. Elsewhere on Plaza Mayor, *Hostal La Cadena* and *Restaurante Pizarro* do normal-size meals, *Cafétería Nuria* has salads and egg dishes for 500 to 900 ptas and meat and fish from 900 ptas, *Bar La Victoria* has a range of breakfasts including 'English' for 225 to 550 ptas, and *Bar Pillete* is the classiest café and has the best position.

Café-Bar El Escudo up the hill on Plaza Santiago has moderately priced raciones and platos combinados.

The *Parador de Trujillo* has an excellent restaurant, but you're looking at around 4000 ptas for a full meal.

Getting There & Away
The estación de autobuses (☎ 927 32 05 00) is 500m south of Plaza Mayor, on Carretera de Mérida. At least six buses daily run to/from Cáceres (45 minutes; 400 ptas), Badajoz and Madrid (2½ to four hours; 1985 ptas), and four or more to/from Mérida (1¼ hours; 830 ptas). For buses to/from Villarreal de San Carlos (for Parque Natural Monfragüe) and Plasencia, see the Parque Natural Monfragüe section.

GUADALUPE
Tucked away among the picturesque hills of eastern Extremadura – an extension of those in western Castilla-La Mancha – the attractive old village of Guadalupe is home to an important and interesting monastery housing a statuette of the Virgin, Nuestra Señora de Guadalupe, which for centuries has been one of Spain's and Latin America's most revered. Lovers of remote country can drive or walk off from Guadalupe into craggy sierras divided by deep, green valleys with chestnut and oak woodlands as well as olive groves and vineyards.

Orientation & Information
Buses stop opposite the ayuntamiento on Avenida Conde de Barcelona, a two-minute

Extremadura & America

Many extremeños jumped at the opportunities opened up by Columbus' discovery of the Americas in 1492.

In 1501 Fray Nicolás de Ovando from Cáceres was named governor of the Indies by the Catholic Monarchs. He set up his capital, Santo Domingo, on the Caribbean island of Hispaniola. With him went 2500 followers, many of them from Extremadura, including Francisco Pizarro, an illegitimate son of a minor noble family from Trujillo. In 1504, Hernán Cortés, from a similar family in Medellín, east of Mérida, arrived in Santo Domingo too.

Both young men prospered in the new world. Cortés took part in the conquest of Cuba in 1511 and settled there to raise livestock and trade the gold mined by the Indians whose labour he had been granted. Pizarro, in 1513, accompanied Vasco Núñez de Balboa (from Jerez de los Caballeros in south-west Extremadura) to Darién (Panama), where they discovered the Pacific Ocean. Pizarro eventually rose to be mayor of the town of Panama.

In 1519 Cortés led a small expedition to what's now Mexico, which was rumoured to be full of gold and silver. By 1524, with a combination of incredible fortitude, cunning, luck and ruthlessness, Cortés and his band had subdued the mighty Aztec empire. Though initially named governor of what he had conquered, Cortés soon found royal officials arriving to usurp his authority. He came back to Spain in 1528 to see King Carlos I, who confirmed him as captain general of Nueva España but not as governor. Cortés returned to Mexico in 1530 but, increasingly discontented, returned again to Spain in 1540, this time to a cool reception. He never went back to Mexico, dying in a village near Sevilla in 1547. There's a monument to him in Medellín.

Pizarro, obsessed by tales of another empire of silver and gold south of Panama, formed in 1524 a partnership with two other colonists, Diego de Almagro and the priest Hernando de Luque, to search for this. In 1526 they reached the Inca town of Tumbes, on the coast of Peru. But, unable to gain the support of their governor in Panama for a bigger expedition, in 1529 Pizarro followed Cortés' trail back to Spain to see the king, bringing llamas and other

---

walk from the central Plaza de Santa María de Guadalupe (or Plaza Mayor). The monastery rises above the plaza. The helpful tourist office (☎ 927 15 41 28) on the plaza normally is open Tuesday to Friday from 9 am to 2 pm and 5 to 7.30 pm and holidays and one day of each weekend from 9.15 am to 2 pm. Centro Hispano bank on Calle del Licenciado Gregorio López has an ATM. Around the centre are numerous craft and souvenir shops.

Real Monasterio de Santa María de Guadalupe

The monastery was founded in 1340 by Alfonso XI on a site where a shepherd had not long before found an effigy of the Virgin that had been hidden years earlier by Christians fleeing from the Muslims. The monastery became one of Spain's most important pilgrimage sites and an important centre for the study of medicine.

In the 15th and 16th centuries, the Virgin of Guadalupe was so revered that she was made patron of all the territories conquered by Spain in America. On 29 July 1496 Columbus' Indian servants were baptised in the fountain in front of the monastery, an event registered in the monastery's first book of baptisms.

The monastery is open daily from 9.30 am to 1 pm and 3.30 to 6.30 pm. It costs nothing to enter the church, with the Virgin's image, a 12th century Romanesque work occupying the place of honour in the

Extremadura & America

gifts. He met Cortés in Toledo, won royal backing for his project, and got himself named, in advance, governor of what was to be called Nueva Castilla.

Before returning to Panama, Pizarro visited Trujillo, where he received a hero's welcome and picked up his four half-brothers – Hernando, Juan and Gonzalo Pizarro and Martín de Alcántara – and other relatives and friends. Their expedition finally set off from Panama in 1531, with just 180 men and 37 horses. With a perhaps even more incredible combination of the factors by which Cortés had succeeded in Mexico, Pizarro crossed the Andes and managed to capture the Inca emperor Atahualpa in Cajamarca despite his having an army of 30,000 on hand. The Inca empire, with its capital in Cuzco, extended from Colombia to Chile. Atahualpa offered to buy his freedom by filling with gold the room where he was held. The conquistadors took the gold but the following year executed Atahualpa.

Few of their leaders survived to enjoy their spoils for long. By the time the last Inca resistance had been quelled in 1545, Francisco and Juan Pizarro, Martín de Alcántara and Diego de Almagro had all been killed in Inca revolts or in their own quarrels (Francisco is buried in Lima cathedral). In 1548 Gonzalo Pizarro, too, was executed, after rebelling against the new Spanish viceroy.

Other extremeño members of the expedition did survive to make their mark elsewhere. In about 1540 Hernando de Soto, from either Jerez de los Caballeros or nearby Barcarrota (both places claim him), became the first European to discover the Mississippi. Shortly afterwards Francisco de Orellana, from Trujillo, found the Amazon, floating down it by raft for eight months from the Andes to the Atlantic.

Altogether 600 or 700 people from Trujillo made their way to the Americas in the 16th century. So it's hardly surprising that there are at least seven Trujillos in North, Central and South America today. There are even more Guadalupes, for conquistadors and colonists from all over Spain took with them the cult of the Virgen de Guadalupe in eastern Extremadura. The cult of the Virgen de Guadalupe remains widespread in Latin America today.

---

retablo, but the one-hour guided tour of other rooms (300 ptas) shouldn't be missed.

At the centre of the monastery is a 15th century **mudéjar cloister**, off which are three museums. The **Museo de Bordados** contains wonderfully embroidered altar cloths and vestments, including cloaks which belonged to the Catholic Monarchs; the **Museo de Libros Miniados** has a fine collection of illuminated choral song books from the 15th century on; and the **Museo de Pintura y Escultura** includes paintings by El Greco and Goya and a beautiful little ivory crucifixion attributed to Michelangelo. The superbly decorated baroque **Sacristía** is hung with 11 paintings by Zurbarán and a lantern captured from the Turkish flagship

at the Battle of Lepanto (1571). The **Relicario-Tesoro** houses a variety of other treasures including an exquisite baroque chandelier, a 200,000-pearl cape for the Virgin, and the jewel-encrusted crown with which Alfonso XIII crowned her *Reina de las Españas* (Queen of the Hispanic Countries) in 1928. Finally the tour reaches the **Camarín**, a room behind the church's retablo, where the image of the Virgin is revolved for the faithful to contemplate her at close quarters and kiss a fragment of her mantle.

Hiking

The tourist office has printed material on walks in the area, including an informative leaflet in Spanish on the Ruta de Isabel la Católica, a marked cross-country route of about 12km to Cañamero village, south-west of Guadalupe.

Special Events
There are fiestas and processions during Semana Santa and on 8 and 30 September and 12 October. At such times it's essential to book accommodation in advance.

Places to Stay
Camping Las Villuercas (☎ *927 36 71 39)* has a pretty site in a river valley a short distance off the C-401, 3km below Guadalupe. It's open all year and has a bar, restaurant and swimming pool.

There's no shortage of places to stay in the village, all a short walk from the monastery. The following prices are for singles/doubles with bath or shower: *Pensión Tena* (☎ *927 36 71 04, Calle Ventilla 1)* 2000/3000 ptas; *Mesón Típico Isabel* (☎ *927 36 71 26, Plaza de Santa María de Guadalupe 13)* 3000/4000 ptas plus IVA; *Hostal Lujuan* (☎ *927 36 71 70, Calle del Licenciado Gregorio López 19)* 3000/4000 ptas plus IVA; *Hostal Cerezo* (☎ *927 36 73 79, Calle del Licenciado Gregorio López 12)* 2800/4200 ptas plus IVA; and *Hostal Cerezo II* (☎ *927 15 41 77, Plaza de Santa María de Guadalupe 33)* 3000/5000 ptas plus IVA.

Parador Zurbarán (☎ *927 36 70 75, Calle Marqués de la Romana 12)*, a converted 15th century hospital opposite the monastery, has singles/doubles from 10,800/13,500 ptas plus IVA. Much better value is *Hospedería del Real Monasterio* (☎ *927 36 70 00, Plaza de Su Majestad El Rey Juan Carlos I)*. This hotel, centred on the monastery's beautiful 16th century Gothic cloister, has rooms for 5000/7000 ptas plus IVA, but you should book ahead.

Places to Eat
Numerous cafés and restaurants around the centre offer *menús* for 1100 ptas or so. The *Hospedería del Real Monasterio* has a *menú* for 2100 ptas plus IVA, and a bar opening on the spectacular Gothic cloister which you should go out of your way to visit.

The *parador* has a rather sedate restaurant with a *menú* for 3250 ptas plus IVA, but you're likely to have a much better time at *Mesón El Cordero (Calle Convento 2)* near the Hospedería del Real Monasterio. It's probably the best restaurant in town and specialises in *cordero asado en horno de leña* (roast lamb from a wood-fired oven) for 1550 ptas. Alternatively, there's a 2120 ptas set *menú*.

Getting There & Away
To/from Cáceres (960 ptas) and Trujillo there are two buses Monday to Friday, and one on Sunday. To/from Mérida or Badajoz, you need to change buses at Miajadas (estación de autobuses ☎ 927 34 82 09), served by two buses a day to/from Guadalupe. Two daily buses (one on Sunday) run to/from Madrid (2100 ptas) via Talavera de la Reina. The tourist office has timetables.

Southern Extremadura

MÉRIDA
Mérida stands on the site of the Roman Augusta Emerita, founded in 25 BC for veterans of Rome's campaigns in Cantabria. It became the capital of the Roman province of Lusitania, and with more than 40,000 inhabitants was the largest Roman city on the Iberian Peninsula and its political and cultural hub. Mérida remained an important city under the Visigoths and held out against the Muslims until 713, after which it fell into decline. This continued after the Reconquista by Alfonso IX in 1230 as the inhabitants moved away, leaving Mérida abandoned until the era of the Catholic Monarchs.

Today, Mérida has more Roman ruins than anywhere else in Spain, around which a lively city of 52,000 people has grown up. Since 1983 it has been the seat of the Junta de Extremadura, the Extremadura regional government.

Orientation

The train station on Calle Cardero is a 10 minute walk from the central Plaza de España. Much of the accommodation lies between the two.

From the estación de autobuses, on Avenida de la Libertad on the southern side of the Río Guadiana, it's a 20 minute walk, but you have a spectacular view of the Puente Romano from the modern suspension bridge.

The most important Roman ruins are on the eastern side of town, but all are within walking distance. Pedestrianised Calle Santa Eulalia, heading north from Plaza de España, is the main shopping street.

Information

The helpful tourist office (☎ 924 31 53 53) on Avenida José Álvarez Saenz de Buruaga is right by the gates to the Roman theatre

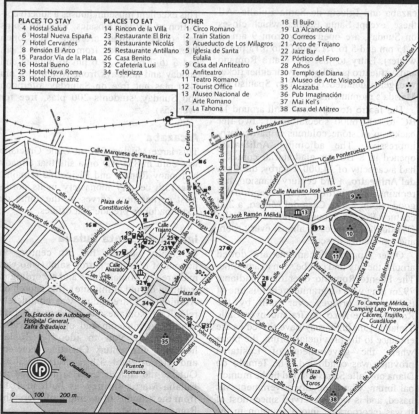

MÉRIDA

PLACES TO STAY	PLACES TO EAT	OTHER	
4 Hostal Salud	14 Rincon de la Villa	1 Circo Romano	18 El Bujío
6 Hostal Nueva España	23 Restaurante El Briz	2 Train Station	19 La Alcandoria
7 Hotel Cervantes	24 Restaurante Nicolás	3 Acueducto de Los Milagros	20 Correos
8 Pensión El Arco	25 Restaurante Antillano	5 Iglesia de Santa	21 Arco de Trajano
15 Parador Vía de la Plata	26 Casa Benito	Eulalia	22 Jazz Bar
16 Hostal Bueno	32 Cafetería Lusi	9 Casa del Anfiteatro	27 Pórtico del Foro
29 Hotel Nova Roma	34 Telepizza	10 Anfiteatro	28 Athos
33 Hotel Emperatriz		11 Teatro Romano	30 Templo de Diana
		12 Tourist Office	31 Museo de Arte Visigodo
		13 Museo Nacional de	35 Alcazaba
		Arte Romano	36 Pub Imaginación
		17 La Tahona	37 Mai Kel's
			38 Casa del Mitreo

EXTREMADURA

and amphitheatre. It is open daily from 9 am to 1.45 pm, plus Monday to Friday from 5 to 7.15 pm (4 to 6.15 pm in winter).

Several banks on Plaza de España and the streets north off it have ATMs. The main correos (postcode 06800) is on Plaza de la Constitución. For an ambulance call ☎ 924 38 10 18. The Hospital General (☎ 924 38 10 00) is on Calle Enrique Sánchez de León, south-west of the bus station.

Roman Remains

For 750 ptas (375 ptas for EU citizens with a student or Euro26 card) you can buy a ticket for the Teatro Romano, Anfiteatro, Casa del Anfiteatro, Casa del Mitreo, Alcazaba and Iglesia de Santa Eulalia. All these, except Santa Eulalia, which closes on Sunday, are open daily from 9 am to 1.45 pm and 5 to 7.15 pm (4 to 6.15 pm in winter). Entry to just the Teatro Romano and Anfiteatro is 600 ptas. With either ticket you get a detailed booklet in Spanish on Mérida's monuments.

The **Teatro Romano** was built around 15 BC to seat 6000 spectators. Its two-tier backdrop of stone columns is particularly impressive. The adjoining **Anfiteatro**, opened in 8 BC for gladiatorial contests, had a capacity of 14,000. Nearby, the **Casa del Anfiteatro**, a 3rd century mansion, has remains of paintings and exceptionally good mosaics. The **Casa del Mitreo**, a 2nd century Roman suburban house on Calle Oviedo, has mosaics in almost every room and top-quality frescoes.

Other Roman monuments are dotted around the city and can be seen at any time. The **Puente Romano** over the Guadiana, 792m long with 60 granite arches, is one of the longest bridges ever built by the Romans. The **Arco de Trajano** over Calle Trajano, 15m high, may have served as the entrance to the provincial forum, the plaza where the government of Lusitania province was conducted. The **Templo de Diana** on Calle Sagasta stood in the municipal forum, where the city government was based, and is well preserved since most of it was incorporated into a mansion in the 16th century. The restored **Pórtico del Foro**, the municipal forum's portico, is nearby on Calle Sagasta.

North-east of the amphitheatre, on Avenida Juan Carlos I, are the grassed-over remains of the 1st century **Circo Romano**, the only surviving hippodrome of its kind in Spain. It could accommodate 30,000 spectators and may sometimes have been filled with water for spectacles involving ships.

The remains of the **Acueducto de Los Milagros** off Calle Marquesa de Pinares are highly favoured by nesting storks.

Museo Nacional de Arte Romano

This excellent museum houses a superb collection of statues, mosaics, frescoes, coins and other Roman artefacts. It's open Tuesday to Saturday from 10 am to 2 pm and 5 to 7 pm (4 to 6 pm in winter) and Sunday and holidays from 10 am to 2 pm (400 ptas but free on Saturday afternoon and Sunday, students 200 ptas, free for over-65s).

Alcazaba

This large Muslim fort on Calle Graciano was built in 835 AD on a site that already had many Roman and Visigothic remains. The 15th century monastery in its north-west corner now serves as the Junta de Extremadura's presidential offices.

Iglesia de Santa Eulalia

Originally built in the 5th century in honour of Mérida's patron saint (who was martyred in Roman times and according to tradition buried at this site), this church on Avenida de Extremadura was completely rebuilt in Romanesque style in the 13th century. A museum and open excavated areas enable you to identify Roman houses, a 4th century Christian cemetery and the original 5th century basilica. Outside the church, the Hornito de Santa Eulalia Martir shrine was built in 1612 from the remains of a temple of Mars, the Roman war god.

Museo de Arte Visigodo

Many of the Visigothic objects unearthed in Mérida are exhibited in this museum just off Plaza de España, open daily except Monday (free).

Special Events

The prestigious Festival de Teatro Clásico at the Roman theatre in July and early August features Greek, Roman and more recent drama classics. Mérida lets its hair down a little later than most of Extremadura, in its Feria de Septiembre.

Places to Stay

Camping Mérida (☎ 924 30 34 53) on Carretera de Madrid, at Km 336.6, 2km east of town, is open all year at 475 ptas plus IVA per person, per tent and per car. A nicer site, a little cheaper but only open from April to mid-September, is *Camping Lago Proserpina (☎ 924 31 32 36)*, 5km north of Mérida by a reservoir that is still held back by a Roman dam.

Pensión El Arco (☎ 924 31 83 21, Calle Miguel de Cervantes 16) is great value and deservedly popular with backpackers: spotless singles/doubles cost 1800/3500 ptas with shared bathroom. *Hostal Bueno (☎ 924 30 29 77, Calle Calvario 9)* is also good, at 2500/4500 ptas. Nearly all rooms have private bathroom; the modernised ones upstairs are the best.

Hostal Salud (☎ 924 31 22 59, Calle Vespasiano 41), a five minute walk from the train station, has decent rooms with bath for 2800/4800 ptas. *Hostal Nueva España (☎ 924 31 33 55, Avenida de Extremadura 6)* has simple rooms with bath for 2600/4800 ptas.

The more upmarket *Hotel Cervantes (☎ 924 31 49 61, Calle Camilo José Cela 8)* has comfortable rooms for 6000/9000 ptas plus IVA. The international-style *Hotel Nova Roma (☎ 924 31 12 61, Calle Suárez Somonte 42)* charges 8000/11,295 ptas plus IVA, but *Hotel Emperatriz (☎ 924 31 31 11, Plaza de España 19)*, a former palace, is far preferable, with rooms for 8000/12,000 ptas plus IVA.

Parador Vía de la Plata (☎ 924 31 38 00, Plaza de la Constitución 3) has rooms for 9200/16,500 plus IVA. Originally part of the Roman provincial forum, it has subsequently been a mosque, a convent and an asylum.

Places to Eat

Telepizza on Plaza de España has fast pizzas from 685 ptas. *Rincón de la Villa* bar, conveniently situated at the top of Calle Santa Eulalia, does excellent toasted *bocadillos de jamón* for 200 ptas.

Casa Benito on Calle San Francisco is a great old-style wood-panelled bar and restaurant, decked with bullfight photos and posters, doing meat, sheep cheese and other local fare at reasonable prices as tapas, raciones or main dishes.

There are three good eateries in a line on Calle Felix Valverde Lillo. *Restaurante El Briz* at No 5 does a great *montado de lomo* (pork loin sandwich) for 350 ptas and has a restaurant at the back with a *menú* for 1350 ptas. Next door, the upmarket *Restaurante Nicolás* has a 2000 ptas *menú*. *Restaurante Antillano* at No 15 is popular with locals and has a *menú* for just 1200 ptas.

Parador Vía de la Plata has a *menú* for 3500 ptas plus IVA featuring specialities such as marinated partridge, but best of all is the *Hotel Emperatriz's* stylish courtyard restaurant, with a 1900 ptas *menú* ranging from regional specialities to bacon, eggs and chips. *Cafetería Lusi* at the back of this hotel does a three-course *menú* for 990 ptas (1100 ptas if you sit at the tables outside on Plaza de Santa Clara).

Entertainment

La Alcandoria and *El Bujío* bars on Calle Holguín and *La Tahona* on Calle Alvarado have varied live music some nights – usually Thursday or Friday – and nearby is the classy late-night *Jazz Bar*, just off Plaza de la Constitucíon. Calle John Lennon, south-east of Plaza de España, has a line of late-night music bars – including *Pub Imaginacíon* – and a large disco, *Mai Kel's*, open Friday and Saturday from 11 pm until

5 am. Three blocks away at Calle Baños 29 is *Athos*, the only gay bar in Extremadura – or so they claim – featuring a late-night bar, hard-core videos and a somewhat raunchy dance floor.

Getting There & Away

Bus From the estación de autobuses (☎ 924 37 14 04) at least seven daily buses run to Badajoz (665 ptas), Sevilla (1575 to 1690 ptas) and Madrid (from 2720 ptas) and at least four to Cáceres (650 ptas) and Trujillo (830 ptas). Daily buses also go to Lisbon, Barcelona, Cordoba, Jabugo, Huelva, Ayamonte, Plasencia and Salamanca.

Train There are at least four trains a day to/from Badajoz (one hour; 395 to 1100 ptas); and two or more to Cáceres (one hour; 500 to 1200 ptas), Ciudad Real, Madrid (five to six hours; 2840 to 4000 ptas), Plasencia, Zafra and Barcelona. One daily train runs to/from Sevilla (4½ hours; 1720 ptas). The station is on ☎ 924 31 81 09.

BADAJOZ

Badajoz, the provincial capital of the southern half of Extremadura, straddles the Río Guadiana just 4km from Portugal. It's an old but now sprawling and industrial city of 123,000 people, visited by few travellers who are not heading to or from Portugal. The centre was probably once handsome, but now most of it is either modern but uninspired or old but dilapidated. Dilapidation plumbs amazing depths in the streets below the old Muslim Alcazaba (Fort), especially on Plaza Alta. However you might find Badajoz's unpretentiousness vaguely refreshing. It has two good art museums too.

Formerly the capital of a Muslim taifa, Badajoz was conquered by Alfonso IX of León in 1230 and subsequently became the scene of much military conflict. It was first occupied by Portugal in 1385, and again in 1396, 1542 and 1660. It was besieged during the War of the Spanish Succession, and three times by the French in the Peninsular War. In 1812 the French were driven out by the British in a bloody battle which cost 6000 lives. In the civil war, the Nationalists carried out atrocious massacres when they took Badajoz in 1936.

Orientation

Plaza de España, around the cathedral, is the centre of the old town; west of it are narrow pedestrianised streets, with a number of places to eat and drink. The main commercial centre is to the south, around Avenida Juan Carlos I and Paseo de San Francisco.

The estación de autobuses on Calle José Rebollo López is 1km south of the centre. The train station, on Avenida de Carolina Coronado, is 1.5km north-west of the centre, across the river.

Information

Tourist Office The helpful municipal tourist office (☎ 924 22 49 81) on Pasaje de San Juan, just off Plaza de España, is open Monday to Friday from 8 am to 3 pm and sometime Saturday from 9 am to 1 pm. For regional information, the Junta de Extremadura tourist office (☎ 924 22 27 63) is at Plaza de la Libertad 3, just south-west of Paseo de San Francisco. It is open Monday to Friday from 9 am to 2 pm and 5 to 7.30 pm and weekends from 9 am to 2 pm.

Money There are plenty of banks, many with ATMs, on Plaza de España, Plaza de Minayo, Paseo de San Francisco and elsewhere.

Post & Communications The main correos (postcode 06080) is on Plaza de la Libertad.

Medical Services The Cruz Roja (☎ 924 22 22 22) is south of the centre at Calle del Museo 5. The Hospital Provincial San Sebastián (☎ 924 22 47 43) is at Plaza de Minayo 2.

Things to See

The **Catedral de San Juan** on Plaza de España was built on the site of a mosque in

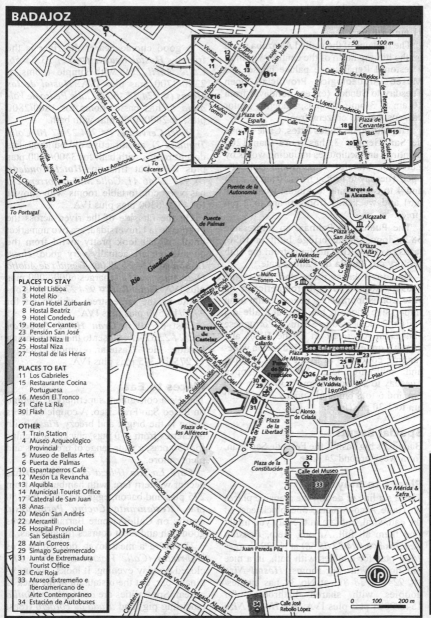

BADAJOZ

To Cáceres

To Portugal

To Mérida & Zafra

PLACES TO STAY
2   Hotel Lisboa
3   Hotel Río
7   Gran Hotel Zurbarán
8   Hostal Beatriz
9   Hotel Condedu
19 Hotel Cervantes
23 Pensión San José
24 Hostal Niza II
25 Hostal Niza
27 Hostal de las Heras

PLACES TO EAT
11 Los Gabrieles
15 Restaurante Cocina
     Portuguesa
16 Mesón El Tronco
21 Café La Ria
30 Flash

OTHER
1   Train Station
4   Museo Arqueológico
     Provincial
5   Museo de Bellas Artes
6   Puerta de Palmas
10 Espantaperros Café
12 Mesón La Revancha
13 Alquibla
14 Municipal Tourist Office
17 Catedral de San Juan
18 Anas
20 Mesón San Andrés
22 Mercantil
26 Hospital Provincial
     San Sebastián
28 Main Correos
29 Simago Supermercado
31 Junta de Extremadura
     Tourist Office
32 Cruz Roja
33 Museo Extremeño e
     Iberoamericano de
     Arte Contemporáneo
34 Estación de Autobuses

EXTREMADURA

the 13th century but has been much altered since. It's open Tuesday to Saturday from 11 am to 1 pm.

The remains of the walled **Alcazaba** stand on the hill top north of the centre. Within it, a restored Renaissance palace houses the **Museo Arqueológico Provincial**, open Tuesday to Sunday (except holidays) from 10 am to 3 pm (200 ptas, students, senior citizens and EU citizens free).

The **Museo de Bellas Artes**, Calle Duque de San Germán 3, has more than 1200 paintings and sculptures including works by Zurbarán, Morales, Picasso and Dalí. It's open Tuesday to Friday from 10 am to 2 pm and 4 to 6 pm (June to August from 6 to 8 pm) and weekends from 10 am to 2 pm (free).

The **Puente de Palmas**, an impressive 582m-long granite bridge built in 1596, leads over the Río Guadiana from the 16th century city **Puerta de Palmas** gate.

Badajoz's latest pride and joy is the **Museo Extremeño e Iberoamericano de Arte Contemporáneo**, a new museum in an impressive modern building at Calle del Museo 2, dedicated to Spanish, Portuguese and Latin American art of the 1980s and 90s. It's quite a surprise to find such a wide-ranging collection of avant-garde painting and sculpture here. MEIAC is open Tuesday to Saturday from 10.30 am to 1.30 pm and 6 to 8 pm, and Sunday from 10.30 am to 1.30 pm (free).

Special Events

Badajoz's big bash is the Feria de San Juan, for a week around 24 June.

Places to Stay

There's a line of decent inexpensive places on Calle Arco-Agüero, one block east of the cathedral, but late in the day you might find them all full. Among them, *Pensión San José* (☎ 924 22 05 68) at No 39 charges 2500 ptas for doubles with bath, in a nice old house with big rooms; *Hostal Niza* (☎ 924 22 38 81) at No 34 has singles/doubles with shared bathrooms for 1542/2804 ptas plus IVA; and *Hostal Niza II* (☎ 924 22 31 73) at No 45 has good rooms with bath for 3271/5600 ptas plus IVA.

A good choice nearer the river is the friendly *Hostal Beatriz* (☎ 924 23 35 56, Calle Abril 20), with simple rooms at 2300/3700 ptas plus IVA. *Hostal de las Heras* (☎ 924 22 40 14, Calle Pedro de Valdivia 6) has basic rooms for 1800/2800 ptas, or 2800/4000 ptas with bath.

Hotel Cervantes (☎ 924 22 37 10, Calle Trinidad 2), an attractive old building, has decent rooms with bath for 3400/4700 ptas plus IVA, but fills up. *Hotel Condedu* (☎ 924 22 46 41, Calle Muñoz Torrero 29) has very comfortable rooms with shower for 4700/6300 ptas plus IVA.

On the far side of the river, across the Puente de la Universidad, are two upmarket hotels which look pretty awful from the outside but are actually very good. *Hotel Lisboa* (☎ 924 27 29 00, Avenida de Adolfo Díaz Ambrona 13) charges 6000/8000 ptas plus IVA. *Hotel Río* (☎ 924 27 26 00) is opposite on the same street, with rooms for 9975/14,500 ptas plus IVA.

Best of all is *Gran Hotel Zurbarán* (☎ 924 22 37 41), closer to the centre facing Parque de Castelar, which charges 11,275/18,375 ptas plus IVA.

Places to Eat

There's a convenient supermarket, *Simago* on Paseo San Francisco. A couple of doors along is the bright and breezy *Flash*, with omelettes from 450 ptas, chicken and chips for 650 ptas, a wide range of breakfasts and plenty more.

Café La Ria (Plaza de España 7) has decent western fare, with hamburgers from 275 ptas and bacon, eggs and chips for 750 ptas. *Restaurante Cocina Portuguesa*, nearby on Calle Vicente Barrantes, serves good fish and meat courses for 900 ptas.

If you're a meat-lover, don't miss *Los Gabrieles* (Calle Vicente Barrantes 21), closed Sunday evening. It looks like an ordinary bar, but the restaurant at the back is a treat. Specialities are *asado de cochinillo* (suckling pig) and *asado de cordero* (roast lamb), both 1700 ptas, but there are cheaper options. *Mesón El Tronco (Calle Muñoz Torrero 16A)* specialises in regional food, and does a brisk trade with a *menú* for 1000 ptas, many mains for 900 to 1600 ptas, good bocadillos and raciones in the bar, and free tapas with drinks.

The Gran Hotel Zurbarán has a range of eating options, with the excellent but very expensive *Los Monjes Zurbarán* restaurant at the top of its range.

Across the river, *Hotel Río* has a popular medium-priced restaurant.

Entertainment

Late-night bars are scattered around the streets near the cathedral. Among the liveliest are the pub-like *Anas* on Plaza de Cervantes and *Espantaperros Café* on Calle Hernán Cortés, the huge *Mercantil* music bar on Calle Zurbarán, *Mesón La Revancha* on Calle Felipe Checa and the more upmarket *Mesón San Andrés (Calle Madre de Dios 4)*. A fine hangout is *Alquibla*, a cool, moody jazz and blues bar on Calle Virgen de la Soledad.

Getting There & Away

Bus From the estación de autobuses (☎ 924 25 86 61), at least seven daily buses run to Mérida (665 ptas), Trujillo (1215 to 1510 ptas) and Madrid (3195 to 3740 ptas), five or more to Zafra (750 ptas) and Sevilla (1680 ptas), four to Lisbon (2100 ptas) and at least two each to Cáceres (825 ptas), Plasencia, Salamanca, Córdoba and Barcelona.

Train There are four or more trains a day to Mérida, two or three each to Barcelona, Ciudad Real and Madrid (five to eight hours; 3900 to 4400 ptas); one or two to Cáceres (1¾ hours; 1600 to 1800 ptas); and one (except Saturday) to Plasencia. The 8.15 am train from Badajoz connects at Mérida with a train for Sevilla (six hours). Two trains a day run to Lisbon (five to six hours). The station is on ☎ 924 27 18 62.

Getting Around

To get into town from the train station, take bus No 1 to Calle Alonso de Celada, just off Paseo de San Francisco. From the bus station, bus No 4 goes to Plaza de España. Buses run every half-hour throughout the day.

ZAFRA

The pretty town of Zafra, 66km south of Mérida, originally a Muslim settlement known as Zafar, is a convenient stop between Badajoz or Mérida and Sevilla. It's also a base for exploring Extremadura's little visited far south.

The tourist office (☎ 924 55 10 36), on the central Plaza de España, is open Monday to Friday from 11 am to 2 pm and 5 to 7 pm and weekends and holidays from 11 am to 2 pm.

Zafra's 15th century **castle**, now a parador, was built over the former Muslim *alcázar* (fortress) by order of Lorenzo Suárez de Figueroa, the first Conde de Feria. His descendants commissioned Juan de Herrera to design the Renaissance marble patio. The town's most interesting squares are **Plaza Grande** and the adjoining **Plaza Chica**, both with arcades and cafés.

Places to Stay & Eat

Pensión Carmen (☎ 924 55 14 39, Avenida de la Estación 9), about 250m east of Plaza de España, has decent rooms for 2400/4800 ptas, and a moderately priced restaurant.

There's no shortage of mid-range hotels. *Hotel Las Palmeras (☎ 924 55 22 08, Plaza Grande 14)* has rooms with bath for 2968/5936 ptas plus IVA. *Hotel Don Quijote (☎ 924 55 47 71, Calle Huelva 3)*, just off Plaza Grande, has rooms for 5000/8500 ptas plus IVA. Both have restaurants with *menús* for about 1000 ptas.

Hotel Huerta Honda (☎ 924 55 41 00, Calle López Asme 30), just west of the parador, has good rooms for 5500/9200 ptas plus IVA, a nice patio and bar with tapas, and main courses for 1600 to 2500 ptas in its stylish *Restaurante Barbacana*. *Parador Hernán Cortés (☎ 924 55 45 40,*

EXTREMADURA

Plaza del Corazón de María 7) has rooms for 14,000/17,500 ptas plus IVA and the restaurant in its marble patio does a *menú* for 3500 ptas plus IVA.

Getting There & Away

The estación de autobuses (☎ 924 55 39 07) is on Carretera Badajoz-Granada, about 500m north-east of the centre, and the train station (☎ 924 55 02 15) is 1.5km south-east of the centre at the end of Avenida de la Estación. One or two trains a day run to Cáceres, Huelva, Madrid, Mérida, Plasencia and Sevilla.

AROUND ZAFRA

Those with a yearning to get off the beaten track have much scope down here. Apart from the main roads to Sevilla and Córdoba, other roads through the rolling Sierra Morena into Andalucía head south-west through Fregenal de la Sierra into northern Huelva province and south-east into the Parque Natural Sierra Norte in

Sevilla province. Trains bound for Huelva and Sevilla also go through these regions.

In **Fregenal de la Sierra** you'll find a castle and adjoining church, both dating from the 13th century, together with a bull-ring and market square in an unusual grouping. Walled **Jerez de los Caballeros**, 42km west of Zafra, was a cradle of conquistadors (see the boxed text 'Extremadura & America') and has a Knights Templar castle and several handsome churches, three of them with towers copying the Giralda in Sevilla. There's a tourist office (☎ 924 73 03 72) at Plaza de San Agustín 1.

Feria, 4km off the Badajoz-Zafra road about 20km from Zafra, is dominated by an impressive hill-top 15th century castle. Just outside **Casas de Reina** on the Guadalcanal road are impressive remains of a Roman theatre and a hill-top Muslim castle.

The tourist offices in Zafra and Jerez de los Caballeros can put you in the picture about other interesting spots to visit. Fregenal de la Sierra, Jerez de los Caballeros and Almendralejo have hostales and hotels.

EXTREMADURA

Language

SPANISH
Pronunciation

Spanish pronunciation isn't difficult, given that many Spanish sounds are similar to their English counterparts, and there's a clear and consistent relationship between pronunciation and spelling. If you stick to the following rules you should have very few problems making yourself understood.

Vowels

Unlike English, each of the vowels in Spanish has a uniform pronunciation which doesn't vary. For example, the Spanish 'a' has one pronunciation rather than the numerous pronunciations we find in English, such as 'cat', 'cake', 'cart', 'care', 'call'. Many Spanish words have a written accent. The acute accent (as in *días*) generally indicates a stressed syllable and doesn't change the sound of the vowel. Vowels are pronounced clearly even if they are in unstressed positions or at the end of a word.

a	as the 'u' in 'nut', or a shorter sound than the 'a' in 'art'
e	as in 'met'
i	somewhere between the 'i' in 'marine' and the 'i' in 'flip'
o	similar to the 'o' in 'hot'
u	as the 'oo' in 'hoof'

Consonants

Some Spanish consonants are the same as their English counterparts. The pronunciation of other consonants varies according to which vowel follows and also according to which part of Spain you happen to be in. The Spanish alphabet also contains three consonants that are not found within the English alphabet: **ch**, **ll** and **ñ**.

b	softer than in English; sometimes as in 'be' when initial or preceded by a nasal

c	a hard 'c' as in 'cat' when followed by **a**, **o**, **u** or a consonant; as the 'th' in 'thin' before **e** and **i**
ch	as in 'church'
d	as in 'do' when initial; elsewhere as the 'th' in 'then'
g	as in 'get' when initial and before **a**, **o** and **u**; elsewhere much softer. Before **e** or **i** it's a harsh, breathy sound, similar to the 'h' in 'hit'
h	silent
j	a harsh, guttural sound similar to the 'ch' in Scottish *loch*
ll	as the 'lli' in 'million'; some people pronounce it rather like the 'y' in 'yellow'
ñ	a nasal sound, as the 'ni' in 'onion'
q	as the 'k' in 'kick'; 'q' is always followed by a silent **u** and is combined only with the vowels **e** (as in *que*) and **i** (as in *qui*)
r	a rolled 'r' sound; longer and stronger when initial or doubled
s	as in 'see'
v	the same sound as **b**
x	as the 'ks' sound in 'taxi' when between two vowels; as the 's' in 'see' when preceding a consonant
z	as the 'th' in 'thin'

Semiconsonant

Spanish also has the semiconsonant **y**. When at the end of a word or when standing alone as a conjunction it's pronounced like the Spanish **i**. As a consonant, it's somewhere between the 'y' in 'yonder' and the 'g' in 'beige', depending on the region.

Greetings & Civilities

Hello/Goodbye.	*¡Hola!/¡Adiós!*
Yes/No.	*Sí/No.*
Please.	*Por favor.*
Thank you.	*Gracias.*
That's fine/ You're welcome.	*De nada.*
Excuse me.	*Perdón/Perdoneme.*
I'm sorry. (excuse me, forgive me)	*Lo siento/ Discúlpeme.*

Useful Phrases

Do you speak English?	Habla inglés?
Does anyone speak English?	Hay alguien que hable inglés?
I understand.	Entiendo.
I don't understand.	No entiendo.
Please write that down.	Puede escribirlo, por favor?
How much is it?	¿Cuánto cuesta?/ ¿Cuánto vale?
Just a minute.	Un momento.
What's your name?	¿Cómo se llama?
My name is ...	Me llamo ...

Signs

ENTRADA	Entrance
SALIDA	Exit
OCUPADO, COMPLETO	Full, No Vacancies
INFORMACIÓN	Information
ABIERTO	Open
CERRADO	Closed
PROHIBIDO	Prohibited
COMISARÍA	Police Station
HABITACIONES LIBRES	Rooms Available
SERVICIOS/ASEOS	Toilets
HOMBRES	Men
MUJERES	Women

Getting Around

What time does the ... leave/arrive?	¿A qué hora sale/ llega el ...?
boat	barco
bus (city)	autobús, bus
bus (intercity)	autocar
train	tren
tram	tranvía
next	próximo
first	primer
last	último
I'd like a ... ticket.	Quisiera un billete ...
one-way	sencillo/de sólo ida
return	de ida y vuelta
1st class	primera clase
2nd class	segunda clase
left luggage	consigna
timetable	horario
bus stop	parada de autobus
train station	estación (de ferrocarril)
the underground	el metro
I'd like to hire a car/bicycle.	Quisiera alquilar un coche/una bicicleta.
I want to go to ...	Quiero ir a ...
Can you show me (on the map)?	Me puede indicar (en el mapa)?
Where is ...?	¿Dónde está ...?
far/near	lejos/cerca

Go straight ahead.	Siga/Vaya todo derecho.
Turn left.	Gire a la izquierda.
Turn right.	Gire a la derecha/ recto.

Around Town

I'm looking for ...	Estoy buscando ...
a bank	un banco
the city centre	el centro de la ciudad
the ... embassy	la embajada ...
my hotel	mi hotel
the market	el mercado
the police	la policía
the post office	los correos
public toilets	los servicios/ aseos públicos
the telephone centre	el locutorio
the tourist office	la oficina de turismo
the beach	la playa
the bridge	el puente
the castle	el castillo
the cathedral	la catedral
the church	la iglesia
the hospital	el hospital
the lake	el lago
the main square	la plaza mayor
the mosque	la mezquita

the old city	la ciudad antigua/ el casco antiguo
the palace	el palacio
the ruins	las ruinas
the sea	el mar
the square	la plaza
the tower	la torre
What time does it open/close?	¿A qué hora abren/cierran?

Accommodation

hotel	hotel
guesthouse	pensión/casa de huéspedes
youth hostel	albergue juvenil
camping ground	camping
Where is a cheap hotel?	Dónde hay un hotel barato?
What's the address?	Cuál es la dirección?
Could you write it down, please?	Puede escribirla, por favor?
Do you have any rooms available?	¿Tiene habitaciones libres?
a bed	una cama
a single room	una habitación individual
a double room	una habitación doble
a room with a bathroom	una habitación con baño
to share a dorm	compartir un dormitorio
for/one two nights	para una/dos noches
How much is it ...?	¿Cuánto cuesta ...?
per night	por noche
per person	por persona
Is breakfast included?	¿Incluye el desayuno?
Can I see it?	Puedo verla?
Where is the bathroom?	Dónde está el baño?

Food

breakfast	desayuno
lunch	almuerzo/comida
dinner	cena

I'd like the set lunch.	Quisiera el menú del día.
Is service included?	El servicio está incluido?
I'm a vegetarian.	Soy vegetariano/ vegetariana. (m/f)

Time, Days & Numbers

What time is it?	¿Qué hora es?
today	hoy
tomorrow	mañana
yesterday	ayer
in the morning	de la mañana
in the afternoon	de la tarde
in the evening	de la noche
Monday	lunes
Tuesday	martes
Wednesday	miércoles
Thursday	jueves
Friday	viernes
Saturday	sábado
Sunday	domingo
January	enero
February	febrero
March	marzo
April	abril
May	mayo
June	junio
July	julio
August	agosto
September	setiembre/septiembre
October	octubre
November	noviembre
December	diciembre

0	cero
1	uno, una
2	dos
3	tres
4	cuatro
5	cinco
6	seis
7	siete
8	ocho
9	nueve
10	diez
100	cien/ciento
1000	mil
one million	un millón

Emergencies

Help!	¡Socorro!/¡Auxilio!
Call a doctor!	¡Llame a un doctor!
Call the police!	¡Llame a la policía!
Go away!	¡Váyase!
I'm lost.	Estoy perdido/a.

Health

I'm ...	Soy...
diabetic	diabético/a
epileptic	epiléptico/a
asthmatic	asmático/a
I'm allergic ...	Soy alérgico/a ...
to antibiotics	a los antibióticos
to penicillin	a la penicilina
antiseptic	antiséptico
aspirin	aspirina
condoms	preservativos/ condones
contraceptive	anticonceptivo
diarrhoea	diarrea
medicine	medicamento
nausea	náusea
sunblock cream	crema protectora contra el sol
tampons	tampones

BASQUE

The Basque language is one of the oldest in the world, and a key to primitive Europe. It's the oldest surviving pre-Indo-European language in Europe; Hungarian and Finnish arrived considerably later. In a territory straddling France and Spain, and divided by the Pyrenees, Basque is spoken by 800,000 of the 2.4 million people who live in the territory known in Basque as Euskadi.

Pronunciation

An English-speaker shouldn't have many difficulties with Basque pronunciation. There are no written accents, and stress is flexible. Vowels are pronounced as in Castilian. There are two distinct 'r' sounds to be aware of: one, much as the English 'r' when at the beginning or middle of a word; and the other, like a cross between the Scottish 'r' and the growl of a two-stroke motorbike: 'r-r-r-r-r-r'. Consonants are pronounced as in English with the exception of the following:

g	always hard, as in 'goat'
h	silent in the País Vasco; as the 'h' in 'hat' in French Basque Country
rr	the growly 'r'
tx/ts	as the 'ch' in 'chew'
tz	as the 'tz' in 'tzetze'
x	as the 'sh' in 'ship'
z	as the 's' in 'sun'

Basics

Hi!	Kaixo!
Good morning.	Egunon.
Good night.	Gabon.
Goodbye.	Agur.
See you later.	Gero arte.
Please.	Mesedez.
Thank you.	Eskerrik asko.
Excuse me.	Parkatu.
How do you say that in Basque?	Nola esaten da hori euskaraz?

Finding Your Way

Where's the toilet, please?	Non dago komuna, mesedez?
At the end.	Azkenean.
Straight ahead.	Zuzen-zuzenian.
On the left.	Ezkerretara.
On the right.	Eskuinetara.

Small Talk

How are you?	Zer moduz?
Very well, thanks.	Oso ongi, eskerrik asko.
What's your name?	Nola duzu izena?
I'm called John.	Nire izena Jon da.
Where are you from?	Nongoa zara?
I'm from ...	Ni ... naiz.

Food

Waiter!	Aizan!/Aizak! (f/m)
I'd like ...	... nahi nuke.
a beer.	garagardo bat
a bottle of wine	botila bat ardo

beefsteak with chips	*xerra patata frijituekin*
a little bread	*ogi piska bat*
water	*ura*
mineral water	*metalura*
fish	*arraina*
vegetables	*barazkiak*

CATALAN

Catalan is one of the Romance, or neo-Latin, languages such as French, Italian, Portuguese, Romanian and Spanish. It's not a dialect of any other language and its nearest relative is Occitan, spoken colloquially in southern France. It's the mother tongue of up to seven million people, most of whom also speak at least one other language. It has a number of local dialect variations: in Catalunya, most of Valencia, the Islas Baleares, the strip of Aragón that borders Catalunya, Andorra, Roussillon (in France), and in and around L'Alguer (Alghero) in Sardinia.

Pronunciation

Catalan sounds are not hard for an English-speaker to pronounce but you should note that vowels will vary according to whether they occur in stressed or unstressed syllables.

Vowels

a	stressed, as in 'far'; unstressed, as in 'about'
e	stressed, as in 'pet'; unstressed, as the 'e' in 'open'
i	as the 'i' in 'machine'
o	stressed, as in 'pot'; unstressed, as the 'oo' in 'zoo'.
u	as the 'u' in 'humid'

Consonants

b	pronounced 'p' at the end of a word
c	hard before **a**, **o**, and **u**; soft before **e** and **i**
ç	like 'ss'
d	pronounced 't' at the end of a word
g	hard before **a**, **o** and **u**; before **e** and **i**, as the 's' in measure
h	silent
j	as the 's' in 'pleasure'

r	as in 'red' in the middle of a word; silent at the end
rr	the roll of the tongue 'r', at the beginning of a word; 'rr' in the middle of a word
s	as in 'so' at the beginning of a word; as 'z' in the middle of a word
v	in Barcelona it's pronounced as 'b'; as 'v' in some other areas
x	mostly as in English but sometimes as 'sh'

Other letters are pronounced approximately as in English. There are, however, a few odd combinations:

ll	repeat the 'l'
tx	like 'ch'
qu	like 'k'

Basics

Hi!	*Hola!*
Good morning/ Goodbye.	*Bon dia.*
Good afternoon.	*Bona tarda.*
Good night.	*Bona nit.*
Goodbye.	*Adéu.*
See you later.	*A reveure.*
Please.	*Sisplau/Si us plau.*
Thank you.	*Gràcies.*
Thank you very much.	*Moltes gràcies.*
You're welcome.	*De res, company.*
Excuse me.	*Perdoni.*
How much is it?	*Quant val?*
Do you speak English?	*Parla anglès?*
Could you speak in Castilian please?	*Pot parlar castellà sisplau?*
I understand.	*Ho entenc.*
I don't understand.	*No ho entenc.*
How do you say that in Catalan?	*Com es diu això en català?*
today	*avui*
tomorrow	*demà*

Finding Your Way

Where's the toilet, please?	*On és el lavabo, si us plau?*
At the end.	*Al fons.*

| On the left. | A mà esquerra. |
| On the right. | A la dreta.` |

Small Talk

I'd like you to meet ...	Li presento ...
Pleased to meet you.	Molt de gust.
Delighted!	Encantat/ Encantada. (m/f)
What's new?	Què hi ha?
How are you?	Com esteu?
Very well, thanks.	Molt bé, gràcies.
Take care.	Passi-ho bé.
What's your name?	Com es diu?
My name is ...	Em dic ...
I like ...	M'agrada ...
OK.	Val/D'acord.
Where are you from?	D'on ets?

I'm from ...	Sóc de ...
UK	Anglaterra
USA	Amèrica
New Zealand	Nova Zelanda
Australia	Austràlia

Food

Catalan food is among the best in Spain. For names and descriptions of typical dishes, see the boxed aside in the Barcelona chapter.

breakfast	esmorzar
lunch	dinar
dinner	sopar

| Waiter! | Cambrer! |
| Can I see the menu please? | Puc veure el menú, sisplau? |

I'd like ..., please.	Voldira ... si us plau.
a little bread	una mica de pa
a drop of wine (No byo here!)	un glop de vi
a bottle	una ampolla
a beer	una cervesa

| I'm vegetarian. | Soc vegetarià. |

GALICIAN

The language of the natives of Galicia tends not to be promoted as vigorously as Basque or Catalan. Although signs in Galician (galego to the locals) have popped up all over the region, you'll generally hear Castilian spoken, not Galician. As you get further off the beaten track, your chances of encountering people who prefer not to speak Castilian will grow. A close cousin of Portuguese, Galician is nevertheless distinct from its neighbour.

Useful Phrases

Hello!	Ola!
Goodbye.	Adeus/Até logo.
See you later.	Vemos-nos.
Please.	Por favor.
Thank you.	Gracias/Graciñas.
That's fine/ You're welcome.	De nada.
What's your name?	Como se chama?
My name is ...	Chamo-me ...
Excuse me/Sorry.	Perdoa.
Do you speak English?	Falas inglés?
I don't understand.	Non entendo.
Please write that down.	Por favor, pódemo escribir?
How do I get to ...?	Como se vai a ...?
When does the bus/ train arrive/leave?	A qué hora chega/ sae o autobús/tren?
Where is a cheap hotel?	Onda hay un hotel/ unha fonda?
I'm looking for ...	Estou buscando ...
What's the address?	Cal é o enderezo?
What time is it?	Qué hora é?

| open | aberto |
| closed | pechado |

Emergencies	
Help!	Socorro!
Call a doctor!	Chame un doctor/ médico!
Call the police!	Chame a policia!
Go away!	Vaite!

Glossary

Unless otherwise indicated, these terms are in Castilian Spanish. See the following Food Glossary for help in decoding menus.

abierto – open
abogado de oficio – duty solicitor
acequia – Islamic-era canals
aficionado – enthusiast
agroturismo – another word for *turismo rural*
ajuntament – Catalan for city or town hall
altar mayor – high altar
albergue – refuge
albergue juvenil – youth hostel; not to be confused with **hostal**
alcalde – mayor
alcázar – Muslim-era fortress
alfiz – rectangular frame about the top of an arch in Islamic architecture
alud – avalanche
años de hambre – literally 'years of hunger'; a period in the late 1940s when Spain was hit by a UN-sponsored trade boycott
apartado de correos – post office box
apnea – snorkelling
armadura – wooden *mudéjar* ceiling, especially one like an inverted ship's hull
arroyo – stream
artesonado – *mudéjar* wooden ceiling with interlaced beams leaving a pattern of spaces for decoration
auto de fe – elaborate execution ceremony staged by the Inquisition
autonomía – autonomous community or region: Spain's 50 *provincias* are grouped into 17 of these
autopista – tollway
autovía – toll-free dual-carriage highway
AVE – Tren de Alta Velocidad Español; high-speed train
ayuntamiento – city or town hall
azulejo – glazed tile

bakalao – ear-splitting Spanish techno music (not to be confused with *bacalao*, salted cod)
balcón – balcony
baño completo – full bathroom, with a toilet, shower and/or bath, and basin
barrio – district, quarter (of a town or city)
biblioteca – library
bici todo terreno – mountain bike
bodega – literally, a cellar (especially a wine cellar); also means a winery, or a traditional wine bar likely to serve wine from the barrel

bomberos – fire brigade
bota – sherry cask or animal-skin wine vessel
botijo – jug, usually an earthenware one
BTT – abbreviation for *bici todo terreno*
buceo – scuba diving
buzón – yellow street postboxes

cajero automático – automatic teller machine (ATM)
calle – street
callejón – lane
cama – bed
cambio – in general, change; also currency exchange
campings – officially graded camp sites
caña – a beer in a small glass
cante hondo – literally 'deep song'; song of the *gitano*
capeas – amateur bullfights
capilla – chapel
capilla mayor – chapel containing the high altar of a church
carmen – walled villa with gardens, in Granada
carnaval – carnival; a period of fancy-dress parades and merrymaking in many places, usually ending on the Tuesday 47 days before Easter Sunday
carretera – highway
carta – menu
casa de huéspedes/hospedajes – guesthouse
casa de labranza – a *casa rural* in Cantabria
casa de pagès – a *casa rural* in Catalunya
casa rural – a village or country house or farmstead with rooms to let
casco – literally, helmet; often used to refer to the old part of a city (more correctly, *casco antiguo/histórico/viejo*)
castellers – Catalan human-castle builders
castillo – castle
castro – Celtic or Celtiberian fortified village
catedral – cathedral
cava – Spanish equivalent of champagne
caza – hunting
centro de salud – health centre
cercanías – local trains serving big cities' suburbs and nearby towns
cerrado – closed
certificado – certified mail
cervecería – beer bar
chato – glass
churrigueresque – ornate style of baroque architecture named after the brothers Alberto and José Churriguera

cigarrales – country estates

claustro – cloister

CNIG – Centro Nacional de Información Geográfica; producers of good quality maps

cofradía – same as *hermandad*

colegiata – collegiate church

coll, collado – Catalan for a mountain pass

comarca – district, a grouping of municipios

comedor – dining room

comisaría – National Police station

completo – full

comunidad – fixed charge for maintenance of rental accommodation (sometimes included in the rent)

comunidad autónoma – same as *autonomía*

condones – condoms

conquistador – adventurer; pilgrim

consigna – left-luggage office or lockers

converso – Jew who converted to Christianity in medieval Spain

copas – drinks (literally, glasses); *ir de copas* is to go out for a few drinks

cordillera – mountain chain

coro – choir (part of a church, usually in the middle)

correos – post office

corrida de toros – bullfight

Cortes – parliament

costa – coast

cruceiro – standing crucifix found at many cross-roads in Galicia

cuenta – bill (check)

cuesta – lane (usually on a hill)

custodia – monstrance

día del espectador – cut-price ticket day at cinemas (literally 'viewer's day')

diapositiva – slide film

DELE – Diploma de Español como Lengua Extranjera; language qualification recognised by the Spanish government

dolmen – prehistoric megalithic tomb

ducha – shower

duro – literally, hard; also a common name for a 5 ptas coin

embalse – reservoir

embarcadero – pier or landing stage

encierro – running of bulls Pamplona-style (also happens in many other places around Spain)

entrada – entrance

ermita – hermitage or chapel

església – Catalan for *iglesia*

estació – Catalan for *estación*

estación de autobuses – bus station

estación de esquí – ski station or resort

estación de ferrocarril – train station

estación marítima – ferry terminal

estanco – tobacconist shop

extremeño – Extremaduran; a native of Extremadura

farmacia – pharmacy

faro – lighthouse

feria – fair; can refer to trade fairs as well as to city, town or village fairs which are basically several days of merrymaking; can also mean a bullfight or festival stretching over days or weeks

ferrocarril – railway

fiesta – festival, public holiday or party

fin de semana – weekend

flamenco – means flamingo and Flemish as well as flamenco music and dance

fútbol – football (soccer)

gaditano – person from Cádiz

gaita – Galician version of the bagpipes

gallego – Galician; a native of Galicia

garum – a spicy, vitamin-rich sauce made from fish entrails in Roman Andalucía, used as a seasoning or tonic

gatos – literally 'cats'; also a colloquial name for *madrileños*

gitanos – the Roma people (formerly known as the Gypsies)

glorieta – big roundabout

GRs – senderos de Gran Recorrido; extensive network of long-distance paths

guardia civil – police

gusanitos – corn puffs sold at *kioscos*

habitaciones libres – literally 'rooms available'

hermandad – brotherhood, in particular one that takes part in religious processions

hórreo – Galician or Asturian grain store

hostal – commercial establishment providing accommodation in the one to three star category; not to be confused with *albergue juvenil*

hostal-residencia – *hostal* without any kind of restaurant

huerta – market garden; orchard

humedal – wetland

iglesia – church

infanta – princess

infante – prince

IVA – impuesto sobre el valor añadido, or value-added tax

judería – Jewish *barrio* in medieval Spain

kioscos – kiosk; newspaper stand
la gente guapa – literally 'the beautiful people'
lavabo – washbasin
lavandería – laundrette
librería – bookshop
lidia – the art of bullfighting
lista de correos – poste restante
litera – couchette or sleeping carriage
llegada – arrival
locutorio – private telephone centre
luz – electricity

macarras – Madrid's rough but (usually) likable lads
madrileño – a person from Madrid
madrugada – the 'early hours', from around 3 am to dawn – a pretty lively time in some Spanish cities!
manchego – La Manchan; a person from La Mancha
marcha – action, life, 'the scene'
marisquería – seafood eatery
mas tasa – plus tax
medina – Arabic word for town or city
menú – short form for menú del día
menú del día – fixed-price meal available at lunchtime, sometimes in the evening too; often called just a menú
mercadillo – flea market
mercado – market
mercat – Catalan for mercado
meseta – the high tableland of central Spain
mihrab – prayer niche in a mosque indicating the direction of Mecca
mirador – lookout point
modernisme – literally, modernism; the architectural and artistic style, influenced by Art Nouveau and sometimes known as Catalan modernism, whose leading practitioner was Antoni Gaudí
modernista – an exponent of modernisme
mojito – popular Cuban-based rum concoction
morería – former Islamic quarter in a town
morisco – a Muslim converted (often only superficially) to Christianity in medieval Spain
moro – 'Moor' or Muslim (usually in a medieval context)
movida – similar to marcha; a zona de movida is an area of a town where lively bars and maybe discos are clustered
Mozarab – Christian living under Muslim rule in medieval Spain; those who left for Christian territory often took their Islamic-influenced Mozarabic style of architecture and decoration with them
mozarabic – style of architecture developed by mozarabs, Christians living under Islamic rule, adopting elements of classic Islamic construction to Christian architecture

mudéjar – a Muslim living under Christian rule in medieval Spain; also refers to their decorative style of architecture
muralla – city wall
museo – museum
muelle – wharf or pier
municipio – municipality, Spain's basic local administrative unit
museu – Catalan for museo
muwallad – descendant of Christians who converted to Islam in medieval Spain

nezakalturismoa – Basque for turismo rural

objetos perdidos – lost and found office
oficina de turismo – tourist office; also oficina de información turística

Páginas Amarillas – phone directory (the 'Yellow Pages')
Pantocrator – Christ the All-Ruler or Christ in Majesty, a central emblem of Romanesque art
parador – one of a chain of luxurious state-owned hotels, many of them in historic buildings
parque nacional – national park; strictly controlled protected area
parque naturale – natural park; protected environmental area
pasos – figures carried in Semana Santa parades
peña – a club, usually of flamenco aficionados or Real Madrid or Barcelona football fans; sometimes a dining club
pensión – pension
pinchadiscos – DJs
pinchos – Basque for tapas
piscina – swimming pool
plateresque – early phase of Renaissance architecture noted for its intricately decorated façades
platja – Catalan for playa
plato combinado – literally 'combined plate', a largish serve of meat/seafood/omelette with trimmings
playa – beach
plaza de toros – bullring
plaza mayor – main plaza
porrón – jug with a long, thin spout through which you (try to) pour wine into your mouth
port – port or mountain pass (Catalan)
PRs – senderos de Pequeño Recorrido; footpaths for day or weekend hikes
presa – dam
preservativos – condoms
prohibido – prohibited
pronunciamiento – pronouncement of military rebellion

provincia – province; Spain is divided into 50 of them

pueblo – village

puente – bridge; also means the extra day or two off that many people take when a holiday falls close to a weekend

puerta – gate or door

puerto – port or mountain pass

RACE – Real Automóvil Club de España

ración – meal-sized serve of *tapas*

rastro – flea market, car-boot (trunk) sale

REAJ – Red Española de Albergues Juveniles, the Spanish HI youth hostel network

Reconquista – the Christian reconquest of the Iberian Peninsula from the Muslims (8th to 15th centuries)

refugi – Catalan for *refugio*

refugio – shelter or refuge, especially a mountain refuge with basic accommodation for hikers

reja – grille, especially a wrought-iron one dividing a chapel from the rest of a church

RENFE – Red Nacional de los Ferrocarriles Españoles; the national rail network

Reservas Nacionales de Caza – national hunting reserves

retablo – altarpiece

Reyes Católicos – Catholic Monarchs; Isabel and Fernando

ría – estuary

río – river

riu – Catalan for river

rodalies – Catalan for *cercanías*

romería – festive pilgrimage or procession

ronda – ring road

sacristía – sacristy, the part of a church in which vestments, sacred objects and other valuables are kept

sala capitular – chapterhouse

salida – exit or departure

Semana Santa – Holy Week, the week leading up to Easter Sunday

Sephardic Jews – Jews of Spanish origin

servicios – toilets

sevillana – Andalucian classical dance

SGE – Servicio Geográfico del Ejécito (Army Geographic Service); producers of good quality maps

sida – AIDS

sidra – cider

sidrería – cider bar

sierra – mountain range

s/m – on menus, an abbreviation for *según mercado*, meaning 'according to market price'

s/n – sin numero (without number), sometimes seen in addresses

supermercado – supermarket

tablao – tourist-oriented flamenco performances

taifa – small Muslim kingdom in medieval Spain

tapas – bar snacks traditionally served on a saucer or lid *(tapa)*

taquilla – ticket window

tarjeta de crédito – credit card

tarjeta de residencia – residence card

tarjeta telefónica – phonecard

techumbre – roof, or specifically a common type of *armadura*

temporada alta/media/baja – high/mid/low season

terraza – terrace; often means a café's or bar's outdoor tables

tertulia – informal discussion group or other regular social gathering

tetería – teahouse, usually in Middle Eastern style with low seats round low tables

tienda – shop or tent

topoguías – detailed Spanish walking guides

torno – revolving counter in a convent by which nuns can sell cakes, sweets and other products to the public without being seen

transept – either of the two wings of a cruciform church at right angles to the nave

trascoro – screen behind the *coro*

trono – literally, throne; can also mean the platform an image is carried on in a religious procession

turismo – means both tourism and saloon car; *el turismo* can also mean the tourist office

turismo rural – rural tourism: usually refers to accommodation in *casas rurales* and associated activities such as walking and horse riding

tympanum – semi-circle above the main entrance of a church

urbanització – Catalan for *urbanización*

urbanización – suburban housing development

urgencia – emergency

vall – Catalan for *valle*

valle – valley

v.o. – abbreviation of versión original; a foreign-language film subtitled in Spanish

zona de acampada – country camp site with no facilities, no supervision and no charge; also called *área de acampada*

Food Glossary

Spain has such huge variety in food and food terminology from place to place that you could travel the country for years and still find unfamiliar items on every menu. This is nothing new: Don Quijote visited one inn which had nothing to offer except a type of fish which 'they call *abadejo* in Castilla, *bacalao* in Andalucía, in other parts *curadillo* and in others *truchuela*'. Still, you should be able to decipher a good half of most worthwhile menus with the help of the following lists:

Ways of Cooking & Preparing Food
a la brasa – chargrilled
a la parrilla – grilled
a la plancha – grilled on a hotplate
a la vasca – with parsley, garlic and peas; a Basque green sauce
adobo – a marinade of vinegar, salt, lemon and spices, usually for fish before frying
ahumado/a – smoked
albóndiga – meatball or fishball
aliño – anything in a vinegar and oil dressing
allioli – garlic mayonnaise
asado – roasted
caldereta – stew
caldo – broth, stock, consommé
casero/a – home-made
cazuela – casserole
cocido – cooked; also hotpot/stew
crudo – raw
escabeche – a marinade of oil, vinegar and water for pickling perishables, usually fish or seafood
estofado – stew
flamenquín – rolled and crumbed veal or ham, deep fried
frito – fried
gratinada – au gratin
guiso – stew
horno – oven
horneado – baked
olla – pot
paella – rice, seafood and meat dish
pavía – battered fish or seafood
pil pil – garlic sauce usually spiked with chilli
potaje – stew
rebozado – battered and fried
relleno – stuffed

salado – salted, salty
seco – dry, dried
zarzuela – fish stew

Basics
aceite (de oliva) – (olive) oil
ajo – garlic
arroz – rice
azúcar – sugar
bollo – bread roll
confitura – jam
espagueti – spaghetti
fideo – vermicelli noodles
harina – flour
macarrones – macaroni
mayonesa – mayonnaise
mermelada – jam
miel – honey
mollete – soft bread roll
pan – bread
panecillo – bread roll
pimienta – pepper
sal – salt
salsa – sauce
soja – soy
tostada – toasted roll
trigo – wheat
vinagre – vinegar

Sopas (Soups), Entremeses (Starters) & Meriendas (Snacks)
bocadillo – bread roll with filling
ensalada – salad
entremeses – hors d'oeuvres
gazpacho – cold, blended soup of tomatoes, peppers, cucumber, onions, garlic, lemon and breadcrumbs
montadito – small bread roll with filling, or a small sandwich, or an open sandwich – often toasted
pincho – a tapa-sized portion of food, or a *pinchito* (see Carne & Aves)
sopa de ajo – garlic soup
tabla – selection of cold meats and cheeses
tapa – snack on a saucer

Frutas (Fruit)
aceituna – olive
aguacate – avocado
cereza – cherry
chirimoya – custard apple, a tropical fruit

977

frambuesa – raspberry
fresa – strawberry
granada – pomegranate
higo – fig
lima – lime
limón – lemon
mandarina – tangerine
manzana – apple
manzanilla – a type of olive (also means camomile and a type of sherry)
melocotón – peach
melón – melon
naranja – orange
pasa – raisin
piña – pineapple
plátano – banana
sandía – watermelon
uva – grape

Vegetales/Verduras/Hortalizas (Vegetables)

alcachofa – artichoke
berenjena – aubergine, eggplant
calabacín – zucchini, courgette
calabaza – pumpkin
cebolla – onion
champiñones – mushrooms
col – cabbage
coliflor – cauliflower
espárragos – asparagus
espinacas – spinach
guindilla – chilli pepper
guisante – pea
hongo – wild mushroom
judías blancas – butter beans
judías verdes – green beans
lechuga – lettuce
maíz – sweet corn
patata – potato
patatas a lo pobre – poor man's potatoes (potato dish with peppers and garlic)
patatas bravas – spicy fried potatoes
patatas fritas – chips, French fries
pimiento – pepper, capsicum
puerro – leek
seta – wild mushroom
tomate – tomato
verdura – green vegetable
zanahoria – carrot

Legumbres (Pulses) & Nueces (Nuts)

almendra – almond
alubia – dried bean
anacardo – cashew nut
cacahuete – peanut

faba – type of dried bean
garbanzo – chickpea
haba – broad bean
lentejas – lentils
nuez – nut, also walnut
piñón – pine nut
pipa – sunflower seed

Pescados (Fish)

aguja – swordfish
anchoa – tinned anchovy
atún – tuna
bacalao – salted cod
boquerones – fresh anchovies
caballa – mackerel
chanquetes – whitebait (illegal, but not uncommon)
dorada – sea bass
lenguado – sole
merluza – hake
mojama – cured tuna
pescadilla – whiting
pez espada – swordfish
platija – flounder
rape – monkfish
rosada – ocean catfish, wolf-fish
salmón – salmon
salmonete – red mullet
sardina – sardine
trucha – trout

Mariscos (Seafood)

almejas – clams
calamares – squid
camarón – small prawn, shrimp
cangrejo – crab
cangrejo de río – crayfish
carabinero – large prawn
chipirón – small squid
choco – cuttlefish
cigala – crayfish (lobster)
gamba – prawn
langosta – spiny lobster
langostino – large prawn
mejillones – mussels
ostra – oyster
peregrina – scallop
pulpo – octopus
puntillita/o – small squid, fried whole
sepia – cuttlefish
venera – scallop
vieira – scallop

Carne (Meat) & Aves (Poultry)

beicon – bacon (usually thinly sliced and prepackaged; see *tocino*)

bistek – thin beef steak
butifarra – thick sausage (to be cooked)
cabra – goat
cabrito – kid, baby goat
callos – tripe
carne de monte – 'mountain meat' such as venison or wild boar
caza – hunt, game
cerdo – pig, pork
chacinas – cured pork meats
charcutería – cured pork meats
chivo – kid, baby goat
chorizo – red sausage
chuleta – chop, cutlet
churrasco – slabs of grilled meat or ribs in a tangy sauce, popular in Galicia
conejo – rabbit
cordero – lamb
codorniz – quail
embutidos – the many varieties of sausage
faisán – pheasant
filete – fillet
hamburguesa – hamburger
hígado – liver
jabalí – wild boar
jamón (serrano) – ham (mountain-cured)
lengua – tongue
lomo – loin (of pork unless specified otherwise), usually the cheapest meat dish on the menu
longaniza – dark pork sausage
morcilla – blood sausage, ie black pudding
pajarito – small bird
paloma – pigeon
pato – duck
pavo – turkey
pechuga – breast, of poultry
perdiz – partridge
picadillo – minced meat
pierna – leg
pinchito – Moroccan-style kebab
pollo – chicken
rabo (de toro) – (ox) tail

riñón – kidney
salchicha – fresh pork sausage
salchichón – cured sausage
sesos – brains
solomillo – sirloin (usually of pork)
ternera – beef, veal
tocino – bacon (usually thick; see beicon)
vaca, carne de – beef
venado – venison

Productos Lácteos (Dairy Products) & Huevos (Eggs)

leche – milk
mantequilla – butter
nata – cream
queso – cheese
revuelto de ... – eggs scrambled with ...
tortilla – omelette
tortilla española – potato omelette
yogur – yoghurt

Postres (Desserts) & Dulces (Sweet Things)

churro – long, deep-fried doughnut
galleta – biscuit, cookie
helado – ice cream
natilla – custards
pastel – pastry, cake
tarta – cake
torta – round flat bun, cake
turrón – almond nougat or rich chocolatey sweets that appear at Christmas
yema – candied egg yolk

Other

caracol – snail
empanada – pie
hierba buena/menta – mint
migas – fried breadcrumb dish

Acknowledgments

THANKS

Many thanks to the travellers who used the last edition and wrote to us with helpful hints, useful advice and interesting anecdotes:

Herbert J Addison, Brian Agnew, Jeff Adams, Alf, Julia Fueyo Alvarez, Joel Amy, Patty Andersen, Seonaid Anderson, James Anderson, Phillip Andre, D Andrew, Cathy Anstey, Emanuela Appetiti, Lynda Appleby, O Arav, Febe Armendariz, Marcos Arzua, Greg Ashforth, Anni Baker, Emma Baker, J Baranowski, G Barnes, Mark Baroni, Jochen Beier, John Berta, Stav Birnbaum, Polly Bishop, Cassandra Bladen, Henrik Borckdorff, Ann-lise Breuning, Aric Bright, Martin Broeuner, Vicki Brooke, Ronald Burr, Helen Byme, Georgina C, Jeffrey L Campbell, Arno Caras, Eden Carmichael, J Carmody, Rusty Cartmill, Peter Carty, Helen Casey, Mike Cavendish, Allen Chao, Marcel Checa, Wong Wai Cheung, Susan Chin, William Chung-How, Damian Clair, Claudia Coebergh, Richard Collins, Jennifer Coombs, Karen Cooper, Richard Corbett, Jaime Felipe Moreira Cordero, Ed Cowan, Leo Crofts, Cameron Crowe, Maeve Crowley, Alexander Curiss, C M Cuthbertson, Marlene Dalli, Sonja Damboch, Michael Davies, John De Gelleke, Shirley Dobson, Galit & Lior Dor, Jean Dorrell, A Drinkwater, Charles Du Bois, Shirley Duke, Anusha Edwards, Efrat Elron, Sara Esdahl, Sheila Eustace, Adrian R Ferre-D'Amare, Mick Fielden, Minerva Figueroa, Jim Flahaven, Tobias Flaitz, Steven Flanders, Susana Fortini, Michelle Fox, Shawn Francis, Loek Frederiks, Robuta Friend, Sebastian Galka, Lara Punal Garcia, Michael Gardocki, Helen Georghiou, Amy Getchell, M Gething, Brendon Gibson, L E Gilbert, Marten Gillfors, Planet Glassberg, Jill Gonzales, Tricia Goodlet, Adam Goodman, Ian D Goodwin, Alberto Sanz Granda, Laura Greaves, Stephen Grech, Sue & Lou Greenwood, Olav Gressner, Manuel J Grimaldi, Graham Groome, Michael K Gschwind, Gretal Hammond, Les P Harasymek, Leonie Harris, Ghita Harris, Judith Hayes, Brian Haynes, Thomas Haywood, David Healey, Maartje Heerkens, Pippa Hilary, Richard Hill, Ann Hobson, Anne & Harry Hodgkinson, Paul Holloway, Henriette, Henrik & Ulla-Berith Holmgard, Kacey Houston, Alistair How, Sharon Hurst, Paul Ichilcik, Jeroen, Linda Johnson, Karen Jones, J Jones, Catherine Joseph, Saskia Juinen, Ming-Hua Kao, A Keigher, Susan Kelly, Ken, Claire Kennedy, Karen Kepke, Amanda King, Andreas Klahr, Huub Kloosterman, Kathy Knight, Alexandre Lalonde, Suzanne Lampard, Baylor Lancaster, Peter Langdon, Ton Langenhuyzen, Rachel Lee, Martine van der Lee, Rosanna Lee, Janet Lemon, Almond Leung, Rebecca Levin, Dodi Levine, Annie Levy, Simon Li, Li-Chin Lin, Ashley List, Linda Liu, Marc Lobmann, Clive Long, Sam Loose, Kathryn Lovemore, Jim Lowther, Trish Lu, Sabine Ludwig, Mark Lydon, K P Lynch, Maril M, Vivian Mackereth, Orlaith Mannion, Chris Mantz, Dan & Amy Marcus, Juan Martfnez, Dianna Mason, Kate Mathews, Jost Maurin, Ronald L Mayfield, Rene Maynez, Thomas McCarthy, Ross McGregor, Jo McLean, Billy McMillan, Gordon McNenney, Michael Mee, Tania van Megchelen, Jaap Meijer, Tomas Alonso Millan, Amanda Millar, Donna Mitchell, Ann Mocchi, Joaquin Antonio Moliner, Michelvan Montfort, Mauro Moroni, Susan Morris, Marc N, Holly E Neumann, L Nicol, E Nicoletates, Wim Niehaus, Marc Norman, Herman Olij, Chris Onisiphorou, Leo Orenstein, Carmelo Orosz, Benj Osborn, Stephanie Oswald, Nick Parissis, Adam Parker, Vander Goten Pascal, Gordon S Patton, Natasa Pavselj, Sian Perera, Lars Peter, Cianne Philadelphia, Cameron Phillips, Peddo Picaop, Tom Pike, Lucy C Porter, Reg Quelch, Patrick Quigley, Manuel Ramos, Eric Rasmussen, Esther van Rein, Javier Remon, Marie Odiel van Rhyn, Monica Robinson, Angela Rooney, Sandra Ross, Griff Round, Jose Rovira, James Rowley, Catriona Rust, Lorenzo Salvioni, Alan & Valerie Samuel, Malcolm Scott, Jenny Shaw, Diane Shaw, David Sheehan, Bryan Sherman, Valerie Shipp, Frank Sierowski, Gary Simpson, H Simpson, Steve Slittler, Peg Smith, Steve Castroman Souto, Philip B Springer, Melissa Staples, J Starritt, Natalie Stauffer, Jaap Stavenuiter, Bas Steemers, Yvonne Steinmann, Michael Stewart, Volker Stolz, Elin Stuart, Jill Swartz, Tibor Sztaricskai, Oliver Taylor, Frank Van Thillo, Ilonka Tiemens, JohnH Timoney, Travelling Tom, Gregory Tuck, Geoff Turner, Heather Tweddle, Ida M Valero, Zoltan Vamosi, Sabrina Vandierendonck, Jan & Cynthia Vercruysse, Jenny Versloot, Anneke Visser, Frans P de Vries, Andy Wagner, Yolande Wahrmann, Sharon Watson, Barbara Webster, Duncan Webster, Becca & Deborah Weinstein, I Wells, Camilla Wikstrom, Ed Wilde, Arthur Wilkinson, Erik & Mirianne Willemse, DrCliffard Williams, Ann Williams, Amanda Williams, Michael Wimpfheimer, John Winkelman, Alfred Wise, Nat & Helen Wood, Jon Wood, Cliff Woolford, Geoff Yeates, Melanie Yennadhiou, Peterde Youf, Anson Yu and Justin Zaman.

LONELY PLANET

Phrasebooks

L onely Planet phrasebooks are packed with essential words and phrases to help travellers communicate with the locals. With colour tabs for quick reference, an extensive vocabulary and use of script, these handy pocket-sized language guides cover day-to-day travel situations.

- handy pocket-sized books
- easy to understand Pronunciation chapter
- clear & comprehensive Grammar chapter
- romanisation alongside script to allow ease of pronunciation
- script throughout so users can point to phrases for every situation
- full of cultural information and tips for the traveller

'...vital for a real DIY spirit and attitude in language learning'
— *Backpacker*

'the phrasebooks have good cultural backgrounders and offer solid advice for challenging situations in remote locations'
— *San Francisco Examiner*

Arabic (Egyptian) • Arabic (Moroccan) • Australian *(Australian English, Aboriginal and Torres Strait languages)* • Baltic States *(Estonian, Latvian, Lithuanian)* • Bengali • Brazilian • Burmese • Cantonese • Central Asia • Central Europe *(Czech, French, German, Hungarian, Italian, Slovak)* • Eastern Europe *(Bulgarian, Czech, Hungarian, Polish, Romanian, Slovak)* • Ethiopian (Amharic) • Fijian • French • German • Greek • Hill Tribes • Hindi/Urdu • Indonesian • Italian • Japanese • Korean • Lao • Latin American Spanish • Malay • Mandarin • Mediterranean Europe *(Albanian, Croatian, Greek, Italian, Macedonian, Maltese, Serbian, Slovene)* • Mongolian • Nepali • Papua New Guinea • Pilipino (Tagalog) • Quechua • Russian • Scandinavian Europe *(Danish, Finnish, Icelandic, Norwegian, Swedish)* • South-East Asia *(Burmese, Indonesian, Khmer, Lao, Malay, Tagalog Pilipino, Thai, Vietnamese)* • Spanish (Castilian) *(also includes Catalan, Galician and Basque)* • Sri Lanka • Swahili • Thai • Tibetan • Turkish • Ukrainian • USA *(US English, Vernacular, Native American languages, Hawaiian)* • Vietnamese • Western Europe *(Basque, Catalan, Dutch, French, German, Greek, Irish)*

LONELY PLANET

Guides by Region

Lonely Planet is known worldwide for publishing practical, reliable and no-nonsense travel information in our guides and on our Web site. The Lonely Planet list covers just about every accessible part of the world. Currently there are nine series: travel guides, shoestring guides, walking guides, city guides, phrasebooks, audio packs, travel atlases, diving and snorkeling guides and travel literature.

AFRICA Africa – the South ● Africa on a shoestring ● Arabic (Egyptian) phrasebook ● Arabic (Moroccan) phrasebook ● Cairo ● Cape Town ● Central Africa ● East Africa ● Egypt ● Egypt travel atlas ● Ethiopian (Amharic) phrasebook ● The Gambia & Senegal ● Kenya ● Kenya travel atlas ● Malawi, Mozambique & Zambia ● Morocco ● North Africa ● South Africa, Lesotho & Swaziland ● South Africa, Lesotho & Swaziland travel atlas ● Swahili phrasebook ● Trekking in East Africa ● Tunisia ● West Africa ● Zimbabwe, Botswana & Namibia ● Zimbabwe, Botswana & Namibia travel atlas
Travel Literature: The Rainbird: A Central African Journey ● Songs to an African Sunset: A Zimbabwean Story ● Mali Blues: Traveling to an African Beat

AUSTRALIA & THE PACIFIC Australia ● Australian phrasebook ● Bushwalking in Australia ● Bushwalking in Papua New Guinea ● Fiji ● Fijian phrasebook ● Islands of Australia's Great Barrier Reef ● Melbourne ● Micronesia ● New Caledonia ● New South Wales & the ACT ● New Zealand ● Northern Territory ● Outback Australia ● Papua New Guinea ● Papua New Guinea (Pidgin) phrasebook ● Queensland ● Rarotonga & the Cook Islands ● Samoa ● Solomon Islands ● South Australia ● Sydney ● Tahiti & French Polynesia ● Tasmania ● Tonga ● Tramping in New Zealand ● Vanuatu ● Victoria ● Western Australia
Travel Literature: Islands in the Clouds ● Sean & David's Long Drive

CENTRAL AMERICA & THE CARIBBEAN Bahamas and Turks & Caicos ● Bermuda ● Central America on a shoestring ● Costa Rica ● Cuba ● Eastern Caribbean ● Guatemala, Belize & Yucatán: La Ruta Maya ● Jamaica ● Mexico ● Mexico City ● Panama
Travel Literature: Green Dreams: Travels in Central America

EUROPE Amsterdam ● Andalucía ● Austria ● Baltic States phrasebook ● Berlin ● Britain ● Central Europe ● Central Europe phrasebook ● Czech & Slovak Republics ● Denmark ● Dublin ● Eastern Europe ● Eastern Europe phrasebook ● Edinburgh ● Estonia, Latvia & Lithuania ● Europe ● Finland ● France ● French phrasebook ● Germany ● German phrasebook ● Greece ● Greek phrasebook ● Hungary ● Iceland, Greenland & the Faroe Islands ● Ireland ● Italian phrasebook ● Italy ● Lisbon ● London ● Mediterranean Europe ● Mediterranean Europe phrasebook ● Paris ● Poland ● Portugal ● Portugal travel atlas ● Prague ● Romania & Moldova ● Russia, Ukraine & Belarus ● Russian phrasebook ● Scandinavian & Baltic Europe ● Scandinavian Europe phrasebook ● Scotland ● Slovenia ● Spain ● Spanish phrasebook ● St Petersburg ● Switzerland ● Trekking in Spain ● Ukrainian phrasebook ● Vienna ● Walking in Britain ● Walking in Italy ● Walking in Switzerland ● Western Europe ● Western Europe phrasebook
Travel Literature: The Olive Grove: Travels in Greece

INDIAN SUBCONTINENT Bangladesh ● Bengali phrasebook ● Bhutan ● Delhi ● Goa ● Hindi/Urdu phrasebook ● India ● India & Bangladesh travel atlas ● Indian Himalaya ● Karakoram Highway ● Nepal ● Nepali phrasebook ● Pakistan ● Rajasthan ● South India ● Sri Lanka ● Sri Lanka phrasebook ● Trekking in the Indian Himalaya ● Trekking in the Karakoram & Hindukush ● Trekking in the Nepal Himalaya
Travel Literature: In Rajasthan ● Shopping for Buddhas

LONELY PLANET

Mail Order

Lonely Planet products are distributed worldwide. They are also available by mail order from Lonely Planet, so if you have difficulty finding a title please write to us. North and South American residents should write to 150 Linden St, Oakland, CA 94607, USA; European and African residents should write to 10a Spring Place, London NW5 3BH, UK; and residents of other countries to PO Box 617, Hawthorn, Victoria 3122, Australia.

ISLANDS OF THE INDIAN OCEAN Madagascar & Comoros • Maldives • Mauritius, Réunion & Seychelles

MIDDLE EAST & CENTRAL ASIA Arab Gulf States • Central Asia • Central Asia phrasebook • Iran • Israel & the Palestinian Territories • Israel & the Palestinian Territories travel atlas • Istanbul • Jerusalem • Jordan & Syria • Jordan, Syria & Lebanon travel atlas • Lebanon • Middle East on a shoestring • Turkey • Turkish phrasebook • Turkey travel atlas • Yemen
Travel Literature: The Gates of Damascus • Kingdom of the Film Stars: Journey into Jordan

NORTH AMERICA Alaska • Backpacking in Alaska • Baja California • California & Nevada • Canada • Florida • Hawaii • Honolulu • Los Angeles • Miami • New England USA • New Orleans • New York City • New York, New Jersey & Pennsylvania • Pacific Northwest USA • Rocky Mountain States • San Francisco • Seattle • Southwest USA • USA phrasebook • Washington, DC & the Capital Region
Travel Literature: Drive Thru America

NORTH-EAST ASIA Beijing • Cantonese phrasebook • China • Hong Kong • Hong Kong, Macau & Guangzhou • Japan • Japanese phrasebook • Japanese audio pack • Korea • Korean phrasebook • Kyoto • Mandarin phrasebook • Mongolia • Mongolian phrasebook • North-East Asia on a shoestring • Seoul • South-West China • Taiwan • Tibet • Tibetan phrasebook • Tokyo
Travel Literature: Lost Japan

SOUTH AMERICA Argentina, Uruguay & Paraguay • Bolivia • Brazil • Brazilian phrasebook • Buenos Aires • Chile & Easter Island • Chile & Easter Island travel atlas • Colombia • Ecuador & the Galapagos Islands • Latin American Spanish phrasebook • Peru • Quechua phrasebook • Rio de Janeiro • South America on a shoestring • Trekking in the Patagonian Andes • Venezuela
Travel Literature: Full Circle: A South American Journey

SOUTH-EAST ASIA Bali & Lombok • Bangkok • Burmese phrasebook • Cambodia • Hill Tribes phrasebook • Ho Chi Minh City • Indonesia • Indonesian phrasebook • Indonesian audio pack • Jakarta • Java • Laos • Lao phrasebook • Laos travel atlas • Malay phrasebook • Malaysia, Singapore & Brunei • Myanmar (Burma) • Philippines • Pilipino (Tagalog) phrasebook • Singapore • South-East Asia on a shoestring • South-East Asia phrasebook • Thailand • Thailand's Islands & Beaches • Thailand travel atlas • Thai phrasebook • Thai audio pack • Vietnam • Vietnamese phrasebook • Vietnam travel atlas

---

ALSO AVAILABLE: Antarctica • Brief Encounters: Stories of Love, Sex & Travel • Chasing Rickshaws • Not the Only Planet: Travel Stories from Science Fiction • Travel with Children • Traveller's Tales

Lonely Planet Journeys

JOURNEYS is a unique collection of travel writing – published by the company that understands travel better than anyone else. It is a series for anyone who has ever experienced - or dreamed of – the magical moment when they encountered a strange culture or saw a place for the first time. They are tales to read while you're planning a trip, while you're on the road or while you're in an armchair in front of a fire.

These outstanding titles explore our planet through the eyes of a diverse group of international writers. JOURNEYS books catch the spirit of a place, illuminate a culture, recount a crazy adventure or introduce a fascinating way of life. They always entertain, and always enrich the experience of travel.

MALI BLUES
Traveling to an African Beat
Lieve Joris (translated by Sam Garrett)

Drought, rebel uprisings, ethnic conflict: these are the predominant images of West Africa. But as Lieve Joris travels in Senegal, Mauritania and Mali, she meets survivors, fascinating individuals charting new ways of living between tradition and modernity. With her remarkable gift for drawing out people's stories, Joris brilliantly captures the rhythms of a world that refuses to give in.

THE GATES OF DAMASCUS
Lieve Joris (translated by Sam Garrett)

This best-selling book is a beautifully drawn portrait of day-to-day life in modern Syria. Through her intimate contact with local people, Lieve Joris draws us into the fascinating world that lies behind the gates of Damascus. Hala's husband is a political prisoner, jailed for his opposition to the Assad regime; through the author's friendship with Hala we see how Syrian politics impacts on the lives of ordinary people.

THE OLIVE GROVE
Travels in Greece
Katherine Kizilos

Katherine Kizilos travels to fabled islands, troubled border zones and her family's village deep in the mountains. She vividly evokes breathtaking landscapes, generous people and passionate politics, capturing the complexities of a country she loves.

'beautifully captures the real tensions of Greece' – *Sunday Times*

KINGDOM OF THE FILM STARS
Journey into Jordan
Annie Caulfield

Kingdom of the Film Stars is a travel book and a love story. With honesty and humour, Annie Caulfield writes of travelling in Jordan and falling in love with a Bedouin with film-star looks.

She offers fascinating insights into the country – from the tent life of traditional women to the hustle of downtown Amman – and unpicks tight-woven western myths about the Arab world.

LONELY PLANET

Lonely Planet Travel Atlases

L onely Planet has long been famous for the number and quality of its guidebook maps. Now we've gone one step further and produced a handy companion series: Lonely Planet travel atlases – maps of a country produced in book form.

Unlike other maps, which look good but lead travellers astray, our travel atlases have been researched on the road by Lonely Planet's experienced team of writers. All details are carefully checked to ensure the atlas corresponds with the equivalent Lonely Planet guidebook.

- full-colour throughout
- maps researched and checked by Lonely Planet authors
- place names correspond with Lonely Planet guidebooks
- no confusing spelling differences
- legend and travelling information in English, French, German, Japanese and Spanish
- size: 230 x 160 mm

Available now: Chile & Easter Island • Egypt • India & Bangladesh • Israel & the Palestinian Territories • Jordan, Syria & Lebanon • Kenya • Laos • Portugal • South Africa, Lesotho & Swaziland • Thailand • Turkey • Vietnam • Zimbabwe, Botswana & Namibia

Lonely Planet TV Series & Videos

L onely Planet travel guides have been brought to life on television screens around the world. Like our guides, the programs are based on the joy of independent travel, and look honestly at some of the most exciting, picturesque and frustrating places in the world. Each show is presented by one of three travellers from Australia, England or the USA and combines an innovative mixture of video, Super-8 film, atmospheric soundscapes and original music.

Videos of each episode – containing additional footage not shown on television – are available from good book and video shops, but the availability of individual videos varies with regional screening schedules.

Video destinations include: Alaska • American Rockies • Australia – The South-East • Baja California & the Copper Canyon • Brazil • Central Asia • Chile & Easter Island • Corsica, Sicily & Sardinia – The Mediterranean Islands • East Africa (Tanzania & Zanzibar) • Ecuador & the Galapagos Islands • Greenland & Iceland • Indonesia • Israel & the Sinai Desert • Jamaica • Japan • La Ruta Maya • Morocco • New York • North India • Pacific Islands (Fiji, Solomon Islands & Vanuatu) • South India • South West China • Turkey • Vietnam • West Africa • Zimbabwe, Botswana & Namibia

The Lonely Planet TV series is produced by: Pilot Productions
The Old Studio
18 Middle Row
London W10 5AT, UK

Lonely Planet On-line
www.lonelyplanet.com *or* **AOL keyword: lp**

Whether you've just begun planning your next trip, or you're chasing down specific info on currency regulations or visa requirements, check out Lonely Planet On-line for up-to-the minute travel information.

As well as mini guides to more than 250 destinations, you'll find maps, photos, travel news, health and visa updates, travel advisories, and discussion of the ecological and political issues you need to be aware of as you travel. You'll also find timely upgrades to popular guidebooks which you can print out and stick in the back of your book.

There's also an on-line travellers' forum where you can share your experience of life on the road, meet travel companions and ask other travellers for their recommendations and advice.

And of course we have a complete and up-to-date list of all Lonely Planet travel products including travel guides, diving and snorkeling guides, phrasebooks, atlases, travel literature and videos, and a simple on-line ordering facility if you can't find the book you want elsewhere.

Lonely Planet Diving & Snorkeling Guides

Known for indispensible guidebooks to destinations all over the world, Lonely Planet's Pisces Books are the most popular series of diving and snorkeling titles available.

There are three series: **Diving & Snorkeling Guides**, **Shipwreck Diving** series and **Dive Into History**. Full colour throughout, the **Diving & Snorkeling Guides** combine quality photographs with detailed descriptions of the best dive sites for each location, giving divers a glimpse of what they can expect both on land and in water. The **Dive Into History** series is perfect for the adventure diver or armchair traveller. The **Shipwreck Diving** series provides all the details for exploring the most interesting wrecks in the Atlantic and Pacific oceans. The list also includes underwater nature and technical guides.

LONELY PLANET

FREE Lonely Planet Newsletters

We love hearing from you and think you'd like to hear from us.

Planet Talk

Our FREE quarterly printed newsletter is full of tips from travellers and anecdotes from Lonely Planet guidebook authors. Every issue is packed with up-to-date travel news and advice, and includes:

- a postcard from Lonely Planet co-founder Tony Wheeler
- a swag of mail from travellers
- a look at life on the road through the eyes of a Lonely Planet author
- topical health advice
- prizes for the best travel yarn
- news about forthcoming Lonely Planet events
- a complete list of Lonely Planet books and other titles

To join our mailing list, residents of the UK, Europe and Africa can email us at go@lonelyplanet.co.uk; residents of North and South America can email us at info@lonelyplanet.com; the rest of the world can email us at talk2us@lonelyplanet.com.au, or contact any Lonely Planet office.

Comet

Our FREE monthly email newsletter brings you all the latest travel news, features, interviews, competitions, destination ideas, travellers' tips & tales, Q&As, raging debates and related links. Find out what's new on the Lonely Planet Web site and which books are about to hit the shelves.

Subscribe from your desktop: www.lonelyplanet.com/comet

Index

Text

Bold indicates maps.
Italics indicates boxed text.

Bold indicates maps.
Italics indicates boxed text.

Bold indicates maps.
Italics indicates boxed text.

Bold indicates maps.
Italics indicates boxed text.

Bold indicates maps.
Italics indicates boxed text.

Boxed Text

MAP LEGEND

BOUNDARIES

................International
................State
................Disputed

HYDROGRAPHY

................Coastline
................River, Creek
................River Flow
................Lake
................Salt Lake
................Spring, Rapids
................Swamp
................Waterfalls

CAPITAL ....National Capital
CAPITAL ....State Capital
CITY ....City
Town ....Town
Village ....Village
○ ....Point of Interest

■ ....Place to Stay
▲ ....Camping Ground
⌂ ....Caravan Park
⌂ ⌂ ....Hut, Shelter

▼ ....Place to Eat
♥ ....Pub, Bar or Disco

ROUTES & TRANSPORT

................Freeway
................Highway
................Major Road
................Unsealed Road
................City Highway
................City Road
................City Street, with Steps
................City Lane

................Pedestrian Mall
................Tunnel
................Train Route & Station
................Metro & Station
................Tramway
................Cable Car or Chairlift
................Walking Track, Route
................Ferry Route

AREA FEATURES

................Building
................Park, Gardens
................Cemetery
................Market
................Pedestrian Mall
................Urban Area

MAP SYMBOLS

✈ ....Airport
................Ancient or City Wall
∴ ....Archaeological Site
⊖ ....Bank
................Beach
................Cave or Cavern
................Castle or Fort
................Church or Monastery
................Cliff or Escarpment
⊘ ....Embassy
⊕ ....Hospital
................Lighthouse
※ ....Lookout
................Mosque
⌖ ....Monument
▲ ....Mountain

🏛 ....Museum
................National Park
)(................Pass
★ ....Police Station
................Post Office
◆ ....Shopping Centre
................Ski field
................Stately Home
................Swimming Pool
................Synagogue
................Telephone
................Temple, Classical
................Temple
ⓘ ....Tourist Information
................Transport
................Vineyard

LONELY PLANET OFFICES

Australia
PO Box 617, Hawthorn 3122, Victoria
tel: (03) 9819 1877 fax: (03) 9819 6459
e-mail: talk2us@lonelyplanet.com.au

USA
150 Linden St, Oakland, CA 94607
tel: (510) 893 8555 TOLL FREE: 800 275-8555
fax: (510) 893 8572
e-mail: info@lonelyplanet.com

UK
10a Spring Place, London, NW5 3BH
tel: (0171) 428 4800 fax: (0170) 428 4828
e-mail: go@lonelyplanet.co.uk

France
1 rue du Dahomey, 75011 Paris
tel: 01 55 25 33 00 fax: 01 55 25 33 01
e-mail: bip@lonelyplanet.fr

World Wide Web: www.lonelyplanet.com or AOL keyword: lp
Lonely Planet Images: lpi@lonelyplanet.com.au